SHONEN JUMP MANGA

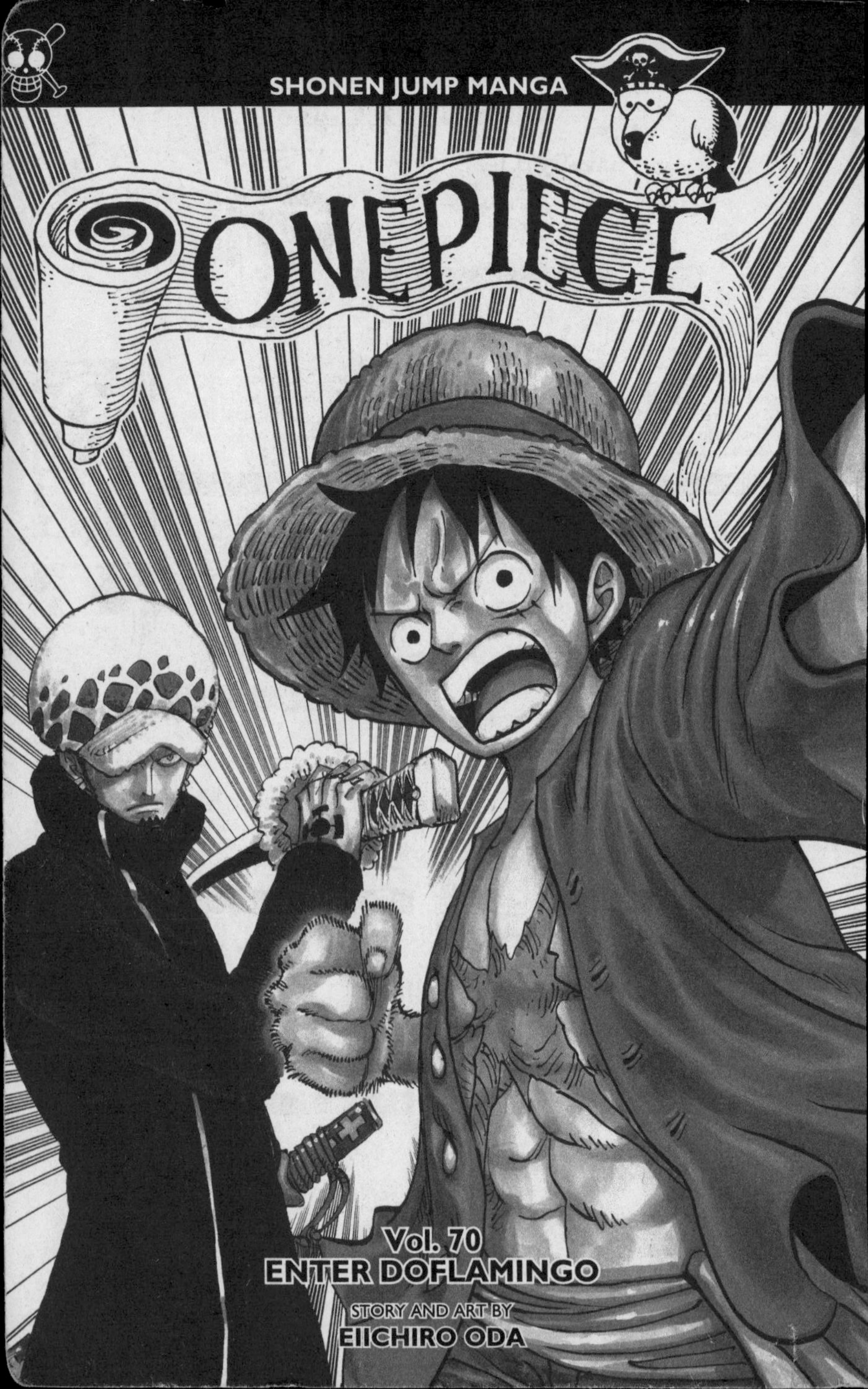
ONE PIECE
Vol. 70
ENTER DOFLAMINGO
STORY AND ART BY
EIICHIRO ODA

The Straw Hat Crew

Monkey D. Luffy
A young man who dreams of becoming the Pirate King. After training with Rayleigh, he and his crew head for the New World!

Captain, Bounty: 400 million berries

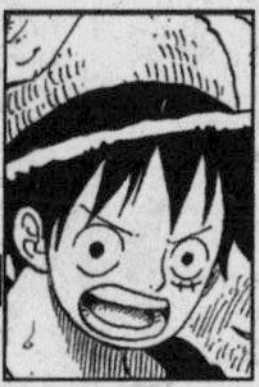

Roronoa Zolo
He swallowed his pride and asked to be trained by Mihawk on Gloom Island before reuniting with the rest of the crew.

Fighter, Bounty: 120 million berries

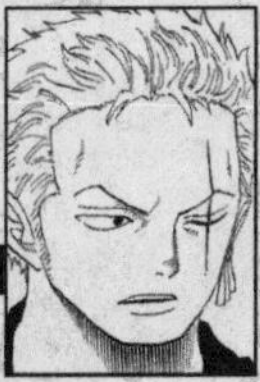

Tony Tony Chopper
After researching powerful medicine in Birdie Kingdom, he reunites with the rest of the crew.

Ship's Doctor, Bounty: 50 berries

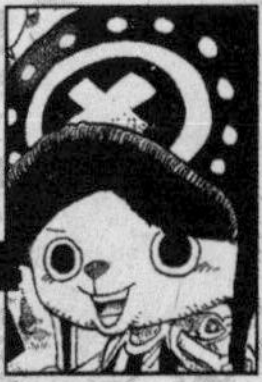

Nami
She studied the weather of the New World on the small Sky Island Weatheria, a place where weather is studied as a science.

Navigator, Bounty: 16 million berries

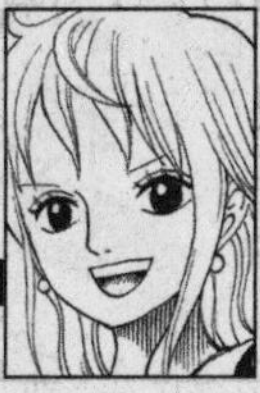

Nico Robin
She spent her time in Baltigo with the leader of the Revolutionary Army: Luffy's father, Dragon.

Archeologist, Bounty: 80 million berries

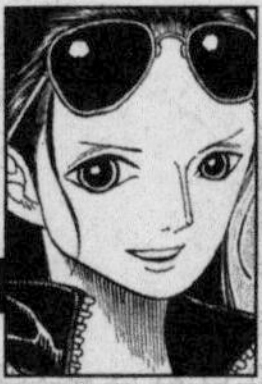

Usopp
He trained under Heracles at the Bowin Islands to become the King of Snipers.

Sniper, Bounty: 30 million berries

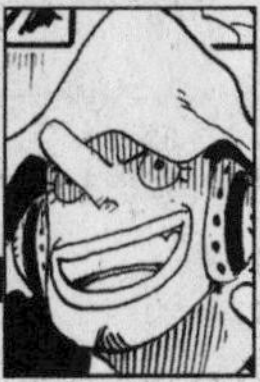

Franky
He modified himself in Future Land Baldimore and turned himself into Armored Franky before reuniting with the rest of the crew.

Shipwright, Bounty: 44 million berries

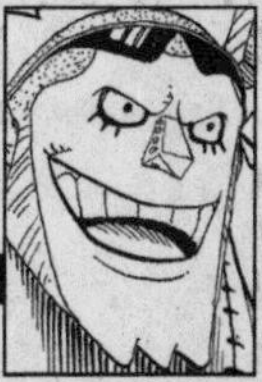

Sanji
After fighting the New Kama Karate masters in the Kamabakka Kingdom, he returned to the crew.

Cook, Bounty: 77 million berries

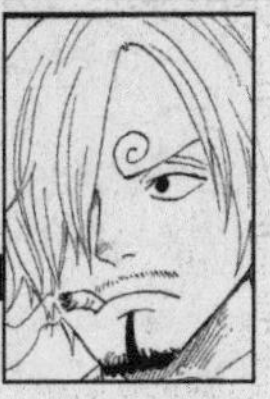

Brook
After being captured and used as a freak show by the Longarm Tribe, he became a famous rock star called "Soul King" Brook.

Musician, Bounty: 33 million berries

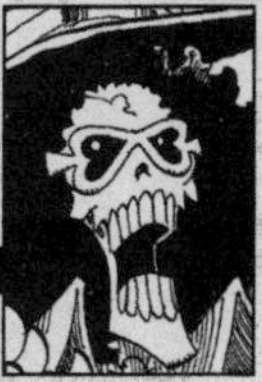

THE STORY OF ONE PIECE • VOLUME 70 •

Shanks
One of the Four Emperors. He continues to wait for Luffy in the second half of the Grand Line, called the New World.
Captain of the Red-Haired Pirates

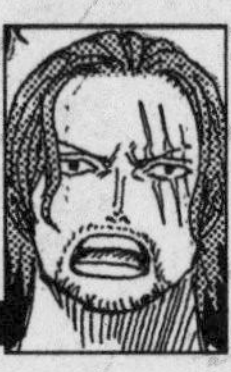

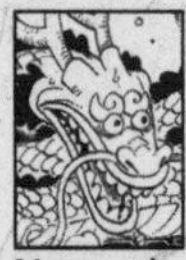

Momonosuke
Kin'emon's Son, Dragon

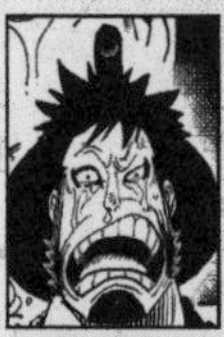

Foxfire Kin'emon
Samurai of Wano

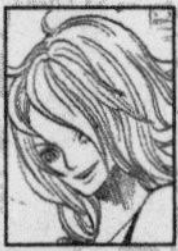

Monet
Harpy

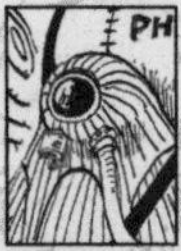
PH

Caesar's Guards
Caesar's followers

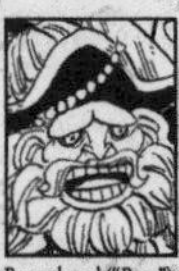

Brownbeard ("Boss")
Punk Hazard Patrol

Punk Hazard

Naval G-5:
5th Branch of the Naval Grand Line

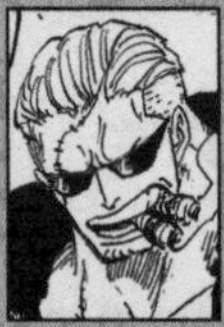

White Chase Smoker
G-5 Vice Admiral

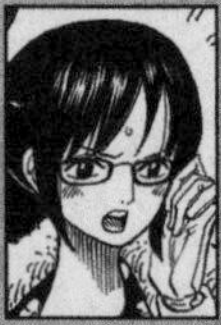

Tashigi
G-5 Captain

Master Caesar Clown
Dr. Vegapunk's former colleague. An authority on weapons of mass murder, now wanted by the government.
Former gov't scientist

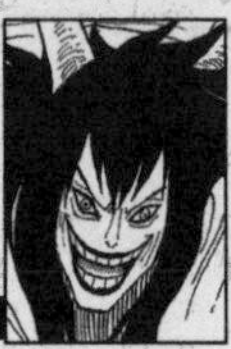

Vice Admiral Vergo
A Navy officer who secretly works for Doflamingo's organization. He helped orchestrate the child abductions.
G-5 Commander

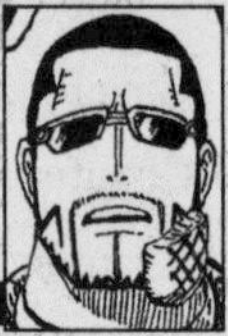

Don Quixote Doflamingo (Joker)
One of the Seven Warlords of the sea and a weapons broker. He works under the alias of "Joker."
Pirate, Warlord

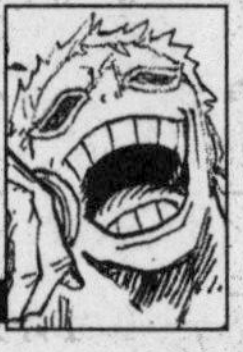

Trafalgar Law
The Surgeon of Death, wielder of the Op-Op Fruit's powers. One of the Seven Warlords of the Sea.
Pirate, Warlord

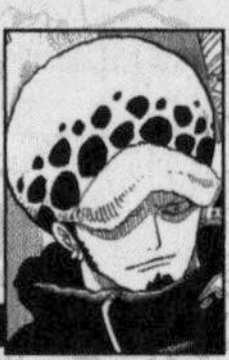

Having finished their two years of training, the Straw Hat crew reunites on the Sabaody Archipelago. They set sail more determined than ever to reach the New World!

The crew lands on Punk Hazard, where the mad scientist and wanted man Caesar Clown rules over the ruins of a government laboratory. With the arrival of the newly appointed Warlord of the Sea Trafalgar Law, the Straw Hats, and the pursuing Navy, the island bursts into chaos! At Law's suggestion, Luffy forms a new pirate alliance for the purpose of capturing Caesar and bringing down one of the mighty Four Emperors. Capturing Caesar would effectively cut off his employer Doflamingo's supply of "Smile," the artificial Devil Fruit being offered to the Emperor in question. Luffy and crew's journey into the new era begins by throwing a wrench into this heinous scheme...

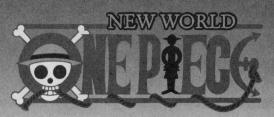

Vol. 70
Enter Doflamingo

CONTENTS

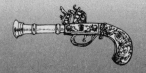

Chapter 691: KING OF THE LAND OF THE DEAD

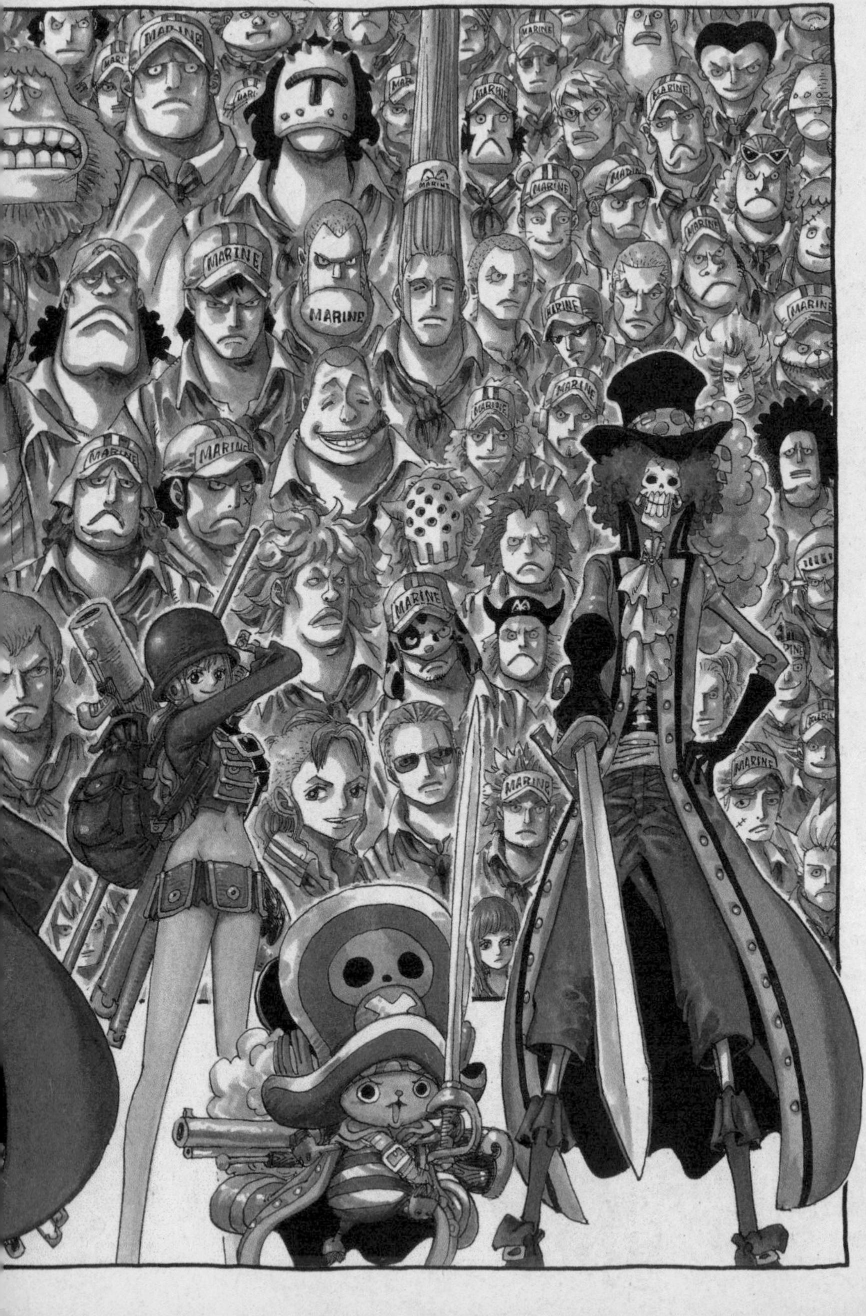

OF THE LAND OF THE DEAD

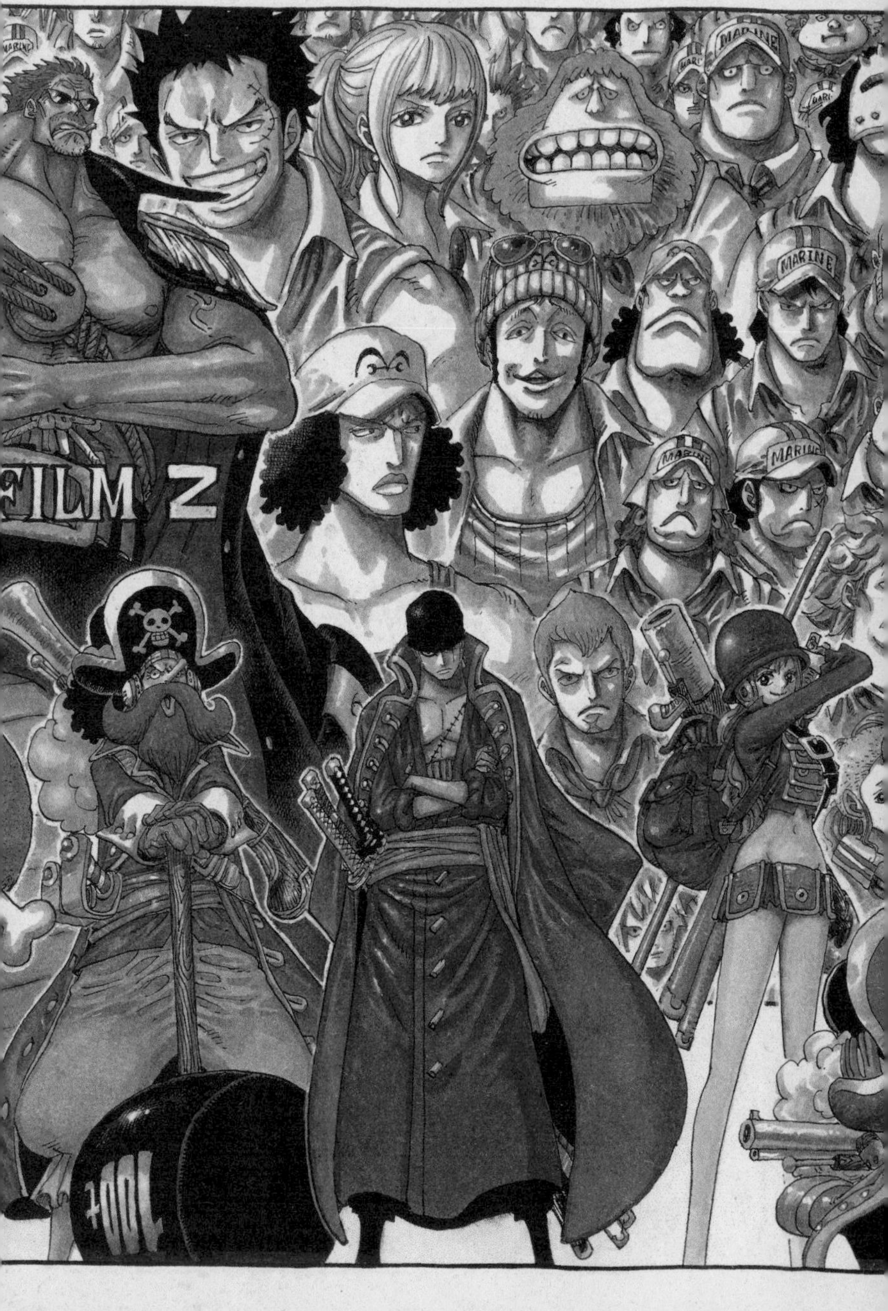
MARINE
FILM Z

Chapter 691: KING

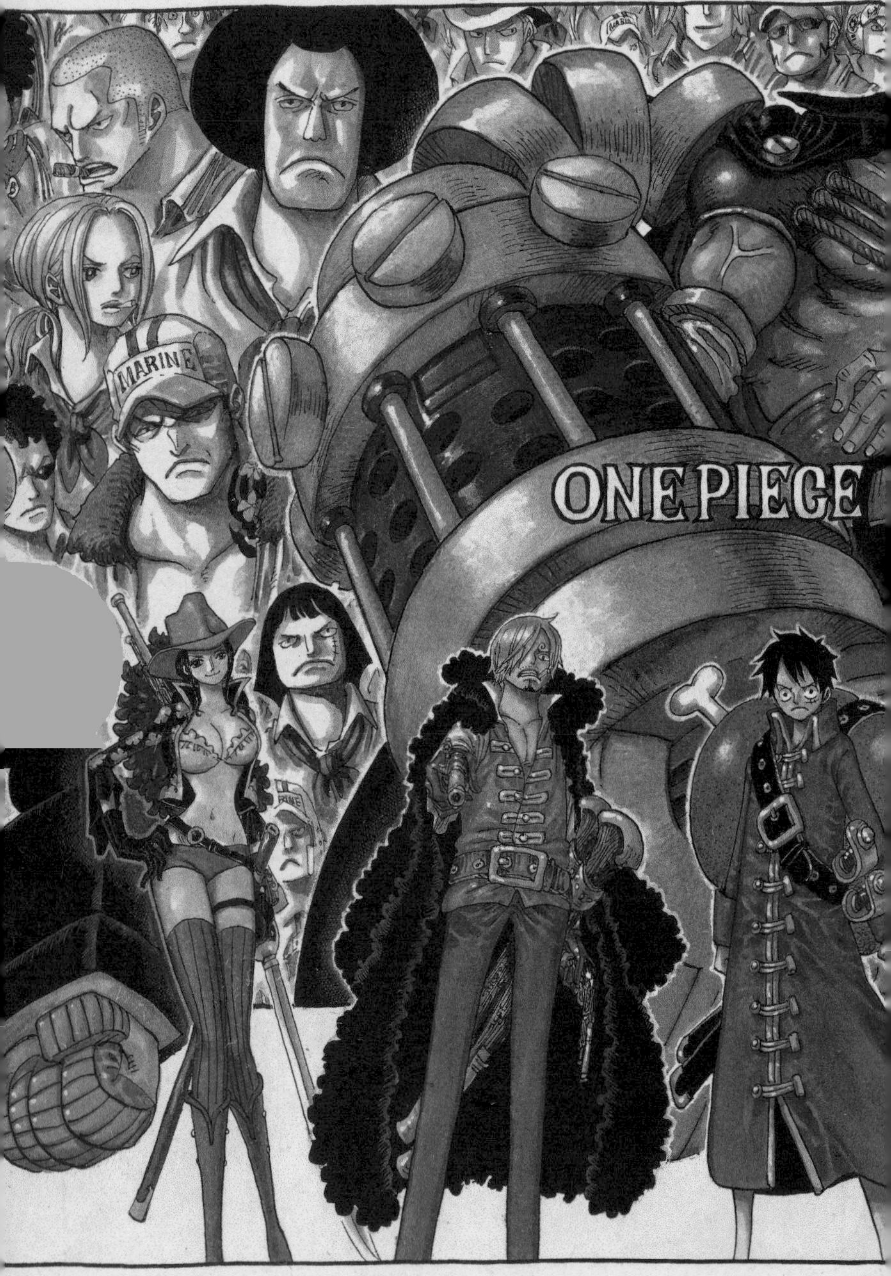
ONE PIECE
MARINE

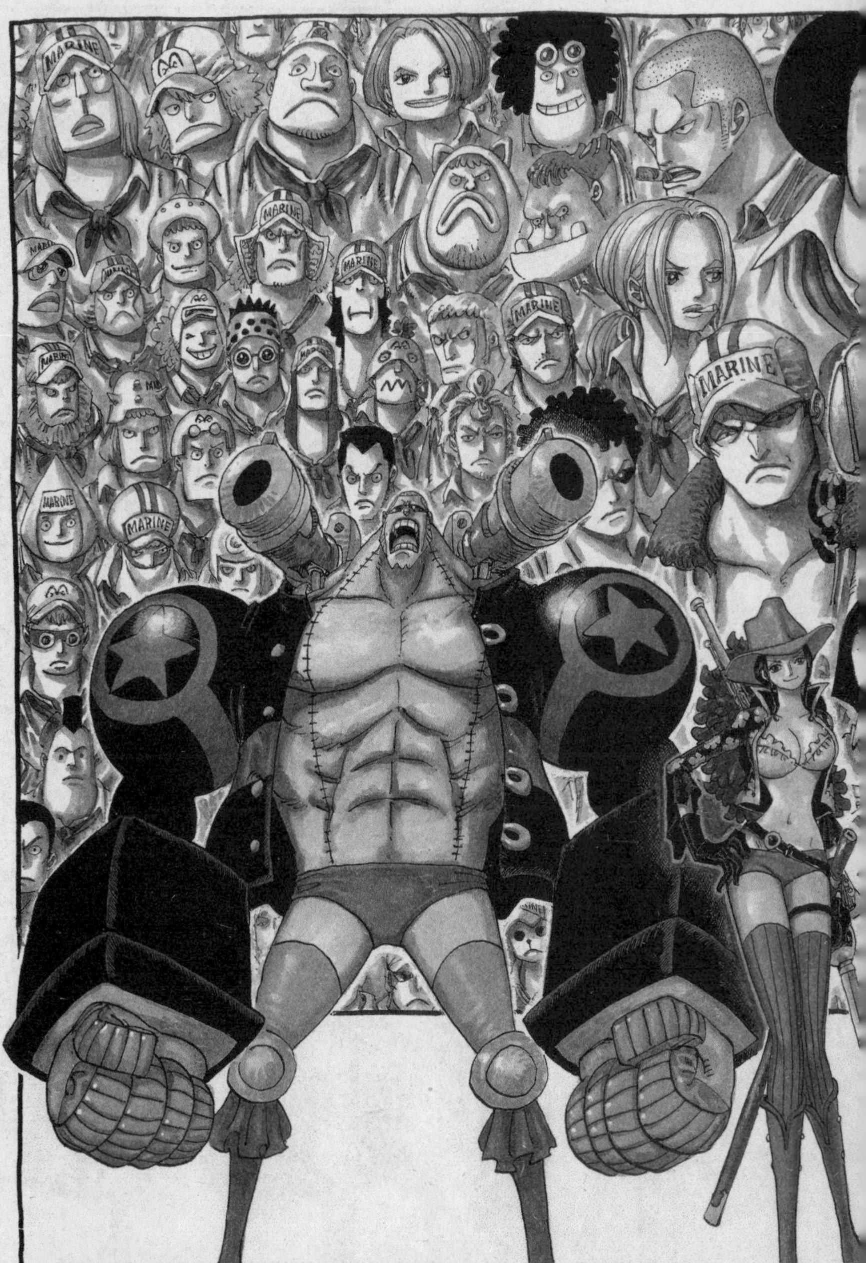
MARINE
MARINE
MARINE
MARINE
MARINE
MARINE

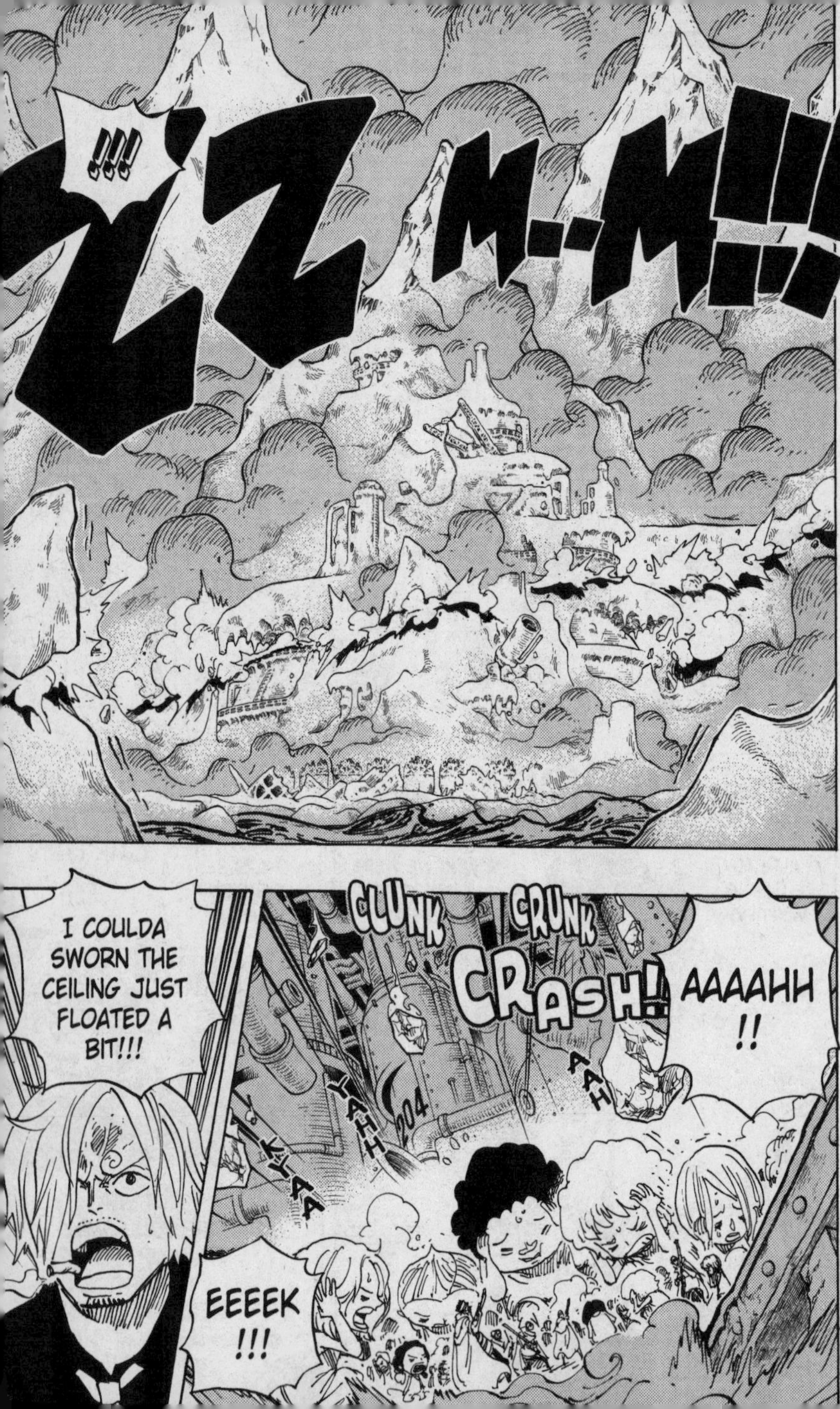
!!!
ZZM-M!!!
AAAAHH !!
CRUNK
CLUNK
CRASH!
AAH
YAHH
KYAA
EEEEK !!!
I COULDA SWORN THE CEILING JUST FLOATED A BIT!!!

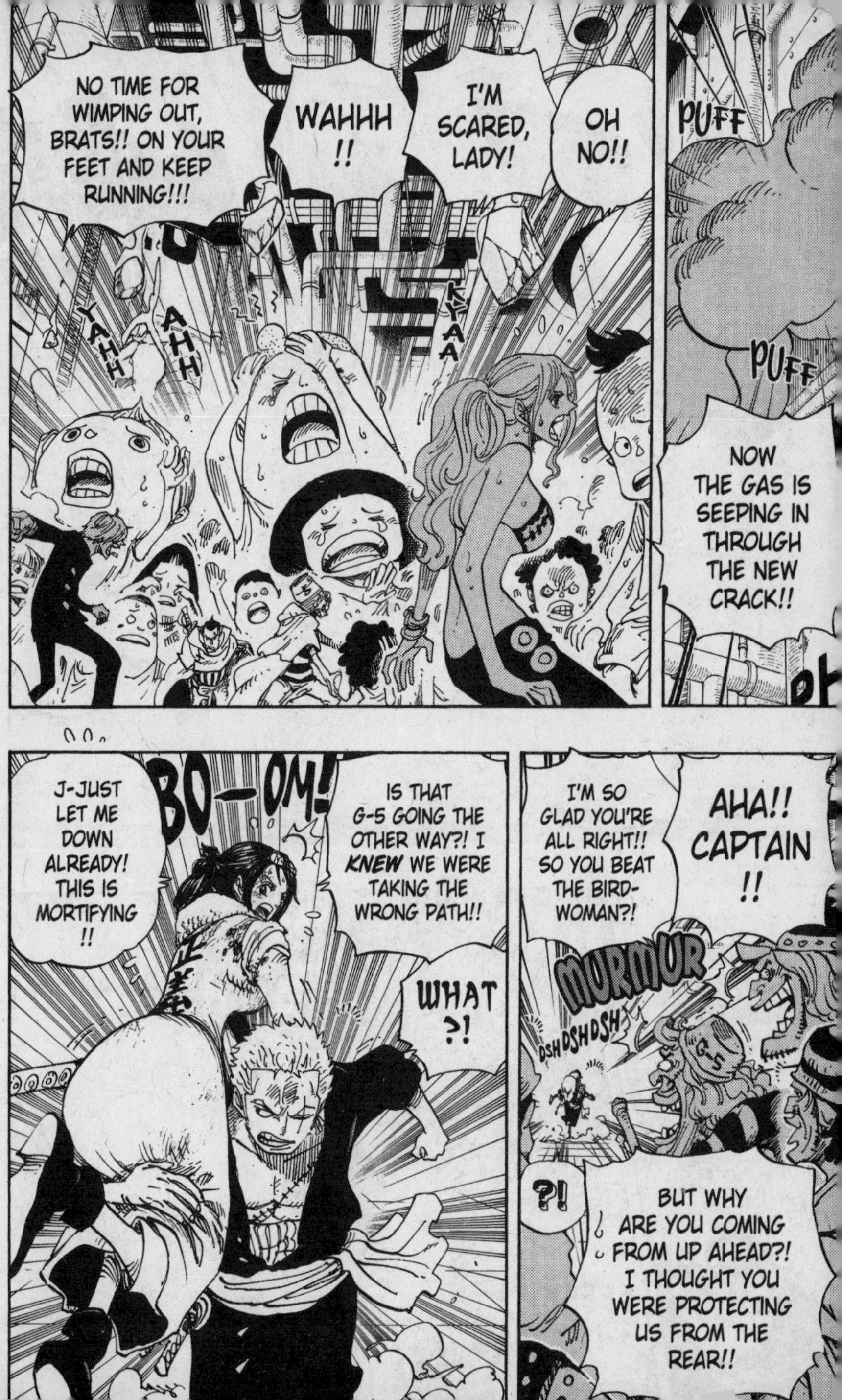
PUFF
PUFF
NOW THE GAS IS SEEPING IN THROUGH THE NEW CRACK!!
OH NO!!
I'M SCARED, LADY!
WAHHH!!
NO TIME FOR WIMPING OUT, BRATS!! ON YOUR FEET AND KEEP RUNNING!!!
KYAA
AHH
YAHH
AHA!! CAPTAIN!!
I'M SO GLAD YOU'RE ALL RIGHT!! SO YOU BEAT THE BIRD-WOMAN?!
MURMUR
DSH DSH DSH
?!
BUT WHY ARE YOU COMING FROM UP AHEAD?! I THOUGHT YOU WERE PROTECTING US FROM THE REAR!!
BO-OM!
IS THAT G-5 GOING THE OTHER WAY?! I KNEW WE WERE TAKING THE WRONG PATH!!
J-JUST LET ME DOWN ALREADY! THIS IS MORTIFYING!!
WHAT?!

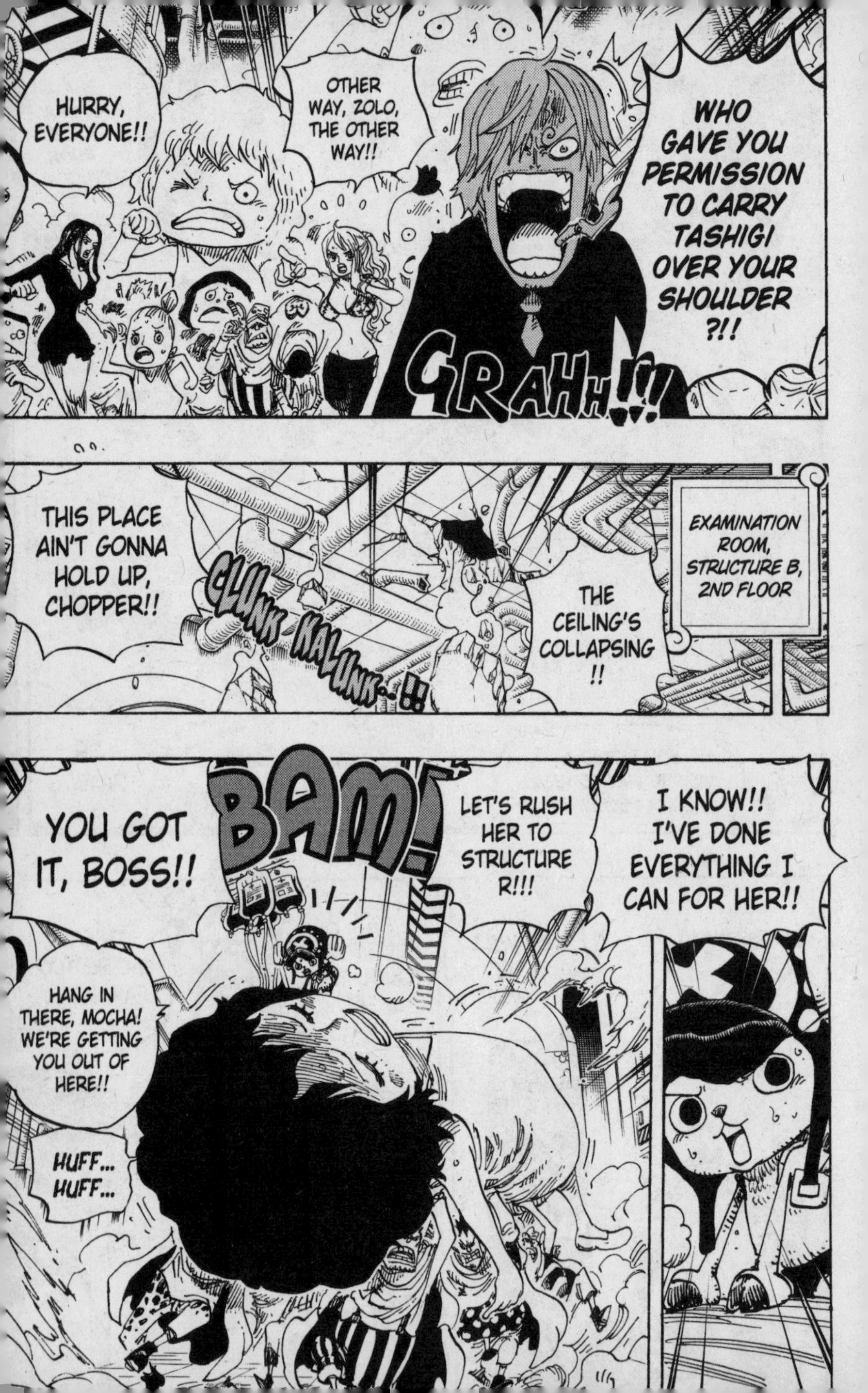
WHO GAVE YOU PERMISSION TO CARRY TASHIGI OVER YOUR SHOULDER ?!!
GRAHH!!!
OTHER WAY, ZOLO, THE OTHER WAY!!
HURRY, EVERYONE!!
EXAMINATION ROOM, STRUCTURE B, 2ND FLOOR
THE CEILING'S COLLAPSING !!
CLUNK KALUNK..!!
THIS PLACE AIN'T GONNA HOLD UP, CHOPPER!!
I KNOW!! I'VE DONE EVERYTHING I CAN FOR HER!!
LET'S RUSH HER TO STRUCTURE R!!!
BAM!
YOU GOT IT, BOSS!!
HANG IN THERE, MOCHA! WE'RE GETTING YOU OUT OF HERE!!
HUFF... HUFF...

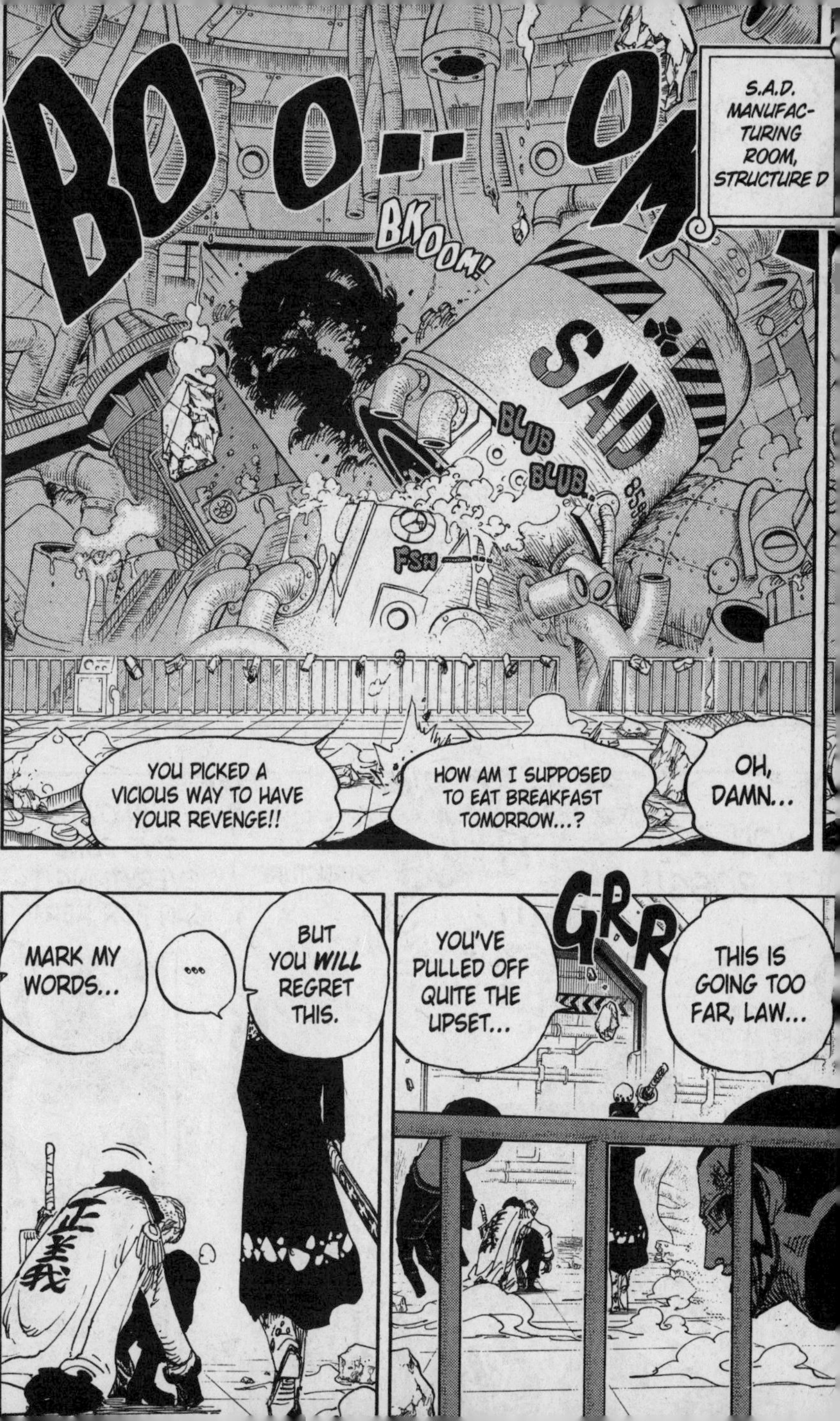
S.A.D. MANUFAC-TURING ROOM, STRUCTURE D
BOO--OM
BKOOM!
SAD
BLUB
BLUB...
FSH
OH, DAMN...
HOW AM I SUPPOSED TO EAT BREAKFAST TOMORROW...?
YOU PICKED A VICIOUS WAY TO HAVE YOUR REVENGE!!
THIS IS GOING TOO FAR, LAW...
GRR
YOU'VE PULLED OFF QUITE THE UPSET...
BUT YOU *WILL* REGRET THIS.
...
MARK MY WORDS...

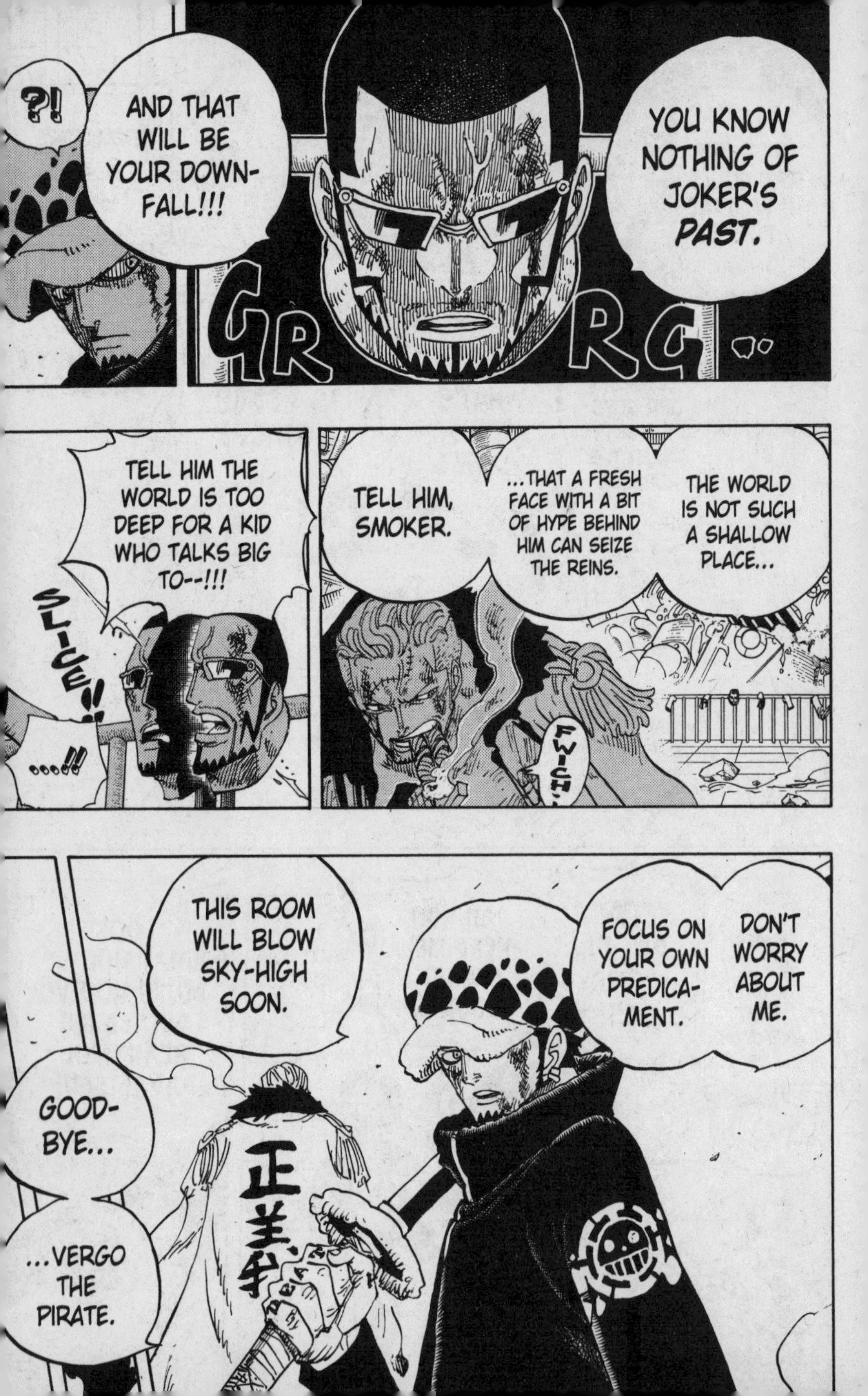
YOU KNOW NOTHING OF JOKER'S PAST.
GRRG..
AND THAT WILL BE YOUR DOWN-FALL!!!
?!
THE WORLD IS NOT SUCH A SHALLOW PLACE...
...THAT A FRESH FACE WITH A BIT OF HYPE BEHIND HIM CAN SEIZE THE REINS.
TELL HIM, SMOKER.
FWICH..
TELL HIM THE WORLD IS TOO DEEP FOR A KID WHO TALKS BIG TO--!!!
SLICE!!
...!!
DON'T WORRY ABOUT ME.
FOCUS ON YOUR OWN PREDICA-MENT.
THIS ROOM WILL BLOW SKY-HIGH SOON.
GOOD-BYE...
...VERGO THE PIRATE.
正義

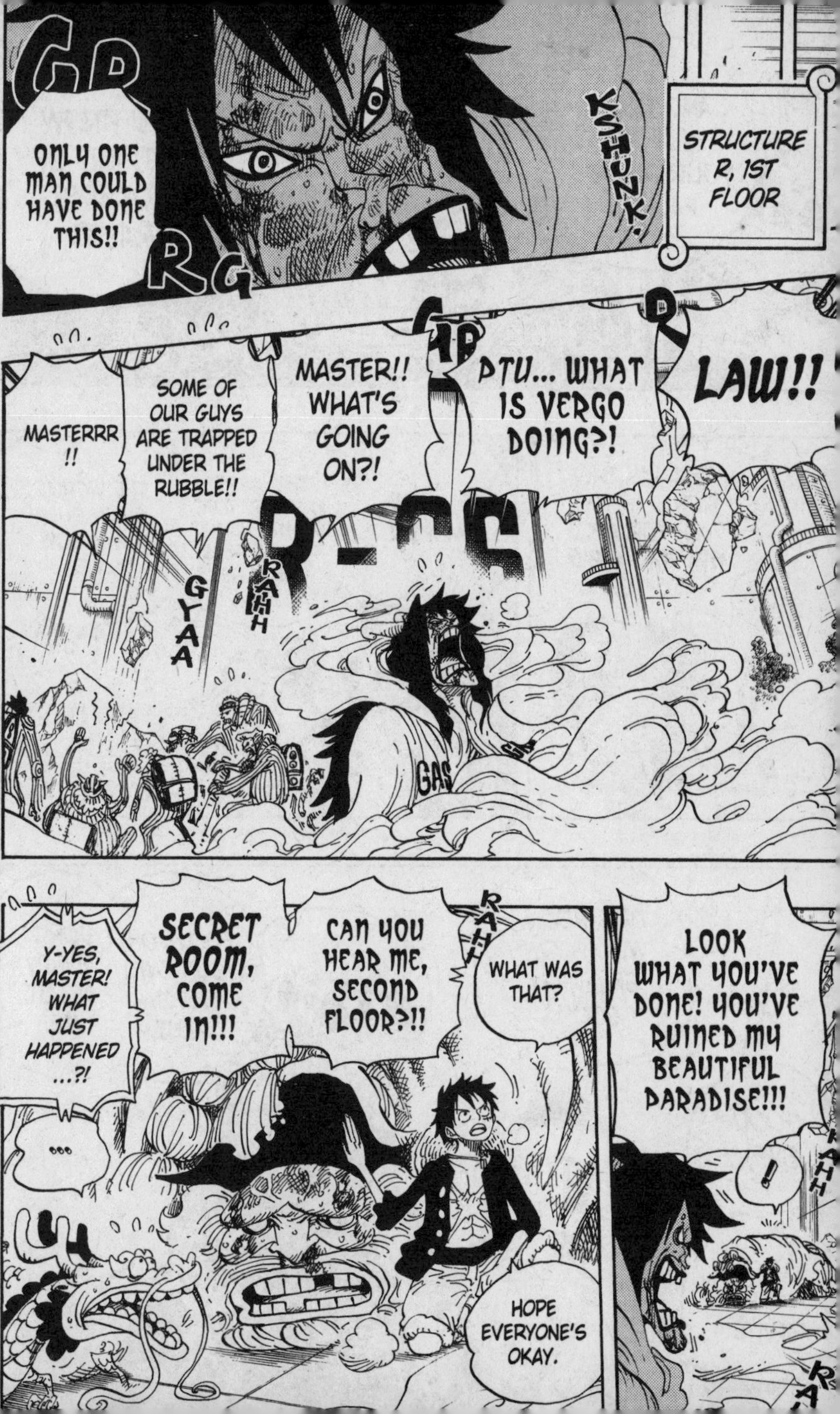
STRUCTURE R, 1ST FLOOR
KSHUNK
GR
ONLY ONE MAN COULD HAVE DONE THIS!!
RG
LAW!!
R
PTU... WHAT IS VERGO DOING?!
GR
MASTER!! WHAT'S GOING ON?!
SOME OF OUR GUYS ARE TRAPPED UNDER THE RUBBLE!!
MASTERRR !!
RAHHH
GYAA
GAS
LOOK WHAT YOU'VE DONE! YOU'VE RUINED MY BEAUTIFUL PARADISE!!!
!
RAHH
RAHH
WHAT WAS THAT?
CAN YOU HEAR ME, SECOND FLOOR?!!
SECRET ROOM, COME IN!!!
Y-YES, MASTER! WHAT JUST HAPPENED ...?!
...
HOPE EVERYONE'S OKAY.

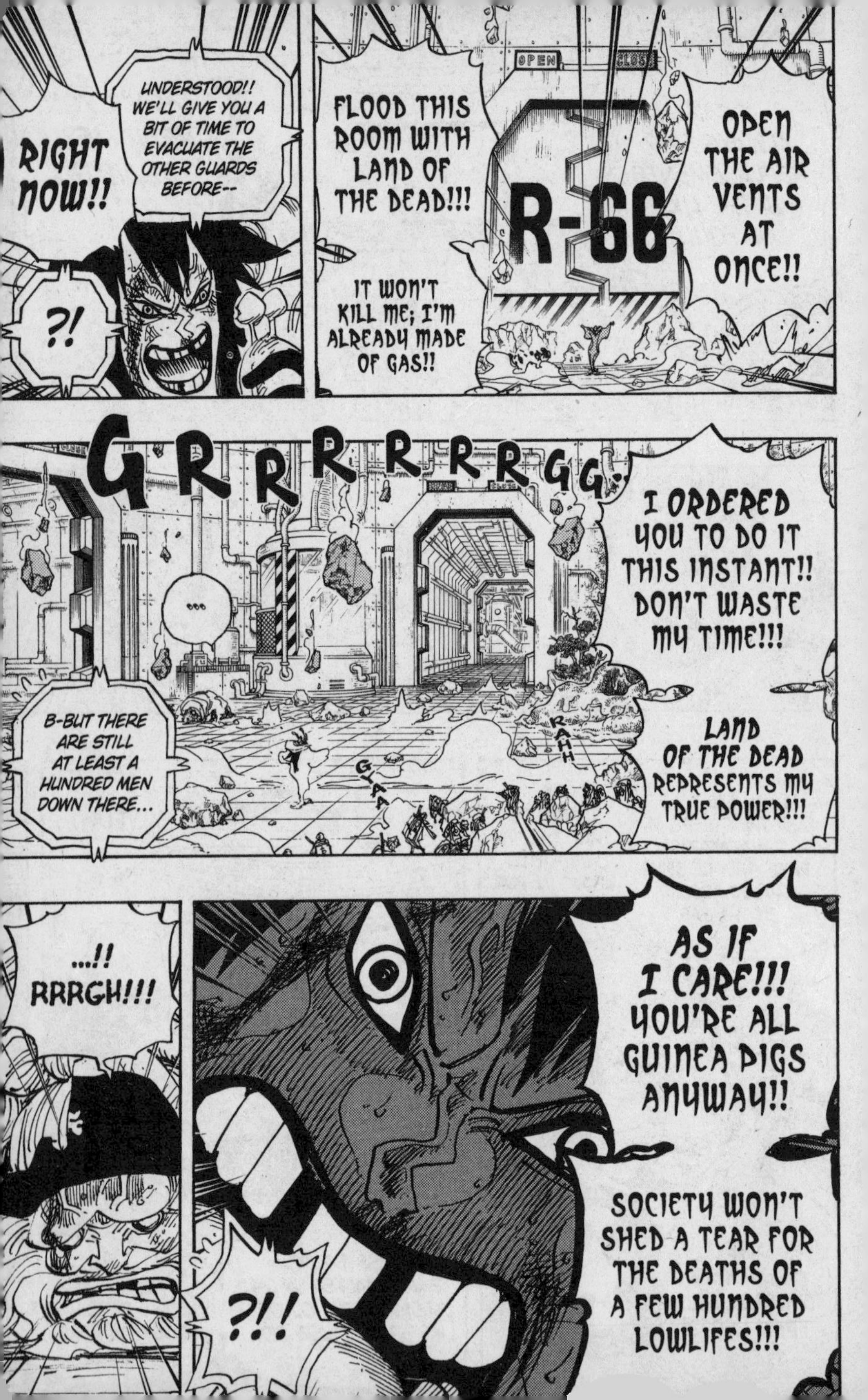
OPEN
CLOS
OPEN THE AIR VENTS AT ONCE!!
R-66
FLOOD THIS ROOM WITH LAND OF THE DEAD!!!
IT WON'T KILL ME; I'M ALREADY MADE OF GAS!!
UNDERSTOOD!! WE'LL GIVE YOU A BIT OF TIME TO EVACUATE THE OTHER GUARDS BEFORE--
RIGHT NOW!!
?!
GRRRRRRGG
I ORDERED YOU TO DO IT THIS INSTANT!! DON'T WASTE MY TIME!!!
LAND OF THE DEAD REPRESENTS MY TRUE POWER!!!
RAHH
GYAA
...
B-BUT THERE ARE STILL AT LEAST A HUNDRED MEN DOWN THERE...
AS IF I CARE!!! YOU'RE ALL GUINEA PIGS ANYWAY!!
SOCIETY WON'T SHED A TEAR FOR THE DEATHS OF A FEW HUNDRED LOWLIFES!!!
?!!
...!! RRRGH!!!

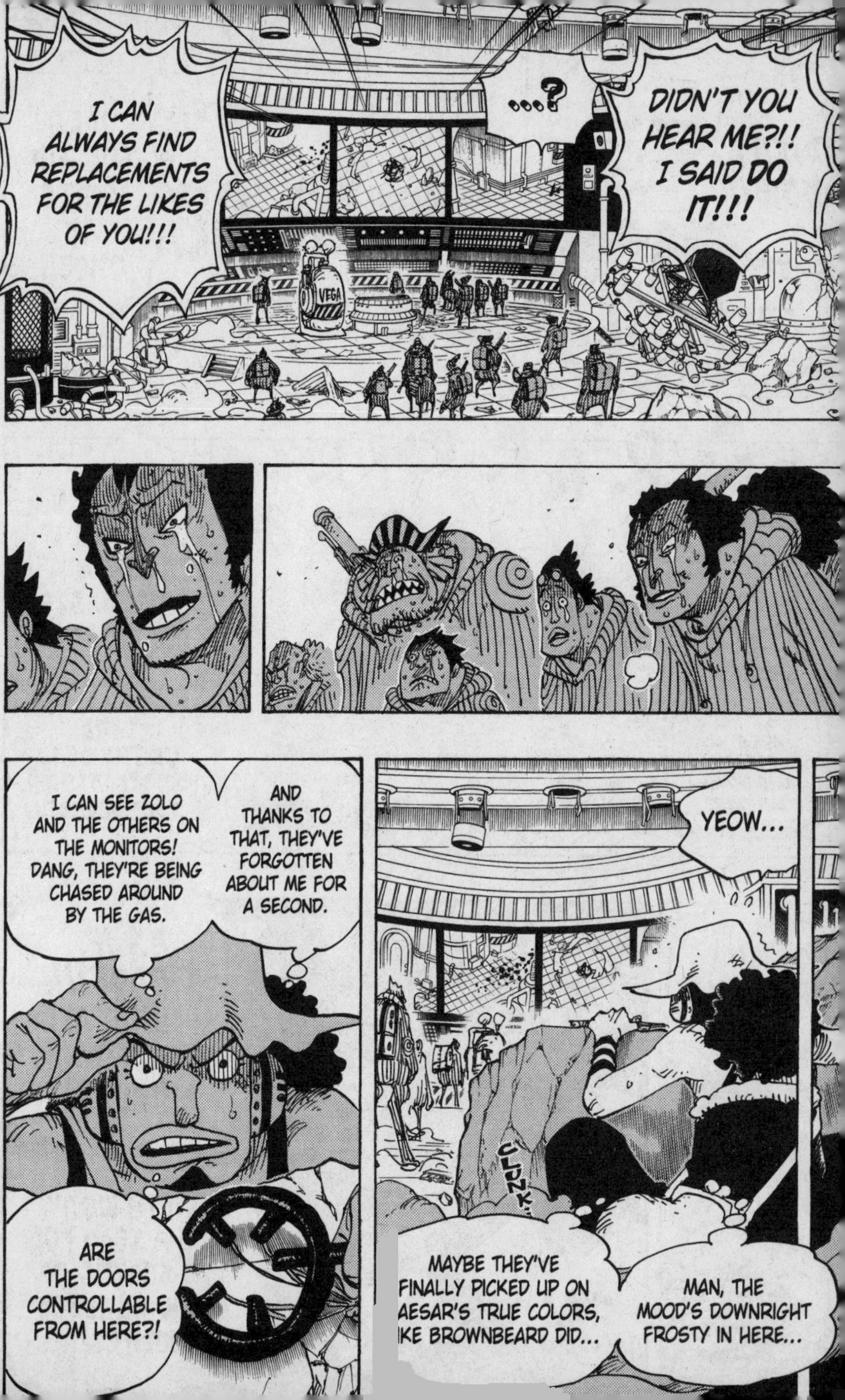
DIDN'T YOU HEAR ME?!! I SAID DO IT!!!
...?
I CAN ALWAYS FIND REPLACEMENTS FOR THE LIKES OF YOU!!!
VEGA
YEOW...
CLUNK...
MAN, THE MOOD'S DOWNRIGHT FROSTY IN HERE...
MAYBE THEY'VE FINALLY PICKED UP ON AESAR'S TRUE COLORS, IKE BROWNBEARD DID...
I CAN SEE ZOLO AND THE OTHERS ON THE MONITORS! DANG, THEY'RE BEING CHASED AROUND BY THE GAS.
AND THANKS TO THAT, THEY'VE FORGOTTEN ABOUT ME FOR A SECOND.
ARE THE DOORS CONTROLLABLE FROM HERE?!

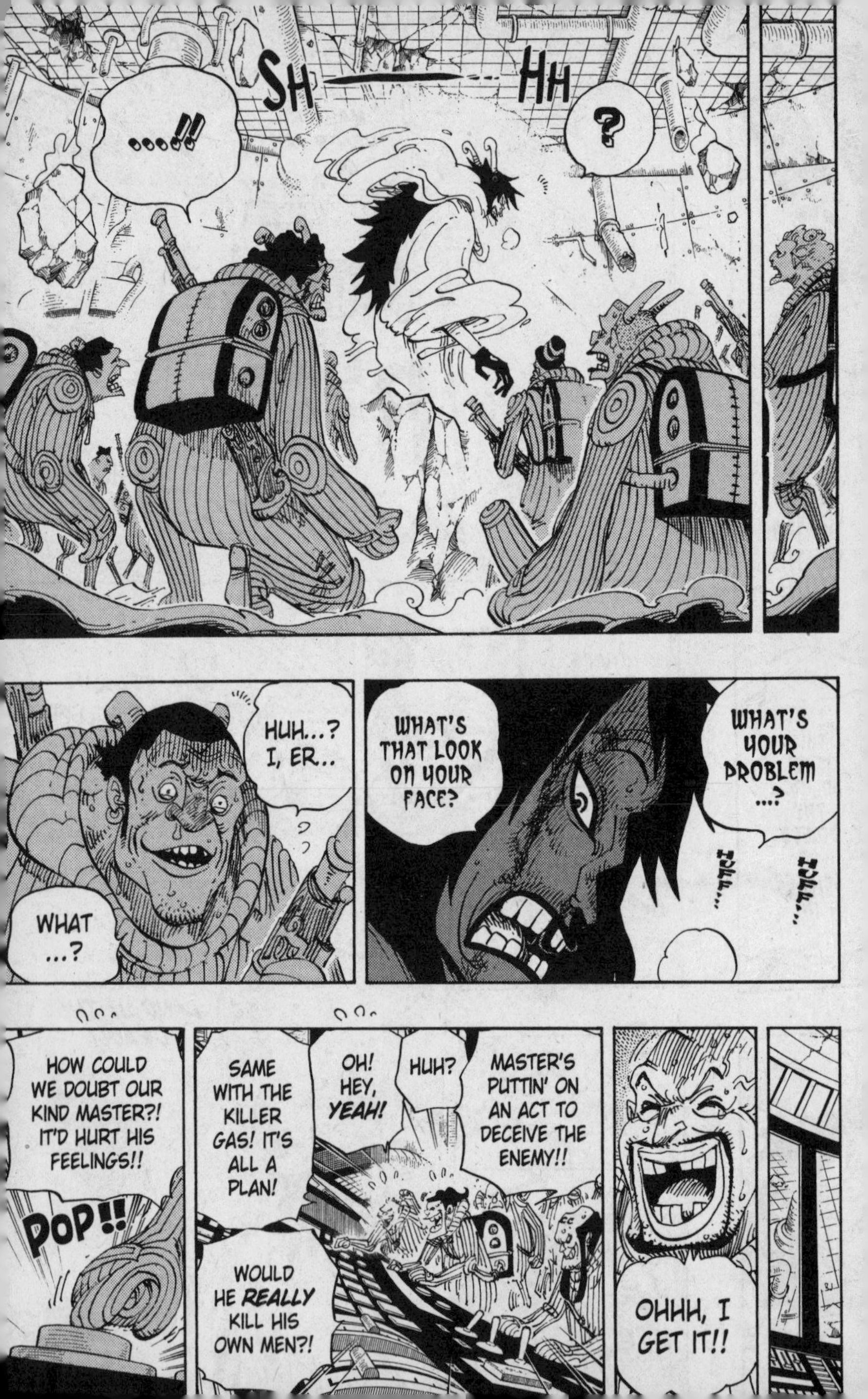
SH—HH
?
....!!
WHAT'S YOUR PROBLEM ...?
HUFF... HUFF...
WHAT'S THAT LOOK ON YOUR FACE?
HUH...? I, ER..
WHAT ...?
OHHH, I GET IT!!
MASTER'S PUTTIN' ON AN ACT TO DECEIVE THE ENEMY!!
HUH?
OH! HEY, YEAH!
SAME WITH THE KILLER GAS! IT'S ALL A PLAN!
WOULD HE REALLY KILL HIS OWN MEN?!
HOW COULD WE DOUBT OUR KIND MASTER?! IT'D HURT HIS FEELINGS!!
POP!!

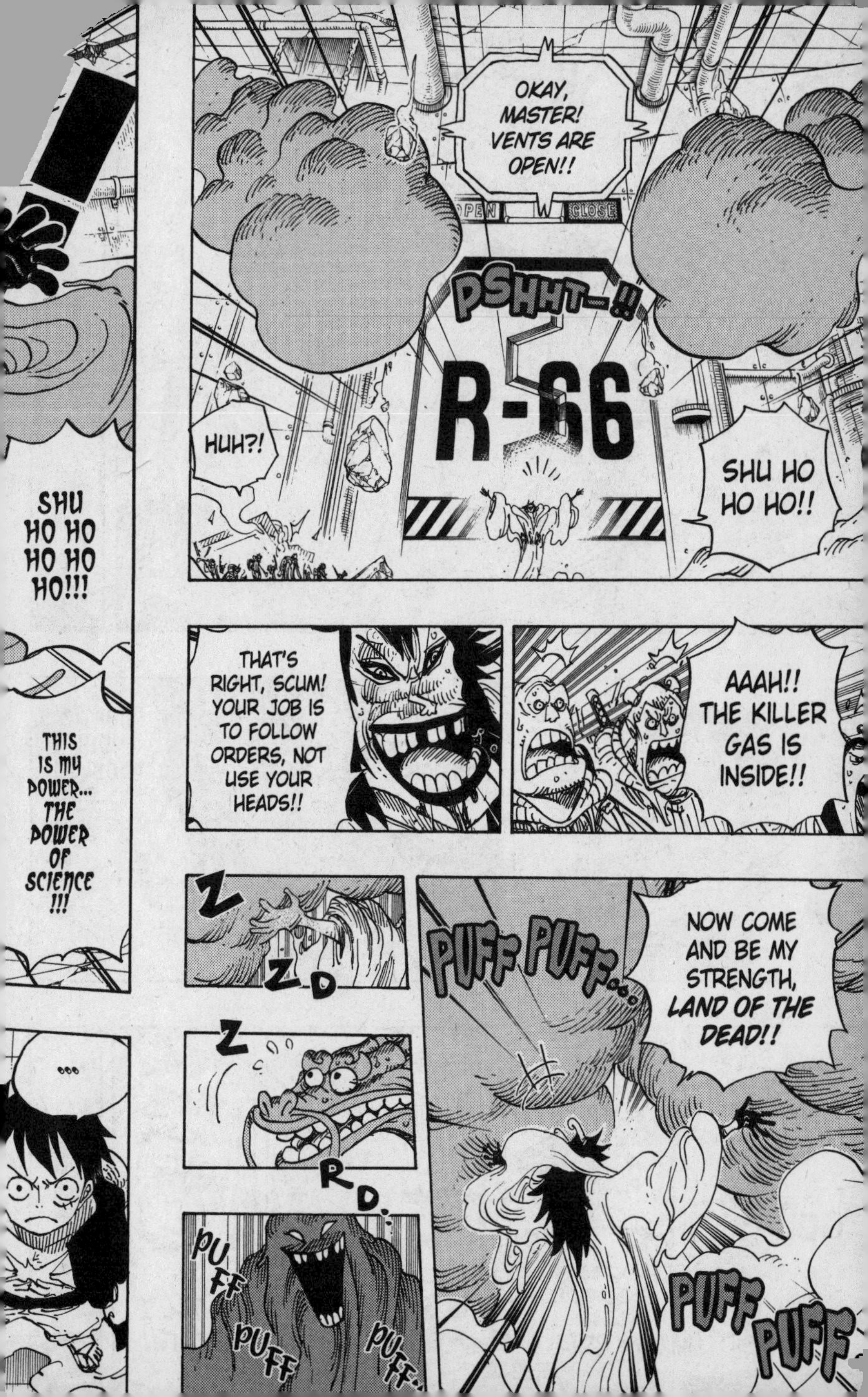
OKAY, MASTER! VENTS ARE OPEN!!
OPEN
CLOSE
PSHHT--!!
SHU HO HO HO!!
R-66
HUH?!
AAAH!! THE KILLER GAS IS INSIDE!!
THAT'S RIGHT, SCUM! YOUR JOB IS TO FOLLOW ORDERS, NOT USE YOUR HEADS!!
NOW COME AND BE MY STRENGTH, LAND OF THE DEAD!!
PUFF PUFF...
PUFF PUFF
Z
Z D
Z
R D..
PUFF
PUFF
PUFF...
SHU HO HO HO HO HO!!!
THIS IS MY POWER... THE POWER OF SCIENCE!!!
...

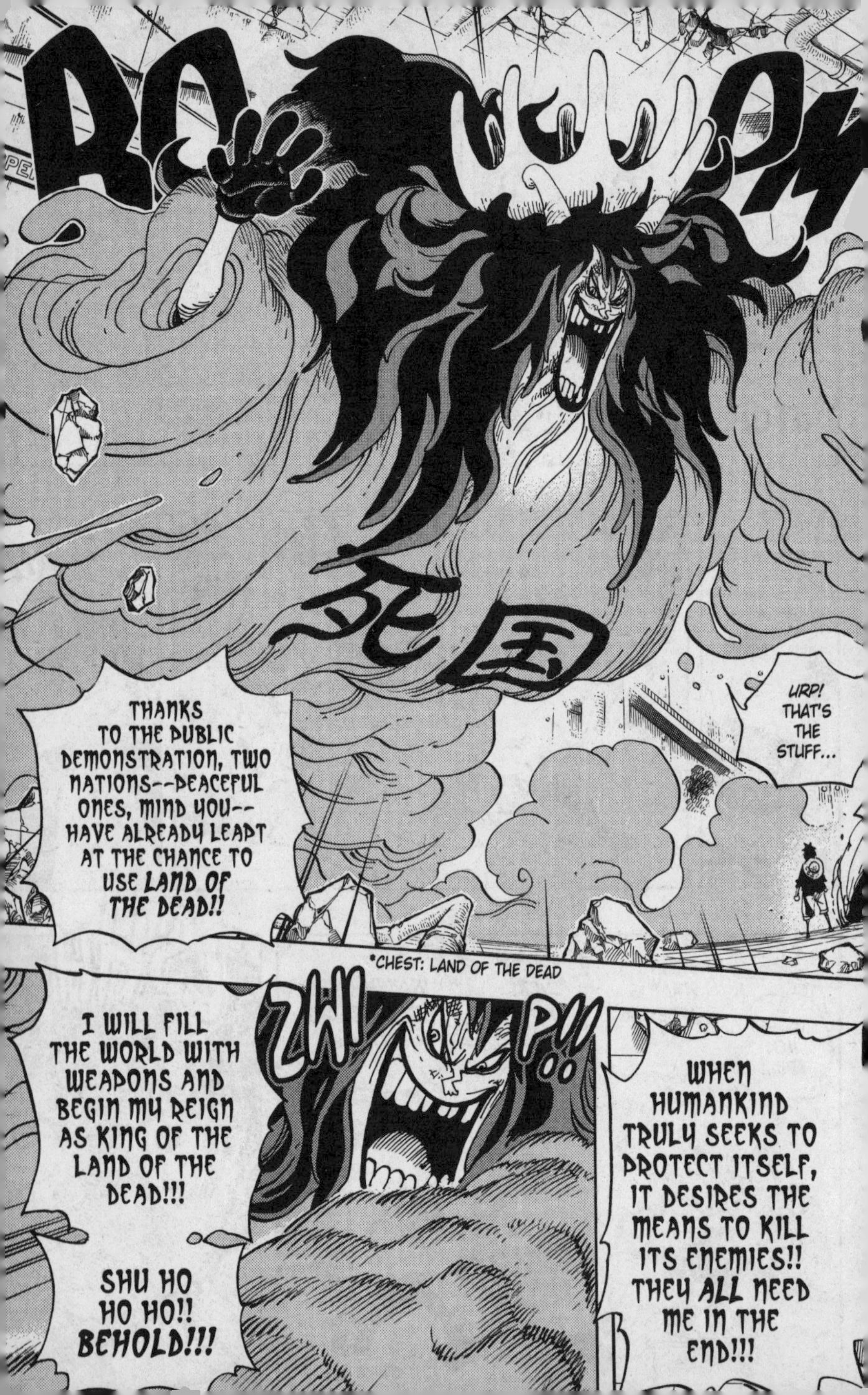
URP! THAT'S THE STUFF...
死国
THANKS TO THE PUBLIC DEMONSTRATION, TWO NATIONS--PEACEFUL ONES, MIND YOU--HAVE ALREADY LEAPT AT THE CHANCE TO USE LAND OF THE DEAD!!
*CHEST: LAND OF THE DEAD
WHEN HUMANKIND TRULY SEEKS TO PROTECT ITSELF, IT DESIRES THE MEANS TO KILL ITS ENEMIES!! THEY ALL NEED ME IN THE END!!!
ZWIP!!
I WILL FILL THE WORLD WITH WEAPONS AND BEGIN MY REIGN AS KING OF THE LAND OF THE DEAD!!!
SHU HO HO HO!! BEHOLD!!!

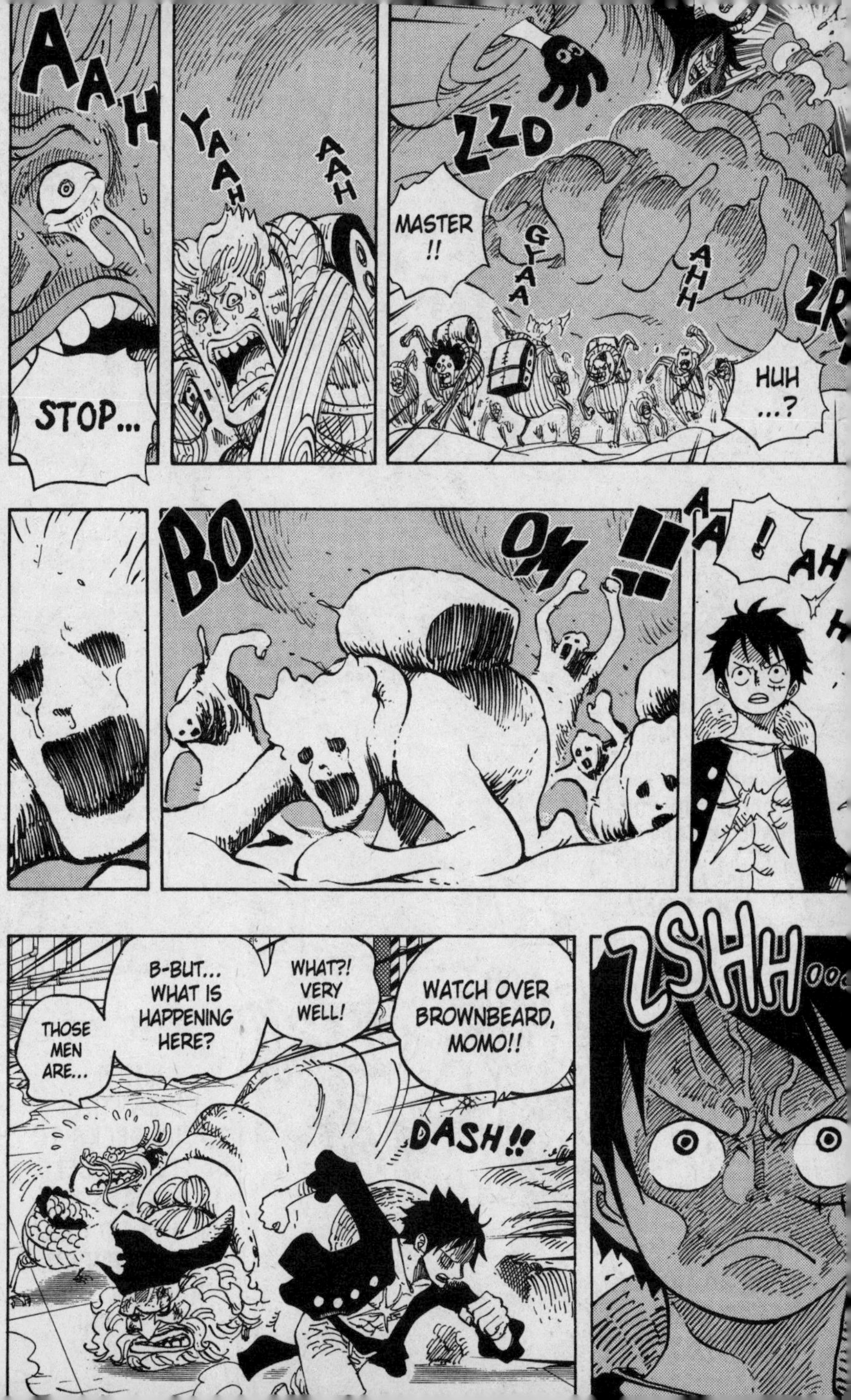
ZZD
ZR
HUH ...?
AHH
MASTER !!
GYAA
AAH
YAAH
AAH
STOP...
AA
!
AHH
BOOM!!
ZSHH...
WATCH OVER BROWNBEARD, MOMO!!
WHAT?! VERY WELL!
B-BUT... WHAT IS HAPPENING HERE?
THOSE MEN ARE...
DASH!!

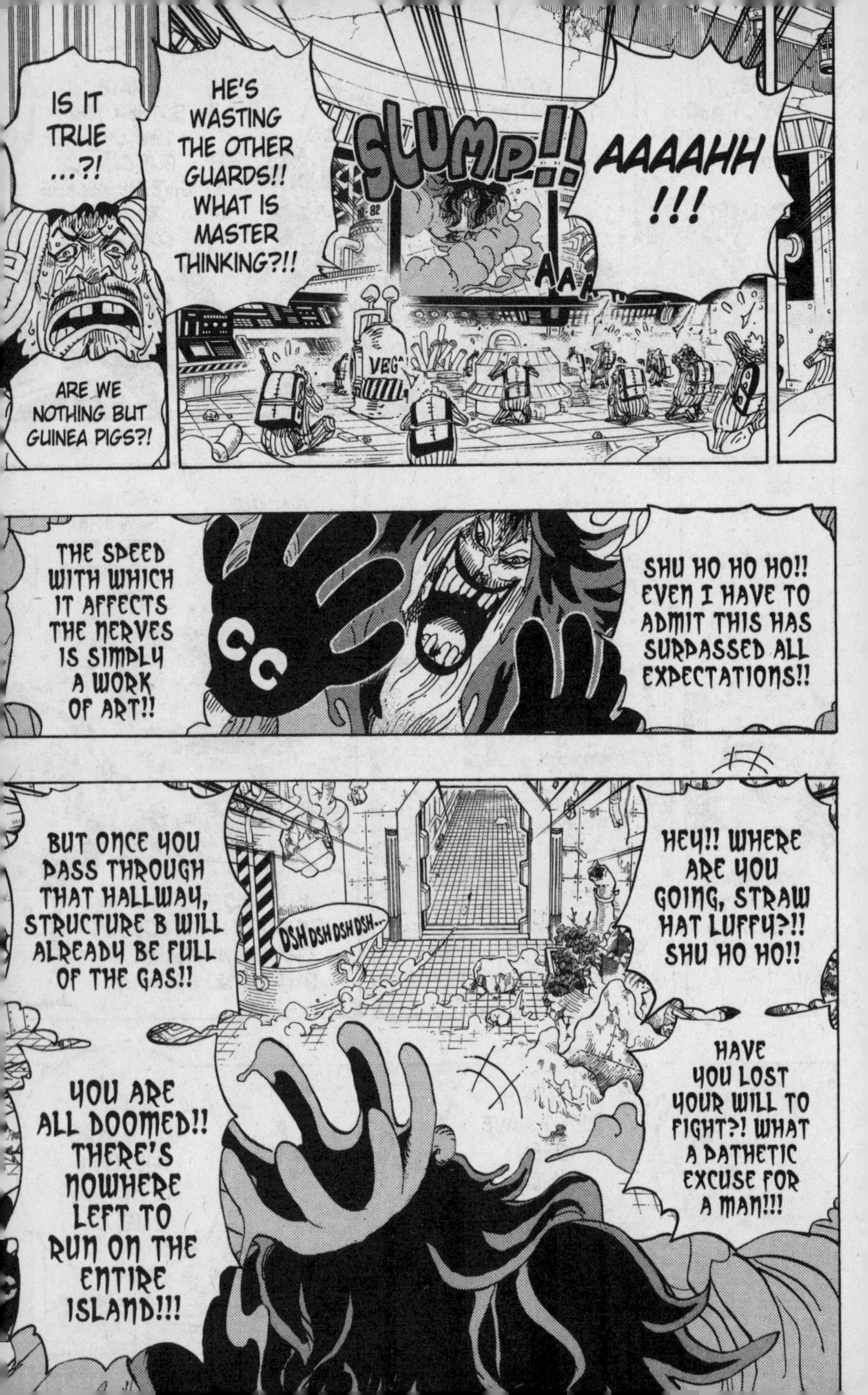
AAAAHH!!!
SLUMP!!
AAA
HE'S WASTING THE OTHER GUARDS!! WHAT IS MASTER THINKING?!!
IS IT TRUE ...?!
ARE WE NOTHING BUT GUINEA PIGS?!
SHU HO HO HO!! EVEN I HAVE TO ADMIT THIS HAS SURPASSED ALL EXPECTATIONS!!
THE SPEED WITH WHICH IT AFFECTS THE NERVES IS SIMPLY A WORK OF ART!!
HEY!! WHERE ARE YOU GOING, STRAW HAT LUFFY?!! SHU HO HO!!
BUT ONCE YOU PASS THROUGH THAT HALLWAY, STRUCTURE B WILL ALREADY BE FULL OF THE GAS!!
DSH DSH DSH DSH...
HAVE YOU LOST YOUR WILL TO FIGHT?! WHAT A PATHETIC EXCUSE FOR A MAN!!!
YOU ARE ALL DOOMED!! THERE'S NOWHERE LEFT TO RUN ON THE ENTIRE ISLAND!!!

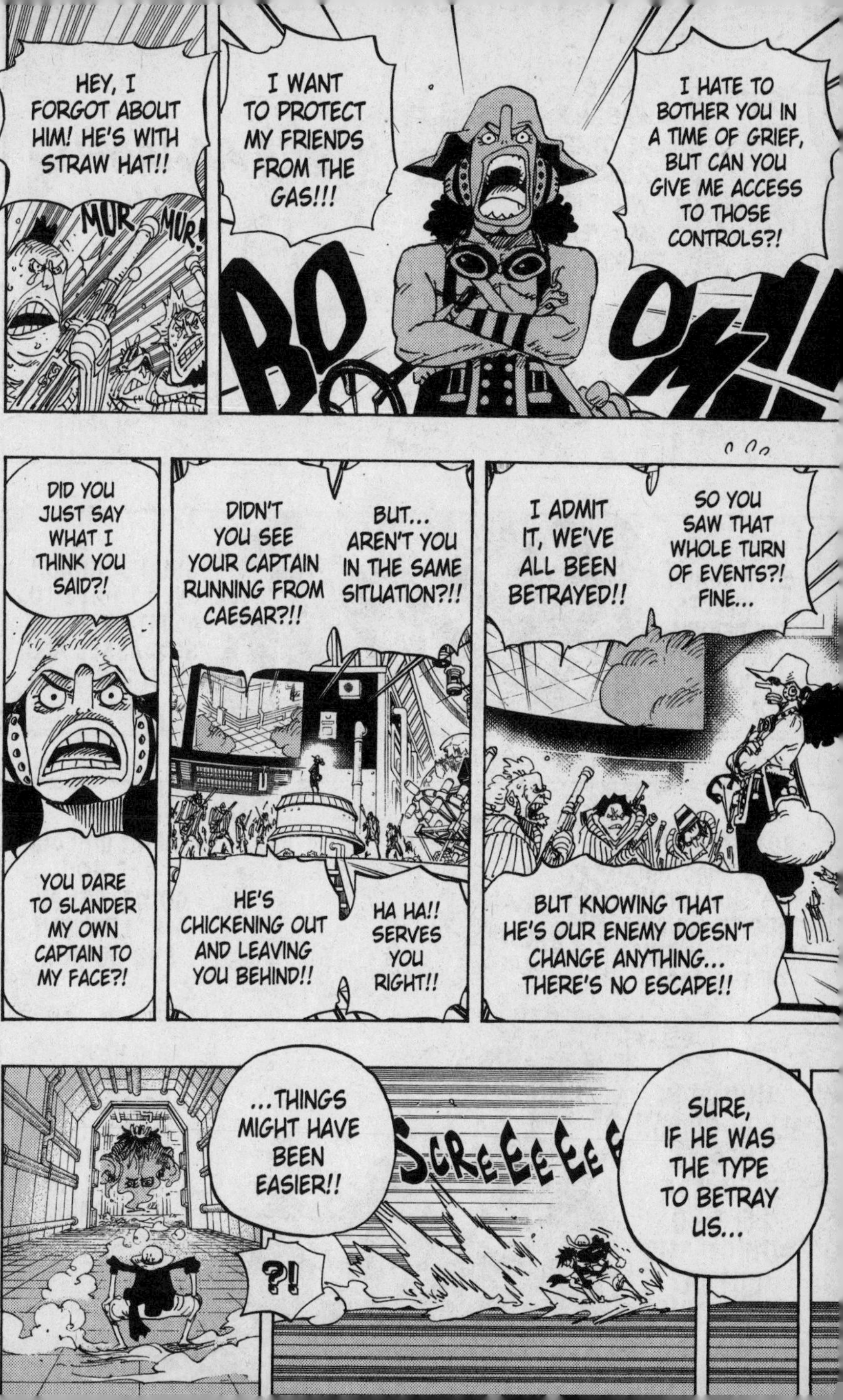
I HATE TO BOTHER YOU IN A TIME OF GRIEF, BUT CAN YOU GIVE ME ACCESS TO THOSE CONTROLS?!
I WANT TO PROTECT MY FRIENDS FROM THE GAS!!!
BOOOH
HEY, I FORGOT ABOUT HIM! HE'S WITH STRAW HAT!!
MUR MUR!
SO YOU SAW THAT WHOLE TURN OF EVENTS?! FINE...
I ADMIT IT, WE'VE ALL BEEN BETRAYED!!
BUT KNOWING THAT HE'S OUR ENEMY DOESN'T CHANGE ANYTHING... THERE'S NO ESCAPE!!
BUT... AREN'T YOU IN THE SAME SITUATION?!!
DIDN'T YOU SEE YOUR CAPTAIN RUNNING FROM CAESAR?!!
HA HA!! SERVES YOU RIGHT!!
HE'S CHICKENING OUT AND LEAVING YOU BEHIND!!
DID YOU JUST SAY WHAT I THINK YOU SAID?!
YOU DARE TO SLANDER MY OWN CAPTAIN TO MY FACE?!
SURE, IF HE WAS THE TYPE TO BETRAY US...
...THINGS MIGHT HAVE BEEN EASIER!!
SCREEEEEE
?!

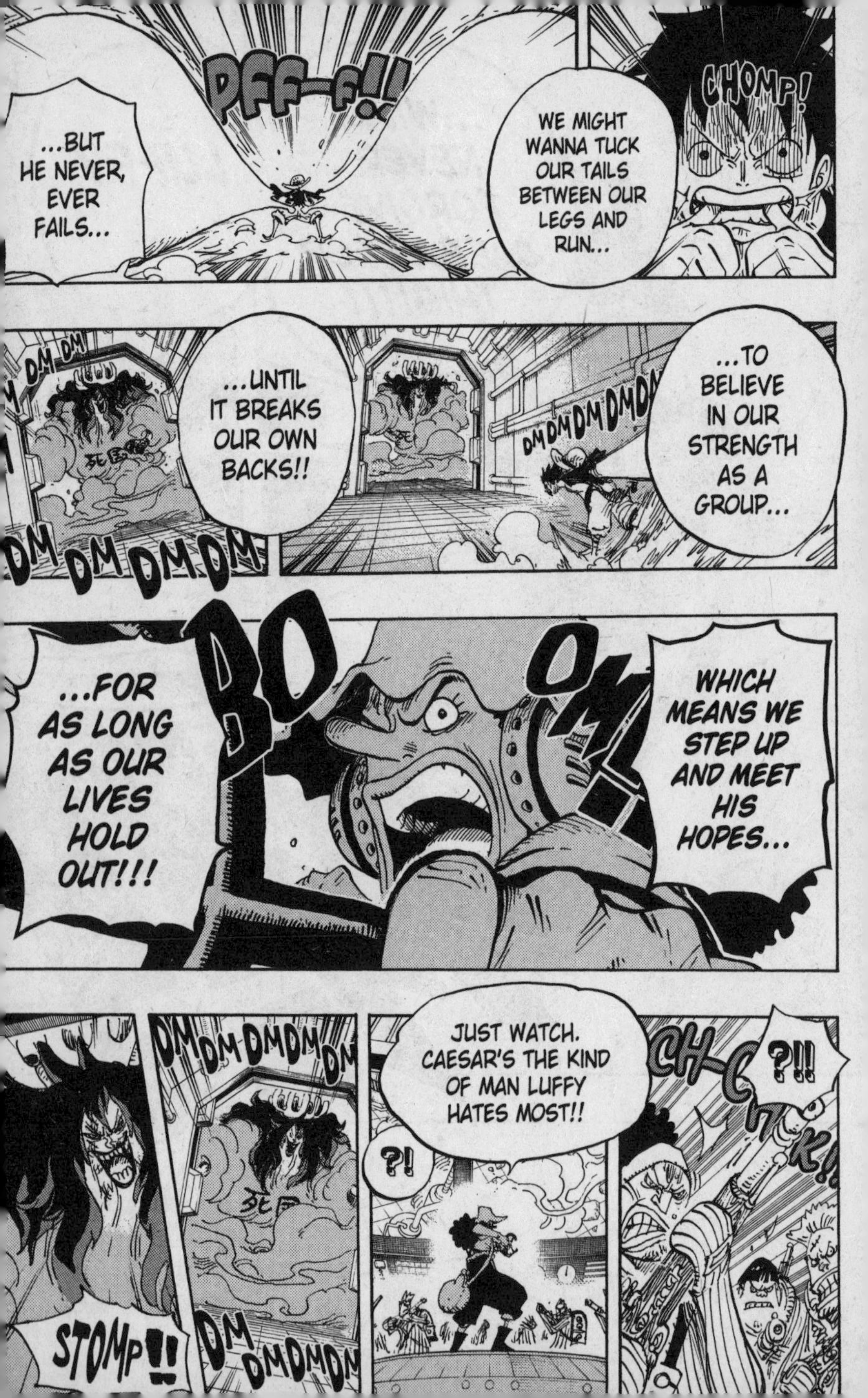
CHOMP!
WE MIGHT WANNA TUCK OUR TAILS BETWEEN OUR LEGS AND RUN...
PFF—F!!
...BUT HE NEVER, EVER FAILS...
...TO BELIEVE IN OUR STRENGTH AS A GROUP...
DM DM DM DM DMDM
...UNTIL IT BREAKS OUR OWN BACKS!!
DM DM DM
DM DM DMDM
WHICH MEANS WE STEP UP AND MEET HIS HOPES...
BOOM
...FOR AS LONG AS OUR LIVES HOLD OUT!!!
?!!
CH-CHK!!
JUST WATCH. CAESAR'S THE KIND OF MAN LUFFY HATES MOST!!
?!
DM DM DMDMDM DM
DM DMDMDM
STOMP!!

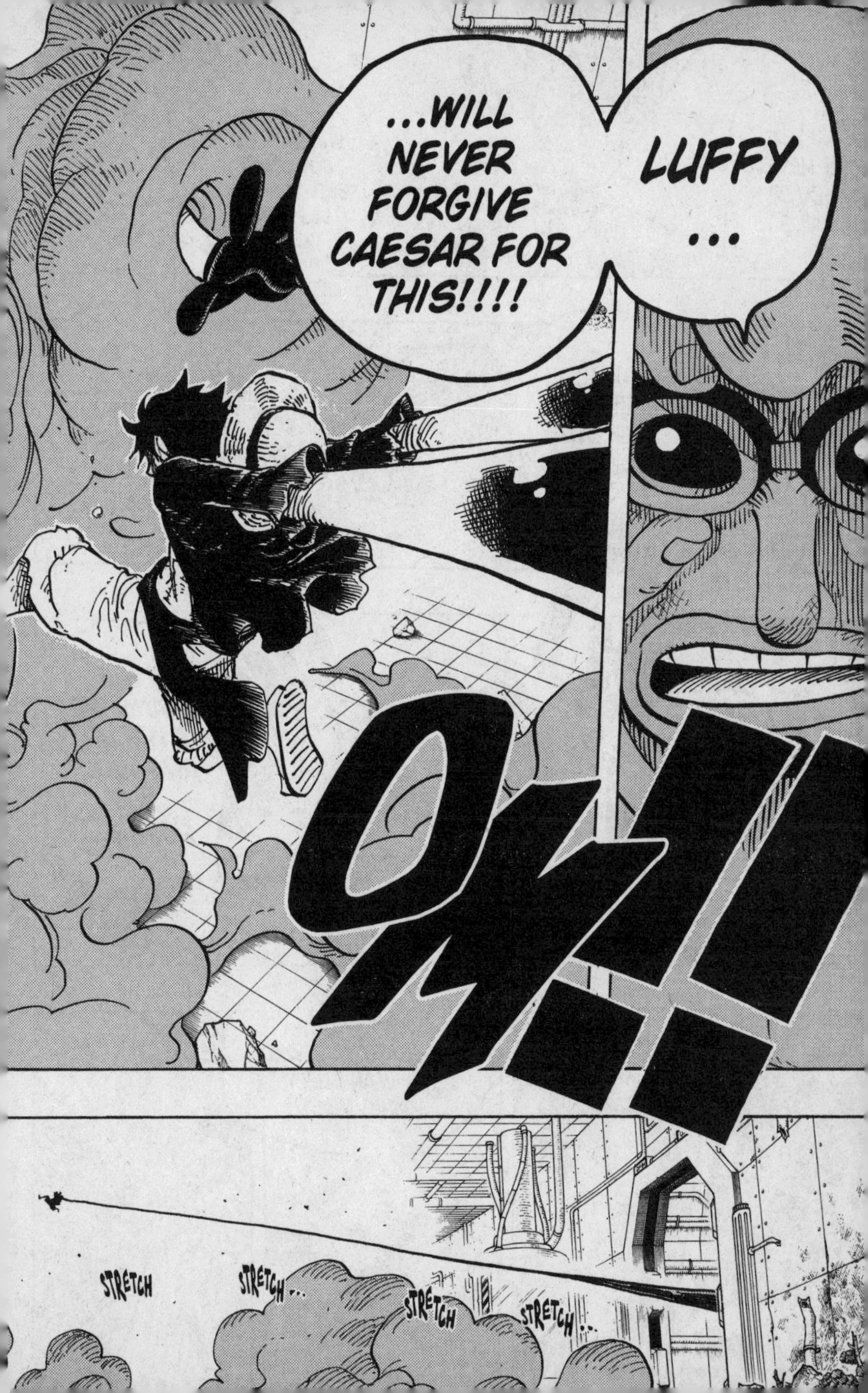
LUFFY ...
...WILL NEVER FORGIVE CAESAR FOR THIS!!!!
OH!!
STRETCH...
STRETCH
STRETCH...
STRETCH

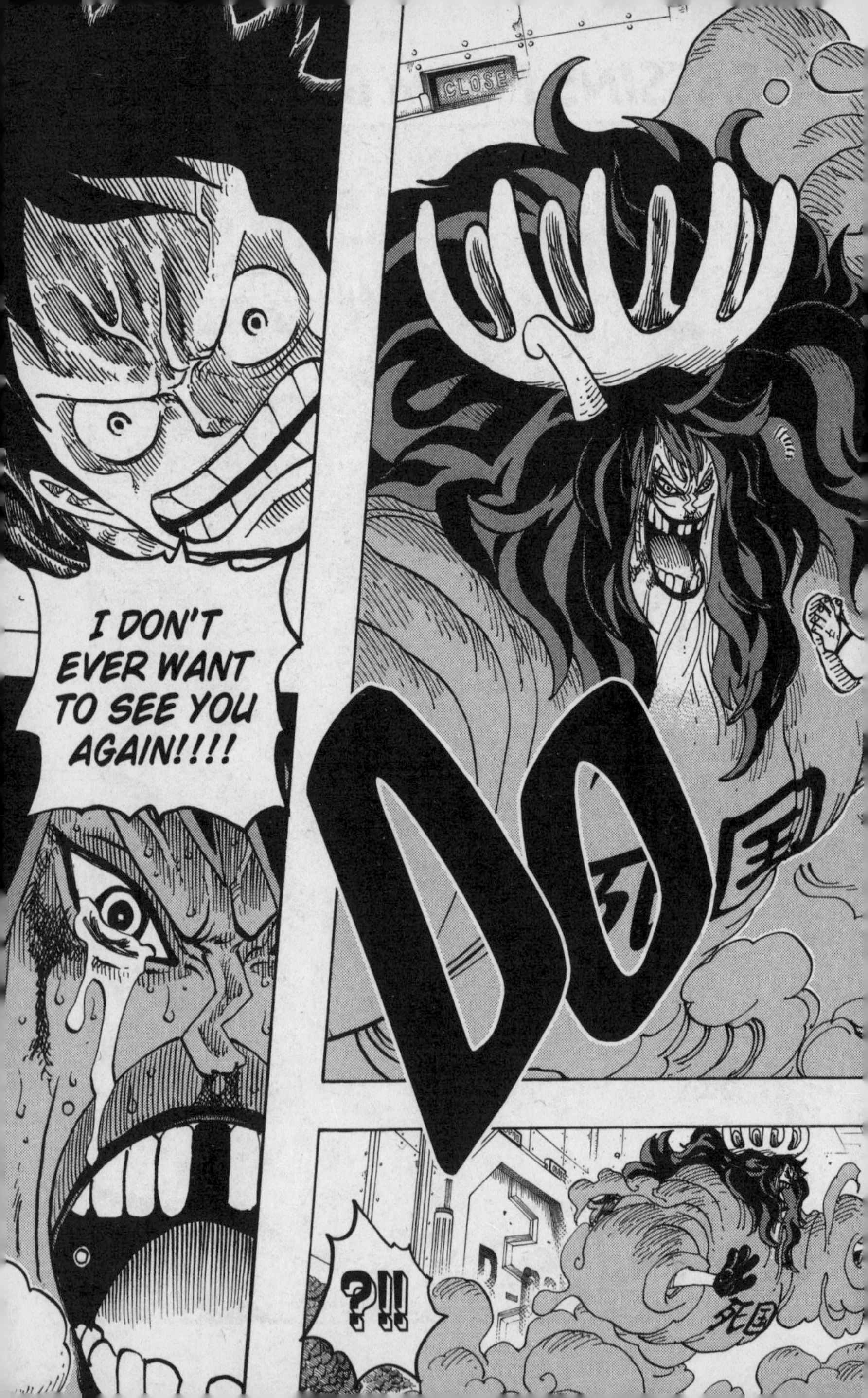
DO
?!!
I DON'T EVER WANT TO SEE YOU AGAIN!!!!

ASSASSINS FROM DRESSROSA

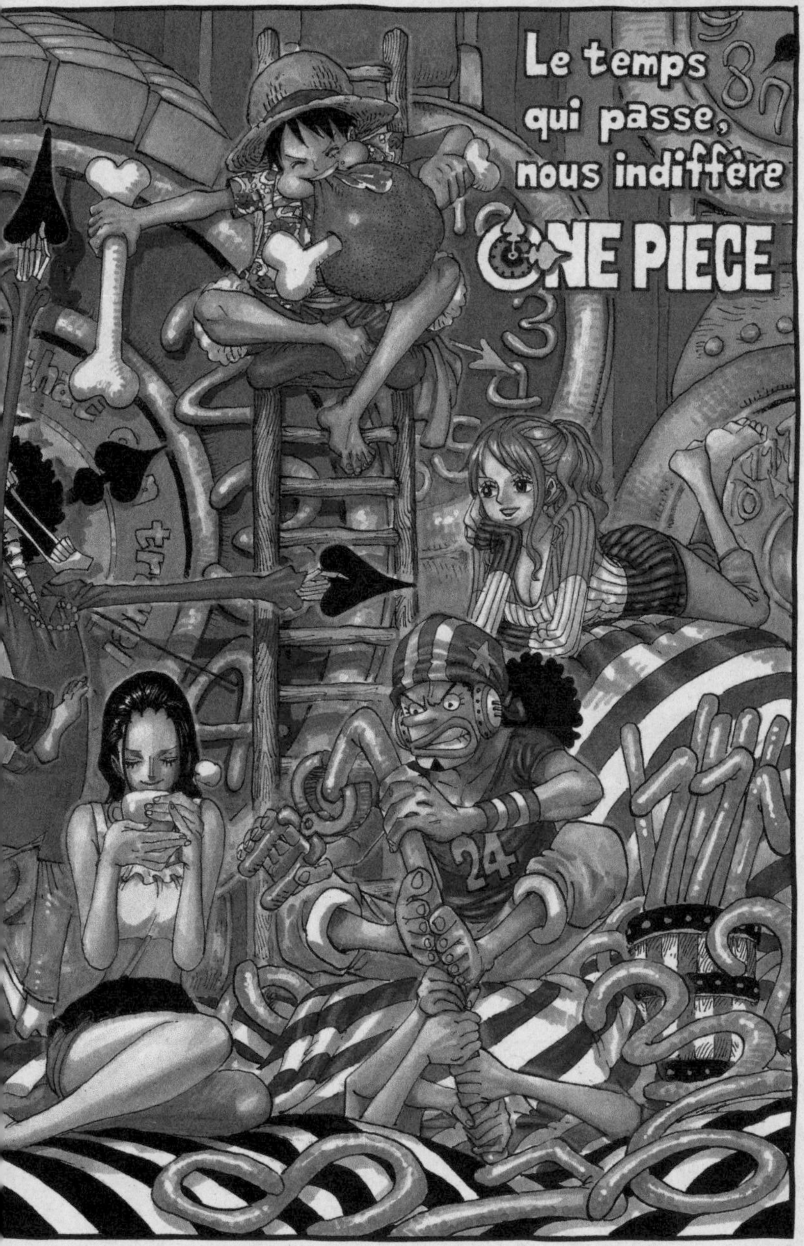
Le temps qui passe, nous indiffère
ONE PIECE

Chapter 692:

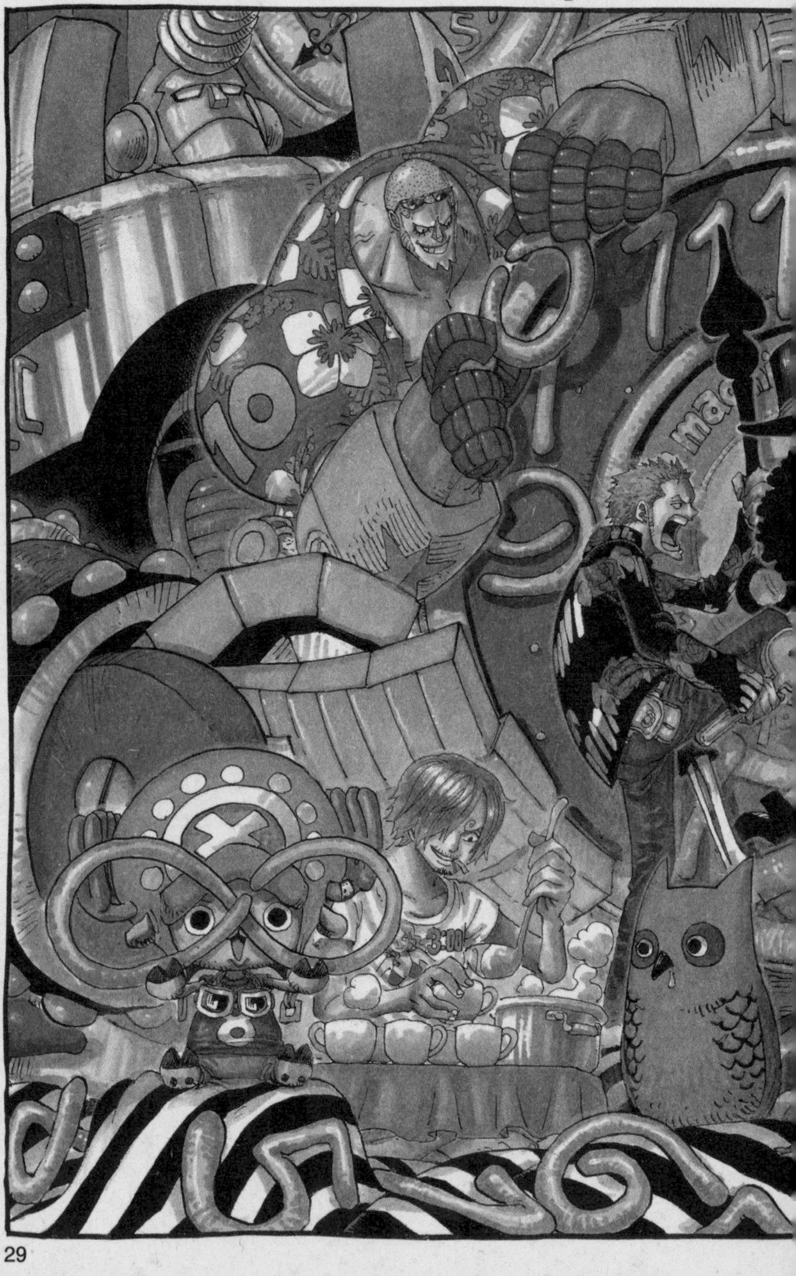

vol. 70
ONE PIECE

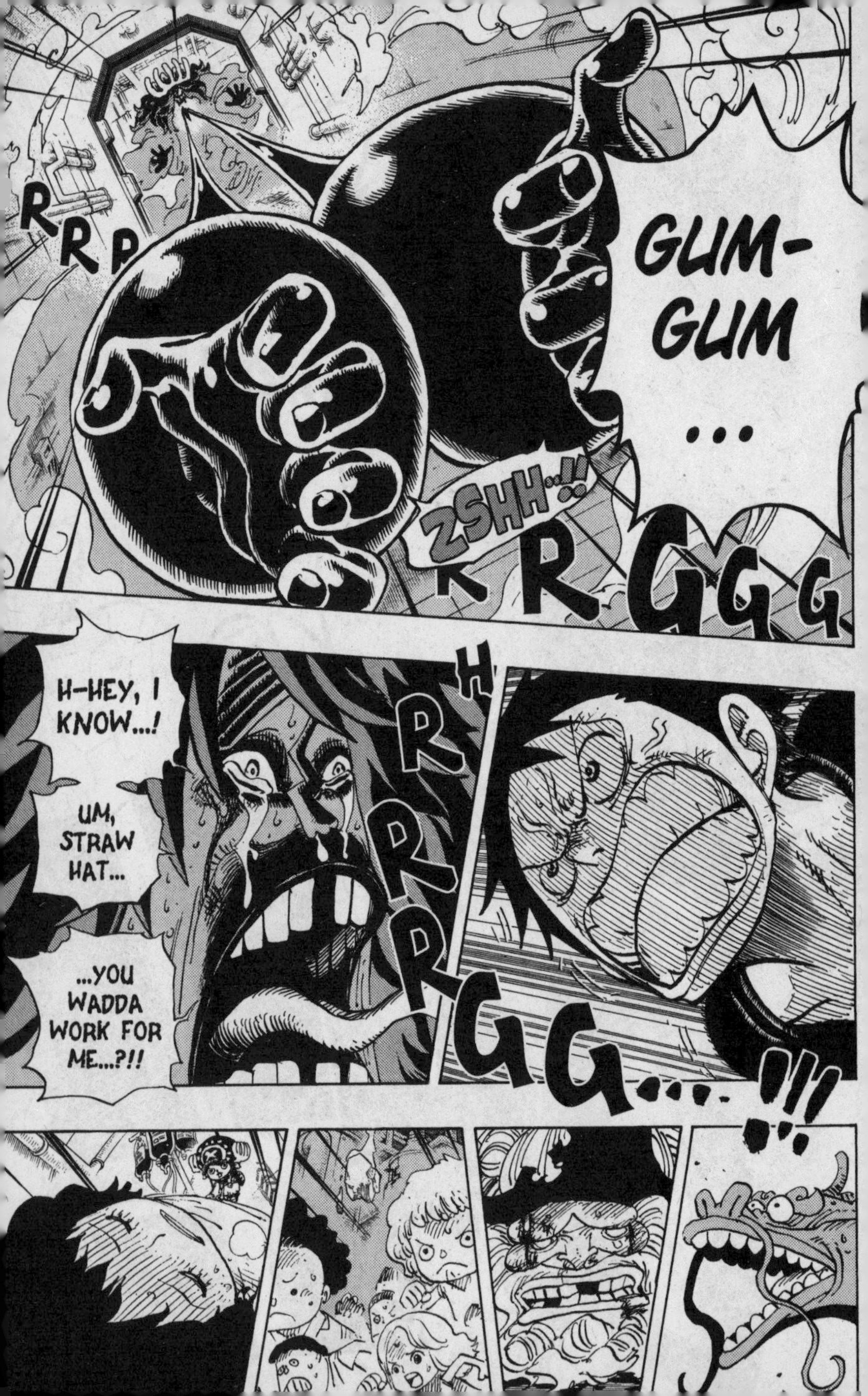
GUM-GUM ...
RRR
ZSHH..!!
RRGGGG
HRRRRGG...!!!
H-HEY, I KNOW...!
UM, STRAW HAT...
...YOU WADDA WORK FOR ME...?!!

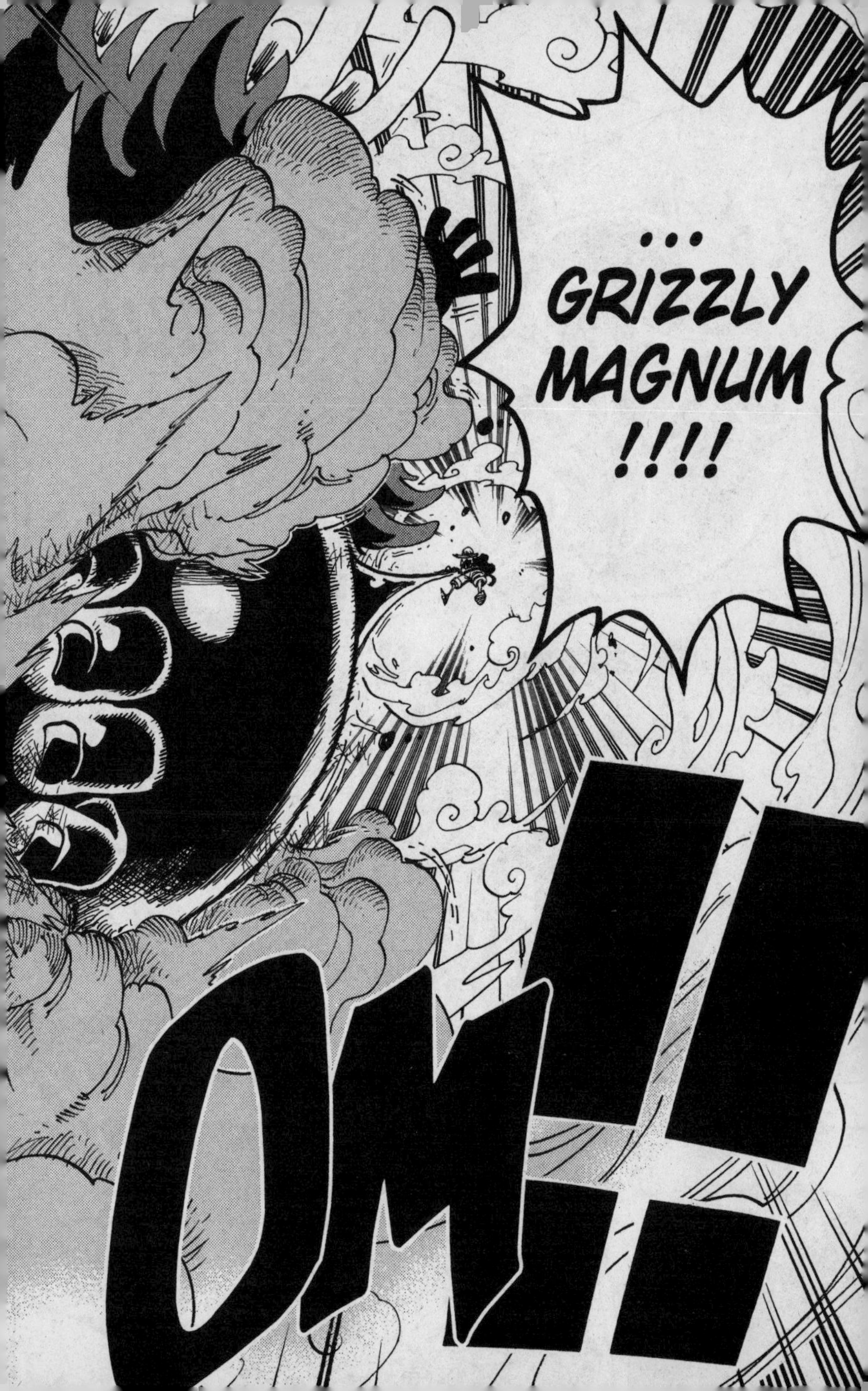
...GRIZZLY MAGNUM !!!!
OM!!!!

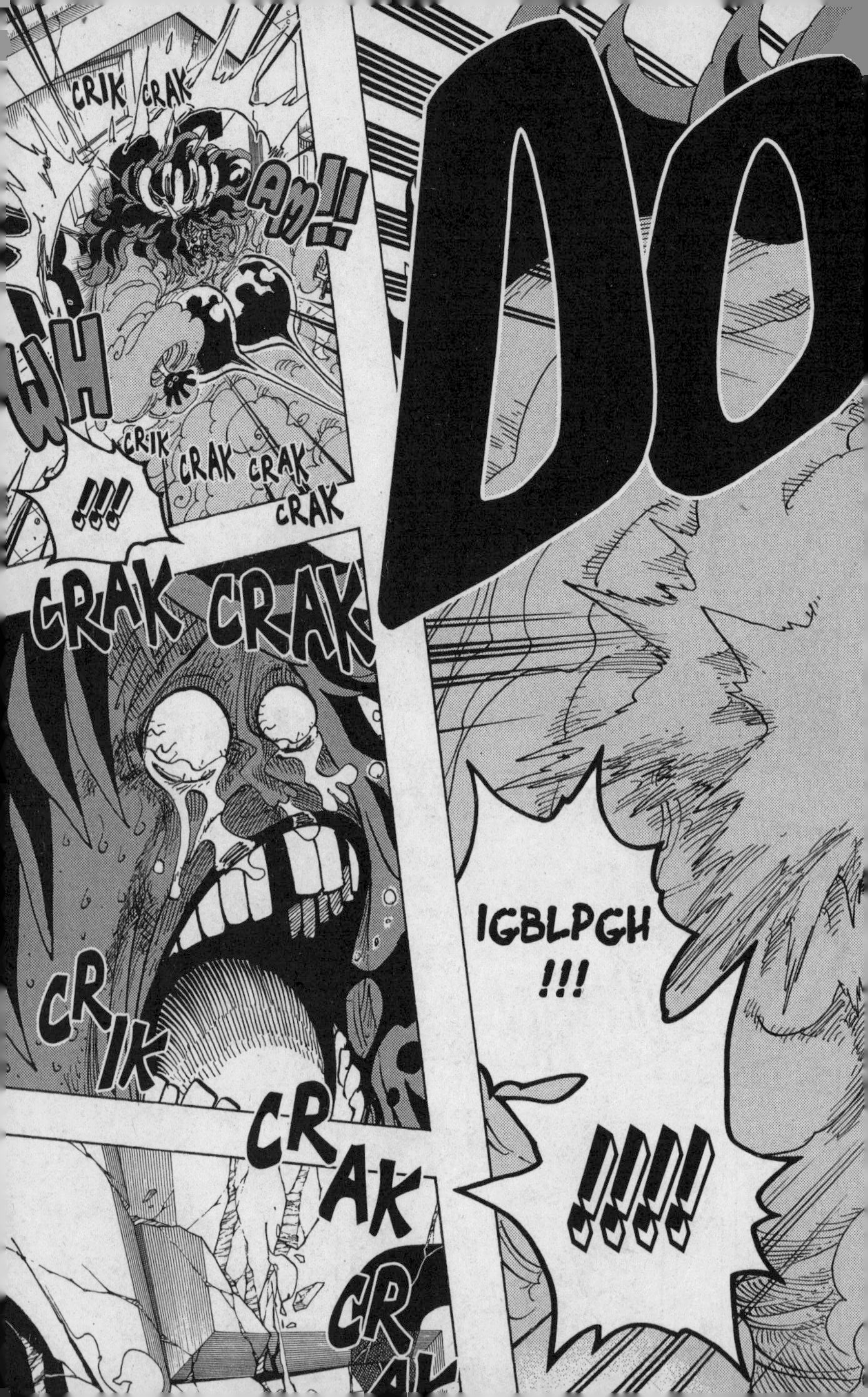
DO
IGBLPGH
!!!
!!!!!
CRIK CRAK
AM!!
WH
CRIK
CRAK CRAK
CRAK
!!!
CRAK CRAK
CRIK
CRAK
CR

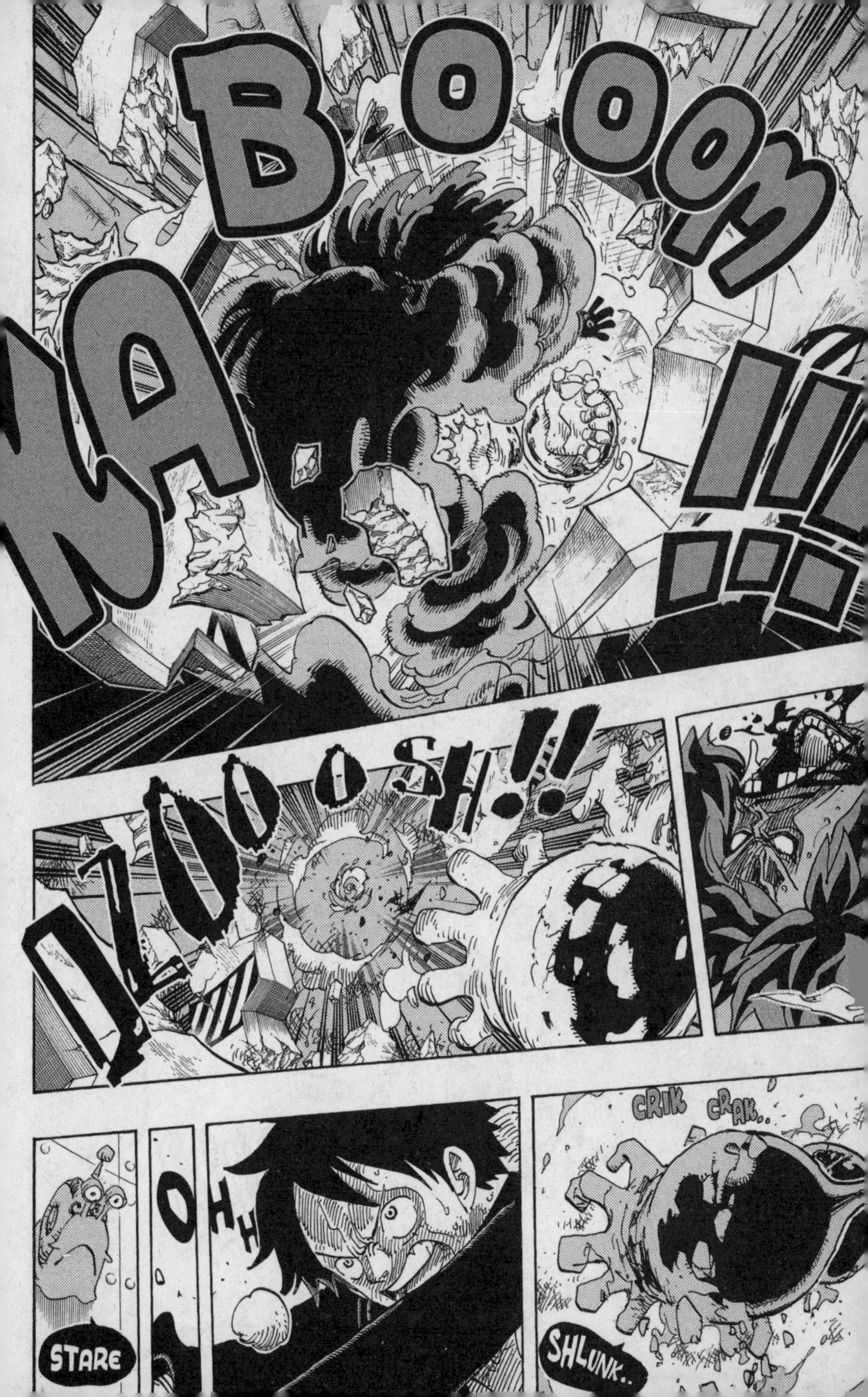
KA-BOOOM!!!
ZOOOSH!!
CRIK CRAK..
SHLUNK..
OHH
STARE

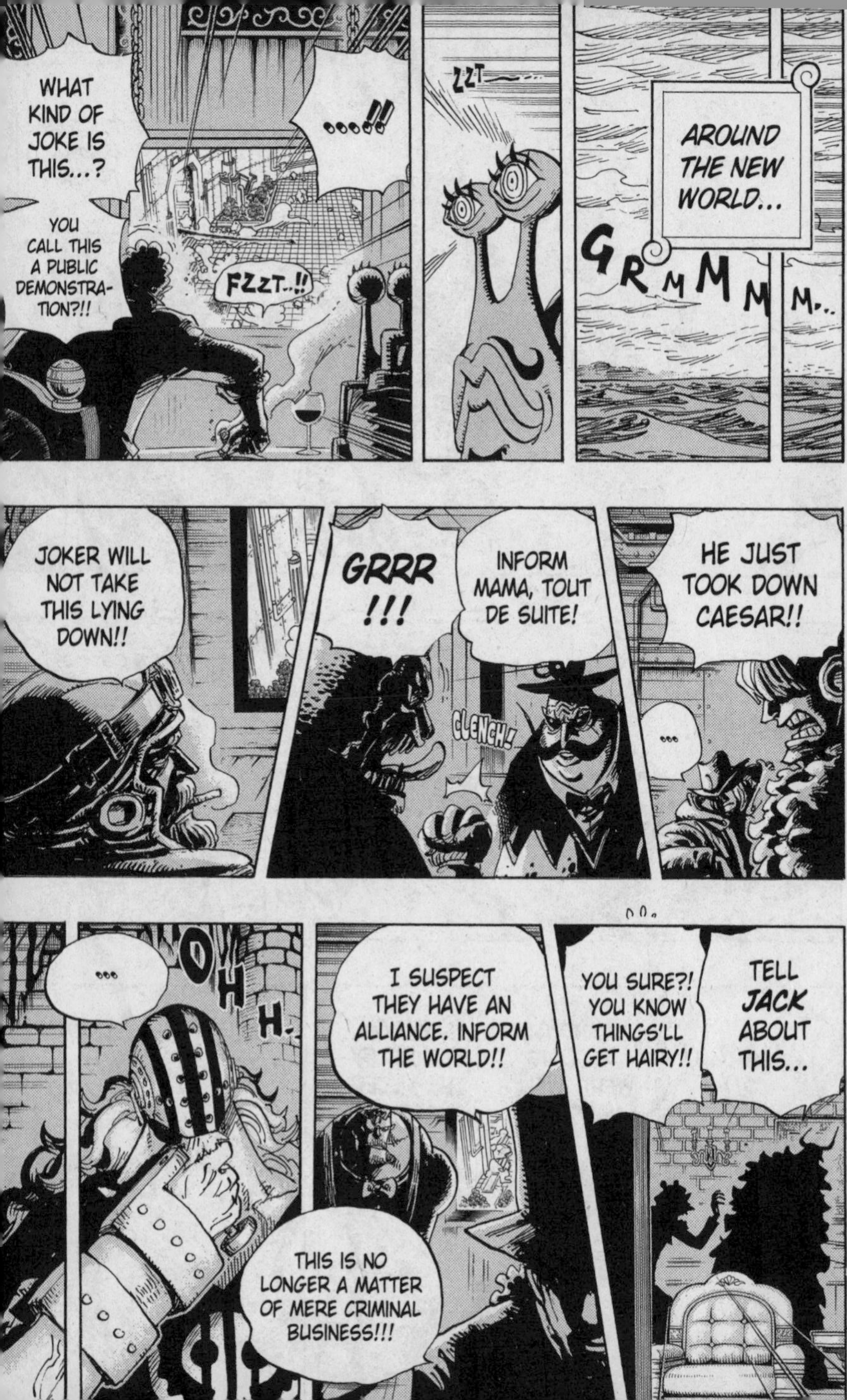
AROUND THE NEW WORLD...
GRMMMMM..
ZZT—
...!!
WHAT KIND OF JOKE IS THIS...?
YOU CALL THIS A PUBLIC DEMONSTRATION?!!
FZZT..!!
HE JUST TOOK DOWN CAESAR!!
...
INFORM MAMA, TOUT DE SUITE!
GRRR!!!
CLENCH!
JOKER WILL NOT TAKE THIS LYING DOWN!!
TELL JACK ABOUT THIS...
YOU SURE?! YOU KNOW THINGS'LL GET HAIRY!!
I SUSPECT THEY HAVE AN ALLIANCE. INFORM THE WORLD!!
THIS IS NO LONGER A MATTER OF MERE CRIMINAL BUSINESS!!!
OHH.
...

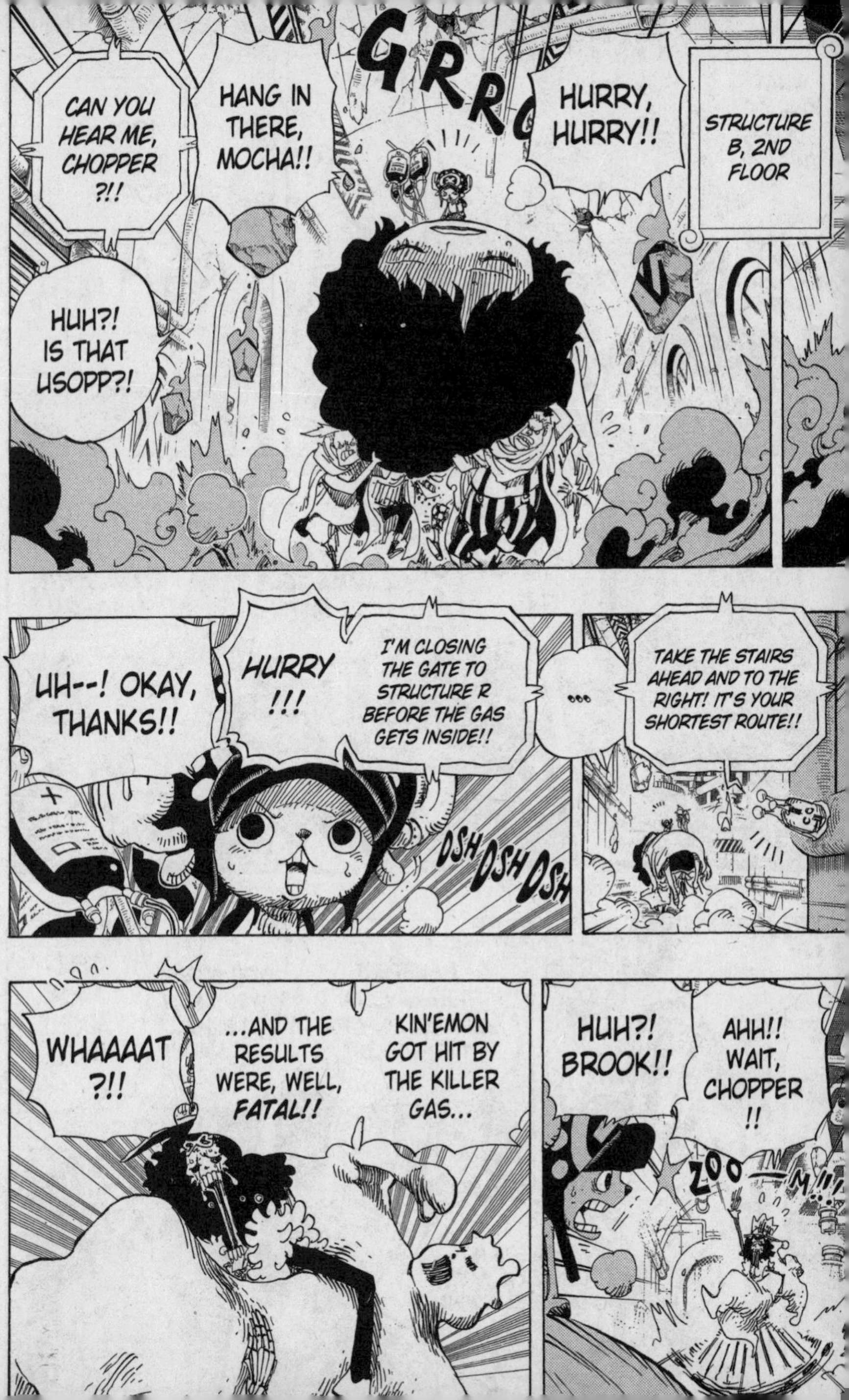
STRUCTURE B, 2ND FLOOR
HURRY, HURRY!!
GRRO
HANG IN THERE, MOCHA!!
CAN YOU HEAR ME, CHOPPER ?!!
HUH?! IS THAT USOPP?!
TAKE THE STAIRS AHEAD AND TO THE RIGHT! IT'S YOUR SHORTEST ROUTE!!
...
I'M CLOSING THE GATE TO STRUCTURE R BEFORE THE GAS GETS INSIDE!!
HURRY !!!
UH--! OKAY, THANKS!!
DSH DSH DSH
AHH!! WAIT, CHOPPER !!
HUH?! BROOK!!
ZOOOM!!
KIN'EMON GOT HIT BY THE KILLER GAS...
...AND THE RESULTS WERE, WELL, FATAL!!
WHAAAAT ?!!

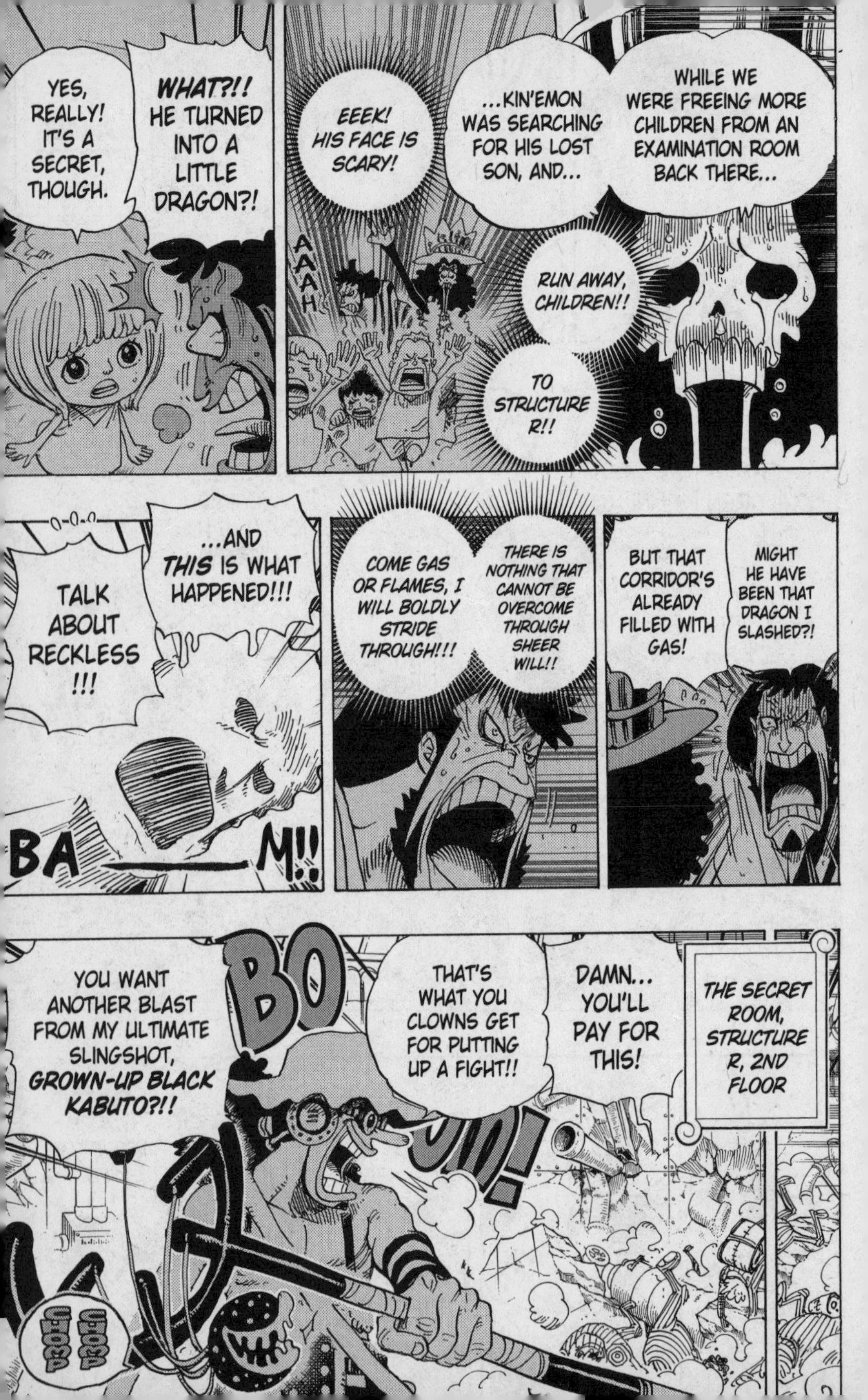
WHILE WE WERE FREEING MORE CHILDREN FROM AN EXAMINATION ROOM BACK THERE...
...KIN'EMON WAS SEARCHING FOR HIS LOST SON, AND...
RUN AWAY, CHILDREN!!
TO STRUCTURE R!!
EEEK! HIS FACE IS SCARY!
AAAH
WHAT?!! HE TURNED INTO A LITTLE DRAGON?!
YES, REALLY! IT'S A SECRET, THOUGH.
MIGHT HE HAVE BEEN THAT DRAGON I SLASHED?!
BUT THAT CORRIDOR'S ALREADY FILLED WITH GAS!
THERE IS NOTHING THAT CANNOT BE OVERCOME THROUGH SHEER WILL!!
COME GAS OR FLAMES, I WILL BOLDLY STRIDE THROUGH!!!
...AND THIS IS WHAT HAPPENED!!!
TALK ABOUT RECKLESS!!!
BA—M!!
THE SECRET ROOM, STRUCTURE R, 2ND FLOOR
DAMN... YOU'LL PAY FOR THIS!
THAT'S WHAT YOU CLOWNS GET FOR PUTTING UP A FIGHT!!
BO
YOU WANT ANOTHER BLAST FROM MY ULTIMATE SLINGSHOT, GROWN-UP BLACK KABUTO?!!

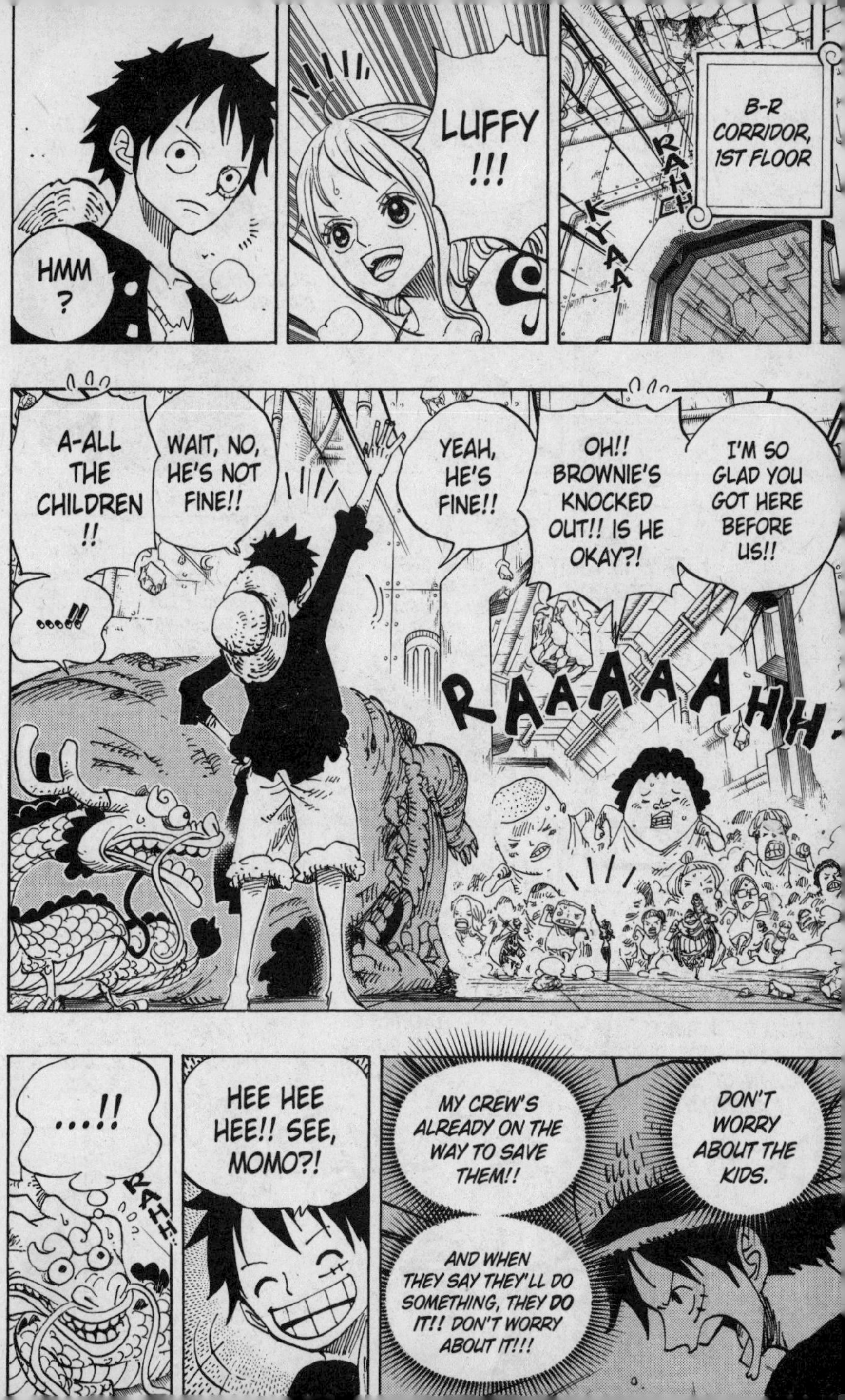
B-R CORRIDOR, 1ST FLOOR
RAHH
KYAA
LUFFY!!!
HMM?
I'M SO GLAD YOU GOT HERE BEFORE US!!
OH!! BROWNIE'S KNOCKED OUT!! IS HE OKAY?!
YEAH, HE'S FINE!!
WAIT, NO, HE'S NOT FINE!!
A-ALL THE CHILDREN!!
....!!
RAAAAAHH
DON'T WORRY ABOUT THE KIDS.
MY CREW'S ALREADY ON THE WAY TO SAVE THEM!!
AND WHEN THEY SAY THEY'LL DO SOMETHING, THEY DO IT!! DON'T WORRY ABOUT IT!!!
HEE HEE HEE!! SEE, MOMO?!
...!!
RAHH

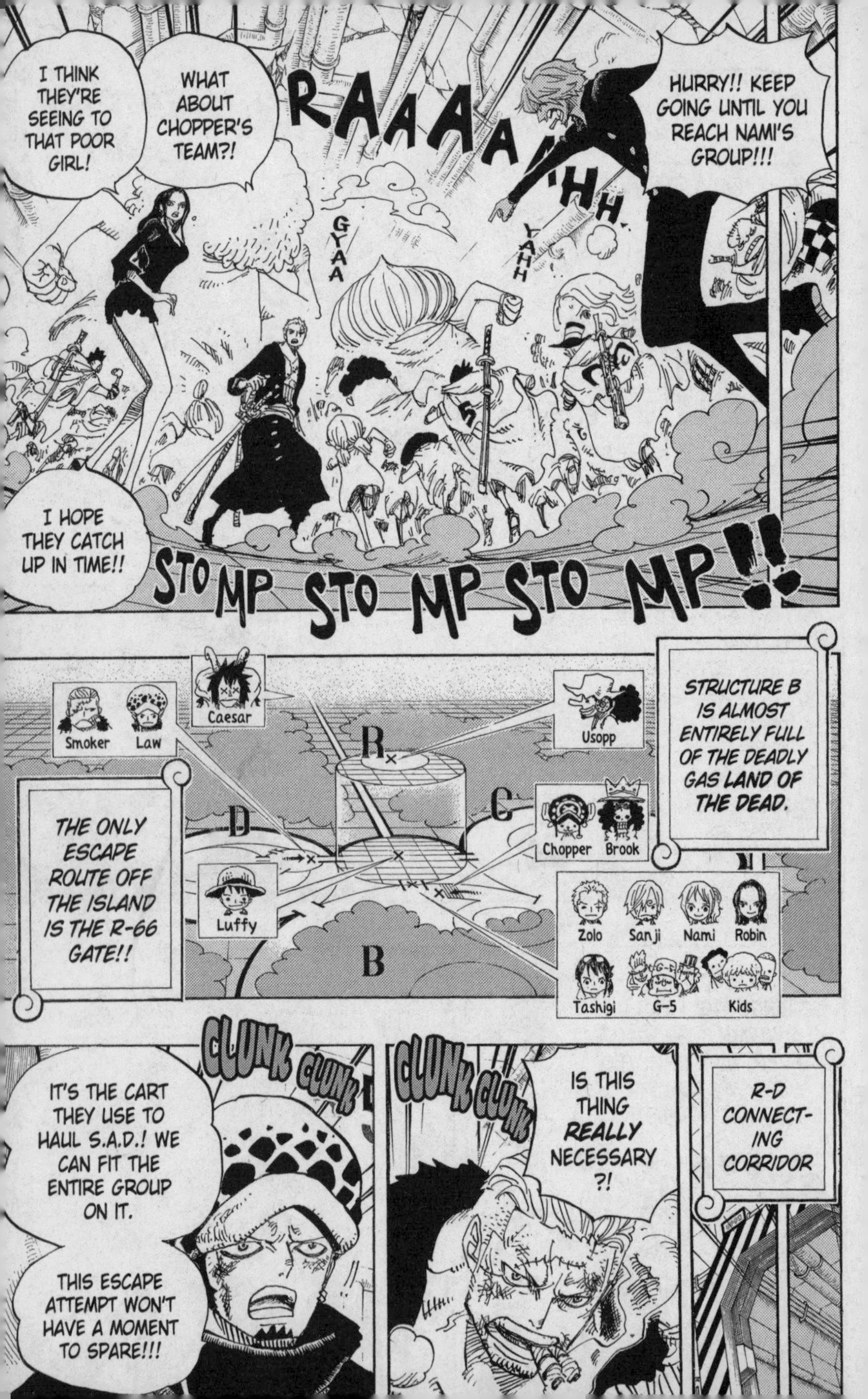
HURRY!! KEEP GOING UNTIL YOU REACH NAMI'S GROUP!!!
RAAAAAHH
YAHH
GYAA
WHAT ABOUT CHOPPER'S TEAM?!
I THINK THEY'RE SEEING TO THAT POOR GIRL!
I HOPE THEY CATCH UP IN TIME!!
STOMP STOMP STOMP!!
STRUCTURE B IS ALMOST ENTIRELY FULL OF THE DEADLY GAS LAND OF THE DEAD.
Usopp
Caesar
Smoker Law
R
C
Chopper Brook
D
Zolo Sanji Nami Robin
Tashigi G-5 Kids
Luffy
B
THE ONLY ESCAPE ROUTE OFF THE ISLAND IS THE R-66 GATE!!
R-D CONNECTING CORRIDOR
IS THIS THING REALLY NECESSARY?!
CLUNK CLUNK
CLUNK CLUNK
IT'S THE CART THEY USE TO HAUL S.A.D.! WE CAN FIT THE ENTIRE GROUP ON IT.
THIS ESCAPE ATTEMPT WON'T HAVE A MOMENT TO SPARE!!!

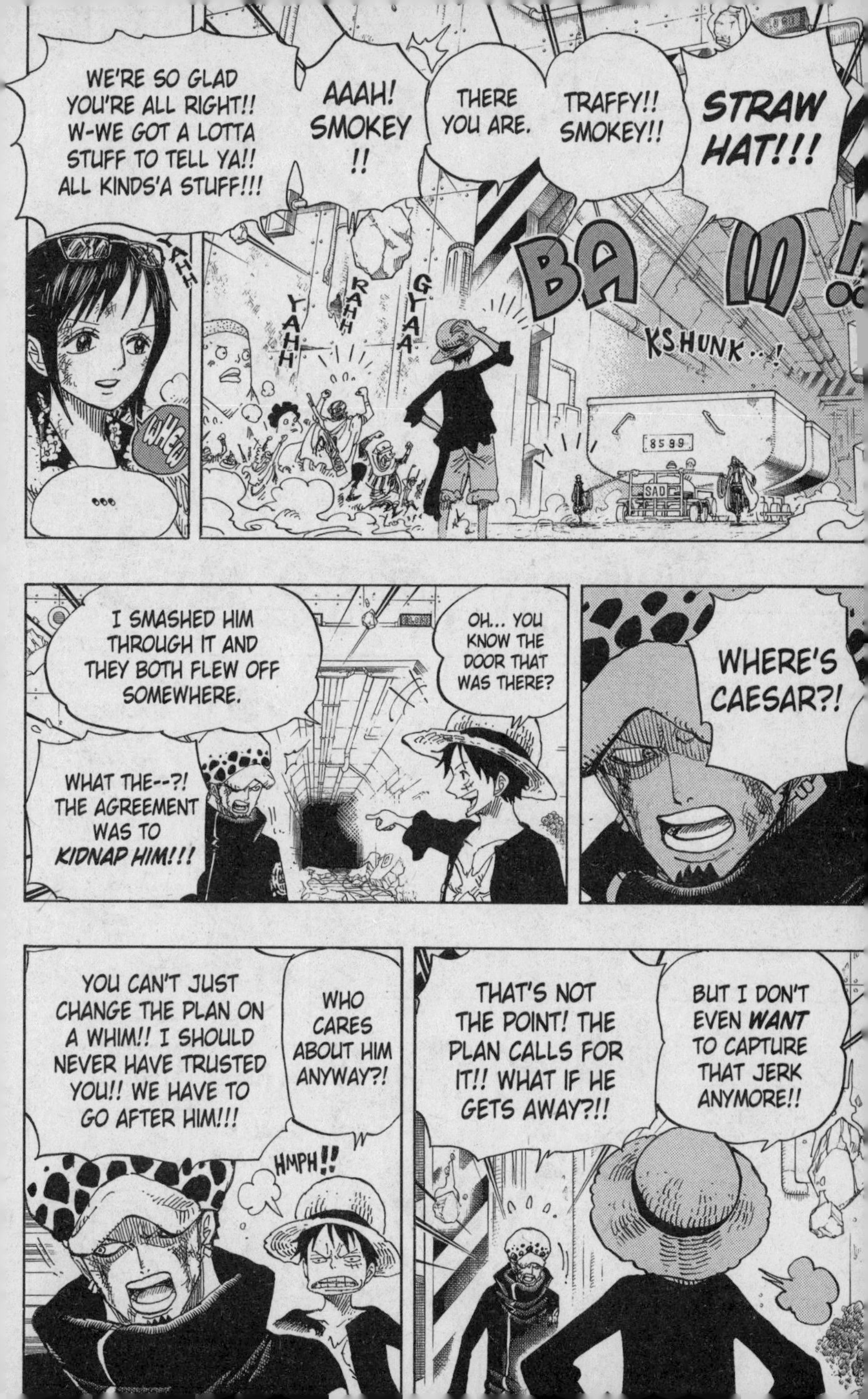
STRAW HAT!!!
TRAFFY!! SMOKEY!!
THERE YOU ARE.
AAAH! SMOKEY !!
WE'RE SO GLAD YOU'RE ALL RIGHT!! W-WE GOT A LOTTA STUFF TO TELL YA!! ALL KINDS'A STUFF!!!
BAM!!
KSHUNK...!
GYAA
RAHH
YAHH
YAHH
WHEW
...
WHERE'S CAESAR?!
OH... YOU KNOW THE DOOR THAT WAS THERE?
I SMASHED HIM THROUGH IT AND THEY BOTH FLEW OFF SOMEWHERE.
WHAT THE--?! THE AGREEMENT WAS TO KIDNAP HIM!!!
BUT I DON'T EVEN WANT TO CAPTURE THAT JERK ANYMORE!!
THAT'S NOT THE POINT! THE PLAN CALLS FOR IT!! WHAT IF HE GETS AWAY?!!
WHO CARES ABOUT HIM ANYWAY?!
HMPH!!
YOU CAN'T JUST CHANGE THE PLAN ON A WHIM!! I SHOULD NEVER HAVE TRUSTED YOU!! WE HAVE TO GO AFTER HIM!!!

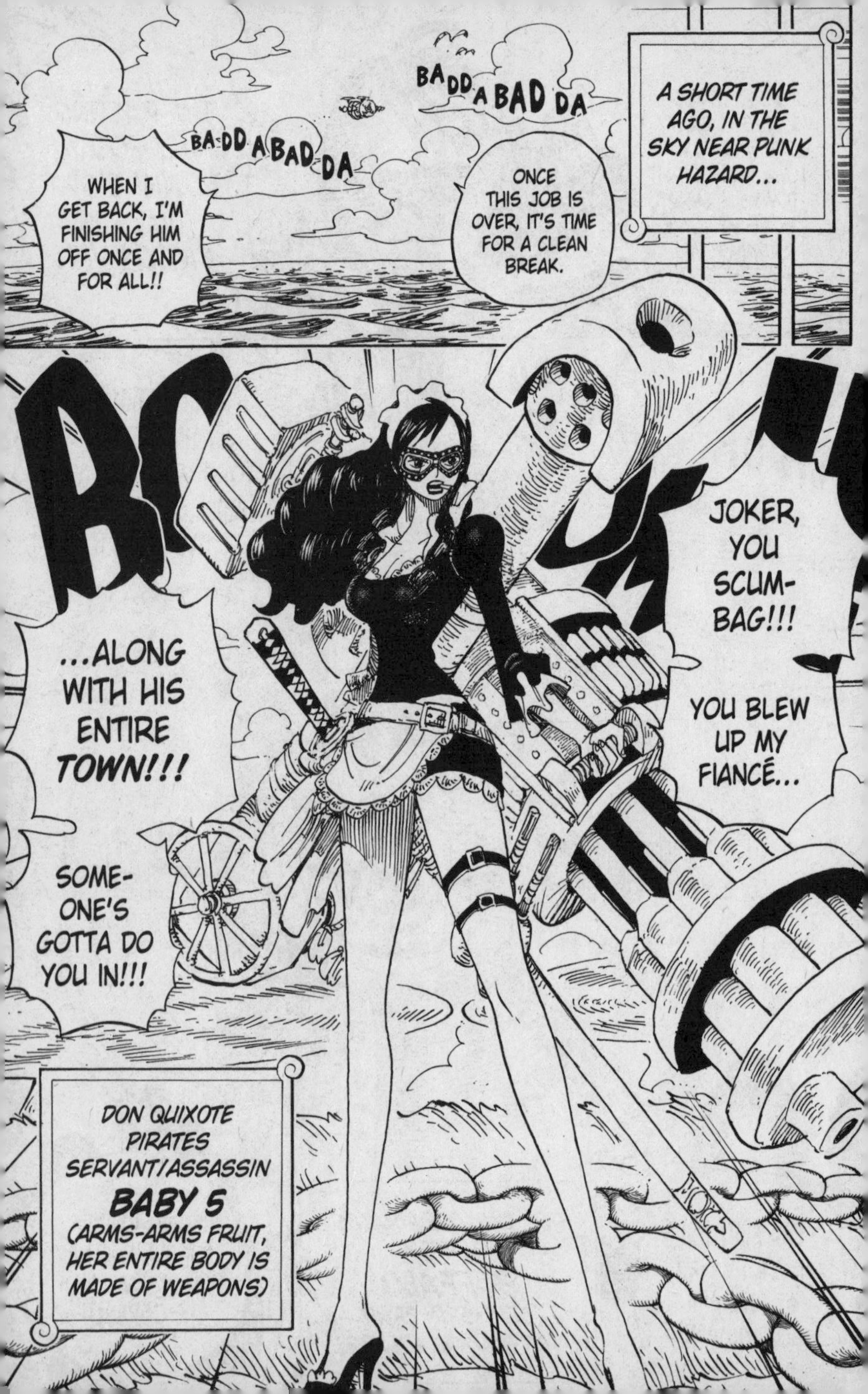
A SHORT TIME AGO, IN THE SKY NEAR PUNK HAZARD...
BADDA BAD DA
ONCE THIS JOB IS OVER, IT'S TIME FOR A CLEAN BREAK.
BADDA BAD DA
WHEN I GET BACK, I'M FINISHING HIM OFF ONCE AND FOR ALL!!
JOKER, YOU SCUM-BAG!!!
YOU BLEW UP MY FIANCÉ...
...ALONG WITH HIS ENTIRE TOWN!!!
SOME-ONE'S GOTTA DO YOU IN!!!
DON QUIXOTE PIRATES SERVANT/ASSASSIN BABY 5 (ARMS-ARMS FRUIT, HER ENTIRE BODY IS MADE OF WEAPONS)

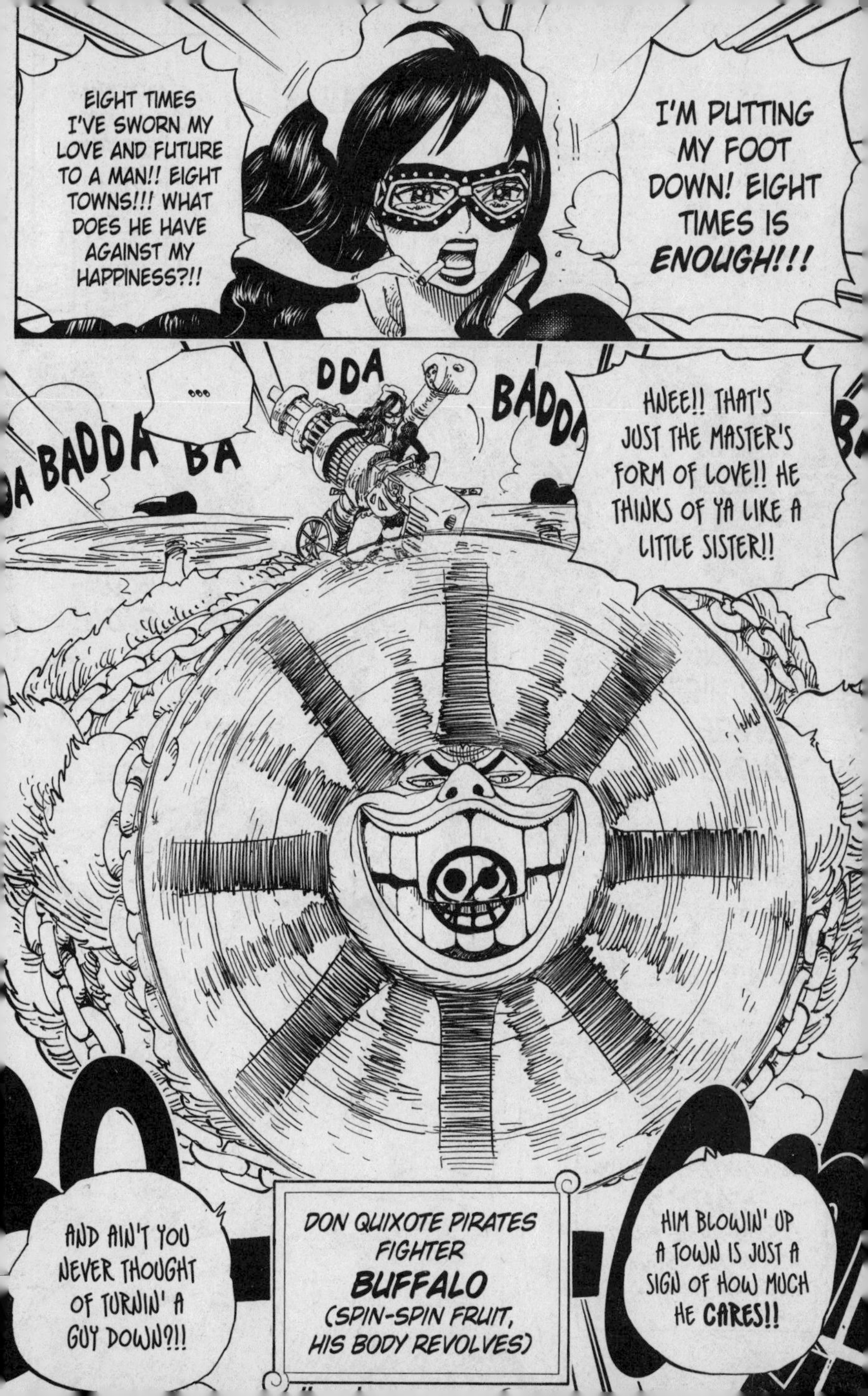
I'M PUTTING MY FOOT DOWN! EIGHT TIMES IS ENOUGH!!!
EIGHT TIMES I'VE SWORN MY LOVE AND FUTURE TO A MAN!! EIGHT TOWNS!!! WHAT DOES HE HAVE AGAINST MY HAPPINESS?!!
HNEE!! THAT'S JUST THE MASTER'S FORM OF LOVE!! HE THINKS OF YA LIKE A LITTLE SISTER!!
BADD
DDA
...
DA BADDA BA
HIM BLOWIN' UP A TOWN IS JUST A SIGN OF HOW MUCH HE CARES!!
DON QUIXOTE PIRATES FIGHTER
BUFFALO
(SPIN-SPIN FRUIT, HIS BODY REVOLVES)
AND AIN'T YOU NEVER THOUGHT OF TURNIN' A GUY DOWN?!!

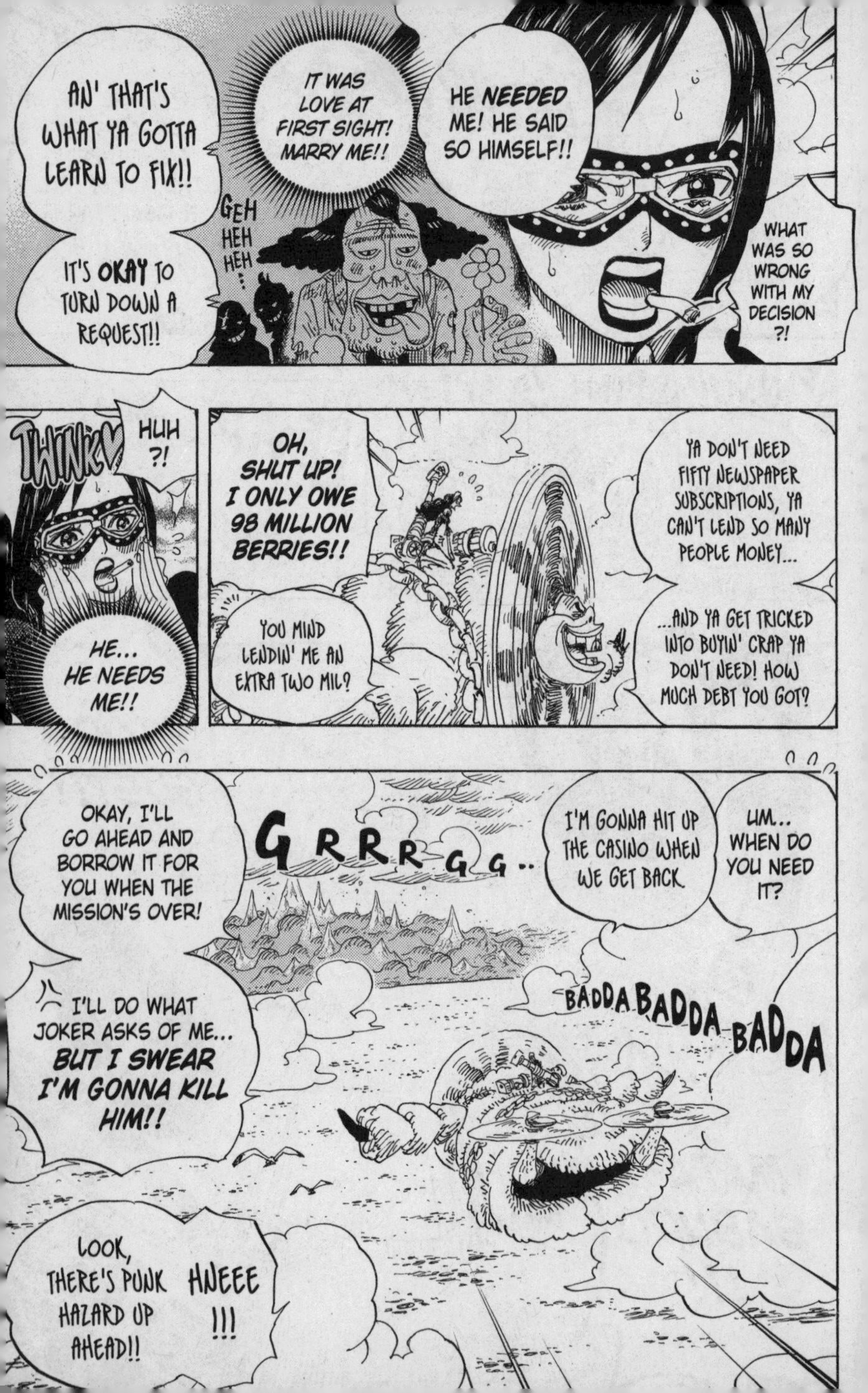
WHAT WAS SO WRONG WITH MY DECISION?!
HE NEEDED ME! HE SAID SO HIMSELF!!
IT WAS LOVE AT FIRST SIGHT! MARRY ME!!
GEH HEH HEH...
AN' THAT'S WHAT YA GOTTA LEARN TO FIX!!
IT'S OKAY TO TURN DOWN A REQUEST!!
YA DON'T NEED FIFTY NEWSPAPER SUBSCRIPTIONS, YA CAN'T LEND SO MANY PEOPLE MONEY...
...AND YA GET TRICKED INTO BUYIN' CRAP YA DON'T NEED! HOW MUCH DEBT YOU GOT?
OH, SHUT UP! I ONLY OWE 98 MILLION BERRIES!!
YOU MIND LENDIN' ME AN EXTRA TWO MIL?
THINK♥
HUH?!
HE... HE NEEDS ME!!
UM.. WHEN DO YOU NEED IT?
I'M GONNA HIT UP THE CASINO WHEN WE GET BACK
OKAY, I'LL GO AHEAD AND BORROW IT FOR YOU WHEN THE MISSION'S OVER!
GRRRRGG..
BADDA BADDA BADDA
I'LL DO WHAT JOKER ASKS OF ME... BUT I SWEAR I'M GONNA KILL HIM!!
HNEEE!!!
LOOK, THERE'S PUNK HAZARD UP AHEAD!!

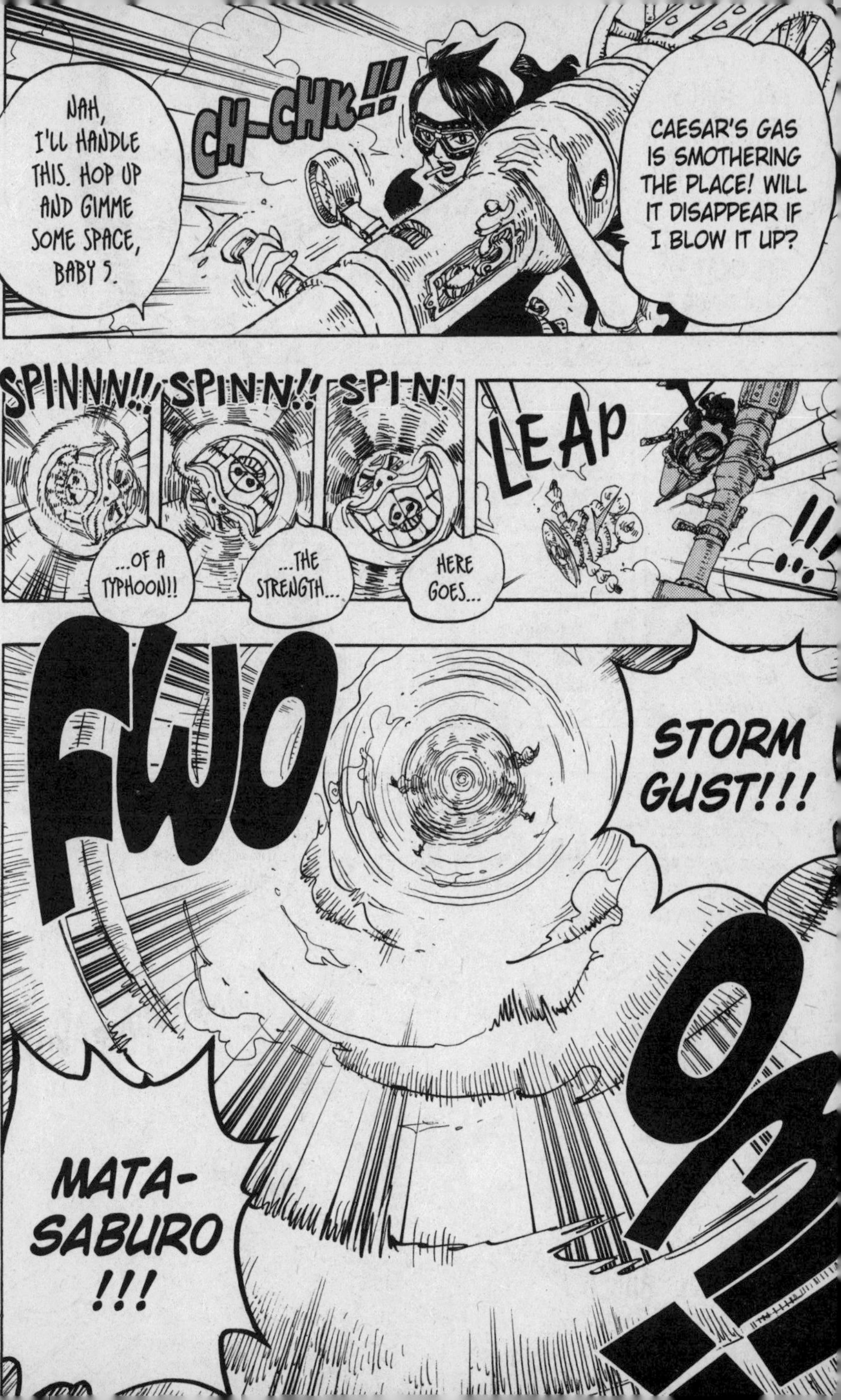
CAESAR'S GAS IS SMOTHERING THE PLACE! WILL IT DISAPPEAR IF I BLOW IT UP?
CH-CHK!!
NAH, I'LL HANDLE THIS. HOP UP AND GIMME SOME SPACE, BABY 5.
LEAP
SPIN!
HERE GOES...
SPINN!!
...THE STRENGTH...
SPINNN!!
...OF A TYPHOON!!
STORM GUST!!!
FWO
MATA-SABURO!!!

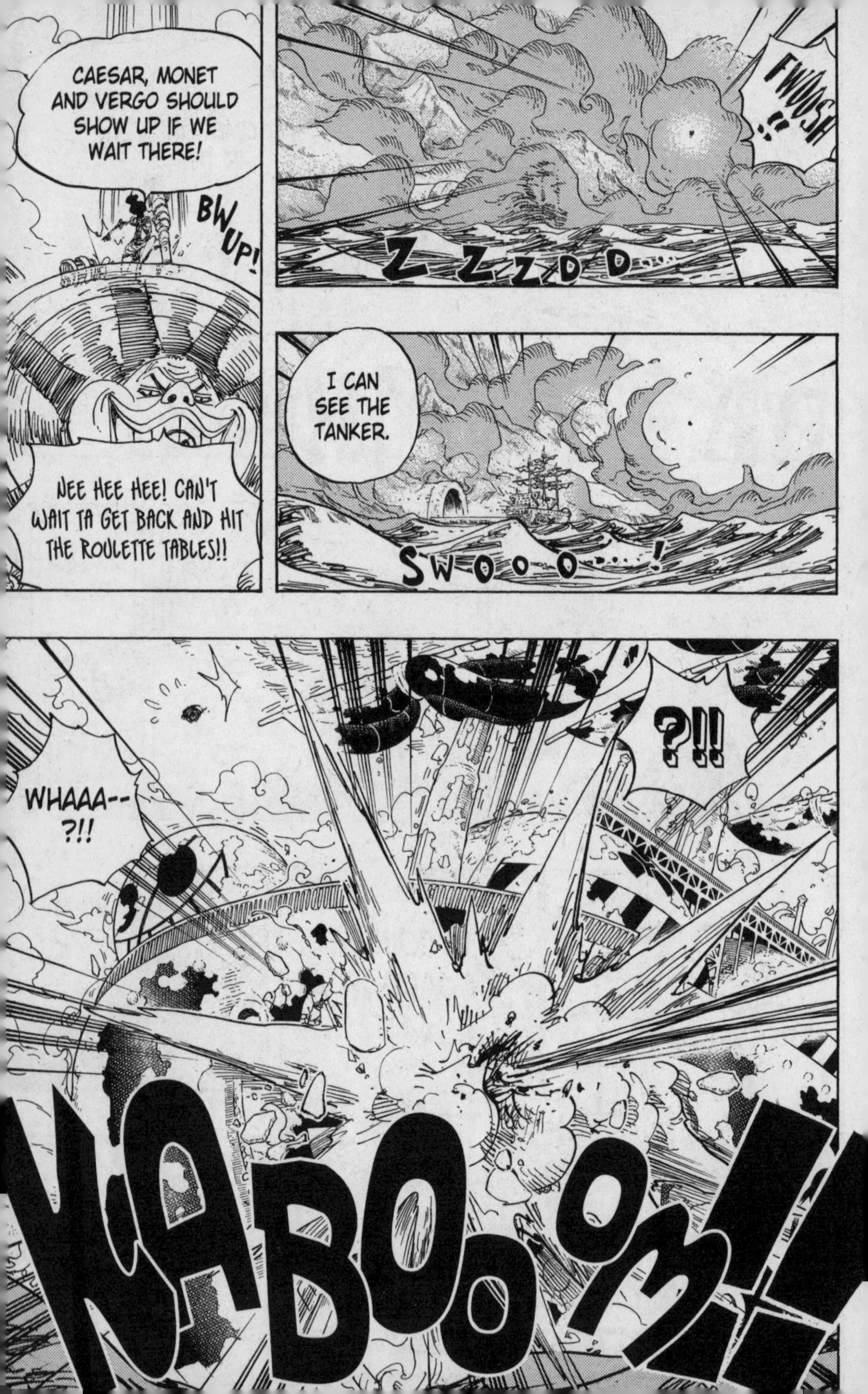
FWOOSH ...!!
ZZZDD...
I CAN SEE THE TANKER.
SWOOO...!
CAESAR, MONET AND VERGO SHOULD SHOW UP IF WE WAIT THERE!
BWUP!
NEE HEE HEE! CAN'T WAIT TA GET BACK AND HIT THE ROULETTE TABLES!!
?!!
WHAAA-- ?!!
KABOOM!!

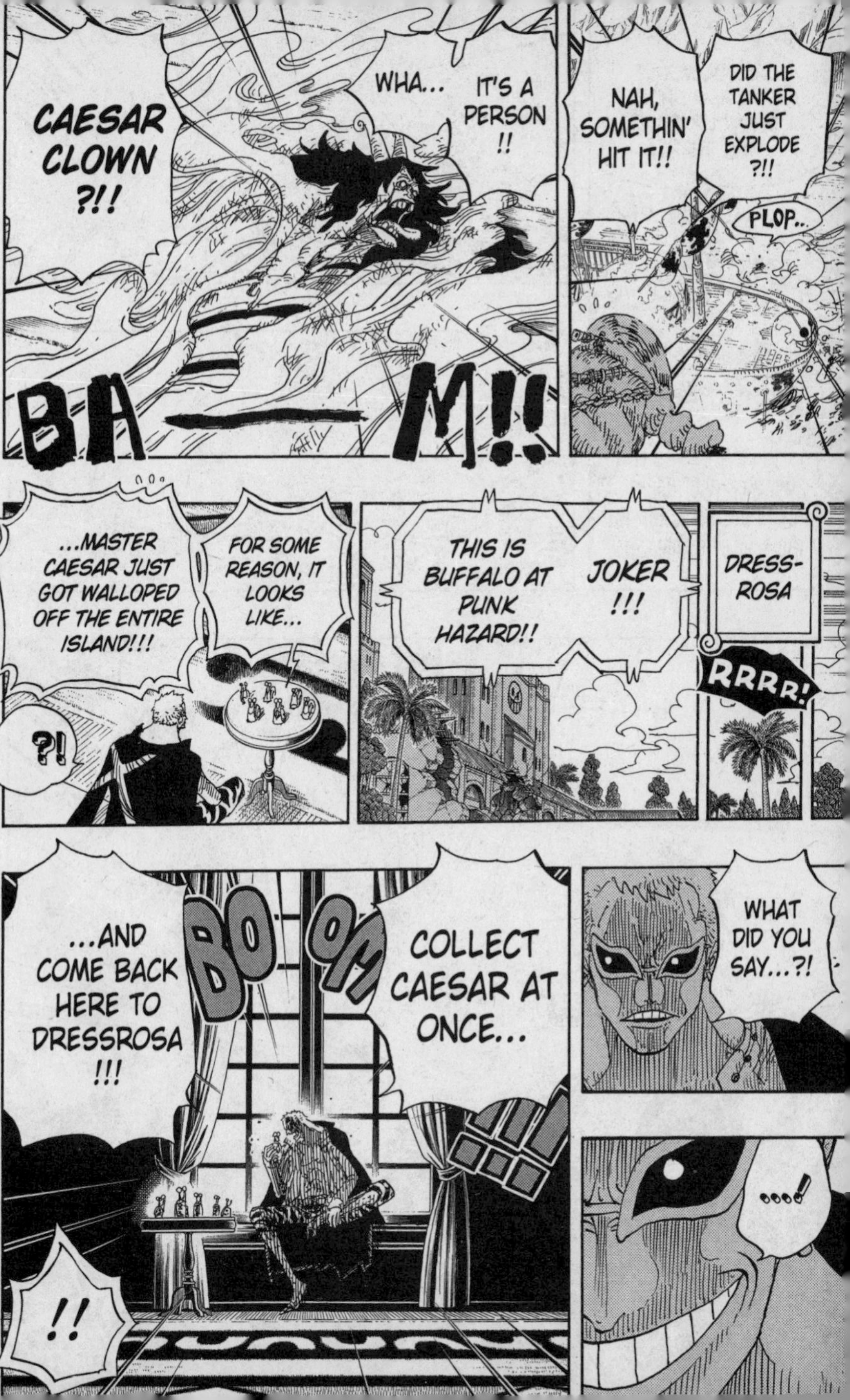
DID THE TANKER JUST EXPLODE ?!!
NAH, SOMETHIN' HIT IT!!
PLOP...
IT'S A PERSON !!
WHA...
CAESAR CLOWN ?!!
BA—M!!
DRESS-ROSA
RRRR!
JOKER !!!
THIS IS BUFFALO AT PUNK HAZARD!!
FOR SOME REASON, IT LOOKS LIKE...
...MASTER CAESAR JUST GOT WALLOPED OFF THE ENTIRE ISLAND!!!
?!
WHAT DID YOU SAY...?!
...!
COLLECT CAESAR AT ONCE...
BOOM
...AND COME BACK HERE TO DRESSROSA !!!
!!

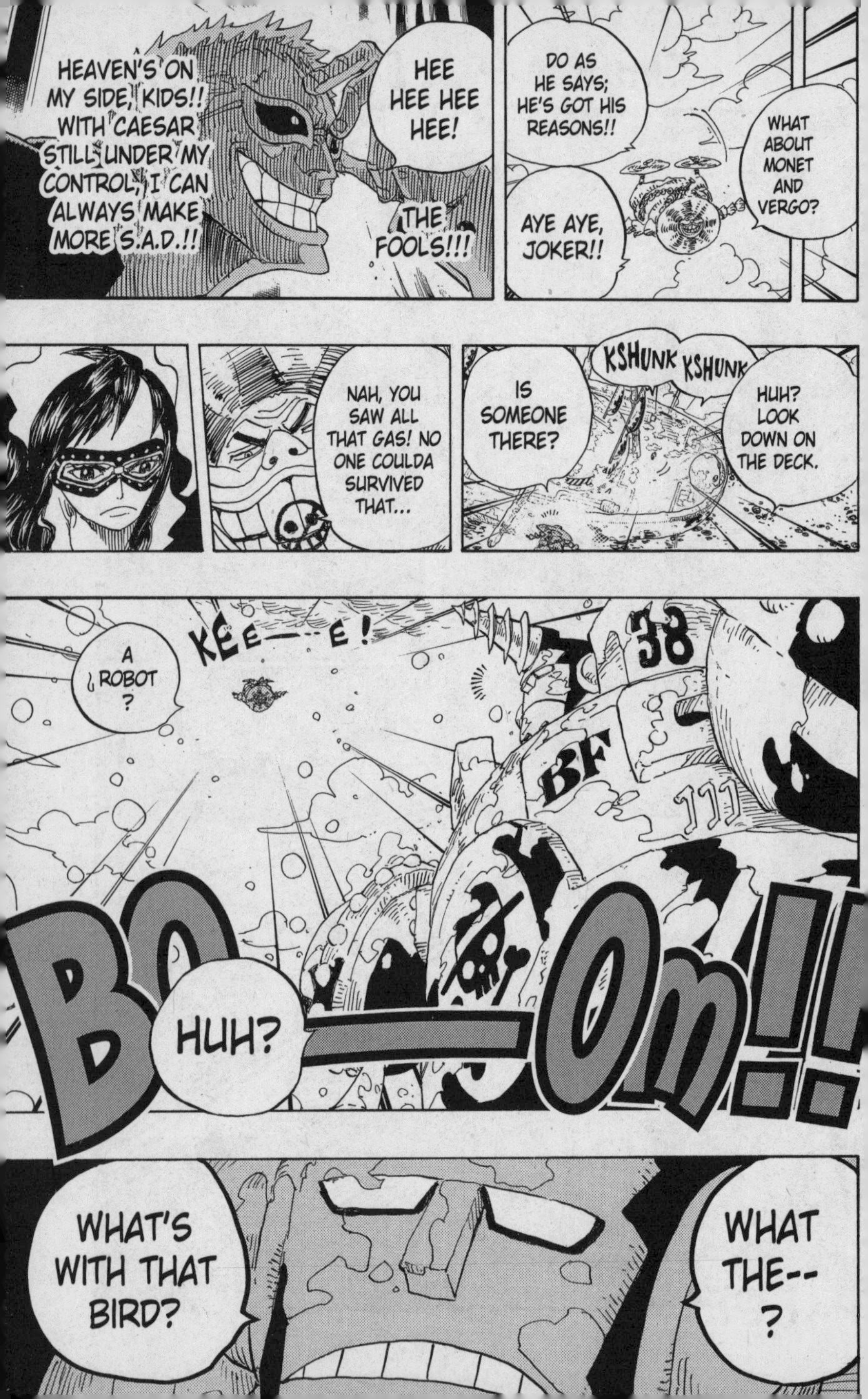
DO AS HE SAYS; HE'S GOT HIS REASONS!!
WHAT ABOUT MONET AND VERGO?
AYE AYE, JOKER!!
HEE HEE HEE HEE!
THE FOOLS!!!
HEAVEN'S ON MY SIDE, KIDS!! WITH CAESAR STILL UNDER MY CONTROL, I CAN ALWAYS MAKE MORE S.A.D.!!
KSHUNK KSHUNK
HUH? LOOK DOWN ON THE DECK.
IS SOMEONE THERE?
NAH, YOU SAW ALL THAT GAS! NO ONE COULDA SURVIVED THAT...
38
BF
KEE——E!
¿A ROBOT?
BO——OM!!
HUH?
WHAT THE--?
WHAT'S WITH THAT BIRD?

Chapter 693: DIE FOR ME

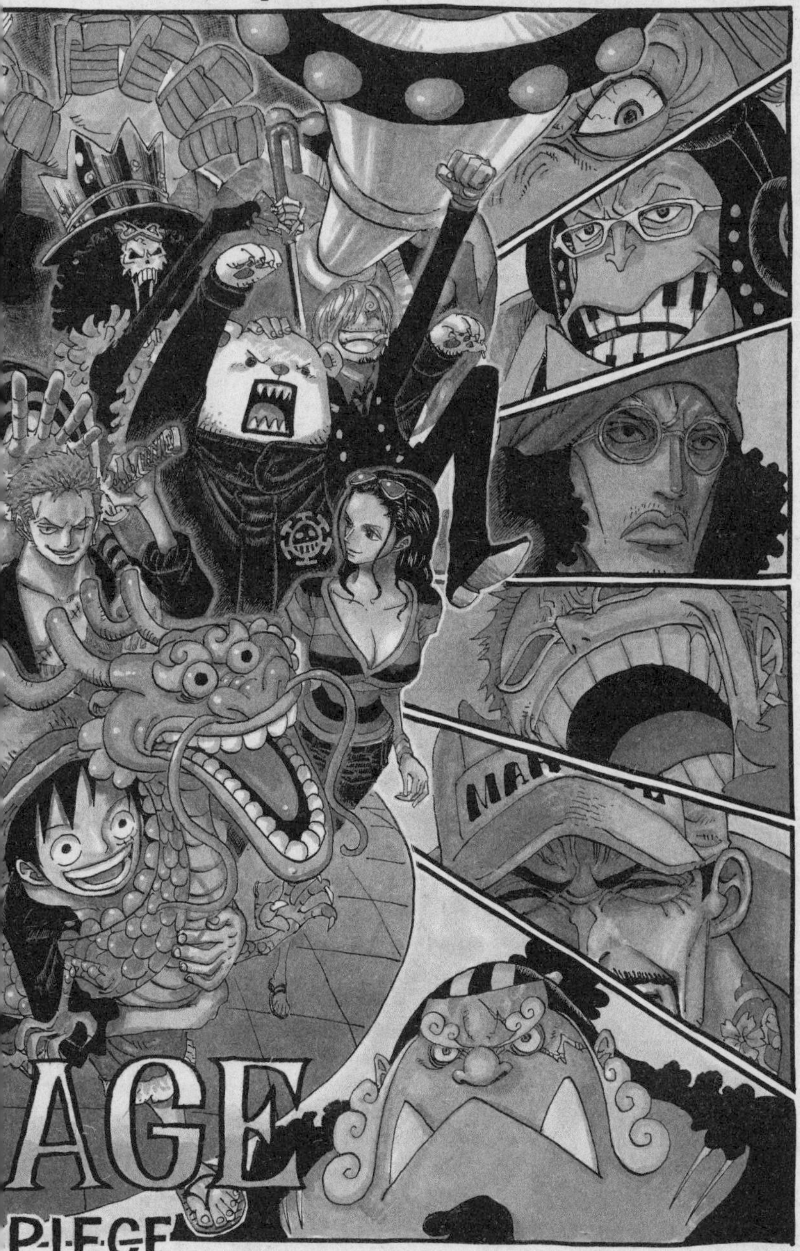

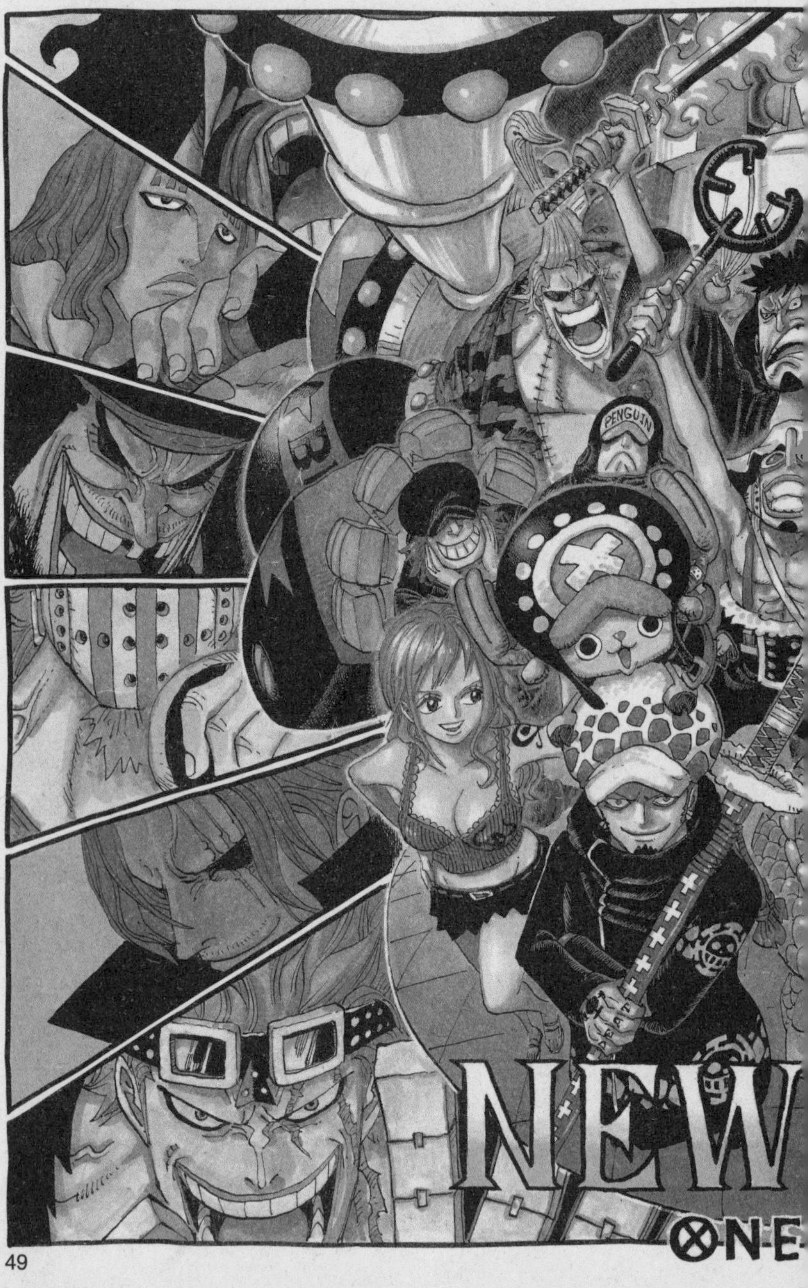

PENGUIN
NEW
ONE

vol. 70
ONE PIECE

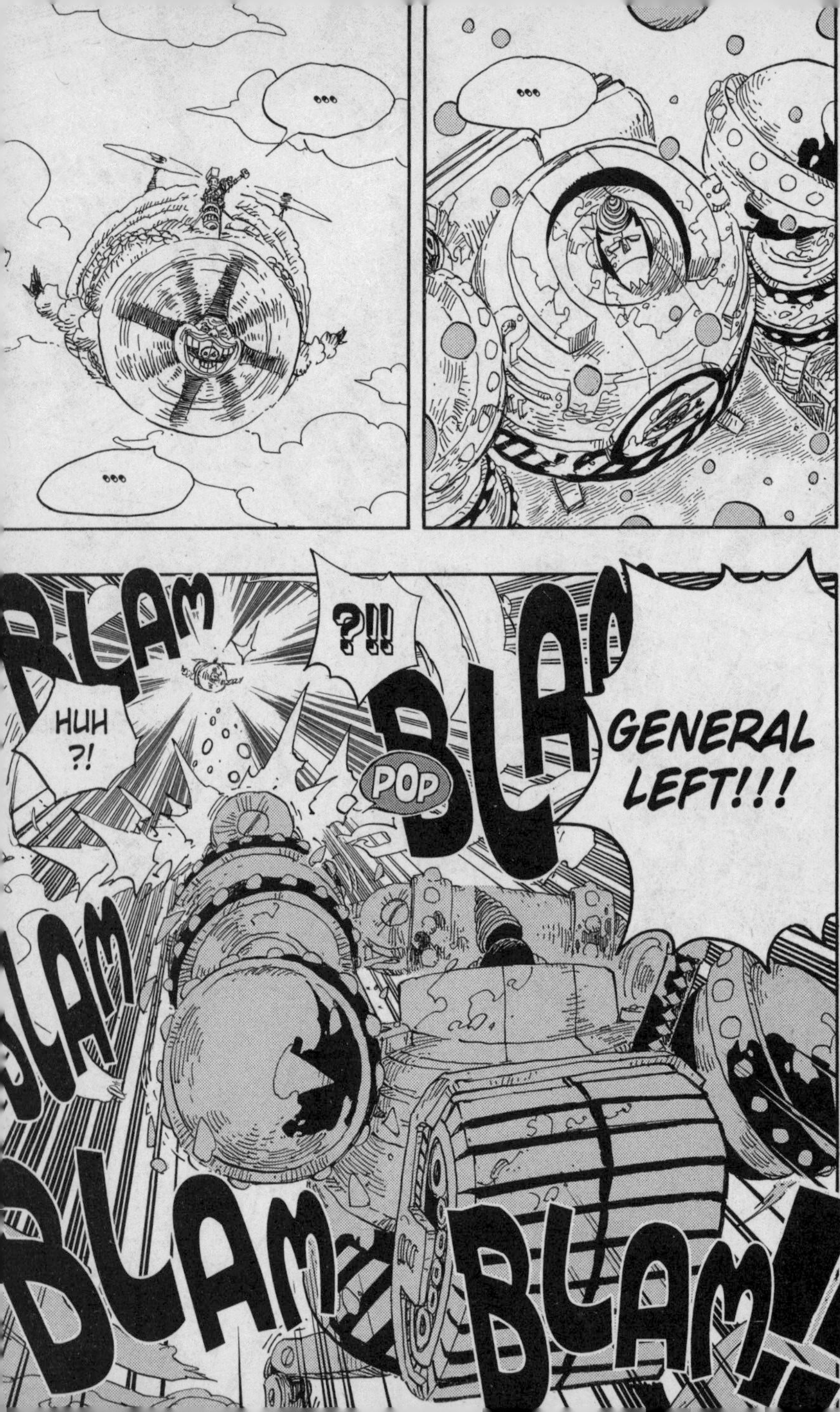
...
...
...
GENERAL LEFT!!!
?!!
POP
BLAM
HUH ?!
BLAM!!
BLAM

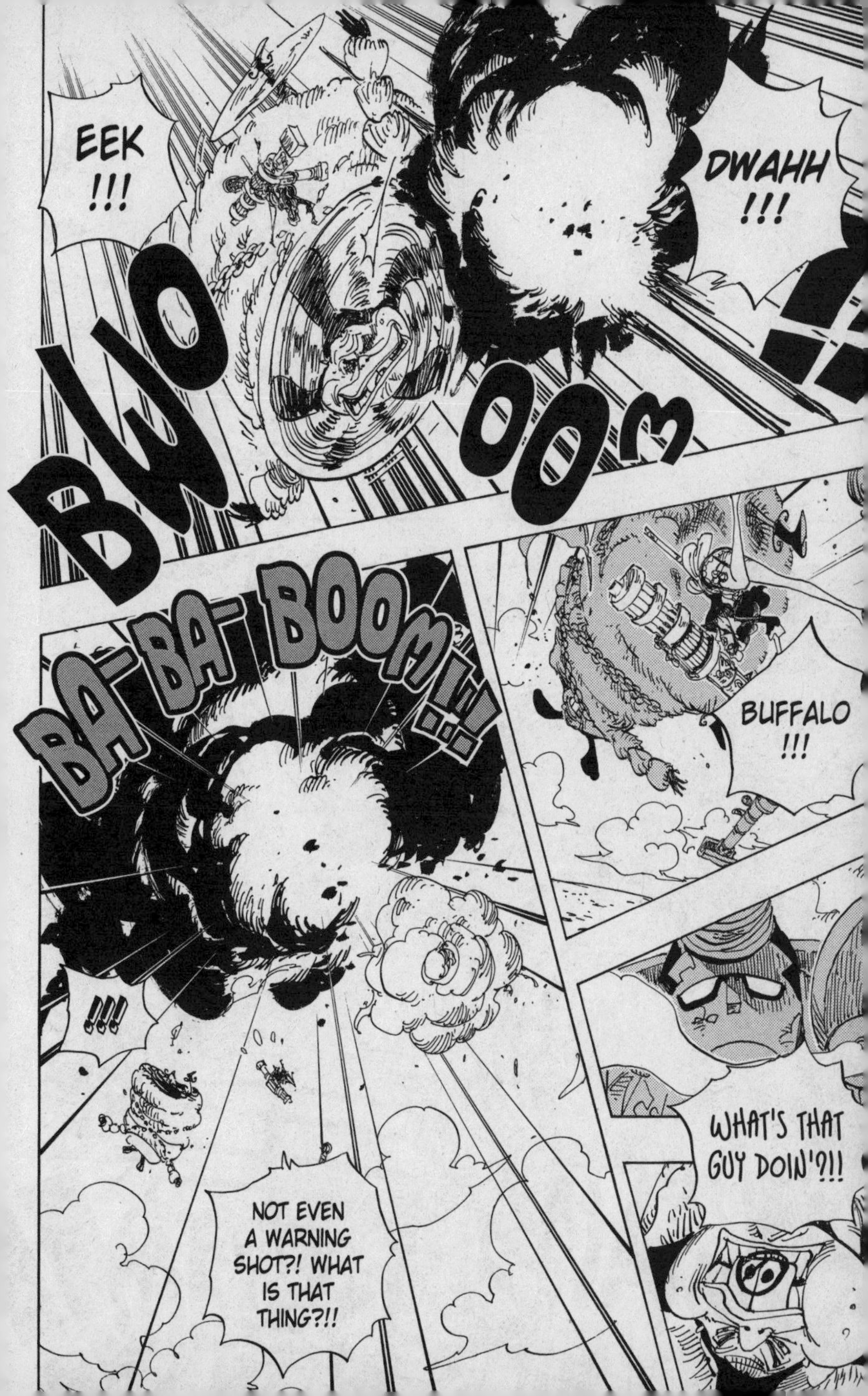
DWAHH !!!
BWOOOM
EEK !!!
BUFFALO !!!
WHAT'S THAT GUY DOIN'?!!
BA-BA-BOOM!!!
!!!
NOT EVEN A WARNING SHOT?! WHAT IS THAT THING?!!

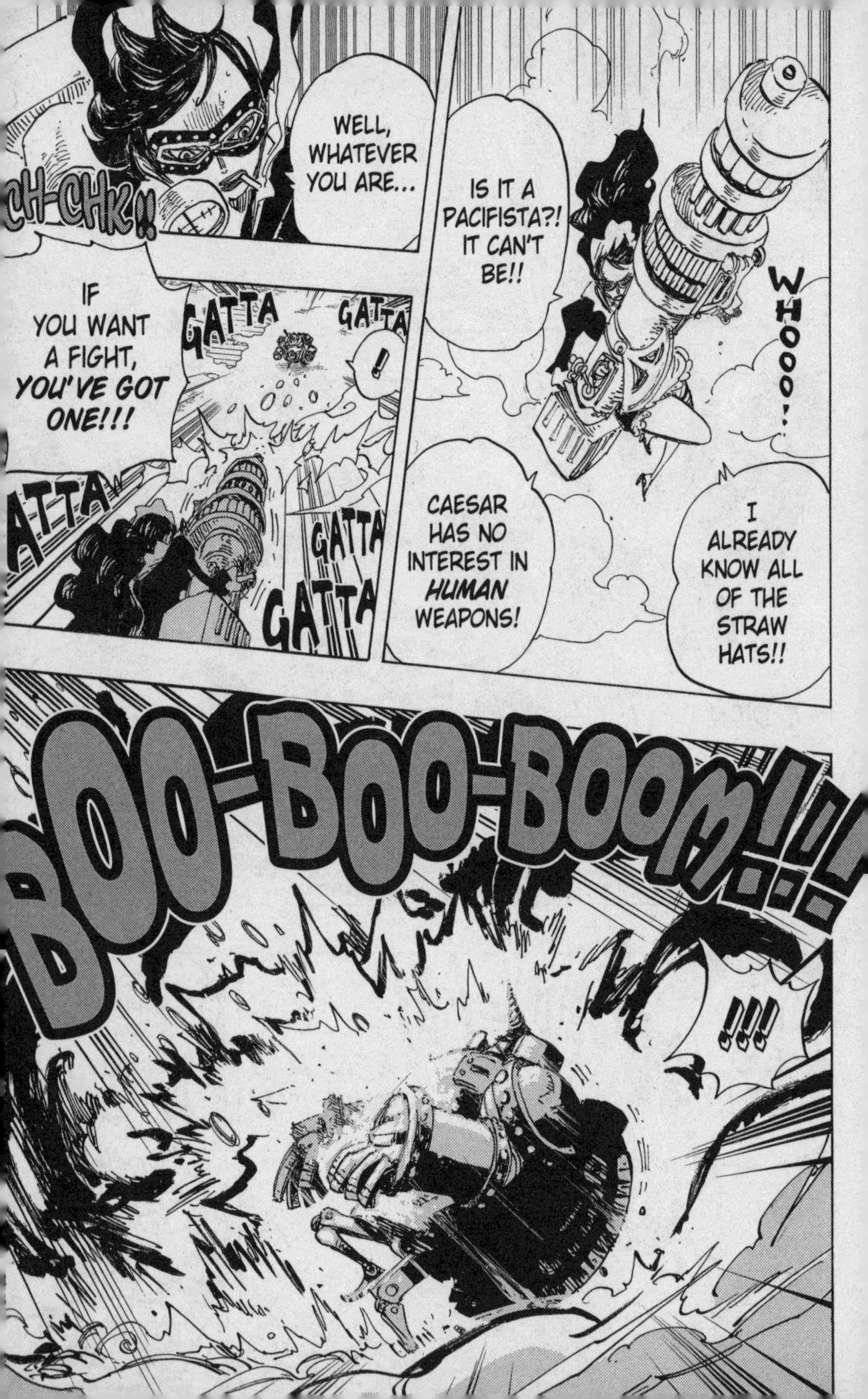
IS IT A PACIFISTA?! IT CAN'T BE!!
WHOOO!!
I ALREADY KNOW ALL OF THE STRAW HATS!!
CAESAR HAS NO INTEREST IN *HUMAN* WEAPONS!
WELL, WHATEVER YOU ARE...
CH-CHK!!
GATTA
GATTA
!
IF YOU WANT A FIGHT, *YOU'VE GOT ONE!!!*
GATTA
GATTA
GATTA
GATTA
BOO-BOO-BOOM!!!
!!!

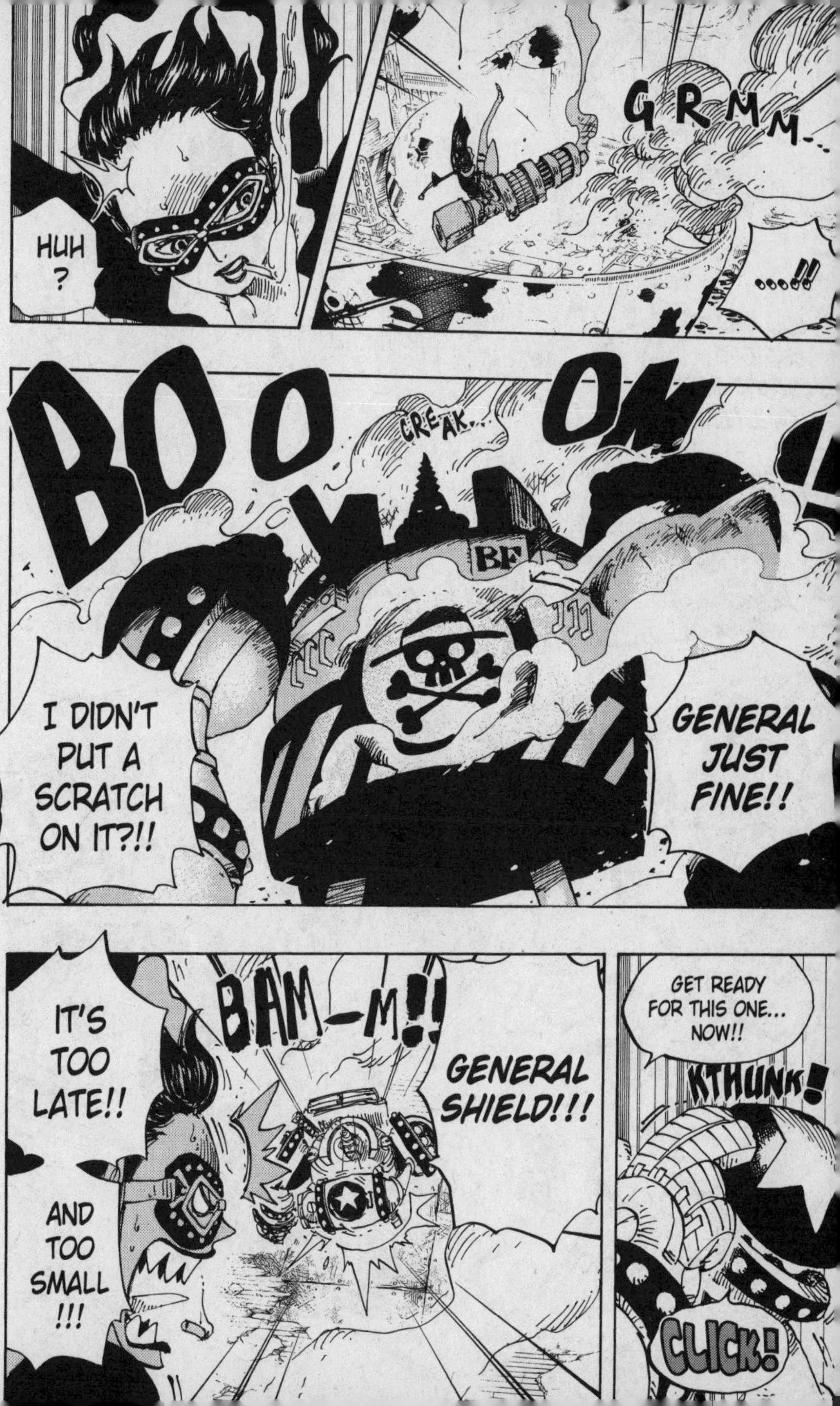
GRMMM...
....!!
HUH?
BOOOM!!
CREAK...
GENERAL JUST FINE!!
I DIDN'T PUT A SCRATCH ON IT?!!
GET READY FOR THIS ONE... NOW!!
KTHUNK!
CLICK!
BAM-M!!
GENERAL SHIELD!!!
IT'S TOO LATE!!
AND TOO SMALL!!!

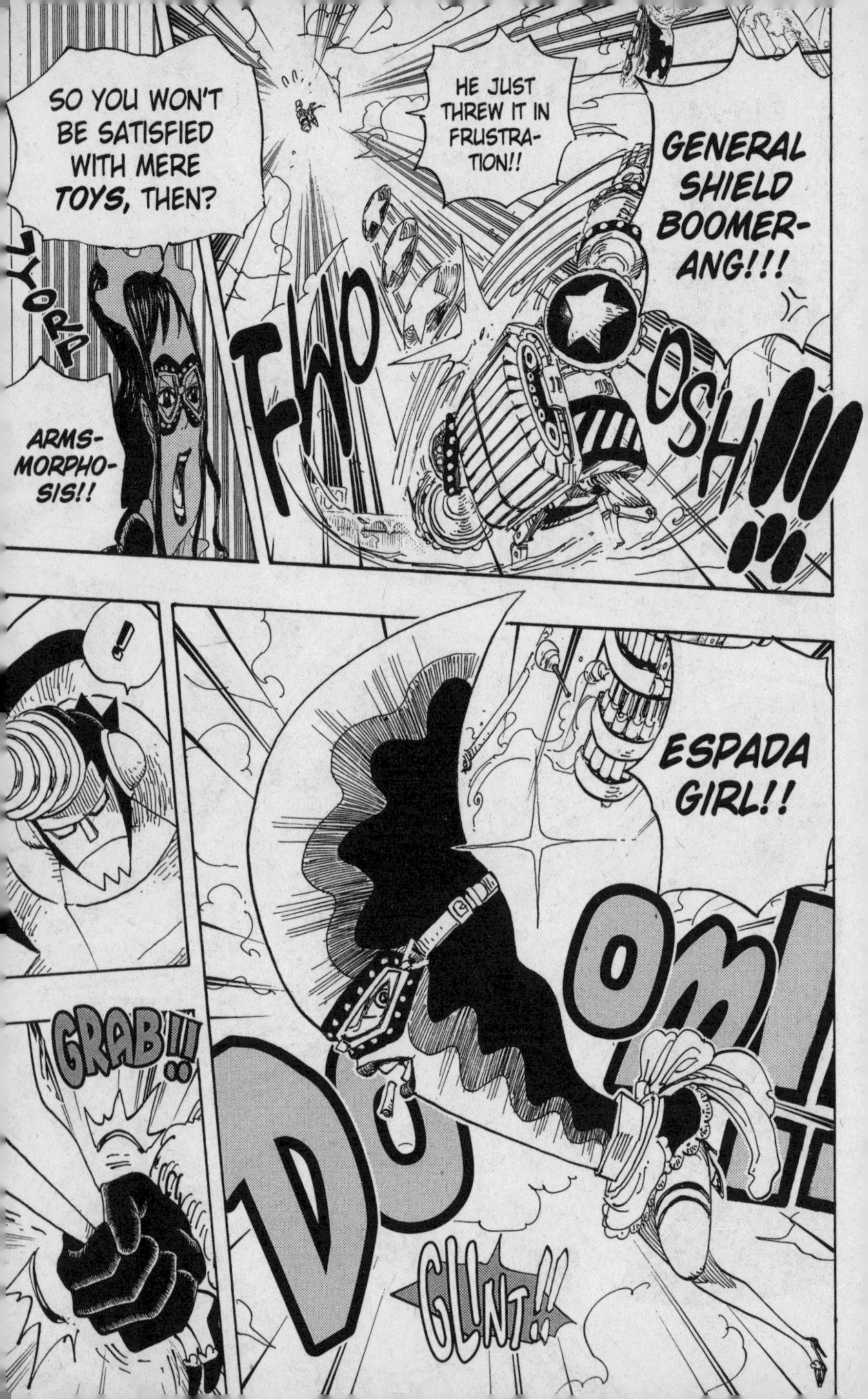
GENERAL SHIELD BOOMERANG!!!
FWOOSH!!!
HE JUST THREW IT IN FRUSTRATION!!
SO YOU WON'T BE SATISFIED WITH MERE TOYS, THEN?
YORP
ARMS-MORPHOSIS!!
ESPADA GIRL!!
DOOM!
GLINT!!
!
GRAB!!

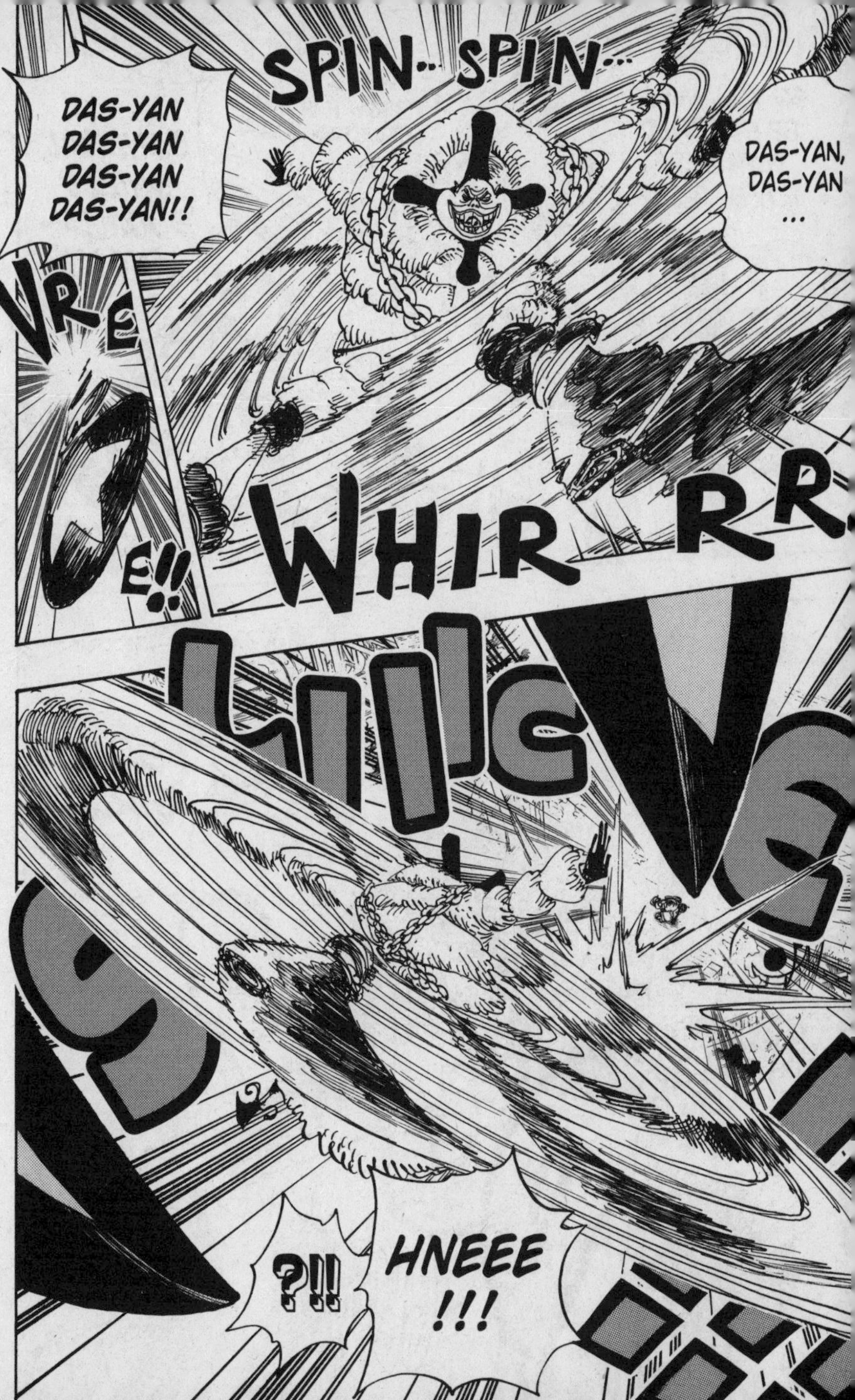

DAS-YAN, DAS-YAN ...
SPIN... SPIN...
DAS-YAN DAS-YAN DAS-YAN DAS-YAN!!
WHIRRR...
VREE!!
HNEEE !!!
?!!

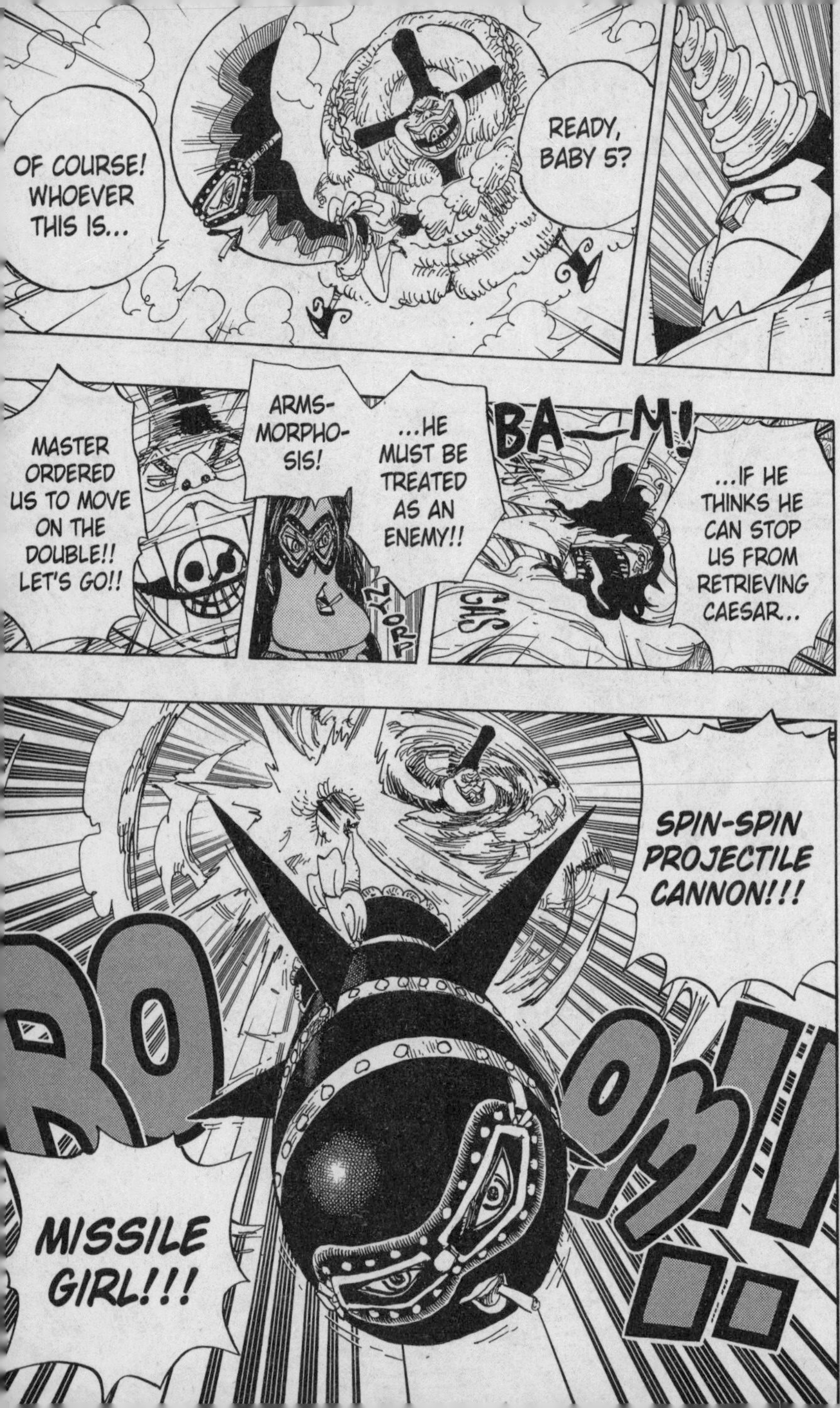
READY, BABY 5?
OF COURSE! WHOEVER THIS IS...
BA-M!
...IF HE THINKS HE CAN STOP US FROM RETRIEVING CAESAR...
GAS
...HE MUST BE TREATED AS AN ENEMY!!
ARMS-MORPHO-SIS!
ZYORP
MASTER ORDERED US TO MOVE ON THE DOUBLE!! LET'S GO!!
SPIN-SPIN PROJECTILE CANNON!!!
BOOM!!
MISSILE GIRL!!!

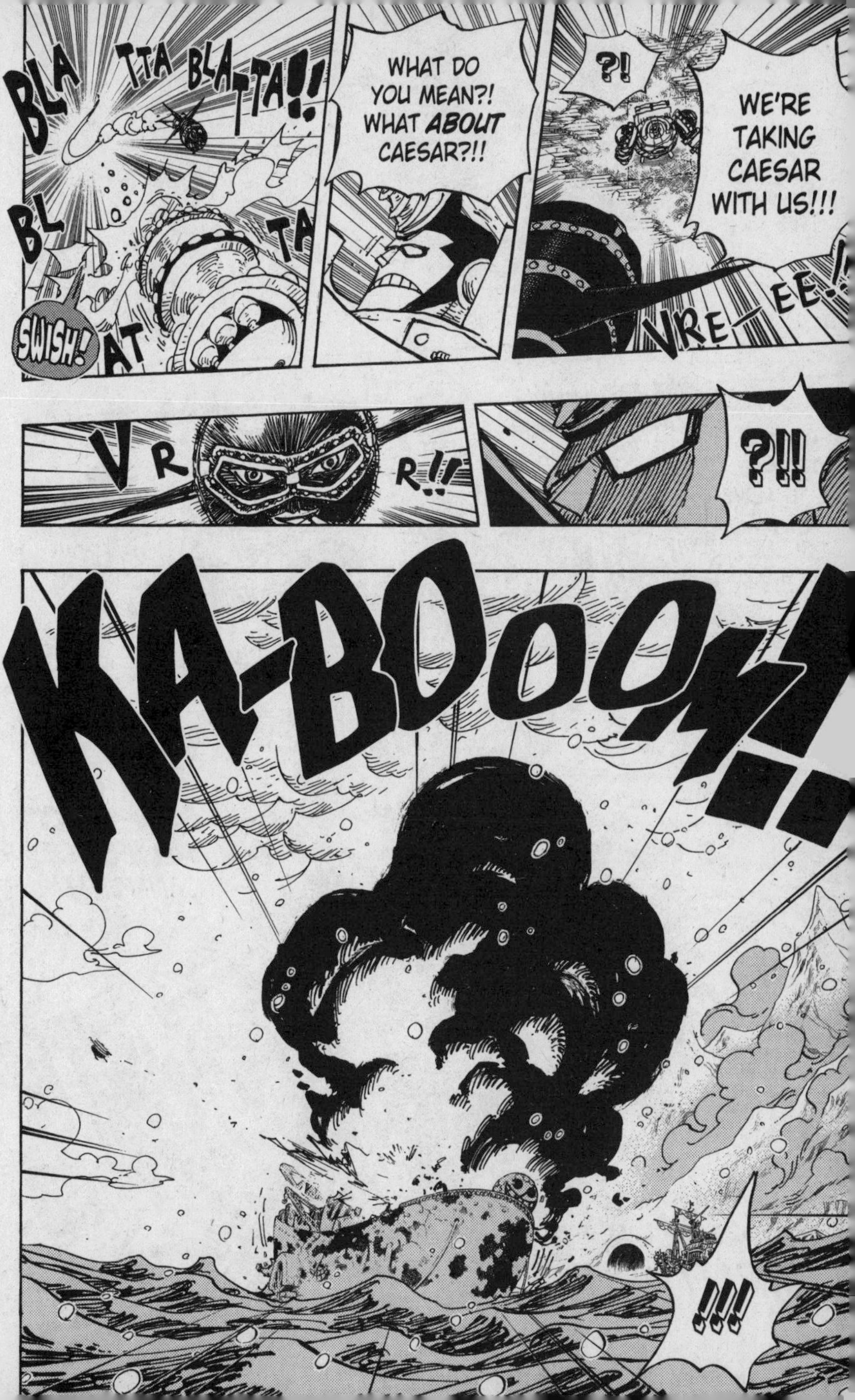
?!
WE'RE TAKING CAESAR WITH US!!!
VRE—EE!!
WHAT DO YOU MEAN?! WHAT *ABOUT* CAESAR?!!
BLATTA BLATTA!!
BLATTA
SWISH!
?!!
VRR!!
KA-BOOOM!!
!!!

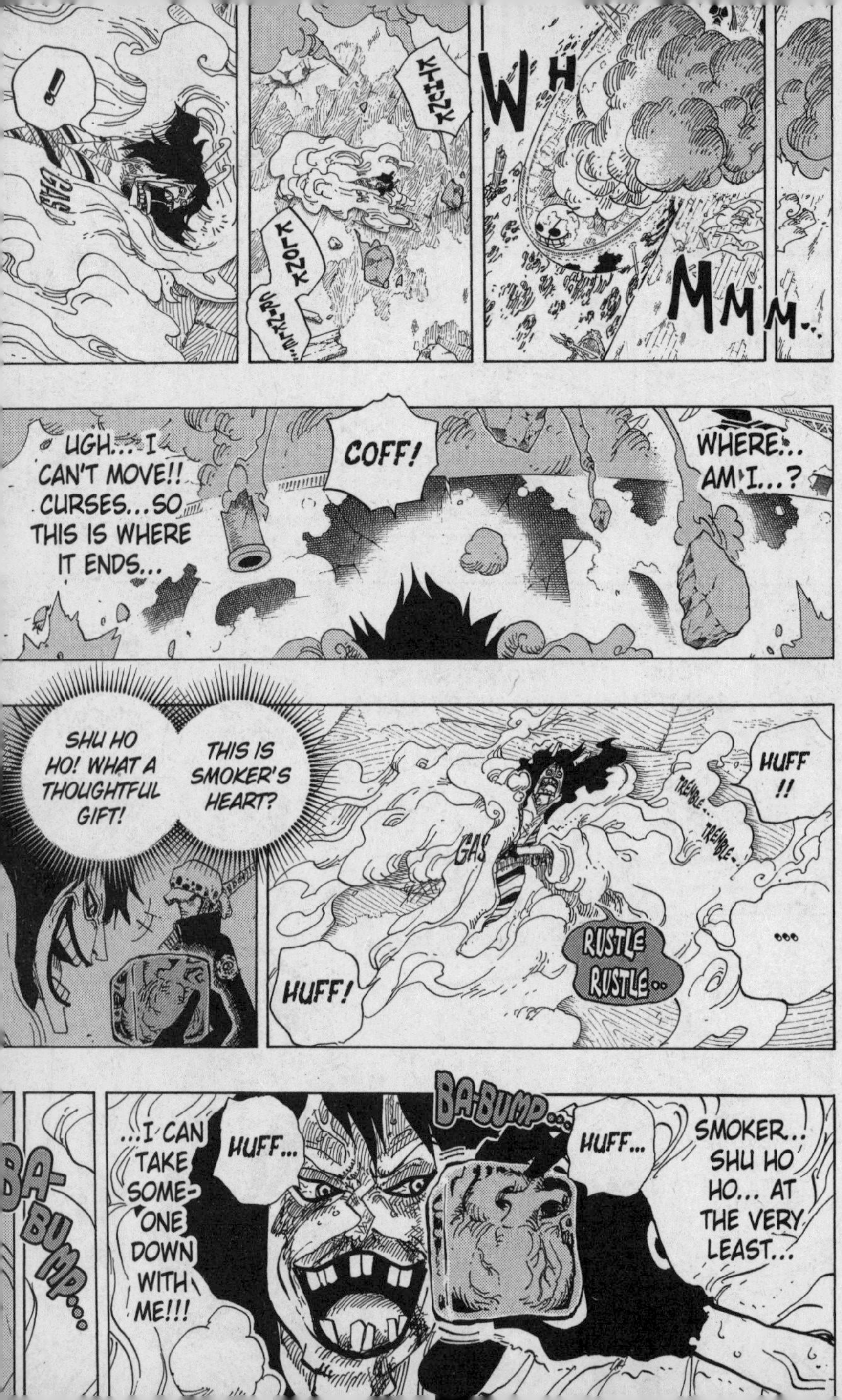
WH
MMM...
KTHUNK
KLONK
CRINKLE...
!
GAS
WHERE... AM I...?
COFF!
UGH... I CAN'T MOVE!! CURSES...SO THIS IS WHERE IT ENDS...
HUFF !!
TREMBLE...
TREMBLE...
GAS
...
RUSTLE RUSTLE..
HUFF!
THIS IS SMOKER'S HEART?
SHU HO HO! WHAT A THOUGHTFUL GIFT!
SMOKER.. SHU HO HO... AT THE VERY LEAST...
HUFF...
BA-BUMP...
HUFF...
...I CAN TAKE SOME-ONE DOWN WITH ME!!!
BA-BUMP...

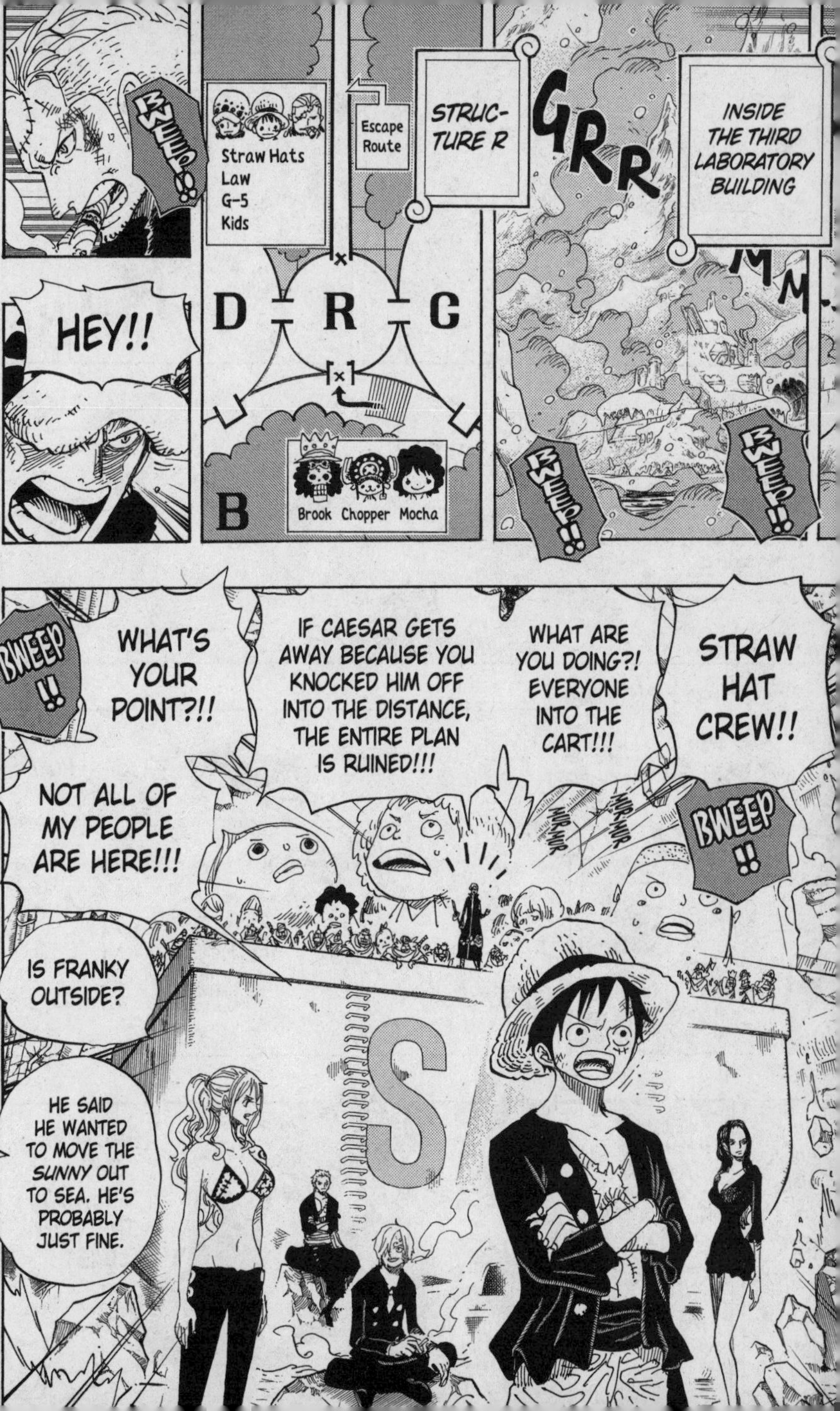
INSIDE THE THIRD LABORATORY BUILDING
GRR
MMN
BWEEP!!
BWEEP!!
STRUC-TURE R
Escape Route
Straw Hats
Law
G-5
Kids
D
R
C
B
Brook Chopper Mocha
BWEEP!!
HEY!!
STRAW HAT CREW!!
BWEEP!!
WHAT ARE YOU DOING?! EVERYONE INTO THE CART!!!
MUR MUR
MUR MUR
IF CAESAR GETS AWAY BECAUSE YOU KNOCKED HIM OFF INTO THE DISTANCE, THE ENTIRE PLAN IS RUINED!!!
WHAT'S YOUR POINT?!!
BWEEP!!
NOT ALL OF MY PEOPLE ARE HERE!!!
IS FRANKY OUTSIDE?
HE SAID HE WANTED TO MOVE THE SUNNY OUT TO SEA. HE'S PROBABLY JUST FINE.

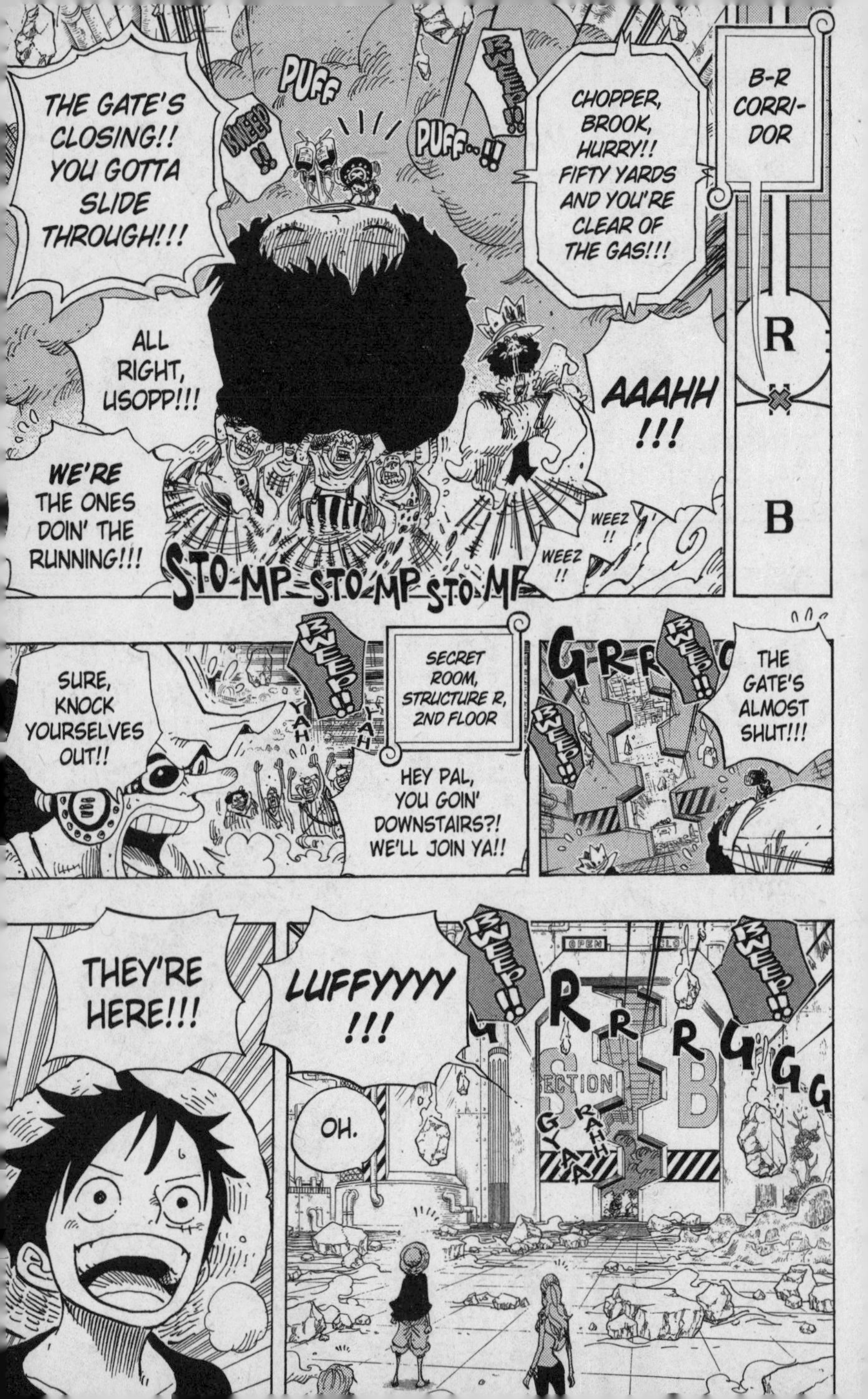
B-R CORRIDOR
R
B
CHOPPER, BROOK, HURRY!! FIFTY YARDS AND YOU'RE CLEAR OF THE GAS!!!
BWEEP!!
PUFF...!!
PUFF
BWEEP!!
THE GATE'S CLOSING!! YOU GOTTA SLIDE THROUGH!!!
AAAHH!!!
ALL RIGHT, USOPP!!!
WEEZ!!
WEEZ!!
WE'RE THE ONES DOIN' THE RUNNING!!!
STOMP STOMP STOMP
THE GATE'S ALMOST SHUT!!!
BWEEP!!
GRRR
BWEEP!!
SECRET ROOM, STRUCTURE R, 2ND FLOOR
BWEEP!!
YAH
YAH
HEY PAL, YOU GOIN' DOWNSTAIRS?! WE'LL JOIN YA!!
SURE, KNOCK YOURSELVES OUT!!
BWEEP!!
RRRRGGGG
BWEEP!!
SECTION B
GYAA
RAHH
LUFFYYYY!!!
OH.
THEY'RE HERE!!!

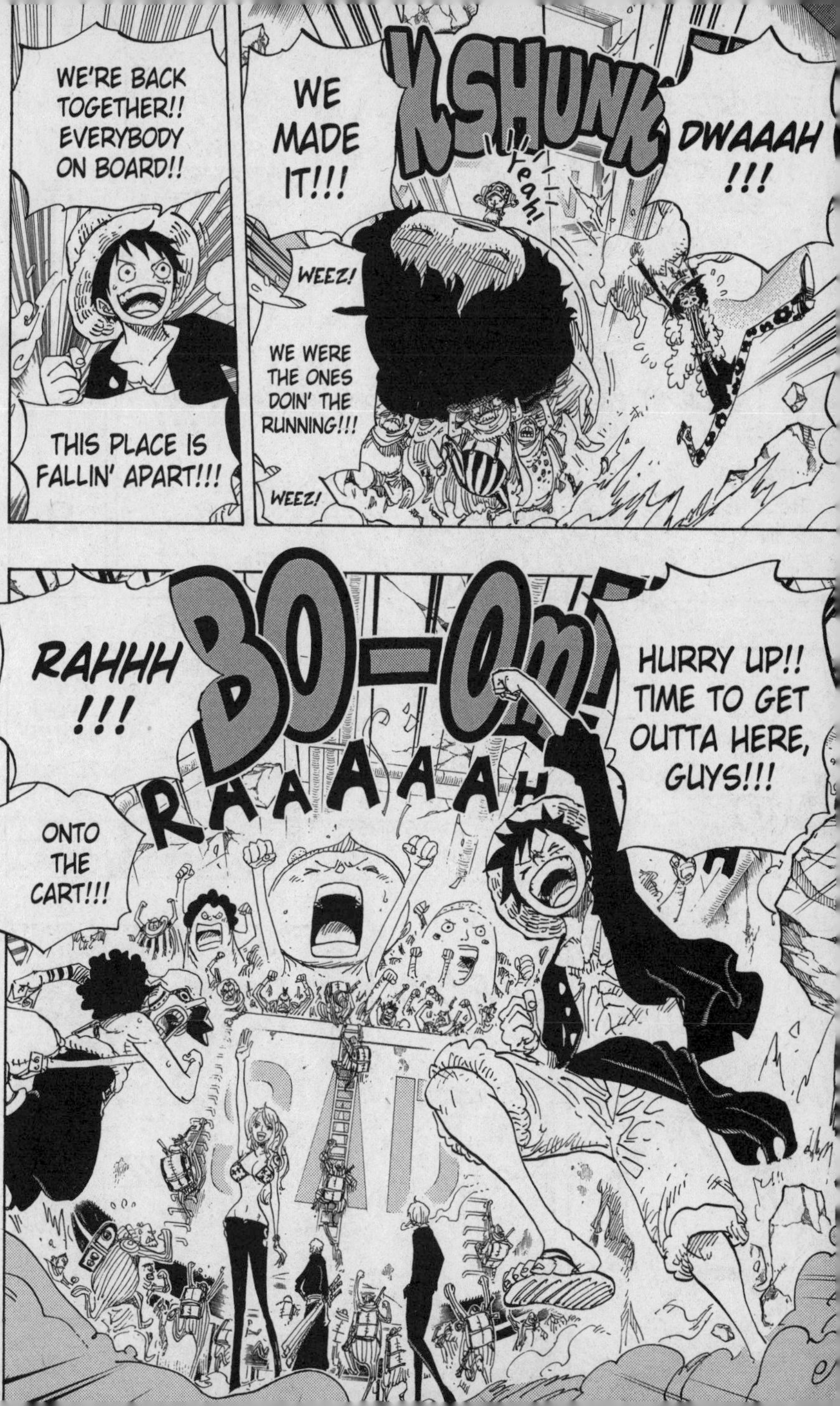
DWAAAH !!!
K-SHUNK
Yeah!
WE MADE IT!!!
WEEZ!
WE WERE THE ONES DOIN' THE RUNNING!!!
WEEZ!
WE'RE BACK TOGETHER!! EVERYBODY ON BOARD!!
THIS PLACE IS FALLIN' APART!!!
HURRY UP!! TIME TO GET OUTTA HERE, GUYS!!!
BO-OM!
RAAAAAH
RAHHH !!!
ONTO THE CART!!!

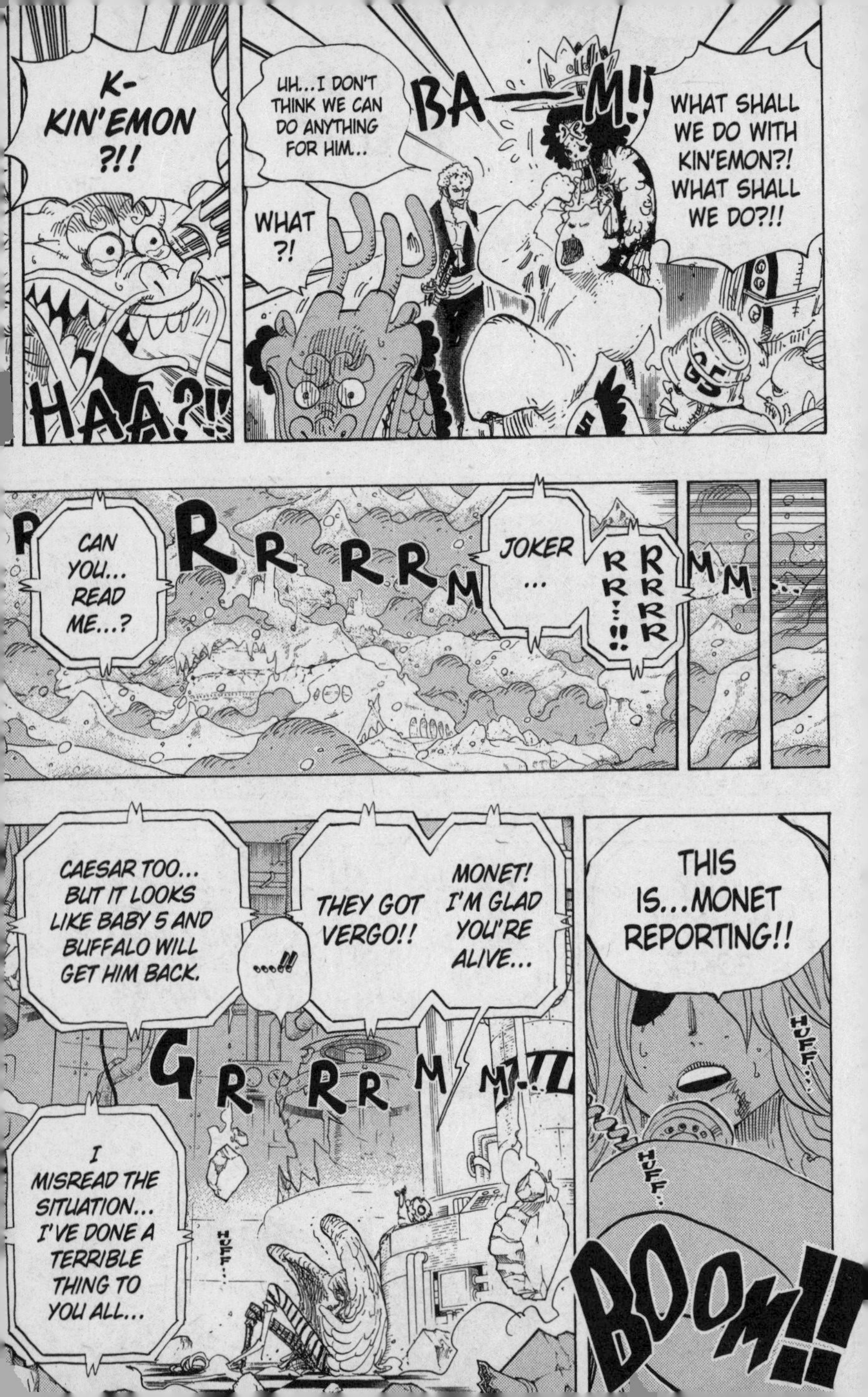
WHAT SHALL WE DO WITH KIN'EMON?! WHAT SHALL WE DO?!!
BA-M!!
UH...I DON'T THINK WE CAN DO ANYTHING FOR HIM...
WHAT ?!
K-KIN'EMON ?!!
HAA?!!
RRRRRRRR!!
MM
JOKER ...
RRRRRM
CAN YOU... READ ME...?
THIS IS...MONET REPORTING!!
HUFF...
HUFF...
BOOM!!
MONET! I'M GLAD YOU'RE ALIVE...
THEY GOT VERGO!!
...!!
CAESAR TOO... BUT IT LOOKS LIKE BABY 5 AND BUFFALO WILL GET HIM BACK.
GRRRRMM
I MISREAD THE SITUATION... I'VE DONE A TERRIBLE THING TO YOU ALL...
HUFF...

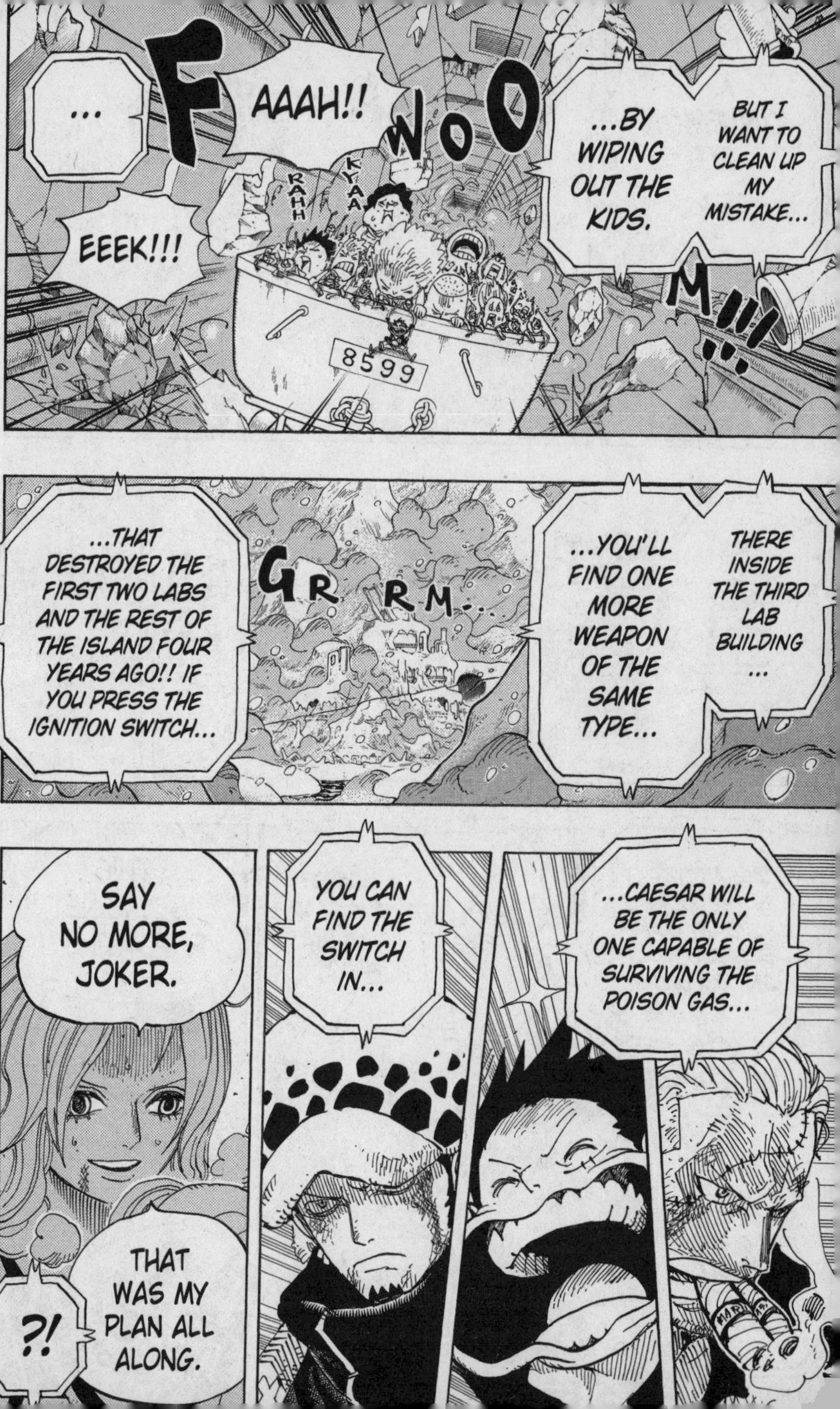
BUT I WANT TO CLEAN UP MY MISTAKE...
...BY WIPING OUT THE KIDS.
FWOOM!!!
AAAH!!
KYAA
RAHH
...
EEEK!!!
8599
THERE INSIDE THE THIRD LAB BUILDING ...
...YOU'LL FIND ONE MORE WEAPON OF THE SAME TYPE...
GRRM...
...THAT DESTROYED THE FIRST TWO LABS AND THE REST OF THE ISLAND FOUR YEARS AGO!! IF YOU PRESS THE IGNITION SWITCH...
...CAESAR WILL BE THE ONLY ONE CAPABLE OF SURVIVING THE POISON GAS...
YOU CAN FIND THE SWITCH IN...
SAY NO MORE, JOKER.
THAT WAS MY PLAN ALL ALONG.
?!

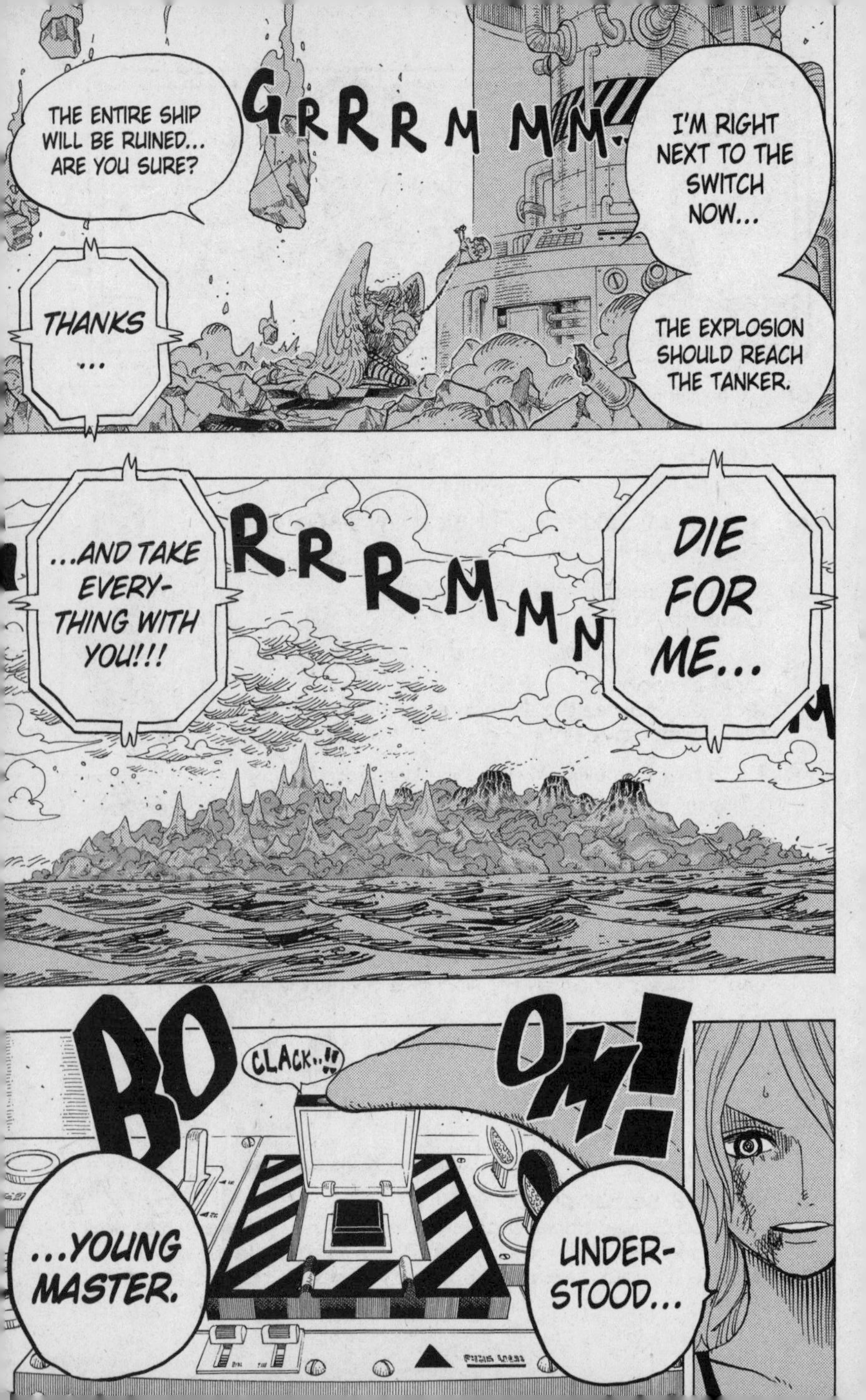
I'M RIGHT NEXT TO THE SWITCH NOW...
THE EXPLOSION SHOULD REACH THE TANKER.
GRRRRM MM
THE ENTIRE SHIP WILL BE RUINED... ARE YOU SURE?
THANKS ...
DIE FOR ME...
RRRRMMMN
...AND TAKE EVERY-THING WITH YOU!!!
UNDER-STOOD...
BOOM!
CLACK..!!
...YOUNG MASTER.

SBS Question Corner

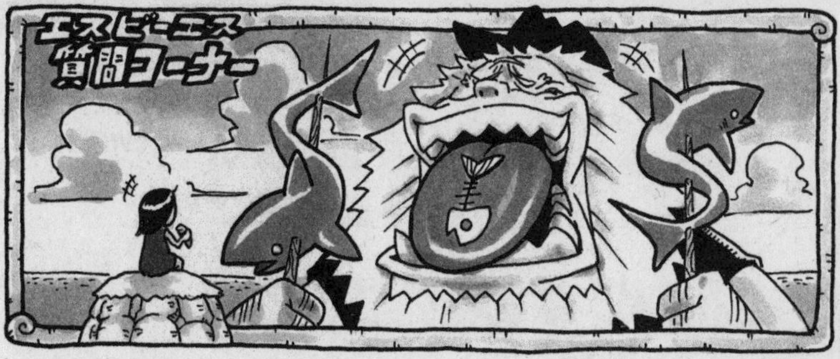
エスビーエス
質問コーナー

(Hippo Iron, Saitama)

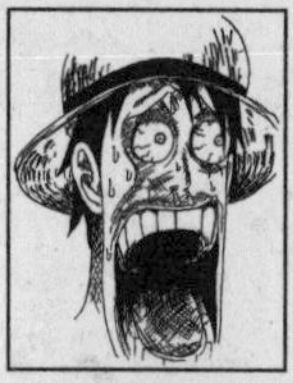

Q: Who's going to slip in the first "Start the SBS!!" this volume? I can't wait to find out...
Oh! It's me.

--Nomi

A: You just said it!! That's my face on the right!!

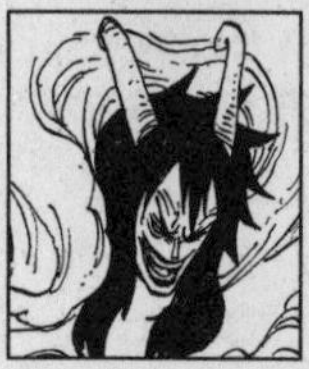

Q: Take this, Odacchi!
Land of Nothing!

--I'm the Master

A: Urk!! I...I can't...!!
Hrg...can't...breathe...!! I...can breathe?
Okay, next question.

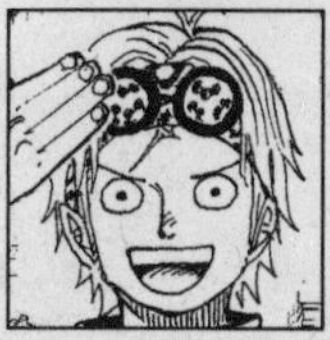

Q: Um...I have a problem. My *One Piece*-loving friend keeps telling me that I look just like Koby. What should I do about this? (cries)
You have to take responsibility!! (angry)

--Yuminami Kobayashi Pigeon

A: What?! Wow, you're really angry! What's so bad about that? Koby's gotten so much cooler lately! I just... can't take responsibility for this. I mean, who's saying this to you?

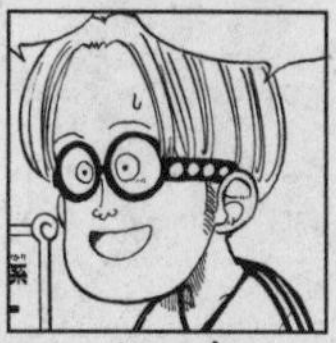

Q: Odacchi!! Hey, Odacchi! One of my friends totally looks like Koby!!! But he's really angry at you because of it, so watch out!!! Anyway, here's my question.♪ In Chapter 653...

--Yuminami Kobayashi Cat

A: Wait a second!! It's you!!
I was totally getting chewed out because you keep teasing the kid in the previous letter!! What's the big idea?! And looking at your pen names...you two seem to get along just fine!

Chapter 694:
THE MOST DANGEROUS MAN

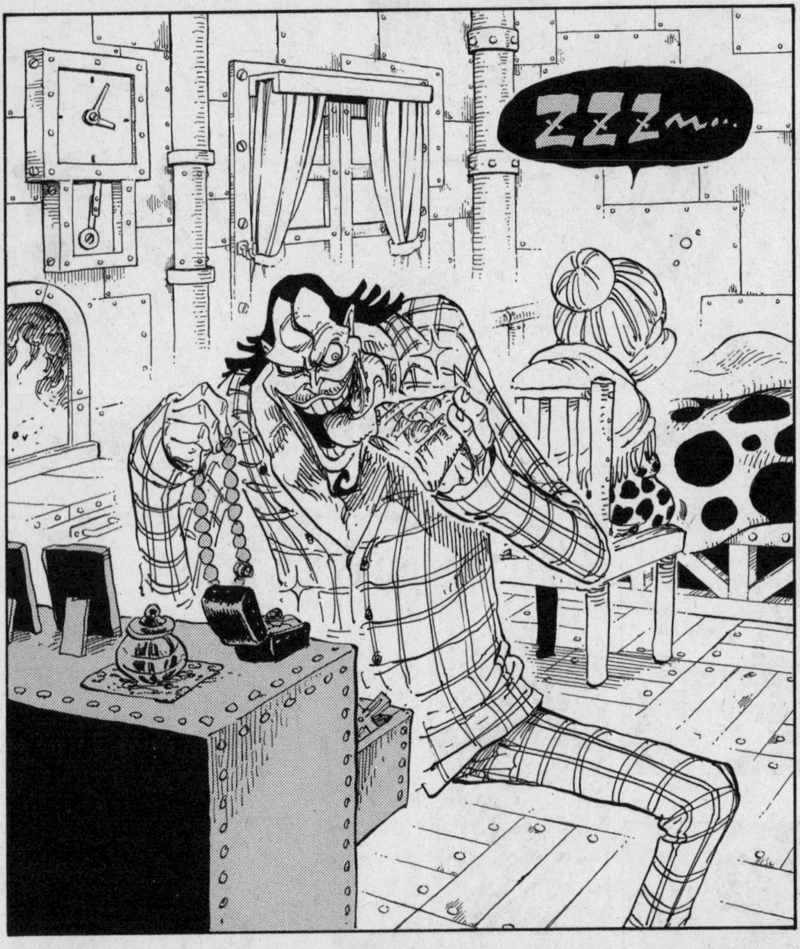
ZZZm...

CARIBOU'S NEW WORLD KEE HEE HEE, VOL. 16: "HELPIN' HIMSELF TO THE OLD HAG'S MEAT PIE AND CHEAP JEWELRY"

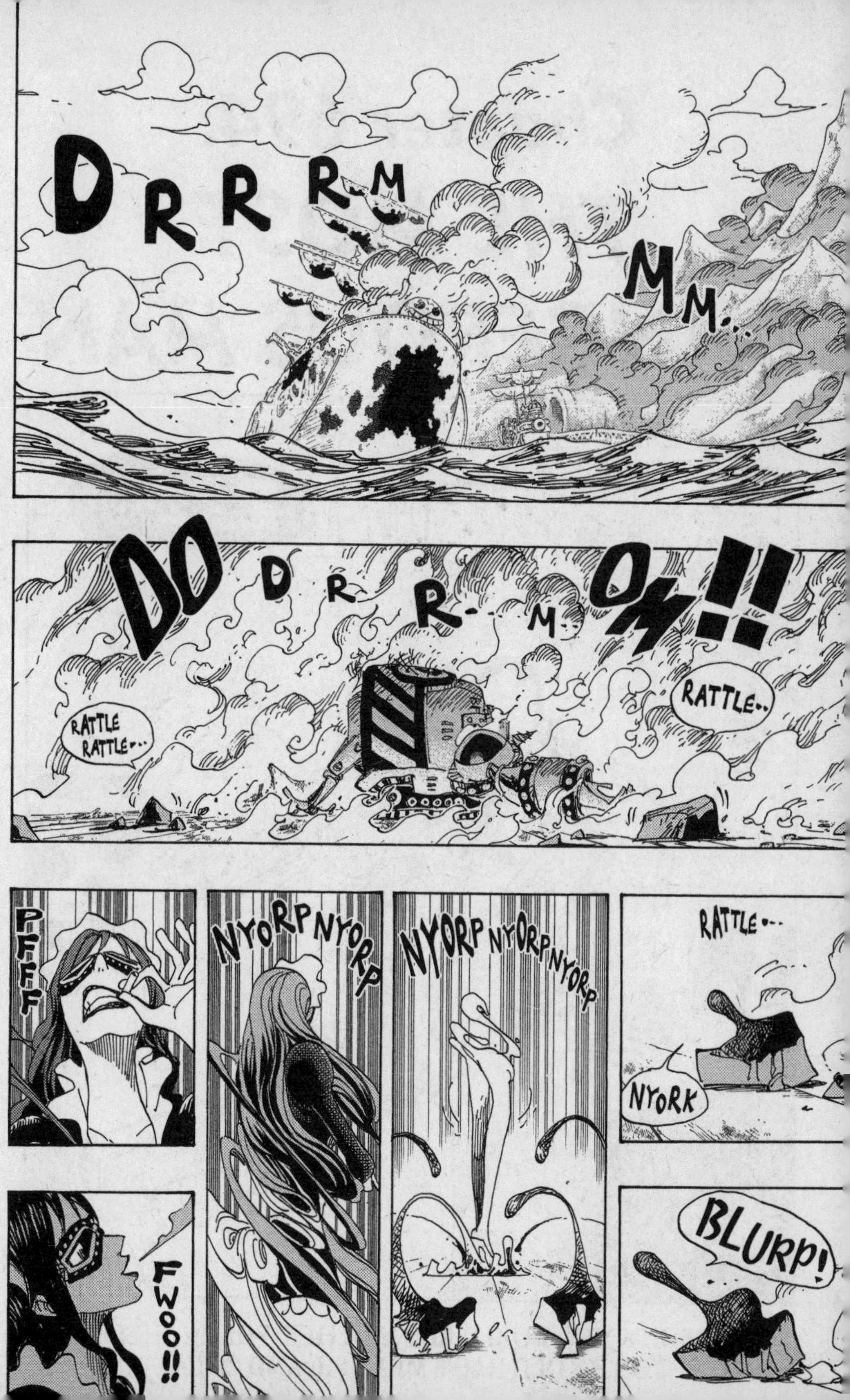
DRRRM
MM...
DODRRM OM!!
RATTLE..
RATTLE RATTLE...
RATTLE...
NYORK
BLURP!
NYORP NYORPNYORPNYORP
NYORPNYORP
PFFF
FWOO!!

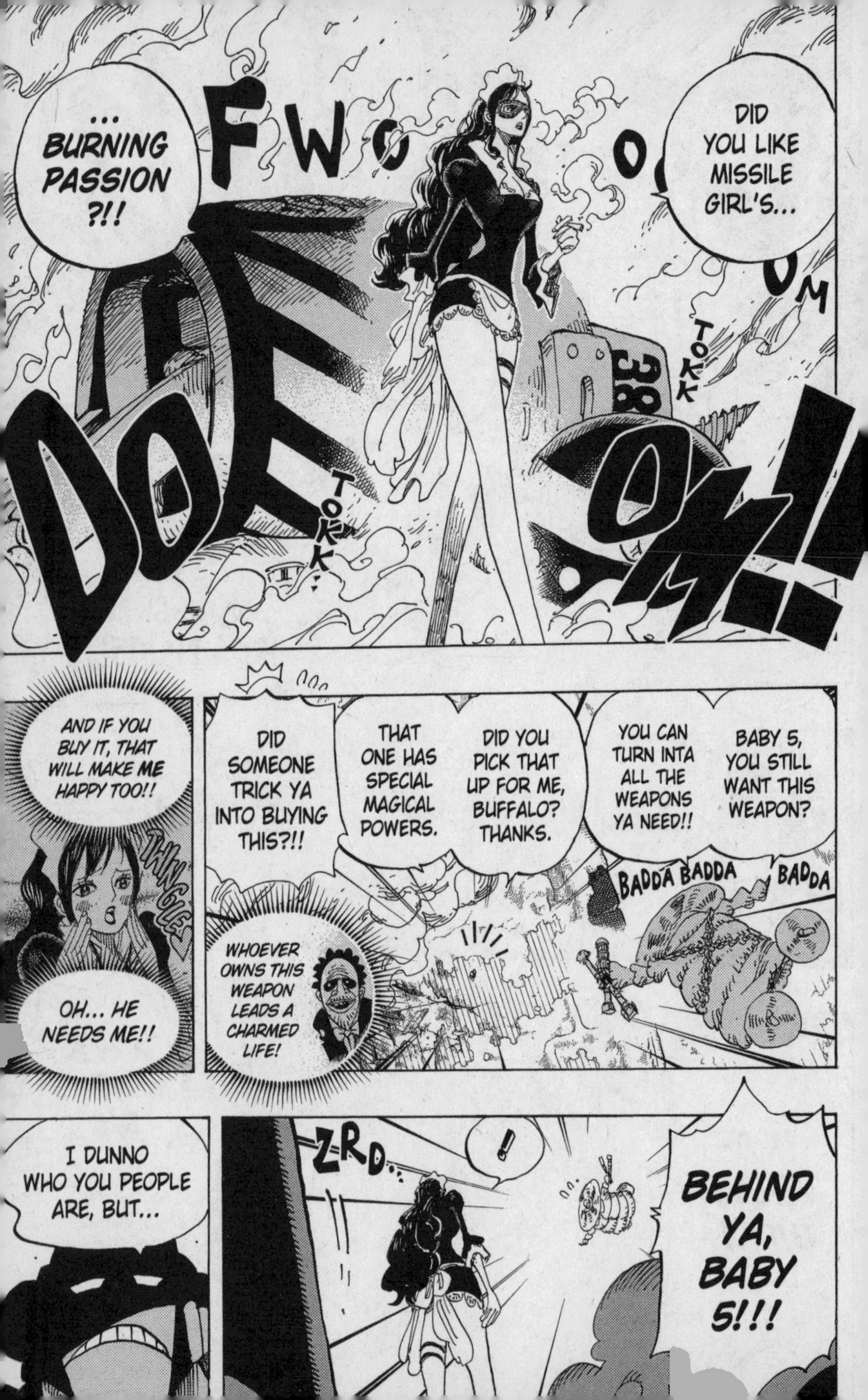
DID YOU LIKE MISSILE GIRL'S...
FWOOOOM
... BURNING PASSION ?!!
TOKK TOKK
TOKK TOKK
DOOOM!!
BABY 5, YOU STILL WANT THIS WEAPON?
YOU CAN TURN INTA ALL THE WEAPONS YA NEED!!
BADDA BADDA BADDA
DID YOU PICK THAT UP FOR ME, BUFFALO? THANKS.
THAT ONE HAS SPECIAL MAGICAL POWERS.
DID SOMEONE TRICK YA INTO BUYING THIS?!!
WHOEVER OWNS THIS WEAPON LEADS A CHARMED LIFE!
AND IF YOU BUY IT, THAT WILL MAKE ME HAPPY TOO!!
THINGLE
OH... HE NEEDS ME!!
BEHIND YA, BABY 5!!!
!
ZRD...
I DUNNO WHO YOU PEOPLE ARE, BUT...

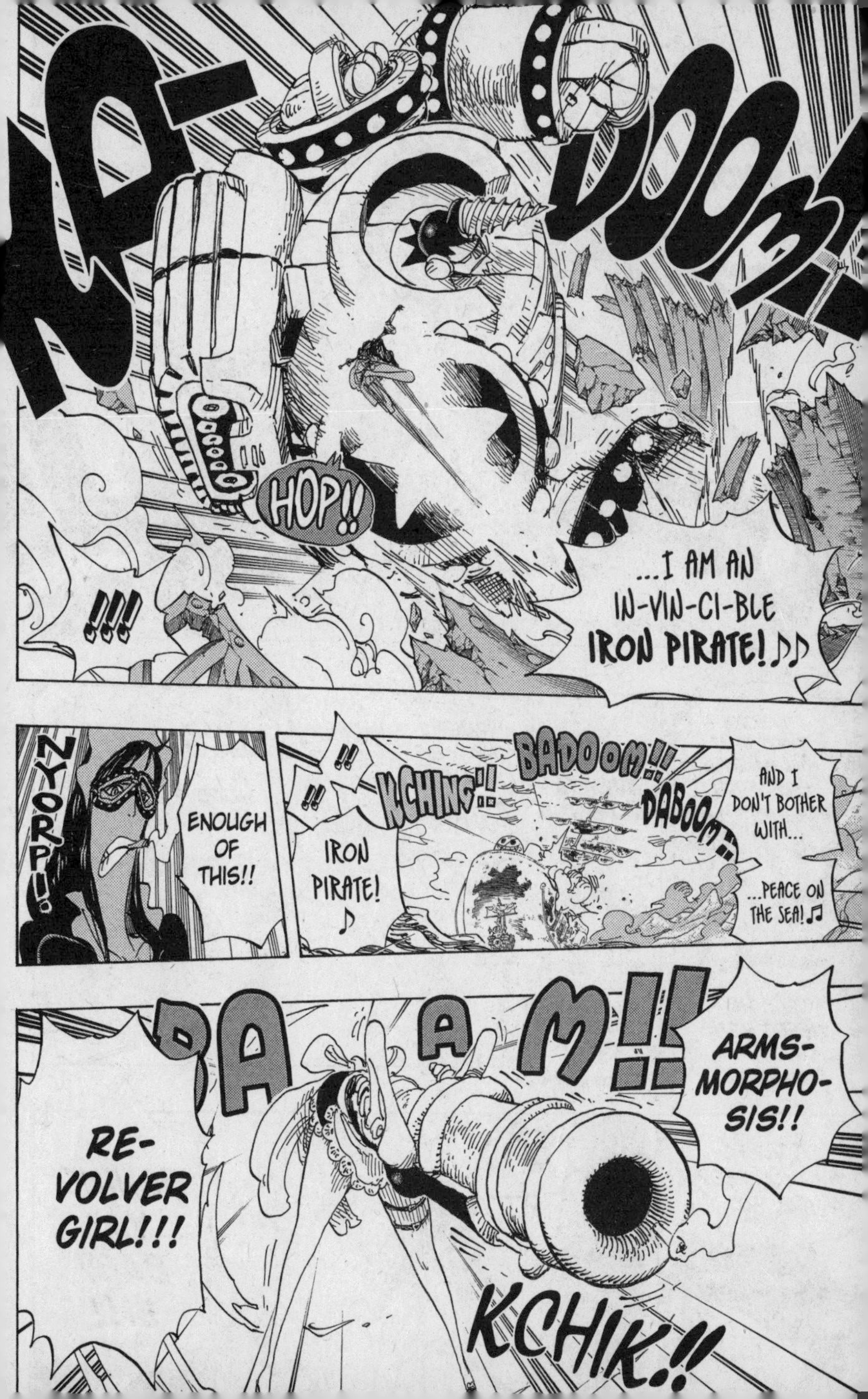
DOOM!!
...I AM AN IN-VIN-CI-BLE IRON PIRATE! ♪♪
HOP!!
!!!
BADOOM!!
AND I DON'T BOTHER WITH...
DABOOM!!
...PEACE ON THE SEA! ♫
KCHING!!
!!
!!
IRON PIRATE! ♪
ENOUGH OF THIS!!
NYORP!!
ARMS-MORPHO-SIS!!
BAAM!!
RE-VOLVER GIRL!!!
KCHIK!!

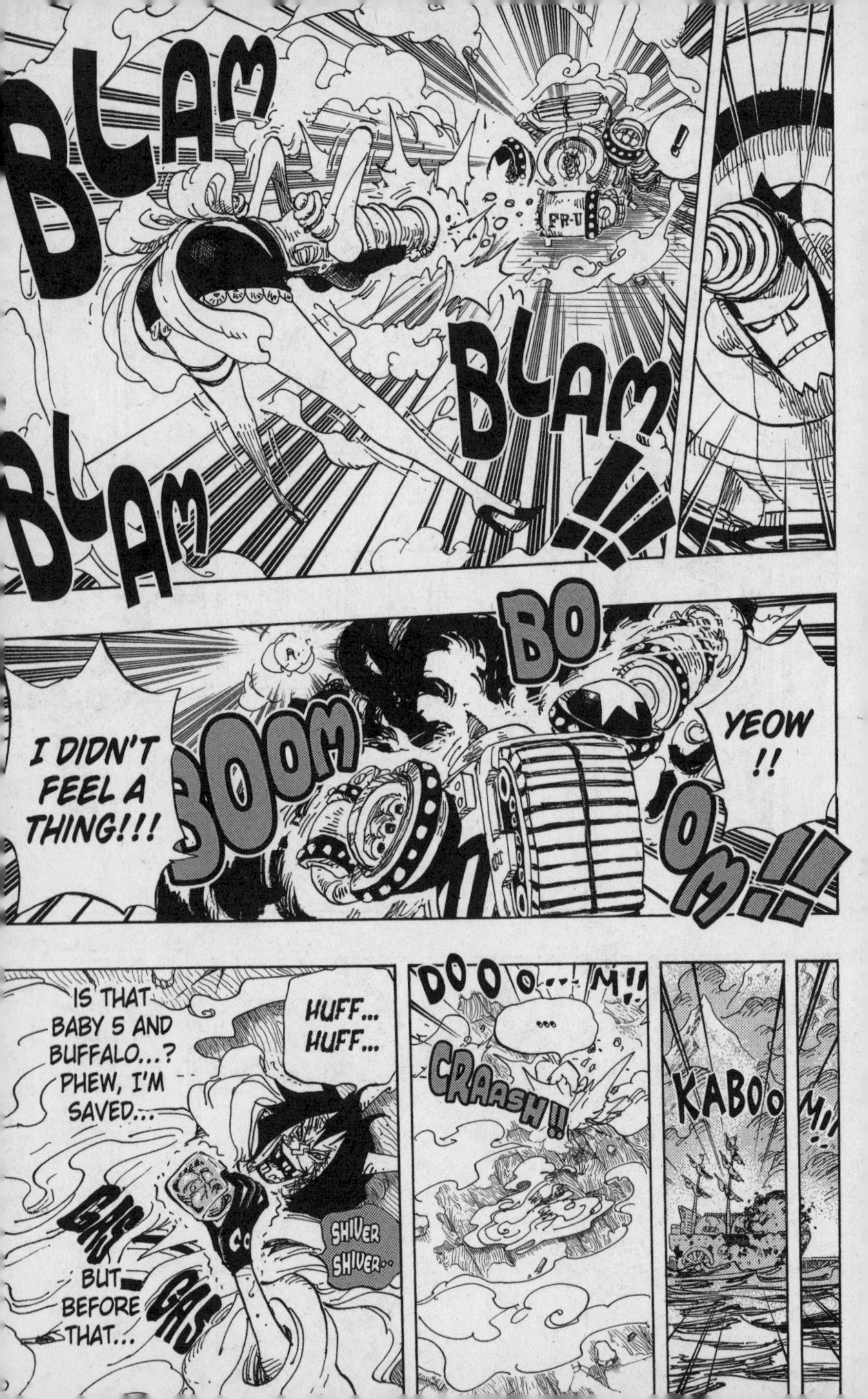
!
BLAM
BLAM
BLAM!!!
YEOW!!
BO
OM!!
BOOM
I DIDN'T FEEL A THING!!!
KABOOM!!
DOOO...M!!
...
CRAASH!!
HUFF... HUFF...
IS THAT BABY 5 AND BUFFALO...? PHEW, I'M SAVED...
SHIVER SHIVER...
GAS GAS
BUT BEFORE THAT...

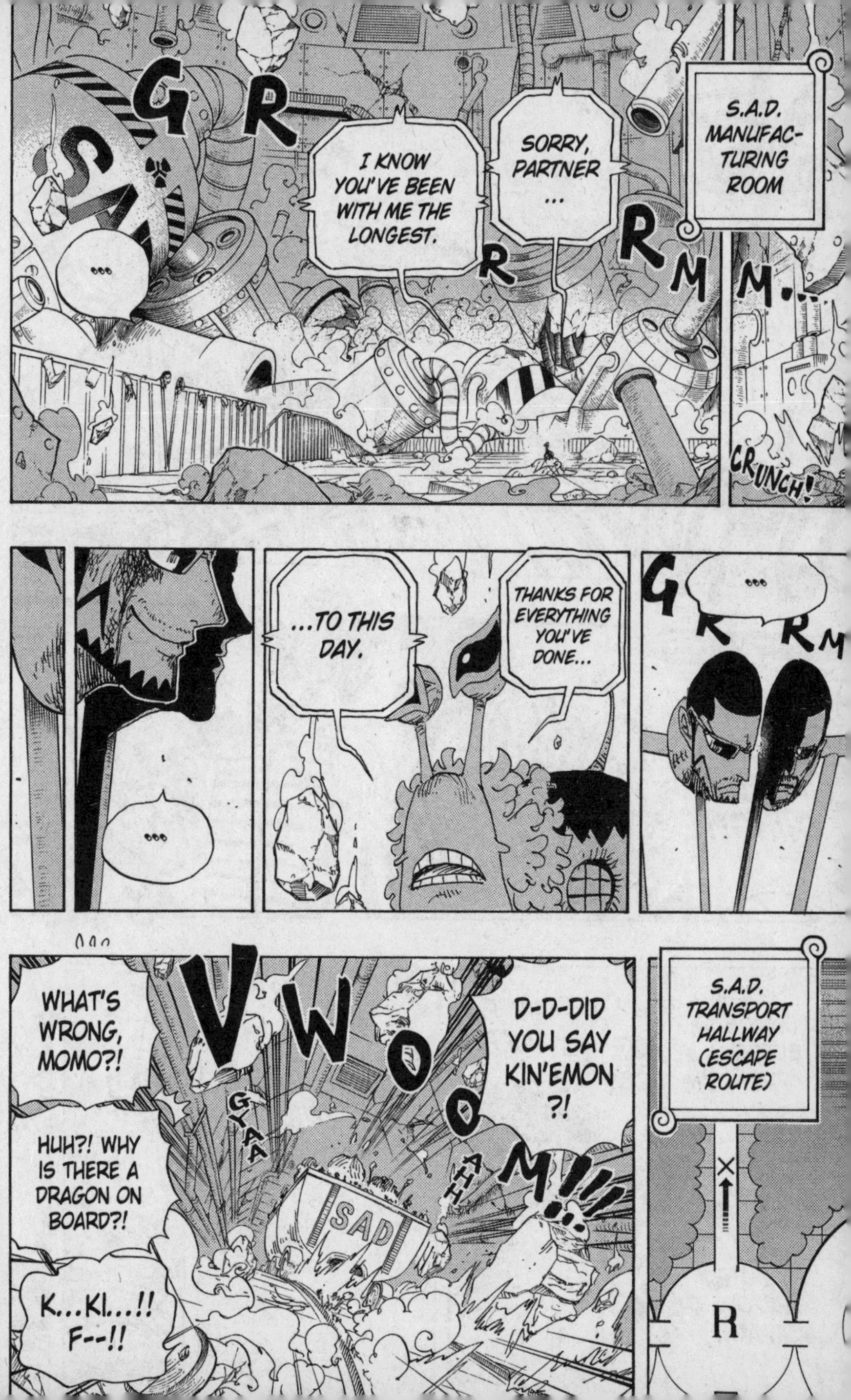

S.A.D. MANUFACTURING ROOM
M...
CRUNCH!
SORRY, PARTNER ...
I KNOW YOU'VE BEEN WITH ME THE LONGEST.
...
GRRRM
...
GRRM
THANKS FOR EVERYTHING YOU'VE DONE...
...TO THIS DAY.
...
S.A.D. TRANSPORT HALLWAY (ESCAPE ROUTE)
R
D-D-DID YOU SAY KIN'EMON ?!
VWOOOM!!!
GYAA
AHH
SAD
WHAT'S WRONG, MOMO?!
HUH?! WHY IS THERE A DRAGON ON BOARD?!
K...KI...!! F--!!

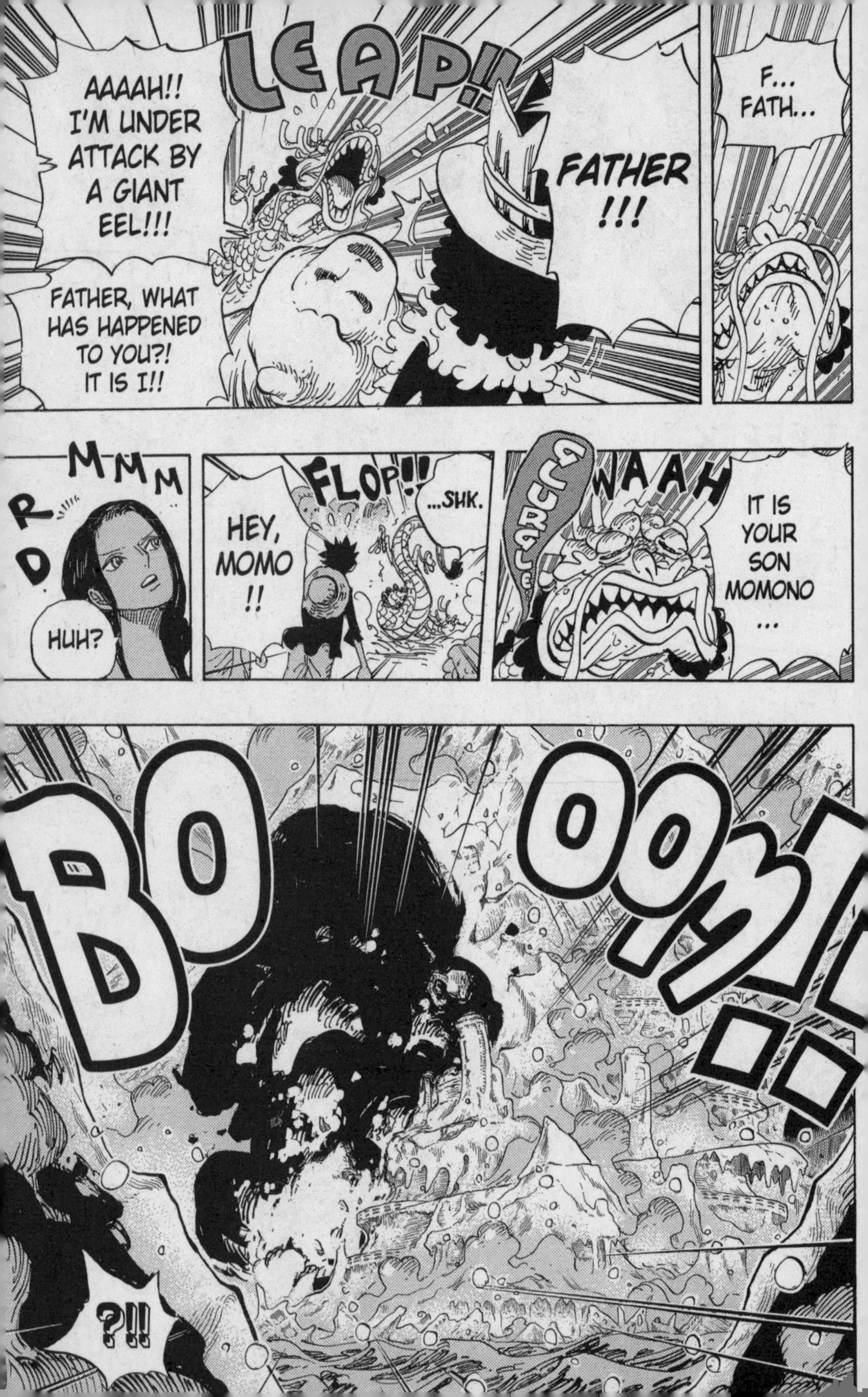
F...
FATH...
LEAP!!
FATHER!!!
AAAAH!! I'M UNDER ATTACK BY A GIANT EEL!!!
FATHER, WHAT HAS HAPPENED TO YOU?! IT IS I!!
WAAH
GURGLE
IT IS YOUR SON MOMONO...
FLOP!!
...SHK.
HEY, MOMO!!
RMMMMD
HUH?
BOOOM!!
?!!

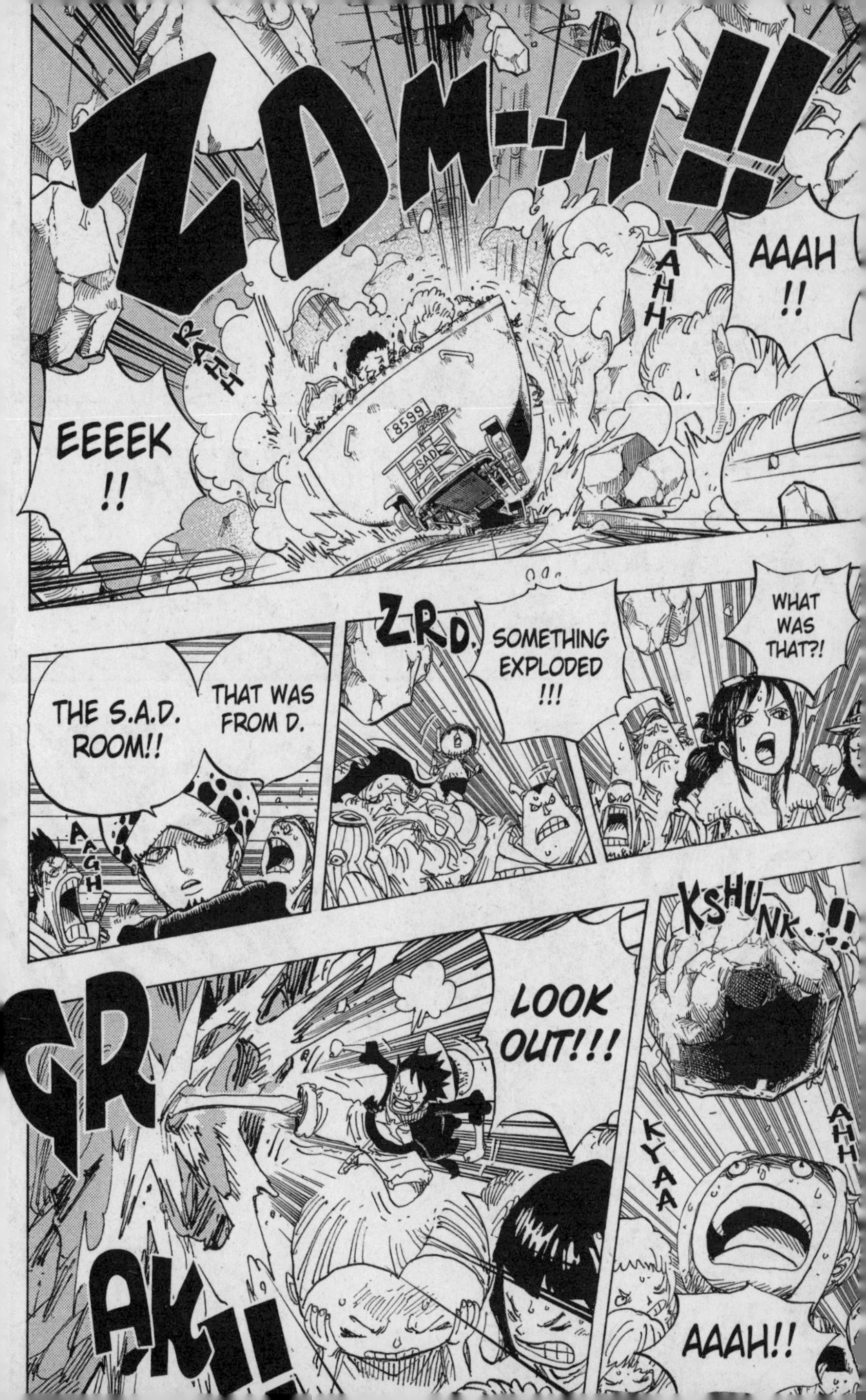
ZDM-M!!
AAAH!!
YAHH
RAHH
EEEEK!!
WHAT WAS THAT?!
SOMETHING EXPLODED!!!
ZRD.
THAT WAS FROM D.
THE S.A.D. ROOM!!
AAGH
KSHUNK..!!
AHH
KYAA
AAAH!!
LOOK OUT!!!
GRAK!!

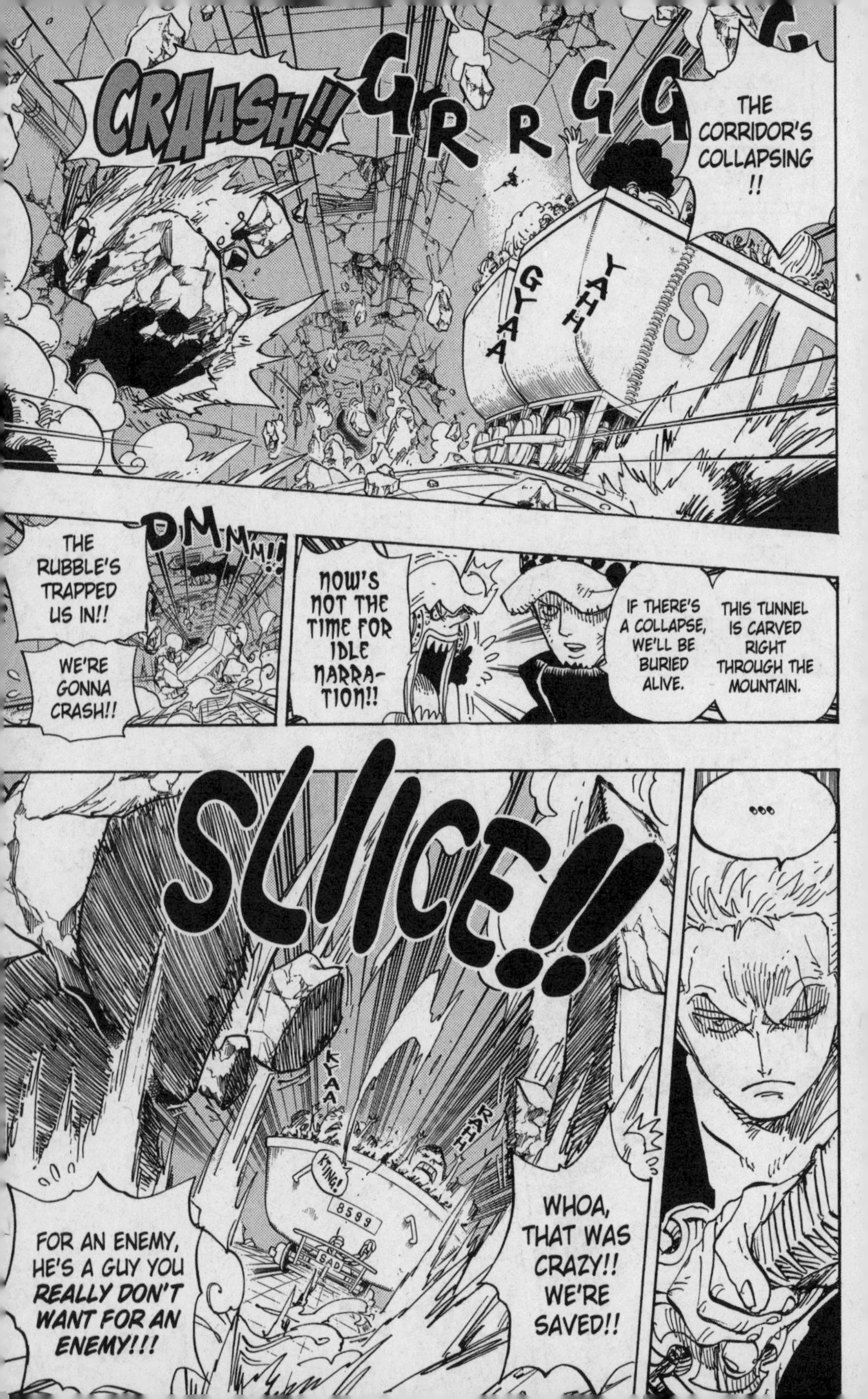
THE CORRIDOR'S COLLAPSING!!
YAHH
GYAAA
SAD
GRRGGG
CRAASH!!
THIS TUNNEL IS CARVED RIGHT THROUGH THE MOUNTAIN.
IF THERE'S A COLLAPSE, WE'LL BE BURIED ALIVE.
NOW'S NOT THE TIME FOR IDLE NARRATION!!
DMMM!!
THE RUBBLE'S TRAPPED US IN!!
WE'RE GONNA CRASH!!
...
SLIICE!!
KYAA
RAHH
KTING!
8599
SAD
WHOA, THAT WAS CRAZY!! WE'RE SAVED!!
FOR AN ENEMY, HE'S A GUY YOU *REALLY DON'T WANT FOR AN ENEMY!!!*

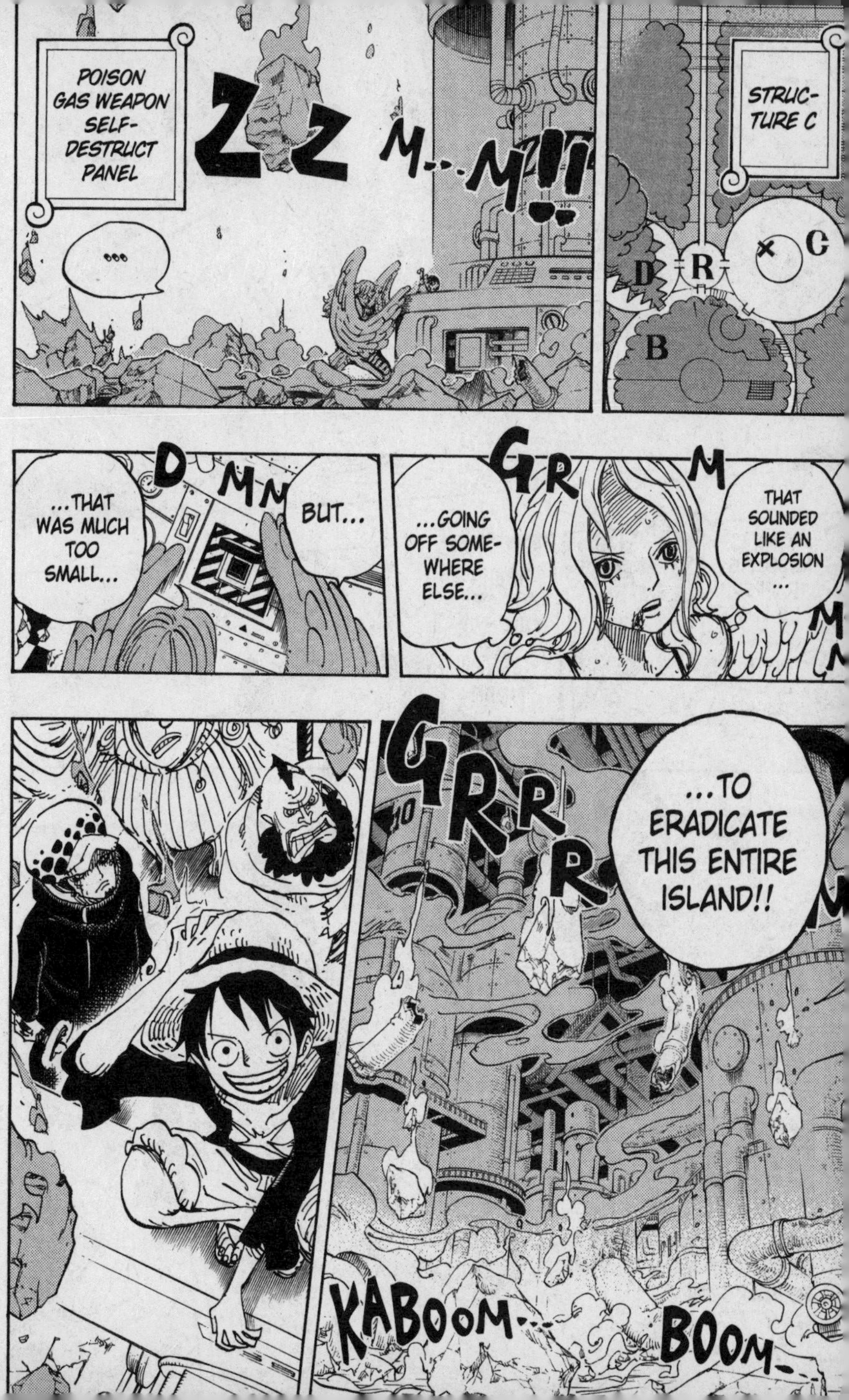
STRUC-TURE C
D
R
C
B
POISON GAS WEAPON SELF-DESTRUCT PANEL
ZZ
M...M!!
...
GR
M
THAT SOUNDED LIKE AN EXPLOSION ...
...GOING OFF SOME-WHERE ELSE...
DMM
BUT...
...THAT WAS MUCH TOO SMALL...
GRRRR
...TO ERADICATE THIS ENTIRE ISLAND!!
KABOOM...
BOOM..

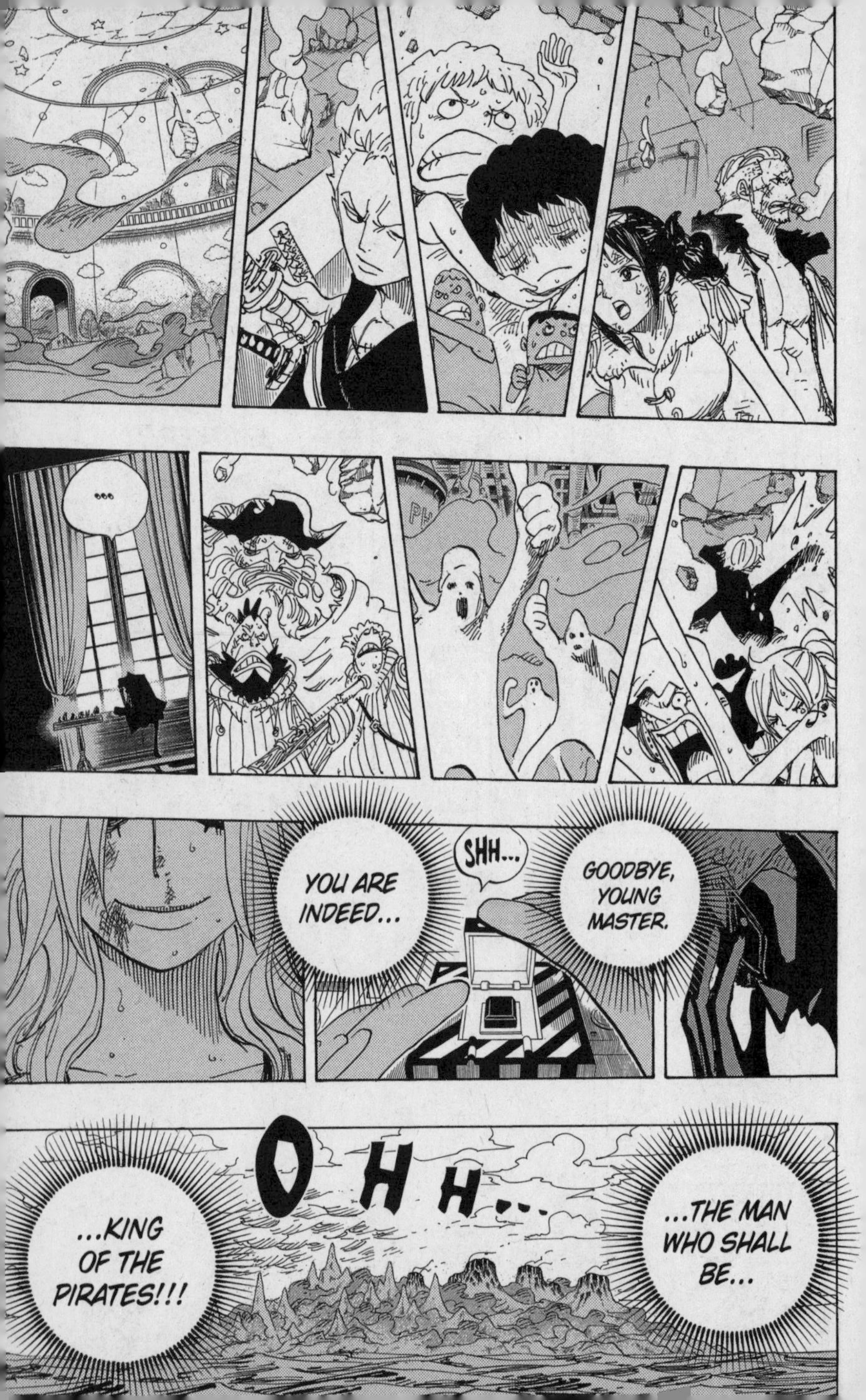
...
GOODBYE, YOUNG MASTER.
SHH...
YOU ARE INDEED...
...THE MAN WHO SHALL BE...
OHH...
...KING OF THE PIRATES!!!

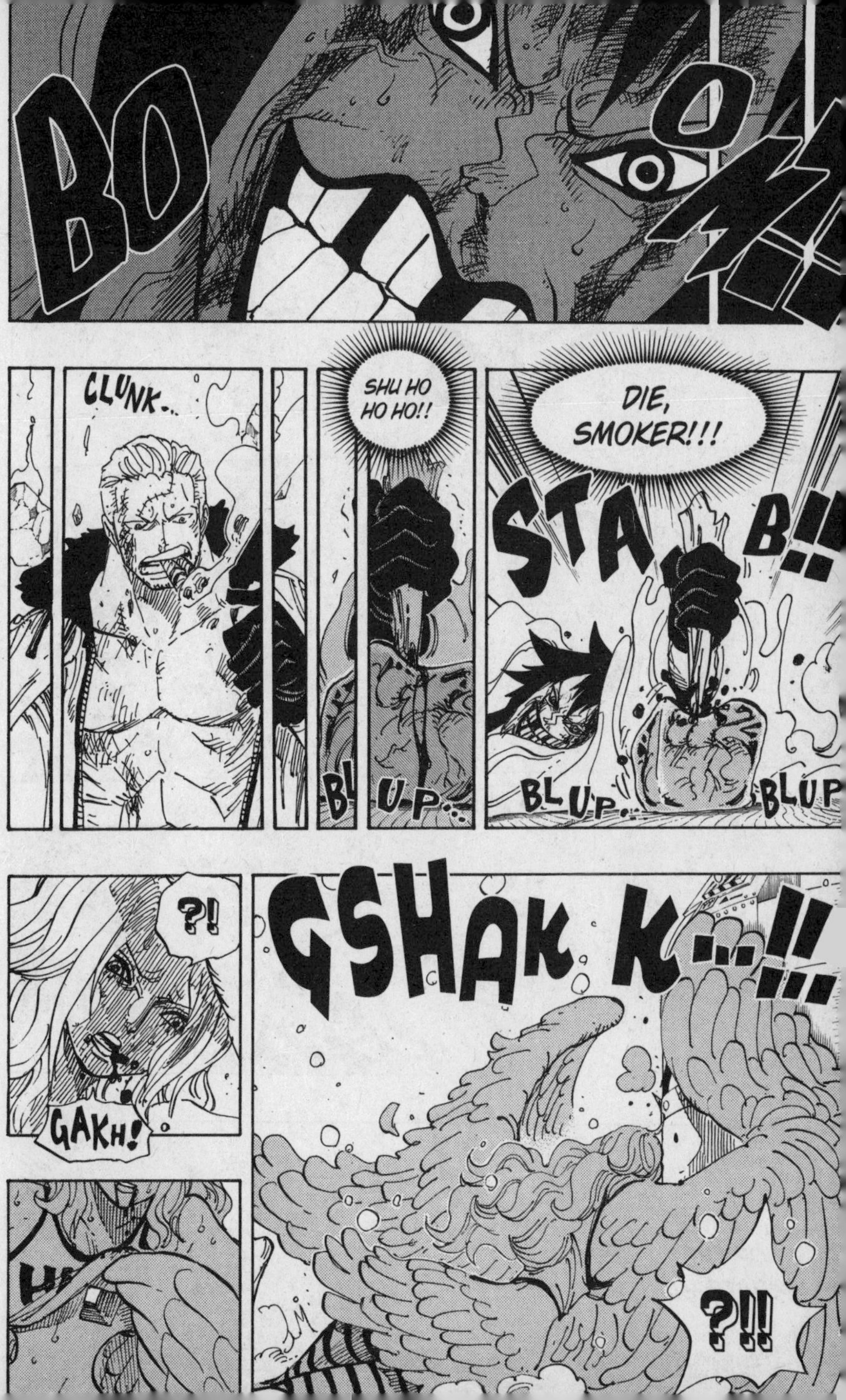
BOOM!!
DIE, SMOKER!!!
STAB!!
BLUP
BLUP..
SHU HO HO HO!!
BLUP...
CLUNK...
GSHAKK...!!
?!!
?!
GAKH!

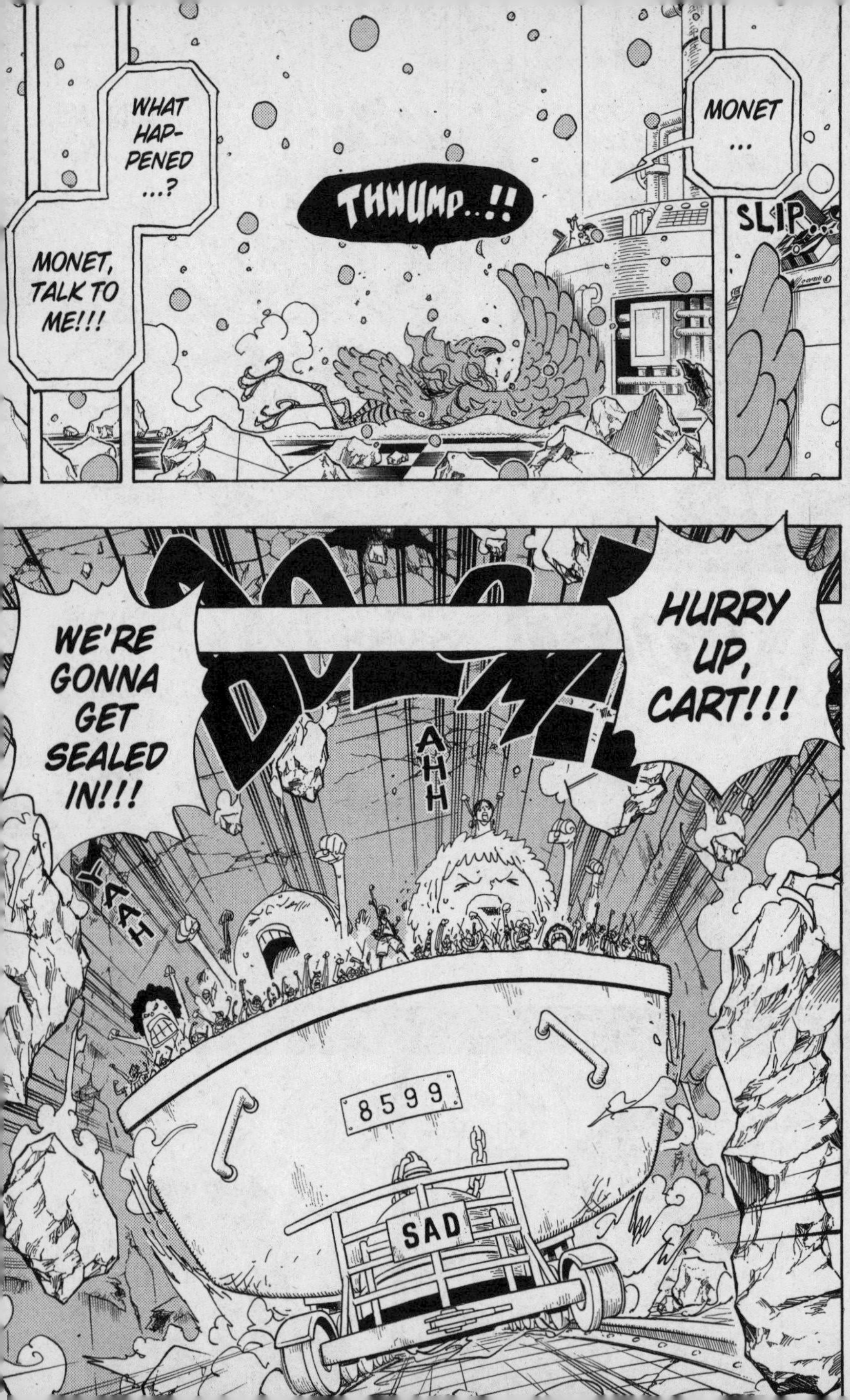
MONET ...
SLIP
THWUMP..!!
WHAT HAP-PENED ...?
MONET, TALK TO ME!!!
HURRY UP, CART!!!
AHH
YAAH
WE'RE GONNA GET SEALED IN!!!
8599
SAD

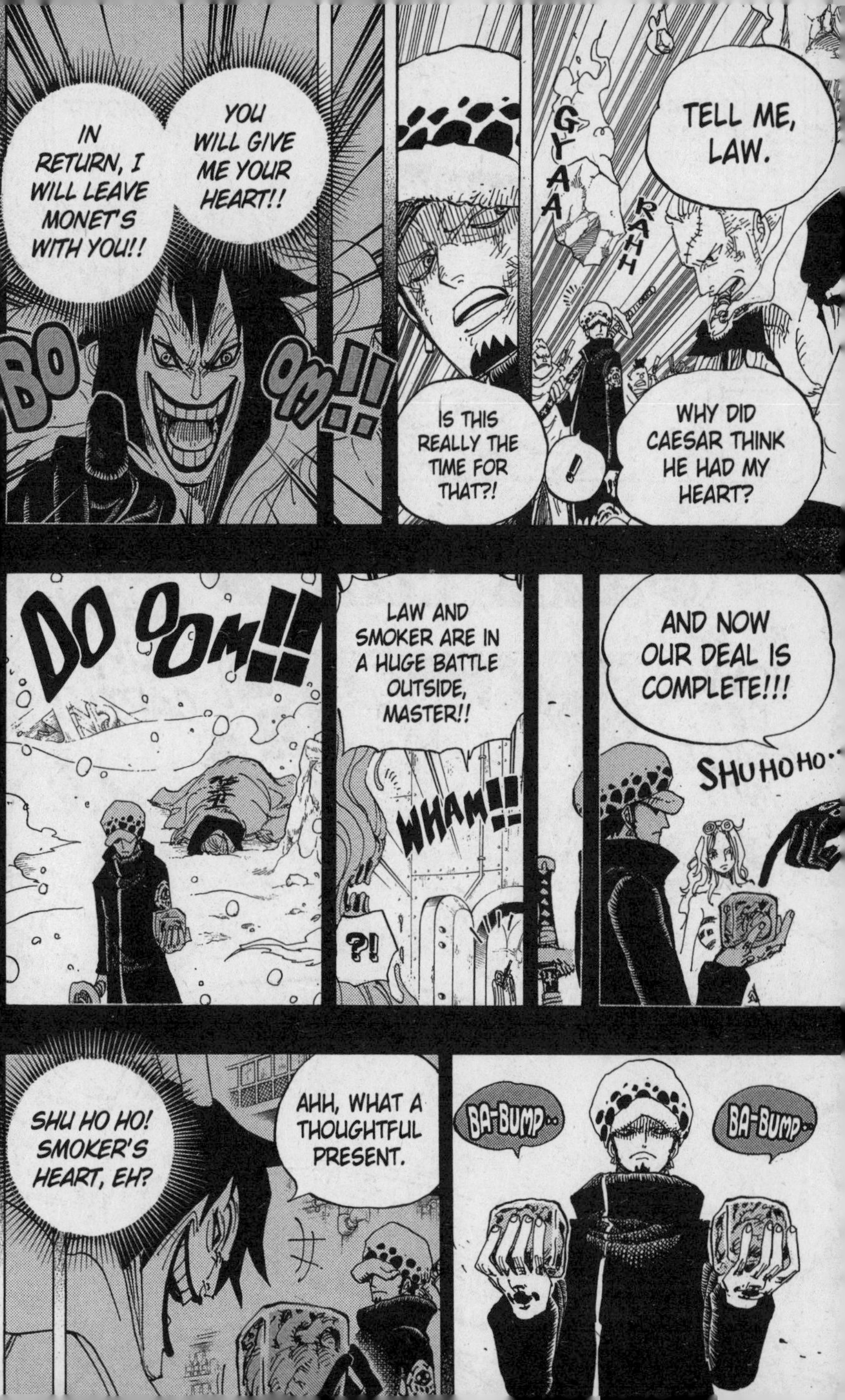
TELL ME, LAW.
GYAA
RAHH
WHY DID CAESAR THINK HE HAD MY HEART?
!
IS THIS REALLY THE TIME FOR THAT?!
YOU WILL GIVE ME YOUR HEART!!
IN RETURN, I WILL LEAVE MONET'S WITH YOU!!
BOOM!!
AND NOW OUR DEAL IS COMPLETE!!!
SHUHOHO..
LAW AND SMOKER ARE IN A HUGE BATTLE OUTSIDE, MASTER!!
WHAM!!
?!
DOOOM!!
BA-BUMP..
BA-BUMP..
AHH, WHAT A THOUGHTFUL PRESENT.
SHU HO HO! SMOKER'S HEART, EH?

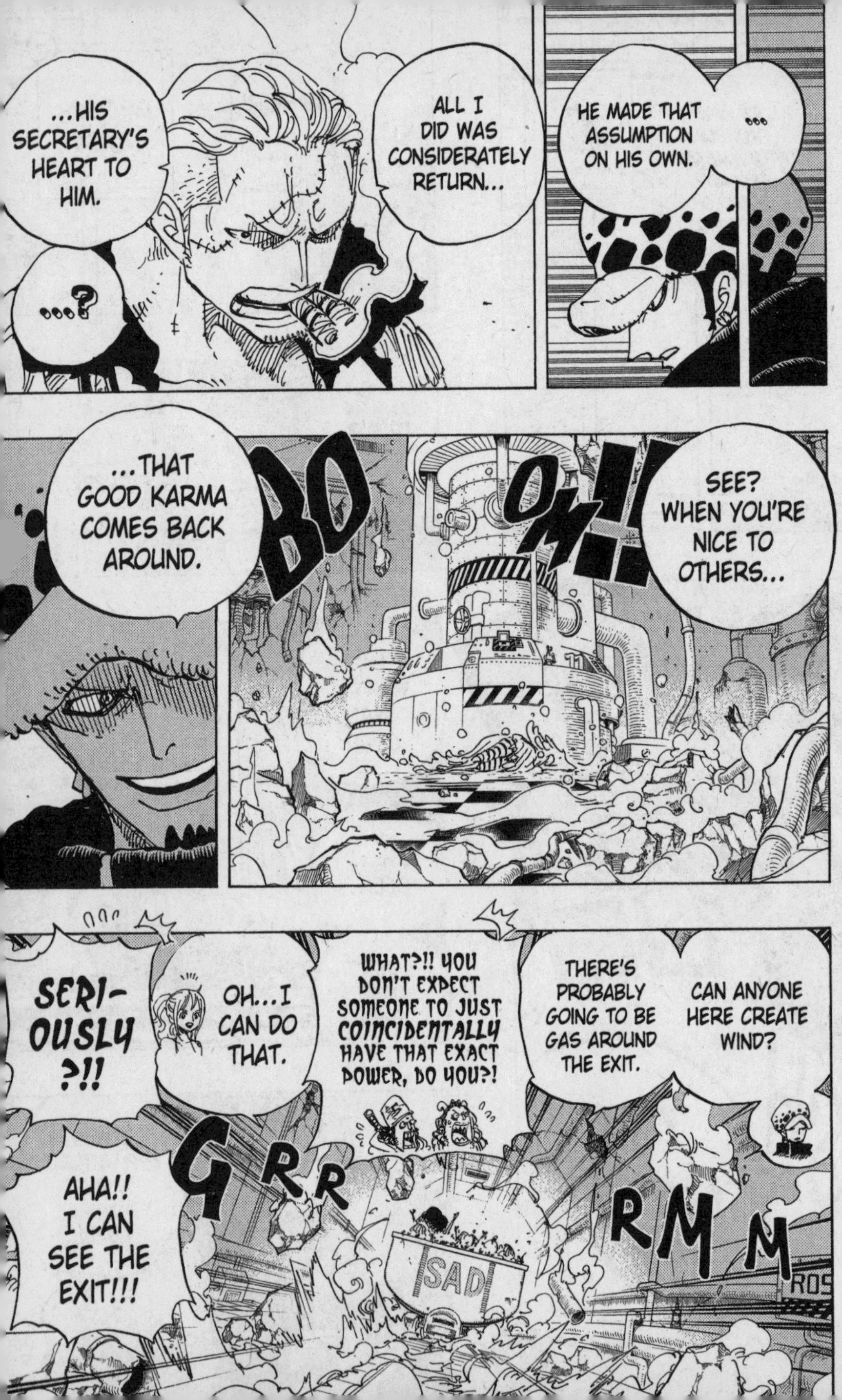
...
HE MADE THAT ASSUMPTION ON HIS OWN.
ALL I DID WAS CONSIDERATELY RETURN...
...HIS SECRETARY'S HEART TO HIM.
...?
SEE? WHEN YOU'RE NICE TO OTHERS...
BOOM!!
...THAT GOOD KARMA COMES BACK AROUND.
CAN ANYONE HERE CREATE WIND?
THERE'S PROBABLY GOING TO BE GAS AROUND THE EXIT.
WHAT?!! YOU DON'T EXPECT SOMEONE TO JUST COINCIDENTALLY HAVE THAT EXACT POWER, DO YOU?!
OH...I CAN DO THAT.
SERI-OUSLY?!!
RMM
GRR
AHA!! I CAN SEE THE EXIT!!!
SAD
ROS

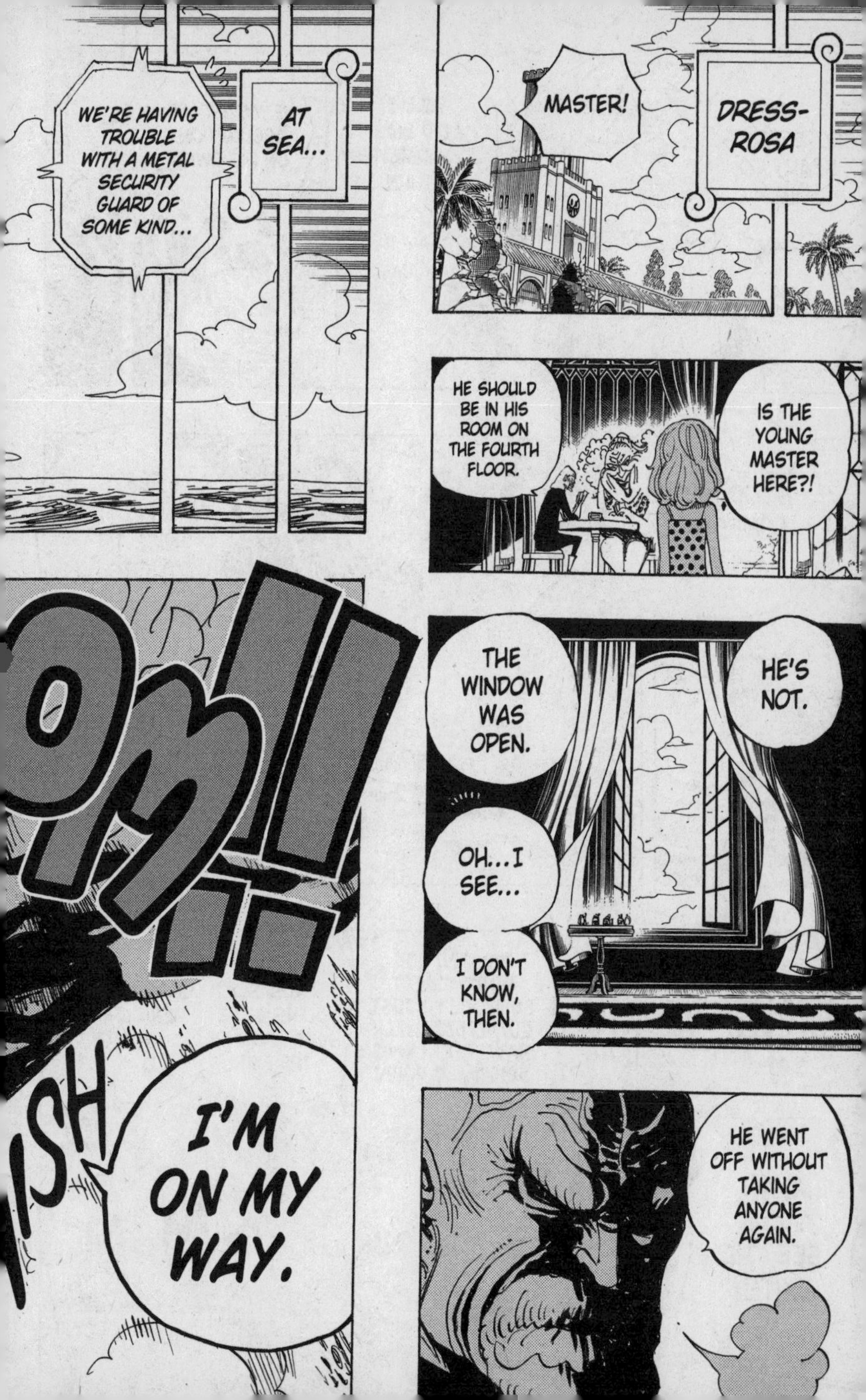
DRESS-ROSA
MASTER!
IS THE YOUNG MASTER HERE?!
HE SHOULD BE IN HIS ROOM ON THE FOURTH FLOOR.
AT SEA...
WE'RE HAVING TROUBLE WITH A METAL SECURITY GUARD OF SOME KIND...
HE'S NOT.
THE WINDOW WAS OPEN.
OH...I SEE...
I DON'T KNOW, THEN.
HE WENT OFF WITHOUT TAKING ANYONE AGAIN.
I'M ON MY WAY.

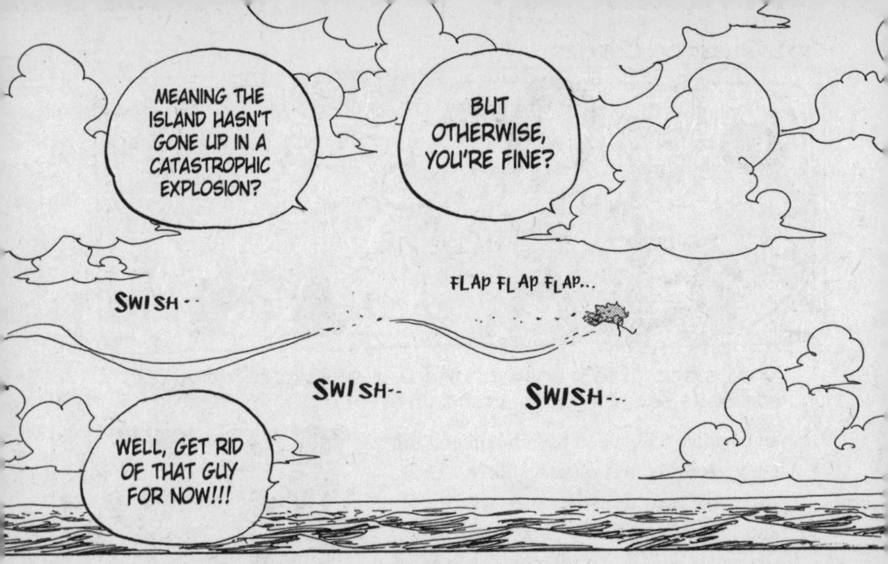
BUT OTHERWISE, YOU'RE FINE?
MEANING THE ISLAND HASN'T GONE UP IN A CATASTROPHIC EXPLOSION?
FLAP FLAP FLAP...
SWISH--
SWISH---
SWISH--
WELL, GET RID OF THAT GUY FOR NOW!!!
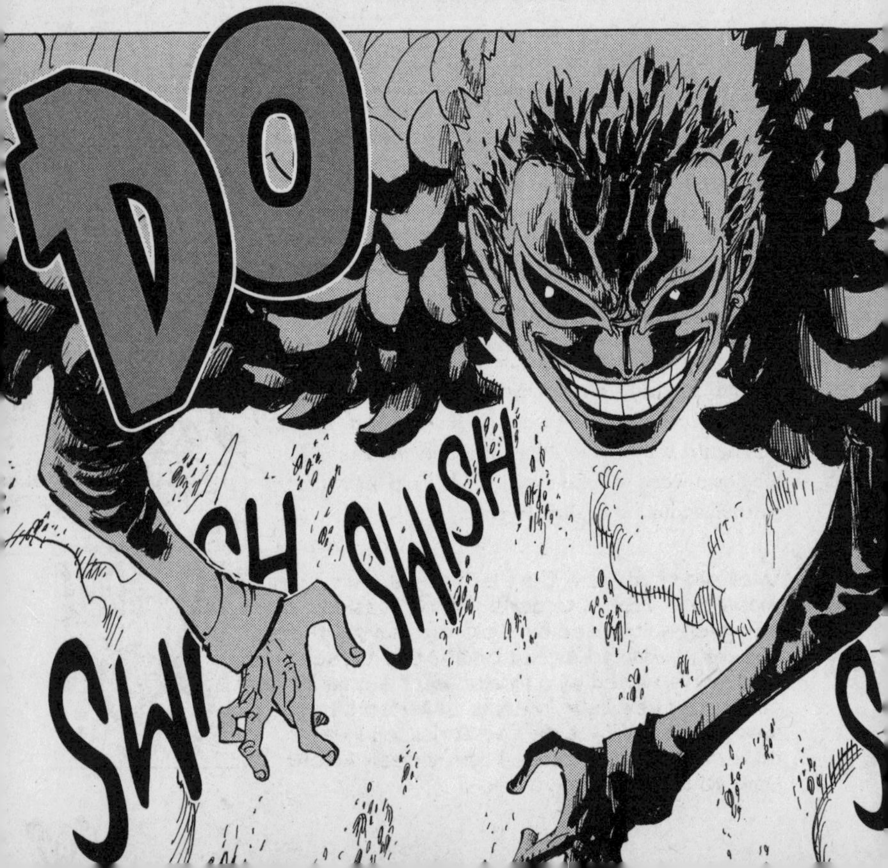
DO
SWISH
SWISH

SBS Question Corner

質問コーナー
想像すんな!!!!
エス
ドロ
ビー
ドロ
エス

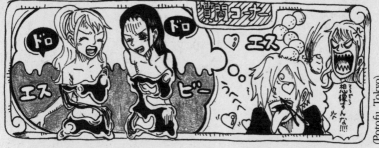

(Potofu, Tokyo)

A: Well, since I didn't answer the last question from the previous section, let's start with that.

SO WILL I.
WELL, WITH THIS MANY PROMISES...
SQUEEZE!!
...I'M SURE IT WILL BE FULFILLED!

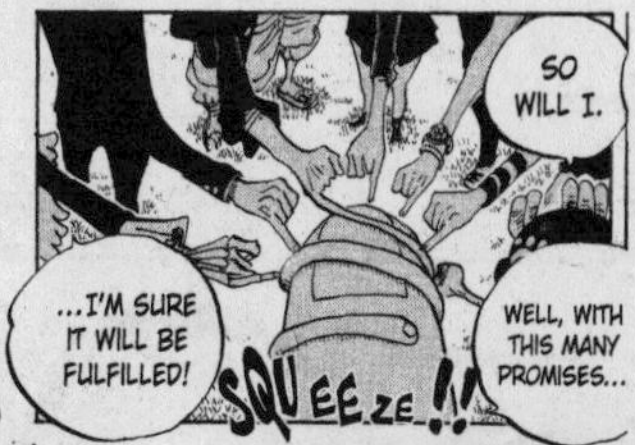

Q: In Chapter 653, when Shirahoshi and the crew promised to go on a walk in a real forest the next time they met, why did Zolo and Franky not do the pinky promise?!

--Yuminami Kobayashi Cat

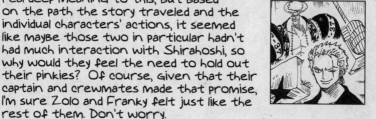

A: Hmm. Seems like many people were bothered by this. There's no real deep meaning to this, but based on the path the story traveled and the individual characters' actions, it seemed like maybe those two in particular hadn't had much interaction with Shirahoshi, so why would they feel the need to hold out their pinkies? Of course, given that their captain and crewmates made that promise, I'm sure Zolo and Franky felt just like the rest of them. Don't worry.

Q: In Chapter 692, there's a scene where Nami and Luffy reunite. You can see a stocky-looking sailor who appears to be carrying Tashigi on his shoulder. That's her, right?! Why is she riding him? She told Zolo, "Let me down when we find my men." Is Zolo really that worried about her health? Heehee.

--Someta

BO—OM!

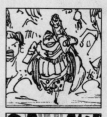

A: Well spotted. Yes, that is Tashigi. But that wasn't on Zolo's orders. I think Tashigi being embarrassed by Zolo was simply that she didn't want her subordinates to see her being helped by a pirate. But being carried by her own men is different. I suppose she might be embarrassed in a different way, though. I don't really know how young women think.

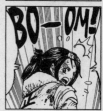

Chapter 695:
LEAVE IT TO US!!!

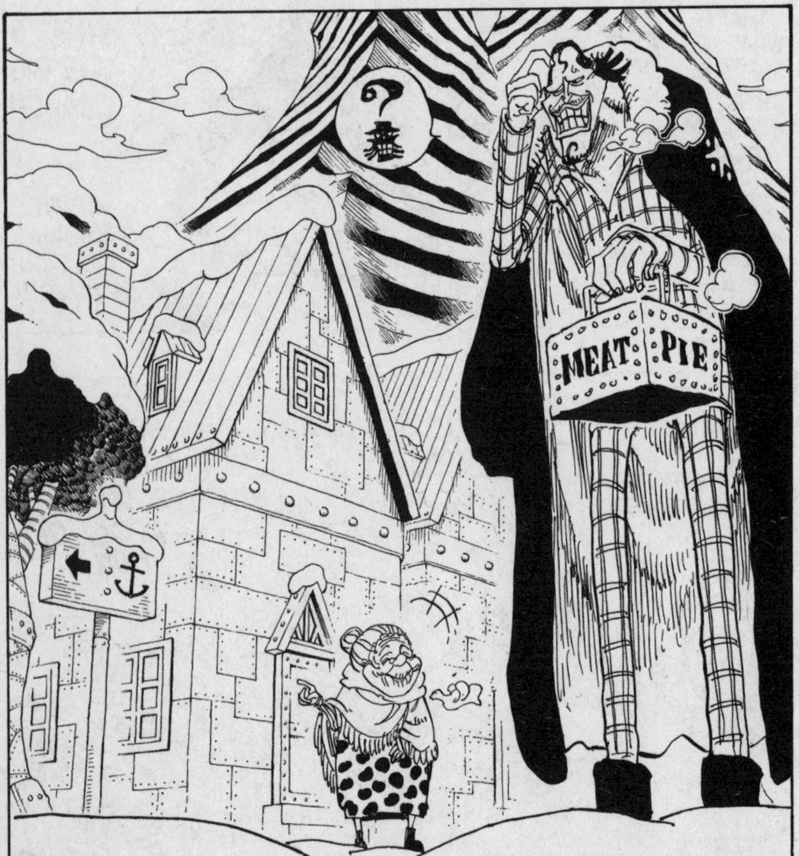
MEAT PIE

CARIBOU'S NEW WORLD KEE HEE HEE, VOL. 17: "CARIBOU GETS A MEAT PIE FOR THE ROAD—THE PORT IS THAT WAY"

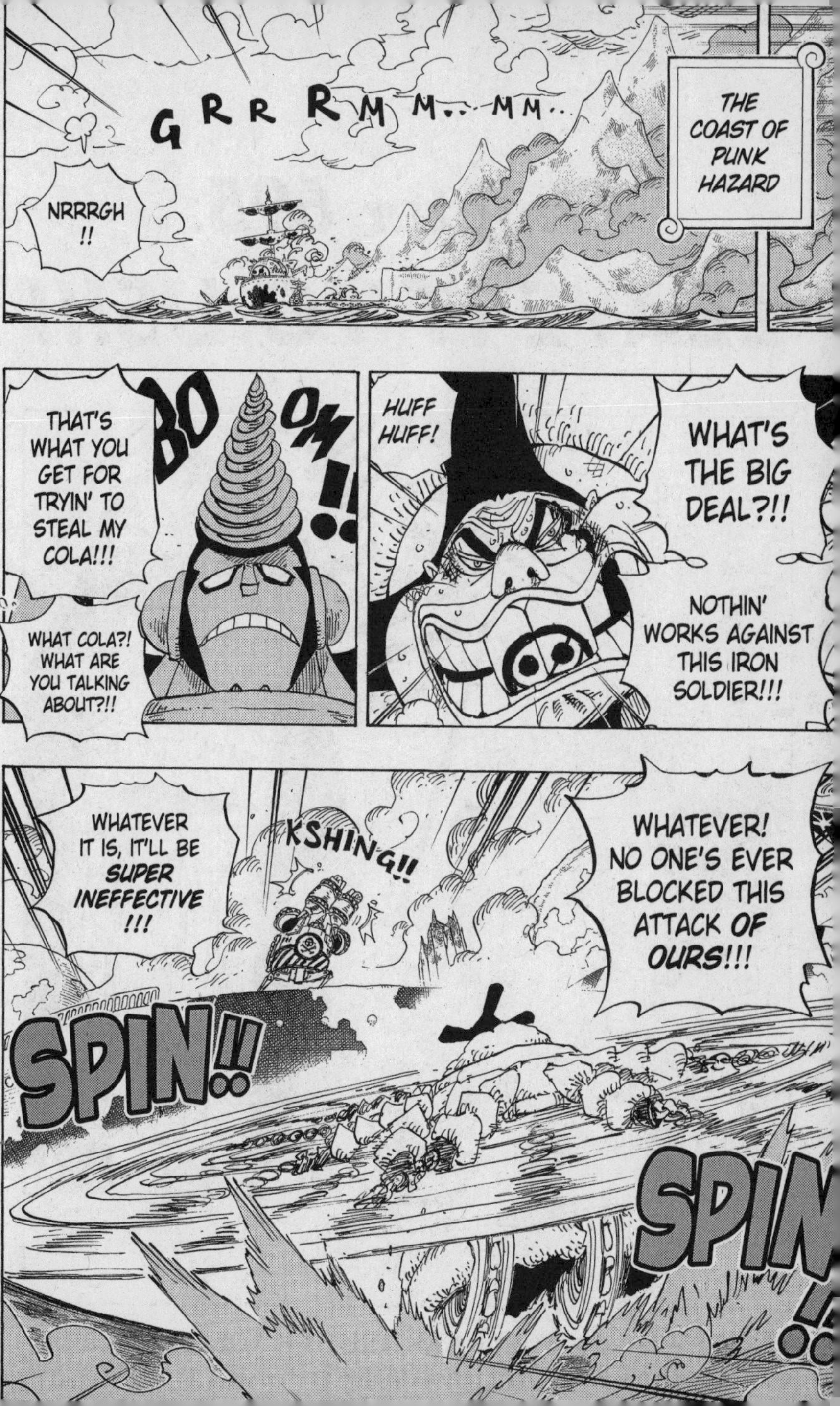

THE COAST OF PUNK HAZARD
G R R R M M M.. MM..
NRRRGH !!
WHAT'S THE BIG DEAL?!!
NOTHIN' WORKS AGAINST THIS IRON SOLDIER!!!
HUFF HUFF!
BOOM!!
THAT'S WHAT YOU GET FOR TRYIN' TO STEAL MY COLA!!!
WHAT COLA?! WHAT ARE YOU TALKING ABOUT?!!
WHATEVER! NO ONE'S EVER BLOCKED THIS ATTACK OF OURS!!!
KSHING!!
WHATEVER IT IS, IT'LL BE SUPER INEFFECTIVE !!!
SPIN!!
SPIN!!

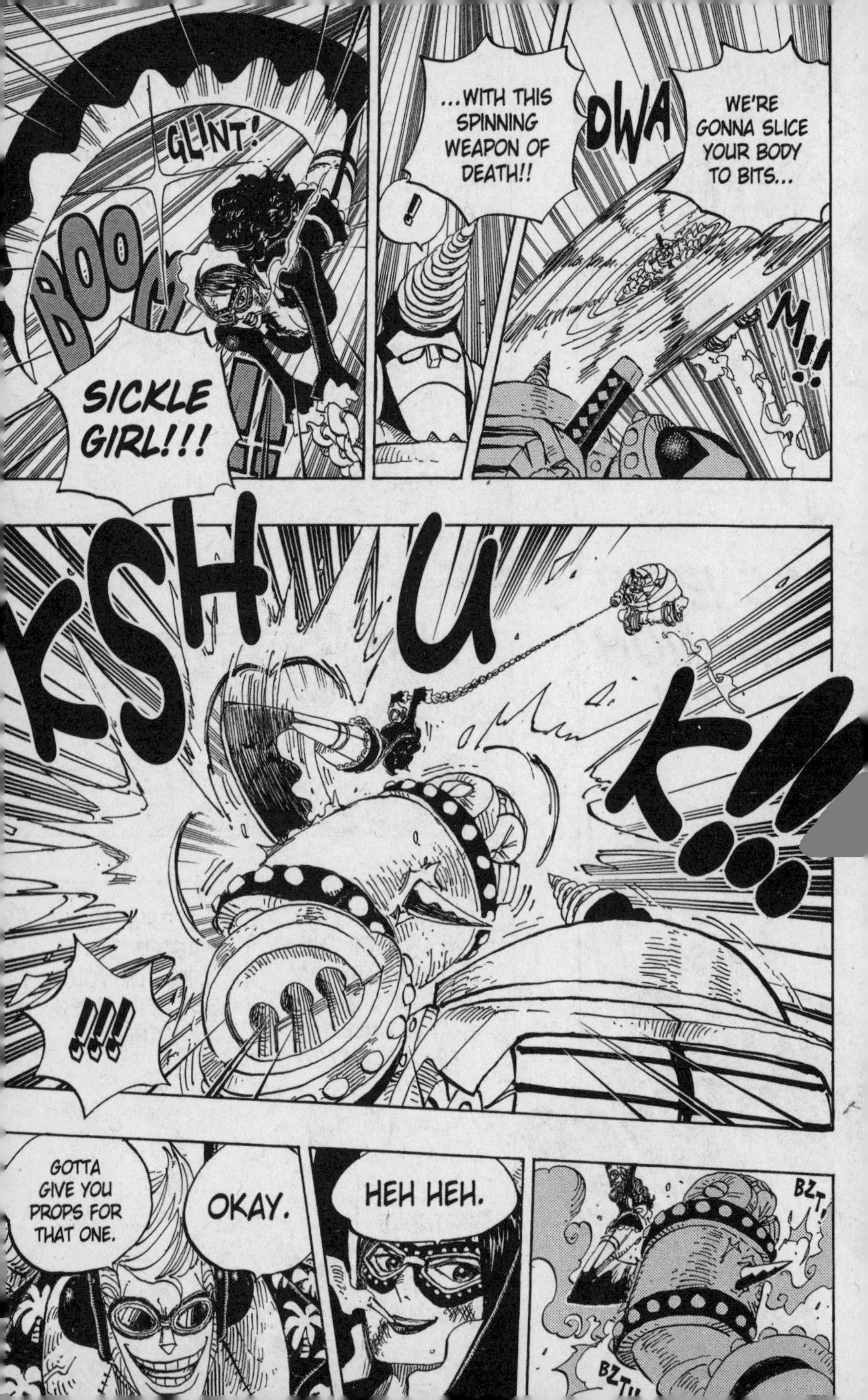
WE'RE GONNA SLICE YOUR BODY TO BITS...
DWA
...WITH THIS SPINNING WEAPON OF DEATH!!
!
M!!
GLINT!
SICKLE GIRL!!!
KSHUNK!!
!!!
BZT!
BZT!!
HEH HEH.
OKAY.
GOTTA GIVE YOU PROPS FOR THAT ONE.

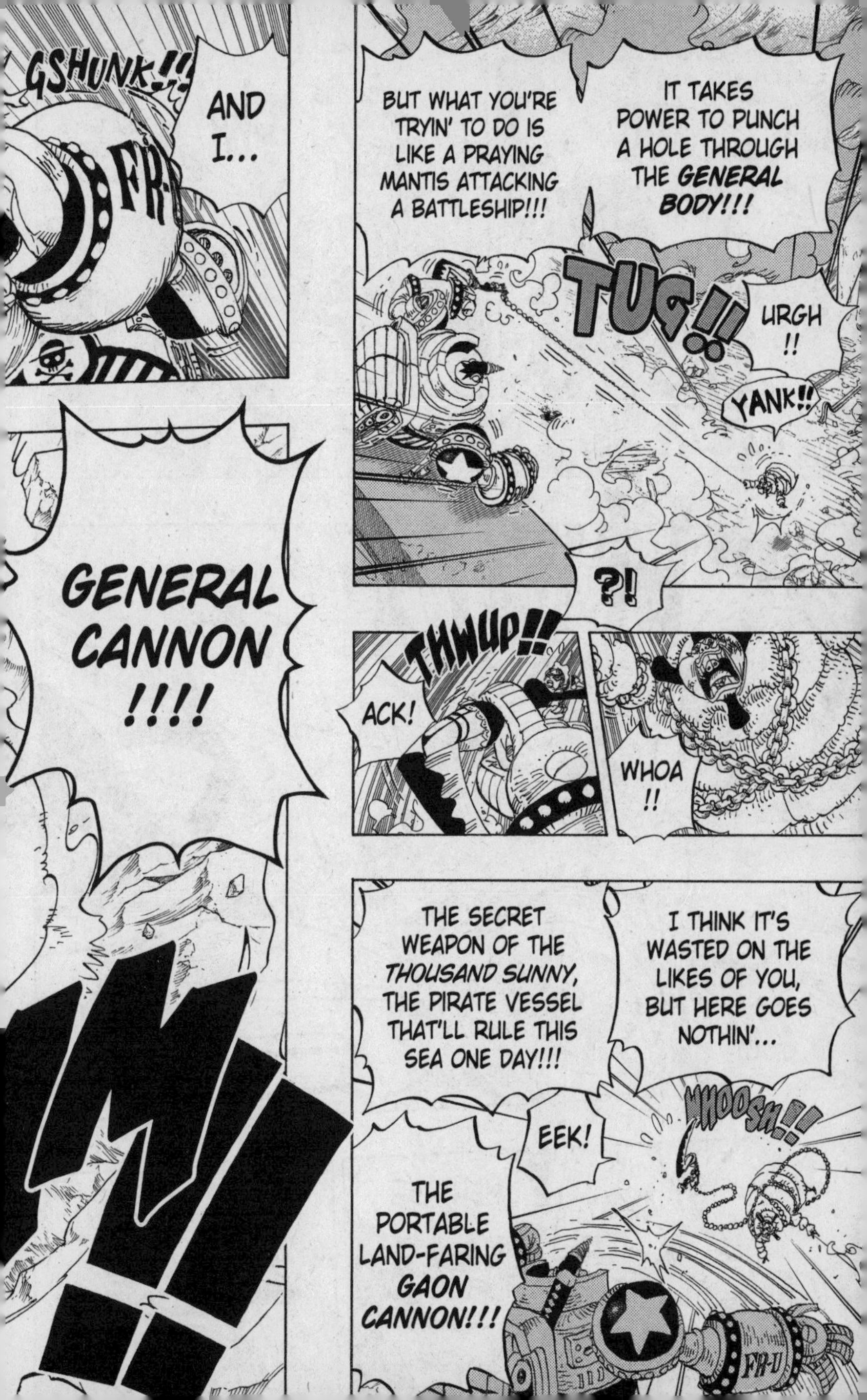
IT TAKES POWER TO PUNCH A HOLE THROUGH THE GENERAL BODY!!!
BUT WHAT YOU'RE TRYIN' TO DO IS LIKE A PRAYING MANTIS ATTACKING A BATTLESHIP!!!
TUG!!
URGH!!
YANK!!
?!
WHOA!!
THWUP!!
ACK!
I THINK IT'S WASTED ON THE LIKES OF YOU, BUT HERE GOES NOTHIN'...
THE SECRET WEAPON OF THE THOUSAND SUNNY, THE PIRATE VESSEL THAT'LL RULE THIS SEA ONE DAY!!!
WHOOSH!!
EEK!
THE PORTABLE LAND-FARING GAON CANNON!!!
GSHUNK!!!
AND I...
GENERAL CANNON!!!!

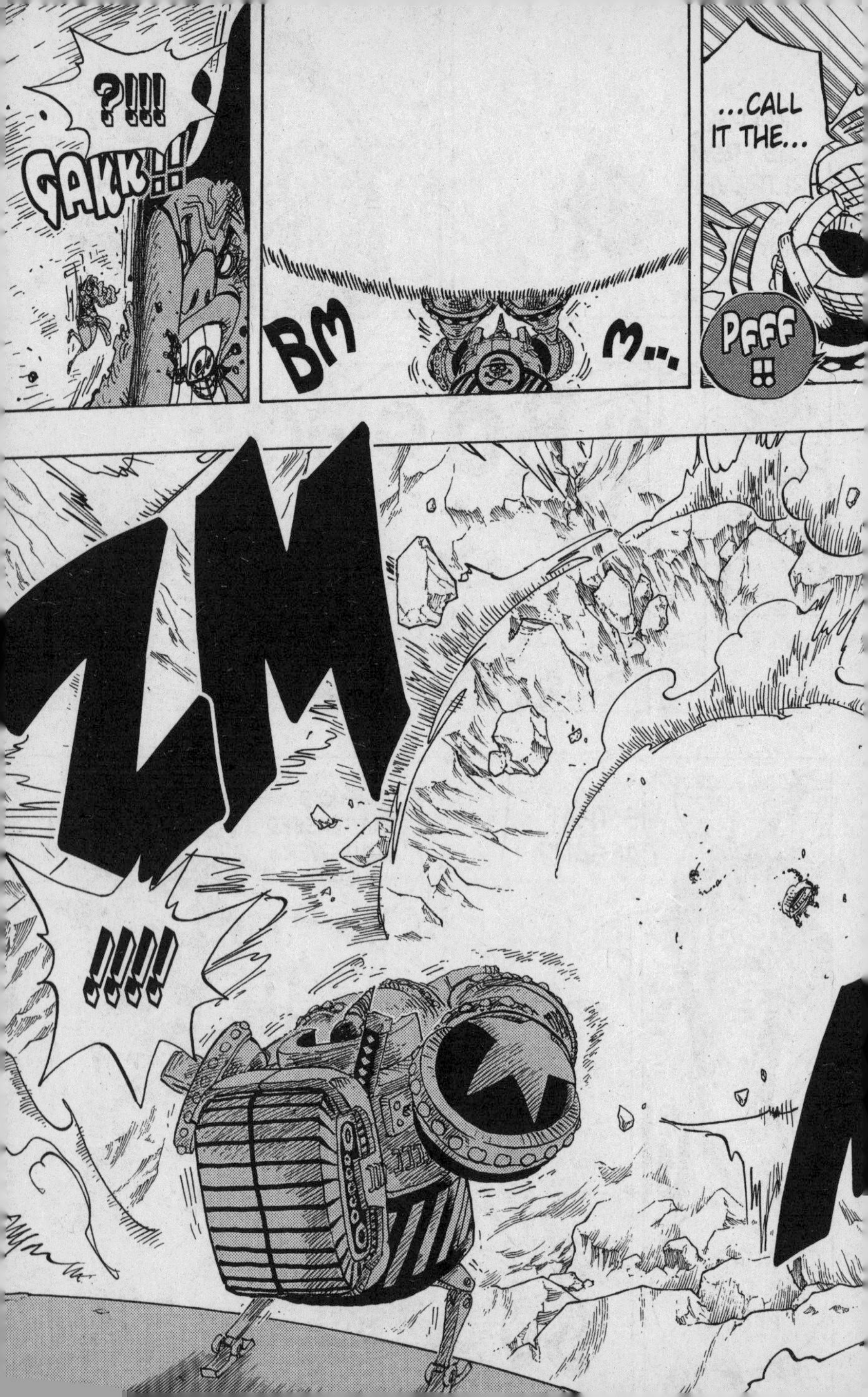
...CALL IT THE...
PFFF!!
BM
M...
?!!!
GAKK!!
ZM
!!!!

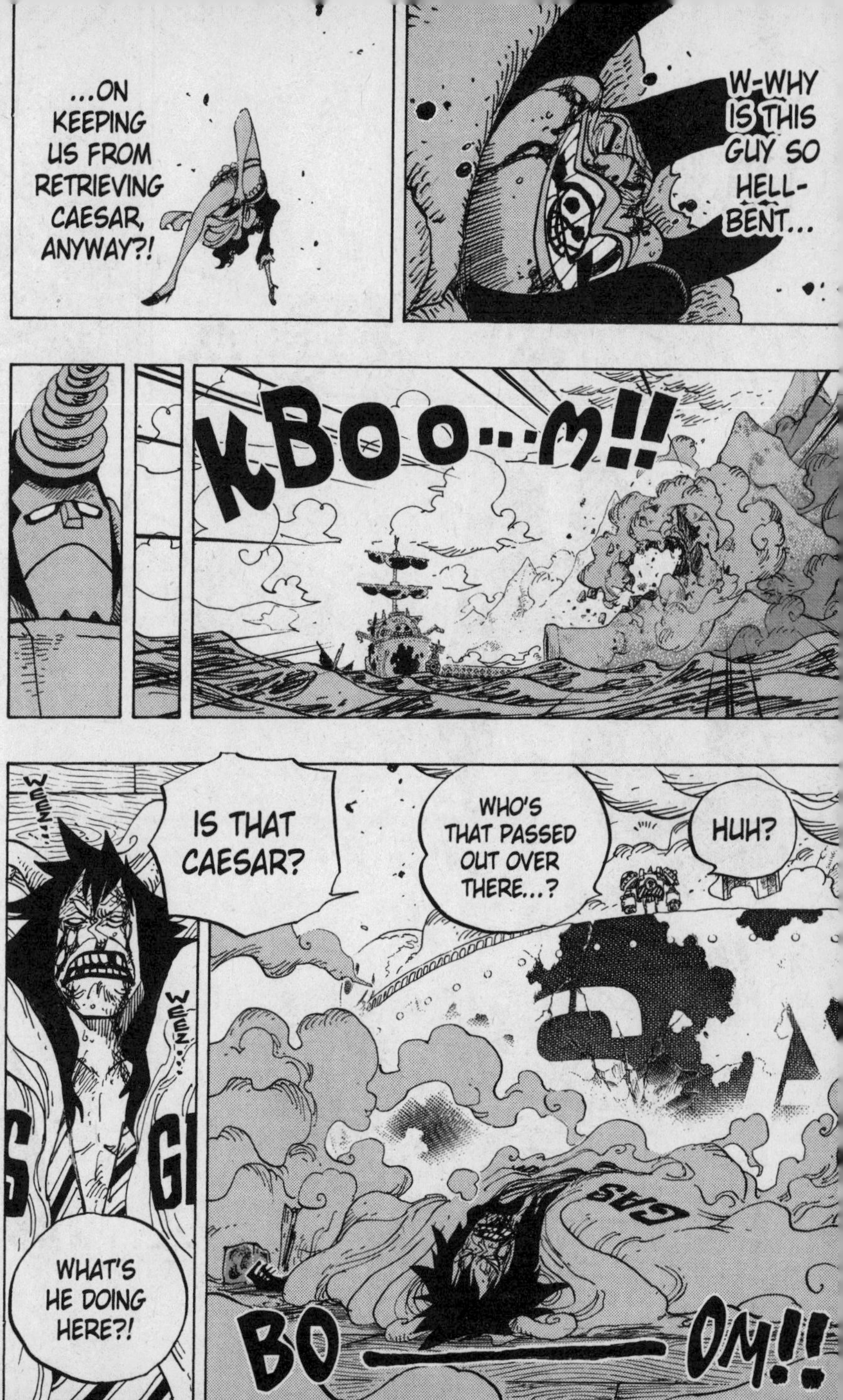
W-WHY IS THIS GUY SO HELL-BENT...
...ON KEEPING US FROM RETRIEVING CAESAR, ANYWAY?!
KBOO...M!!
HUH?
WHO'S THAT PASSED OUT OVER THERE...?
IS THAT CAESAR?
WEEZ...
WEEZ...
WHAT'S HE DOING HERE?!
BO——OM!!

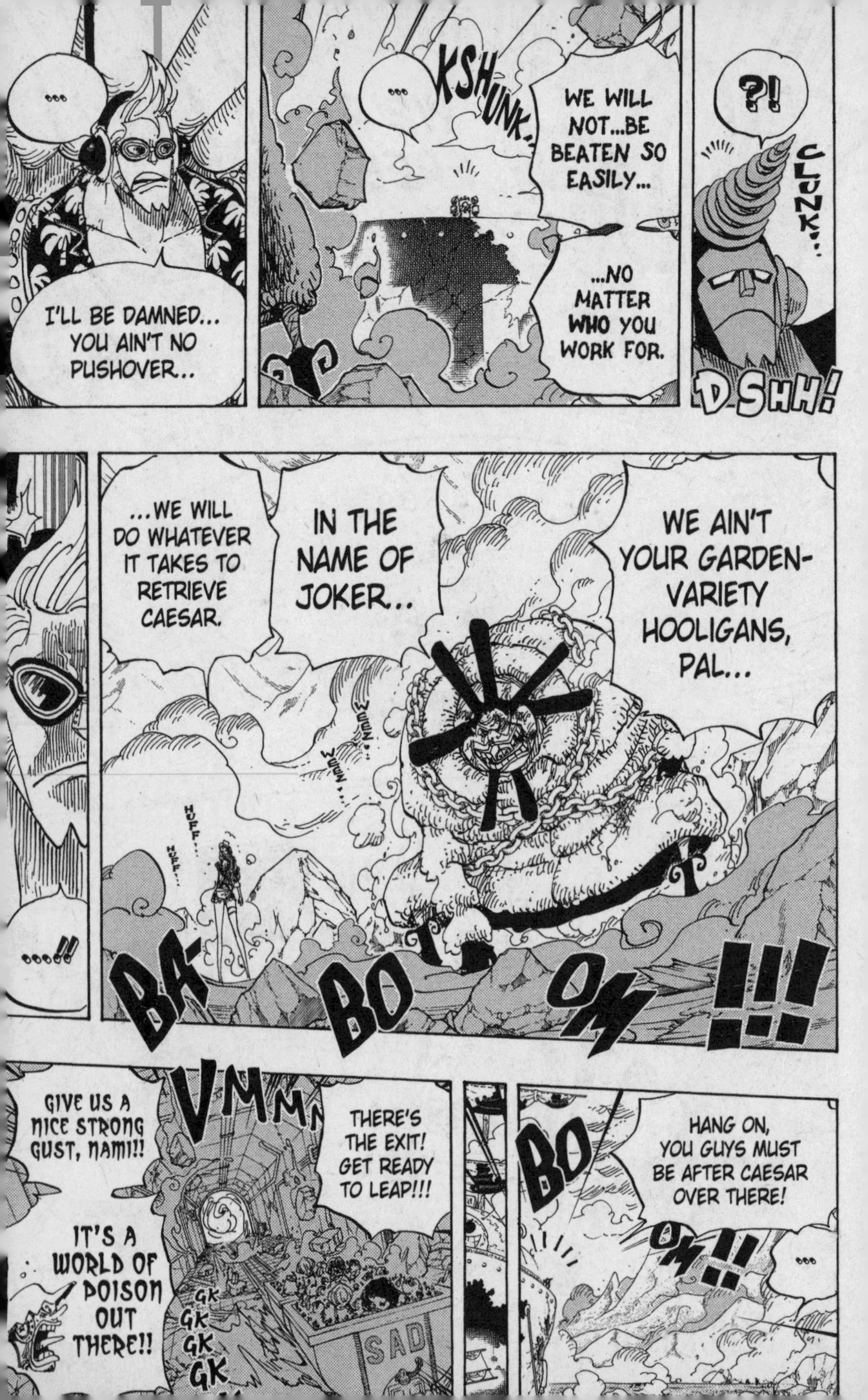
?!
CLUNK...
DSHH!
WE WILL NOT...BE BEATEN SO EASILY...
KSHUNK...
...
...NO MATTER WHO YOU WORK FOR.
...
I'LL BE DAMNED... YOU AIN'T NO PUSHOVER...
WE AIN'T YOUR GARDEN-VARIETY HOOLIGANS, PAL...
IN THE NAME OF JOKER...
...WE WILL DO WHATEVER IT TAKES TO RETRIEVE CAESAR.
WEEN...
WEEN...
HUFF...
HUFF...
BA-BOOM!!!
...!!
HANG ON, YOU GUYS MUST BE AFTER CAESAR OVER THERE!
BO
OM!!
...
THERE'S THE EXIT! GET READY TO LEAP!!!
VMMN
GIVE US A NICE STRONG GUST, NAMI!!
IT'S A WORLD OF POISON OUT THERE!!
GK
GK
GK
GK
SAD

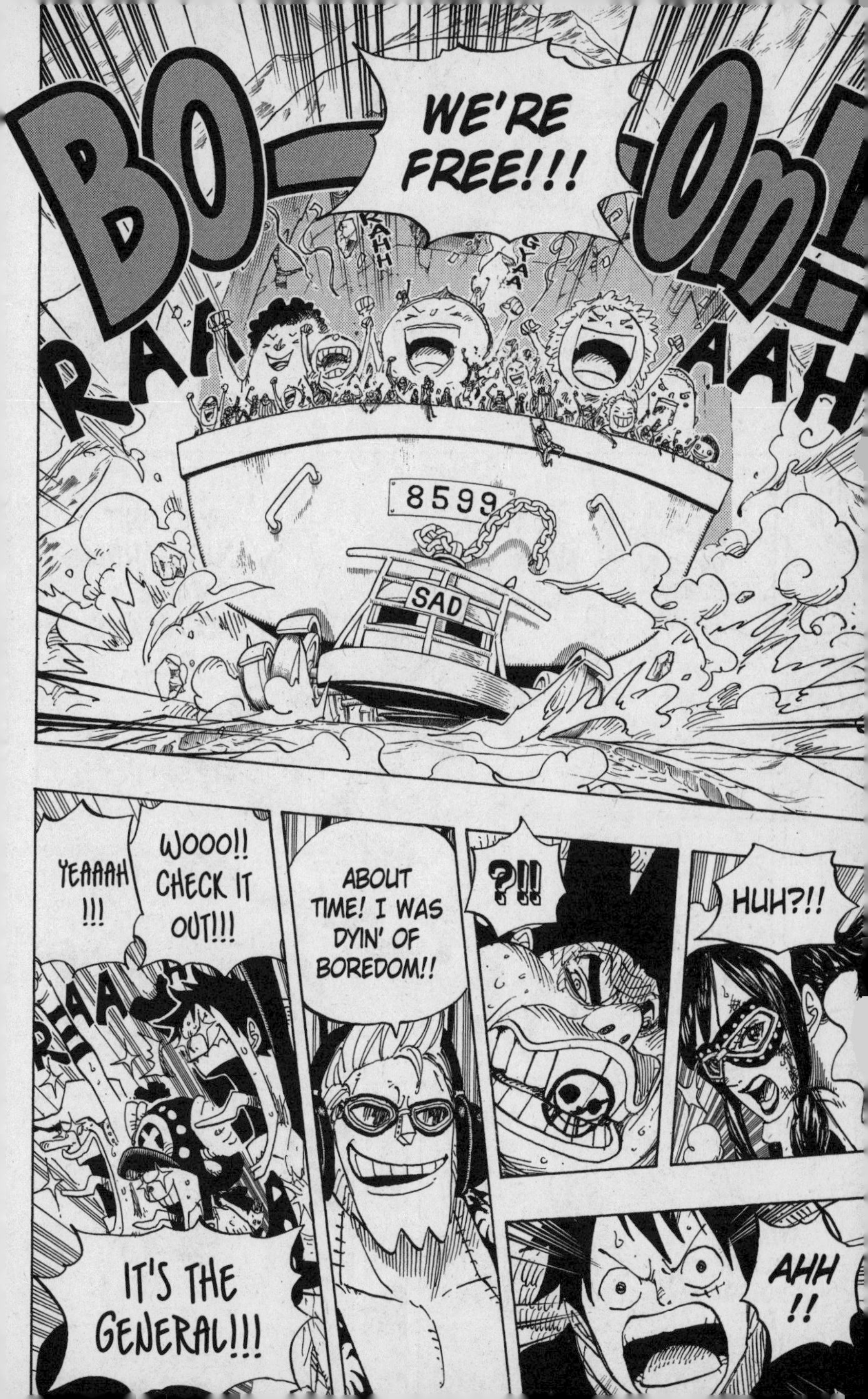

BO-OM!!
WE'RE FREE!!!
RAAAH
KAHHH
GYAA
HUH?!!
?!!
AHH !!
ABOUT TIME! I WAS DYIN' OF BOREDOM!!
WOOO!! CHECK IT OUT!!!
YEAAAH !!!
RAAAH
IT'S THE GENERAL!!!

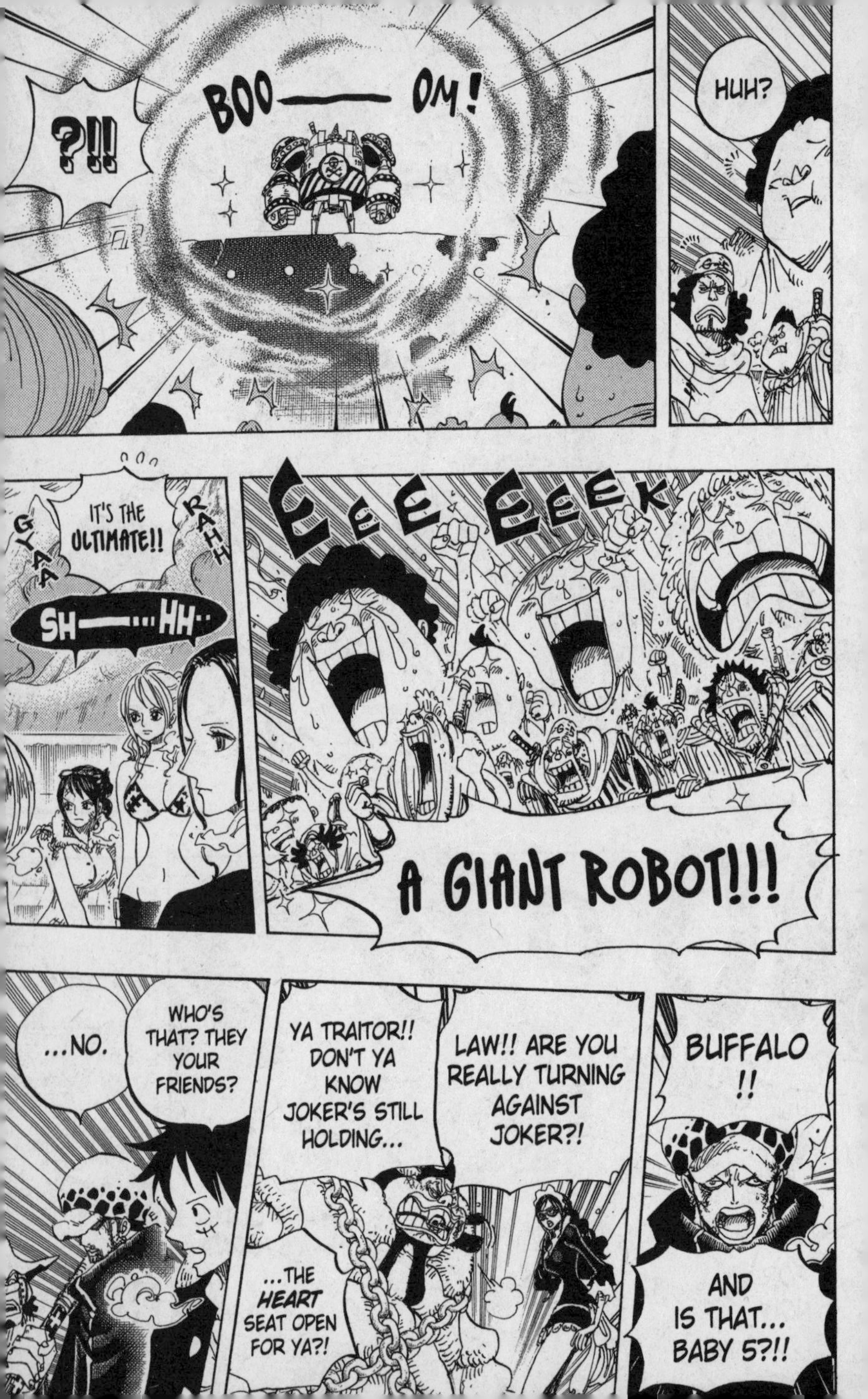
HUH?
BOO——OM!
?!!
EEEEEK
A GIANT ROBOT!!!
RAHH
IT'S THE ULTIMATE!!
GYAA
SH——...HH..
BUFFALO!!
AND IS THAT... BABY 5?!!
LAW!! ARE YOU REALLY TURNING AGAINST JOKER?!
YA TRAITOR!! DON'T YA KNOW JOKER'S STILL HOLDING...
...THE HEART SEAT OPEN FOR YA?!
WHO'S THAT? THEY YOUR FRIENDS?
...NO.

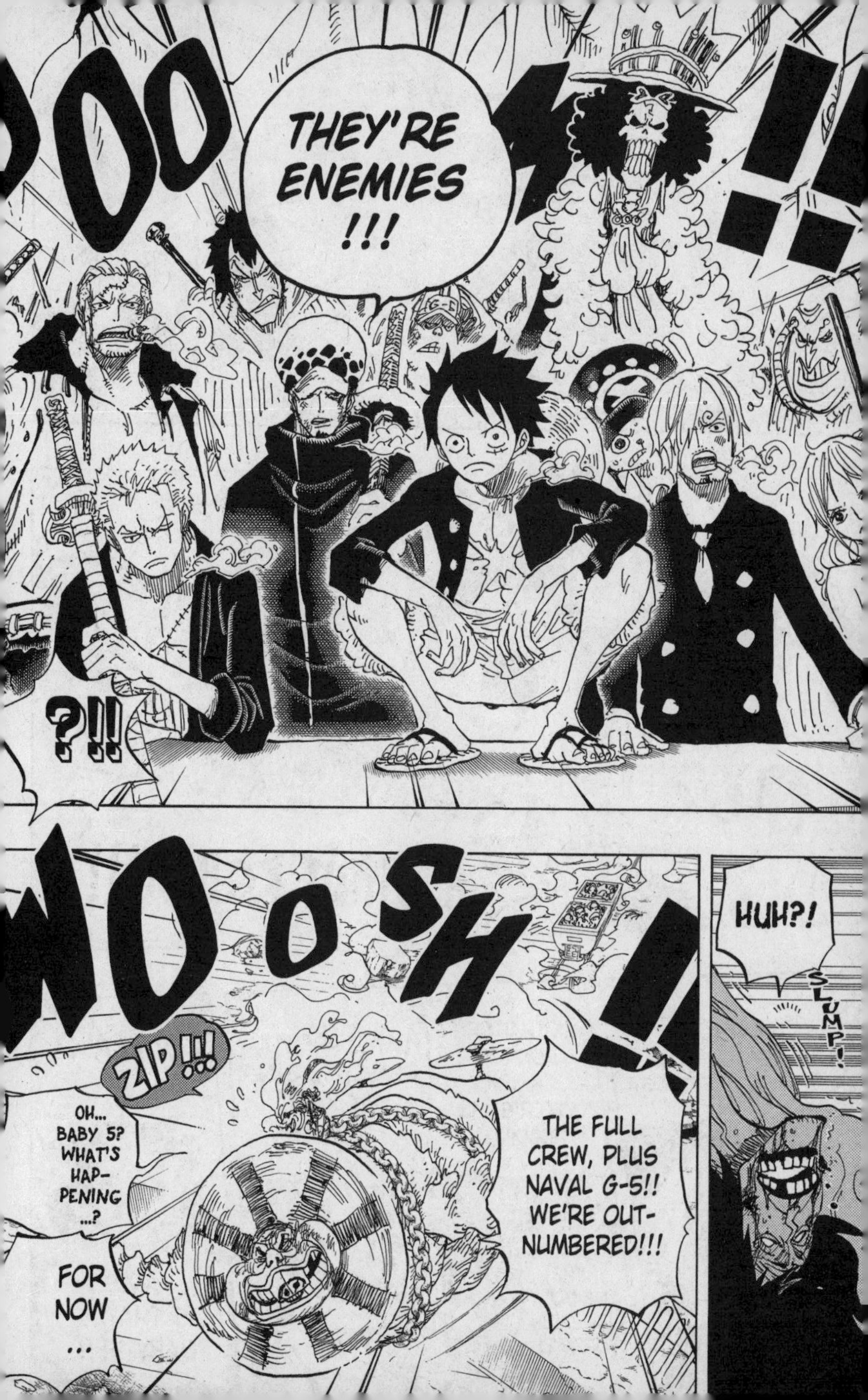
THEY'RE ENEMIES !!!
?!!
HUH?!
SLUMP!
WOOSH!!
THE FULL CREW, PLUS NAVAL G-5!! WE'RE OUT-NUMBERED!!!
ZIP!!!
OH... BABY 5? WHAT'S HAP-PENING ...?
FOR NOW ...

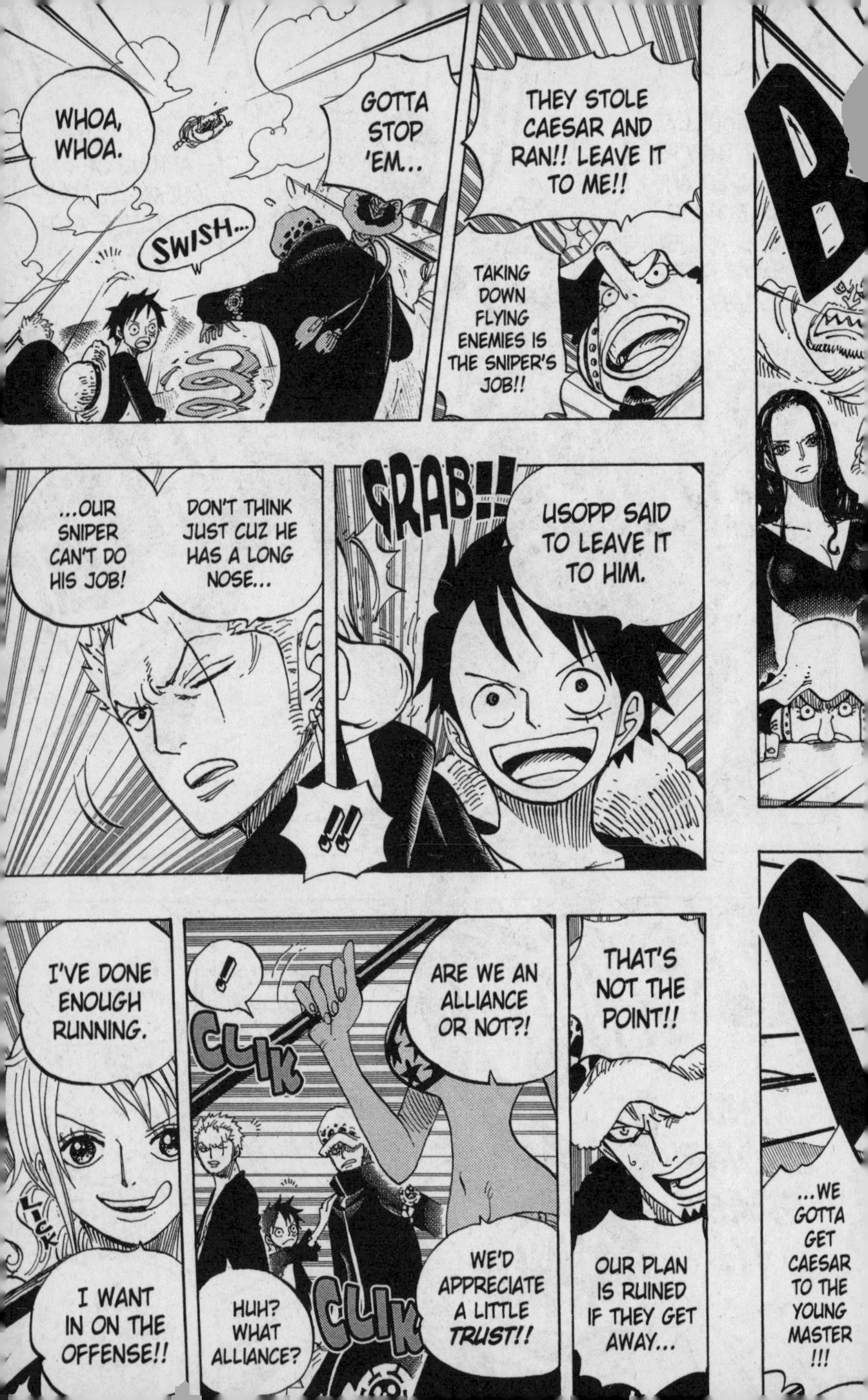
...WE GOTTA GET CAESAR TO THE YOUNG MASTER!!!
THEY STOLE CAESAR AND RAN!! LEAVE IT TO ME!!
TAKING DOWN FLYING ENEMIES IS THE SNIPER'S JOB!!
GOTTA STOP 'EM...
SWISH...
WHOA, WHOA.
GRAB!!
USOPP SAID TO LEAVE IT TO HIM.
!!
DON'T THINK JUST CUZ HE HAS A LONG NOSE...
...OUR SNIPER CAN'T DO HIS JOB!
THAT'S NOT THE POINT!!
OUR PLAN IS RUINED IF THEY GET AWAY...
ARE WE AN ALLIANCE OR NOT?!
!
CLIK
WE'D APPRECIATE A LITTLE TRUST!!
HUH? WHAT ALLIANCE?
CLIK
I'VE DONE ENOUGH RUNNING.
LICK
I WANT IN ON THE OFFENSE!!

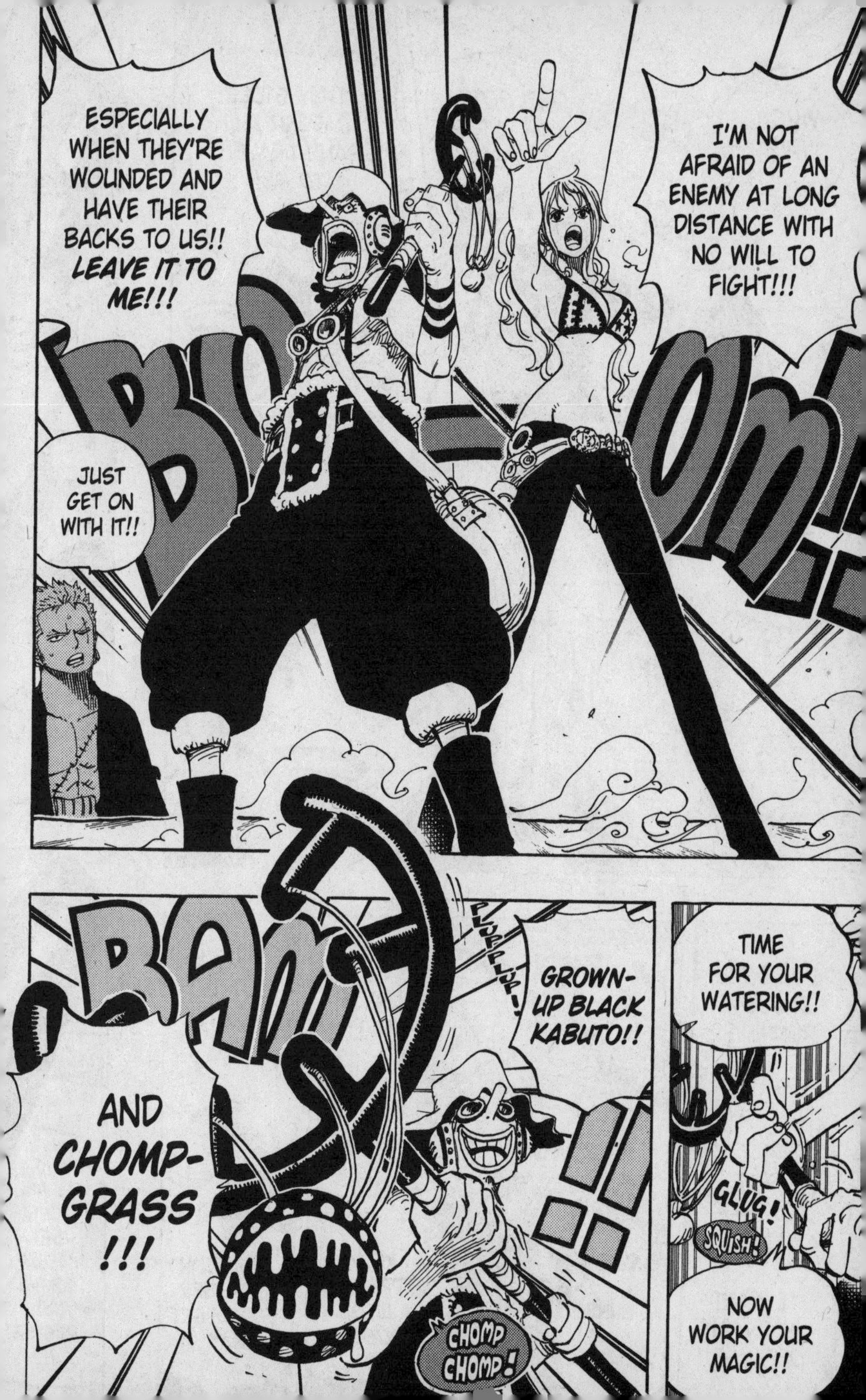

I'M NOT AFRAID OF AN ENEMY AT LONG DISTANCE WITH NO WILL TO FIGHT!!!
ESPECIALLY WHEN THEY'RE WOUNDED AND HAVE THEIR BACKS TO US!! LEAVE IT TO ME!!!
JUST GET ON WITH IT!!
TIME FOR YOUR WATERING!!
GLUG!
SQUISH!
NOW WORK YOUR MAGIC!!
PLUP PLUP!
GROWN-UP BLACK KABUTO!!
AND CHOMP-GRASS!!!
CHOMP CHOMP!

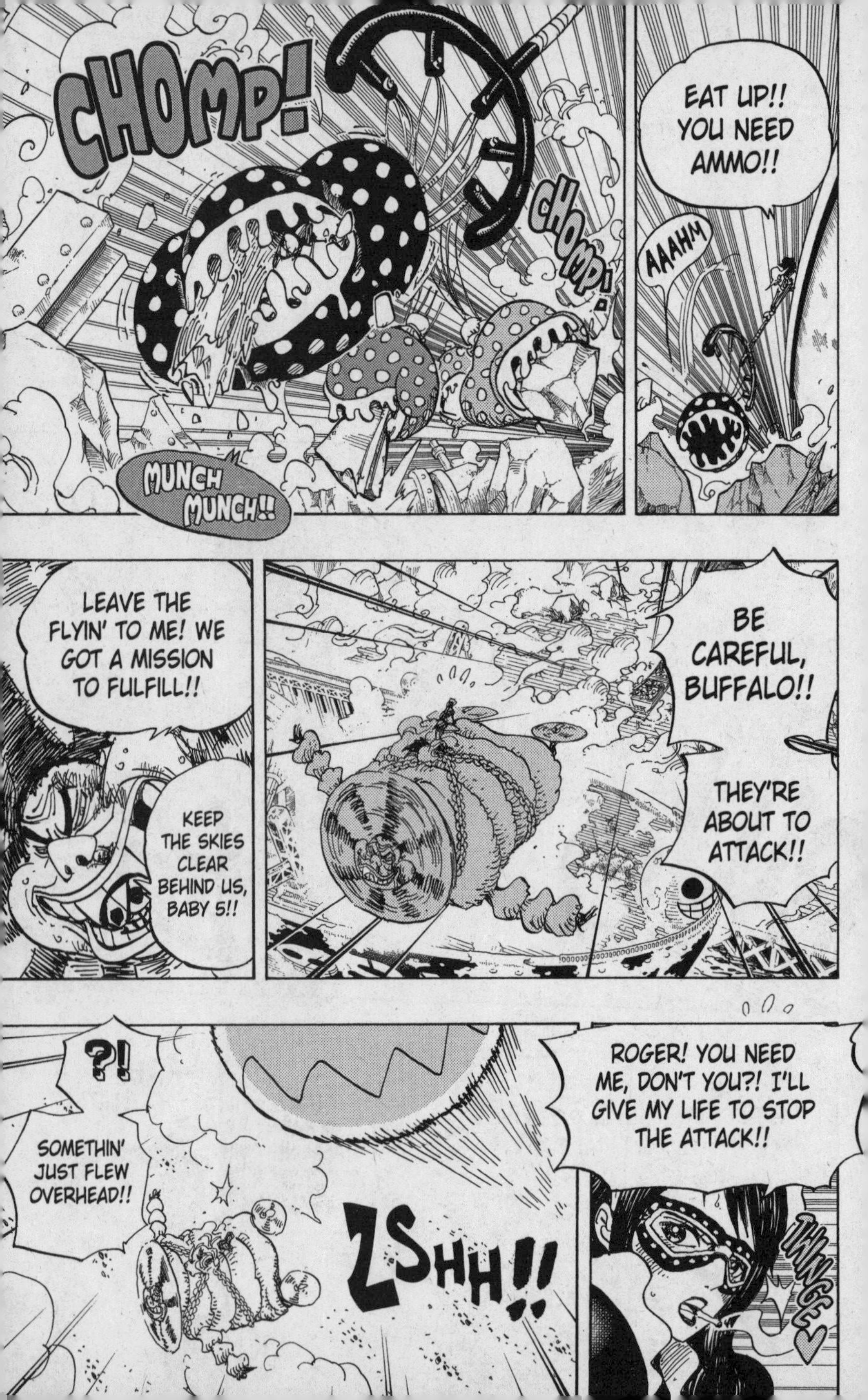
EAT UP!! YOU NEED AMMO!!
AAAHM
CHOMP!
CHOMP!
MUNCH MUNCH!!
BE CAREFUL, BUFFALO!!
THEY'RE ABOUT TO ATTACK!!
LEAVE THE FLYIN' TO ME! WE GOT A MISSION TO FULFILL!!
KEEP THE SKIES CLEAR BEHIND US, BABY 5!!
ROGER! YOU NEED ME, DON'T YOU?! I'LL GIVE MY LIFE TO STOP THE ATTACK!!
TWINGE♥
ZSHH!!
?!
SOMETHIN' JUST FLEW OVERHEAD!!

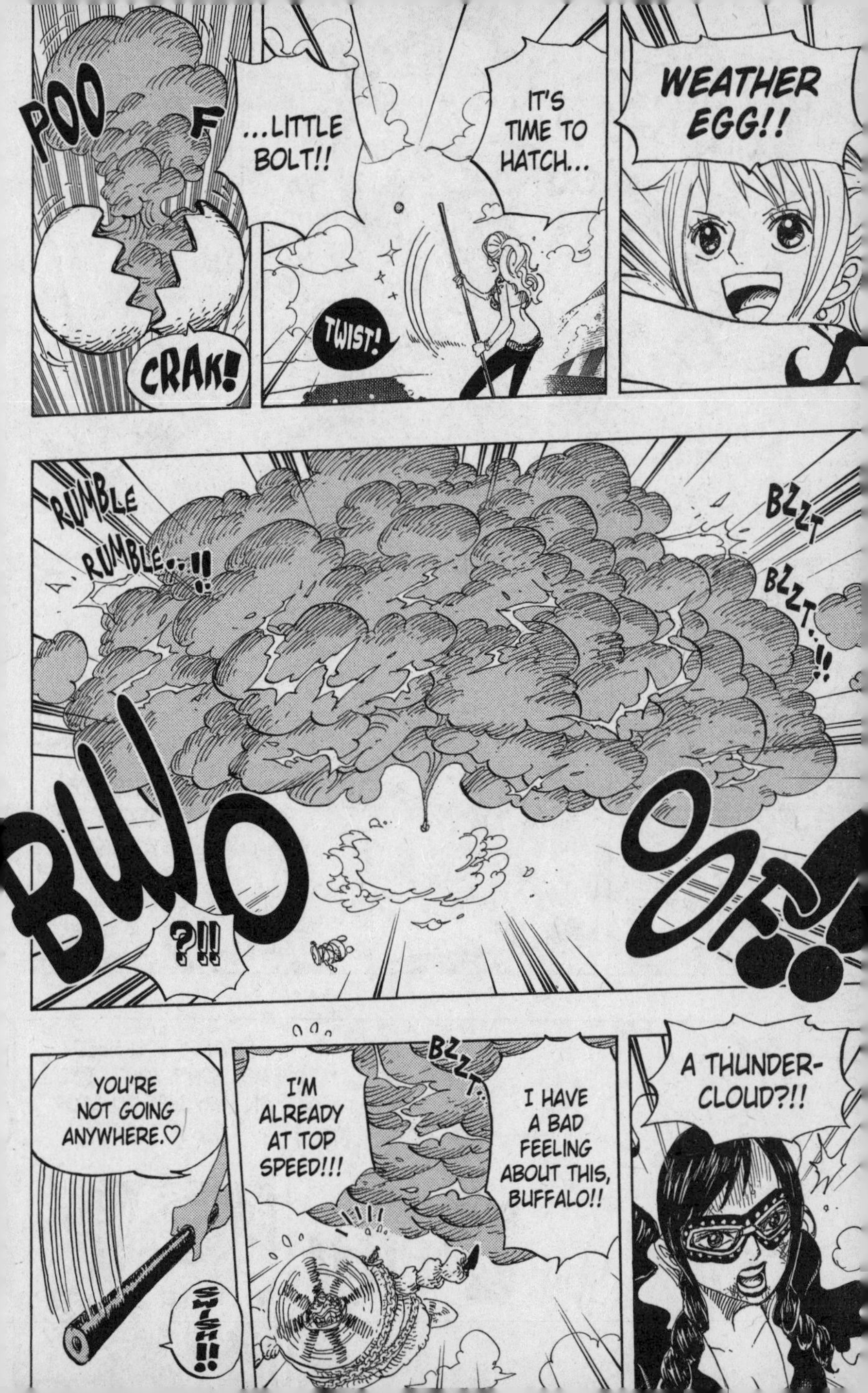
WEATHER EGG!!
IT'S TIME TO HATCH...
...LITTLE BOLT!!
TWIST!
POOF
CRAK!
BZZT
BZZT...!!
RUMBLE RUMBLE...!!
BUOOF!!
?!!
A THUNDER-CLOUD?!!
I HAVE A BAD FEELING ABOUT THIS, BUFFALO!!
BZZT...
I'M ALREADY AT TOP SPEED!!!
YOU'RE NOT GOING ANYWHERE.♡
SWISH!!

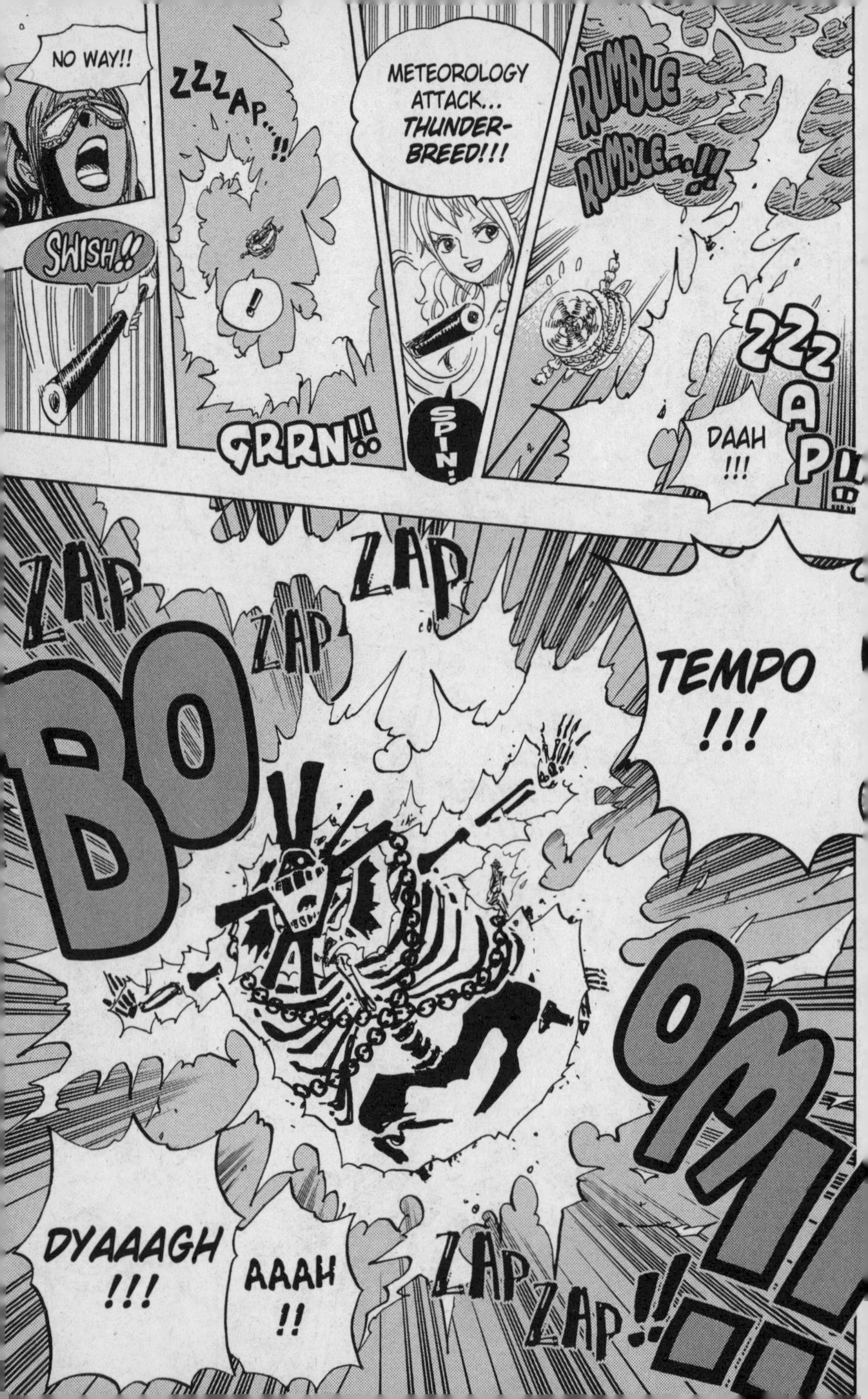
RUMBLE RUMBLE...!!
ZZZAP!!
DAAH!!!
METEOROLOGY ATTACK... THUNDER-BREED!!!
SPIN!
ZZZAP...!!
!
GRRN!!
NO WAY!!
SWISH!!
TEMPO!!!
ZAP
ZAP
ZAP
BOOM!!
ZAP ZAP!!
AAAH!!
DYAAAGH!!!

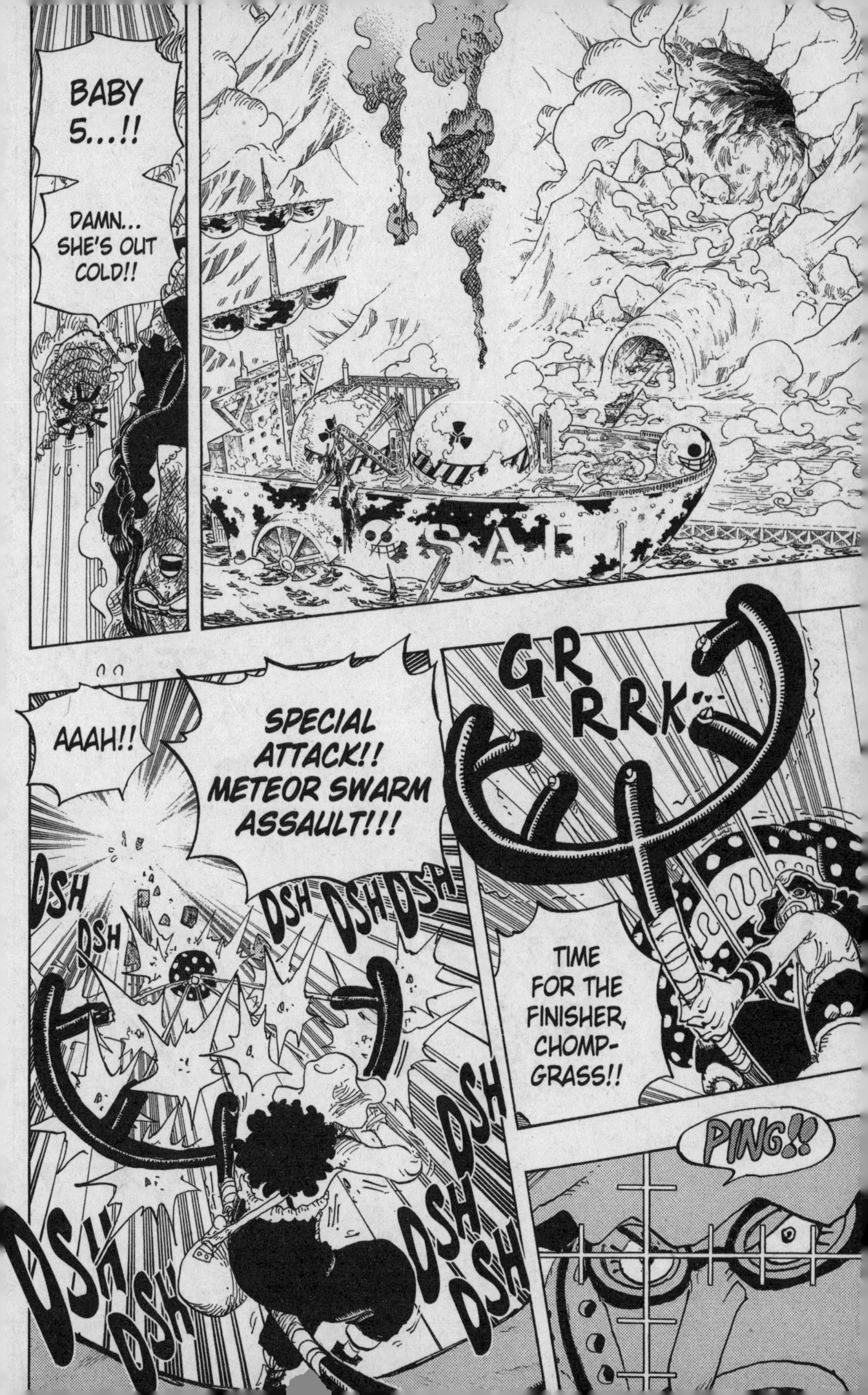
BABY 5...!!
DAMN... SHE'S OUT COLD!!
GR RRK...
TIME FOR THE FINISHER, CHOMP-GRASS!!
PING!!
AAAH!!
SPECIAL ATTACK!! METEOR SWARM ASSAULT!!!
DSH DSH DSH DSH
DSH DSH
DSH DSH DSH
DSH DSH
DSH DSH

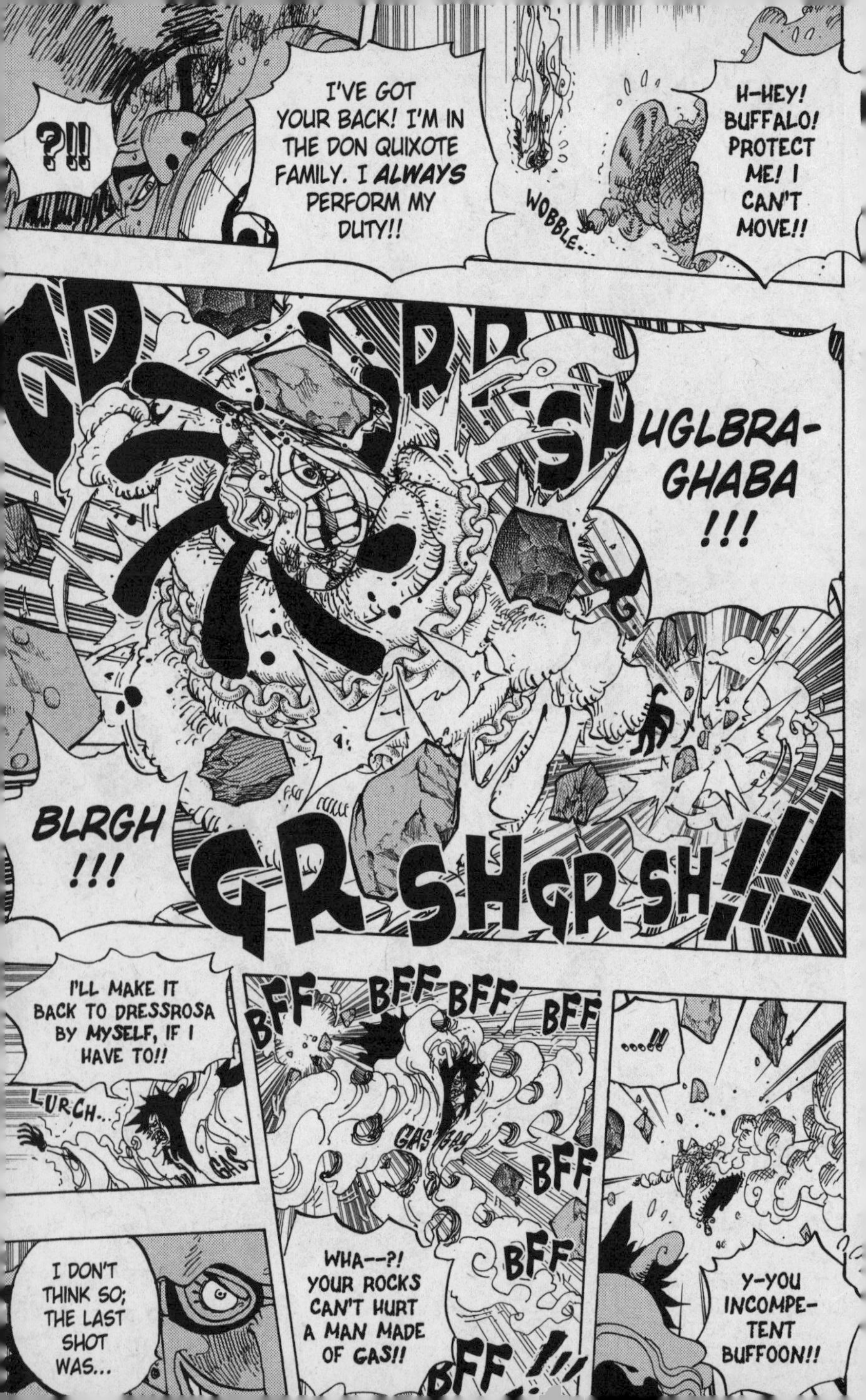
H-HEY! BUFFALO! PROTECT ME! I CAN'T MOVE!!
WOBBLE...
I'VE GOT YOUR BACK! I'M IN THE DON QUIXOTE FAMILY. I ALWAYS PERFORM MY DUTY!!
?!!
UGLBRA-GHABA!!!
GRSHGRSH!!!
BLRGH!!!
...!!
Y-YOU INCOMPETENT BUFFOON!!
BFF BFF BFF BFF
GAS GAS
BFF
BFF
WHA--?! YOUR ROCKS CAN'T HURT A MAN MADE OF GAS!!
BFF!!!
I'LL MAKE IT BACK TO DRESSROSA BY MYSELF, IF I HAVE TO!!
LURCH...
GAS
I DON'T THINK SO; THE LAST SHOT WAS...

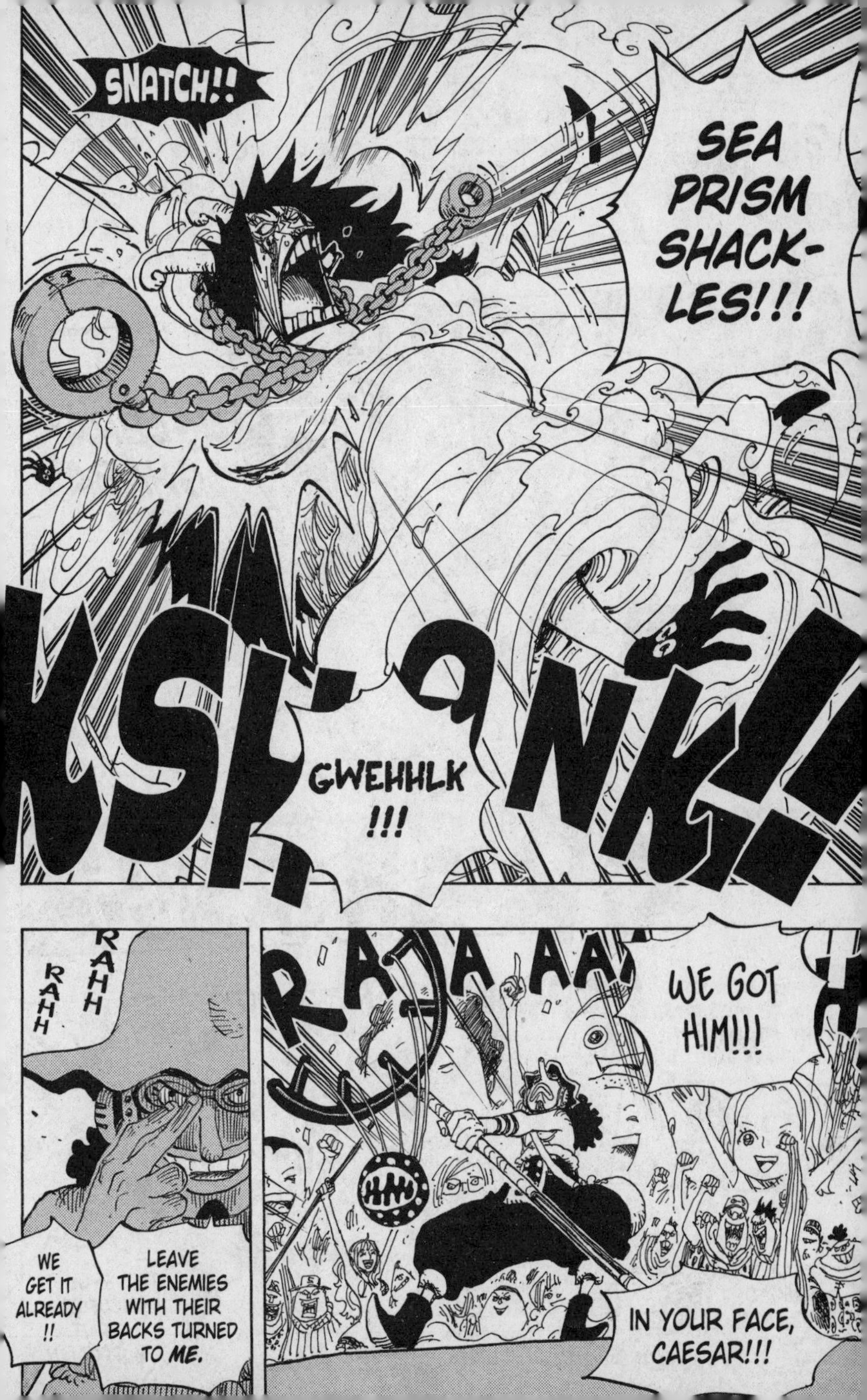

SEA PRISM SHACK-LES!!!
SNATCH!!
KSH-ANK!!
GWEHHLK !!!
RAAAA
WE GOT HIM!!!
IN YOUR FACE, CAESAR!!!
RAHH
RAHH
LEAVE THE ENEMIES WITH THEIR BACKS TURNED TO *ME.*
WE GET IT ALREADY !!

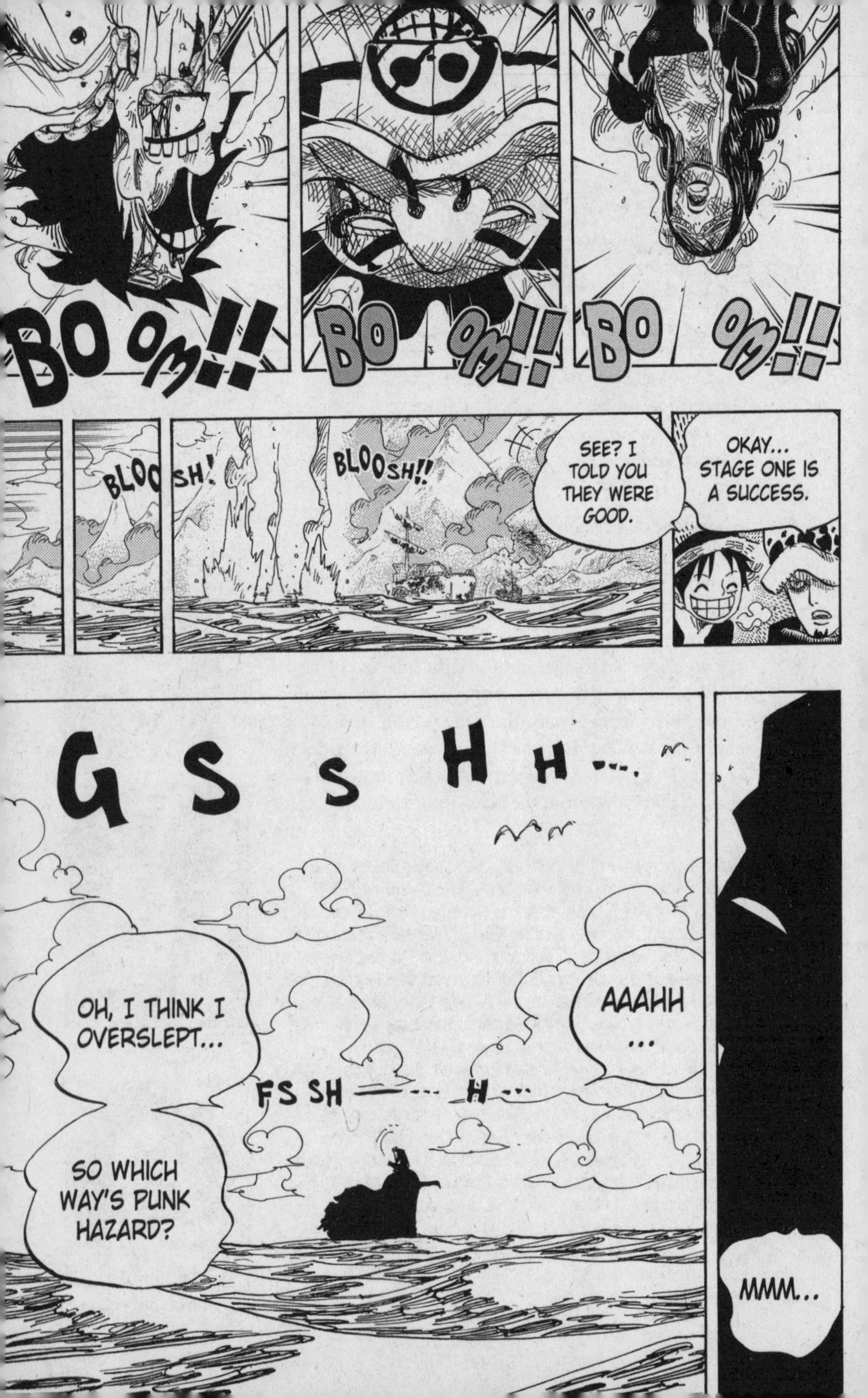
BOOM!!
BOOM!!
BOOM!!
OKAY... STAGE ONE IS A SUCCESS.
SEE? I TOLD YOU THEY WERE GOOD.
BLOOSH!!
BLOOSH!
MMM...
GSSHH...
AAAHH...
OH, I THINK I OVERSLEPT...
FSSH—...H...
SO WHICH WAY'S PUNK HAZARD?

SBS Question Corner

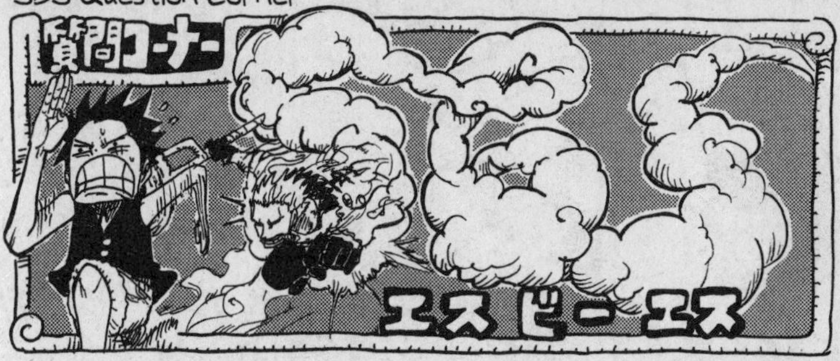

質問コーナー
エスビーエス

(Ponio, Aichi)

Q: In the last panel of the tenth page of Chapter 602 (Volume 61), she says, "Creatures I've never seen before! One, two, three, four..." So that would be Brook, Franky, Chopper, and who?

--Chopper's Friend's Owner

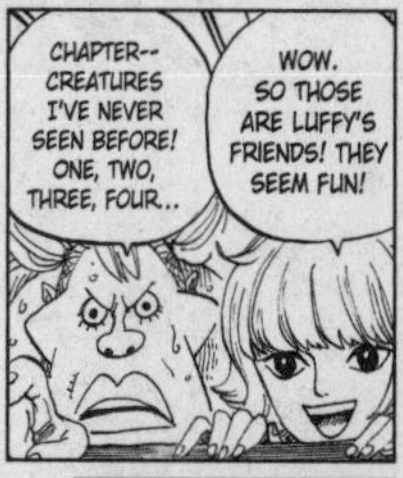

WOW. SO THOSE ARE LUFFY'S FRIENDS! THEY SEEM FUN!
CHAPTER-- CREATURES I'VE NEVER SEEN BEFORE! ONE, TWO, THREE, FOUR...

A: I'm assuming it'sSanji with a bizarre look on his face.

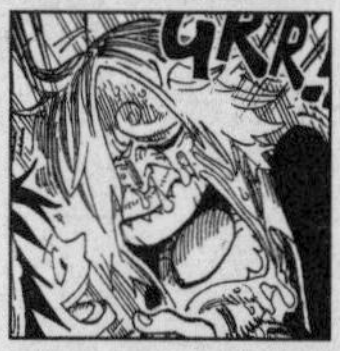

Q: Hello! I'm usually a graphic-novel-only reader, but I heard about how incredible this color chapter cover was, and rushed out to buy the issue of Jump with Chapter 691 (^_^). And I just so happened to spot, on the right edge over Brook's shoulder, among all the younger versions of the Naval officers, what appears to be the same person who was to the right of Ivankov on the page after Whitebeard's order to "back up Luffy with all you've got." Is that really the same person?!! Did he go from the Navy to being a pirate?!!

--Anri

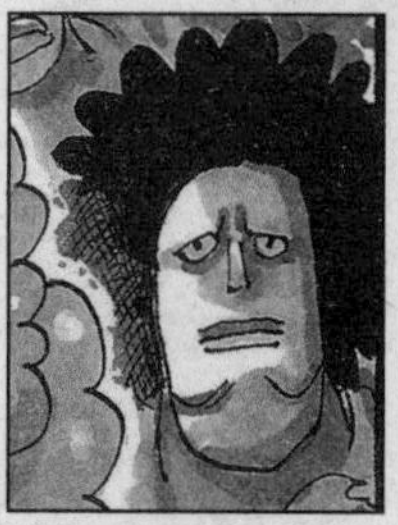

Chapter 691, cover

A: That's very well spotted. So how does the same face show up in both the Navy and a pirate crew? Well, there was a fellow originally introduced in the book One Piece Green (in Japan) as "Pirate Captain Andre," a member of Whitebeard's fleet. But the people I drew in the Chapter 691 cover illustration are all past versions of Navy officers. The guy with the same face shown here is actually still in the Navy, and his name is Kandre. A few years ago during the Paramount War arc, I'm pretty sure I drew Kandre as well, fighting on the side of the Navy--search for him if you're bored sometime! You see, the twin brothers Andre and Kandre were forced to fight against each other in the big war!!

It's a very boring and pointless story!!

But thanks for spotting them!

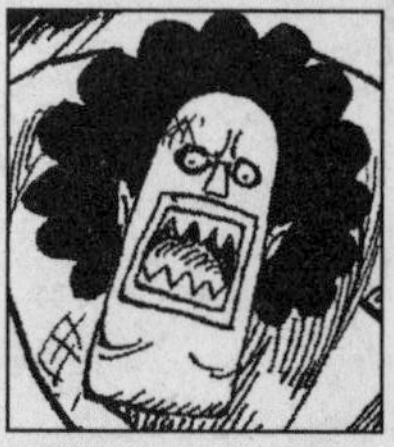

Volume 58, p.138

Chapter 696:

ALIGNMENT OF INTERESTS

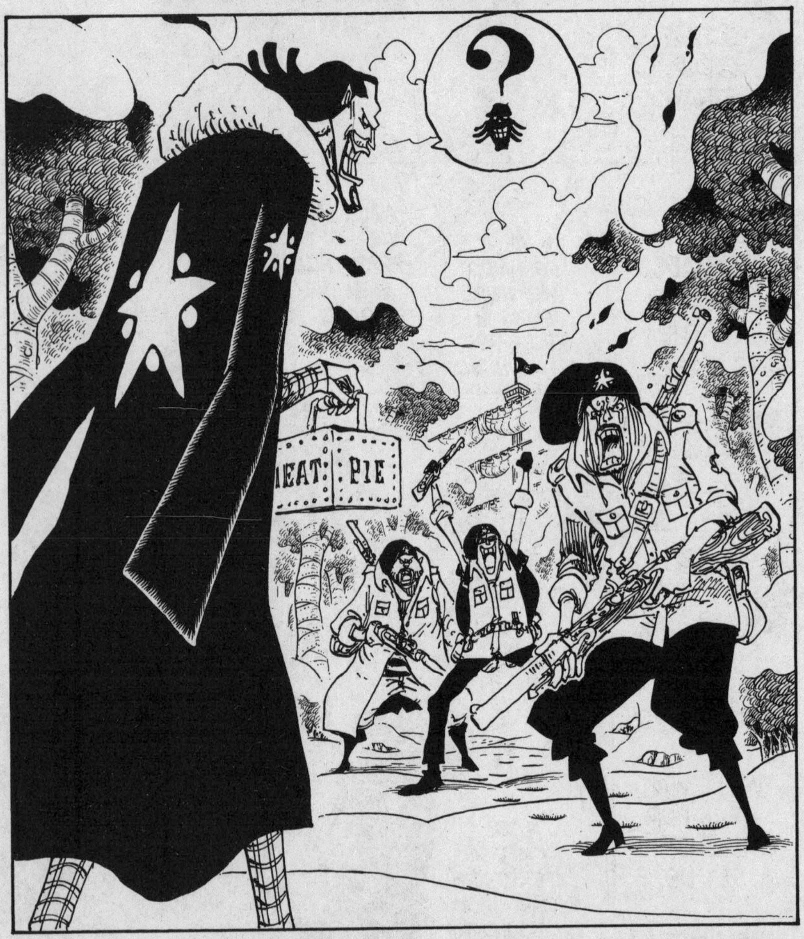
?
MEAT PIE

CARIBOU'S NEW WORLD KEE HEE HEE, VOL. 18: "ON THE ROAD TO PORT, A VOICE CALLS OUT, "CAPTAIN GOBBLE!!""

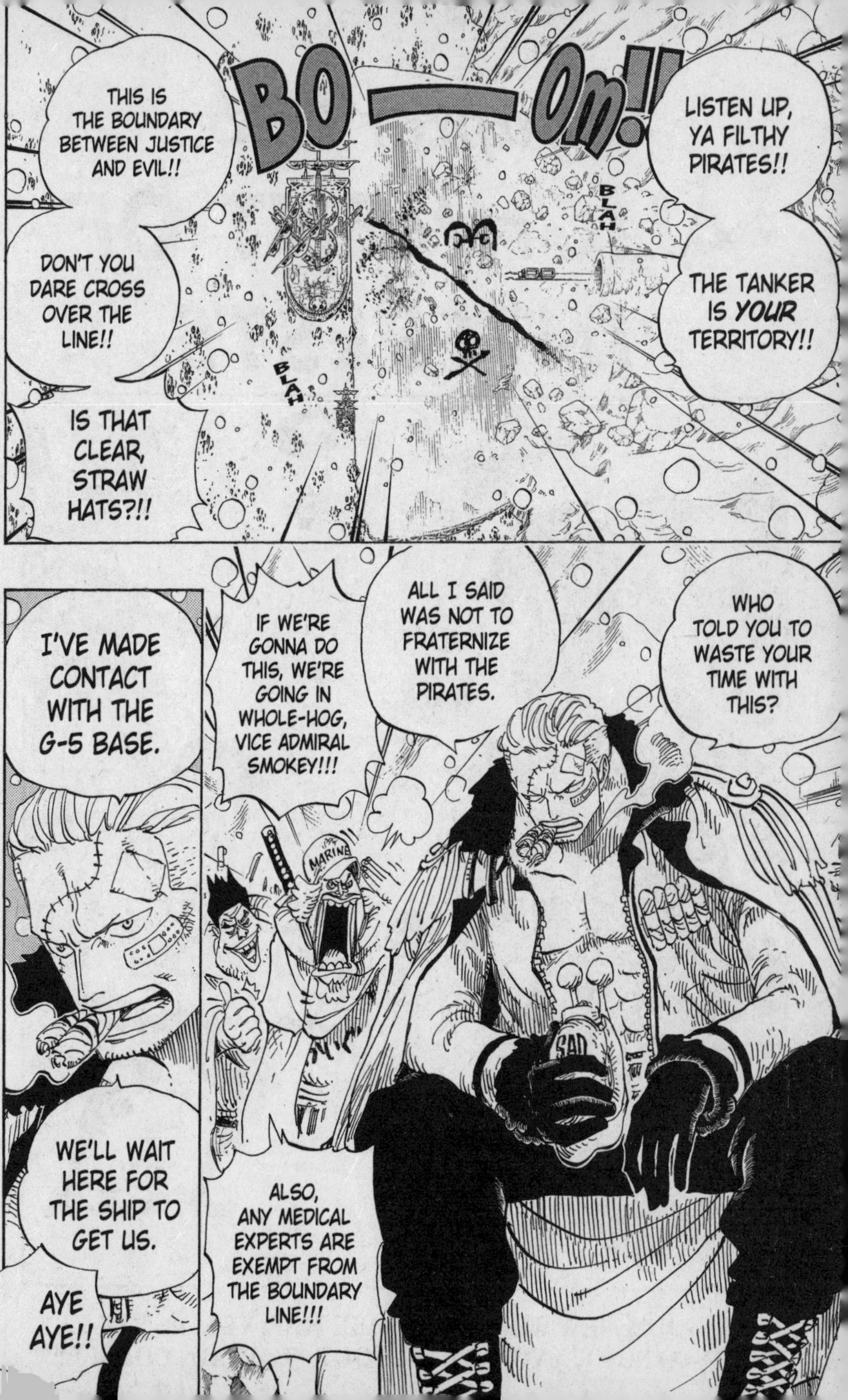
LISTEN UP, YA FILTHY PIRATES!!
THE TANKER IS YOUR TERRITORY!!
BO——OM!!
BLAH
BLAH
THIS IS THE BOUNDARY BETWEEN JUSTICE AND EVIL!!
DON'T YOU DARE CROSS OVER THE LINE!!
IS THAT CLEAR, STRAW HATS?!!
WHO TOLD YOU TO WASTE YOUR TIME WITH THIS?
ALL I SAID WAS NOT TO FRATERNIZE WITH THE PIRATES.
IF WE'RE GONNA DO THIS, WE'RE GOING IN WHOLE-HOG, VICE ADMIRAL SMOKEY!!!
MARINE
SAD
ALSO, ANY MEDICAL EXPERTS ARE EXEMPT FROM THE BOUNDARY LINE!!!
I'VE MADE CONTACT WITH THE G-5 BASE.
WE'LL WAIT HERE FOR THE SHIP TO GET US.
AYE AYE!!

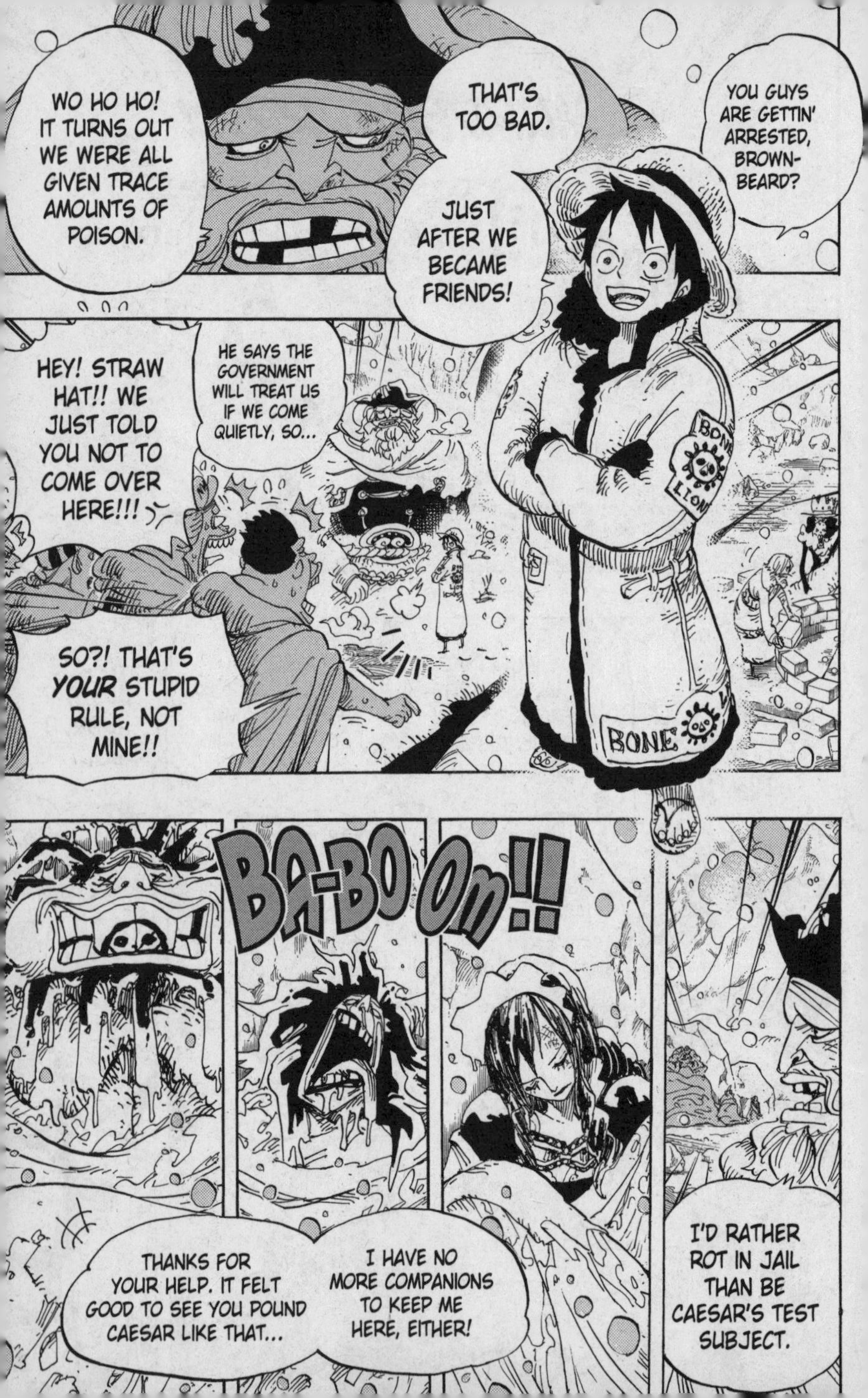
YOU GUYS ARE GETTIN' ARRESTED, BROWN-BEARD?
THAT'S TOO BAD.
JUST AFTER WE BECAME FRIENDS!
WO HO HO! IT TURNS OUT WE WERE ALL GIVEN TRACE AMOUNTS OF POISON.
HE SAYS THE GOVERNMENT WILL TREAT US IF WE COME QUIETLY, SO...
HEY! STRAW HAT!! WE JUST TOLD YOU NOT TO COME OVER HERE!!!
SO?! THAT'S *YOUR* STUPID RULE, NOT MINE!!
BONE
LION
BONE
I'D RATHER ROT IN JAIL THAN BE CAESAR'S TEST SUBJECT.
I HAVE NO MORE COMPANIONS TO KEEP ME HERE, EITHER!
BA-BOOm!!
THANKS FOR YOUR HELP. IT FELT GOOD TO SEE YOU POUND CAESAR LIKE THAT...

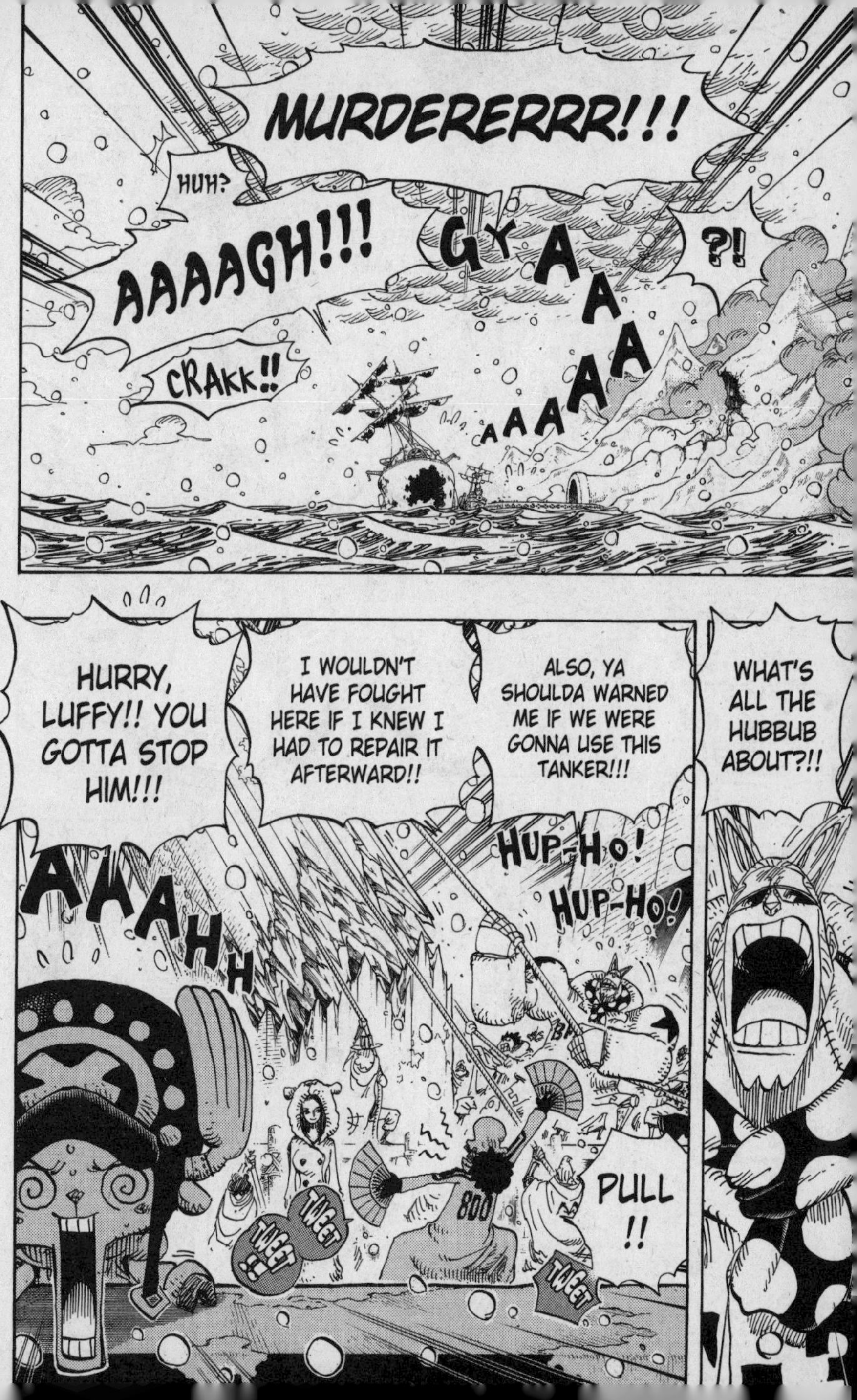
?!
MURDERERRR!!!
HUH?
GYAAAAAAAAA
AAAAGH!!!
CRAKK!!
WHAT'S ALL THE HUBBUB ABOUT?!!
ALSO, YA SHOULDA WARNED ME IF WE WERE GONNA USE THIS TANKER!!!
I WOULDN'T HAVE FOUGHT HERE IF I KNEW I HAD TO REPAIR IT AFTERWARD!!
HURRY, LUFFY!! YOU GOTTA STOP HIM!!!
HUP-HO!
HUP-HO!
AAAHH
PULL!!
TWEET
TWEET
TWEET

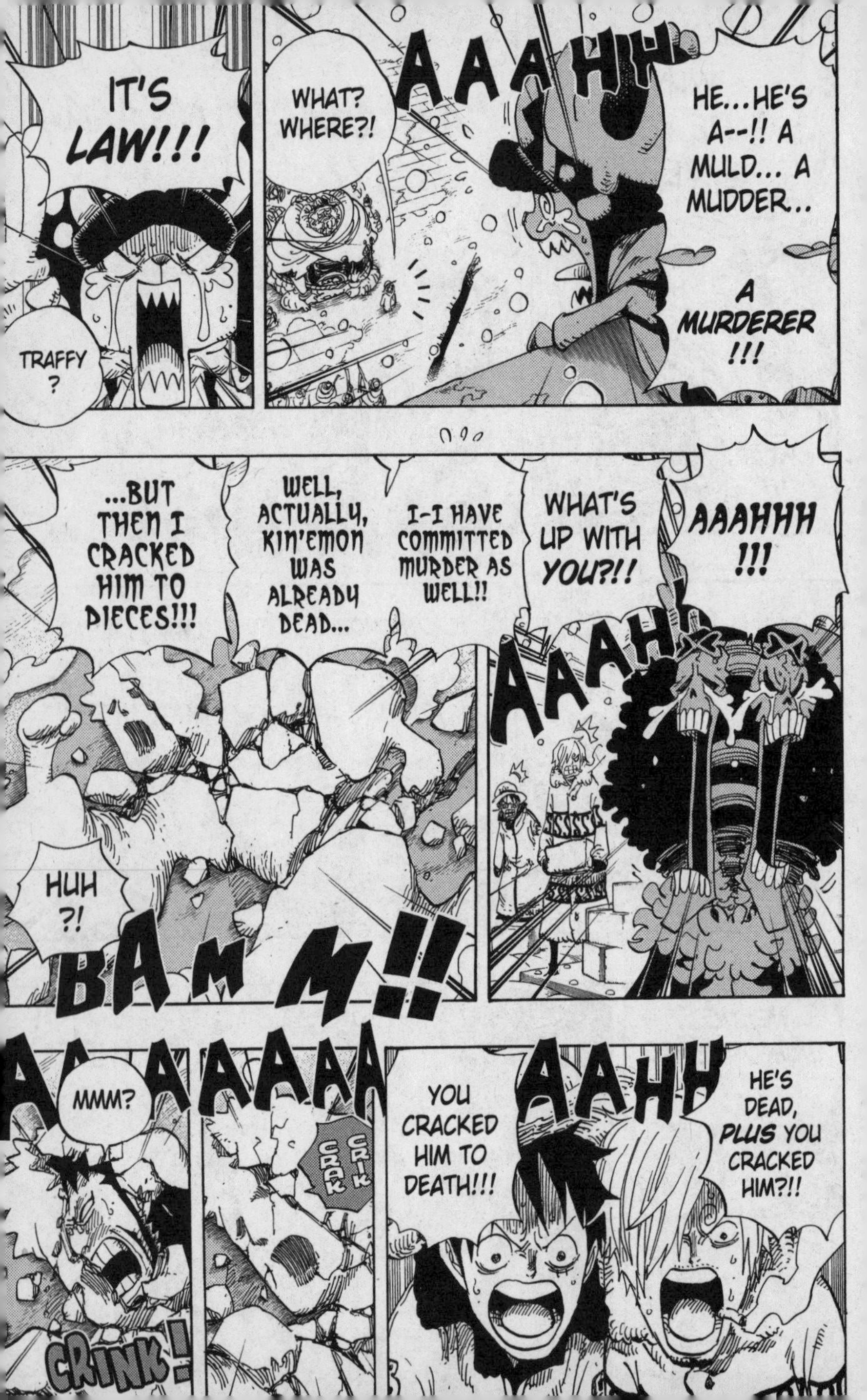
AAAHH
HE...HE'S A--!! A MULD... A MUDDER...
A MURDERER !!!
WHAT? WHERE?!
IT'S LAW!!!
TRAFFY ?
AAAHHH !!!
WHAT'S UP WITH YOU?!!
AAAH
I-I HAVE COMMITTED MURDER AS WELL!!
WELL, ACTUALLY, KIN'EMON WAS ALREADY DEAD...
...BUT THEN I CRACKED HIM TO PIECES!!!
HUH ?!
BAMM!!
AAHH
HE'S DEAD, PLUS YOU CRACKED HIM?!!
YOU CRACKED HIM TO DEATH!!!
CRAK CRIK
AAAAAAA
MMM?
CRINK!

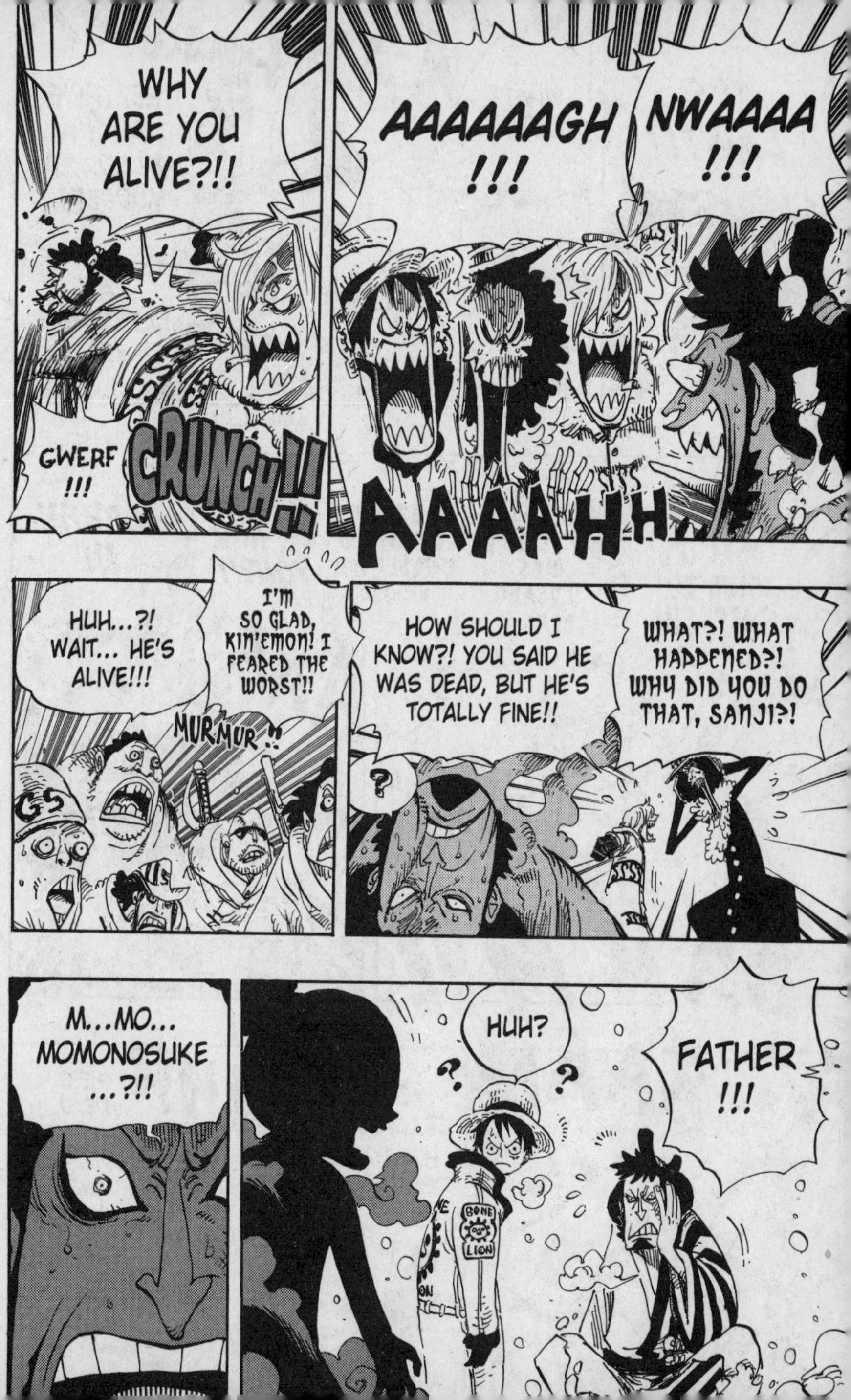
NWAAAA !!!
AAAAAAGH !!!
AAAAHH
WHY ARE YOU ALIVE?!!
CRUNCH!!
GWERF !!!
WHAT?! WHAT HAPPENED?! WHY DID YOU DO THAT, SANJI?!
HOW SHOULD I KNOW?! YOU SAID HE WAS DEAD, BUT HE'S TOTALLY FINE!!
?
I'M SO GLAD, KIN'EMON! I FEARED THE WORST!!
HUH...?! WAIT... HE'S ALIVE!!!
MURMUR
FATHER !!!
HUH?
? ?
BONE LION
M...MO... MOMONOSUKE ...?!!

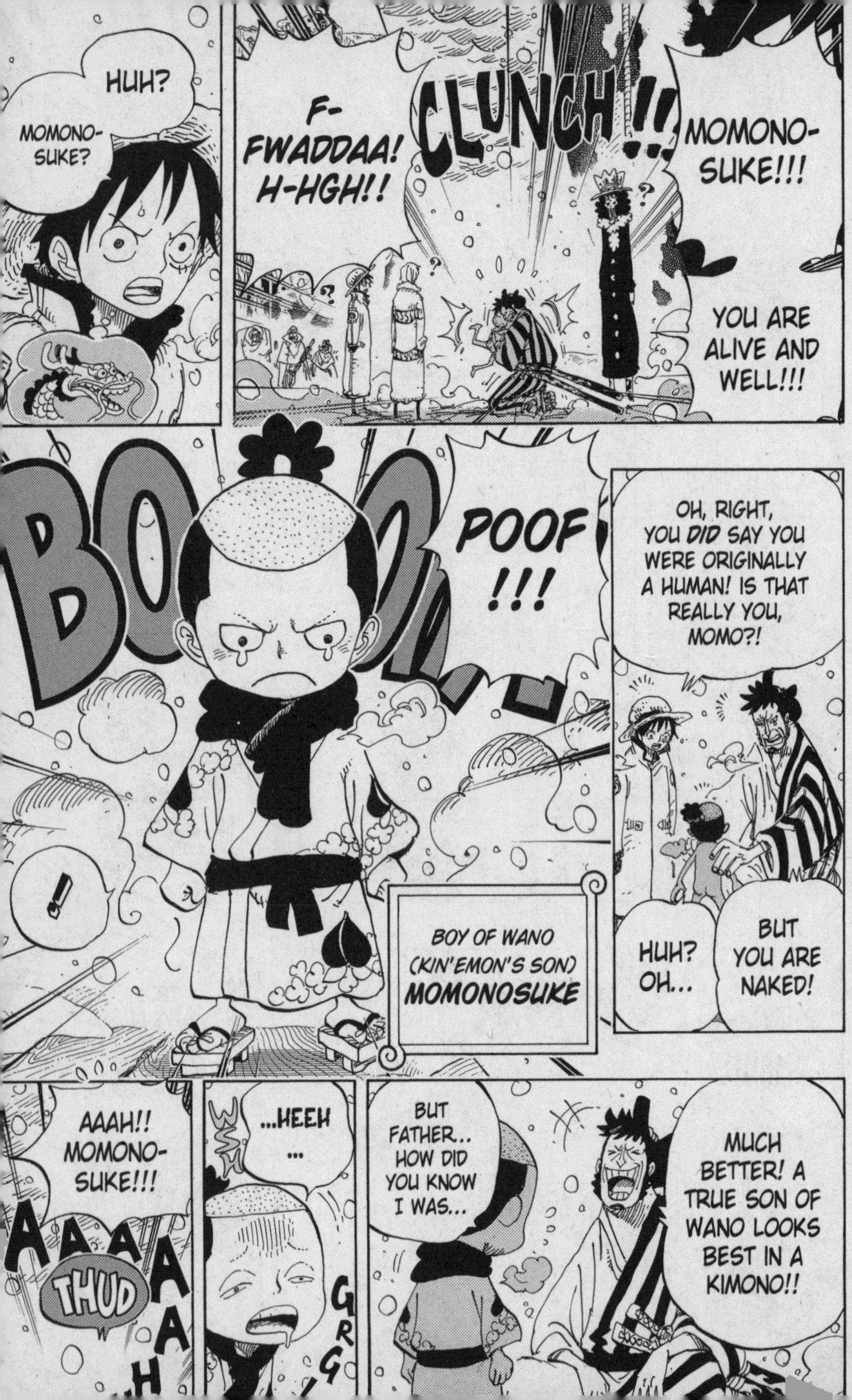
MOMONO-SUKE!!!
CLUNCH!!!
F-FWADDAA! H-HGH!!
YOU ARE ALIVE AND WELL!!!
HUH?
MOMONO-SUKE?
OH, RIGHT, YOU DID SAY YOU WERE ORIGINALLY A HUMAN! IS THAT REALLY YOU, MOMO?!
BUT YOU ARE NAKED!
HUH? OH...
POOF!!!
!
BOY OF WANO (KIN'EMON'S SON) MOMONOSUKE
MUCH BETTER! A TRUE SON OF WANO LOOKS BEST IN A KIMONO!!
BUT FATHER... HOW DID YOU KNOW I WAS...
...HEEH ...
AAAH!! MOMONO-SUKE!!!
THUD

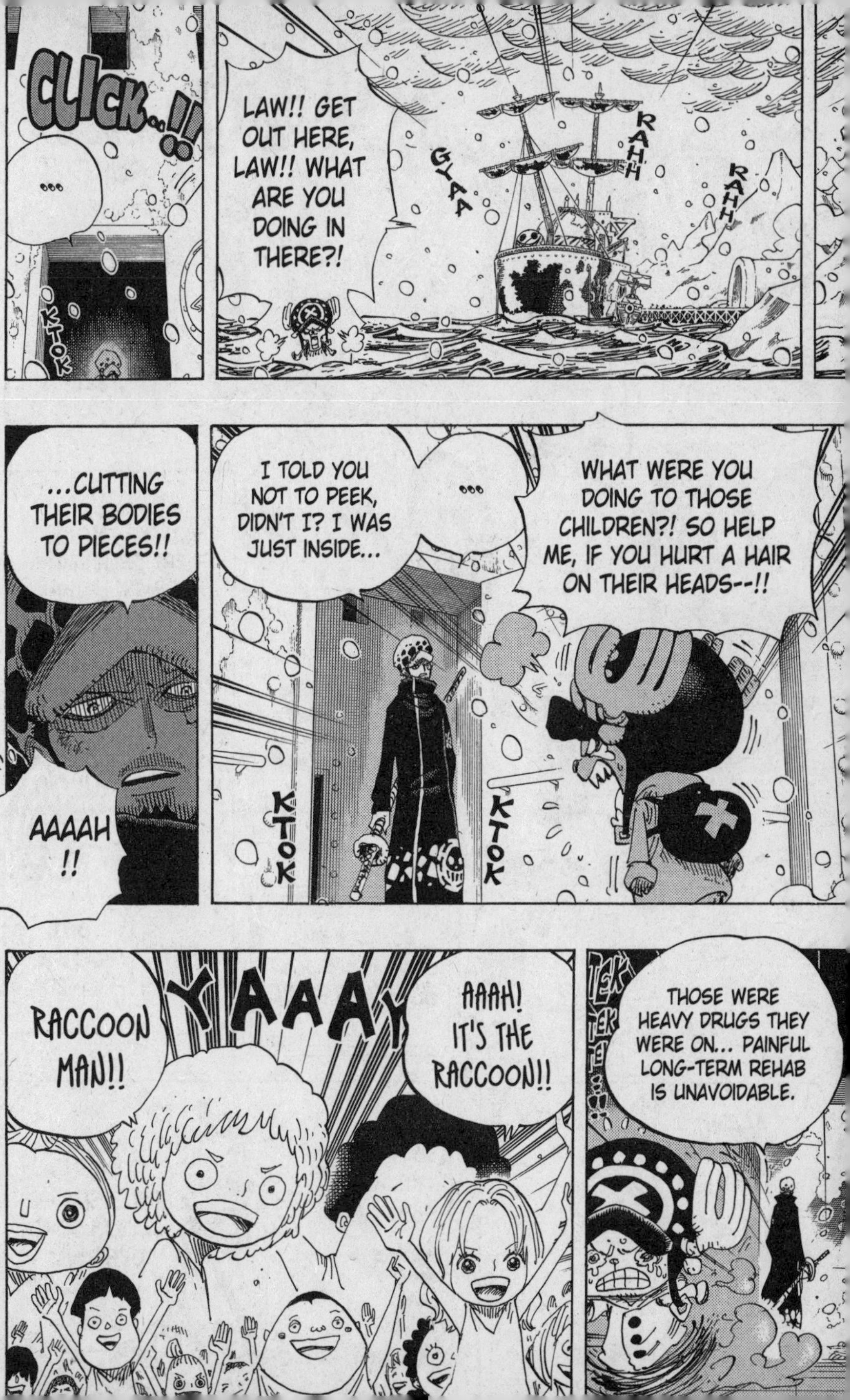
LAW!! GET OUT HERE, LAW!! WHAT ARE YOU DOING IN THERE?!
RAHH
RAHH
GYAA
CLICK..!!
...
KTOK
WHAT WERE YOU DOING TO THOSE CHILDREN?! SO HELP ME, IF YOU HURT A HAIR ON THEIR HEADS--!!
...
I TOLD YOU NOT TO PEEK, DIDN'T I? I WAS JUST INSIDE...
KTOK
KTOK
...CUTTING THEIR BODIES TO PIECES!!
AAAAH !!
THOSE WERE HEAVY DRUGS THEY WERE ON... PAINFUL LONG-TERM REHAB IS UNAVOIDABLE.
TEK TEK
AAAH! IT'S THE RACCOON!!
YAAAY
RACCOON MAN!!

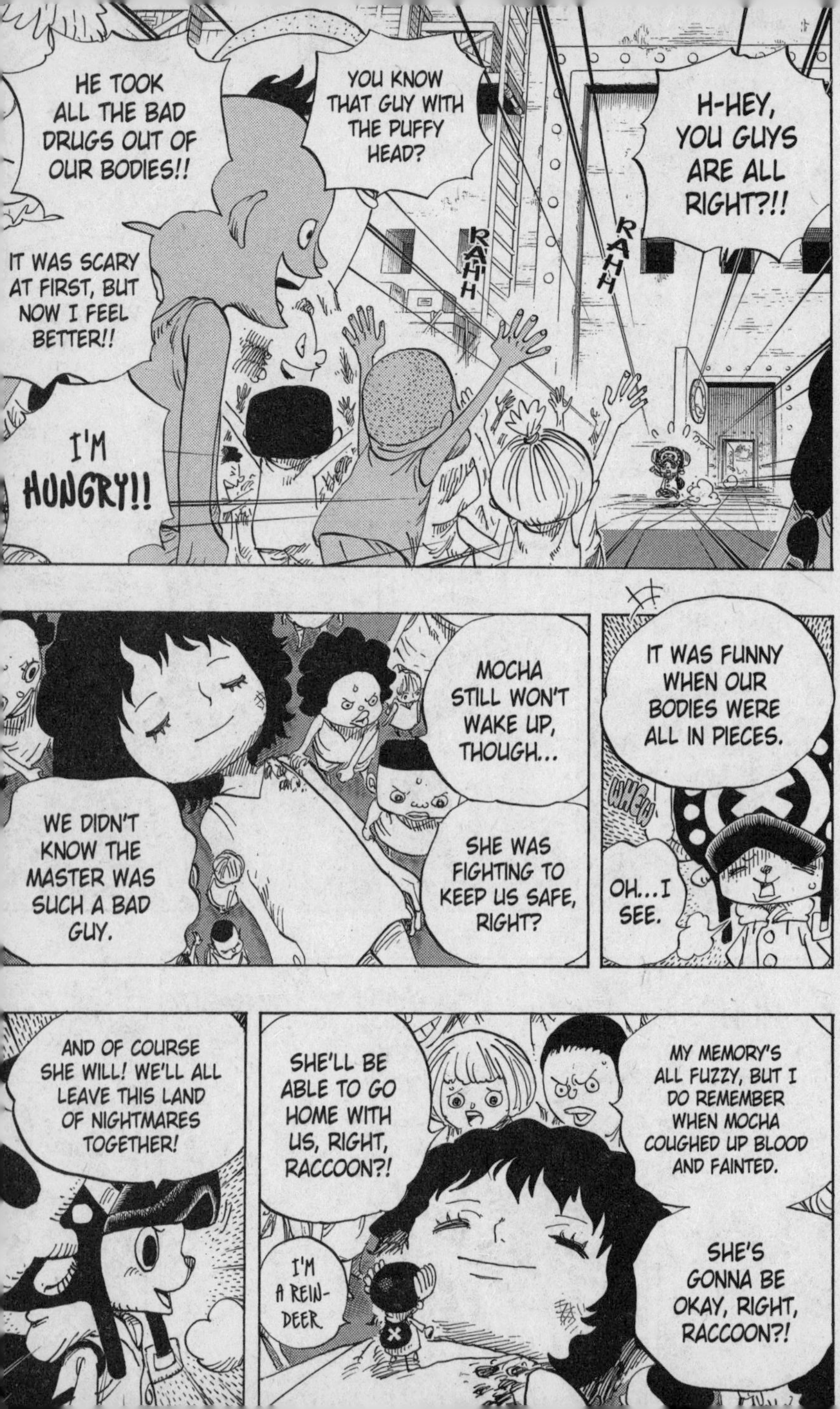
H-HEY, YOU GUYS ARE ALL RIGHT?!!
RAHHH
RAHHH
YOU KNOW THAT GUY WITH THE PUFFY HEAD?
HE TOOK ALL THE BAD DRUGS OUT OF OUR BODIES!!
IT WAS SCARY AT FIRST, BUT NOW I FEEL BETTER!!
I'M HUNGRY!!
IT WAS FUNNY WHEN OUR BODIES WERE ALL IN PIECES.
WHEW
OH...I SEE.
MOCHA STILL WON'T WAKE UP, THOUGH...
SHE WAS FIGHTING TO KEEP US SAFE, RIGHT?
WE DIDN'T KNOW THE MASTER WAS SUCH A BAD GUY.
MY MEMORY'S ALL FUZZY, BUT I DO REMEMBER WHEN MOCHA COUGHED UP BLOOD AND FAINTED.
SHE'S GONNA BE OKAY, RIGHT, RACCOON?!
SHE'LL BE ABLE TO GO HOME WITH US, RIGHT, RACCOON?!
I'M A REIN-DEER.
AND OF COURSE SHE WILL! WE'LL ALL LEAVE THIS LAND OF NIGHTMARES TOGETHER!

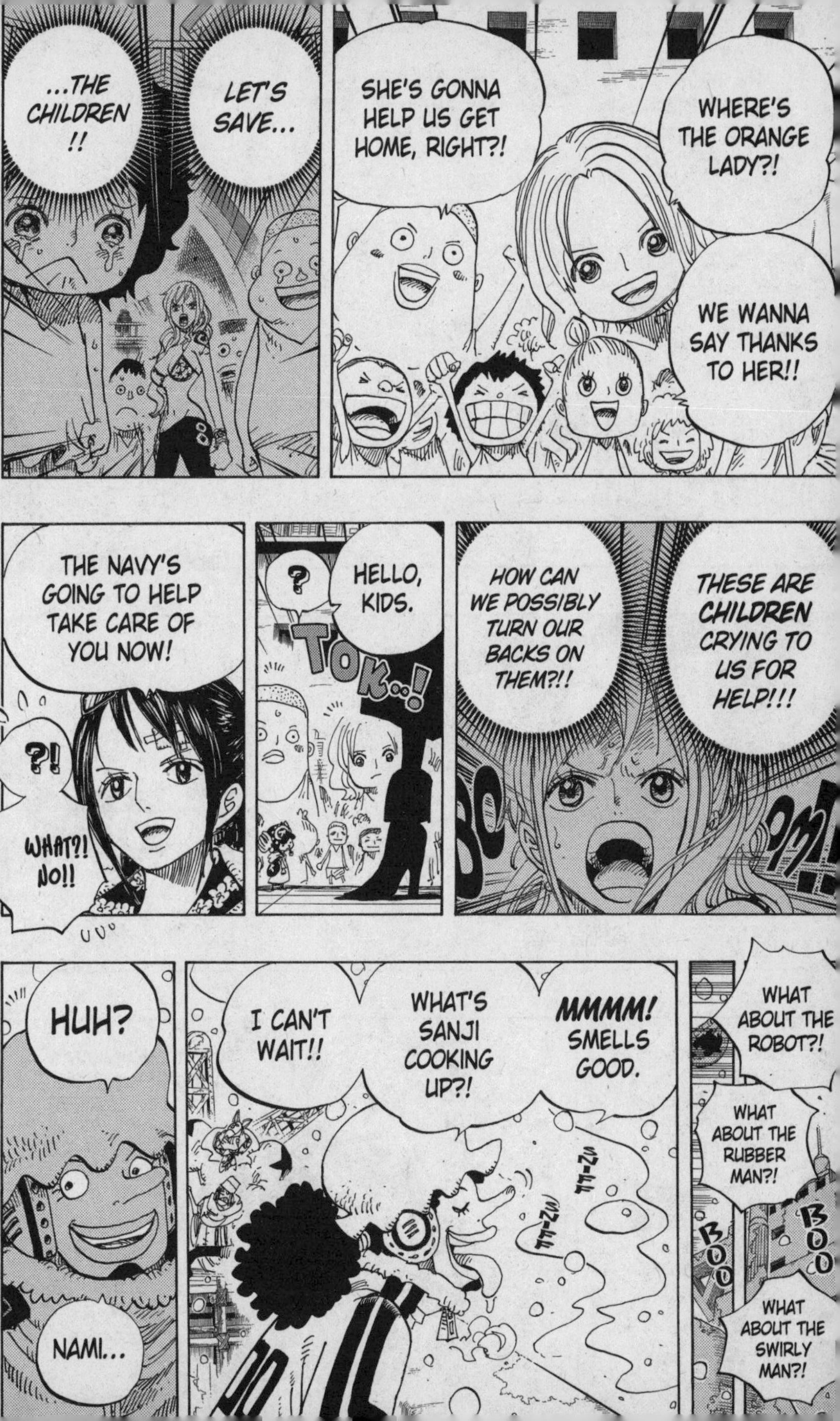
WHERE'S THE ORANGE LADY?!
WE WANNA SAY THANKS TO HER!!
SHE'S GONNA HELP US GET HOME, RIGHT?!
LET'S SAVE...
...THE CHILDREN !!
THESE ARE CHILDREN CRYING TO US FOR HELP!!!
HOW CAN WE POSSIBLY TURN OUR BACKS ON THEM?!!
HELLO, KIDS.
?
TOK..!
THE NAVY'S GOING TO HELP TAKE CARE OF YOU NOW!
?!
WHAT?! NO!!
WHAT ABOUT THE ROBOT?!
WHAT ABOUT THE RUBBER MAN?!
BOO
BOO
WHAT ABOUT THE SWIRLY MAN?!
MMMM! SMELLS GOOD.
WHAT'S SANJI COOKING UP?!
I CAN'T WAIT!!
SNIFF
SNIFF
HUH?
NAMI...

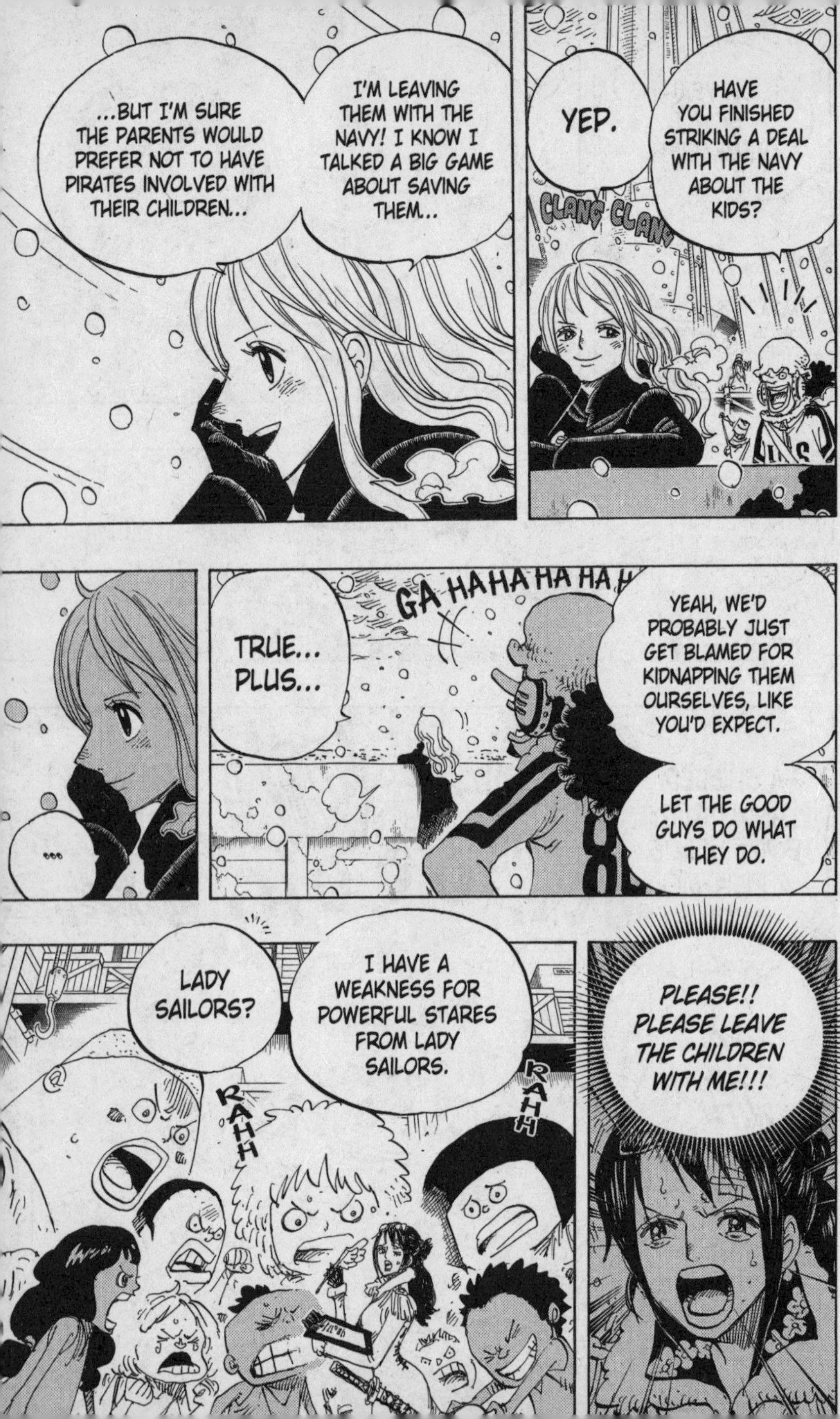
HAVE YOU FINISHED STRIKING A DEAL WITH THE NAVY ABOUT THE KIDS?
YEP.
CLANG CLANG
I'M LEAVING THEM WITH THE NAVY! I KNOW I TALKED A BIG GAME ABOUT SAVING THEM...
...BUT I'M SURE THE PARENTS WOULD PREFER NOT TO HAVE PIRATES INVOLVED WITH THEIR CHILDREN...
GA HAHA HA HA H
YEAH, WE'D PROBABLY JUST GET BLAMED FOR KIDNAPPING THEM OURSELVES, LIKE YOU'D EXPECT.
LET THE GOOD GUYS DO WHAT THEY DO.
TRUE... PLUS...
...
PLEASE!! PLEASE LEAVE THE CHILDREN WITH ME!!!
RAHH
I HAVE A WEAKNESS FOR POWERFUL STARES FROM LADY SAILORS.
LADY SAILORS?
RAHH

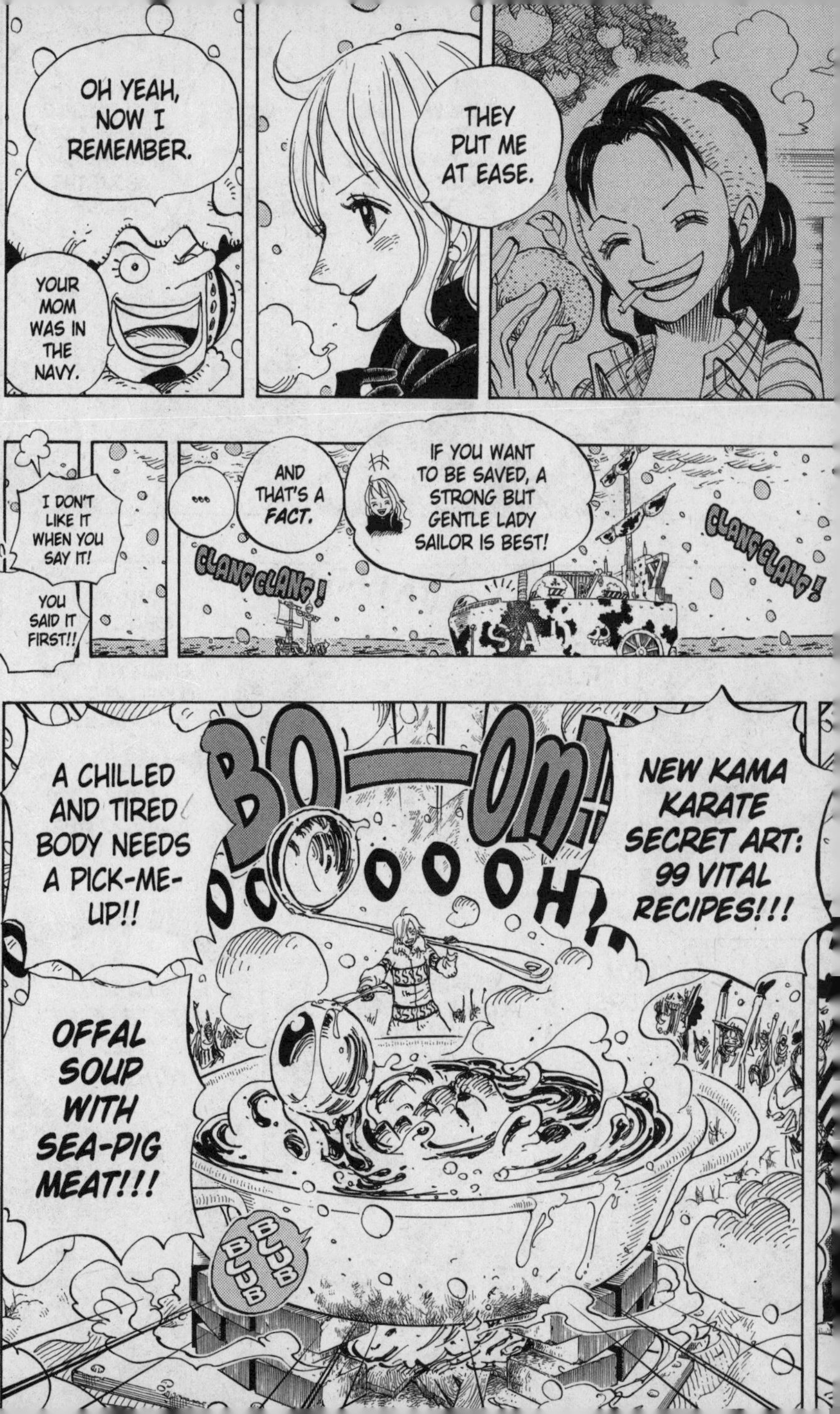
THEY PUT ME AT EASE.
OH YEAH, NOW I REMEMBER.
YOUR MOM WAS IN THE NAVY.
CLANG CLANG!
IF YOU WANT TO BE SAVED, A STRONG BUT GENTLE LADY SAILOR IS BEST!
AND THAT'S A FACT.
CLANG CLANG!
...
I DON'T LIKE IT WHEN YOU SAY IT!
YOU SAID IT FIRST!!
NEW KAMA KARATE SECRET ART: 99 VITAL RECIPES!!!
BO—OM!
OOOOOOH!!
A CHILLED AND TIRED BODY NEEDS A PICK-ME-UP!!
OFFAL SOUP WITH SEA-PIG MEAT!!!
BLUB BLUB

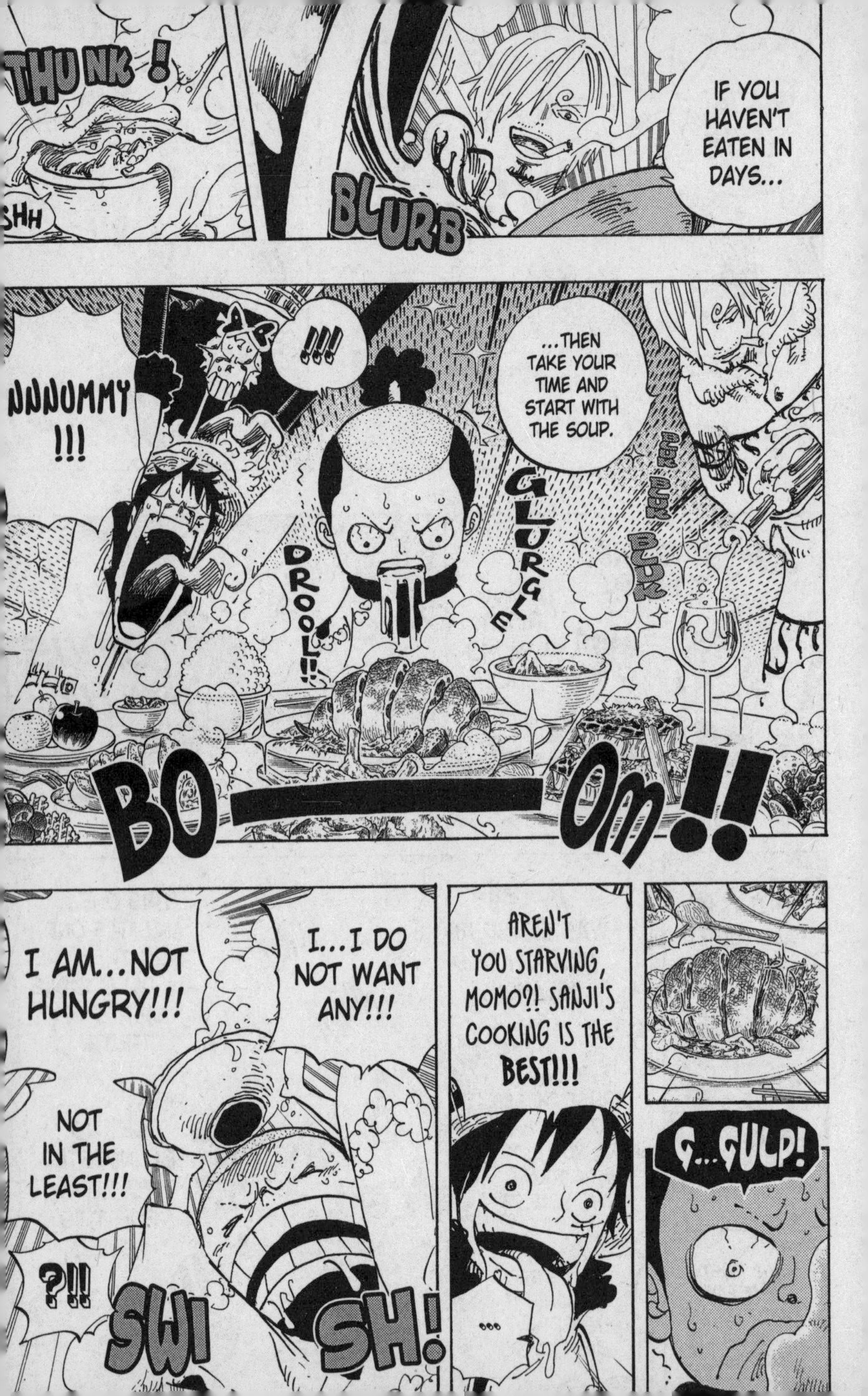
IF YOU HAVEN'T EATEN IN DAYS...
BLURB
THUNK!
SHH
...THEN TAKE YOUR TIME AND START WITH THE SOUP.
BLUK
GLURGLE
DROOL!!
!!!
NNNUMMY!!!
BO—OM!!
G...GULP!
AREN'T YOU STARVING, MOMO?! SANJI'S COOKING IS THE BEST!!!
...
I...I DO NOT WANT ANY!!!
I AM...NOT HUNGRY!!!
NOT IN THE LEAST!!!
?!!
SWISH!

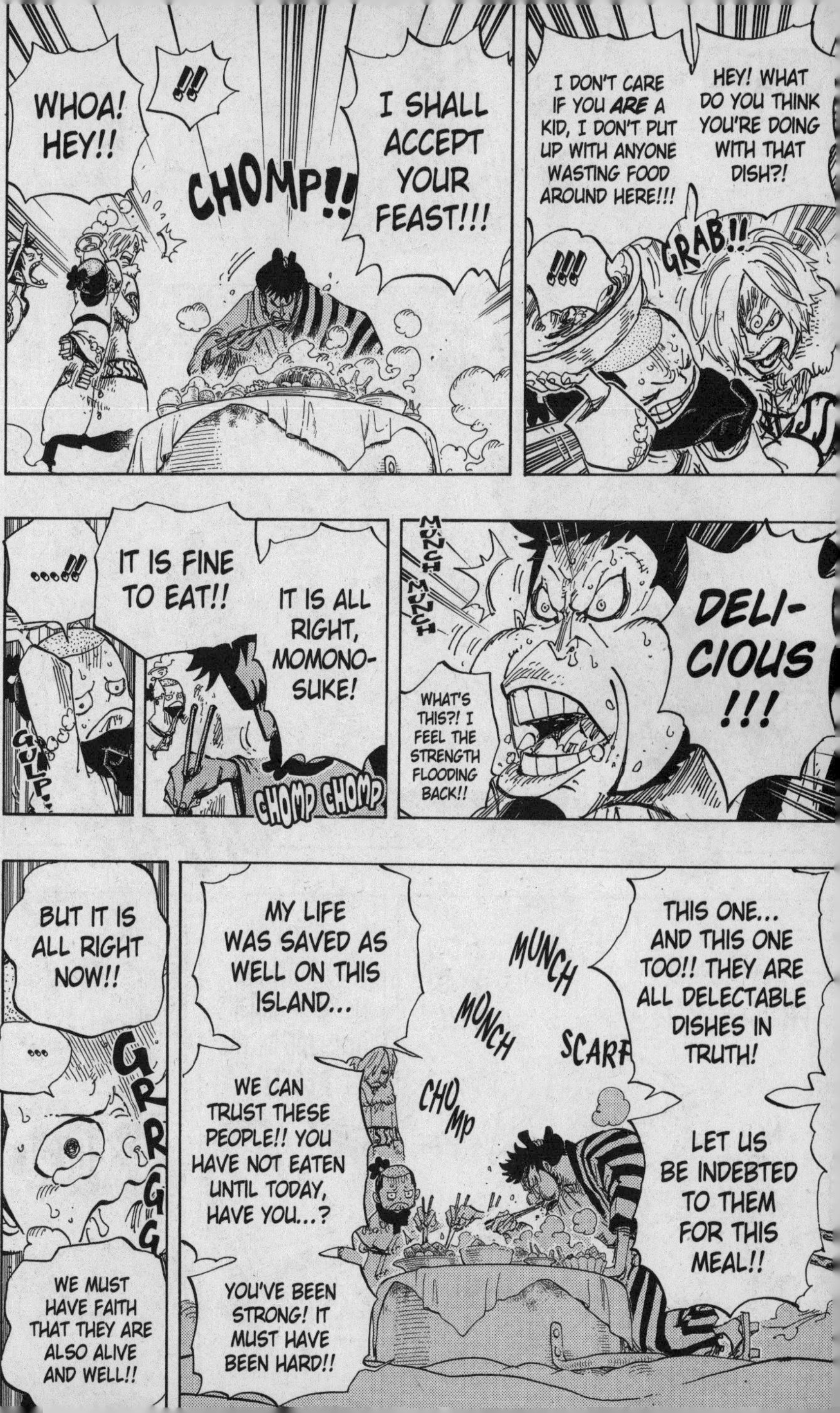
HEY! WHAT DO YOU THINK YOU'RE DOING WITH THAT DISH?!
I DON'T CARE IF YOU *ARE* A KID, I DON'T PUT UP WITH ANYONE WASTING FOOD AROUND HERE!!!
GRAB!!
!!!
I SHALL ACCEPT YOUR FEAST!!!
!!
CHOMP!!
WHOA! HEY!!
DELI-CIOUS!!!
MUNCH MUNCH
WHAT'S THIS?! I FEEL THE STRENGTH FLOODING BACK!!
IT IS ALL RIGHT, MOMONOSUKE!
CHOMP CHOMP
IT IS FINE TO EAT!!
...!!
GULP!!
THIS ONE... AND THIS ONE TOO!! THEY ARE ALL DELECTABLE DISHES IN TRUTH!
MY LIFE WAS SAVED AS WELL ON THIS ISLAND...
MUNCH
MUNCH
SCARF
CHOMP
LET US BE INDEBTED TO THEM FOR THIS MEAL!!
WE CAN TRUST THESE PEOPLE!! YOU HAVE NOT EATEN UNTIL TODAY, HAVE YOU...?
YOU'VE BEEN STRONG! IT MUST HAVE BEEN HARD!!
BUT IT IS ALL RIGHT NOW!!
...
GRRRGG
WE MUST HAVE FAITH THAT THEY ARE ALSO ALIVE AND WELL!!

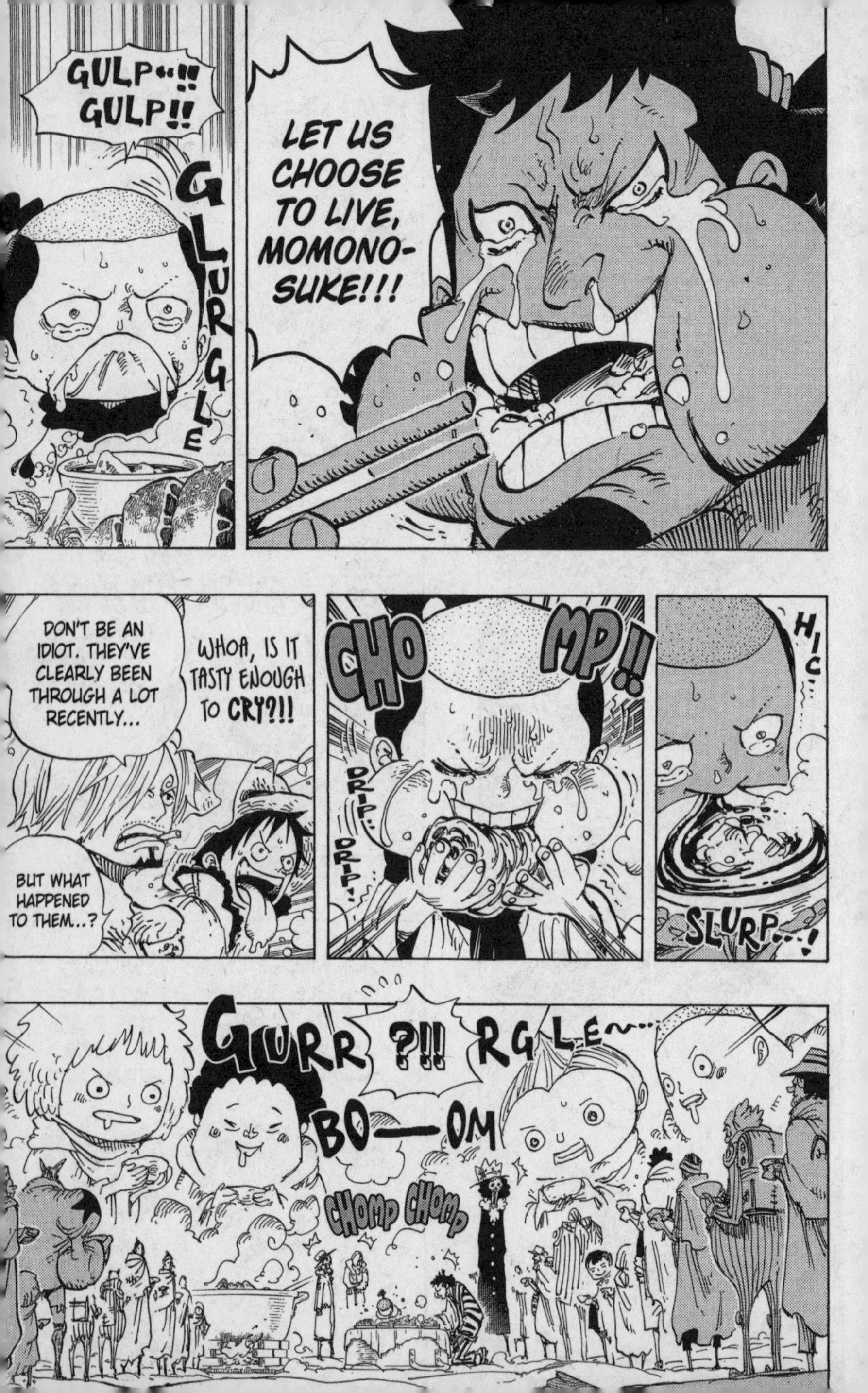
LET US CHOOSE TO LIVE, MOMONOSUKE!!!
GULP··!! GULP!!
GLURGLE
HIC...
SLURP...!
CHOMP!!
DRIP... DRIP...
WHOA, IS IT TASTY ENOUGH TO CRY?!!
DON'T BE AN IDIOT. THEY'VE CLEARLY BEEN THROUGH A LOT RECENTLY...
BUT WHAT HAPPENED TO THEM...?
GURR RGLE~...
?!!
BO—OM
CHOMP CHOMP

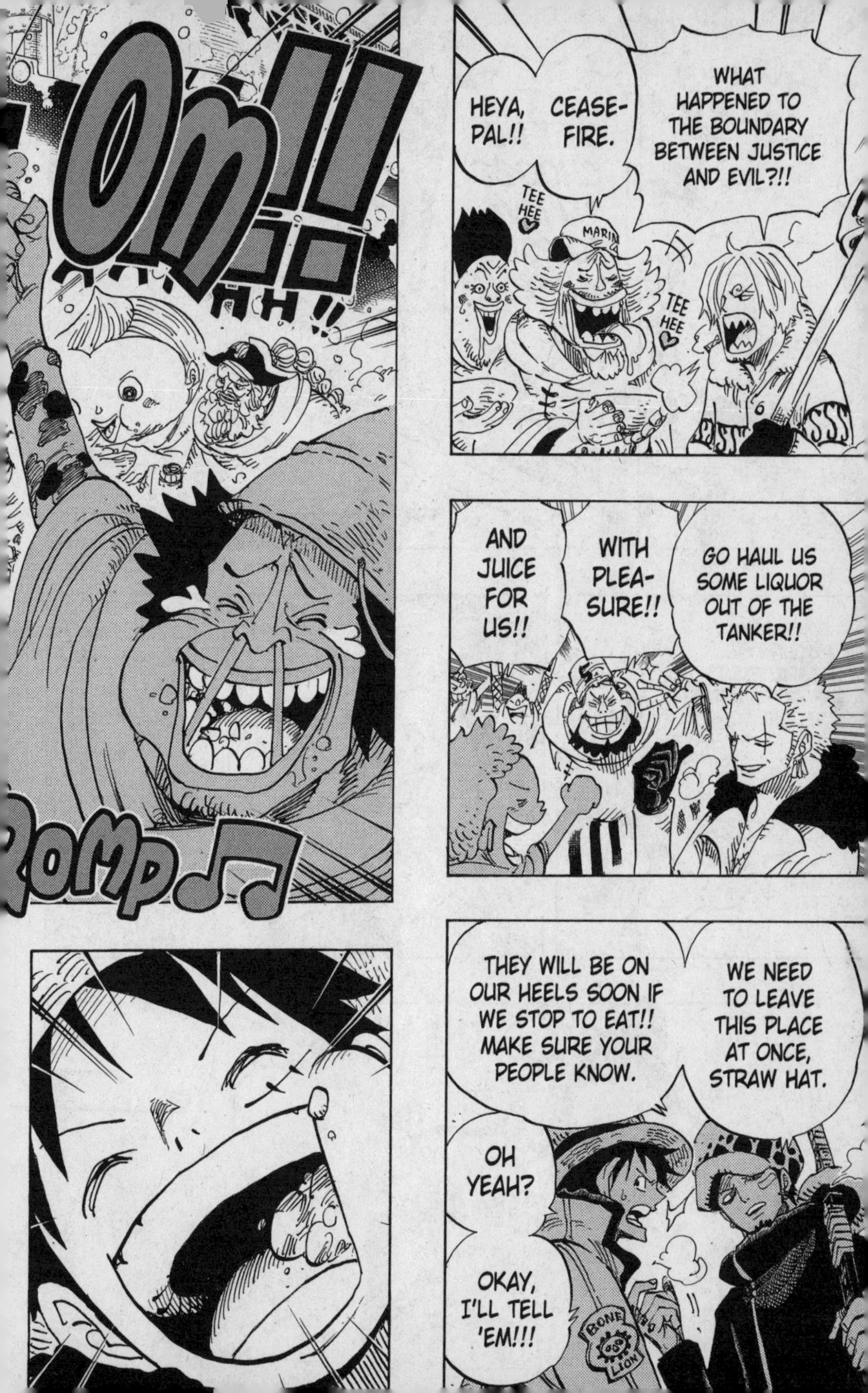
WHAT HAPPENED TO THE BOUNDARY BETWEEN JUSTICE AND EVIL?!!
CEASE-FIRE.
HEYA, PAL!!
TEE HEE
TEE HEE
GO HAUL US SOME LIQUOR OUT OF THE TANKER!!
WITH PLEA-SURE!!
AND JUICE FOR US!!
OM!!
ROMP
WE NEED TO LEAVE THIS PLACE AT ONCE, STRAW HAT.
THEY WILL BE ON OUR HEELS SOON IF WE STOP TO EAT!! MAKE SURE YOUR PEOPLE KNOW.
OH YEAH?
OKAY, I'LL TELL 'EM!!!
BONE LION

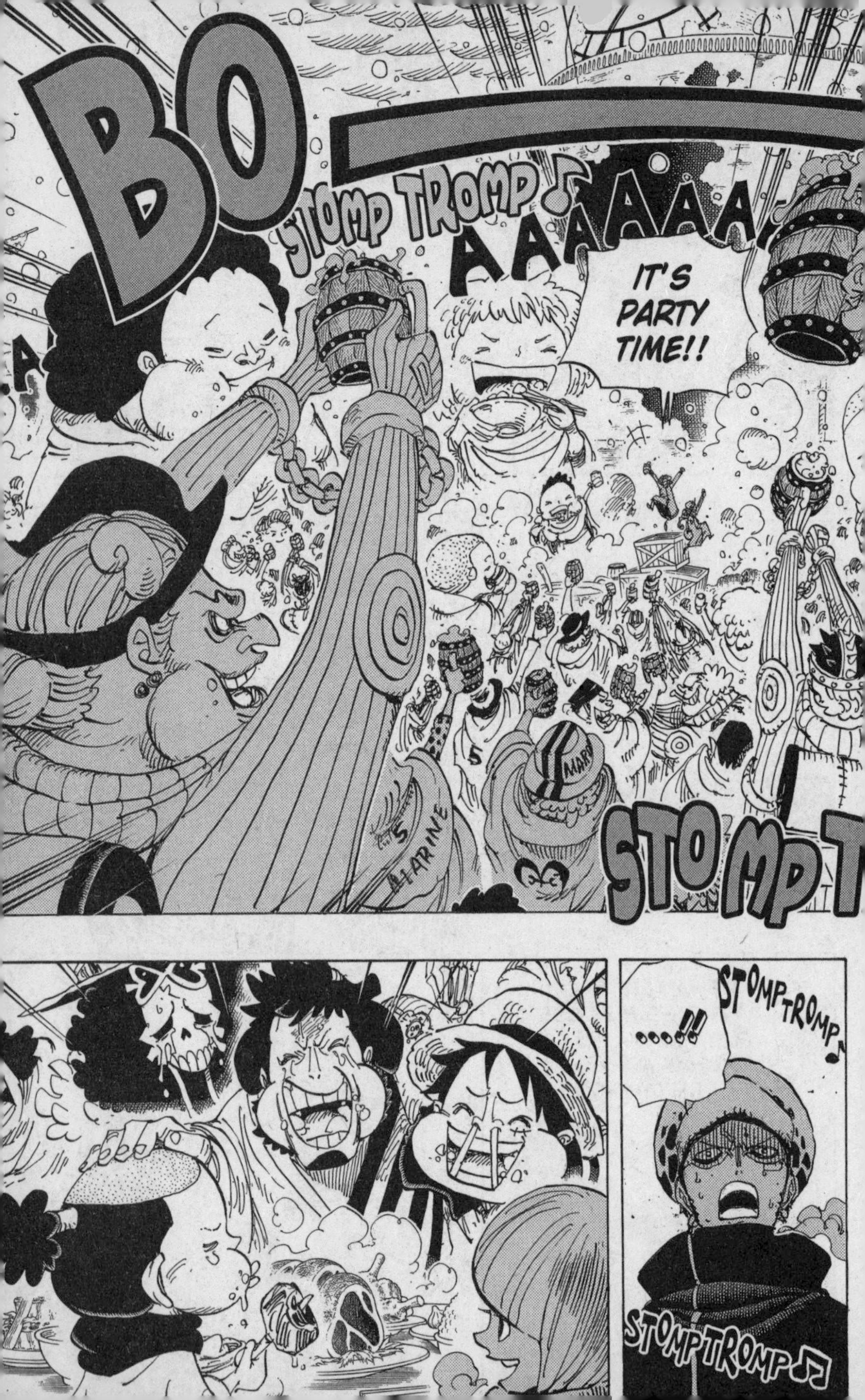
BO————AAAAAA
STOMP TROMP♪
IT'S PARTY TIME!!
STOMP T
STOMP TROMP♪
....!!
STOMP TROMP♫

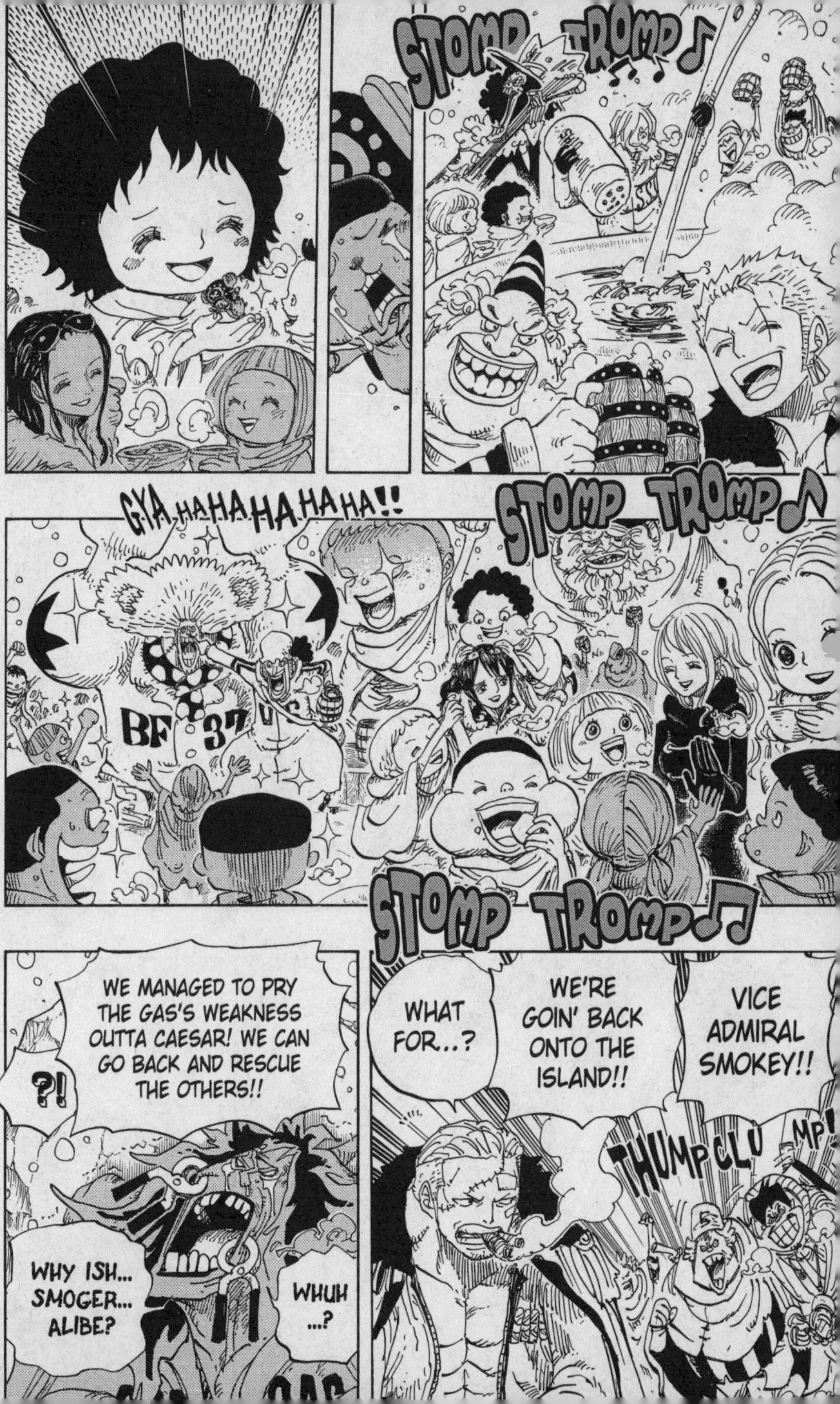
STOMP TROMP♪
STOMP TROMP♪
GYAHAHAHAHAHAHA!!
STOMP TROMP♪♫
VICE ADMIRAL SMOKEY!!
WE'RE GOIN' BACK ONTO THE ISLAND!!
WHAT FOR...?
THUMP CLUMP!
WE MANAGED TO PRY THE GAS'S WEAKNESS OUTTA CAESAR! WE CAN GO BACK AND RESCUE THE OTHERS!!
?!
WHUH ...?
WHY ISH... SMOGER... ALIBE?

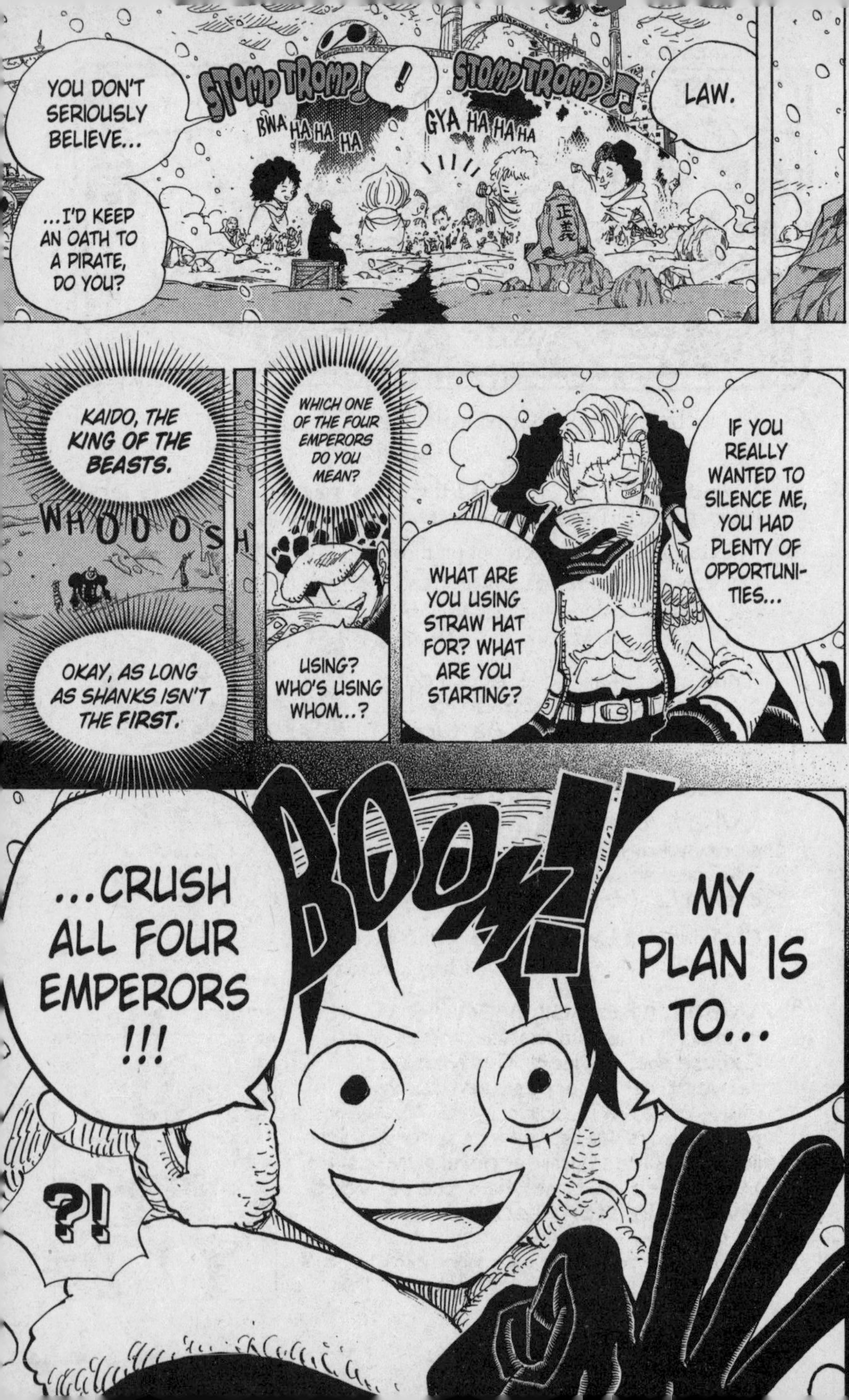
LAW.
STOMP TROMP ♫
!
GYA HA HA HA
STOMP TROMP ♪
BWA HA HA HA
YOU DON'T SERIOUSLY BELIEVE...
...I'D KEEP AN OATH TO A PIRATE, DO YOU?
IF YOU REALLY WANTED TO SILENCE ME, YOU HAD PLENTY OF OPPORTUNITIES...
WHAT ARE YOU USING STRAW HAT FOR? WHAT ARE YOU STARTING?
WHICH ONE OF THE FOUR EMPERORS DO YOU MEAN?
USING? WHO'S USING WHOM...?
KAIDO, THE KING OF THE BEASTS.
WHOOOOSH
OKAY, AS LONG AS SHANKS ISN'T THE FIRST.
MY PLAN IS TO...
BOOM!
...CRUSH ALL FOUR EMPERORS!!!
?!

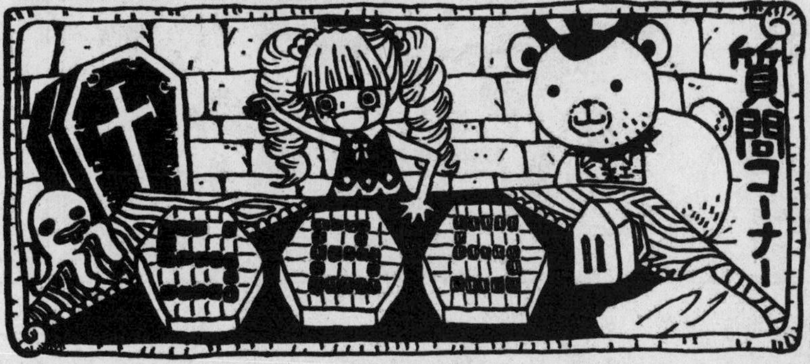
SBS
質問コーナー

(Misapero, Fukui)

Q: Odacchi, speak in Kansai dialect!

--Enoki

A: Whaaat? I cain't do that! It's jes' plain impossible, ya jerk! I cain't do it!! Don't make me whupyer behind!!

Q: The crew's hair has to grow out on those long voyages, right? Does someone give the rest haircuts? Nami or Robin, perhaps?

--I Want to be a Hairdresser

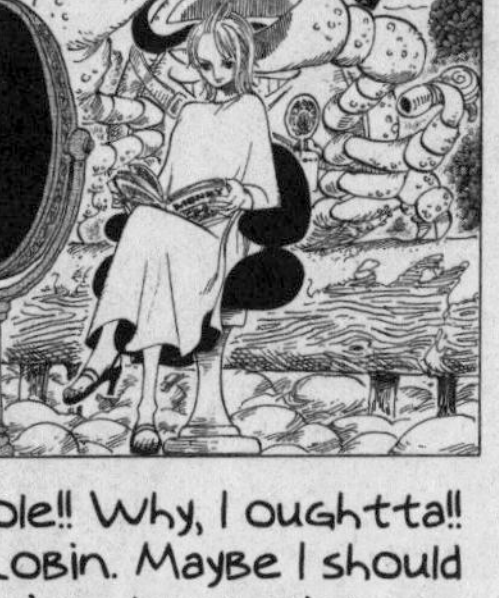

A: True, their hair does grow out. So who gives haircuts on the crew? Why, it's Zolo. He turns on the rest and goes, "Tiger Trap!!" Just kidding!! What the hell, man?!! I'm gonnawhupyer behind!! Shut yerpiehole!! Why, I oughtta!! The real answer is prolly Usopp or Robin. Maybe I should draw a heart-warmin' picture of a haircut someday.

Q: Can I drink the bath water after Nami's been in it?

--ChageroKiyomizu

A: What the hell, man?!! What in tarnation are you thinkin'?! This is a manga for all ages!! Excuse me, officer! This man's a pervert, can ya arrest him for me? Huh? What'm I holding, ya say? Why, it's a pretty lady's flute. What's wrong with lickin' it whiles I walk around plum-naked? What--hey! Not me! He's the pervert, I swear! No, stop!? I got deadlines ta meet!

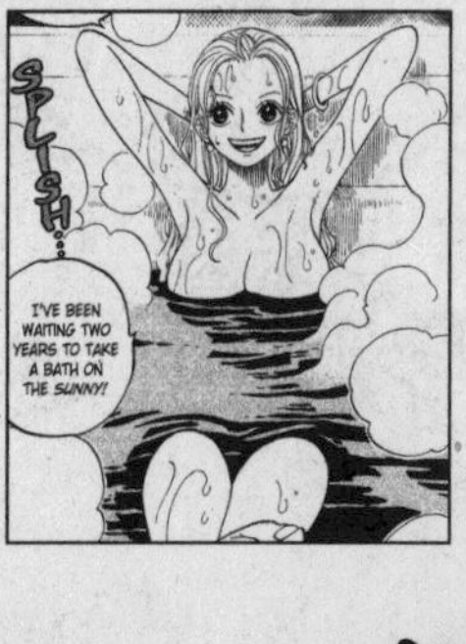
SPLISH...
I'VE BEEN WAITING TWO YEARS TO TAKE A BATH ON THE SUNNY!

What?! Impersonation of a Kansai resident?! What's that s'pose ta mean?! Who cares?! No, look, the readers put me up to it...

Chapter 697:
A DEAL

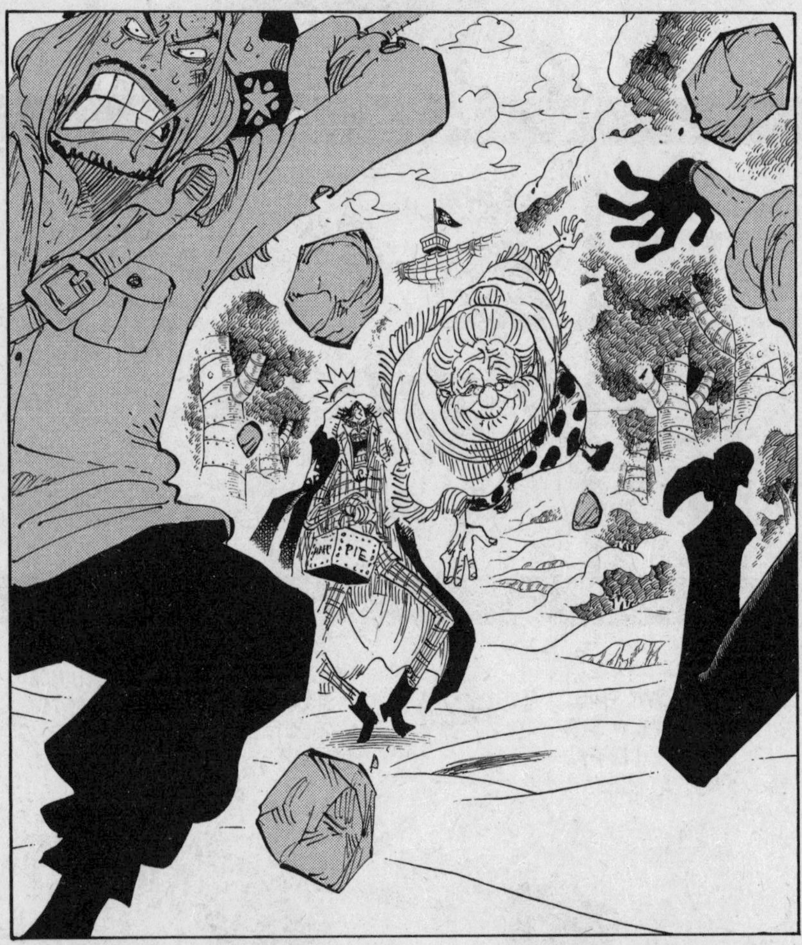
PIE

CARIBOU'S NEW WORLD KEE HEE HEE, VOL. 19: "THE OLD HAG DRIVES OFF THE MYSTERIOUS SOLDIERS"

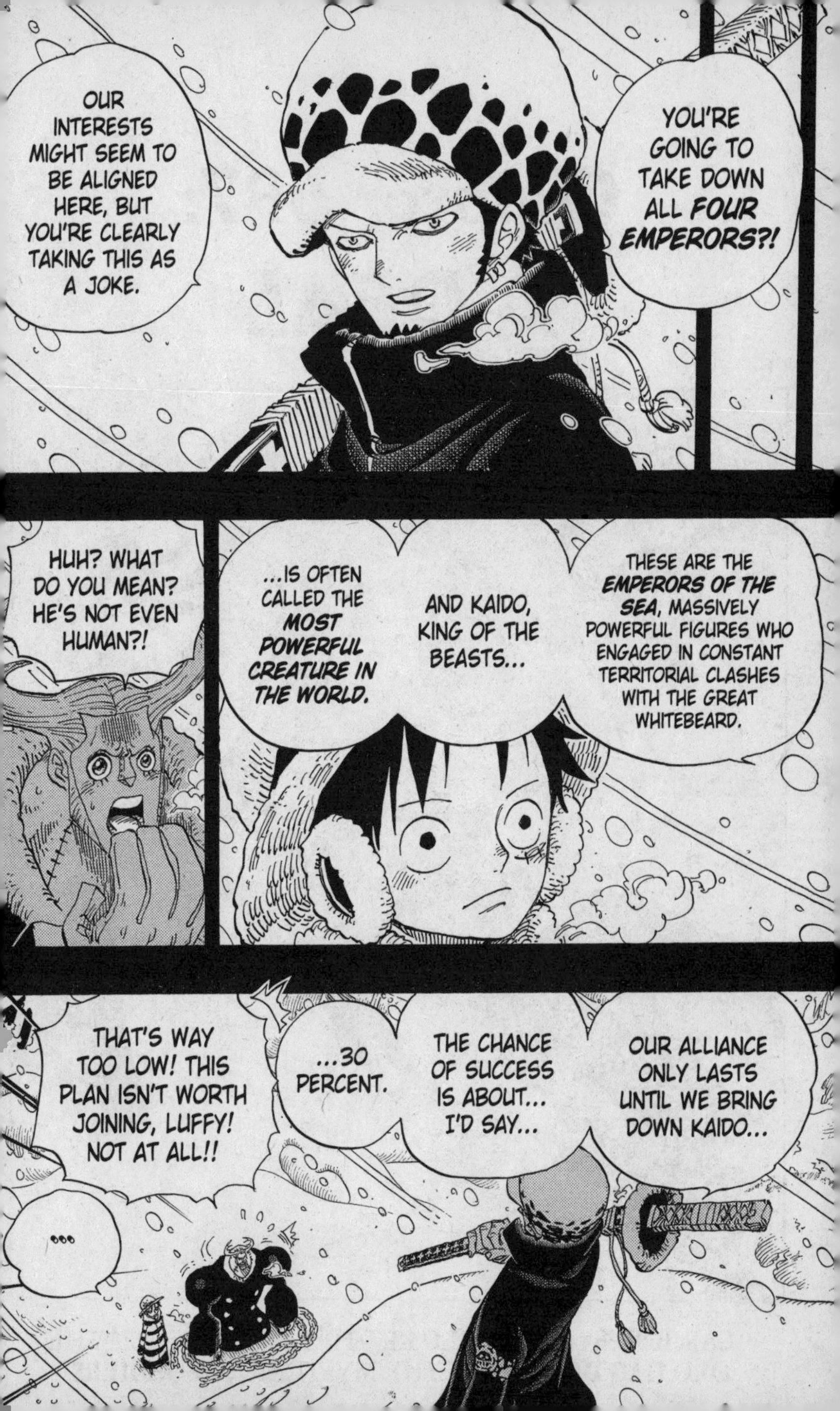
YOU'RE GOING TO TAKE DOWN ALL *FOUR EMPERORS?!*
OUR INTERESTS MIGHT SEEM TO BE ALIGNED HERE, BUT YOU'RE CLEARLY TAKING THIS AS A JOKE.
THESE ARE THE *EMPERORS OF THE SEA*, MASSIVELY POWERFUL FIGURES WHO ENGAGED IN CONSTANT TERRITORIAL CLASHES WITH THE GREAT WHITEBEARD.
AND KAIDO, KING OF THE BEASTS...
...IS OFTEN CALLED THE *MOST POWERFUL CREATURE IN THE WORLD.*
HUH? WHAT DO YOU MEAN? HE'S NOT EVEN HUMAN?!
OUR ALLIANCE ONLY LASTS UNTIL WE BRING DOWN KAIDO...
THE CHANCE OF SUCCESS IS ABOUT... I'D SAY...
...30 PERCENT.
THAT'S WAY TOO LOW! THIS PLAN ISN'T WORTH JOINING, LUFFY! NOT AT ALL!!
...

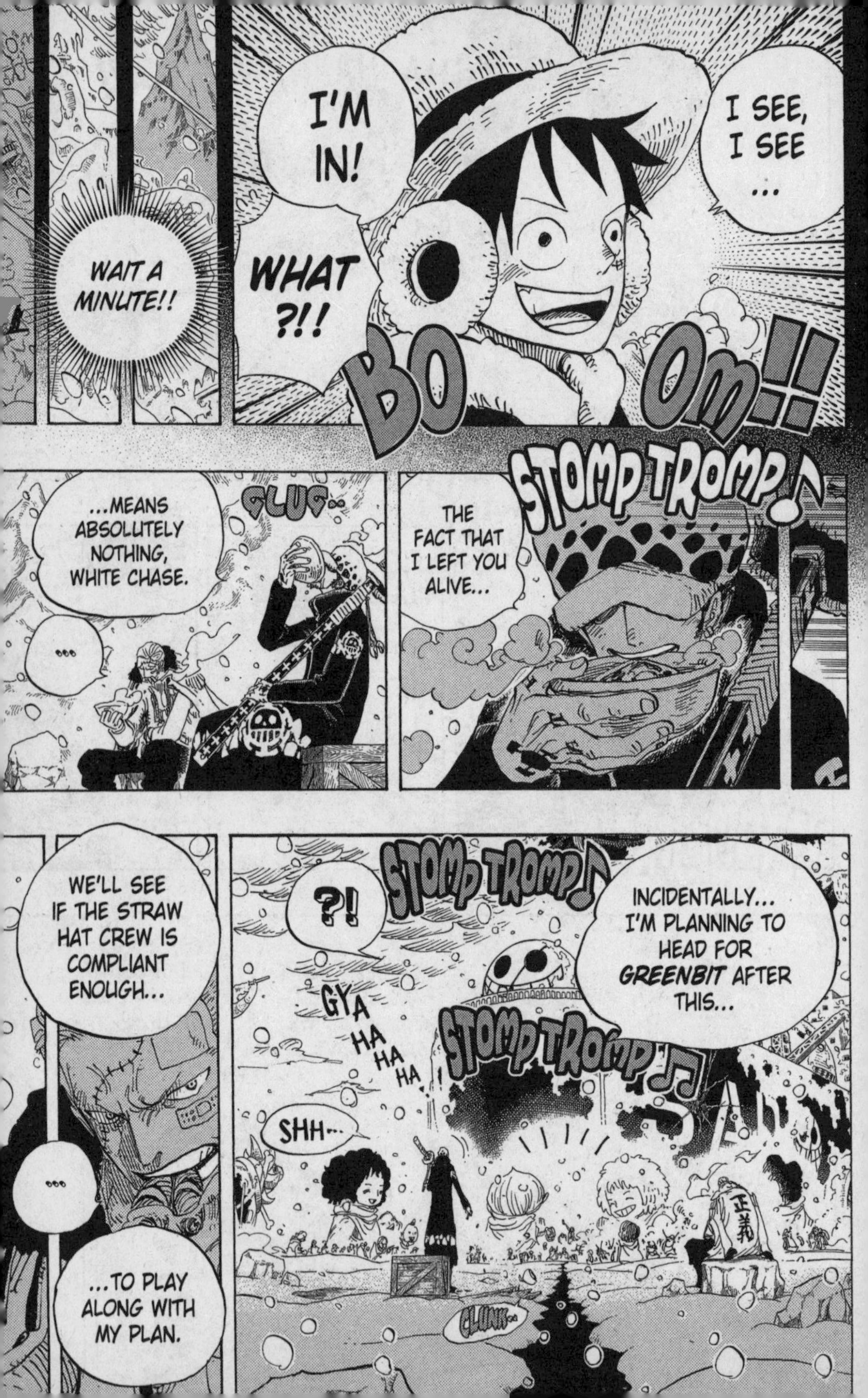

I SEE, I SEE ...
I'M IN!
WHAT ?!!
BOOM!!
WAIT A MINUTE!!
STOMP TROMP♪
THE FACT THAT I LEFT YOU ALIVE...
GLUG...
...MEANS ABSOLUTELY NOTHING, WHITE CHASE.
...
STOMP TROMP♪
INCIDENTALLY... I'M PLANNING TO HEAD FOR GREENBIT AFTER THIS...
?!
GYAHAHAHAHA
STOMP TROMP♪
SHH...
CLINK...
WE'LL SEE IF THE STRAW HAT CREW IS COMPLIANT ENOUGH...
...
...TO PLAY ALONG WITH MY PLAN.

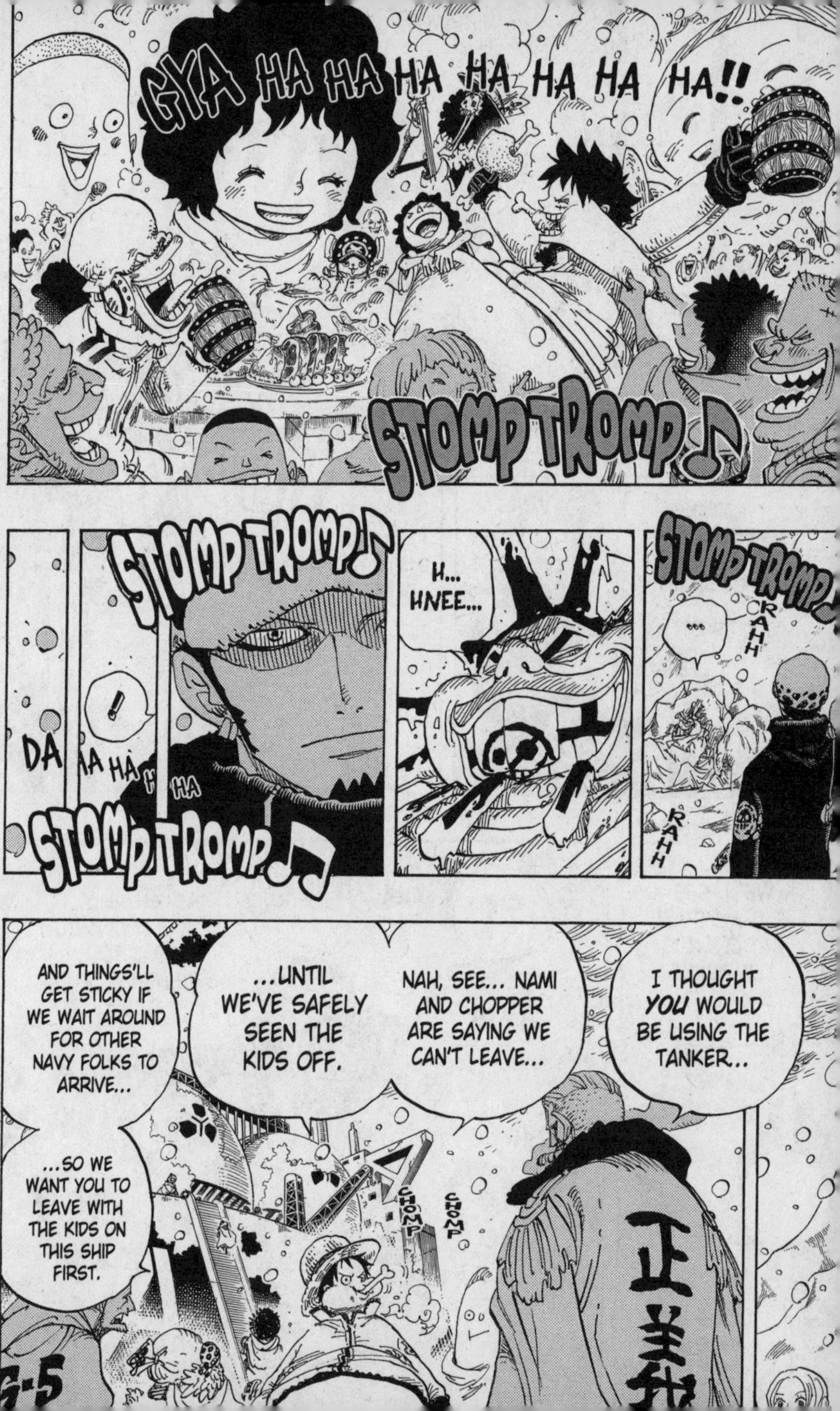
GYA HA HA HA HA HA HA HA!!
STOMP TROMP ♪
STOMP TROMP ♪
...
RAHH
RAHH
H... HNEE...
STOMP TROMP ♪
!
DA HA HA HA HA
STOMP TROMP ♪
I THOUGHT YOU WOULD BE USING THE TANKER...
NAH, SEE... NAMI AND CHOPPER ARE SAYING WE CAN'T LEAVE...
...UNTIL WE'VE SAFELY SEEN THE KIDS OFF.
CHOMP
CHOMP
AND THINGS'LL GET STICKY IF WE WAIT AROUND FOR OTHER NAVY FOLKS TO ARRIVE...
...SO WE WANT YOU TO LEAVE WITH THE KIDS ON THIS SHIP FIRST.

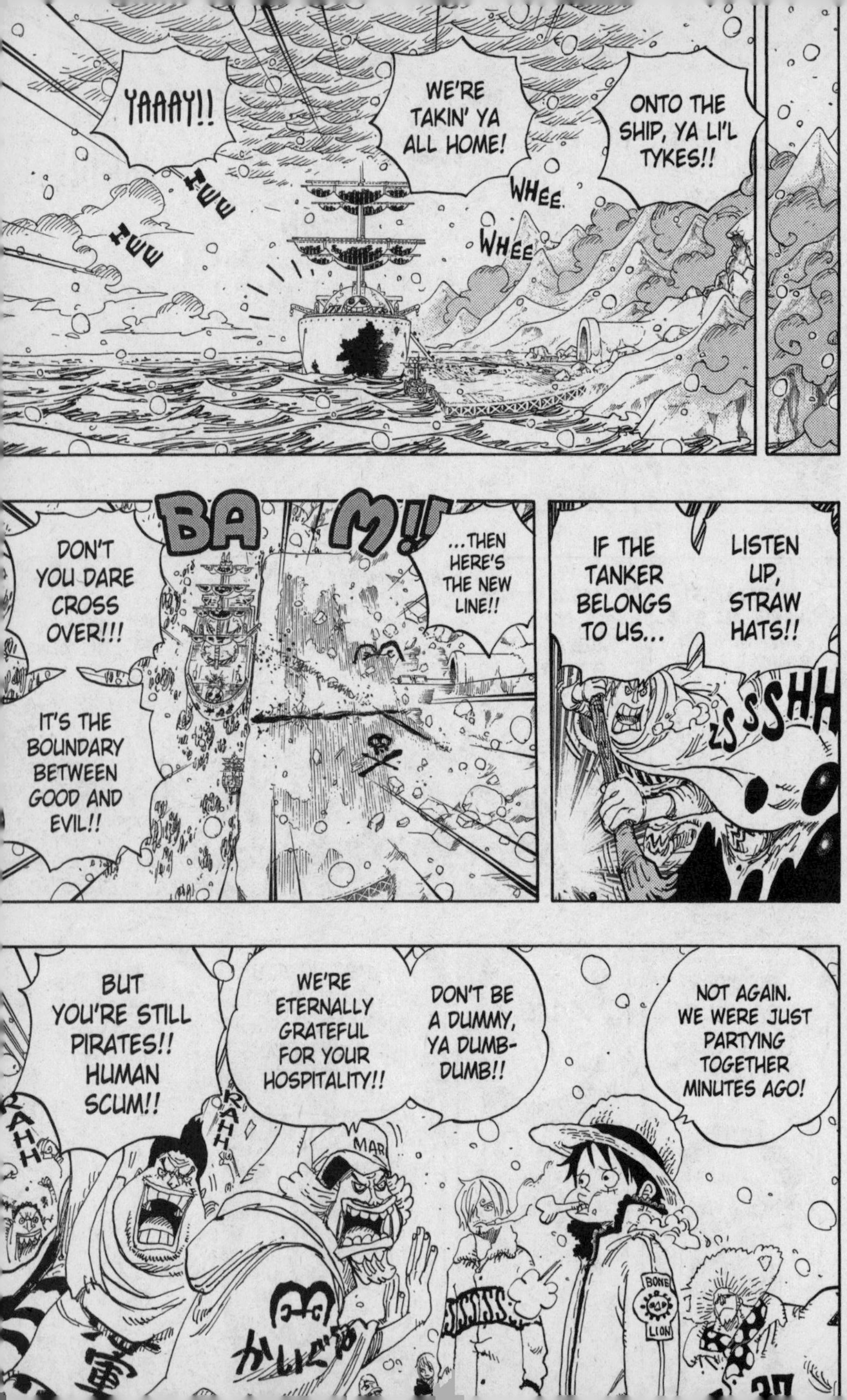
ONTO THE SHIP, YA LI'L TYKES!!
WE'RE TAKIN' YA ALL HOME!
YAAAY!!
WHEE
WHEE
LISTEN UP, STRAW HATS!!
IF THE TANKER BELONGS TO US...
ZSSSHH
...THEN HERE'S THE NEW LINE!!
BAM!!
DON'T YOU DARE CROSS OVER!!!
IT'S THE BOUNDARY BETWEEN GOOD AND EVIL!!
NOT AGAIN. WE WERE JUST PARTYING TOGETHER MINUTES AGO!
DON'T BE A DUMMY, YA DUMB-DUMB!!
WE'RE ETERNALLY GRATEFUL FOR YOUR HOSPITALITY!!
BUT YOU'RE STILL PIRATES!! HUMAN SCUM!!
RAHH
RAHH

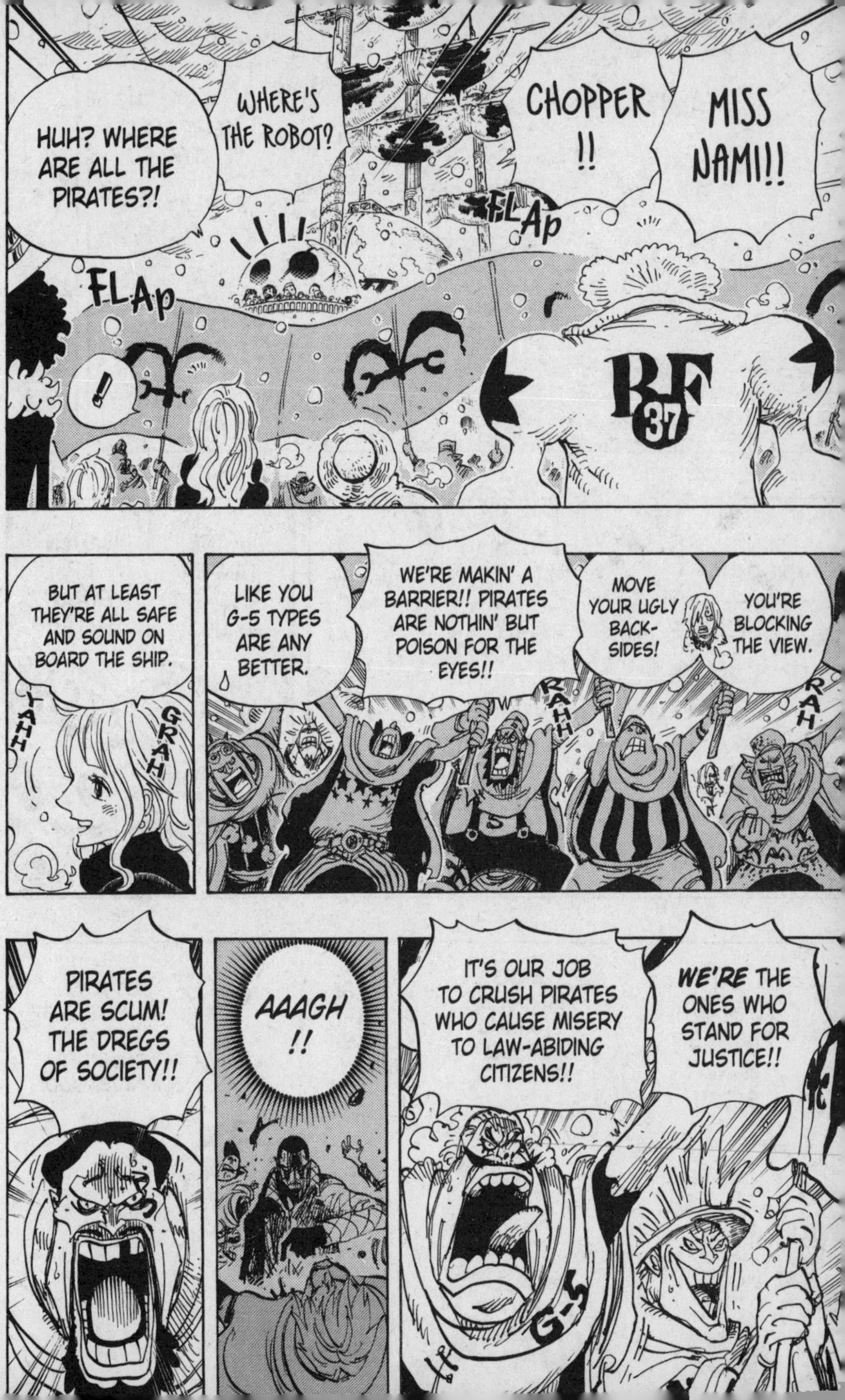
MISS NAMI!!
CHOPPER!!
FLAp
WHERE'S THE ROBOT?
HUH? WHERE ARE ALL THE PIRATES?!
FLAp
!
BF 37
YOU'RE BLOCKING THE VIEW.
MOVE YOUR UGLY BACK-SIDES!
RAH
RAHH
WE'RE MAKIN' A BARRIER!! PIRATES ARE NOTHIN' BUT POISON FOR THE EYES!!
LIKE YOU G-5 TYPES ARE ANY BETTER.
BUT AT LEAST THEY'RE ALL SAFE AND SOUND ON BOARD THE SHIP.
GRAH
YAHH
WE'RE THE ONES WHO STAND FOR JUSTICE!!
IT'S OUR JOB TO CRUSH PIRATES WHO CAUSE MISERY TO LAW-ABIDING CITIZENS!!
G-5
AAAGH!!
PIRATES ARE SCUM! THE DREGS OF SOCIETY!!

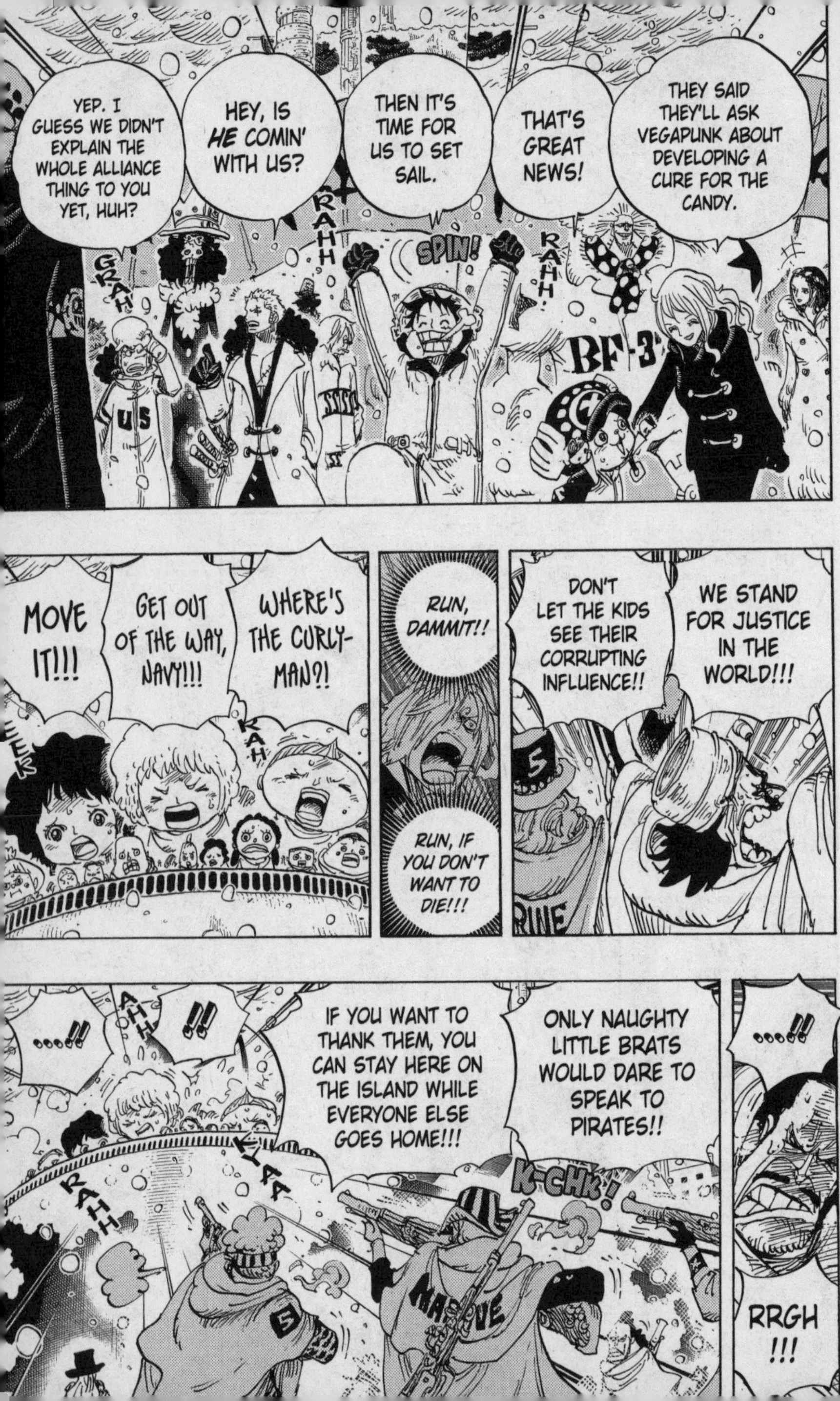
THEY SAID THEY'LL ASK VEGAPUNK ABOUT DEVELOPING A CURE FOR THE CANDY.
THAT'S GREAT NEWS!
RAHH!
SPIN!
THEN IT'S TIME FOR US TO SET SAIL.
RAHH
HEY, IS HE COMIN' WITH US?
YEP. I GUESS WE DIDN'T EXPLAIN THE WHOLE ALLIANCE THING TO YOU YET, HUH?
GRAH
WE STAND FOR JUSTICE IN THE WORLD!!!
DON'T LET THE KIDS SEE THEIR CORRUPTING INFLUENCE!!
RUN, DAMMIT!!
RUN, IF YOU DON'T WANT TO DIE!!!
WHERE'S THE CURLY-MAN?!
KRAH
GET OUT OF THE WAY, NAVY!!!
MOVE IT!!!
.....!!
RRGH!!!
ONLY NAUGHTY LITTLE BRATS WOULD DARE TO SPEAK TO PIRATES!!
K-CHK!
IF YOU WANT TO THANK THEM, YOU CAN STAY HERE ON THE ISLAND WHILE EVERYONE ELSE GOES HOME!!!
!!
AHH
.....!!
KYAA
RAHH

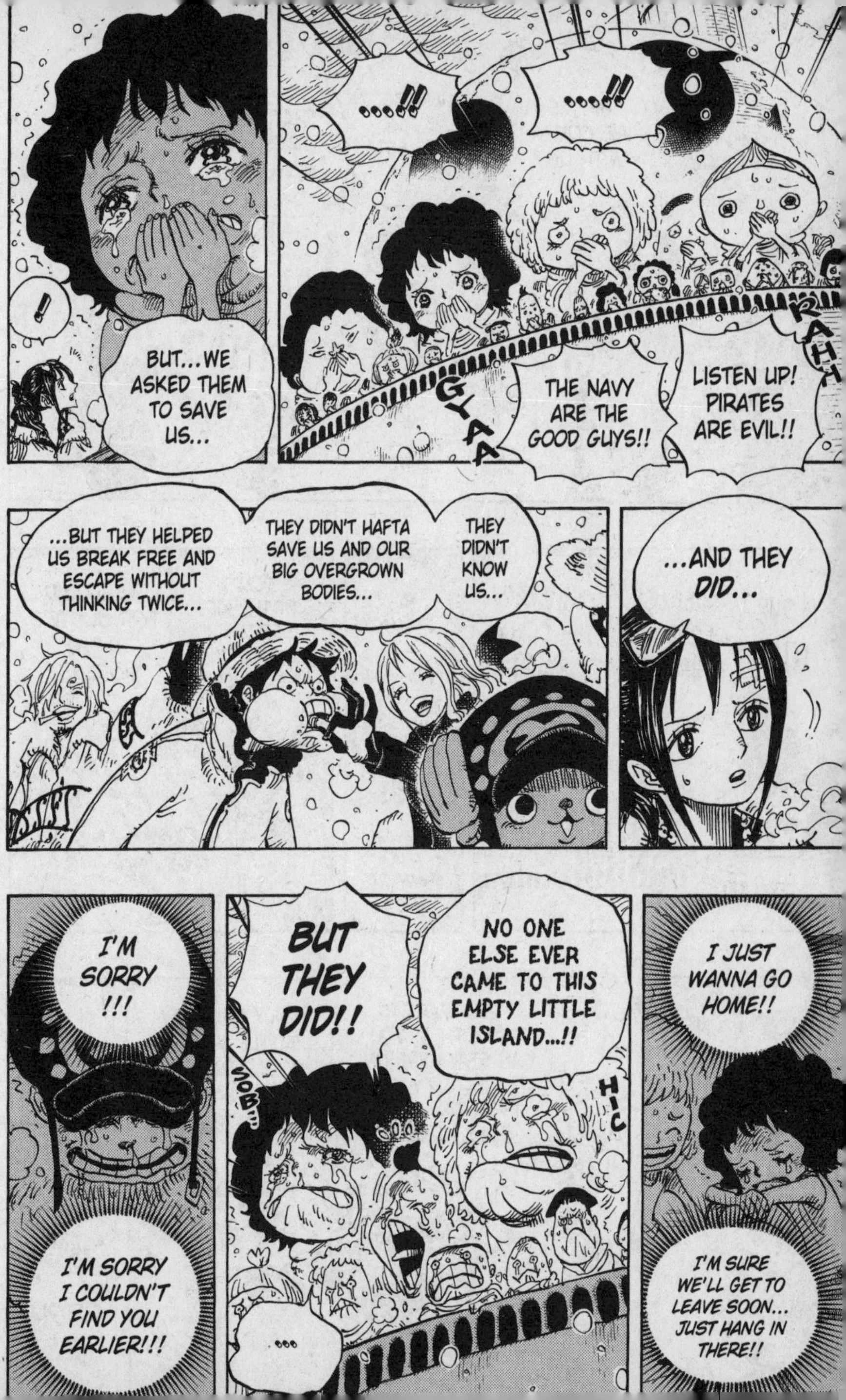
...!!
...!!
RAHH
LISTEN UP! PIRATES ARE EVIL!!
THE NAVY ARE THE GOOD GUYS!!
GYAA
!
BUT...WE ASKED THEM TO SAVE US...
...AND THEY DID...
THEY DIDN'T KNOW US...
THEY DIDN'T HAFTA SAVE US AND OUR BIG OVERGROWN BODIES...
...BUT THEY HELPED US BREAK FREE AND ESCAPE WITHOUT THINKING TWICE...
I JUST WANNA GO HOME!!
I'M SURE WE'LL GET TO LEAVE SOON... JUST HANG IN THERE!!
NO ONE ELSE EVER CAME TO THIS EMPTY LITTLE ISLAND...!!
HIC
BUT THEY DID!!
SOB
...
I'M SORRY!!!
I'M SORRY I COULDN'T FIND YOU EARLIER!!!

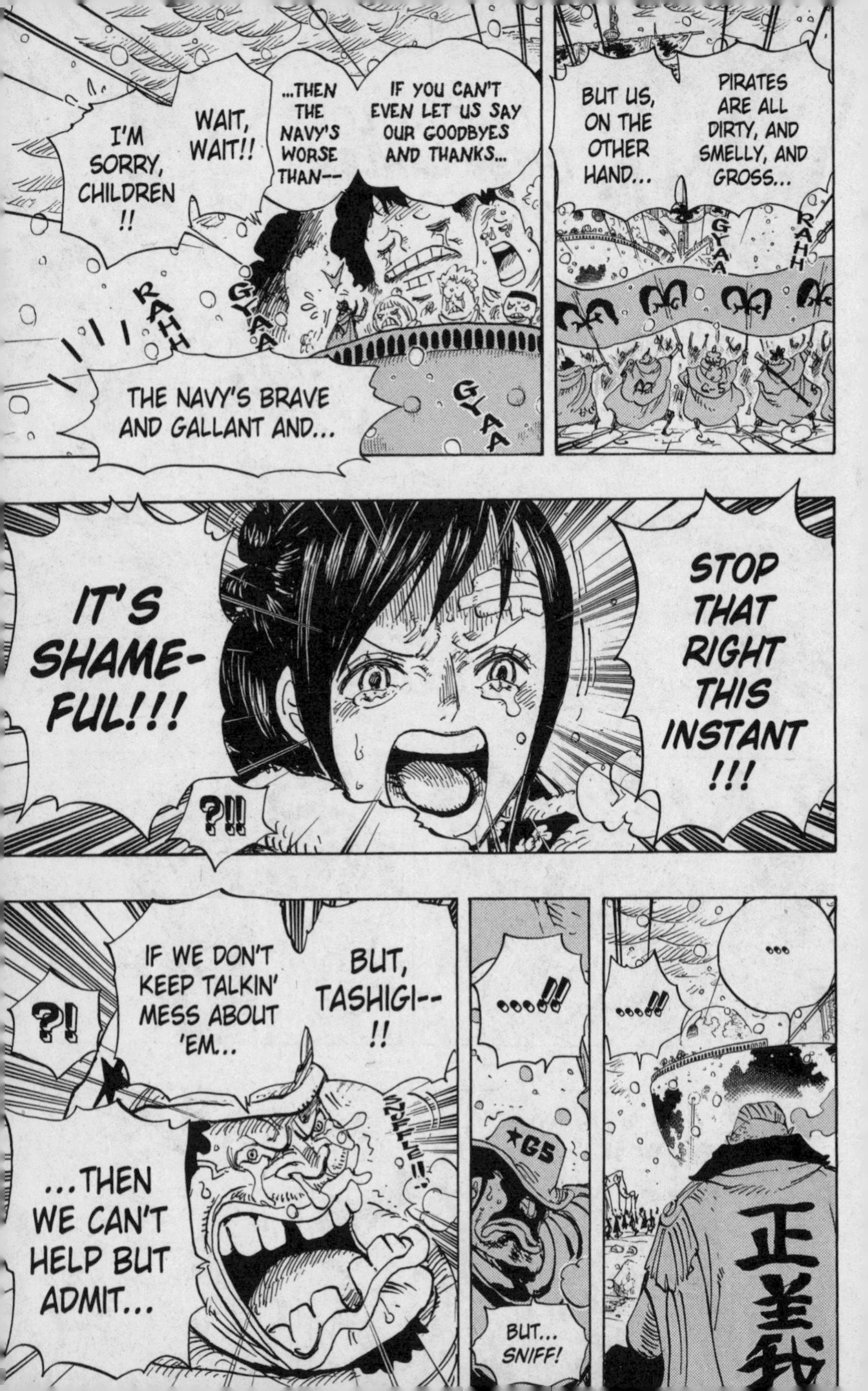
PIRATES ARE ALL DIRTY, AND SMELLY, AND GROSS...
BUT US, ON THE OTHER HAND...
RAHH
GYAA
IF YOU CAN'T EVEN LET US SAY OUR GOODBYES AND THANKS...
...THEN THE NAVY'S WORSE THAN--
WAIT, WAIT!!
I'M SORRY, CHILDREN!!
GYAA
RAHH
THE NAVY'S BRAVE AND GALLANT AND...
GYAA
STOP THAT RIGHT THIS INSTANT!!!
IT'S SHAMEFUL!!!
?!!
...
...!!
...!!
BUT... SNIFF!
BUT, TASHIGI--!!
IF WE DON'T KEEP TALKIN' MESS ABOUT 'EM...
?!
SNIFFLE!!
...THEN WE CAN'T HELP BUT ADMIT...
正義

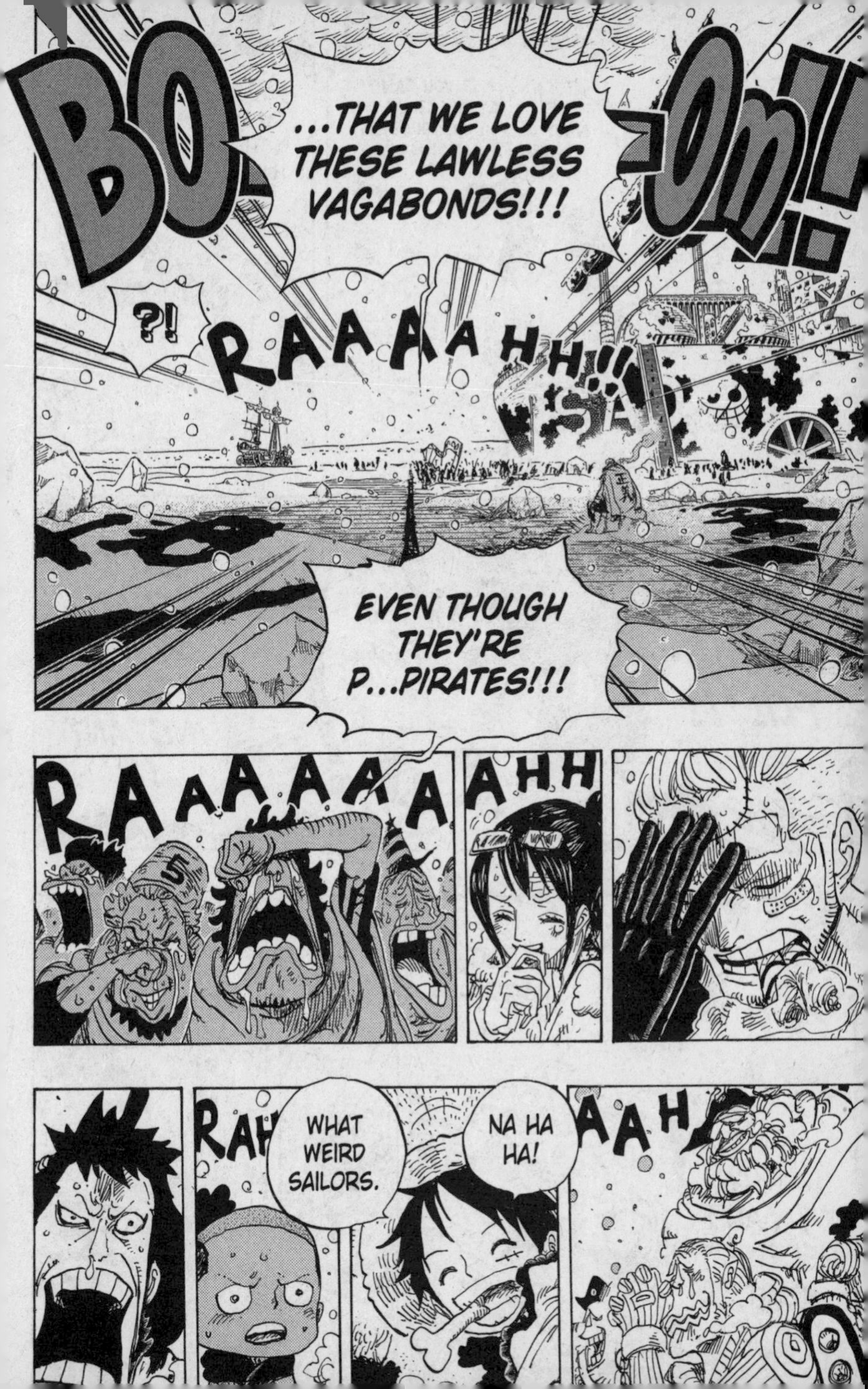
BOOM!!
...THAT WE LOVE THESE LAWLESS VAGABONDS!!!
RAAAAAHH!!!
?!
EVEN THOUGH THEY'RE P...PIRATES!!!
RAAAAAAAAHH
AAH
NA HA HA!
WHAT WEIRD SAILORS.
RAH

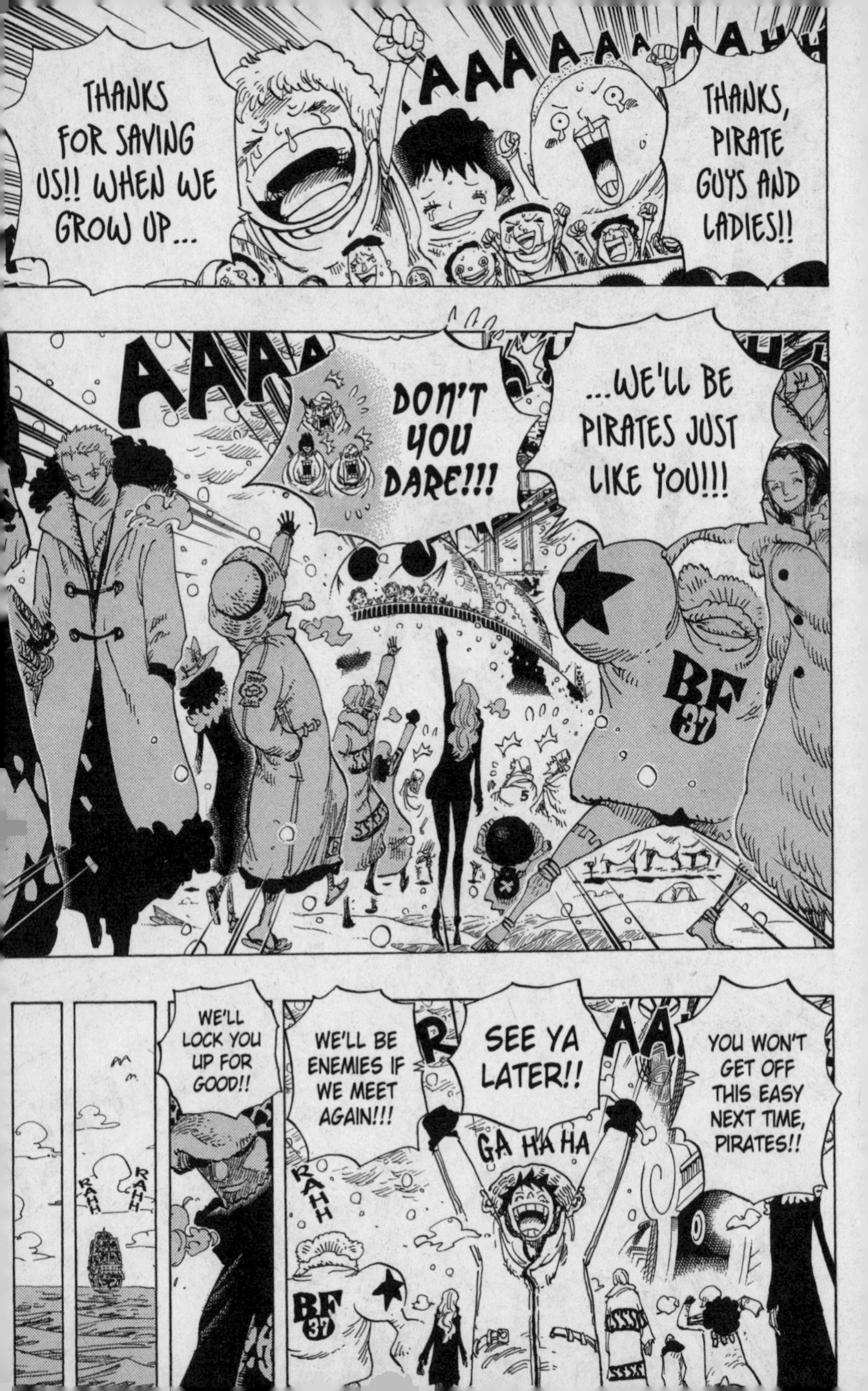
THANKS, PIRATE GUYS AND LADIES!!
THANKS FOR SAVING US!! WHEN WE GROW UP...
...WE'LL BE PIRATES JUST LIKE YOU!!!
DON'T YOU DARE!!!
YOU WON'T GET OFF THIS EASY NEXT TIME, PIRATES!!
SEE YA LATER!!
GA HA HA
WE'LL BE ENEMIES IF WE MEET AGAIN!!!
RAHH
WE'LL LOCK YOU UP FOR GOOD!!
RAHH
RAHH

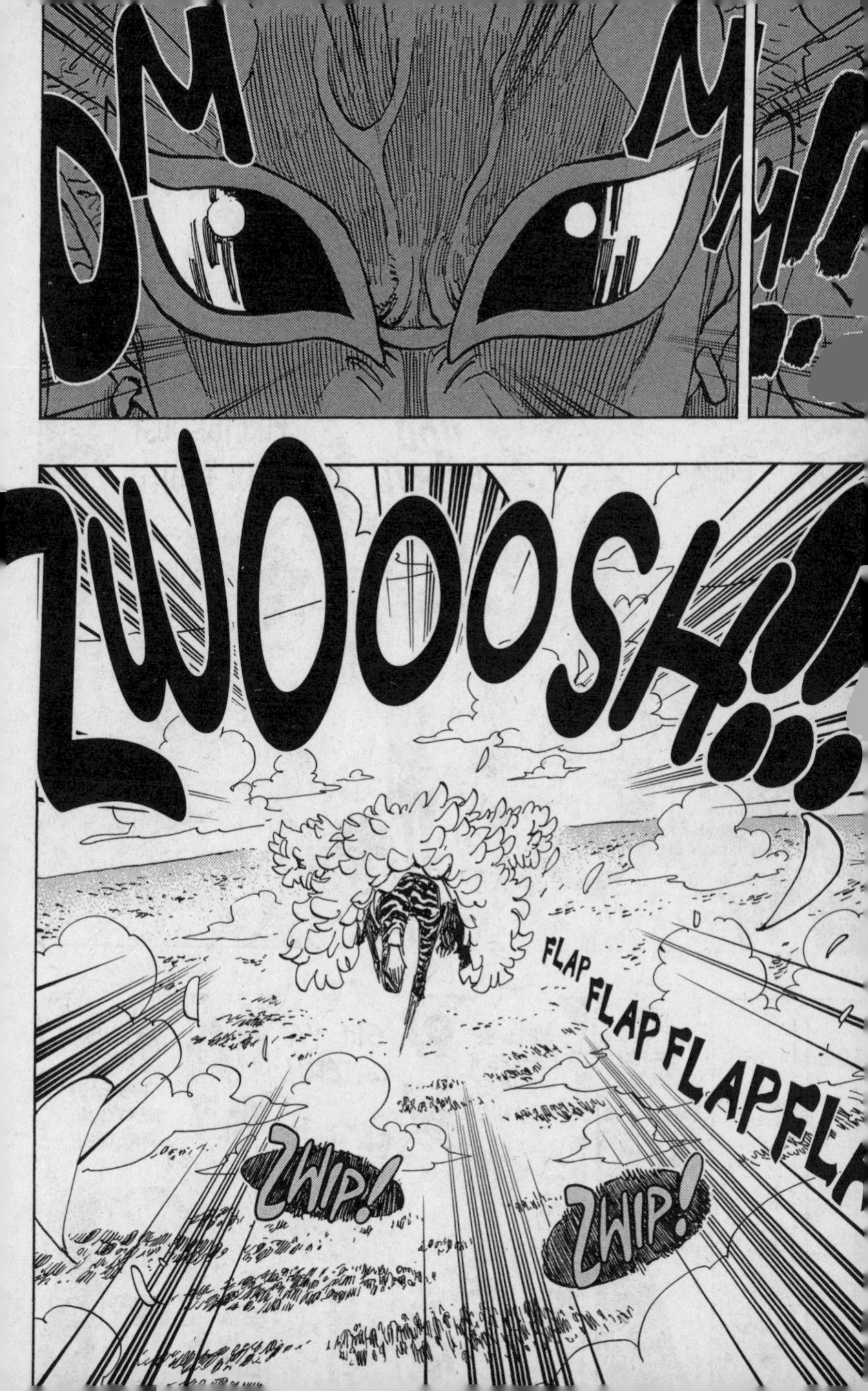
ZWOOSH!!
FLAP FLAP FLAP FLAP
ZWIP!
ZWIP!

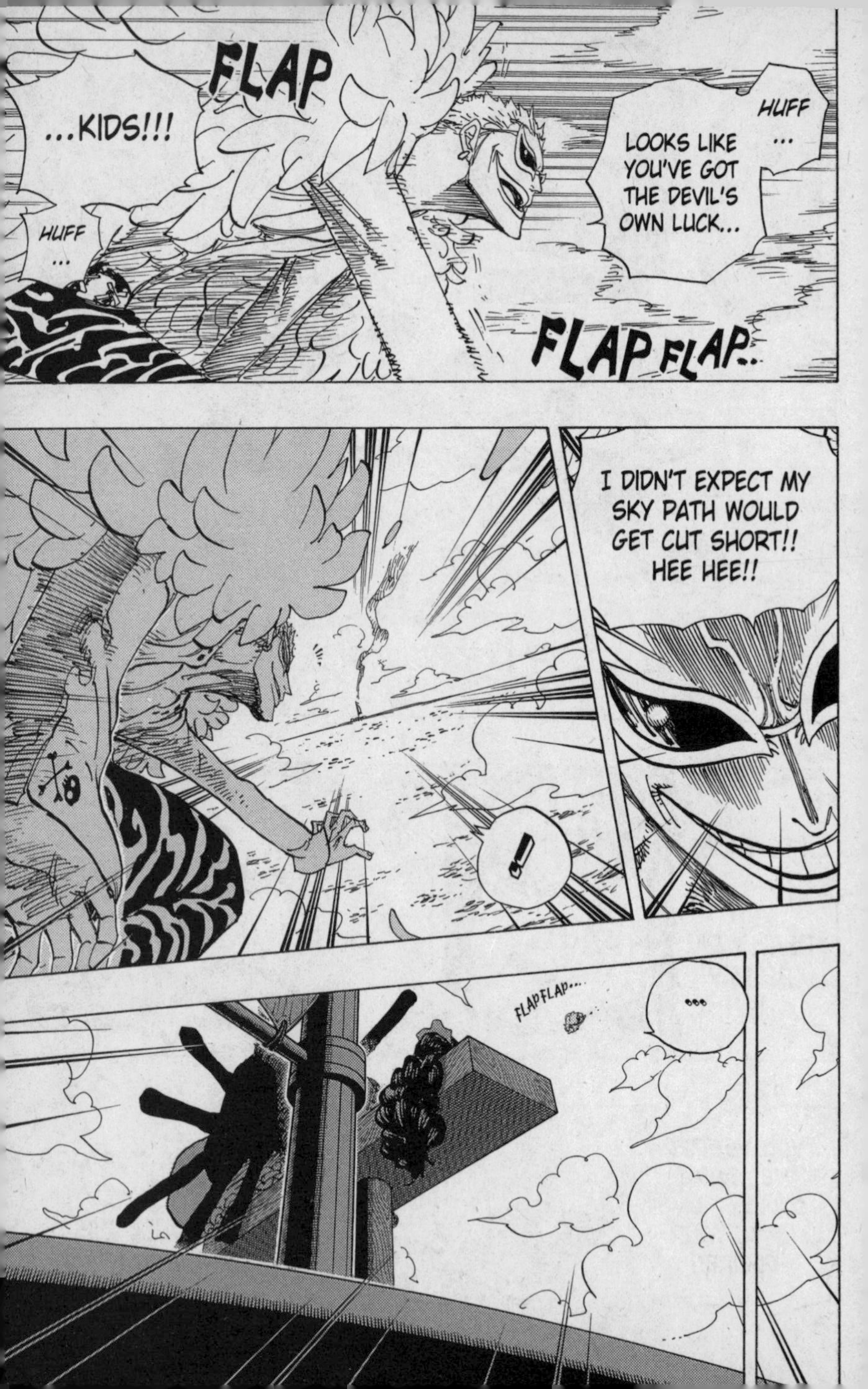
HUFF ...
LOOKS LIKE YOU'VE GOT THE DEVIL'S OWN LUCK...
FLAP
...KIDS!!!
HUFF ...
FLAP FLAP...
I DIDN'T EXPECT MY SKY PATH WOULD GET CUT SHORT!! HEE HEE!!
!
...
FLAPFLAP...

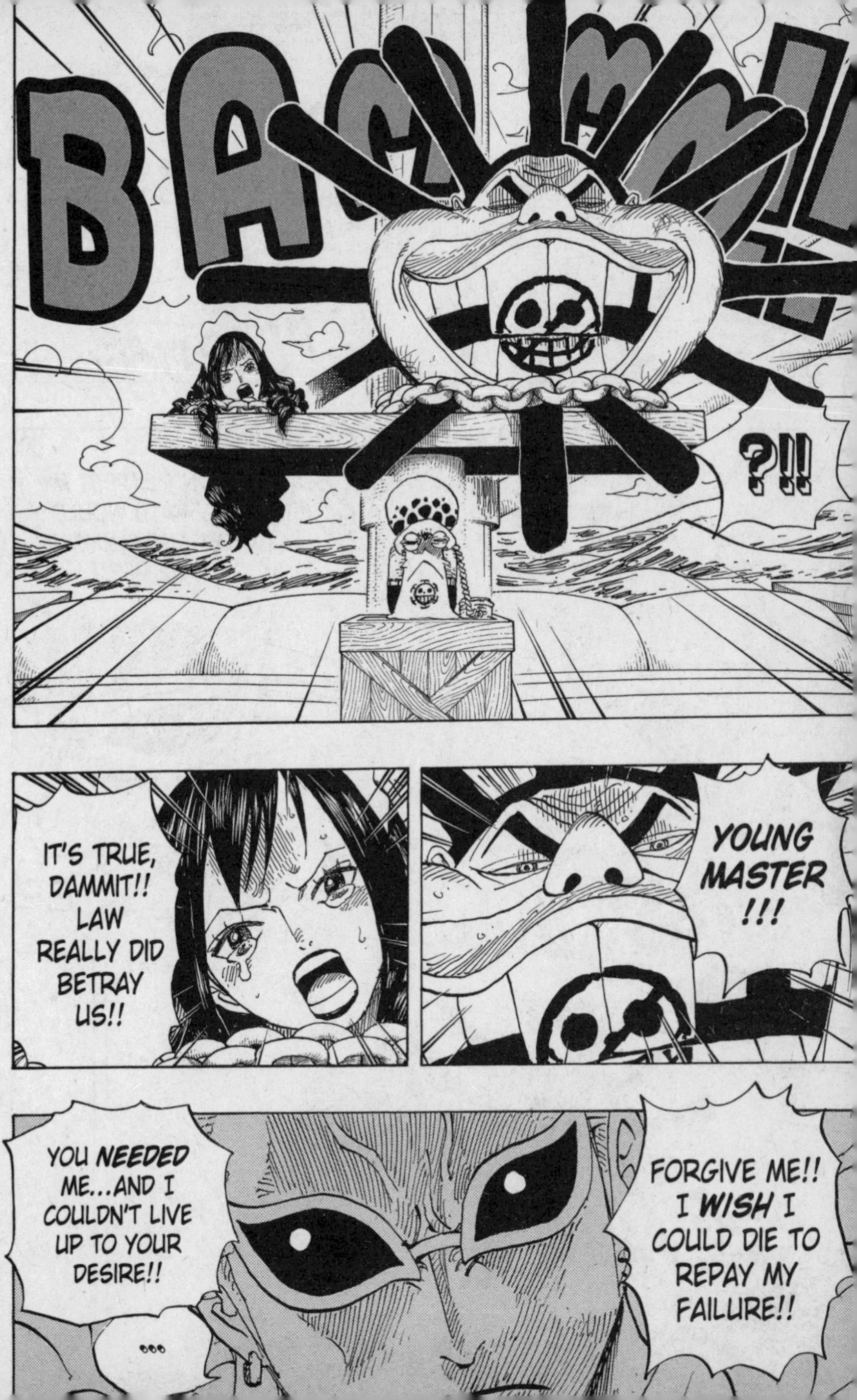
BAGMMM!
?!!
YOUNG MASTER!!!
IT'S TRUE, DAMMIT!! LAW REALLY DID BETRAY US!!
FORGIVE ME!! I *WISH* I COULD DIE TO REPAY MY FAILURE!!
YOU *NEEDED* ME...AND I COULDN'T LIVE UP TO YOUR DESIRE!!
...

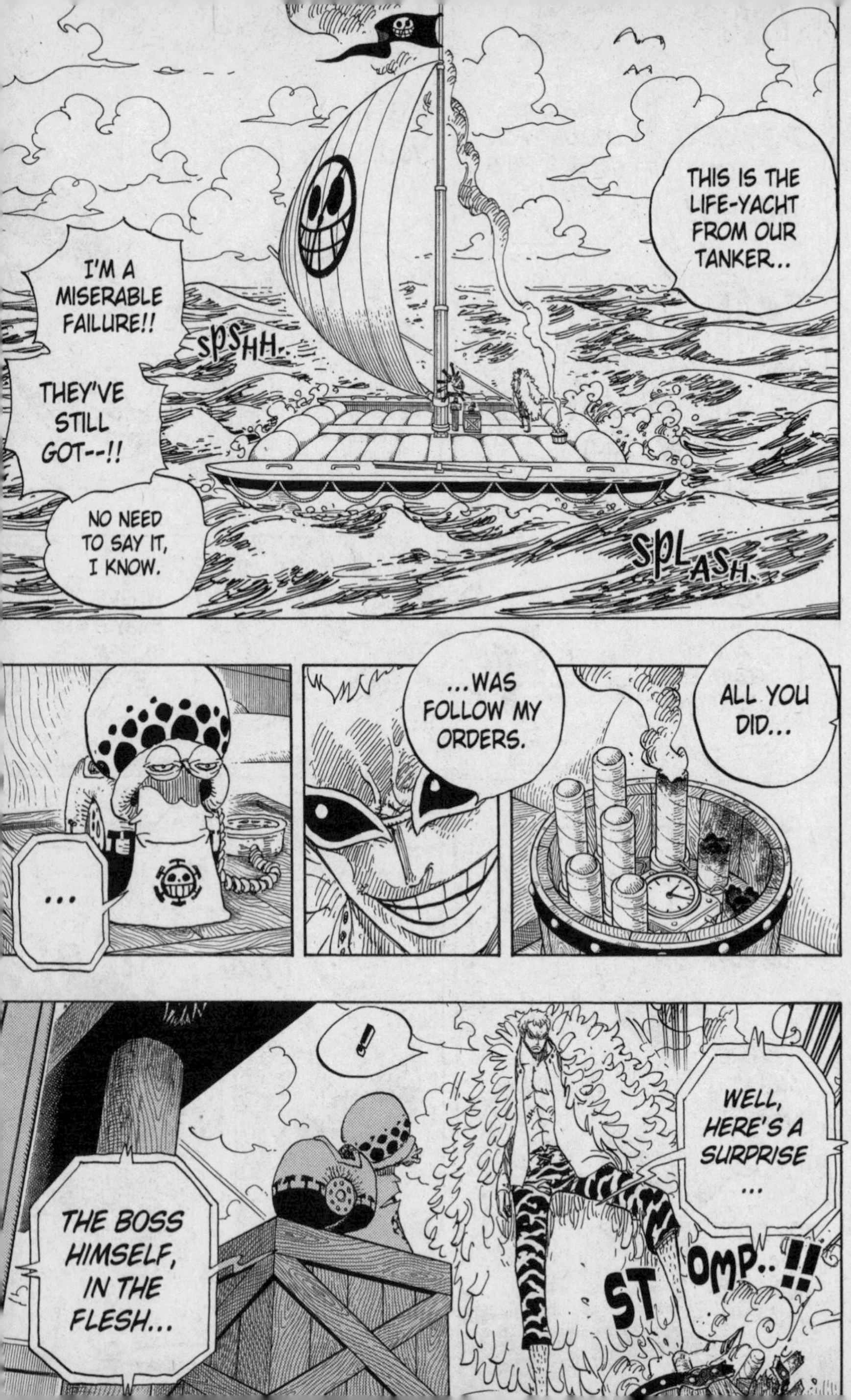
THIS IS THE LIFE-YACHT FROM OUR TANKER...
I'M A MISERABLE FAILURE!!
SPSHH...
THEY'VE STILL GOT--!!
NO NEED TO SAY IT, I KNOW.
SPLASH.
ALL YOU DID...
...WAS FOLLOW MY ORDERS.
...
WELL, HERE'S A SURPRISE...
!
STOMP..!!
THE BOSS HIMSELF, IN THE FLESH...

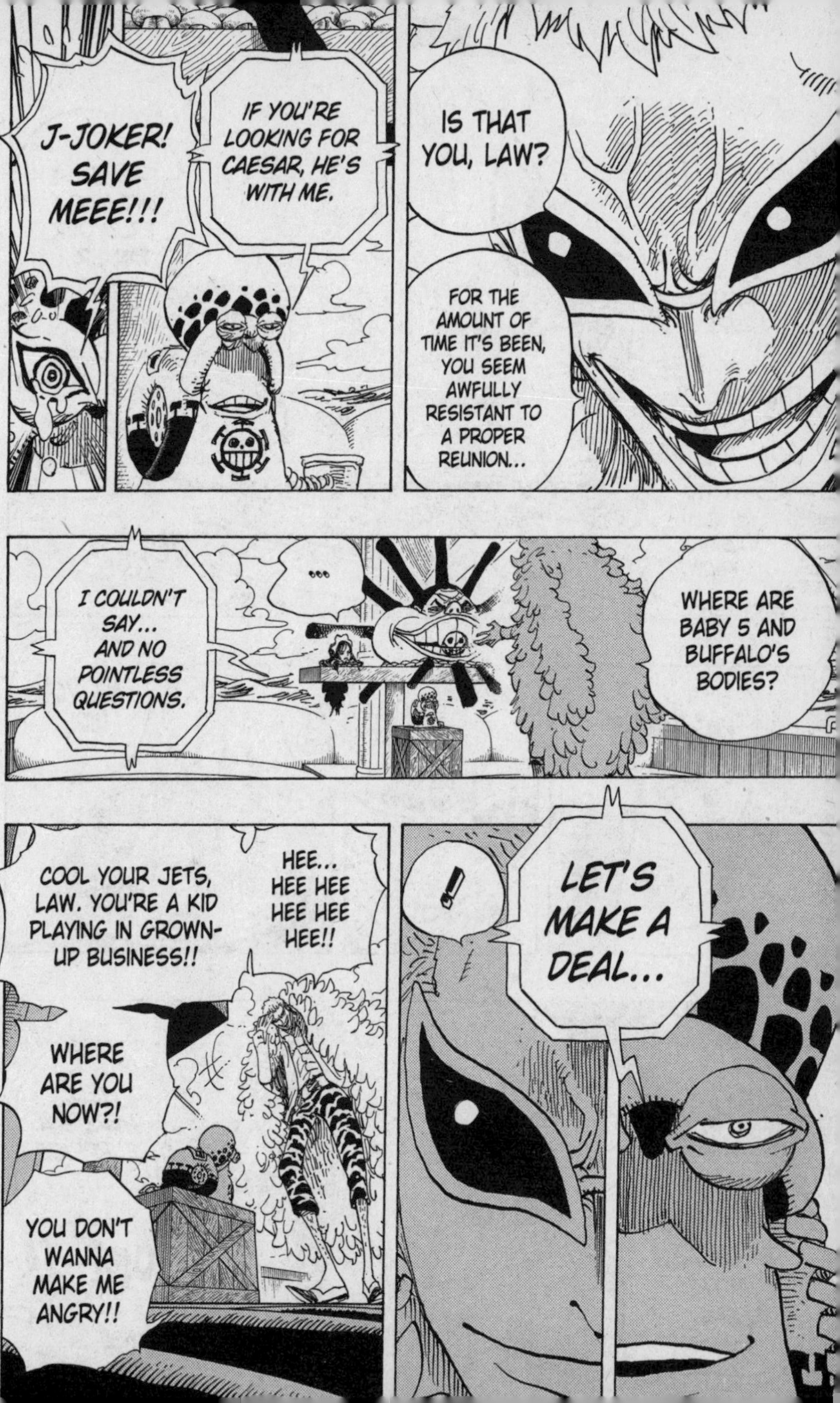
IS THAT YOU, LAW?
FOR THE AMOUNT OF TIME IT'S BEEN, YOU SEEM AWFULLY RESISTANT TO A PROPER REUNION...
IF YOU'RE LOOKING FOR CAESAR, HE'S WITH ME.
J-JOKER! SAVE MEEE!!!
WHERE ARE BABY 5 AND BUFFALO'S BODIES?
...
I COULDN'T SAY... AND NO POINTLESS QUESTIONS.
!
LET'S MAKE A DEAL...
HEE... HEE HEE HEE HEE HEE!!
COOL YOUR JETS, LAW. YOU'RE A KID PLAYING IN GROWN-UP BUSINESS!!
WHERE ARE YOU NOW?!
YOU DON'T WANNA MAKE ME ANGRY!!

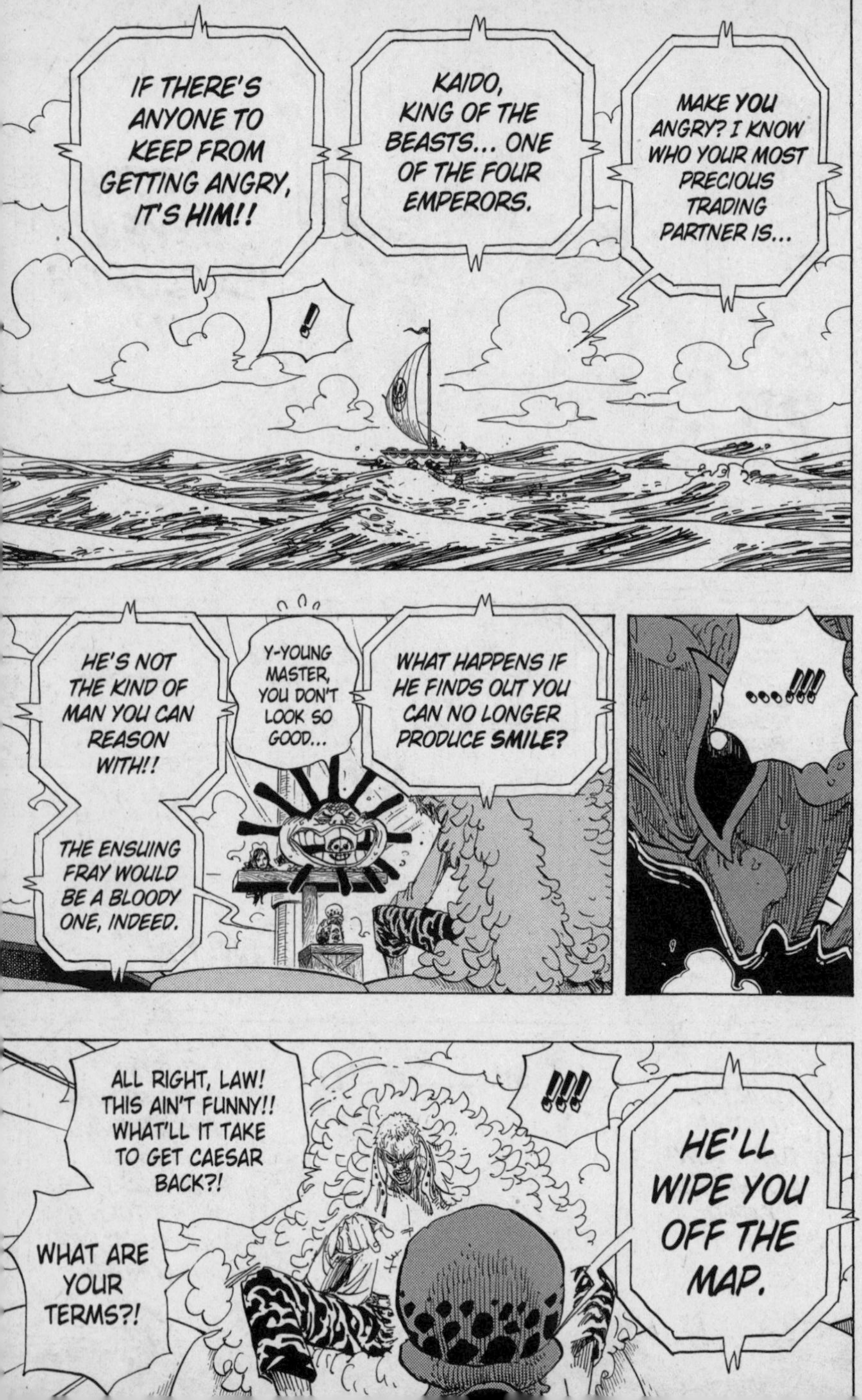
MAKE YOU ANGRY? I KNOW WHO YOUR MOST PRECIOUS TRADING PARTNER IS...
KAIDO, KING OF THE BEASTS... ONE OF THE FOUR EMPERORS.
IF THERE'S ANYONE TO KEEP FROM GETTING ANGRY, IT'S HIM!!
!
...!!!
WHAT HAPPENS IF HE FINDS OUT YOU CAN NO LONGER PRODUCE SMILE?
Y-YOUNG MASTER, YOU DON'T LOOK SO GOOD...
HE'S NOT THE KIND OF MAN YOU CAN REASON WITH!!
THE ENSUING FRAY WOULD BE A BLOODY ONE, INDEED.
HE'LL WIPE YOU OFF THE MAP.
!!!
ALL RIGHT, LAW! THIS AIN'T FUNNY!! WHAT'LL IT TAKE TO GET CAESAR BACK?!
WHAT ARE YOUR TERMS?!

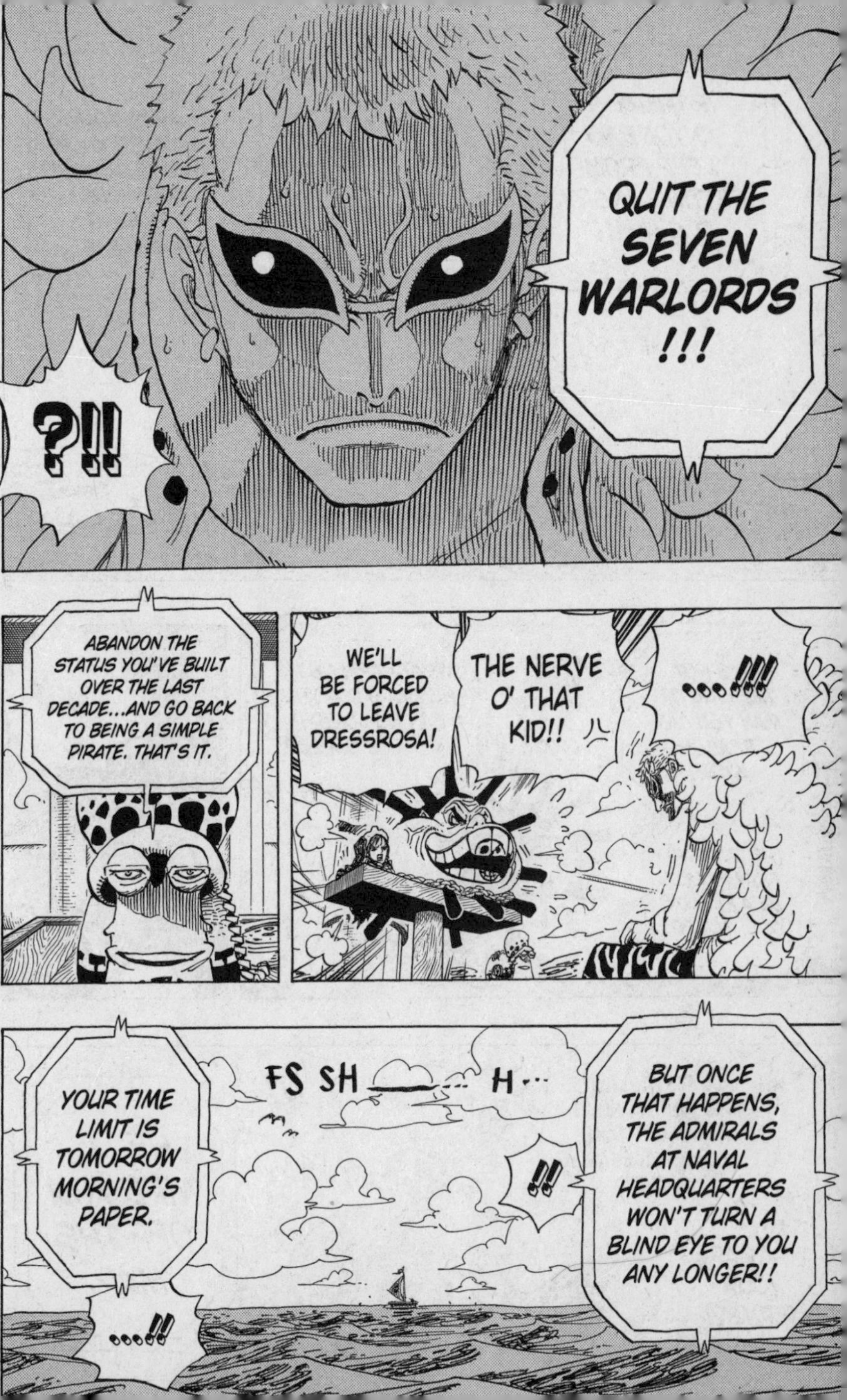
QUIT THE SEVEN WARLORDS!!!
?!!
...!!!
THE NERVE O' THAT KID!!
WE'LL BE FORCED TO LEAVE DRESSROSA!
ABANDON THE STATUS YOU'VE BUILT OVER THE LAST DECADE...AND GO BACK TO BEING A SIMPLE PIRATE. THAT'S IT.
BUT ONCE THAT HAPPENS, THE ADMIRALS AT NAVAL HEADQUARTERS WON'T TURN A BLIND EYE TO YOU ANY LONGER!!
!!
FS SH—H...
YOUR TIME LIMIT IS TOMORROW MORNING'S PAPER.
...!!

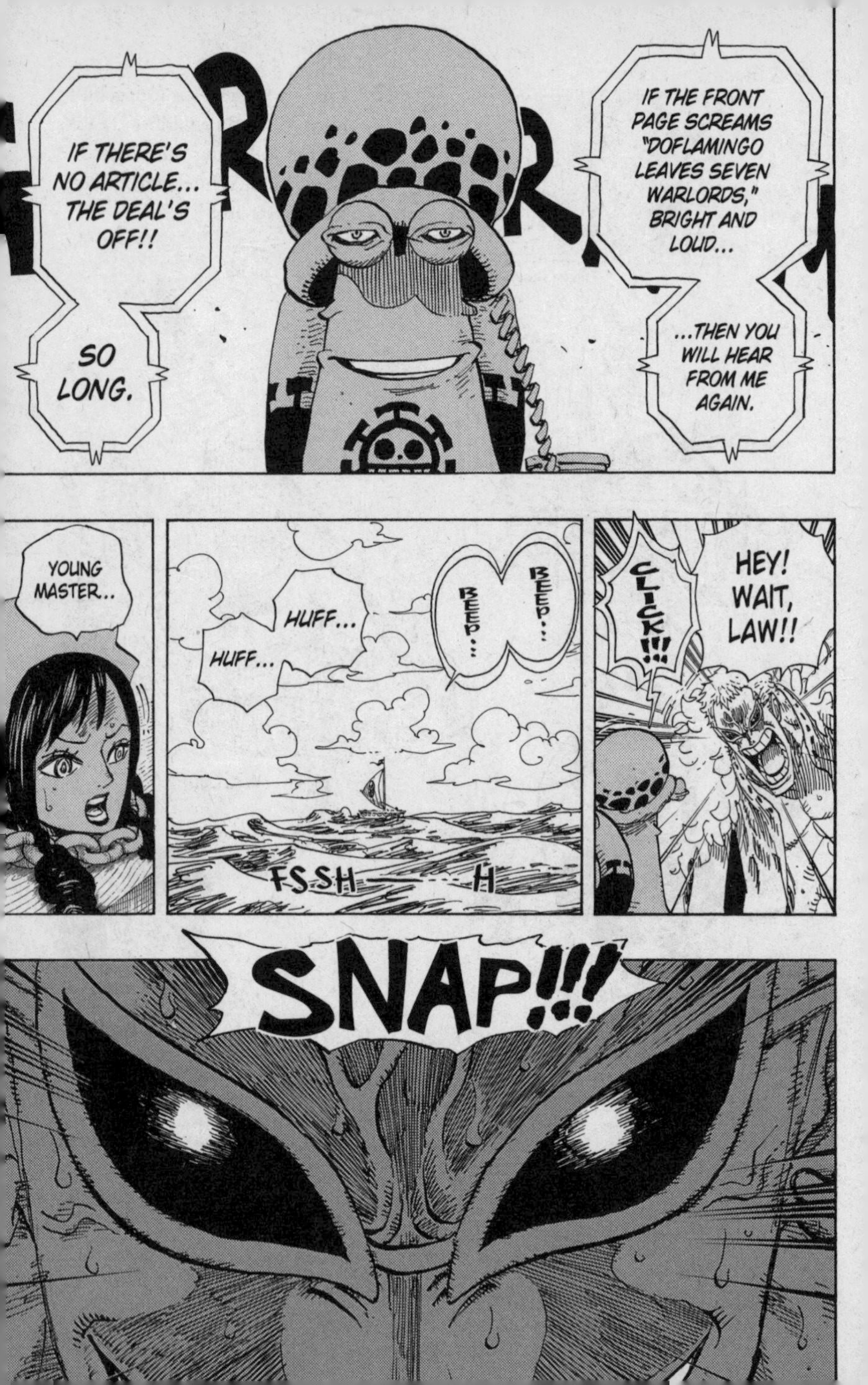
IF THE FRONT PAGE SCREAMS "DOFLAMINGO LEAVES SEVEN WARLORDS," BRIGHT AND LOUD...
...THEN YOU WILL HEAR FROM ME AGAIN.
IF THERE'S NO ARTICLE... THE DEAL'S OFF!!
SO LONG.
HEY! WAIT, LAW!!
CLICK!!!
BEEP... BEEP...
HUFF... HUFF...
FSSH——H
YOUNG MASTER...
SNAP!!!

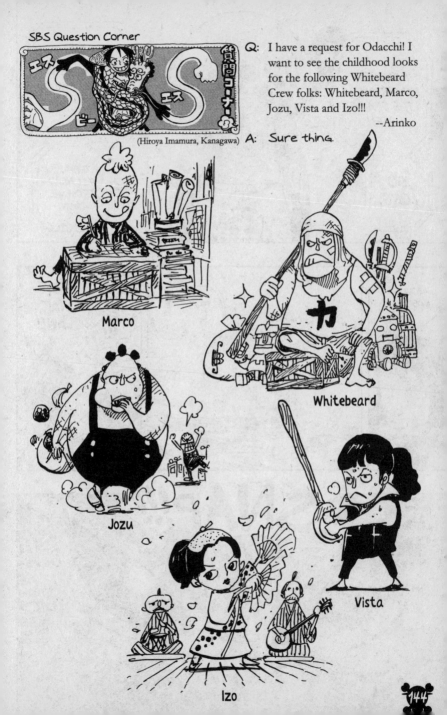

SBS Question Corner

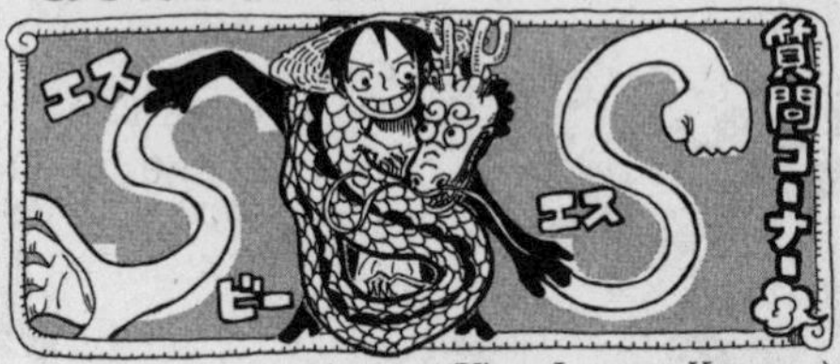
エス
ビー
エス
質問コーナー

(Hiroya Imamura, Kanagawa)

Q: I have a request for Odacchi! I want to see the childhood looks for the following Whitebeard Crew folks: Whitebeard, Marco, Jozu, Vista and Izo!!!

--Arinko

A: Sure thing.

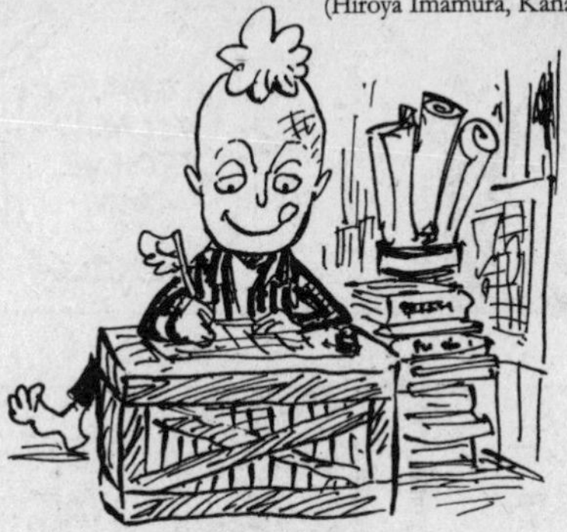

Marco

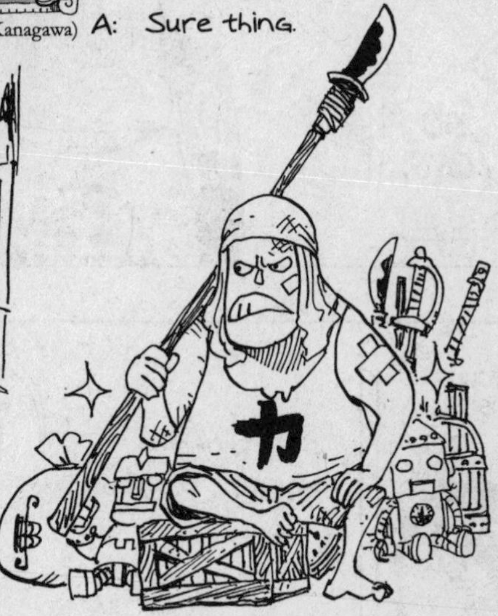

Whitebeard

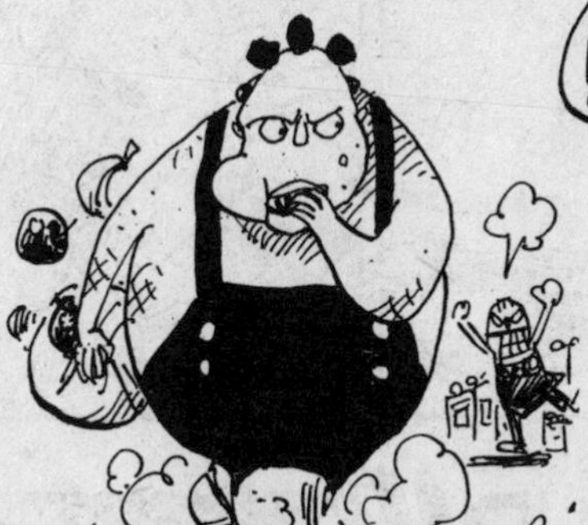

Jozu

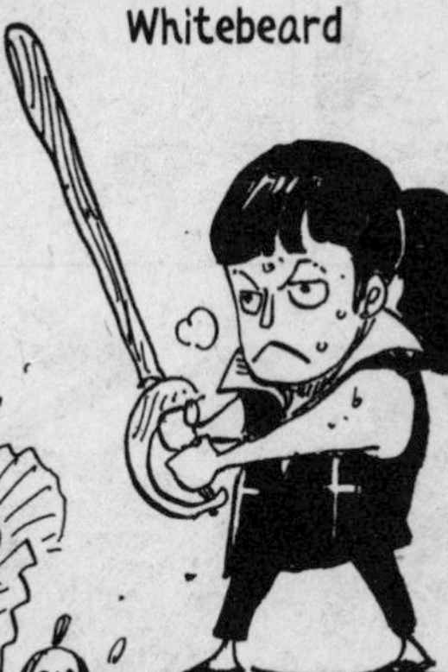

Vista

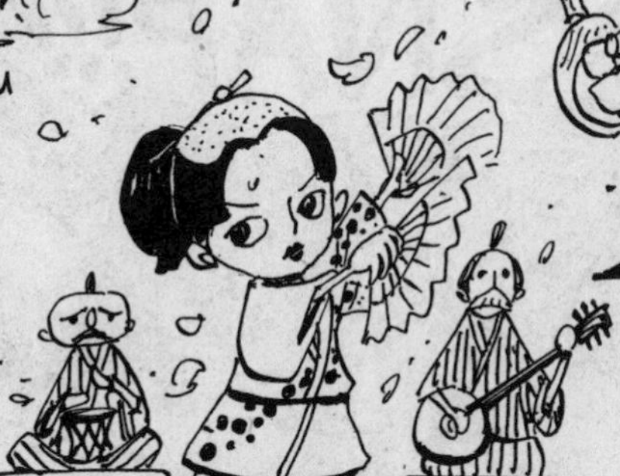

Izo

Chapter 698:
ENTER DOFLAMINGO

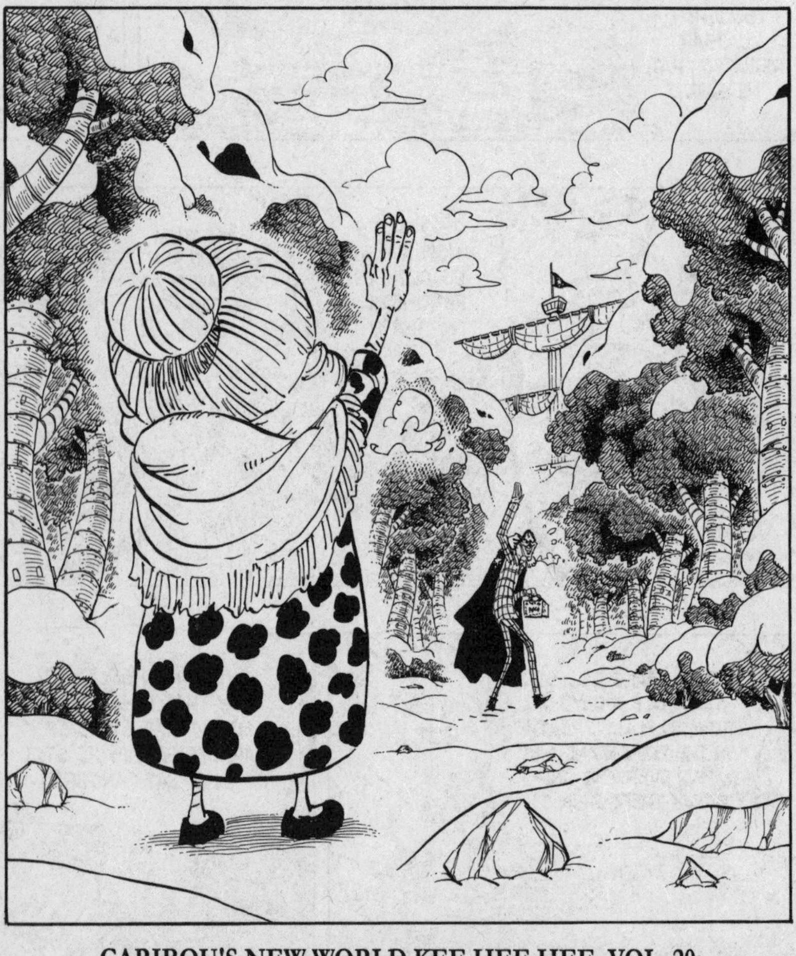

CARIBOU'S NEW WORLD KEE HEE HEE, VOL. 20:
"TO THE PORT"

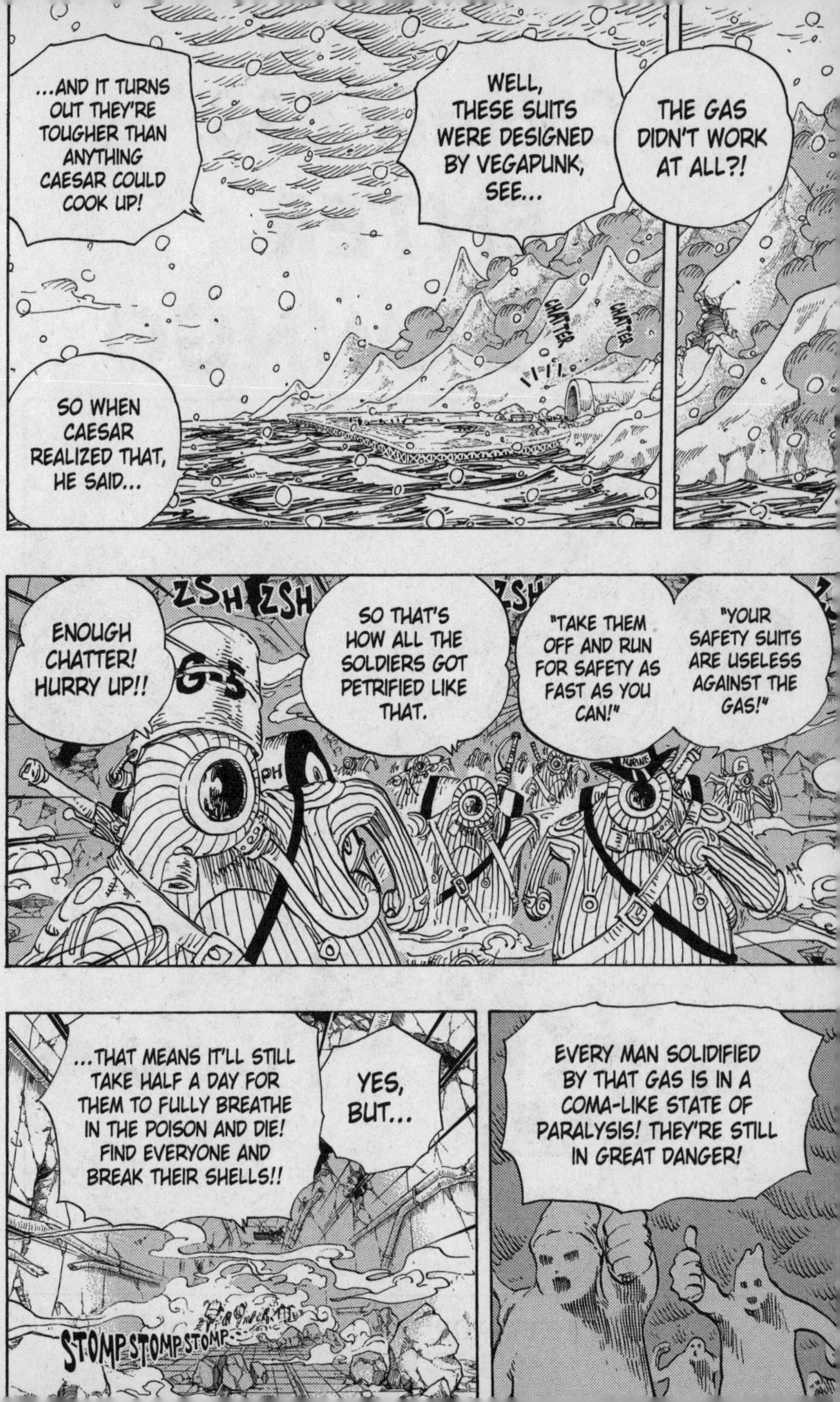
THE GAS DIDN'T WORK AT ALL?!
WELL, THESE SUITS WERE DESIGNED BY VEGAPUNK, SEE...
...AND IT TURNS OUT THEY'RE TOUGHER THAN ANYTHING CAESAR COULD COOK UP!
CHATTER
CHATTER
SO WHEN CAESAR REALIZED THAT, HE SAID...
ZSH
"YOUR SAFETY SUITS ARE USELESS AGAINST THE GAS!"
"TAKE THEM OFF AND RUN FOR SAFETY AS FAST AS YOU CAN!"
SO THAT'S HOW ALL THE SOLDIERS GOT PETRIFIED LIKE THAT.
ZSH
ZSH
ENOUGH CHATTER! HURRY UP!!
G-5
PH
EVERY MAN SOLIDIFIED BY THAT GAS IS IN A COMA-LIKE STATE OF PARALYSIS! THEY'RE STILL IN GREAT DANGER!
YES, BUT...
...THAT MEANS IT'LL STILL TAKE HALF A DAY FOR THEM TO FULLY BREATHE IN THE POISON AND DIE! FIND EVERYONE AND BREAK THEIR SHELLS!!
STOMP STOMP STOMP

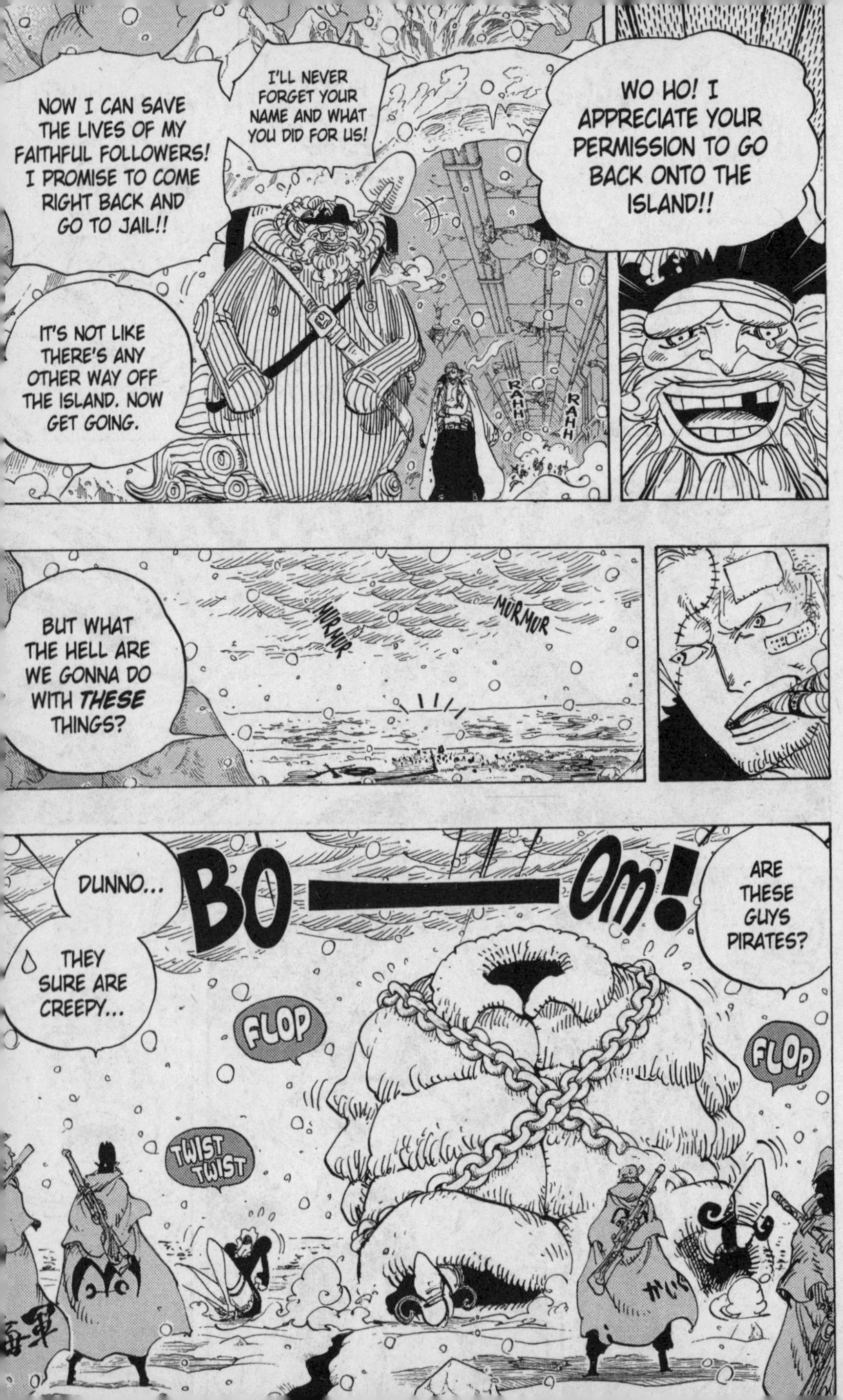
WO HO! I APPRECIATE YOUR PERMISSION TO GO BACK ONTO THE ISLAND!!
I'LL NEVER FORGET YOUR NAME AND WHAT YOU DID FOR US!
NOW I CAN SAVE THE LIVES OF MY FAITHFUL FOLLOWERS! I PROMISE TO COME RIGHT BACK AND GO TO JAIL!!
RAHH
RAHH
IT'S NOT LIKE THERE'S ANY OTHER WAY OFF THE ISLAND. NOW GET GOING.
MURMUR
MURMUR
BUT WHAT THE HELL ARE WE GONNA DO WITH *THESE* THINGS?
ARE THESE GUYS PIRATES?
BO——OM!
FLOP
DUNNO...
THEY SURE ARE CREEPY...
FLOP
TWIST TWIST

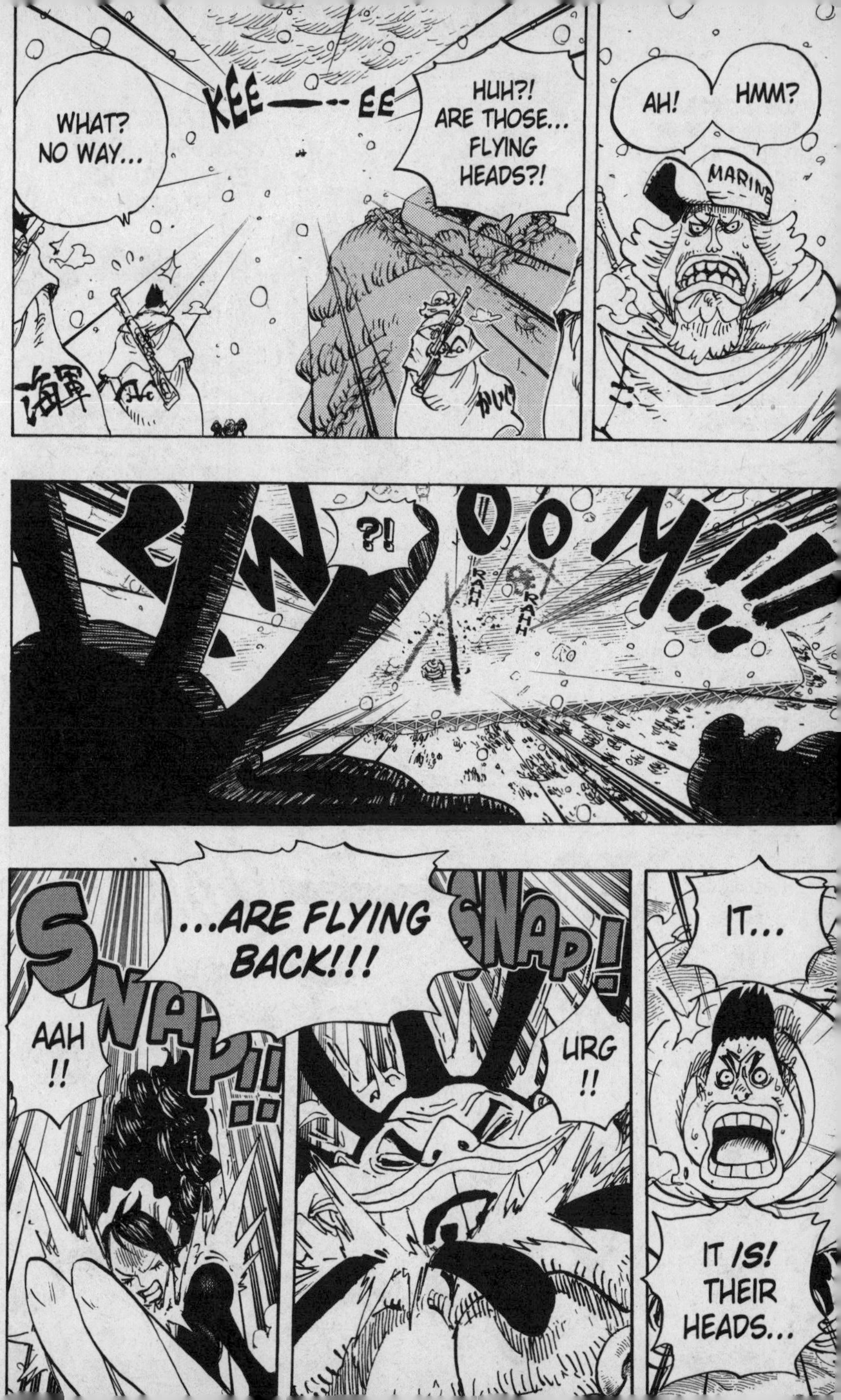
HMM?
AH!
MARINE
HUH?! ARE THOSE... FLYING HEADS?!
KEE---EE
WHAT? NO WAY...
海軍
?!
RAHH
RAHH
IT...
IT IS! THEIR HEADS...
...ARE FLYING BACK!!!
SNAP!
URG!!
SNAP!!
AAH!!

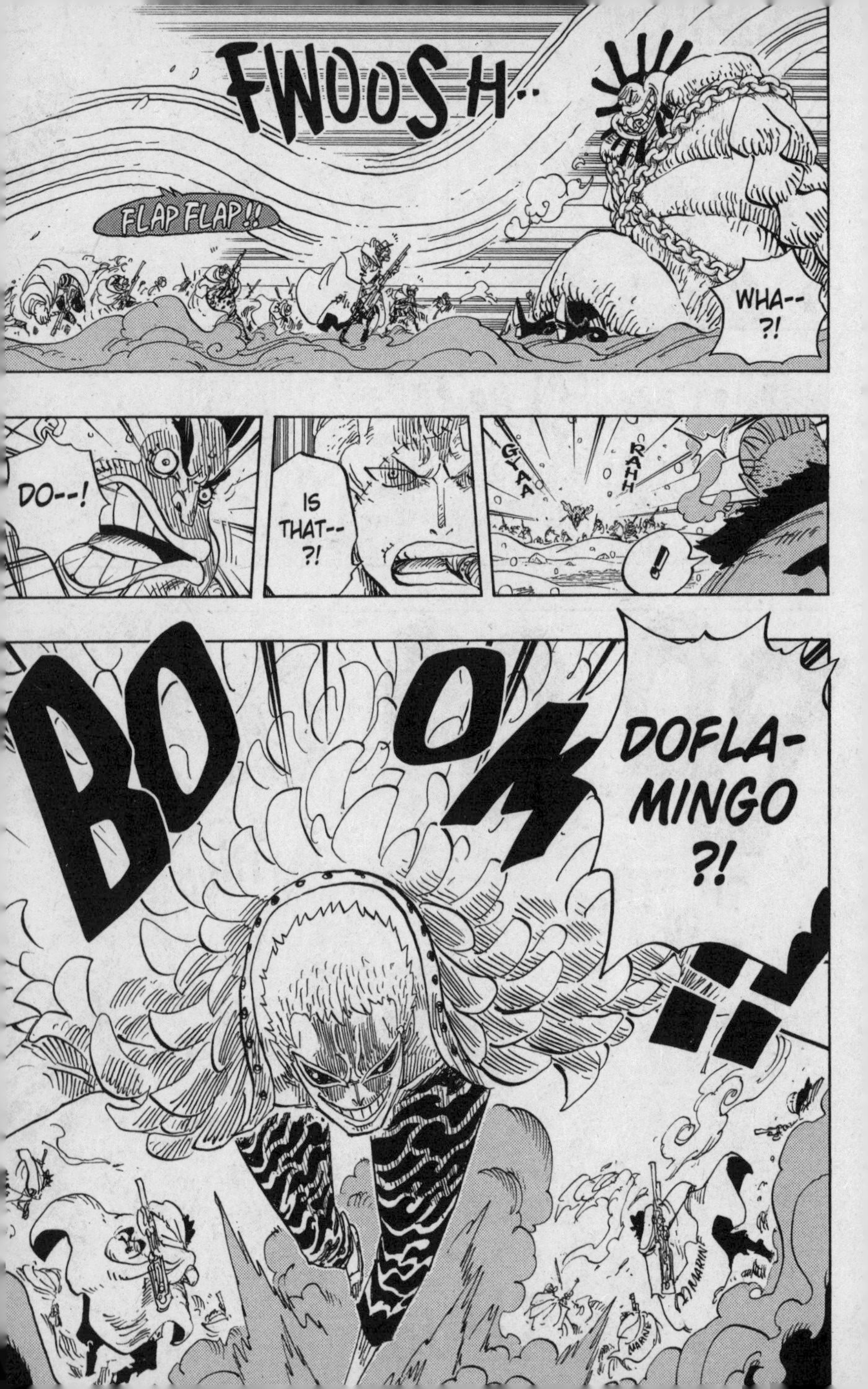

FWOOSH..
WHA--?!
FLAP FLAP!!
RAHH
GYAA
!
IS THAT--?!
DO--!
DOFLA-MINGO?!
BOOM
!!

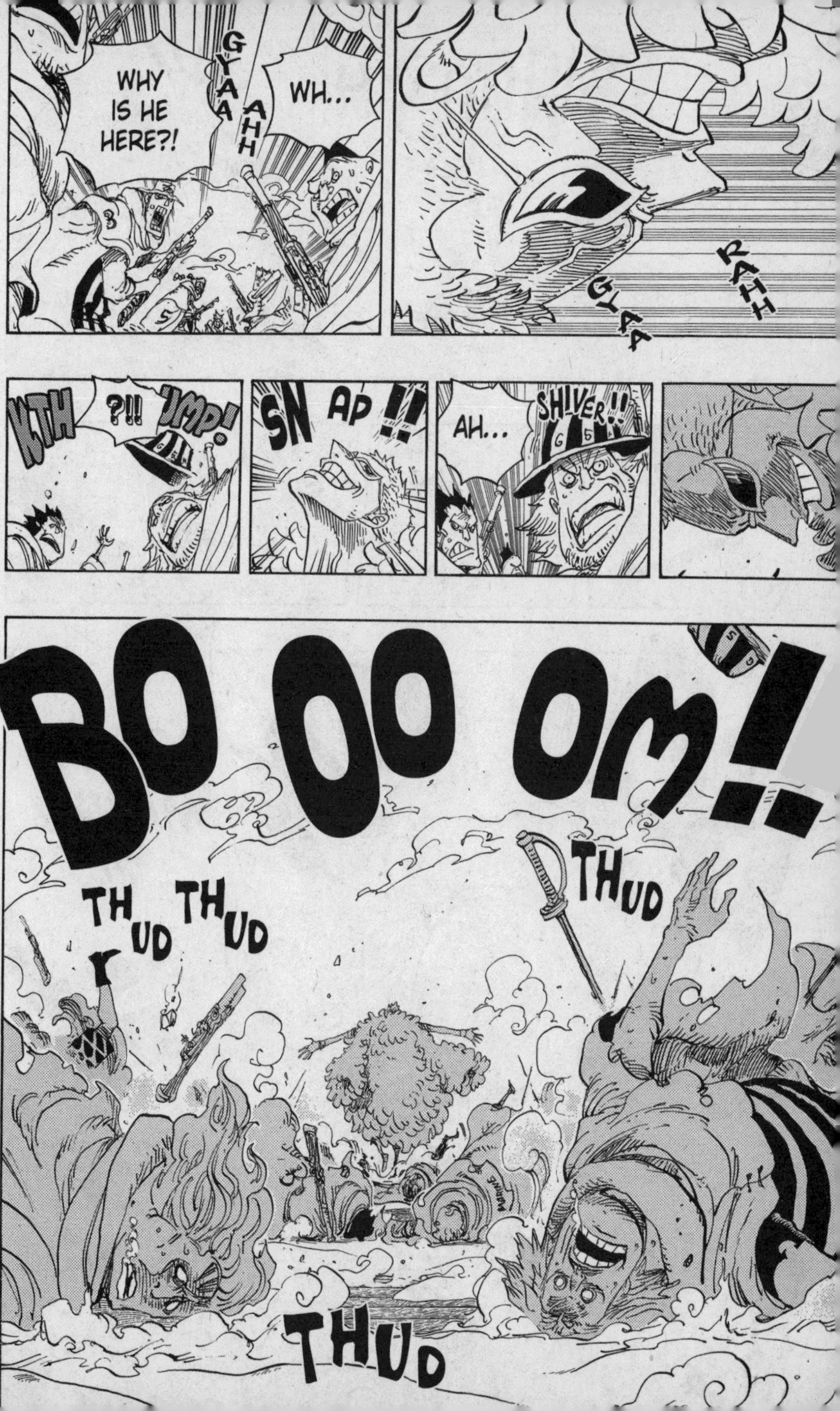
GYAA
RAHH
WH...
GYAAAHH
WHY IS HE HERE?!
SHIVER!!
AH...
SNAP!!
?!!
BOOOOM!!
THUD
THUD
THUD
THUD

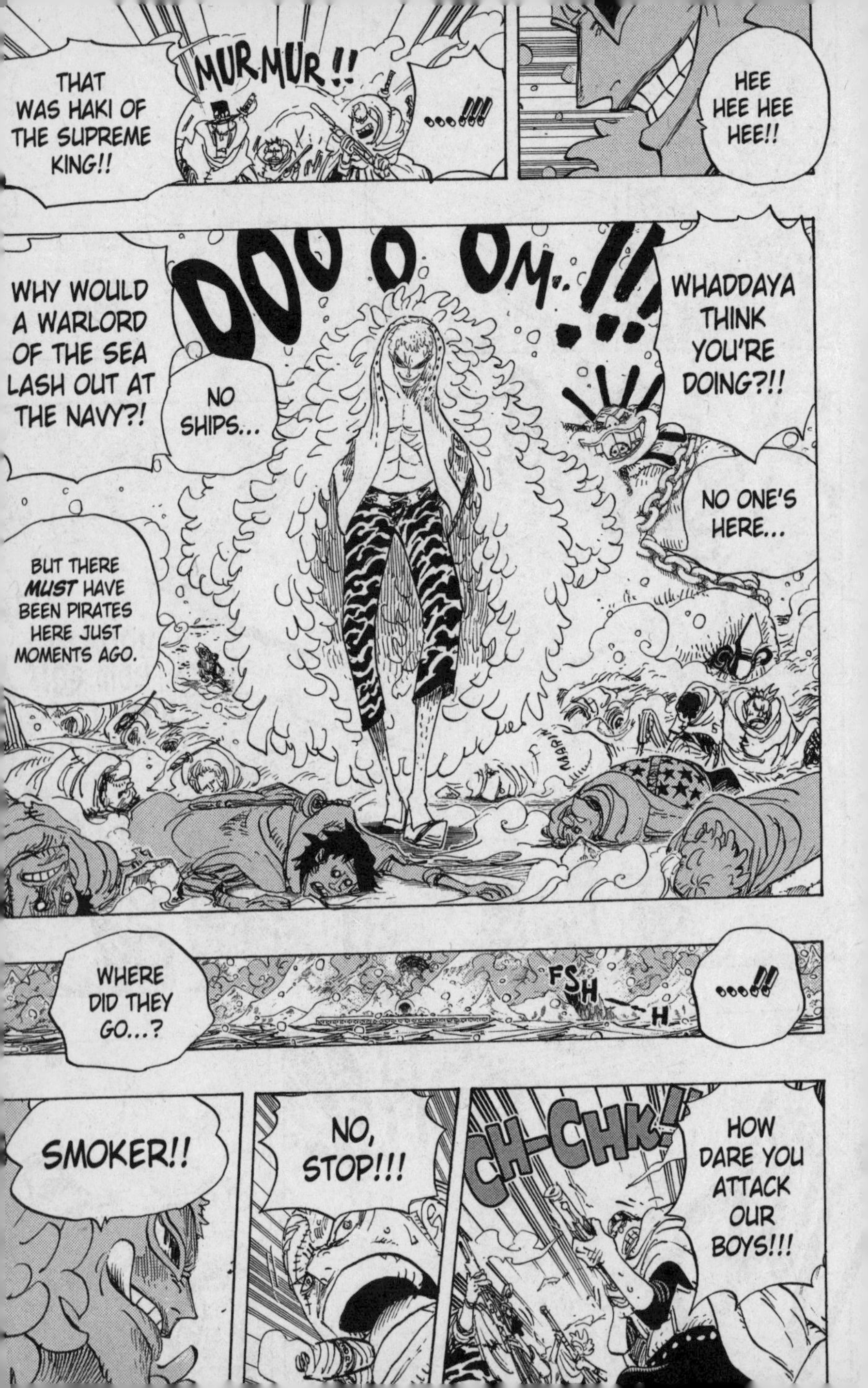
HEE HEE HEE HEE!!
MURMUR!!
...!!!
THAT WAS HAKI OF THE SUPREME KING!!
DOOOOM..!!
WHADDAYA THINK YOU'RE DOING?!!
WHY WOULD A WARLORD OF THE SEA LASH OUT AT THE NAVY?!
NO SHIPS...
NO ONE'S HERE...
BUT THERE *MUST* HAVE BEEN PIRATES HERE JUST MOMENTS AGO.
...!!
FSH—H
WHERE DID THEY GO...?
CH-CHK!
HOW DARE YOU ATTACK OUR BOYS!!!
NO, STOP!!!
SMOKER!!

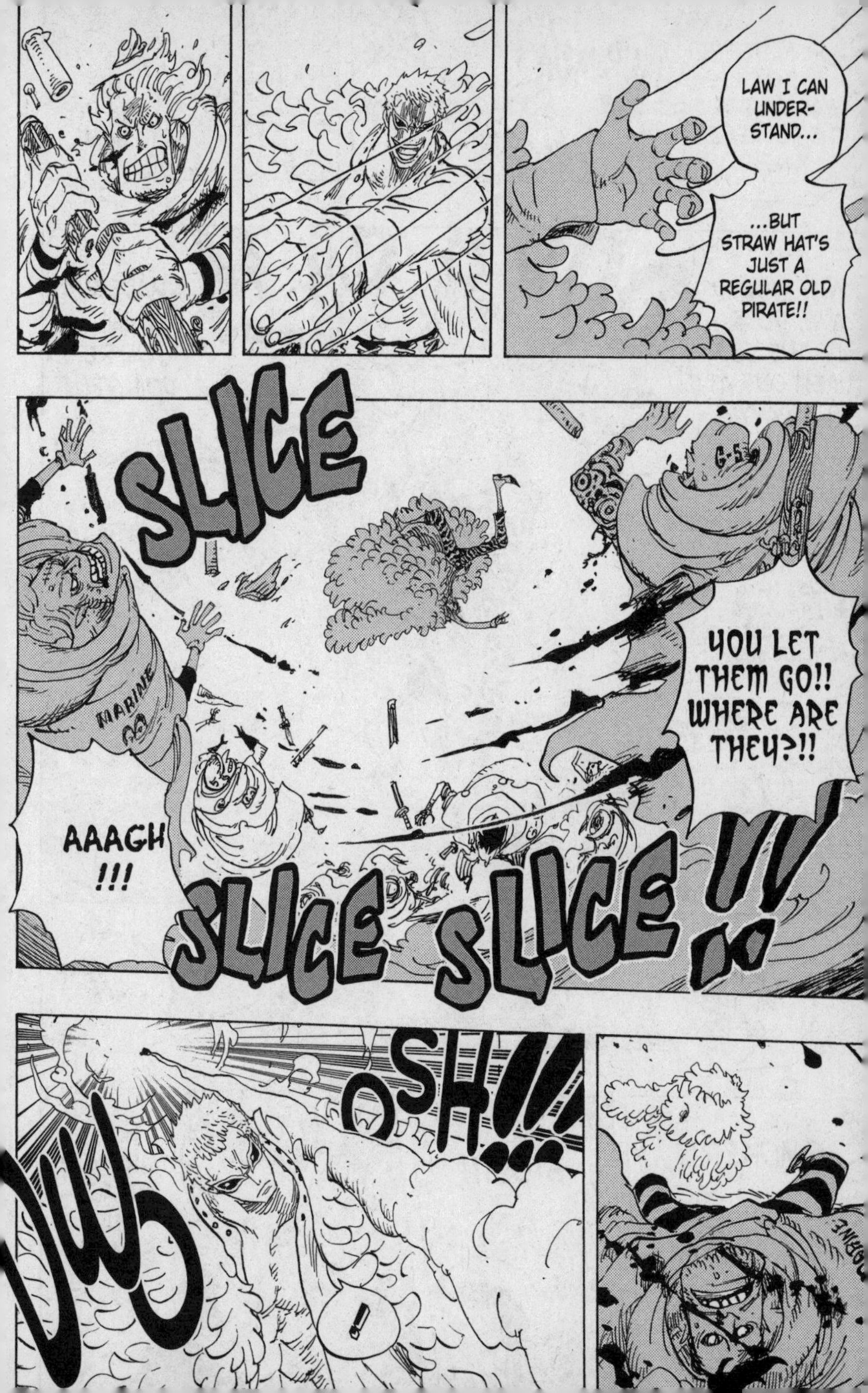
LAW I CAN UNDER-STAND...
...BUT STRAW HAT'S JUST A REGULAR OLD PIRATE!!
YOU LET THEM GO!! WHERE ARE THEY?!!
SLICE
AAAGH !!!
SLICE SLICE!!
OSH!!!
!

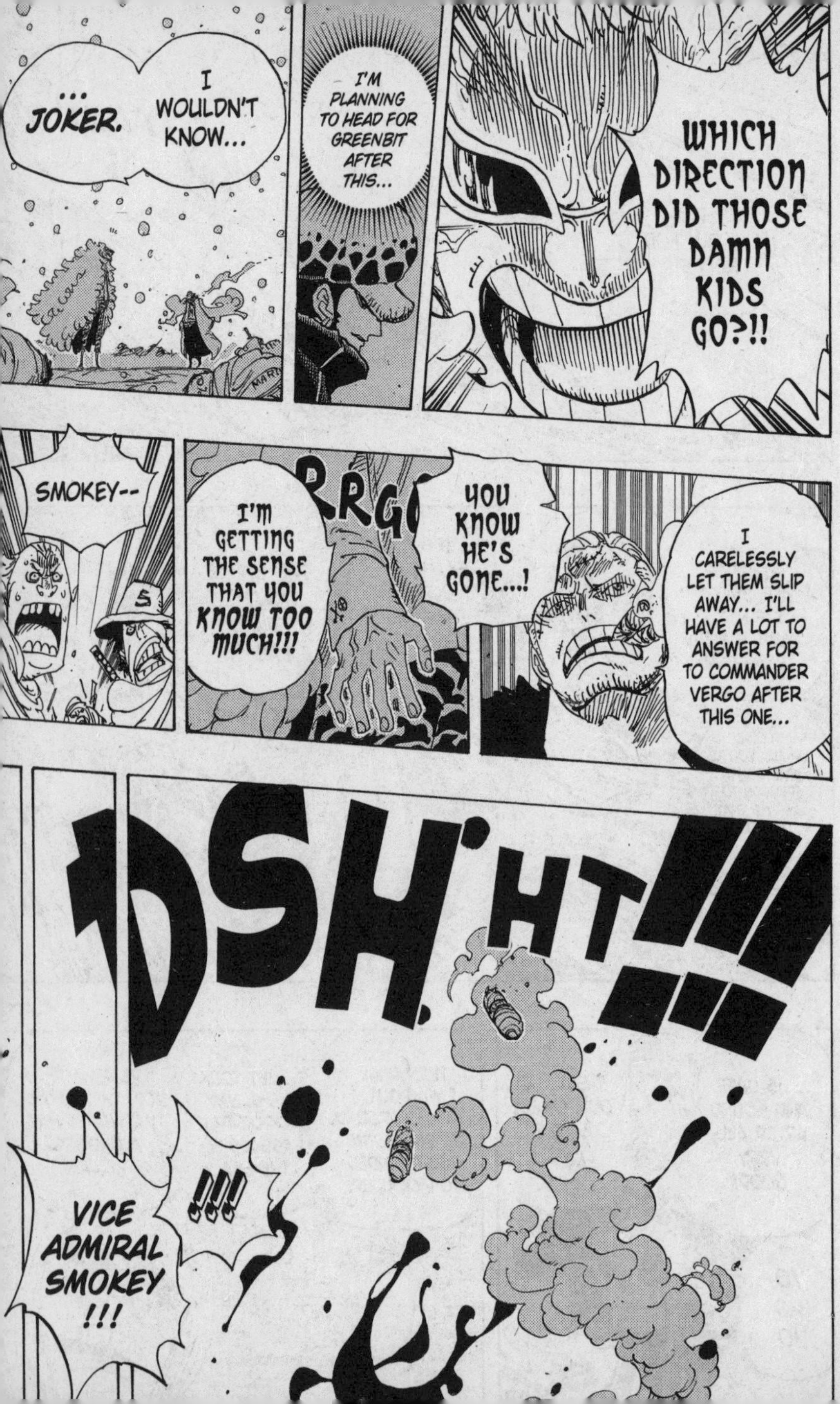
WHICH DIRECTION DID THOSE DAMN KIDS GO?!!
I'M PLANNING TO HEAD FOR GREENBIT AFTER THIS...
I WOULDN'T KNOW...
...JOKER.
I CARELESSLY LET THEM SLIP AWAY... I'LL HAVE A LOT TO ANSWER FOR TO COMMANDER VERGO AFTER THIS ONE...
YOU KNOW HE'S GONE...!
RRGO
I'M GETTING THE SENSE THAT YOU KNOW TOO MUCH!!!
SMOKEY--
DSHHT!!!
!!!
VICE ADMIRAL SMOKEY!!!

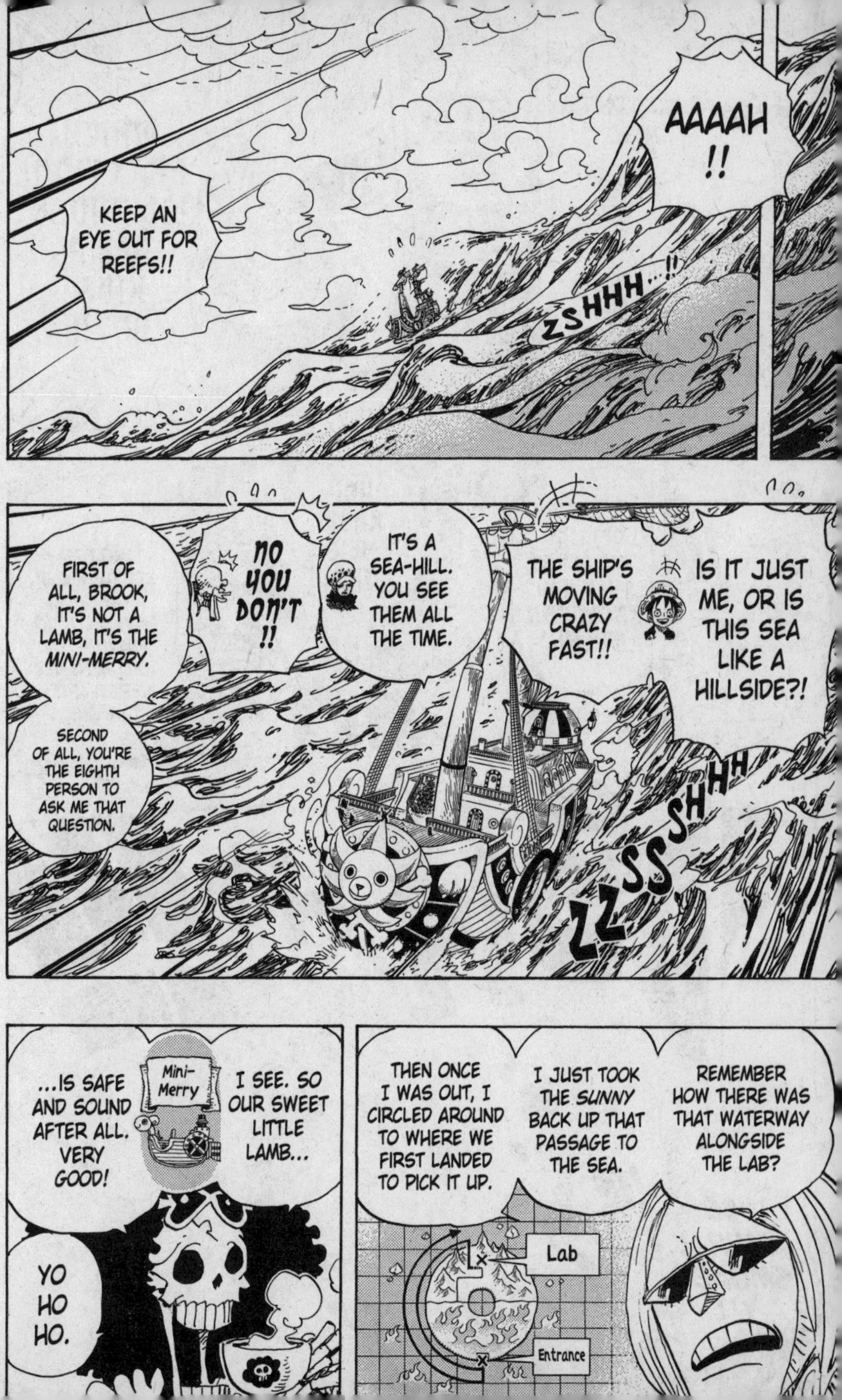
AAAAH!!
ZSHHH...!!
KEEP AN EYE OUT FOR REEFS!!
IS IT JUST ME, OR IS THIS SEA LIKE A HILLSIDE?!
THE SHIP'S MOVING CRAZY FAST!!
IT'S A SEA-HILL. YOU SEE THEM ALL THE TIME.
NO YOU DON'T!!
FIRST OF ALL, BROOK, IT'S NOT A LAMB, IT'S THE *MINI-MERRY*.
SECOND OF ALL, YOU'RE THE EIGHTH PERSON TO ASK ME THAT QUESTION.
ZZSSSHHH
REMEMBER HOW THERE WAS THAT WATERWAY ALONGSIDE THE LAB?
I JUST TOOK THE *SUNNY* BACK UP THAT PASSAGE TO THE SEA.
THEN ONCE I WAS OUT, I CIRCLED AROUND TO WHERE WE FIRST LANDED TO PICK IT UP.
Lab
Entrance
I SEE. SO OUR SWEET LITTLE LAMB...
Mini-Merry
...IS SAFE AND SOUND AFTER ALL. VERY GOOD!
YO HO HO.

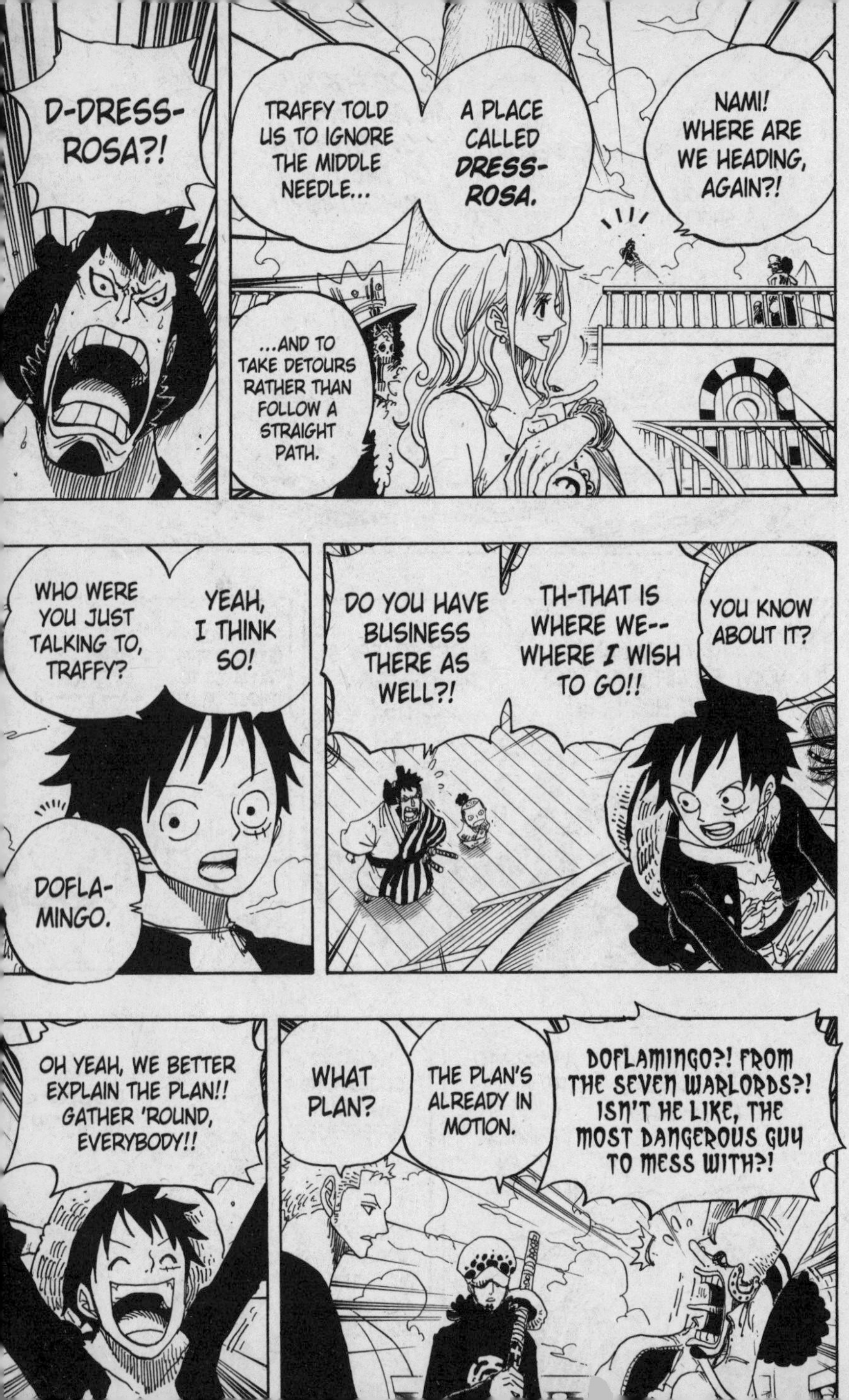
NAMI! WHERE ARE WE HEADING, AGAIN?!
A PLACE CALLED DRESS-ROSA.
TRAFFY TOLD US TO IGNORE THE MIDDLE NEEDLE...
...AND TO TAKE DETOURS RATHER THAN FOLLOW A STRAIGHT PATH.
D-DRESS-ROSA?!
YOU KNOW ABOUT IT?
TH-THAT IS WHERE WE-- WHERE I WISH TO GO!!
DO YOU HAVE BUSINESS THERE AS WELL?!
YEAH, I THINK SO!
WHO WERE YOU JUST TALKING TO, TRAFFY?
DOFLA-MINGO.
DOFLAMINGO?! FROM THE SEVEN WARLORDS?! ISN'T HE LIKE, THE MOST DANGEROUS GUY TO MESS WITH?!
THE PLAN'S ALREADY IN MOTION.
WHAT PLAN?
OH YEAH, WE BETTER EXPLAIN THE PLAN!! GATHER 'ROUND, EVERYBODY!!

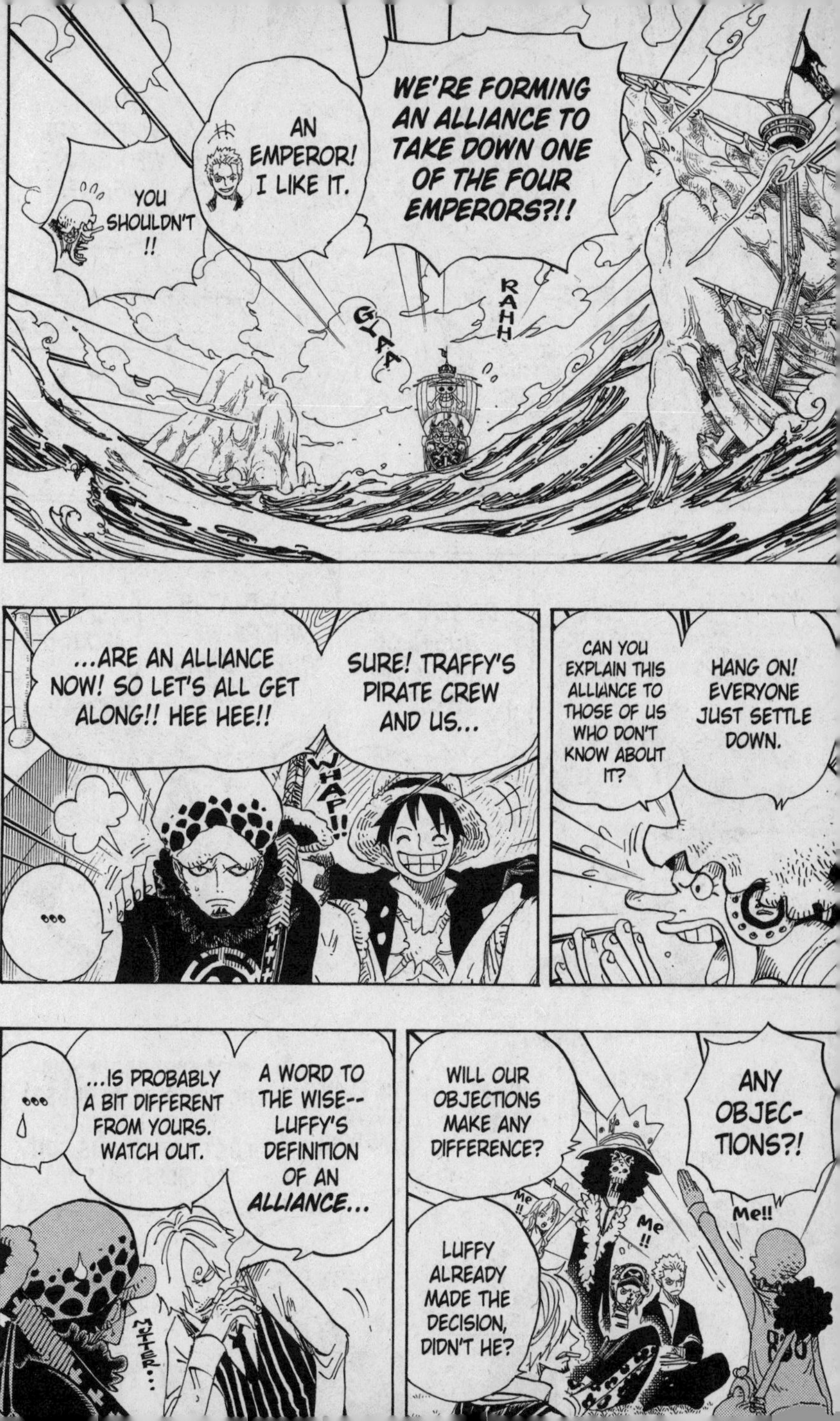
WE'RE FORMING AN ALLIANCE TO TAKE DOWN ONE OF THE FOUR EMPERORS?!!
AN EMPEROR! I LIKE IT.
YOU SHOULDN'T !!
RAHH
GYAA
HANG ON! EVERYONE JUST SETTLE DOWN.
CAN YOU EXPLAIN THIS ALLIANCE TO THOSE OF US WHO DON'T KNOW ABOUT IT?
SURE! TRAFFY'S PIRATE CREW AND US...
...ARE AN ALLIANCE NOW! SO LET'S ALL GET ALONG!! HEE HEE!!
WHAP!!
...
ANY OBJEC- TIONS?!
Me!!
WILL OUR OBJECTIONS MAKE ANY DIFFERENCE?
Me !!
Me !!
LUFFY ALREADY MADE THE DECISION, DIDN'T HE?
A WORD TO THE WISE-- LUFFY'S DEFINITION OF AN ALLIANCE...
...IS PROBABLY A BIT DIFFERENT FROM YOURS. WATCH OUT.
...
MUTTER...

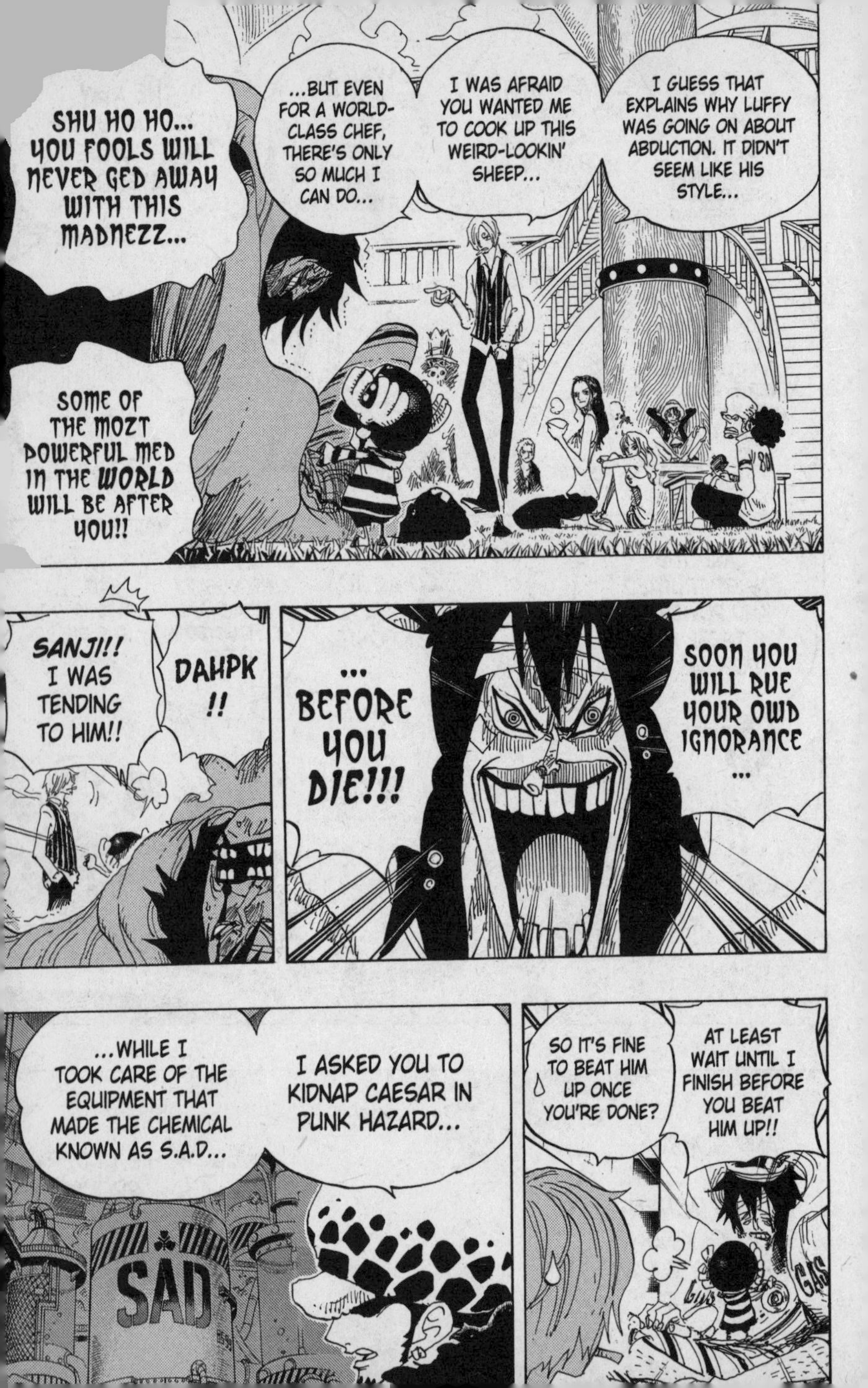
I GUESS THAT EXPLAINS WHY LUFFY WAS GOING ON ABOUT ABDUCTION. IT DIDN'T SEEM LIKE HIS STYLE...
I WAS AFRAID YOU WANTED ME TO COOK UP THIS WEIRD-LOOKIN' SHEEP...
...BUT EVEN FOR A WORLD-CLASS CHEF, THERE'S ONLY SO MUCH I CAN DO...
SHU HO HO... YOU FOOLS WILL NEVER GED AWAY WITH THIS MADNEZZ...
SOME OF THE MOZT POWERFUL MED IN THE WORLD WILL BE AFTER YOU!!
SOON YOU WILL RUE YOUR OWD IGNORANCE ...
... BEFORE YOU DIE!!!
DAHPK !!
SANJI!! I WAS TENDING TO HIM!!
AT LEAST WAIT UNTIL I FINISH BEFORE YOU BEAT HIM UP!!
SO IT'S FINE TO BEAT HIM UP ONCE YOU'RE DONE?
GAS
I ASKED YOU TO KIDNAP CAESAR IN PUNK HAZARD...
...WHILE I TOOK CARE OF THE EQUIPMENT THAT MADE THE CHEMICAL KNOWN AS S.A.D...
SAD

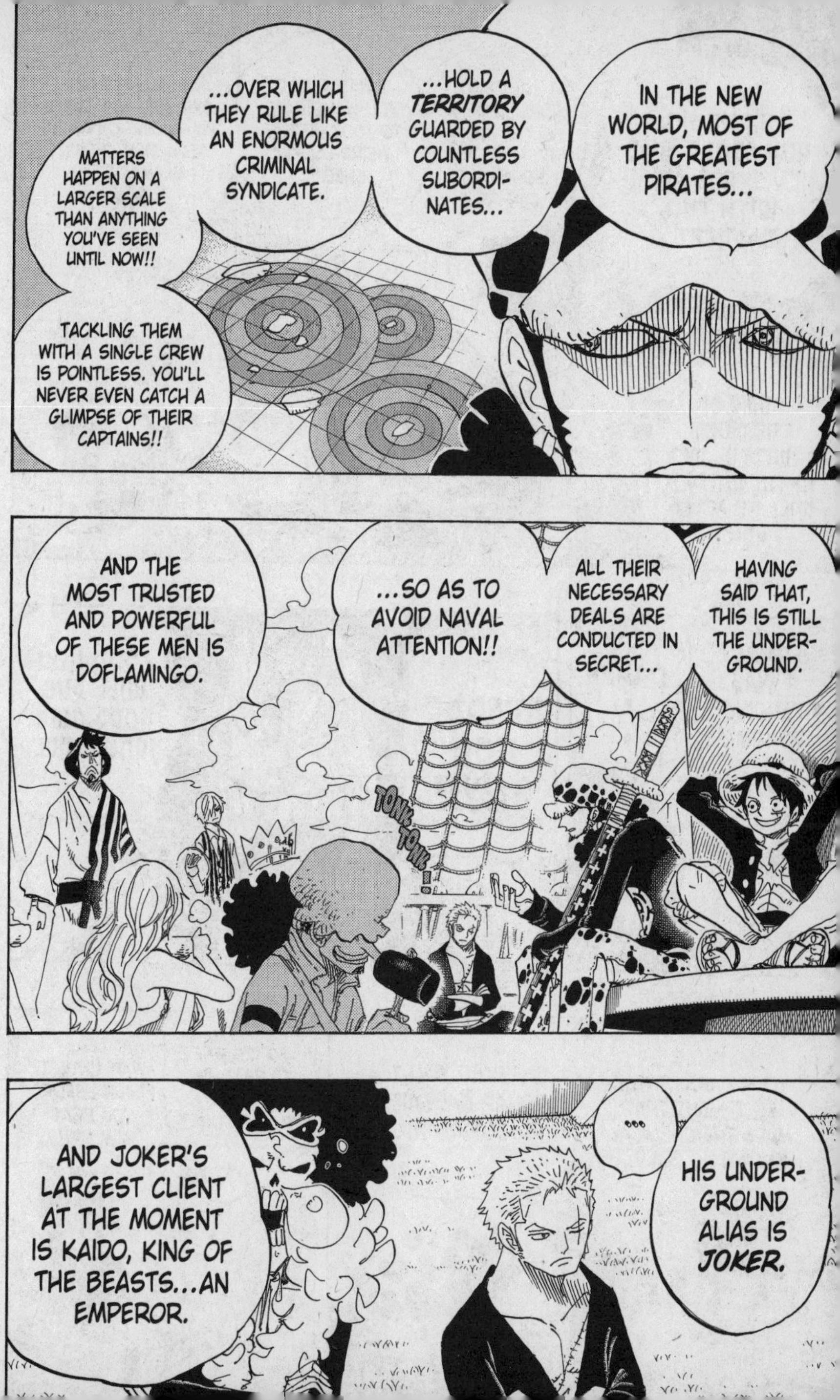
IN THE NEW WORLD, MOST OF THE GREATEST PIRATES...
...HOLD A TERRITORY GUARDED BY COUNTLESS SUBORDINATES...
...OVER WHICH THEY RULE LIKE AN ENORMOUS CRIMINAL SYNDICATE.
MATTERS HAPPEN ON A LARGER SCALE THAN ANYTHING YOU'VE SEEN UNTIL NOW!!
TACKLING THEM WITH A SINGLE CREW IS POINTLESS. YOU'LL NEVER EVEN CATCH A GLIMPSE OF THEIR CAPTAINS!!
HAVING SAID THAT, THIS IS STILL THE UNDERGROUND.
ALL THEIR NECESSARY DEALS ARE CONDUCTED IN SECRET...
...SO AS TO AVOID NAVAL ATTENTION!!
AND THE MOST TRUSTED AND POWERFUL OF THESE MEN IS DOFLAMINGO.
TONK TONK
HIS UNDERGROUND ALIAS IS JOKER.
...
AND JOKER'S LARGEST CLIENT AT THE MOMENT IS KAIDO, KING OF THE BEASTS...AN EMPEROR.

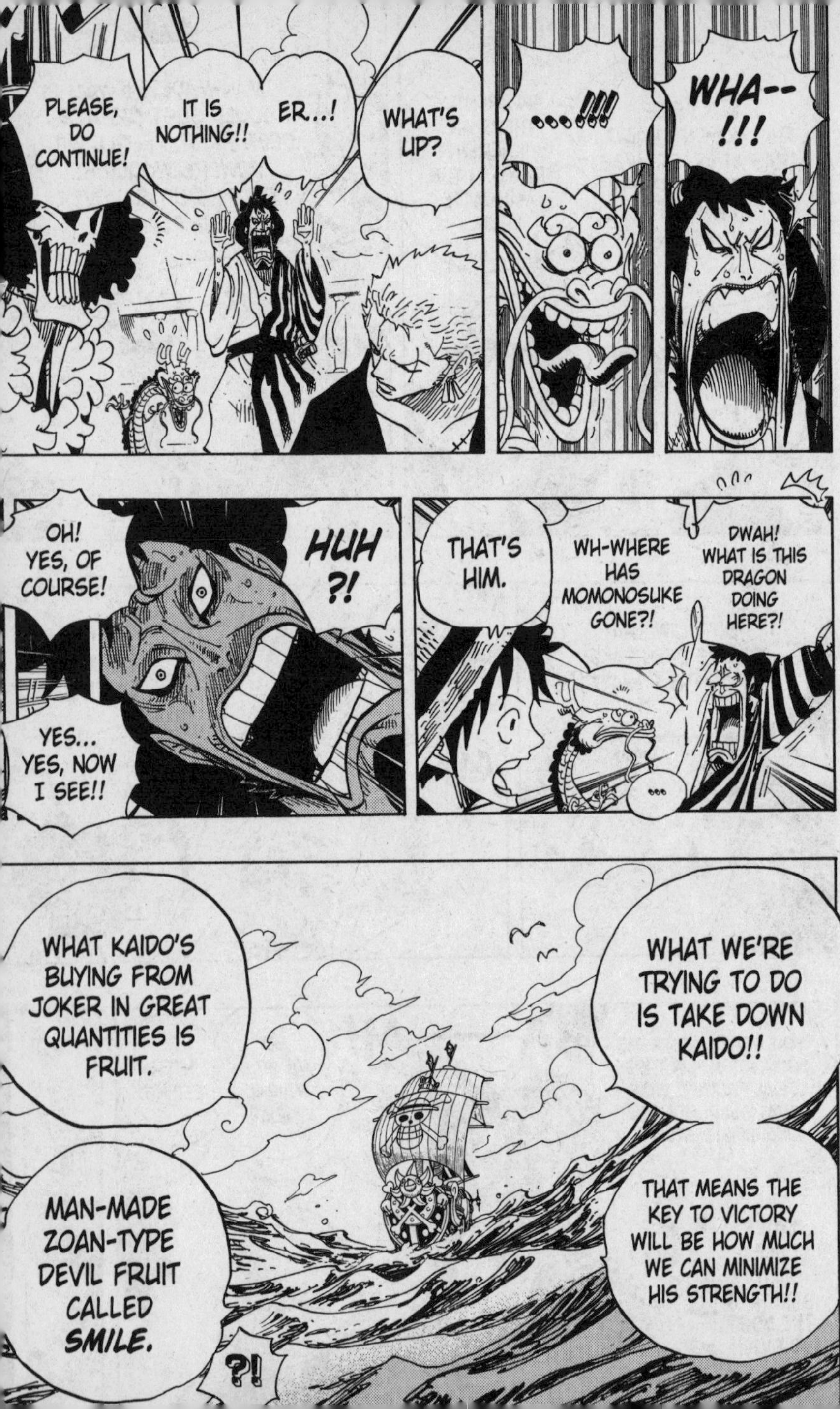
WHA-- !!!
...!!!
WHAT'S UP?
ER...!
IT IS NOTHING!!
PLEASE, DO CONTINUE!
DWAH! WHAT IS THIS DRAGON DOING HERE?!
WH-WHERE HAS MOMONOSUKE GONE?!
THAT'S HIM.
...
HUH ?!
OH! YES, OF COURSE!
YES... YES, NOW I SEE!!
WHAT WE'RE TRYING TO DO IS TAKE DOWN KAIDO!!
WHAT KAIDO'S BUYING FROM JOKER IN GREAT QUANTITIES IS FRUIT.
THAT MEANS THE KEY TO VICTORY WILL BE HOW MUCH WE CAN MINIMIZE HIS STRENGTH!!
MAN-MADE ZOAN-TYPE DEVIL FRUIT CALLED **SMILE.**
?!

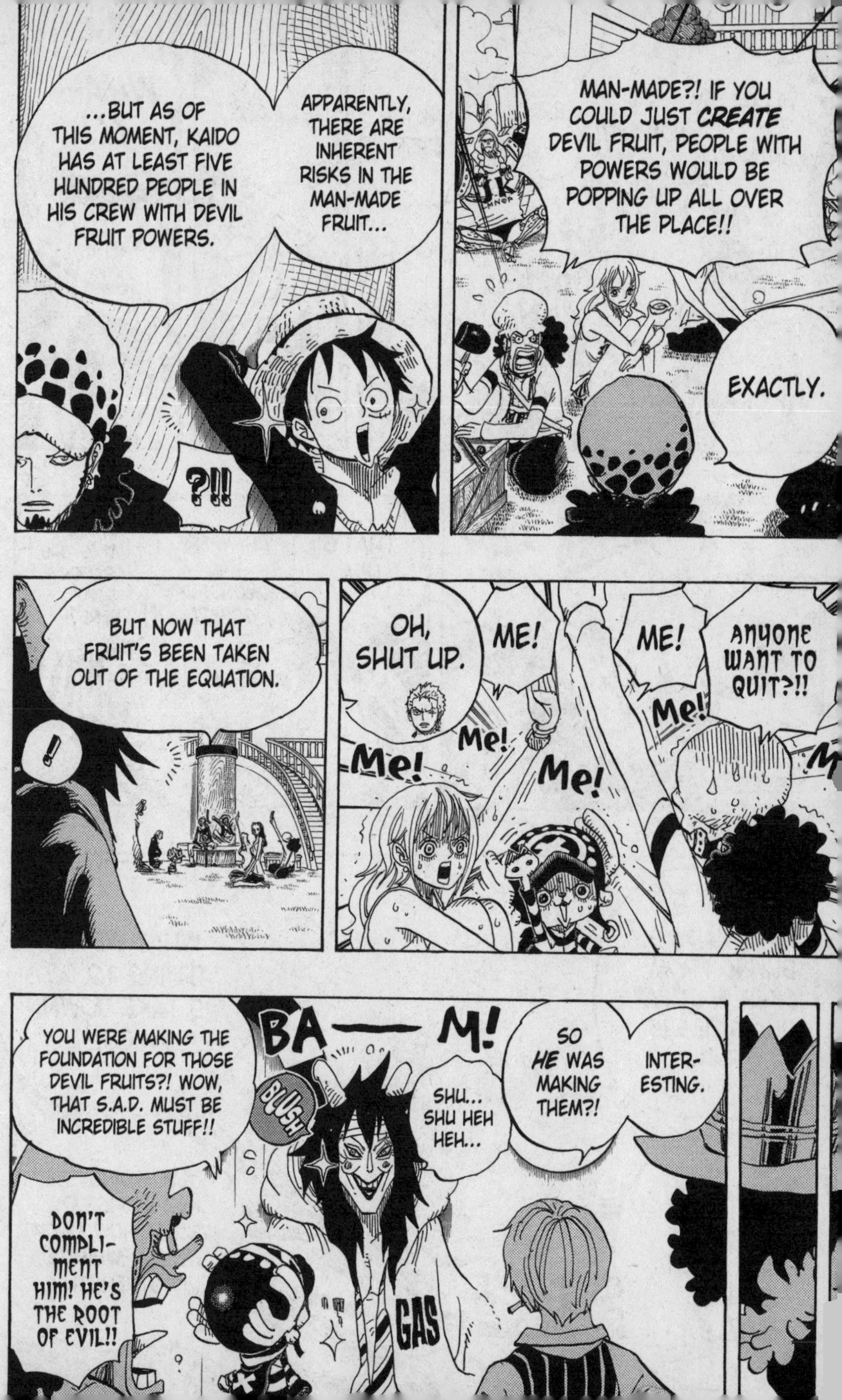
MAN-MADE?! IF YOU COULD JUST *CREATE* DEVIL FRUIT, PEOPLE WITH POWERS WOULD BE POPPING UP ALL OVER THE PLACE!!
EXACTLY.
APPARENTLY, THERE ARE INHERENT RISKS IN THE MAN-MADE FRUIT...
...BUT AS OF THIS MOMENT, KAIDO HAS AT LEAST FIVE HUNDRED PEOPLE IN HIS CREW WITH DEVIL FRUIT POWERS.
?!!
ANYONE WANT TO QUIT?!!
ME!
Me!
ME!
OH, SHUT UP.
Me!
Me!
Me!
BUT NOW THAT FRUIT'S BEEN TAKEN OUT OF THE EQUATION.
!
INTER-ESTING.
SO *HE* WAS MAKING THEM?!
SHU... SHU HEH HEH...
BA—M!
BLUSH
YOU WERE MAKING THE FOUNDATION FOR THOSE DEVIL FRUITS?! WOW, THAT S.A.D. MUST BE INCREDIBLE STUFF!!
DON'T COMPLIMENT HIM! HE'S THE ROOT OF EVIL!!
GAS

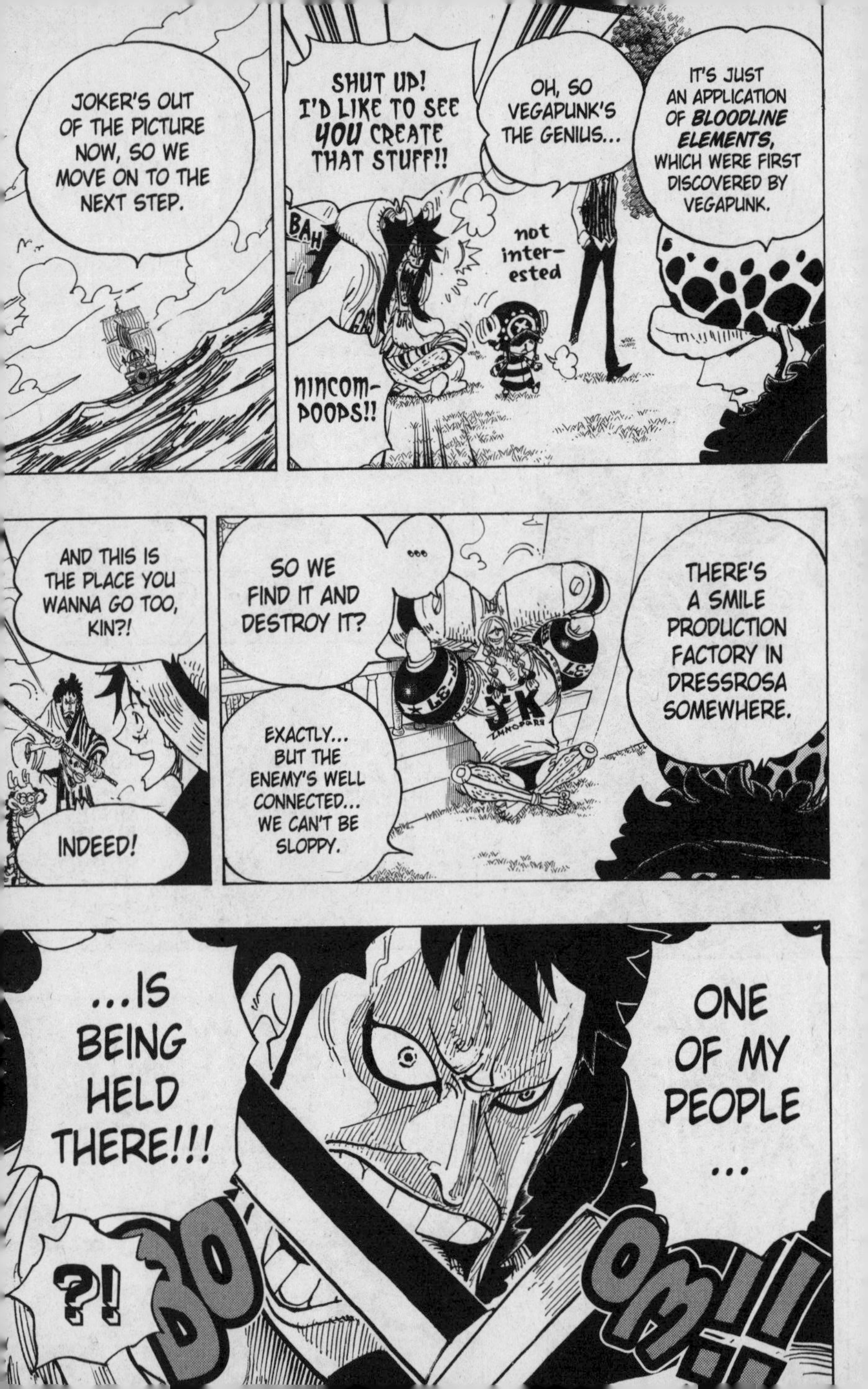
IT'S JUST AN APPLICATION OF BLOODLINE ELEMENTS, WHICH WERE FIRST DISCOVERED BY VEGAPUNK.
OH, SO VEGAPUNK'S THE GENIUS...
SHUT UP! I'D LIKE TO SEE YOU CREATE THAT STUFF!!
BAH
not interested
nincompoops!!
JOKER'S OUT OF THE PICTURE NOW, SO WE MOVE ON TO THE NEXT STEP.
THERE'S A SMILE PRODUCTION FACTORY IN DRESSROSA SOMEWHERE.
...
SO WE FIND IT AND DESTROY IT?
EXACTLY... BUT THE ENEMY'S WELL CONNECTED... WE CAN'T BE SLOPPY.
AND THIS IS THE PLACE YOU WANNA GO TOO, KIN?!
INDEED!
ONE OF MY PEOPLE ...
...IS BEING HELD THERE!!!
?!
BOOM!!

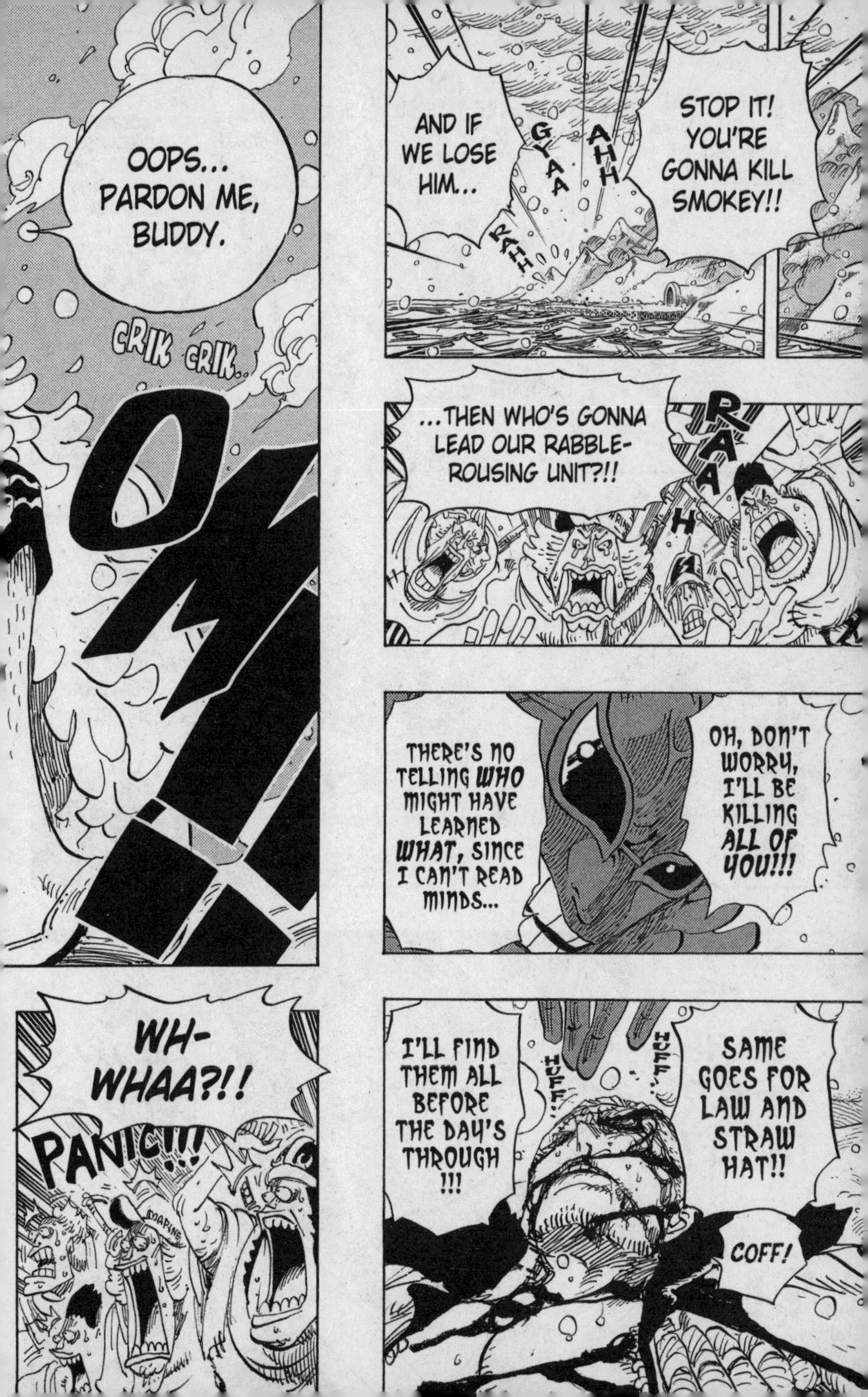
STOP IT! YOU'RE GONNA KILL SMOKEY!!
AHH
GYAA
AND IF WE LOSE HIM...
RAHH
...THEN WHO'S GONNA LEAD OUR RABBLE-ROUSING UNIT?!!
RAAAH
OH, DON'T WORRY, I'LL BE KILLING ALL OF YOU!!!
THERE'S NO TELLING WHO MIGHT HAVE LEARNED WHAT, SINCE I CAN'T READ MINDS...
OOPS... PARDON ME, BUDDY.
CRIK CRIK
SAME GOES FOR LAW AND STRAW HAT!!
HUFF
HUFF
I'LL FIND THEM ALL BEFORE THE DAY'S THROUGH!!!
COFF!
WH- WHAA?!!
PANIC!!!

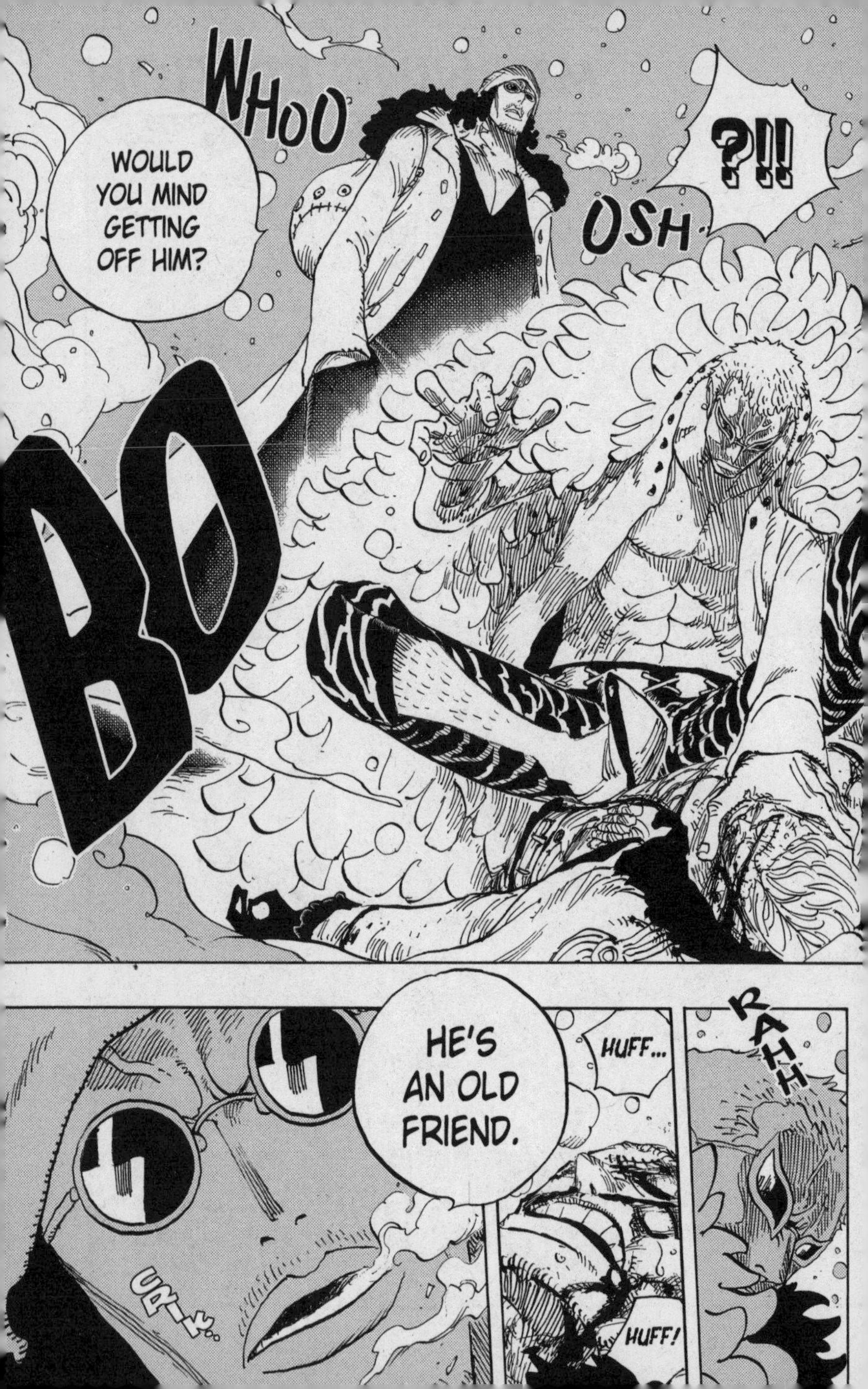
?!!
OSH
WHOO
WOULD YOU MIND GETTING OFF HIM?
BO
RAHH
HUFF...
HUFF!
HE'S AN OLD FRIEND.

MORNING EDITION

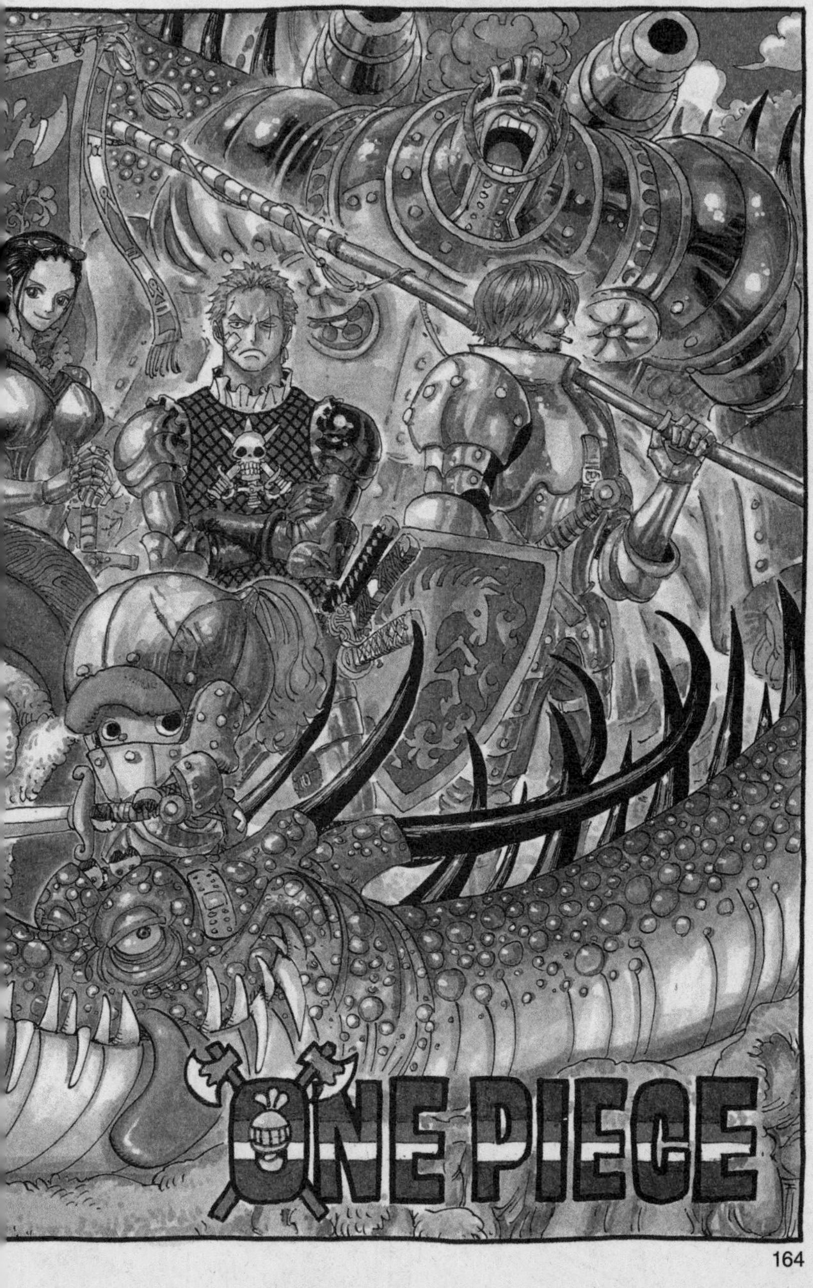
ONE PIECE

Chapter 699:

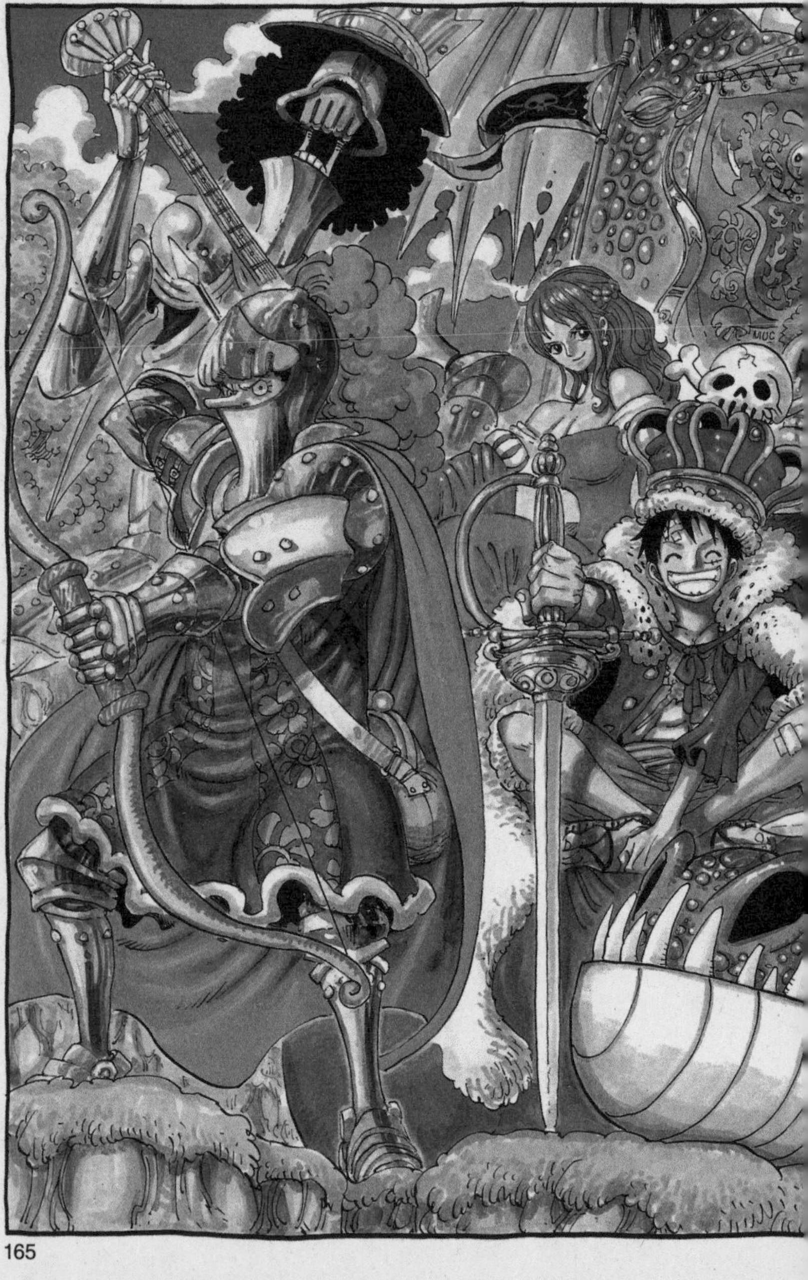

vol. 70
ONE PIECE

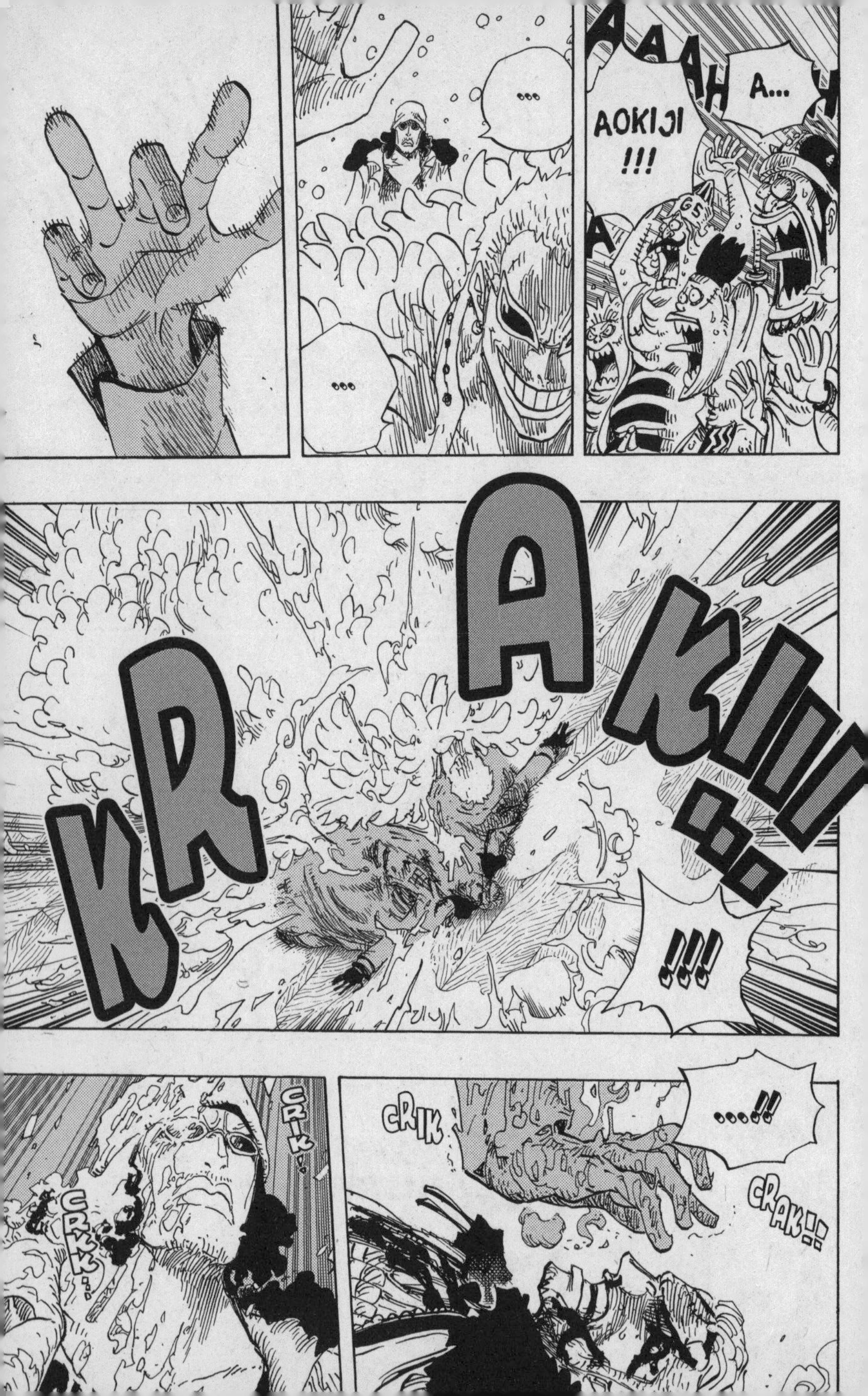
AAAH
A...
AOKIJI!!!
...
...
KRAK!!!
!!!
CRIK
....!!
CRAK!!
CRIK!
CRIK..

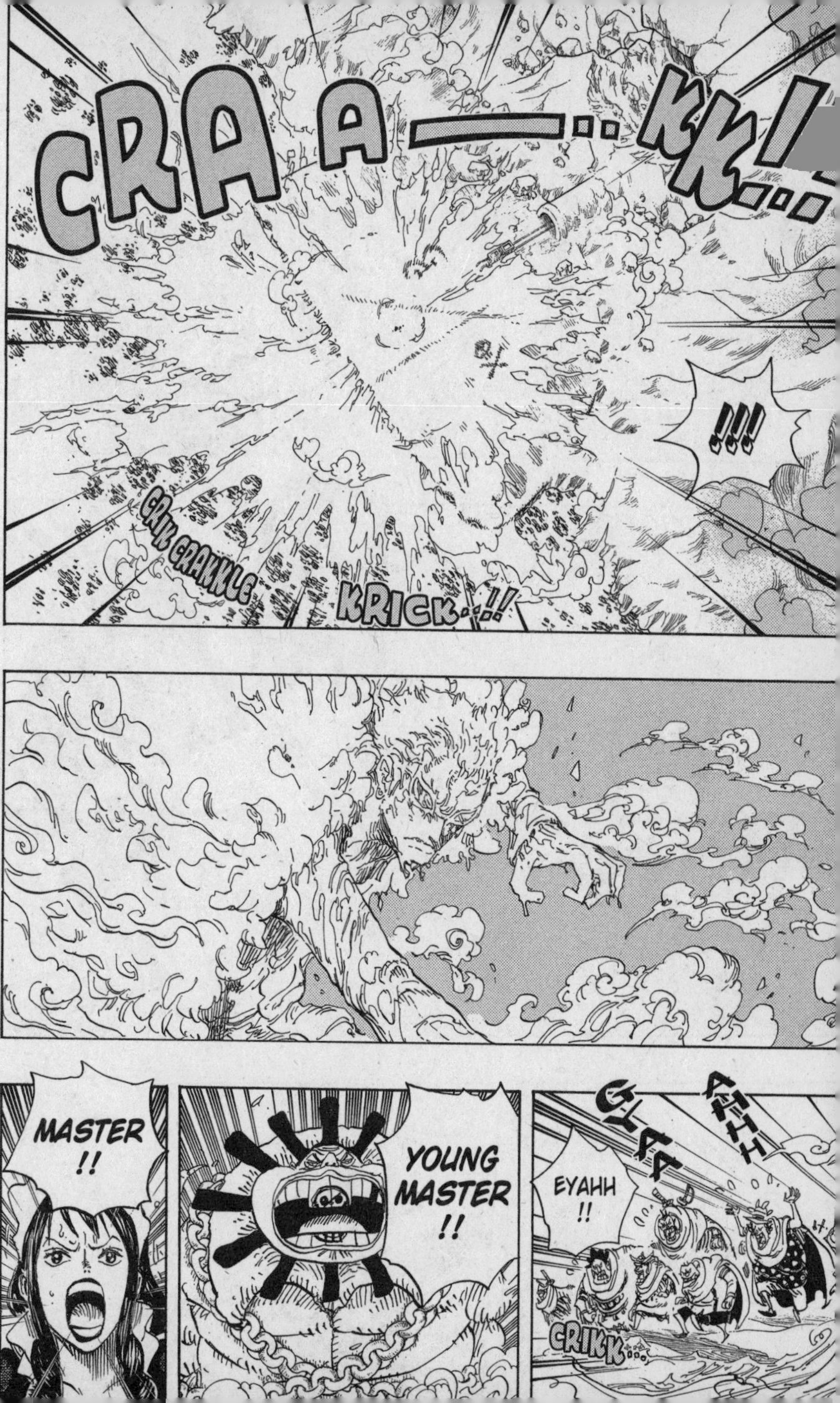
CRAA——..KK!...
!!!
KRICK..!!
CRIK CRAKKLE
GYAAAHHH
EYAHH !!
CRIKK...
YOUNG MASTER !!
MASTER !!

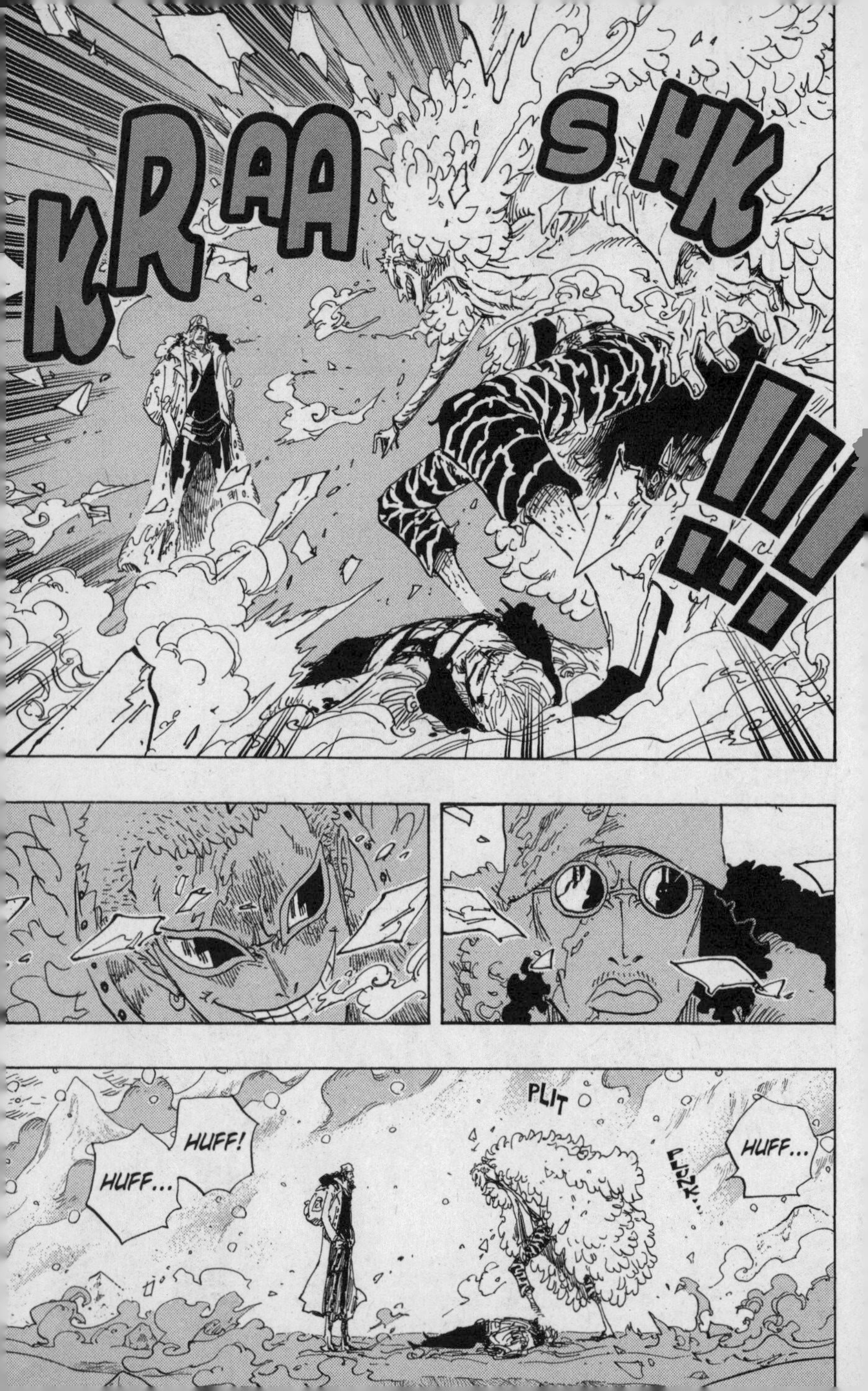
KRAASHK
!!
HUFF...
PLUNK...
PLIT
HUFF!
HUFF...

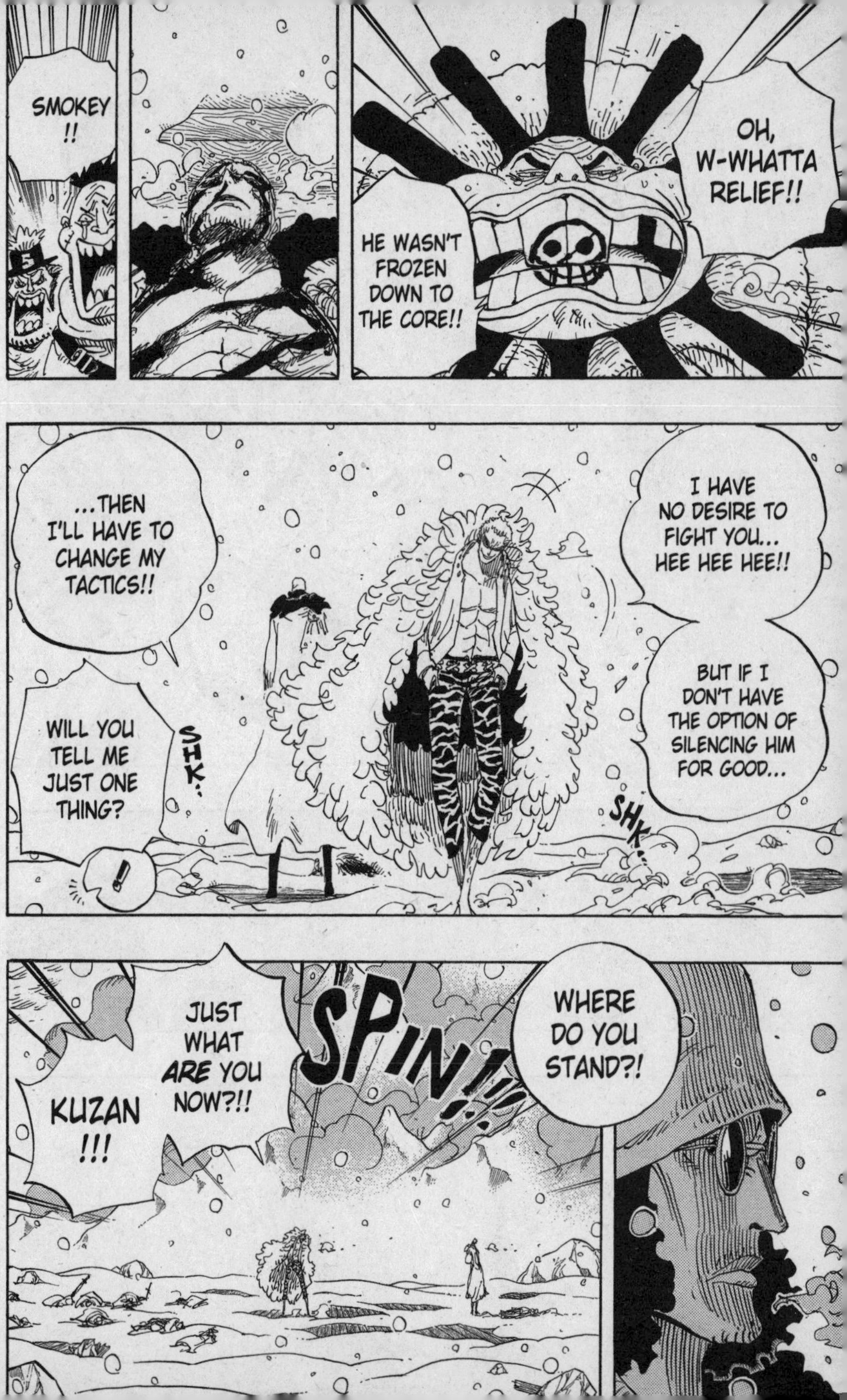
OH, W-WHATTA RELIEF!!
HE WASN'T FROZEN DOWN TO THE CORE!!
SMOKEY !!
I HAVE NO DESIRE TO FIGHT YOU... HEE HEE HEE!!
BUT IF I DON'T HAVE THE OPTION OF SILENCING HIM FOR GOOD...
SHK...
...THEN I'LL HAVE TO CHANGE MY TACTICS!!
SHK...
WILL YOU TELL ME JUST ONE THING?
!
WHERE DO YOU STAND?!
SPIN!!!
JUST WHAT ARE YOU NOW?!!
KUZAN !!!

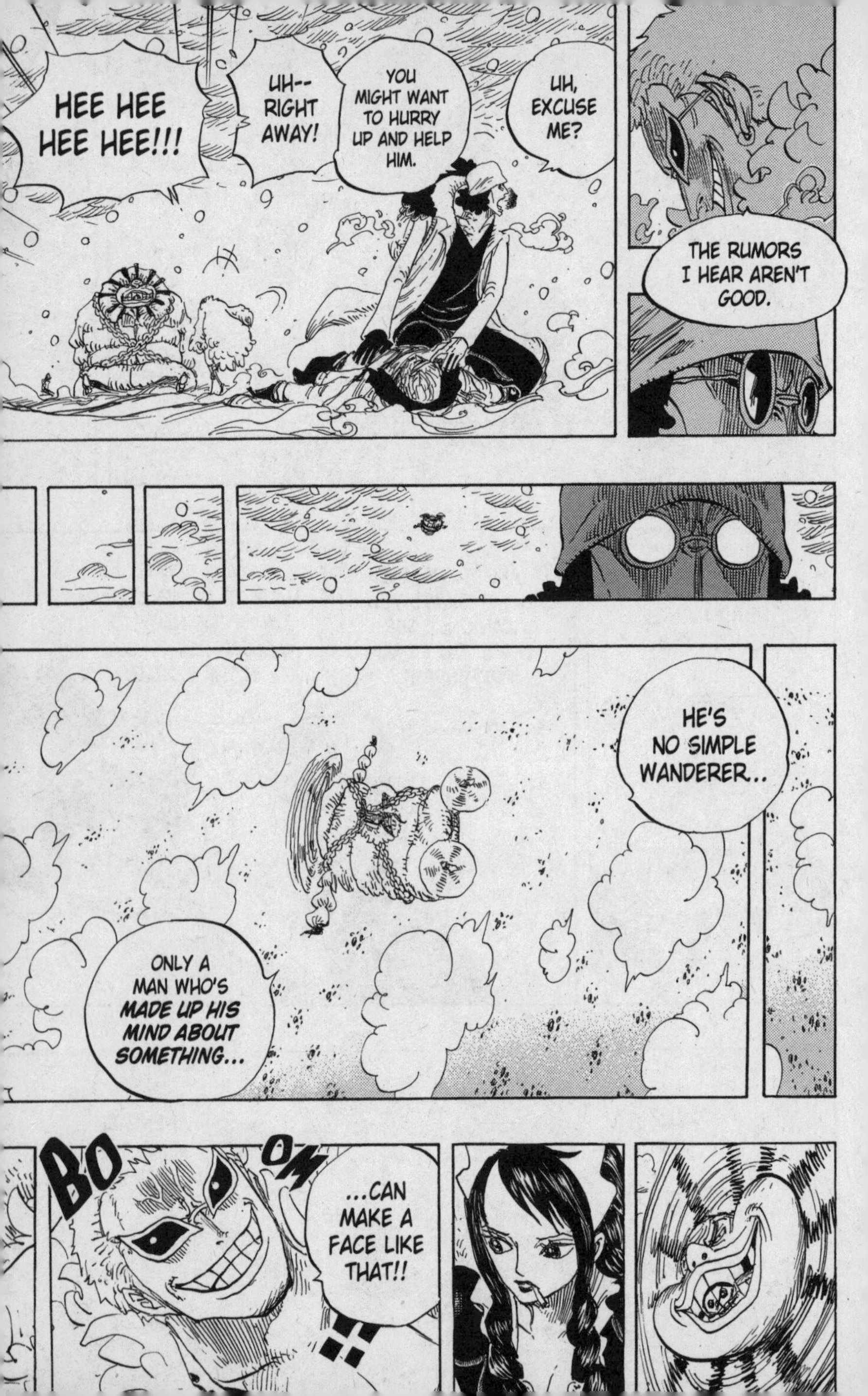
THE RUMORS I HEAR AREN'T GOOD.
UH, EXCUSE ME?
YOU MIGHT WANT TO HURRY UP AND HELP HIM.
UH-- RIGHT AWAY!
HEE HEE HEE HEE!!!
HE'S NO SIMPLE WANDERER..
ONLY A MAN WHO'S *MADE UP HIS MIND ABOUT SOMETHING*...
...CAN MAKE A FACE LIKE THAT!!
BOOM

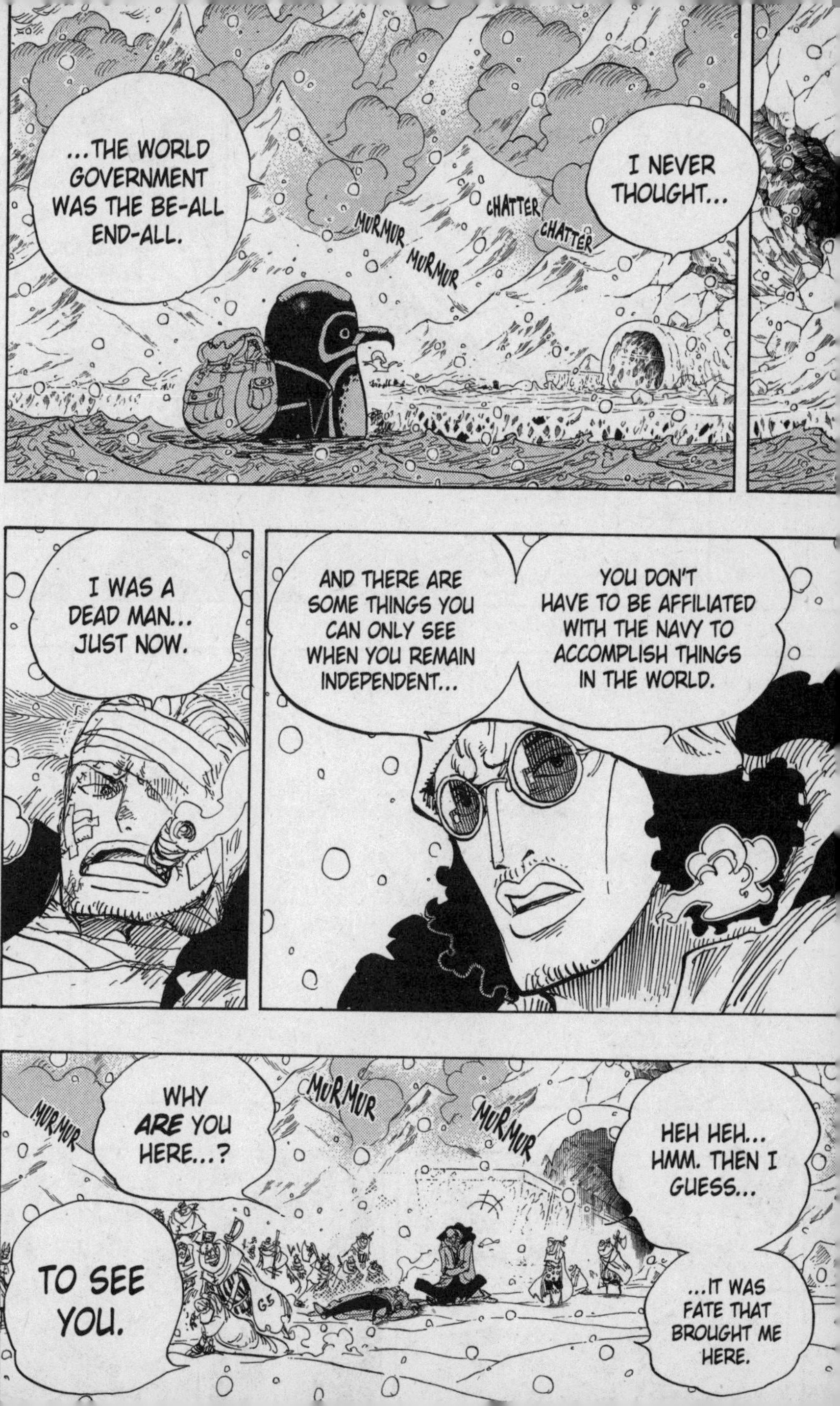
I NEVER THOUGHT...
CHATTER
CHATTER
MURMUR
MURMUR
...THE WORLD GOVERNMENT WAS THE BE-ALL END-ALL.
YOU DON'T HAVE TO BE AFFILIATED WITH THE NAVY TO ACCOMPLISH THINGS IN THE WORLD.
AND THERE ARE SOME THINGS YOU CAN ONLY SEE WHEN YOU REMAIN INDEPENDENT...
I WAS A DEAD MAN... JUST NOW.
HEH HEH... HMM. THEN I GUESS...
...IT WAS FATE THAT BROUGHT ME HERE.
MURMUR
MURMUR
WHY ***ARE*** YOU HERE...?
MURMUR
TO SEE YOU.

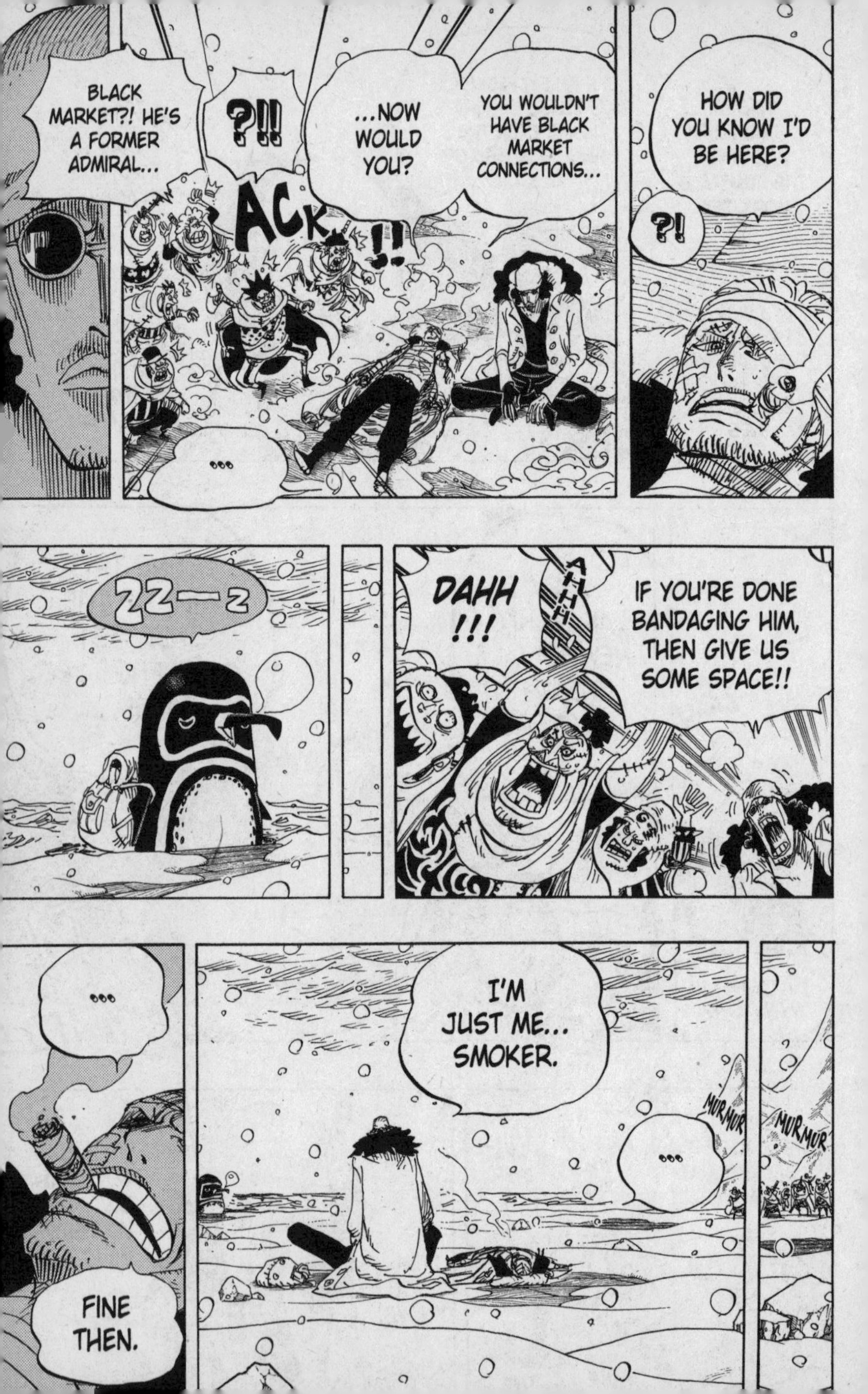
HOW DID YOU KNOW I'D BE HERE?
?!
YOU WOULDN'T HAVE BLACK MARKET CONNECTIONS...
...NOW WOULD YOU?
?!!
ACK
!!
...
BLACK MARKET?! HE'S A FORMER ADMIRAL...
IF YOU'RE DONE BANDAGING HIM, THEN GIVE US SOME SPACE!!
AHHHH
DAHH !!!
ZZ—z
MUR MUR
MUR MUR
I'M JUST ME... SMOKER.
...
...
FINE THEN.

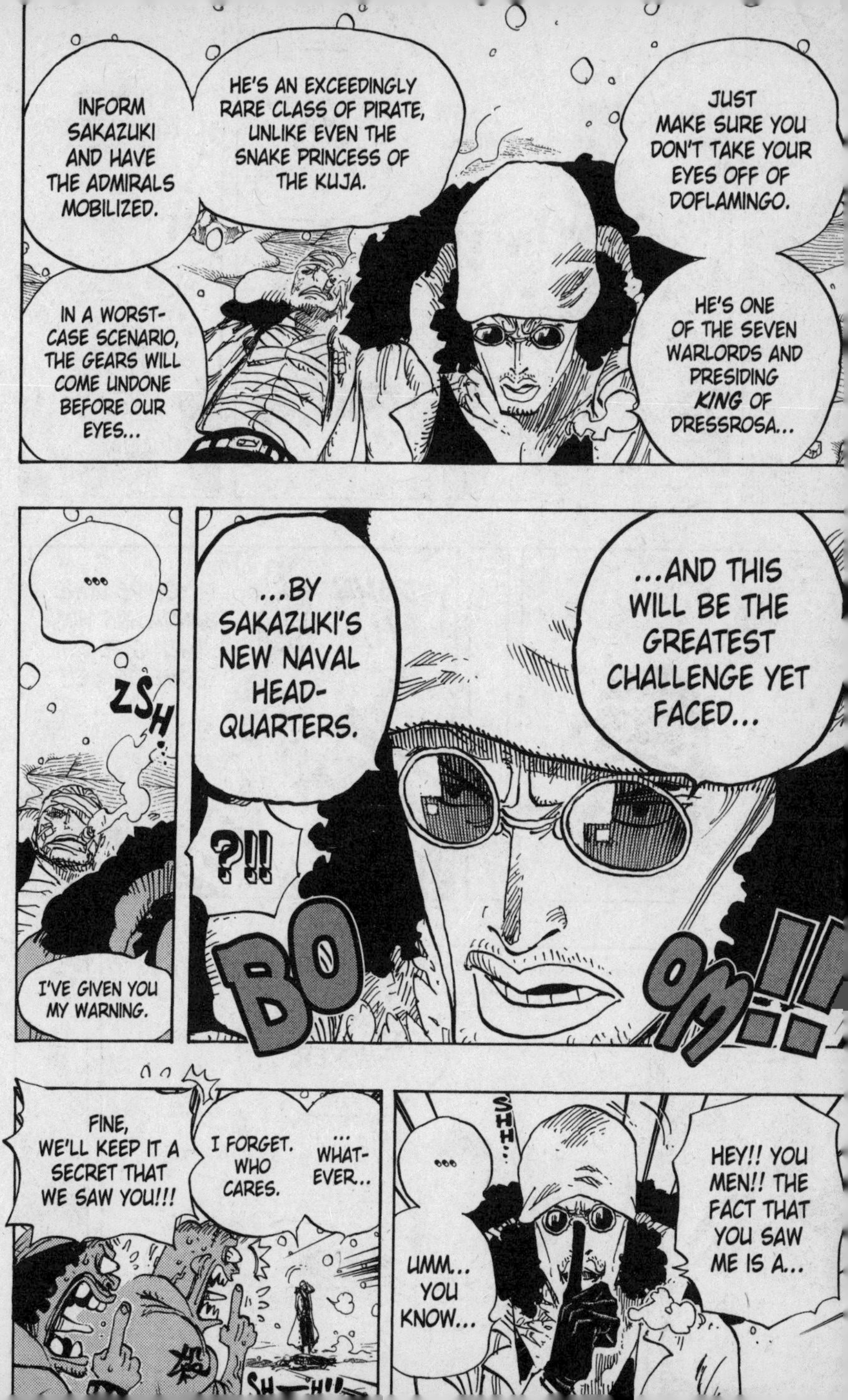
JUST MAKE SURE YOU DON'T TAKE YOUR EYES OFF OF DOFLAMINGO.
HE'S ONE OF THE SEVEN WARLORDS AND PRESIDING KING OF DRESSROSA...
HE'S AN EXCEEDINGLY RARE CLASS OF PIRATE, UNLIKE EVEN THE SNAKE PRINCESS OF THE KUJA.
INFORM SAKAZUKI AND HAVE THE ADMIRALS MOBILIZED.
IN A WORST-CASE SCENARIO, THE GEARS WILL COME UNDONE BEFORE OUR EYES...
...AND THIS WILL BE THE GREATEST CHALLENGE YET FACED...
...BY SAKAZUKI'S NEW NAVAL HEAD-QUARTERS.
?!!
BOOM!!
...
ZSH
I'VE GIVEN YOU MY WARNING.
HEY!! YOU MEN!! THE FACT THAT YOU SAW ME IS A...
SHH..
...
UMM... YOU KNOW...
... WHAT-EVER...
I FORGET. WHO CARES.
FINE, WE'LL KEEP IT A SECRET THAT WE SAW YOU!!!
SH—H!!

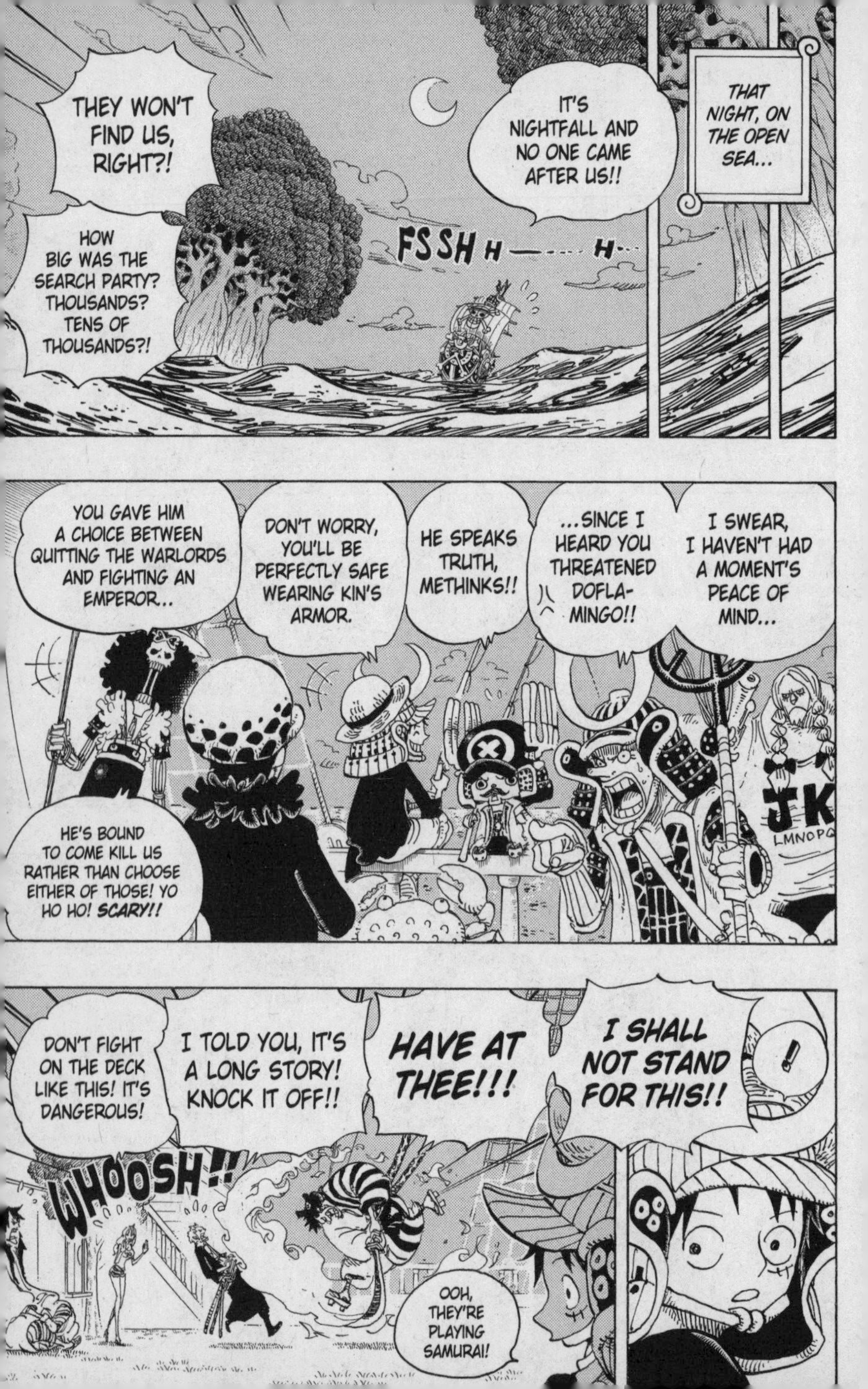
THAT NIGHT, ON THE OPEN SEA...
IT'S NIGHTFALL AND NO ONE CAME AFTER US!!
FSSHH—H
THEY WON'T FIND US, RIGHT?!
HOW BIG WAS THE SEARCH PARTY? THOUSANDS? TENS OF THOUSANDS?!
I SWEAR, I HAVEN'T HAD A MOMENT'S PEACE OF MIND...
...SINCE I HEARD YOU THREATENED DOFLAMINGO!!
JK
LMNOPQ
HE SPEAKS TRUTH, METHINKS!!
DON'T WORRY, YOU'LL BE PERFECTLY SAFE WEARING KIN'S ARMOR.
YOU GAVE HIM A CHOICE BETWEEN QUITTING THE WARLORDS AND FIGHTING AN EMPEROR...
HE'S BOUND TO COME KILL US RATHER THAN CHOOSE EITHER OF THOSE! YO HO HO! SCARY!!
!
I SHALL NOT STAND FOR THIS!!
HAVE AT THEE!!!
I TOLD YOU, IT'S A LONG STORY! KNOCK IT OFF!!
DON'T FIGHT ON THE DECK LIKE THIS! IT'S DANGEROUS!
WHOOSH!!
OOH, THEY'RE PLAYING SAMURAI!

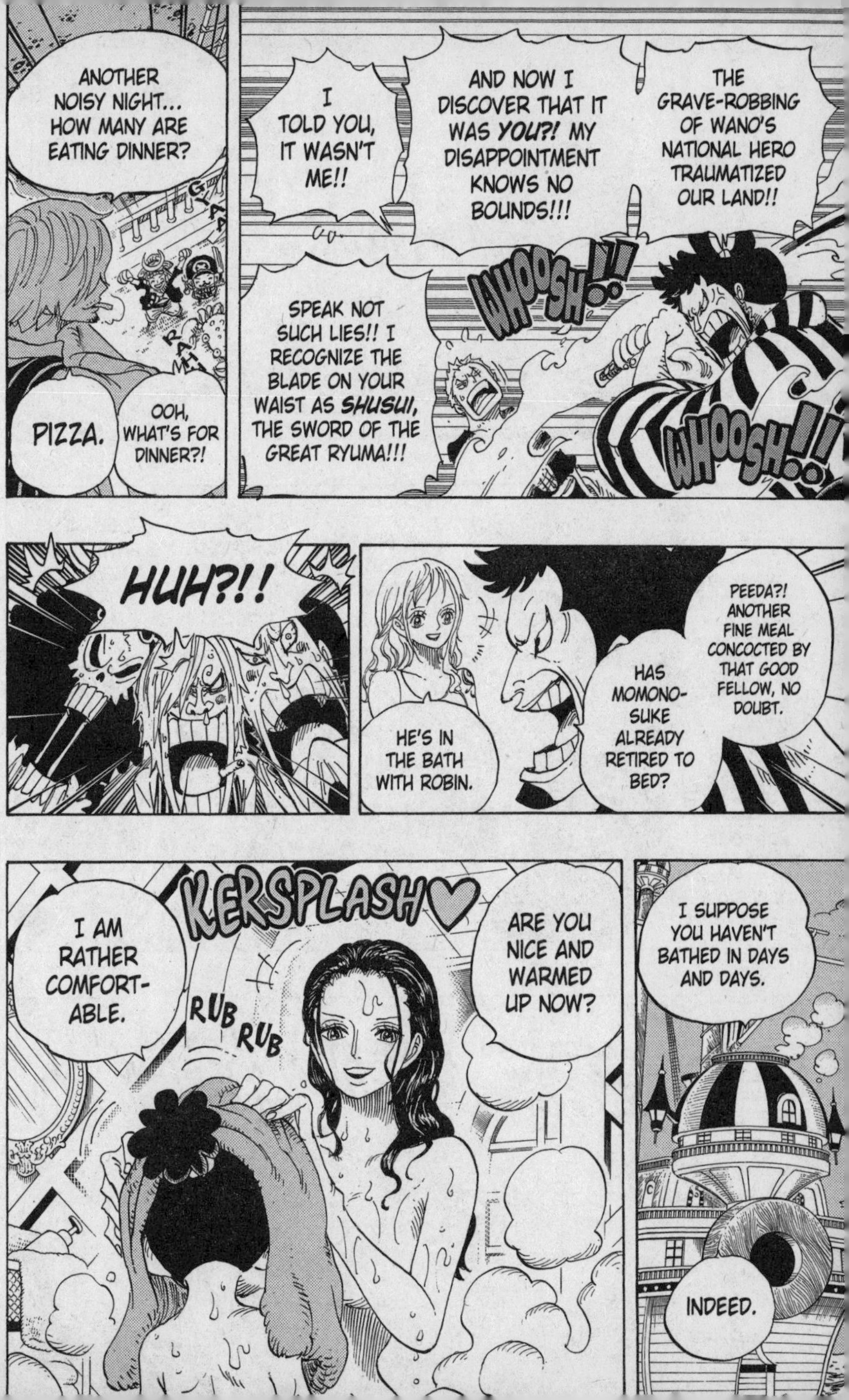
THE GRAVE-ROBBING OF WANO'S NATIONAL HERO TRAUMATIZED OUR LAND!!
AND NOW I DISCOVER THAT IT WAS YOU?! MY DISAPPOINTMENT KNOWS NO BOUNDS!!!
I TOLD YOU, IT WASN'T ME!!
WHOOSH!!
SPEAK NOT SUCH LIES!! I RECOGNIZE THE BLADE ON YOUR WAIST AS SHUSUI, THE SWORD OF THE GREAT RYUMA!!!
WHOOSH!!
ANOTHER NOISY NIGHT... HOW MANY ARE EATING DINNER?
OOH, WHAT'S FOR DINNER?!
PIZZA.
PEEDA?! ANOTHER FINE MEAL CONCOCTED BY THAT GOOD FELLOW, NO DOUBT.
HAS MOMONOSUKE ALREADY RETIRED TO BED?
HE'S IN THE BATH WITH ROBIN.
HUH?!!
I SUPPOSE YOU HAVEN'T BATHED IN DAYS AND DAYS.
INDEED.
KERSPLASH♥
ARE YOU NICE AND WARMED UP NOW?
I AM RATHER COMFORTABLE.
RUB RUB

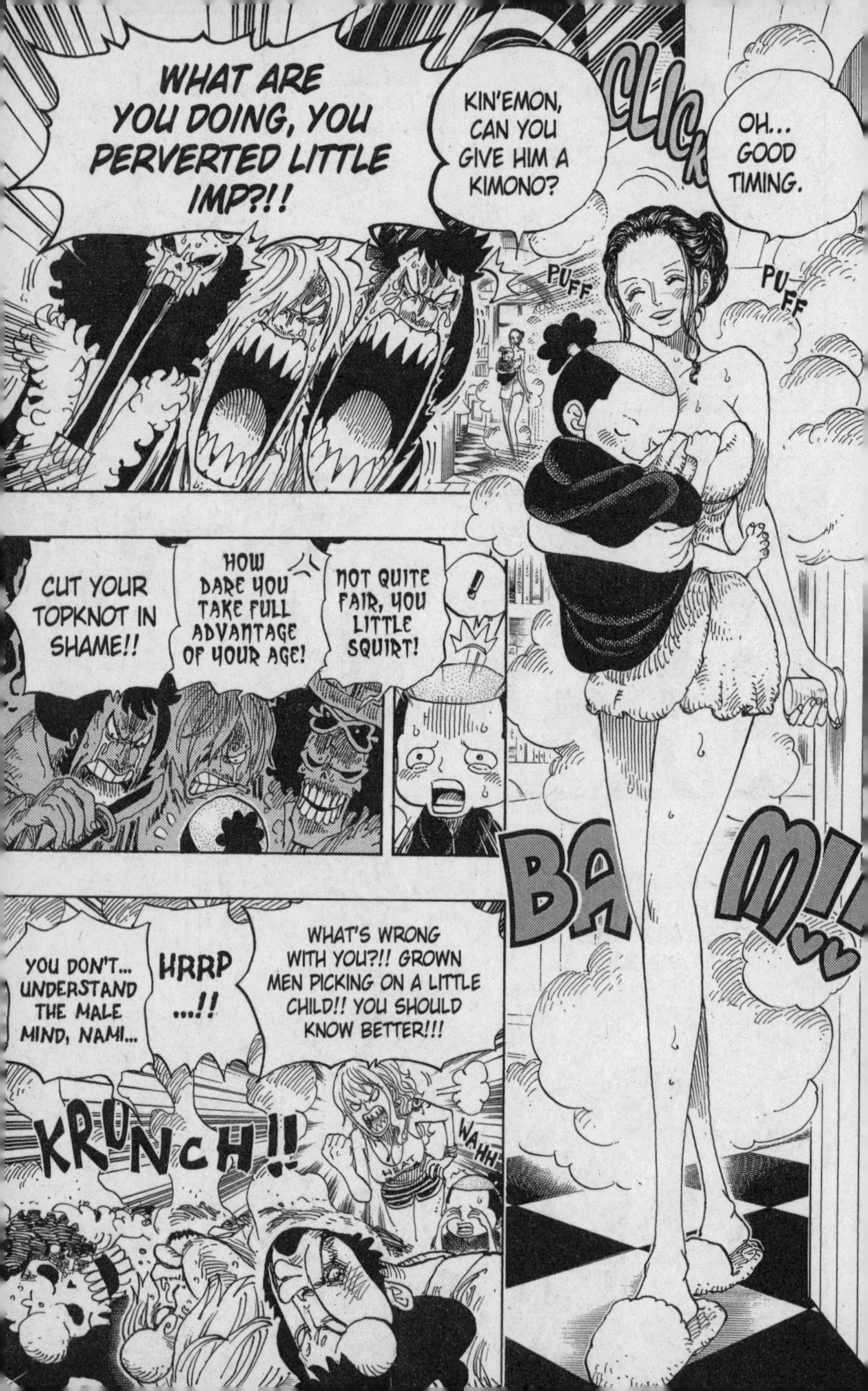
CLICK
OH... GOOD TIMING.
KIN'EMON, CAN YOU GIVE HIM A KIMONO?
PUFF
PUFF
BAM!!
WHAT ARE YOU DOING, YOU PERVERTED LITTLE IMP?!!
!
NOT QUITE FAIR, YOU LITTLE SQUIRT!
HOW DARE YOU TAKE FULL ADVANTAGE OF YOUR AGE!
CUT YOUR TOPKNOT IN SHAME!!
WHAT'S WRONG WITH YOU?!! GROWN MEN PICKING ON A LITTLE CHILD!! YOU SHOULD KNOW BETTER!!!
HRRP ...!!
YOU DON'T... UNDERSTAND THE MALE MIND, NAMI...
KRUNCH!!
WAHH

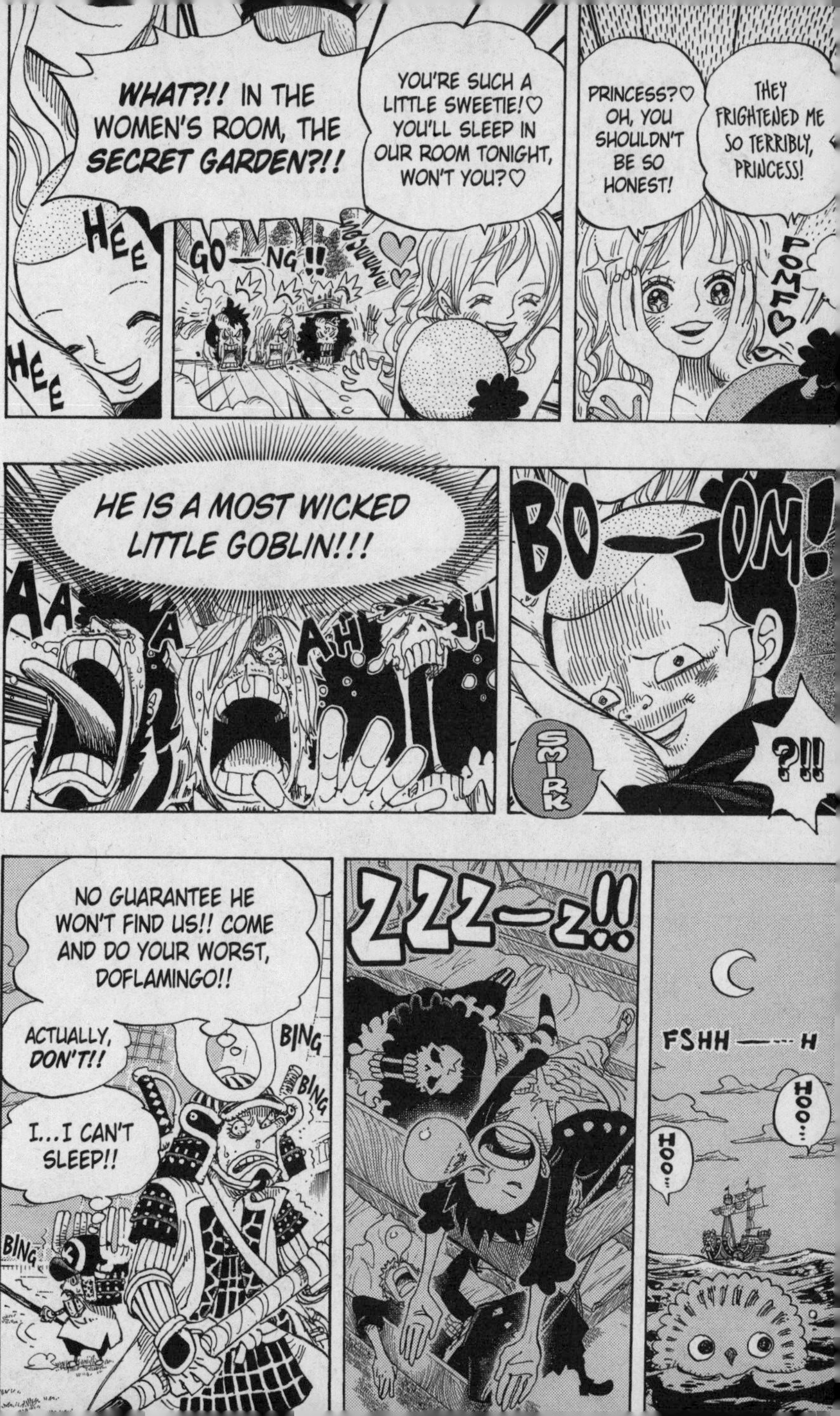
THEY FRIGHTENED ME SO TERRIBLY, PRINCESS!
PRINCESS?♡ OH, YOU SHOULDN'T BE SO HONEST!
POMF♡
YOU'RE SUCH A LITTLE SWEETIE!♡ YOU'LL SLEEP IN OUR ROOM TONIGHT, WON'T YOU?♡
GO—NG!!
WHAT?!! IN THE WOMEN'S ROOM, THE SECRET GARDEN?!!
HEE
HEE
BO—OM!
SMIRK
?!!
HE IS A MOST WICKED LITTLE GOBLIN!!!
AAAAH
FSHH—H
HOO...
HOO...
ZZZ—Z!!
NO GUARANTEE HE WON'T FIND US!! COME AND DO YOUR WORST, DOFLAMINGO!!
ACTUALLY, DON'T!!
I...I CAN'T SLEEP!!
BING
BING
BING

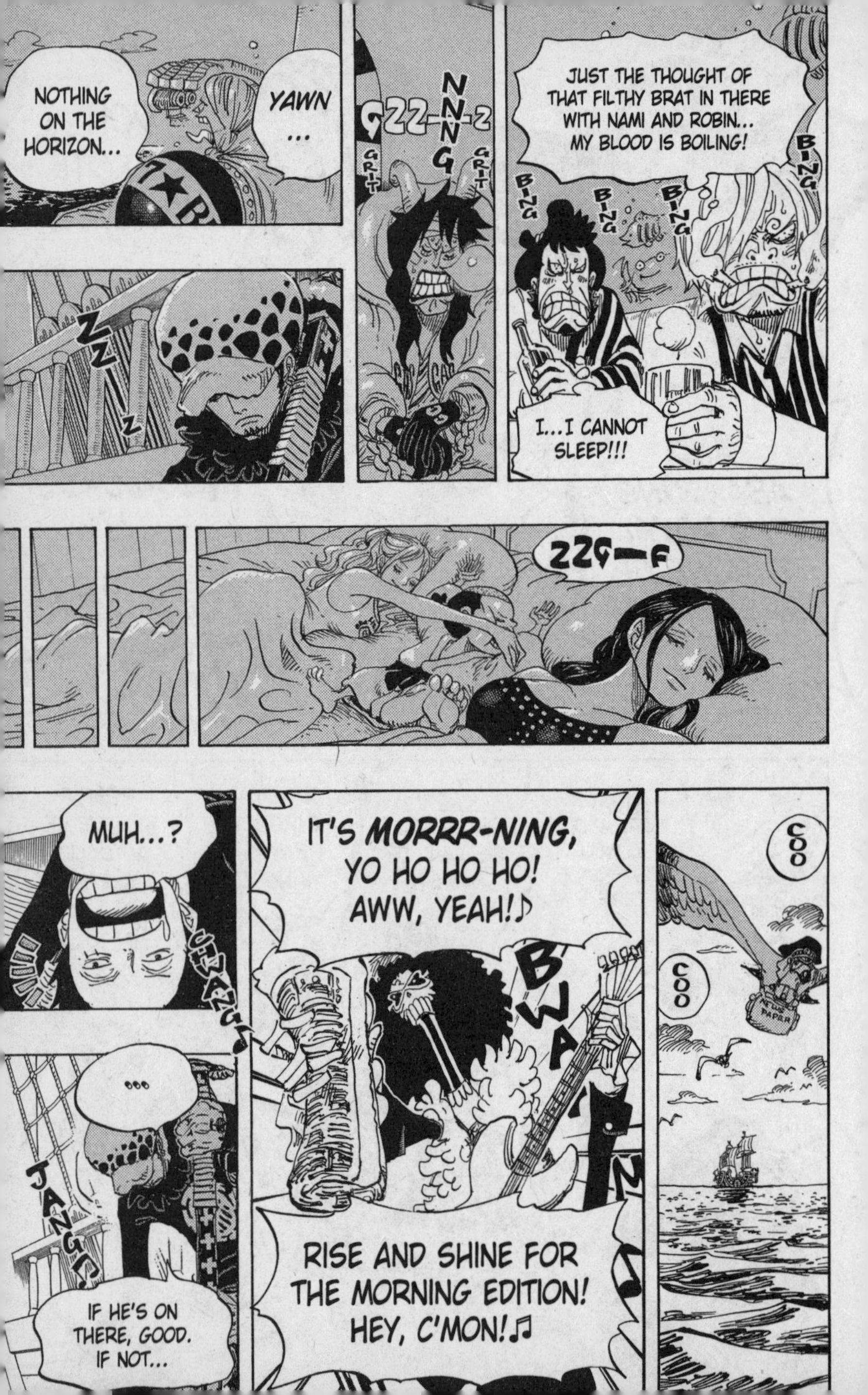
JUST THE THOUGHT OF THAT FILTHY BRAT IN THERE WITH NAMI AND ROBIN... MY BLOOD IS BOILING!
BING
BING
BING
BING
I...I CANNOT SLEEP!!!
GZZ-NNNG-Z
GRIT
GRIT
YAWN ...
NOTHING ON THE HORIZON...
ZZZ
ZZG—F
COO
COO
IT'S MORRR-NING, YO HO HO HO! AWW, YEAH!♪
BWA
RISE AND SHINE FOR THE MORNING EDITION! HEY, C'MON!♫
MUH...?
...
JANG♪
IF HE'S ON THERE, GOOD. IF NOT...

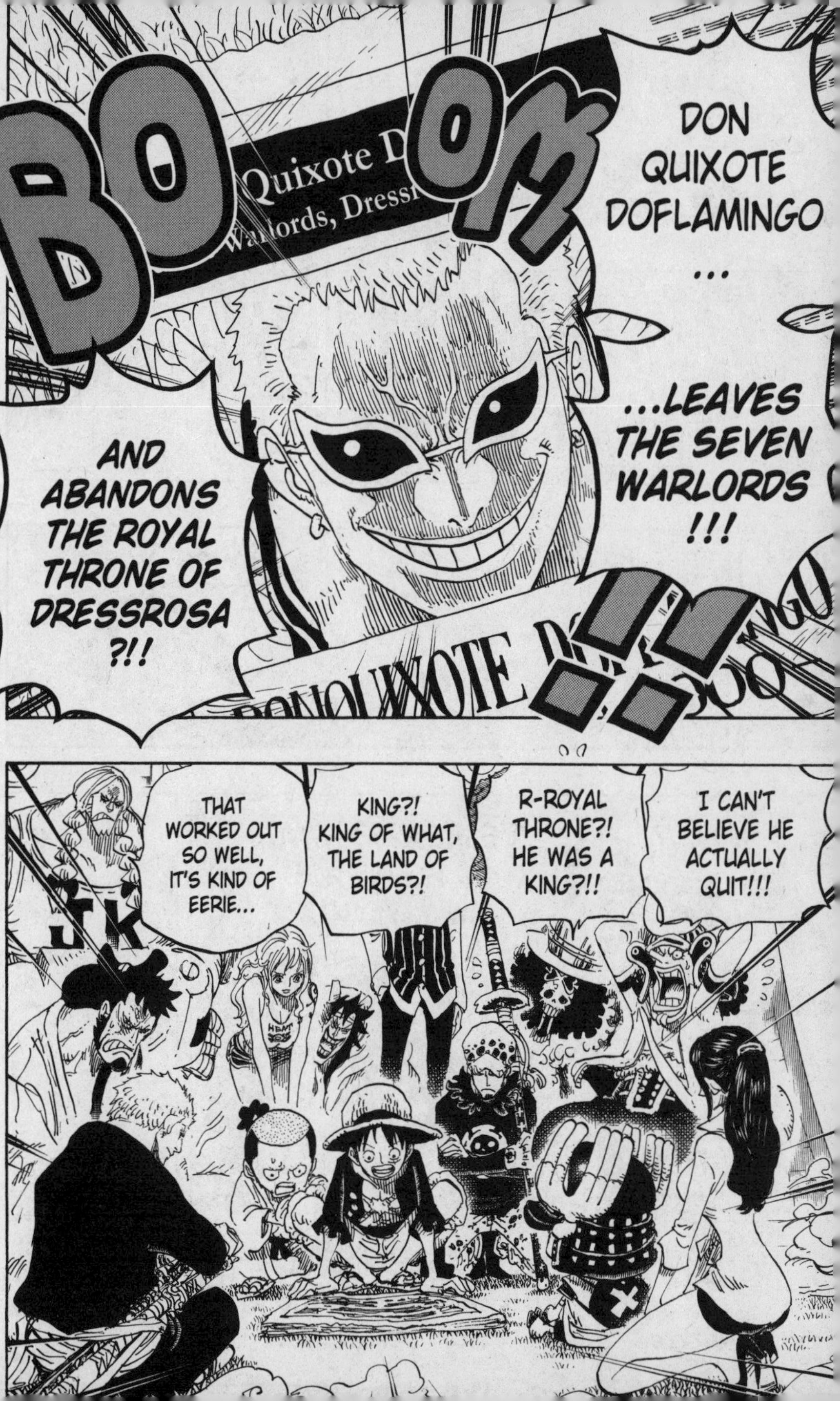
DON QUIXOTE DOFLAMINGO ...
...LEAVES THE SEVEN WARLORDS!!!
Quixote D
Warlords, Dress
BOOM
AND ABANDONS THE ROYAL THRONE OF DRESSROSA?!!
I CAN'T BELIEVE HE ACTUALLY QUIT!!!
R-ROYAL THRONE?! HE WAS A KING?!!
KING?! KING OF WHAT, THE LAND OF BIRDS?!
THAT WORKED OUT SO WELL, IT'S KIND OF EERIE...

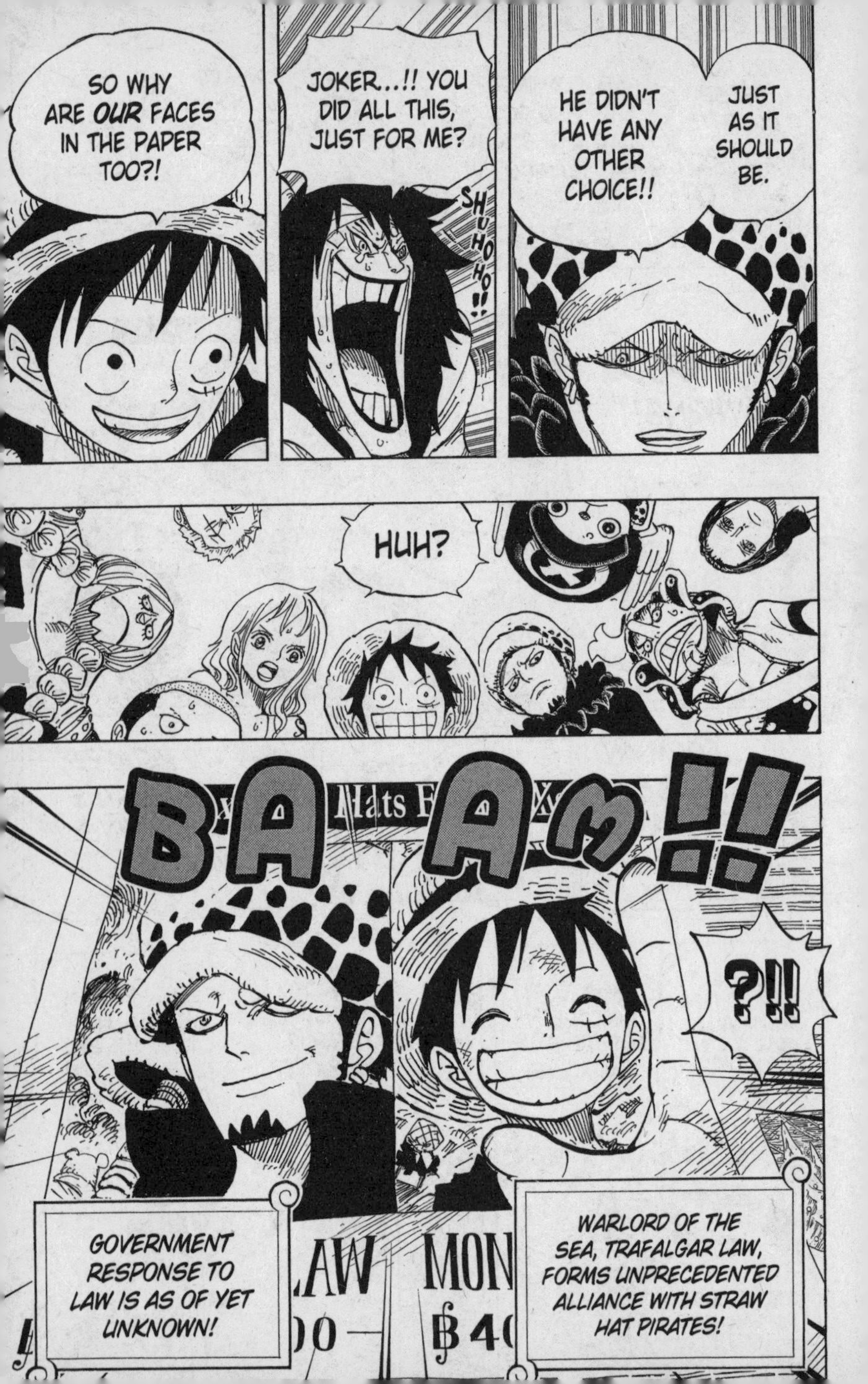
JUST AS IT SHOULD BE.
HE DIDN'T HAVE ANY OTHER CHOICE!!
JOKER...!! YOU DID ALL THIS, JUST FOR ME?
SHUHOHO!!
SO WHY ARE OUR FACES IN THE PAPER TOO?!
HUH?
BAAM!!
?!!
WARLORD OF THE SEA, TRAFALGAR LAW, FORMS UNPRECEDENTED ALLIANCE WITH STRAW HAT PIRATES!
MON
LAW
GOVERNMENT RESPONSE TO LAW IS AS OF YET UNKNOWN!

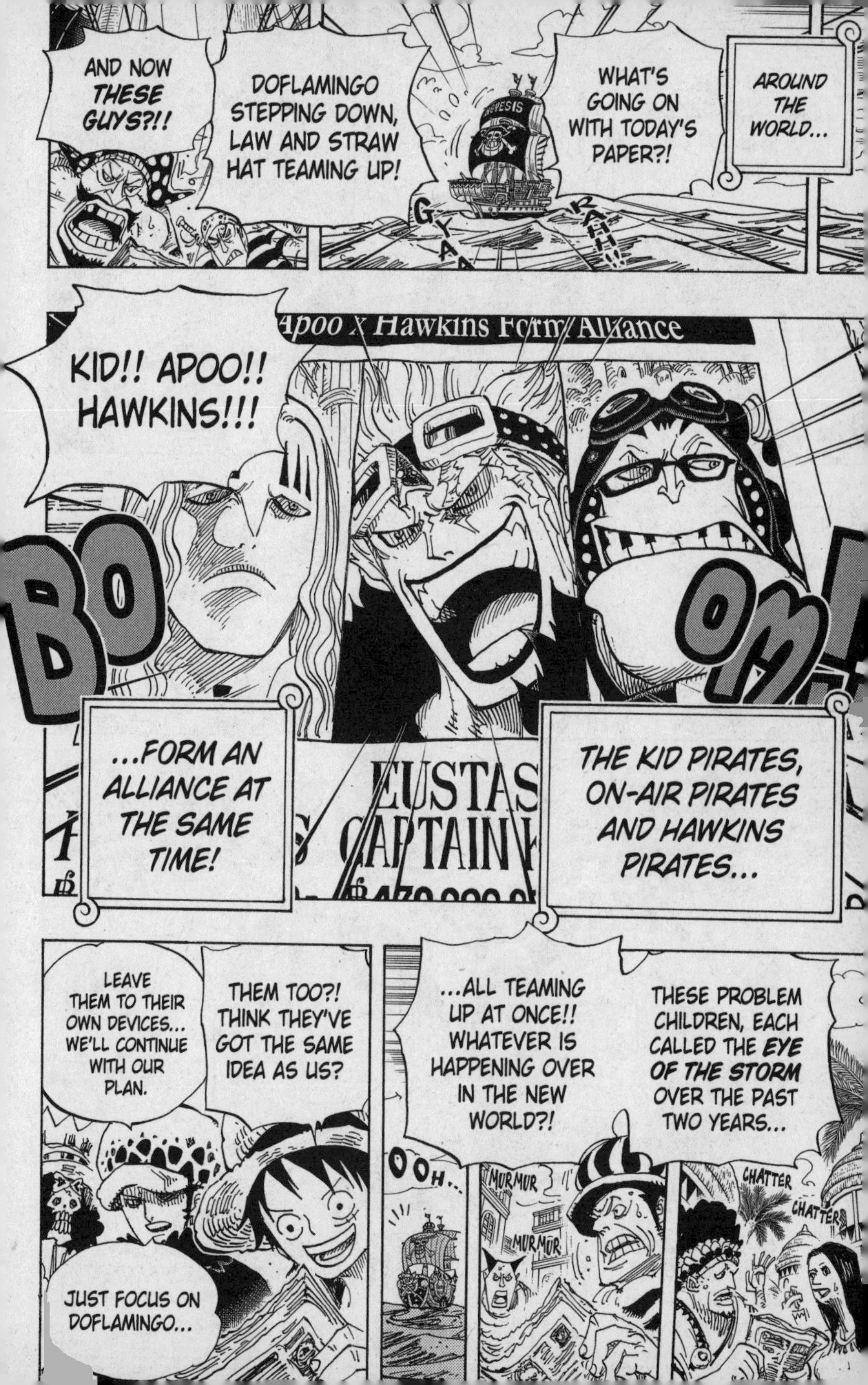
AROUND THE WORLD...
WHAT'S GOING ON WITH TODAY'S PAPER?!
RAHH!!
GYAA
DOFLAMINGO STEPPING DOWN, LAW AND STRAW HAT TEAMING UP!
AND NOW THESE GUYS?!!
Apoo x Hawkins Form Alliance
KID!! APOO!! HAWKINS!!!
BOOM
THE KID PIRATES, ON-AIR PIRATES AND HAWKINS PIRATES...
...FORM AN ALLIANCE AT THE SAME TIME!
THESE PROBLEM CHILDREN, EACH CALLED THE EYE OF THE STORM OVER THE PAST TWO YEARS...
...ALL TEAMING UP AT ONCE!! WHATEVER IS HAPPENING OVER IN THE NEW WORLD?!
CHATTER
CHATTER
MURMUR
MURMUR
OOH...
THEM TOO?! THINK THEY'VE GOT THE SAME IDEA AS US?
LEAVE THEM TO THEIR OWN DEVICES... WE'LL CONTINUE WITH OUR PLAN.
JUST FOCUS ON DOFLAMINGO...

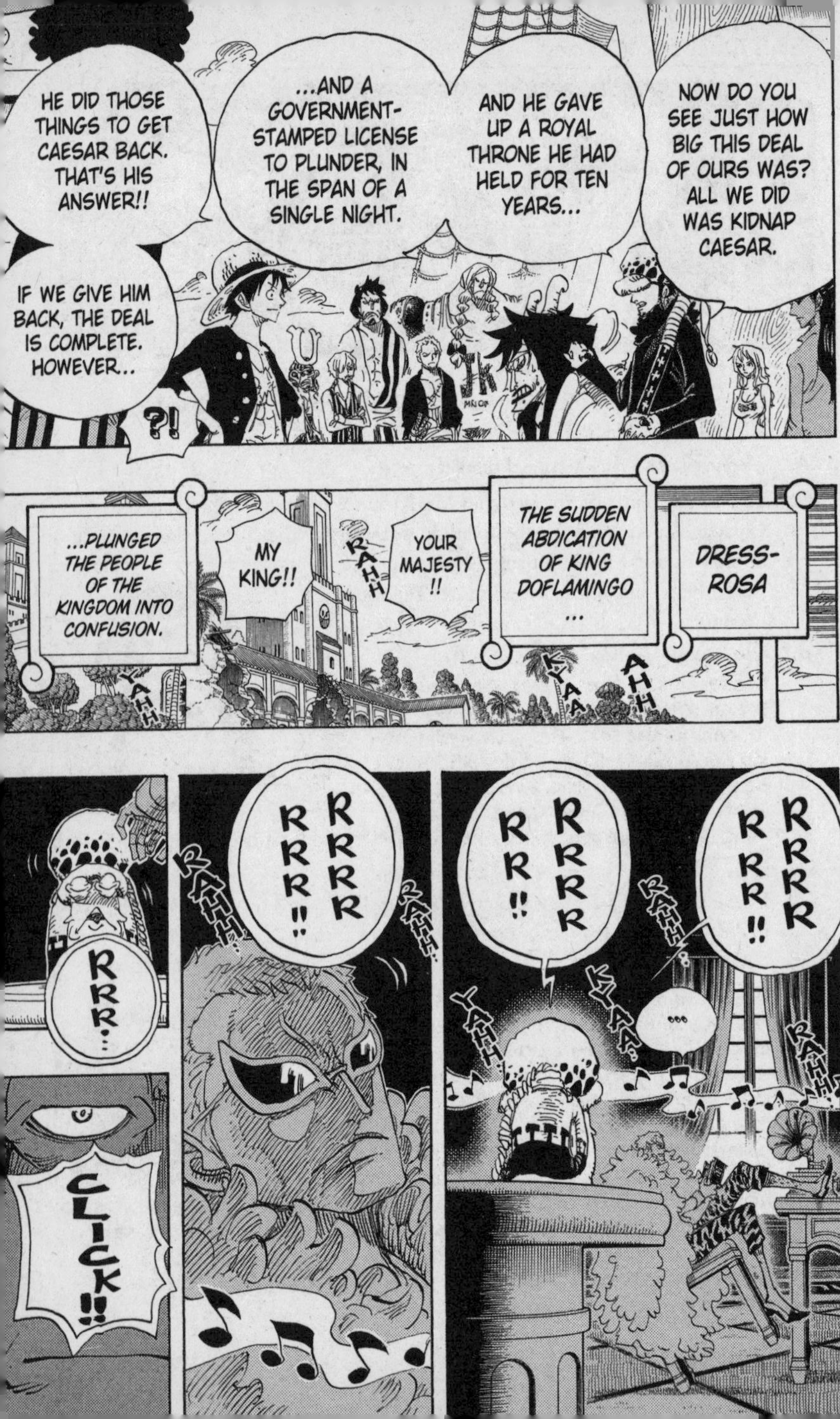
NOW DO YOU SEE JUST HOW BIG THIS DEAL OF OURS WAS? ALL WE DID WAS KIDNAP CAESAR.
AND HE GAVE UP A ROYAL THRONE HE HAD HELD FOR TEN YEARS...
...AND A GOVERNMENT-STAMPED LICENSE TO PLUNDER, IN THE SPAN OF A SINGLE NIGHT.
HE DID THOSE THINGS TO GET CAESAR BACK. THAT'S HIS ANSWER!!
IF WE GIVE HIM BACK, THE DEAL IS COMPLETE. HOWEVER...
?!
DRESS-ROSA
AHH
KYAA
THE SUDDEN ABDICATION OF KING DOFLAMINGO...
YOUR MAJESTY!!
RAHH
MY KING!!
YAHH
...PLUNGED THE PEOPLE OF THE KINGDOM INTO CONFUSION.
RRRRRRRR!!
RAHH
RAHH
...
KYAA
RRRRRRRR!!
YAHH
RRRRRRRR!!
RAHH
RAHH
RRR...
CLICK!!

SBS Question Corner

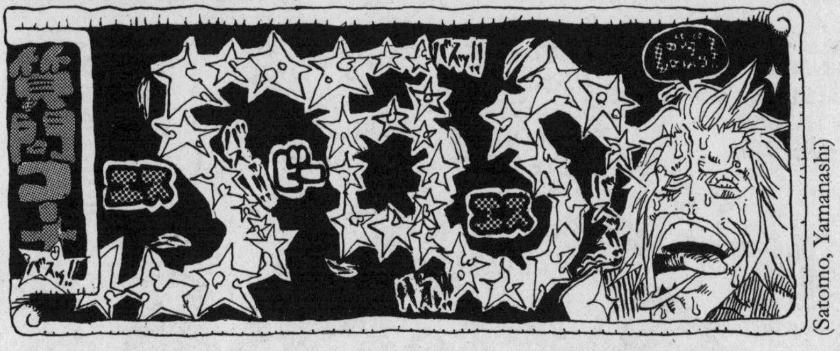

(Satomo, Yamanashi)

Q: What do you think of how young people are driving cars less and less?
--Maeda A.K.A. Kimotowa

A: Hmmmmm... Hmmmm. I don't care.

Q: Tell me the name of the penguin Mr. Kuzan was riding! Is he related to the Galapagos penguin?! Was he treading water under the surface the entire time he was waiting for Mr. Kuzan?! He's so cute, I can't help but want to know more! Tell me!!
--Kunugi

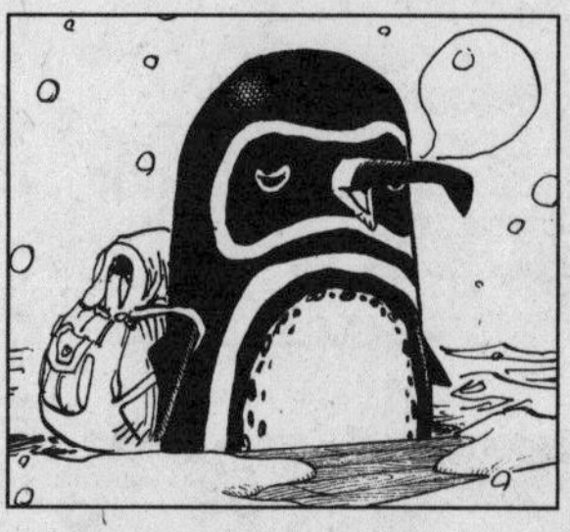

A: Yep, that's a big penguin. He's a member of the "super penguin" species, which is very adept at treading water. He fits well with Kuzan's Chilly-Chilly style, and has been accompanying him since he left the Navy. His name is Camel. Also, he's a hardboiled dude, so don't call him cute or you'll get burned.

Q: I have a question. Is the character of Borsalino based on Kunie Tanaka's role of "Borsalino 2" from the movie *Truck Yaro: Bakuso Ichiban-boshi?*
--AkuaNoichigo

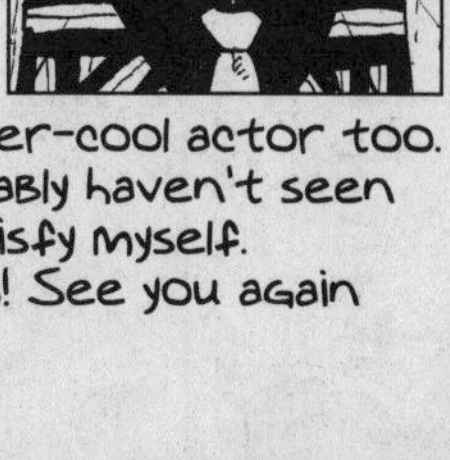

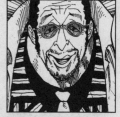

A: You saw that movie?! That's fantastic. It's quite an old film. I wonder if it's out on DVD and Blu-ray now. I have the entire Truck Yaro series on VHS tapes. You are correct, Borsalino comes from that role. There's an Alain Delon film called Borsalino as well, and I suspect that Kunie Tanaka's character was named in homage to that movie. Alain Delon's a super-cool actor too. His movies are older, so most people probably haven't seen them. I don't mind, though. I did this to satisfy myself. That's all for this installment of the SBS! See you again soon!!

Chapter 700:
HIS MOMENTUM

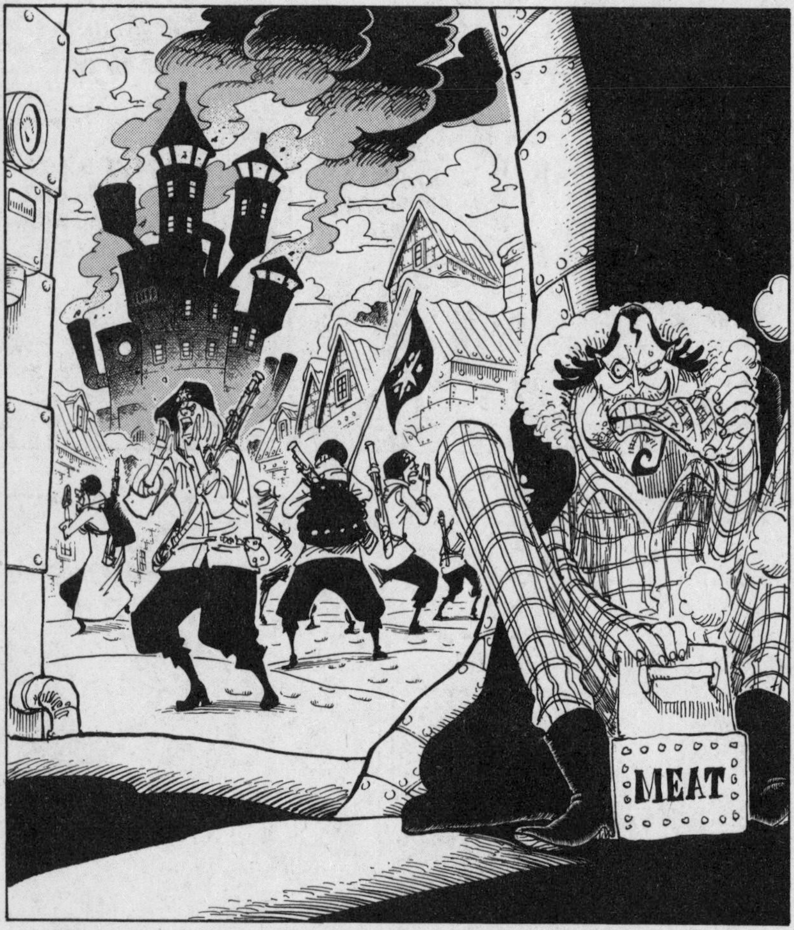
MEAT

CARIBOU'S NEW WORLD KEE HEE HEE, VOL. 21: "GOT CURIOUS AND RETURNED TO TOWN, WHERE I'M A WANTED MAN"

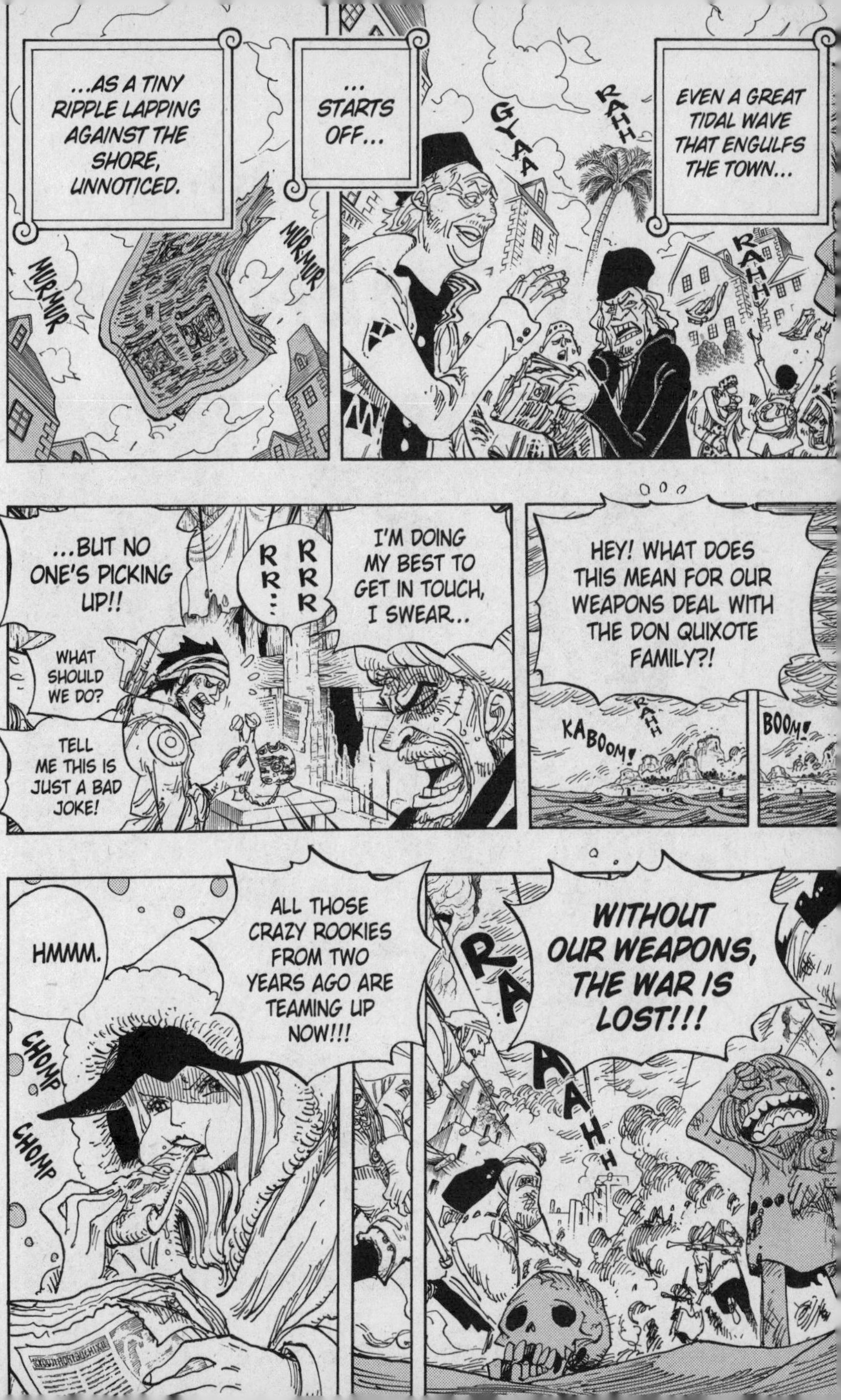
EVEN A GREAT TIDAL WAVE THAT ENGULFS THE TOWN...
RAHH
GYAAA
RAHH
... STARTS OFF...
...AS A TINY RIPPLE LAPPING AGAINST THE SHORE, UNNOTICED.
MUR-MUR
MUR-MUR
HEY! WHAT DOES THIS MEAN FOR OUR WEAPONS DEAL WITH THE DON QUIXOTE FAMILY?!
RAHH
BOOM!
KABOOM!
I'M DOING MY BEST TO GET IN TOUCH, I SWEAR...
RRR
RR...
...BUT NO ONE'S PICKING UP!!
WHAT SHOULD WE DO?
TELL ME THIS IS JUST A BAD JOKE!
WITHOUT OUR WEAPONS, THE WAR IS LOST!!!
RAAAHH
ALL THOSE CRAZY ROOKIES FROM TWO YEARS AGO ARE TEAMING UP NOW!!!
HMMM.
CHOMP
CHOMP

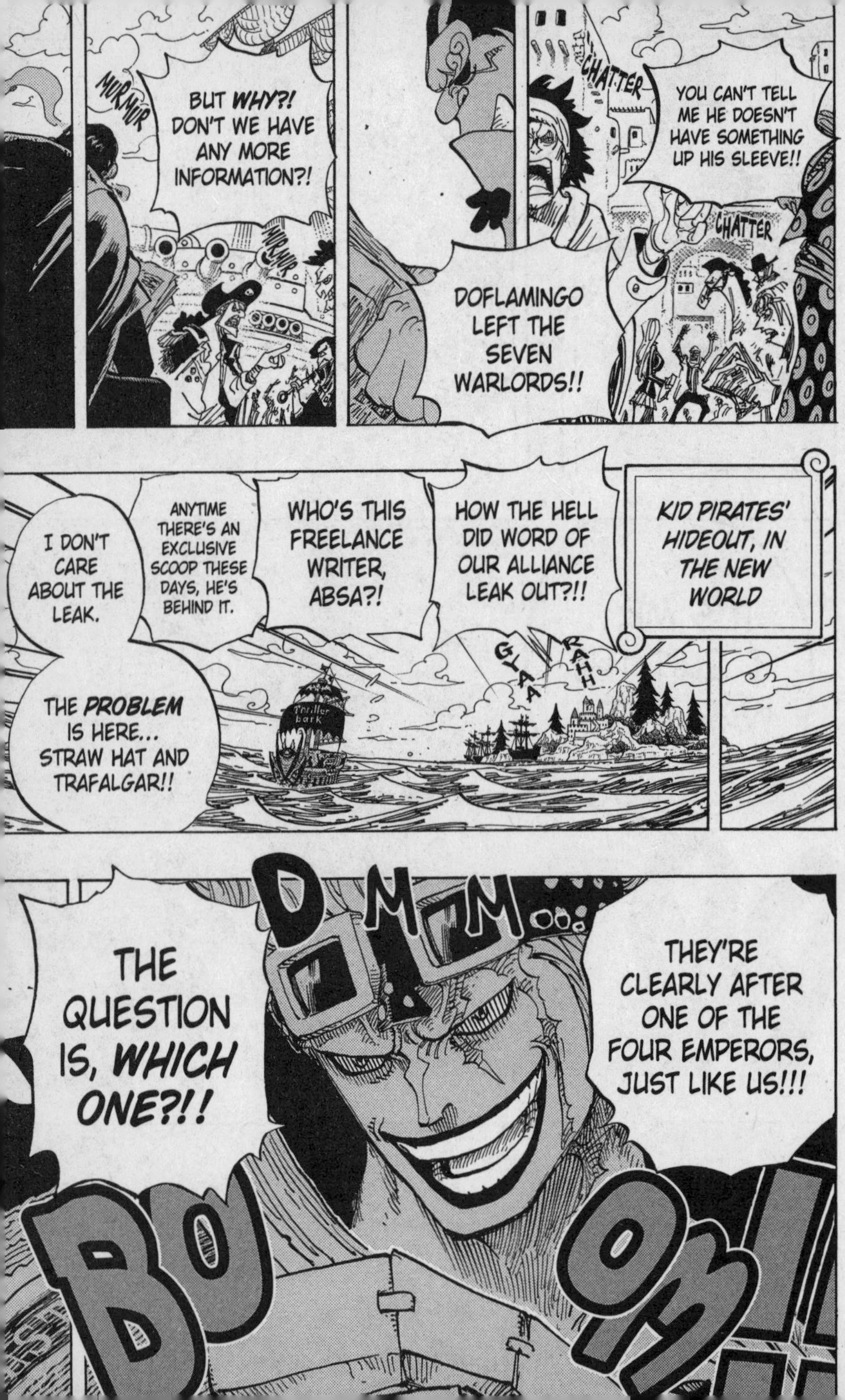
YOU CAN'T TELL ME HE DOESN'T HAVE SOMETHING UP HIS SLEEVE!!
CHATTER
CHATTER
DOFLAMINGO LEFT THE SEVEN WARLORDS!!
MURMUR
BUT WHY?! DON'T WE HAVE ANY MORE INFORMATION?!
MURMUR
KID PIRATES' HIDEOUT, IN THE NEW WORLD
HOW THE HELL DID WORD OF OUR ALLIANCE LEAK OUT?!!
GYAA
RAHH
WHO'S THIS FREELANCE WRITER, ABSA?!
ANYTIME THERE'S AN EXCLUSIVE SCOOP THESE DAYS, HE'S BEHIND IT.
I DON'T CARE ABOUT THE LEAK.
THE PROBLEM IS HERE... STRAW HAT AND TRAFALGAR!!
THEY'RE CLEARLY AFTER ONE OF THE FOUR EMPERORS, JUST LIKE US!!!
DMM
THE QUESTION IS, WHICH ONE?!!
BOOM!!

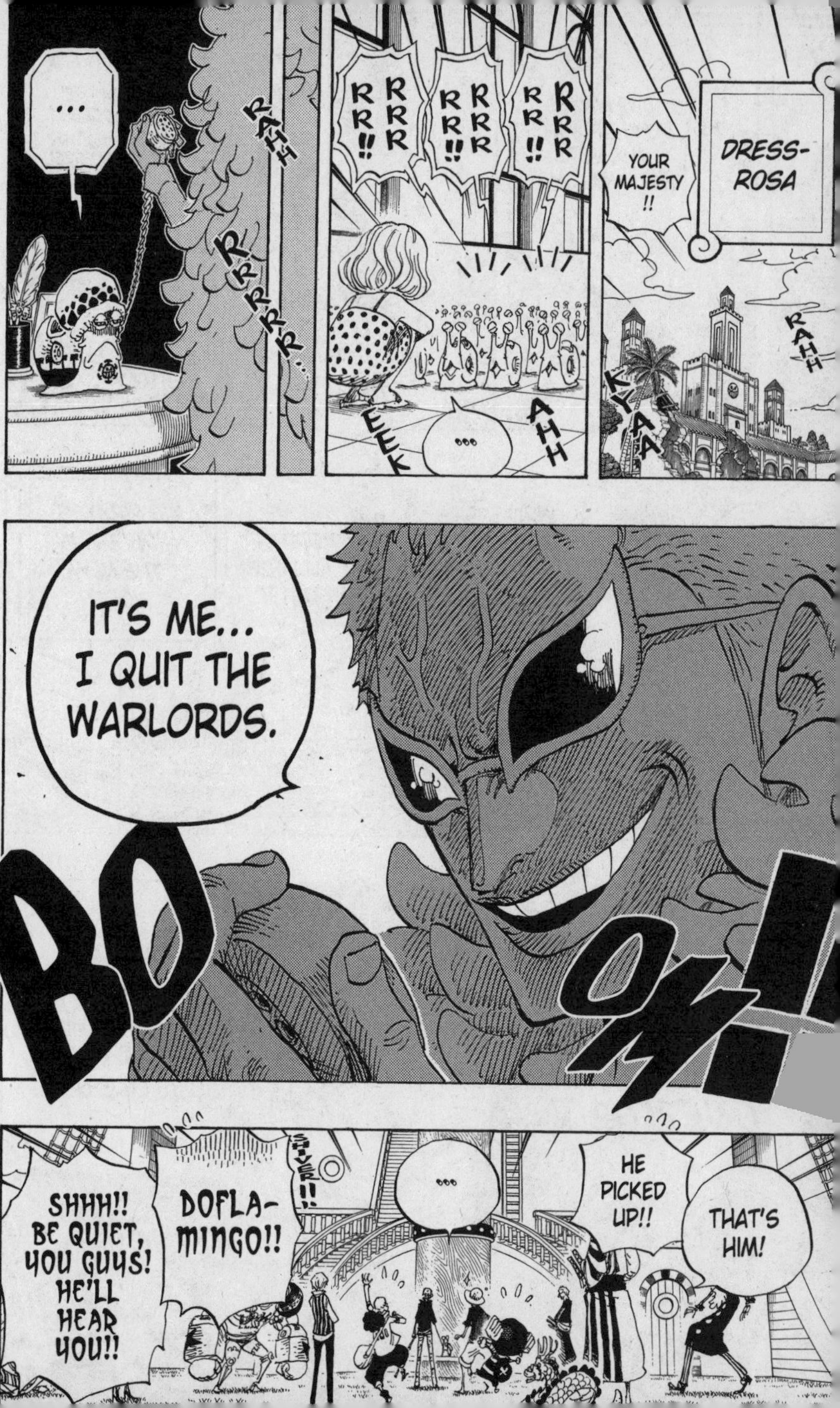
DRESS-ROSA
YOUR MAJESTY!!
RAHH
KYAA
RRRRR!!
RRRRR!!
RRRRR!!
EEEK
...
AHH
...
RAHH
RRRRR...
IT'S ME... I QUIT THE WARLORDS.
BOOM!!
THAT'S HIM!
HE PICKED UP!!
...
SHIVER!!
DOFLAMINGO!!
SHHH!! BE QUIET, YOU GUYS! HE'LL HEAR YOU!!

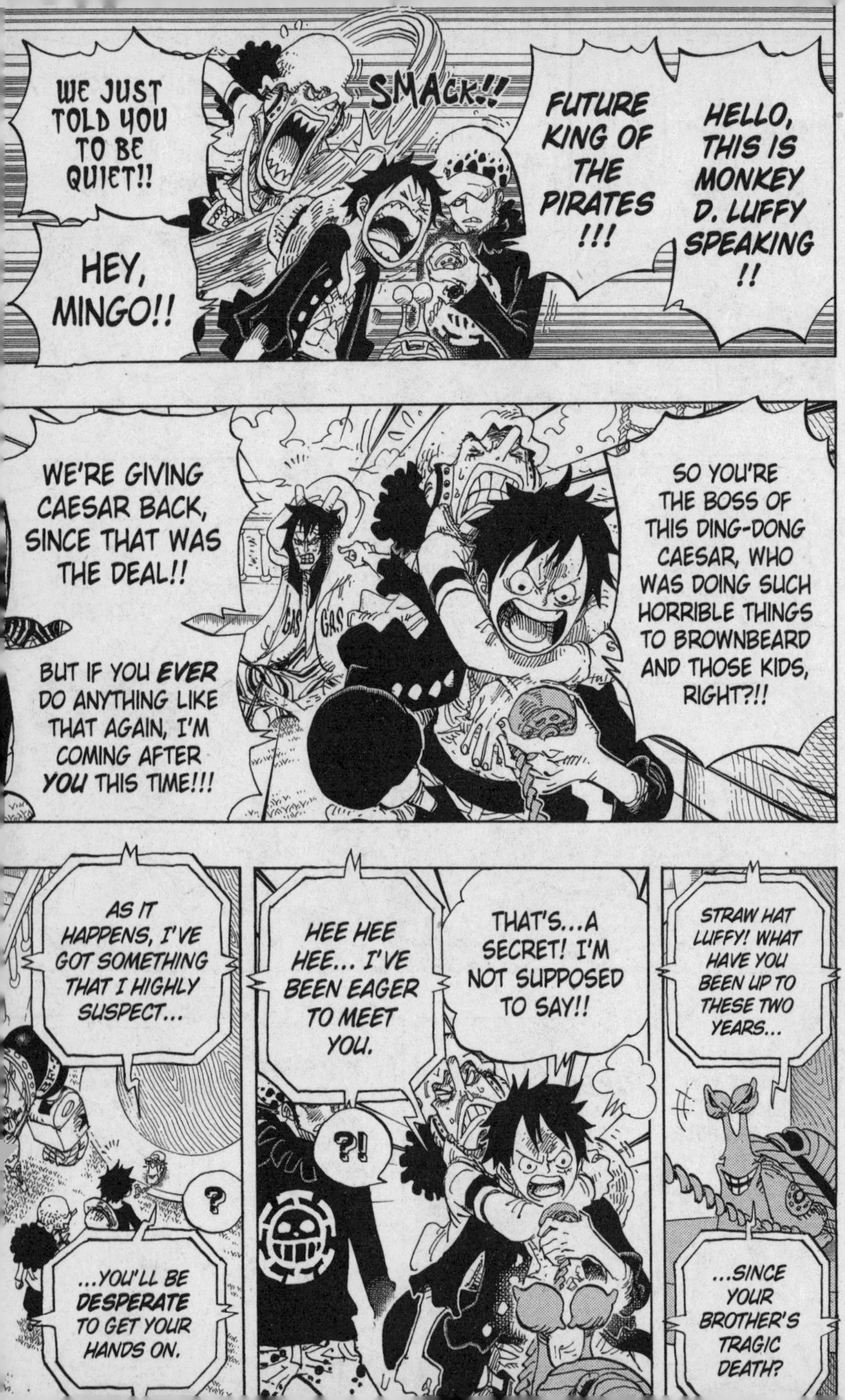
HELLO, THIS IS MONKEY D. LUFFY SPEAKING!!
FUTURE KING OF THE PIRATES!!!
SMACK!!
WE JUST TOLD YOU TO BE QUIET!!
HEY, MINGO!!
SO YOU'RE THE BOSS OF THIS DING-DONG CAESAR, WHO WAS DOING SUCH HORRIBLE THINGS TO BROWNBEARD AND THOSE KIDS, RIGHT?!!
WE'RE GIVING CAESAR BACK, SINCE THAT WAS THE DEAL!!
BUT IF YOU EVER DO ANYTHING LIKE THAT AGAIN, I'M COMING AFTER YOU THIS TIME!!!
STRAW HAT LUFFY! WHAT HAVE YOU BEEN UP TO THESE TWO YEARS...
...SINCE YOUR BROTHER'S TRAGIC DEATH?
THAT'S...A SECRET! I'M NOT SUPPOSED TO SAY!!
HEE HEE HEE... I'VE BEEN EAGER TO MEET YOU.
?!
AS IT HAPPENS, I'VE GOT SOMETHING THAT I HIGHLY SUSPECT...
?
...YOU'LL BE DESPERATE TO GET YOUR HANDS ON.

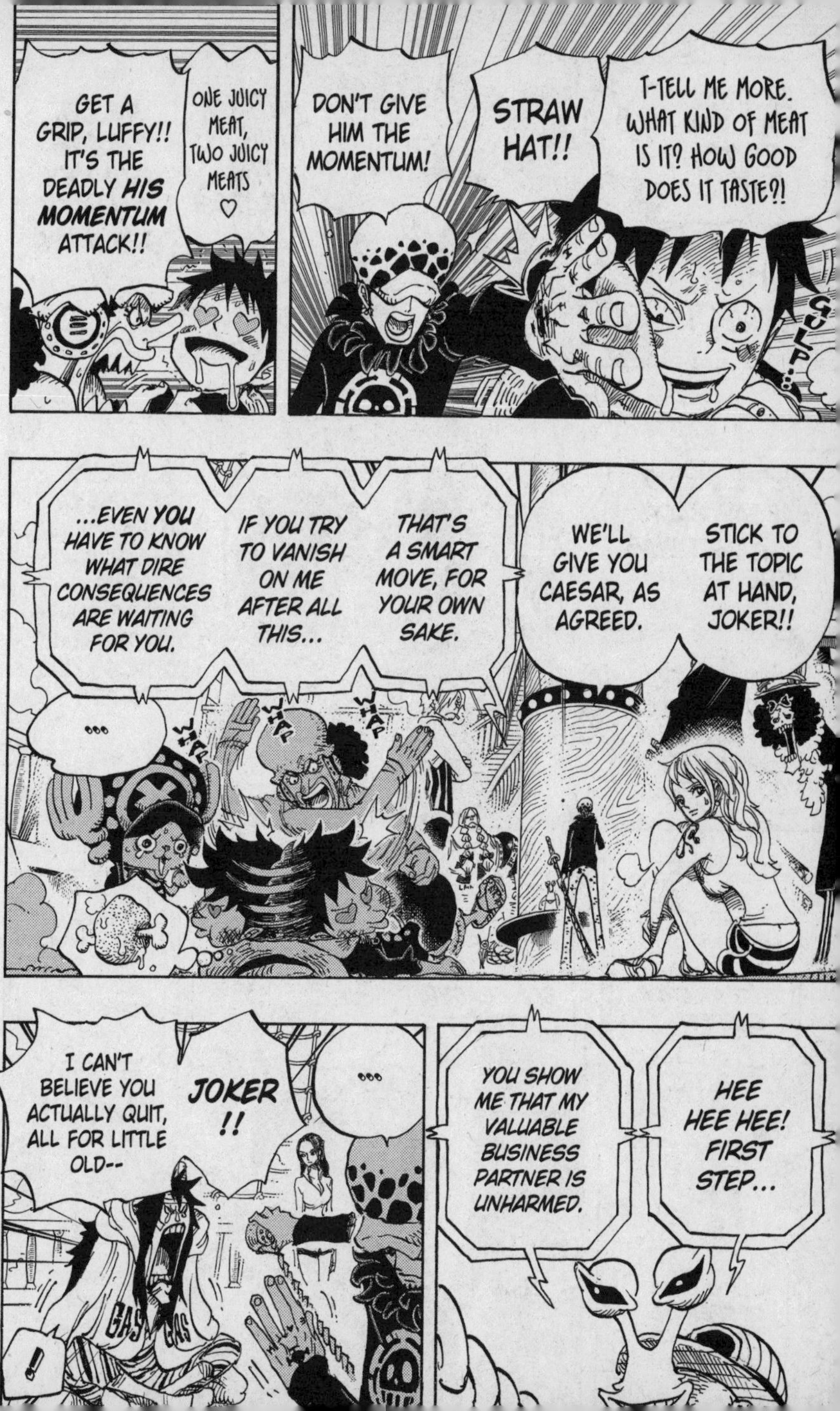
T-TELL ME MORE. WHAT KIND OF MEAT IS IT? HOW GOOD DOES IT TASTE?!
STRAW HAT!!
DON'T GIVE HIM THE MOMENTUM!
GULP...
ONE JUICY MEAT, TWO JUICY MEATS ♡
GET A GRIP, LUFFY!! IT'S THE DEADLY **HIS MOMENTUM** ATTACK!!
STICK TO THE TOPIC AT HAND, JOKER!!
WE'LL GIVE YOU CAESAR, AS AGREED.
THAT'S A SMART MOVE, FOR YOUR OWN SAKE.
IF YOU TRY TO VANISH ON ME AFTER ALL THIS...
...EVEN **YOU** HAVE TO KNOW WHAT DIRE CONSEQUENCES ARE WAITING FOR YOU.
WHAP
WHAP
WHAP
...
HEE HEE HEE! FIRST STEP...
YOU SHOW ME THAT MY VALUABLE BUSINESS PARTNER IS UNHARMED.
...
JOKER!!
I CAN'T BELIEVE YOU ACTUALLY QUIT, ALL FOR LITTLE OLD--
!

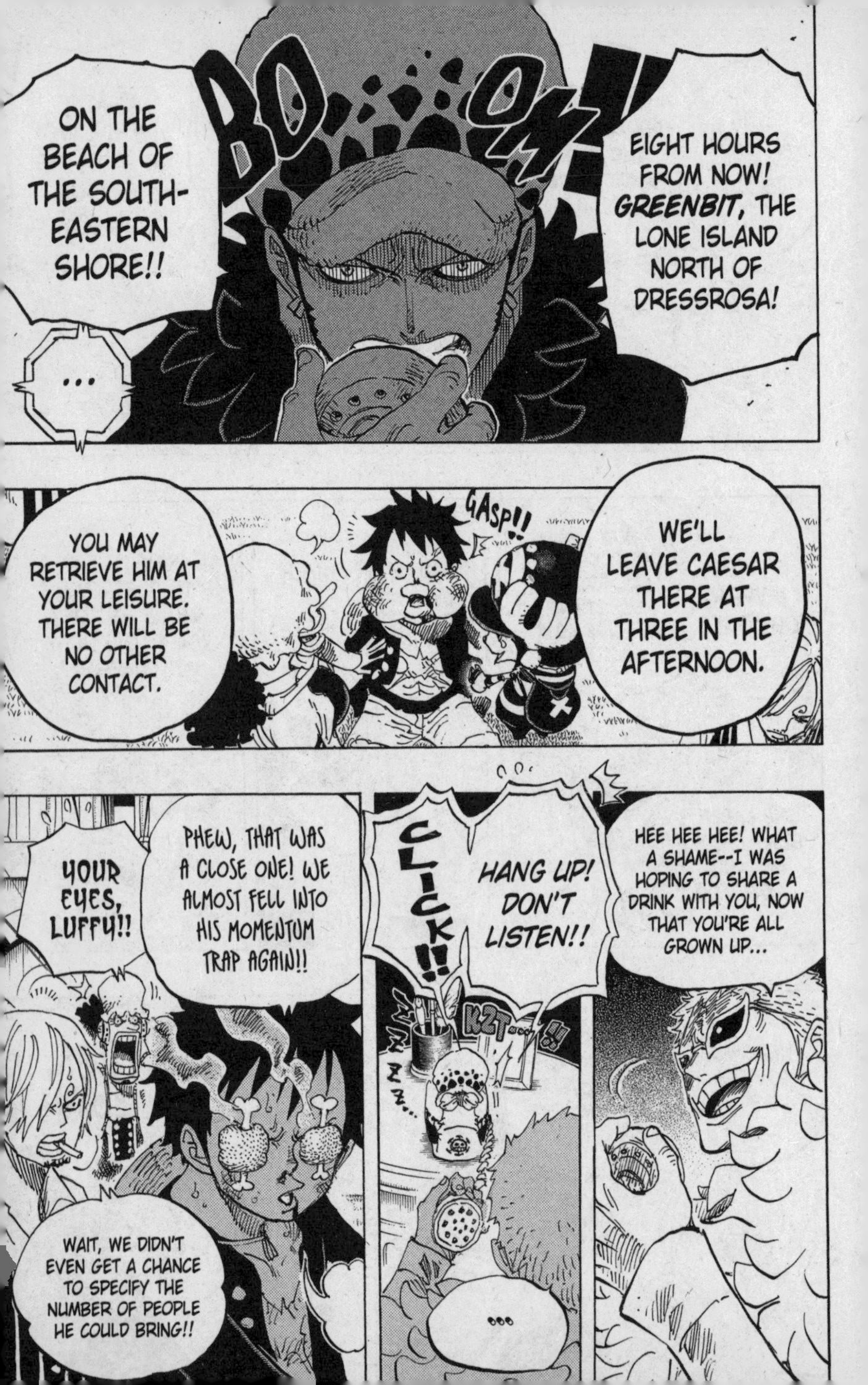
EIGHT HOURS FROM NOW! GREENBIT, THE LONE ISLAND NORTH OF DRESSROSA!
BOOM
ON THE BEACH OF THE SOUTH-EASTERN SHORE!!
...
WE'LL LEAVE CAESAR THERE AT THREE IN THE AFTERNOON.
GASP!!
YOU MAY RETRIEVE HIM AT YOUR LEISURE. THERE WILL BE NO OTHER CONTACT.
HEE HEE HEE! WHAT A SHAME--I WAS HOPING TO SHARE A DRINK WITH YOU, NOW THAT YOU'RE ALL GROWN UP...
HANG UP! DON'T LISTEN!!
CLICK!!
KZT...!!
...
PHEW, THAT WAS A CLOSE ONE! WE ALMOST FELL INTO HIS MOMENTUM TRAP AGAIN!!
YOUR EYES, LUFFY!!
WAIT, WE DIDN'T EVEN GET A CHANCE TO SPECIFY THE NUMBER OF PEOPLE HE COULD BRING!!

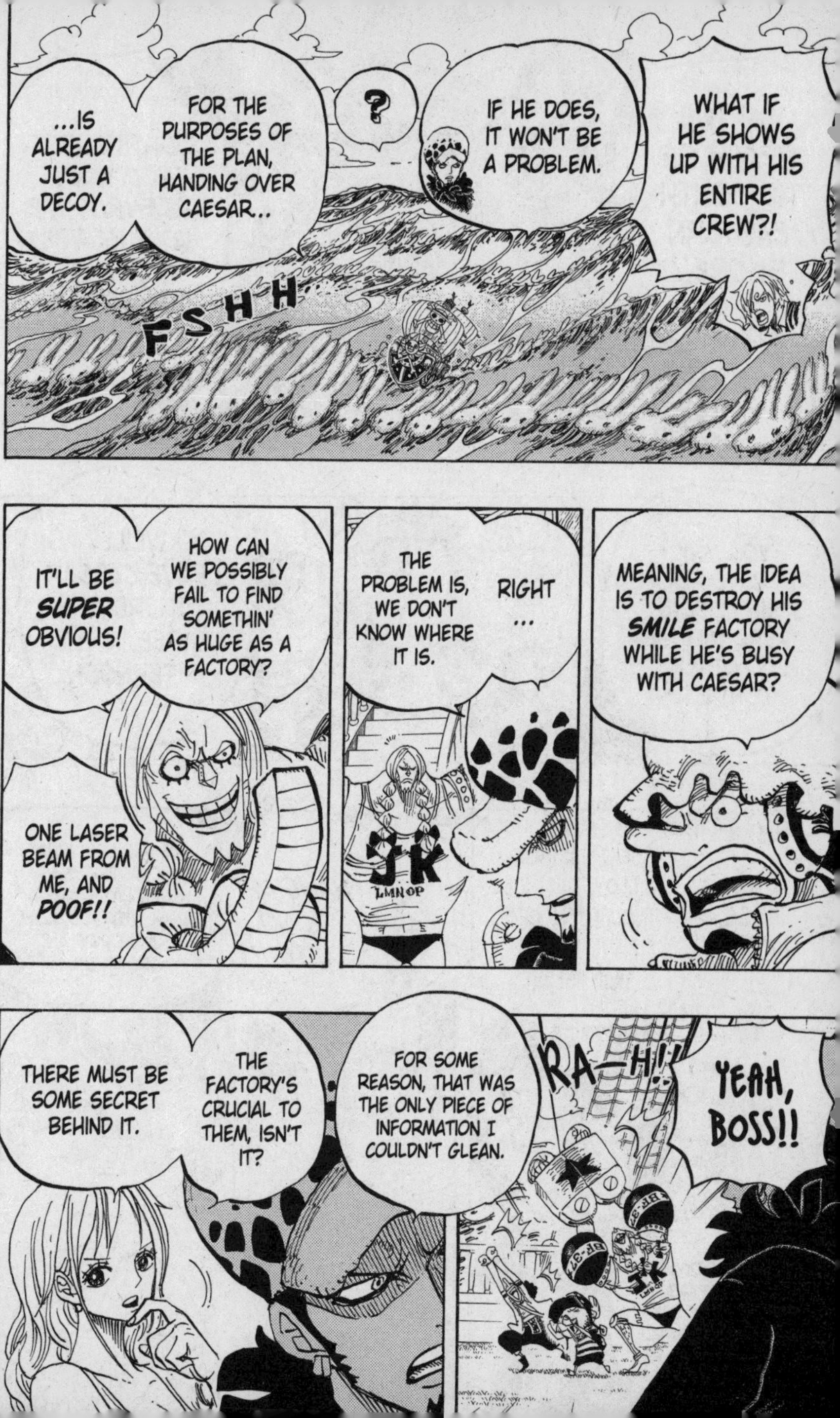
WHAT IF HE SHOWS UP WITH HIS ENTIRE CREW?!
IF HE DOES, IT WON'T BE A PROBLEM.
?
FOR THE PURPOSES OF THE PLAN, HANDING OVER CAESAR...
...IS ALREADY JUST A DECOY.
FSHH
MEANING, THE IDEA IS TO DESTROY HIS *SMILE* FACTORY WHILE HE'S BUSY WITH CAESAR?
RIGHT...
THE PROBLEM IS, WE DON'T KNOW WHERE IT IS.
HOW CAN WE POSSIBLY FAIL TO FIND SOMETHIN' AS HUGE AS A FACTORY?
IT'LL BE *SUPER* OBVIOUS!
ONE LASER BEAM FROM ME, AND *POOF!!*
YEAH, BOSS!!
RA-H!!
FOR SOME REASON, THAT WAS THE ONLY PIECE OF INFORMATION I COULDN'T GLEAN.
THE FACTORY'S CRUCIAL TO THEM, ISN'T IT?
THERE MUST BE SOME SECRET BEHIND IT.

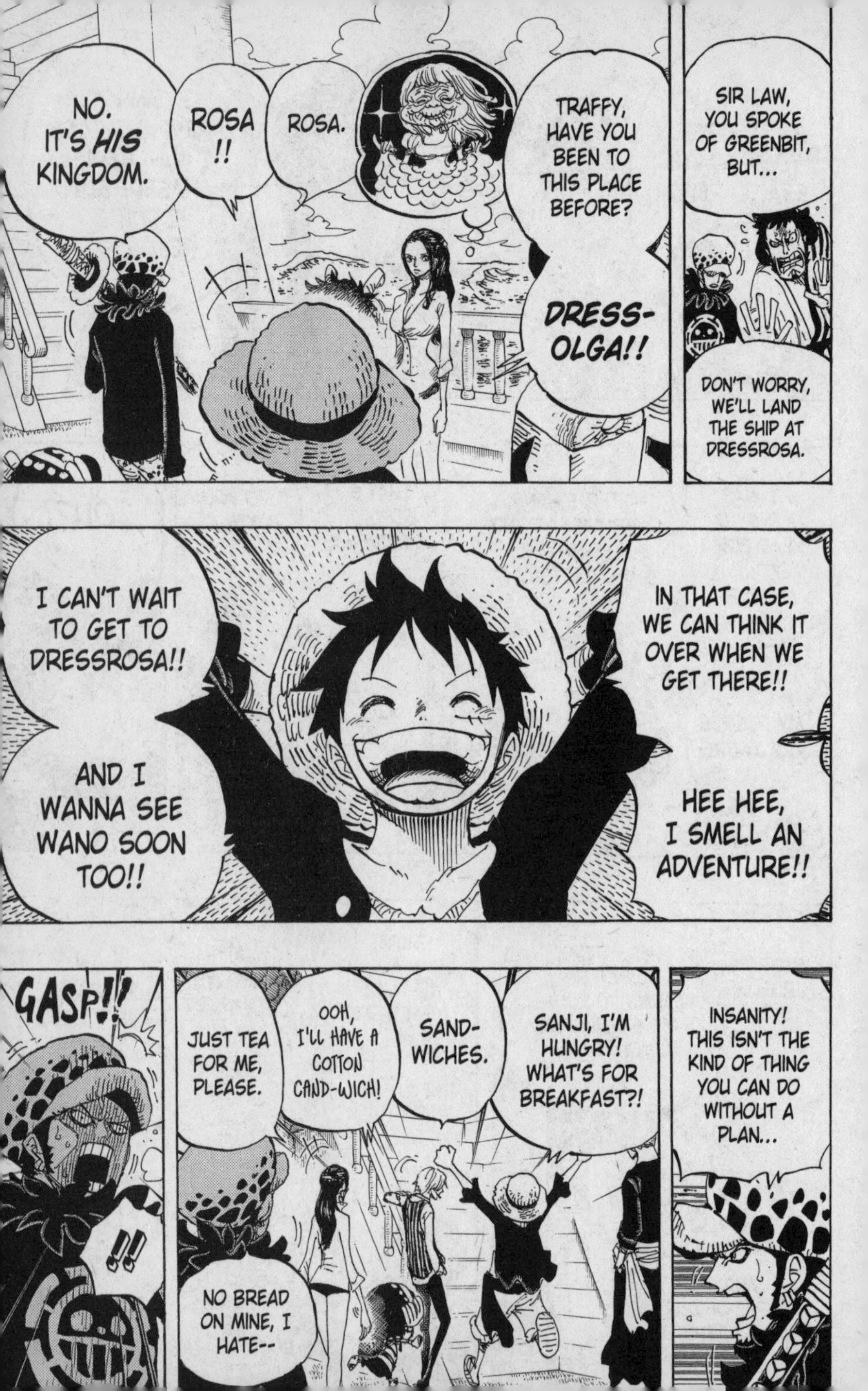
SIR LAW, YOU SPOKE OF GREENBIT, BUT...
DON'T WORRY, WE'LL LAND THE SHIP AT DRESSROSA.
TRAFFY, HAVE YOU BEEN TO THIS PLACE BEFORE?
DRESS-OLGA!!
ROSA.
ROSA !!
NO. IT'S *HIS* KINGDOM.
IN THAT CASE, WE CAN THINK IT OVER WHEN WE GET THERE!!
HEE HEE, I SMELL AN ADVENTURE!!
I CAN'T WAIT TO GET TO DRESSROSA!!
AND I WANNA SEE WANO SOON TOO!!
INSANITY! THIS ISN'T THE KIND OF THING YOU CAN DO WITHOUT A PLAN...
SANJI, I'M HUNGRY! WHAT'S FOR BREAKFAST?!
SAND-WICHES.
OOH, I'LL HAVE A COTTON CAND-WICH!
JUST TEA FOR ME, PLEASE.
NO BREAD ON MINE, I HATE--
GASP!!
!!

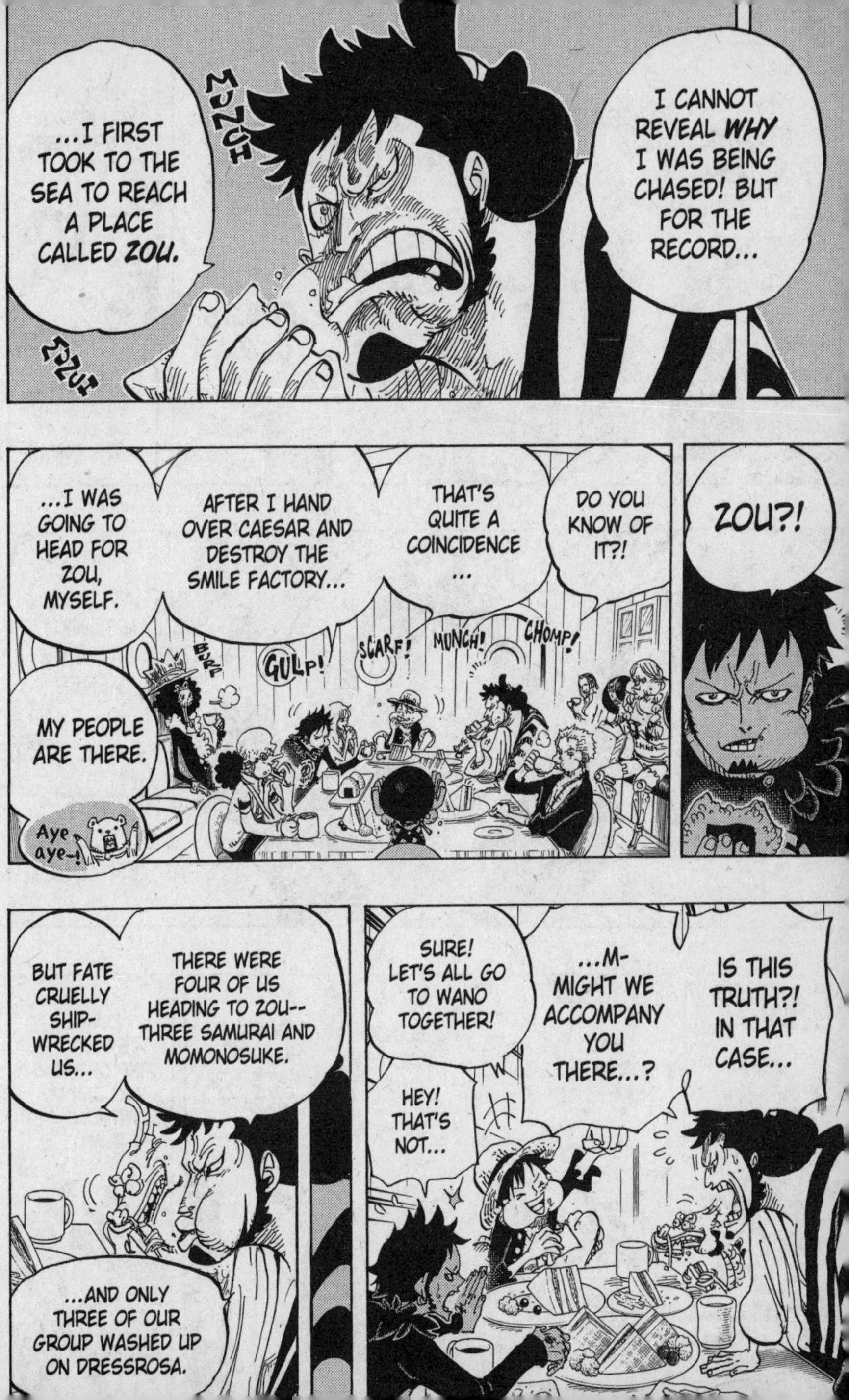
I CANNOT REVEAL *WHY* I WAS BEING CHASED! BUT FOR THE RECORD...
...I FIRST TOOK TO THE SEA TO REACH A PLACE CALLED **ZOU**.
MUNCH
MUNCH
ZOU?!
DO YOU KNOW OF IT?!
THAT'S QUITE A COINCIDENCE ...
AFTER I HAND OVER CAESAR AND DESTROY THE SMILE FACTORY...
...I WAS GOING TO HEAD FOR ZOU, MYSELF.
CHOMP!
MUNCH!
SCARF!
GULP!
BURP
MY PEOPLE ARE THERE.
Aye aye-!
IS THIS TRUTH?! IN THAT CASE...
...M-MIGHT WE ACCOMPANY YOU THERE...?
SURE! LET'S ALL GO TO WANO TOGETHER!
HEY! THAT'S NOT...
THERE WERE FOUR OF US HEADING TO ZOU-- THREE SAMURAI AND MOMONOSUKE.
BUT FATE CRUELLY SHIP-WRECKED US...
...AND ONLY THREE OF OUR GROUP WASHED UP ON DRESSROSA.

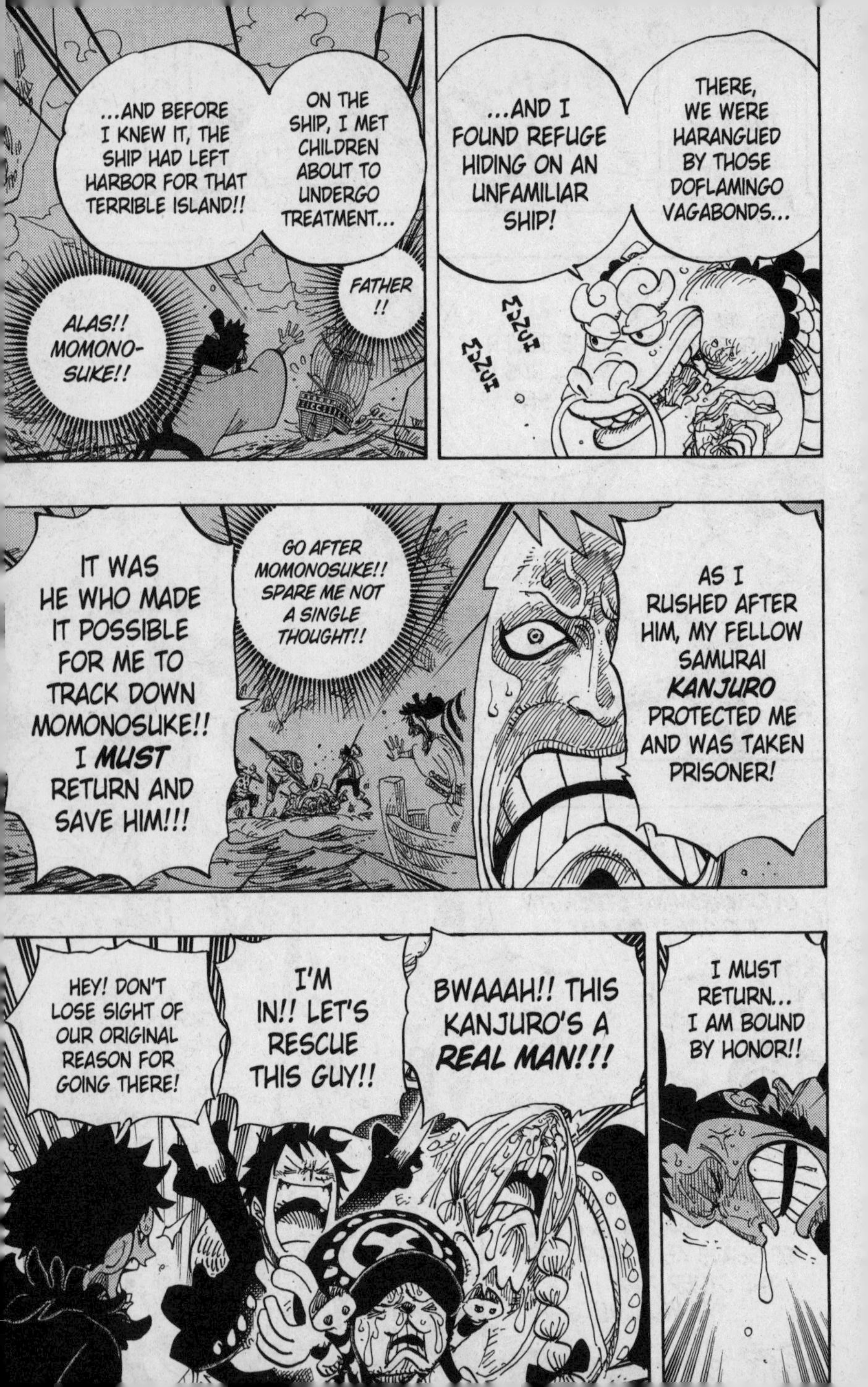
THERE, WE WERE HARANGUED BY THOSE DOFLAMINGO VAGABONDS...
...AND I FOUND REFUGE HIDING ON AN UNFAMILIAR SHIP!
ON THE SHIP, I MET CHILDREN ABOUT TO UNDERGO TREATMENT...
...AND BEFORE I KNEW IT, THE SHIP HAD LEFT HARBOR FOR THAT TERRIBLE ISLAND!!
FATHER!!
ALAS!! MOMONOSUKE!!
AS I RUSHED AFTER HIM, MY FELLOW SAMURAI KANJURO PROTECTED ME AND WAS TAKEN PRISONER!
GO AFTER MOMONOSUKE!! SPARE ME NOT A SINGLE THOUGHT!!
IT WAS HE WHO MADE IT POSSIBLE FOR ME TO TRACK DOWN MOMONOSUKE!! I MUST RETURN AND SAVE HIM!!!
I MUST RETURN... I AM BOUND BY HONOR!!
BWAAAH!! THIS KANJURO'S A REAL MAN!!!
I'M IN!! LET'S RESCUE THIS GUY!!
HEY! DON'T LOSE SIGHT OF OUR ORIGINAL REASON FOR GOING THERE!

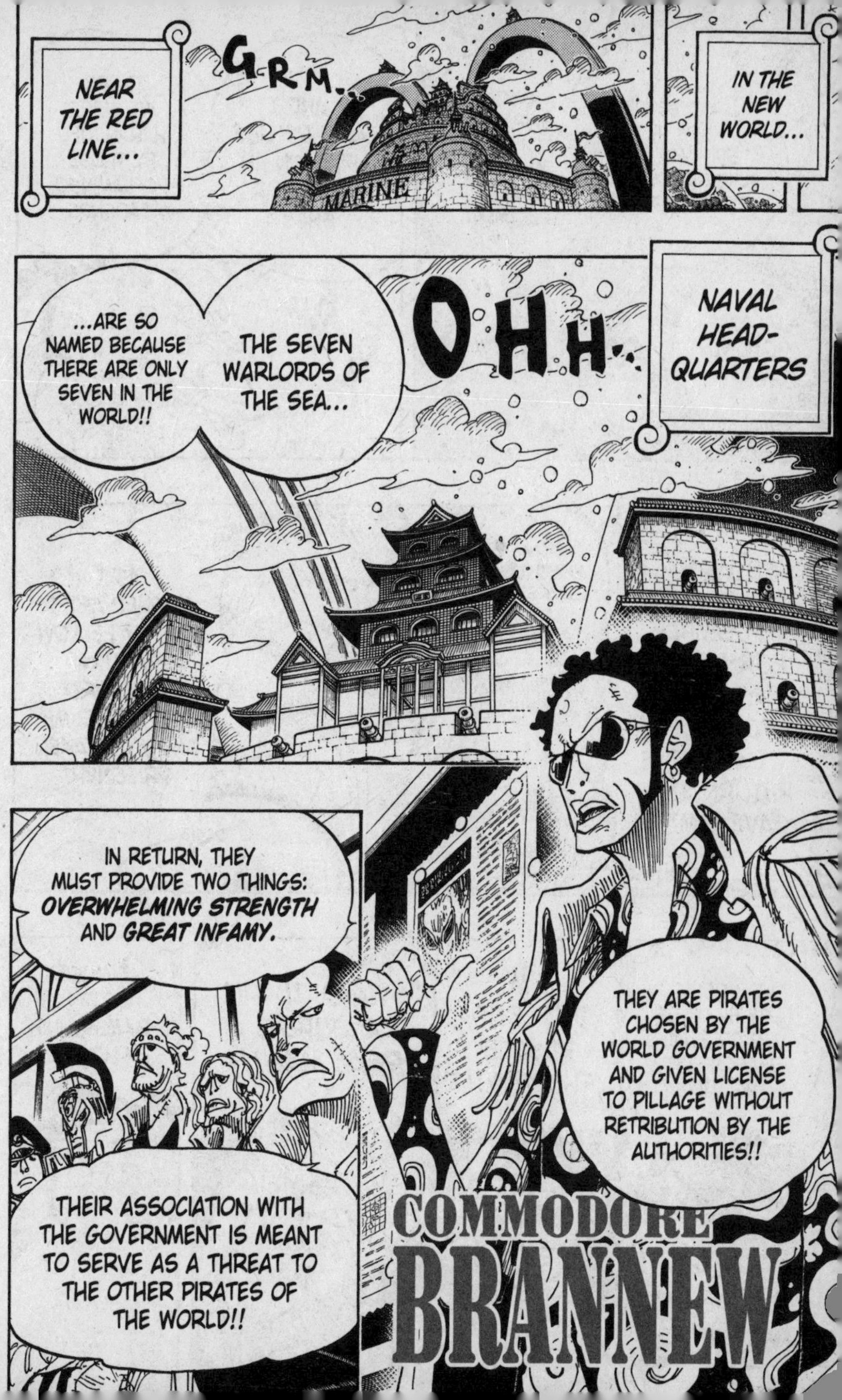
IN THE NEW WORLD...
NEAR THE RED LINE...
GRM..
MARINE
NAVAL HEAD-QUARTERS
OHH..
THE SEVEN WARLORDS OF THE SEA...
...ARE SO NAMED BECAUSE THERE ARE ONLY SEVEN IN THE WORLD!!
COMMODORE BRANNEW
THEY ARE PIRATES CHOSEN BY THE WORLD GOVERNMENT AND GIVEN LICENSE TO PILLAGE WITHOUT RETRIBUTION BY THE AUTHORITIES!!
IN RETURN, THEY MUST PROVIDE TWO THINGS: ***OVERWHELMING STRENGTH*** AND ***GREAT INFAMY.***
THEIR ASSOCIATION WITH THE GOVERNMENT IS MEANT TO SERVE AS A THREAT TO THE OTHER PIRATES OF THE WORLD!!

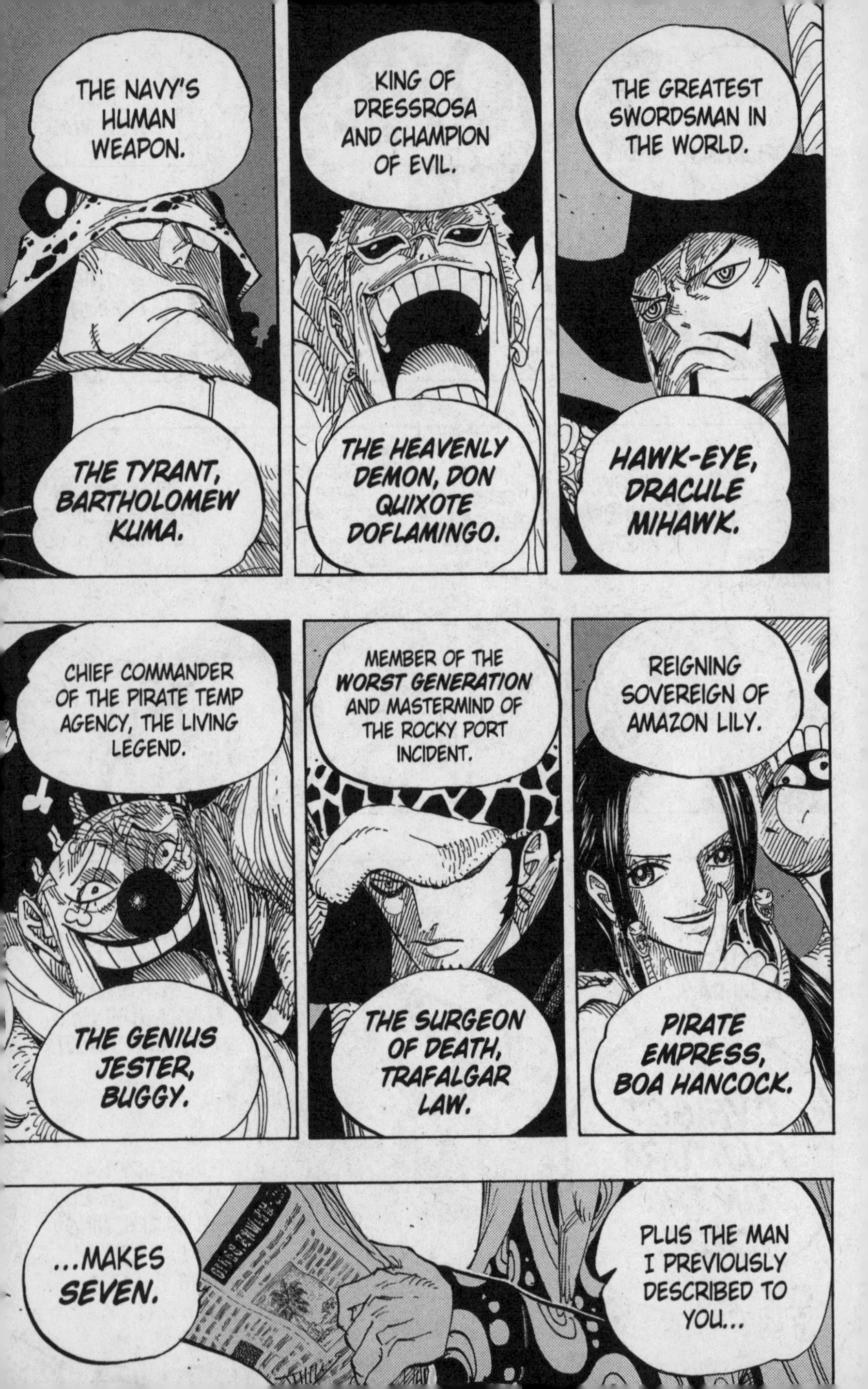
THE GREATEST SWORDSMAN IN THE WORLD.
HAWK-EYE, DRACULE MIHAWK.
KING OF DRESSROSA AND CHAMPION OF EVIL.
THE HEAVENLY DEMON, DON QUIXOTE DOFLAMINGO.
THE NAVY'S HUMAN WEAPON.
THE TYRANT, BARTHOLOMEW KUMA.
REIGNING SOVEREIGN OF AMAZON LILY.
PIRATE EMPRESS, BOA HANCOCK.
MEMBER OF THE WORST GENERATION AND MASTERMIND OF THE ROCKY PORT INCIDENT.
THE SURGEON OF DEATH, TRAFALGAR LAW.
CHIEF COMMANDER OF THE PIRATE TEMP AGENCY, THE LIVING LEGEND.
THE GENIUS JESTER, BUGGY.
PLUS THE MAN I PREVIOUSLY DESCRIBED TO YOU...
...MAKES SEVEN.

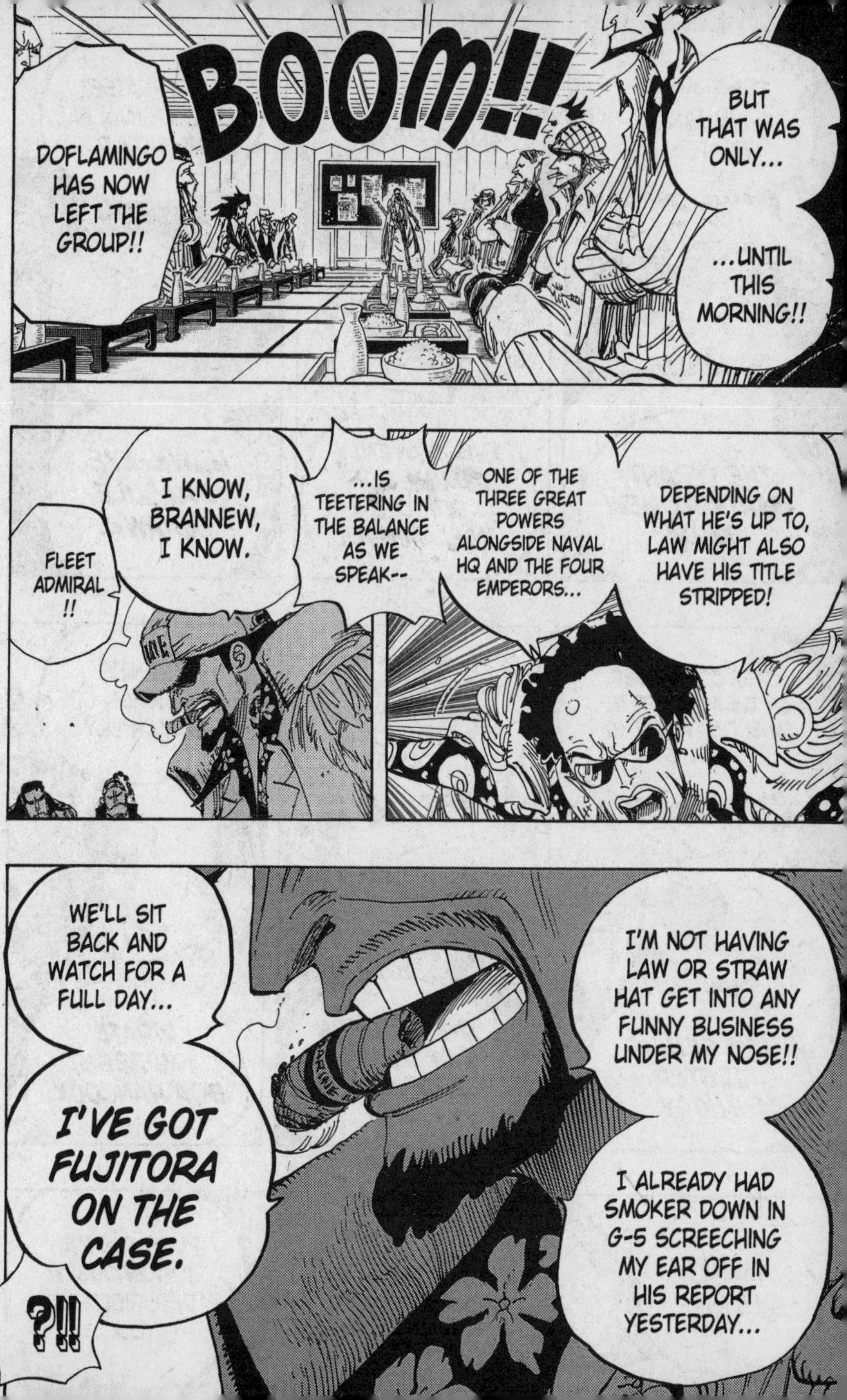
BUT THAT WAS ONLY...
...UNTIL THIS MORNING!!
BOOM!!
DOFLAMINGO HAS NOW LEFT THE GROUP!!
DEPENDING ON WHAT HE'S UP TO, LAW MIGHT ALSO HAVE HIS TITLE STRIPPED!
ONE OF THE THREE GREAT POWERS ALONGSIDE NAVAL HQ AND THE FOUR EMPERORS...
...IS TEETERING IN THE BALANCE AS WE SPEAK--
I KNOW, BRANNEW, I KNOW.
FLEET ADMIRAL!!
I'M NOT HAVING LAW OR STRAW HAT GET INTO ANY FUNNY BUSINESS UNDER MY NOSE!!
I ALREADY HAD SMOKER DOWN IN G-5 SCREECHING MY EAR OFF IN HIS REPORT YESTERDAY...
WE'LL SIT BACK AND WATCH FOR A FULL DAY...
I'VE GOT FUJITORA ON THE CASE.
?!!

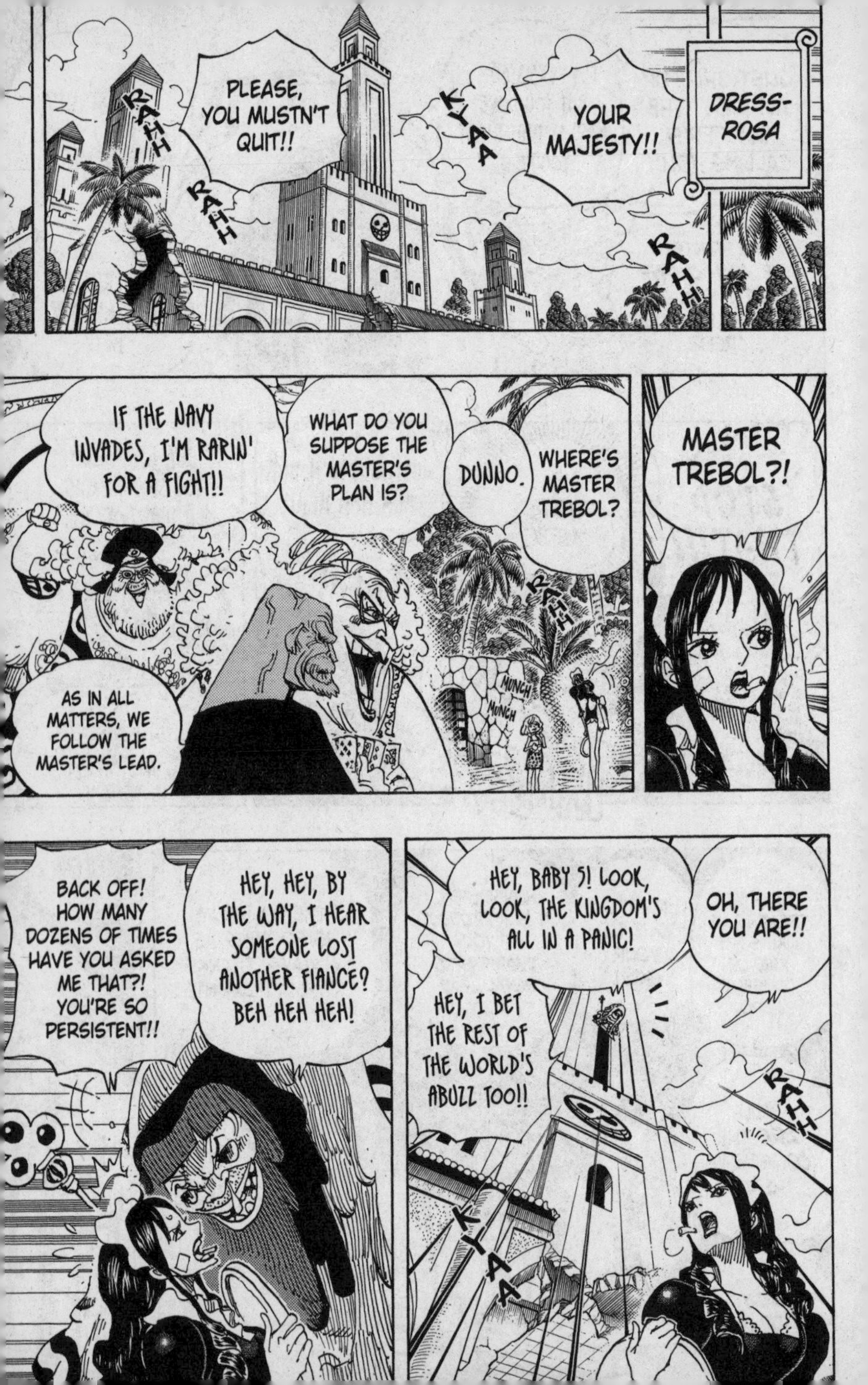

DRESS-ROSA
YOUR MAJESTY!!
KYAA
PLEASE, YOU MUSTN'T QUIT!!
RAHH
RAHH
RAHH
MASTER TREBOL?!
WHERE'S MASTER TREBOL?
DUNNO.
WHAT DO YOU SUPPOSE THE MASTER'S PLAN IS?
IF THE NAVY INVADES, I'M RARIN' FOR A FIGHT!!
RAHH
MUNCH
MUNCH
AS IN ALL MATTERS, WE FOLLOW THE MASTER'S LEAD.
OH, THERE YOU ARE!!
HEY, BABY 5! LOOK, LOOK, THE KINGDOM'S ALL IN A PANIC!
HEY, I BET THE REST OF THE WORLD'S ABUZZ TOO!!
RAHH
KYAA
HEY, HEY, BY THE WAY, I HEAR SOMEONE LOST ANOTHER FIANCÉ? BEH HEH HEH!
BACK OFF! HOW MANY DOZENS OF TIMES HAVE YOU ASKED ME THAT?! YOU'RE SO PERSISTENT!!

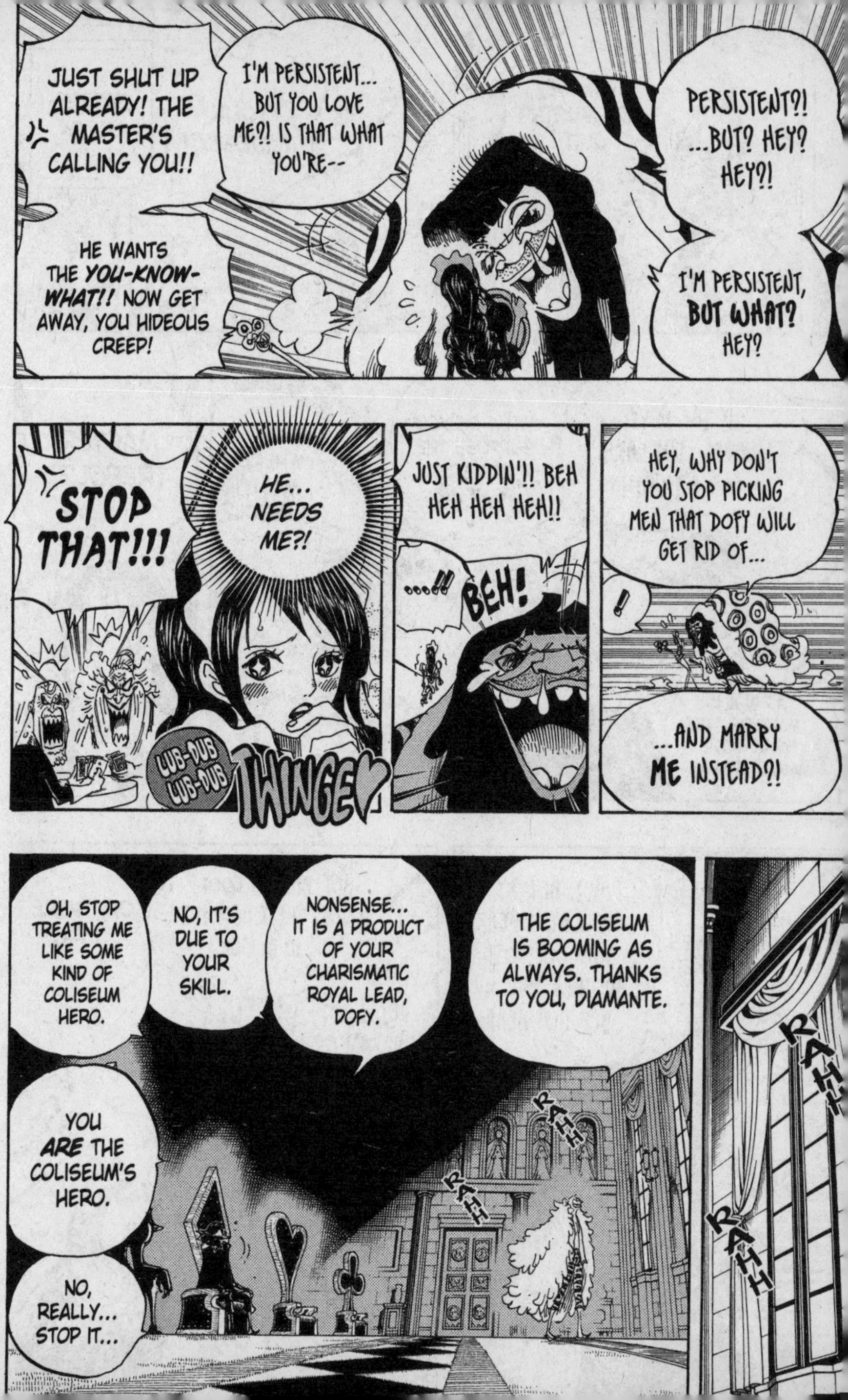
PERSISTENT?! ...BUT? HEY? HEY?!
I'M PERSISTENT, BUT WHAT? HEY?
I'M PERSISTENT... BUT YOU LOVE ME?! IS THAT WHAT YOU'RE--
JUST SHUT UP ALREADY! THE MASTER'S CALLING YOU!!
HE WANTS THE YOU-KNOW-WHAT!! NOW GET AWAY, YOU HIDEOUS CREEP!
HEY, WHY DON'T YOU STOP PICKING MEN THAT DOFY WILL GET RID OF...
!
...AND MARRY ME INSTEAD?!
JUST KIDDIN'!! BEH HEH HEH HEH!!
BEH!
...!!
HE... NEEDS ME?!
STOP THAT!!!
LUB-DUB LUB-DUB
THINGE
RAHH
RAHH
THE COLISEUM IS BOOMING AS ALWAYS. THANKS TO YOU, DIAMANTE.
NONSENSE... IT IS A PRODUCT OF YOUR CHARISMATIC ROYAL LEAD, DOFY.
NO, IT'S DUE TO YOUR SKILL.
OH, STOP TREATING ME LIKE SOME KIND OF COLISEUM HERO.
RAHH
RAHH
YOU ARE THE COLISEUM'S HERO.
NO, REALLY... STOP IT...

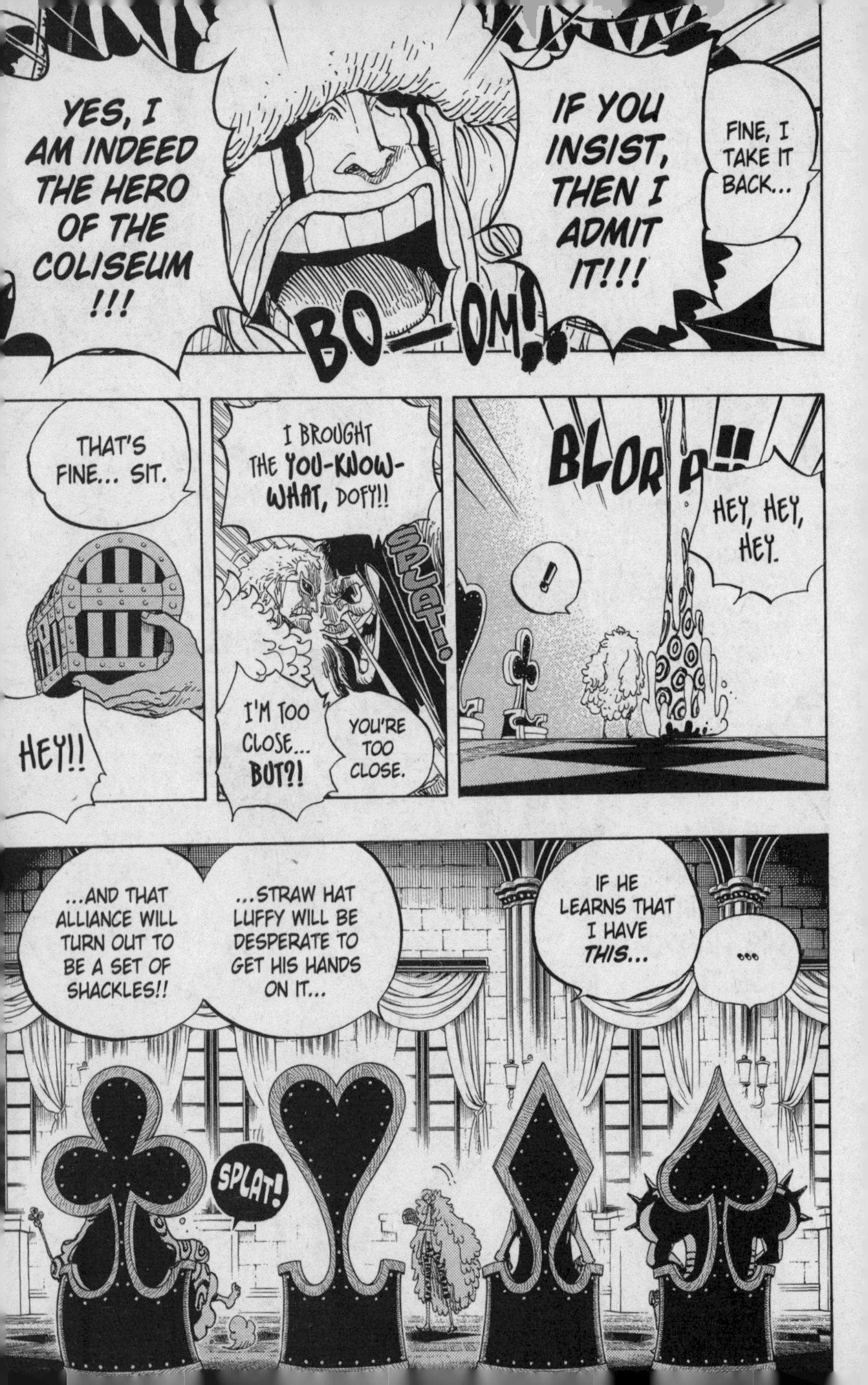
FINE, I TAKE IT BACK...
IF YOU INSIST, THEN I ADMIT IT!!!
BO—OM!!
YES, I AM INDEED THE HERO OF THE COLISEUM!!!
BLORP!!
HEY, HEY, HEY.
!
I BROUGHT THE YOU-KNOW-WHAT, DOFY!!
SPLAT!
YOU'RE TOO CLOSE.
I'M TOO CLOSE... BUT?!
THAT'S FINE... SIT.
HEY!!
...
IF HE LEARNS THAT I HAVE THIS...
...STRAW HAT LUFFY WILL BE DESPERATE TO GET HIS HANDS ON IT...
...AND THAT ALLIANCE WILL TURN OUT TO BE A SET OF SHACKLES!!
SPLAT!

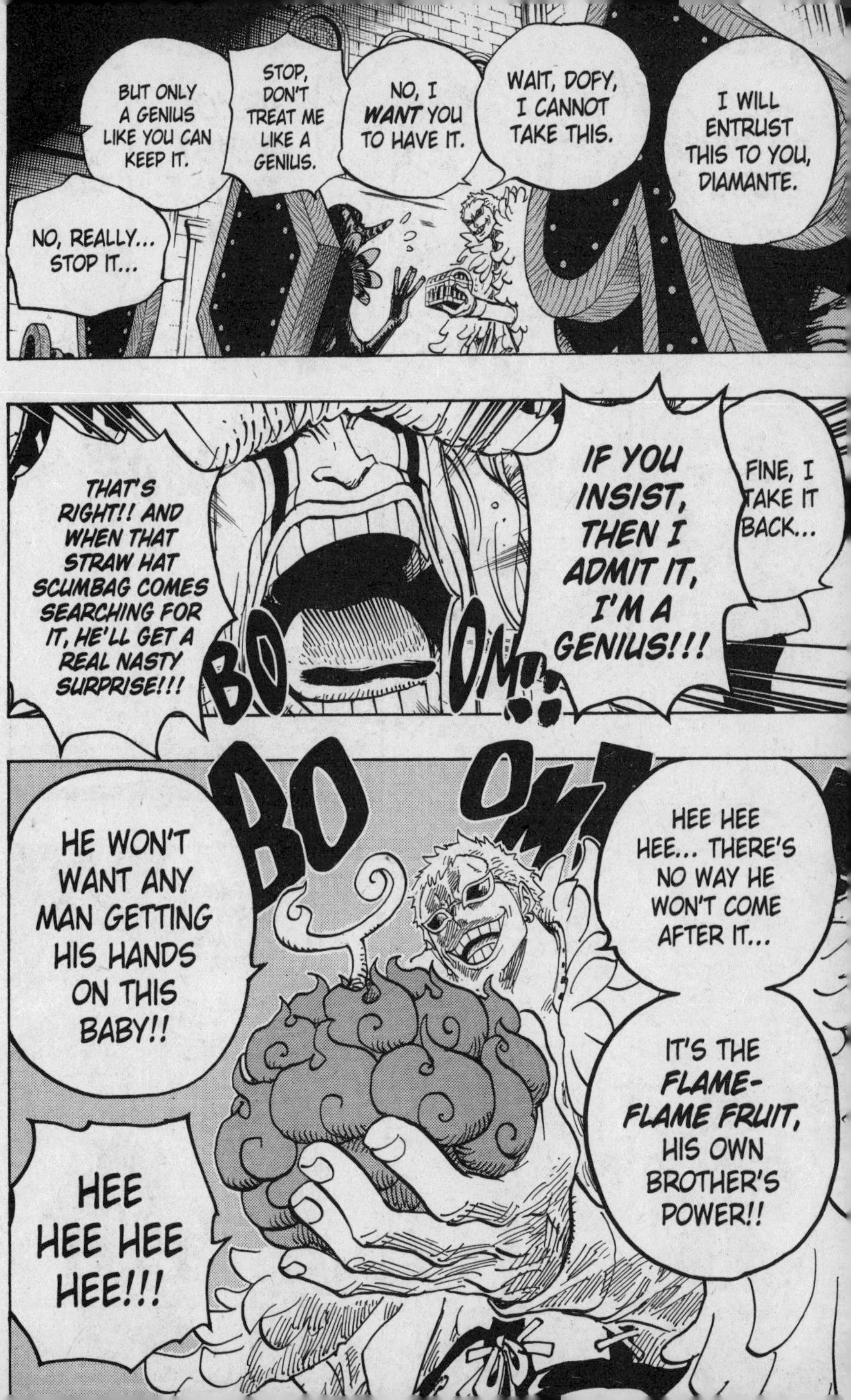
I WILL ENTRUST THIS TO YOU, DIAMANTE.
WAIT, DOFY, I CANNOT TAKE THIS.
NO, I *WANT* YOU TO HAVE IT.
STOP, DON'T TREAT ME LIKE A GENIUS.
BUT ONLY A GENIUS LIKE YOU CAN KEEP IT.
NO, REALLY... STOP IT...
FINE, I TAKE IT BACK...
IF YOU INSIST, THEN I ADMIT IT, I'M A GENIUS!!!
BOOM!!
THAT'S RIGHT!! AND WHEN THAT STRAW HAT SCUMBAG COMES SEARCHING FOR IT, HE'LL GET A REAL NASTY SURPRISE!!!
BOOM
HEE HEE HEE... THERE'S NO WAY HE WON'T COME AFTER IT...
IT'S THE *FLAME-FLAME FRUIT*, HIS OWN BROTHER'S POWER!!
HE WON'T WANT ANY MAN GETTING HIS HANDS ON THIS BABY!!
HEE HEE HEE HEE!!!

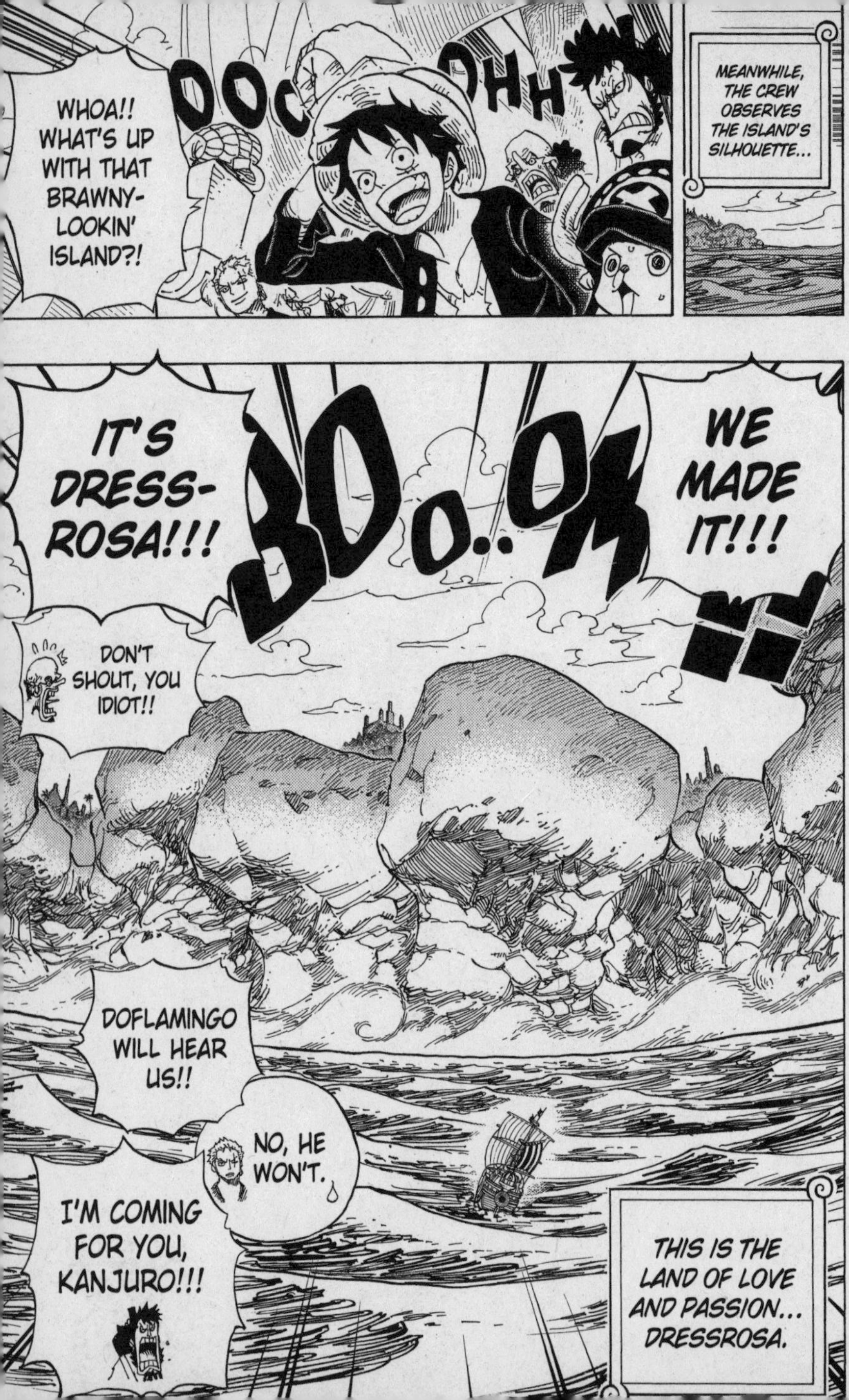
MEANWHILE, THE CREW OBSERVES THE ISLAND'S SILHOUETTE...
DOOOHH
WHOA!! WHAT'S UP WITH THAT BRAWNY-LOOKIN' ISLAND?!
WE MADE IT!!!
BOO..OM
IT'S DRESS-ROSA!!!
DON'T SHOUT, YOU IDIOT!!
DOFLAMINGO WILL HEAR US!!
NO, HE WON'T.
I'M COMING FOR YOU, KANJURO!!!
THIS IS THE LAND OF LOVE AND PASSION... DRESSROSA.

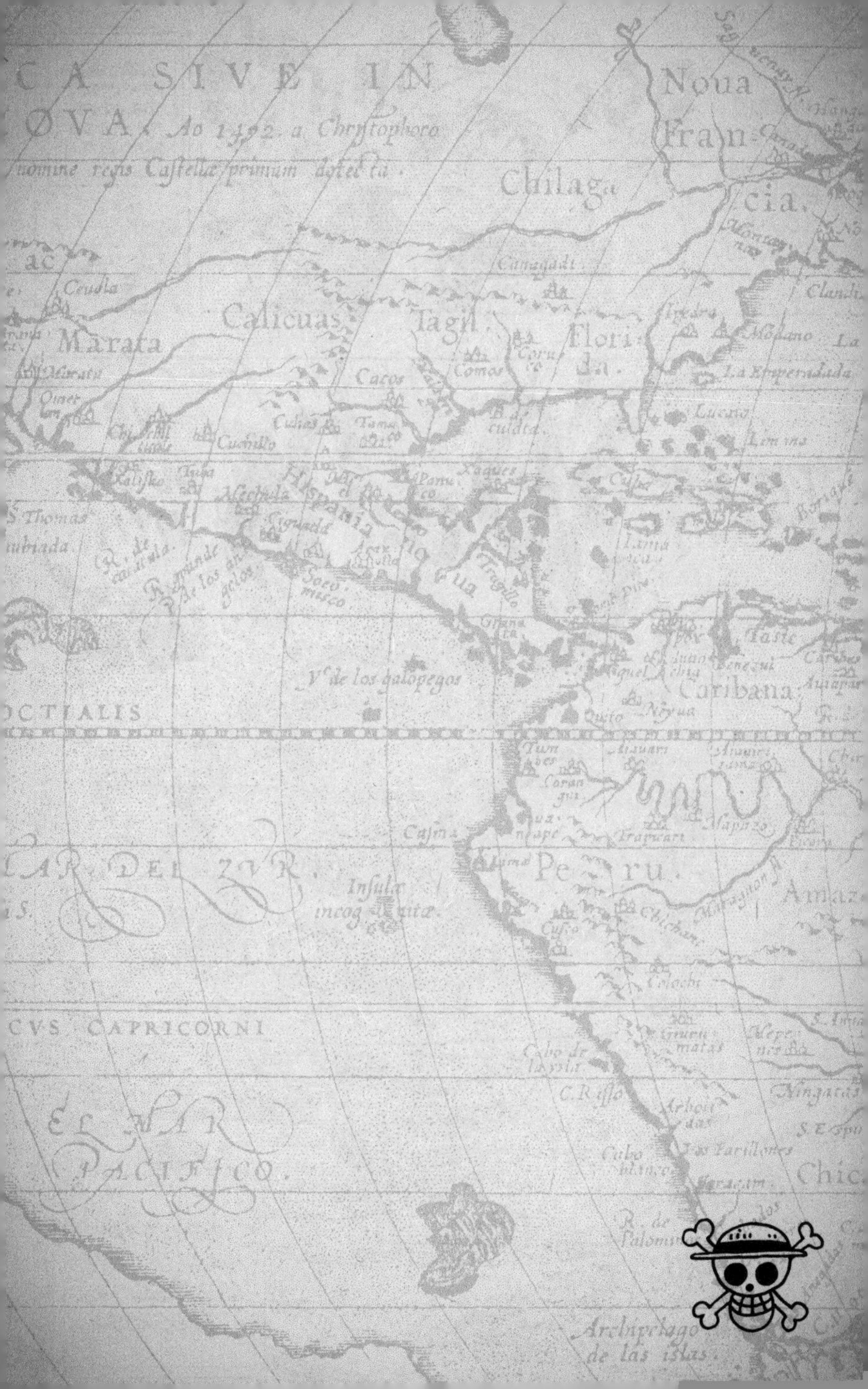

CA SIVE IN
NOVA: Ao 1492 a Chryſtophoro
nomine regis Caſtellæ primum detecta.

Noua Francia.

Chilaga

Canagadi

Calicuas Tagil Florida.

Marata

Cacos

Hispania nova

S. Thomas

Y de los galopegos

OCTIALIS

Caribana

Quito

Peru

MAR DEL ZVR

Inſulæ incognitæ

CVS CAPRICORNI

Cabo de Aguia

C. Riſſo

EL MAR PACIFICO.

Archipelago de las islas.

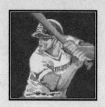

When a new product is selling like hotcakes, they'll say,
"It's a huge hit!" "A mega-hit!" "Smash hit!" "Colossal hit!!"
Which makes me wonder…
Why can't we just call it a home run already?!

Volume 71 is off with the crack of the bat!!

– Eiichiro Oda, 2013

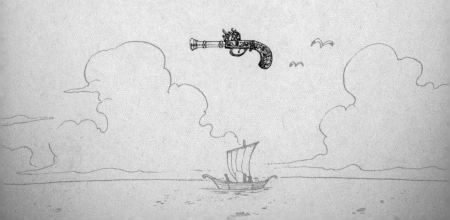

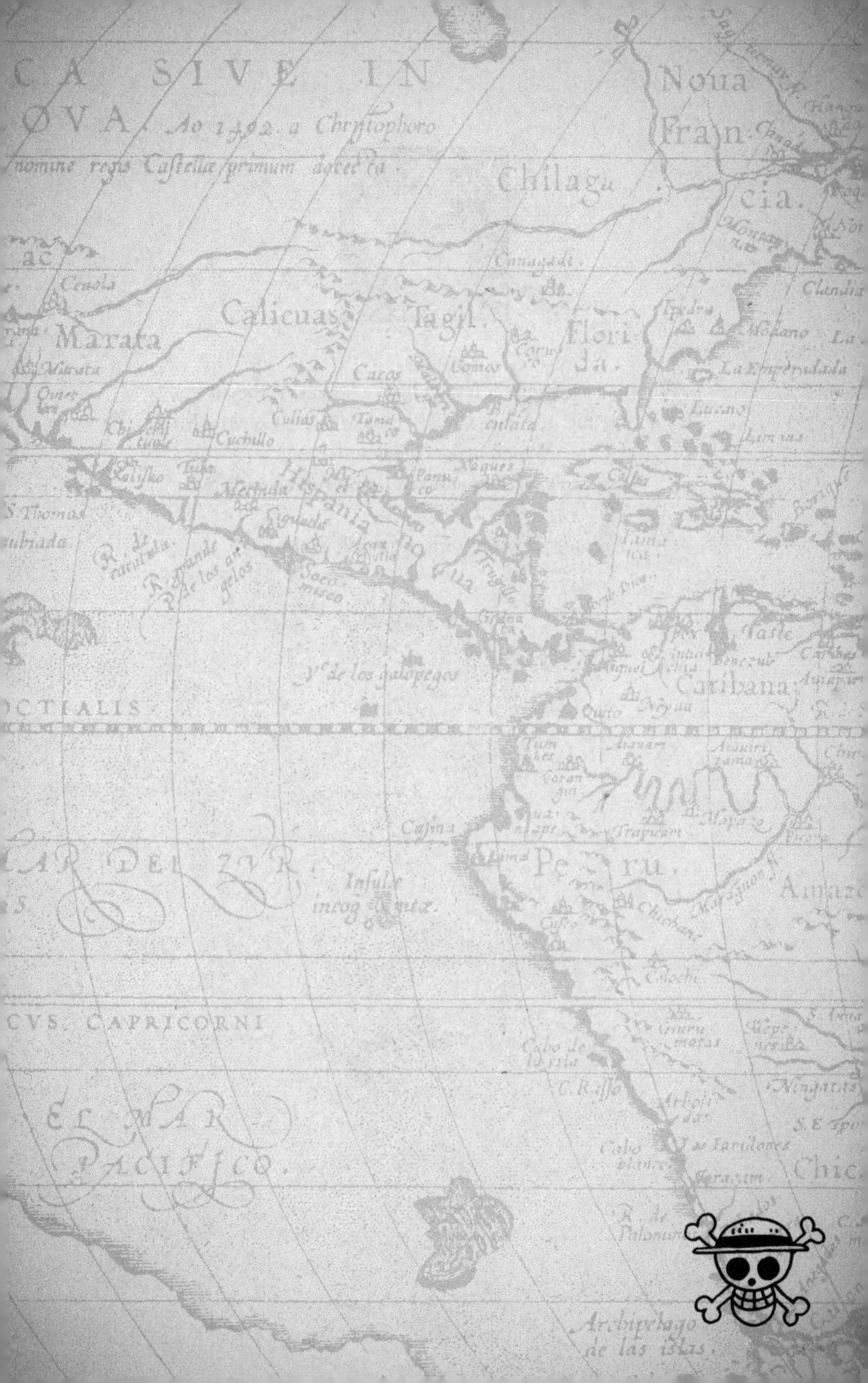

CA SIVE IN
ØVA. Ao 1492 a Chrystophoro
nomine regis Castellæ primum detecta.

Noua
Fran:
cia.

Chilaga

ac

Cenola

Calicuas

Tagil

Flori
da.

Marata

Caccos

Clandia

La

La Espanolada

Culias

Cuchillo

Tana

Lucano

Hispania

Caribana

OCTIALIS

Y de los galopegos

Quito

LAR DEL ZVR

Casna

Pe ru.

Insulæ
incognitæ

Amaz

CVS. CAPRICORNI

EL MAR
PACIFICO.

Cabo de
la stia

C. Rasso

Chica

Archipelago
de las islas.

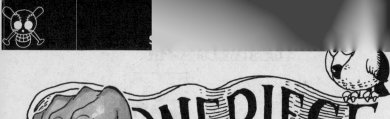

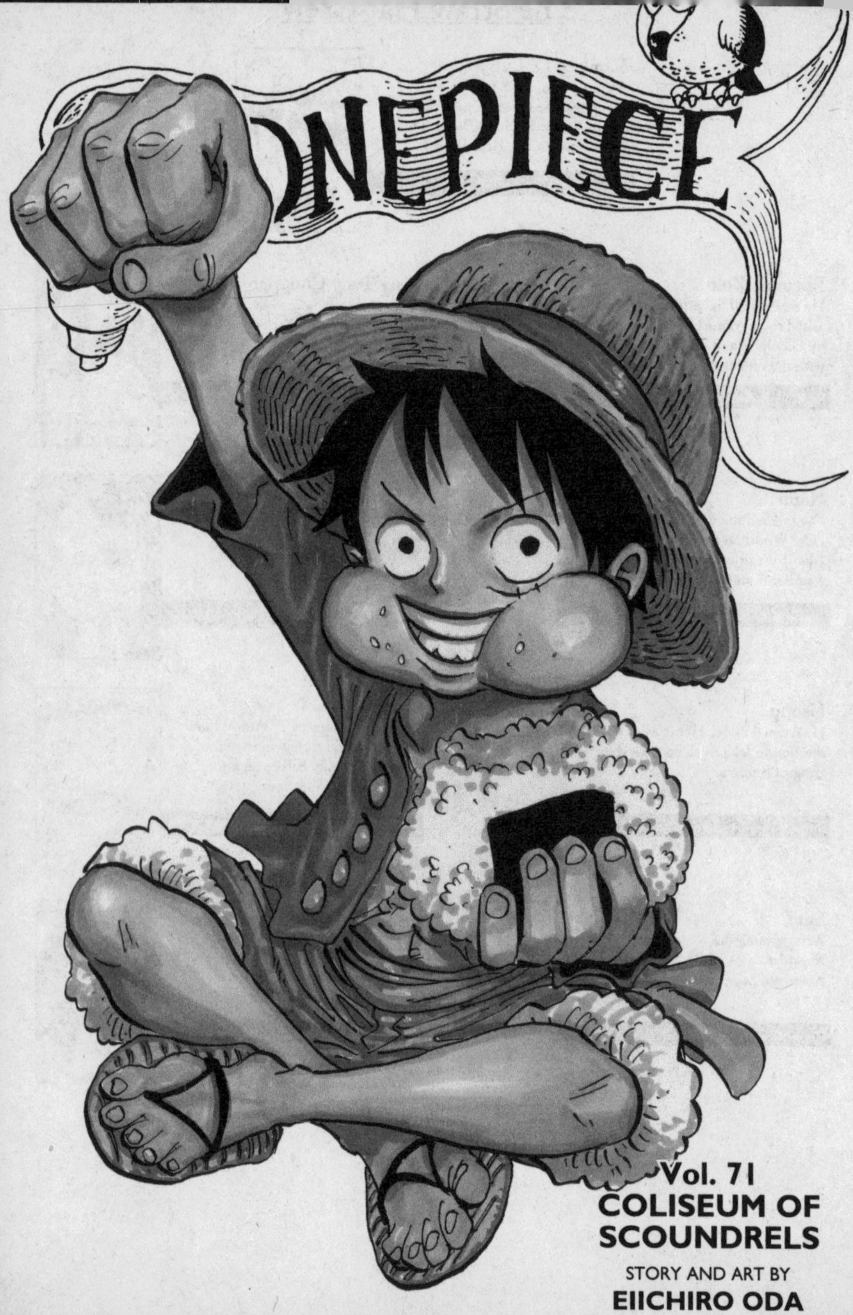
ONEPIECE

Vol. 71
COLISEUM OF SCOUNDRELS

STORY AND ART BY
EIICHIRO ODA

The Straw Hat Crew

Monkey D. Luffy
A young man who dreams of becoming the Pirate King. After training with Rayleigh, he and his crew head for the New World!

Captain, Bounty: 400 million berries

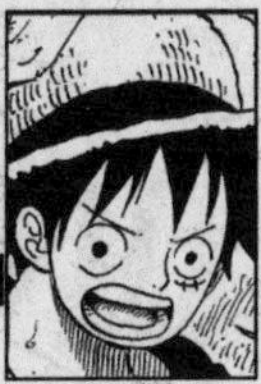

Roronoa Zolo
He swallowed his pride and asked to be trained by Mihawk on Gloom Island before reuniting with the rest of the crew.

Fighter, Bounty: 120 million berries

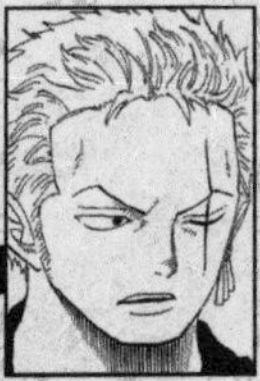

Tony Tony Chopper
After researching powerful medicine in Birdie Kingdom, he reunites with the rest of the crew.

Ship's Doctor, Bounty: 50 berries

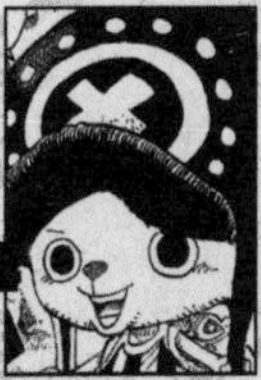

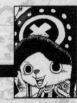

Nami
She studied the weather of the New World on the small Sky Island Weatheria, a place where weather is studied as a science.

Navigator, Bounty: 16 million berries

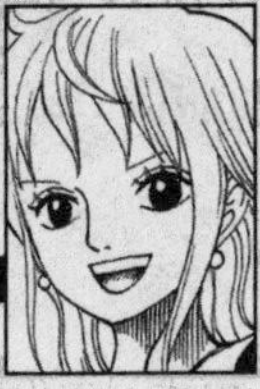

Nico Robin
She spent her time in Baltigo with the leader of the Revolutionary Army: Luffy's father, Dragon.

Archeologist, Bounty: 80 million berries

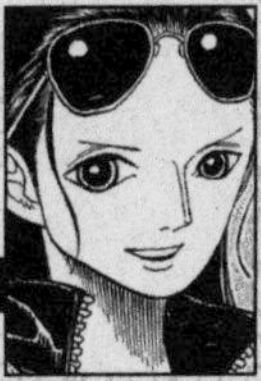

Usopp
He trained under Heracles at the Bowin Islands to become the King of Snipers.

Sniper, Bounty: 30 million berries

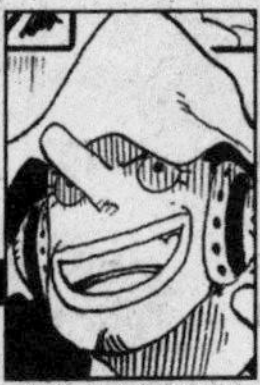

Franky
He modified himself in Future Land Baldimore and turned himself into Armored Franky before reuniting with the rest of the crew.

Shipwright, Bounty: 44 million berries

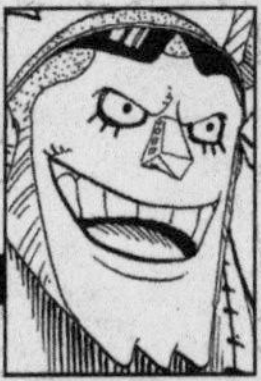

Sanji
After fighting the New Kama Karate masters in the Kamabakka Kingdom, he returned to the crew.

Cook, Bounty: 77 million berries

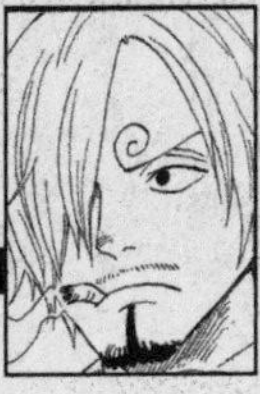

Brook
After being captured and used as a freak show by the Longarm Tribe, he became a famous rock star called "Soul King" Brook.

Musician, Bounty: 33 million berries

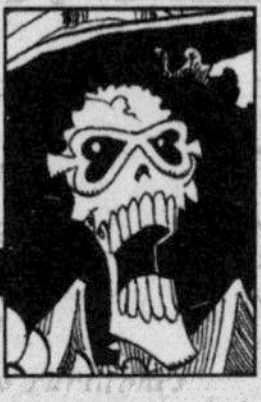

THE STORY OF ONE PIECE · VOLUME 71 ·

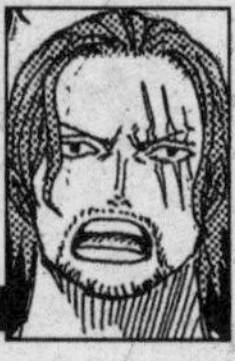

Shanks
One of the Four Emperors. He continues to wait for Luffy in the second half of the Grand Line, called the New World.

Captain of the Red-Haired Pirates

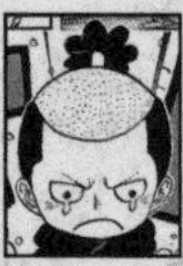

Momonosuke

Kin'emon's Son

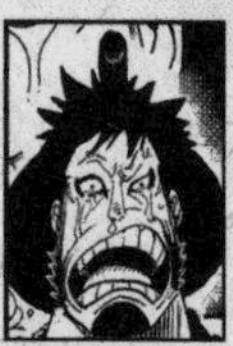

Foxfire Kin'emon

Samurai of Wano

Don Quixote Pirates

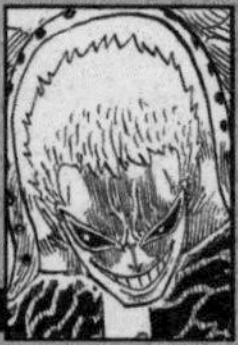

Don Quixote Doflamingo (Joker)
One of the Seven Warlords of the sea and a weapons broker. He works under the alias of "Joker."

Pirate, Warlord (former)

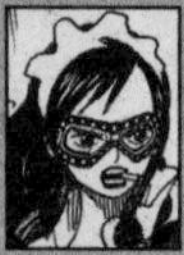

Baby 5

Servant/ Assassin

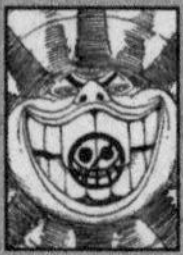

Buffalo

Fighter

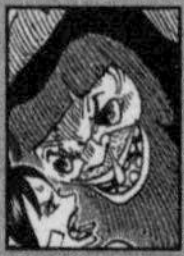

Trebol

?

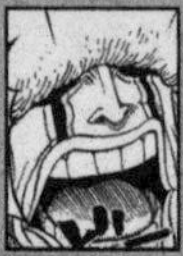

Diamante

?

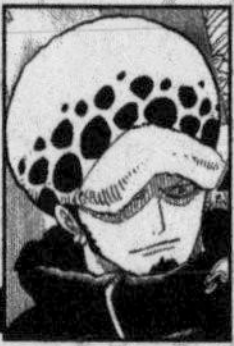

Trafalgar Law
The Surgeon of Death, wielder of the Op-Op Fruit's powers. Currently allied with Luffy.

Pirate, Warlord

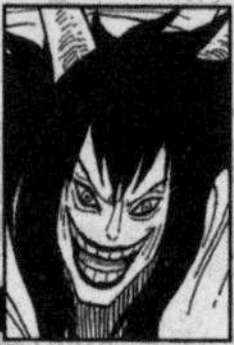

Master Caesar Clown
An authority on weapons of mass murder. Kidnapped by Law in an attempt to goad Doflamingo out of hiding.

Former government scientist

Having finished their two years of training, the Straw Hat crew reunites on the Sabaody Archipelago. They finally reached the New World via Fish-Man Island!

The crew happens across Trafalgar Law on the island of Punk Hazard, run by Caesar Clown. At his suggestion, they form a new pirate alliance that seeks to take down one of the Four Emperors. In order to draw Doflamingo's attention, they must first capture Caesar, who is producing the artificial Devil Fruit that Doflamingo sells to Kaido, a member of the Four Emperors. After a fierce battle, the alliance kidnaps Caesar, then demands that Doflamingo leave the Seven Warlords in return for the scientist. When Doflamingo complies, Law tells him he will hand over Caesar at a small island north of Dressrosa. But somehow, Doflamingo has Ace's Devil Fruit in his possession...

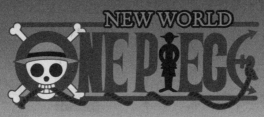

Vol. 71
Coliseum of Scoundrels

CONTENTS

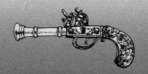

Chapter 701:
ADVENTURE IN THE LAND OF LOVE, PASSION AND TOYS

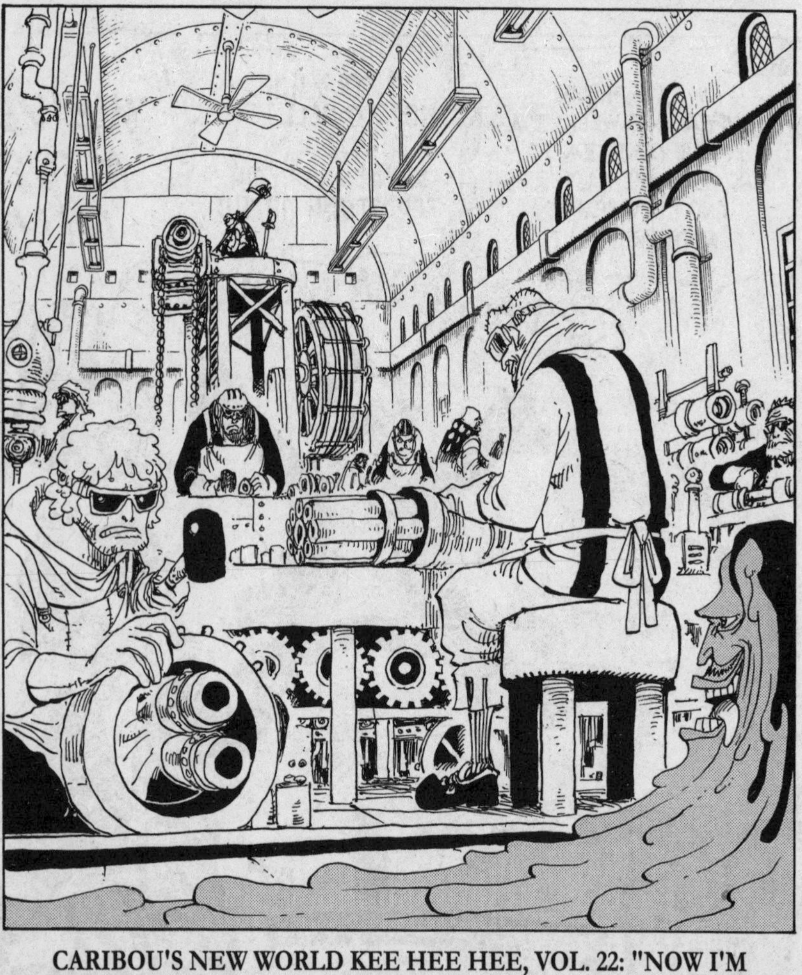

CARIBOU'S NEW WORLD KEE HEE HEE, VOL. 22: "NOW I'M CURIOUS—WHAT'S UP WITH THIS ISLAND'S WEAPON FACTORY?"

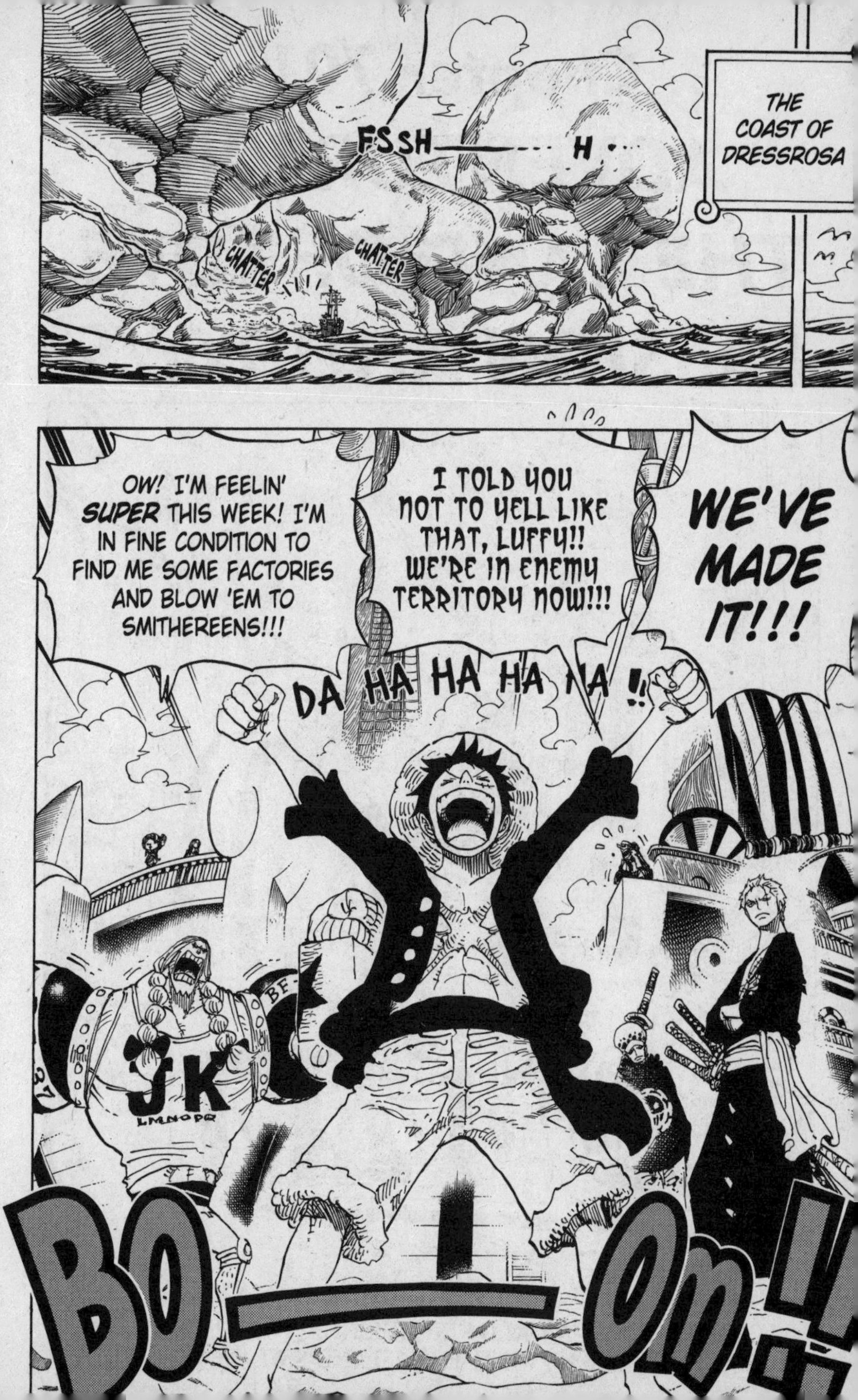
THE COAST OF DRESSROSA
FSSH———H
CHATTER
CHATTER
WE'VE MADE IT!!!
I TOLD YOU NOT TO YELL LIKE THAT, LUFFY!! WE'RE IN ENEMY TERRITORY NOW!!!
OW! I'M FEELIN' SUPER THIS WEEK! I'M IN FINE CONDITION TO FIND ME SOME FACTORIES AND BLOW 'EM TO SMITHEREENS!!!
DA HA HA HA HA!!
BE-
BO——OM!!

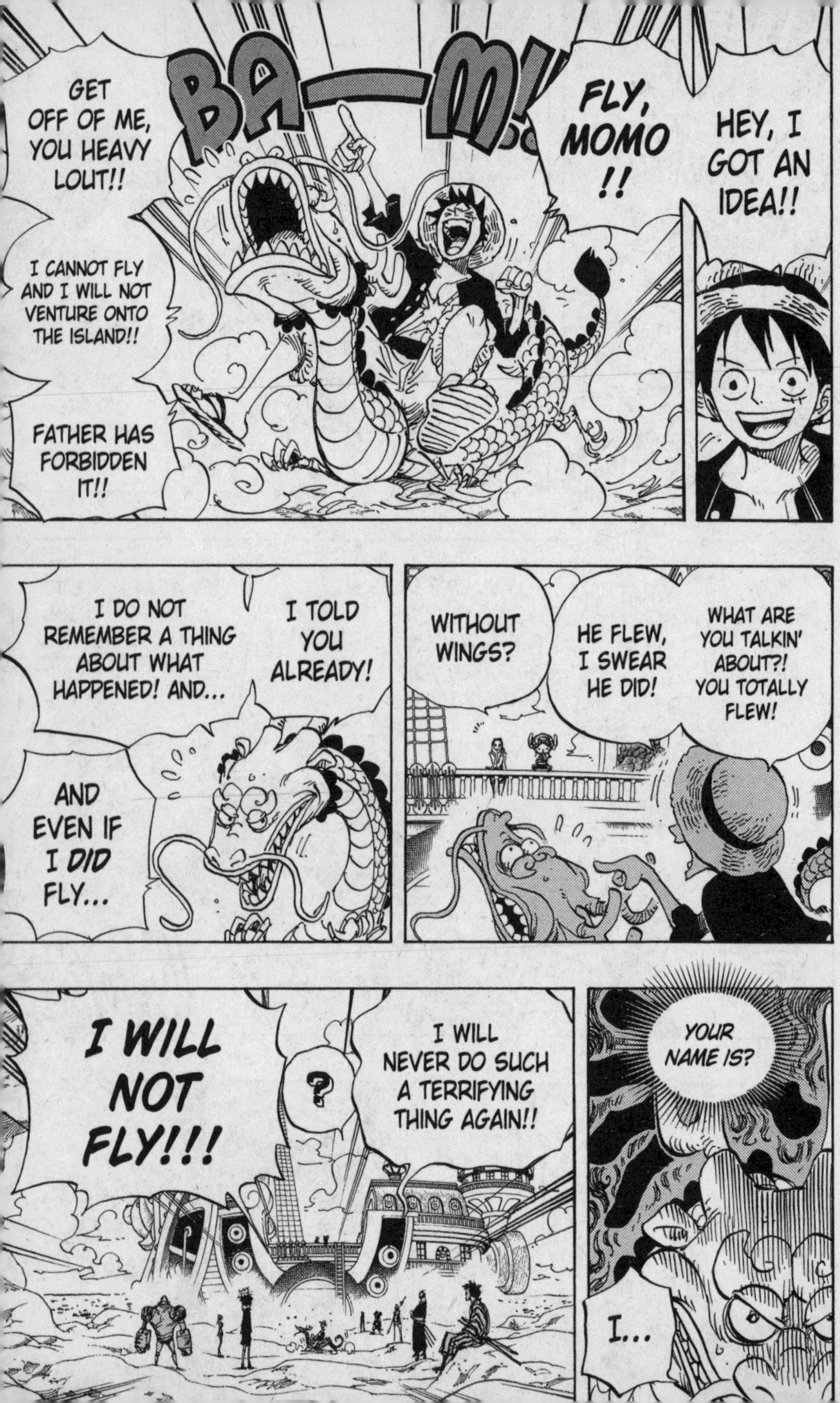
HEY, I GOT AN IDEA!!
FLY, MOMO!!
BA—M!
GET OFF OF ME, YOU HEAVY LOUT!!
I CANNOT FLY AND I WILL NOT VENTURE ONTO THE ISLAND!!
FATHER HAS FORBIDDEN IT!!
WHAT ARE YOU TALKIN' ABOUT?! YOU TOTALLY FLEW!
HE FLEW, I SWEAR HE DID!
WITHOUT WINGS?
I TOLD YOU ALREADY!
I DO NOT REMEMBER A THING ABOUT WHAT HAPPENED! AND...
AND EVEN IF I *DID* FLY...
YOUR NAME IS?
I...
I WILL NEVER DO SUCH A TERRIFYING THING AGAIN!!
?
I WILL NOT FLY!!!

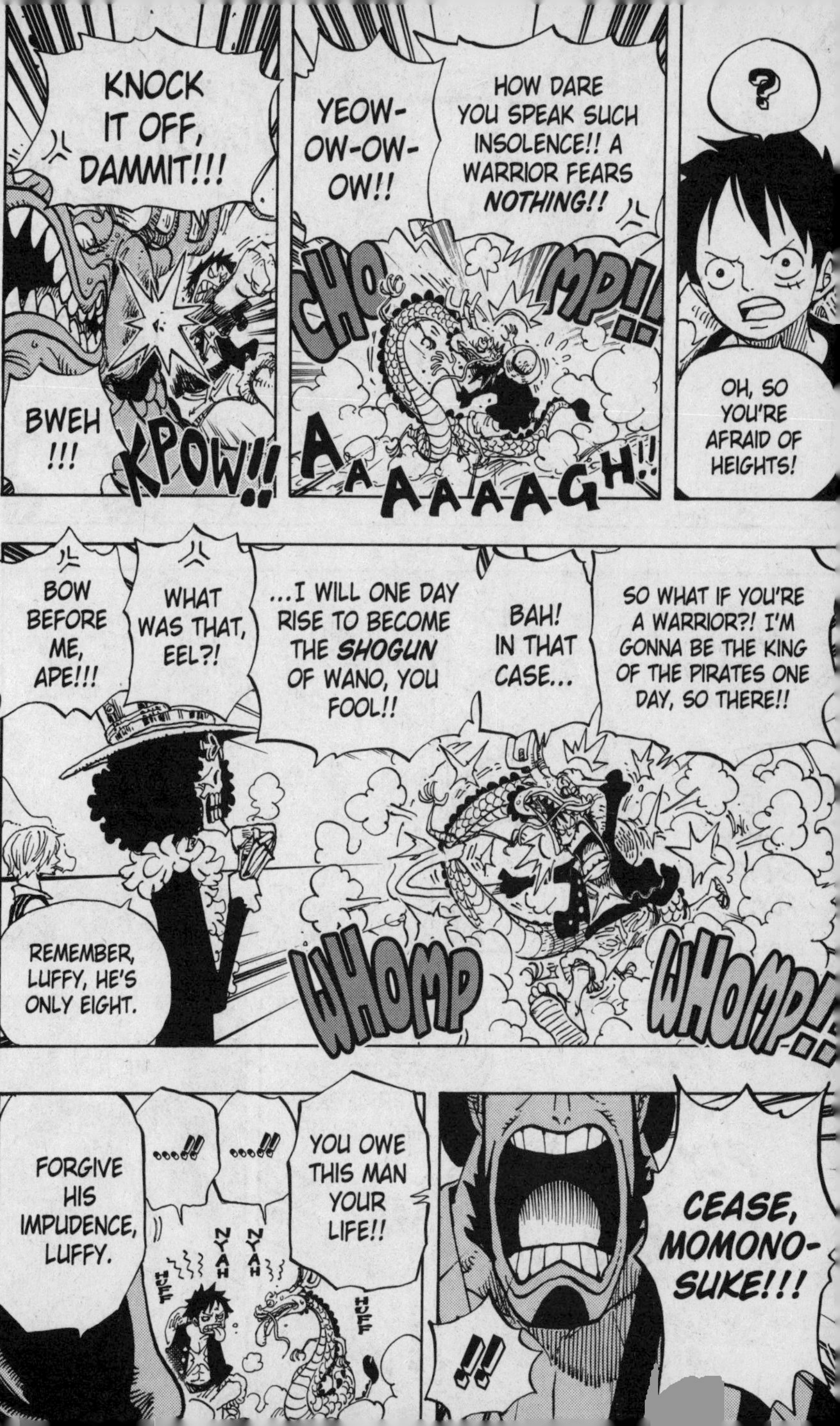
?
OH, SO YOU'RE AFRAID OF HEIGHTS!
HOW DARE YOU SPEAK SUCH INSOLENCE!! A WARRIOR FEARS NOTHING!!
YEOW-OW-OW-OW!!
CHOMP!!
AAAAAAGH!!
KNOCK IT OFF, DAMMIT!!!
BWEH!!!
KPOW!!
SO WHAT IF YOU'RE A WARRIOR?! I'M GONNA BE THE KING OF THE PIRATES ONE DAY, SO THERE!!
BAH! IN THAT CASE...
...I WILL ONE DAY RISE TO BECOME THE SHOGUN OF WANO, YOU FOOL!!
WHAT WAS THAT, EEL?!
BOW BEFORE ME, APE!!!
WHOMP WHOMP!!
REMEMBER, LUFFY, HE'S ONLY EIGHT.
CEASE, MOMONOSUKE!!!
!!
YOU OWE THIS MAN YOUR LIFE!!
...!!
...!!
FORGIVE HIS IMPUDENCE, LUFFY.
HUFF
NYAH
NYAH
HUFF

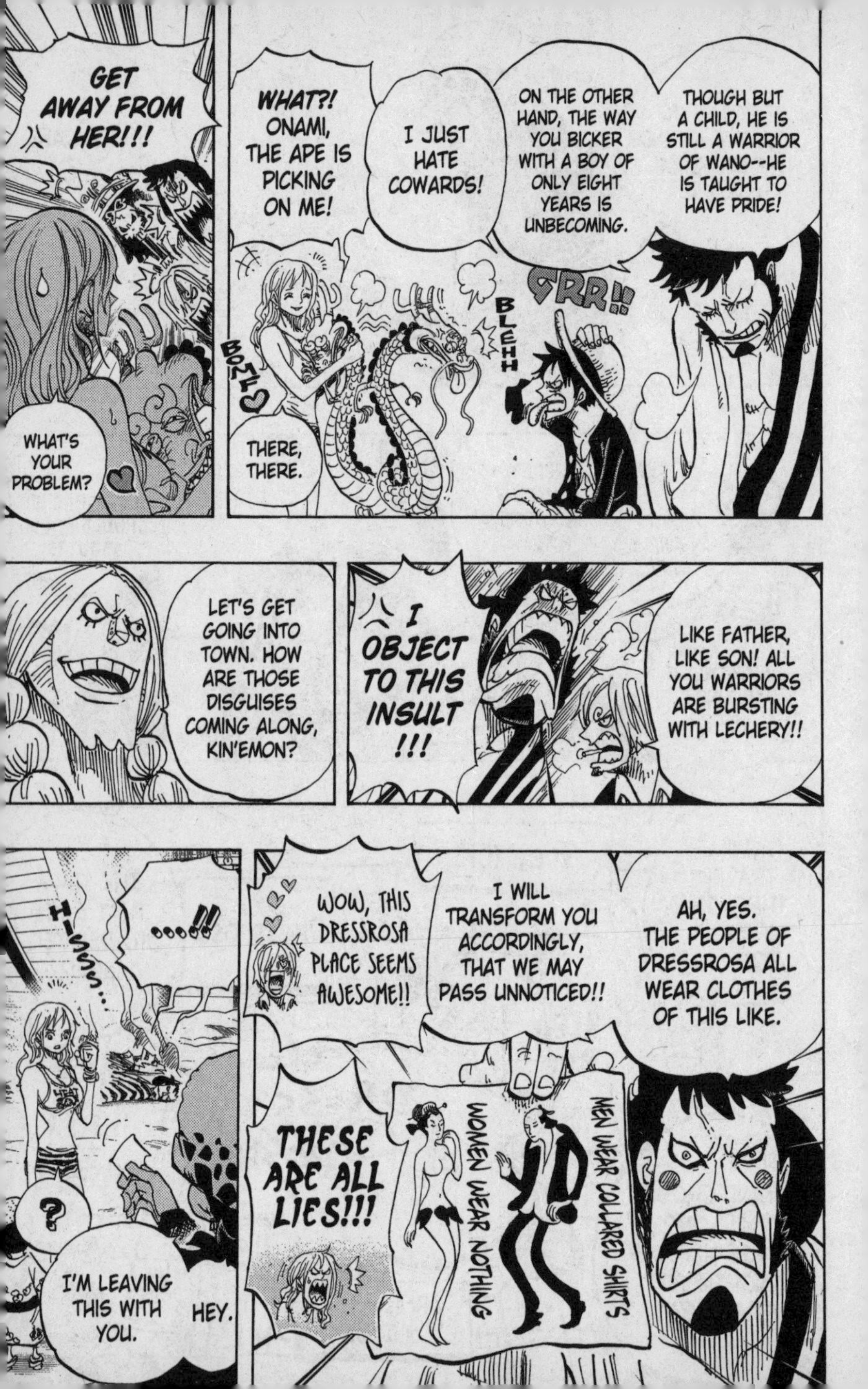
THOUGH BUT A CHILD, HE IS STILL A WARRIOR OF WANO--HE IS TAUGHT TO HAVE PRIDE!
ON THE OTHER HAND, THE WAY YOU BICKER WITH A BOY OF ONLY EIGHT YEARS IS UNBECOMING.
GRR!!
I JUST HATE COWARDS!
BLEHH
WHAT?! ONAMI, THE APE IS PICKING ON ME!
BOMF♥
THERE, THERE.
GET AWAY FROM HER!!!
WHAT'S YOUR PROBLEM?
LIKE FATHER, LIKE SON! ALL YOU WARRIORS ARE BURSTING WITH LECHERY!!
I OBJECT TO THIS INSULT!!!
LET'S GET GOING INTO TOWN. HOW ARE THOSE DISGUISES COMING ALONG, KIN'EMON?
AH, YES. THE PEOPLE OF DRESSROSA ALL WEAR CLOTHES OF THIS LIKE.
I WILL TRANSFORM YOU ACCORDINGLY, THAT WE MAY PASS UNNOTICED!!
WOW, THIS DRESSROSA PLACE SEEMS AWESOME!!
MEN WEAR COLLARED SHIRTS
WOMEN WEAR NOTHING
THESE ARE ALL LIES!!!
...!!
HISSS...
HEY.
I'M LEAVING THIS WITH YOU.
?

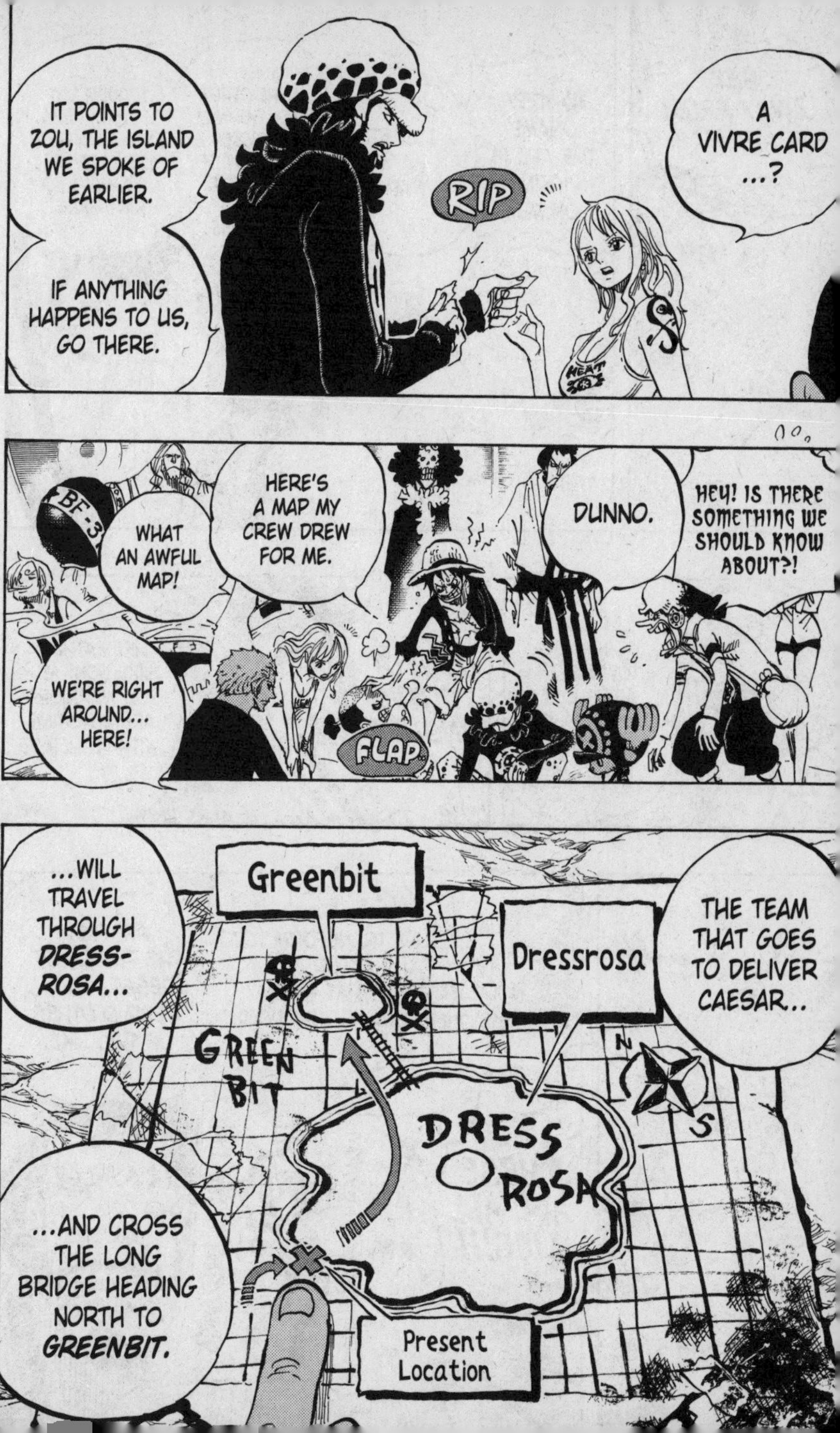
A VIVRE CARD ...?
RIP
IT POINTS TO ZOU, THE ISLAND WE SPOKE OF EARLIER.
IF ANYTHING HAPPENS TO US, GO THERE.
HEY! IS THERE SOMETHING WE SHOULD KNOW ABOUT?!
DUNNO.
HERE'S A MAP MY CREW DREW FOR ME.
WHAT AN AWFUL MAP!
WE'RE RIGHT AROUND... HERE!
FLAP
THE TEAM THAT GOES TO DELIVER CAESAR...
...WILL TRAVEL THROUGH DRESS-ROSA...
Dressrosa
Greenbit
N
S
GREEN BIT
DRESS ROSA
...AND CROSS THE LONG BRIDGE HEADING NORTH TO GREENBIT.
Present Location

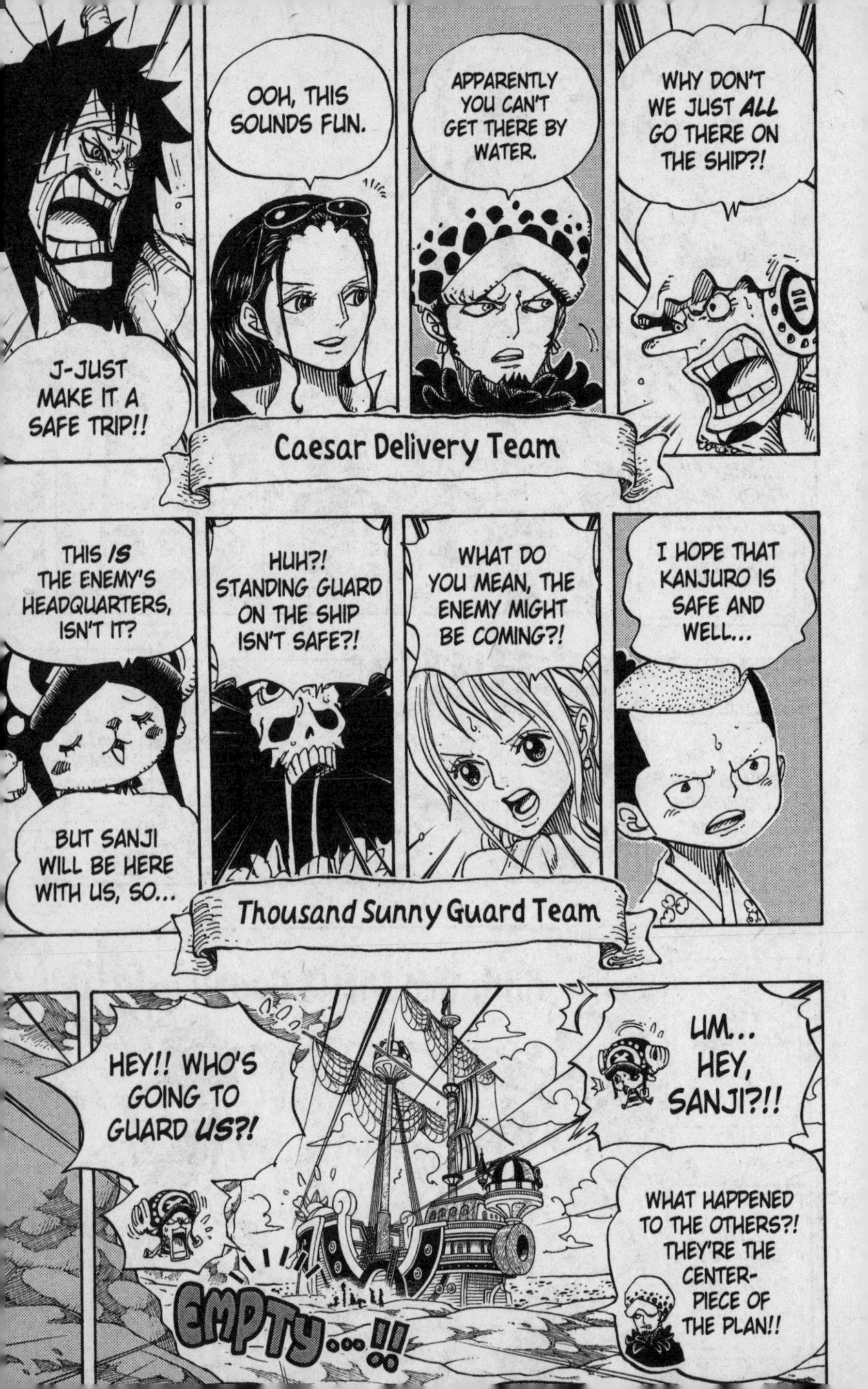
WHY DON'T WE JUST ALL GO THERE ON THE SHIP?!
APPARENTLY YOU CAN'T GET THERE BY WATER.
OOH, THIS SOUNDS FUN.
J-JUST MAKE IT A SAFE TRIP!!
Caesar Delivery Team
I HOPE THAT KANJURO IS SAFE AND WELL...
WHAT DO YOU MEAN, THE ENEMY MIGHT BE COMING?!
HUH?! STANDING GUARD ON THE SHIP ISN'T SAFE?!
THIS IS THE ENEMY'S HEADQUARTERS, ISN'T IT?
BUT SANJI WILL BE HERE WITH US, SO...
Thousand Sunny Guard Team
UM... HEY, SANJI?!!
WHAT HAPPENED TO THE OTHERS?! THEY'RE THE CENTER-PIECE OF THE PLAN!!
HEY!! WHO'S GOING TO GUARD US?!
EMPTY...!!

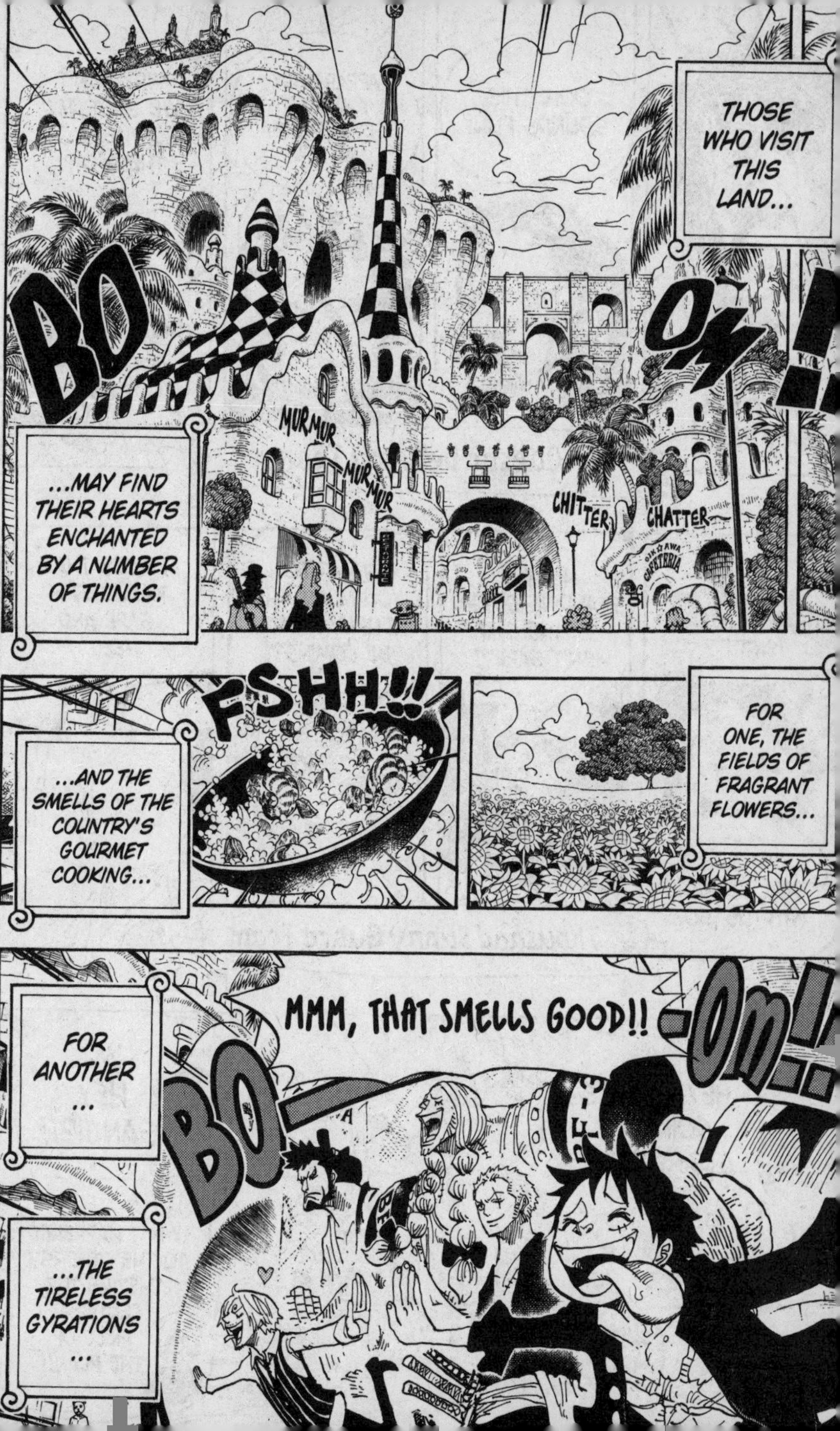
THOSE WHO VISIT THIS LAND...
BO
OM!!
MURMUR
MURMUR
CHITTER
CHATTER
CAFETERIA
...MAY FIND THEIR HEARTS ENCHANTED BY A NUMBER OF THINGS.
FOR ONE, THE FIELDS OF FRAGRANT FLOWERS...
FSHH!!
...AND THE SMELLS OF THE COUNTRY'S GOURMET COOKING...
-OM!!
MMM, THAT SMELLS GOOD!!
FOR ANOTHER ...
BO-
...THE TIRELESS GYRATIONS ...

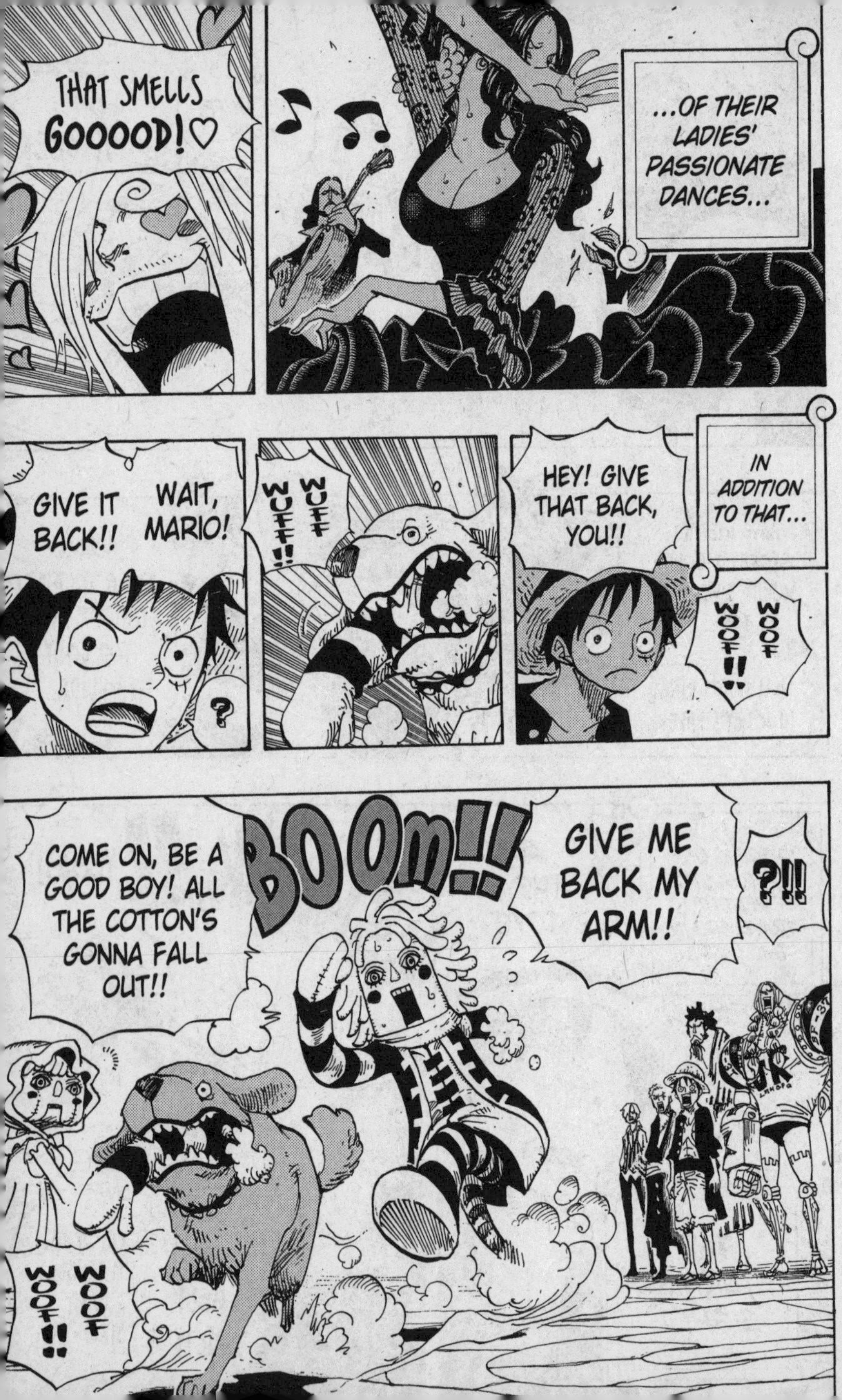
...OF THEIR LADIES' PASSIONATE DANCES...
THAT SMELLS GOOOOD!♡
IN ADDITION TO THAT...
WOOF WOOF!!
HEY! GIVE THAT BACK, YOU!!
WUFF WUFF!!
WAIT, MARIO!
GIVE IT BACK!!
?
?!!
GIVE ME BACK MY ARM!!
BOOM!!
COME ON, BE A GOOD BOY! ALL THE COTTON'S GONNA FALL OUT!!
WOOF WOOF!!

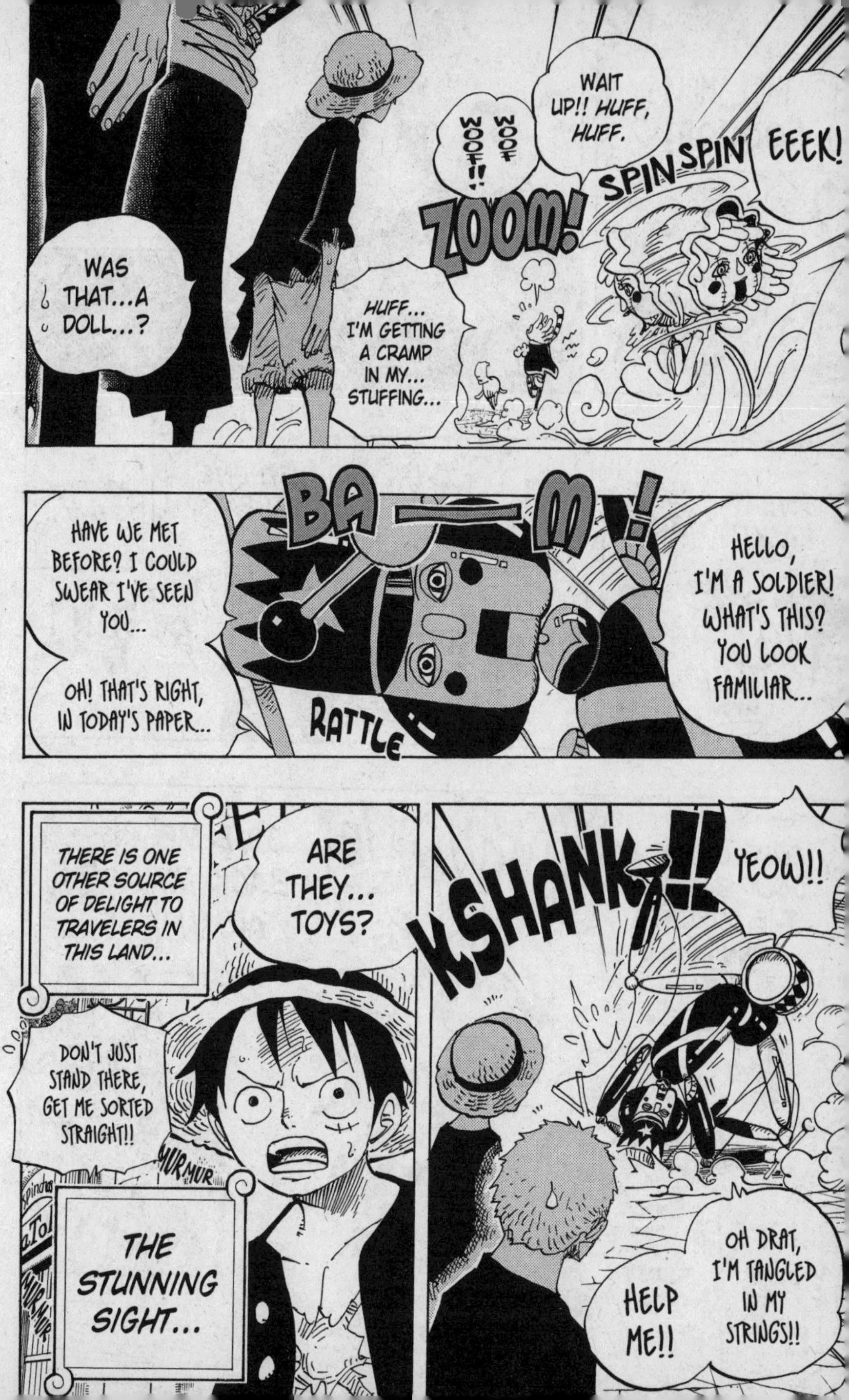
EEEK!
SPIN SPIN
WAIT UP!! HUFF, HUFF.
WOOF WOOF!!
ZOOM!
HUFF... I'M GETTING A CRAMP IN MY... STUFFING...
WAS THAT...A DOLL...?
BA—M!
HELLO, I'M A SOLDIER! WHAT'S THIS? YOU LOOK FAMILIAR...
RATTLE
HAVE WE MET BEFORE? I COULD SWEAR I'VE SEEN YOU...
OH! THAT'S RIGHT, IN TODAY'S PAPER...
YEOW!!
KSHANK!!
OH DRAT, I'M TANGLED IN MY STRINGS!!
HELP ME!!
THERE IS ONE OTHER SOURCE OF DELIGHT TO TRAVELERS IN THIS LAND...
ARE THEY... TOYS?
DON'T JUST STAND THERE, GET ME SORTED STRAIGHT!!
MUR MUR
THE STUNNING SIGHT...

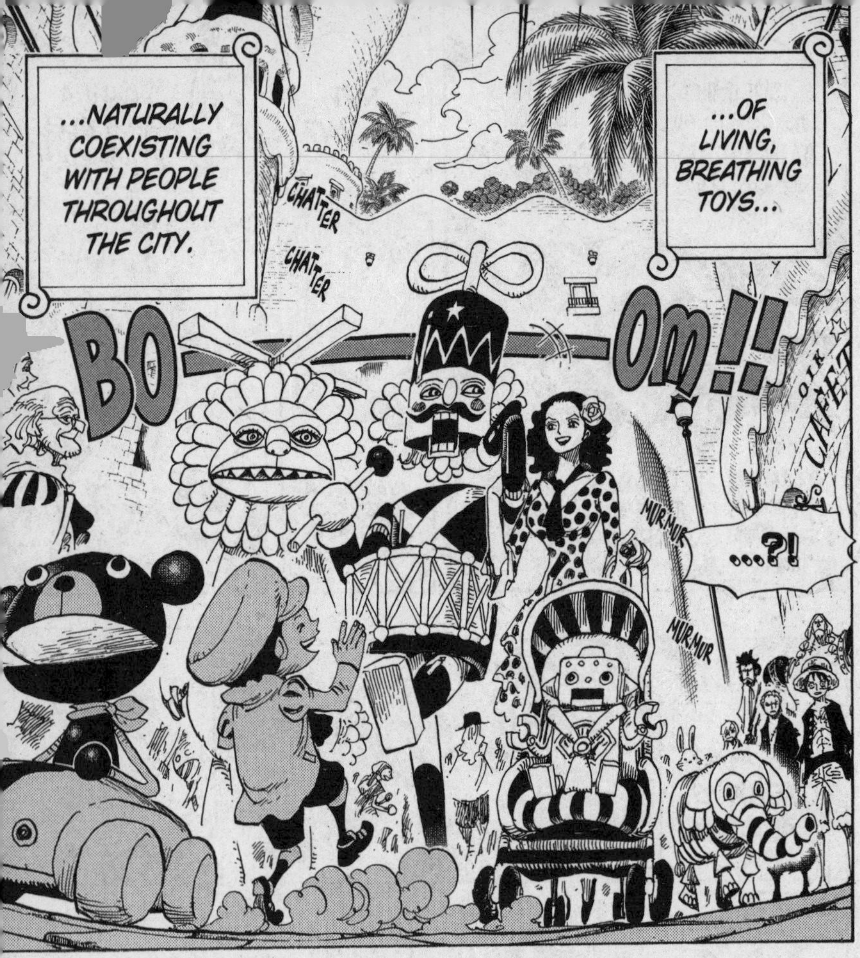
...OF LIVING, BREATHING TOYS...
...NATURALLY COEXISTING WITH PEOPLE THROUGHOUT THE CITY.
CHATTER
CHATTER
BO-OM!!
MURMUR
MURMUR
...?!

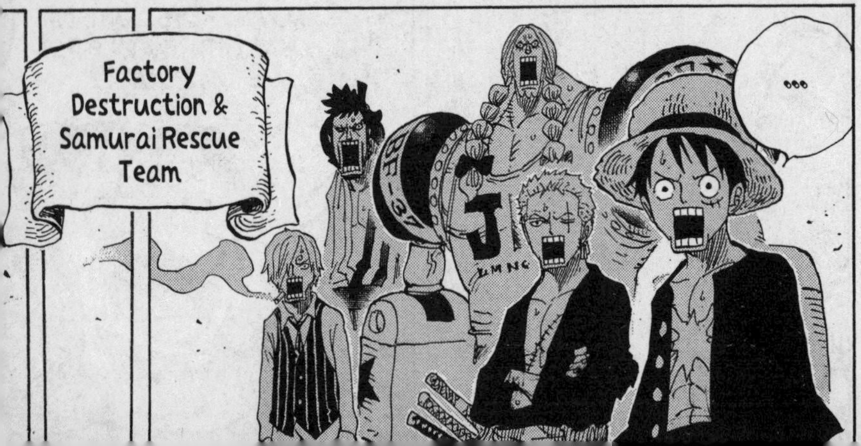
...
Factory Destruction & Samurai Rescue Team

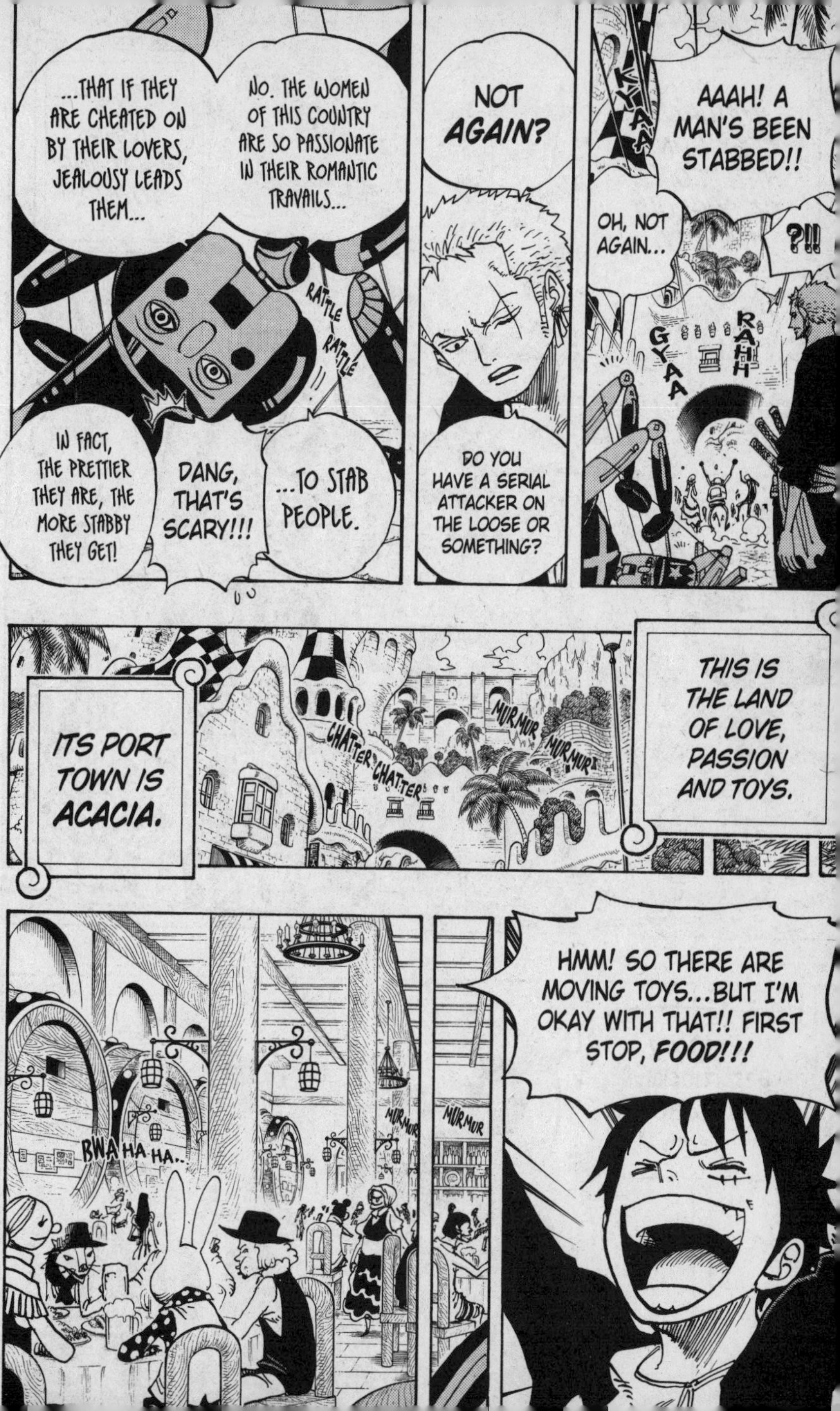
KYAA
AAAH! A MAN'S BEEN STABBED!!
?!!
OH, NOT AGAIN...
GYAA
RAHH
NOT AGAIN?
DO YOU HAVE A SERIAL ATTACKER ON THE LOOSE OR SOMETHING?
NO. THE WOMEN OF THIS COUNTRY ARE SO PASSIONATE IN THEIR ROMANTIC TRAVAILS...
...THAT IF THEY ARE CHEATED ON BY THEIR LOVERS, JEALOUSY LEADS THEM...
RATTLE RATTLE
...TO STAB PEOPLE.
DANG, THAT'S SCARY!!!
IN FACT, THE PRETTIER THEY ARE, THE MORE STABBY THEY GET!
THIS IS THE LAND OF LOVE, PASSION AND TOYS.
MURMUR MURMUR
CHATTER CHATTER
ITS PORT TOWN IS ACACIA.
HMM! SO THERE ARE MOVING TOYS...BUT I'M OKAY WITH THAT!! FIRST STOP, FOOD!!!
MURMUR
MURMUR
BWA HA HA..

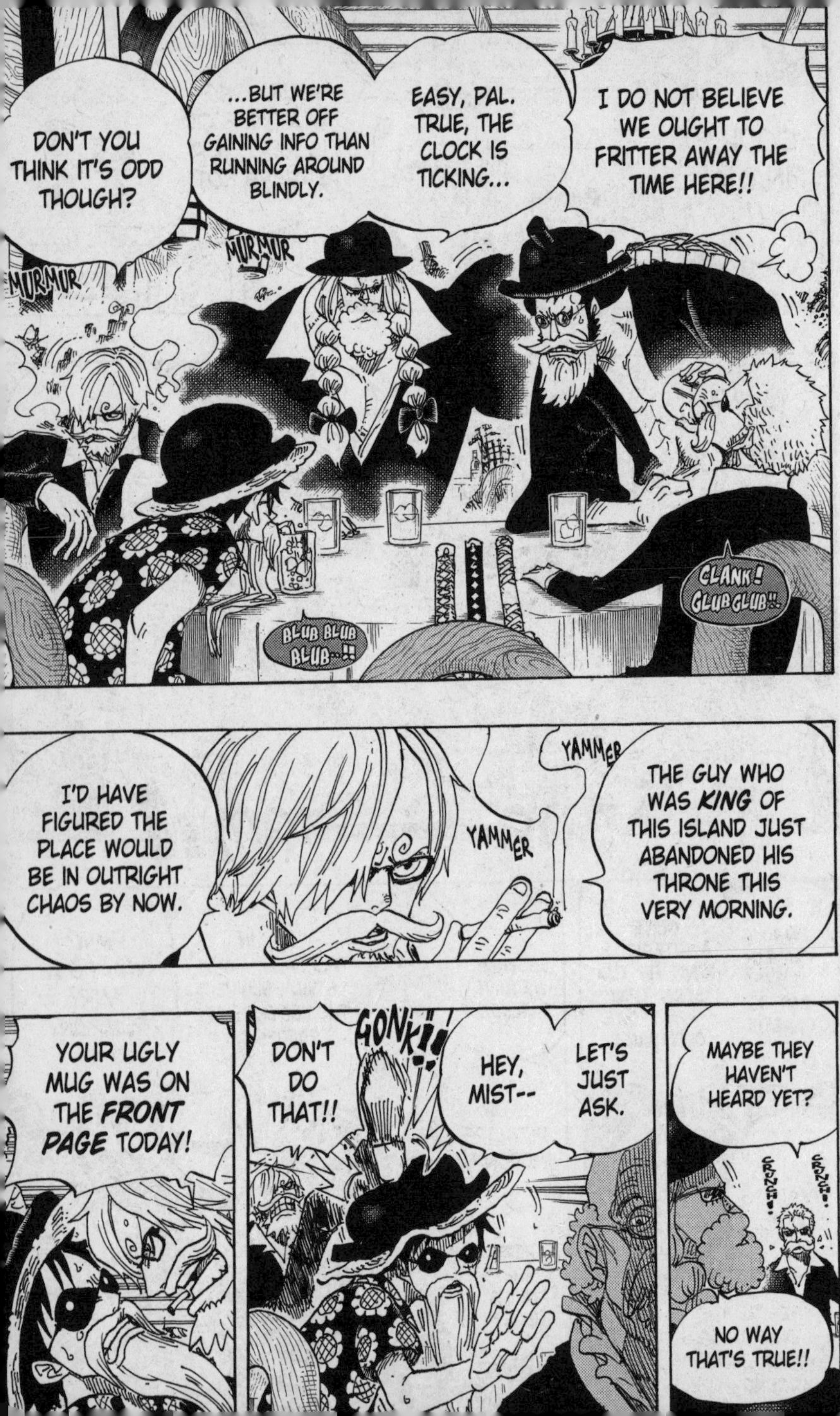
I DO NOT BELIEVE WE OUGHT TO FRITTER AWAY THE TIME HERE!!
EASY, PAL. TRUE, THE CLOCK IS TICKING...
...BUT WE'RE BETTER OFF GAINING INFO THAN RUNNING AROUND BLINDLY.
MURMUR
DON'T YOU THINK IT'S ODD THOUGH?
MURMUR
CLANK! GLUB GLUB!!
BLUB BLUB BLUB...!!
THE GUY WHO WAS *KING* OF THIS ISLAND JUST ABANDONED HIS THRONE THIS VERY MORNING.
YAMMER
YAMMER
I'D HAVE FIGURED THE PLACE WOULD BE IN OUTRIGHT CHAOS BY NOW.
MAYBE THEY HAVEN'T HEARD YET?
CRUNCH!
CRUNCH!
NO WAY THAT'S TRUE!!
LET'S JUST ASK.
HEY, MIST--
GONK!!
DON'T DO THAT!!
YOUR UGLY MUG WAS ON THE *FRONT PAGE* TODAY!

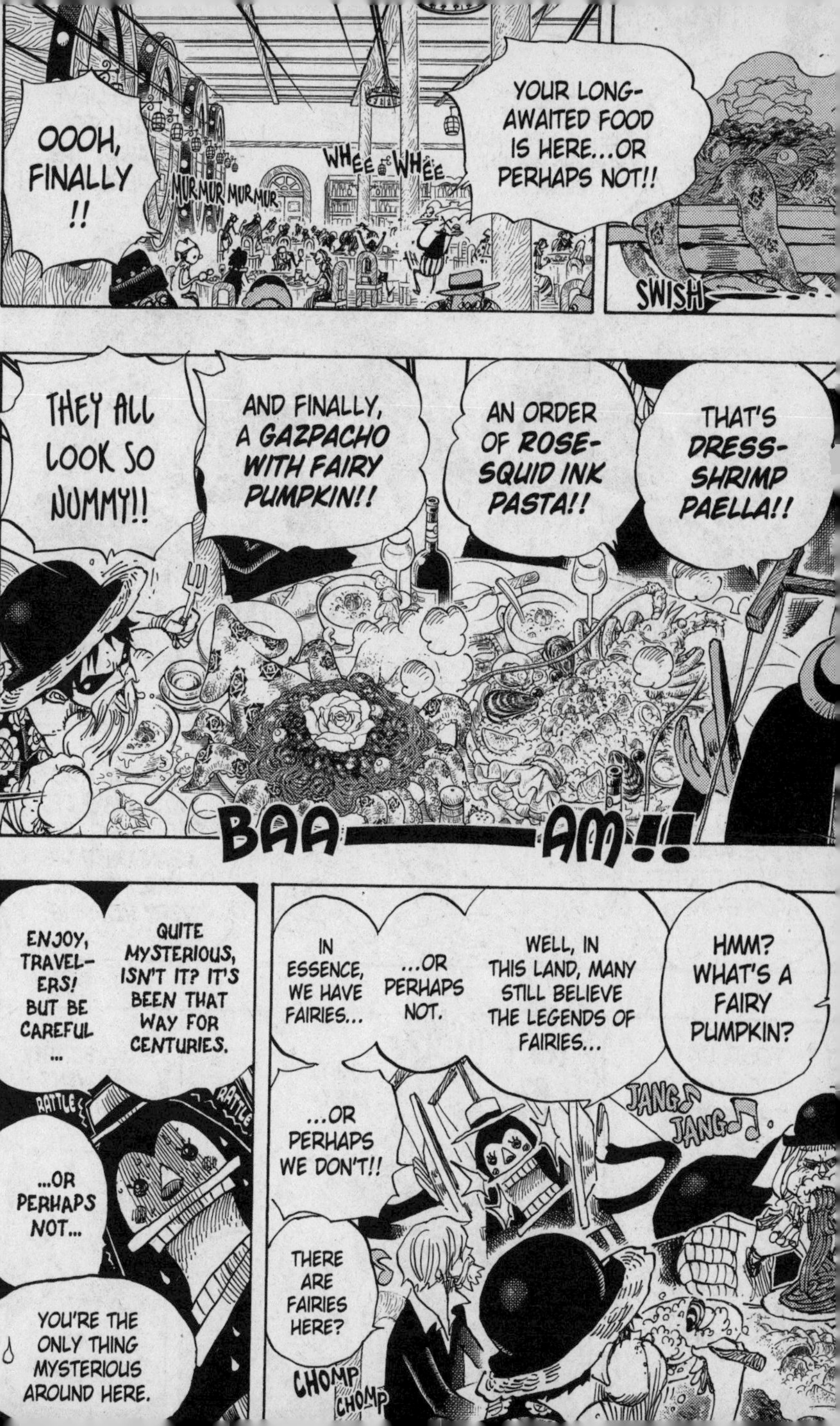
YOUR LONG-AWAITED FOOD IS HERE...OR PERHAPS NOT!!
SWISH
OOOH, FINALLY!!
WHEE WHEE
MURMUR MURMUR
THAT'S *DRESS-SHRIMP PAELLA!!*
AN ORDER OF *ROSE-SQUID INK PASTA!!*
AND FINALLY, A *GAZPACHO WITH FAIRY PUMPKIN!!*
THEY ALL LOOK SO NUMMY!!
BAA—AM!!
HMM? WHAT'S A FAIRY PUMPKIN?
WELL, IN THIS LAND, MANY STILL BELIEVE THE LEGENDS OF FAIRIES...
...OR PERHAPS NOT.
IN ESSENCE, WE HAVE FAIRIES...
JANG JANG
...OR PERHAPS WE DON'T!!
THERE ARE FAIRIES HERE?
CHOMP CHOMP
QUITE MYSTERIOUS, ISN'T IT? IT'S BEEN THAT WAY FOR CENTURIES.
ENJOY, TRAVEL-ERS! BUT BE CAREFUL...
RATTLE RATTLE
...OR PERHAPS NOT...
YOU'RE THE ONLY THING MYSTERIOUS AROUND HERE.

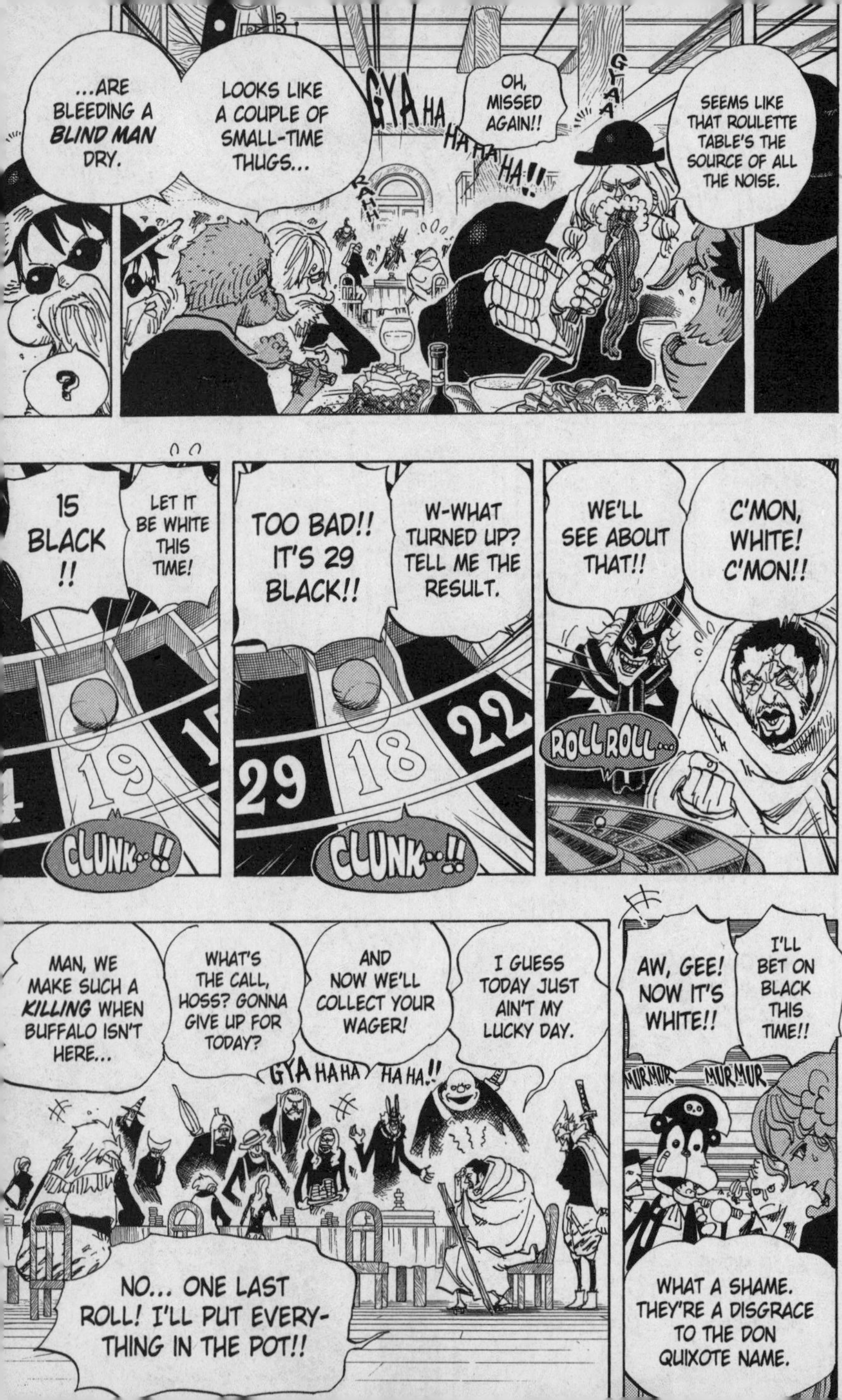
SEEMS LIKE THAT ROULETTE TABLE'S THE SOURCE OF ALL THE NOISE.
GYAAA
OH, MISSED AGAIN!!
GYA HA HA HA HA!!
LOOKS LIKE A COUPLE OF SMALL-TIME THUGS...
RAHH
...ARE BLEEDING A BLIND MAN DRY.
?
C'MON, WHITE! C'MON!!
WE'LL SEE ABOUT THAT!!
ROLL ROLL...
W-WHAT TURNED UP? TELL ME THE RESULT.
TOO BAD!! IT'S 29 BLACK!!
22
18
29
CLUNK..!!
LET IT BE WHITE THIS TIME!
15 BLACK!!
19
CLUNK..!!
I'LL BET ON BLACK THIS TIME!!
AW, GEE! NOW IT'S WHITE!!
MURMUR MURMUR
WHAT A SHAME. THEY'RE A DISGRACE TO THE DON QUIXOTE NAME.
I GUESS TODAY JUST AIN'T MY LUCKY DAY.
AND NOW WE'LL COLLECT YOUR WAGER!
WHAT'S THE CALL, HOSS? GONNA GIVE UP FOR TODAY?
MAN, WE MAKE SUCH A KILLING WHEN BUFFALO ISN'T HERE...
GYA HA HA HA HA!!
NO... ONE LAST ROLL! I'LL PUT EVERYTHING IN THE POT!!

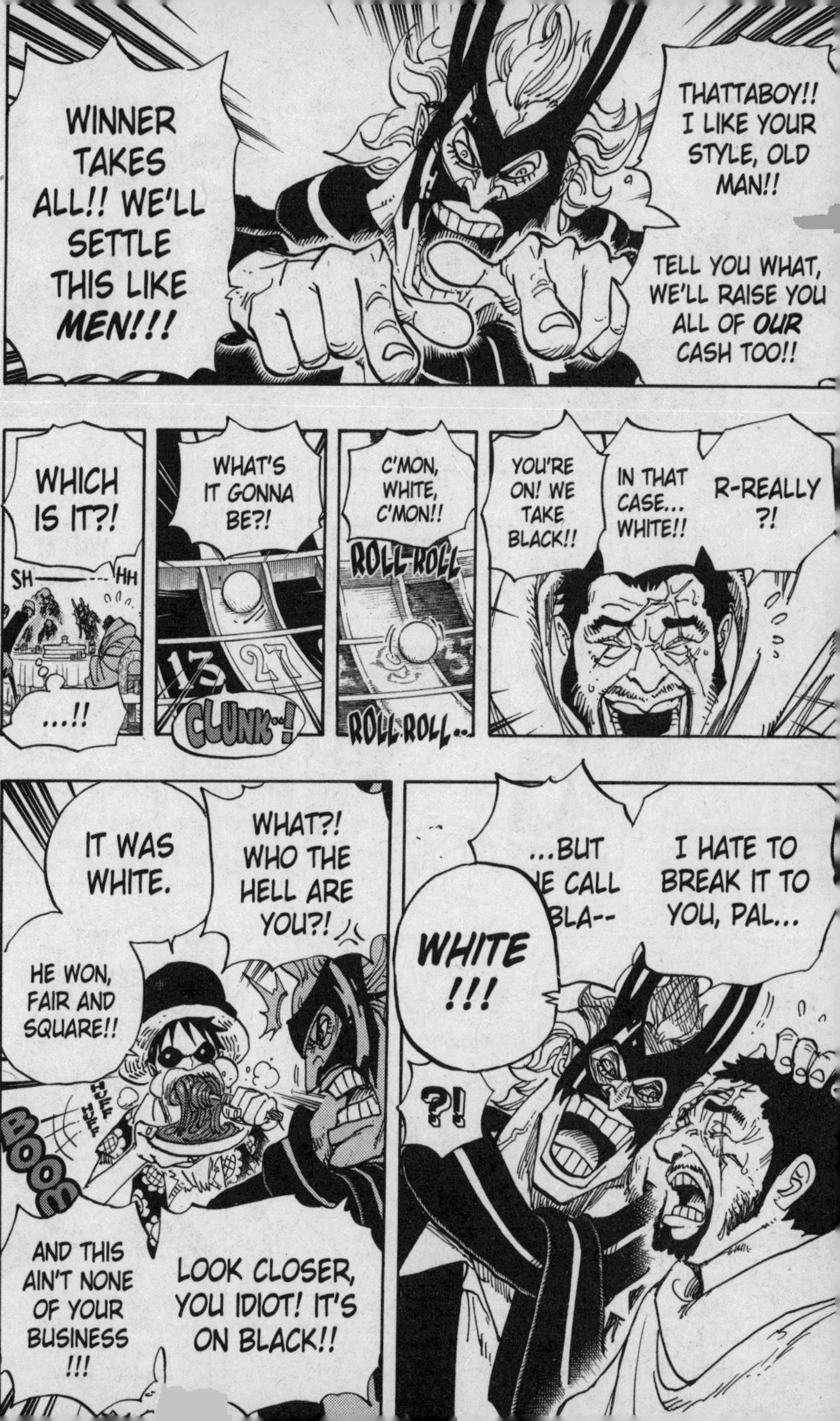
THATTABOY!! I LIKE YOUR STYLE, OLD MAN!!
TELL YOU WHAT, WE'LL RAISE YOU ALL OF OUR CASH TOO!!
WINNER TAKES ALL!! WE'LL SETTLE THIS LIKE MEN!!!
R-REALLY ?!
IN THAT CASE... WHITE!!
YOU'RE ON! WE TAKE BLACK!!
C'MON, WHITE, C'MON!!
ROLL ROLL
ROLL ROLL..
WHAT'S IT GONNA BE?!
CLUNK..!
WHICH IS IT?!
SH———HH
...!!
I HATE TO BREAK IT TO YOU, PAL...
...BUT E CALL BLA--
WHITE !!!
?!
WHAT?! WHO THE HELL ARE YOU?!
IT WAS WHITE.
HE WON, FAIR AND SQUARE!!
HUFF HUFF
BOOM
LOOK CLOSER, YOU IDIOT! IT'S ON BLACK!!
AND THIS AIN'T NONE OF YOUR BUSINESS !!!

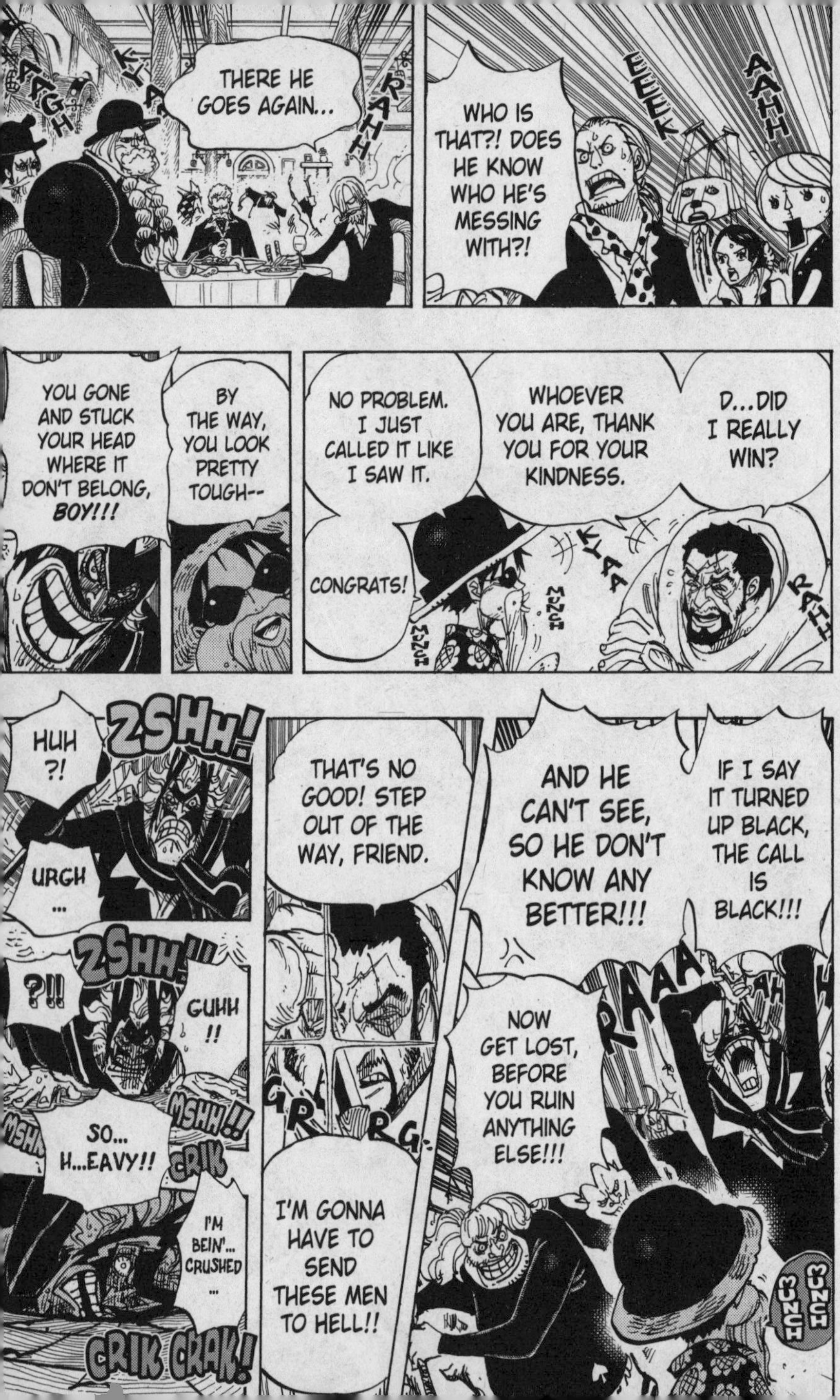
EEEEK
AAHH
WHO IS THAT?! DOES HE KNOW WHO HE'S MESSING WITH?!
THERE HE GOES AGAIN...
AAGH
KYAA
RAHHH
D...DID I REALLY WIN?
WHOEVER YOU ARE, THANK YOU FOR YOUR KINDNESS.
KYAA
NO PROBLEM. I JUST CALLED IT LIKE I SAW IT.
CONGRATS!
MUNCH
MUNCH
BY THE WAY, YOU LOOK PRETTY TOUGH--
YOU GONE AND STUCK YOUR HEAD WHERE IT DON'T BELONG, BOY!!!
IF I SAY IT TURNED UP BLACK, THE CALL IS BLACK!!!
AND HE CAN'T SEE, SO HE DON'T KNOW ANY BETTER!!!
RAAA
NOW GET LOST, BEFORE YOU RUIN ANYTHING ELSE!!!
MUNCH
MUNCH
THAT'S NO GOOD! STEP OUT OF THE WAY, FRIEND.
GR
RG
I'M GONNA HAVE TO SEND THESE MEN TO HELL!!
ZSHH!
HUH ?!
URGH ...
ZSHH!!!
?!!
GUHH !!
MSHH!!
SO... H...EAVY!!
CRIK
I'M BEIN'... CRUSHED ...
CRIK CRAK!

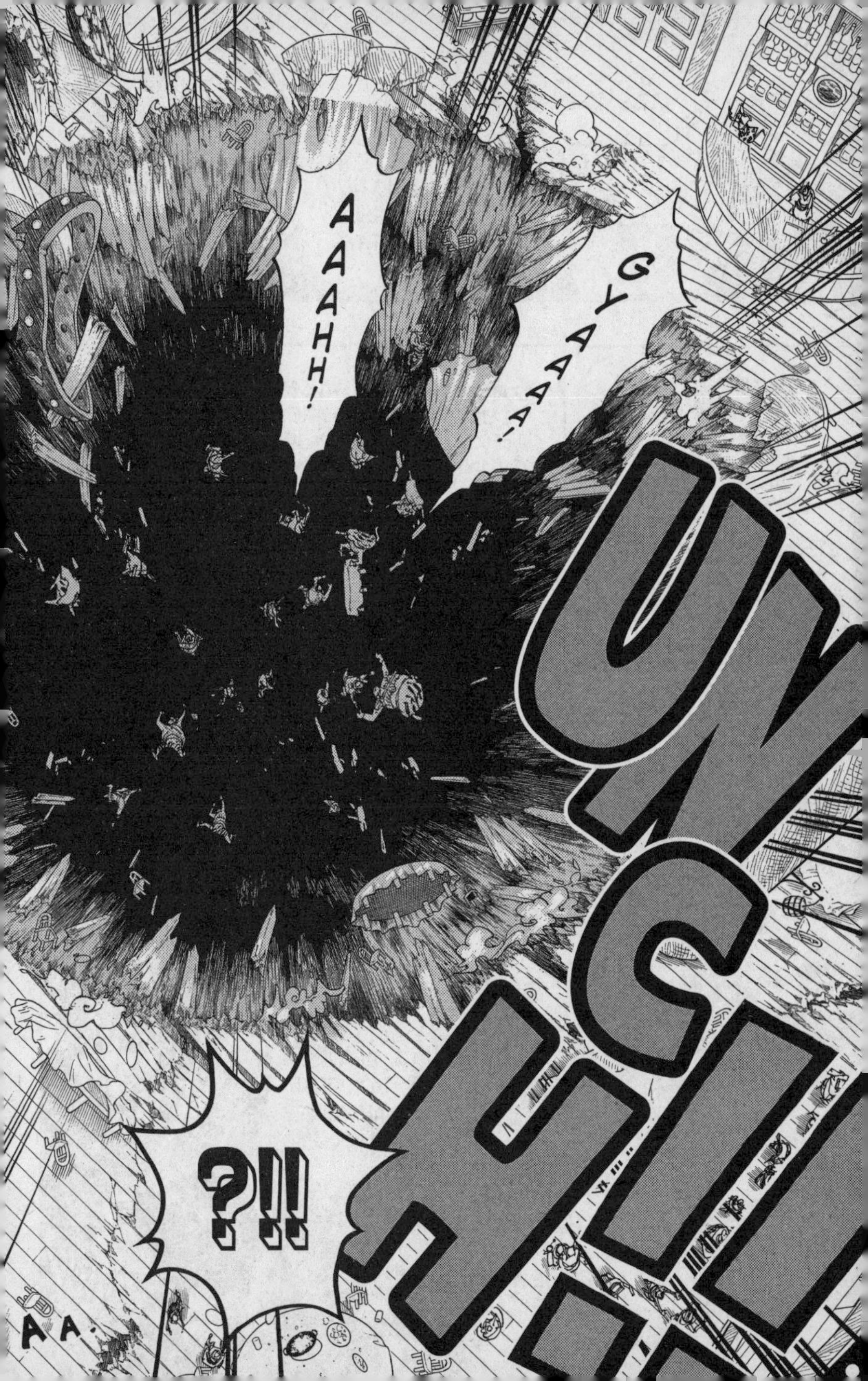
GYAAAAA!
AAAAHH!
?!!
A A

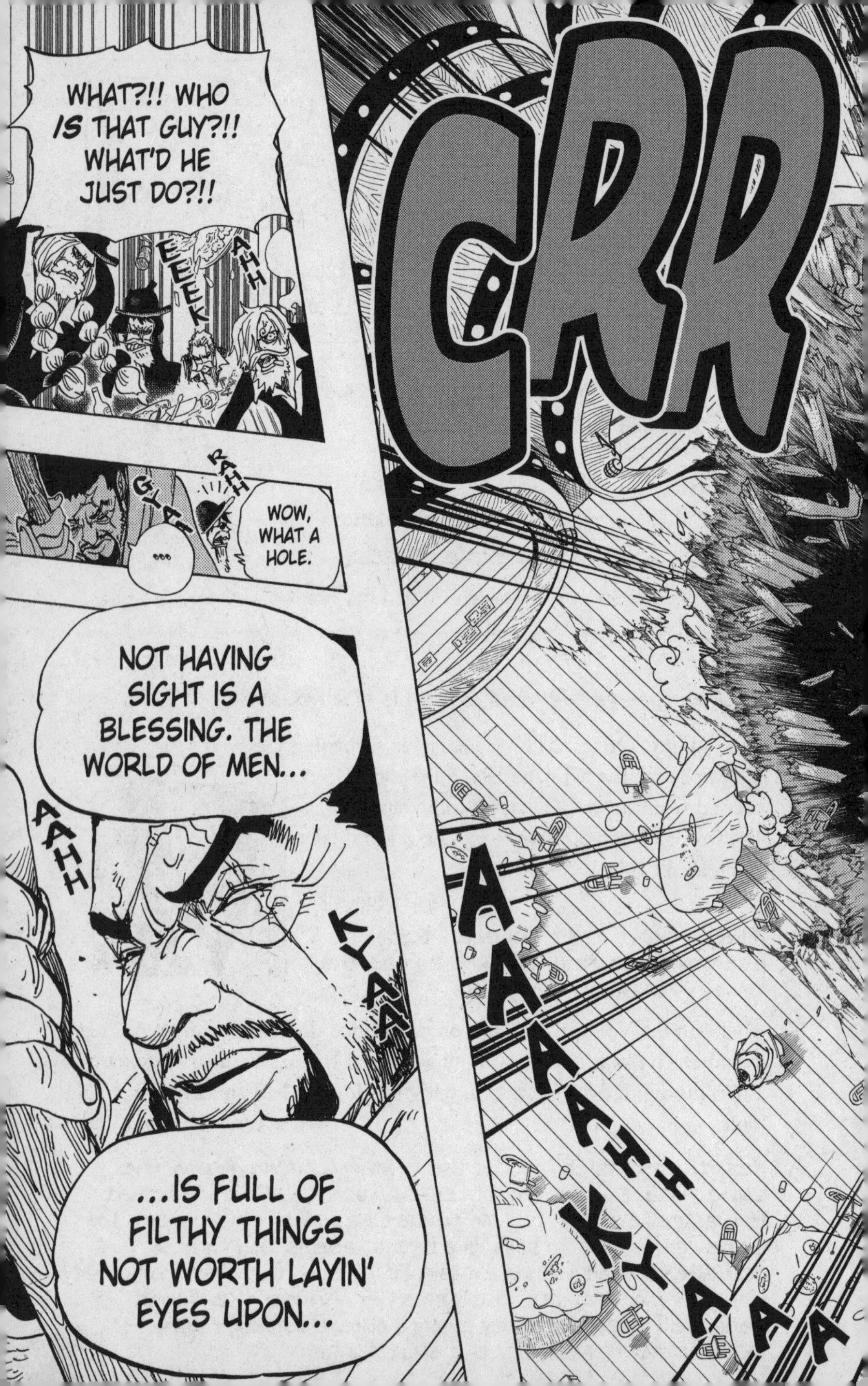
CRR
AAAAAHH
KYAAAA
WHAT?!! WHO *IS* THAT GUY?!! WHAT'D HE JUST DO?!!
EEEEK
AHH
RAHH
WOW, WHAT A HOLE.
...
NOT HAVING SIGHT IS A BLESSING. THE WORLD OF MEN...
AAHH
KYAAA
...IS FULL OF FILTHY THINGS NOT WORTH LAYIN' EYES UPON...

SBS Question Corner

エス
ビー
エス

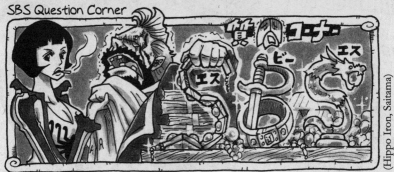

(Hippo Iron, Saitama)

IT'S MR. VERGO TO YOU.
THUMP...

Oda(A): All right! Let's get ready, folks!
"Start!! The SBS!!"
Yahoo!

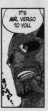

Question(Q): Take it back. That's Mr. SBS.

--Kimurin

A: Oh!! S...sorry... Start the...Mr. SBS...

Q: Question. Question for Odacchi. When did Franky become such a pervert? (^▽^)

--Arabiki Sausage

A: Franky was perverted since his previous life.

Q: I found him, Odacchi!!!!! In fact, it was surprisingly easy. It's him, Kandre!! Volume 57, page 108, third panel, second from the left! That has to be him!! If I'm wrong, then you have to be crazy. I'm totally right, aren't I?!!

--Teaguechikei

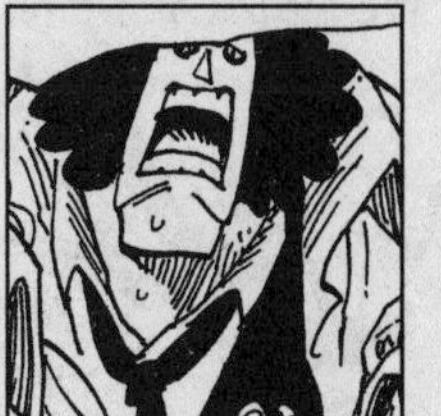

A: That's right. Last volume I told everyone to find him if they had the time. Well, you found him!

Q: Hello! In the Volume 70 SBS, you mentioned the twin brothers Andre/Kandre. That was also famous singer Yosui Inoue's original stage name upon his debut over 40 years ago, right? He even had an afro at the time.

--Was Once a Guitar Lad

A: Yes, that's right. I took the rhyming name from the same place, but as a matter of fact, I had no idea that it was referring to him. I'd just heard the name on TV once years ago. It says that your age is 56, Guitar Lad, so I guess that would explain it, eh? By the way, I originally named Andre after the wrestler Andre the Giant, because I thought they looked alike. Basically, I just make up my names on the spot, ha ha.

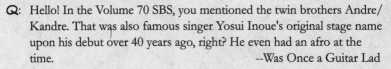

Chapter 702: CORRIDA COLISEUM

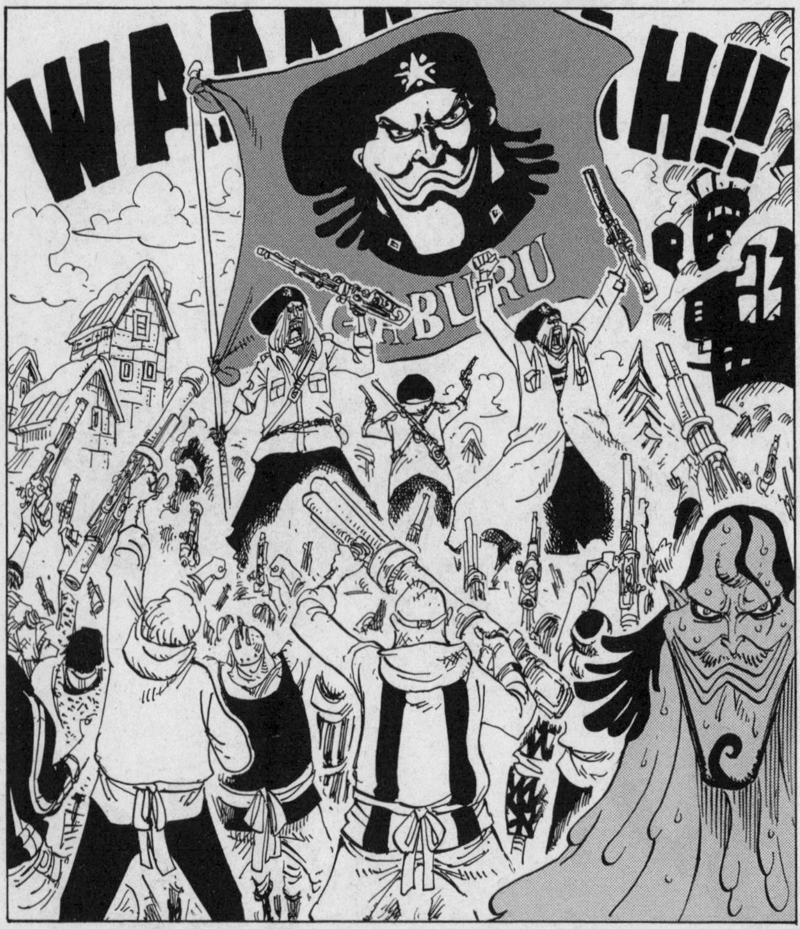
WAAAAAAAH!!
GABURU

CARIBOU'S NEW WORLD KEE HEE HEE, VOL. 23: "PROLETARIATS, GRAB YOUR WEAPONS!! CAPTAIN GABURU, CHILD OF THE REVOLUTION, HAS RETURNED!!!"

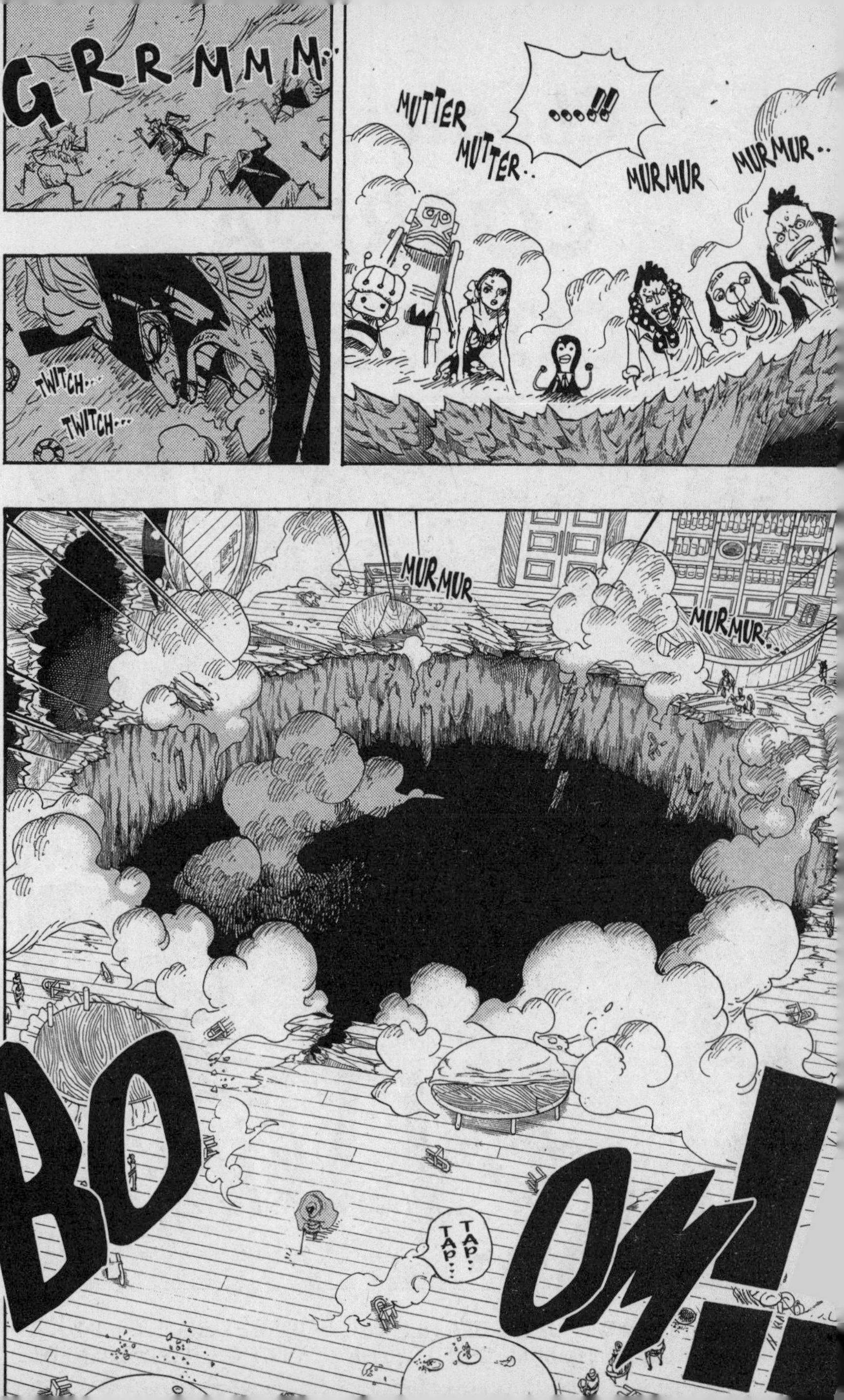
MURMUR..
....!!
MUTTER MUTTER..
MURMUR
GRRMMM..
TWITCH...
TWITCH...
MURMUR...
MURMUR
TAP... TAP...
BOOM!!

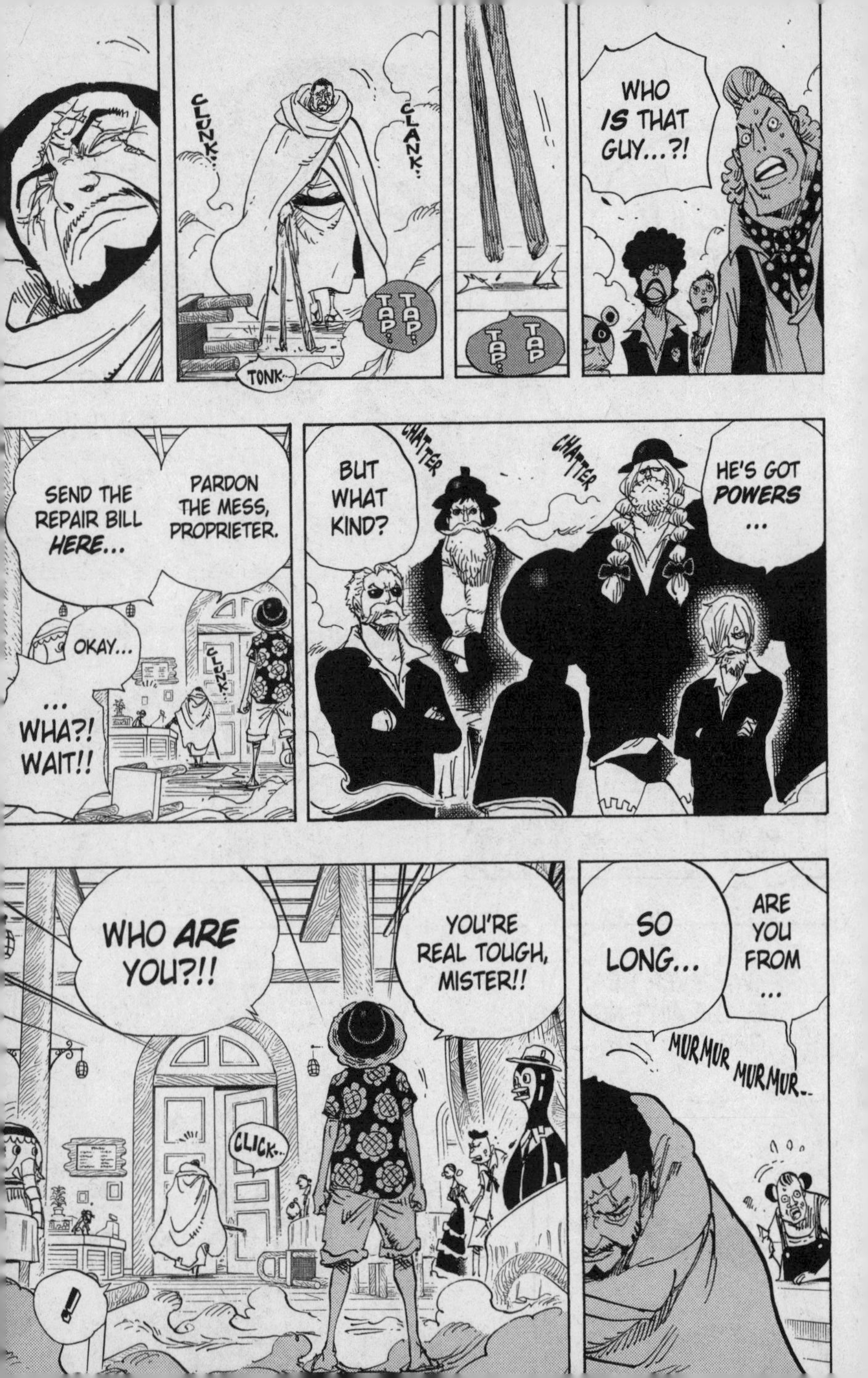
WHO IS THAT GUY...?!
TAP TAP
CLUNK...
CLANK...
TAP TAP
TONK...
HE'S GOT POWERS ...
CHATTER
BUT WHAT KIND?
CHATTER
PARDON THE MESS, PROPRIETER.
SEND THE REPAIR BILL HERE...
OKAY...
CLUNK...
... WHA?! WAIT!!
ARE YOU FROM ...
SO LONG...
MURMUR MURMUR..
YOU'RE REAL TOUGH, MISTER!!
WHO ARE YOU?!!
CLICK..
!

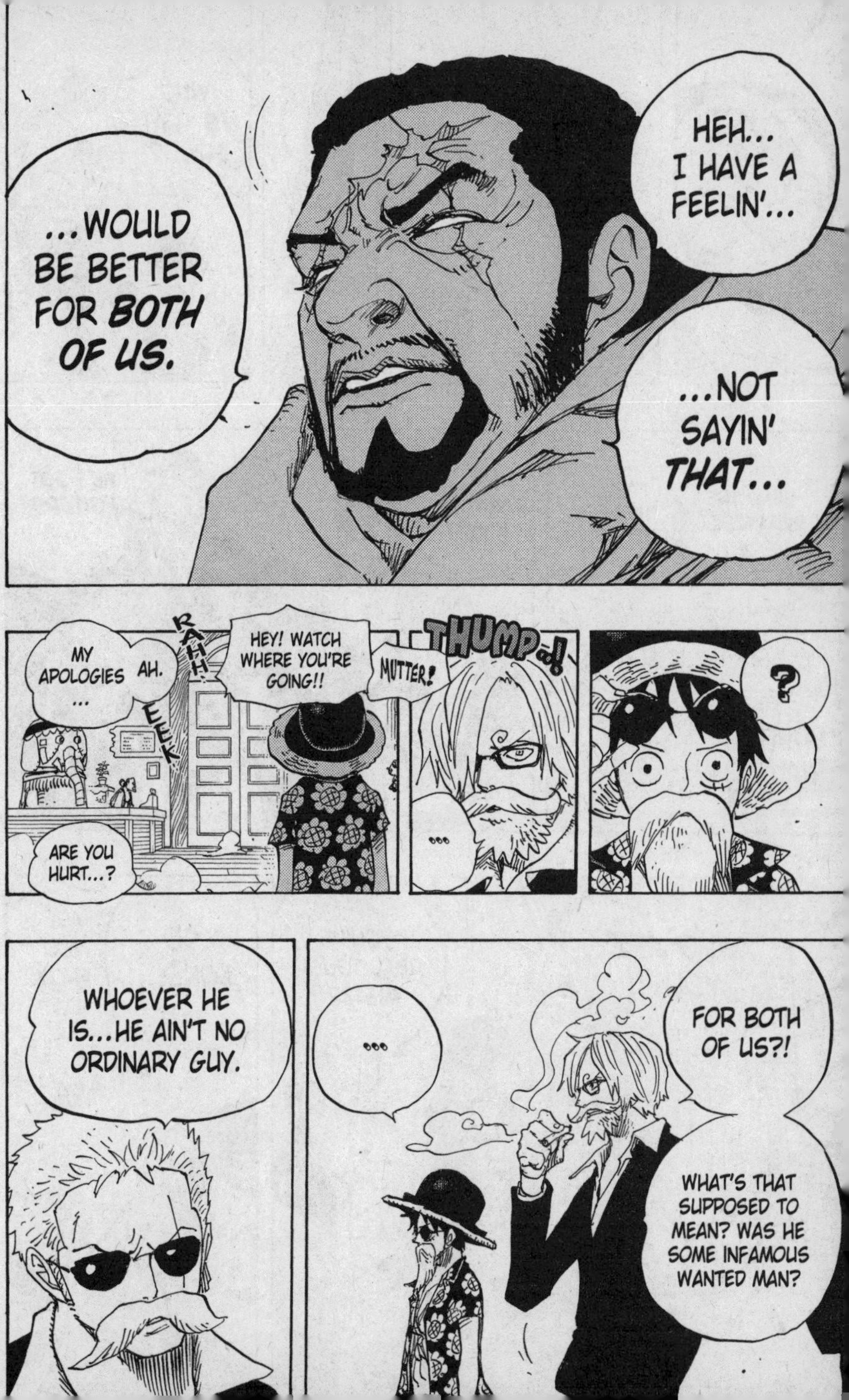
HEH... I HAVE A FEELIN'...
...NOT SAYIN' THAT...
...WOULD BE BETTER FOR *BOTH* OF US.
?
THUMP
...
MUTTER!
HEY! WATCH WHERE YOU'RE GOING!!
RAHHH
AH.
MY APOLOGIES ...
EEEK
ARE YOU HURT...?
FOR BOTH OF US?!
WHAT'S THAT SUPPOSED TO MEAN? WAS HE SOME INFAMOUS WANTED MAN?
...
WHOEVER HE IS...HE AIN'T NO ORDINARY GUY.

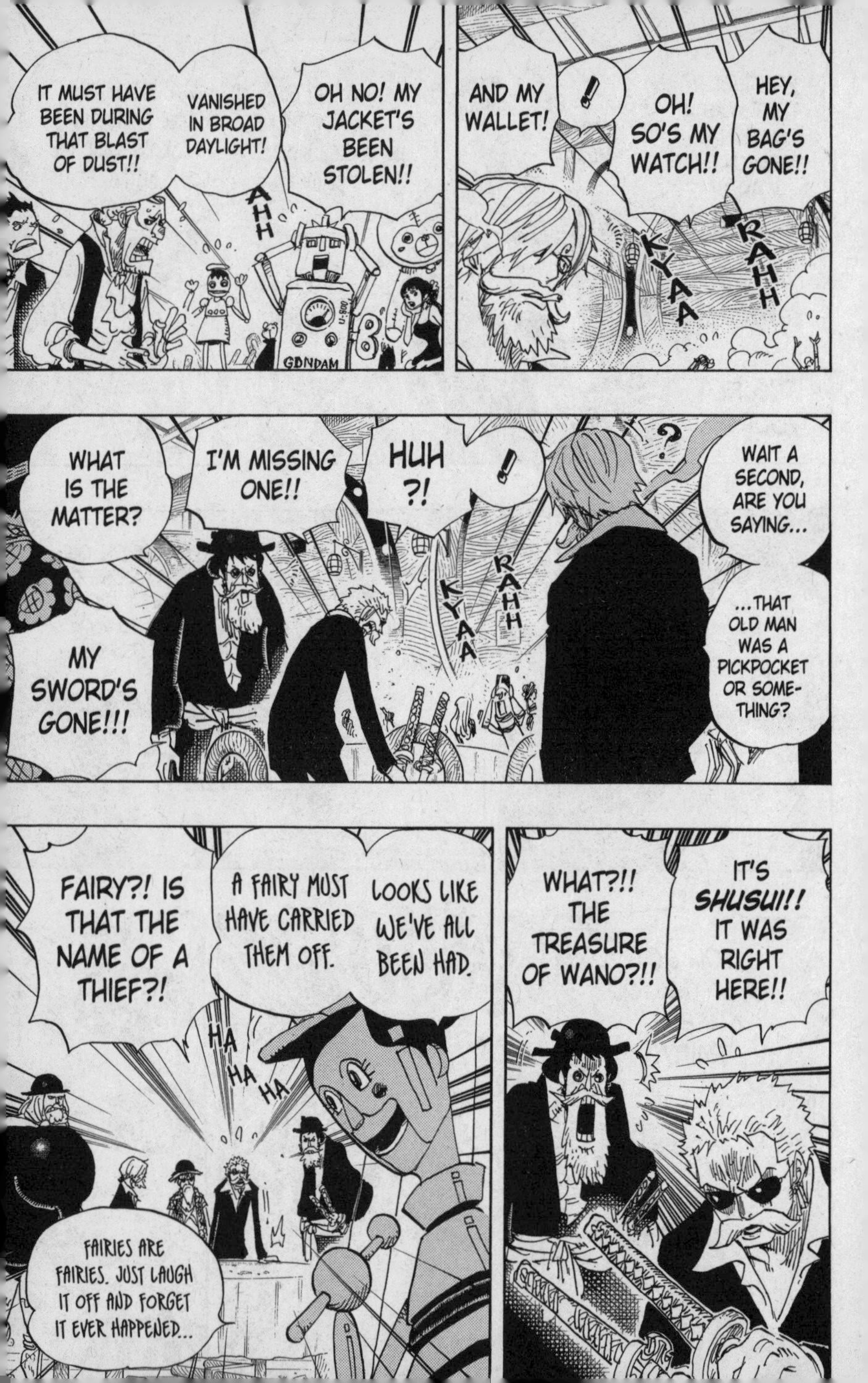
HEY, MY BAG'S GONE!!
RAHH
OH! SO'S MY WATCH!!
KYAA
!
AND MY WALLET!
OH NO! MY JACKET'S BEEN STOLEN!!
AHH
VANISHED IN BROAD DAYLIGHT!
IT MUST HAVE BEEN DURING THAT BLAST OF DUST!!
GDNDAM
WAIT A SECOND, ARE YOU SAYING...
...THAT OLD MAN WAS A PICKPOCKET OR SOME-THING?
?
!
HUH ?!
RAHH
KYAA
I'M MISSING ONE!!
WHAT IS THE MATTER?
MY SWORD'S GONE!!!
IT'S **SHUSUI!!** IT WAS RIGHT HERE!!
WHAT?!! THE TREASURE OF WANO?!!
LOOKS LIKE WE'VE ALL BEEN HAD.
A FAIRY MUST HAVE CARRIED THEM OFF.
FAIRY?! IS THAT THE NAME OF A THIEF?!
HA HA HA
FAIRIES ARE FAIRIES. JUST LAUGH IT OFF AND FORGET IT EVER HAPPENED...

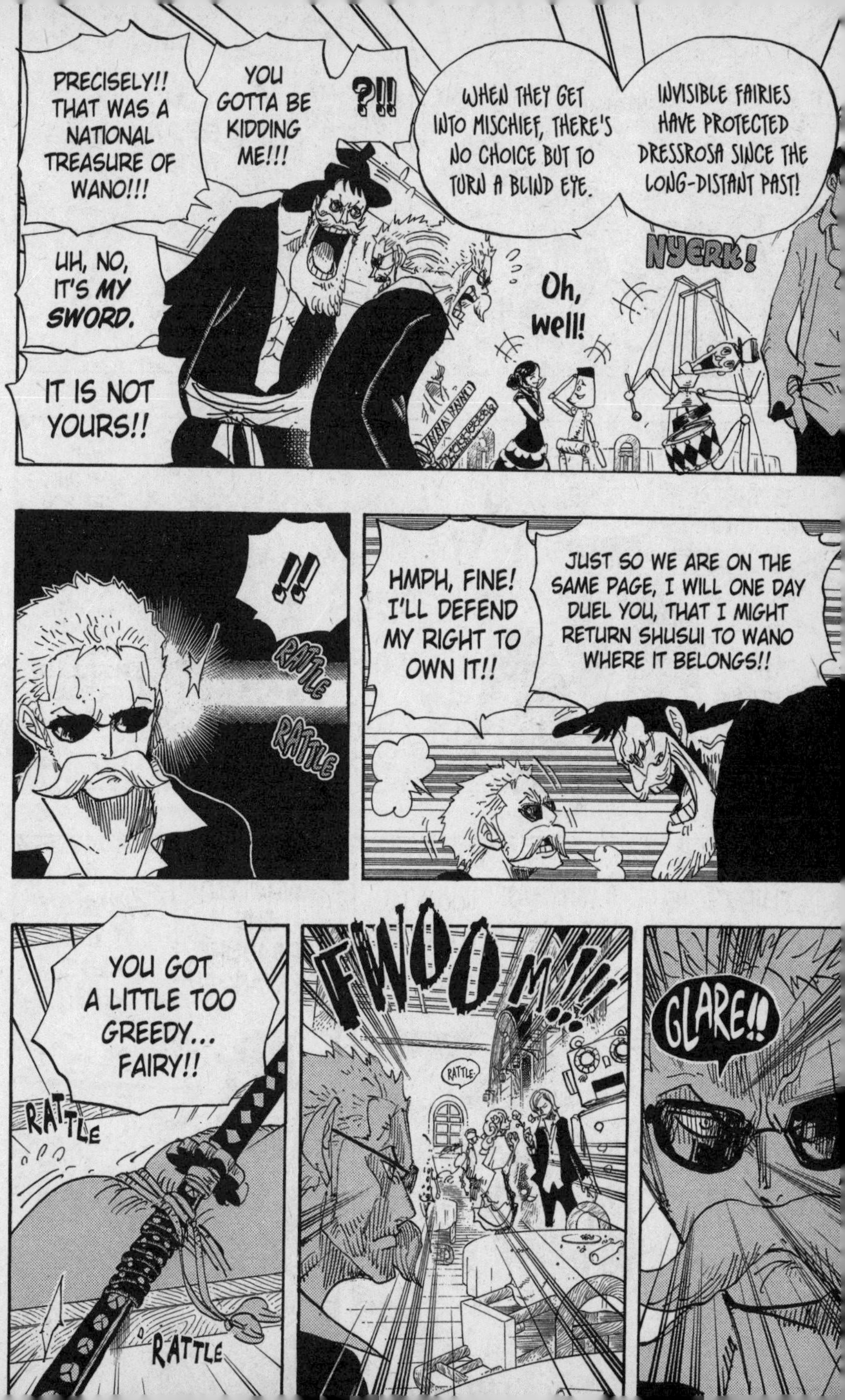
INVISIBLE FAIRIES HAVE PROTECTED DRESSROSA SINCE THE LONG-DISTANT PAST!
WHEN THEY GET INTO MISCHIEF, THERE'S NO CHOICE BUT TO TURN A BLIND EYE.
NYERK!
Oh, well!
?!!
YOU GOTTA BE KIDDING ME!!!
PRECISELY!! THAT WAS A NATIONAL TREASURE OF WANO!!!
UH, NO, IT'S MY SWORD.
IT IS NOT YOURS!!
JUST SO WE ARE ON THE SAME PAGE, I WILL ONE DAY DUEL YOU, THAT I MIGHT RETURN SHUSUI TO WANO WHERE IT BELONGS!!
HMPH, FINE! I'LL DEFEND MY RIGHT TO OWN IT!!
!!
RATTLE
RATTLE
GLARE!!
FWOOM!!!
RATTLE
YOU GOT A LITTLE TOO GREEDY... FAIRY!!
RATTLE
RATTLE

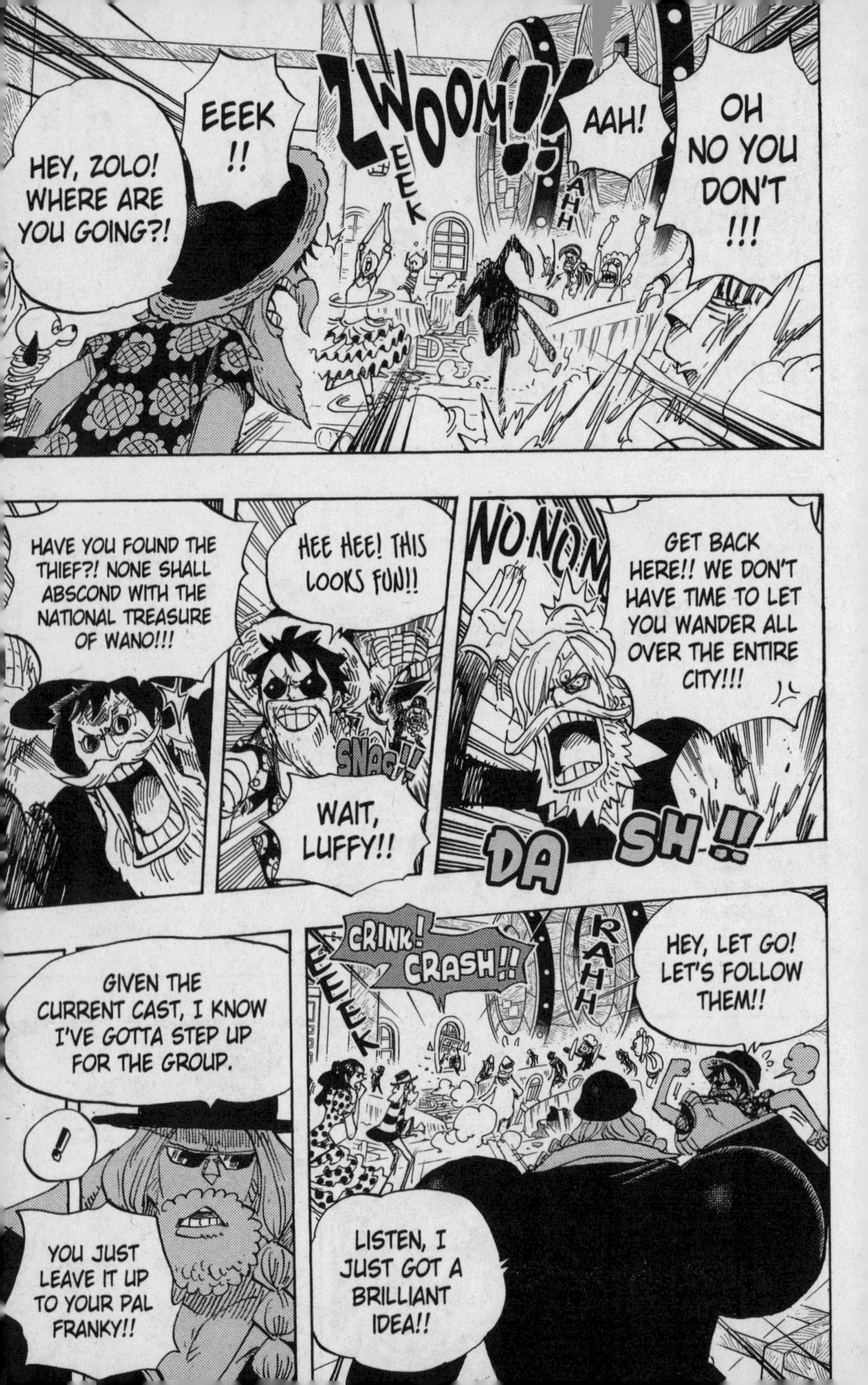
OH NO YOU DON'T!!!
AAH!
ZWOOM!!
EEEK
EEEK !!
HEY, ZOLO! WHERE ARE YOU GOING?!
NO NO NO
GET BACK HERE!! WE DON'T HAVE TIME TO LET YOU WANDER ALL OVER THE ENTIRE CITY!!!
DASH!!
HEE HEE! THIS LOOKS FUN!!
SNAG!!
WAIT, LUFFY!!
HAVE YOU FOUND THE THIEF?! NONE SHALL ABSCOND WITH THE NATIONAL TREASURE OF WANO!!!
HEY, LET GO! LET'S FOLLOW THEM!!
RAHH
CRINK! CRASH!!
EEEK
LISTEN, I JUST GOT A BRILLIANT IDEA!!
GIVEN THE CURRENT CAST, I KNOW I'VE GOTTA STEP UP FOR THE GROUP.
!
YOU JUST LEAVE IT UP TO YOUR PAL FRANKY!!

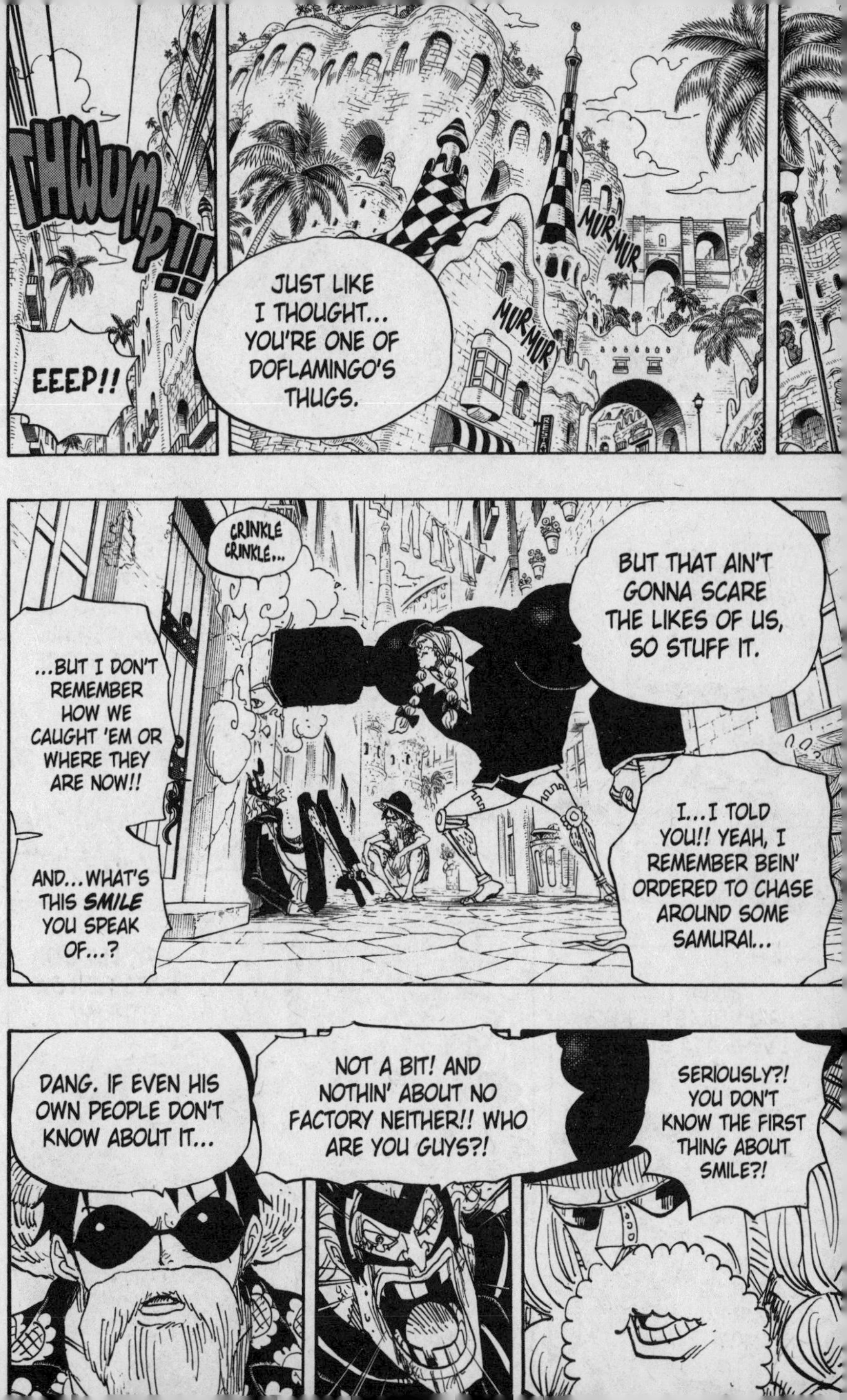
MUR MUR
MUR MUR
JUST LIKE I THOUGHT... YOU'RE ONE OF DOFLAMINGO'S THUGS.
THWUMP!!!
EEEP!!
BUT THAT AIN'T GONNA SCARE THE LIKES OF US, SO STUFF IT.
CRINKLE CRINKLE...
I...I TOLD YOU!! YEAH, I REMEMBER BEIN' ORDERED TO CHASE AROUND SOME SAMURAI...
...BUT I DON'T REMEMBER HOW WE CAUGHT 'EM OR WHERE THEY ARE NOW!!
AND...WHAT'S THIS SMILE YOU SPEAK OF...?
SERIOUSLY?! YOU DON'T KNOW THE FIRST THING ABOUT SMILE?!
NOT A BIT! AND NOTHIN' ABOUT NO FACTORY NEITHER!! WHO ARE YOU GUYS?!
DANG. IF EVEN HIS OWN PEOPLE DON'T KNOW ABOUT IT...

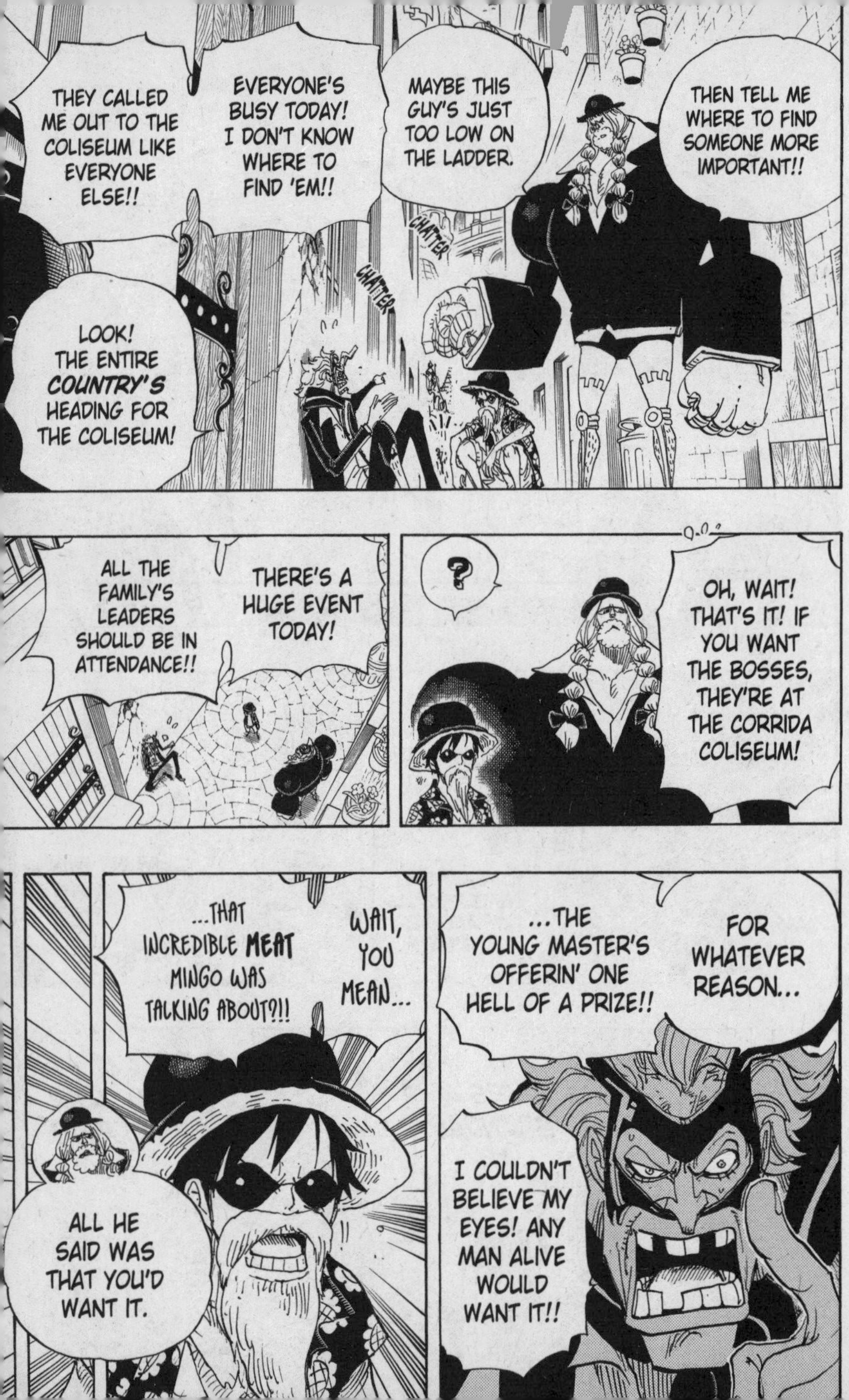
THEN TELL ME WHERE TO FIND SOMEONE MORE IMPORTANT!!
MAYBE THIS GUY'S JUST TOO LOW ON THE LADDER.
EVERYONE'S BUSY TODAY! I DON'T KNOW WHERE TO FIND 'EM!!
THEY CALLED ME OUT TO THE COLISEUM LIKE EVERYONE ELSE!!
CHATTER
CHATTER
LOOK! THE ENTIRE COUNTRY'S HEADING FOR THE COLISEUM!
?
OH, WAIT! THAT'S IT! IF YOU WANT THE BOSSES, THEY'RE AT THE CORRIDA COLISEUM!
THERE'S A HUGE EVENT TODAY!
ALL THE FAMILY'S LEADERS SHOULD BE IN ATTENDANCE!!
FOR WHATEVER REASON...
...THE YOUNG MASTER'S OFFERIN' ONE HELL OF A PRIZE!!
I COULDN'T BELIEVE MY EYES! ANY MAN ALIVE WOULD WANT IT!!
WAIT, YOU MEAN...
...THAT INCREDIBLE MEAT MINGO WAS TALKING ABOUT?!!
ALL HE SAID WAS THAT YOU'D WANT IT.

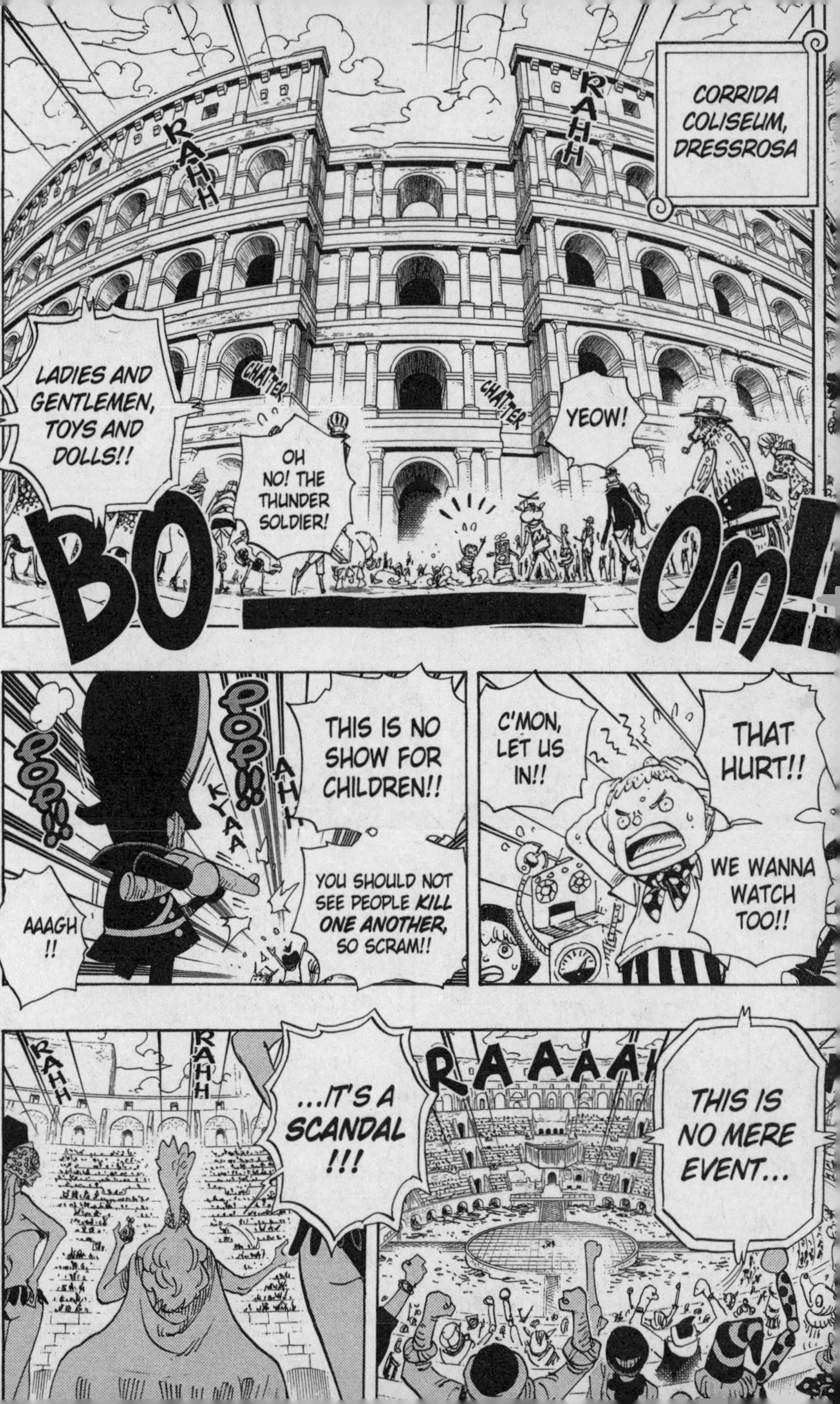

CORRIDA COLISEUM, DRESSROSA
RAHH
RAHH
YEOW!
CHATTER
CHATTER
OH NO! THE THUNDER SOLDIER!
LADIES AND GENTLEMEN, TOYS AND DOLLS!!
BO—OM!!
THAT HURT!!
C'MON, LET US IN!!
WE WANNA WATCH TOO!!
THIS IS NO SHOW FOR CHILDREN!!
AHHK
KYAA
POP!!
POP!!
YOU SHOULD NOT SEE PEOPLE *KILL ONE ANOTHER*, SO SCRAM!!
AAAGH!!
THIS IS NO MERE EVENT...
RAAAA
...IT'S A SCANDAL!!!
RAHH
RAHH

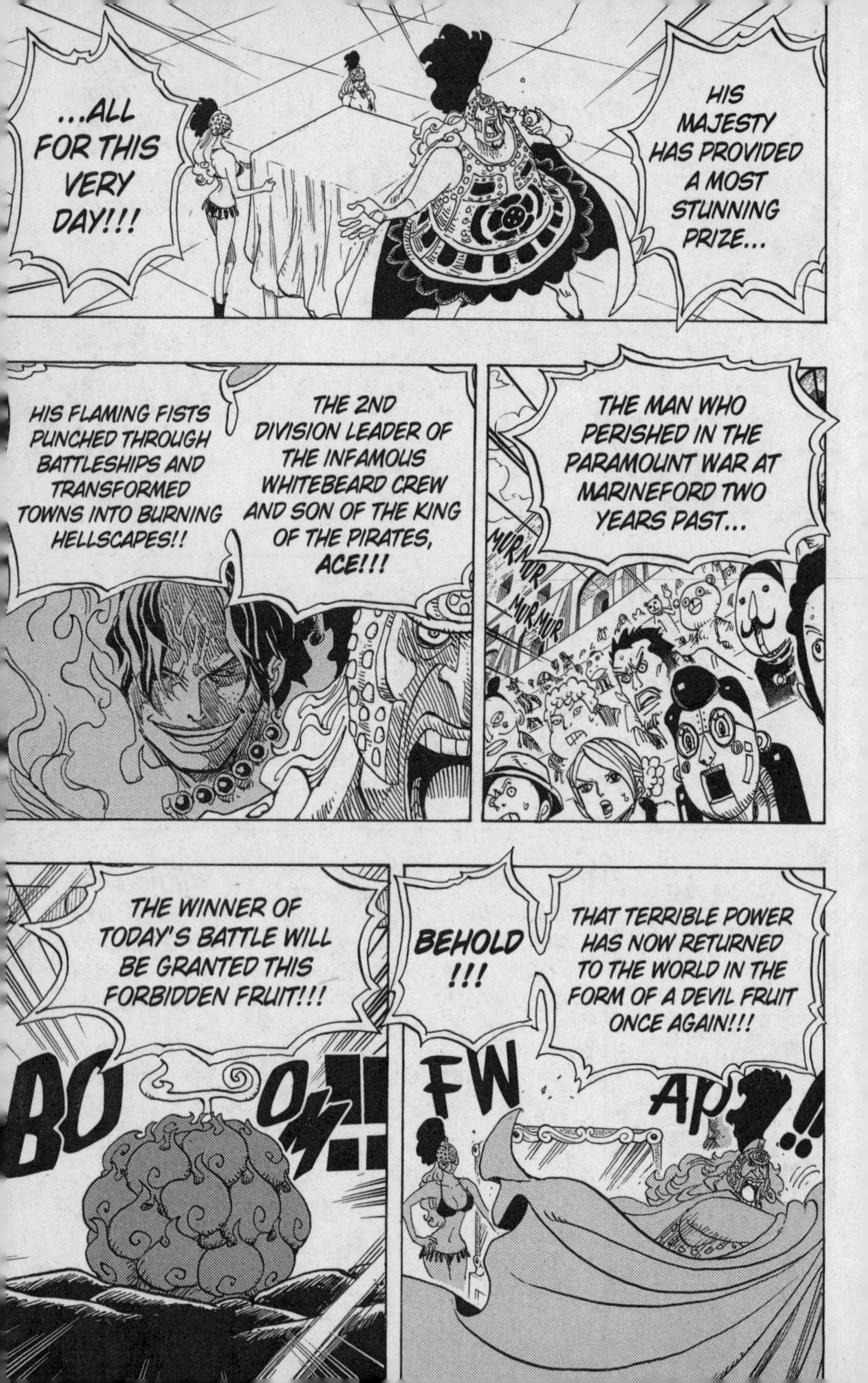
HIS MAJESTY HAS PROVIDED A MOST STUNNING PRIZE...
...ALL FOR THIS VERY DAY!!!
THE MAN WHO PERISHED IN THE PARAMOUNT WAR AT MARINEFORD TWO YEARS PAST...
MUR MUR
MURMUR
THE 2ND DIVISION LEADER OF THE INFAMOUS WHITEBEARD CREW AND SON OF THE KING OF THE PIRATES, ACE!!!
HIS FLAMING FISTS PUNCHED THROUGH BATTLESHIPS AND TRANSFORMED TOWNS INTO BURNING HELLSCAPES!!
THAT TERRIBLE POWER HAS NOW RETURNED TO THE WORLD IN THE FORM OF A DEVIL FRUIT ONCE AGAIN!!!
BEHOLD!!!
FW AP!!
THE WINNER OF TODAY'S BATTLE WILL BE GRANTED THIS FORBIDDEN FRUIT!!!
BO OM!!

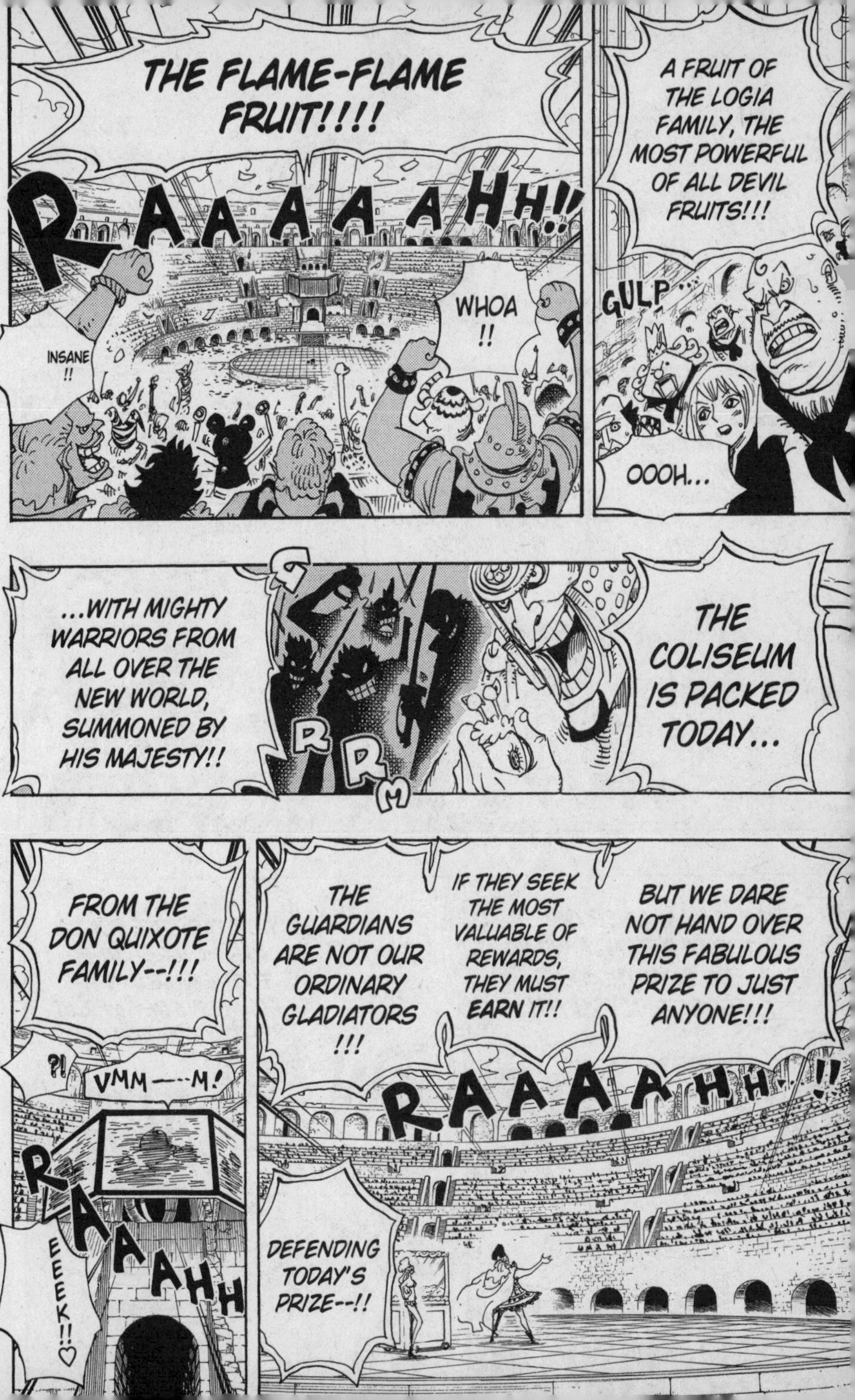
A FRUIT OF THE LOGIA FAMILY, THE MOST POWERFUL OF ALL DEVIL FRUITS!!!
GULP...
OOOH...
THE FLAME-FLAME FRUIT!!!!
RAAAAAHH!!
WHOA !!
INSANE !!
THE COLISEUM IS PACKED TODAY...
GRRM
...WITH MIGHTY WARRIORS FROM ALL OVER THE NEW WORLD, SUMMONED BY HIS MAJESTY!!
BUT WE DARE NOT HAND OVER THIS FABULOUS PRIZE TO JUST ANYONE!!!
IF THEY SEEK THE MOST VALUABLE OF REWARDS, THEY MUST EARN IT!!
THE GUARDIANS ARE NOT OUR ORDINARY GLADIATORS!!!
RAAAAAHH..!!
DEFENDING TODAY'S PRIZE--!!
FROM THE DON QUIXOTE FAMILY--!!!
?!
VMM---M!
RAAAHH
EEEEK!!♡

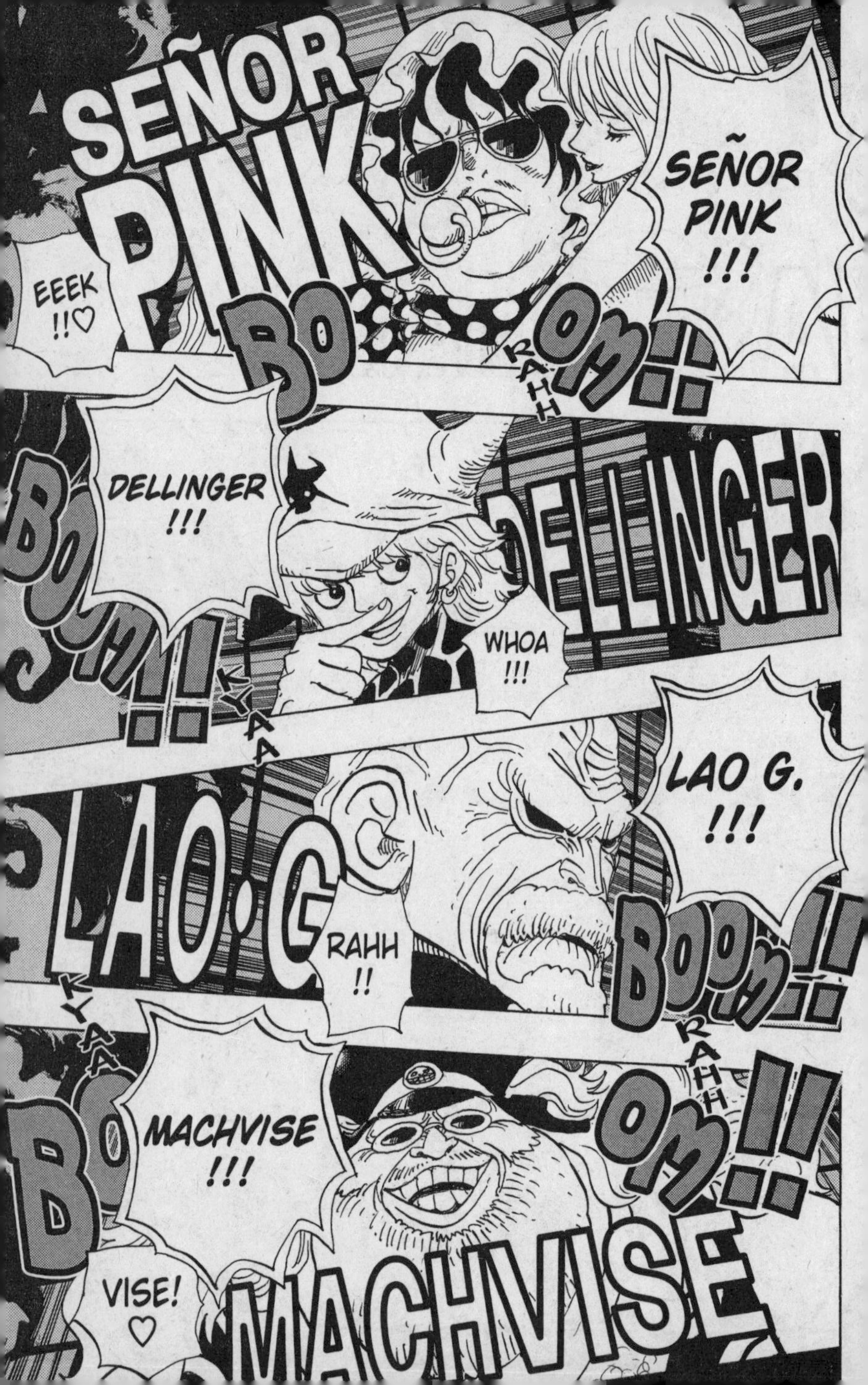
SEÑOR PINK !!!
SEÑOR PINK
RAHH
BOOM!!
EEEK !!♡
DELLINGER
WHOA !!!
DELLINGER !!!
BOOM!!
KYAA
LAO G. !!!
BOOM!!
RAHH
LAO.G
RAHH !!
KYAA
BOOM!!
RAHH
MACHVISE !!!
MACHVISE
VISE! ♡

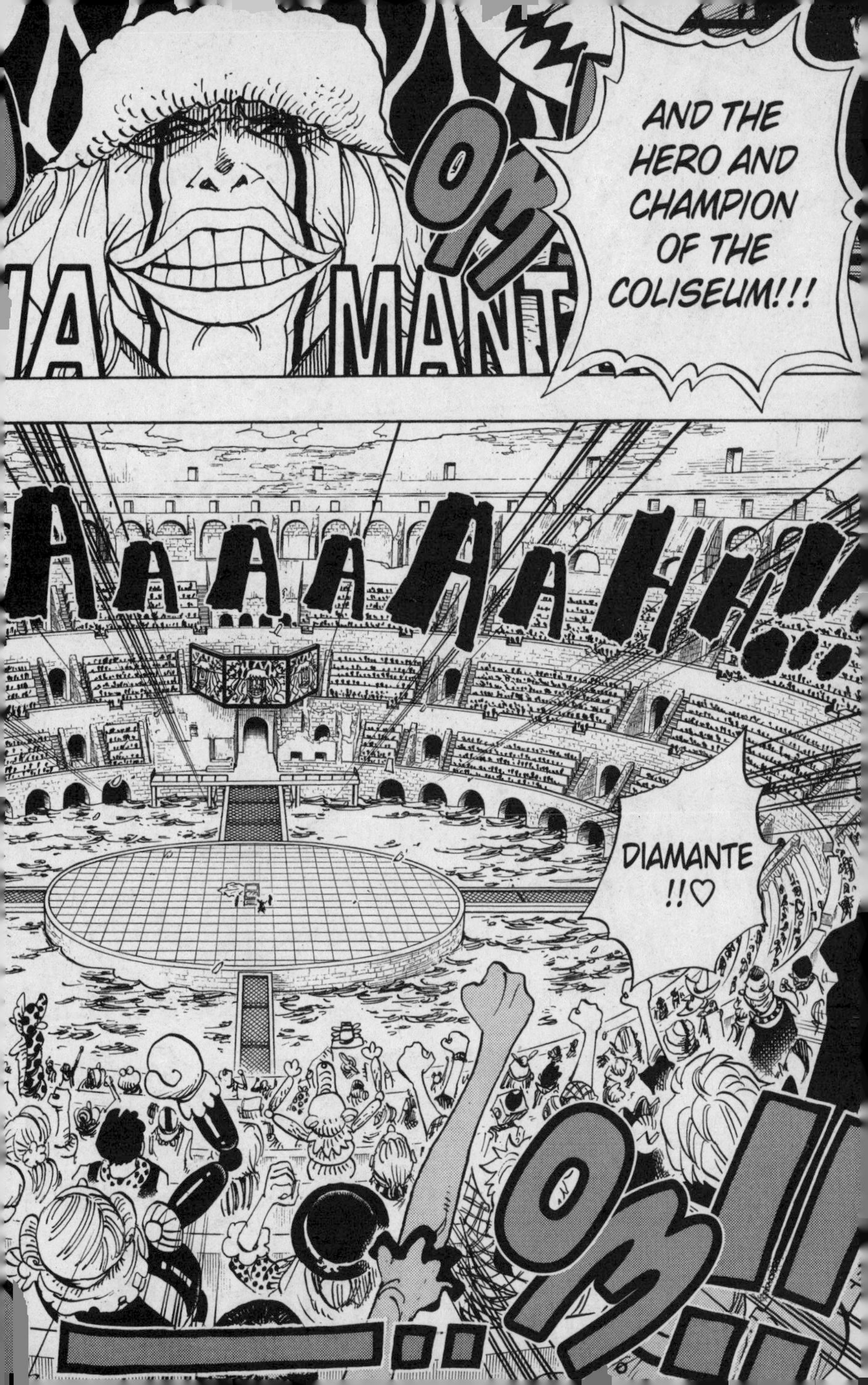
AND THE HERO AND CHAMPION OF THE COLISEUM!!!
DIAMANTE !!♡

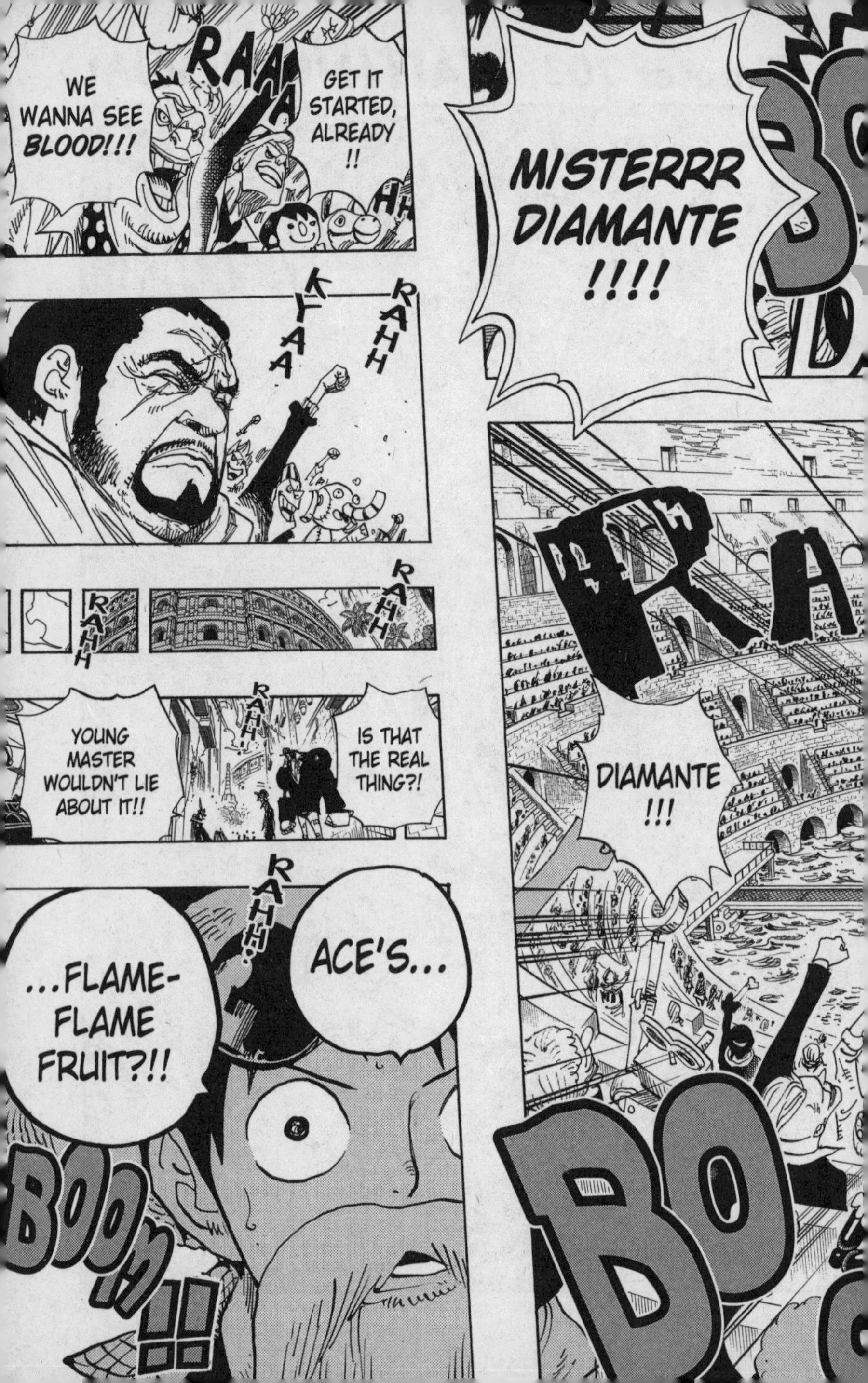

MISTERRR DIAMANTE!!!!
RAA
DIAMANTE!!!
BO
GET IT STARTED, ALREADY!!
RAAA
WE WANNA SEE BLOOD!!!
RAHH
KYAAA
RAHH
RAHH
IS THAT THE REAL THING?!
RAHH
YOUNG MASTER WOULDN'T LIE ABOUT IT!!
RAHH
ACE'S...
...FLAME-FLAME FRUIT?!!
BOOM!!

Chapter 703: WAITING ROOM

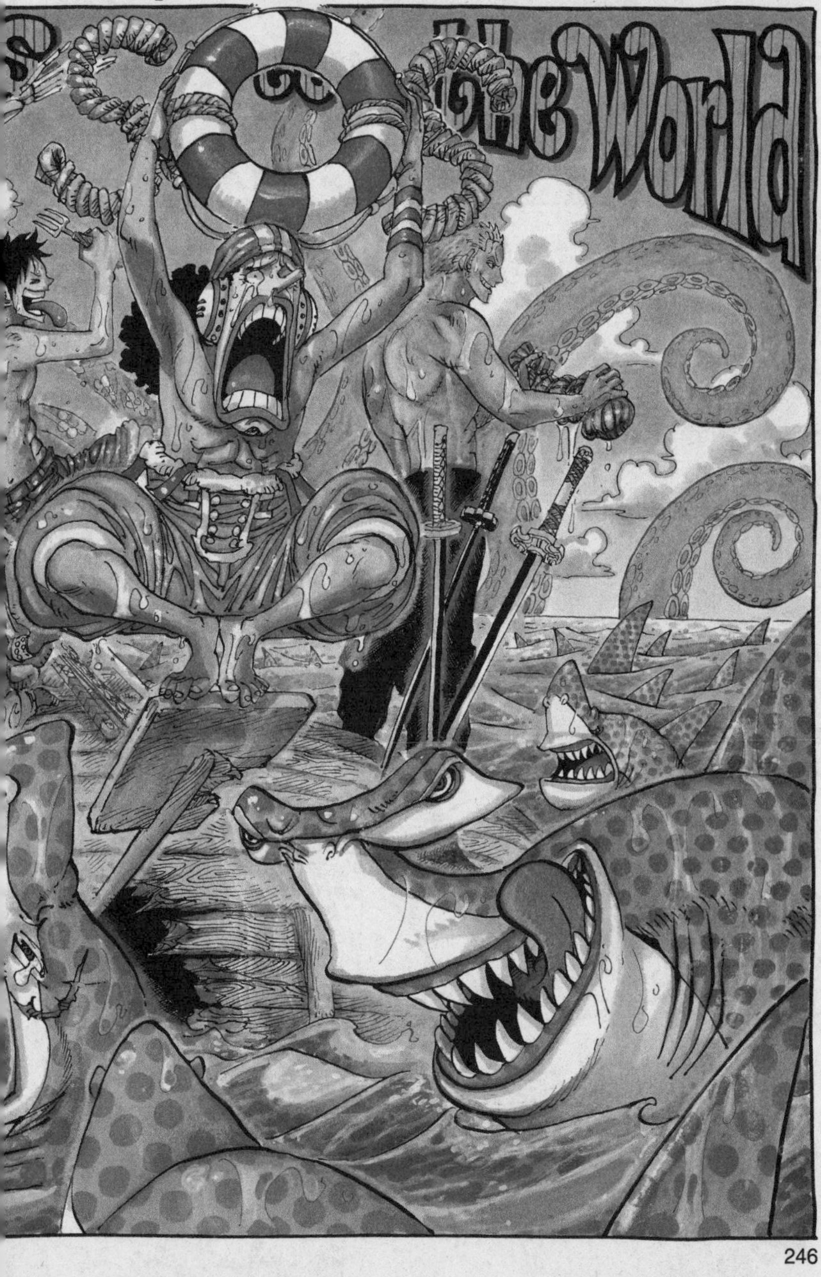

the World

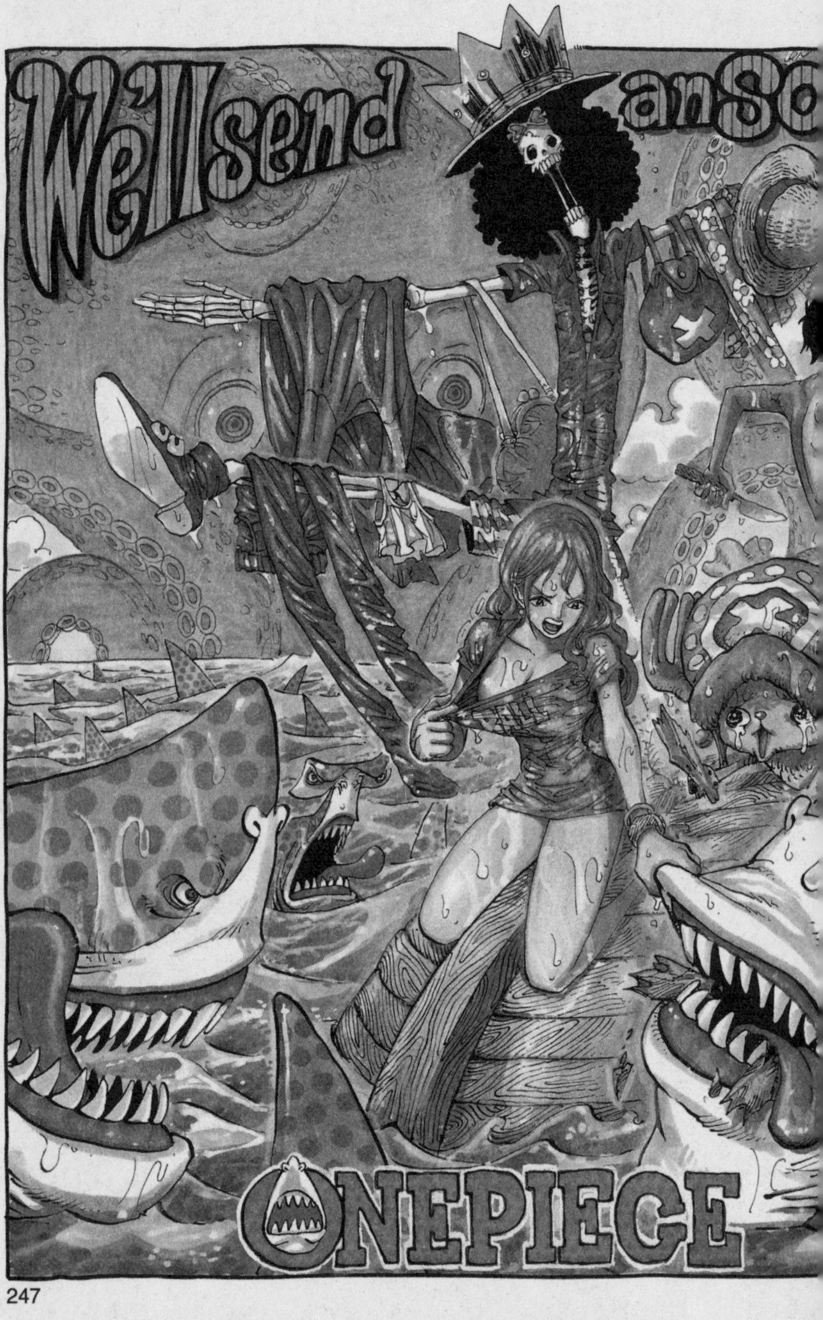
We'll send
an SO
ONE PIECE

vol. 71
ONE PIECE

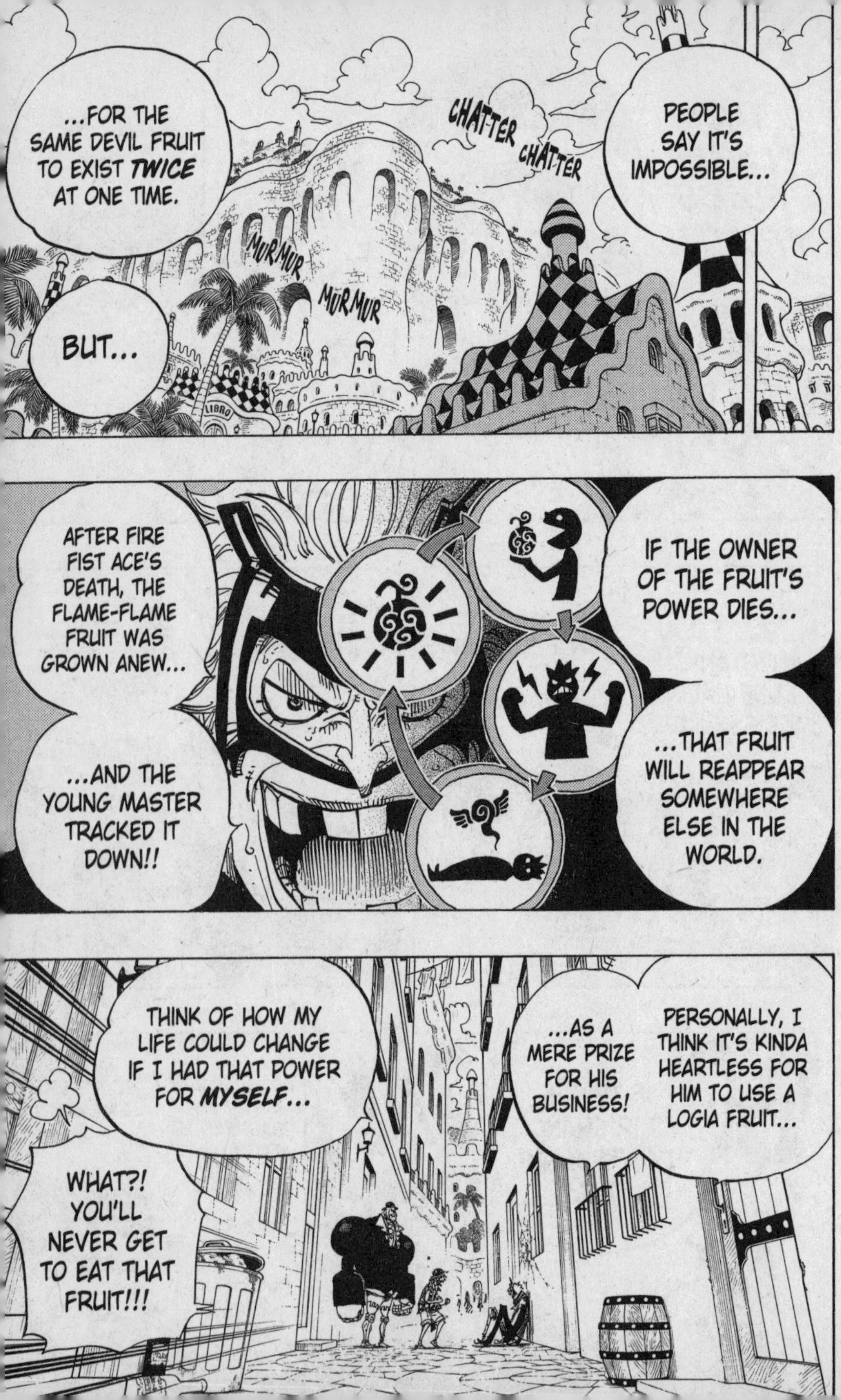
PEOPLE SAY IT'S IMPOSSIBLE...
CHATTER CHATTER
...FOR THE SAME DEVIL FRUIT TO EXIST *TWICE* AT ONE TIME.
MURMUR MURMUR
LIBRO
BUT...
IF THE OWNER OF THE FRUIT'S POWER DIES...
...THAT FRUIT WILL REAPPEAR SOMEWHERE ELSE IN THE WORLD.
AFTER FIRE FIST ACE'S DEATH, THE FLAME-FLAME FRUIT WAS GROWN ANEW...
...AND THE YOUNG MASTER TRACKED IT DOWN!!
PERSONALLY, I THINK IT'S KINDA HEARTLESS FOR HIM TO USE A LOGIA FRUIT...
...AS A MERE PRIZE FOR HIS BUSINESS!
THINK OF HOW MY LIFE COULD CHANGE IF I HAD THAT POWER FOR *MYSELF*...
WHAT?! YOU'LL NEVER GET TO EAT THAT FRUIT!!!

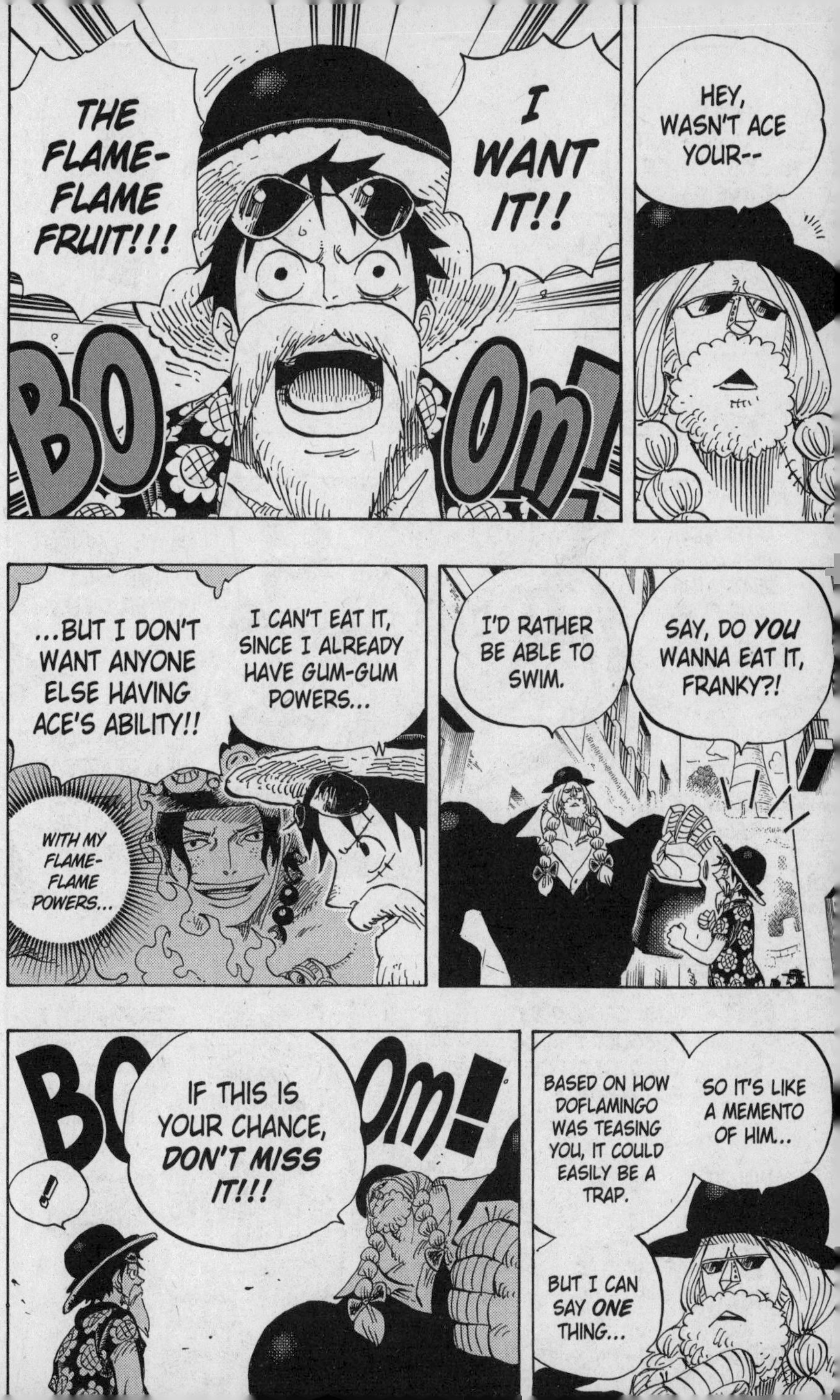
HEY, WASN'T ACE YOUR--
I WANT IT!!
THE FLAME-FLAME FRUIT!!!
BOOM!
SAY, DO YOU WANNA EAT IT, FRANKY?!
I'D RATHER BE ABLE TO SWIM.
I CAN'T EAT IT, SINCE I ALREADY HAVE GUM-GUM POWERS...
...BUT I DON'T WANT ANYONE ELSE HAVING ACE'S ABILITY!!
WITH MY FLAME-FLAME POWERS...
SO IT'S LIKE A MEMENTO OF HIM...
BASED ON HOW DOFLAMINGO WAS TEASING YOU, IT COULD EASILY BE A TRAP.
BUT I CAN SAY ONE THING...
BOOM!
IF THIS IS YOUR CHANCE, DON'T MISS IT!!!
!

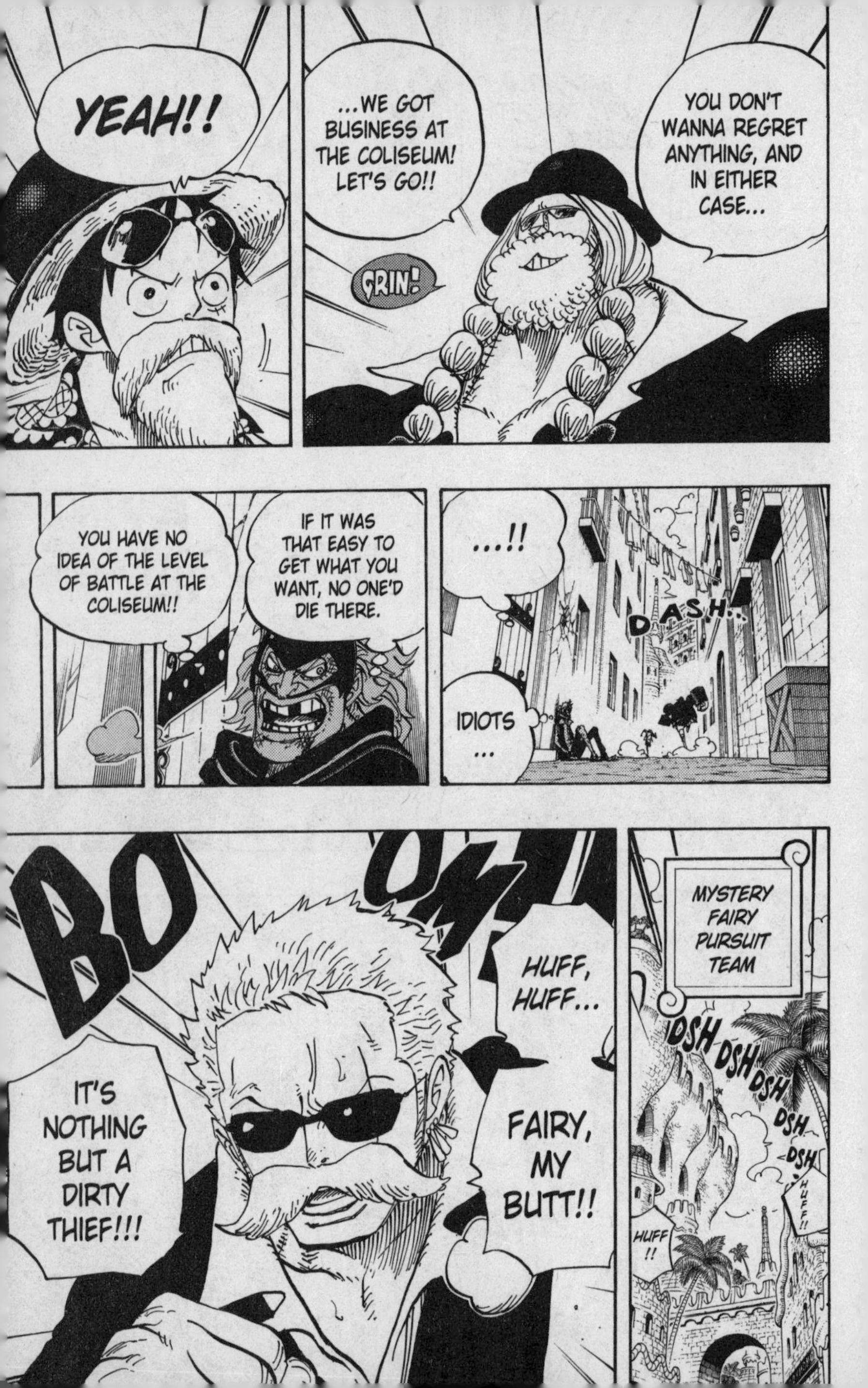
YOU DON'T WANNA REGRET ANYTHING, AND IN EITHER CASE...
...WE GOT BUSINESS AT THE COLISEUM! LET'S GO!!
GRIN!
YEAH!!
...!!
DASH..
IDIOTS ...
IF IT WAS THAT EASY TO GET WHAT YOU WANT, NO ONE'D DIE THERE.
YOU HAVE NO IDEA OF THE LEVEL OF BATTLE AT THE COLISEUM!!
MYSTERY FAIRY PURSUIT TEAM
DSH DSH DSH DSH DSH
HUFF!!
HUFF!!
BOOM
HUFF, HUFF...
FAIRY, MY BUTT!!
IT'S NOTHING BUT A DIRTY THIEF!!!

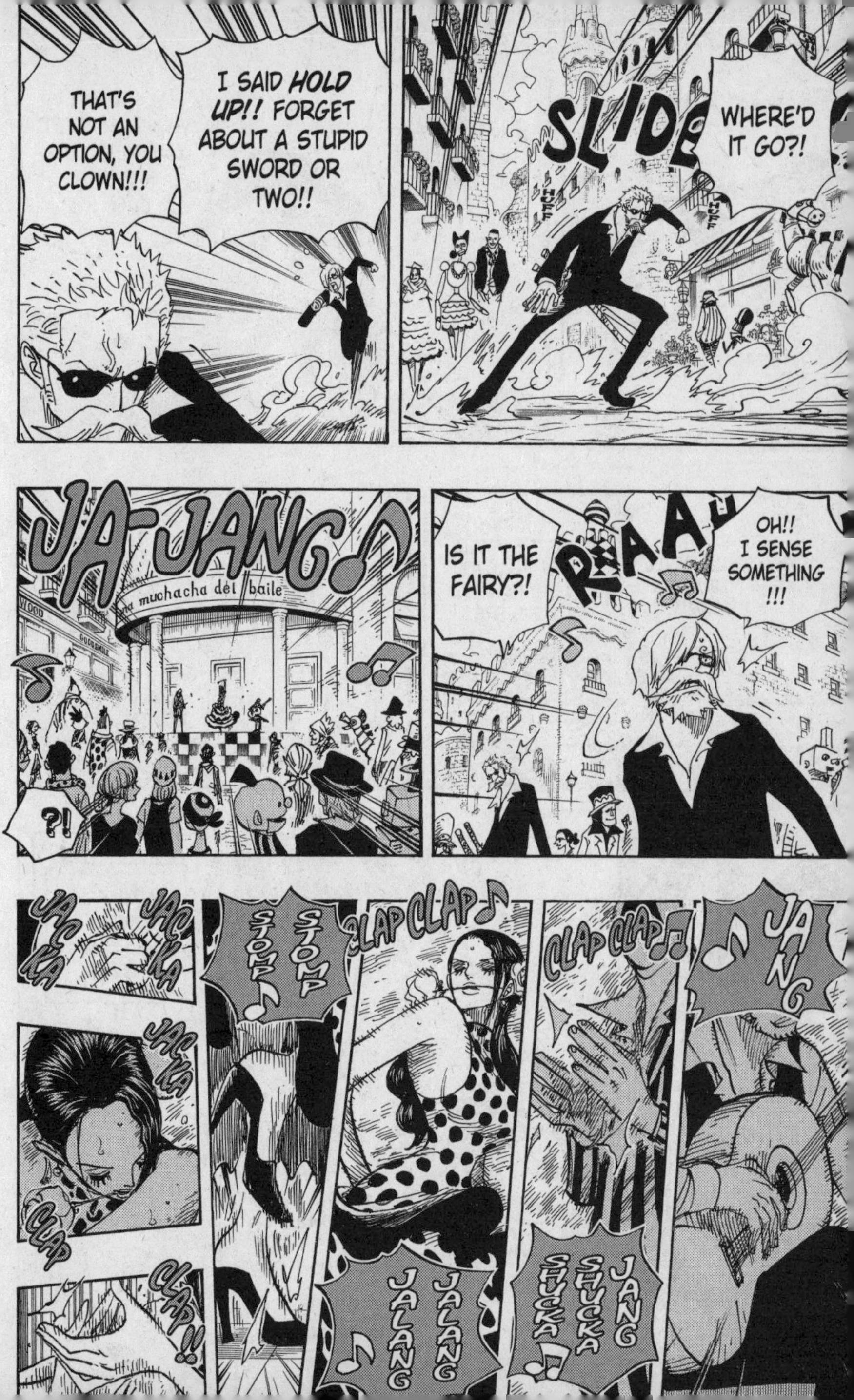
WHERE'D IT GO?!
SLIDE
HUFF
HUFF
I SAID *HOLD UP!!* FORGET ABOUT A STUPID SWORD OR TWO!!
THAT'S NOT AN OPTION, YOU CLOWN!!!
OH!! I SENSE SOMETHING!!!
RAAA
IS IT THE FAIRY?!
JA-JANG♪
muchacha del baile
?!
JANG
CLAP CLAP♪
JANG SHUCKA SHUCKA
CLAP CLAP♪
JALANG JALANG
STOMP STOMP
JACKA JACKA
JACKA
CLAP
CLAP!!

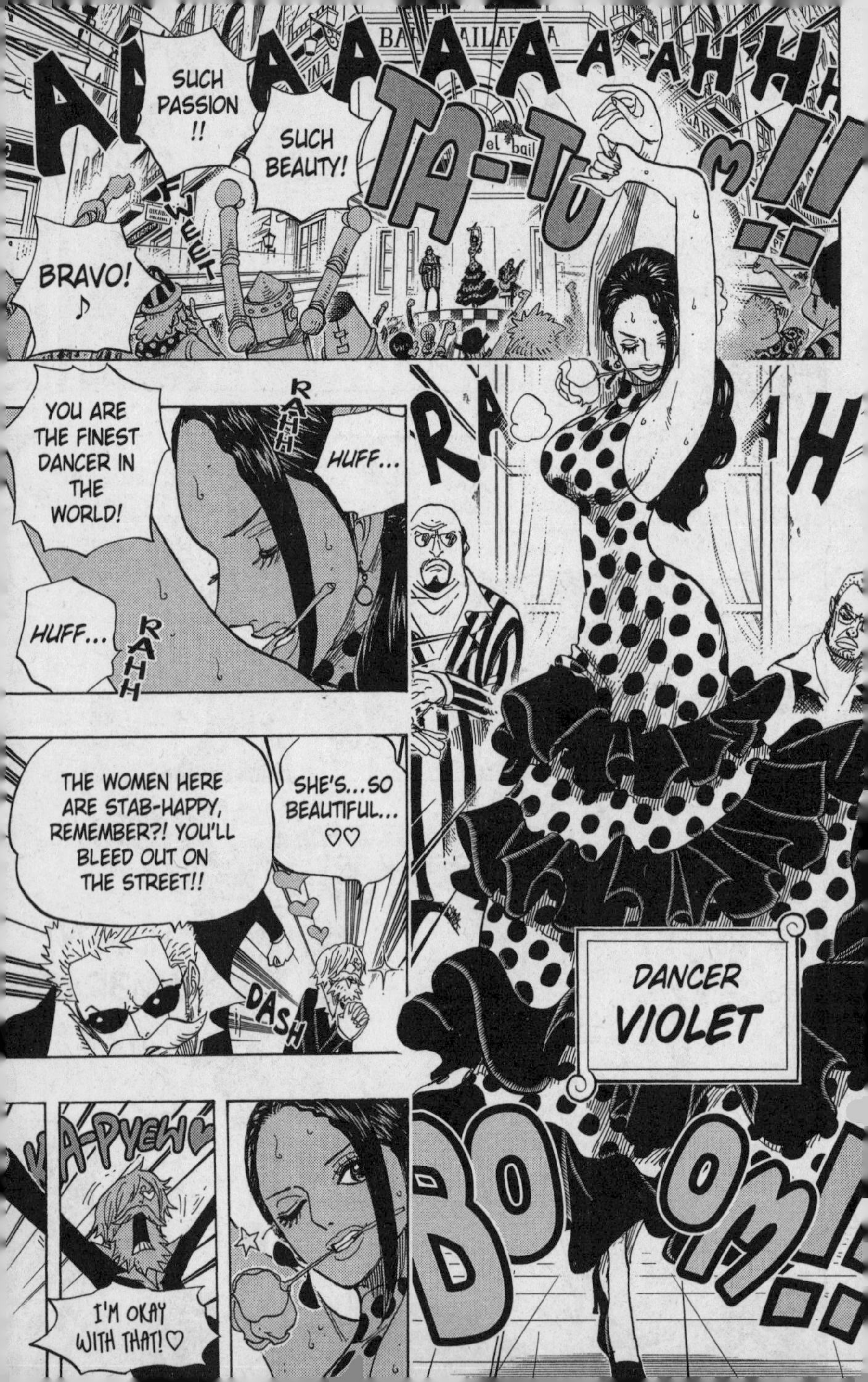
AAAAAAAHH
TA-TUM!!
SUCH BEAUTY!
SUCH PASSION!!
FWEET
BRAVO! ♪
RAAAH
DANCER VIOLET
BOOOM!!
HUFF...
RAHH
YOU ARE THE FINEST DANCER IN THE WORLD!
HUFF...
RAHH
SHE'S...SO BEAUTIFUL... ♡♡
THE WOMEN HERE ARE STAB-HAPPY, REMEMBER?! YOU'LL BLEED OUT ON THE STREET!!
DASH
VA-PYEW♡
I'M OKAY WITH THAT!♡

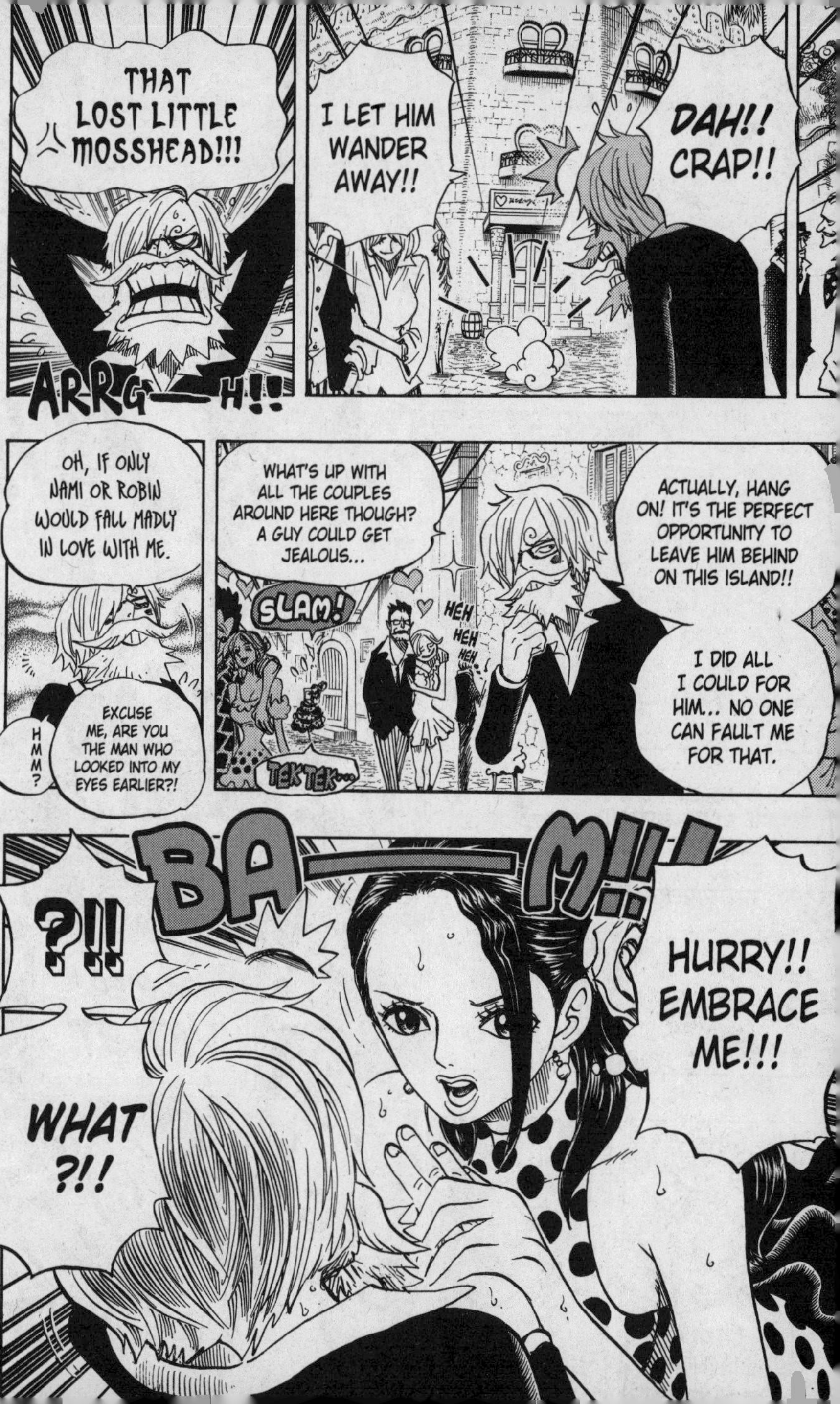
DAH!! CRAP!!
I LET HIM WANDER AWAY!!
THAT LOST LITTLE MOSSHEAD!!!
ARRG—H!!
ACTUALLY, HANG ON! IT'S THE PERFECT OPPORTUNITY TO LEAVE HIM BEHIND ON THIS ISLAND!!
I DID ALL I COULD FOR HIM... NO ONE CAN FAULT ME FOR THAT.
WHAT'S UP WITH ALL THE COUPLES AROUND HERE THOUGH? A GUY COULD GET JEALOUS...
HEH HEH HEH..!
SLAM!
TEKTEK...
OH, IF ONLY NAMI OR ROBIN WOULD FALL MADLY IN LOVE WITH ME.
EXCUSE ME, ARE YOU THE MAN WHO LOOKED INTO MY EYES EARLIER?!
HMM?
BA—M!!
HURRY!! EMBRACE ME!!!
?!!
WHAT?!!

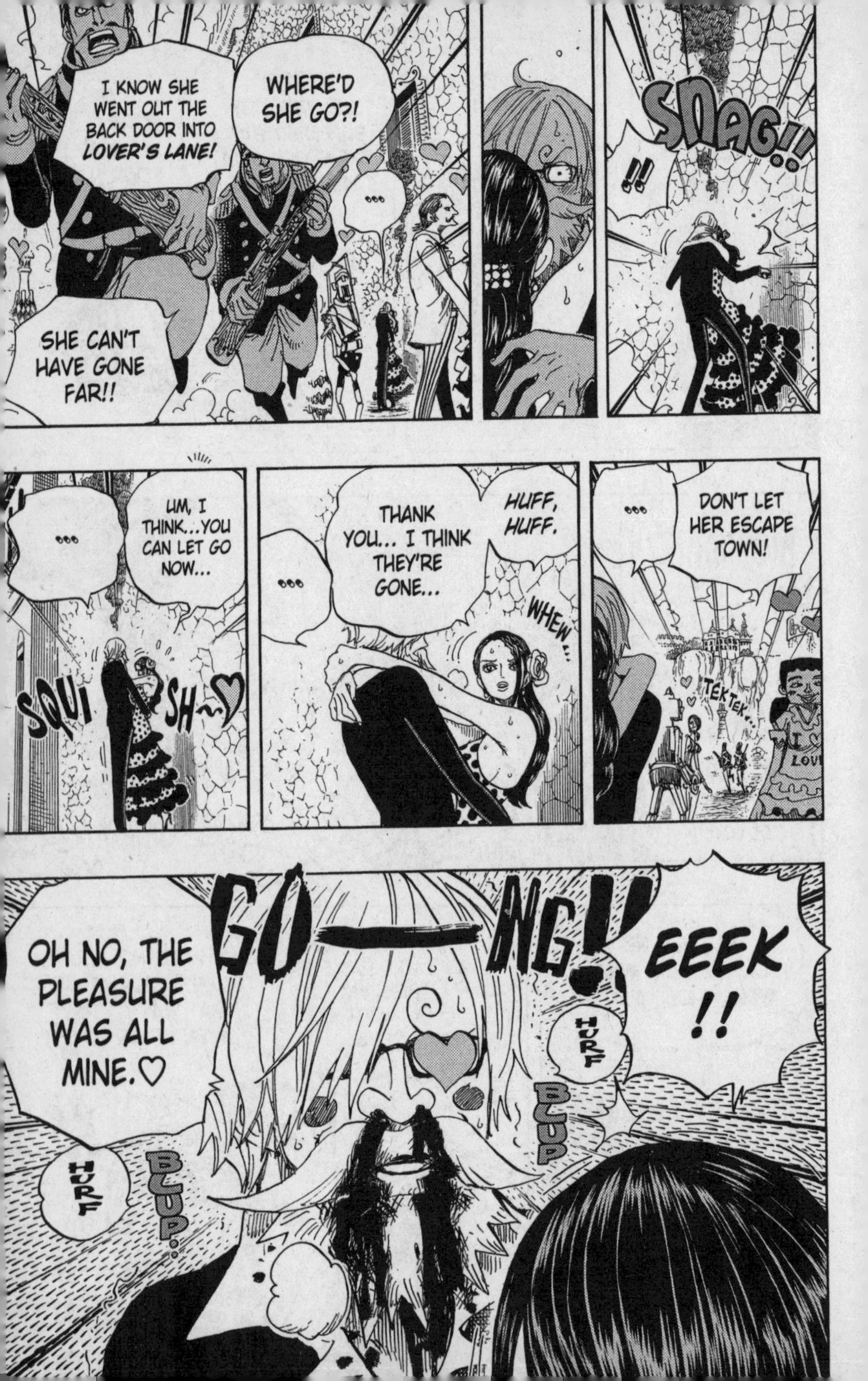
SNAG!!
!!
WHERE'D SHE GO?!
I KNOW SHE WENT OUT THE BACK DOOR INTO LOVER'S LANE!
...
SHE CAN'T HAVE GONE FAR!!
DON'T LET HER ESCAPE TOWN!
...
TEKTEK...
LOVE
HUFF, HUFF.
THANK YOU... I THINK THEY'RE GONE...
...
WHEW...
UM, I THINK...YOU CAN LET GO NOW...
...
SQUISH~♡
EEEK!!
GO—NG!!
HURF
BLUP
OH NO, THE PLEASURE WAS ALL MINE.♡
HURF
BLUP..

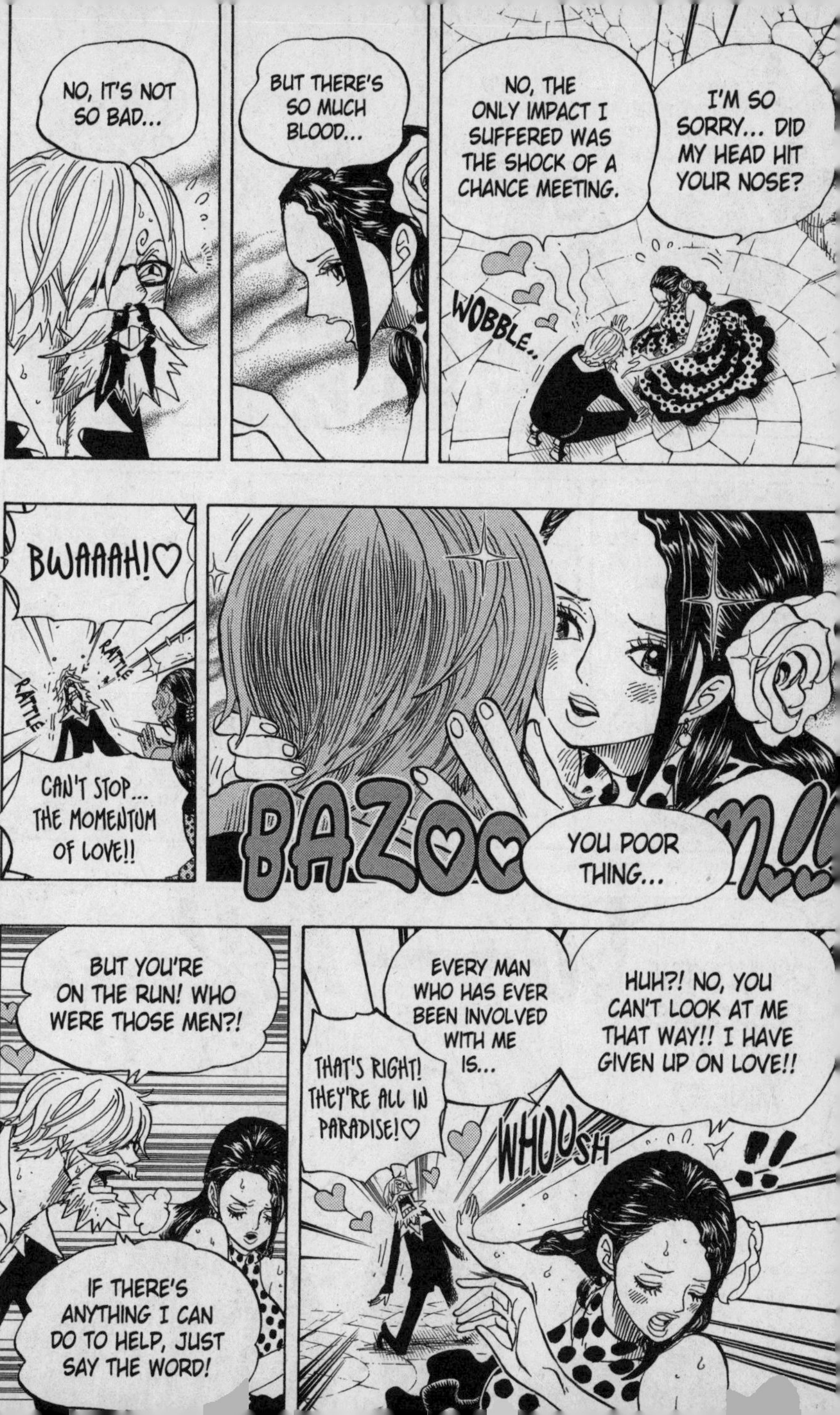
I'M SO SORRY... DID MY HEAD HIT YOUR NOSE?
NO, THE ONLY IMPACT I SUFFERED WAS THE SHOCK OF A CHANCE MEETING.
WOBBLE...
BUT THERE'S SO MUCH BLOOD...
NO, IT'S NOT SO BAD...
YOU POOR THING...
BWAAAH!♡
RATTLE
RATTLE
CAN'T STOP... THE MOMENTUM OF LOVE!!
HUH?! NO, YOU CAN'T LOOK AT ME THAT WAY!! I HAVE GIVEN UP ON LOVE!!
EVERY MAN WHO HAS EVER BEEN INVOLVED WITH ME IS...
THAT'S RIGHT! THEY'RE ALL IN PARADISE!♡
WHOOSH
BUT YOU'RE ON THE RUN! WHO WERE THOSE MEN?!
IF THERE'S ANYTHING I CAN DO TO HELP, JUST SAY THE WORD!

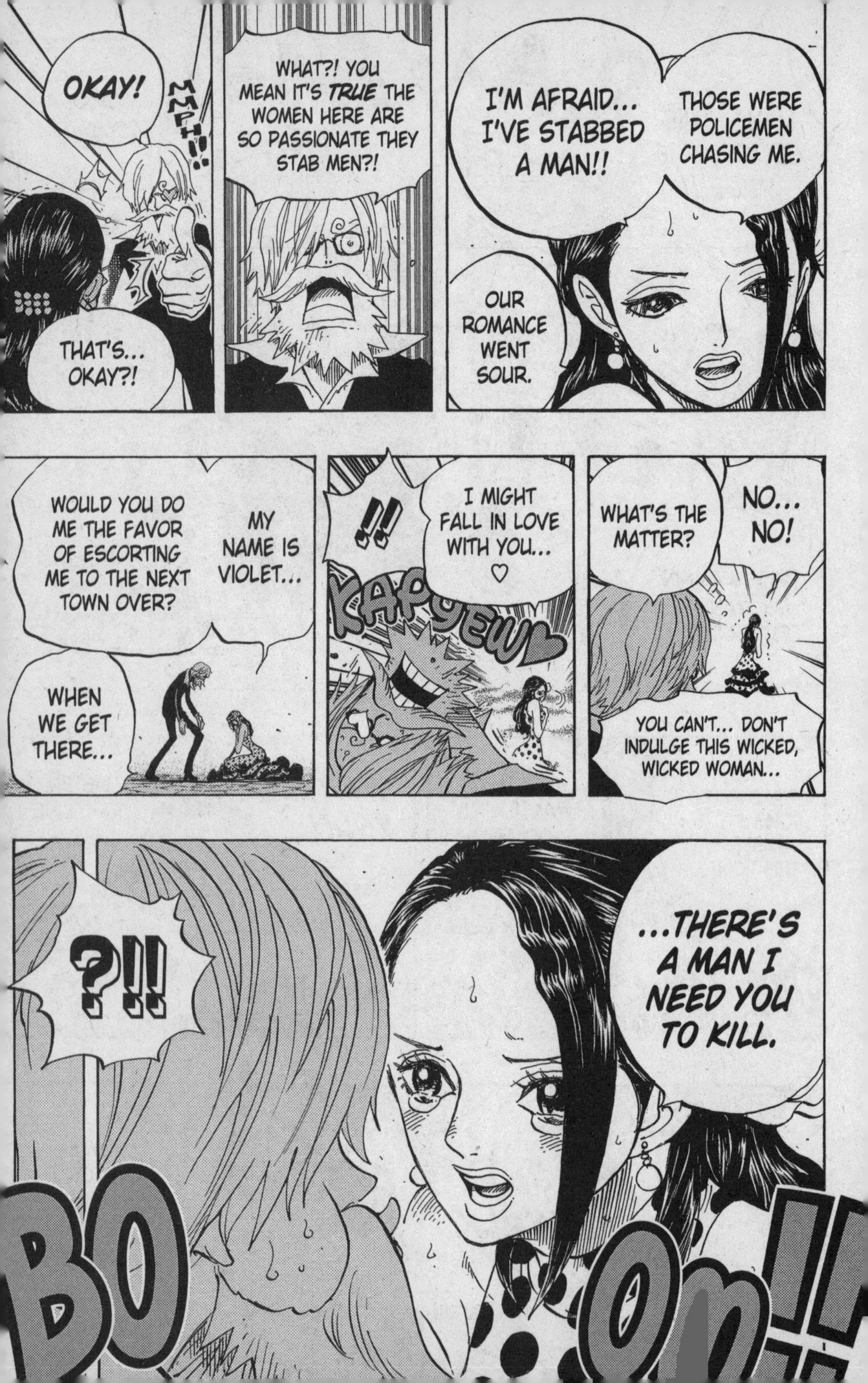
THOSE WERE POLICEMEN CHASING ME.
I'M AFRAID... I'VE STABBED A MAN!!
OUR ROMANCE WENT SOUR.
WHAT?! YOU MEAN IT'S *TRUE* THE WOMEN HERE ARE SO PASSIONATE THEY STAB MEN?!
OKAY!
MMPH!!
THAT'S... OKAY?!
NO... NO!
WHAT'S THE MATTER?
YOU CAN'T... DON'T INDULGE THIS WICKED, WICKED WOMAN...
I MIGHT FALL IN LOVE WITH YOU... ♡
!!
KAPYEW♥
MY NAME IS VIOLET...
WOULD YOU DO ME THE FAVOR OF ESCORTING ME TO THE NEXT TOWN OVER?
WHEN WE GET THERE...
...THERE'S A MAN I NEED YOU TO KILL.
?!!
BOOM!!

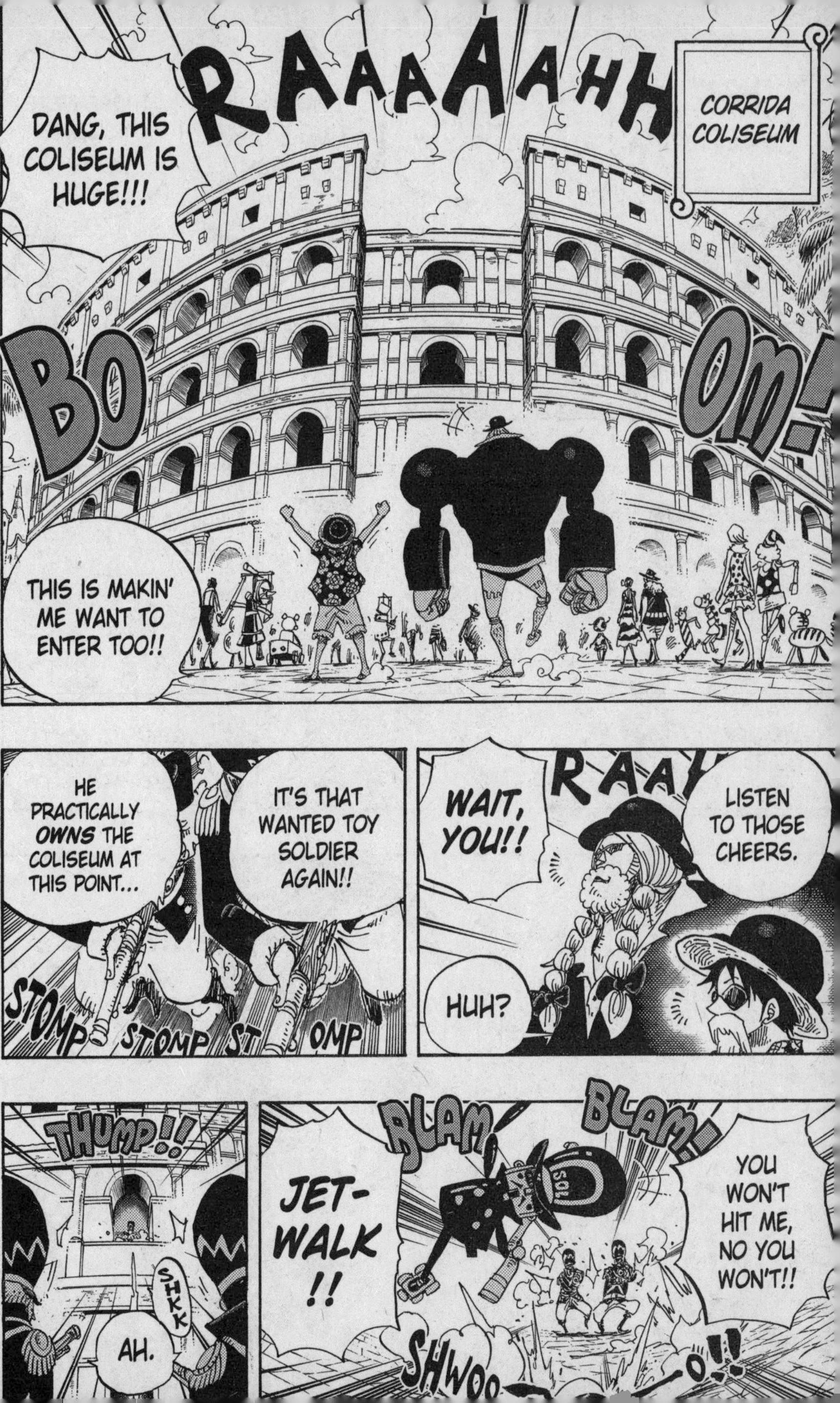
CORRIDA COLISEUM
RAAAAAHH
DANG, THIS COLISEUM IS HUGE!!!
BOOM!!
THIS IS MAKIN' ME WANT TO ENTER TOO!!
RAA
LISTEN TO THOSE CHEERS.
WAIT, YOU!!
HUH?
IT'S THAT WANTED TOY SOLDIER AGAIN!!
HE PRACTICALLY *OWNS* THE COLISEUM AT THIS POINT...
STOMP STOMP ST OMP
BLAM BLAM
YOU WON'T HIT ME, NO YOU WON'T!!
JET-WALK!!
SHWOO—O!!
THUMP!!
SHKK
AH.

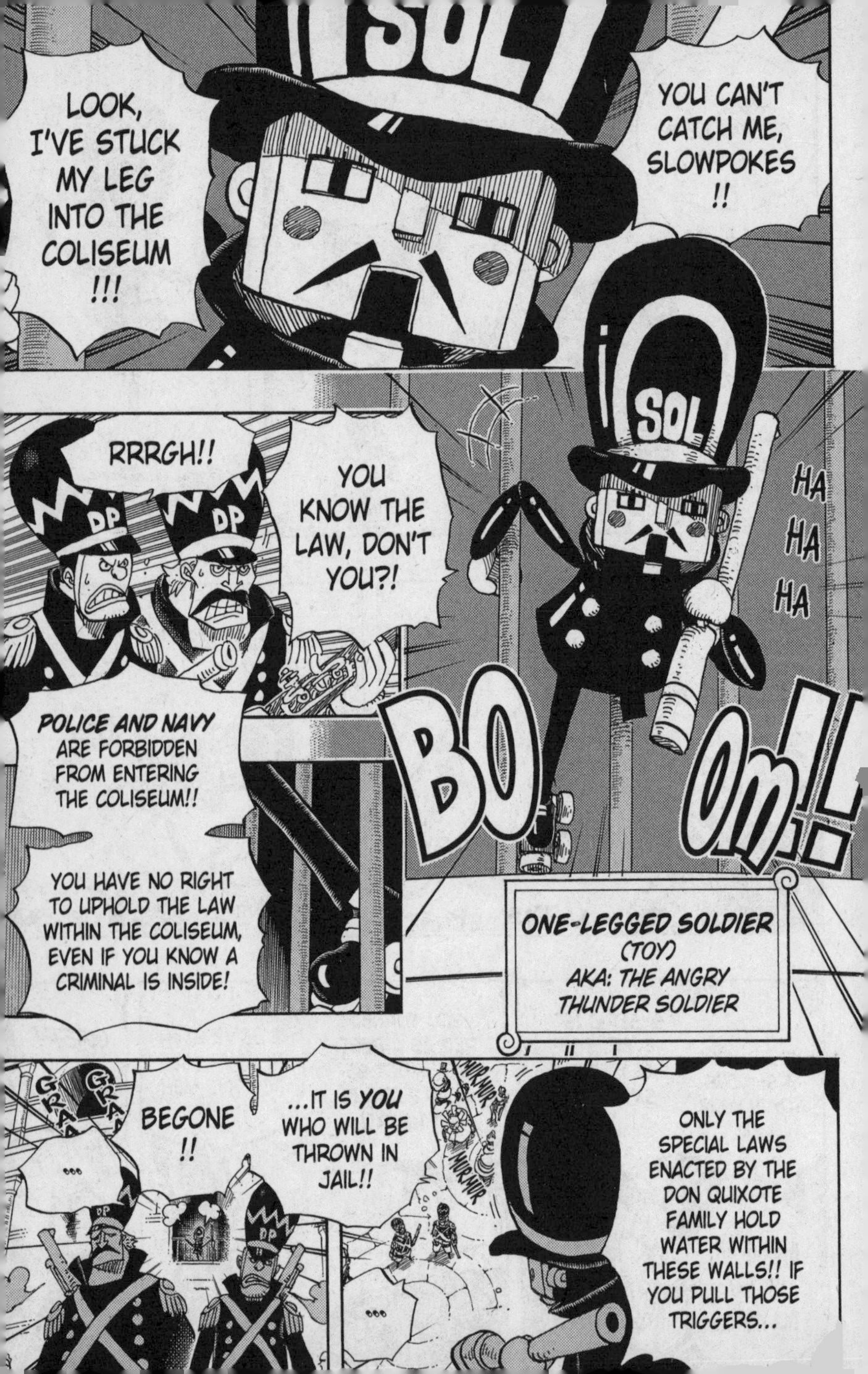
YOU CAN'T CATCH ME, SLOWPOKES!!
LOOK, I'VE STUCK MY LEG INTO THE COLISEUM!!!
HA HA HA
BOOM!!
ONE-LEGGED SOLDIER (TOY) AKA: THE ANGRY THUNDER SOLDIER
YOU KNOW THE LAW, DON'T YOU?!
RRRGH!!
POLICE AND NAVY ARE FORBIDDEN FROM ENTERING THE COLISEUM!!
YOU HAVE NO RIGHT TO UPHOLD THE LAW WITHIN THE COLISEUM, EVEN IF YOU KNOW A CRIMINAL IS INSIDE!
ONLY THE SPECIAL LAWS ENACTED BY THE DON QUIXOTE FAMILY HOLD WATER WITHIN THESE WALLS!! IF YOU PULL THOSE TRIGGERS...
MUR MUR
MUR MUR
...IT IS *YOU* WHO WILL BE THROWN IN JAIL!!
...
BEGONE!!
GRA GRA
...

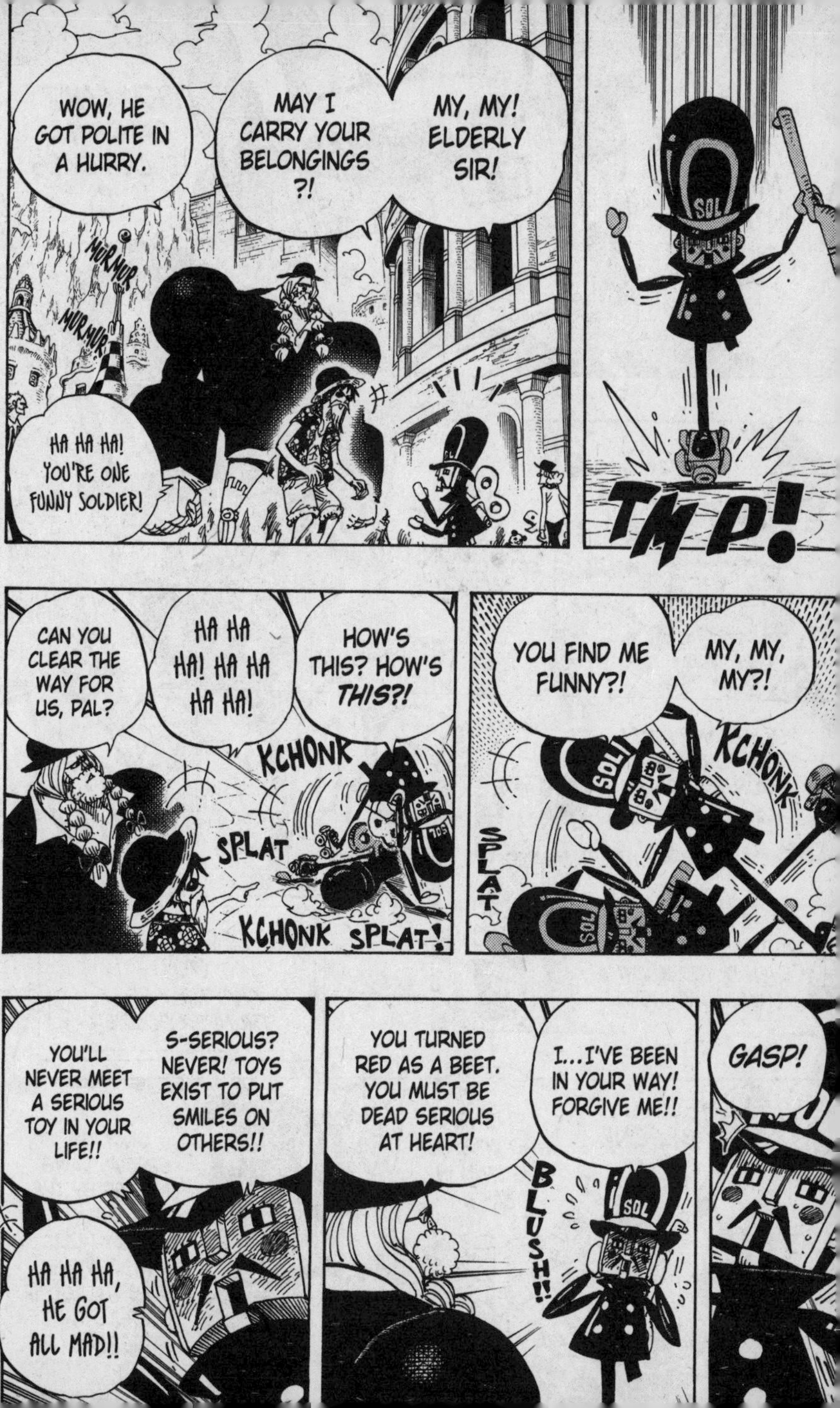
TMP!
MY, MY! ELDERLY SIR!
MAY I CARRY YOUR BELONGINGS?!
WOW, HE GOT POLITE IN A HURRY.
MURMUR
MURMUR
HA HA HA! YOU'RE ONE FUNNY SOLDIER!
MY, MY, MY?!
YOU FIND ME FUNNY?!
KCHONK
SPLAT
HOW'S THIS? HOW'S *THIS?!*
HA HA HA! HA HA HA HA!
CAN YOU CLEAR THE WAY FOR US, PAL?
KCHONK
SPLAT
KCHONK SPLAT!
GASP!
I...I'VE BEEN IN YOUR WAY! FORGIVE ME!!
YOU TURNED RED AS A BEET. YOU MUST BE DEAD SERIOUS AT HEART!
BLUSH!!
S-SERIOUS? NEVER! TOYS EXIST TO PUT SMILES ON OTHERS!!
YOU'LL NEVER MEET A SERIOUS TOY IN YOUR LIFE!!
HA HA HA, HE GOT ALL MAD!!

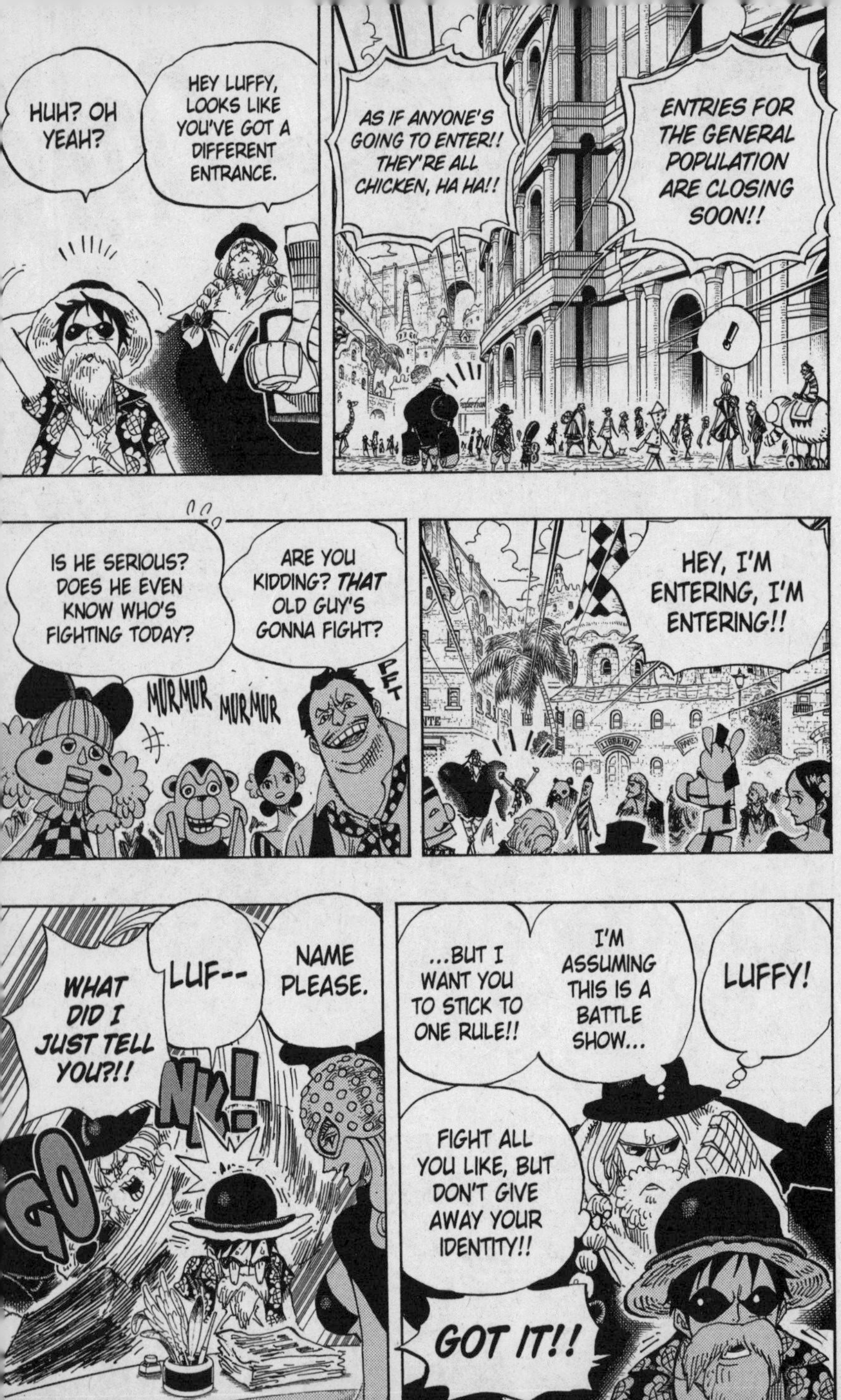
ENTRIES FOR THE GENERAL POPULATION ARE CLOSING SOON!!
AS IF ANYONE'S GOING TO ENTER!! THEY'RE ALL CHICKEN, HA HA!!
!
HEY LUFFY, LOOKS LIKE YOU'VE GOT A DIFFERENT ENTRANCE.
HUH? OH YEAH?
HEY, I'M ENTERING, I'M ENTERING!!
ARE YOU KIDDING? THAT OLD GUY'S GONNA FIGHT?
PFT
IS HE SERIOUS? DOES HE EVEN KNOW WHO'S FIGHTING TODAY?
MURMUR MURMUR
LUFFY!
I'M ASSUMING THIS IS A BATTLE SHOW...
...BUT I WANT YOU TO STICK TO ONE RULE!!
FIGHT ALL YOU LIKE, BUT DON'T GIVE AWAY YOUR IDENTITY!!
GOT IT!!
NAME PLEASE.
LUF--
WHAT DID I JUST TELL YOU?!!
GONK!

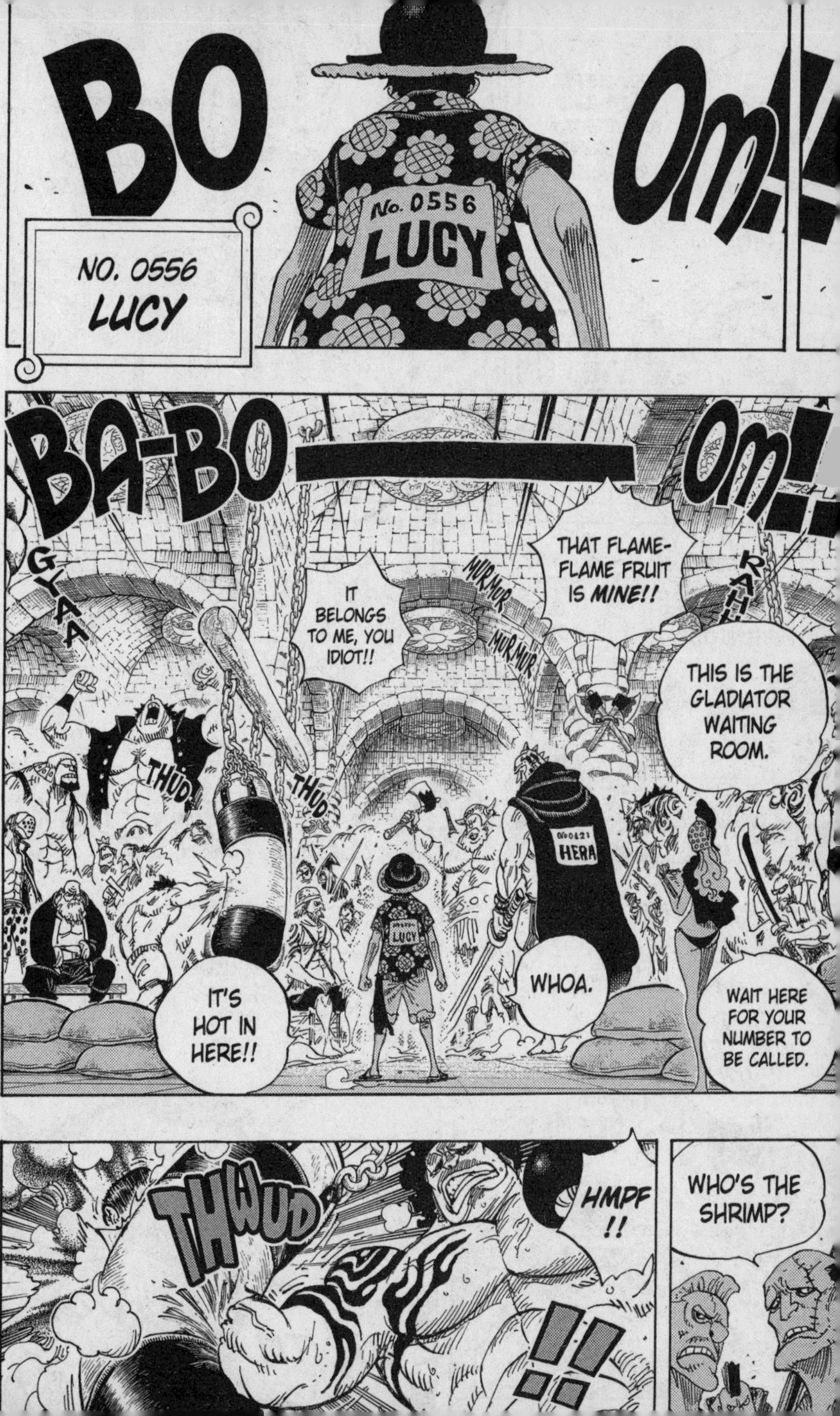
BO Om!!
No. 0556 LUCY
NO. 0556 LUCY
BA-BO——Om!!
RAH!!
THAT FLAME-FLAME FRUIT IS MINE!!
THIS IS THE GLADIATOR WAITING ROOM.
MURMUR MURMUR
IT BELONGS TO ME, YOU IDIOT!!
GYAA
THUD
THUD
HERA
LUCY
WAIT HERE FOR YOUR NUMBER TO BE CALLED.
WHOA.
IT'S HOT IN HERE!!
WHO'S THE SHRIMP?
HMPF!!
THWUD
!!

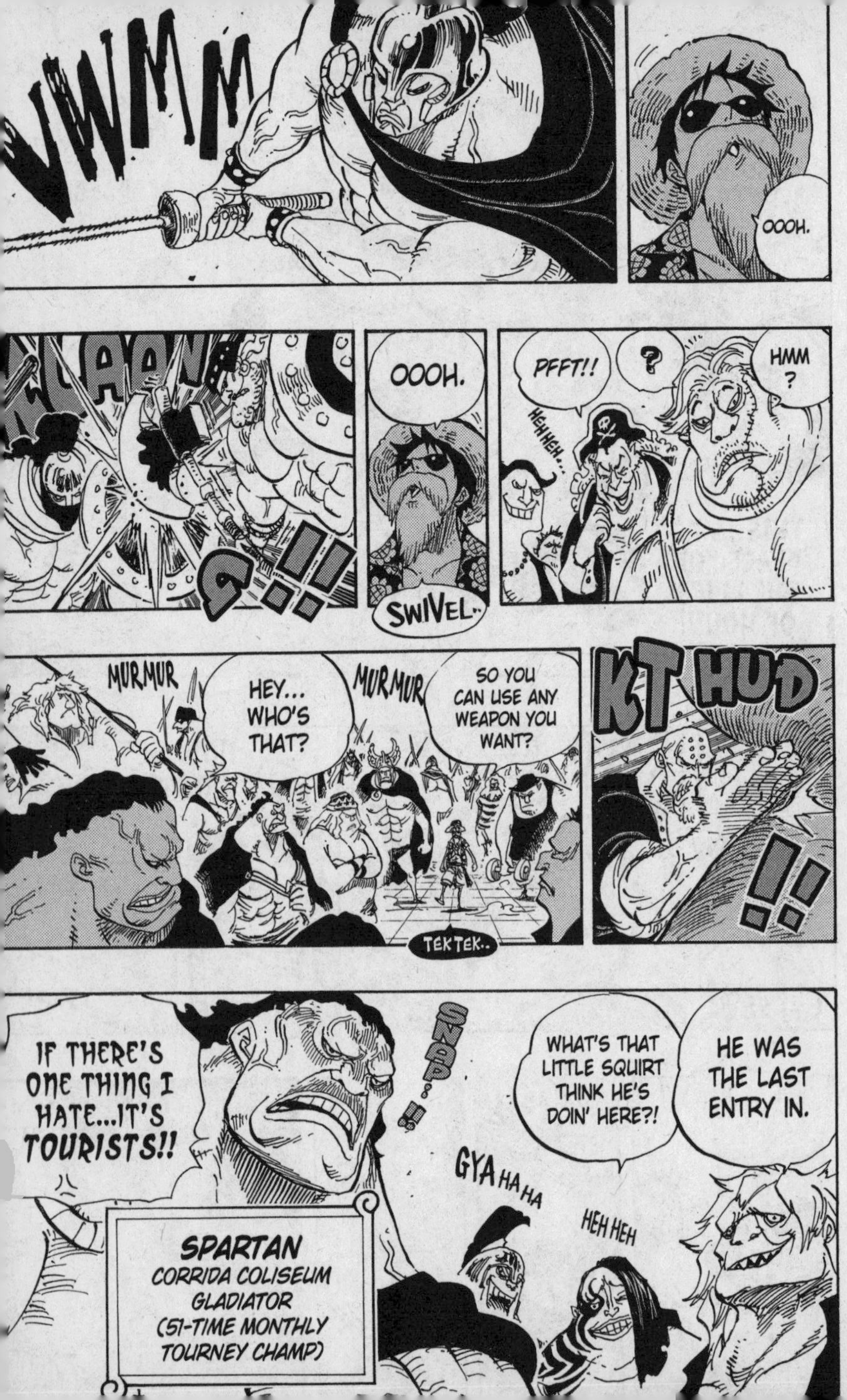
OOOH.
VWMM M
HMM ?
?
PFFT!!
HEH HEH...
OOOH.
SWIVEL..
!!
KT HUD
!!
SO YOU CAN USE ANY WEAPON YOU WANT?
MURMUR
HEY... WHO'S THAT?
MURMUR
TEKTEK..
HE WAS THE LAST ENTRY IN.
WHAT'S THAT LITTLE SQUIRT THINK HE'S DOIN' HERE?!
HEH HEH
GYA HA HA
SNAP..!!
IF THERE'S ONE THING I HATE...IT'S TOURISTS!!
SPARTAN
CORRIDA COLISEUM GLADIATOR
(51-TIME MONTHLY TOURNEY CHAMP)

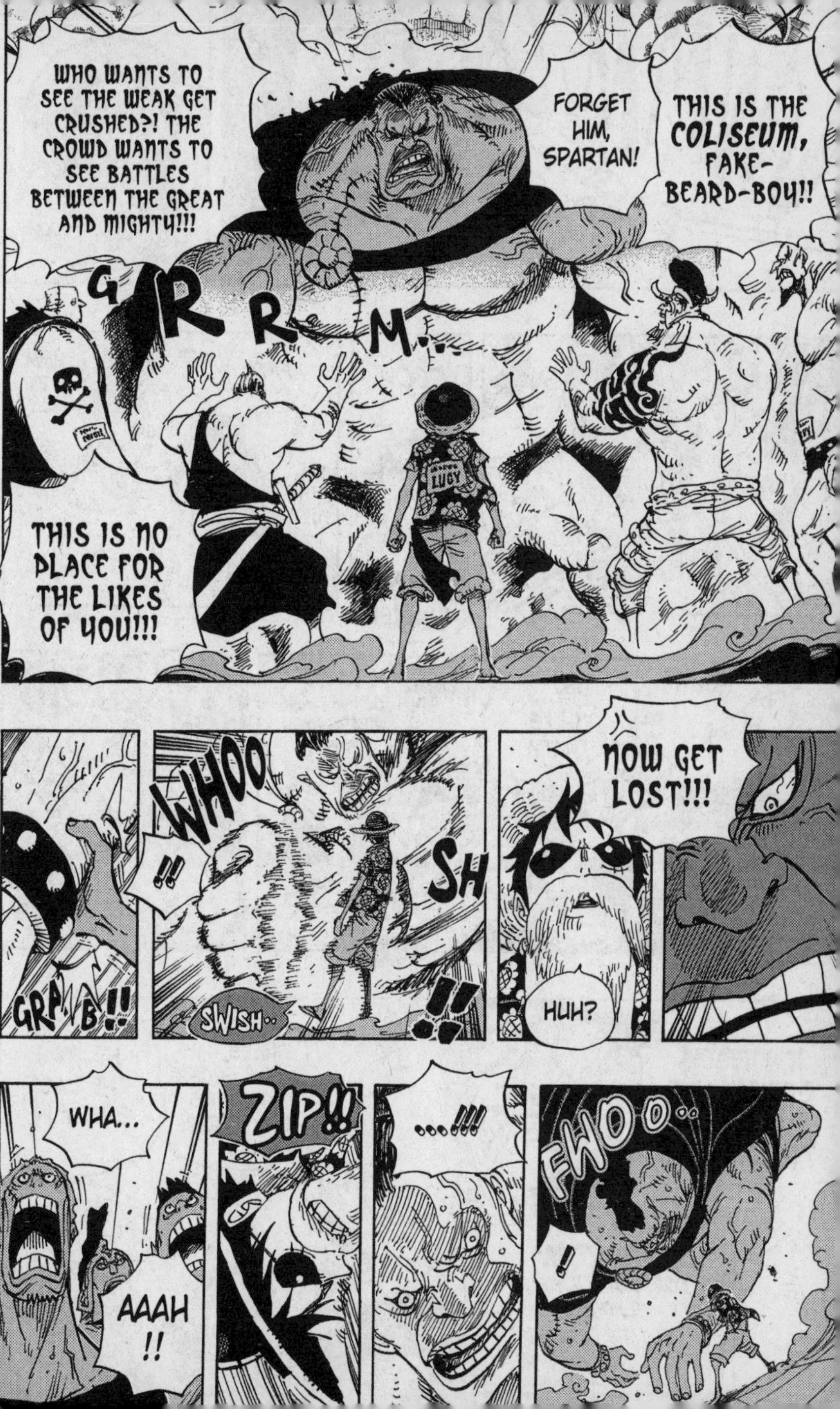
THIS IS THE COLISEUM, FAKE-BEARD-BOY!!
FORGET HIM, SPARTAN!
WHO WANTS TO SEE THE WEAK GET CRUSHED?! THE CROWD WANTS TO SEE BATTLES BETWEEN THE GREAT AND MIGHTY!!!
GRRM...
THIS IS NO PLACE FOR THE LIKES OF YOU!!!
NOW GET LOST!!!
HUH?
WHOOSH!!
!!
SWISH..
GRAB!!
FWOO..
!
...!!!
ZIP!!
WHA...
AAAH!!

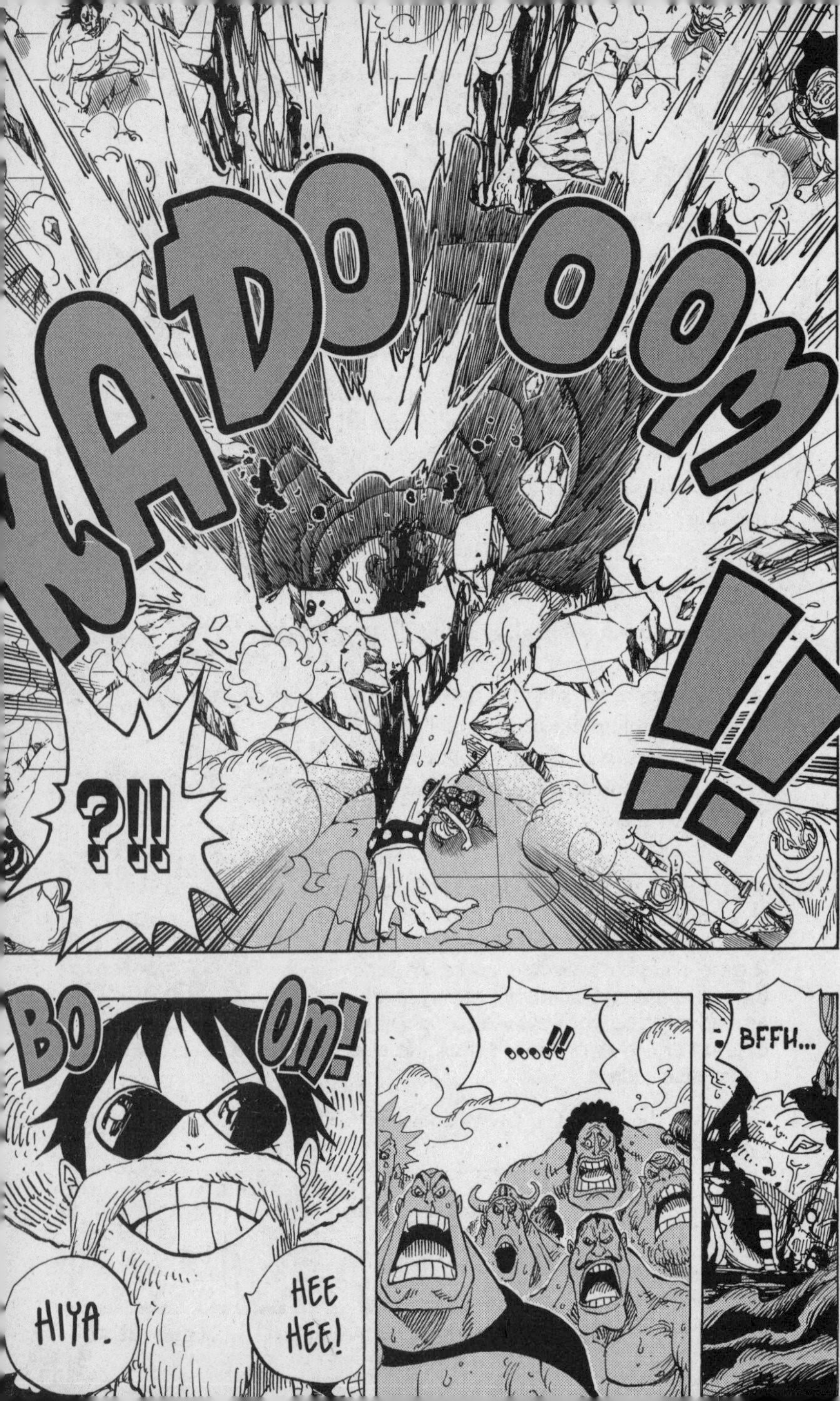
KADOOOM!!
?!!
BFFH...
...!!
BOOM!
HEE HEE!
HIYA.

SBS Question Corner

質問コーナー
エス ビー エス

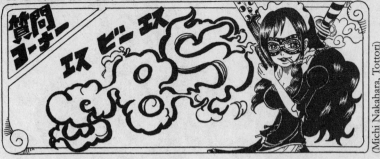

(Michi Nakahara, Tottori)

Q: In Chapter 700--oh! Good evening, Odacchi. In Chapter 700, when Luffy's crew is sailing to Dress~~rosa~~olga, the waves of the sea look like rabbits, but what does Law like to eat aside from rice balls?

--Hasumomo

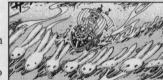

A: Ah, he likes, um...grilled fish! Next question.

Q: I'm curious about something. Robin likes to say scary things out loud. But in her imagination, she's usually thinking of fun, cute things like cats or old ladies in frilly dresses. Why doesn't Robin try to cheer everyone up with her fantasies? That's what I like about Robin.

--Y.O.

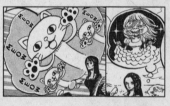

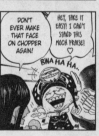

A: Ahh, I see. Yes, good point. Given that she scolded Franky for making weird faces in Chopper's body at Punk Hazard, Robin must really like cute faces. But she's a bit socially clumsy, and her attempts to paint a picture with words end up on the creepy side. She's just one of those ladies.

HEY, TAKE IT EASY! I CAN'T STAND THIS MUCH PRAISE! ♡
DON'T EVER MAKE THAT FACE ON CHOPPER AGAIN!
BWA HA HA..

Q: So, who in the Straw Hat Crew can use Haki? I'm so curious, I can't even cause any love hurricanes.

--Kakuharu

A: It's these three. Inside the parentheses are the types they specialize in.

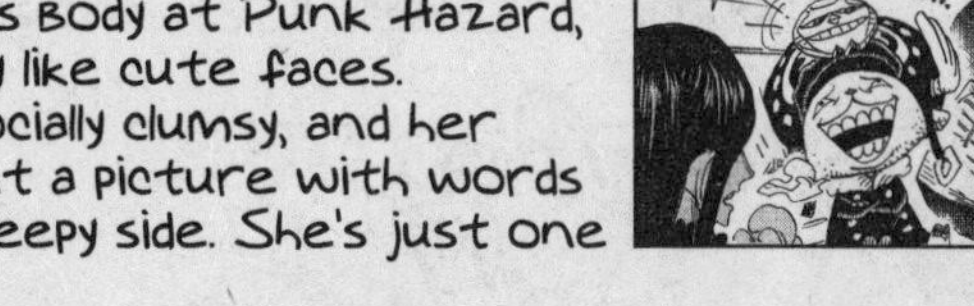

(Supreme King) (Armament) (Observation)

Chapter 704:
LUCY AND THE STATUE OF KYROS

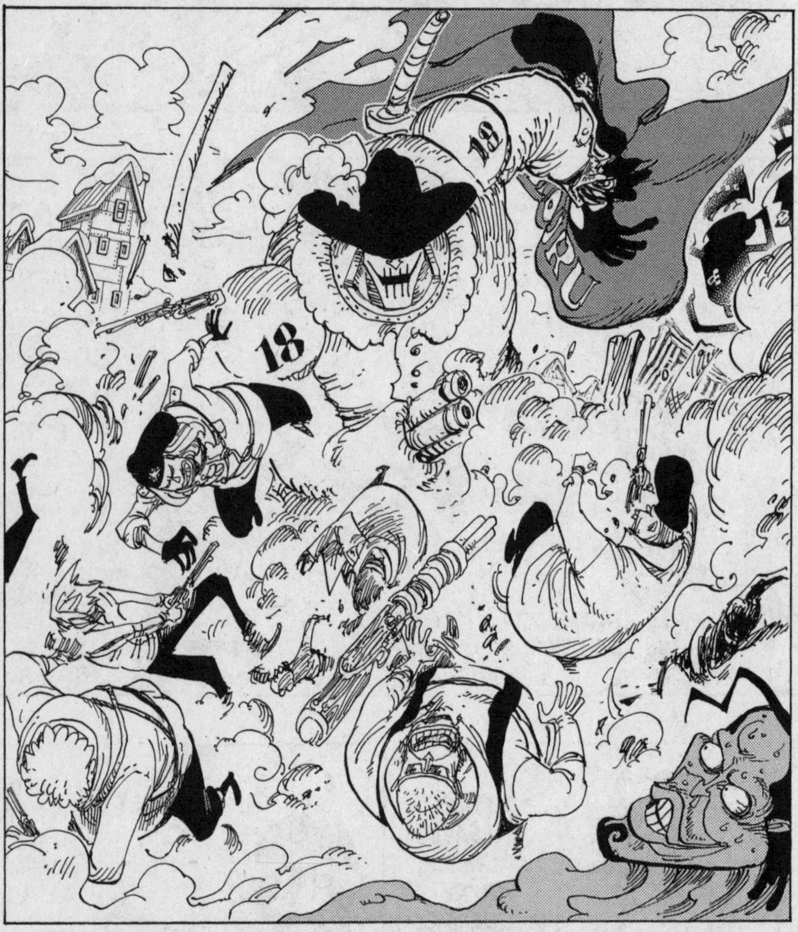
18
18

CARIBOU'S NEW WORLD KEE HEE HEE, VOL. 24
"PROLETARIAT RIOT SUPPRESSED"

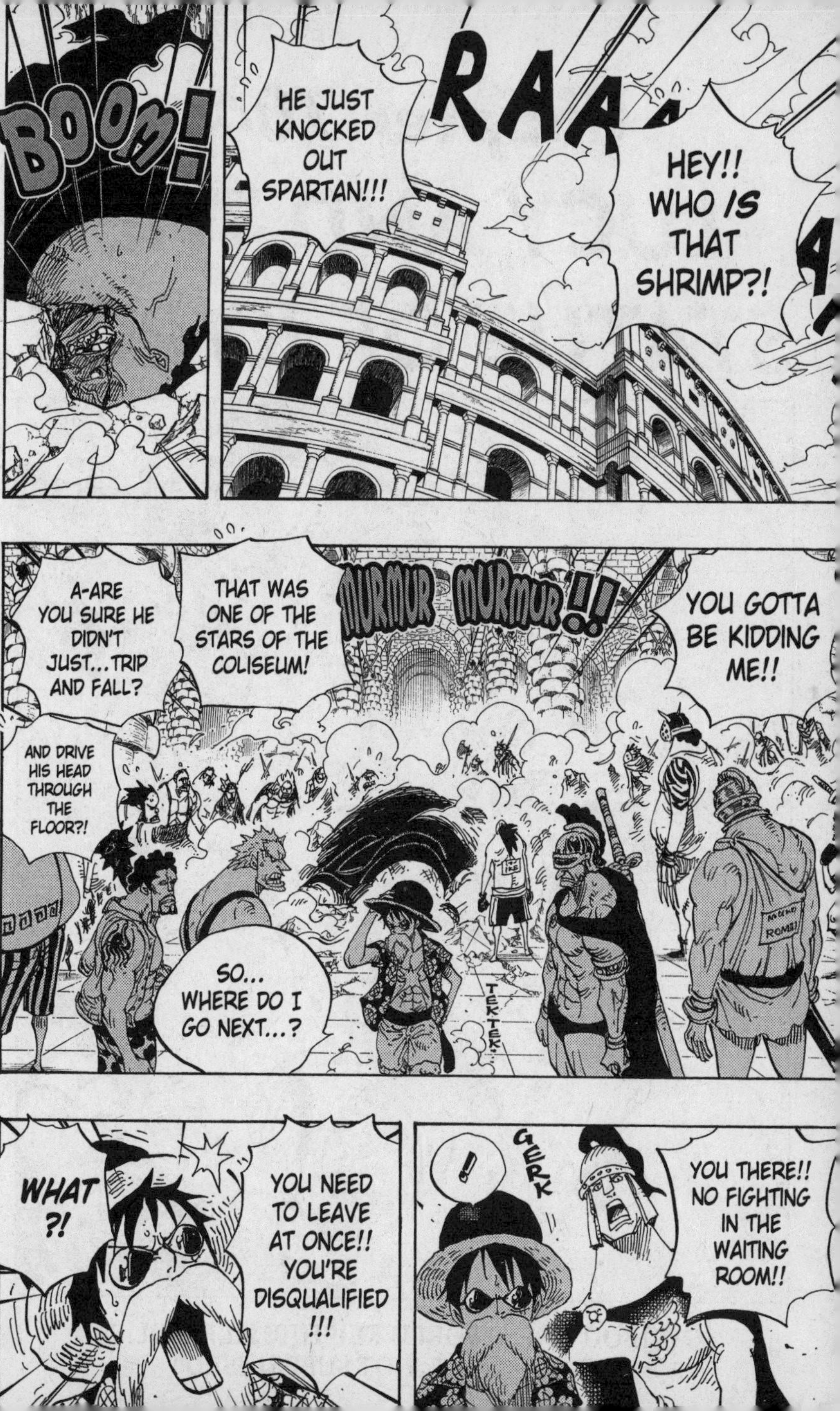
RAAAA
HEY!! WHO IS THAT SHRIMP?!
HE JUST KNOCKED OUT SPARTAN!!!
BOOM!
YOU GOTTA BE KIDDING ME!!
MURMUR MURMUR!!
THAT WAS ONE OF THE STARS OF THE COLISEUM!
A-ARE YOU SURE HE DIDN'T JUST...TRIP AND FALL?
AND DRIVE HIS HEAD THROUGH THE FLOOR?!
TEK TEK
SO... WHERE DO I GO NEXT...?
YOU THERE!! NO FIGHTING IN THE WAITING ROOM!!
GERK
!
YOU NEED TO LEAVE AT ONCE!! YOU'RE DISQUALIFIED!!!
WHAT?!

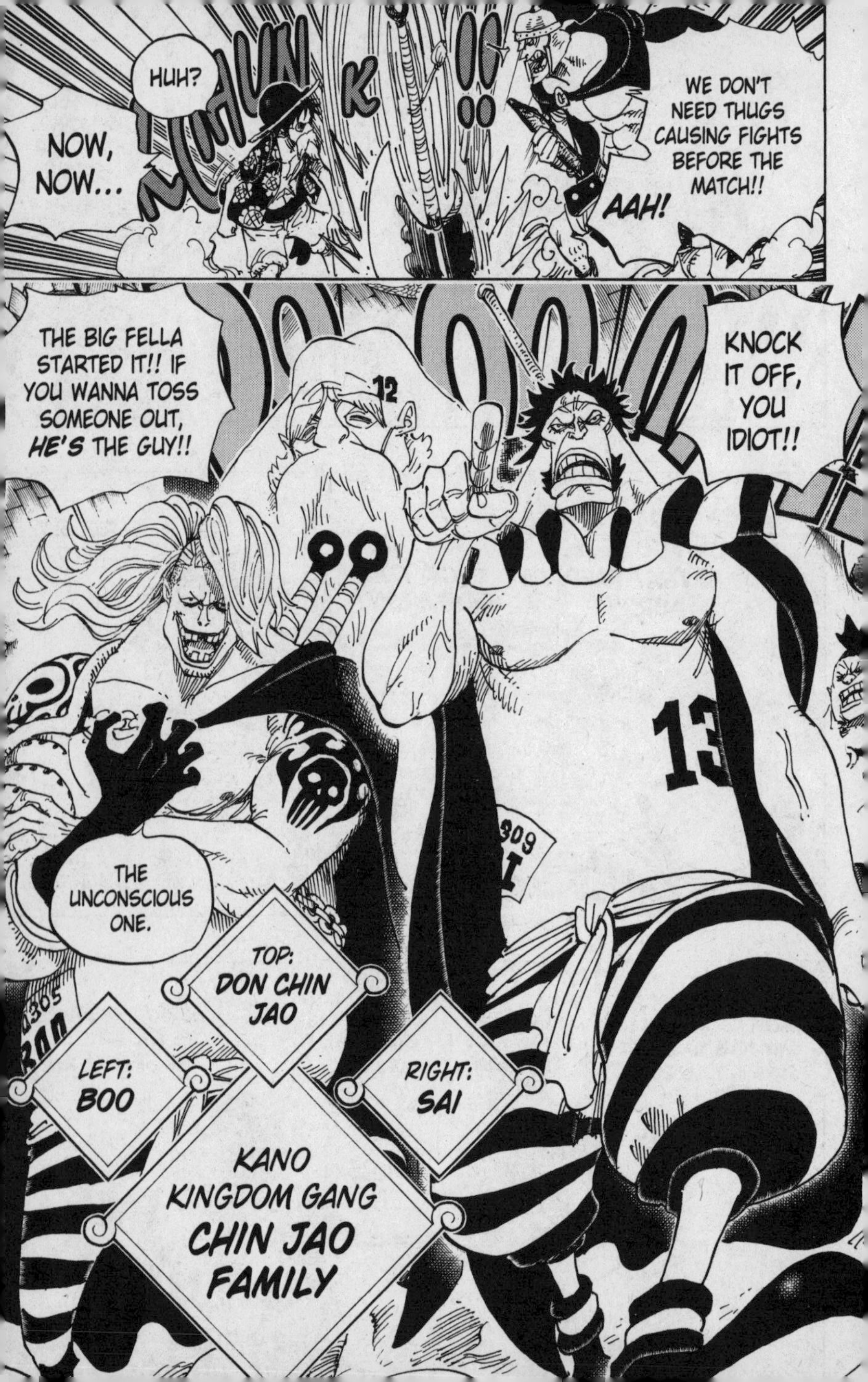
WE DON'T NEED THUGS CAUSING FIGHTS BEFORE THE MATCH!!
AAH!
WHUNK!!
HUH?
NOW, NOW...
KNOCK IT OFF, YOU IDIOT!!
THE BIG FELLA STARTED IT!! IF YOU WANNA TOSS SOMEONE OUT, *HE'S* THE GUY!!
THE UNCONSCIOUS ONE.
TOP: DON CHIN JAO
RIGHT: SAI
LEFT: BOO
KANO KINGDOM GANG CHIN JAO FAMILY

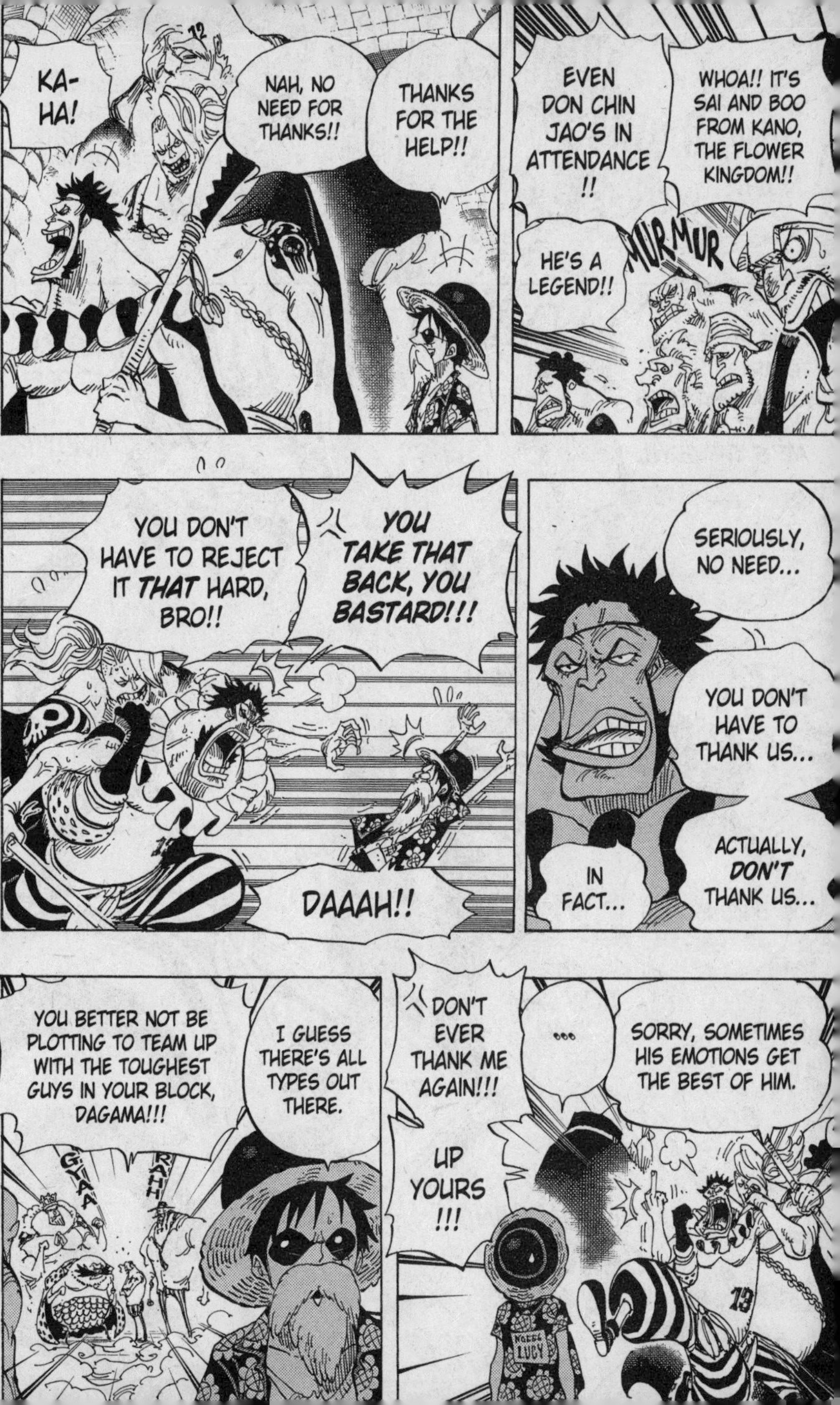
WHOA!! IT'S SAI AND BOO FROM KANO, THE FLOWER KINGDOM!!
EVEN DON CHIN JAO'S IN ATTENDANCE!!
MURMUR
HE'S A LEGEND!!
THANKS FOR THE HELP!!
NAH, NO NEED FOR THANKS!!
KA-HA!
SERIOUSLY, NO NEED...
YOU DON'T HAVE TO THANK US...
IN FACT...
ACTUALLY, *DON'T* THANK US...
YOU TAKE THAT BACK, YOU BASTARD!!!
YOU DON'T HAVE TO REJECT IT *THAT* HARD, BRO!!
DAAAH!!
SORRY, SOMETIMES HIS EMOTIONS GET THE BEST OF HIM.
...
DON'T EVER THANK ME AGAIN!!!
UP YOURS!!!
I GUESS THERE'S ALL TYPES OUT THERE.
YOU BETTER NOT BE PLOTTING TO TEAM UP WITH THE TOUGHEST GUYS IN YOUR BLOCK, DAGAMA!!!
RAHH
GYAA

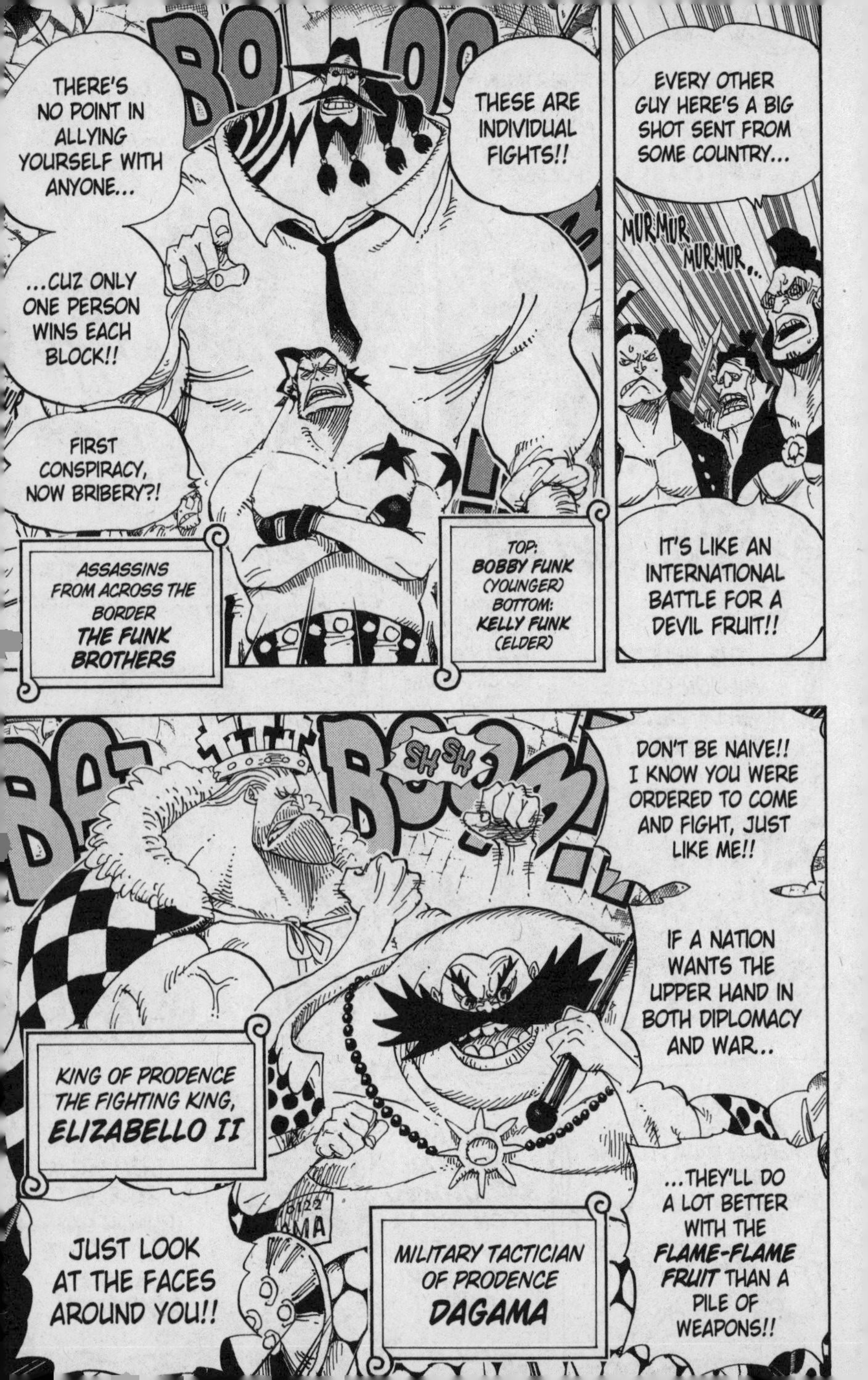
EVERY OTHER GUY HERE'S A BIG SHOT SENT FROM SOME COUNTRY...
MURMUR MURMUR...
IT'S LIKE AN INTERNATIONAL BATTLE FOR A DEVIL FRUIT!!
THESE ARE INDIVIDUAL FIGHTS!!
THERE'S NO POINT IN ALLYING YOURSELF WITH ANYONE...
...CUZ ONLY ONE PERSON WINS EACH BLOCK!!
FIRST CONSPIRACY, NOW BRIBERY?!
TOP: BOBBY FUNK (YOUNGER) BOTTOM: KELLY FUNK (ELDER)
ASSASSINS FROM ACROSS THE BORDER THE FUNK BROTHERS
DON'T BE NAIVE!! I KNOW YOU WERE ORDERED TO COME AND FIGHT, JUST LIKE ME!!
SH SH
IF A NATION WANTS THE UPPER HAND IN BOTH DIPLOMACY AND WAR...
...THEY'LL DO A LOT BETTER WITH THE FLAME-FLAME FRUIT THAN A PILE OF WEAPONS!!
MILITARY TACTICIAN OF PRODENCE DAGAMA
JUST LOOK AT THE FACES AROUND YOU!!
KING OF PRODENCE THE FIGHTING KING, ELIZABELLO II

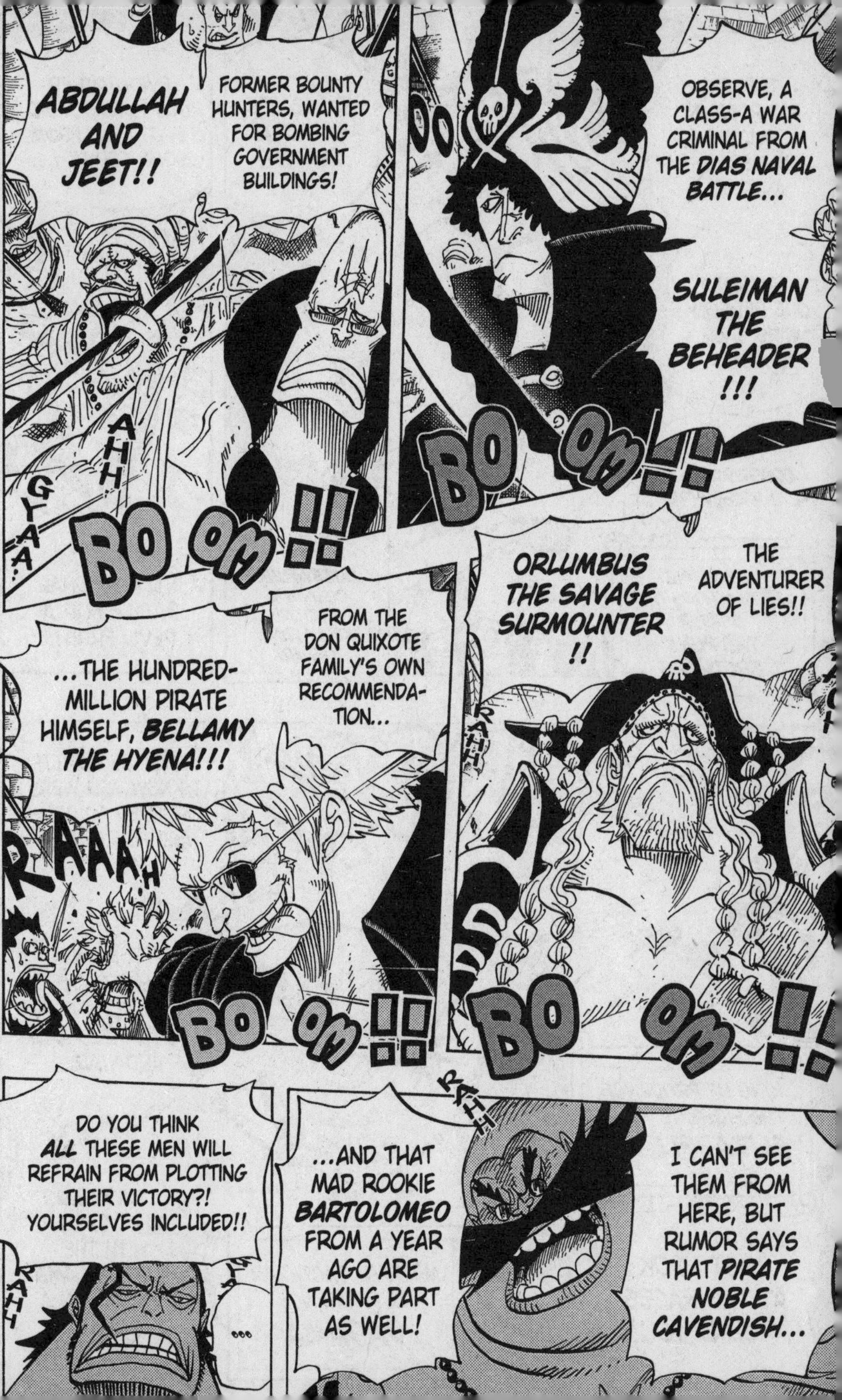
OBSERVE, A CLASS-A WAR CRIMINAL FROM THE DIAS NAVAL BATTLE...
SULEIMAN THE BEHEADER!!!
BOOM!!
FORMER BOUNTY HUNTERS, WANTED FOR BOMBING GOVERNMENT BUILDINGS!
ABDULLAH AND JEET!!
AHH
GYAAA
BOOM!!
THE ADVENTURER OF LIES!!
ORLUMBUS THE SAVAGE SURMOUNTER!!
RAHH
BOOM!!
FROM THE DON QUIXOTE FAMILY'S OWN RECOMMENDATION...
...THE HUNDRED-MILLION PIRATE HIMSELF, BELLAMY THE HYENA!!!
RAAAAH
BOOM!!
RAHH
I CAN'T SEE THEM FROM HERE, BUT RUMOR SAYS THAT PIRATE NOBLE CAVENDISH...
...AND THAT MAD ROOKIE BARTOLOMEO FROM A YEAR AGO ARE TAKING PART AS WELL!
DO YOU THINK ALL THESE MEN WILL REFRAIN FROM PLOTTING THEIR VICTORY?! YOURSELVES INCLUDED!!
RAHH
...

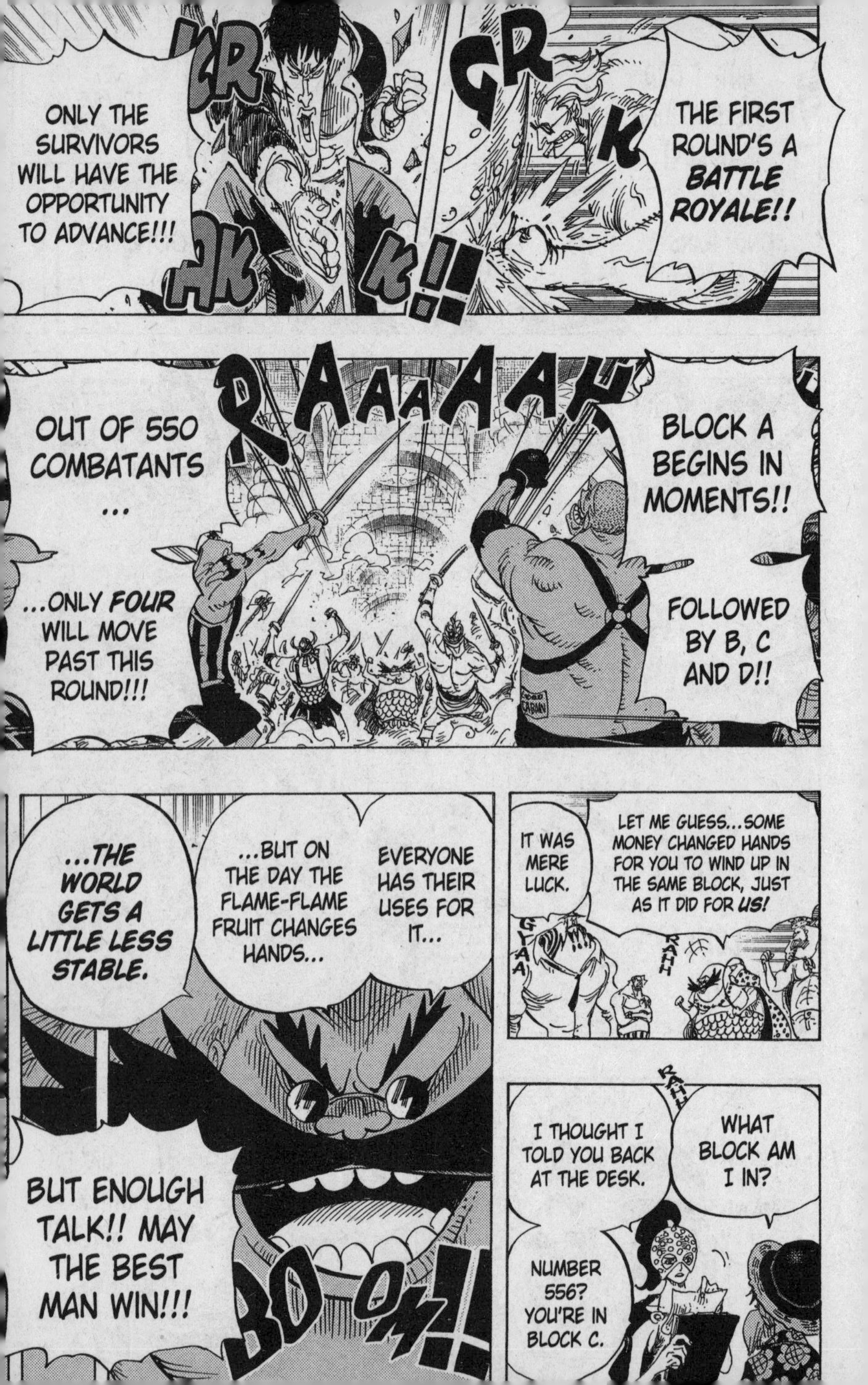
THE FIRST ROUND'S A BATTLE ROYALE!!
GRK!!
ONLY THE SURVIVORS WILL HAVE THE OPPORTUNITY TO ADVANCE!!!
CRAK
BLOCK A BEGINS IN MOMENTS!!
FOLLOWED BY B, C AND D!!
RAAAAAH
OUT OF 550 COMBATANTS ...
...ONLY FOUR WILL MOVE PAST THIS ROUND!!!
LET ME GUESS...SOME MONEY CHANGED HANDS FOR YOU TO WIND UP IN THE SAME BLOCK, JUST AS IT DID FOR US!
IT WAS MERE LUCK.
GYAAA
RAHH
RAHH
WHAT BLOCK AM I IN?
I THOUGHT I TOLD YOU BACK AT THE DESK.
NUMBER 556? YOU'RE IN BLOCK C.
EVERYONE HAS THEIR USES FOR IT...
...BUT ON THE DAY THE FLAME-FLAME FRUIT CHANGES HANDS...
...THE WORLD GETS A LITTLE LESS STABLE.
BUT ENOUGH TALK!! MAY THE BEST MAN WIN!!!
BOOOM!!

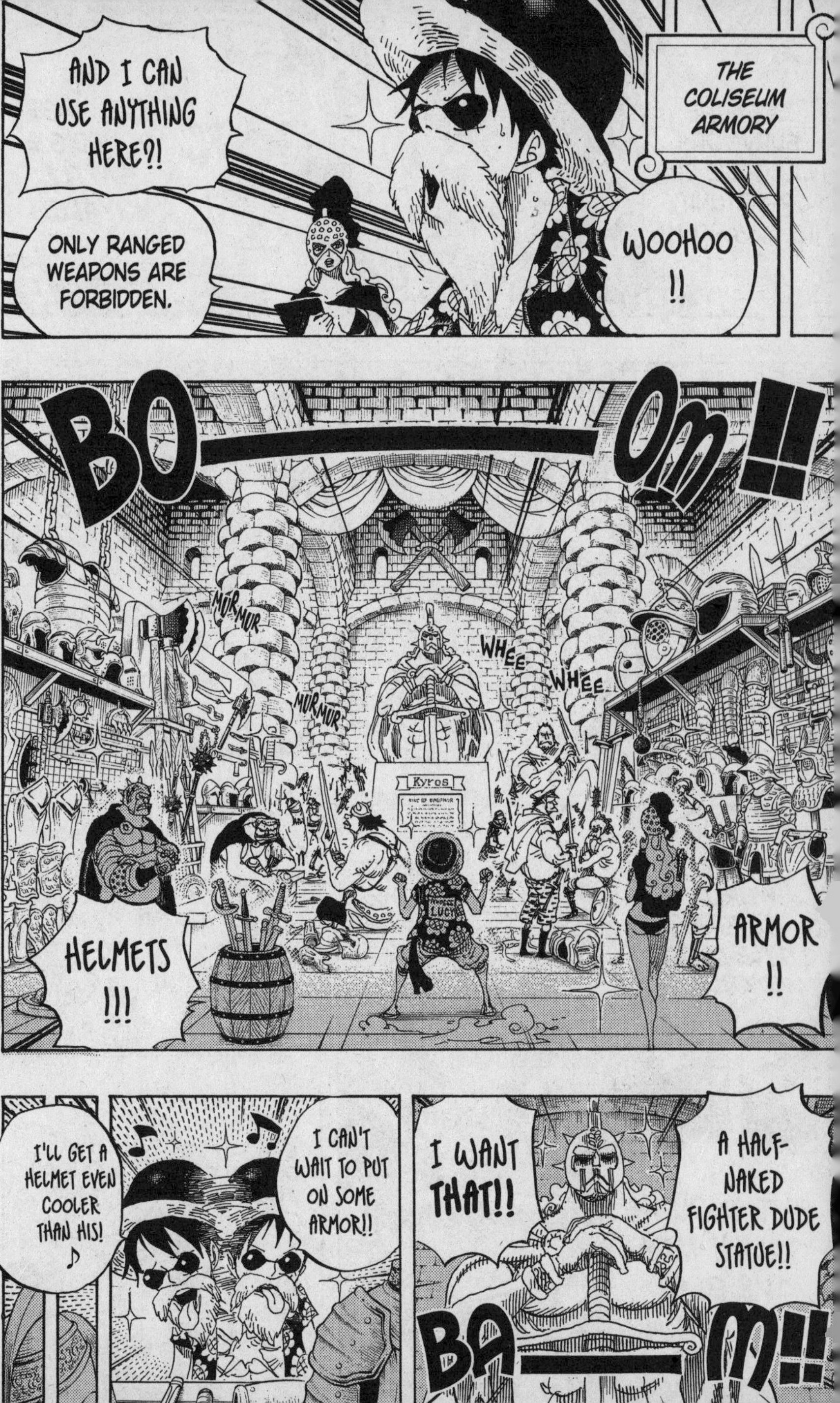
THE COLISEUM ARMORY
AND I CAN USE ANYTHING HERE?!
ONLY RANGED WEAPONS ARE FORBIDDEN.
WOOHOO!!
BO—OM!!
WHEE WHEE
MURMUR
MURMUR
Kyros
ARMOR!!
HELMETS!!!
A HALF-NAKED FIGHTER DUDE STATUE!!
I WANT THAT!!
BA—M!!
I CAN'T WAIT TO PUT ON SOME ARMOR!!
I'LL GET A HELMET EVEN COOLER THAN HIS! ♪

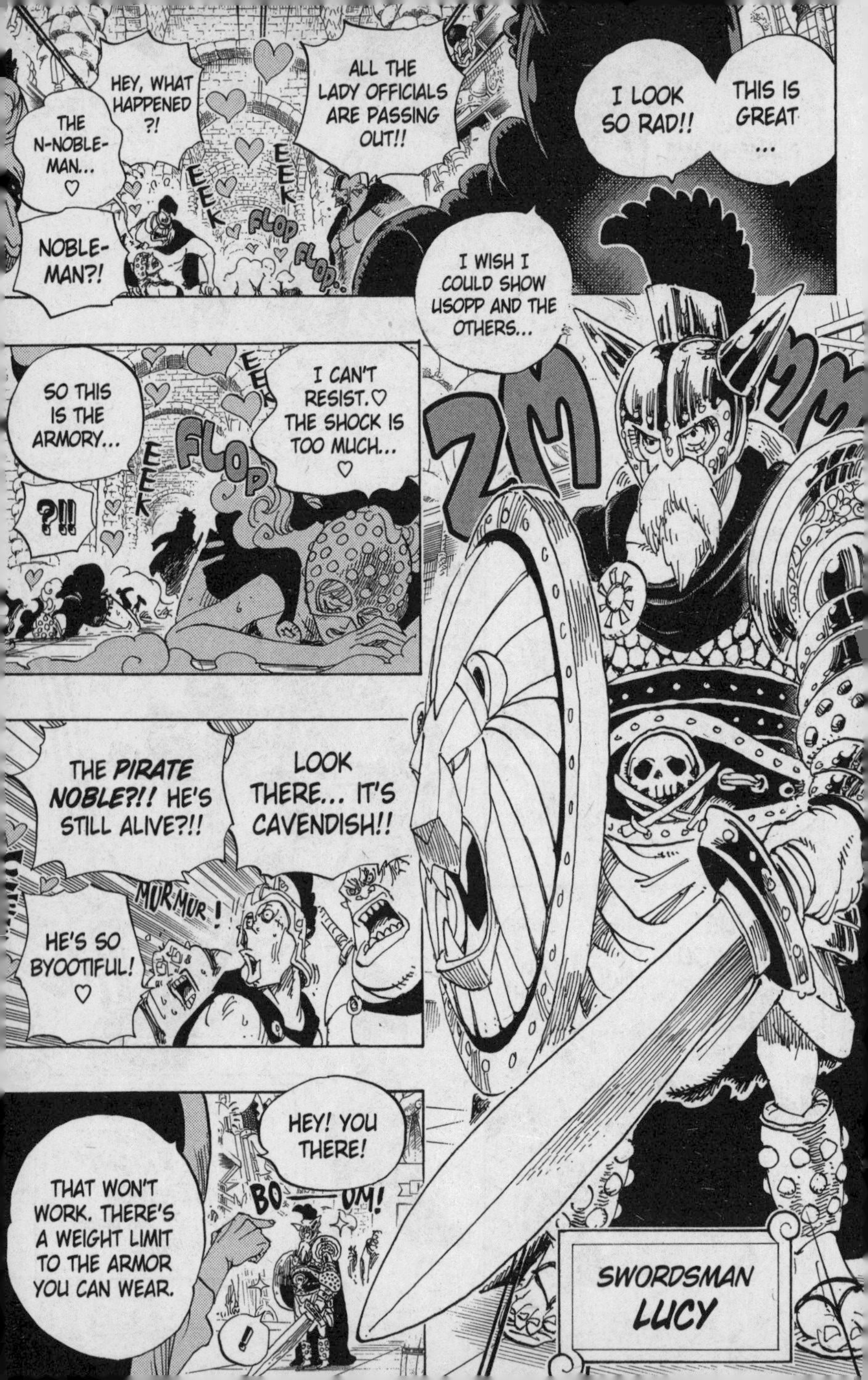
THIS IS GREAT ...
I LOOK SO RAD!!
I WISH I COULD SHOW USOPP AND THE OTHERS...
ZMMM
SWORDSMAN LUCY
ALL THE LADY OFFICIALS ARE PASSING OUT!!
HEY, WHAT HAPPENED ?!
THE N-NOBLE-MAN... ♡
NOBLE-MAN?!
EEK
EEK
FLOP
FLOP
I CAN'T RESIST.♡ THE SHOCK IS TOO MUCH... ♡
EEK
SO THIS IS THE ARMORY...
?!!
FLOP
EEK
LOOK THERE... IT'S CAVENDISH!!
THE *PIRATE NOBLE?!!* HE'S STILL ALIVE?!!
MURMUR!
HE'S SO BYOOTIFUL! ♡
HEY! YOU THERE!
THAT WON'T WORK. THERE'S A WEIGHT LIMIT TO THE ARMOR YOU CAN WEAR.
BO—OM!
!

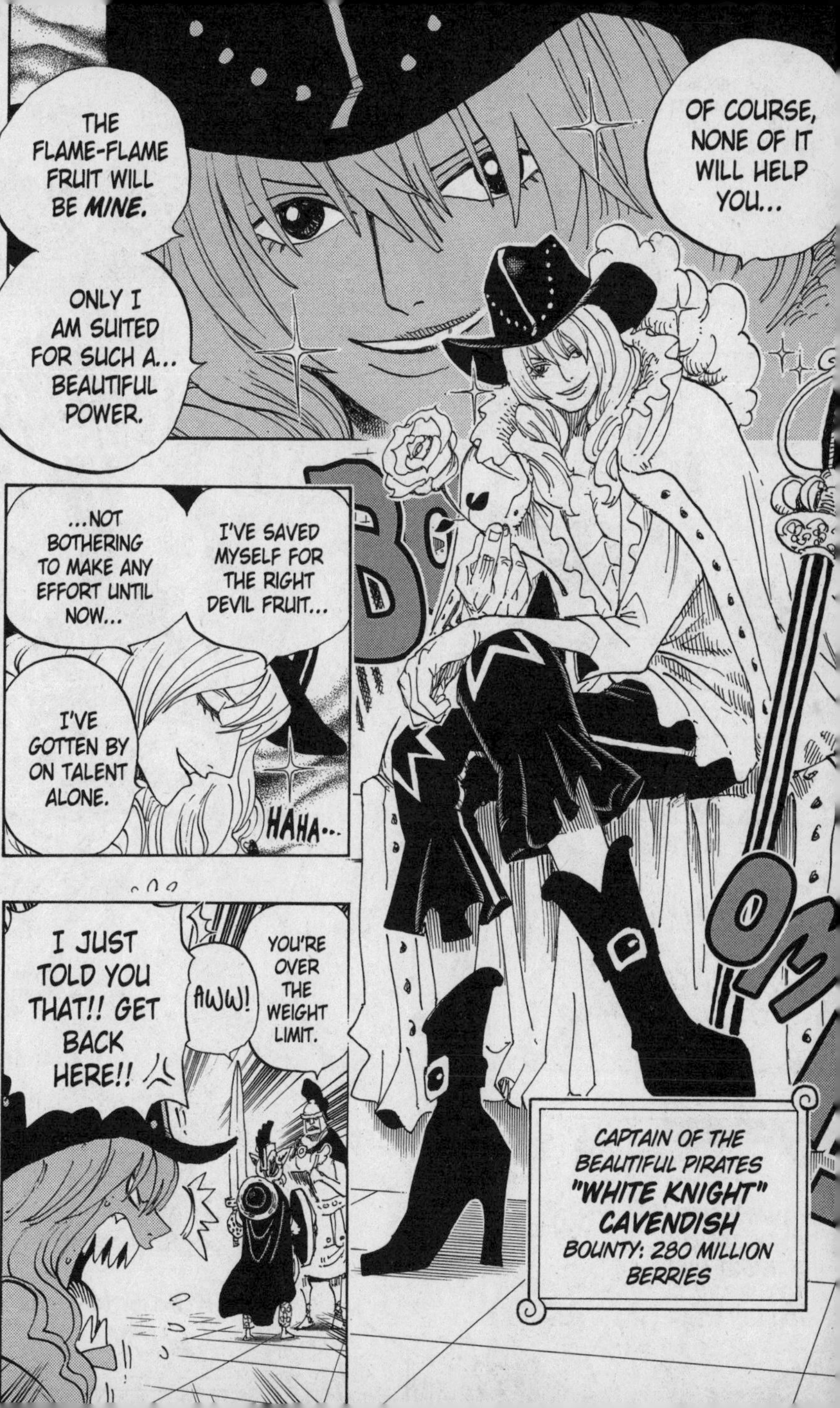
THE FLAME-FLAME FRUIT WILL BE *MINE.*
ONLY I AM SUITED FOR SUCH A... BEAUTIFUL POWER.
OF COURSE, NONE OF IT WILL HELP YOU...
BO
OM
CAPTAIN OF THE BEAUTIFUL PIRATES "WHITE KNIGHT" CAVENDISH BOUNTY: 280 MILLION BERRIES
I'VE SAVED MYSELF FOR THE RIGHT DEVIL FRUIT...
...NOT BOTHERING TO MAKE ANY EFFORT UNTIL NOW...
I'VE GOTTEN BY ON TALENT ALONE.
HAHA...
YOU'RE OVER THE WEIGHT LIMIT.
AWW!
I JUST TOLD YOU THAT!! GET BACK HERE!!

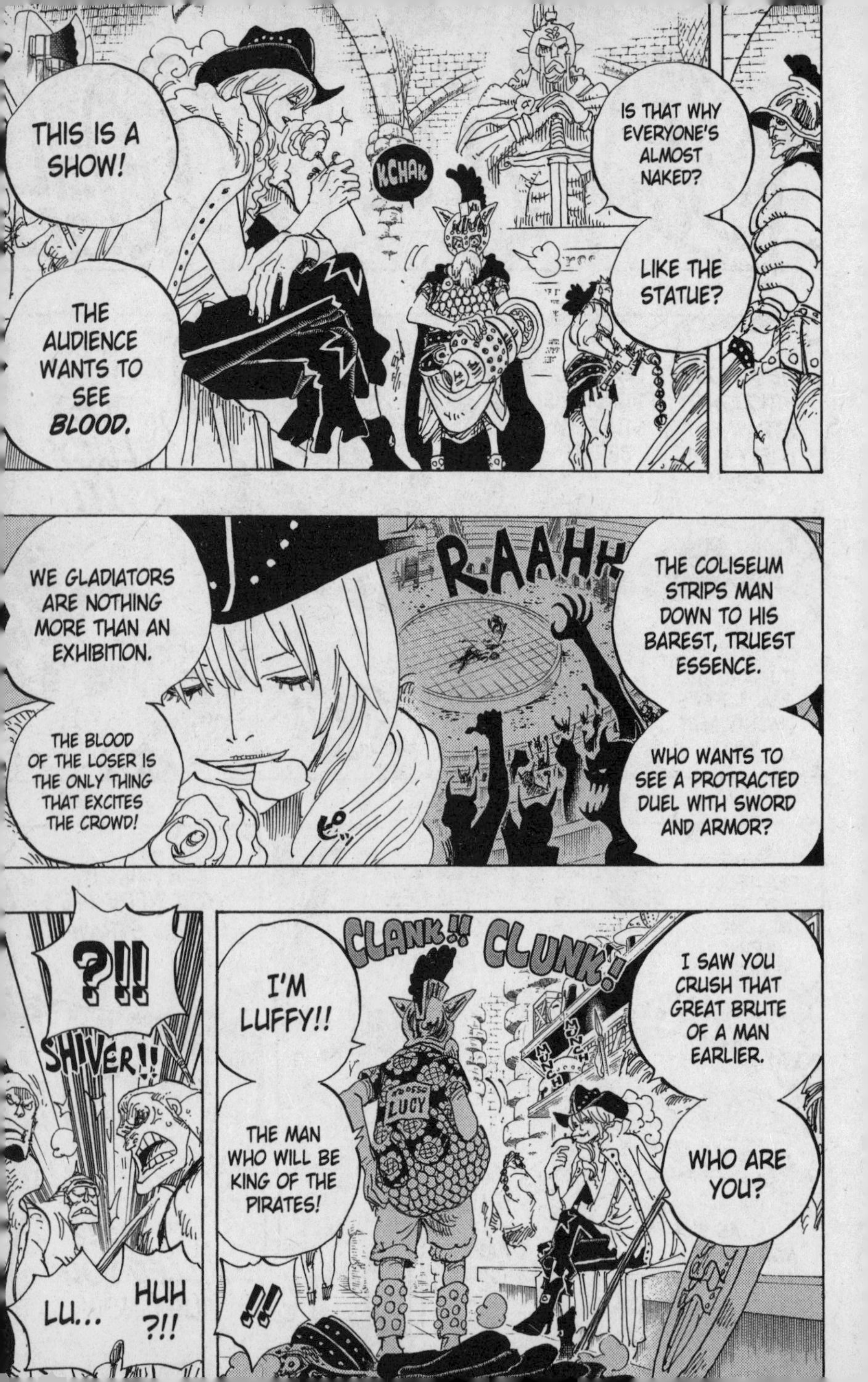
IS THAT WHY EVERYONE'S ALMOST NAKED?
LIKE THE STATUE?
KCHAK
THIS IS A SHOW!
THE AUDIENCE WANTS TO SEE *BLOOD.*
THE COLISEUM STRIPS MAN DOWN TO HIS BAREST, TRUEST ESSENCE.
WHO WANTS TO SEE A PROTRACTED DUEL WITH SWORD AND ARMOR?
RAAHH
WE GLADIATORS ARE NOTHING MORE THAN AN EXHIBITION.
THE BLOOD OF THE LOSER IS THE ONLY THING THAT EXCITES THE CROWD!
CLANK!! CLUNK!
I SAW YOU CRUSH THAT GREAT BRUTE OF A MAN EARLIER.
WHO ARE YOU?
LUCY
I'M LUFFY!!
THE MAN WHO WILL BE KING OF THE PIRATES!
!!
?!!
SHIVER!!
HUH ?!!
LU...

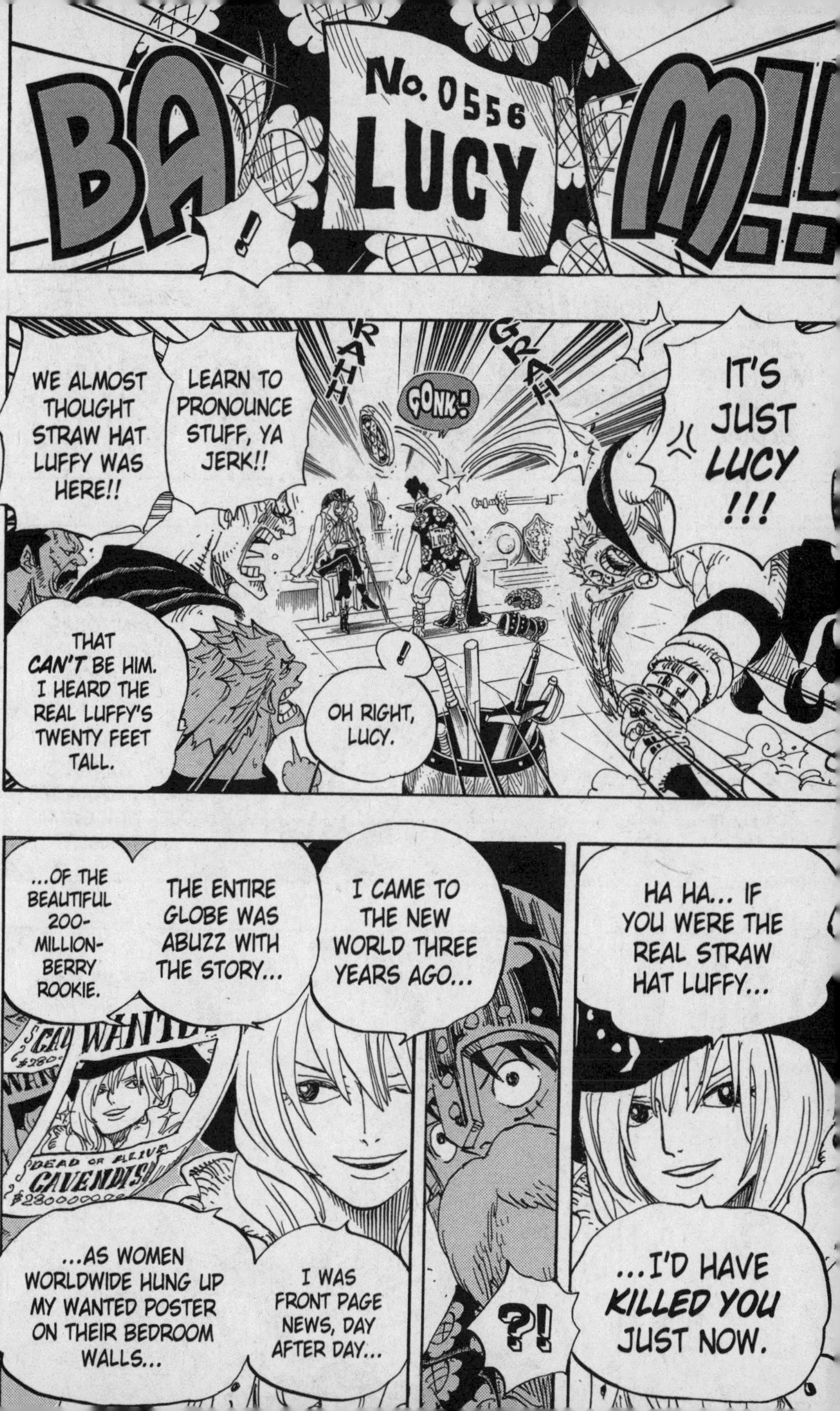
BAM!!
No. 0556
LUCY
!
IT'S JUST LUCY!!!
GRAH
GONK!
RAHH
LEARN TO PRONOUNCE STUFF, YA JERK!!
WE ALMOST THOUGHT STRAW HAT LUFFY WAS HERE!!
!
OH RIGHT, LUCY.
THAT CAN'T BE HIM. I HEARD THE REAL LUFFY'S TWENTY FEET TALL.
HA HA... IF YOU WERE THE REAL STRAW HAT LUFFY...
...I'D HAVE KILLED YOU JUST NOW.
I CAME TO THE NEW WORLD THREE YEARS AGO...
THE ENTIRE GLOBE WAS ABUZZ WITH THE STORY...
...OF THE BEAUTIFUL 200-MILLION-BERRY ROOKIE.
DEAD OR ALIVE
?!
I WAS FRONT PAGE NEWS, DAY AFTER DAY...
...AS WOMEN WORLDWIDE HUNG UP MY WANTED POSTER ON THEIR BEDROOM WALLS...

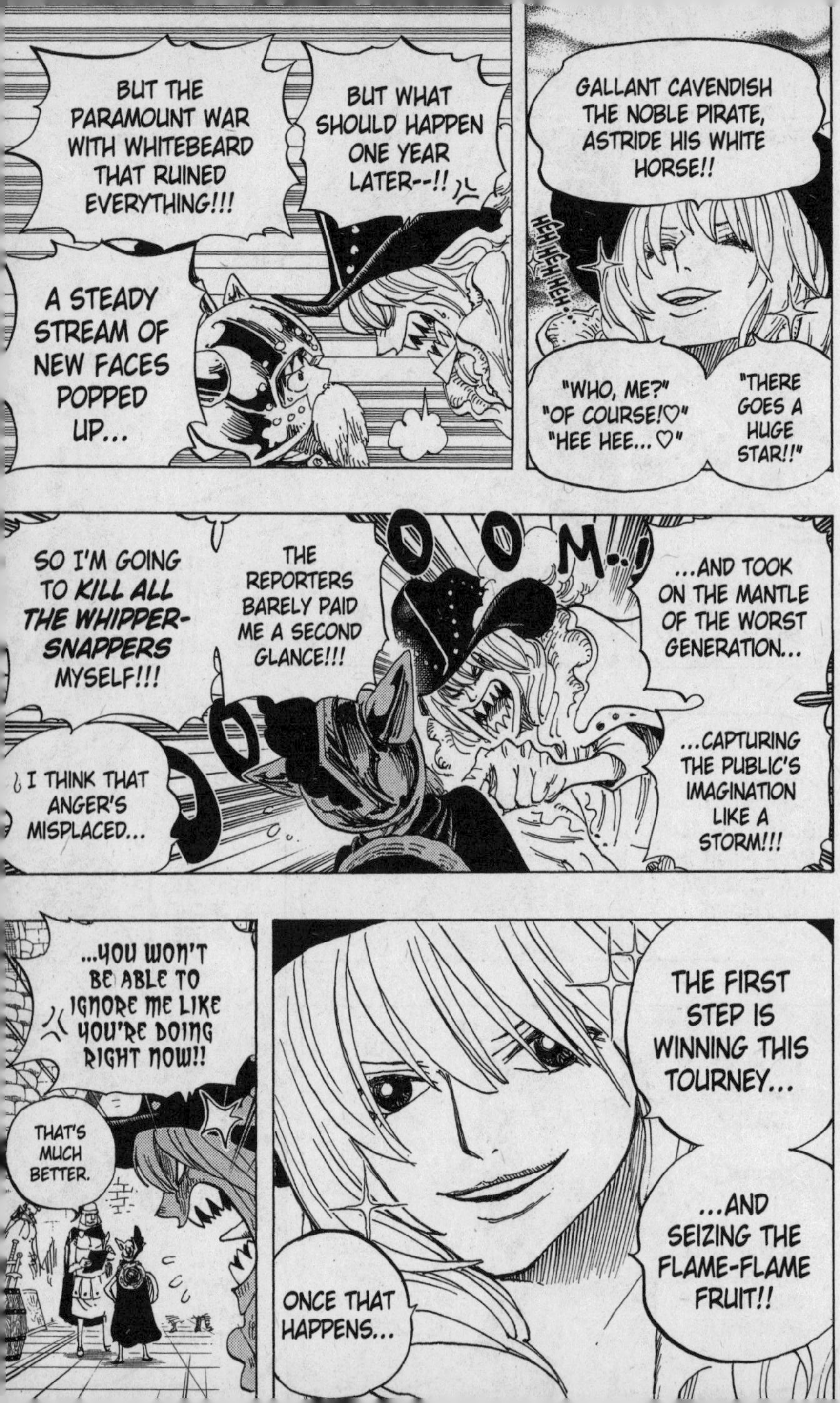
GALLANT CAVENDISH THE NOBLE PIRATE, ASTRIDE HIS WHITE HORSE!!
HEH HEH HEH...
"THERE GOES A HUGE STAR!!"
"WHO, ME?" "OF COURSE!♡" "HEE HEE...♡"
BUT WHAT SHOULD HAPPEN ONE YEAR LATER--!!
BUT THE PARAMOUNT WAR WITH WHITEBEARD THAT RUINED EVERYTHING!!!
A STEADY STREAM OF NEW FACES POPPED UP...
...AND TOOK ON THE MANTLE OF THE WORST GENERATION...
...CAPTURING THE PUBLIC'S IMAGINATION LIKE A STORM!!!
DOOM..
THE REPORTERS BARELY PAID ME A SECOND GLANCE!!!
SO I'M GOING TO KILL ALL THE WHIPPER-SNAPPERS MYSELF!!!
I THINK THAT ANGER'S MISPLACED...
THE FIRST STEP IS WINNING THIS TOURNEY...
...AND SEIZING THE FLAME-FLAME FRUIT!!
ONCE THAT HAPPENS...
...YOU WON'T BE ABLE TO IGNORE ME LIKE YOU'RE DOING RIGHT NOW!!
THAT'S MUCH BETTER.

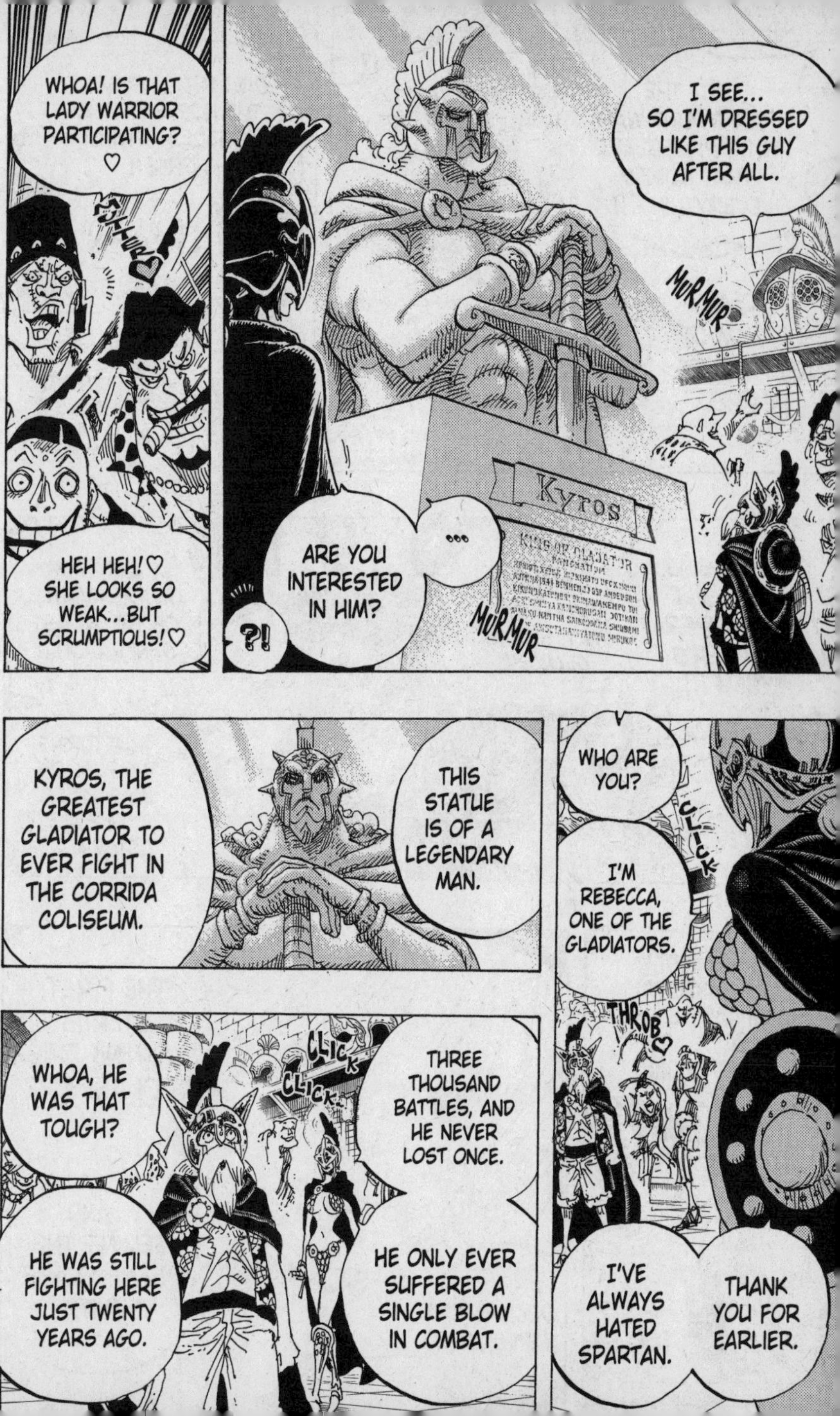
I SEE... SO I'M DRESSED LIKE THIS GUY AFTER ALL.
MURMUR
Kyros
...
ARE YOU INTERESTED IN HIM?
?!
MURMUR
WHOA! IS THAT LADY WARRIOR PARTICIPATING? ♡
HEH HEH! ♡ SHE LOOKS SO WEAK...BUT SCRUMPTIOUS! ♡
WHO ARE YOU?
CLICK
I'M REBECCA, ONE OF THE GLADIATORS.
THROB ♡
THANK YOU FOR EARLIER.
I'VE ALWAYS HATED SPARTAN.
THIS STATUE IS OF A LEGENDARY MAN.
KYROS, THE GREATEST GLADIATOR TO EVER FIGHT IN THE CORRIDA COLISEUM.
THREE THOUSAND BATTLES, AND HE NEVER LOST ONCE.
CLICK
CLICK
WHOA, HE WAS THAT TOUGH?
HE ONLY EVER SUFFERED A SINGLE BLOW IN COMBAT.
HE WAS STILL FIGHTING HERE JUST TWENTY YEARS AGO.

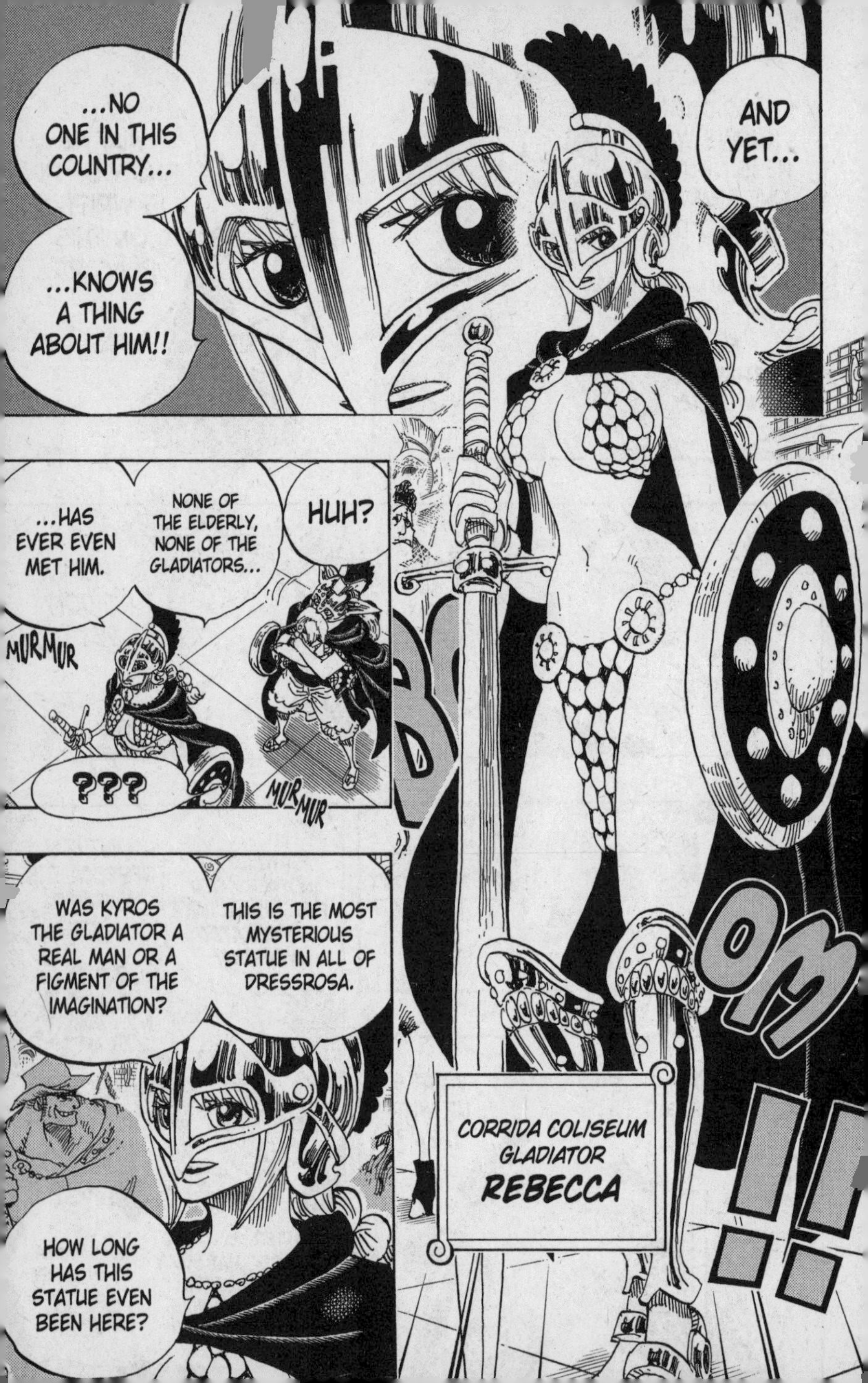
...NO ONE IN THIS COUNTRY...
...KNOWS A THING ABOUT HIM!!
AND YET...
BOOM!!
CORRIDA COLISEUM GLADIATOR REBECCA
HUH?
NONE OF THE ELDERLY, NONE OF THE GLADIATORS...
...HAS EVER EVEN MET HIM.
MURMUR
???
MURMUR
THIS IS THE MOST MYSTERIOUS STATUE IN ALL OF DRESSROSA.
WAS KYROS THE GLADIATOR A REAL MAN OR A FIGMENT OF THE IMAGINATION?
HOW LONG HAS THIS STATUE EVEN BEEN HERE?

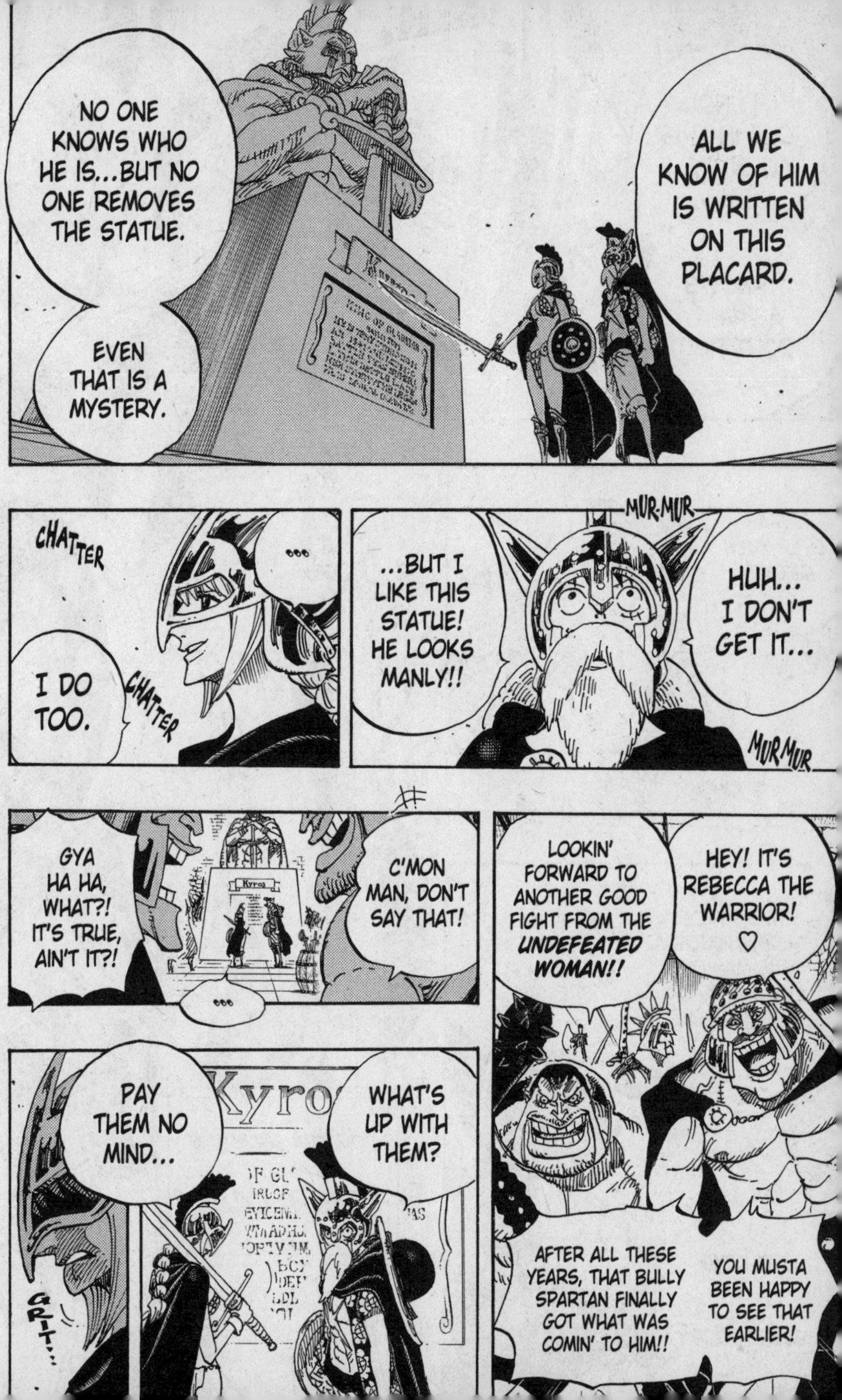
ALL WE KNOW OF HIM IS WRITTEN ON THIS PLACARD.
NO ONE KNOWS WHO HE IS...BUT NO ONE REMOVES THE STATUE.
EVEN THAT IS A MYSTERY.
MUR-MUR
HUH... I DON'T GET IT...
...BUT I LIKE THIS STATUE! HE LOOKS MANLY!!
MURMUR
...
CHATTER
I DO TOO.
CHATTER
HEY! IT'S REBECCA THE WARRIOR! ♡
LOOKIN' FORWARD TO ANOTHER GOOD FIGHT FROM THE ***UNDEFEATED WOMAN!!***
YOU MUSTA BEEN HAPPY TO SEE THAT EARLIER!
AFTER ALL THESE YEARS, THAT BULLY SPARTAN FINALLY GOT WHAT WAS COMIN' TO HIM!!
Kyros
C'MON MAN, DON'T SAY THAT!
GYA HA HA, WHAT?! IT'S TRUE, AIN'T IT?!
...
Kyros
WHAT'S UP WITH THEM?
PAY THEM NO MIND...
GRIT...

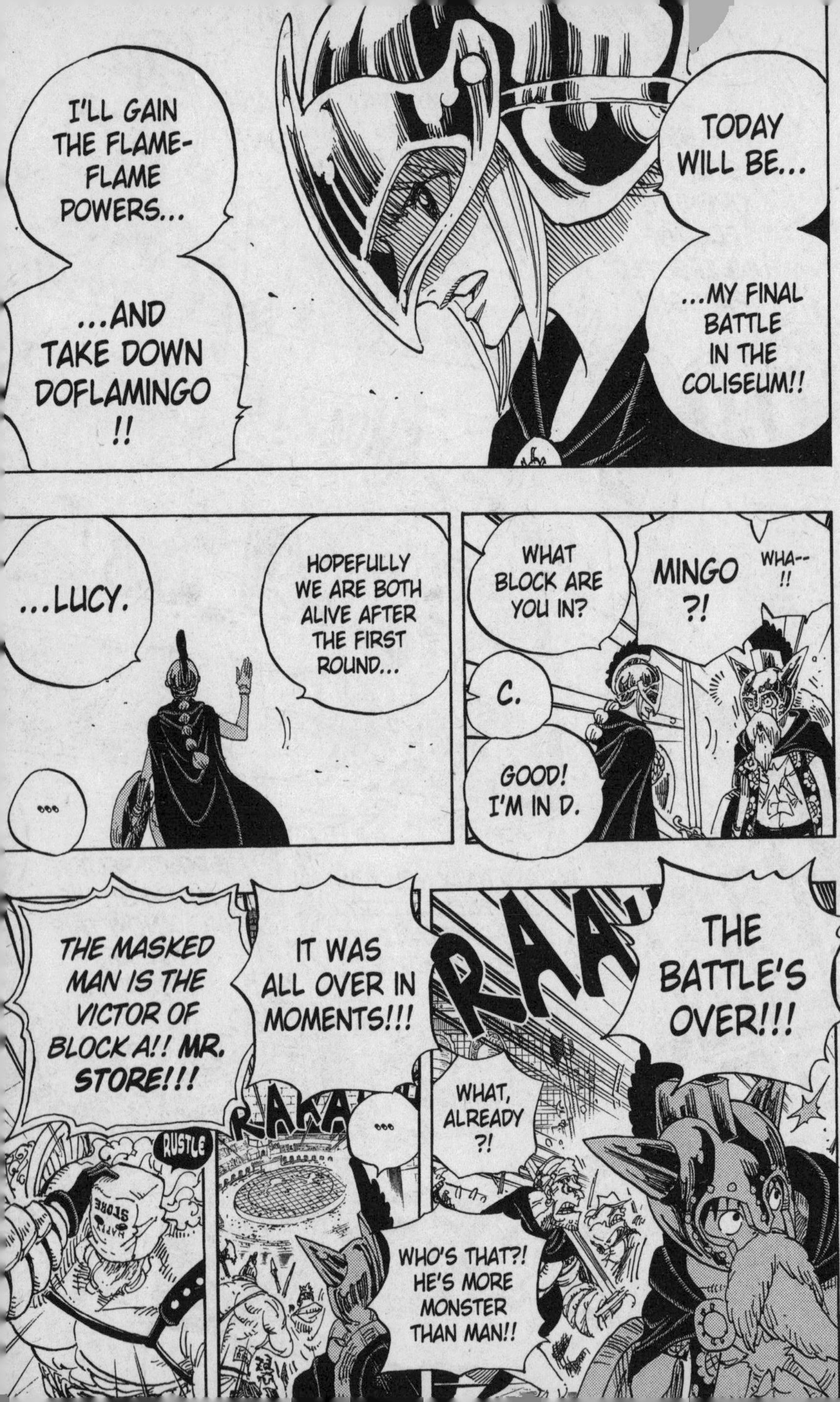
TODAY WILL BE...
...MY FINAL BATTLE IN THE COLISEUM!!
I'LL GAIN THE FLAME-FLAME POWERS...
...AND TAKE DOWN DOFLAMINGO!!
WHA-- !!
MINGO ?!
WHAT BLOCK ARE YOU IN?
C.
GOOD! I'M IN D.
HOPEFULLY WE ARE BOTH ALIVE AFTER THE FIRST ROUND...
...LUCY.
...
THE BATTLE'S OVER!!!
RAA
WHAT, ALREADY ?!
WHO'S THAT?! HE'S MORE MONSTER THAN MAN!!
IT WAS ALL OVER IN MOMENTS!!!
RAA
...
THE MASKED MAN IS THE VICTOR OF BLOCK A!! MR. STORE!!!
RUSTLE

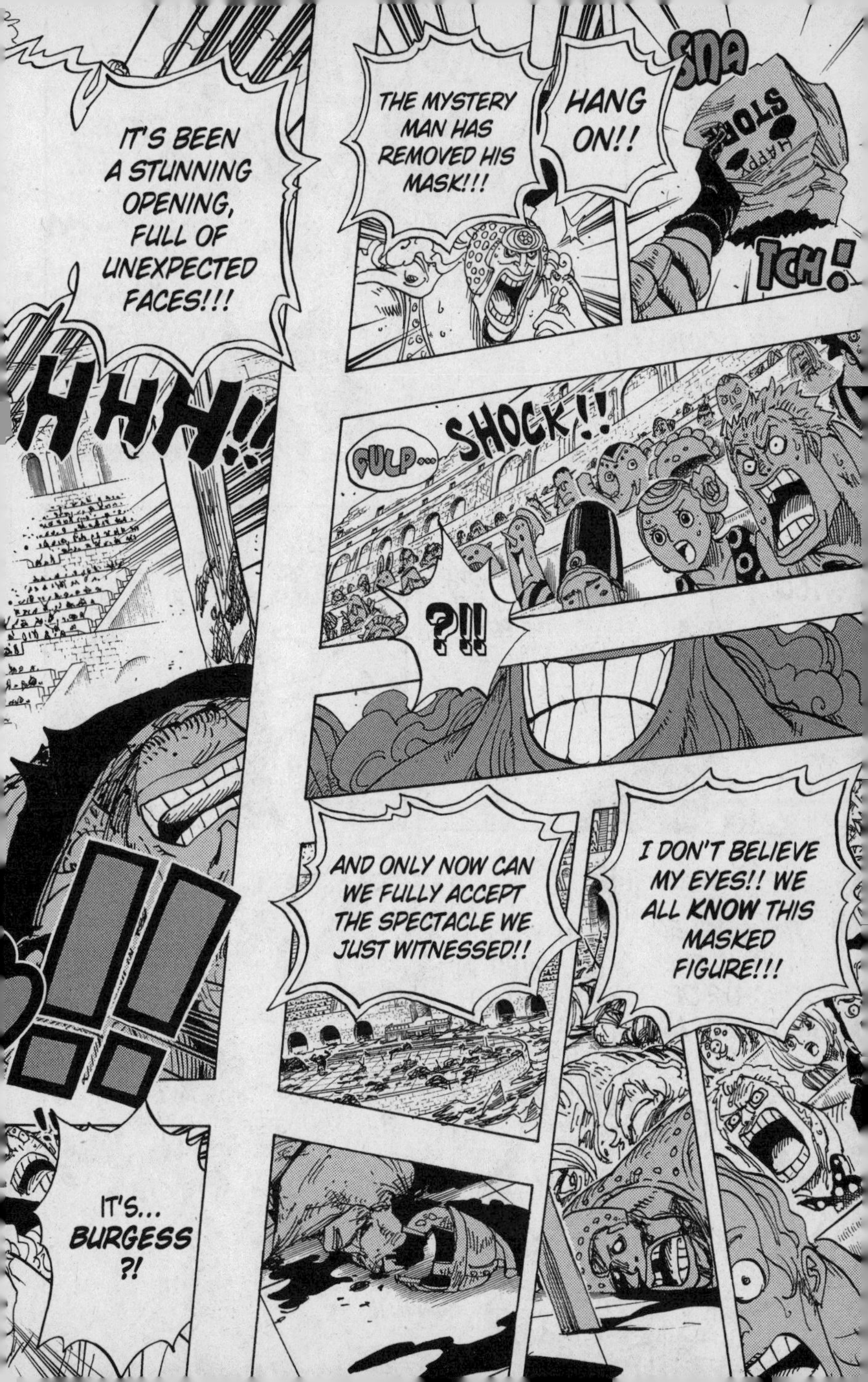
SNA
TCH!
HANG ON!!
THE MYSTERY MAN HAS REMOVED HIS MASK!!!
SHOCK!!
GULP...
?!!
I DON'T BELIEVE MY EYES!! WE ALL KNOW THIS MASKED FIGURE!!!
AND ONLY NOW CAN WE FULLY ACCEPT THE SPECTACLE WE JUST WITNESSED!!
IT'S BEEN A STUNNING OPENING, FULL OF UNEXPECTED FACES!!!
HHH!!
!!
IT'S... BURGESS?!

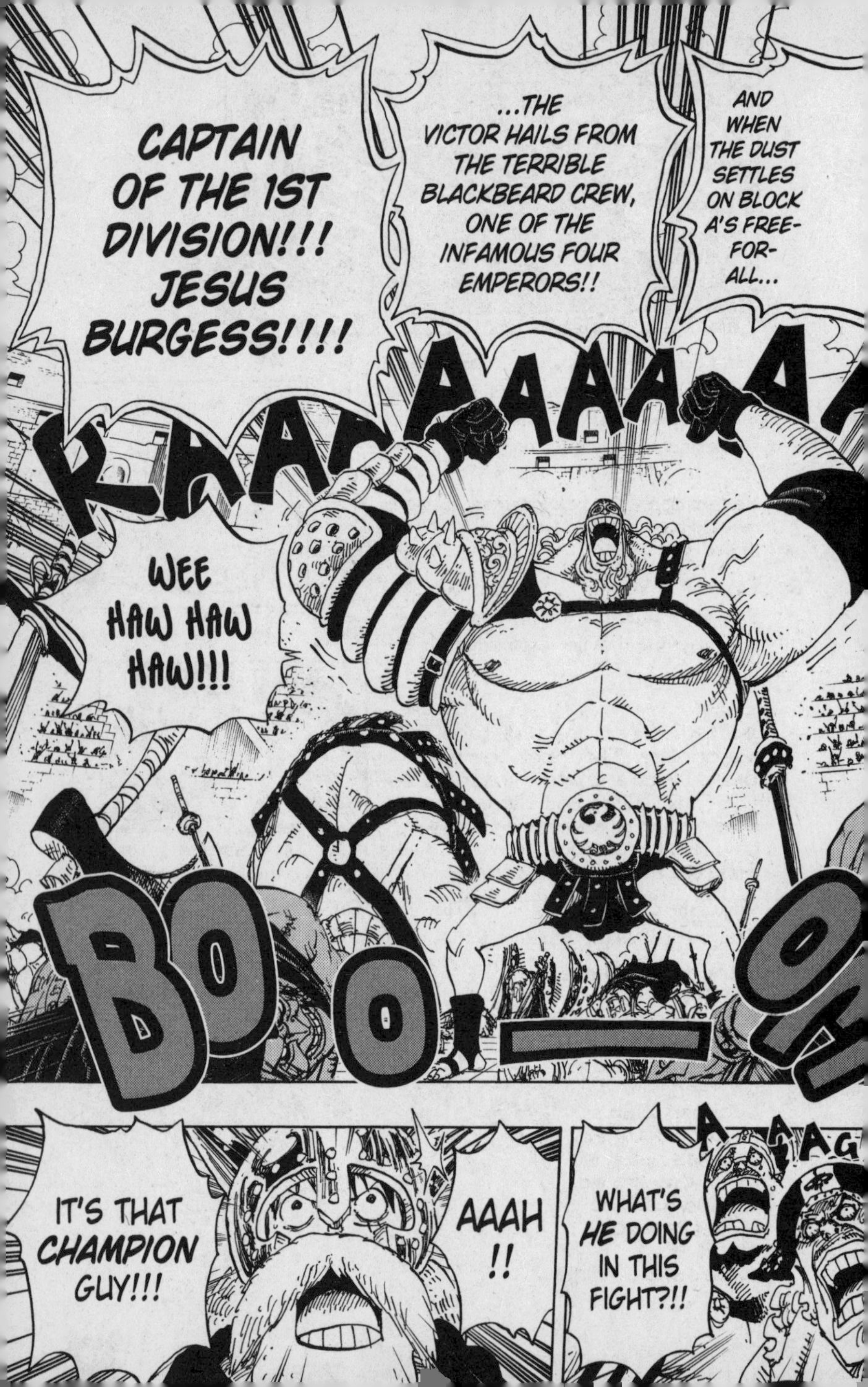
AND WHEN THE DUST SETTLES ON BLOCK A'S FREE-FOR-ALL...
...THE VICTOR HAILS FROM THE TERRIBLE BLACKBEARD CREW, ONE OF THE INFAMOUS FOUR EMPERORS!!
CAPTAIN OF THE 1ST DIVISION!!! JESUS BURGESS!!!!
KAAAAAAA
WEE HAW HAW HAW!!!
BOO—O
WHAT'S HE DOING IN THIS FIGHT?!!
AAAH!!
IT'S THAT CHAMPION GUY!!!

SBS Question Corner

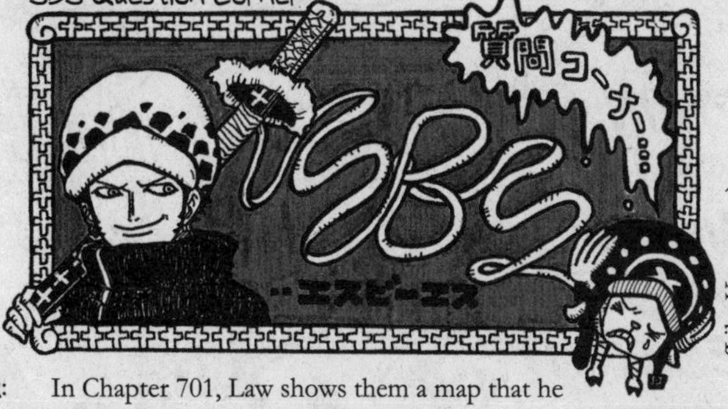

質問コーナー…!!
SBS
エスビーエス

(Lily, Kanagawa)

Q: In Chapter 701, Law shows them a map that he claims his crew prepared for him! Could that be referring to Bepo?!! I mean, that does look like a paw print in the corner, doesn't it?

--T. Takaaki

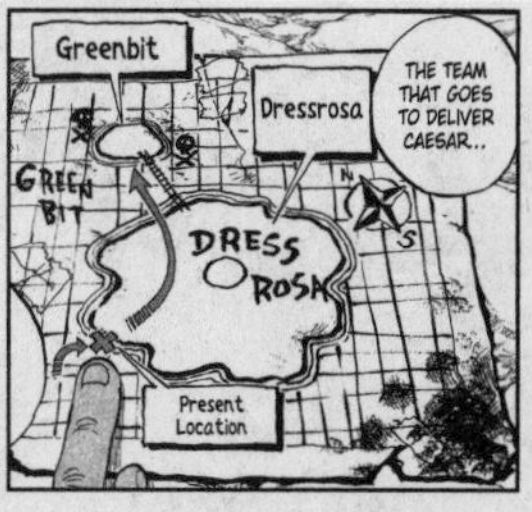

Greenbit
Dressrosa
THE TEAM THAT GOES TO DELIVER CAESAR...
GREEN BIT
DRESS ROSA
N
S
Present Location

A: Yes, it does. And of course, Bepo is the navigator of the Heart Pirates. He drew the map.

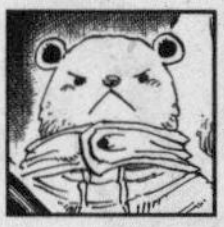

Q: Odacchi! In Volume 70, Chapter 700, Sanji made three rice balls for Law, who hates bread. What was inside each of them?

--Natsuki

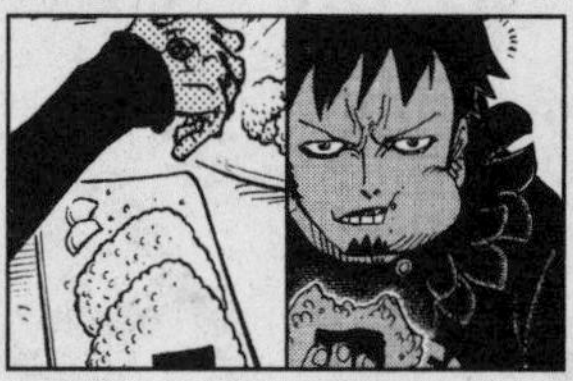

A: Well, the first one was tuna and mayonnaise. The next one was okaka (dried and ground bonito fish with soy sauce), and the last was a super-sour dried plum! By the way, Law also hates sour plums. He had a fight with Sanji a few minutes after that scene.

Q: What's the name of Law's sword? How many tattoos does Law have?! Can you draw all of his tattoos for us, Odacchi?!!! (≧ロ≦)

A: Sure thing. These are from my original sketch notebook. ➡ There's definitely a heart motif going on there. Wonder what's up with that? His katana's name is Kikoku, meaning "demon wail." No special category for it. It's a cursed blade.

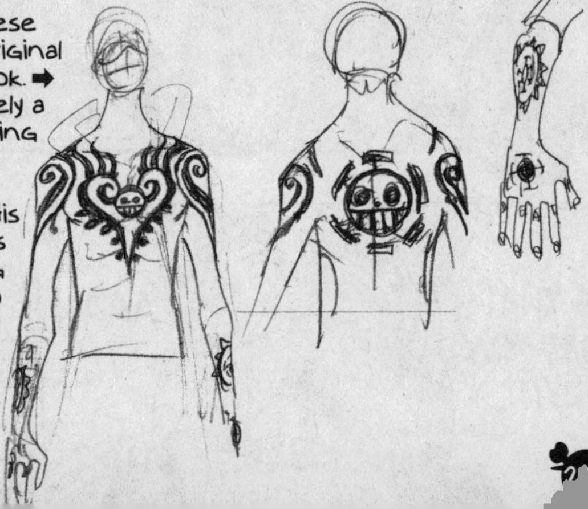

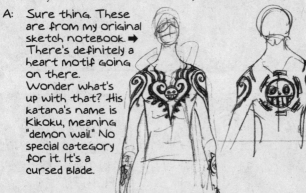

Chapter 705:
MAYNARD THE PURSUER

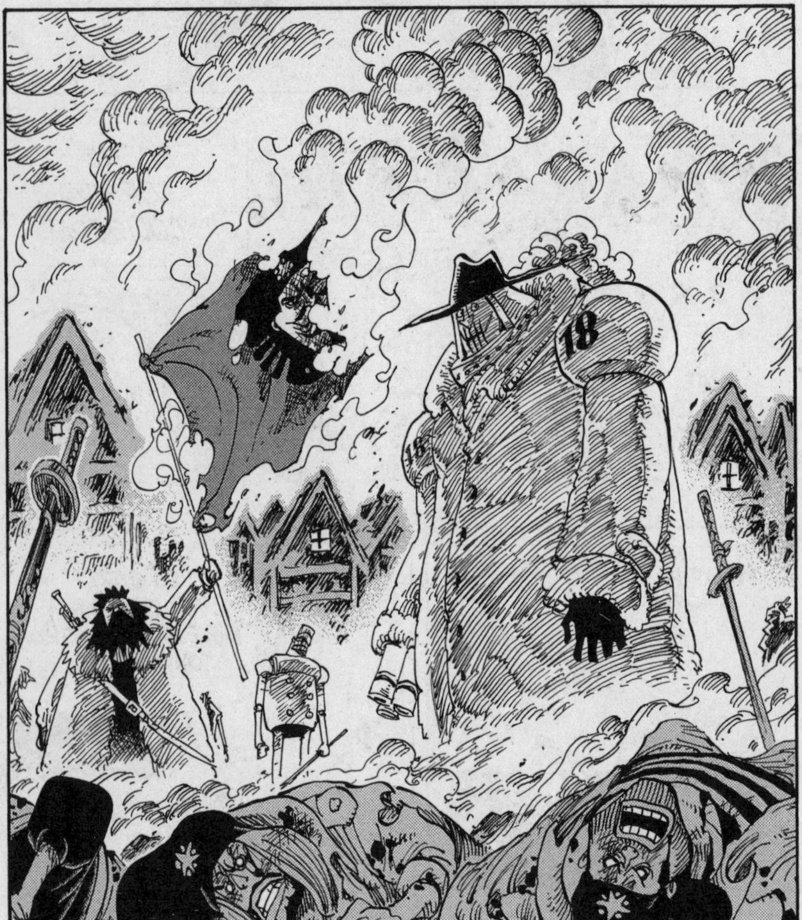

18

CARIBOU'S NEW WORLD KEE HEE HEE, VOL. 25
"AN EXAMPLE TO THE OTHERS"

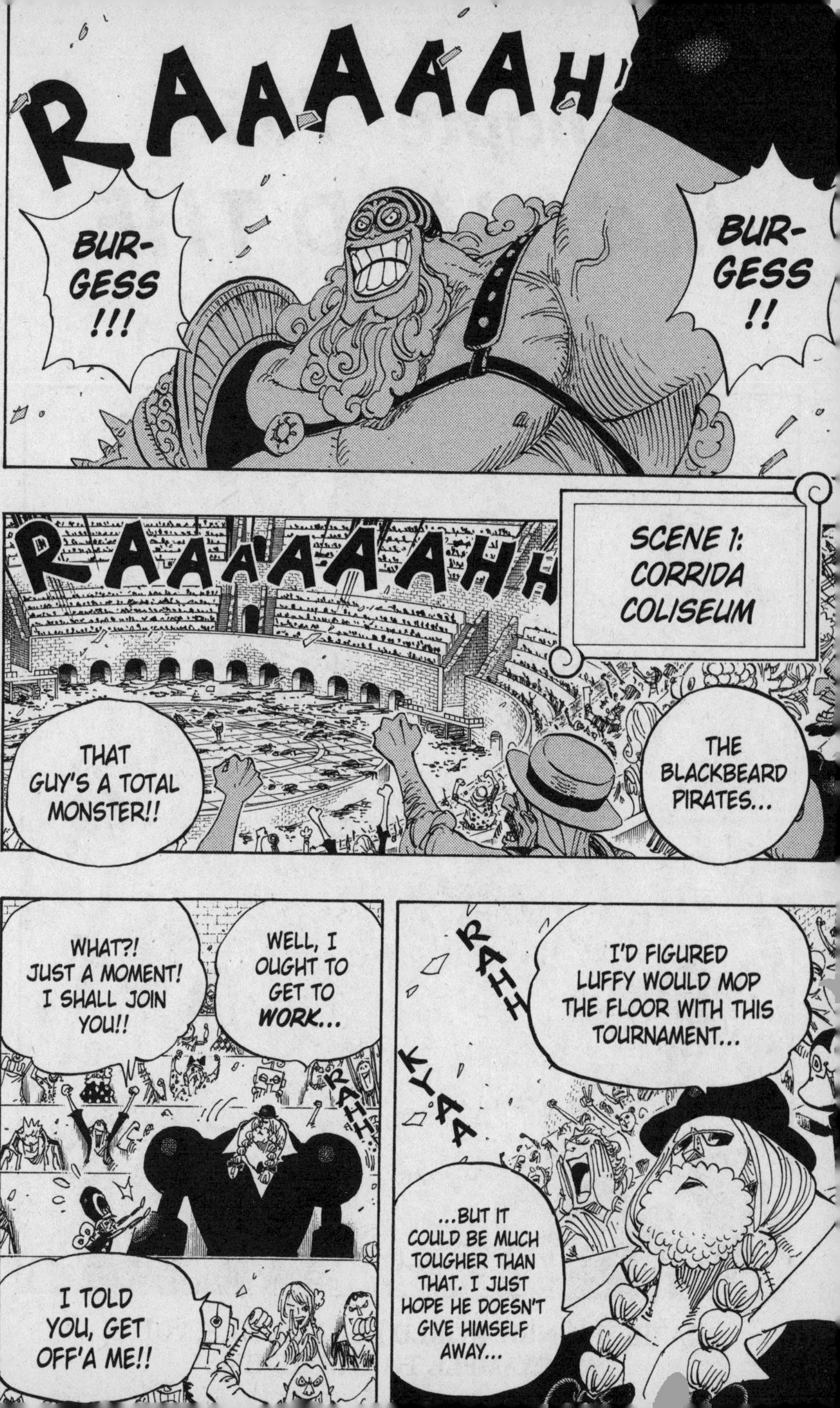
RAAAAAH
BUR-GESS!!
BUR-GESS!!!
SCENE 1: CORRIDA COLISEUM
RAAAAAAHH
THE BLACKBEARD PIRATES...
THAT GUY'S A TOTAL MONSTER!!
RAHH
I'D FIGURED LUFFY WOULD MOP THE FLOOR WITH THIS TOURNAMENT...
KYAA
...BUT IT COULD BE MUCH TOUGHER THAN THAT. I JUST HOPE HE DOESN'T GIVE HIMSELF AWAY...
WELL, I OUGHT TO GET TO **WORK...**
WHAT?! JUST A MOMENT! I SHALL JOIN YOU!!
RAHH
I TOLD YOU, GET OFF'A ME!!

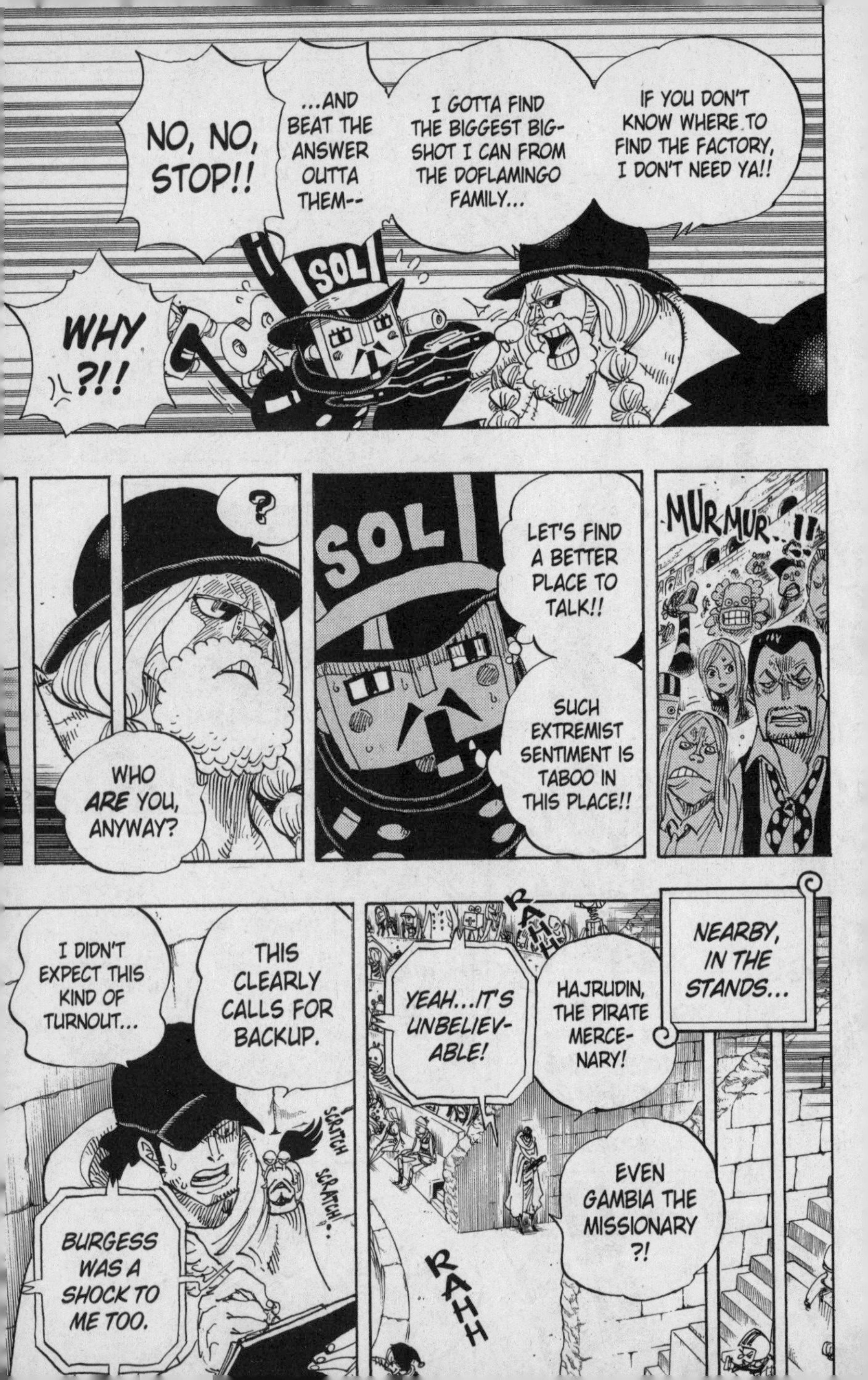
IF YOU DON'T KNOW WHERE TO FIND THE FACTORY, I DON'T NEED YA!!
I GOTTA FIND THE BIGGEST BIG-SHOT I CAN FROM THE DOFLAMINGO FAMILY...
...AND BEAT THE ANSWER OUTTA THEM--
NO, NO, STOP!!
WHY?!!
MURMUR...!!
LET'S FIND A BETTER PLACE TO TALK!!
SUCH EXTREMIST SENTIMENT IS TABOO IN THIS PLACE!!
?
WHO ARE YOU, ANYWAY?
NEARBY, IN THE STANDS...
RAHH
HAJRUDIN, THE PIRATE MERCENARY!
YEAH...IT'S UNBELIEVABLE!
EVEN GAMBIA THE MISSIONARY?!
RAHH
THIS CLEARLY CALLS FOR BACKUP.
I DIDN'T EXPECT THIS KIND OF TURNOUT...
SCRATCH
SCRATCH...
BURGESS WAS A SHOCK TO ME TOO.

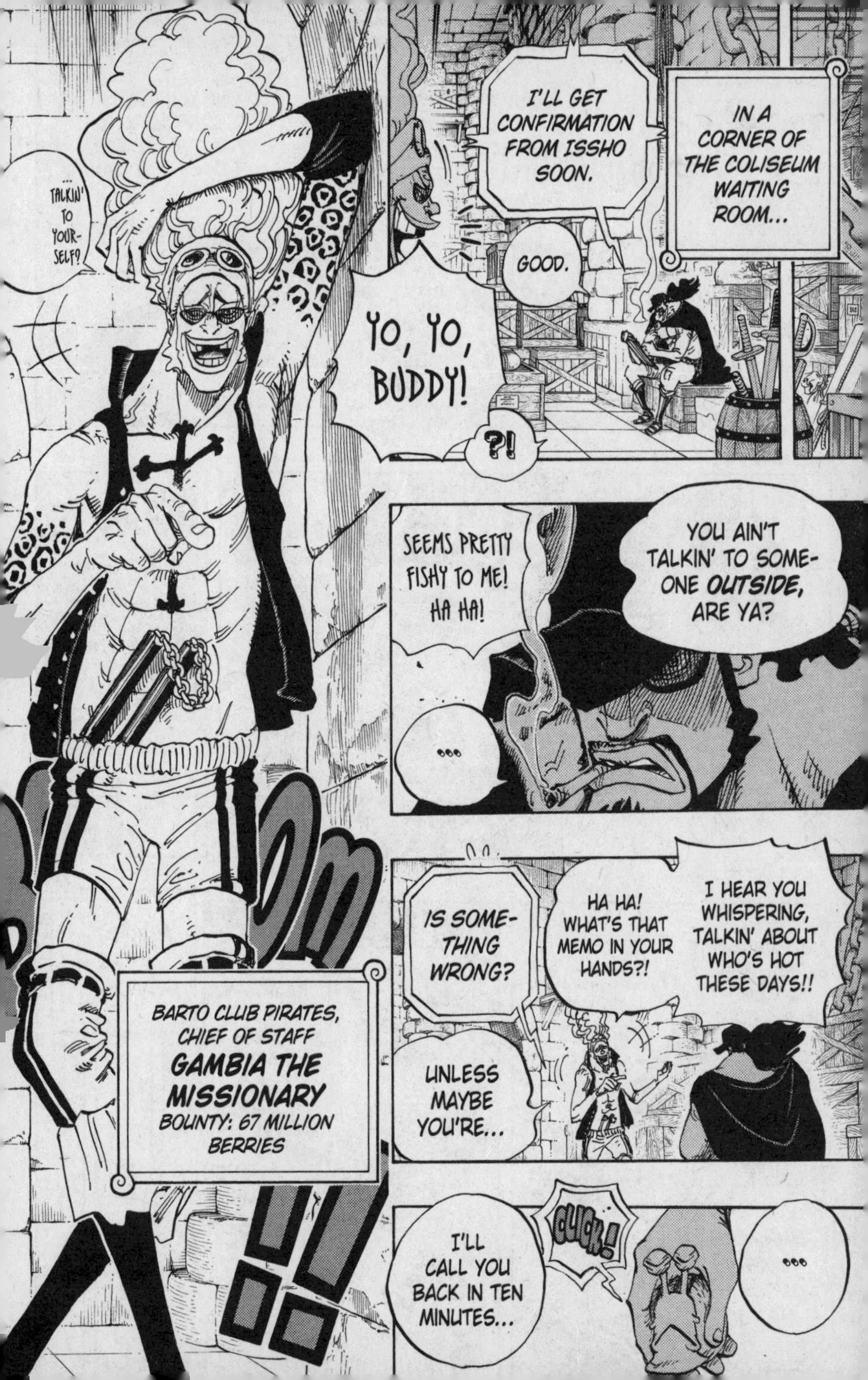

IN A CORNER OF THE COLISEUM WAITING ROOM...
I'LL GET CONFIRMATION FROM ISSHO SOON.
GOOD.
YOU AIN'T TALKIN' TO SOMEONE *OUTSIDE*, ARE YA?
SEEMS PRETTY FISHY TO ME! HA HA!
...
I HEAR YOU WHISPERING, TALKIN' ABOUT WHO'S HOT THESE DAYS!!
HA HA! WHAT'S THAT MEMO IN YOUR HANDS?!
IS SOMETHING WRONG?
UNLESS MAYBE YOU'RE...
...
CLICK!
I'LL CALL YOU BACK IN TEN MINUTES...
YO, YO, BUDDY!
...TALKIN' TO YOURSELF?
?!
BARTO CLUB PIRATES, CHIEF OF STAFF
GAMBIA THE MISSIONARY
BOUNTY: 67 MILLION BERRIES

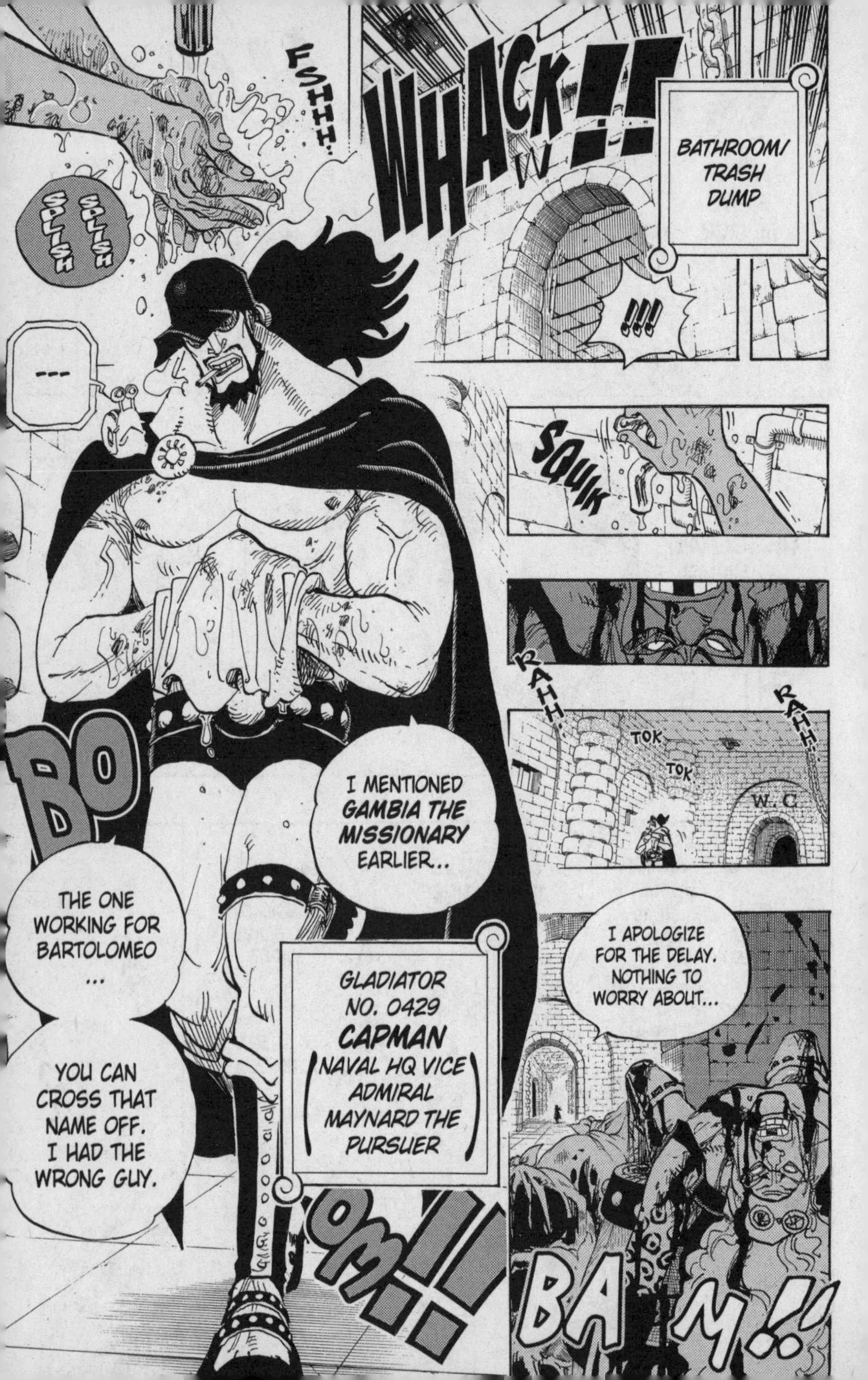
BATHROOM/ TRASH DUMP
WHACK!!
!!!
SQUIK
RAHH
TOK
TOK
W.C
RAHH
I APOLOGIZE FOR THE DELAY. NOTHING TO WORRY ABOUT...
BAM!!
FSHHH
SPLISH SPLISH

I MENTIONED GAMBIA THE MISSIONARY EARLIER...
THE ONE WORKING FOR BARTOLOMEO ...
YOU CAN CROSS THAT NAME OFF. I HAD THE WRONG GUY.
GLADIATOR NO. 0429 CAPMAN (NAVAL HQ VICE ADMIRAL MAYNARD THE PURSUER)
BOOM!!

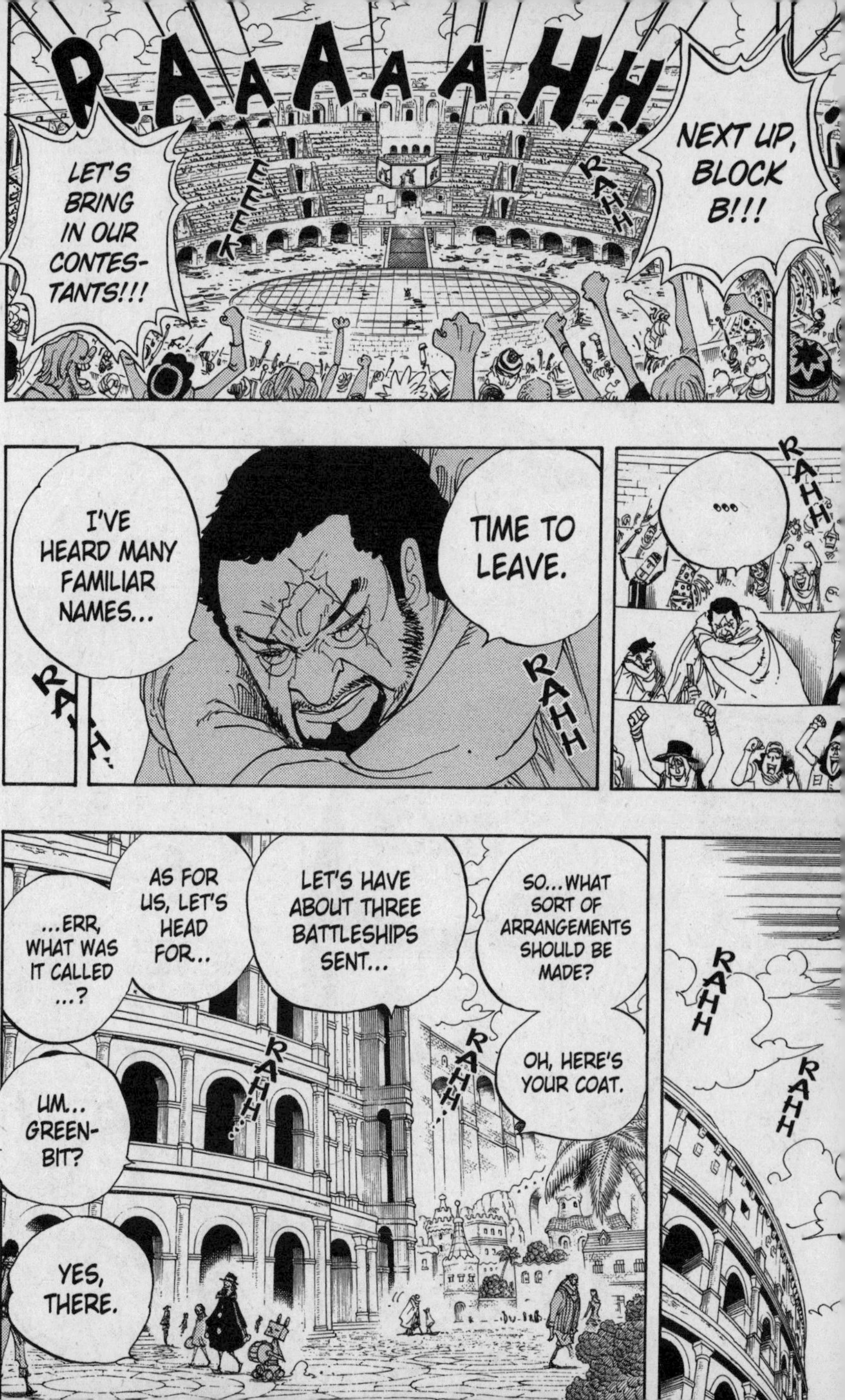
RAAAAAHH
NEXT UP, BLOCK B!!!
RAHH
EEEEK
LET'S BRING IN OUR CONTES-TANTS!!!
RAHH
...
TIME TO LEAVE.
RAHH
I'VE HEARD MANY FAMILIAR NAMES...
RAHH
RAHH
SO...WHAT SORT OF ARRANGEMENTS SHOULD BE MADE?
OH, HERE'S YOUR COAT.
RAHH
LET'S HAVE ABOUT THREE BATTLESHIPS SENT...
RAHH
AS FOR US, LET'S HEAD FOR...
...ERR, WHAT WAS IT CALLED ...?
UM... GREEN-BIT?
YES, THERE.

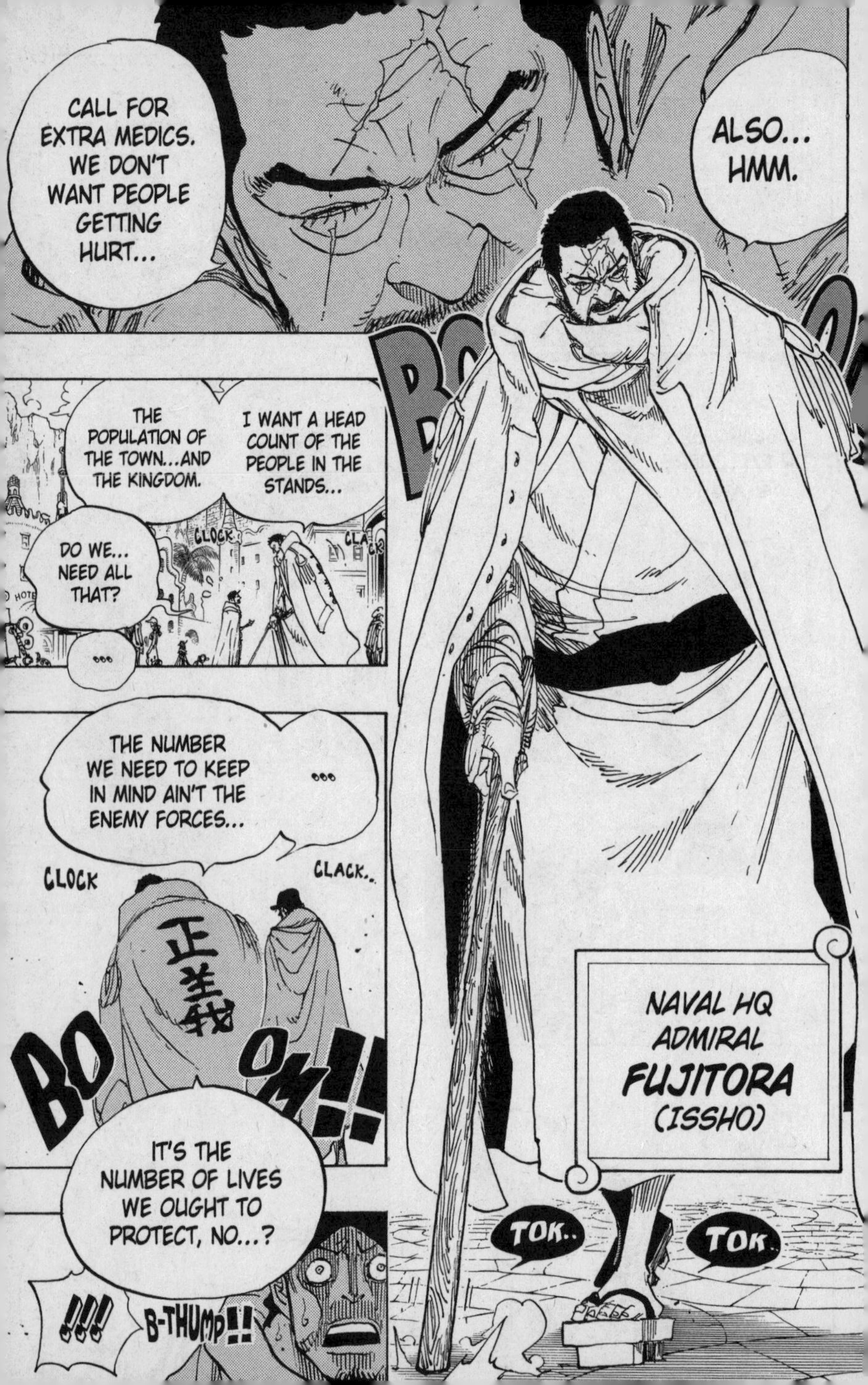
CALL FOR EXTRA MEDICS. WE DON'T WANT PEOPLE GETTING HURT...
ALSO... HMM.
NAVAL HQ ADMIRAL FUJITORA (ISSHO)
TOK..
TOK..
I WANT A HEAD COUNT OF THE PEOPLE IN THE STANDS...
THE POPULATION OF THE TOWN...AND THE KINGDOM.
CLACK
CLOCK
DO WE... NEED ALL THAT?
...
THE NUMBER WE NEED TO KEEP IN MIND AIN'T THE ENEMY FORCES...
...
CLACK..
CLOCK
正義
BOOM!!
IT'S THE NUMBER OF LIVES WE OUGHT TO PROTECT, NO...?
B-THUMP!!
!!!

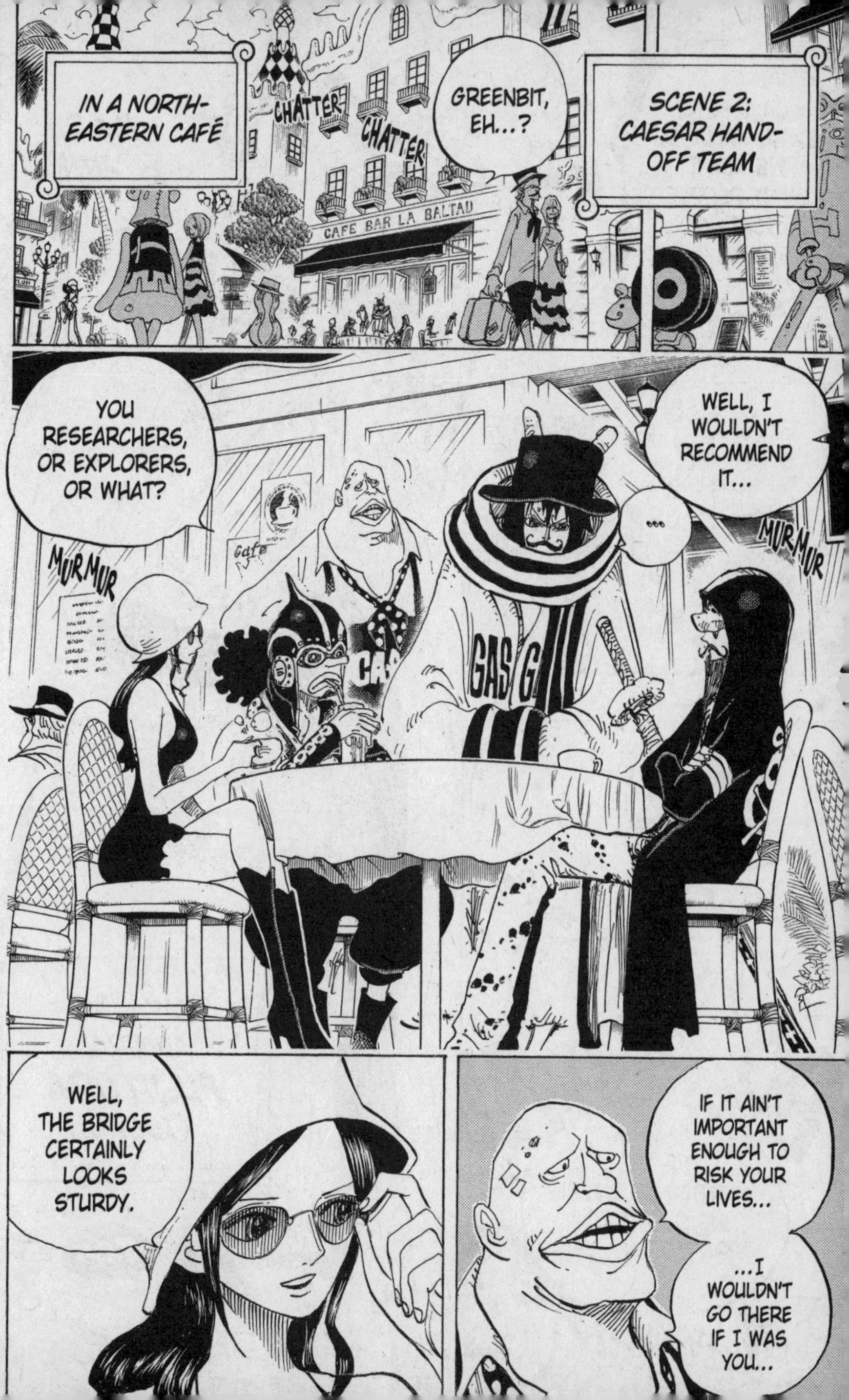
SCENE 2: CAESAR HAND-OFF TEAM
GREENBIT, EH...?
CHATTER
CHATTER
IN A NORTH-EASTERN CAFÉ
CAFE BAR LA BALTAU
WELL, I WOULDN'T RECOMMEND IT...
...
MURMUR
YOU RESEARCHERS, OR EXPLORERS, OR WHAT?
MURMUR
IF IT AIN'T IMPORTANT ENOUGH TO RISK YOUR LIVES...
...I WOULDN'T GO THERE IF I WAS YOU...
WELL, THE BRIDGE CERTAINLY LOOKS STURDY.

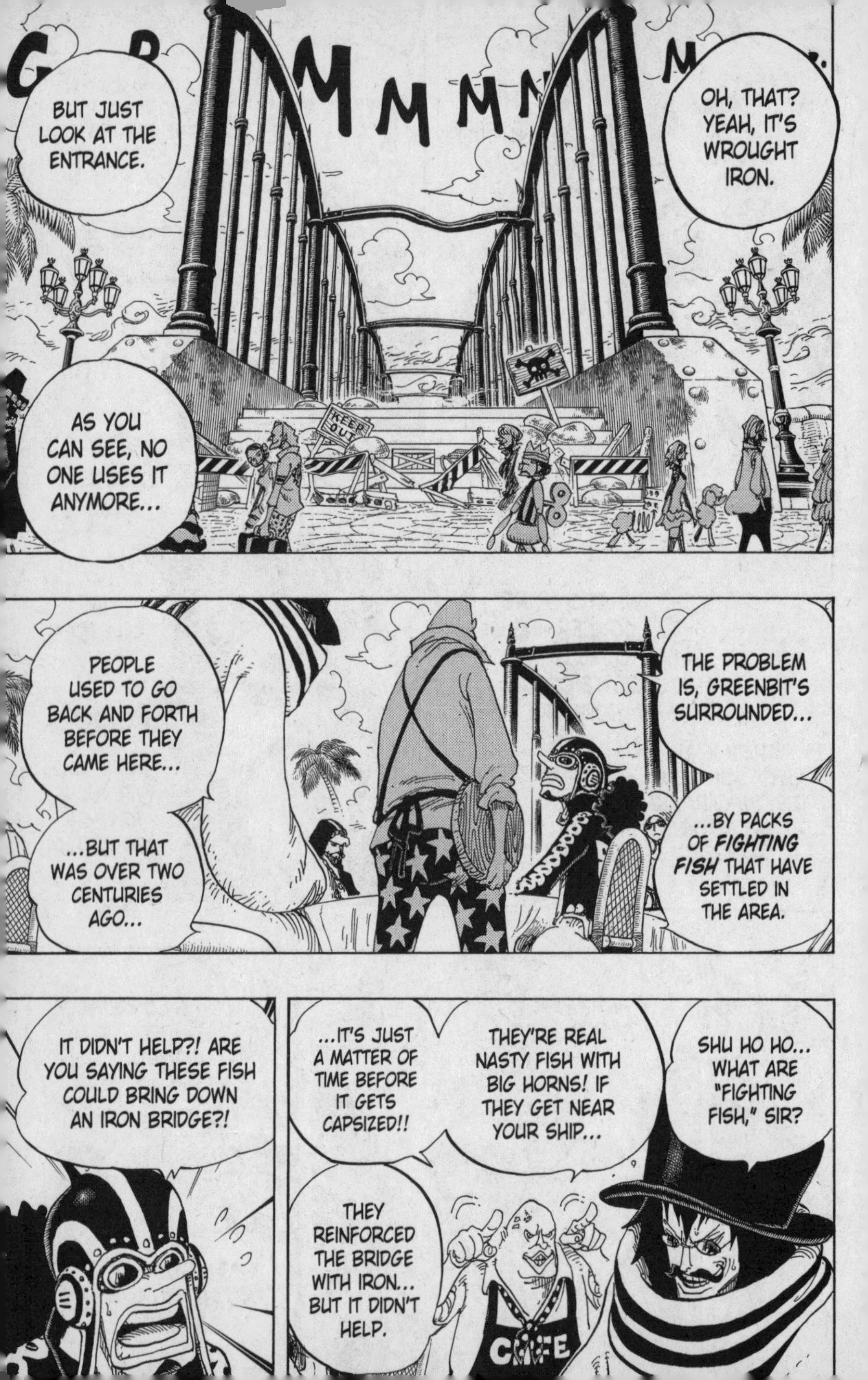
OH, THAT? YEAH, IT'S WROUGHT IRON.
BUT JUST LOOK AT THE ENTRANCE.
KEEP OUT
AS YOU CAN SEE, NO ONE USES IT ANYMORE...
THE PROBLEM IS, GREENBIT'S SURROUNDED...
...BY PACKS OF *FIGHTING FISH* THAT HAVE SETTLED IN THE AREA.
PEOPLE USED TO GO BACK AND FORTH BEFORE THEY CAME HERE...
...BUT THAT WAS OVER TWO CENTURIES AGO...
SHU HO HO... WHAT ARE "FIGHTING FISH," SIR?
THEY'RE REAL NASTY FISH WITH BIG HORNS! IF THEY GET NEAR YOUR SHIP...
...IT'S JUST A MATTER OF TIME BEFORE IT GETS CAPSIZED!!
THEY REINFORCED THE BRIDGE WITH IRON... BUT IT DIDN'T HELP.
CAFE
IT DIDN'T HELP?! ARE YOU SAYING THESE FISH COULD BRING DOWN AN IRON BRIDGE?!

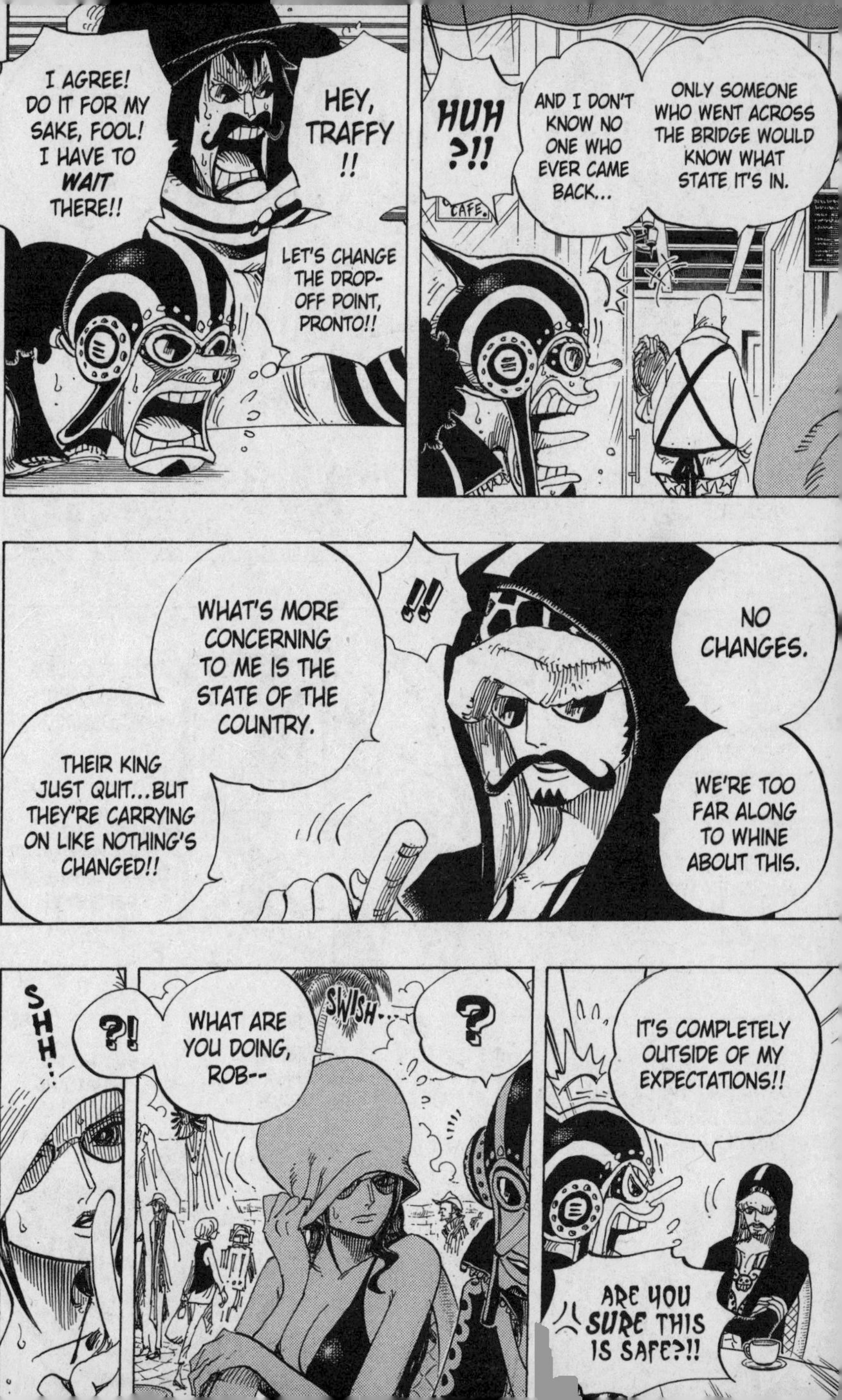
ONLY SOMEONE WHO WENT ACROSS THE BRIDGE WOULD KNOW WHAT STATE IT'S IN.
AND I DON'T KNOW NO ONE WHO EVER CAME BACK...
HUH ?!!
CAFE
HEY, TRAFFY !!
I AGREE! DO IT FOR MY SAKE, FOOL! I HAVE TO WAIT THERE!!
LET'S CHANGE THE DROP-OFF POINT, PRONTO!!
NO CHANGES.
WE'RE TOO FAR ALONG TO WHINE ABOUT THIS.
!!
WHAT'S MORE CONCERNING TO ME IS THE STATE OF THE COUNTRY.
THEIR KING JUST QUIT...BUT THEY'RE CARRYING ON LIKE NOTHING'S CHANGED!!
IT'S COMPLETELY OUTSIDE OF MY EXPECTATIONS!!
ARE YOU SURE THIS IS SAFE?!!
?
SWISH...
WHAT ARE YOU DOING, ROB--
?!
SHH...

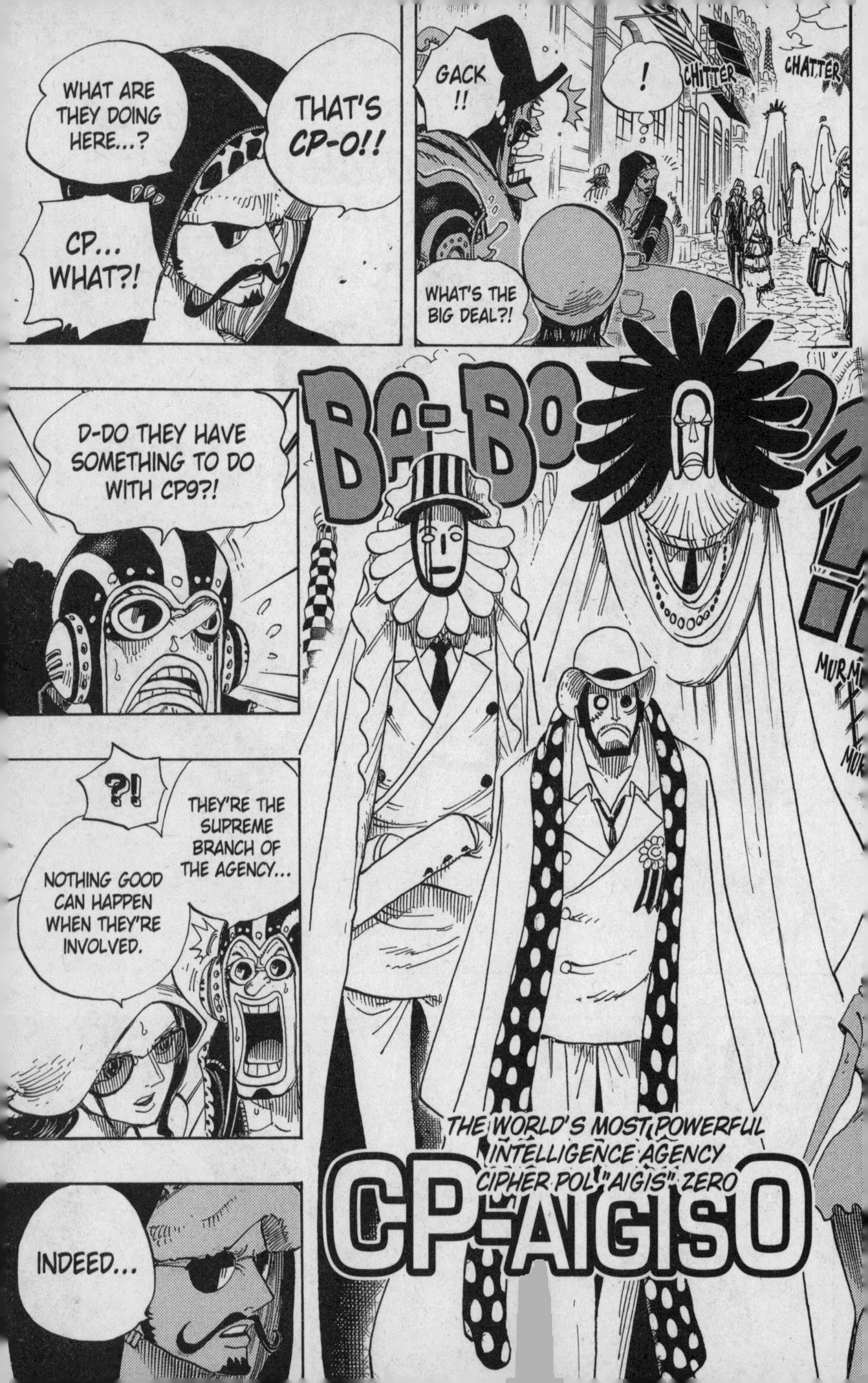
GACK !!
!
CHITTER
CHATTER
WHAT'S THE BIG DEAL?!
THAT'S CP-0!!
WHAT ARE THEY DOING HERE...?
CP... WHAT?!
BA-BO
THE WORLD'S MOST POWERFUL INTELLIGENCE AGENCY CIPHER POL "AIGIS" ZERO
CP-AIGIS0
D-DO THEY HAVE SOMETHING TO DO WITH CP9?!
?!
THEY'RE THE SUPREME BRANCH OF THE AGENCY...
NOTHING GOOD CAN HAPPEN WHEN THEY'RE INVOLVED.
INDEED...

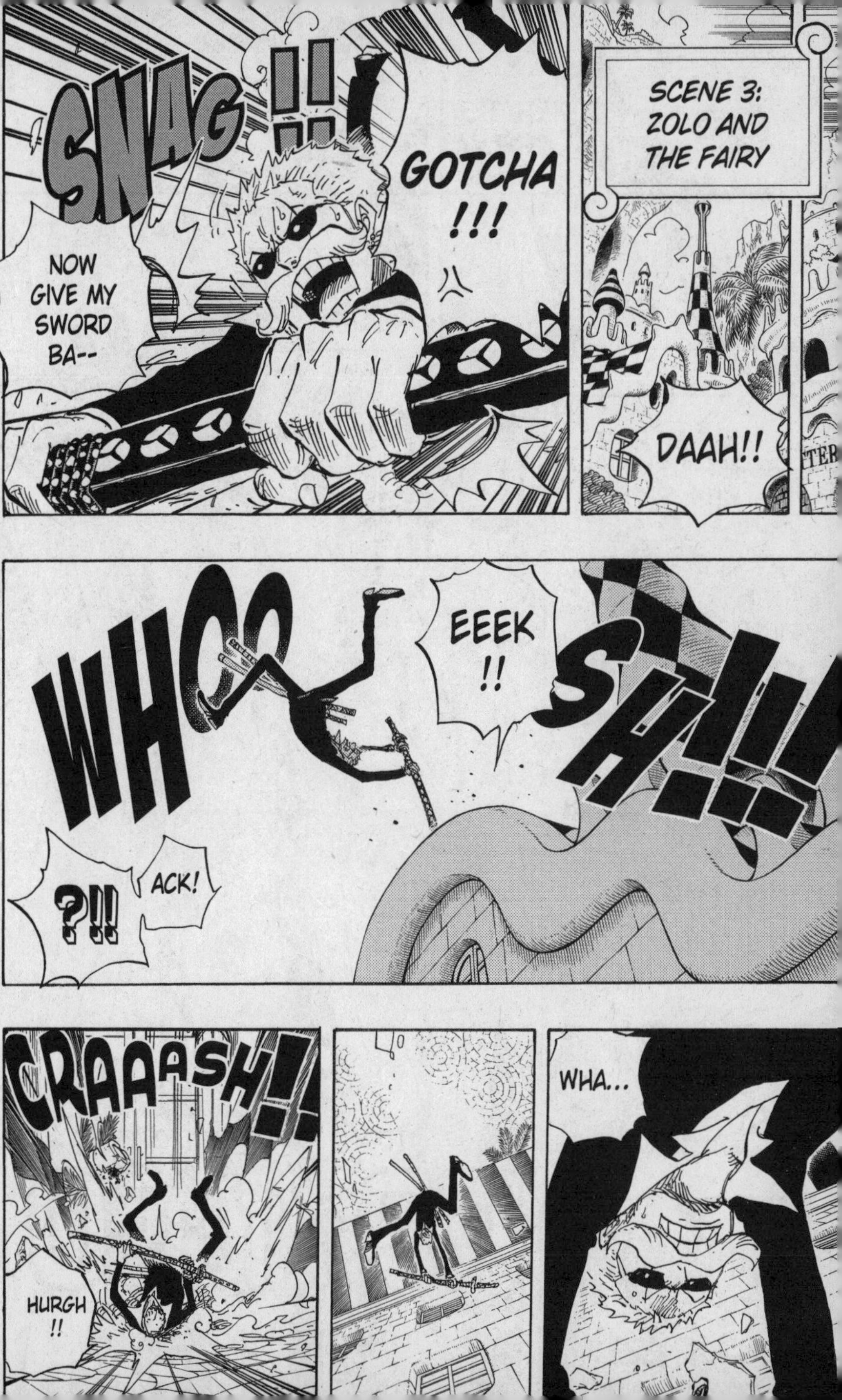
SCENE 3: ZOLO AND THE FAIRY
DAAH!!
GOTCHA!!!
SNAG!!
NOW GIVE MY SWORD BA--
SH!!!
EEEK!!
WHOO
ACK!
?!!
WHA...
CRAAASH!!
HURGH!!

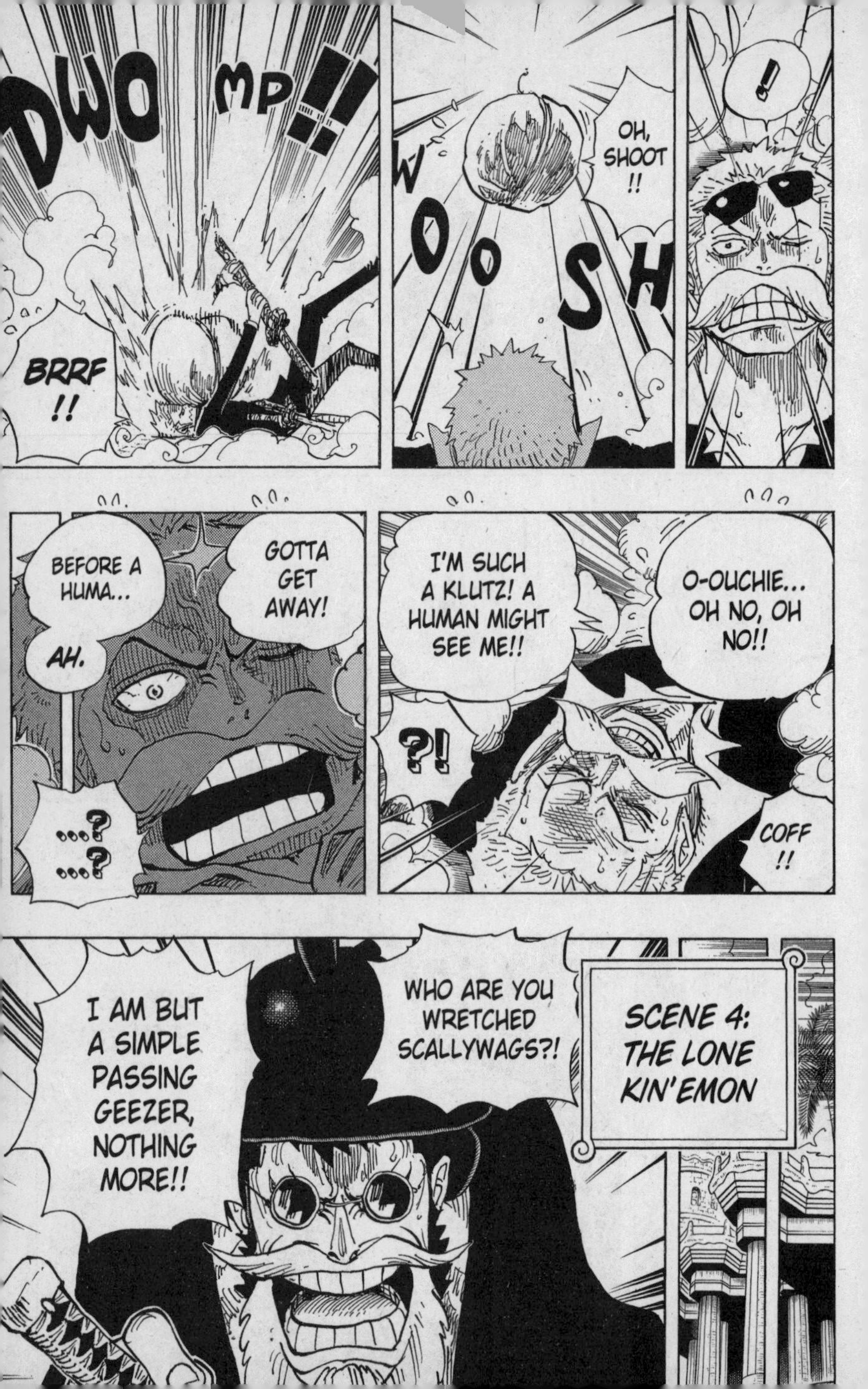
!
OH, SHOOT !!
WOOSH
DWOMP!!
BRRF !!
O-OUCHIE... OH NO, OH NO!!
I'M SUCH A KLUTZ! A HUMAN MIGHT SEE ME!!
?!
COFF !!
GOTTA GET AWAY!
BEFORE A HUMA...
AH.
...? ...?
SCENE 4: THE LONE KIN'EMON
WHO ARE YOU WRETCHED SCALLYWAGS?!
I AM BUT A SIMPLE PASSING GEEZER, NOTHING MORE!!

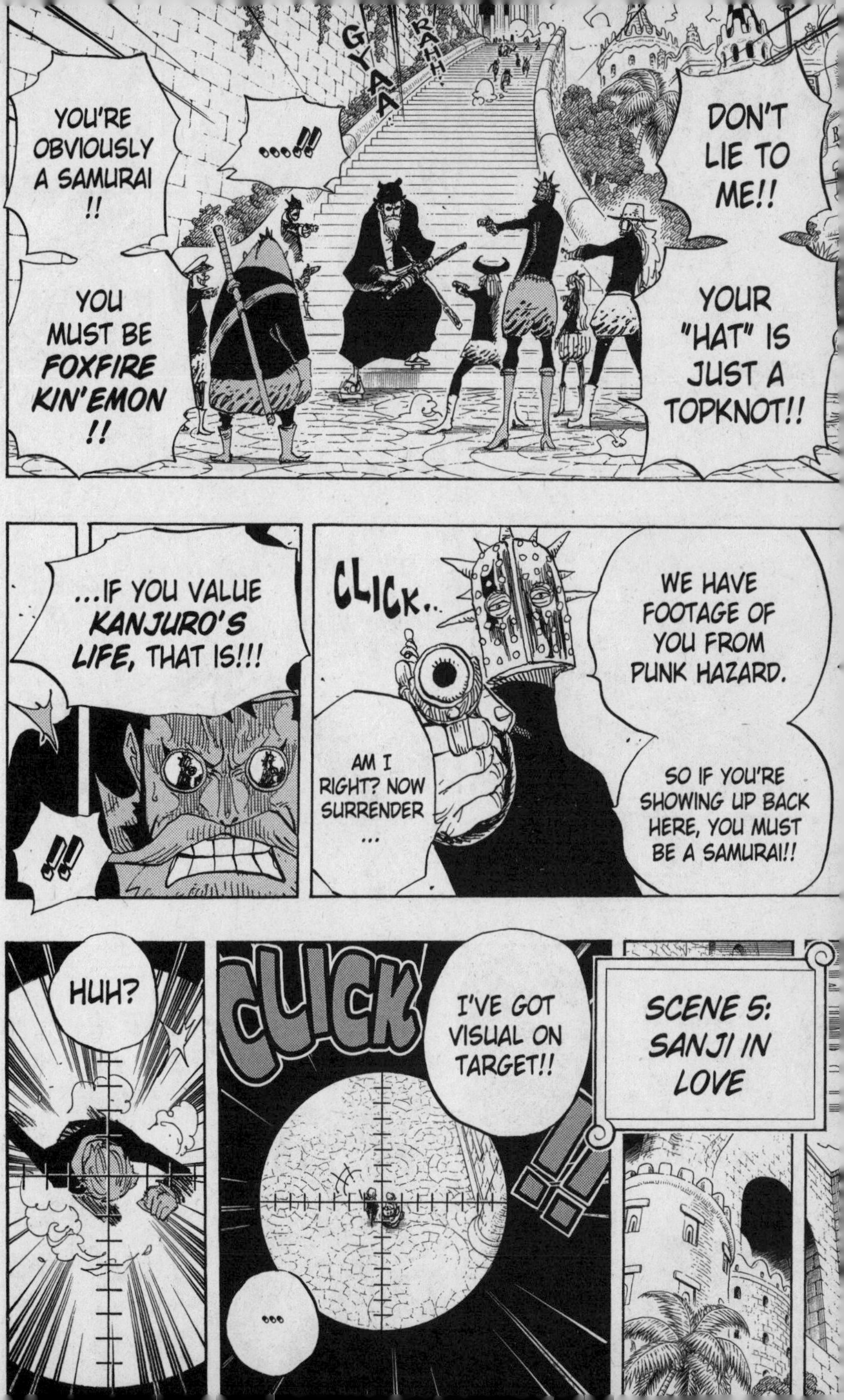
DON'T LIE TO ME!!
YOUR "HAT" IS JUST A TOPKNOT!!
RAHH!
GYAAA
....!!
YOU'RE OBVIOUSLY A SAMURAI!!
YOU MUST BE FOXFIRE KIN'EMON!!
CLICK..
WE HAVE FOOTAGE OF YOU FROM PUNK HAZARD.
SO IF YOU'RE SHOWING UP BACK HERE, YOU MUST BE A SAMURAI!!
AM I RIGHT? NOW SURRENDER ...
...IF YOU VALUE KANJURO'S LIFE, THAT IS!!!
!!
SCENE 5: SANJI IN LOVE
CLICK
I'VE GOT VISUAL ON TARGET!!
...
HUH?

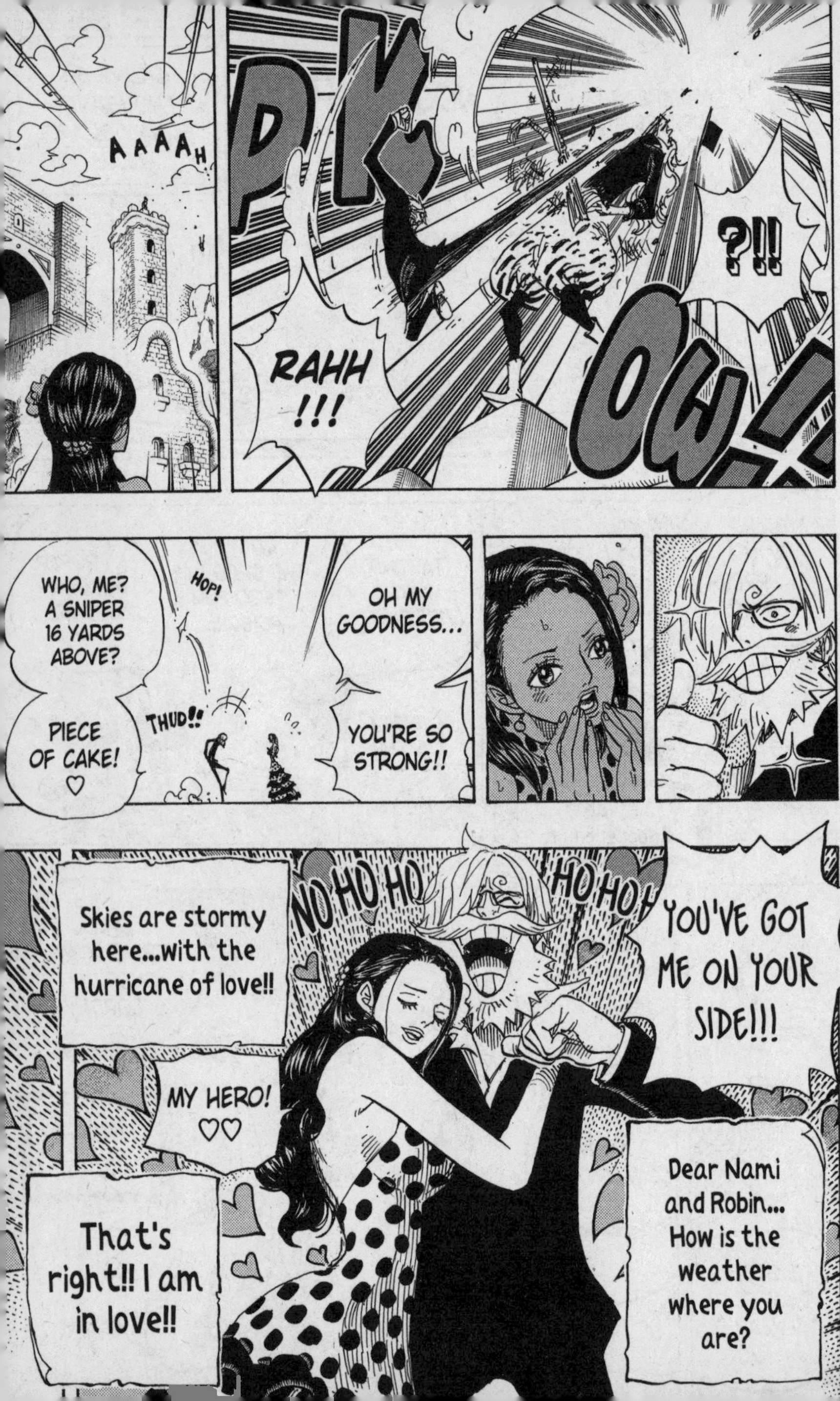
?!!
PK
OW..!
RAHH !!!
AAAAH
OH MY GOODNESS...
YOU'RE SO STRONG!!
HOP!
THUD!!
WHO, ME? A SNIPER 16 YARDS ABOVE?
PIECE OF CAKE! ♡
YOU'VE GOT ME ON YOUR SIDE!!!
NO HO HO HO HO HO
Skies are stormy here...with the hurricane of love!!
Dear Nami and Robin... How is the weather where you are?
MY HERO! ♡♡
That's right!! I am in love!!

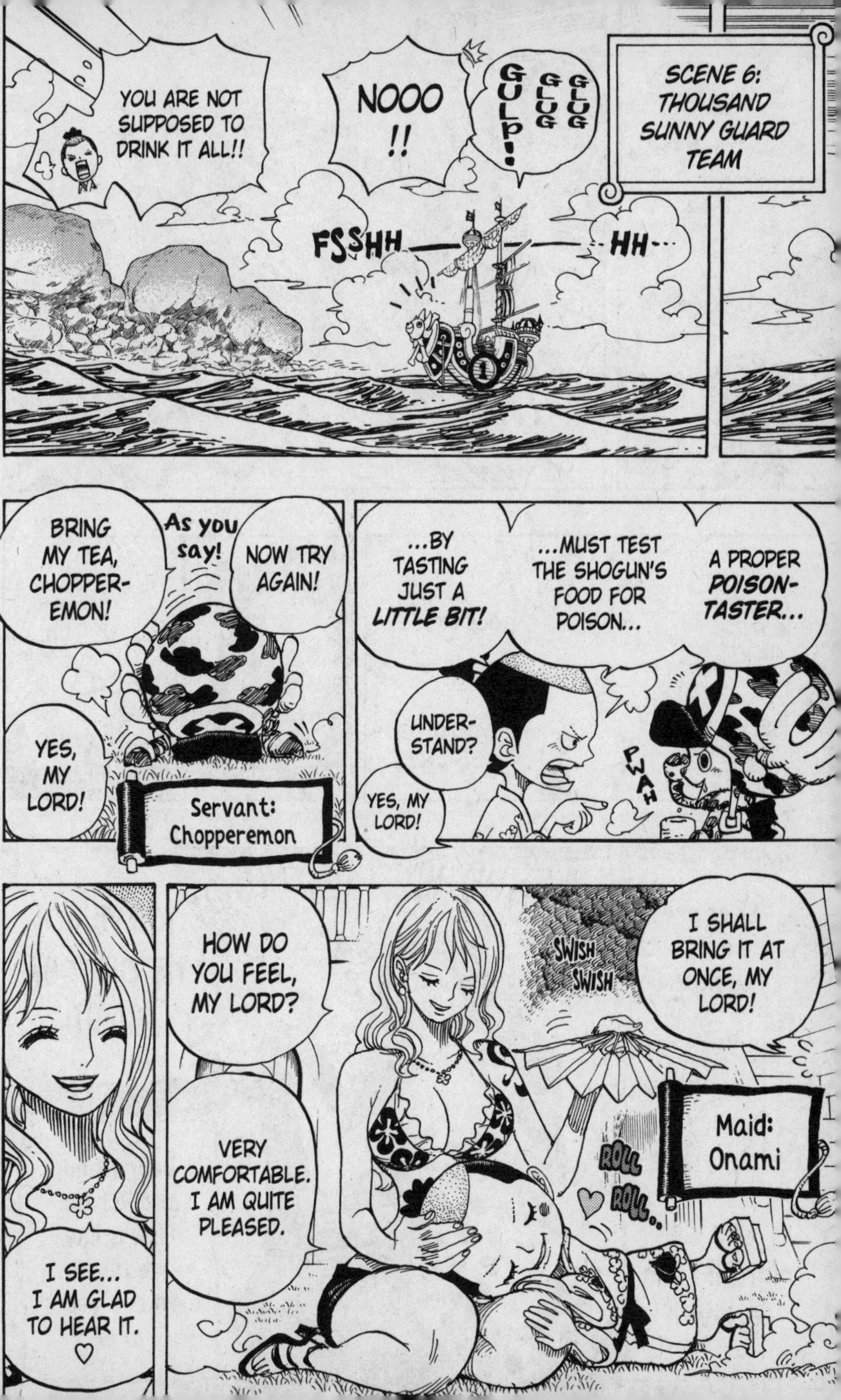
SCENE 6: THOUSAND SUNNY GUARD TEAM
GULP!
GLUG GLUG
NOOO!!
YOU ARE NOT SUPPOSED TO DRINK IT ALL!!
FSSHH---HH...
A PROPER POISON-TASTER...
...MUST TEST THE SHOGUN'S FOOD FOR POISON...
...BY TASTING JUST A LITTLE BIT!
PWAH
UNDER-STAND?
YES, MY LORD!
NOW TRY AGAIN!
As you say!
BRING MY TEA, CHOPPER-EMON!
YES, MY LORD!
Servant: Chopperemon
I SHALL BRING IT AT ONCE, MY LORD!
SWISH SWISH
HOW DO YOU FEEL, MY LORD?
Maid: Onami
ROLL ROLL..
VERY COMFORTABLE. I AM QUITE PLEASED.
I SEE... I AM GLAD TO HEAR IT. ♡

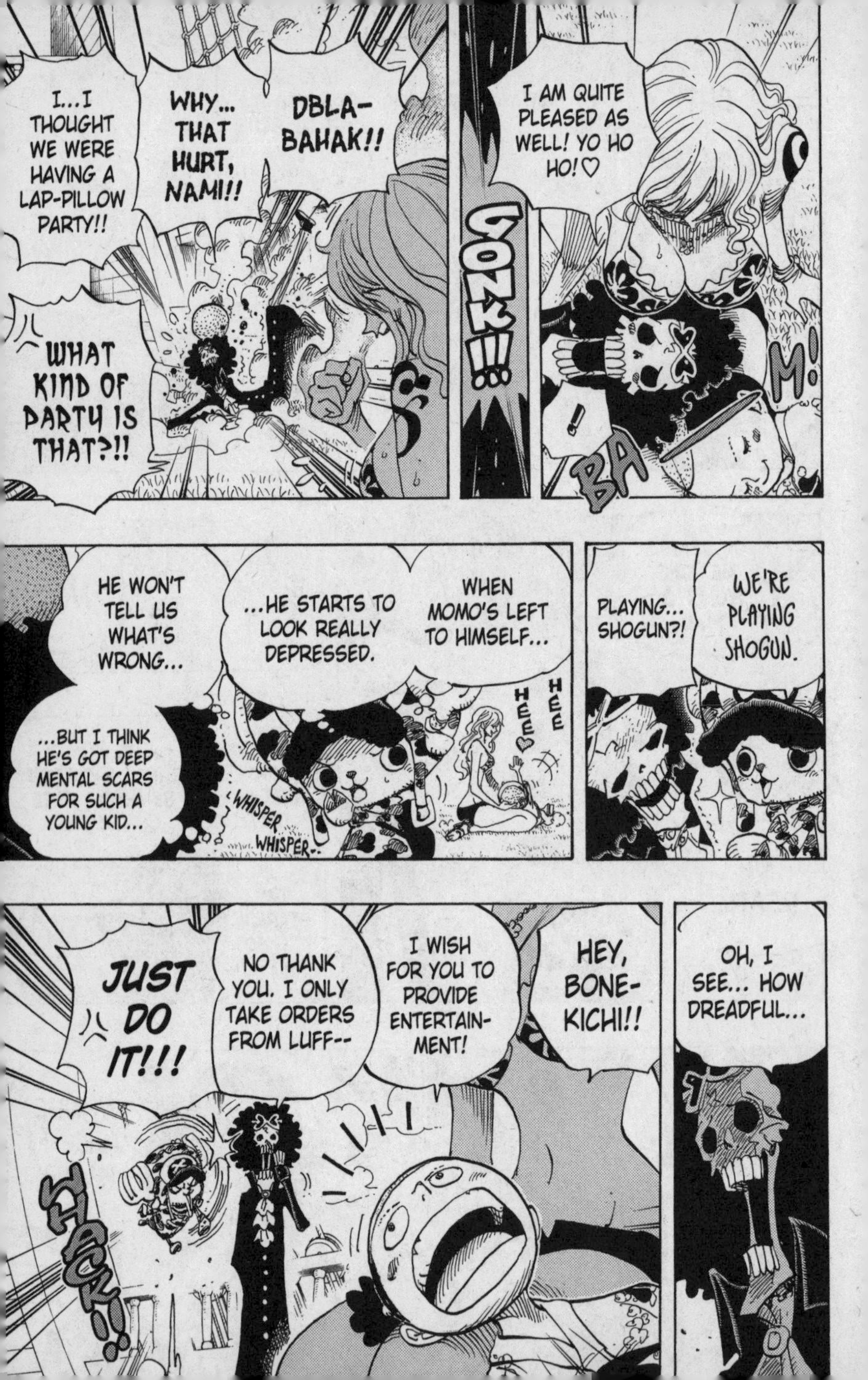
I AM QUITE PLEASED AS WELL! YO HO HO!♡
BAM!
GONK!!!
DBLA-BAHAK!!
WHY... THAT HURT, NAMI!!
I...I THOUGHT WE WERE HAVING A LAP-PILLOW PARTY!!
WHAT KIND OF PARTY IS THAT?!!
WE'RE PLAYING SHOGUN.
PLAYING... SHOGUN?!
WHEN MOMO'S LEFT TO HIMSELF...
...HE STARTS TO LOOK REALLY DEPRESSED.
HE WON'T TELL US WHAT'S WRONG...
HEE HEE
...BUT I THINK HE'S GOT DEEP MENTAL SCARS FOR SUCH A YOUNG KID...
WHISPER WHISPER
OH, I SEE... HOW DREADFUL...
HEY, BONE-KICHI!!
I WISH FOR YOU TO PROVIDE ENTERTAIN-MENT!
NO THANK YOU. I ONLY TAKE ORDERS FROM LUFF--
JUST DO IT!!!
WHACK!!

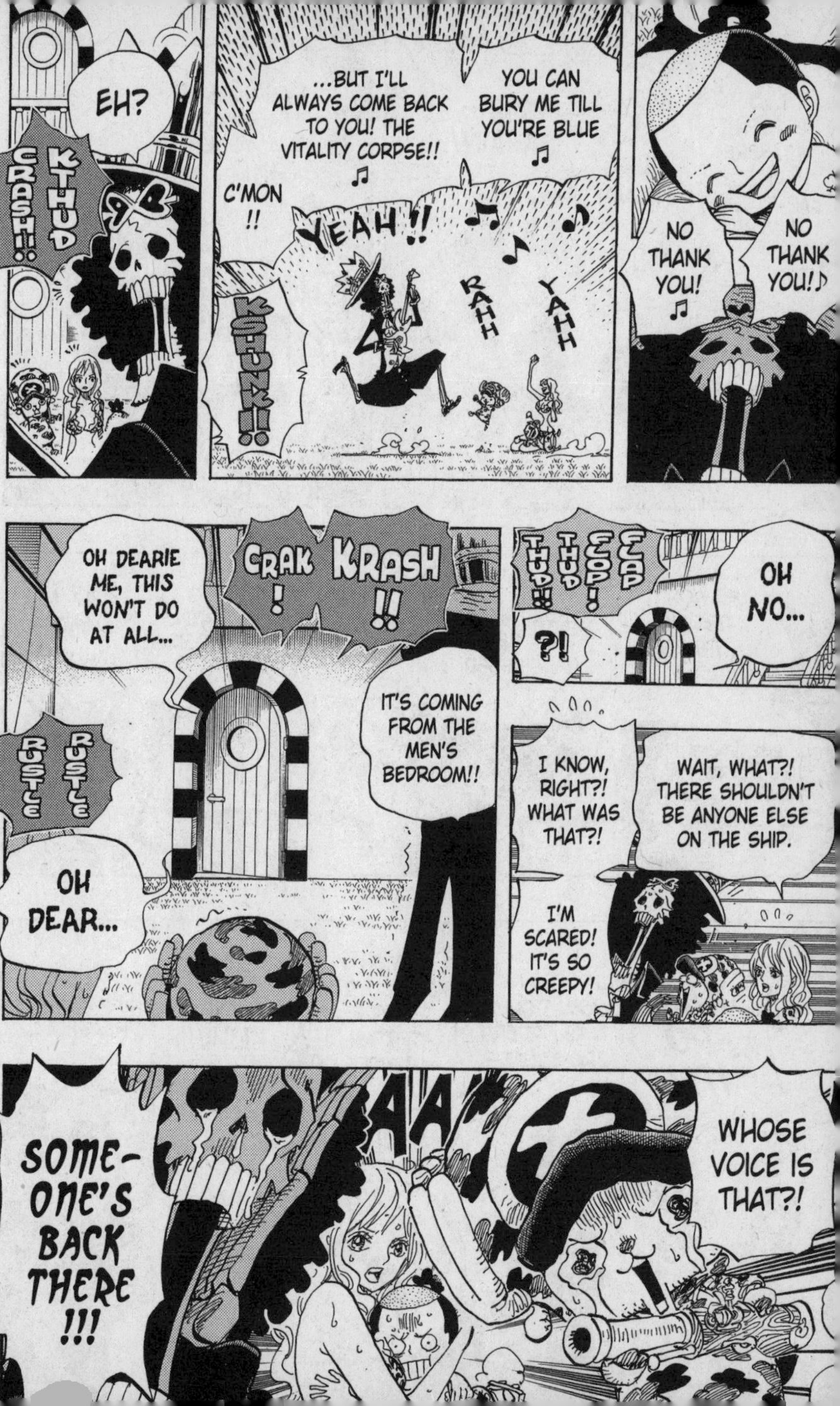
NO THANK YOU!♪
NO THANK YOU! ♫
YOU CAN BURY ME TILL YOU'RE BLUE ♫
...BUT I'LL ALWAYS COME BACK TO YOU! THE VITALITY CORPSE!! ♫
C'MON !!
YEAH!!
RAHH
YAHH
KSHUNK!!
EH?
KTHUD
CRASH!!
OH NO...
CLAP
CLOP!
THUD
THUD!!
?!
WAIT, WHAT?! THERE SHOULDN'T BE ANYONE ELSE ON THE SHIP.
I KNOW, RIGHT?! WHAT WAS THAT?!
I'M SCARED! IT'S SO CREEPY!
KRASH!!
CRAK!
OH DEARIE ME, THIS WON'T DO AT ALL...
IT'S COMING FROM THE MEN'S BEDROOM!!
RUSTLE
RUSTLE
OH DEAR...
WHOSE VOICE IS THAT?!
AAA
SOME-ONE'S BACK THERE!!!

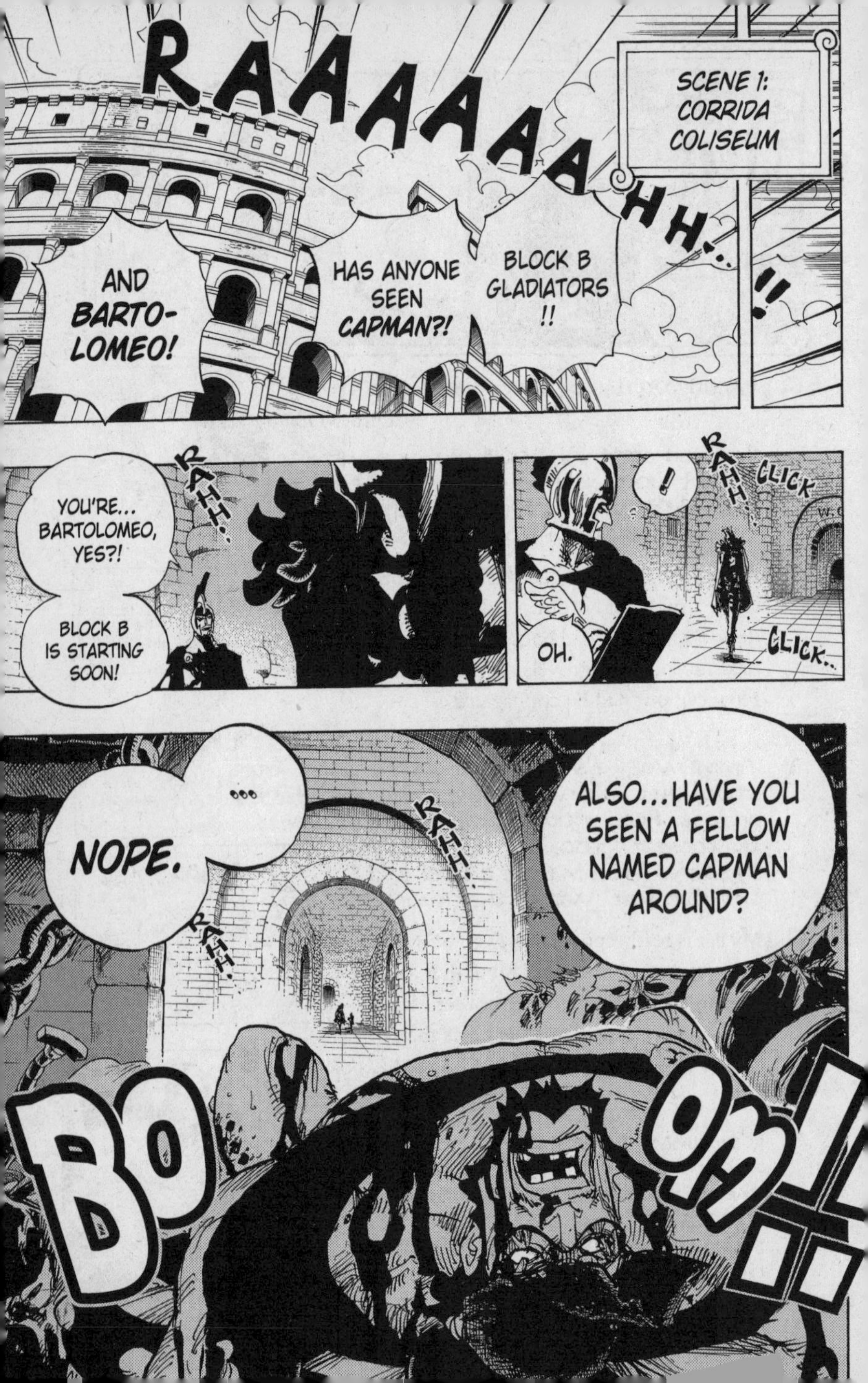
SCENE 1: CORRIDA COLISEUM
RAAAAAAAHH...!!
BLOCK B GLADIATORS !!
HAS ANYONE SEEN CAPMAN?!
AND BARTO-LOMEO!
!
RAHH
CLICK
OH.
CLICK..
RAHH..
YOU'RE... BARTOLOMEO, YES?!
BLOCK B IS STARTING SOON!
ALSO...HAVE YOU SEEN A FELLOW NAMED CAPMAN AROUND?
RAHH..
...
NOPE.
RAHH..
BOOM!!..

質問コーナー
ウイーン
エス
ビー
エス
ガチャン…

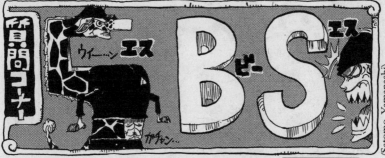

(Satomo, Yamanashi)

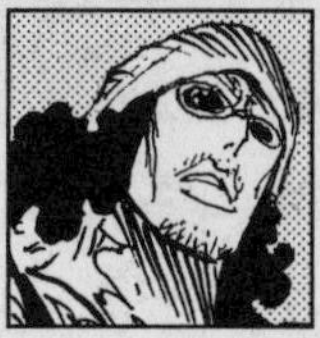

Q: Could you make shaved ice out of Aokiji?

--Dumb Dog

A: Yes, you certainly could. He's ice, after all. But would you really want to eat him? He'd turn back into Aokiji in your tummy, and BOOM! You're possessed.

SHUT UP! I'LL DECIDE WHEN I'VE HAD ENOUGH!
WHAT HARM CAN IT DO?

Q: Our dad loves Whitebeard. Every night, he comes home drunk, and Mom scolds him. He always says, "I'll decide when I've had enough, gurarara!" But then the next morning, he grovels on the ground before her. How can our dad be cool again?

--Piro&Akke

A: Hmm. Well, he's cool partway through your story, but he's not in the morning. Here's an idea. How about if your mom becomes Whitebeard too, and forgives him by saying, "You may be a fool, but I still love you." Would that work?

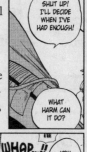

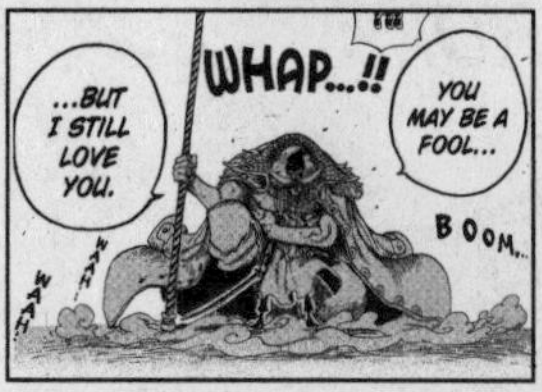

WHAP...!!
YOU MAY BE A FOOL...
...BUT I STILL LOVE YOU.
BOOM..

Q: My cat is really cute; he loves to hop up on your lap out of nowhere. My father (59) likes to lay his head on my mother's lap to get his ears cleaned, but she hates that. What is it about men and lap-pillows?

--Neko Robin

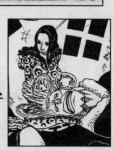

A: It's bumming me out to see so many pathetic dad letters. My theory is that the lap-pillow is a kind of dream, a source of passion. It's like when a climber sees a new mountain to climb. In fact, that's not a theory, it's real!!

Chapter 706:
I AIN'T GONNA LAUGH AT YA

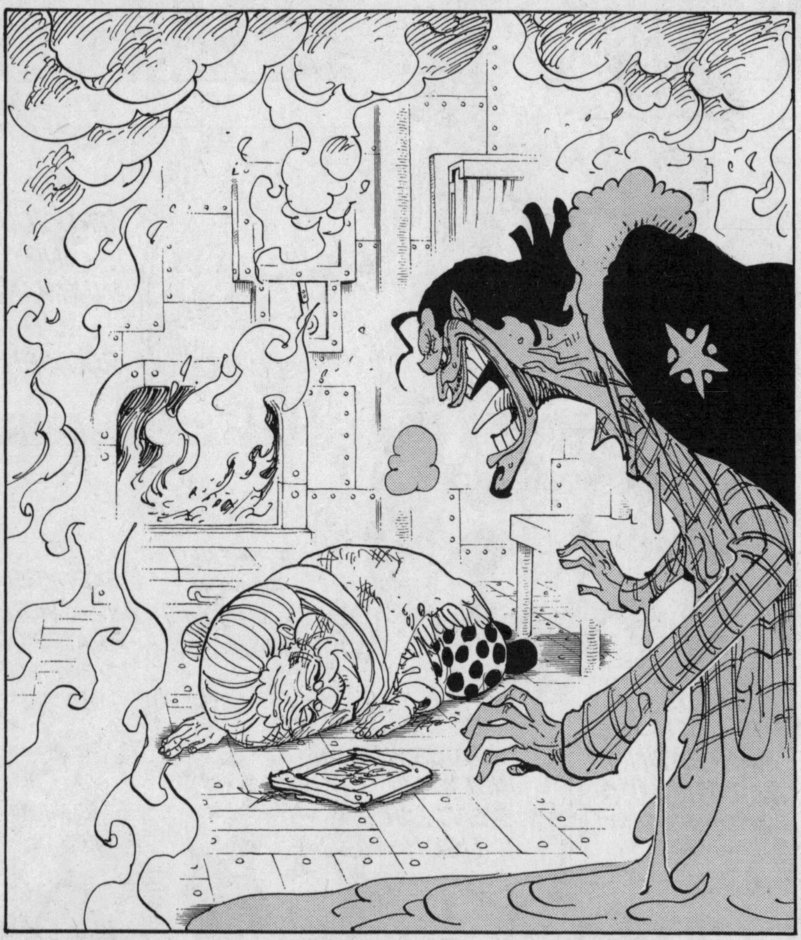

CARIBOU'S NEW WORLD KEE HEE HEE, VOL. 26
"THE OLD HAG LEFT BEHIND WITH A PHOTOGRAPH"

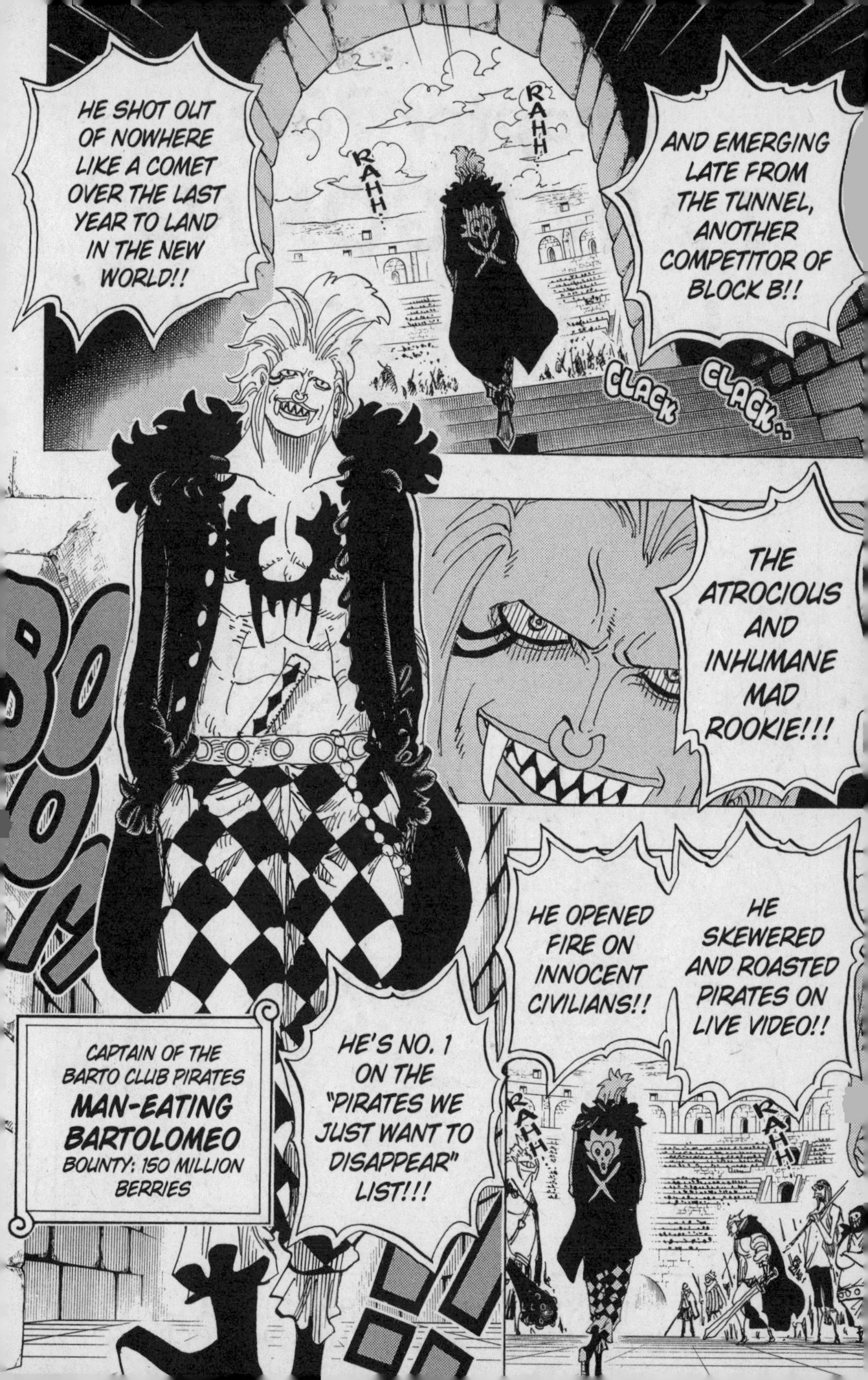

RAHH...
AND EMERGING LATE FROM THE TUNNEL, ANOTHER COMPETITOR OF BLOCK B!!
CLACK CLACK...
RAHH...
HE SHOT OUT OF NOWHERE LIKE A COMET OVER THE LAST YEAR TO LAND IN THE NEW WORLD!!
THE ATROCIOUS AND INHUMANE MAD ROOKIE!!!
HE SKEWERED AND ROASTED PIRATES ON LIVE VIDEO!!
HE OPENED FIRE ON INNOCENT CIVILIANS!!
RAHH...
RAHH...
HE'S NO. 1 ON THE "PIRATES WE JUST WANT TO DISAPPEAR" LIST!!!
CAPTAIN OF THE BARTO CLUB PIRATES
MAN-EATING BARTOLOMEO
BOUNTY: 150 MILLION BERRIES

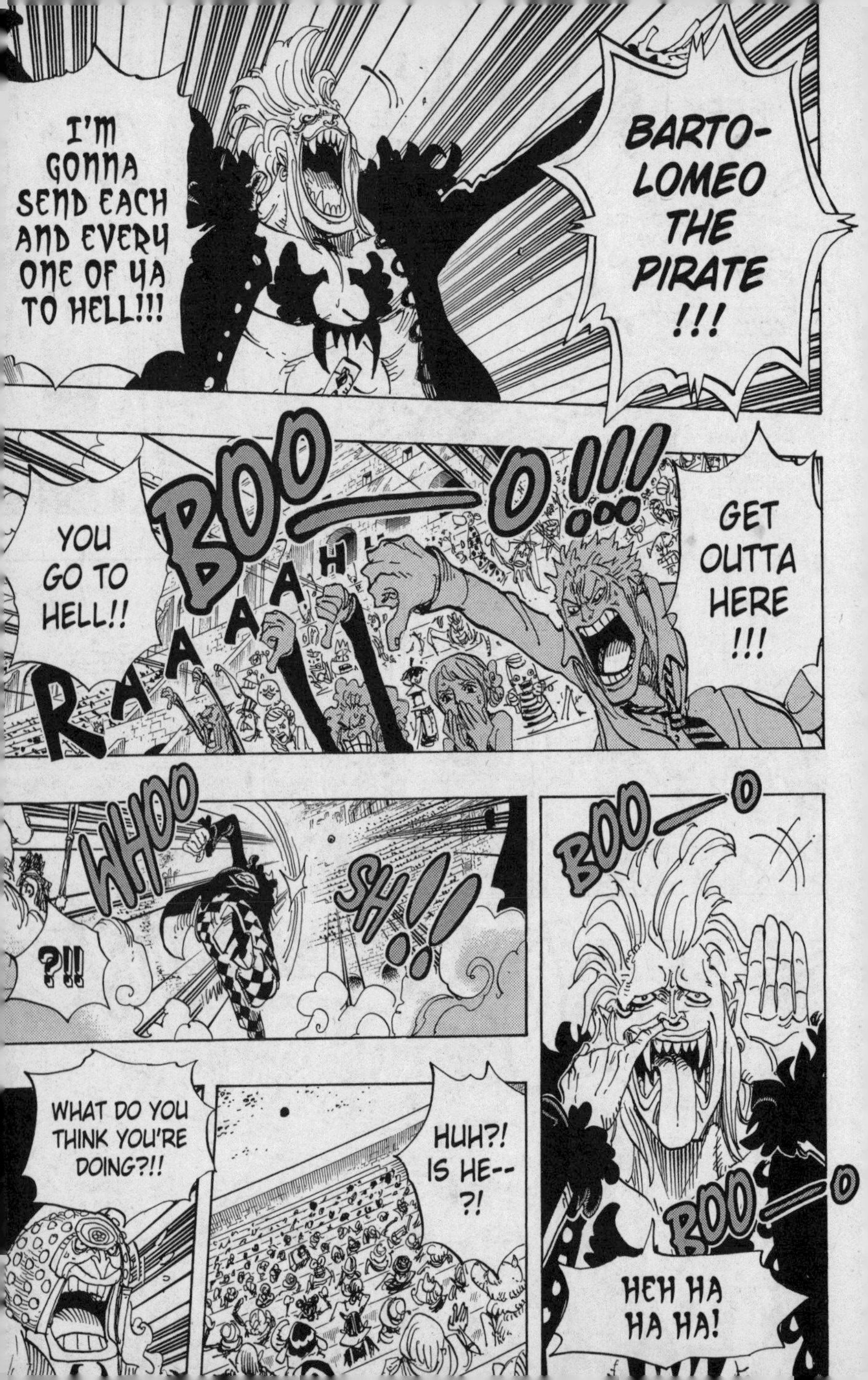
BARTO-LOMEO THE PIRATE!!!
I'M GONNA SEND EACH AND EVERY ONE OF YA TO HELL!!!
GET OUTTA HERE!!!
BOO—O!!!
RAAAAH!
YOU GO TO HELL!!
BOO—O
BOO—O
HEH HA HA HA!
WHOOSH!!
?!!
HUH?! IS HE--?!
WHAT DO YOU THINK YOU'RE DOING?!!

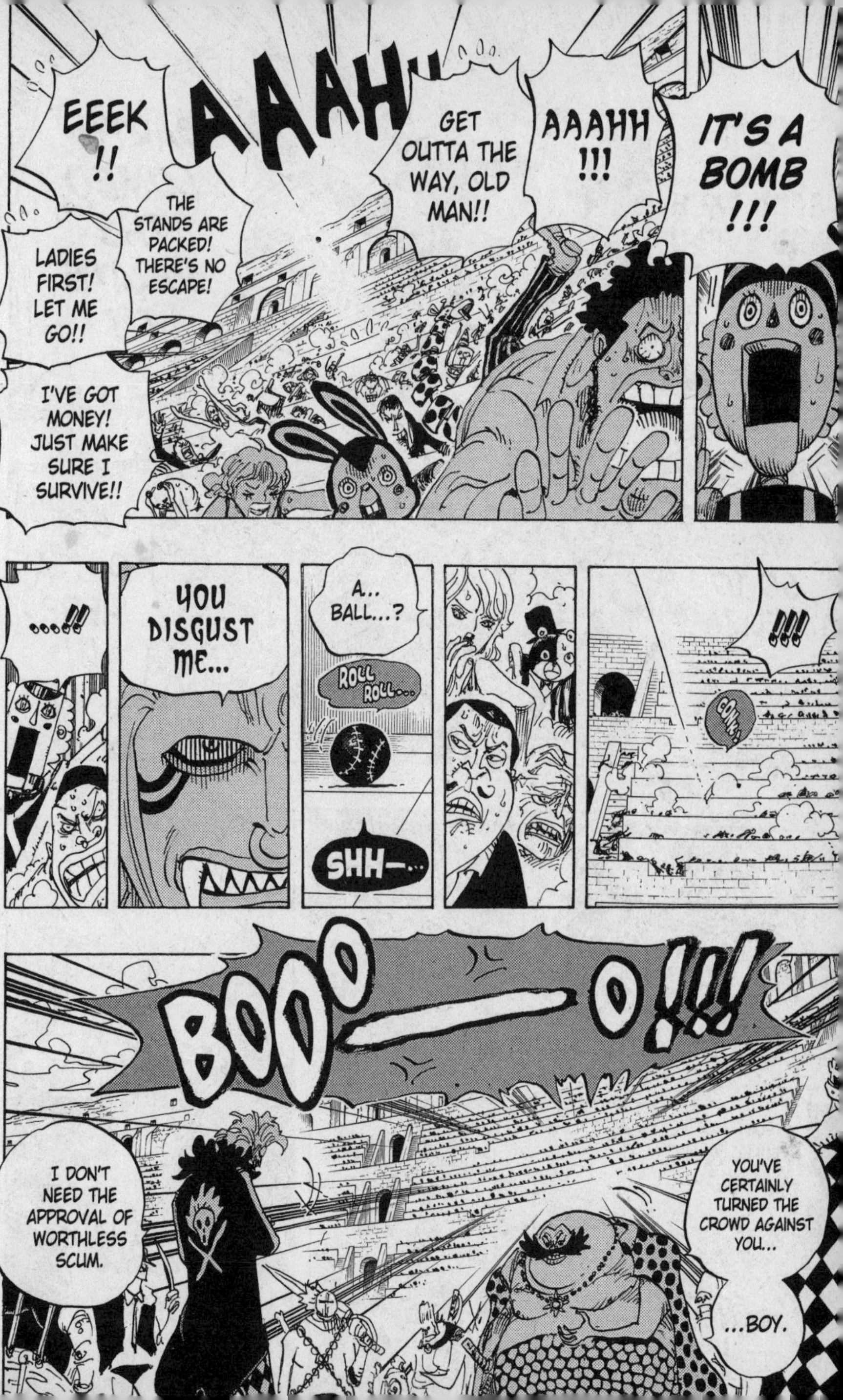
IT'S A BOMB!!!
AAAHH!!!
GET OUTTA THE WAY, OLD MAN!!
AAAH
EEEK!!
THE STANDS ARE PACKED! THERE'S NO ESCAPE!
LADIES FIRST! LET ME GO!!
I'VE GOT MONEY! JUST MAKE SURE I SURVIVE!!
!!!
CONK
A... BALL...?
ROLL ROLL...
SHH—...
YOU DISGUST ME...
...!!
BOOO——O!!!
YOU'VE CERTAINLY TURNED THE CROWD AGAINST YOU...
...BOY.
I DON'T NEED THE APPROVAL OF WORTHLESS SCUM.

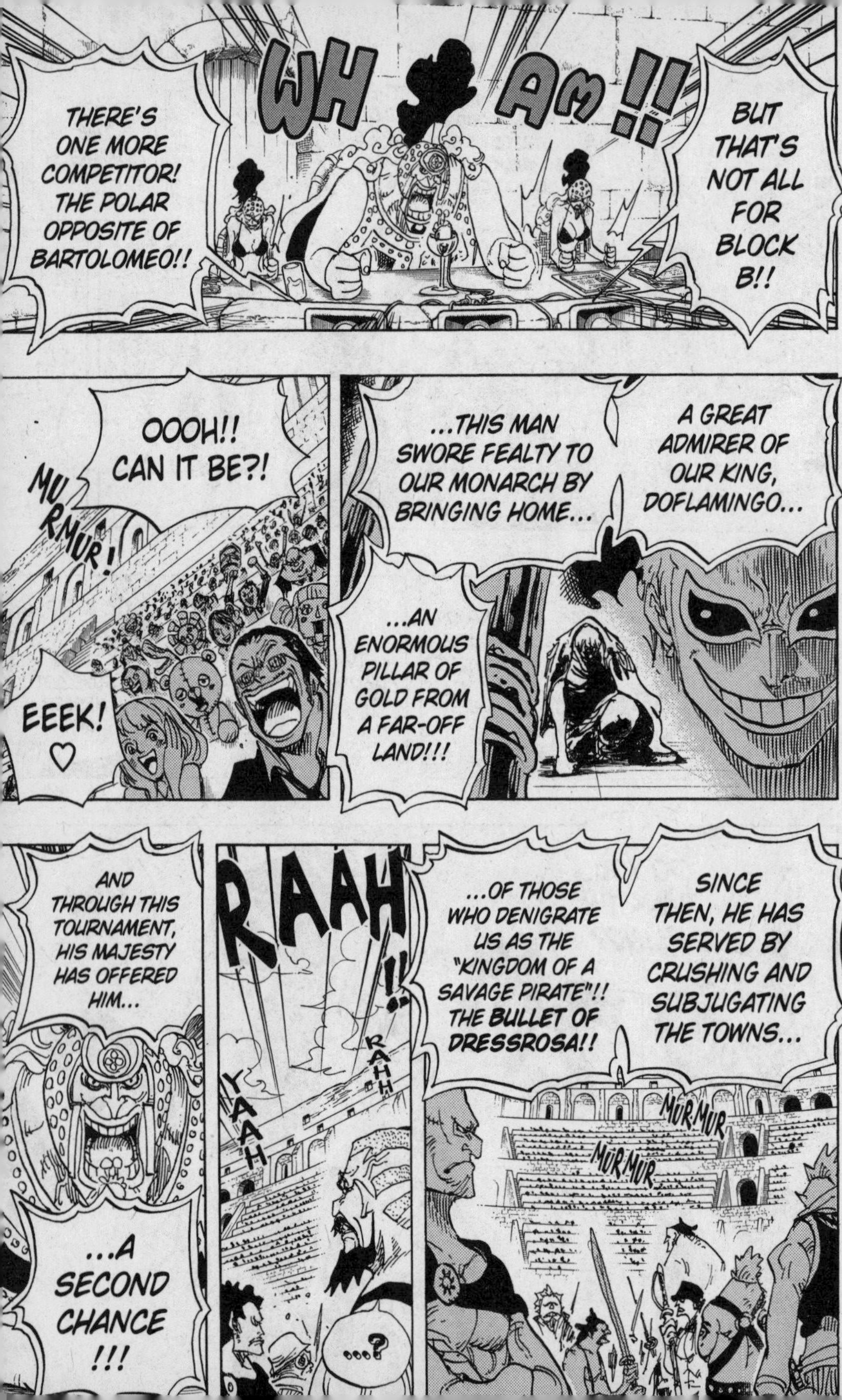
WHAM!!
BUT THAT'S NOT ALL FOR BLOCK B!!
THERE'S ONE MORE COMPETITOR! THE POLAR OPPOSITE OF BARTOLOMEO!!
A GREAT ADMIRER OF OUR KING, DOFLAMINGO...
...THIS MAN SWORE FEALTY TO OUR MONARCH BY BRINGING HOME...
...AN ENORMOUS PILLAR OF GOLD FROM A FAR-OFF LAND!!!
OOOH!! CAN IT BE?!
MURMUR!
EEEK! ♡
SINCE THEN, HE HAS SERVED BY CRUSHING AND SUBJUGATING THE TOWNS...
...OF THOSE WHO DENIGRATE US AS THE "KINGDOM OF A SAVAGE PIRATE"!! THE BULLET OF DRESSROSA!!
MURMUR
MURMUR
RAAAH!!
RAHH
YAAAH
...?
AND THROUGH THIS TOURNAMENT, HIS MAJESTY HAS OFFERED HIM...
...A SECOND CHANCE!!!

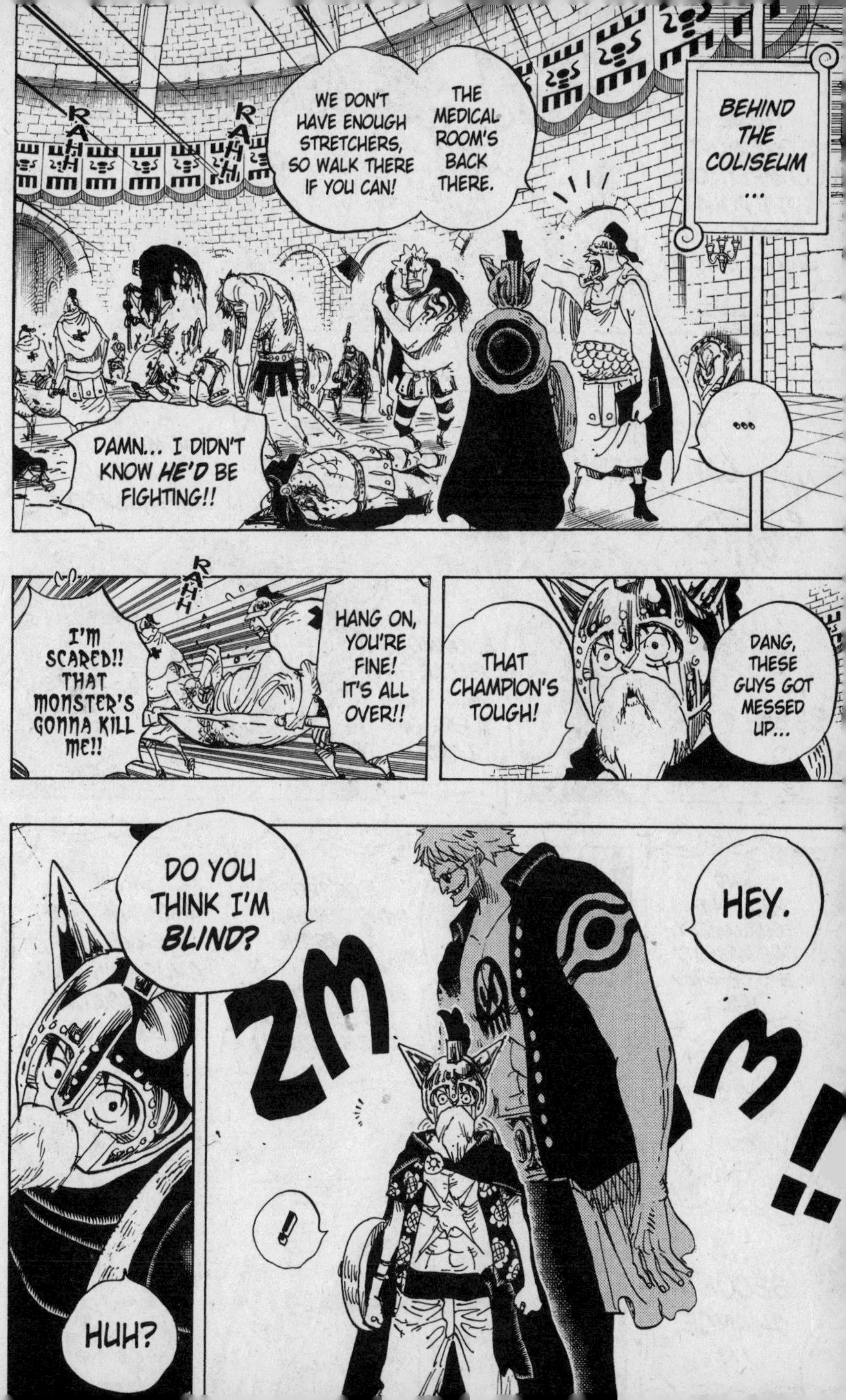
BEHIND THE COLISEUM ...
THE MEDICAL ROOM'S BACK THERE.
WE DON'T HAVE ENOUGH STRETCHERS, SO WALK THERE IF YOU CAN!
RAHH
RAHH
...
DAMN... I DIDN'T KNOW HE'D BE FIGHTING!!
DANG, THESE GUYS GOT MESSED UP...
THAT CHAMPION'S TOUGH!
RAHH
HANG ON, YOU'RE FINE! IT'S ALL OVER!!
I'M SCARED!! THAT MONSTER'S GONNA KILL ME!!
HEY.
ZMM!!
!
DO YOU THINK I'M BLIND?
HUH?

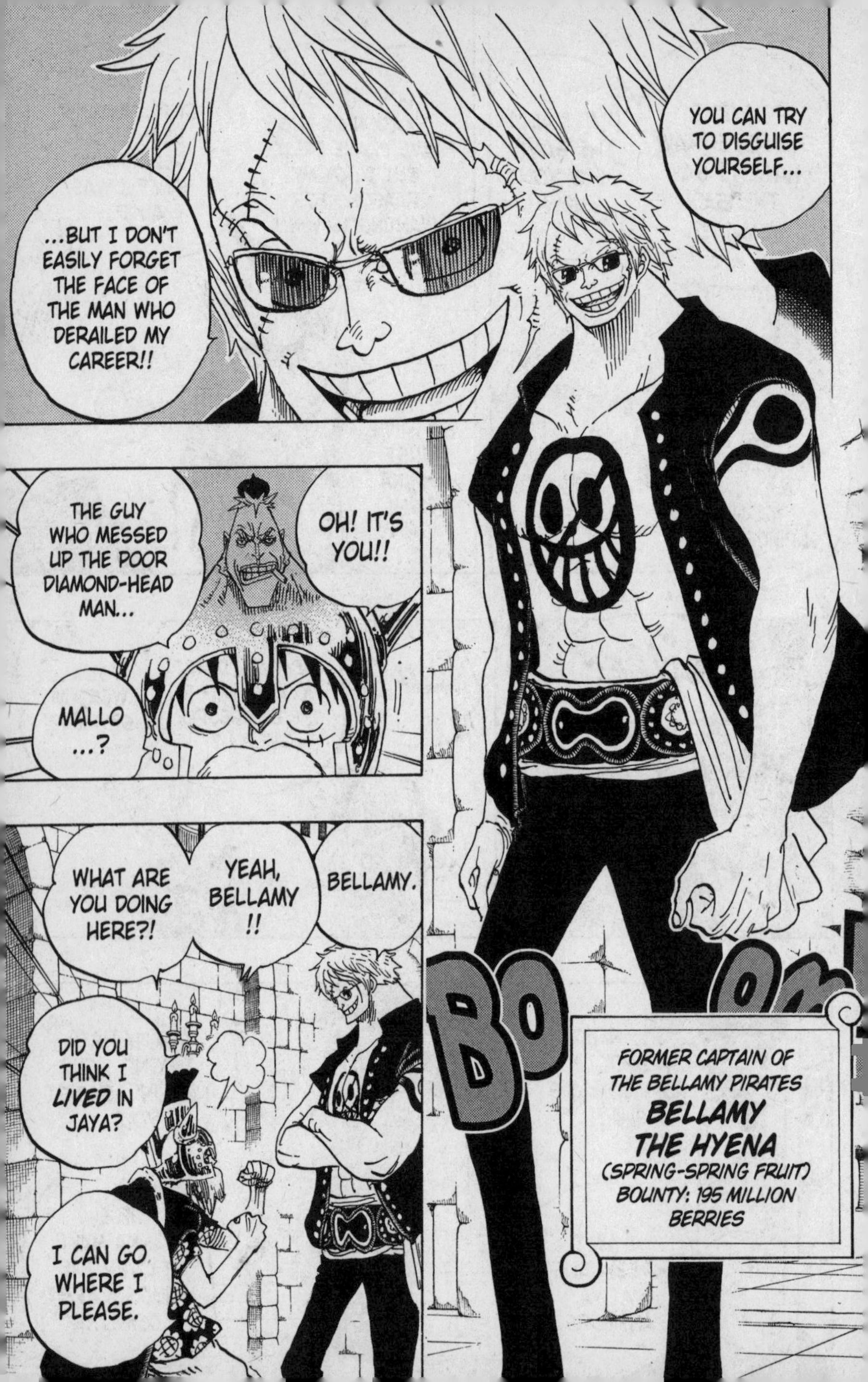
YOU CAN TRY TO DISGUISE YOURSELF...
...BUT I DON'T EASILY FORGET THE FACE OF THE MAN WHO DERAILED MY CAREER!!
BOOM
FORMER CAPTAIN OF THE BELLAMY PIRATES
BELLAMY THE HYENA
(SPRING-SPRING FRUIT)
BOUNTY: 195 MILLION BERRIES
OH! IT'S YOU!!
THE GUY WHO MESSED UP THE POOR DIAMOND-HEAD MAN...
MALLO ...?
BELLAMY.
YEAH, BELLAMY !!
WHAT ARE YOU DOING HERE?!
DID YOU THINK I *LIVED* IN JAYA?
I CAN GO WHERE I PLEASE.

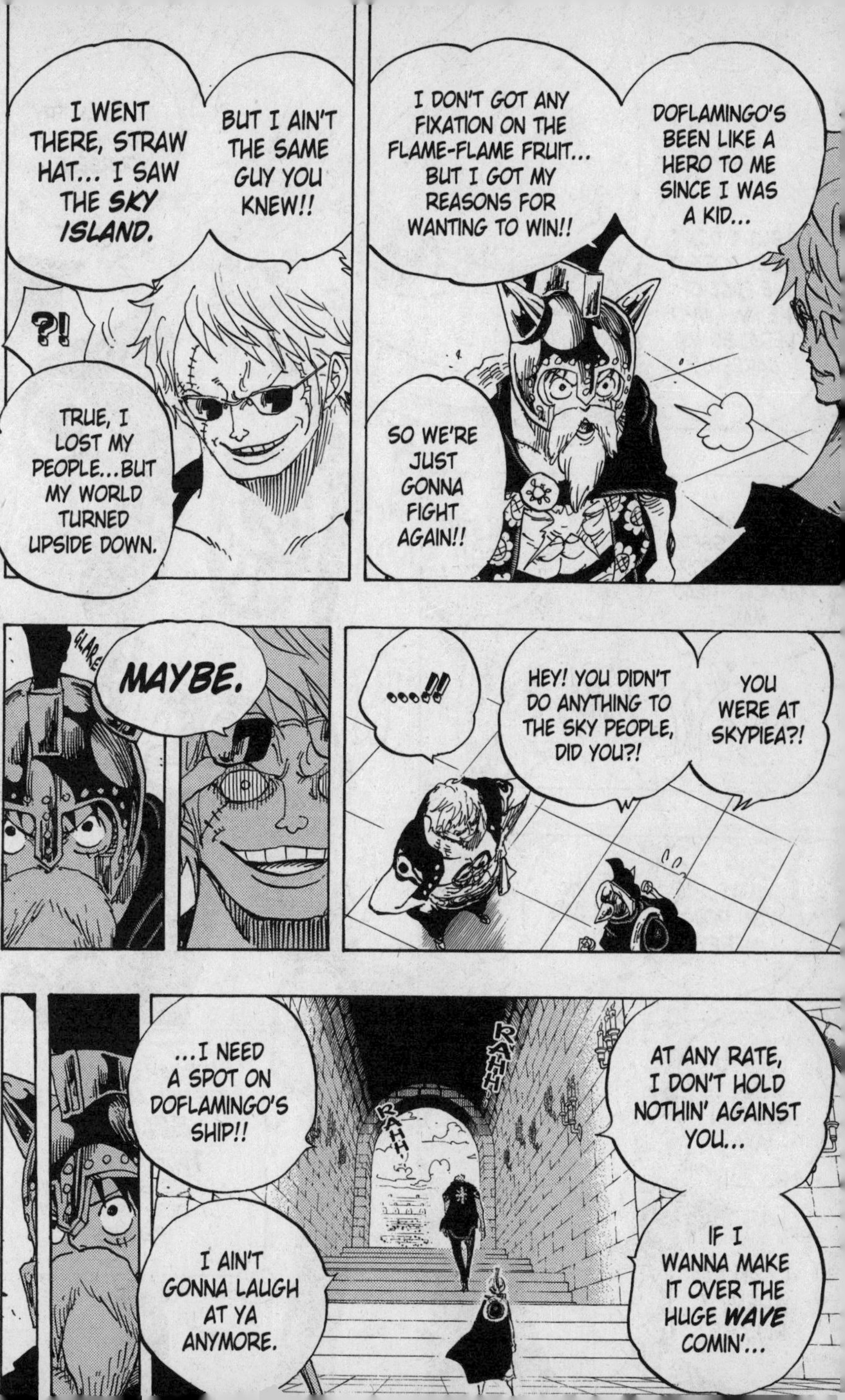
DOFLAMINGO'S BEEN LIKE A HERO TO ME SINCE I WAS A KID...
I DON'T GOT ANY FIXATION ON THE FLAME-FLAME FRUIT... BUT I GOT MY REASONS FOR WANTING TO WIN!!
SO WE'RE JUST GONNA FIGHT AGAIN!!
BUT I AIN'T THE SAME GUY YOU KNEW!!
I WENT THERE, STRAW HAT... I SAW THE SKY ISLAND.
?!
TRUE, I LOST MY PEOPLE...BUT MY WORLD TURNED UPSIDE DOWN.
YOU WERE AT SKYPIEA?!
HEY! YOU DIDN'T DO ANYTHING TO THE SKY PEOPLE, DID YOU?!
...!!
MAYBE.
GLARE
AT ANY RATE, I DON'T HOLD NOTHIN' AGAINST YOU...
IF I WANNA MAKE IT OVER THE HUGE WAVE COMIN'...
RAHH
RAHH
...I NEED A SPOT ON DOFLAMINGO'S SHIP!!
I AIN'T GONNA LAUGH AT YA ANYMORE.

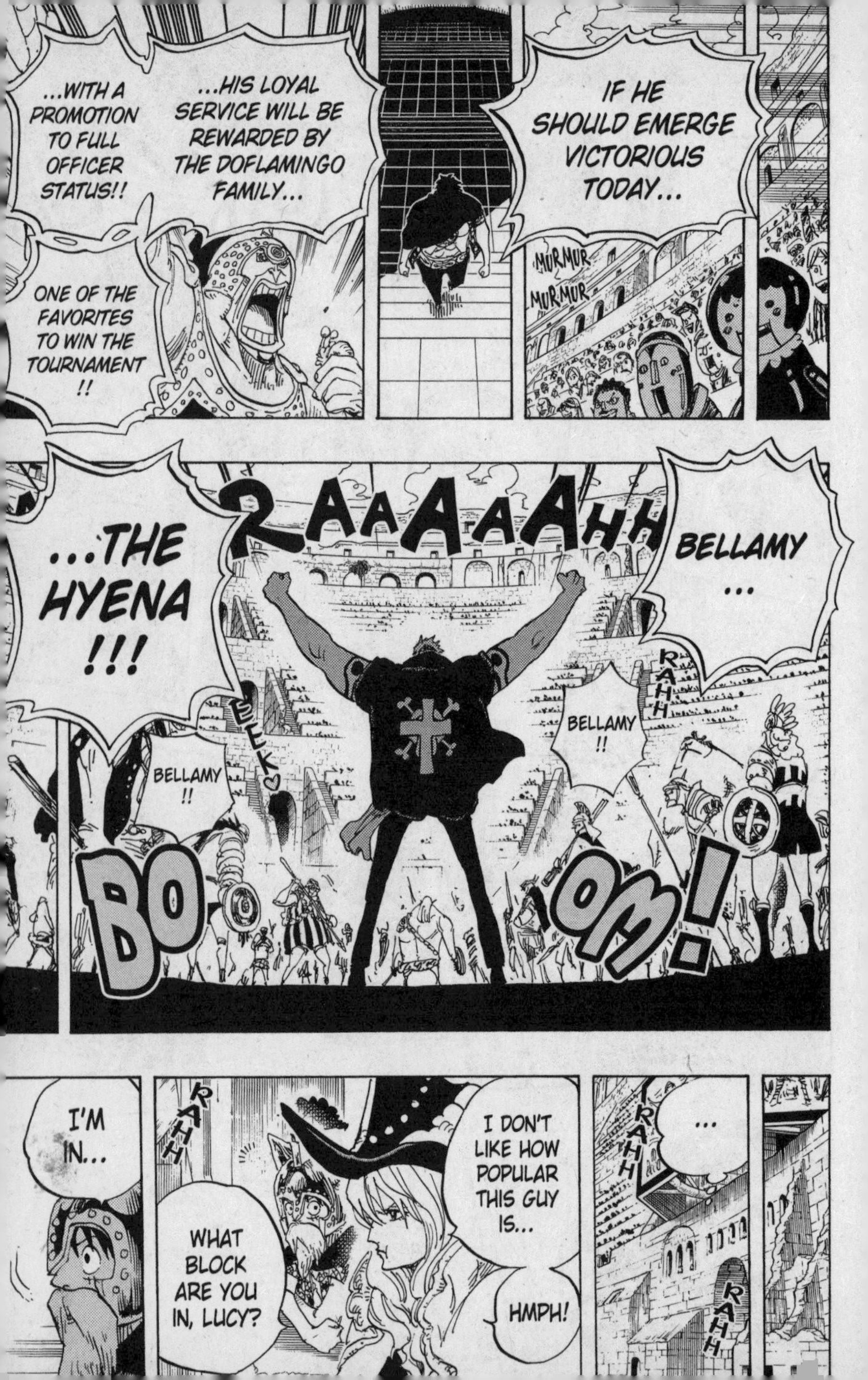
IF HE SHOULD EMERGE VICTORIOUS TODAY...
MURMUR
MURMUR
...HIS LOYAL SERVICE WILL BE REWARDED BY THE DOFLAMINGO FAMILY...
...WITH A PROMOTION TO FULL OFFICER STATUS!!
ONE OF THE FAVORITES TO WIN THE TOURNAMENT!!
BELLAMY...
RAAAAAAHH
...THE HYENA!!!
RAHH
BELLAMY!!
EEK
BELLAMY!!
BOOM!
...
RAHH
RAHH
I DON'T LIKE HOW POPULAR THIS GUY IS...
HMPH!
RAHH
WHAT BLOCK ARE YOU IN, LUCY?
I'M IN...

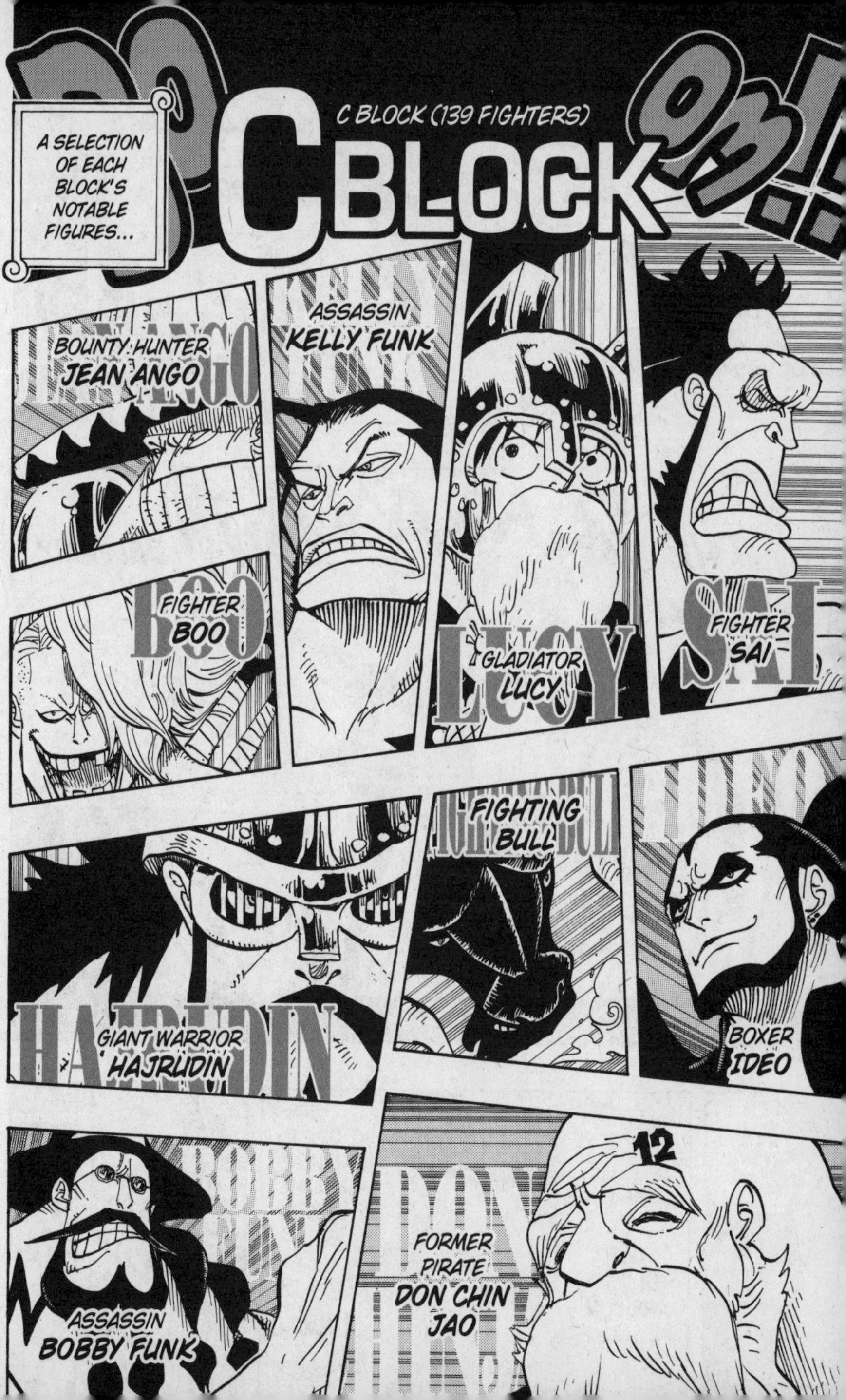
DOOOM!!
C BLOCK (139 FIGHTERS)
C BLOCK
A SELECTION OF EACH BLOCK'S NOTABLE FIGURES...
FIGHTER SAI
GLADIATOR LUCY
ASSASSIN KELLY FUNK
BOUNTY HUNTER JEAN ANGO
FIGHTER BOO
BOXER IDEO
FIGHTING BULL
GIANT WARRIOR HAJRUDIN
FORMER PIRATE DON CHIN JAO
ASSASSIN BOBBY FUNK

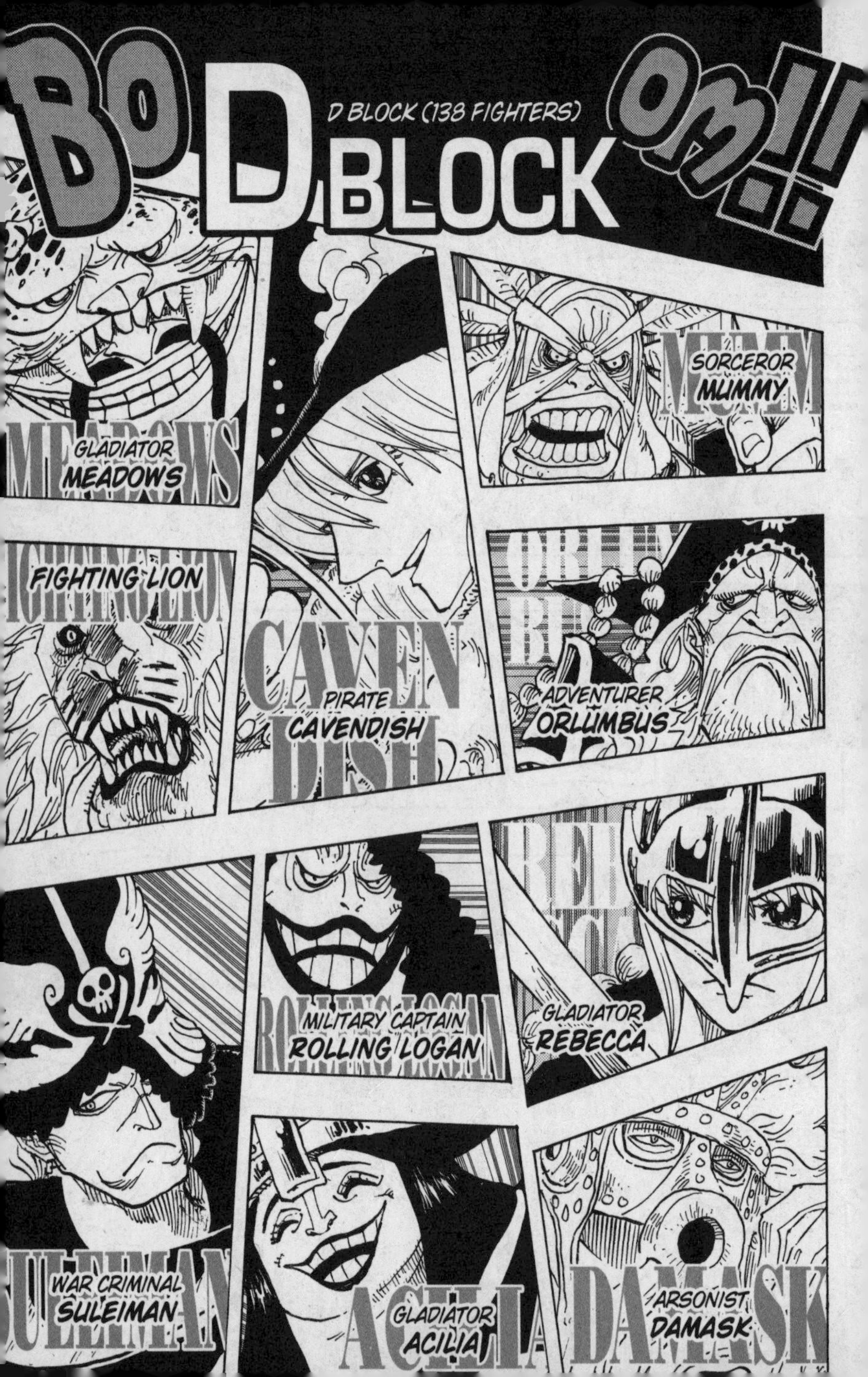
BOOM!!
D BLOCK (138 FIGHTERS)
D BLOCK
SORCEROR MUMMY
ADVENTURER ORLUMBUS
PIRATE CAVENDISH
GLADIATOR MEADOWS
FIGHTING LION
GLADIATOR REBECCA
MILITARY CAPTAIN ROLLING LOGAN
ARSONIST DAMASK
GLADIATOR ACILIA
WAR CRIMINAL SULEIMAN

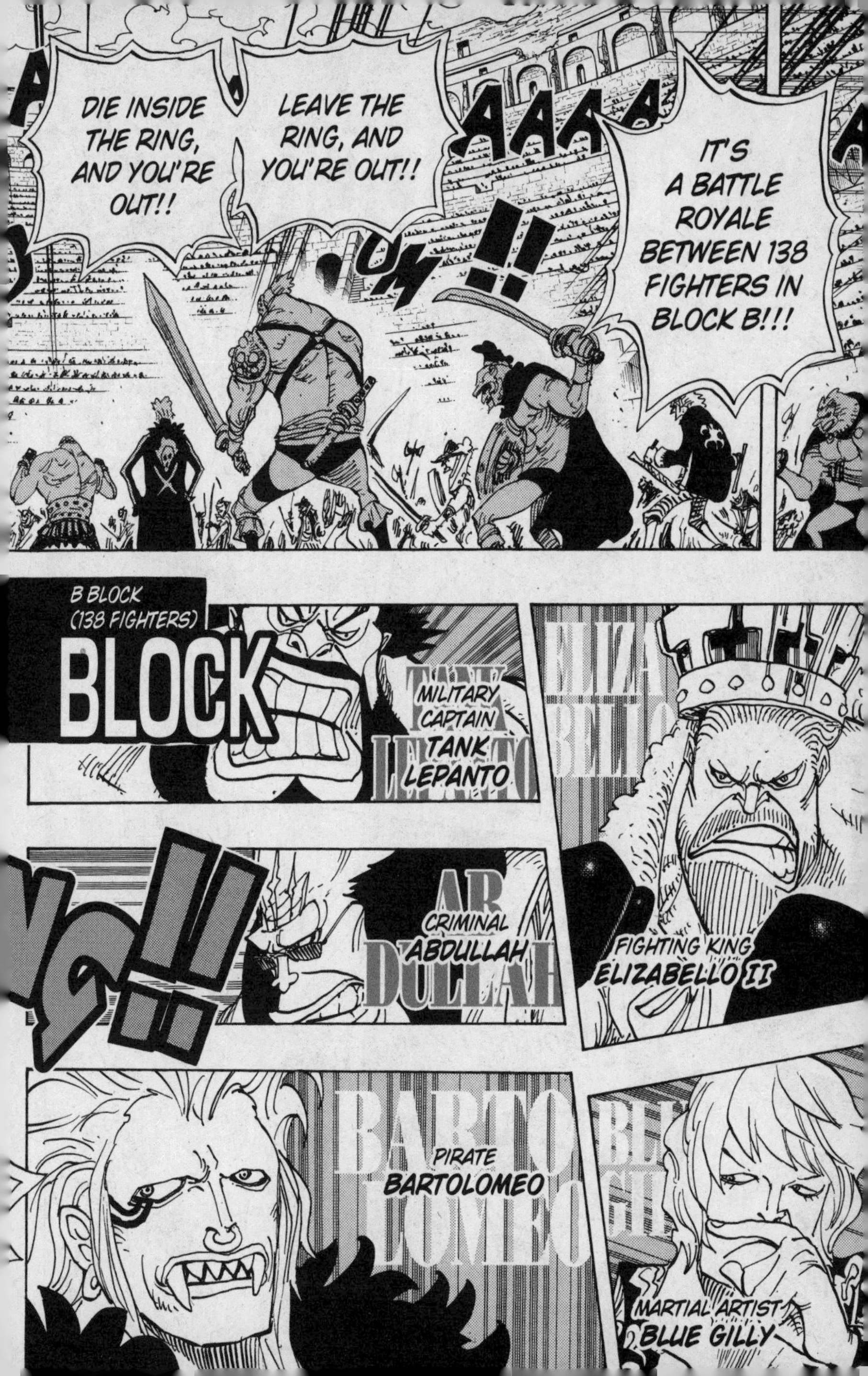

IT'S A BATTLE ROYALE BETWEEN 138 FIGHTERS IN BLOCK B!!!
LEAVE THE RING, AND YOU'RE OUT!!
DIE INSIDE THE RING, AND YOU'RE OUT!!
FIGHTING KING ELIZABELLO II
B BLOCK (138 FIGHTERS)
BLOCK
MILITARY CAPTAIN TANK LEPANTO
CRIMINAL ABDULLAH
MARTIAL ARTIST BLUE GILLY
PIRATE BARTOLOMEO

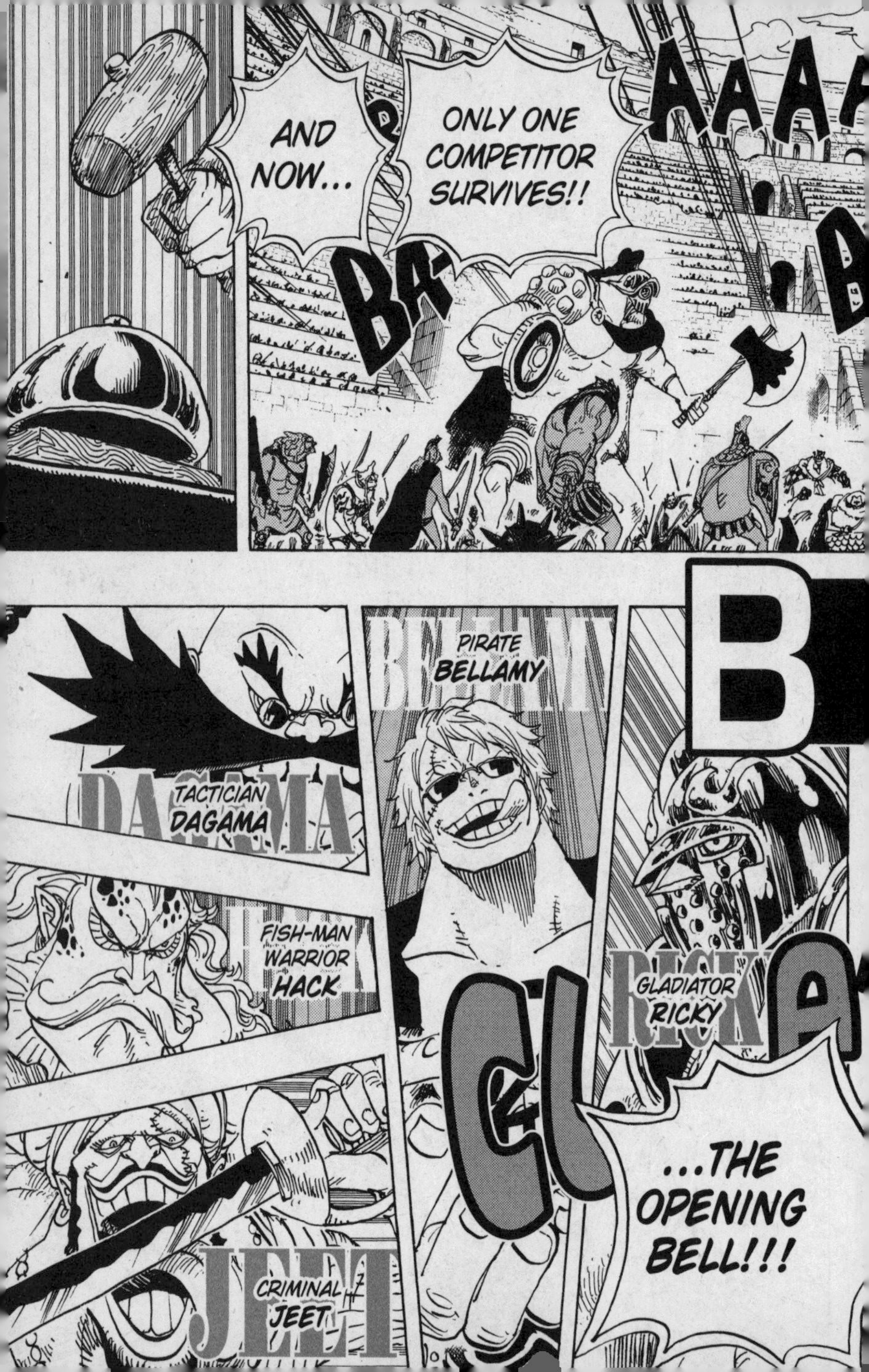
AAAA
AND NOW...
ONLY ONE COMPETITOR SURVIVES!!
BA
B
B
GLADIATOR RICKY
CL
A
...THE OPENING BELL!!!
PIRATE BELLAMY
TACTICIAN DAGAMA
FISH-MAN WARRIOR HACK
CRIMINAL JEET

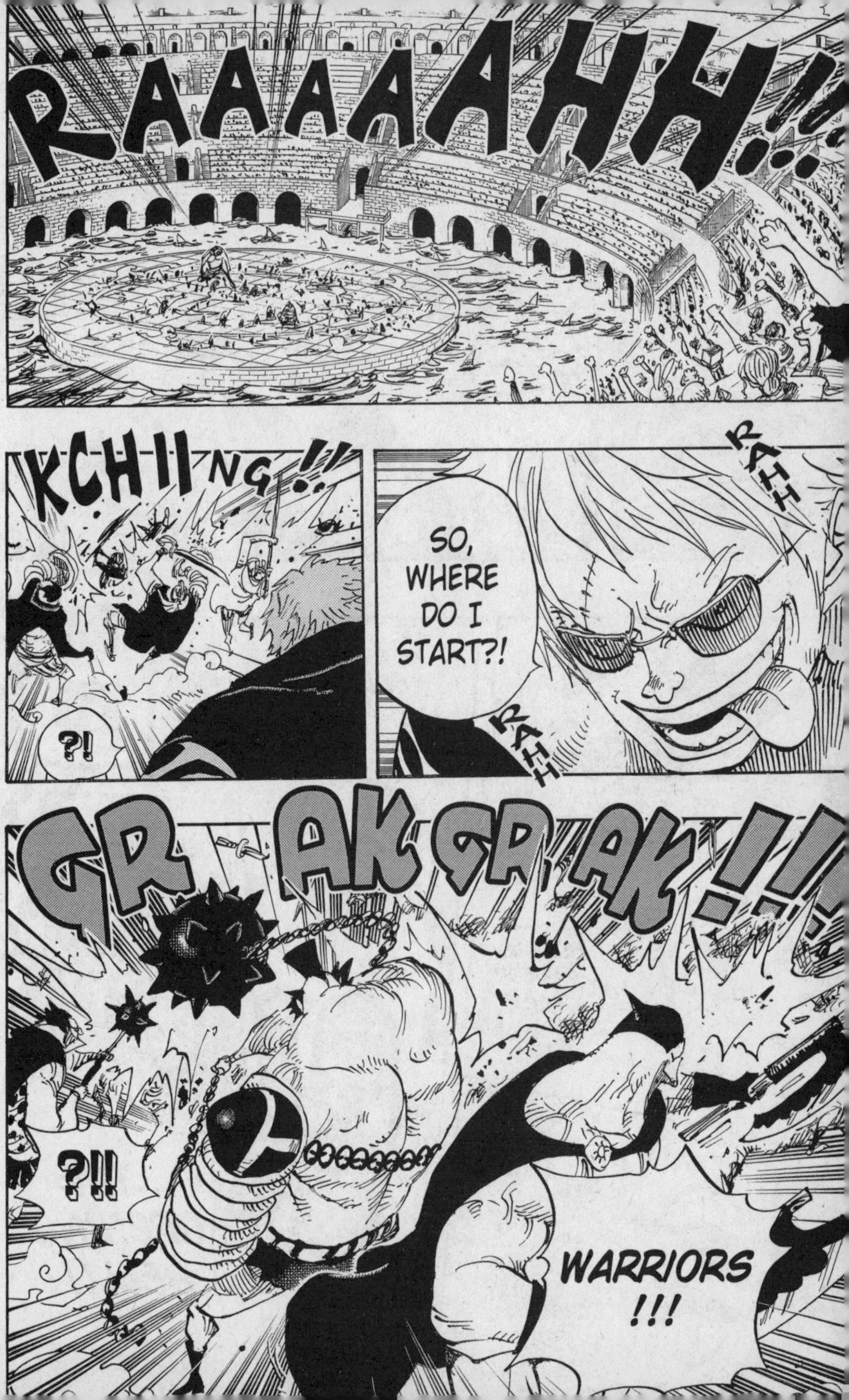
RAAAAAHH!!
RAHH
SO, WHERE DO I START?!
RAHH
KCHIING!!
?!
GRAK GRAK!!!
?!!
WARRIORS!!!

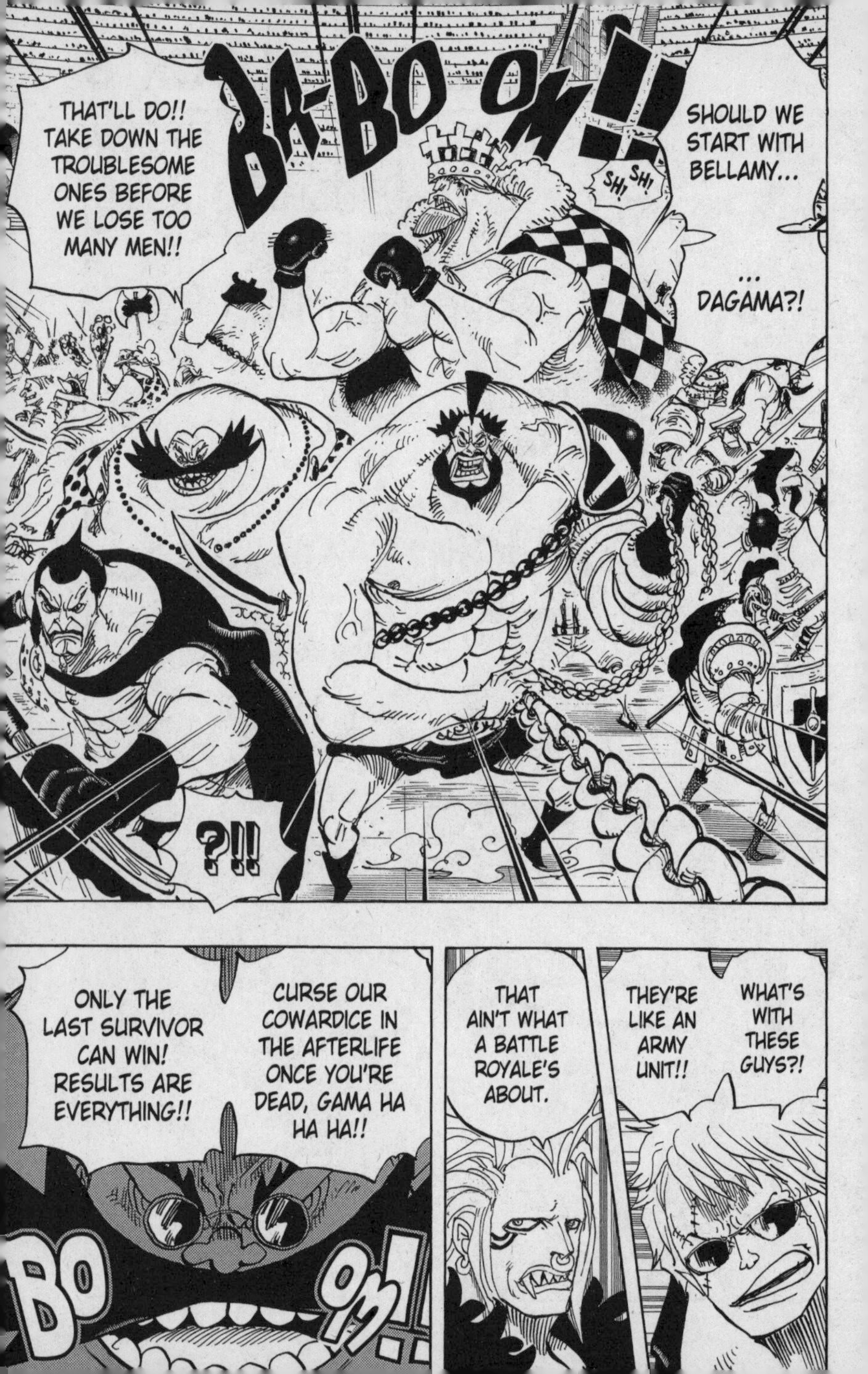
SHOULD WE START WITH BELLAMY...
... DAGAMA?!
SH! SH!
BA-BO OM!!
THAT'LL DO!! TAKE DOWN THE TROUBLESOME ONES BEFORE WE LOSE TOO MANY MEN!!
?!!
WHAT'S WITH THESE GUYS?!
THEY'RE LIKE AN ARMY UNIT!!
THAT AIN'T WHAT A BATTLE ROYALE'S ABOUT.
CURSE OUR COWARDICE IN THE AFTERLIFE ONCE YOU'RE DEAD, GAMA HA HA HA!!
ONLY THE LAST SURVIVOR CAN WIN! RESULTS ARE EVERYTHING!!
BO OM!!

Chapter 707: BLOCK B

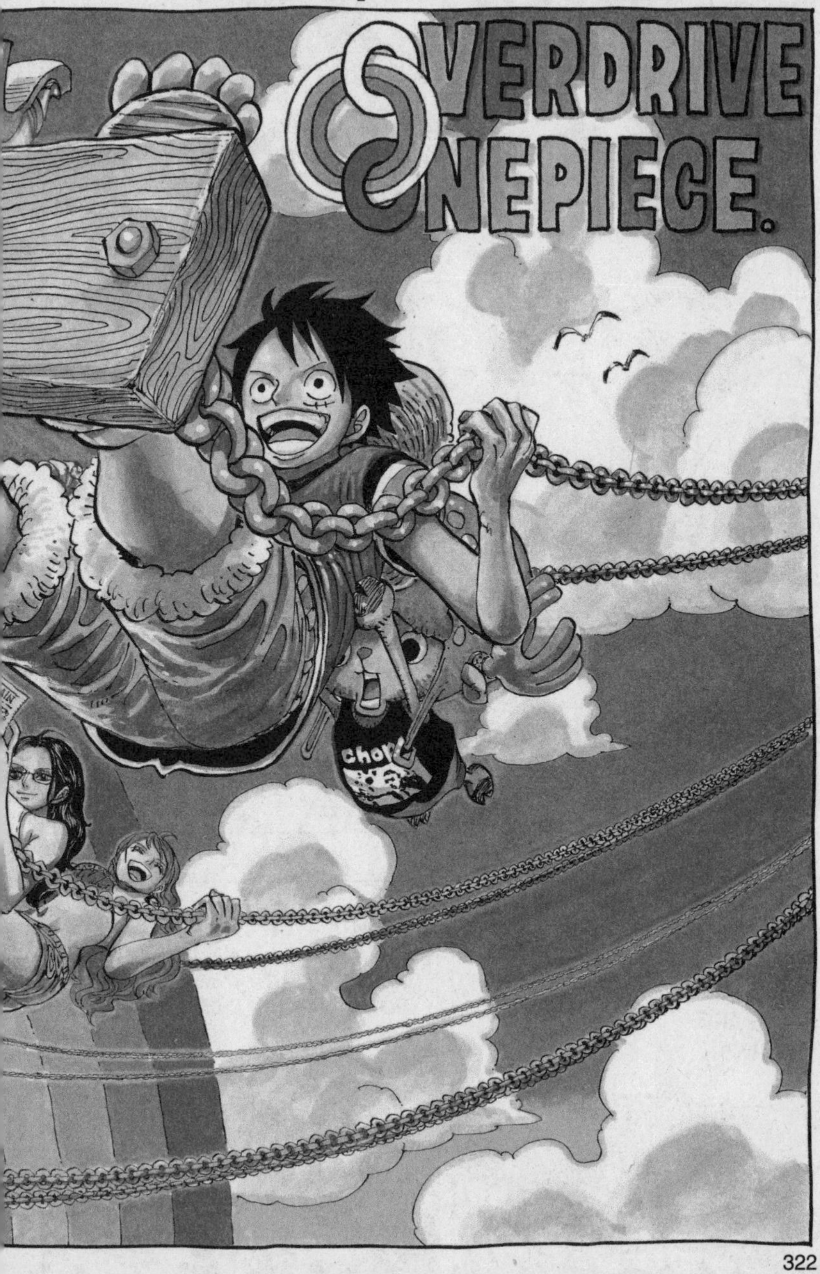
OVERDRIVE
ONEPIECE.
chop

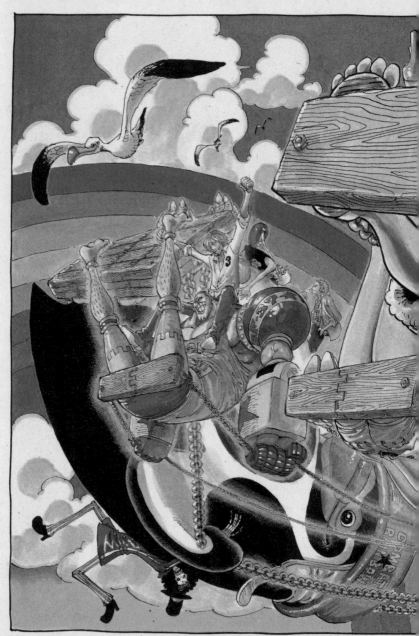

vol. 71
ONE PIECE

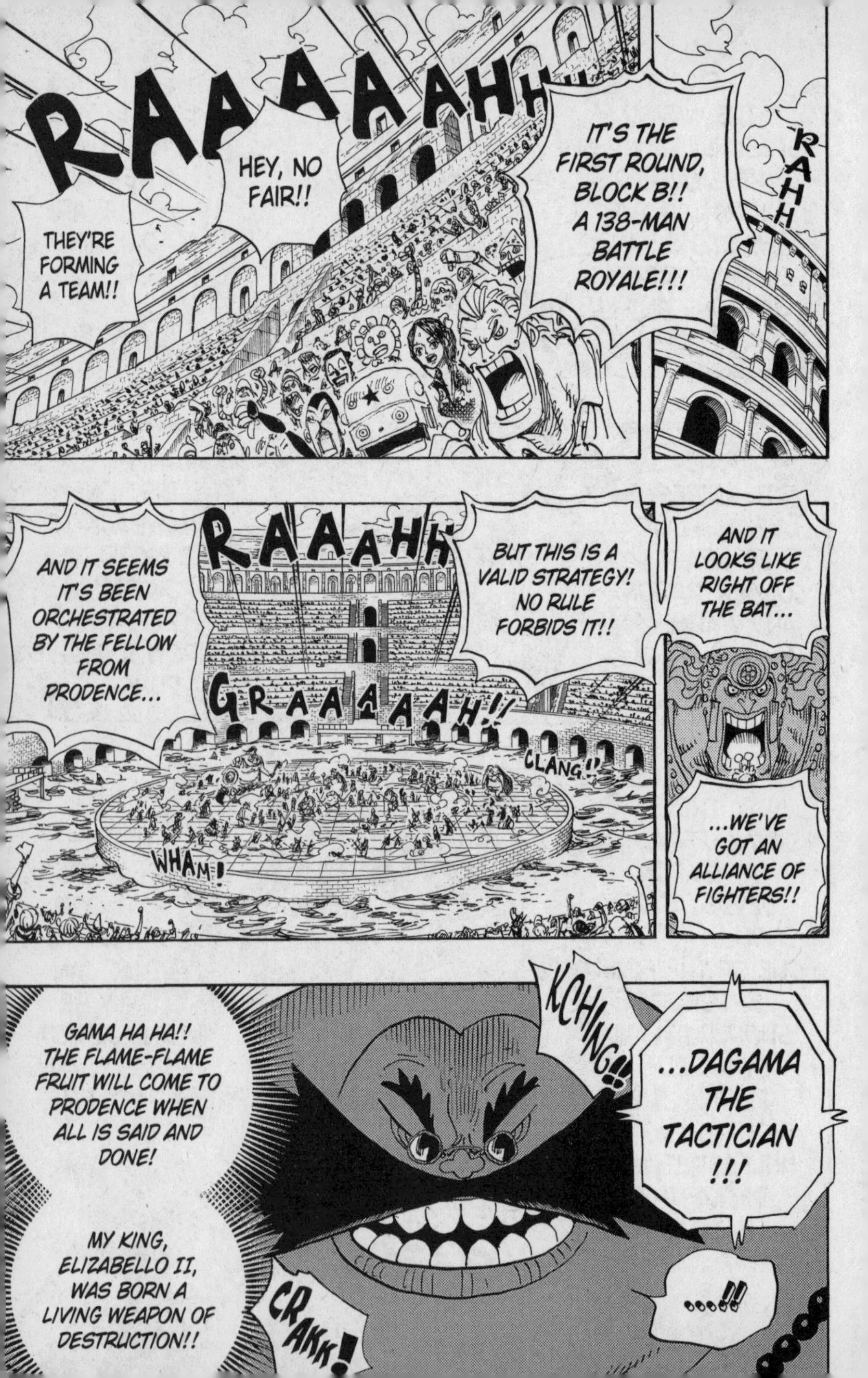

RAHHH
IT'S THE FIRST ROUND, BLOCK B!! A 138-MAN BATTLE ROYALE!!!
RAAAAAHH
HEY, NO FAIR!!
THEY'RE FORMING A TEAM!!
AND IT LOOKS LIKE RIGHT OFF THE BAT...
...WE'VE GOT AN ALLIANCE OF FIGHTERS!!
BUT THIS IS A VALID STRATEGY! NO RULE FORBIDS IT!!
RAAAHH
AND IT SEEMS IT'S BEEN ORCHESTRATED BY THE FELLOW FROM PRODENCE...
GRAAAAAH!!
CLANG!!
WHAM!
...DAGAMA THE TACTICIAN!!!
KCHING!!
GAMA HA HA!! THE FLAME-FLAME FRUIT WILL COME TO PRODENCE WHEN ALL IS SAID AND DONE!
...!!
MY KING, ELIZABELLO II, WAS BORN A LIVING WEAPON OF DESTRUCTION!!
CRAKK!

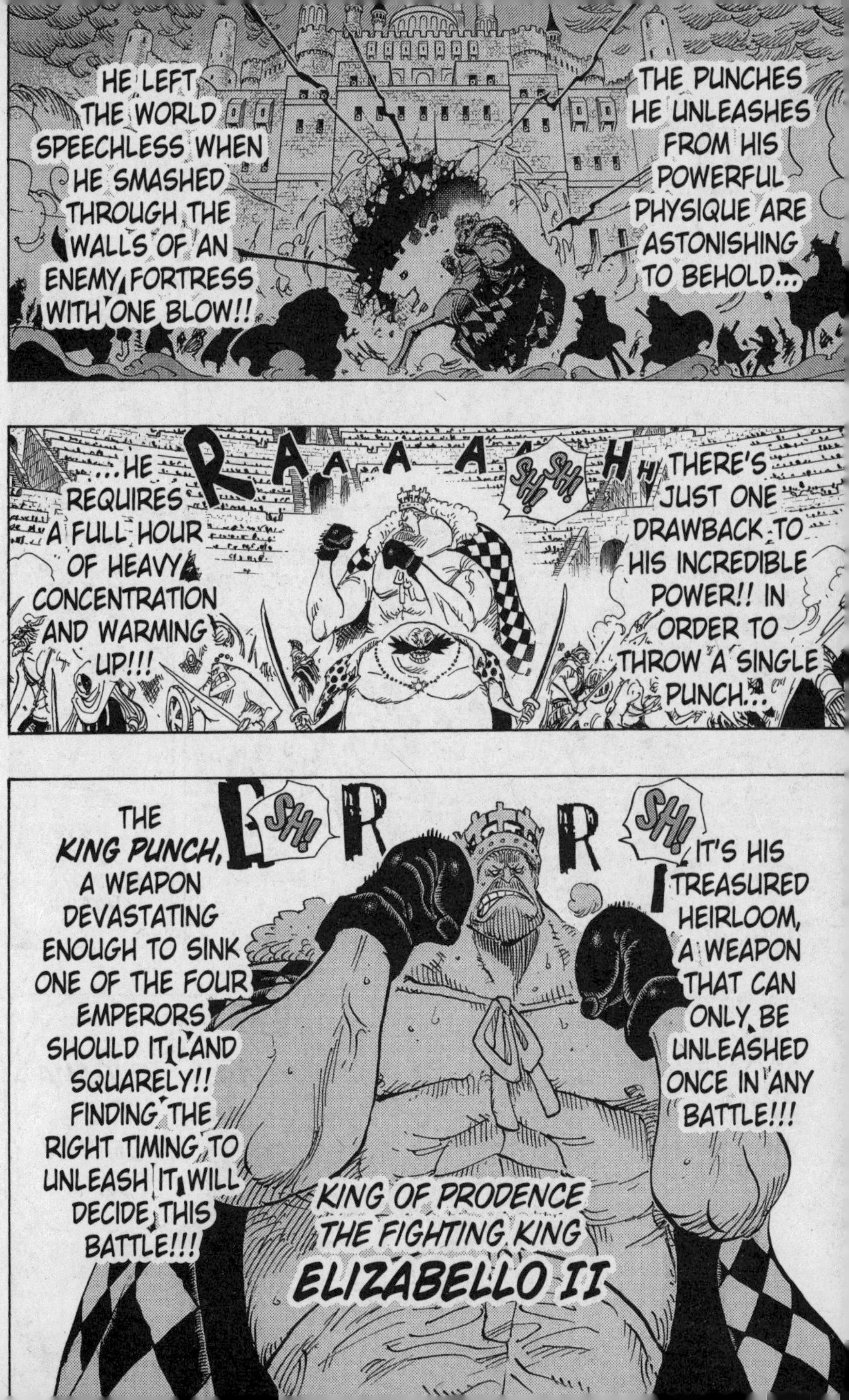
THE PUNCHES HE UNLEASHES FROM HIS POWERFUL PHYSIQUE ARE ASTONISHING TO BEHOLD...
HE LEFT THE WORLD SPEECHLESS WHEN HE SMASHED THROUGH THE WALLS OF AN ENEMY FORTRESS WITH ONE BLOW!!
THERE'S JUST ONE DRAWBACK TO HIS INCREDIBLE POWER!! IN ORDER TO THROW A SINGLE PUNCH...
RAAAAHH
SH! SH!
...HE REQUIRES A FULL HOUR OF HEAVY CONCENTRATION AND WARMING UP!!!
SH!
SH!
IT'S HIS TREASURED HEIRLOOM, A WEAPON THAT CAN ONLY BE UNLEASHED ONCE IN ANY BATTLE!!!
THE *KING PUNCH*, A WEAPON DEVASTATING ENOUGH TO SINK ONE OF THE FOUR EMPERORS SHOULD IT LAND SQUARELY!! FINDING THE RIGHT TIMING TO UNLEASH IT WILL DECIDE THIS BATTLE!!!
KING OF PRODENCE
THE FIGHTING KING
ELIZABELLO II

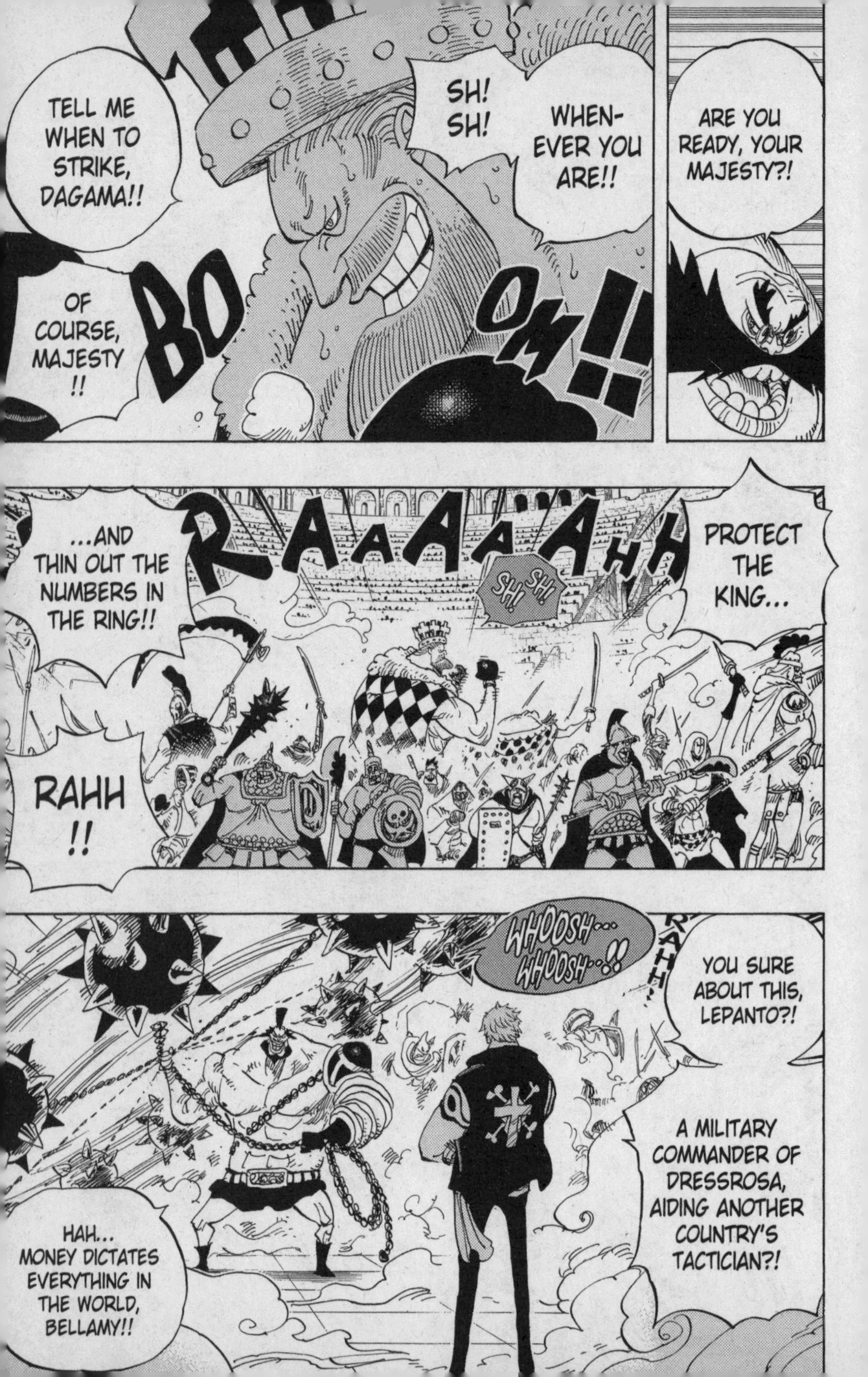
ARE YOU READY, YOUR MAJESTY?!
WHEN-EVER YOU ARE!!
SH! SH!
TELL ME WHEN TO STRIKE, DAGAMA!!
BOOM!!
OF COURSE, MAJESTY!!
PROTECT THE KING...
RAAAAAHH
SH! SH!
...AND THIN OUT THE NUMBERS IN THE RING!!
RAHH!!
RAHH...
WHOOSH... WHOOSH...!!
YOU SURE ABOUT THIS, LEPANTO?!
A MILITARY COMMANDER OF DRESSROSA, AIDING ANOTHER COUNTRY'S TACTICIAN?!
HAH... MONEY DICTATES EVERYTHING IN THE WORLD, BELLAMY!!

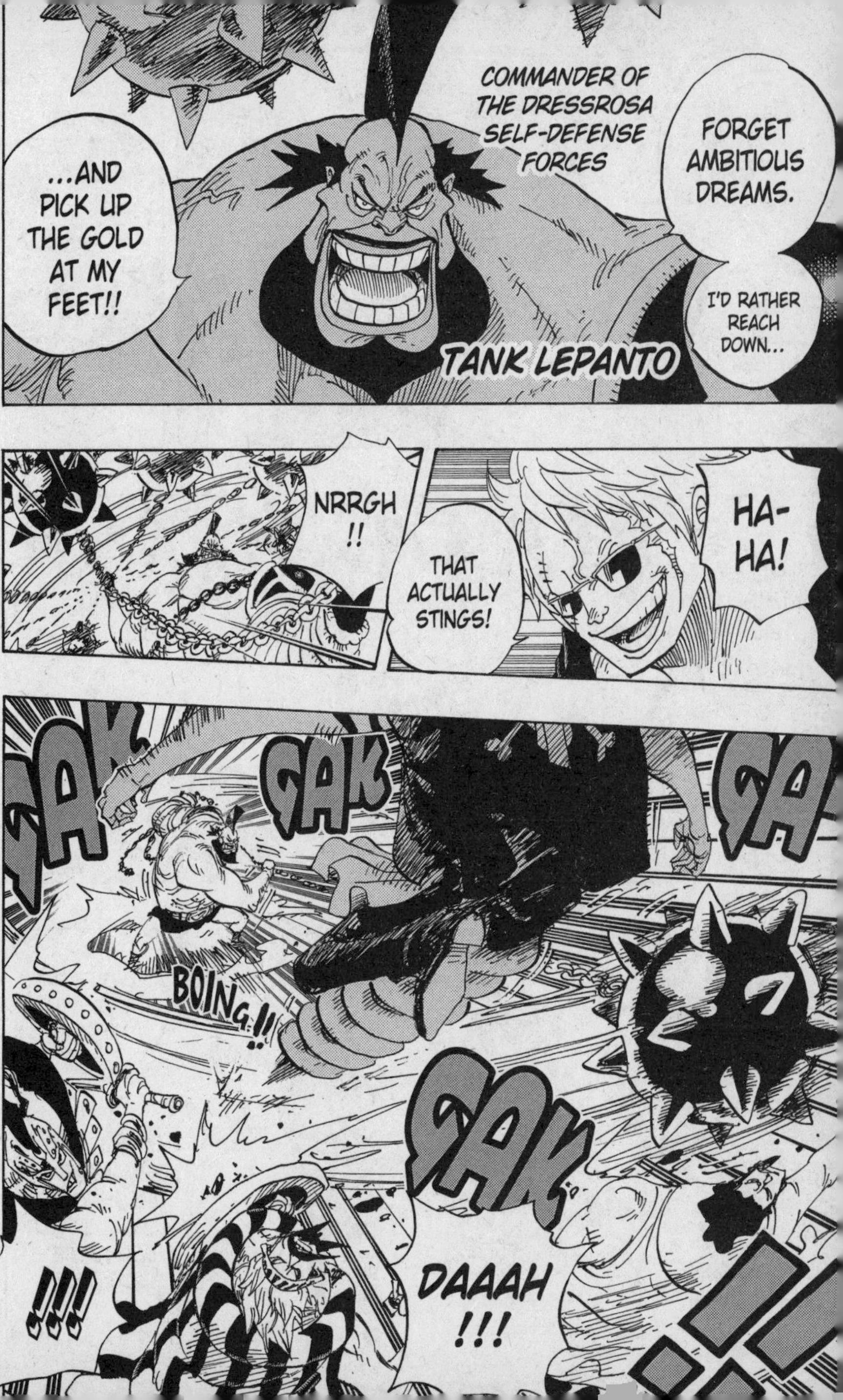
FORGET AMBITIOUS DREAMS.
I'D RATHER REACH DOWN...
COMMANDER OF THE DRESSROSA SELF-DEFENSE FORCES
TANK LEPANTO
...AND PICK UP THE GOLD AT MY FEET!!
HA-HA!
THAT ACTUALLY STINGS!
NRRGH !!
GA-
GAK
GAK
BOING!!
GAK
DAAAH !!!
!!!

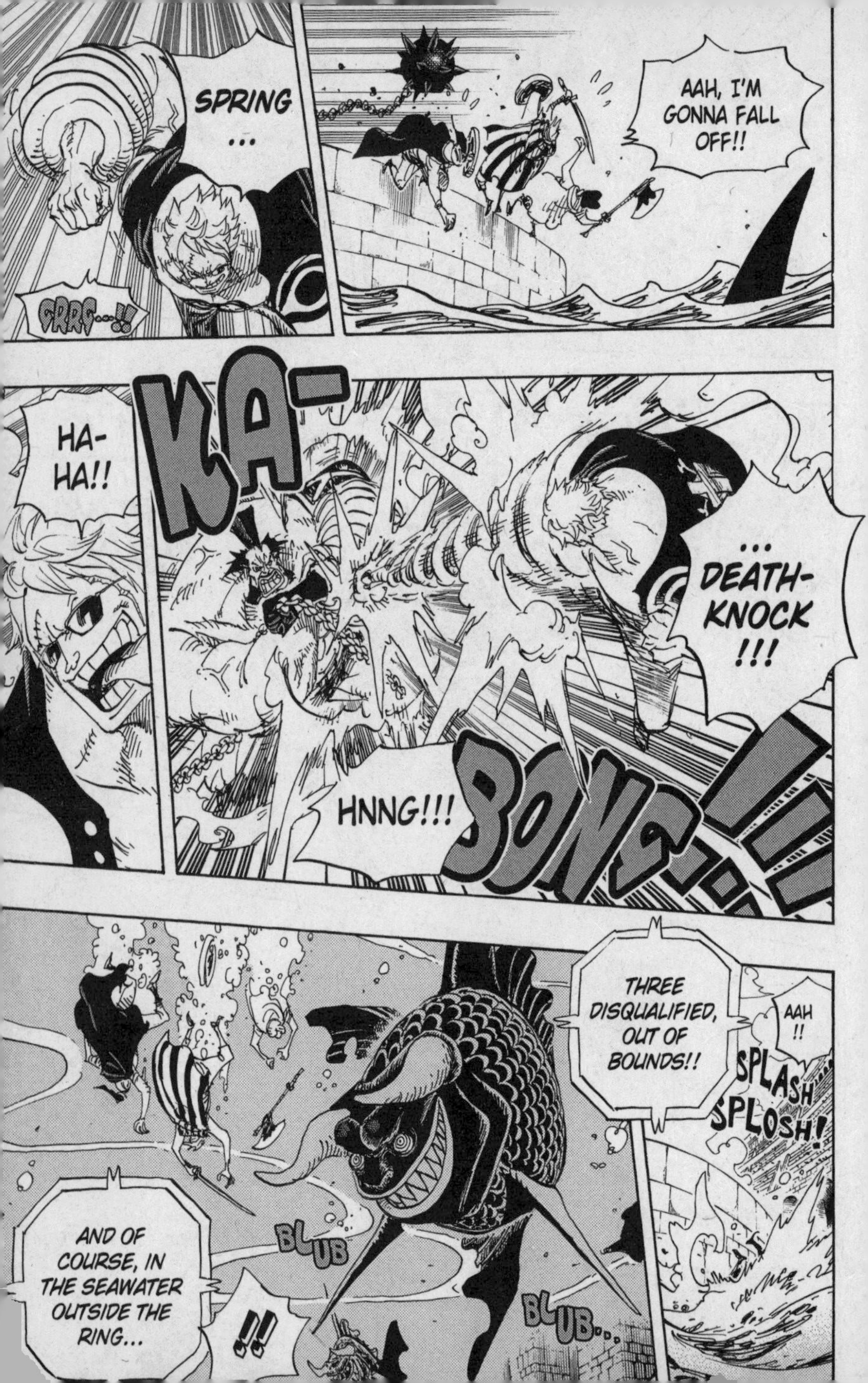
AAH, I'M GONNA FALL OFF!!
SPRING ...
GRRG...!!
KA-
... DEATH-KNOCK !!!
HNNG!!!
BONG...!!!
HA-HA!!
AAH !!
SPLASH... SPLOSH!
THREE DISQUALIFIED, OUT OF BOUNDS!!
AND OF COURSE, IN THE SEAWATER OUTSIDE THE RING...
BLUB
BLUB...
!!

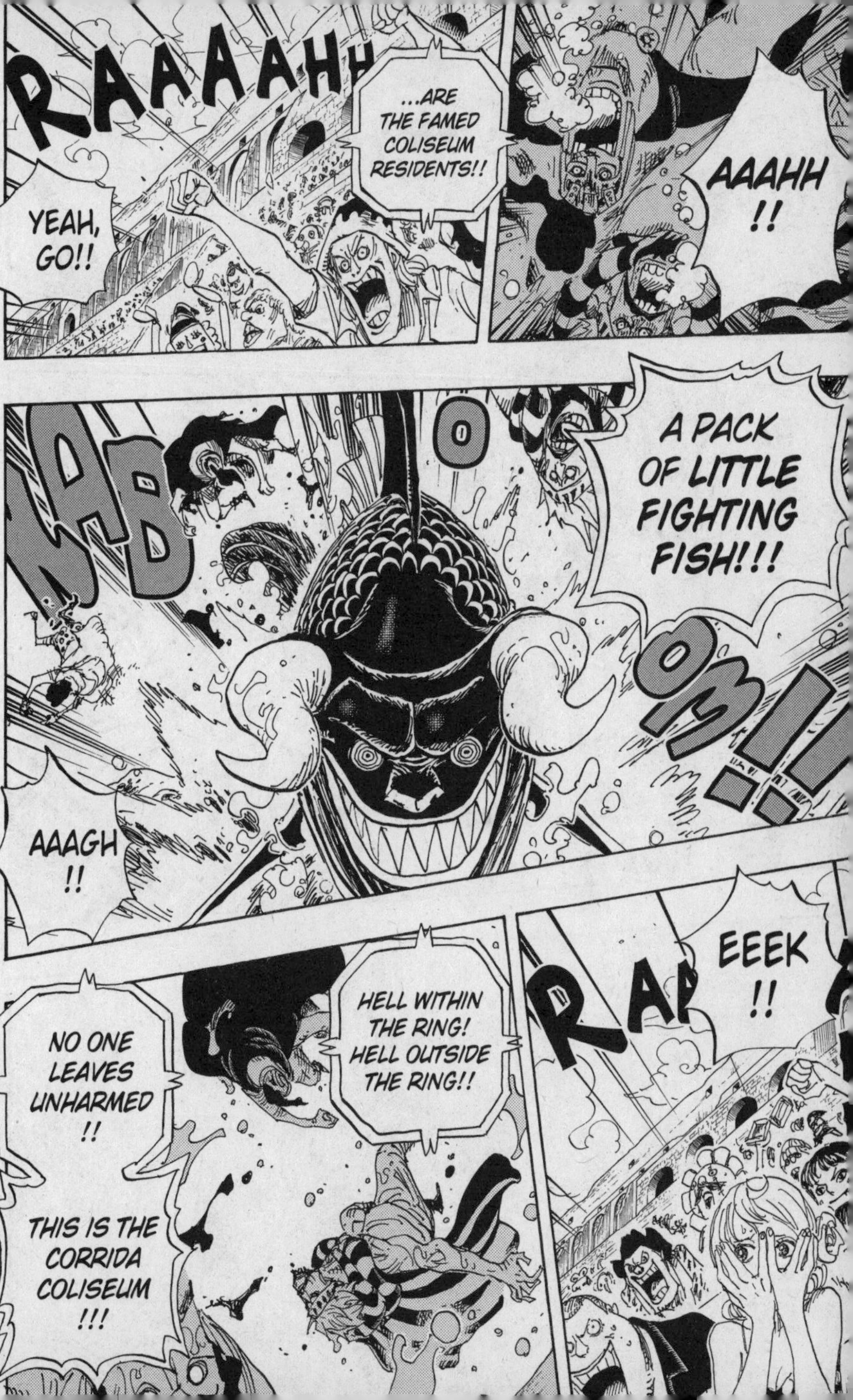
AAAHH !!
...ARE THE FAMED COLISEUM RESIDENTS!!
RAAAAHH
YEAH, GO!!
A PACK OF LITTLE FIGHTING FISH!!!
OM!!
AAAGH !!
EEEK !!
HELL WITHIN THE RING! HELL OUTSIDE THE RING!!
NO ONE LEAVES UNHARMED !!
THIS IS THE CORRIDA COLISEUM !!!

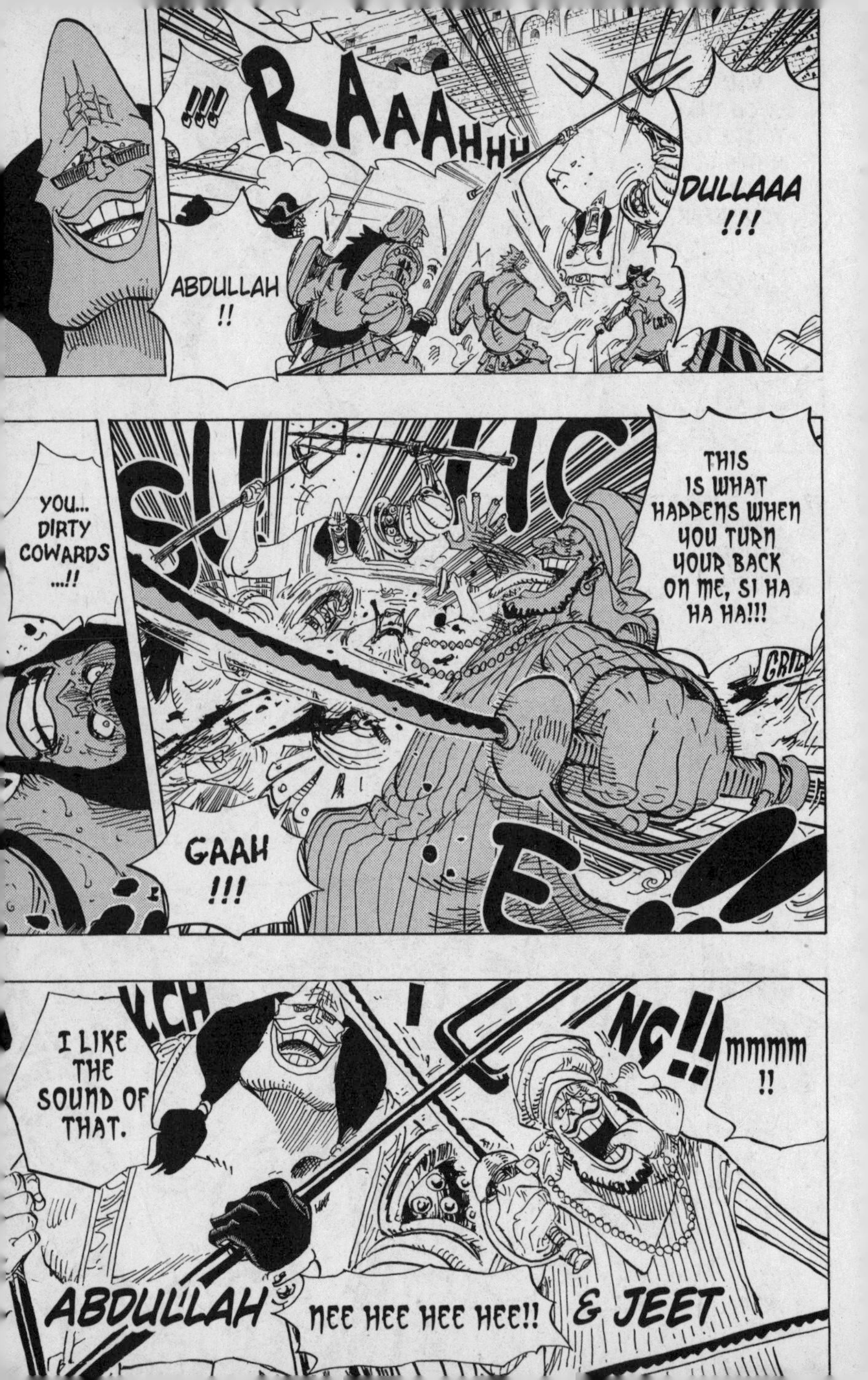
RAAAHHH
DULLAAA!!!
!!!
ABDULLAH!!
THIS IS WHAT HAPPENS WHEN YOU TURN YOUR BACK ON ME, SI HA HA HA!!!
GAAH!!!
YOU... DIRTY COWARDS ...!!
mmmm!!
NG!!
I LIKE THE SOUND OF THAT.
& JEET
NEE HEE HEE HEE!!
ABDULLAH

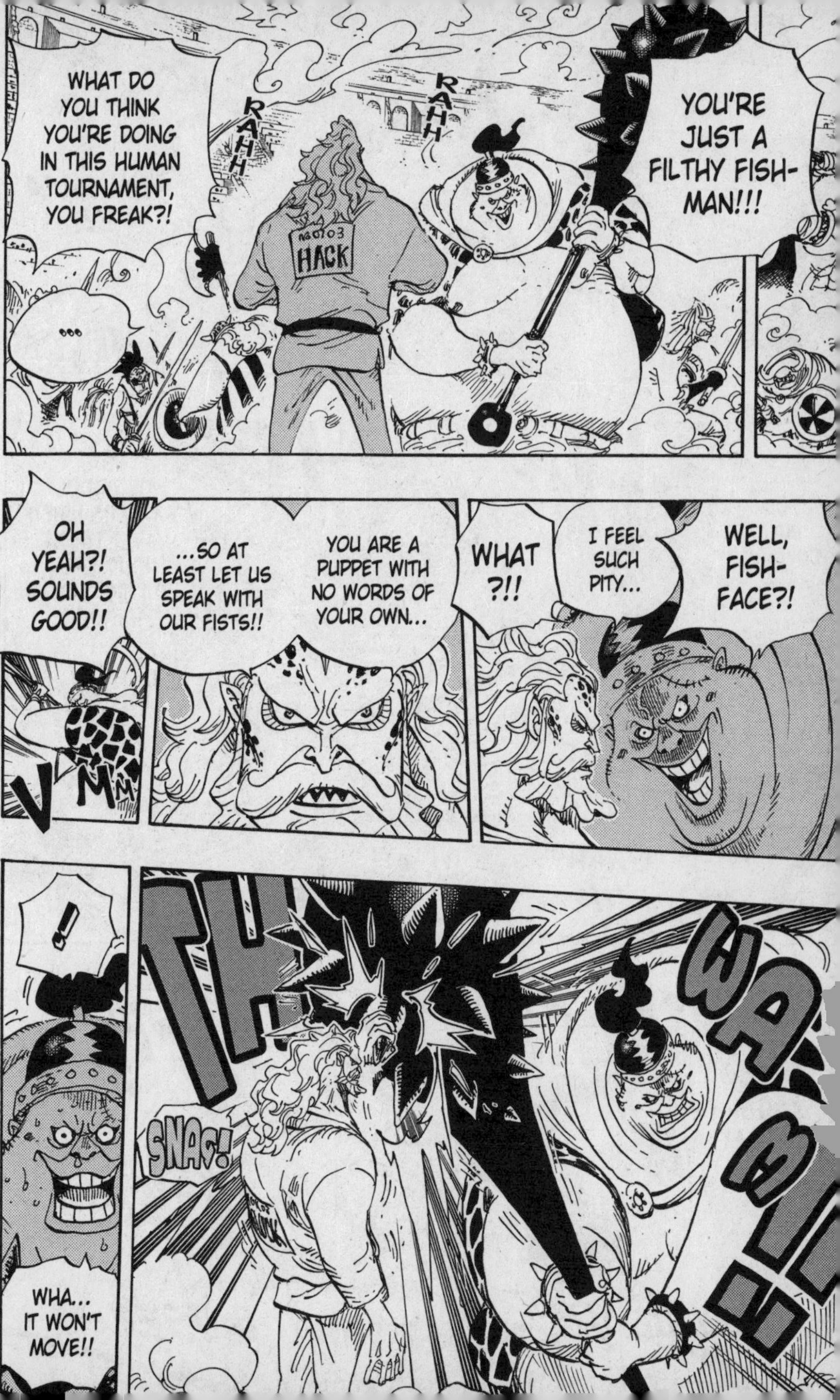
YOU'RE JUST A FILTHY FISH-MAN!!!
RAHH
RAHH
WHAT DO YOU THINK YOU'RE DOING IN THIS HUMAN TOURNAMENT, YOU FREAK?!
HACK
...
WELL, FISH-FACE?!
I FEEL SUCH PITY...
WHAT ?!!
YOU ARE A PUPPET WITH NO WORDS OF YOUR OWN...
...SO AT LEAST LET US SPEAK WITH OUR FISTS!!
OH YEAH?! SOUNDS GOOD!!
VMM
WAM!!
TH
SNAG!
!
WHA... IT WON'T MOVE!!

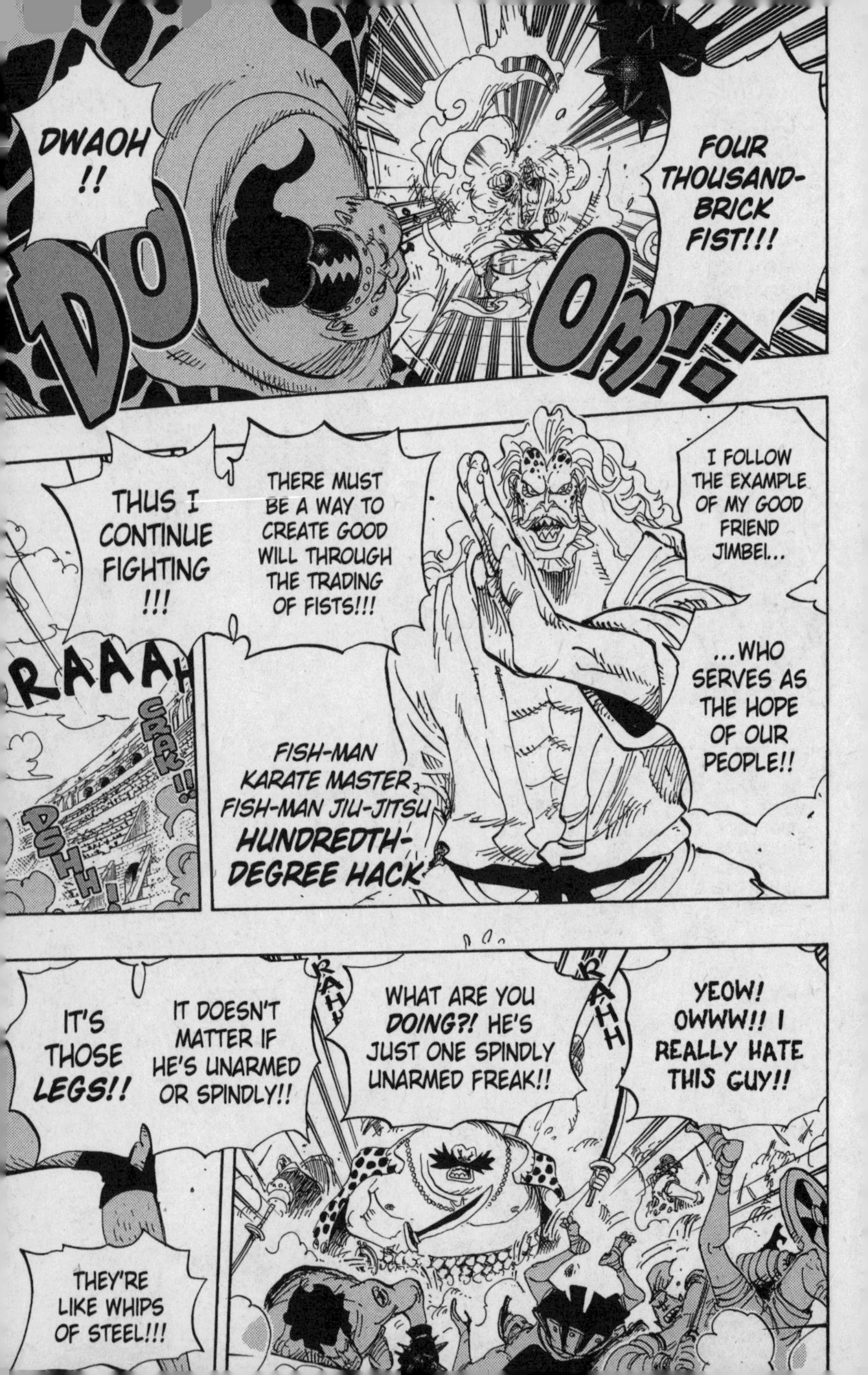
FOUR THOUSAND-BRICK FIST!!!
DWAOH !!
DOOM!!
I FOLLOW THE EXAMPLE OF MY GOOD FRIEND JIMBEI...
...WHO SERVES AS THE HOPE OF OUR PEOPLE!!
THERE MUST BE A WAY TO CREATE GOOD WILL THROUGH THE TRADING OF FISTS!!!
FISH-MAN KARATE MASTER, FISH-MAN JIU-JITSU
HUNDREDTH-DEGREE HACK
THUS I CONTINUE FIGHTING !!!
RAAAH
CRAK!!
PSHH!
YEOW! OWWW!! I REALLY HATE THIS GUY!!
RAHH
WHAT ARE YOU DOING?! HE'S JUST ONE SPINDLY UNARMED FREAK!!
RAHH
IT DOESN'T MATTER IF HE'S UNARMED OR SPINDLY!!
IT'S THOSE LEGS!!
THEY'RE LIKE WHIPS OF STEEL!!!

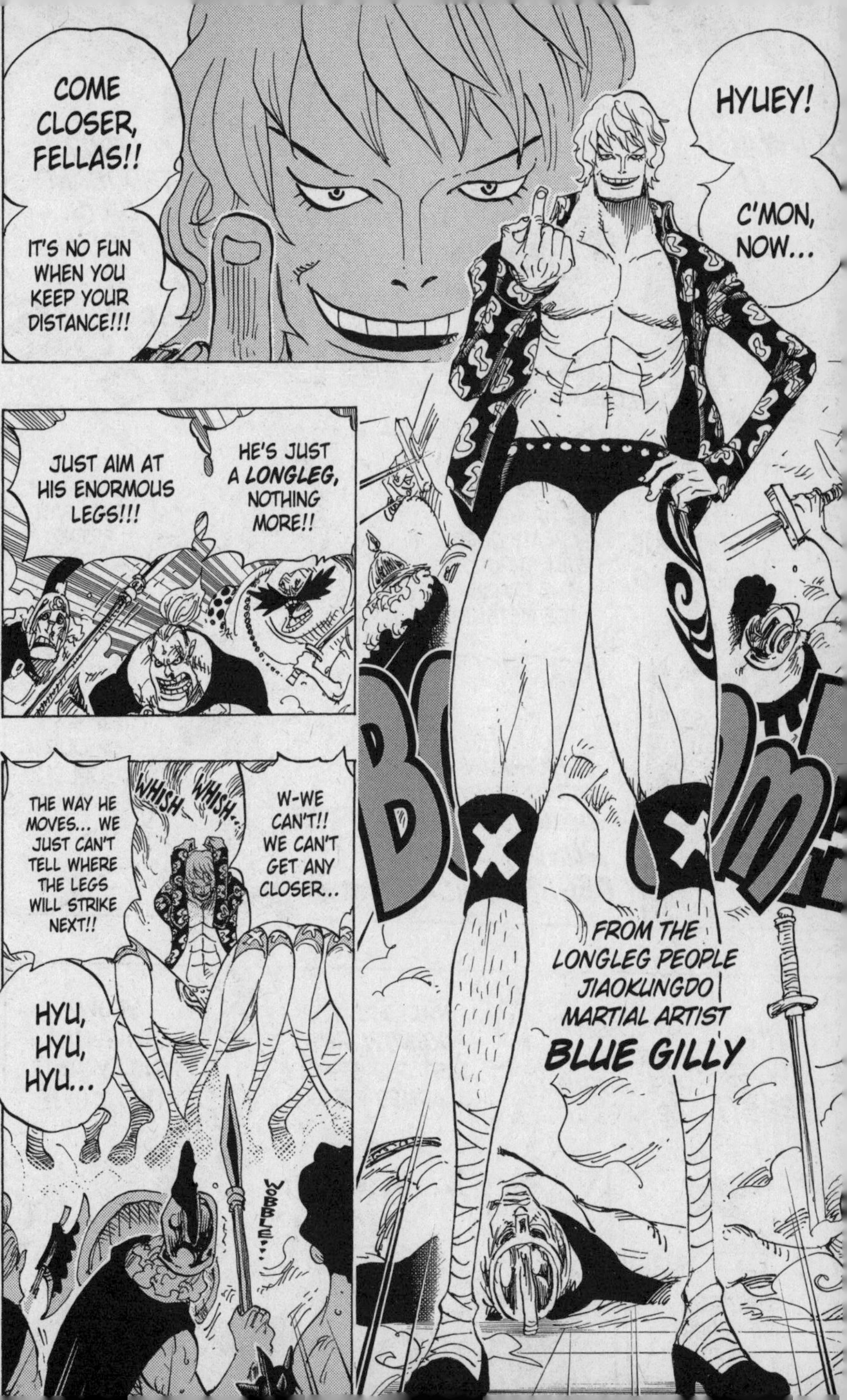
HYUEY!
C'MON, NOW...
FROM THE LONGLEG PEOPLE JIAOKUNGDO MARTIAL ARTIST
BLUE GILLY
COME CLOSER, FELLAS!!
IT'S NO FUN WHEN YOU KEEP YOUR DISTANCE!!!
HE'S JUST A LONGLEG, NOTHING MORE!!
JUST AIM AT HIS ENORMOUS LEGS!!!
WHISH WHISH
W-WE CAN'T!! WE CAN'T GET ANY CLOSER...
THE WAY HE MOVES... WE JUST CAN'T TELL WHERE THE LEGS WILL STRIKE NEXT!!
HYU, HYU, HYU...
WOBBLE...

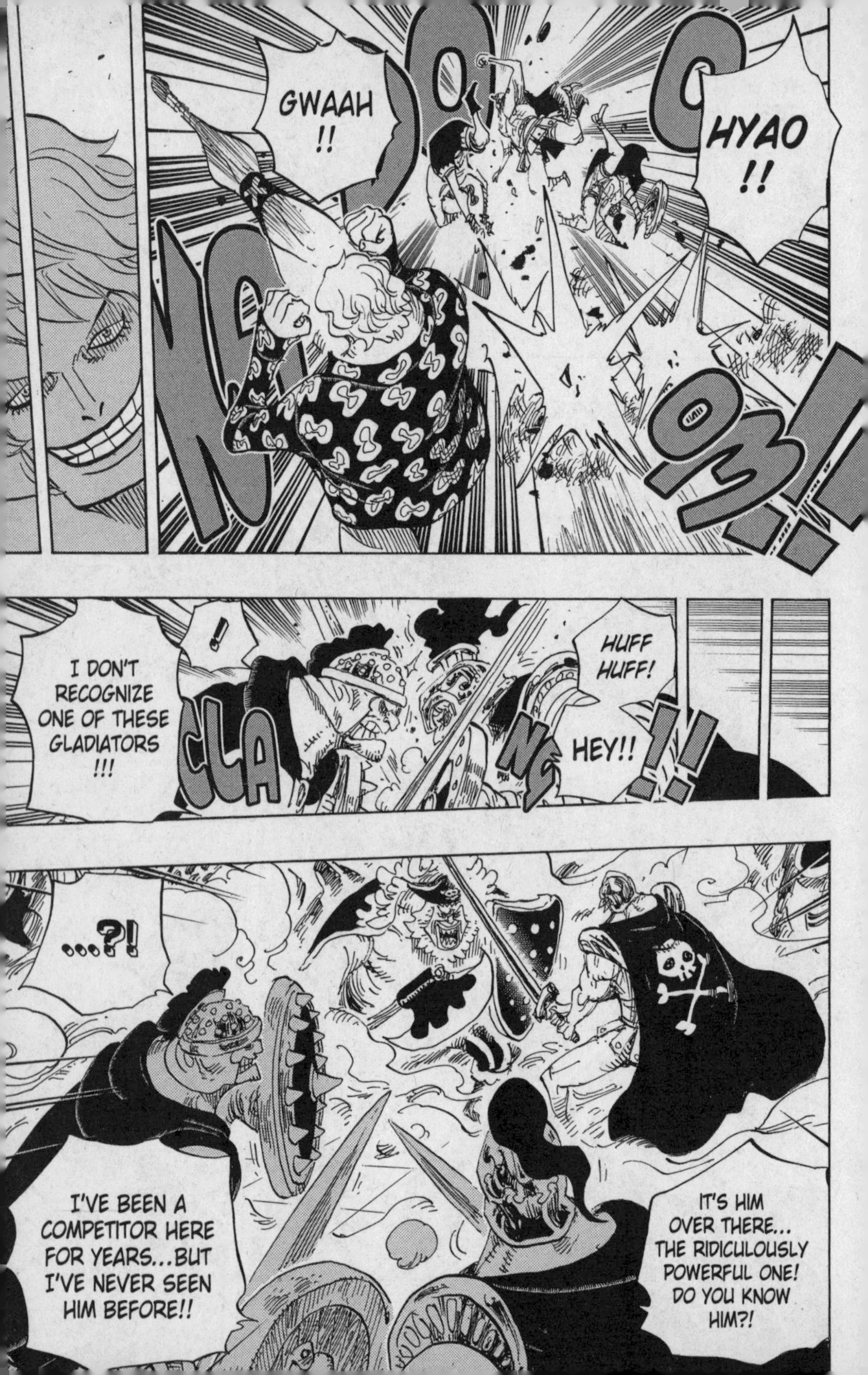
HYAO !!
GWAAH !!
HUFF HUFF!
HEY!!
CLANG
!
I DON'T RECOGNIZE ONE OF THESE GLADIATORS !!!
...?!
IT'S HIM OVER THERE... THE RIDICULOUSLY POWERFUL ONE! DO YOU KNOW HIM?!
I'VE BEEN A COMPETITOR HERE FOR YEARS...BUT I'VE NEVER SEEN HIM BEFORE!!

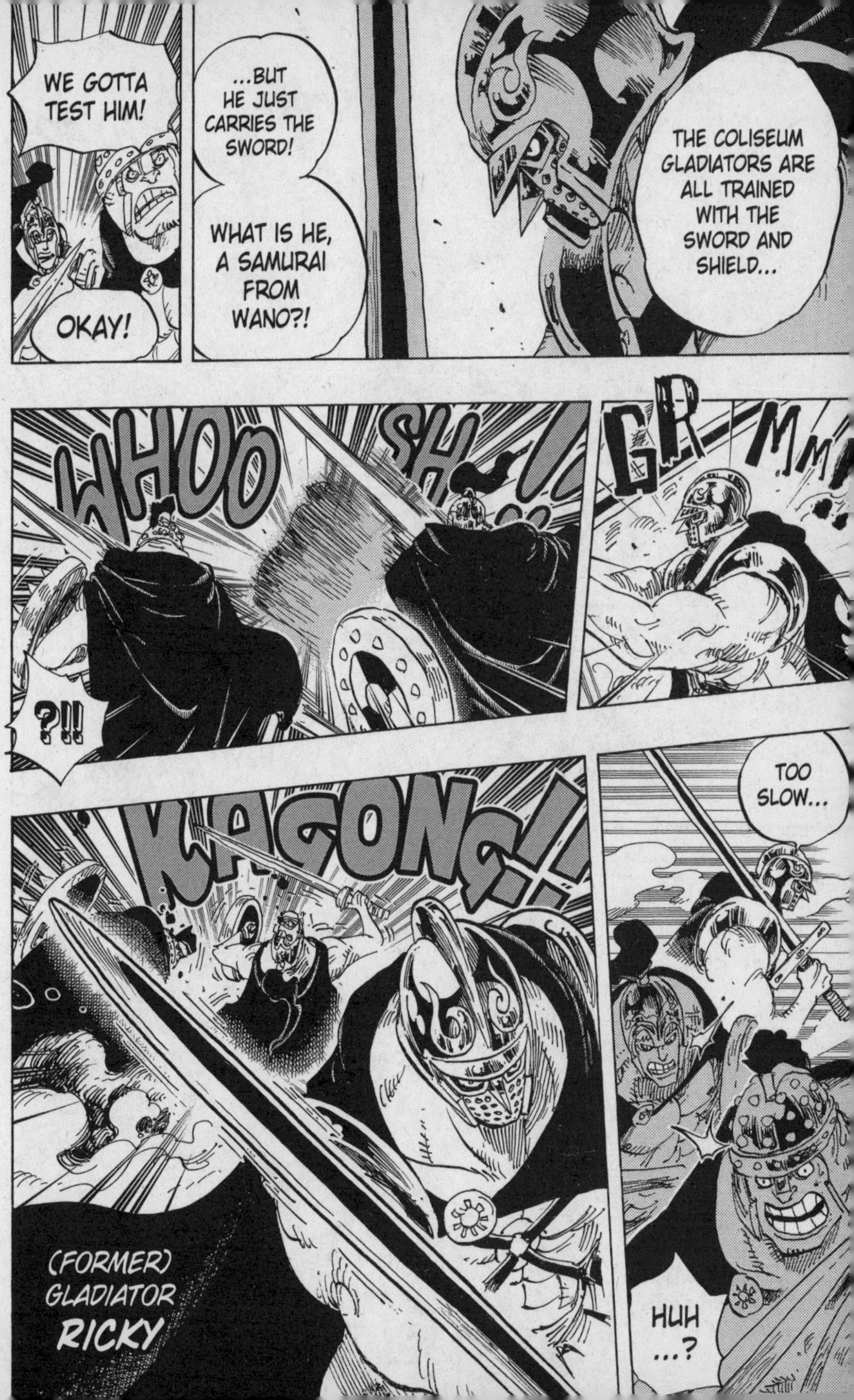
THE COLISEUM GLADIATORS ARE ALL TRAINED WITH THE SWORD AND SHIELD...
...BUT HE JUST CARRIES THE SWORD!
WHAT IS HE, A SAMURAI FROM WANO?!
WE GOTTA TEST HIM!
OKAY!
GR MM
WHOOSH!!
?!!
TOO SLOW...
HUH ...?
KAGONG!!
(FORMER) GLADIATOR RICKY

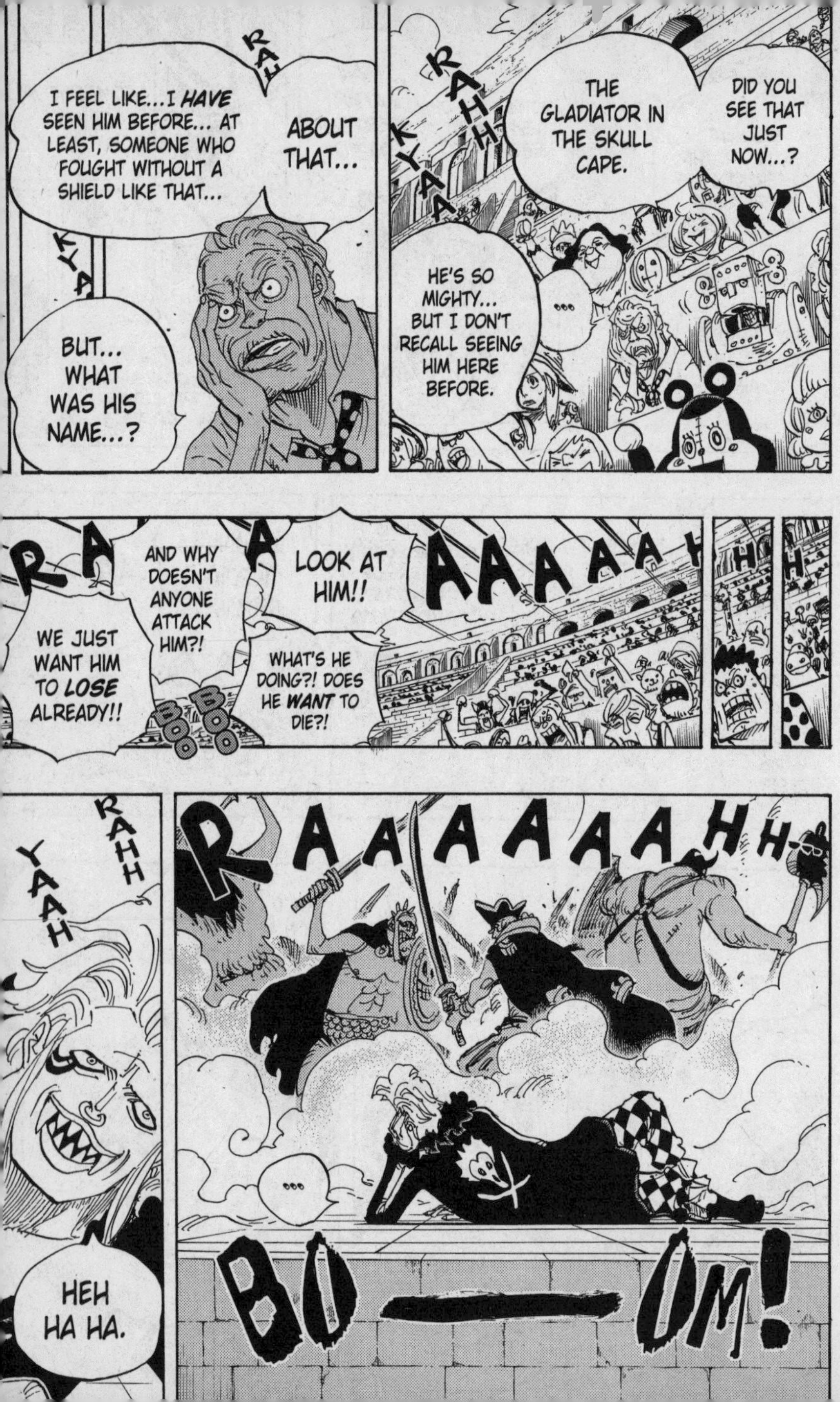

DID YOU SEE THAT JUST NOW...?
THE GLADIATOR IN THE SKULL CAPE.
RAHH
KYAAA
HE'S SO MIGHTY... BUT I DON'T RECALL SEEING HIM HERE BEFORE.
...
RAH
ABOUT THAT...
I FEEL LIKE...I *HAVE* SEEN HIM BEFORE... AT LEAST, SOMEONE WHO FOUGHT WITHOUT A SHIELD LIKE THAT...
KYA
BUT... WHAT WAS HIS NAME...?
H
H
AAAAAH
LOOK AT HIM!!
WHAT'S HE DOING?! DOES HE *WANT* TO DIE?!
A
AND WHY DOESN'T ANYONE ATTACK HIM?!
R A
WE JUST WANT HIM TO *LOSE* ALREADY!!
BOO BOO
RAAAAAAHH
...
BO—OM!
RAHH
YAAH
HEH HA HA.

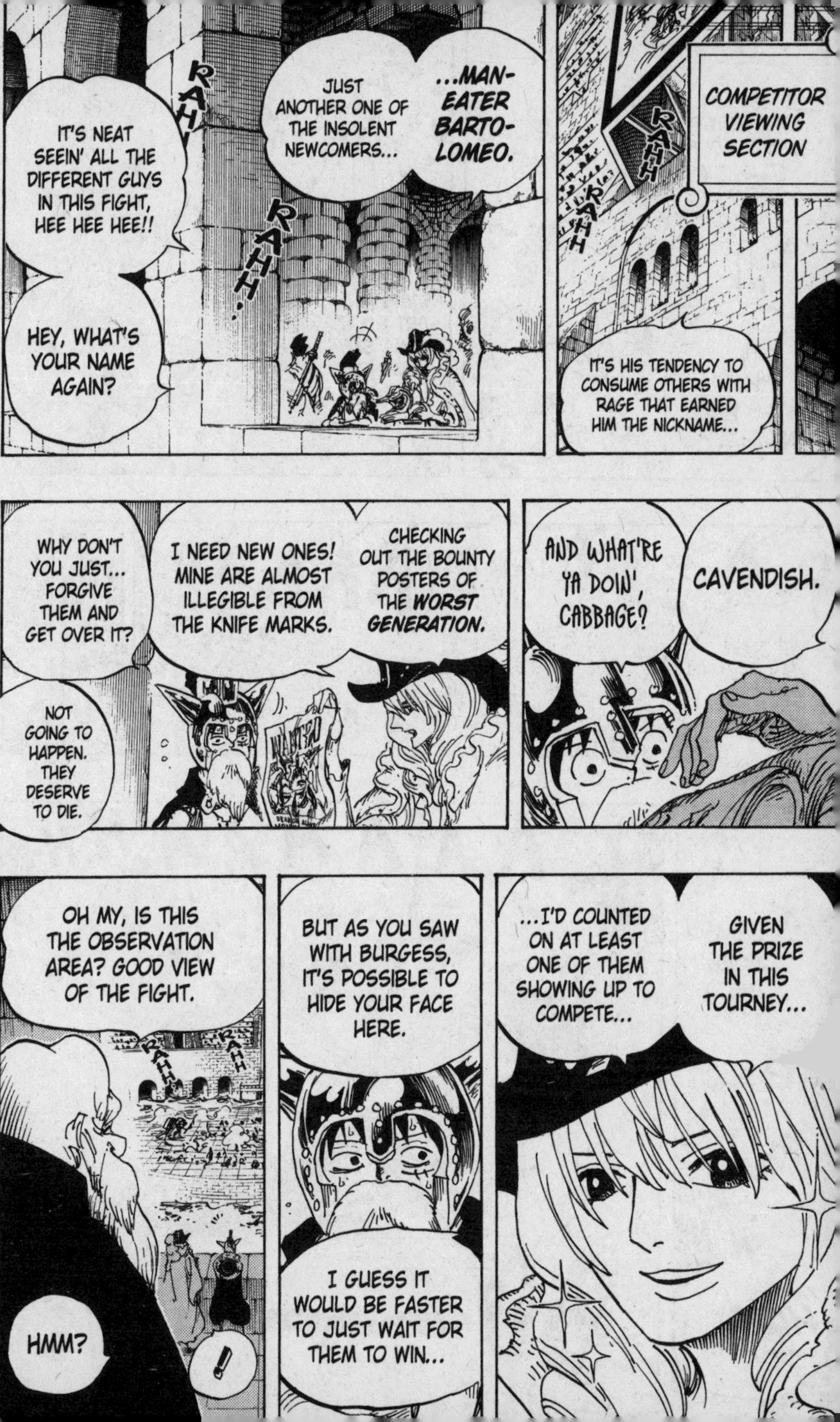
COMPETITOR VIEWING SECTION
RAHH
RAHH
IT'S HIS TENDENCY TO CONSUME OTHERS WITH RAGE THAT EARNED HIM THE NICKNAME...
...MAN-EATER BARTO-LOMEO.
JUST ANOTHER ONE OF THE INSOLENT NEWCOMERS...
RAH!
RAHH!
IT'S NEAT SEEIN' ALL THE DIFFERENT GUYS IN THIS FIGHT, HEE HEE HEE!!
HEY, WHAT'S YOUR NAME AGAIN?
CAVENDISH.
AND WHAT'RE YA DOIN', CABBAGE?
CHECKING OUT THE BOUNTY POSTERS OF THE WORST GENERATION.
I NEED NEW ONES! MINE ARE ALMOST ILLEGIBLE FROM THE KNIFE MARKS.
WHY DON'T YOU JUST... FORGIVE THEM AND GET OVER IT?
NOT GOING TO HAPPEN. THEY DESERVE TO DIE.
GIVEN THE PRIZE IN THIS TOURNEY...
...I'D COUNTED ON AT LEAST ONE OF THEM SHOWING UP TO COMPETE...
BUT AS YOU SAW WITH BURGESS, IT'S POSSIBLE TO HIDE YOUR FACE HERE.
I GUESS IT WOULD BE FASTER TO JUST WAIT FOR THEM TO WIN...
OH MY, IS THIS THE OBSERVATION AREA? GOOD VIEW OF THE FIGHT.
RAHH
RAHH
HMM?
!

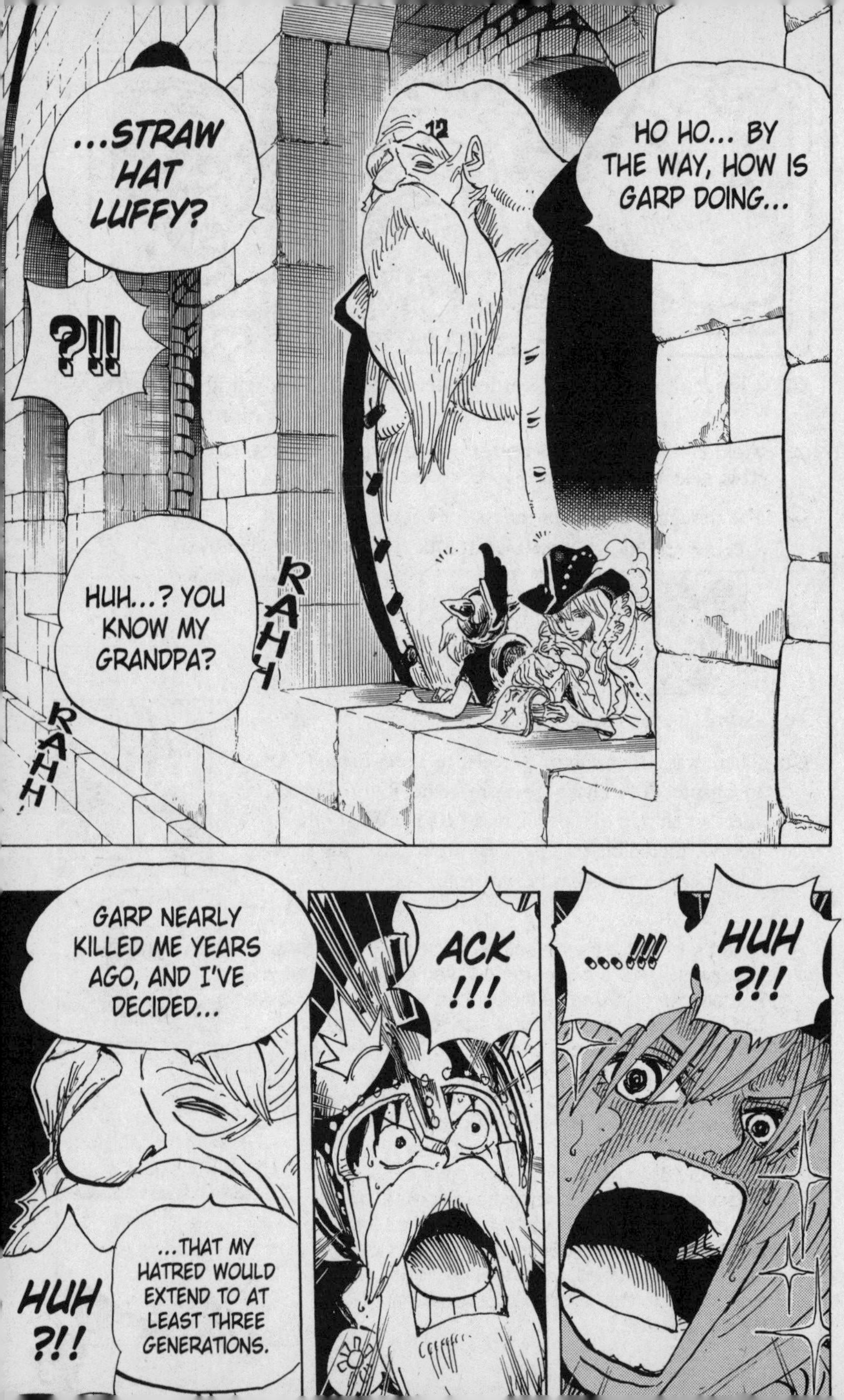
HO HO... BY THE WAY, HOW IS GARP DOING...
...STRAW HAT LUFFY?
?!!
HUH...? YOU KNOW MY GRANDPA?
RAHH
RAHH
HUH ?!!
...!!!
ACK !!!
GARP NEARLY KILLED ME YEARS AGO, AND I'VE DECIDED...
...THAT MY HATRED WOULD EXTEND TO AT LEAST THREE GENERATIONS.
HUH ?!!

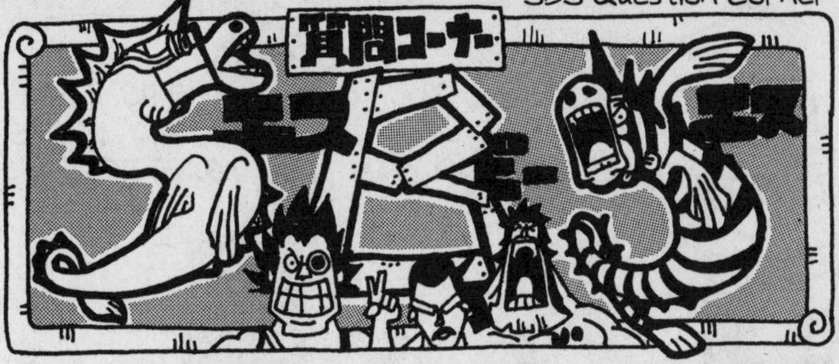
質問コーナー

(Haru, Nagano)

Q: Odacchi, did you eat some toilet paper this morning?

--Haribo Monet

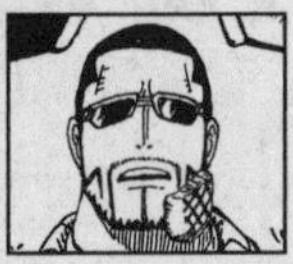

A: Ack!⁉ There's leftover toilet paper stuck on the side of my mouth!⁉ Excuse me.

Q: I've thought of some birthdays for Caesar and Monet!

Caesar: April 9th **Monet: August 27th**

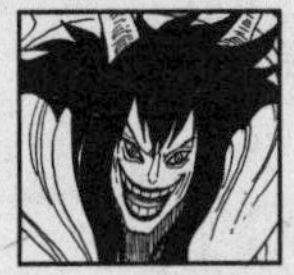

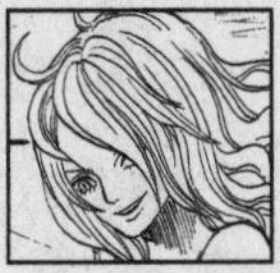

How's that? Is that okay?

--Nakamurider

A: Sure. (picks nose)

Q: There was a mention of a freelance writer named "Absa" in Chapter 700. That's Absalom, right? Right? I mean, there's a ship in that panel, right? Right? What other pervy…incredible scoops, what pervy…moving stories, what pervy articles has he written?

--Makino♡Love

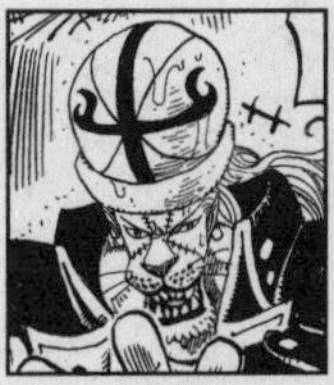

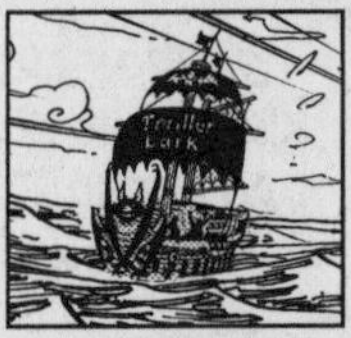

A: That's right, it's Absalom. Doesn't it bring you back? As a matter of fact, he was at the Paramount War. After the battle was over, Doflamingo mentioned something about Moria meeting a strange fate. Why was that, do you suppose? I'm worried about Perona too. Did Moria really die? All we can confirm at this time is that Absalom is using his Clear-Clear Fruit to provide the world with major scoops under the penname "Absa." I'm sure he gets all kinds of pictures. It seems the menfolk enjoy his articles quite a bit. Well, enough of this edition of the Perv-BS! See you next volume!!

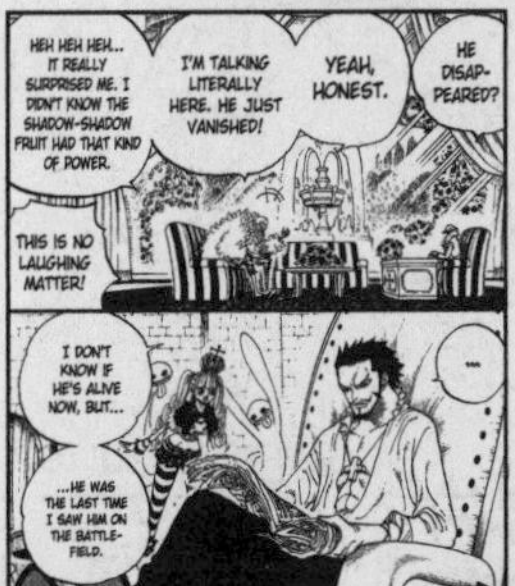
HE DISAP-PEARED?
YEAH, HONEST.
I'M TALKING LITERALLY HERE. HE JUST VANISHED!
HEH HEH HEH… IT REALLY SURPRISED ME. I DIDN'T KNOW THE SHADOW-SHADOW FRUIT HAD THAT KIND OF POWER.
THIS IS NO LAUGHING MATTER!
…
I DON'T KNOW IF HE'S ALIVE NOW, BUT…
…HE WAS THE LAST TIME I SAW HIM ON THE BATTLE-FIELD.

Chapter 708: COLISEUM OF SCOUNDRELS

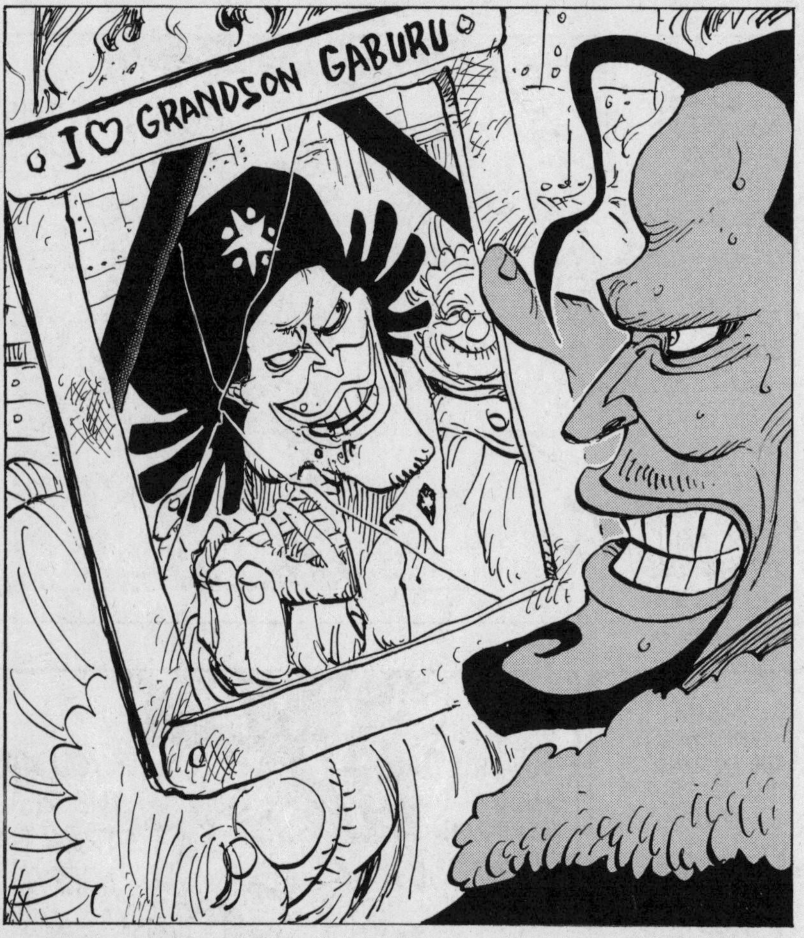
I ♡ GRANDSON GABURU

CARIBOU'S NEW WORLD KEEHEEHEE, VOL. 27 "THE HAG'S DEAD GRANDSON WAS MEAT-PIE-LOVING COMMANDER GABURU"

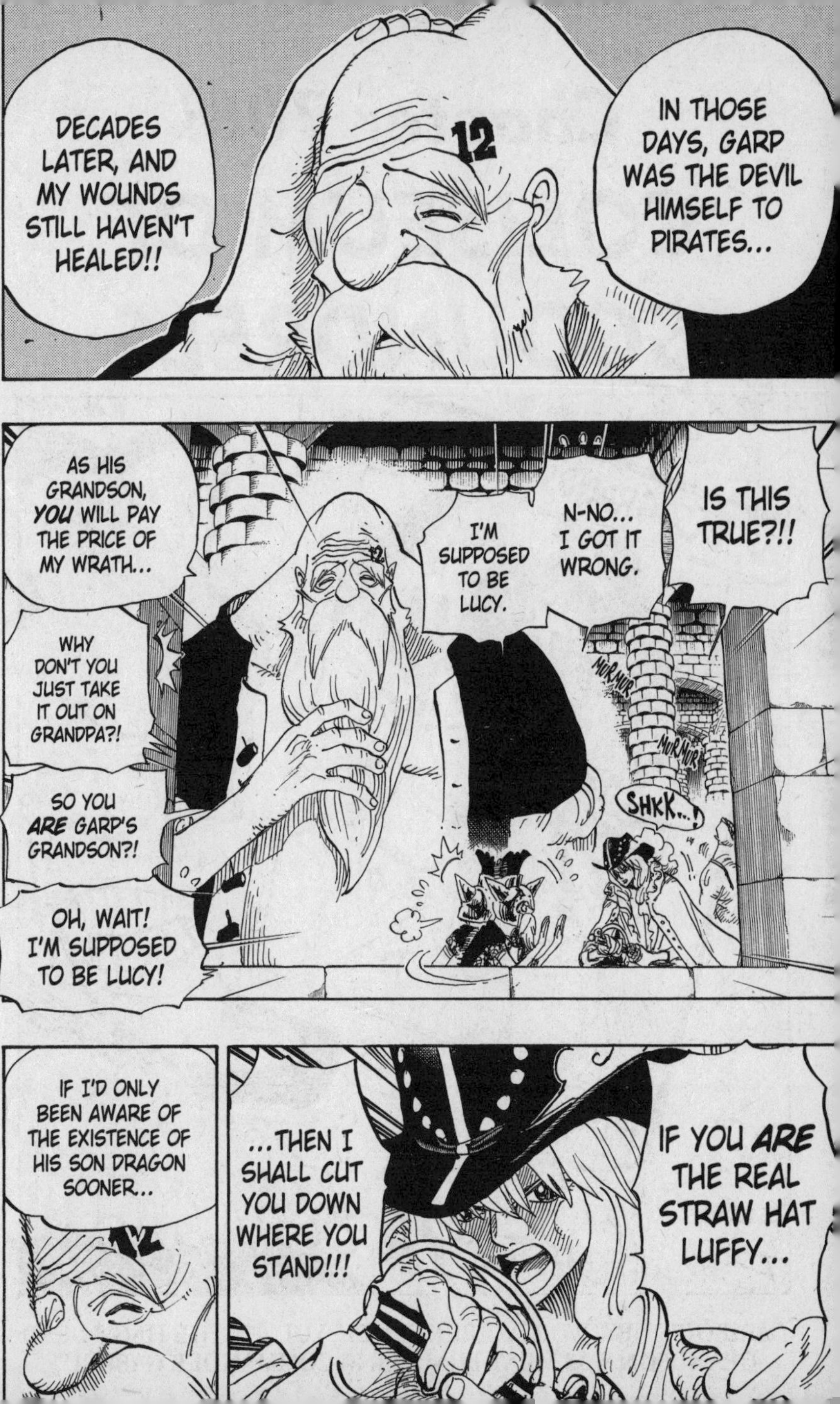
IN THOSE DAYS, GARP WAS THE DEVIL HIMSELF TO PIRATES...
DECADES LATER, AND MY WOUNDS STILL HAVEN'T HEALED!!
IS THIS TRUE?!!
N-NO... I GOT IT WRONG.
I'M SUPPOSED TO BE LUCY.
AS HIS GRANDSON, *YOU* WILL PAY THE PRICE OF MY WRATH...
MURMUR
MURMUR
WHY DON'T YOU JUST TAKE IT OUT ON GRANDPA?!
SHKK...!
SO YOU *ARE* GARP'S GRANDSON?!
OH, WAIT! I'M SUPPOSED TO BE LUCY!
IF YOU *ARE* THE REAL STRAW HAT LUFFY...
...THEN I SHALL CUT YOU DOWN WHERE YOU STAND!!!
IF I'D ONLY BEEN AWARE OF THE EXISTENCE OF HIS SON DRAGON SOONER...

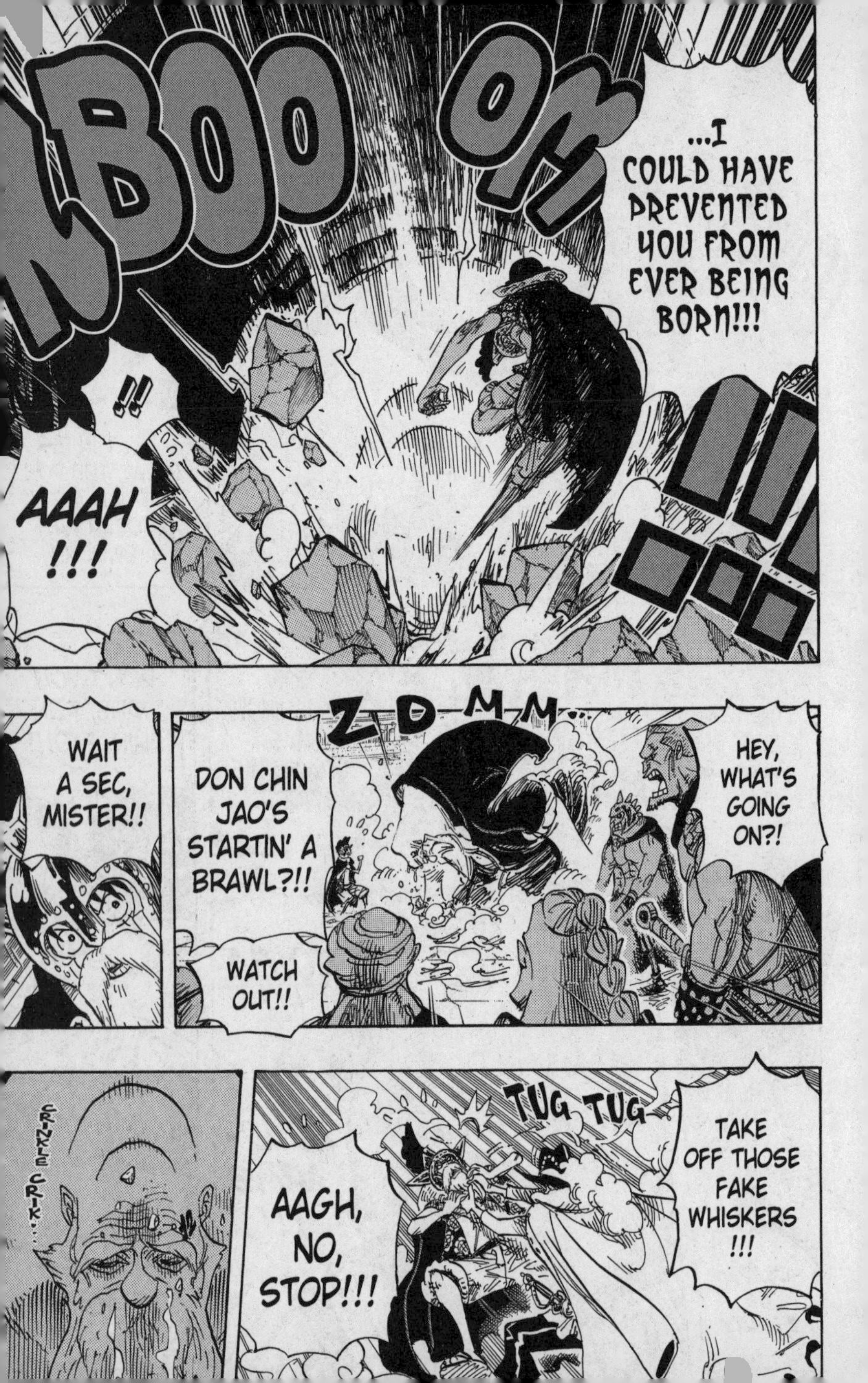

...I COULD HAVE PREVENTED YOU FROM EVER BEING BORN!!!
BOOOM
!!
AAAH !!!
ZDMM..
HEY, WHAT'S GOING ON?!
DON CHIN JAO'S STARTIN' A BRAWL?!!
WATCH OUT!!
WAIT A SEC, MISTER!!
TUG TUG
TAKE OFF THOSE FAKE WHISKERS !!!
AAGH, NO, STOP!!!
CRINKLE CRIK...

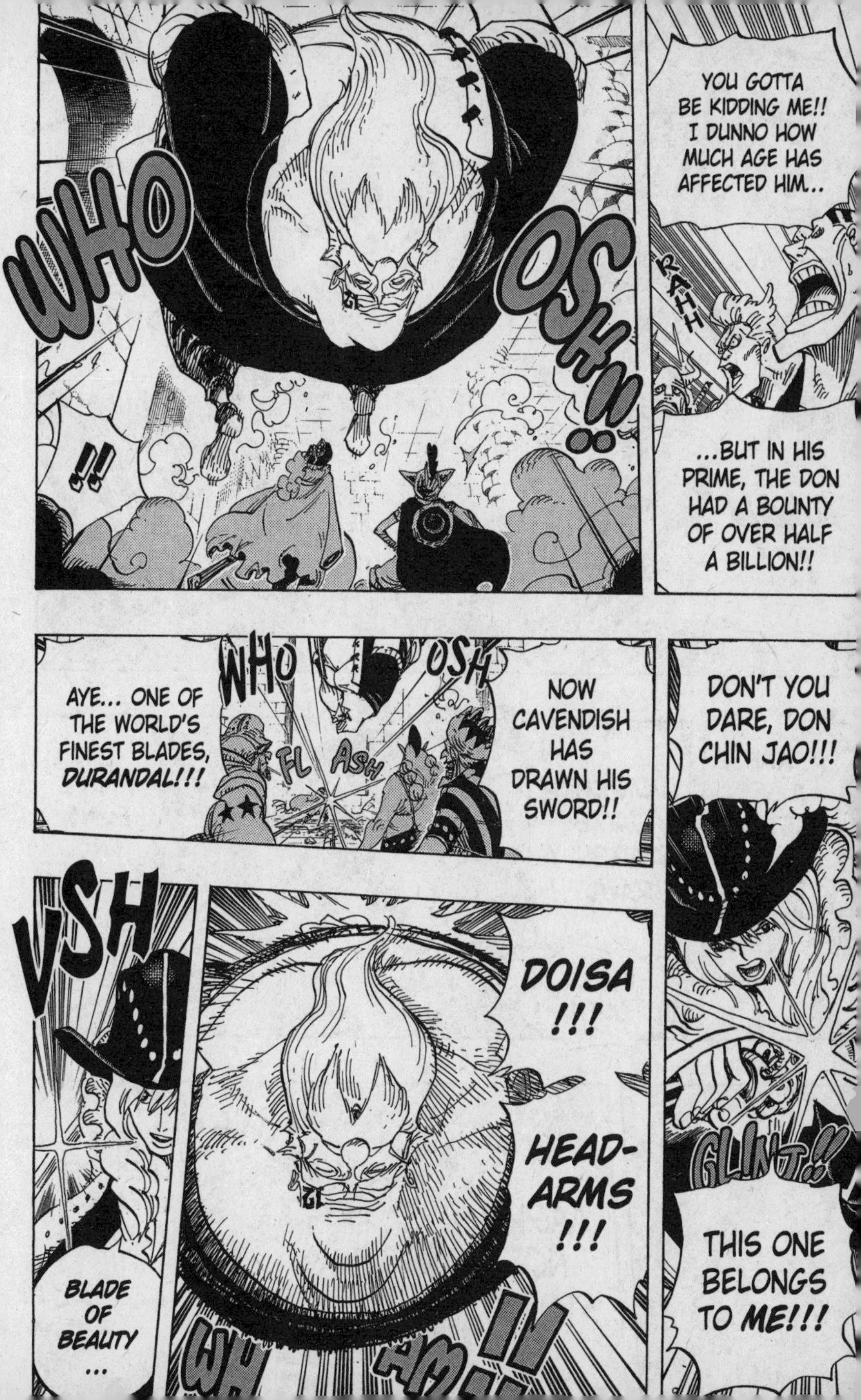

YOU GOTTA BE KIDDING ME!! I DUNNO HOW MUCH AGE HAS AFFECTED HIM...
RAHH
...BUT IN HIS PRIME, THE DON HAD A BOUNTY OF OVER HALF A BILLION!!
WHOOSH!!
!!
DON'T YOU DARE, DON CHIN JAO!!!
GLINT!!
THIS ONE BELONGS TO ME!!!
NOW CAVENDISH HAS DRAWN HIS SWORD!!
WHOOSH
FLASH
AYE... ONE OF THE WORLD'S FINEST BLADES, DURANDAL!!!
DOISA!!!
HEAD-ARMS!!!
VSH
BLADE OF BEAUTY ...

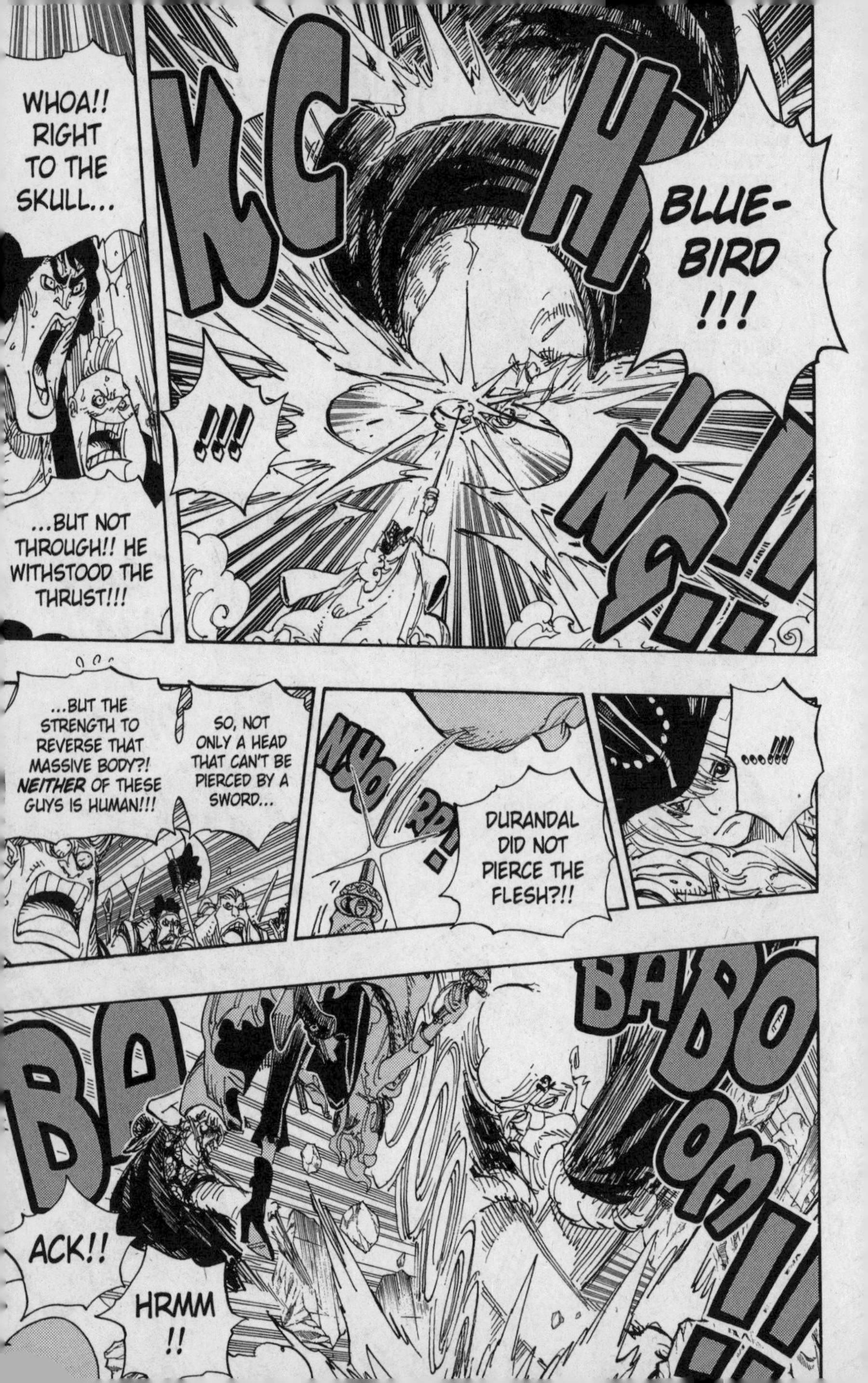
KCHIIING!!
BLUE-BIRD!!!
!!!
WHOA!! RIGHT TO THE SKULL...
...BUT NOT THROUGH!! HE WITHSTOOD THE THRUST!!!
...!!!
NUORP!!
DURANDAL DID NOT PIERCE THE FLESH?!!
SO, NOT ONLY A HEAD THAT CAN'T BE PIERCED BY A SWORD...
...BUT THE STRENGTH TO REVERSE THAT MASSIVE BODY?! *NEITHER* OF THESE GUYS IS HUMAN!!!
BABOOM!!
BA
ACK!!
HRMM!!

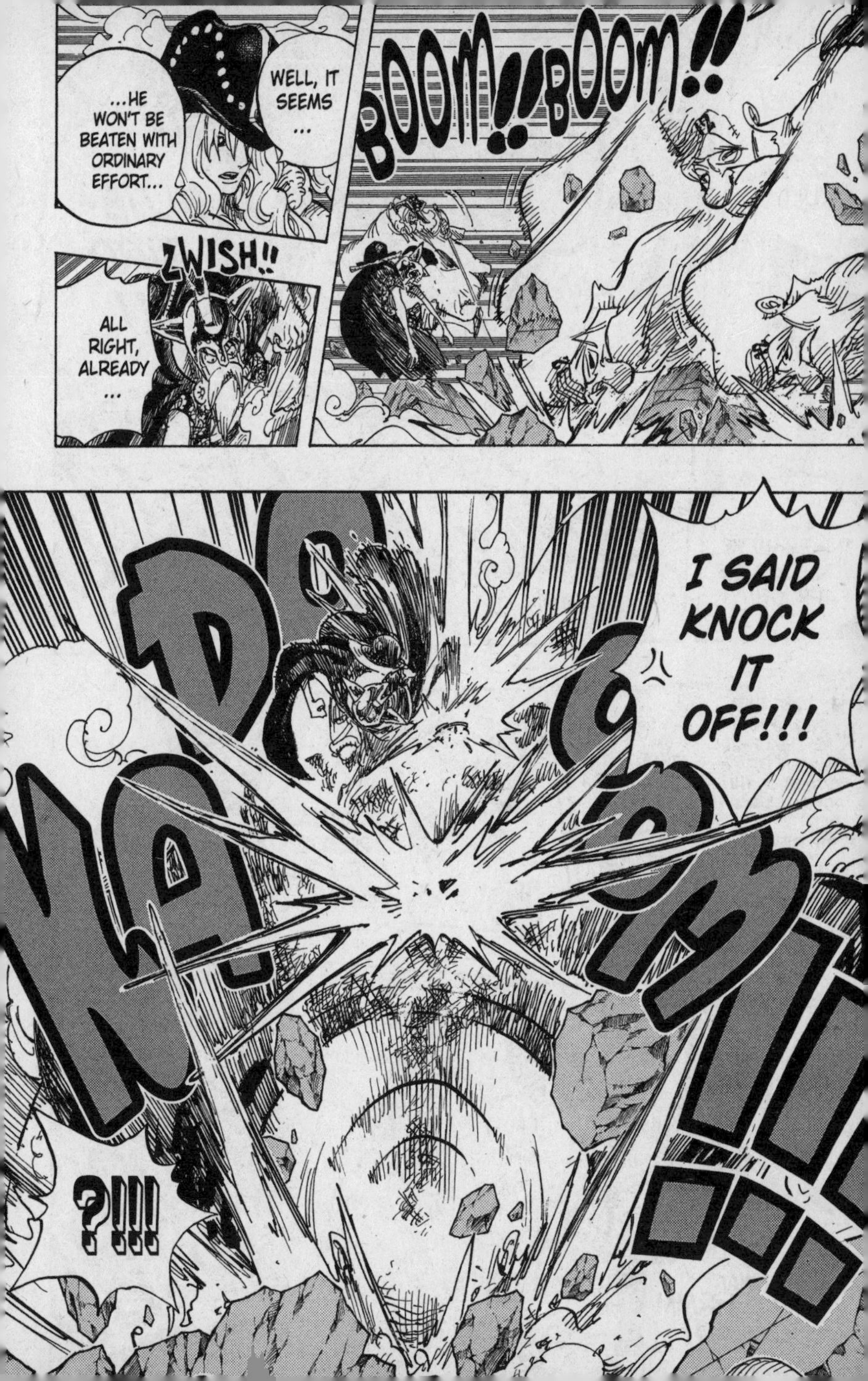
BOOM!! BOOM!!
WELL, IT SEEMS ...
...HE WON'T BE BEATEN WITH ORDINARY EFFORT...
ZWISH!!
ALL RIGHT, ALREADY ...
I SAID KNOCK IT OFF!!!
?!!!

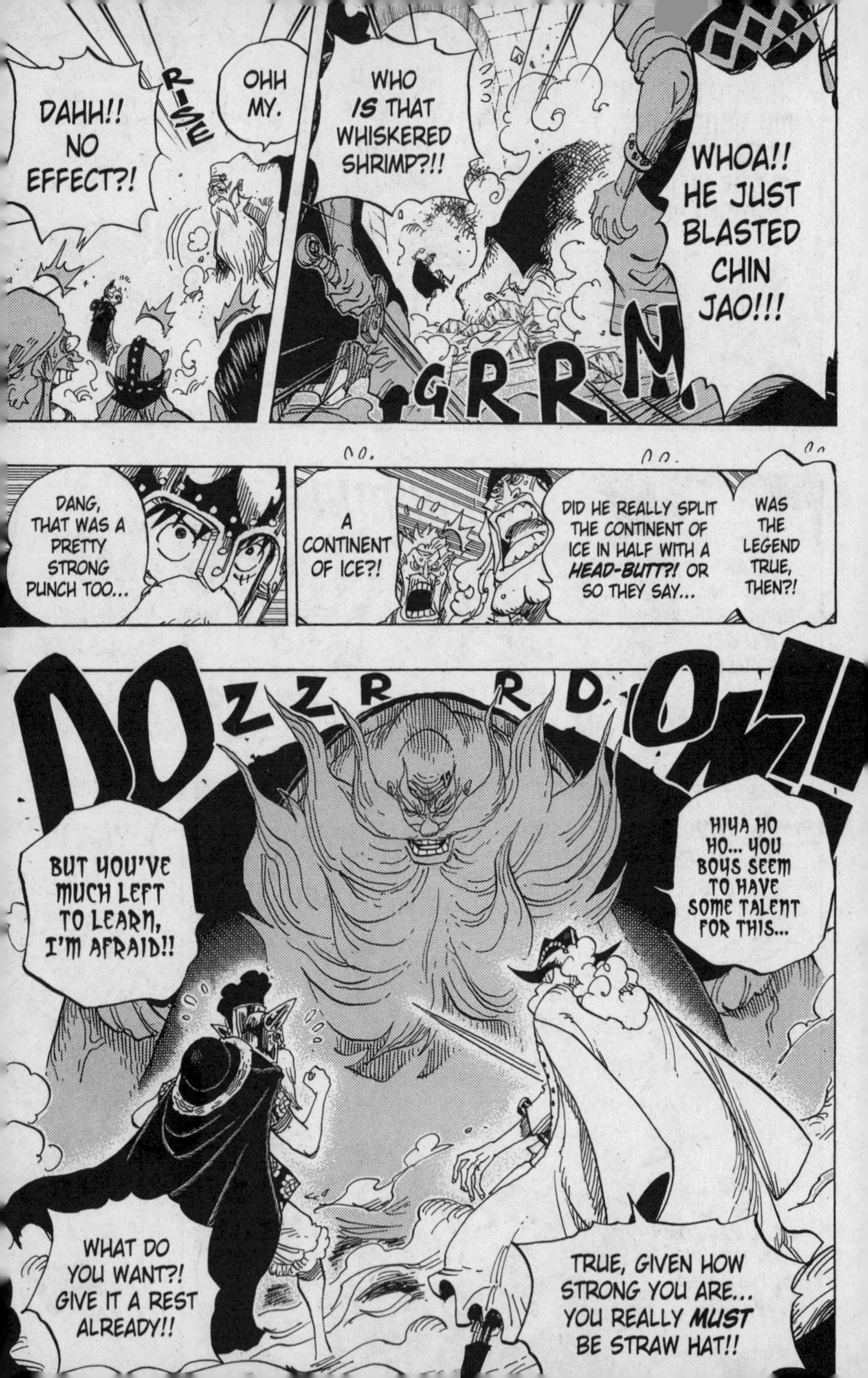

WHO IS THAT WHISKERED SHRIMP?!!
WHOA!! HE JUST BLASTED CHIN JAO!!!
GRRRM.
OHH MY.
RISE
DAHH!! NO EFFECT?!
WAS THE LEGEND TRUE, THEN?!
DID HE REALLY SPLIT THE CONTINENT OF ICE IN HALF WITH A HEAD-BUTT?! OR SO THEY SAY...
A CONTINENT OF ICE?!
DANG, THAT WAS A PRETTY STRONG PUNCH TOO...
DOZZRRDOM!!
HIYA HO HO... YOU BOYS SEEM TO HAVE SOME TALENT FOR THIS...
BUT YOU'VE MUCH LEFT TO LEARN, I'M AFRAID!!
TRUE, GIVEN HOW STRONG YOU ARE... YOU REALLY MUST BE STRAW HAT!!
WHAT DO YOU WANT?! GIVE IT A REST ALREADY!!

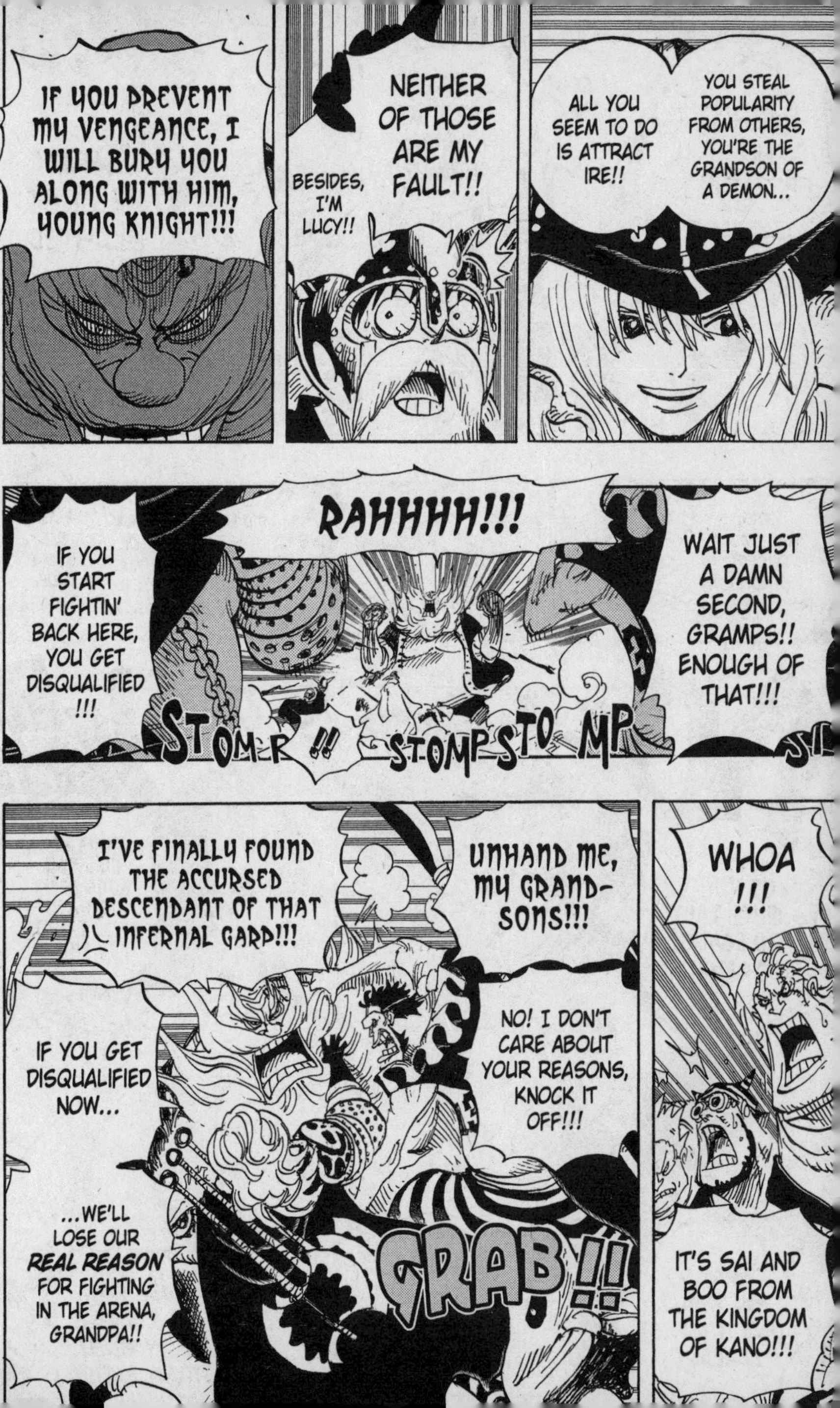
YOU STEAL POPULARITY FROM OTHERS, YOU'RE THE GRANDSON OF A DEMON...
ALL YOU SEEM TO DO IS ATTRACT IRE!!
NEITHER OF THOSE ARE MY FAULT!!
BESIDES, I'M LUCY!!
IF YOU PREVENT MY VENGEANCE, I WILL BURY YOU ALONG WITH HIM, YOUNG KNIGHT!!!
RAHHHH!!!
WAIT JUST A DAMN SECOND, GRAMPS!! ENOUGH OF THAT!!!
IF YOU START FIGHTIN' BACK HERE, YOU GET DISQUALIFIED!!!
STOMP STOMP
STOMP!!
WHOA!!!
IT'S SAI AND BOO FROM THE KINGDOM OF KANO!!!
UNHAND ME, MY GRANDSONS!!!
I'VE FINALLY FOUND THE ACCURSED DESCENDANT OF THAT INFERNAL GARP!!!
NO! I DON'T CARE ABOUT YOUR REASONS, KNOCK IT OFF!!!
IF YOU GET DISQUALIFIED NOW...
GRAB!!
...WE'LL LOSE OUR REAL REASON FOR FIGHTING IN THE ARENA, GRANDPA!!

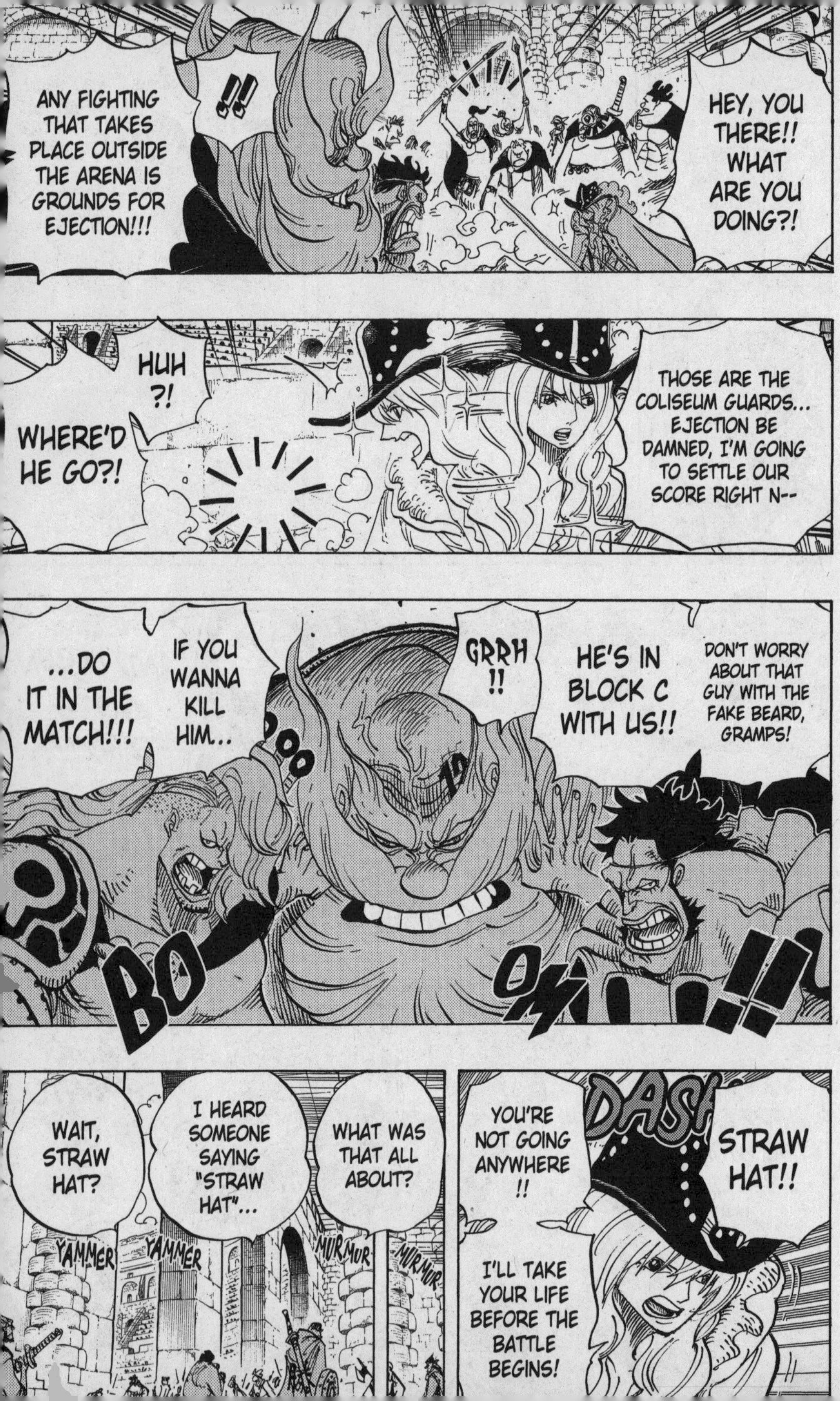
HEY, YOU THERE!! WHAT ARE YOU DOING?!
!!
ANY FIGHTING THAT TAKES PLACE OUTSIDE THE ARENA IS GROUNDS FOR EJECTION!!!
THOSE ARE THE COLISEUM GUARDS... EJECTION BE DAMNED, I'M GOING TO SETTLE OUR SCORE RIGHT N--
HUH ?!
WHERE'D HE GO?!
DON'T WORRY ABOUT THAT GUY WITH THE FAKE BEARD, GRAMPS!
HE'S IN BLOCK C WITH US!!
GRRH !!
IF YOU WANNA KILL HIM...
...DO IT IN THE MATCH!!!
BO
OM!!
DASH
STRAW HAT!!
YOU'RE NOT GOING ANYWHERE !!
I'LL TAKE YOUR LIFE BEFORE THE BATTLE BEGINS!
WHAT WAS THAT ALL ABOUT?
MURMUR
MURMUR
I HEARD SOMEONE SAYING "STRAW HAT"...
WAIT, STRAW HAT?
YAMMER
YAMMER

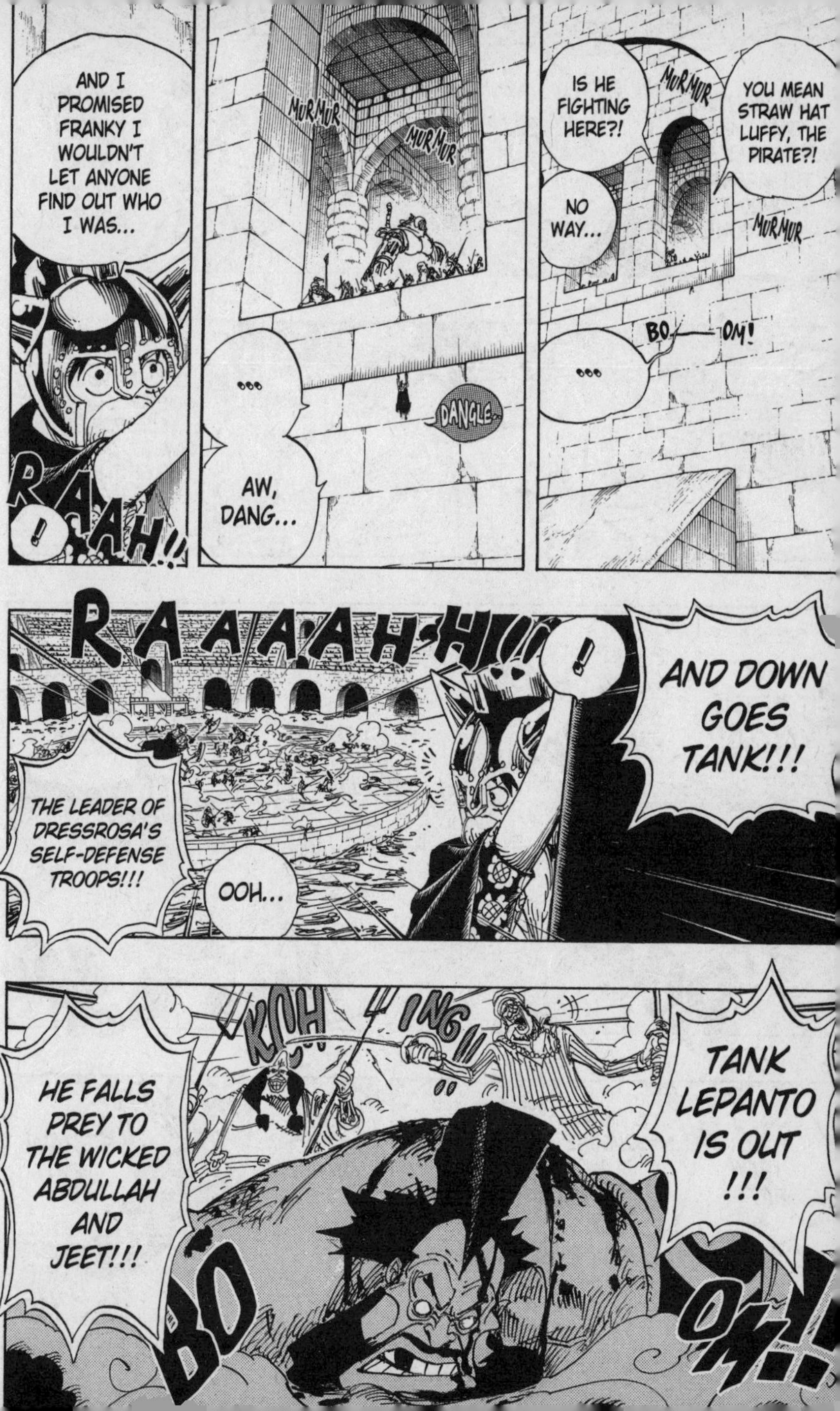

MURMUR
YOU MEAN STRAW HAT LUFFY, THE PIRATE?!
IS HE FIGHTING HERE?!
MURMUR
MURMUR
NO WAY...
BO—OM!
...
MURMUR
MURMUR
...
DANGLE
AW, DANG...
AND I PROMISED FRANKY I WOULDN'T LET ANYONE FIND OUT WHO I WAS...
RAAH!!
!
AND DOWN GOES TANK!!!
!
RAAAAH!!
OOH...
THE LEADER OF DRESSROSA'S SELF-DEFENSE TROOPS!!!
TANK LEPANTO IS OUT !!!
KCH
ING!!
HE FALLS PREY TO THE WICKED ABDULLAH AND JEET!!!
BO
OM!!

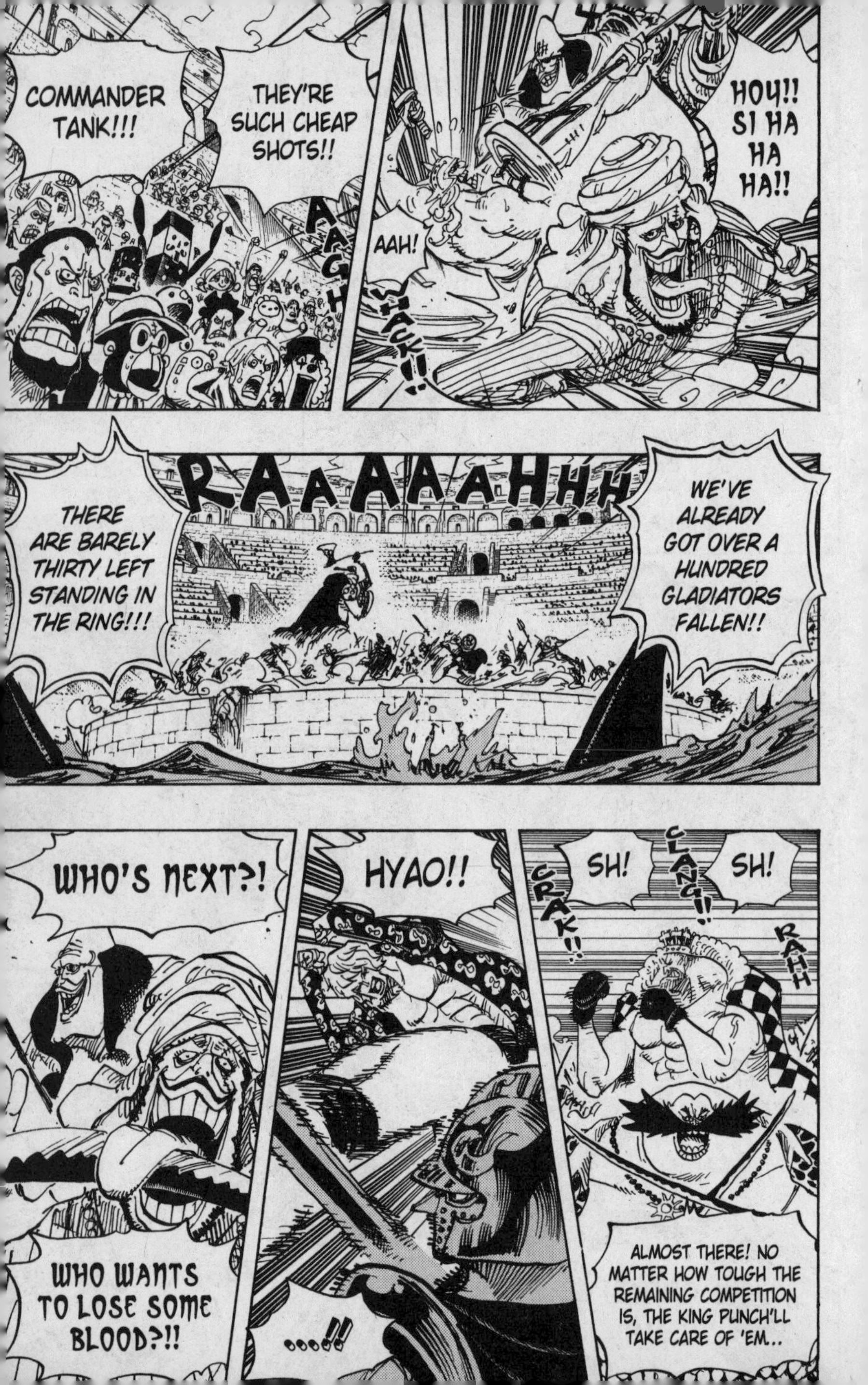
HOY!! SI HA HA HA!!
AAH!
WHACK!!
THEY'RE SUCH CHEAP SHOTS!!
COMMANDER TANK!!!
AAGH
WE'VE ALREADY GOT OVER A HUNDRED GLADIATORS FALLEN!!
RAAAAAHHH
THERE ARE BARELY THIRTY LEFT STANDING IN THE RING!!!
SH!
CLANG!!
SH!
CRAK!!
RAHH
ALMOST THERE! NO MATTER HOW TOUGH THE REMAINING COMPETITION IS, THE KING PUNCH'LL TAKE CARE OF 'EM..
HYAO!!
....!!
WHO'S NEXT?!
WHO WANTS TO LOSE SOME BLOOD?!!

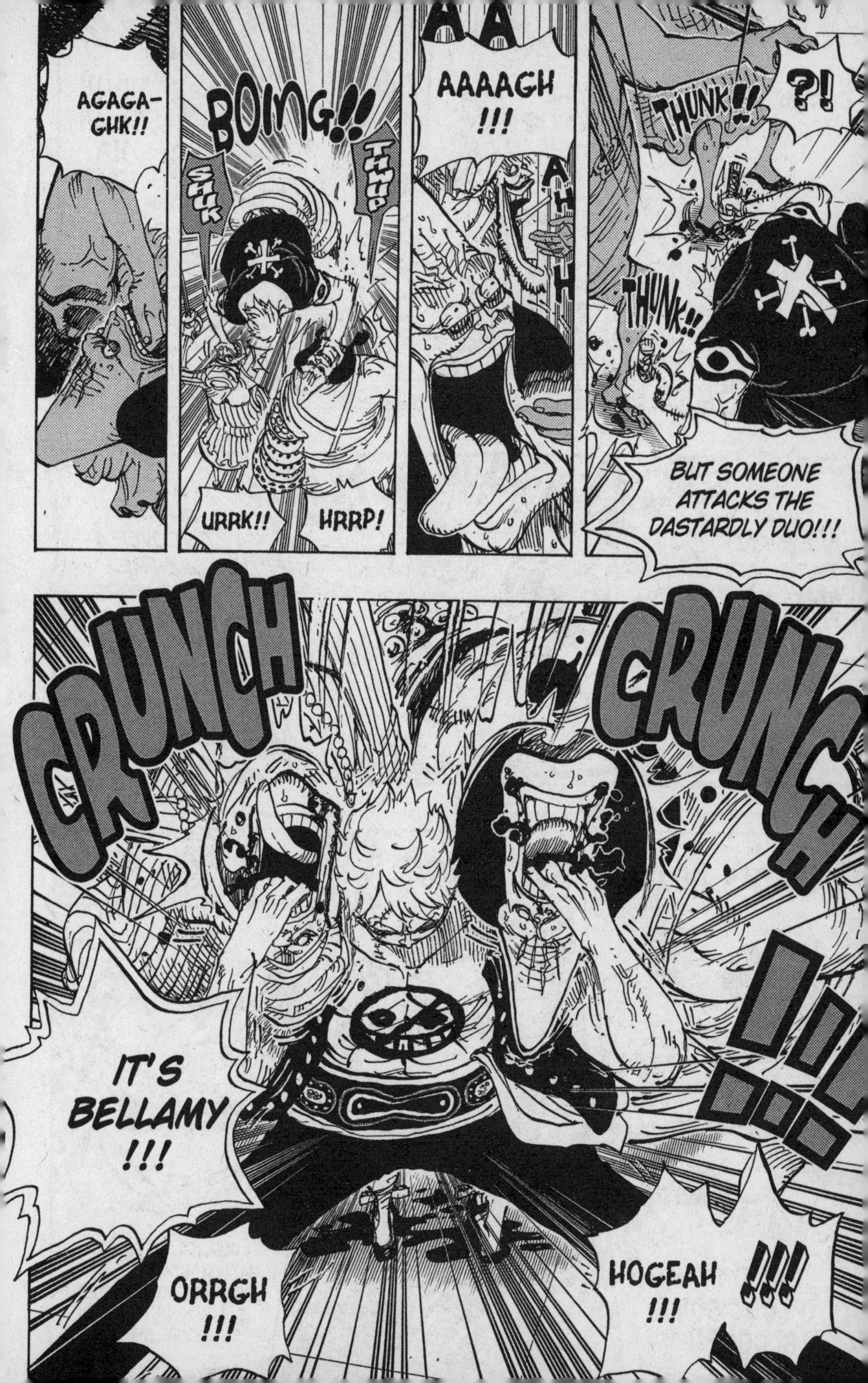
?!
THUNK!!
THUNK!!
BUT SOMEONE ATTACKS THE DASTARDLY DUO!!!
AA
AAAAGH !!!
AHH
BOING!!
THWUD
SHUK
HRRP!
URRK!!
AGAGA-GHK!!
CRUNCH
CRUNCH
!!!
HOGEAH !!!
!!!
IT'S BELLAMY !!!
ORRGH !!!

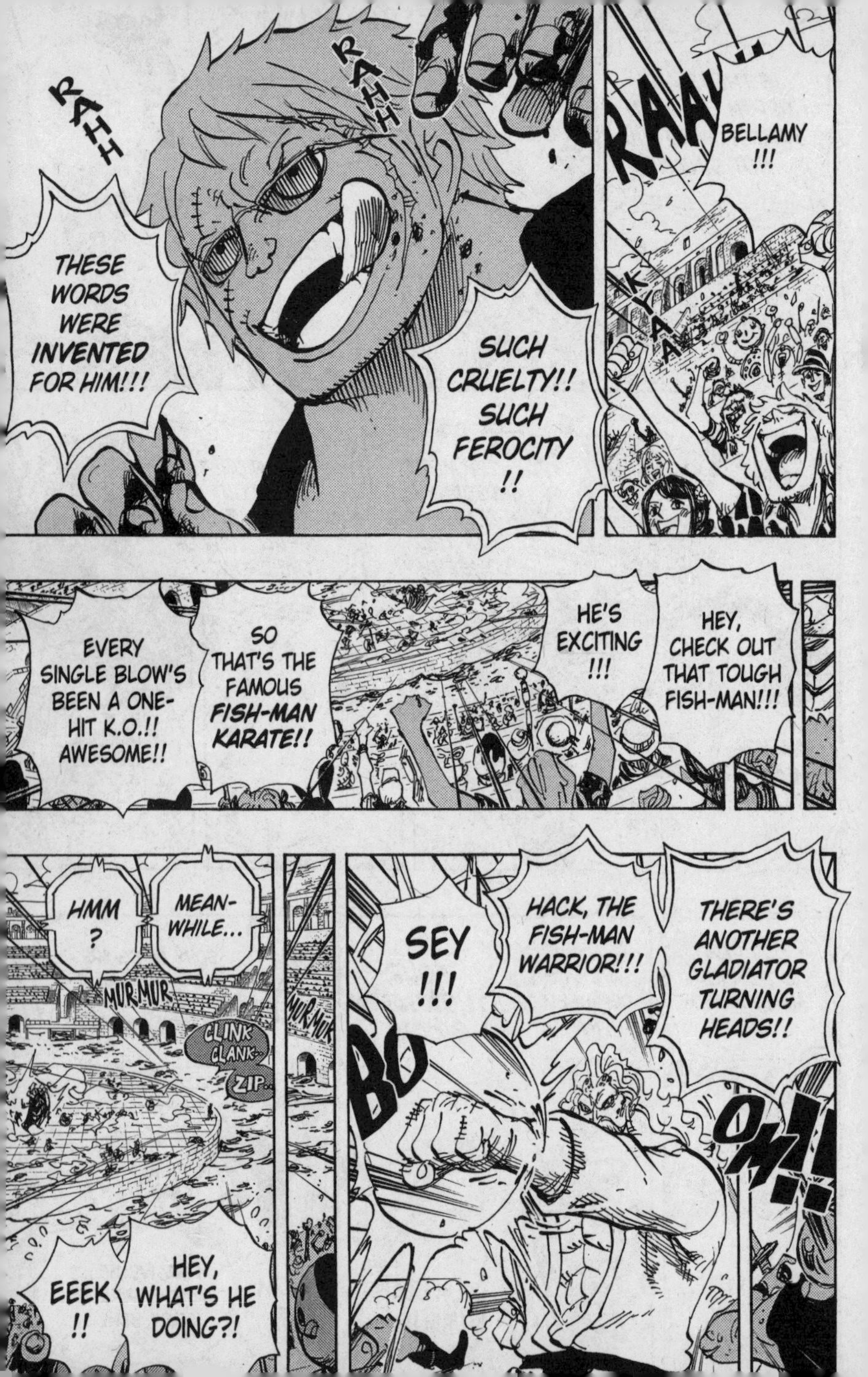
BELLAMY!!!
KYAA
RAHH
SUCH CRUELTY!! SUCH FEROCITY!!
RAHH
THESE WORDS WERE INVENTED FOR HIM!!!
HEY, CHECK OUT THAT TOUGH FISH-MAN!!!
HE'S EXCITING!!!
SO THAT'S THE FAMOUS FISH-MAN KARATE!!
EVERY SINGLE BLOW'S BEEN A ONE-HIT K.O.!! AWESOME!!
THERE'S ANOTHER GLADIATOR TURNING HEADS!!
HACK, THE FISH-MAN WARRIOR!!!
SEY!!!
OH!!
BO
MUR MUR
MEAN-WHILE...
HMM?
MUR MUR
CLINK CLANK..
ZIP..
HEY, WHAT'S HE DOING?!
EEEK!!

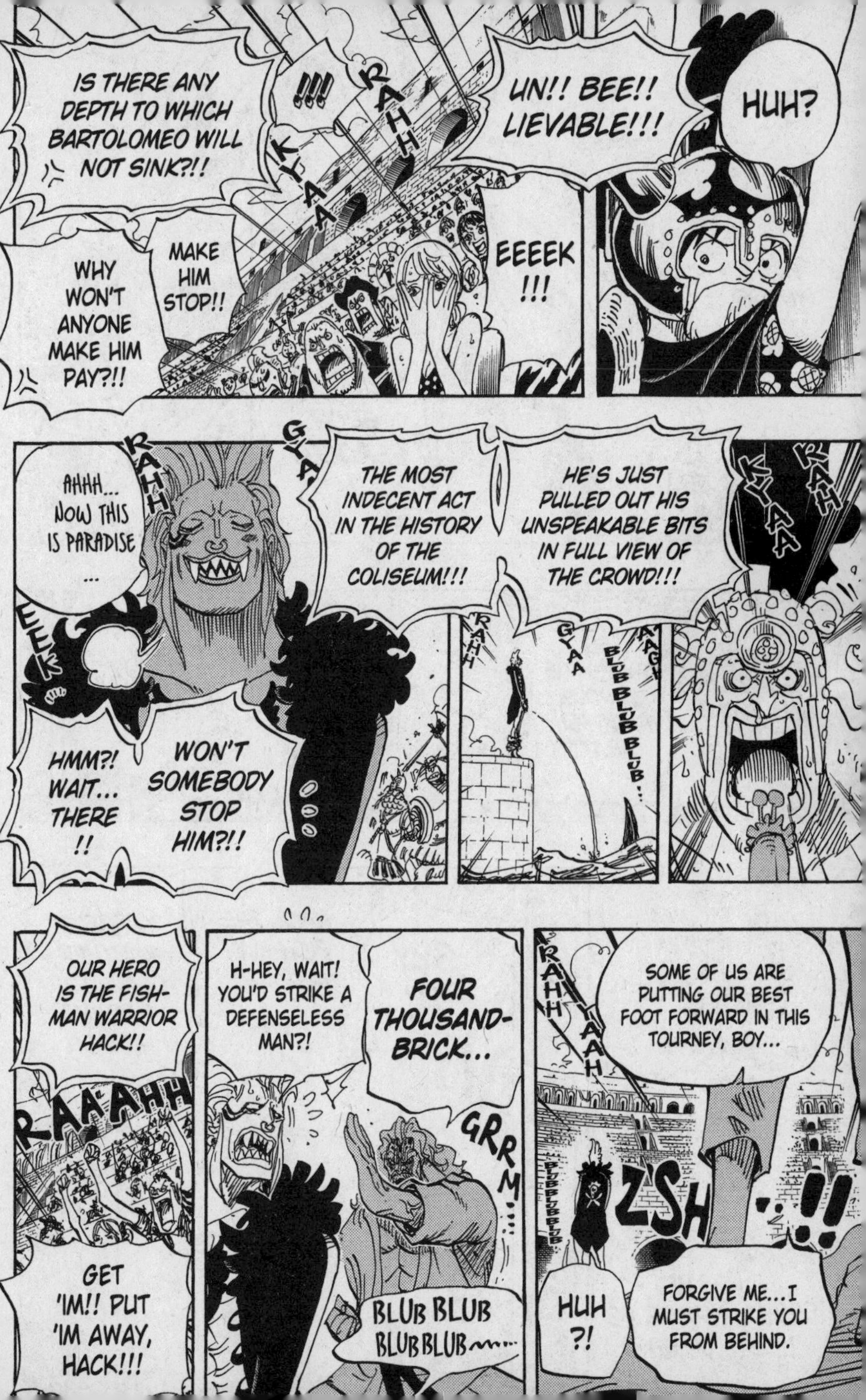
HUH?
UN!! BEE!! LIEVABLE!!!
RAHH
!!!
KYAA
IS THERE ANY DEPTH TO WHICH BARTOLOMEO WILL NOT SINK?!!
EEEEK !!!
MAKE HIM STOP!!
WHY WON'T ANYONE MAKE HIM PAY?!!
KYAA
RAHH
HE'S JUST PULLED OUT HIS UNSPEAKABLE BITS IN FULL VIEW OF THE CROWD!!!
AAGH
GYAA
RAHH
BLUB BLUB BLUB BLUB...
THE MOST INDECENT ACT IN THE HISTORY OF THE COLISEUM!!!
GYAA
RAHH
AHHH... NOW THIS IS PARADISE ...
EEEK
WON'T SOMEBODY STOP HIM?!!
HMM?! WAIT... THERE !!
SOME OF US ARE PUTTING OUR BEST FOOT FORWARD IN THIS TOURNEY, BOY...
RAHH
YAAAH
BLUBBLUBBLUB
Z'SH
..!!
FORGIVE ME...I MUST STRIKE YOU FROM BEHIND.
HUH ?!
FOUR THOUSAND-BRICK...
H-HEY, WAIT! YOU'D STRIKE A DEFENSELESS MAN?!
GRRM...
BLUB BLUB BLUB BLUB~~...
OUR HERO IS THE FISH-MAN WARRIOR HACK!!
RAAAHH
GET 'IM!! PUT 'IM AWAY, HACK!!!

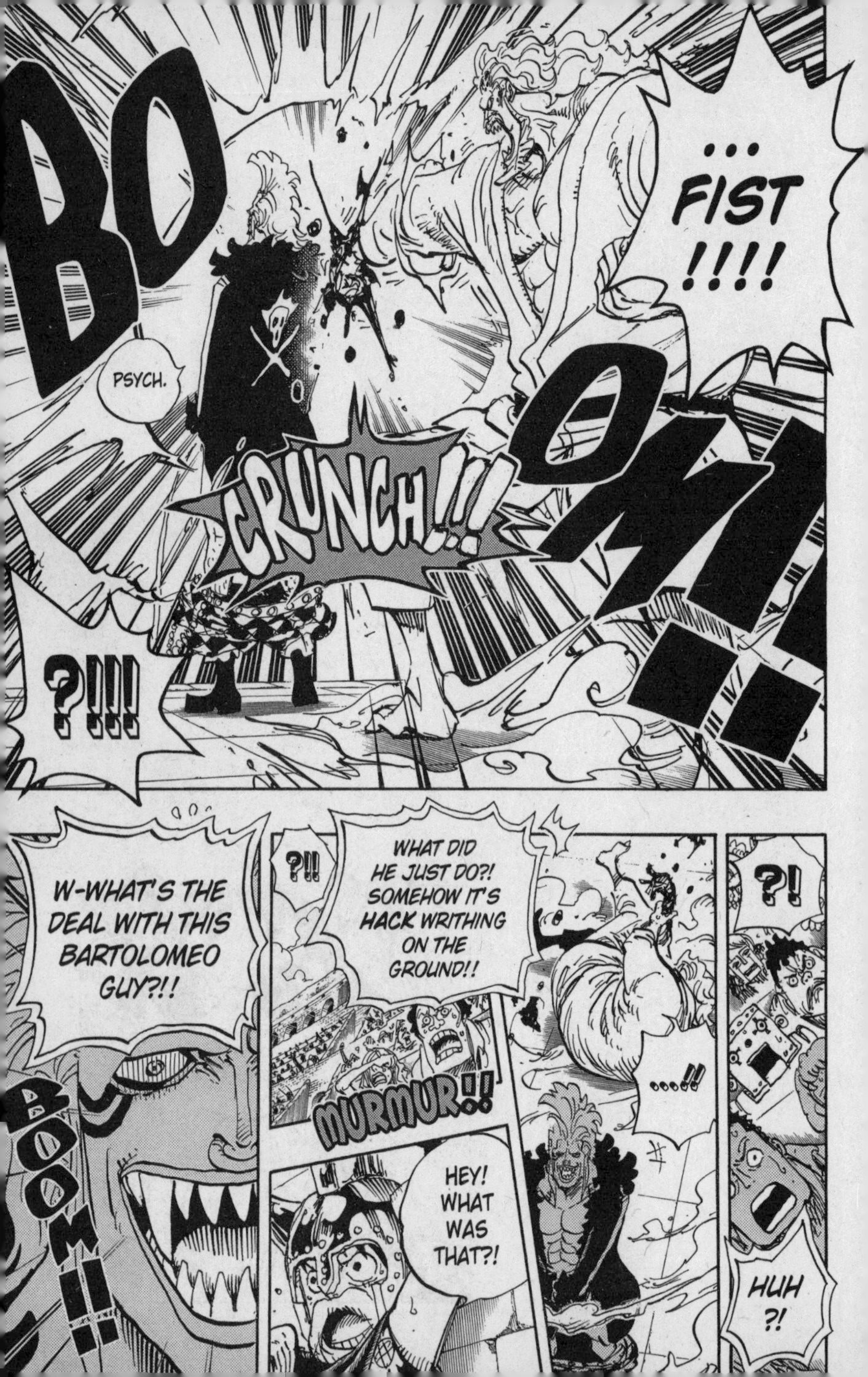
...FIST !!!!
BO
OM!!
PSYCH.
CRUNCH!!!
?!!!
?!
HUH ?!
WHAT DID HE JUST DO?! SOMEHOW IT'S HACK WRITHING ON THE GROUND!!
...!!
?!!
MURMUR!!
HEY! WHAT WAS THAT?!
W-WHAT'S THE DEAL WITH THIS BARTOLOMEO GUY?!!
BOOM!!

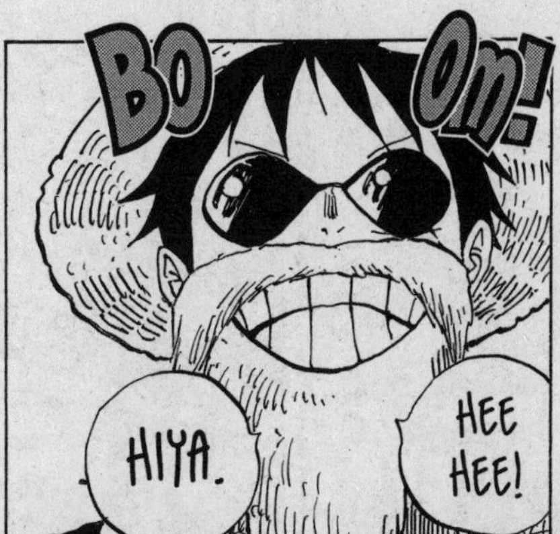
BOOM!
HIYA.
HEE HEE!

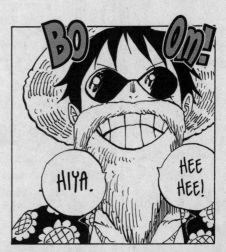

Chapter 709:
KING PUNCH!!

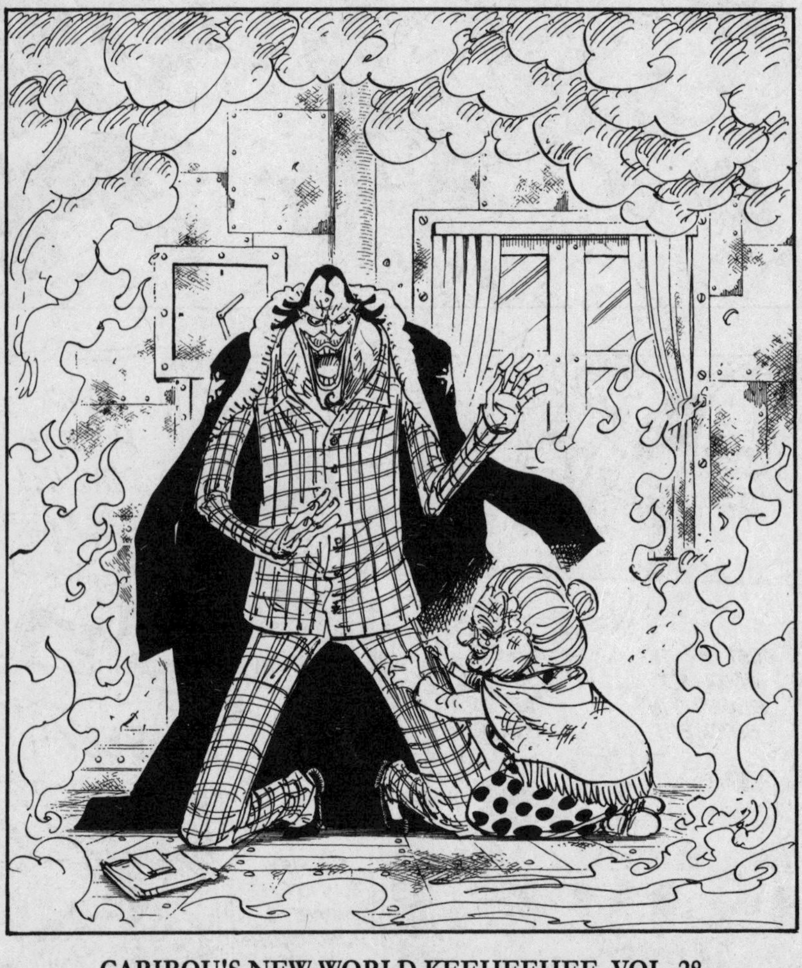

CARIBOU'S NEW WORLD KEEHEEHEE, VOL. 28
"JUST RUN GABURU, YOU MUSTN'T FIGHT ANYMORE"

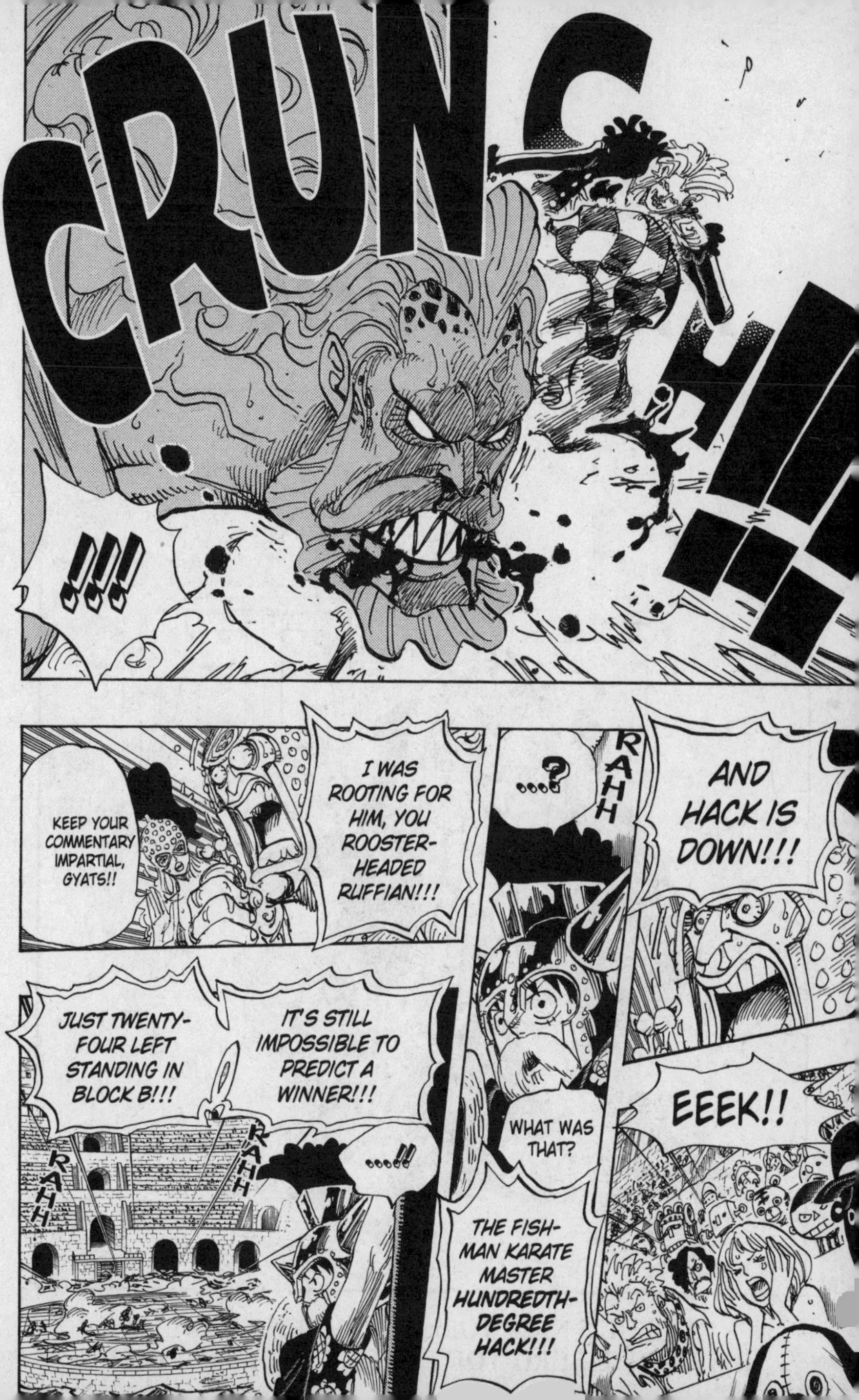
CRUNCH!!!!
!!!
AND HACK IS DOWN!!!
EEEK!!
....?
RAHH
WHAT WAS THAT?
THE FISH-MAN KARATE MASTER HUNDREDTH-DEGREE HACK!!!
I WAS ROOTING FOR HIM, YOU ROOSTER-HEADED RUFFIAN!!!
KEEP YOUR COMMENTARY IMPARTIAL, GYATS!!
IT'S STILL IMPOSSIBLE TO PREDICT A WINNER!!!
JUST TWENTY-FOUR LEFT STANDING IN BLOCK B!!!
RAHH
RAHH
....!!

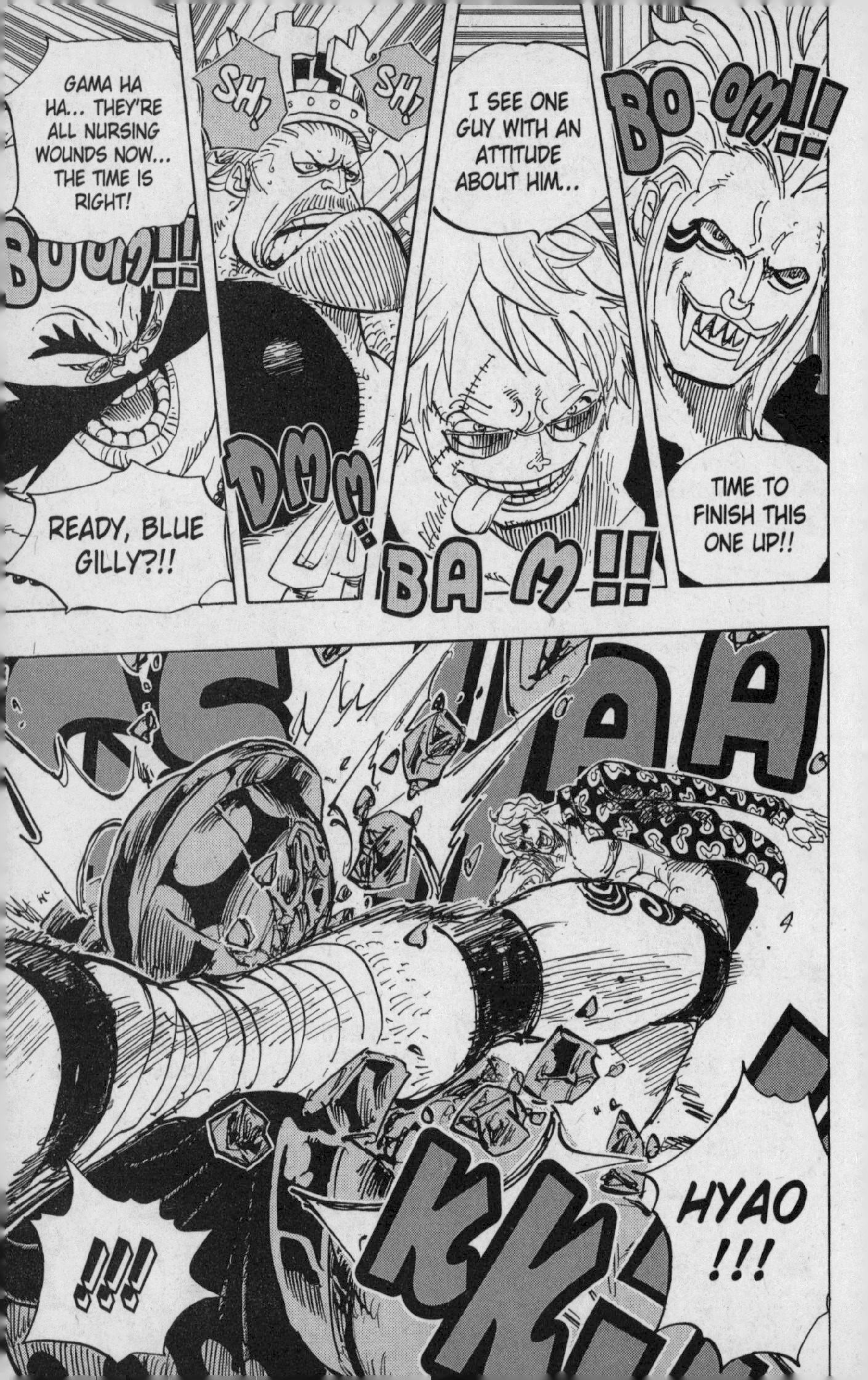
BOOM!!
TIME TO FINISH THIS ONE UP!!
I SEE ONE GUY WITH AN ATTITUDE ABOUT HIM...
BAM!!
SH!
SH!
DMM!
GAMA HA HA... THEY'RE ALL NURSING WOUNDS NOW... THE TIME IS RIGHT!
BOOM!!
READY, BLUE GILLY?!!
HYAO !!!
!!!

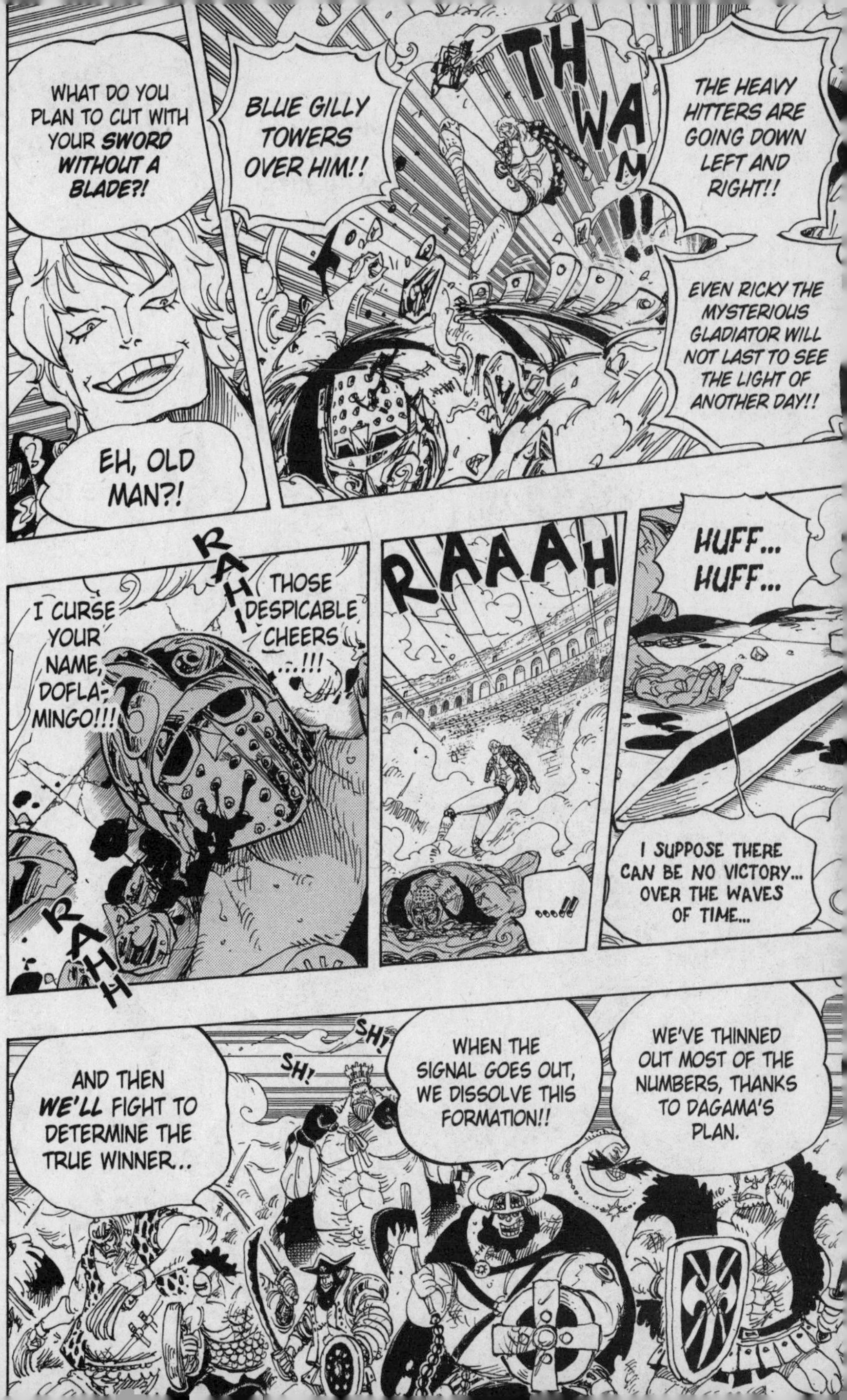
THE HEAVY HITTERS ARE GOING DOWN LEFT AND RIGHT!!
EVEN RICKY THE MYSTERIOUS GLADIATOR WILL NOT LAST TO SEE THE LIGHT OF ANOTHER DAY!!
THWAM!!
BLUE GILLY TOWERS OVER HIM!!
WHAT DO YOU PLAN TO CUT WITH YOUR SWORD WITHOUT A BLADE?!
EH, OLD MAN?!
HUFF... HUFF...
I SUPPOSE THERE CAN BE NO VICTORY... OVER THE WAVES OF TIME...
RAAAH
.....!!
RAH
THOSE DESPICABLE CHEERS ...!!!
I CURSE YOUR NAME, DOFLA-MINGO!!!
RAHH
WE'VE THINNED OUT MOST OF THE NUMBERS, THANKS TO DAGAMA'S PLAN.
WHEN THE SIGNAL GOES OUT, WE DISSOLVE THIS FORMATION!!
SH!
SH!
AND THEN WE'LL FIGHT TO DETERMINE THE TRUE WINNER...

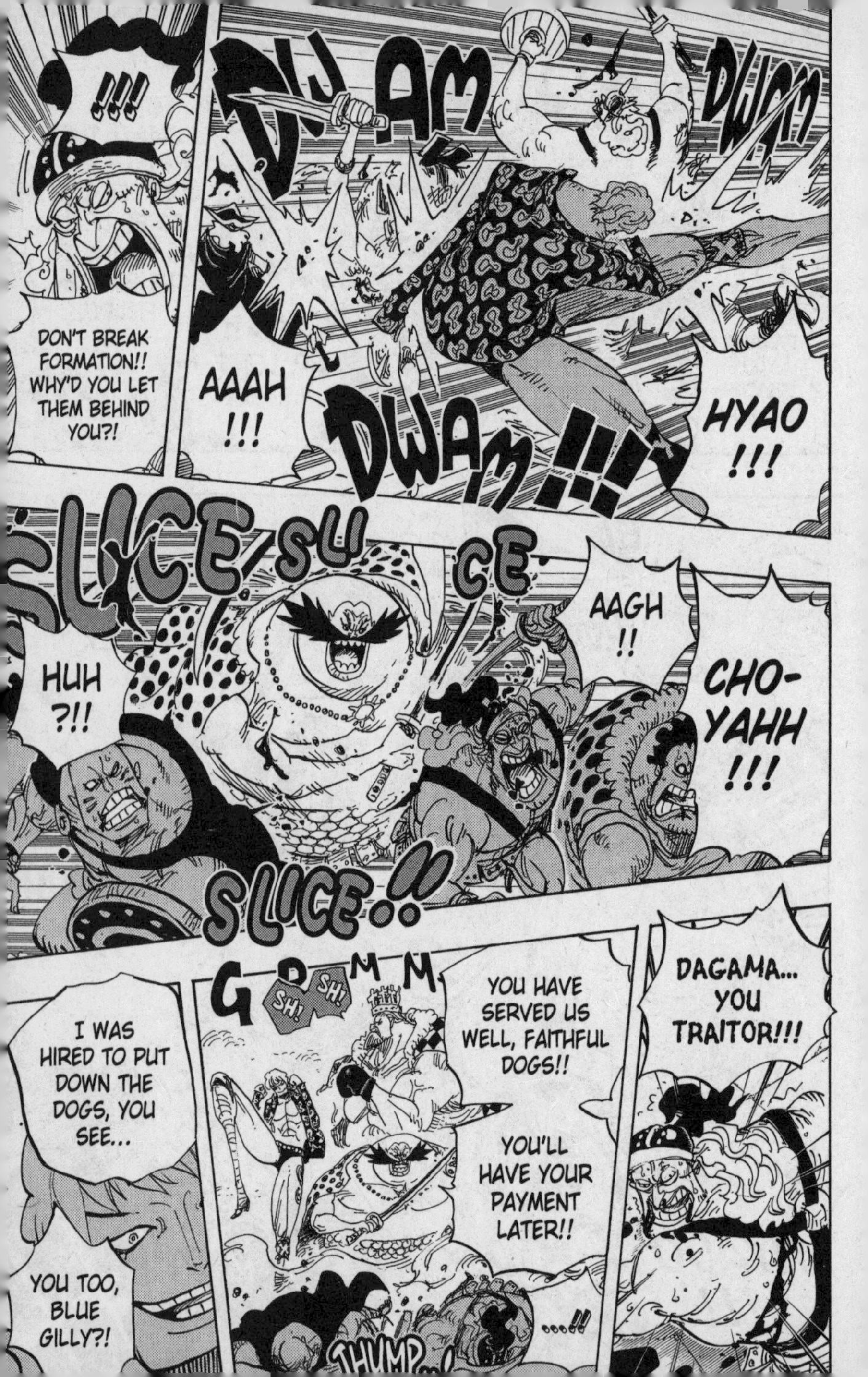
DWAM
HYAO
!!!
AAAH
!!!
DWAM!!!
!!!
DON'T BREAK FORMATION!! WHY'D YOU LET THEM BEHIND YOU?!
SLICE
AAGH
!!
CHO-YAHH
!!!
HUH
?!!
SLICE..!!
DAGAMA... YOU TRAITOR!!!
YOU HAVE SERVED US WELL, FAITHFUL DOGS!!
YOU'LL HAVE YOUR PAYMENT LATER!!
....!!
I WAS HIRED TO PUT DOWN THE DOGS, YOU SEE...
YOU TOO, BLUE GILLY?!

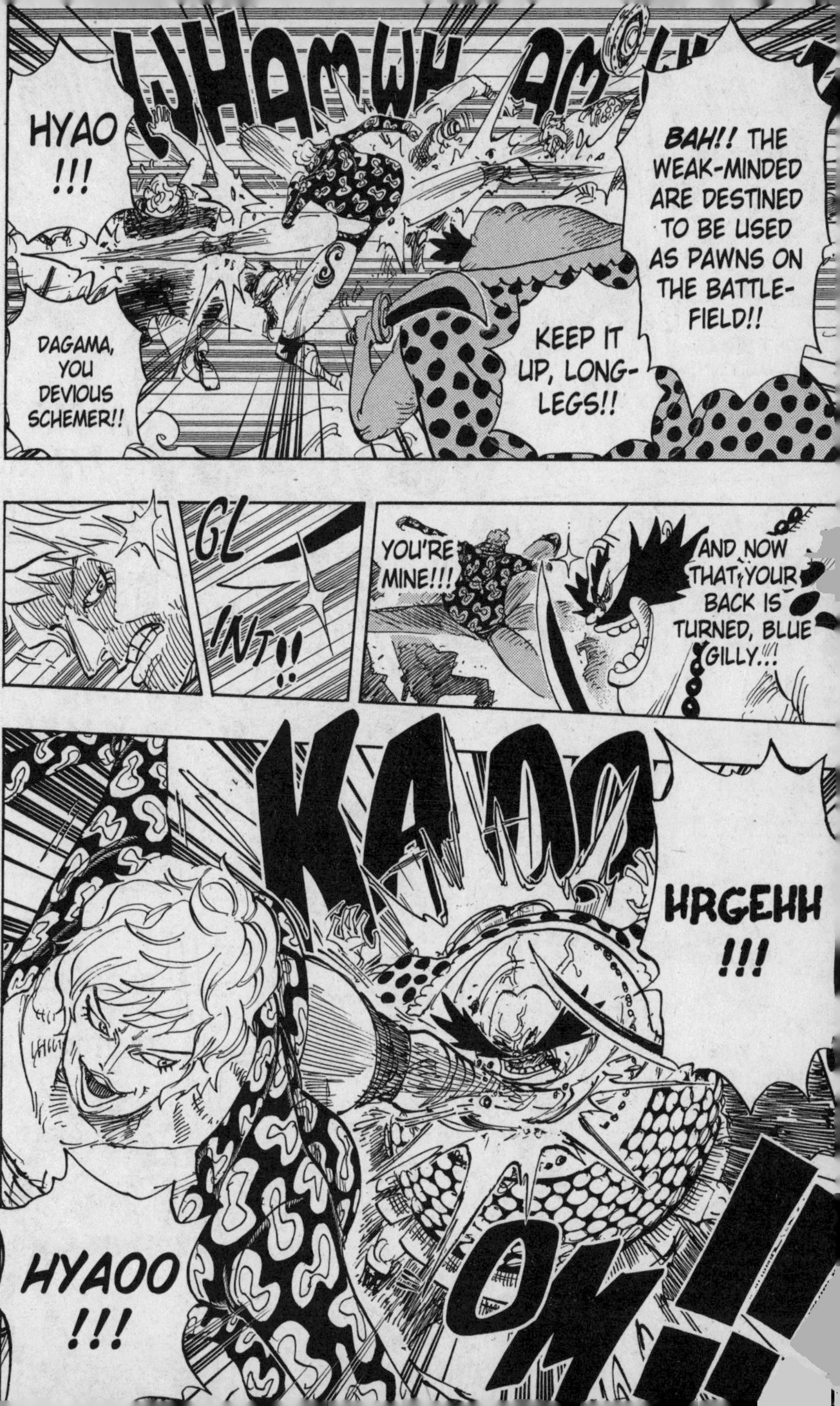
BAH!! THE WEAK-MINDED ARE DESTINED TO BE USED AS PAWNS ON THE BATTLE-FIELD!!
KEEP IT UP, LONG-LEGS!!
WHAM WHAM
HYAO !!!
DAGAMA, YOU DEVIOUS SCHEMER!!
AND NOW THAT YOUR BACK IS TURNED, BLUE GILLY...!!
YOU'RE MINE!!!
GLINT!!
HRGEHH !!!
HYAOO !!!

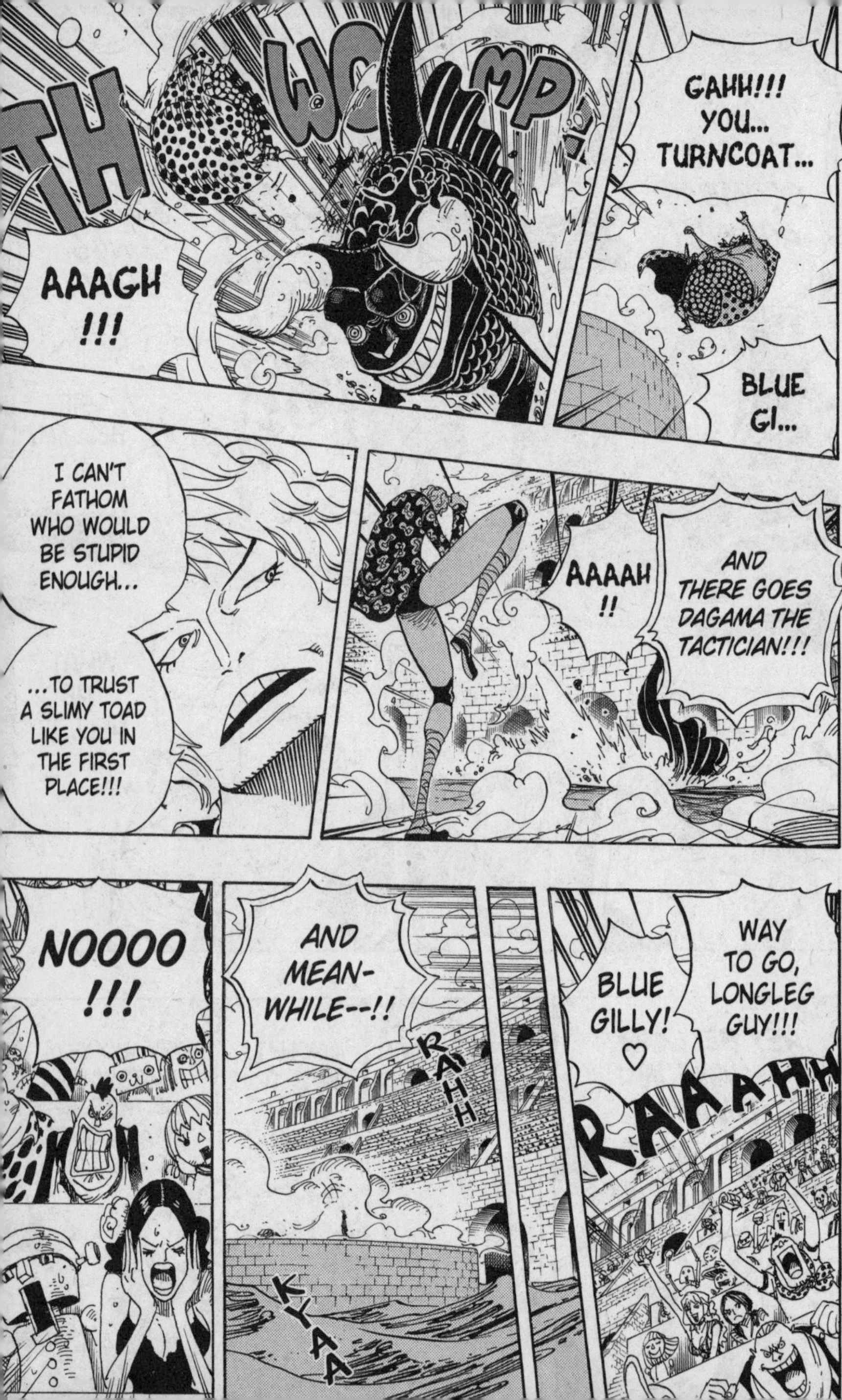
GAHH!!! YOU... TURNCOAT...
BLUE GI...
THWOMP
AAAGH!!!
AND THERE GOES DAGAMA THE TACTICIAN!!!
AAAAH!!
I CAN'T FATHOM WHO WOULD BE STUPID ENOUGH...
...TO TRUST A SLIMY TOAD LIKE YOU IN THE FIRST PLACE!!!
WAY TO GO, LONGLEG GUY!!!
BLUE GILLY! ♡
RAAAAHH
AND MEAN-WHILE--!!
RAHH
KYAA
NOOOO!!!

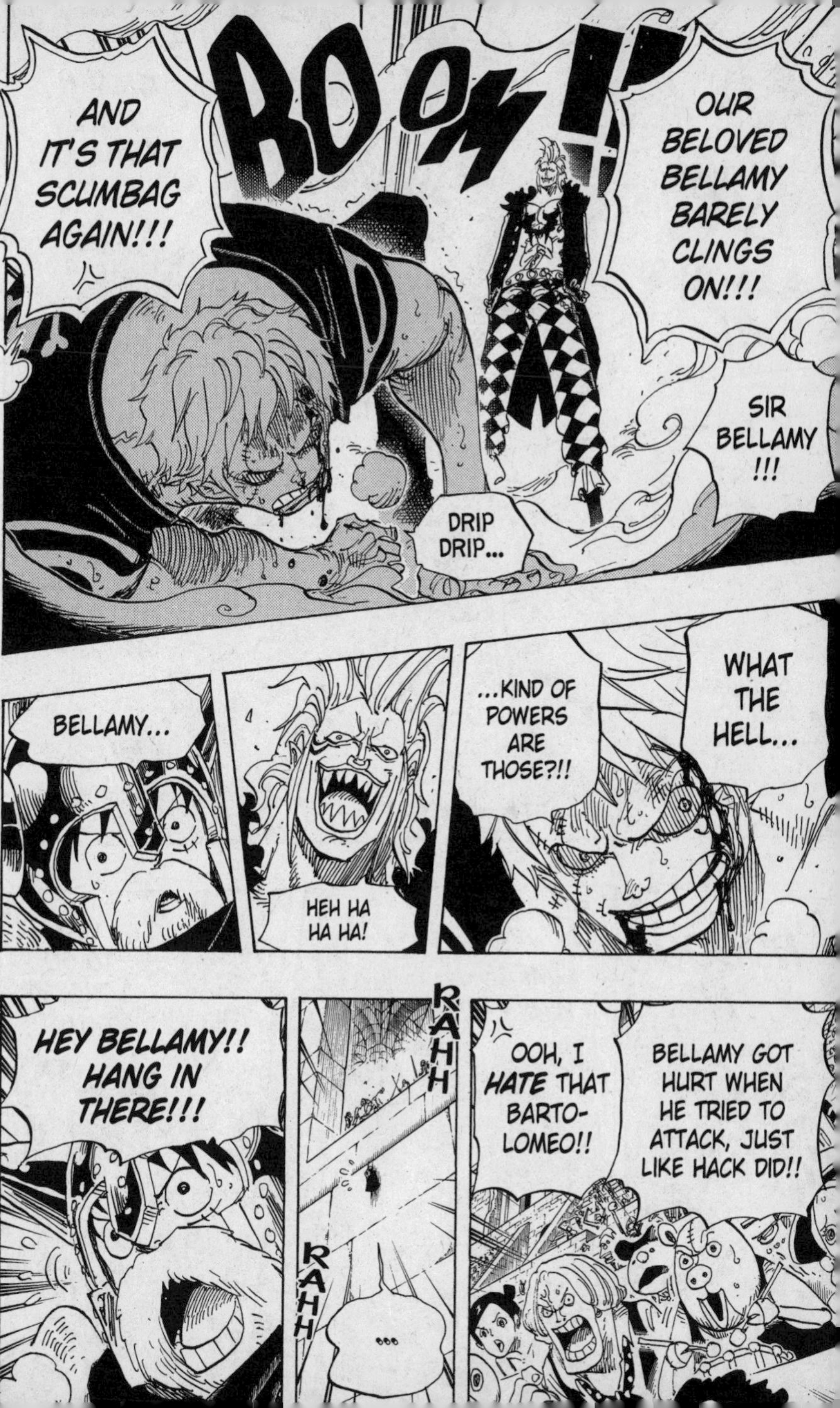
OUR BELOVED BELLAMY BARELY CLINGS ON!!!
BOOM!!
AND IT'S THAT SCUMBAG AGAIN!!!
SIR BELLAMY!!!
DRIP DRIP...
WHAT THE HELL...
...KIND OF POWERS ARE THOSE?!!
HEH HA HA HA!
BELLAMY...
BELLAMY GOT HURT WHEN HE TRIED TO ATTACK, JUST LIKE HACK DID!!
OOH, I *HATE* THAT BARTO-LOMEO!!
RAHH
RAHH
...
HEY BELLAMY!! HANG IN THERE!!!

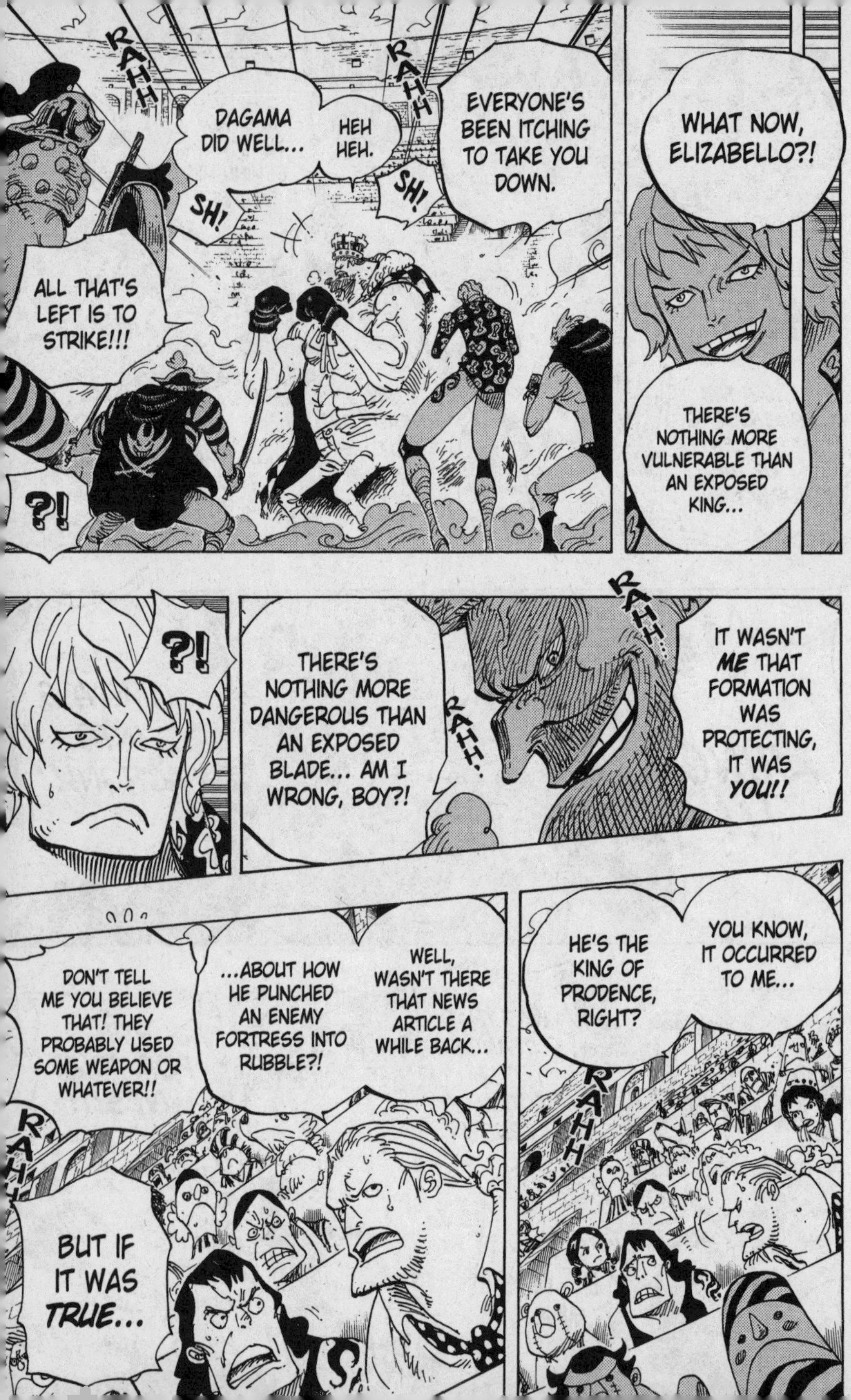
WHAT NOW, ELIZABELLO?!
THERE'S NOTHING MORE VULNERABLE THAN AN EXPOSED KING...
RAHH
EVERYONE'S BEEN ITCHING TO TAKE YOU DOWN.
SH!
RAHH
HEH HEH.
DAGAMA DID WELL...
SH!
ALL THAT'S LEFT IS TO STRIKE!!!
?!
RAHH...
IT WASN'T *ME* THAT FORMATION WAS PROTECTING, IT WAS *YOU!!*
RAHH...
THERE'S NOTHING MORE DANGEROUS THAN AN EXPOSED BLADE... AM I WRONG, BOY?!
?!
YOU KNOW, IT OCCURRED TO ME...
HE'S THE KING OF PRODENCE, RIGHT?
RAHH
WELL, WASN'T THERE THAT NEWS ARTICLE A WHILE BACK...
...ABOUT HOW HE PUNCHED AN ENEMY FORTRESS INTO RUBBLE?!
DON'T TELL ME YOU BELIEVE THAT! THEY PROBABLY USED SOME WEAPON OR WHATEVER!!
RAHH
BUT IF IT WAS *TRUE...*

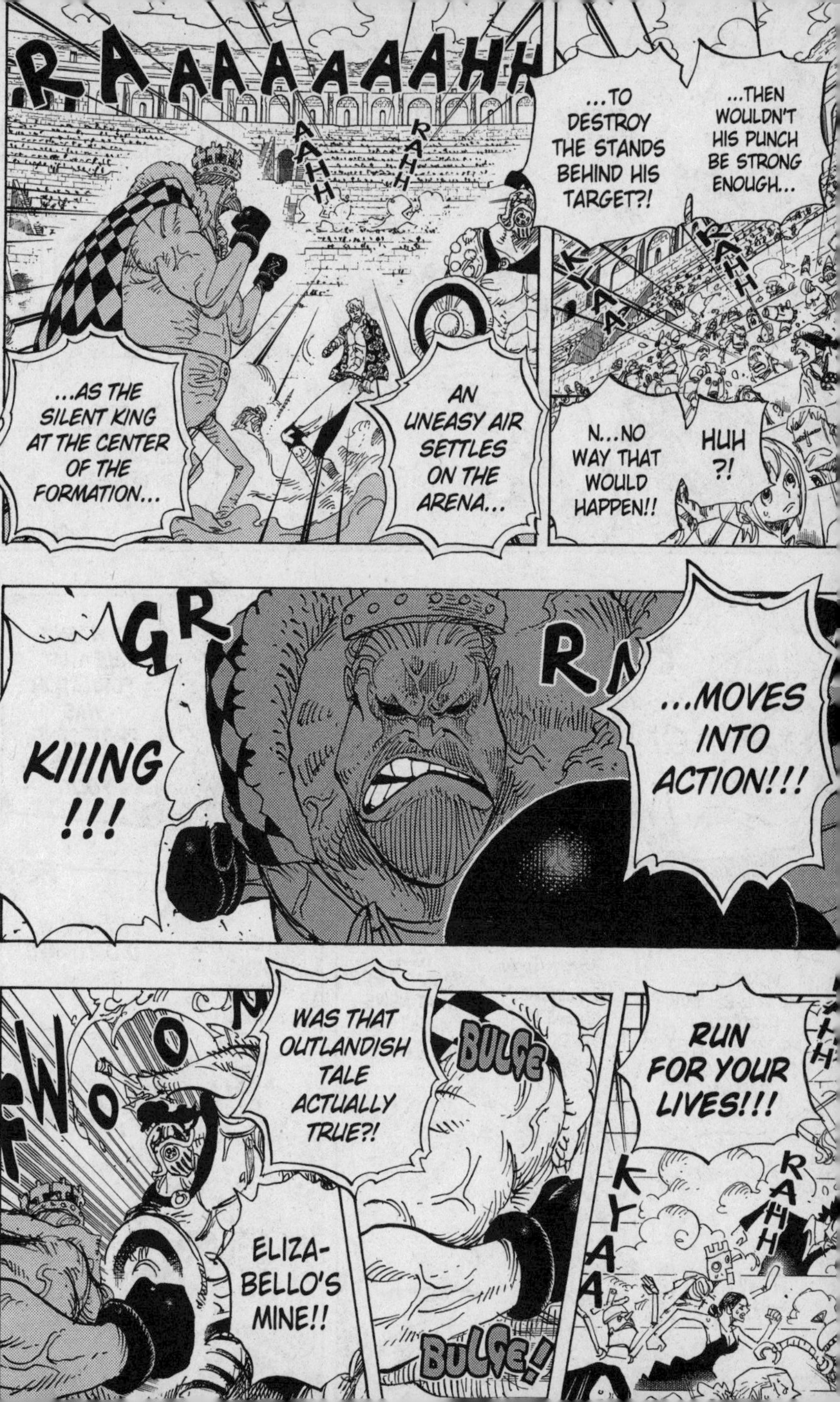
...THEN WOULDN'T HIS PUNCH BE STRONG ENOUGH...
...TO DESTROY THE STANDS BEHIND HIS TARGET?!
RAHH
KYAA
HUH ?!
N...NO WAY THAT WOULD HAPPEN!!
RAAAAAAAHH
RAHH
AAHH
AN UNEASY AIR SETTLES ON THE ARENA...
...AS THE SILENT KING AT THE CENTER OF THE FORMATION...
...MOVES INTO ACTION!!!
RA
GR
KIIING !!!
RUN FOR YOUR LIVES!!!
RAHH
KYAA
WAS THAT OUTLANDISH TALE ACTUALLY TRUE?!
BULGE
BULGE!
FWOOM
ELIZA-BELLO'S MINE!!

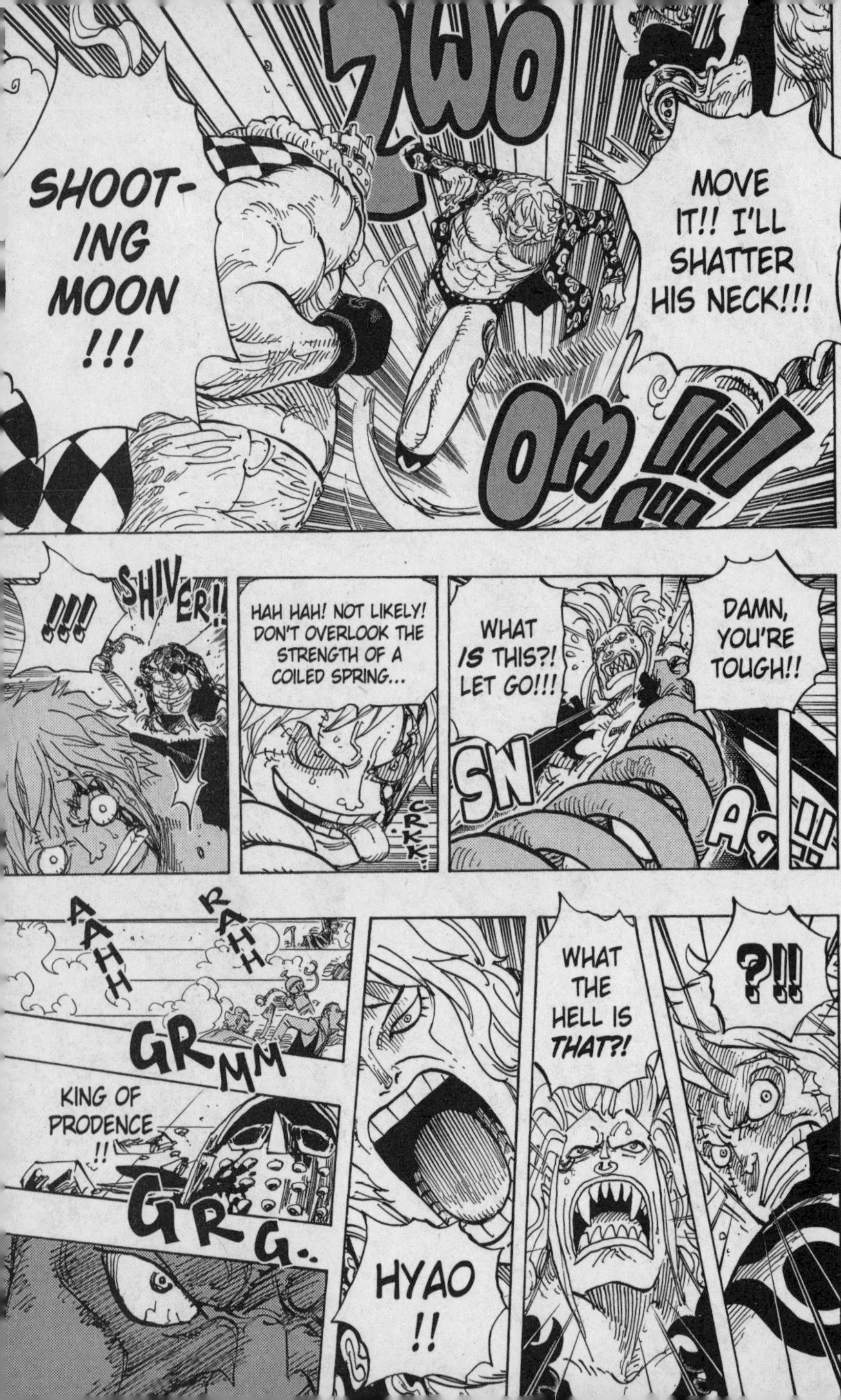
MOVE IT!! I'LL SHATTER HIS NECK!!!
ZWO
OM!!
SHOOT-ING MOON!!!
DAMN, YOU'RE TOUGH!!
WHAT IS THIS?! LET GO!!!
SN
AG!!
HAH HAH! NOT LIKELY! DON'T OVERLOOK THE STRENGTH OF A COILED SPRING...
CRKK
!!!
SHIVER!!
?!!
WHAT THE HELL IS THAT?!
HYAO!!
AAHH
RAHH
GRMM
KING OF PRODENCE!!
GRG..

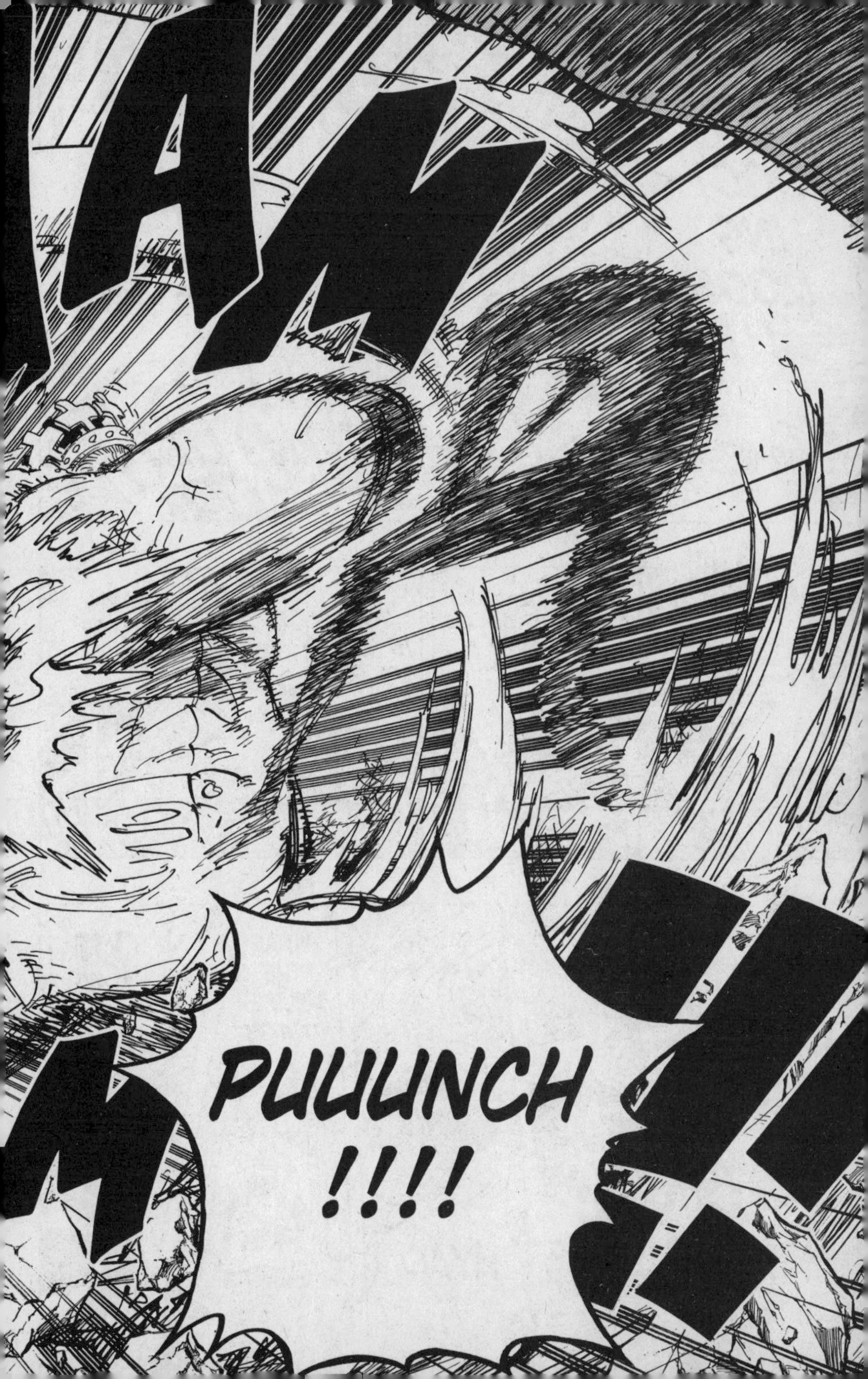
PUUUNCH
!!!!

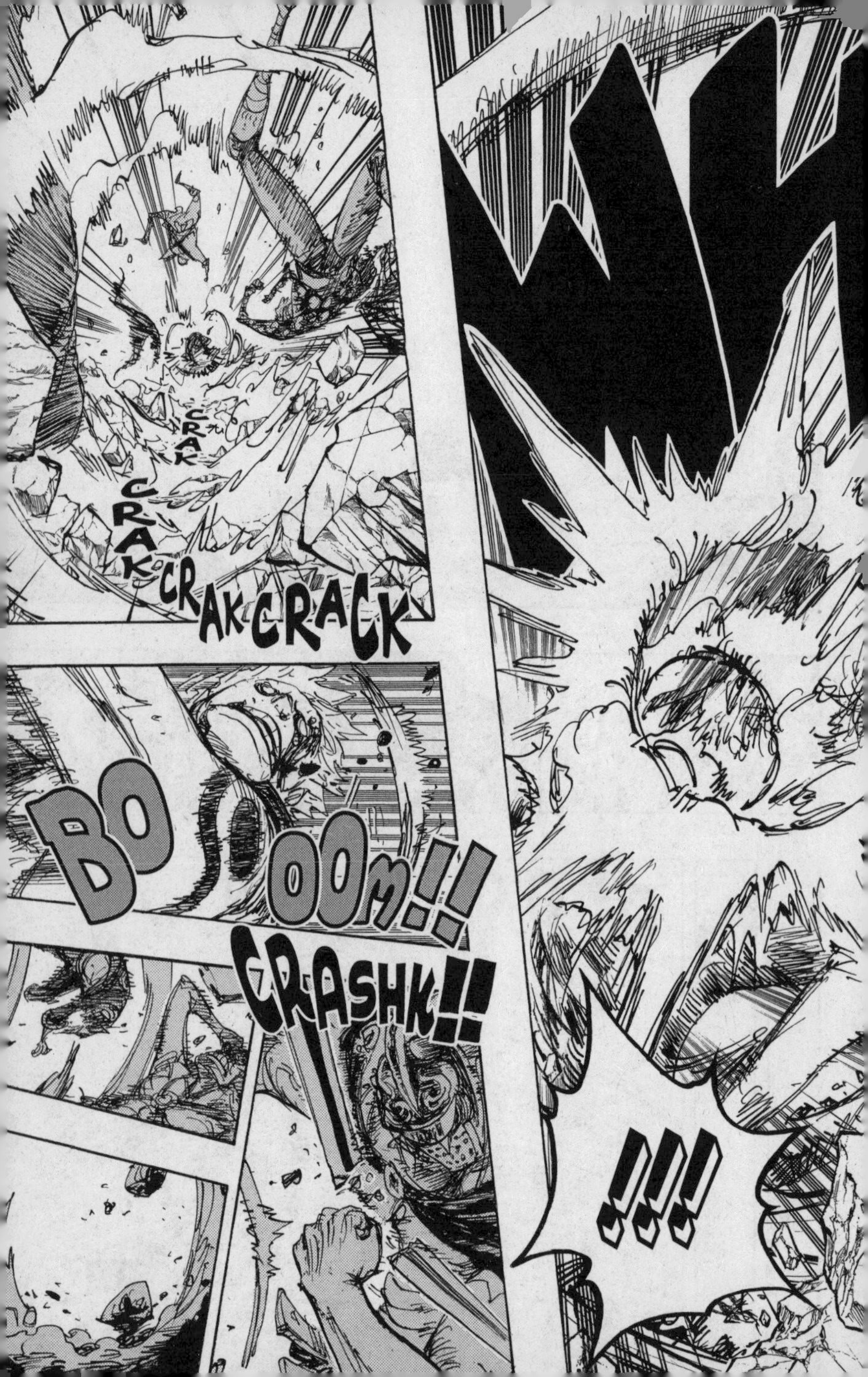
!!!
CRAK
CRAK
CRAK
CRAK
CRACK
BOOOM!!
CRASHK!!

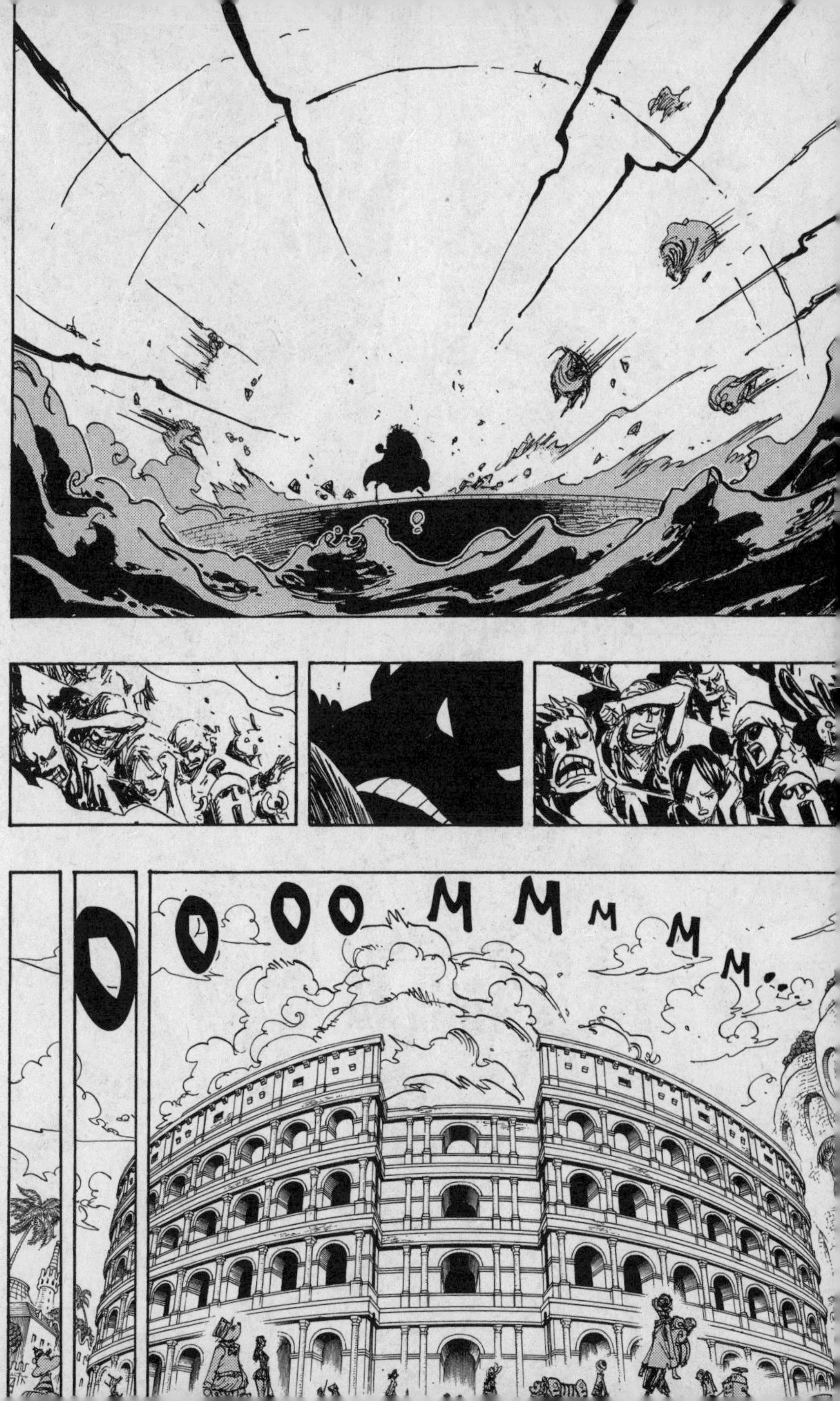
DOOOMMMMM..

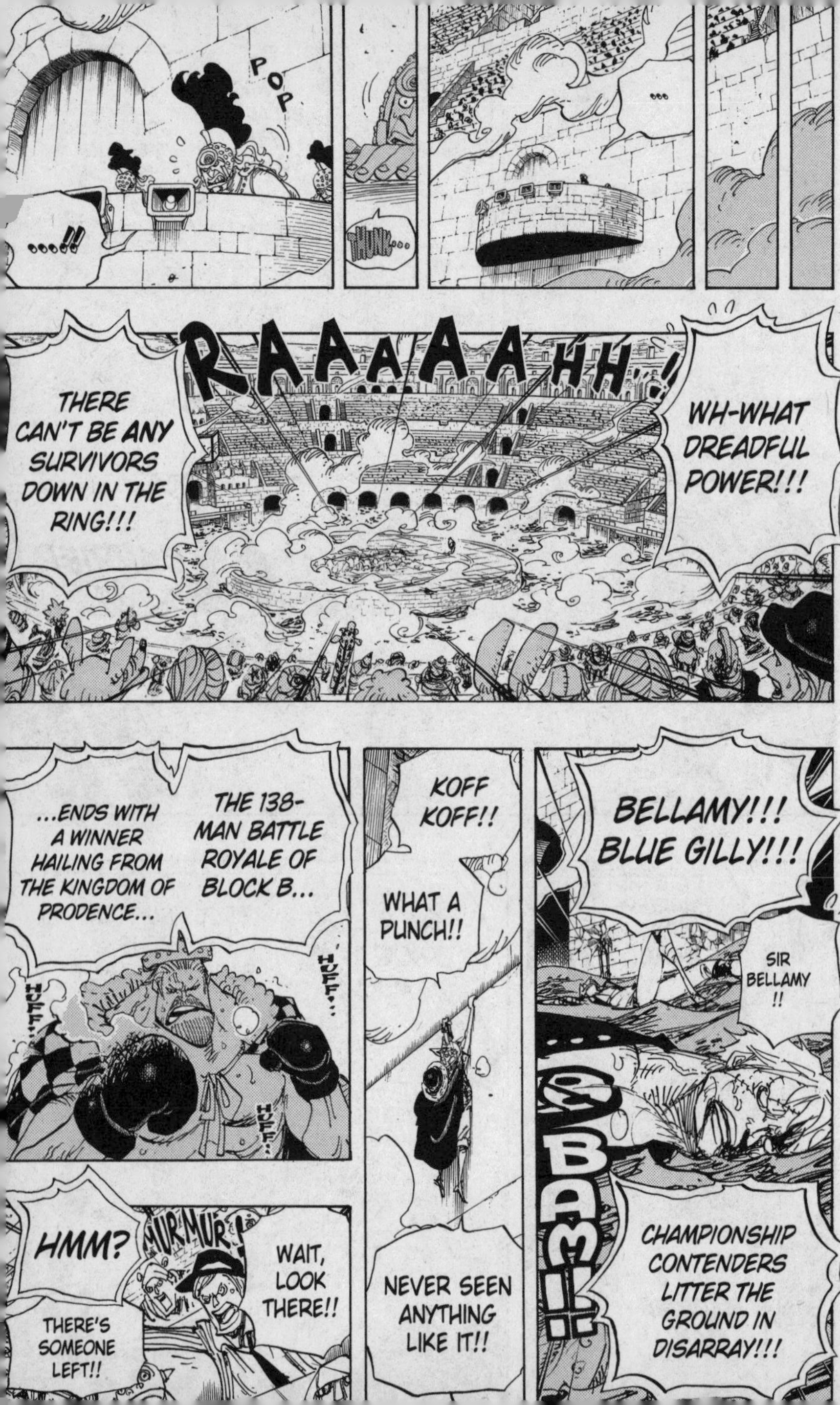
...
THUNK...
POP
....!!
RAAAAAHH!!
WH-WHAT DREADFUL POWER!!!
THERE CAN'T BE ANY SURVIVORS DOWN IN THE RING!!!
BELLAMY!!! BLUE GILLY!!!
SIR BELLAMY !!
BAM!!
CHAMPIONSHIP CONTENDERS LITTER THE GROUND IN DISARRAY!!!
KOFF KOFF!!
WHAT A PUNCH!!
NEVER SEEN ANYTHING LIKE IT!!
THE 138-MAN BATTLE ROYALE OF BLOCK B...
...ENDS WITH A WINNER HAILING FROM THE KINGDOM OF PRODENCE...
HUFF...
HUFF...
HUFF...
WAIT, LOOK THERE!!
MUR MUR
HMM?
THERE'S SOMEONE LEFT!!

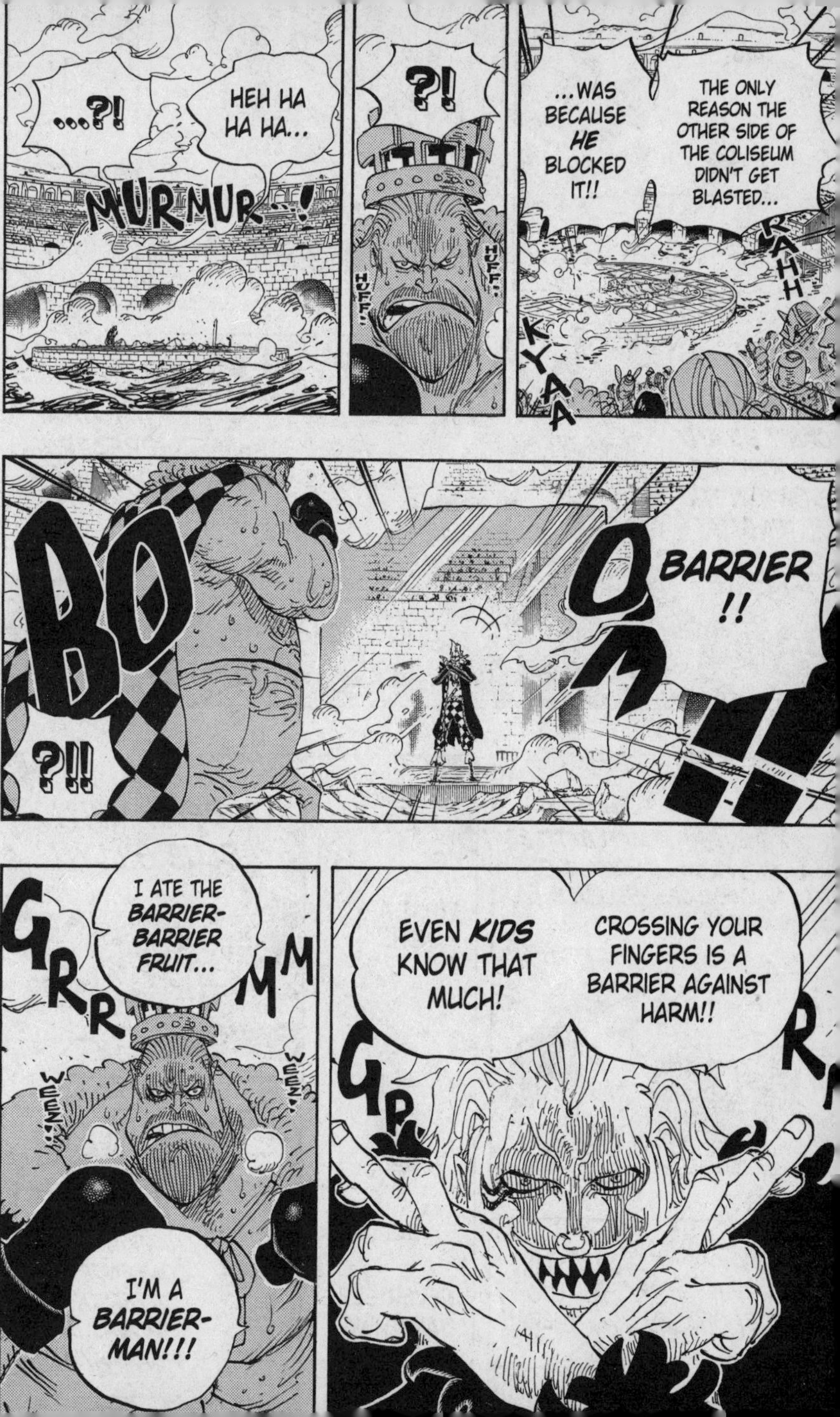
THE ONLY REASON THE OTHER SIDE OF THE COLISEUM DIDN'T GET BLASTED...
...WAS BECAUSE HE BLOCKED IT!!
RAHH
KYAA
?!
HUFF
HUFF
HEH HA HA HA...
...?!
MURMUR...!
BARRIER!!
BOOM
?!!
CROSSING YOUR FINGERS IS A BARRIER AGAINST HARM!!
EVEN KIDS KNOW THAT MUCH!
I ATE THE BARRIER-BARRIER FRUIT...
GRRMM
WEEZ
WEEZ
I'M A BARRIER-MAN!!!

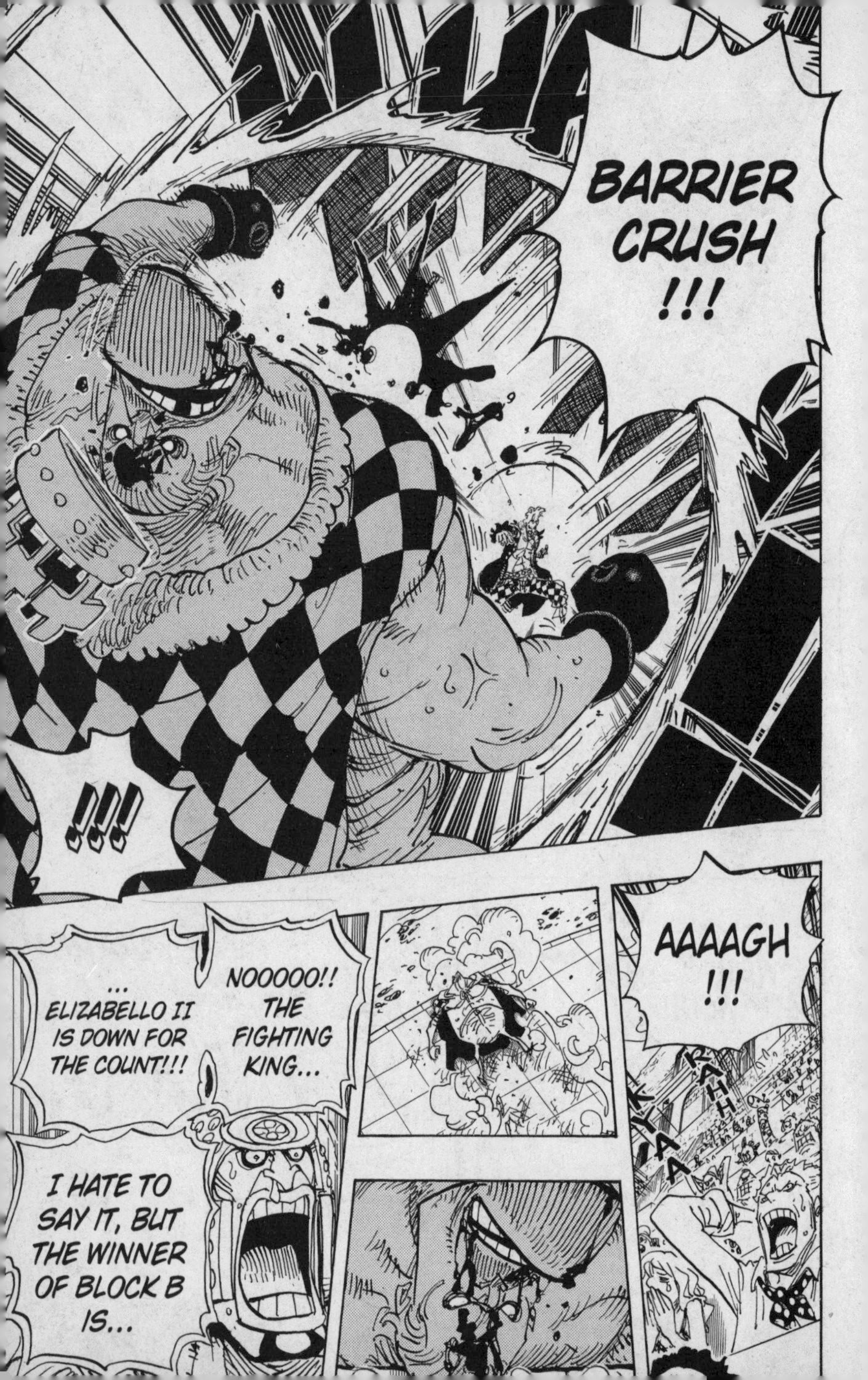
BARRIER CRUSH !!!
!!!
AAAAGH !!!
NOOOOO!! THE FIGHTING KING...
... ELIZABELLO II IS DOWN FOR THE COUNT!!!
I HATE TO SAY IT, BUT THE WINNER OF BLOCK B IS...

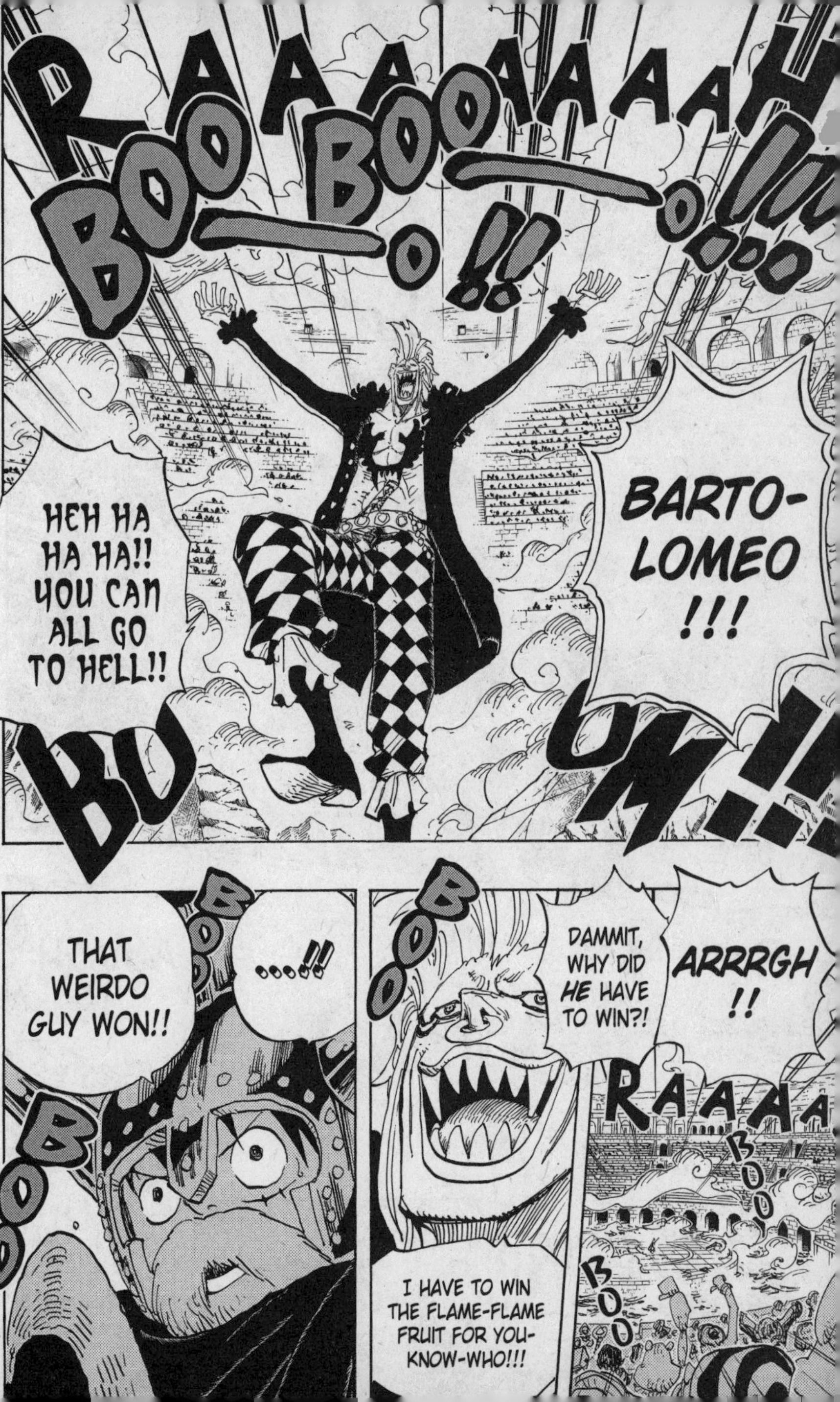

RAAAAAAAH!!
BOO—BOO—O!!
O...
BARTO-LOMEO!!!
HEH HA HA HA!! YOU CAN ALL GO TO HELL!!
UM!!!
BU
RAAAA
BOO
BOO
ARRRGH!!
DAMMIT, WHY DID HE HAVE TO WIN?!
BOO
I HAVE TO WIN THE FLAME-FLAME FRUIT FOR YOU-KNOW-WHO!!!
...!!
THAT WEIRDO GUY WON!!
BOO
BOO

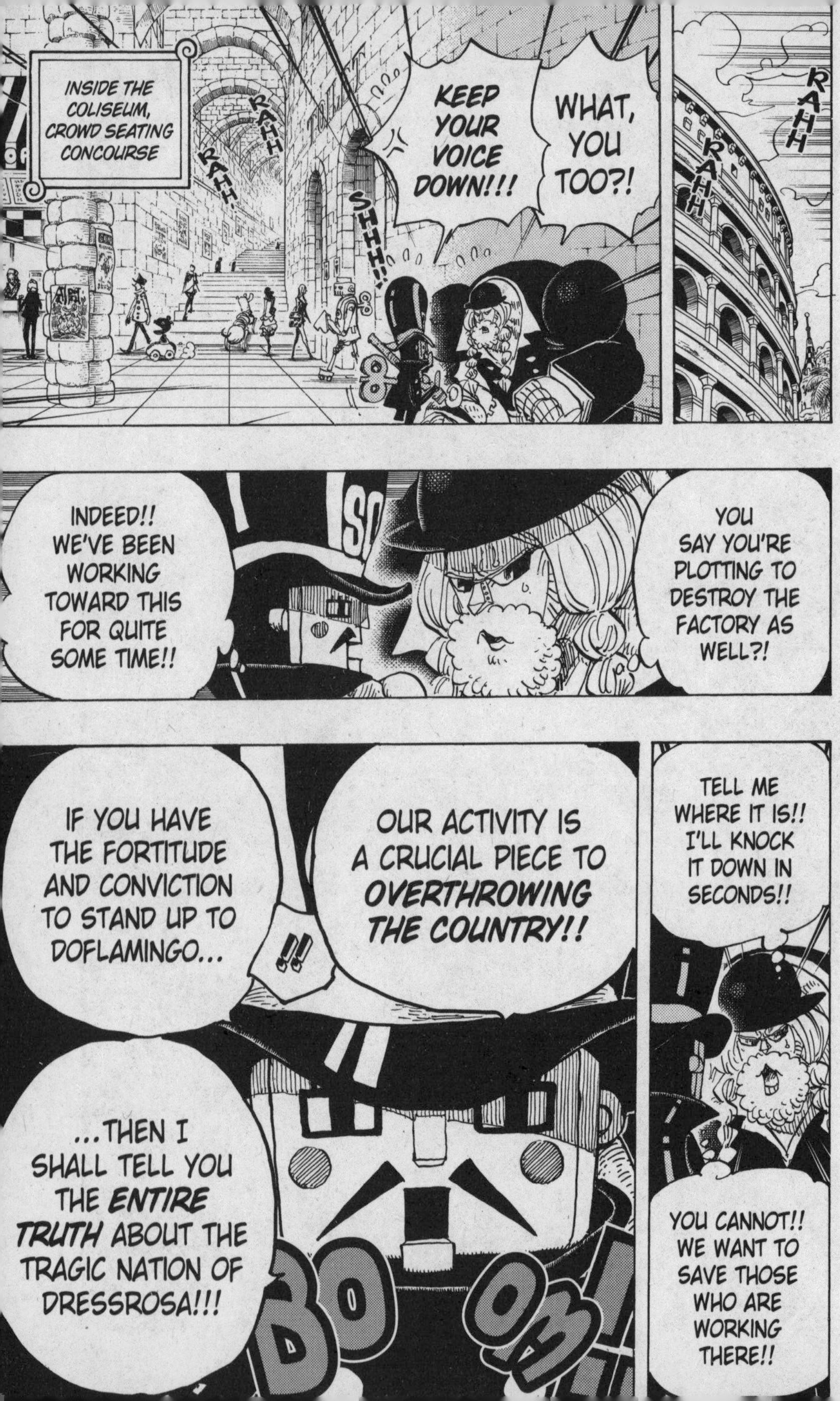
RAHH
RAHH
INSIDE THE COLISEUM, CROWD SEATING CONCOURSE
WHAT, YOU TOO?!
KEEP YOUR VOICE DOWN!!!
SHHHH!!
RAHH
RAHH
YOU SAY YOU'RE PLOTTING TO DESTROY THE FACTORY AS WELL?!
INDEED!! WE'VE BEEN WORKING TOWARD THIS FOR QUITE SOME TIME!!
TELL ME WHERE IT IS!! I'LL KNOCK IT DOWN IN SECONDS!!
YOU CANNOT!! WE WANT TO SAVE THOSE WHO ARE WORKING THERE!!
OUR ACTIVITY IS A CRUCIAL PIECE TO OVERTHROWING THE COUNTRY!!
IF YOU HAVE THE FORTITUDE AND CONVICTION TO STAND UP TO DOFLAMINGO...
!!
...THEN I SHALL TELL YOU THE ENTIRE TRUTH ABOUT THE TRAGIC NATION OF DRESSROSA!!!
BOOM!

Chapter 710: TO GREENBIT

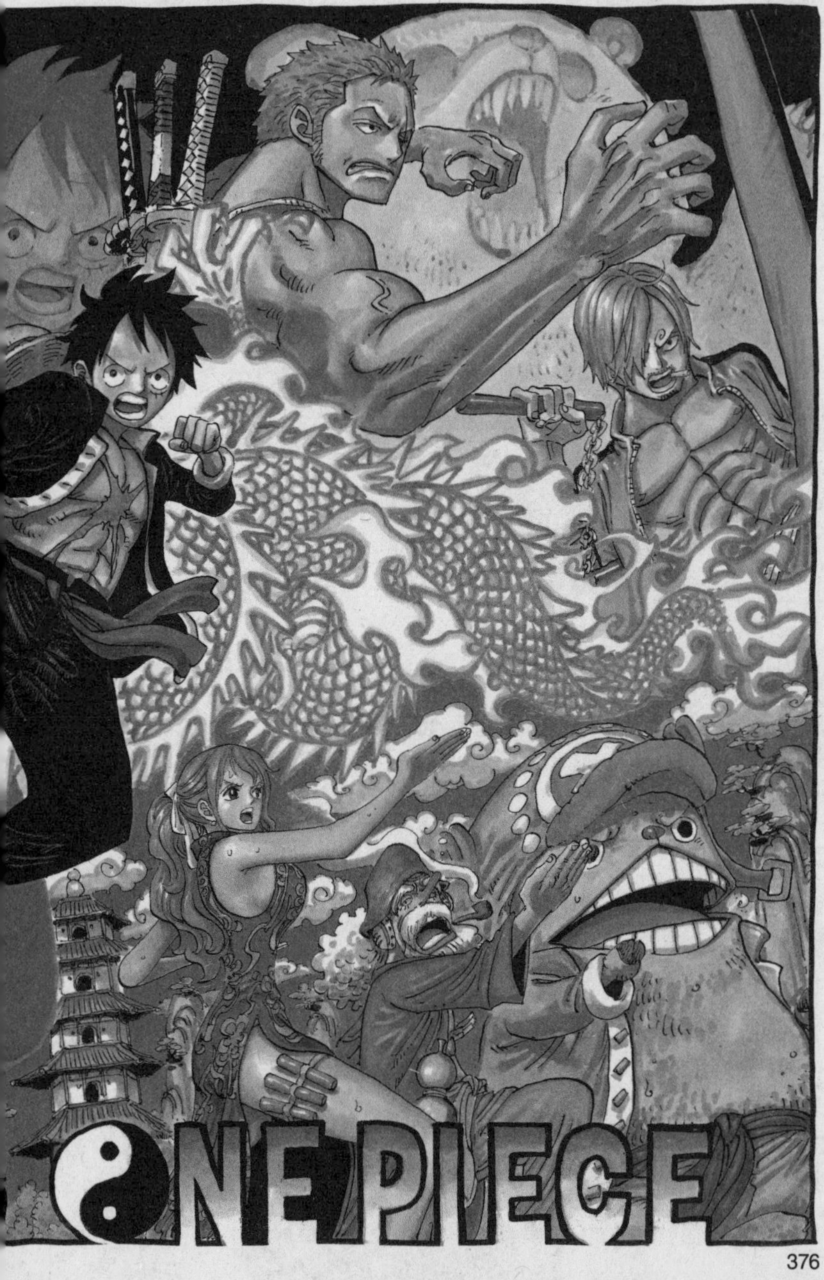
ONE PIECE

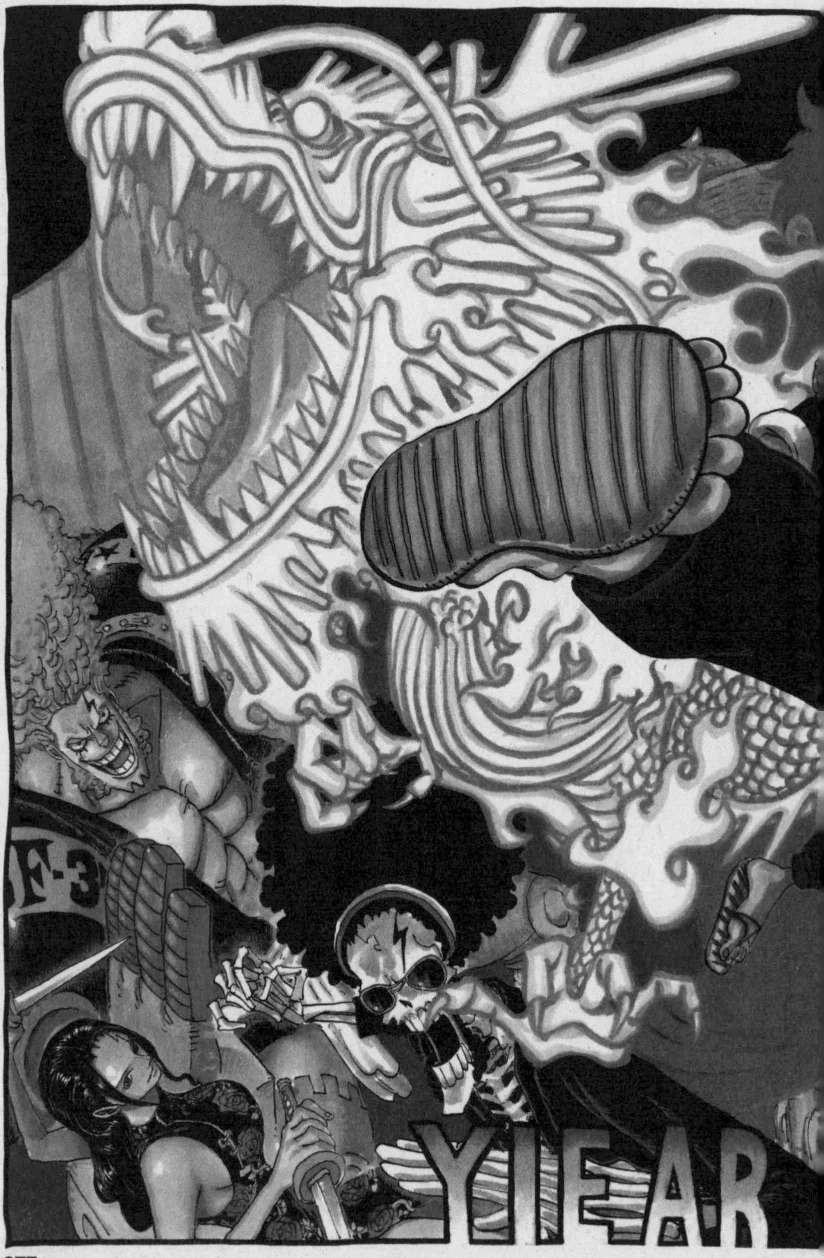
YIEAR

vol.71

ONE PIECE

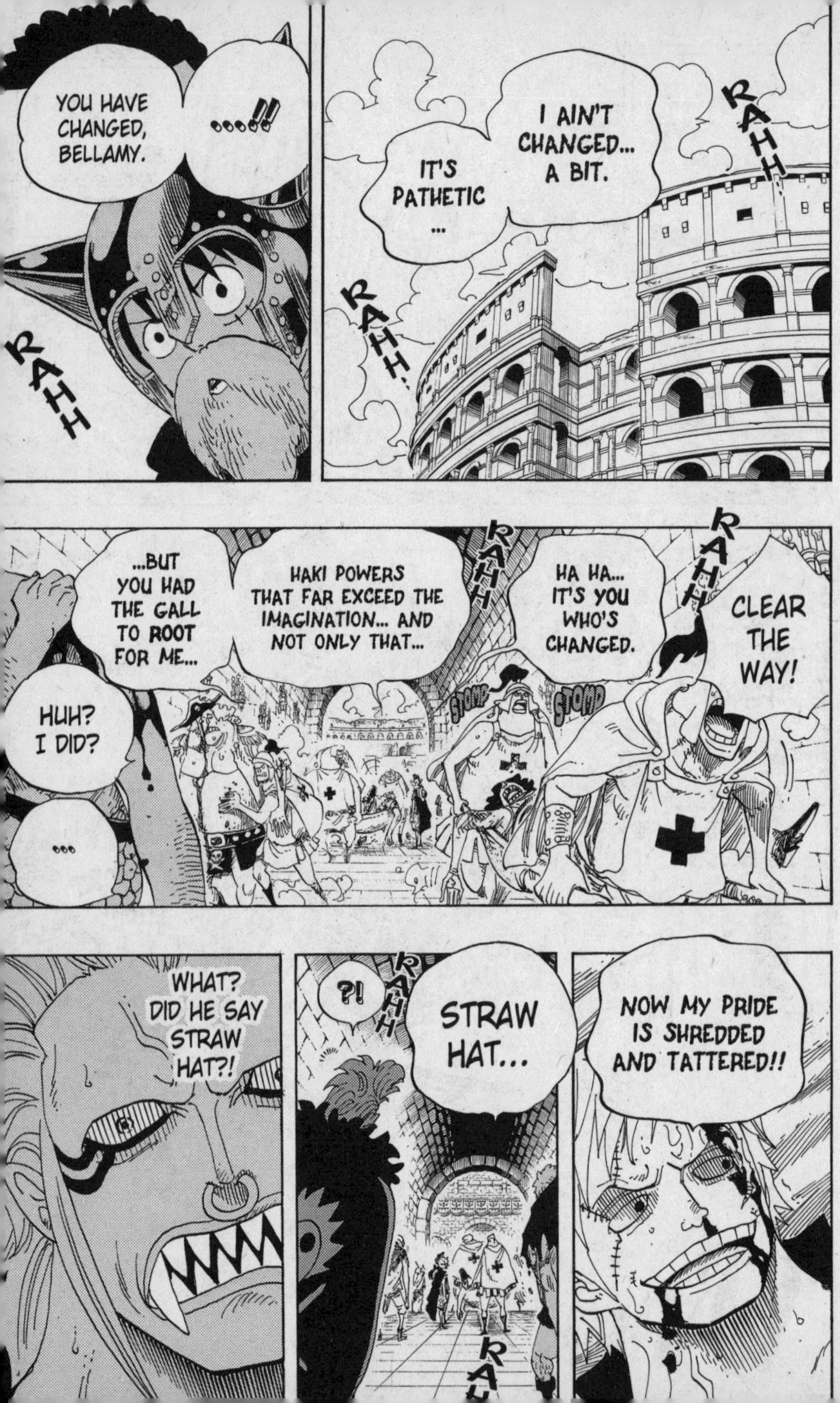
RAHH
I AIN'T CHANGED... A BIT.
IT'S PATHETIC ...
RAHH
....!!
YOU HAVE CHANGED, BELLAMY.
RAHH
RAHH
CLEAR THE WAY!
HA HA... IT'S YOU WHO'S CHANGED.
RAHH
STOMP
STOMP
HAKI POWERS THAT FAR EXCEED THE IMAGINATION... AND NOT ONLY THAT...
...BUT YOU HAD THE GALL TO ROOT FOR ME...
HUH? I DID?
...
NOW MY PRIDE IS SHREDDED AND TATTERED!!
STRAW HAT...
RAHH
?!
RA
WHAT? DID HE SAY STRAW HAT?!

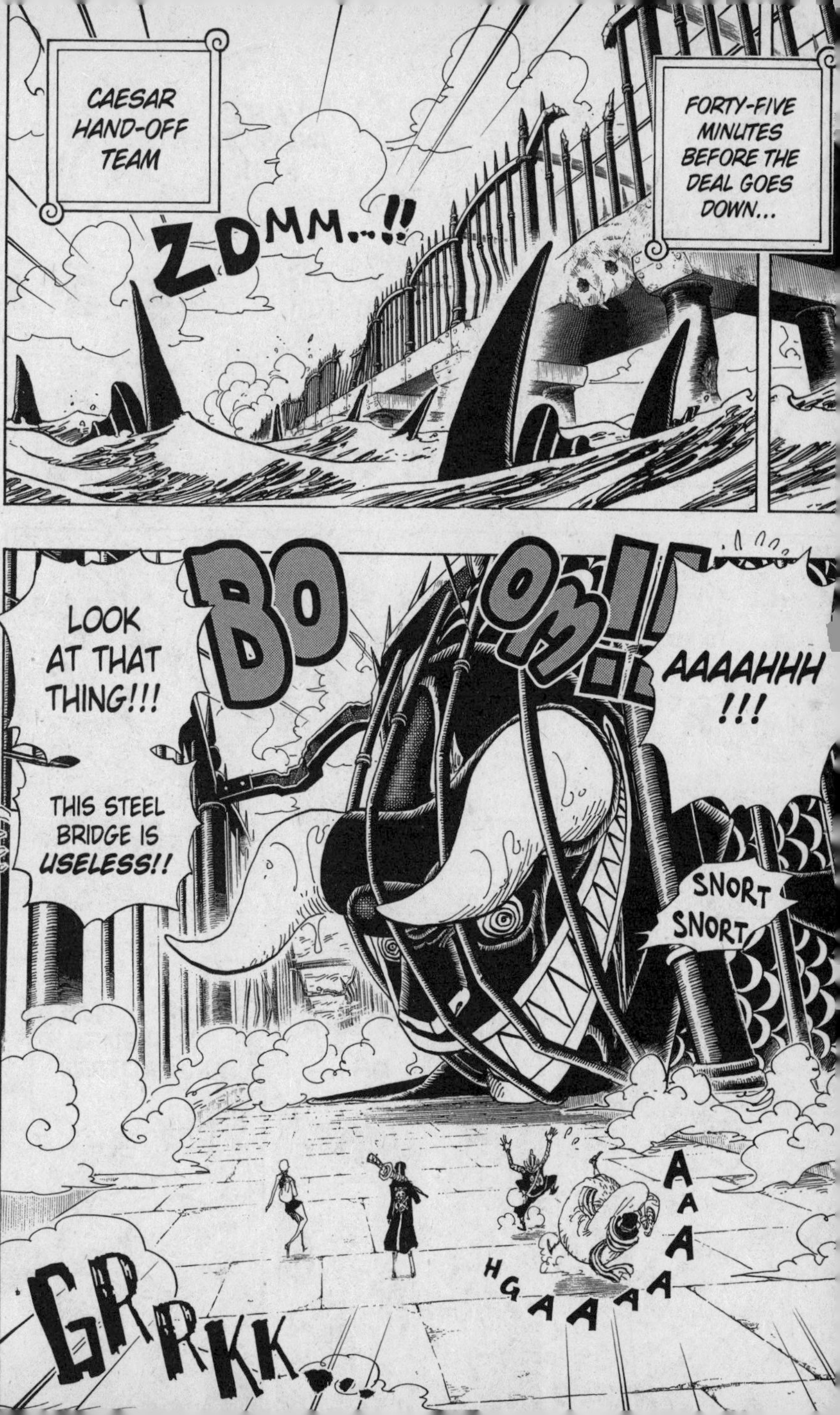
FORTY-FIVE MINUTES BEFORE THE DEAL GOES DOWN...
CAESAR HAND-OFF TEAM
ZDMM...!!
BOOM!!
AAAAHHH!!!
LOOK AT THAT THING!!!
SNORT SNORT
THIS STEEL BRIDGE IS USELESS!!
AAAAA
HGAAAA
GRRKK...

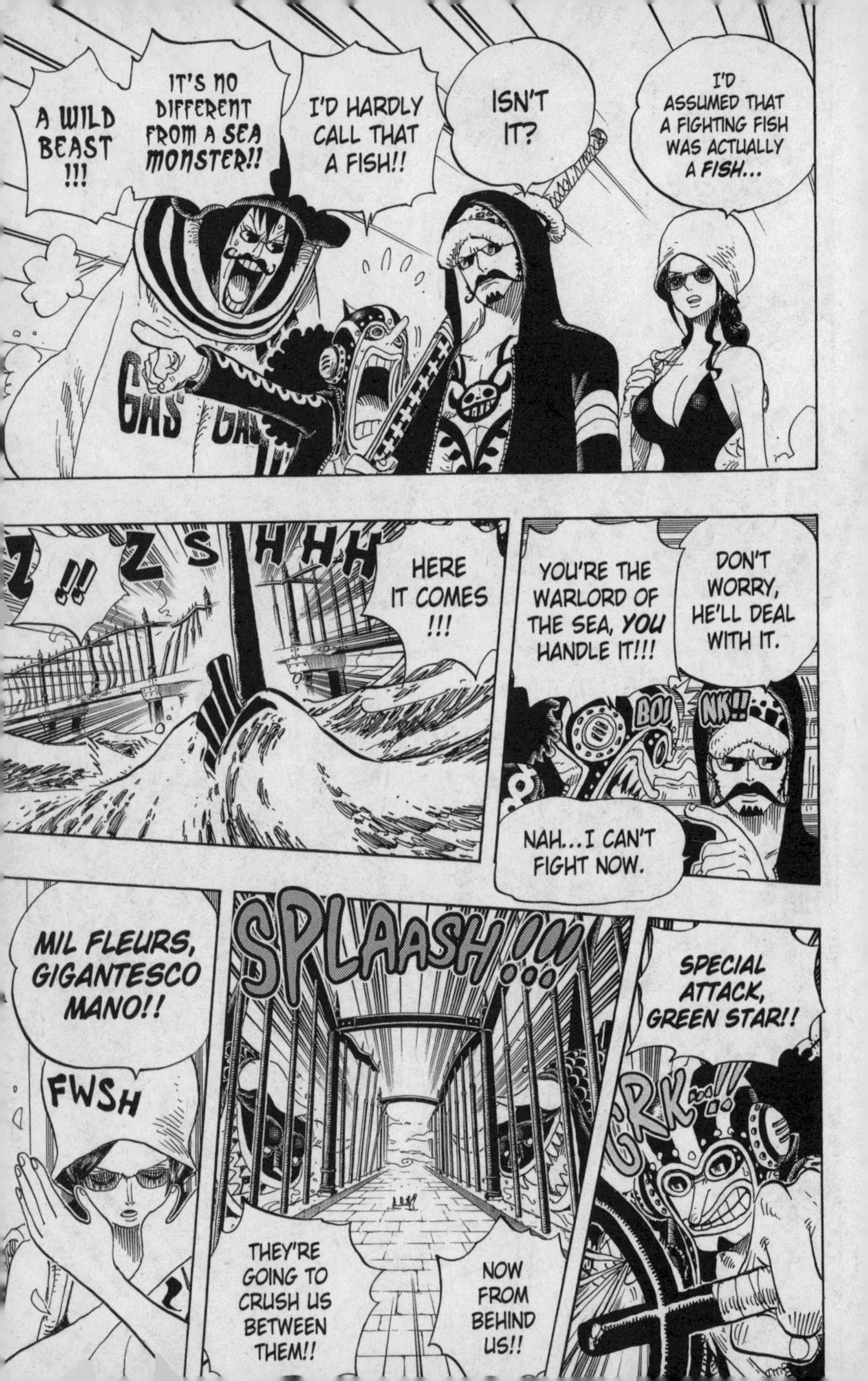
I'D ASSUMED THAT A FIGHTING FISH WAS ACTUALLY A *FISH*...
ISN'T IT?
I'D HARDLY CALL THAT A FISH!!
IT'S NO DIFFERENT FROM A *SEA MONSTER*!!
A WILD BEAST !!!
DON'T WORRY, HE'LL DEAL WITH IT.
YOU'RE THE WARLORD OF THE SEA, *YOU* HANDLE IT!!!
BOINK!!
NAH...I CAN'T FIGHT NOW.
Z!! ZSHHH
HERE IT COMES !!!
SPECIAL ATTACK, GREEN STAR!!
GRK...!!
SPLAASH...!!!
NOW FROM BEHIND US!!
THEY'RE GOING TO CRUSH US BETWEEN THEM!!
MIL FLEURS, GIGANTESCO MANO!!
FWSH

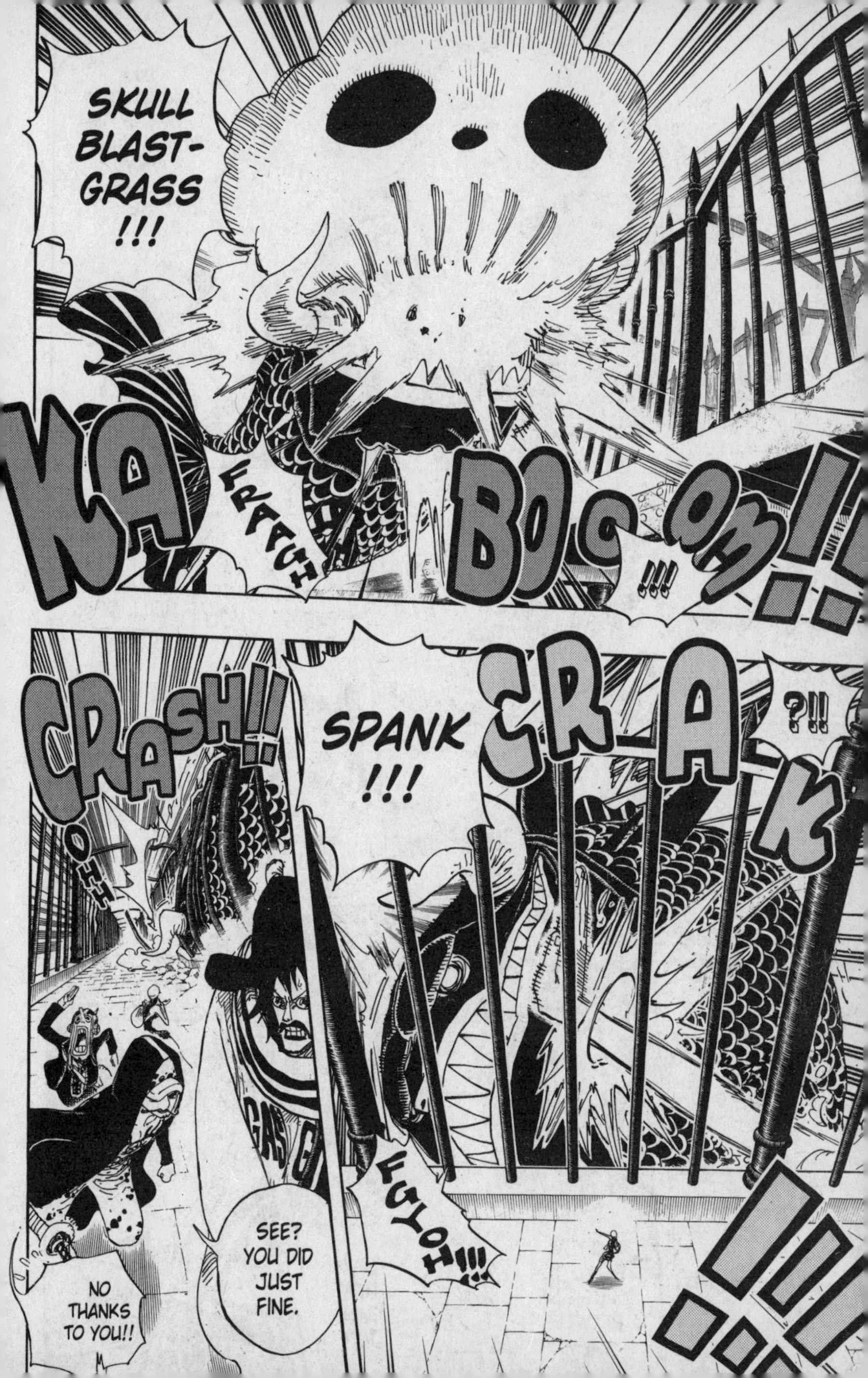
SKULL BLAST-GRASS!!!
FRATCH
KABOOOM!!!
?!!
CRAK
SPANK!!!
FGYOH!!!
SEE? YOU DID JUST FINE.
CRASH!!
OHH
NO THANKS TO YOU!!

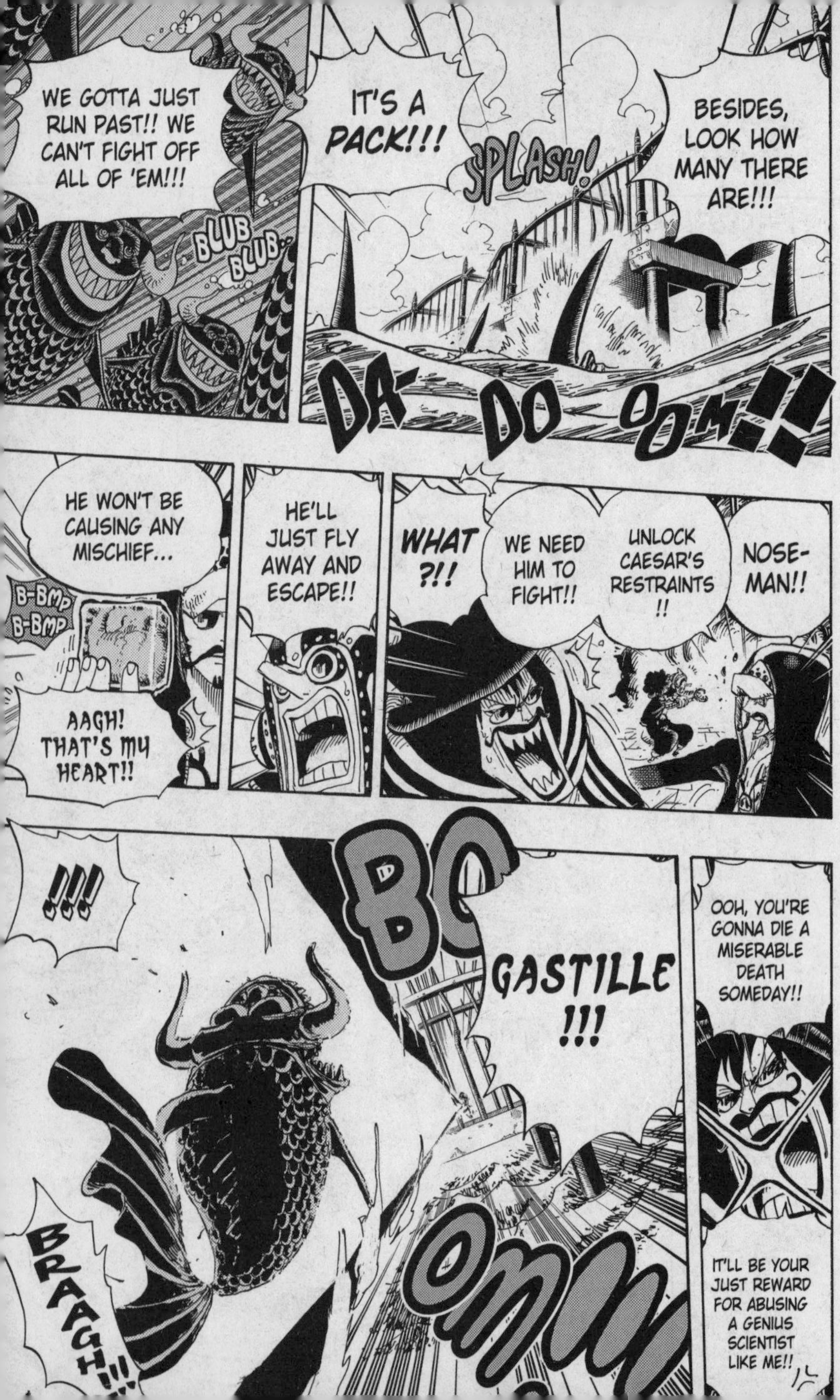
BESIDES, LOOK HOW MANY THERE ARE!!!
SPLASH!
IT'S A PACK!!!
DA-DO OOM!!
WE GOTTA JUST RUN PAST!! WE CAN'T FIGHT OFF ALL OF 'EM!!!
BLUB BLUB
NOSE-MAN!!
UNLOCK CAESAR'S RESTRAINTS!!
WE NEED HIM TO FIGHT!!
WHAT?!!
HE'LL JUST FLY AWAY AND ESCAPE!!
HE WON'T BE CAUSING ANY MISCHIEF...
B-BMP B-BMP
AAGH! THAT'S MY HEART!!
OOH, YOU'RE GONNA DIE A MISERABLE DEATH SOMEDAY!!
IT'LL BE YOUR JUST REWARD FOR ABUSING A GENIUS SCIENTIST LIKE ME!!
GASTILLE!!!
!!!
BRAAGH!!

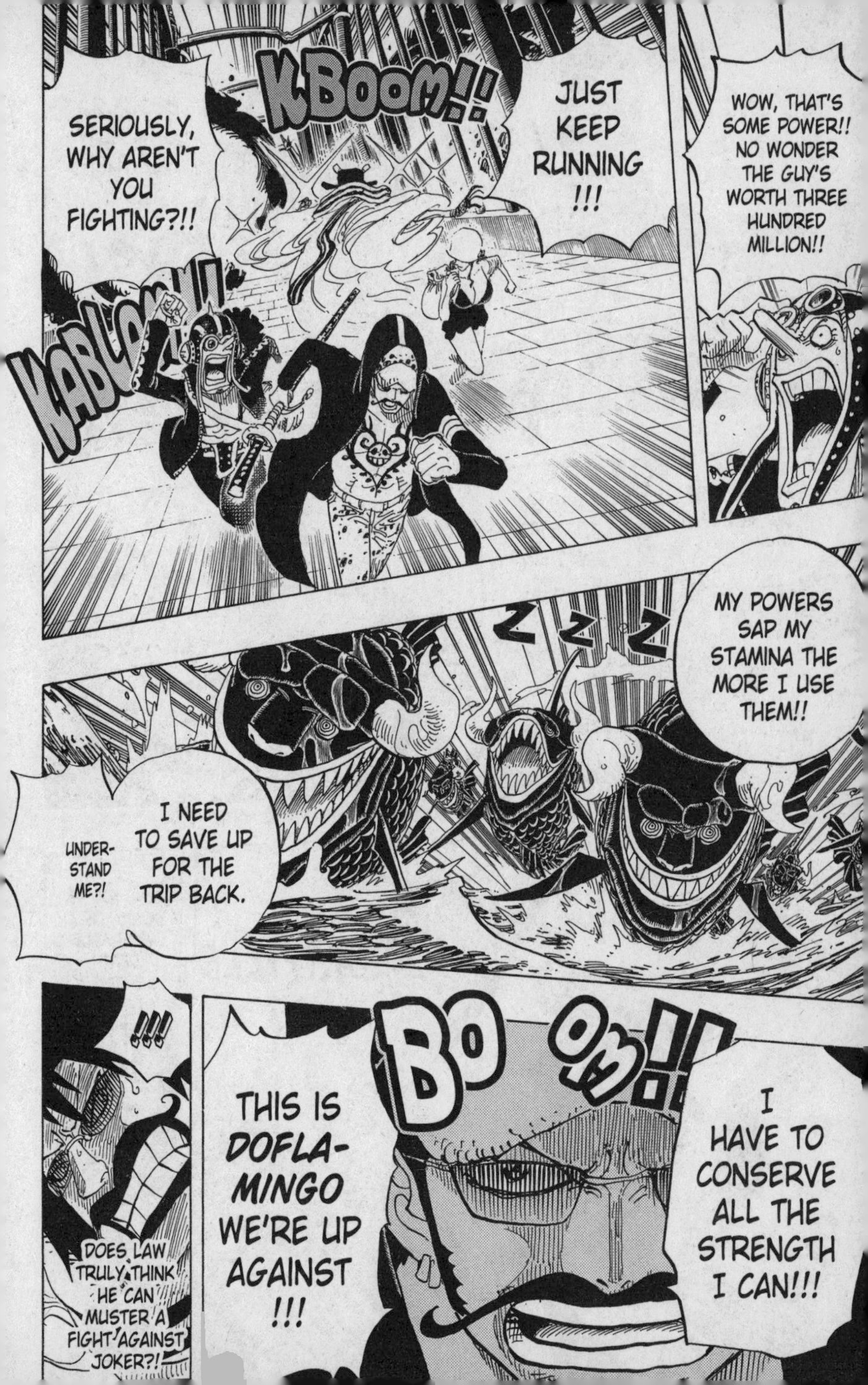
WOW, THAT'S SOME POWER!! NO WONDER THE GUY'S WORTH THREE HUNDRED MILLION!!
KBOOM!!
JUST KEEP RUNNING!!!
SERIOUSLY, WHY AREN'T YOU FIGHTING?!!
KABLOOM!!
Z Z Z
MY POWERS SAP MY STAMINA THE MORE I USE THEM!!
I NEED TO SAVE UP FOR THE TRIP BACK.
UNDER-STAND ME?!
BOOM!!
I HAVE TO CONSERVE ALL THE STRENGTH I CAN!!!
THIS IS *DOFLA-MINGO* WE'RE UP AGAINST!!!
!!!
DOES LAW TRULY THINK HE CAN MUSTER A FIGHT AGAINST JOKER?!

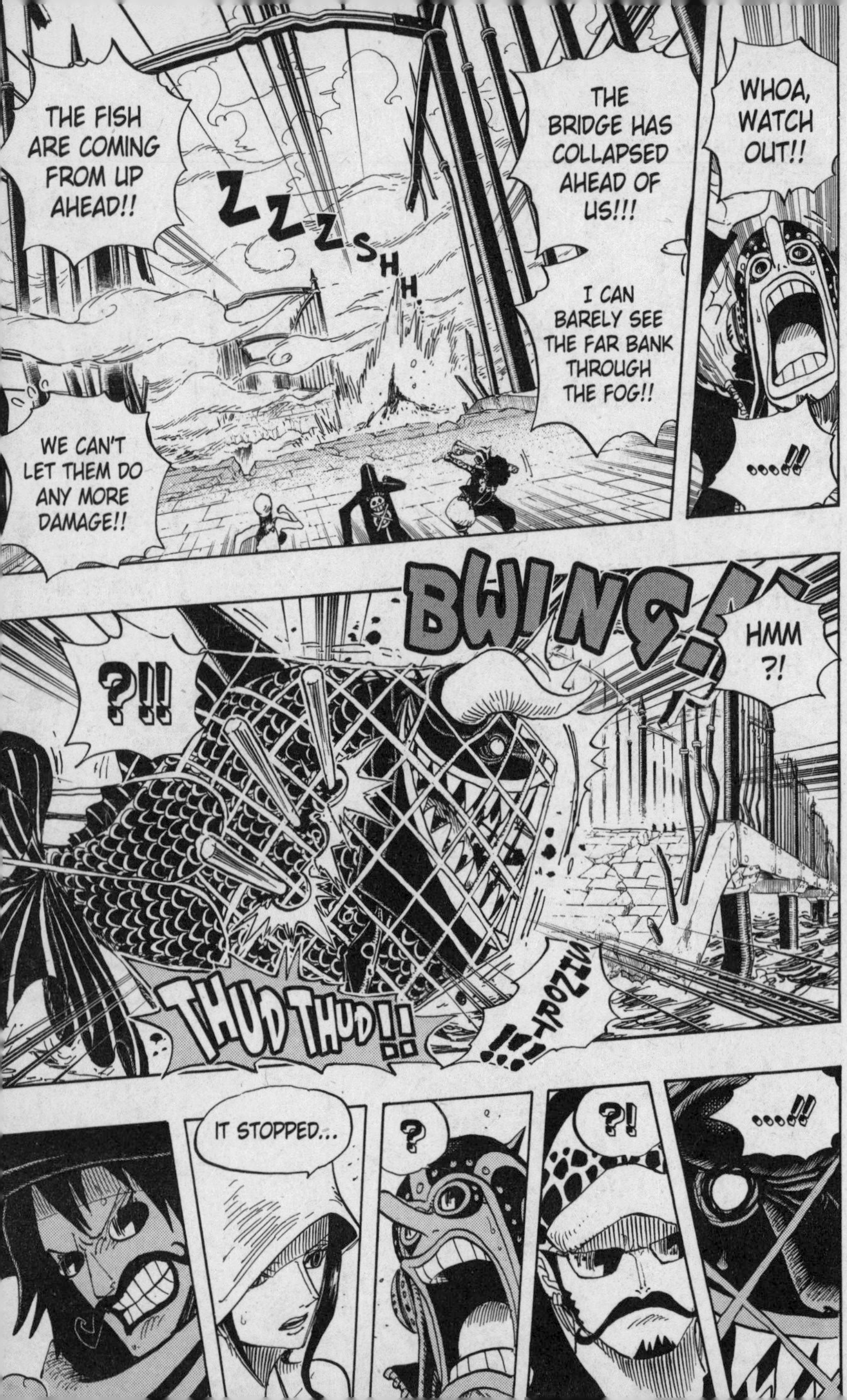
WHOA, WATCH OUT!!
...!!
THE BRIDGE HAS COLLAPSED AHEAD OF US!!!
I CAN BARELY SEE THE FAR BANK THROUGH THE FOG!!
THE FISH ARE COMING FROM UP AHEAD!!
ZZZSHH
WE CAN'T LET THEM DO ANY MORE DAMAGE!!
BWING!
HMM ?!
?!!
THUD THUD!!
...!!
?!
?
IT STOPPED...

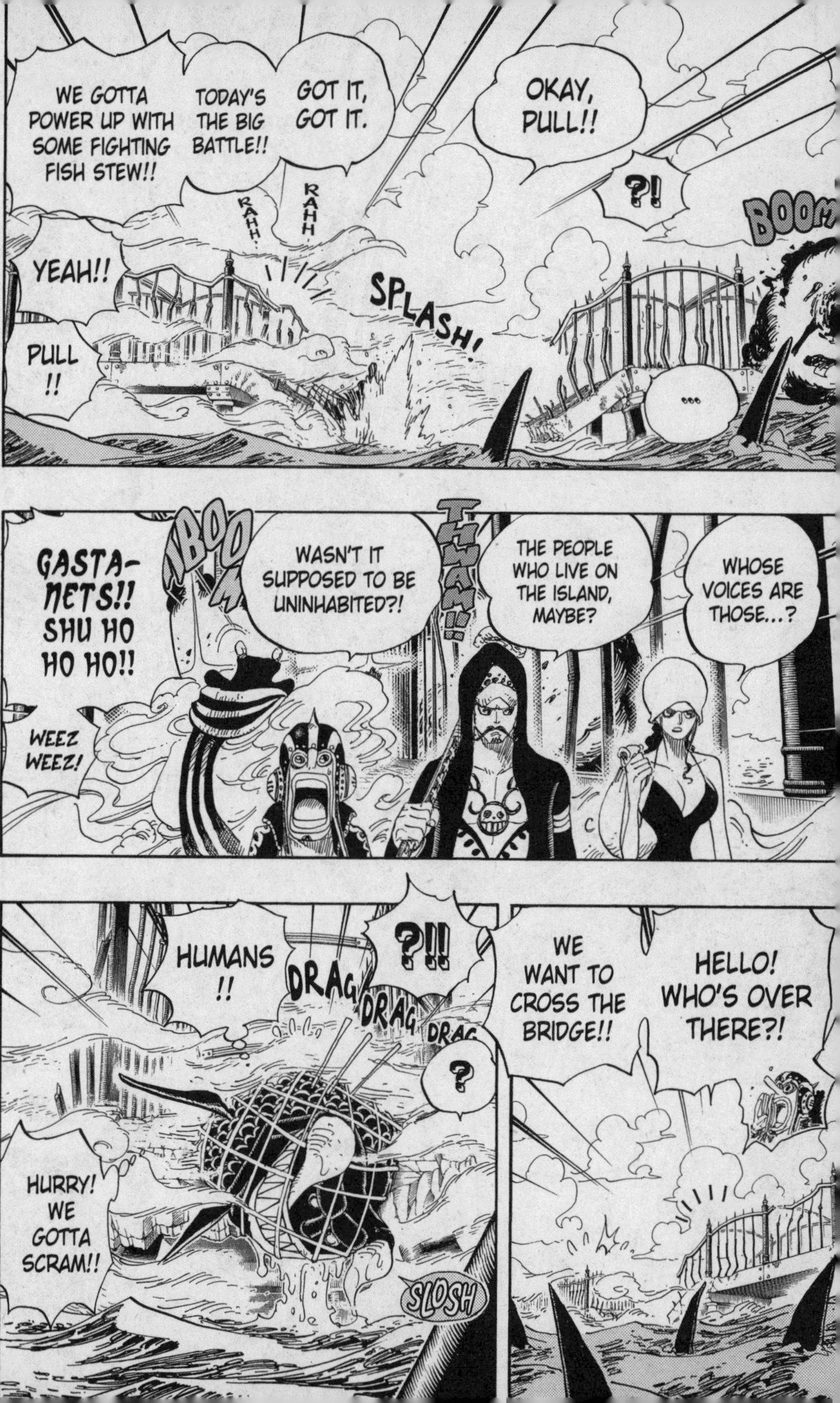
OKAY, PULL!!
?!
BOOM
GOT IT, GOT IT.
TODAY'S THE BIG BATTLE!!
WE GOTTA POWER UP WITH SOME FIGHTING FISH STEW!!
RAHH
RAHH
SPLASH
...
YEAH!!
PULL!!
WHOSE VOICES ARE THOSE...?
THE PEOPLE WHO LIVE ON THE ISLAND, MAYBE?
THWAM!!
WASN'T IT SUPPOSED TO BE UNINHABITED?!
BOOM
GASTA-NETS!! SHU HO HO HO!!
WEEZ WEEZ!
HELLO! WHO'S OVER THERE?!
WE WANT TO CROSS THE BRIDGE!!
?!!
HUMANS!!
DRAG DRAG DRAG
?
HURRY! WE GOTTA SCRAM!!
SLOSH

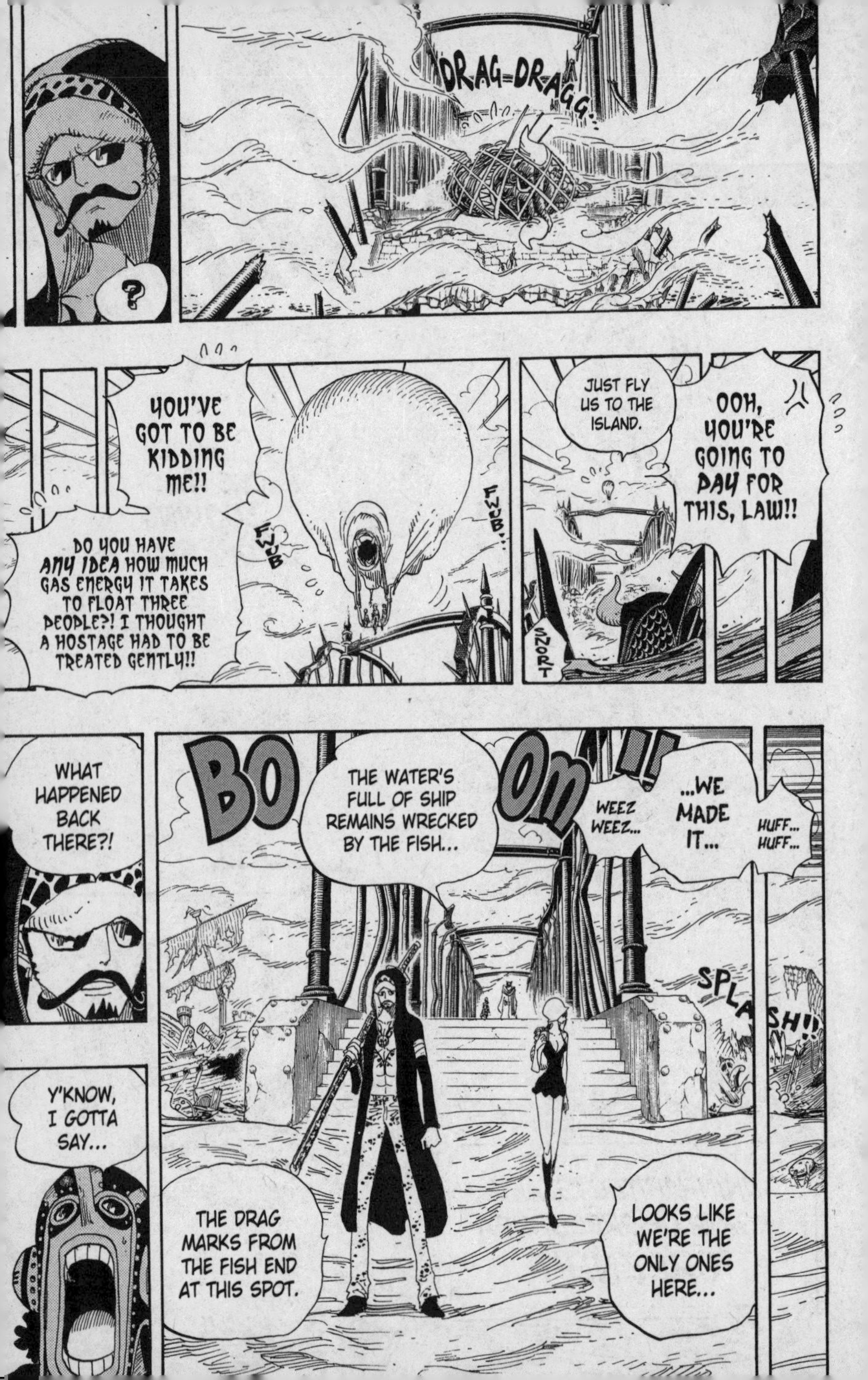
DRAG-DRAGG...
?
JUST FLY US TO THE ISLAND.
OOH, YOU'RE GOING TO PAY FOR THIS, LAW!!
SNORT
FWUB FWUB...
YOU'VE GOT TO BE KIDDING ME!!
DO YOU HAVE ANY IDEA HOW MUCH GAS ENERGY IT TAKES TO FLOAT THREE PEOPLE?! I THOUGHT A HOSTAGE HAD TO BE TREATED GENTLY!!
HUFF... HUFF...
...WE MADE IT...
WEEZ WEEZ...
BOOM!!
THE WATER'S FULL OF SHIP REMAINS WRECKED BY THE FISH...
SPLASH!!
LOOKS LIKE WE'RE THE ONLY ONES HERE...
THE DRAG MARKS FROM THE FISH END AT THIS SPOT.
WHAT HAPPENED BACK THERE?!
Y'KNOW, I GOTTA SAY...

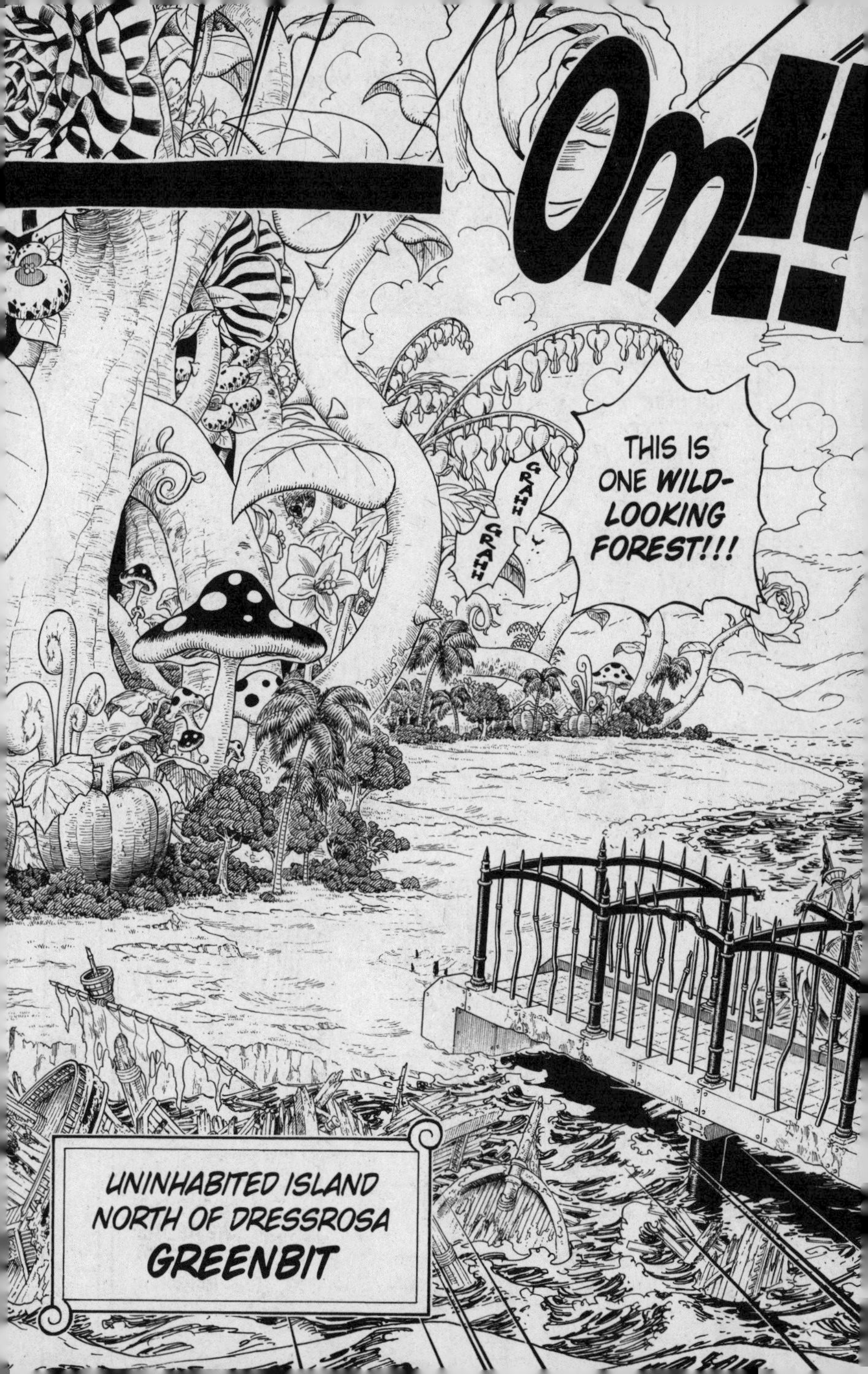
OM!!
THIS IS ONE WILD-LOOKING FOREST!!!
GRAHH GRAHH
UNINHABITED ISLAND NORTH OF DRESSROSA GREENBIT

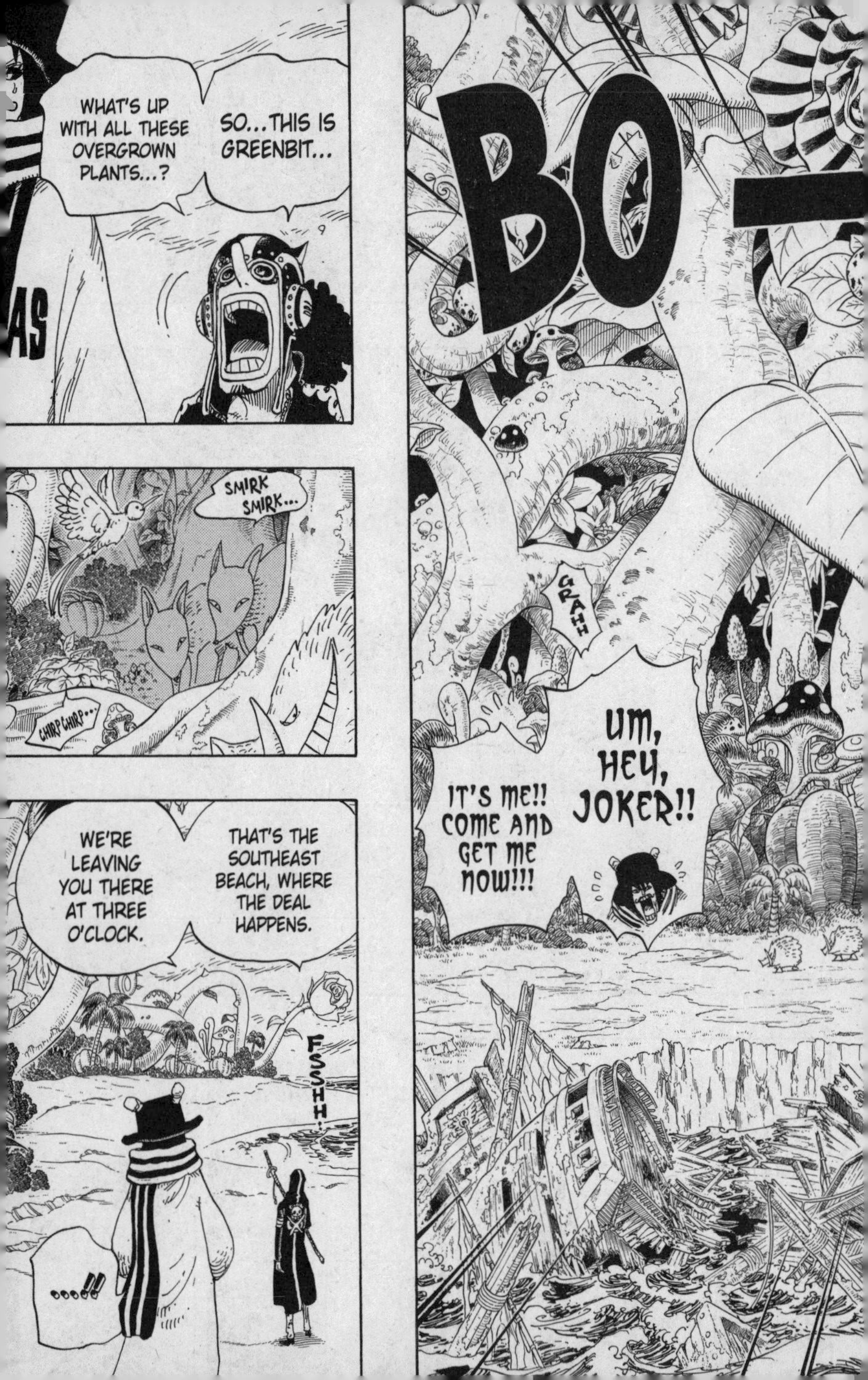
BO-
GRAHH
UM, HEY, JOKER!!
IT'S ME!! COME AND GET ME NOW!!!
SO...THIS IS GREENBIT...
WHAT'S UP WITH ALL THESE OVERGROWN PLANTS...?
SMIRK SMIRK...
CHIRP CHIRP...
THAT'S THE SOUTHEAST BEACH, WHERE THE DEAL HAPPENS.
WE'RE LEAVING YOU THERE AT THREE O'CLOCK.
FSSHH!
....!!

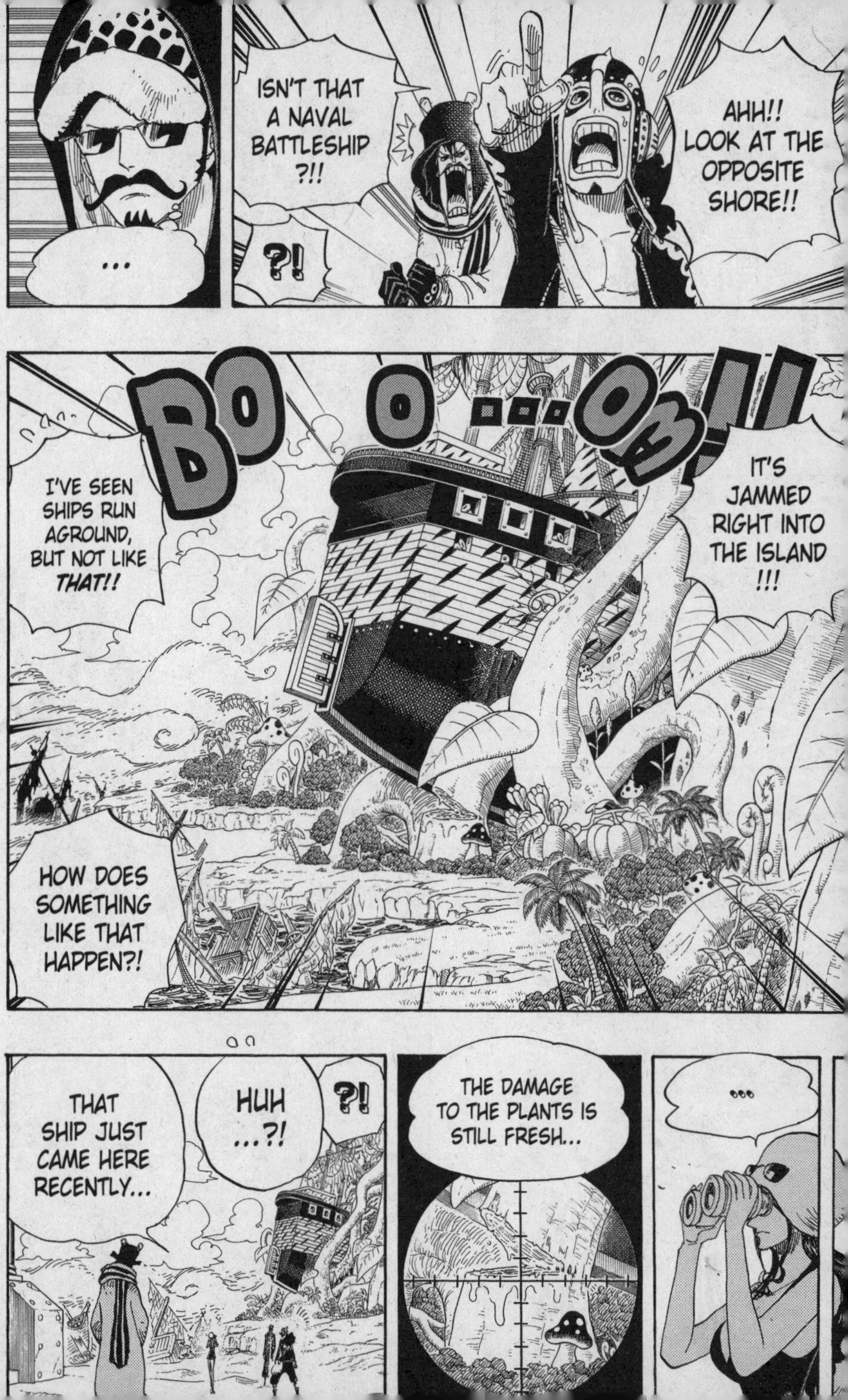
AHH!! LOOK AT THE OPPOSITE SHORE!!
ISN'T THAT A NAVAL BATTLESHIP ?!!
?!
...
BO O ...OM!!
IT'S JAMMED RIGHT INTO THE ISLAND !!!
I'VE SEEN SHIPS RUN AGROUND, BUT NOT LIKE *THAT!!*
HOW DOES SOMETHING LIKE THAT HAPPEN?!
...
THE DAMAGE TO THE PLANTS IS STILL FRESH...
?!
HUH ...?!
THAT SHIP JUST CAME HERE RECENTLY...

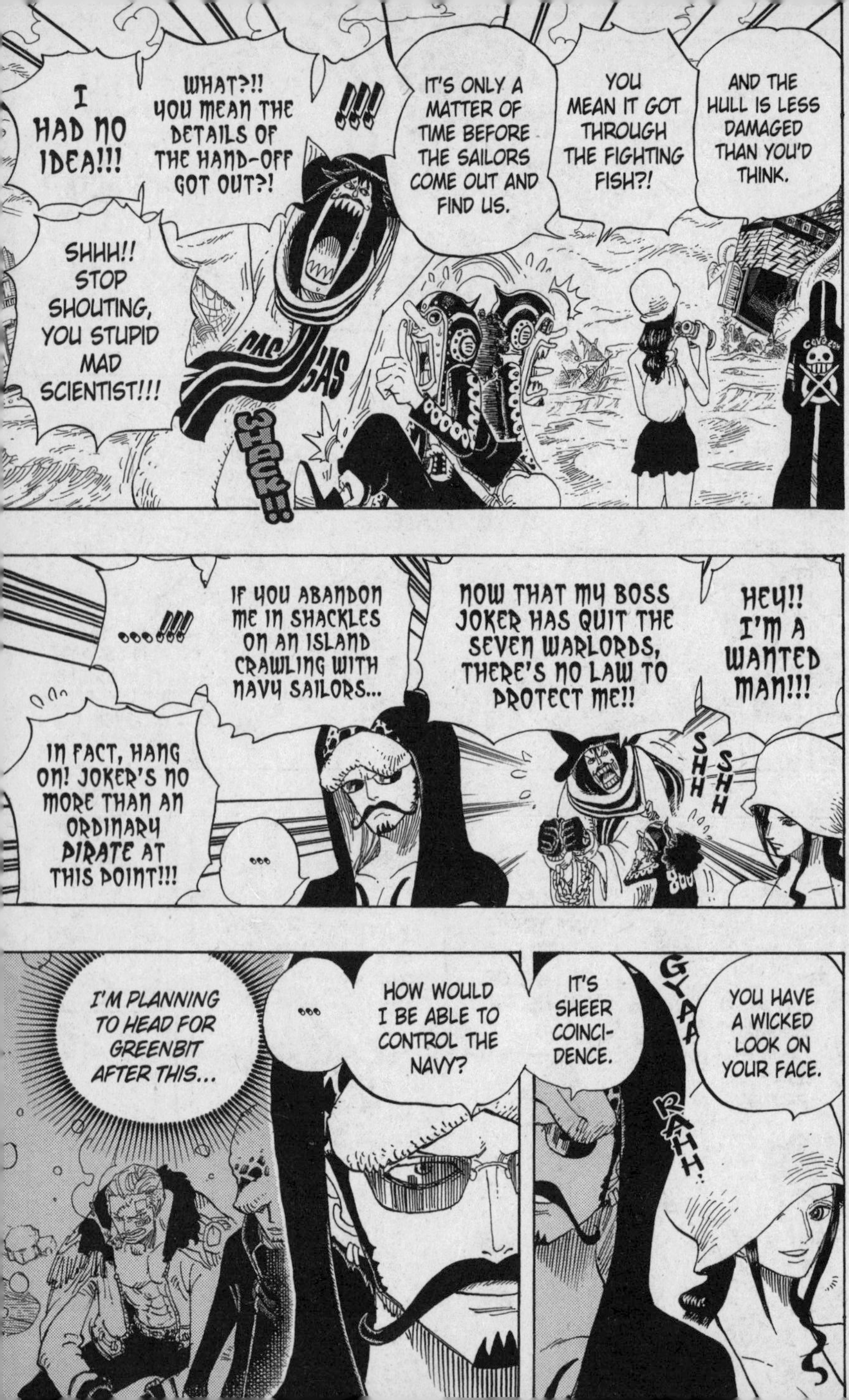
AND THE HULL IS LESS DAMAGED THAN YOU'D THINK.
YOU MEAN IT GOT THROUGH THE FIGHTING FISH?!
IT'S ONLY A MATTER OF TIME BEFORE THE SAILORS COME OUT AND FIND US.
!!!
WHAT?!! YOU MEAN THE DETAILS OF THE HAND-OFF GOT OUT?!
I HAD NO IDEA!!!
SHHH!! STOP SHOUTING, YOU STUPID MAD SCIENTIST!!!
SMACK!!
HEY!! I'M A WANTED MAN!!!
NOW THAT MY BOSS JOKER HAS QUIT THE SEVEN WARLORDS, THERE'S NO LAW TO PROTECT ME!!
SHH
SHH
IF YOU ABANDON ME IN SHACKLES ON AN ISLAND CRAWLING WITH NAVY SAILORS...
...!!!
IN FACT, HANG ON! JOKER'S NO MORE THAN AN ORDINARY PIRATE AT THIS POINT!!!
...
YOU HAVE A WICKED LOOK ON YOUR FACE.
GYAA
RAHH
IT'S SHEER COINCI-DENCE.
HOW WOULD I BE ABLE TO CONTROL THE NAVY?
...
I'M PLANNING TO HEAD FOR GREENBIT AFTER THIS...

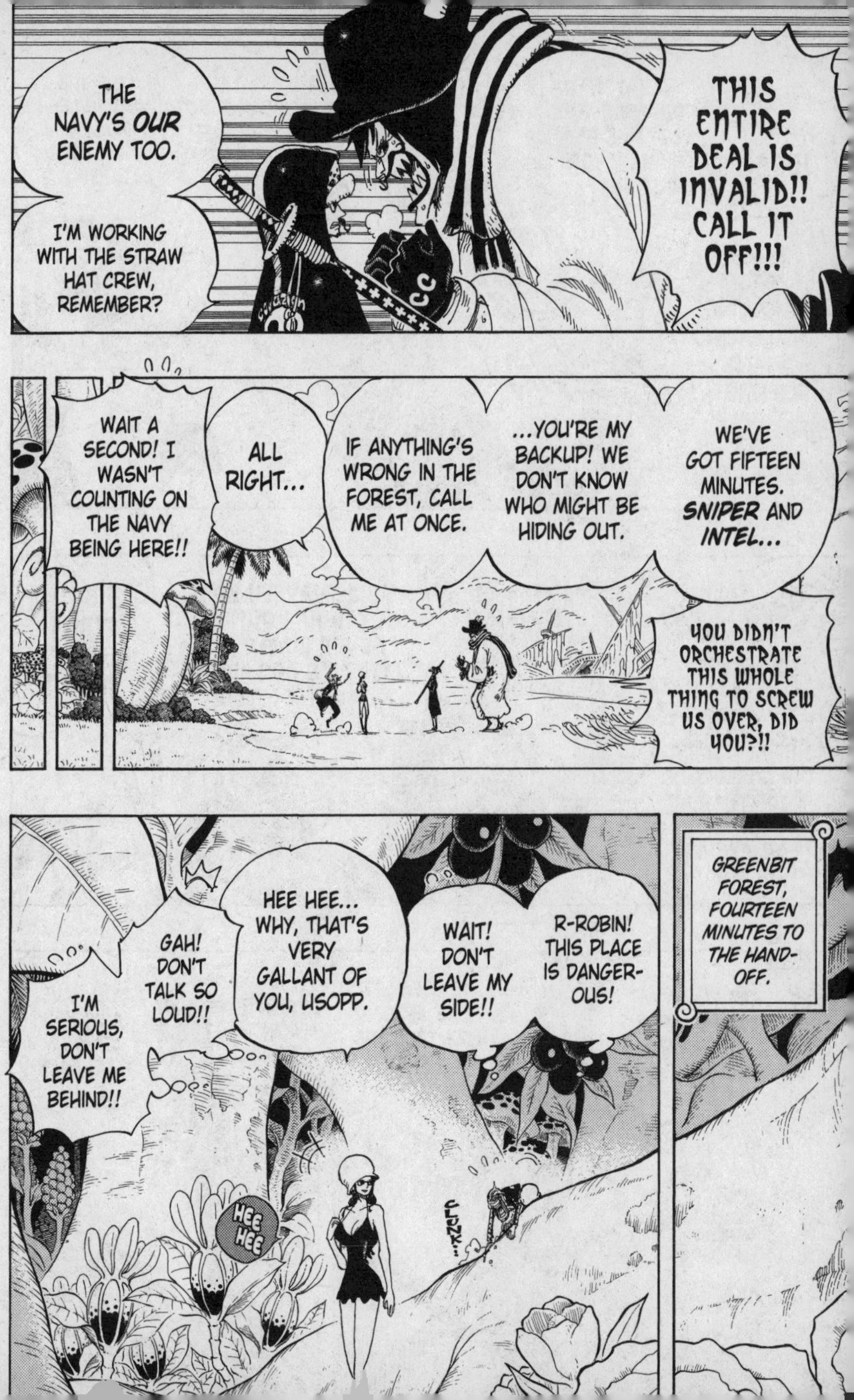
THIS ENTIRE DEAL IS INVALID!! CALL IT OFF!!!
THE NAVY'S OUR ENEMY TOO.
I'M WORKING WITH THE STRAW HAT CREW, REMEMBER?
WE'VE GOT FIFTEEN MINUTES. SNIPER AND INTEL...
...YOU'RE MY BACKUP! WE DON'T KNOW WHO MIGHT BE HIDING OUT.
IF ANYTHING'S WRONG IN THE FOREST, CALL ME AT ONCE.
ALL RIGHT...
WAIT A SECOND! I WASN'T COUNTING ON THE NAVY BEING HERE!!
YOU DIDN'T ORCHESTRATE THIS WHOLE THING TO SCREW US OVER, DID YOU?!!
GREENBIT FOREST, FOURTEEN MINUTES TO THE HAND-OFF.
R-ROBIN! THIS PLACE IS DANGER-OUS!
WAIT! DON'T LEAVE MY SIDE!!
HEE HEE... WHY, THAT'S VERY GALLANT OF YOU, USOPP.
GAH! DON'T TALK SO LOUD!!
I'M SERIOUS, DON'T LEAVE ME BEHIND!!
HEE HEE
CLUNK!!

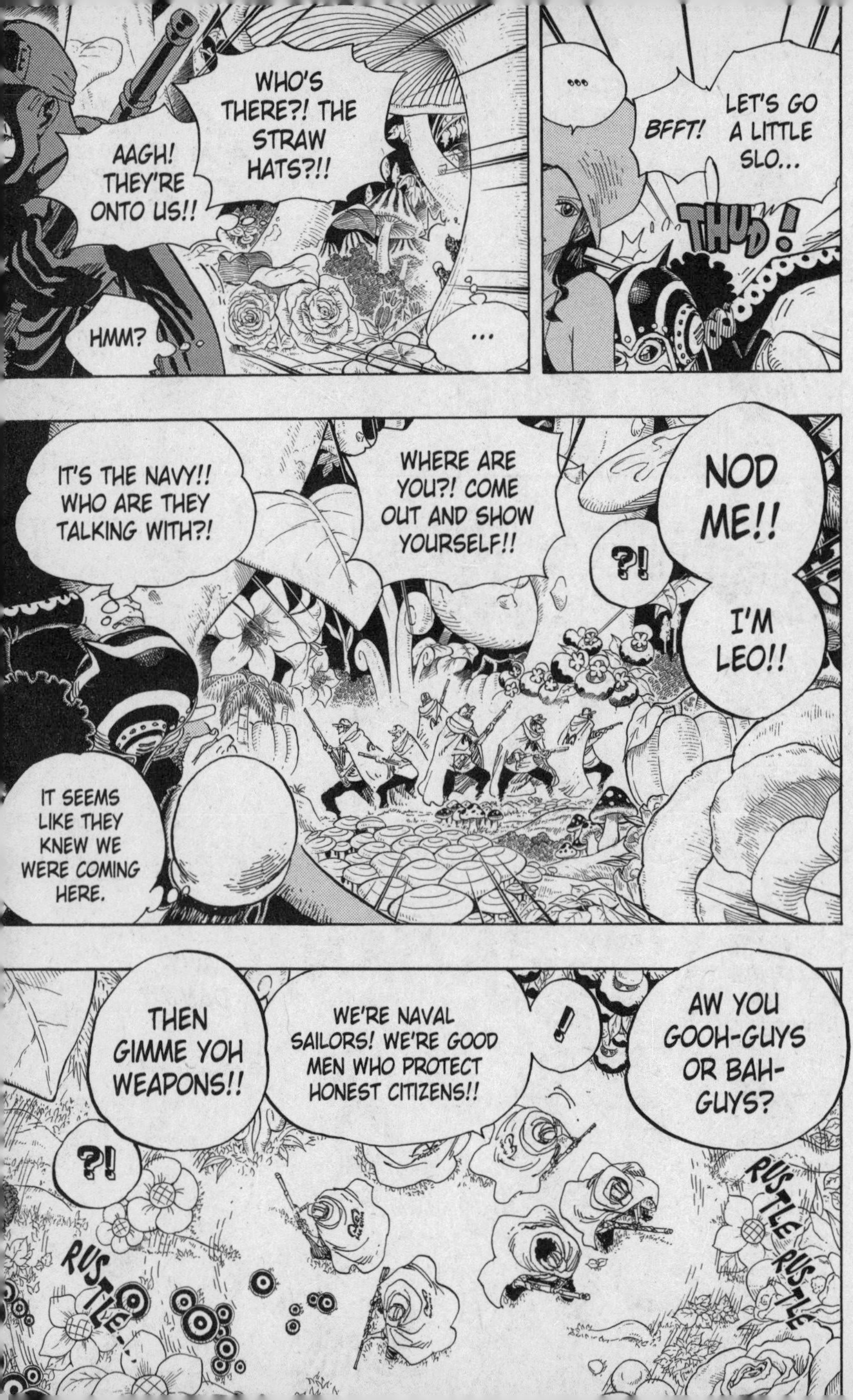
...
LET'S GO A LITTLE SLO...
BFFT!
THUD!
WHO'S THERE?! THE STRAW HATS?!!
AAGH! THEY'RE ONTO US!!
...
HMM?
NOD ME!!
I'M LEO!!
?!
WHERE ARE YOU?! COME OUT AND SHOW YOURSELF!!
IT'S THE NAVY!! WHO ARE THEY TALKING WITH?!
IT SEEMS LIKE THEY KNEW WE WERE COMING HERE.
AW YOU GOOH-GUYS OR BAH-GUYS?
!
WE'RE NAVAL SAILORS! WE'RE GOOD MEN WHO PROTECT HONEST CITIZENS!!
THEN GIMME YOH WEAPONS!!
RUSTLE
RUSTLE
?!
RUSTLE

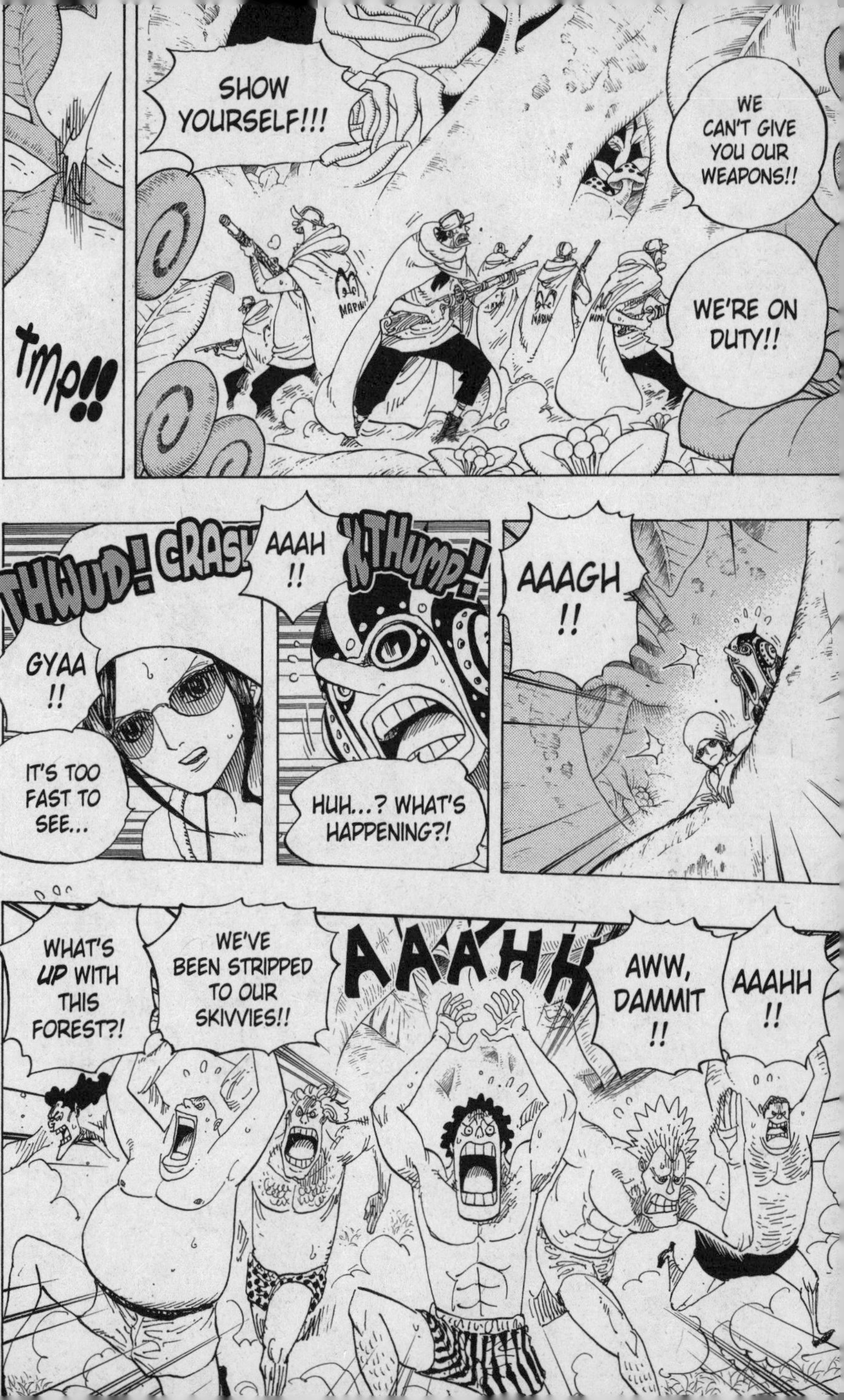
WE CAN'T GIVE YOU OUR WEAPONS!!
WE'RE ON DUTY!!
SHOW YOURSELF!!!
tmp!!
AAAGH !!
'KTHUMP!
AAAH !!
HUH...? WHAT'S HAPPENING?!
THWUD! CRAS
GYAA !!
IT'S TOO FAST TO SEE...
AAAHH !!
AWW, DAMMIT !!
AAAHH
WE'VE BEEN STRIPPED TO OUR SKIVVIES!!
WHAT'S UP WITH THIS FOREST?!

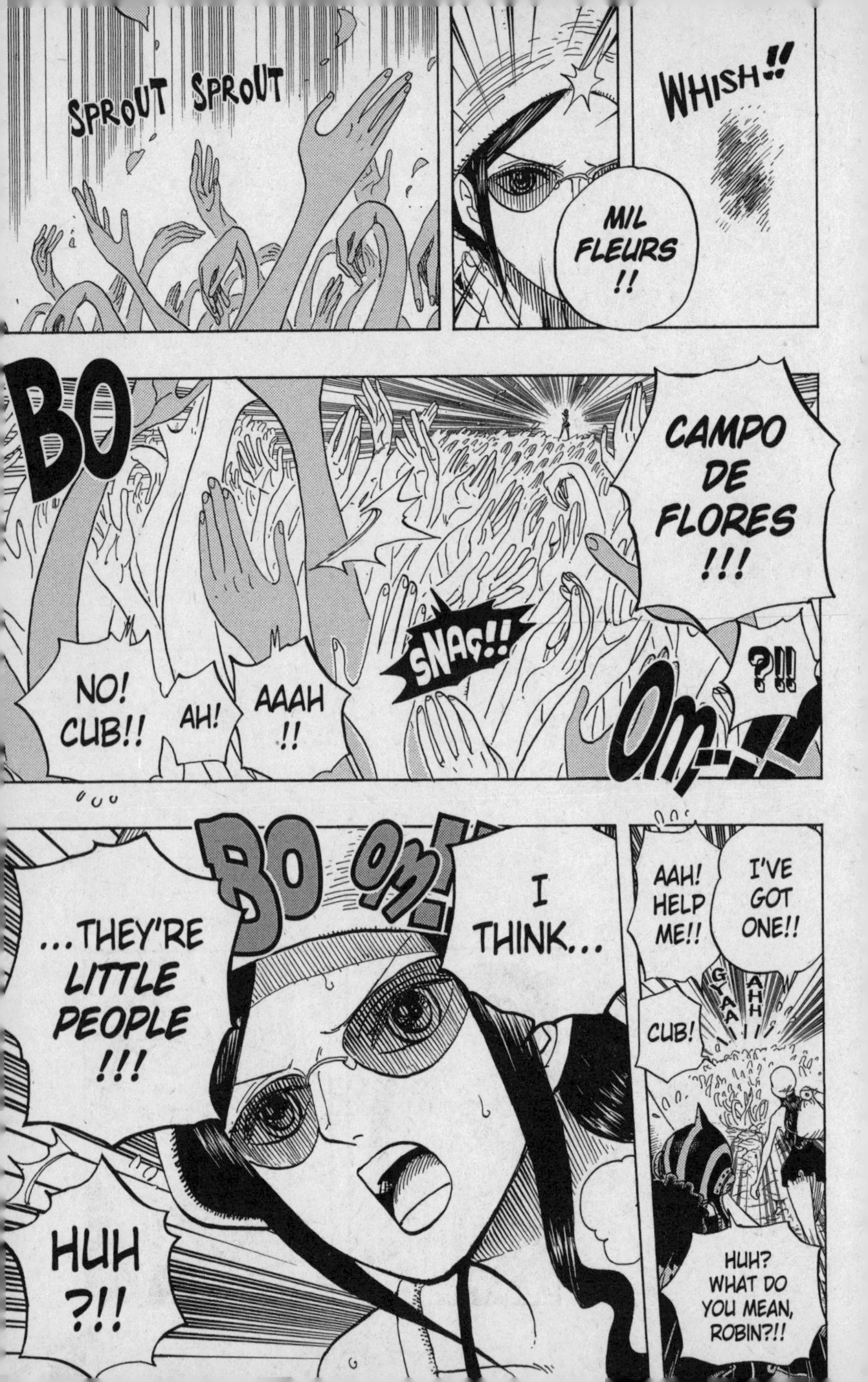
WHISH!!
MIL FLEURS!!
SPROUT SPROUT
CAMPO DE FLORES!!!
?!!
BO OM--!!
SNAG!!
AAAH!!
AH!
NO! CUB!!
I'VE GOT ONE!!
AAH! HELP ME!!
AHH
GYAA
CUB!
HUH? WHAT DO YOU MEAN, ROBIN?!!
BO OM!
I THINK...
...THEY'RE LITTLE PEOPLE!!!
HUH?!!

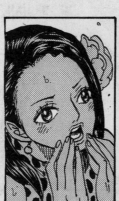
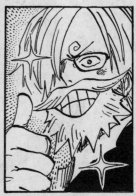

Chapter 711:
ADVENTURE IN THE LAND OF THE LITTLE PEOPLE

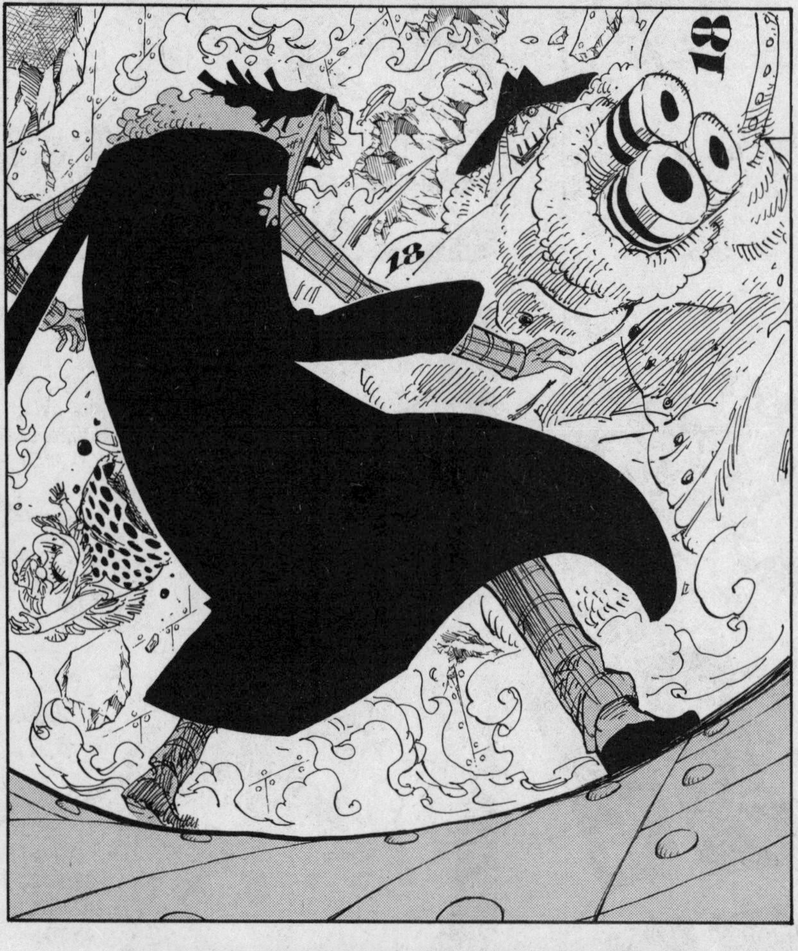
18
18

CARIBOU'S NEW WORLD KEE HEE HEE, VOL. 29:
"THE OLD HAG GETS BLASTED OFF HER FEET"

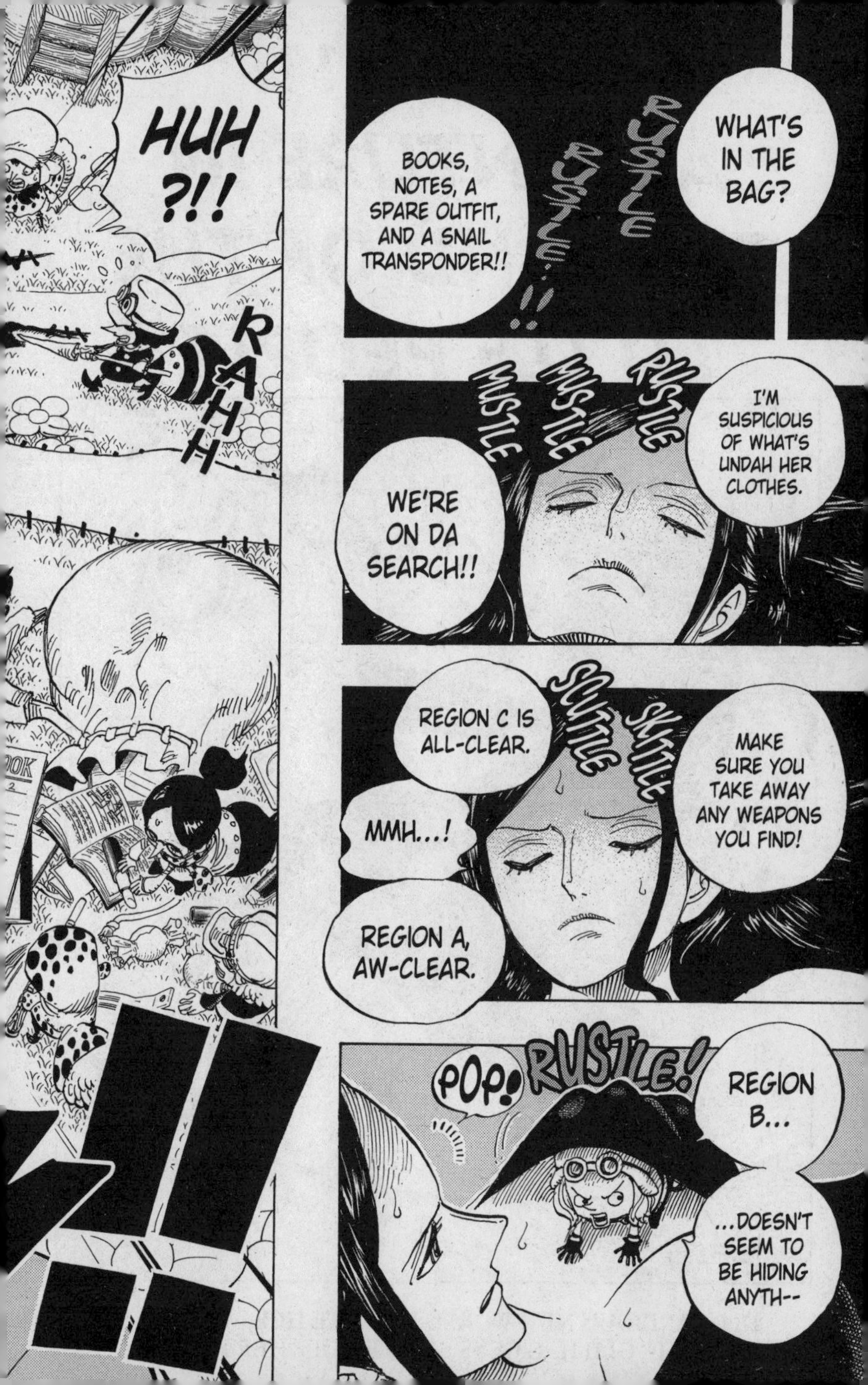
WHAT'S IN THE BAG?
RUSTLE
RUSTLE...!!
BOOKS, NOTES, A SPARE OUTFIT, AND A SNAIL TRANSPONDER!!
I'M SUSPICIOUS OF WHAT'S UNDAH HER CLOTHES.
RUSTLE
MUSTLE
MUSTLE
WE'RE ON DA SEARCH!!
MAKE SURE YOU TAKE AWAY ANY WEAPONS YOU FIND!
SKITTLE
SCUTTLE
REGION C IS ALL-CLEAR.
MMH...!
REGION A, AW-CLEAR.
REGION B...
RUSTLE!
POP!
...DOESN'T SEEM TO BE HIDING ANYTH--
HUH ?!!
RAHHH
!!

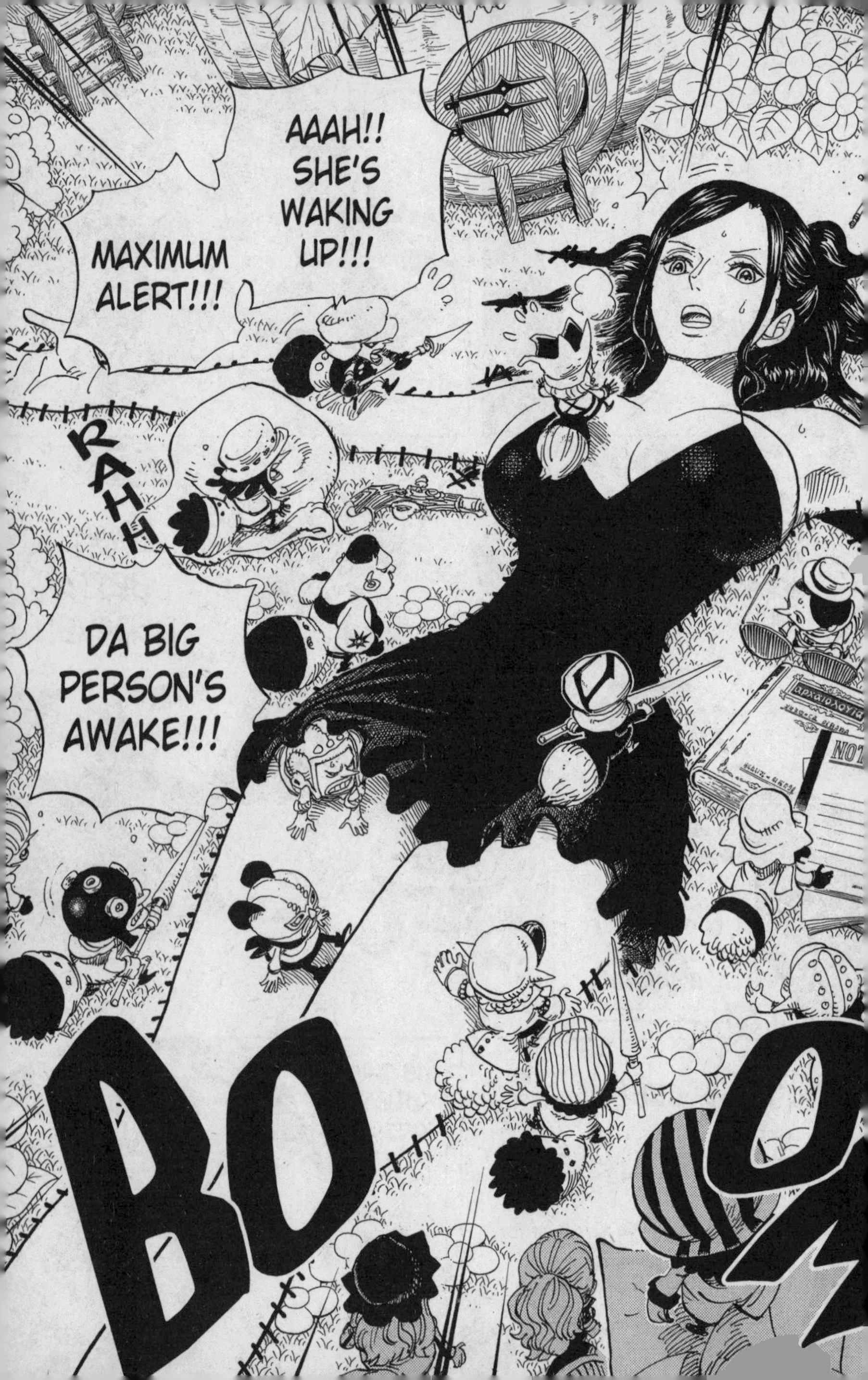
AAAH!! SHE'S WAKING UP!!!
MAXIMUM ALERT!!!
RAHH
DA BIG PERSON'S AWAKE!!!
BO

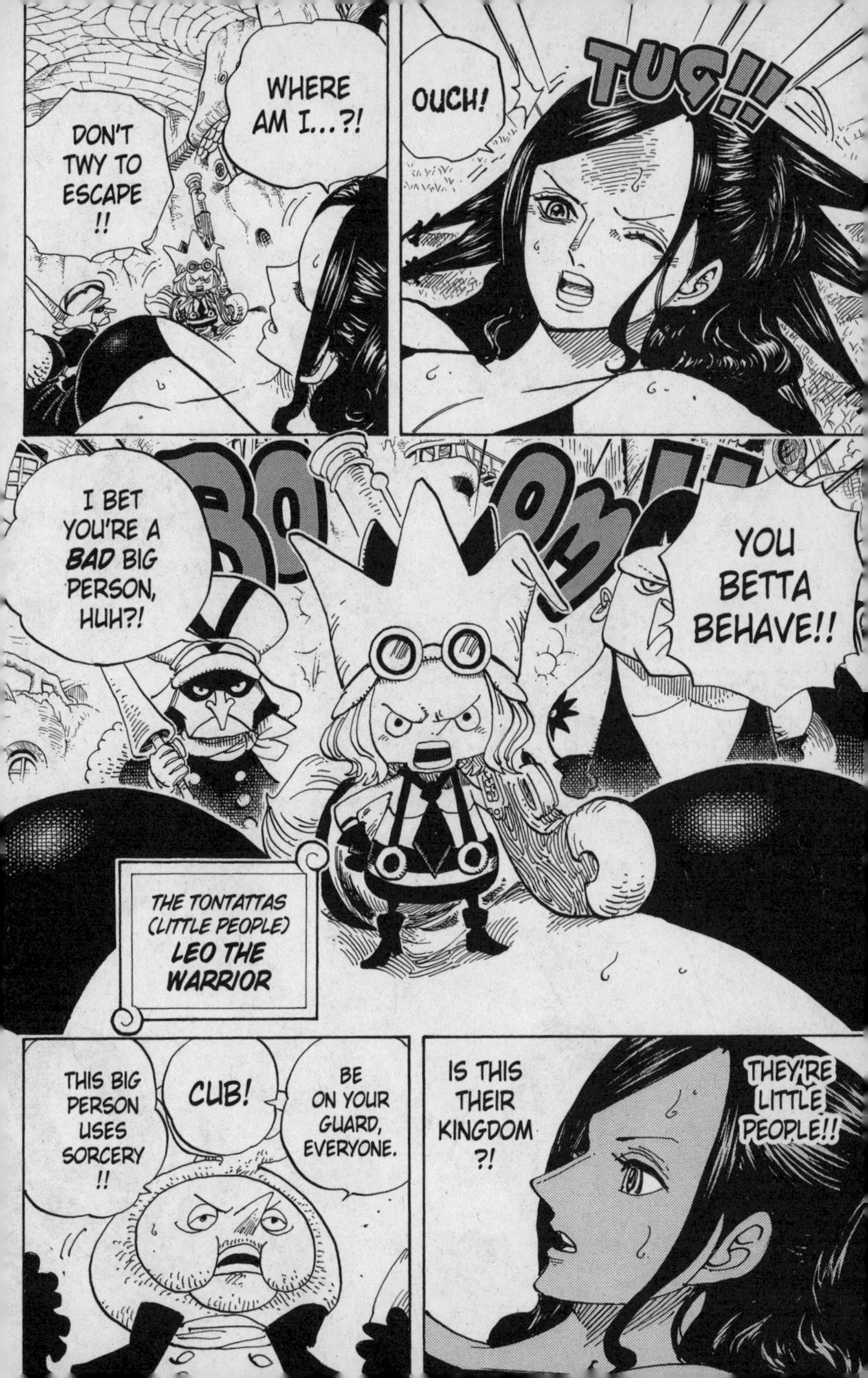
TUG!!
OUCH!
WHERE AM I...?!
DON'T TWY TO ESCAPE!!
BOOM!!
YOU BETTA BEHAVE!!
I BET YOU'RE A *BAD* BIG PERSON, HUH?!
THE TONTATTAS (LITTLE PEOPLE) **LEO THE WARRIOR**
THEY'RE LITTLE PEOPLE!!
IS THIS THEIR KINGDOM ?!
BE ON YOUR GUARD, EVERYONE.
CUB!
THIS BIG PERSON USES SORCERY!!

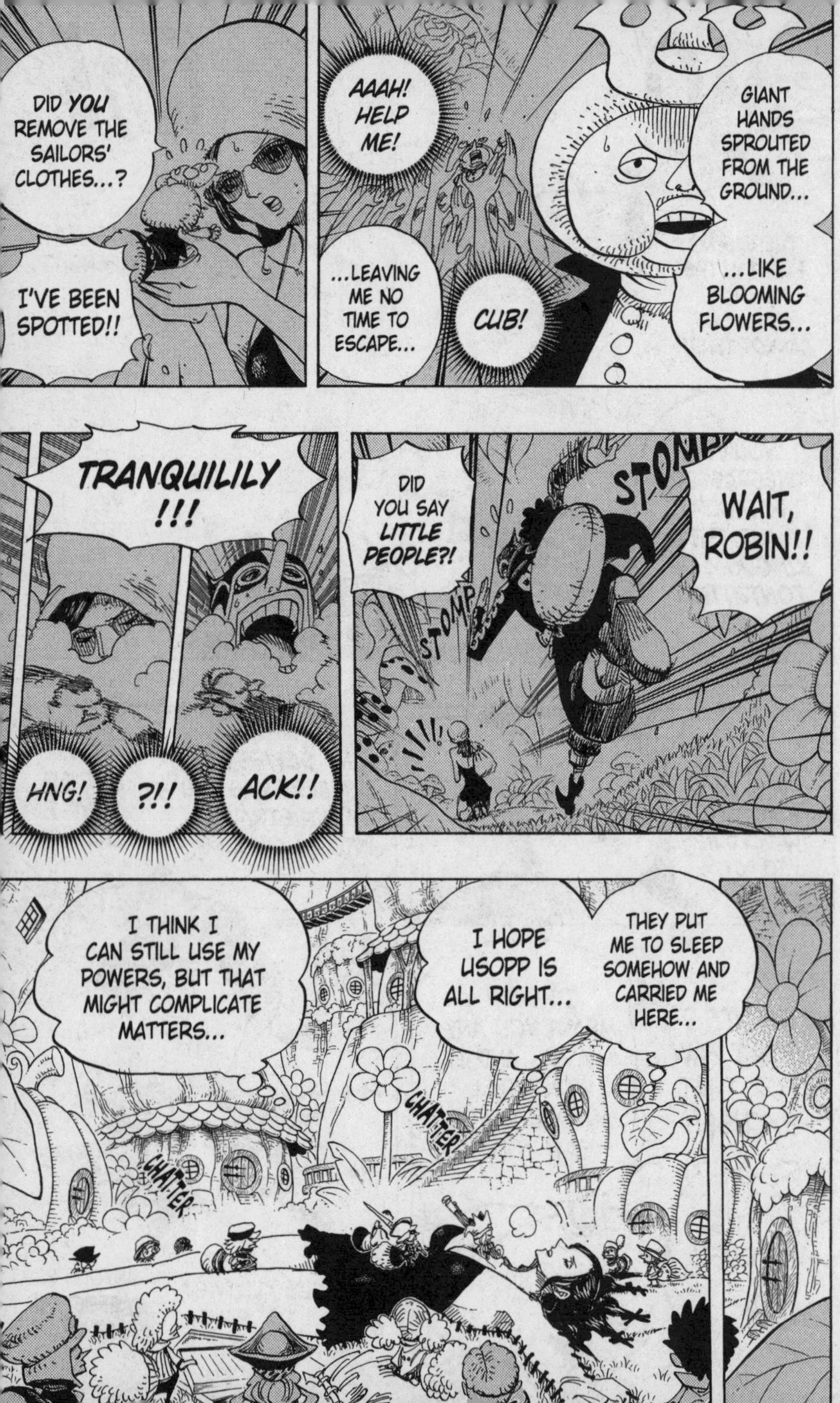

GIANT HANDS SPROUTED FROM THE GROUND...
AAAH! HELP ME!
...LIKE BLOOMING FLOWERS...
CUB!
...LEAVING ME NO TIME TO ESCAPE...
DID YOU REMOVE THE SAILORS' CLOTHES...?
I'VE BEEN SPOTTED!!
WAIT, ROBIN!!
STOMP
DID YOU SAY LITTLE PEOPLE?!
STOMP
STOMP
TRANQUILILY !!!
ACK!!
?!!
HNG!
THEY PUT ME TO SLEEP SOMEHOW AND CARRIED ME HERE...
I HOPE USOPP IS ALL RIGHT...
I THINK I CAN STILL USE MY POWERS, BUT THAT MIGHT COMPLICATE MATTERS...
CHATTER
CHATTER

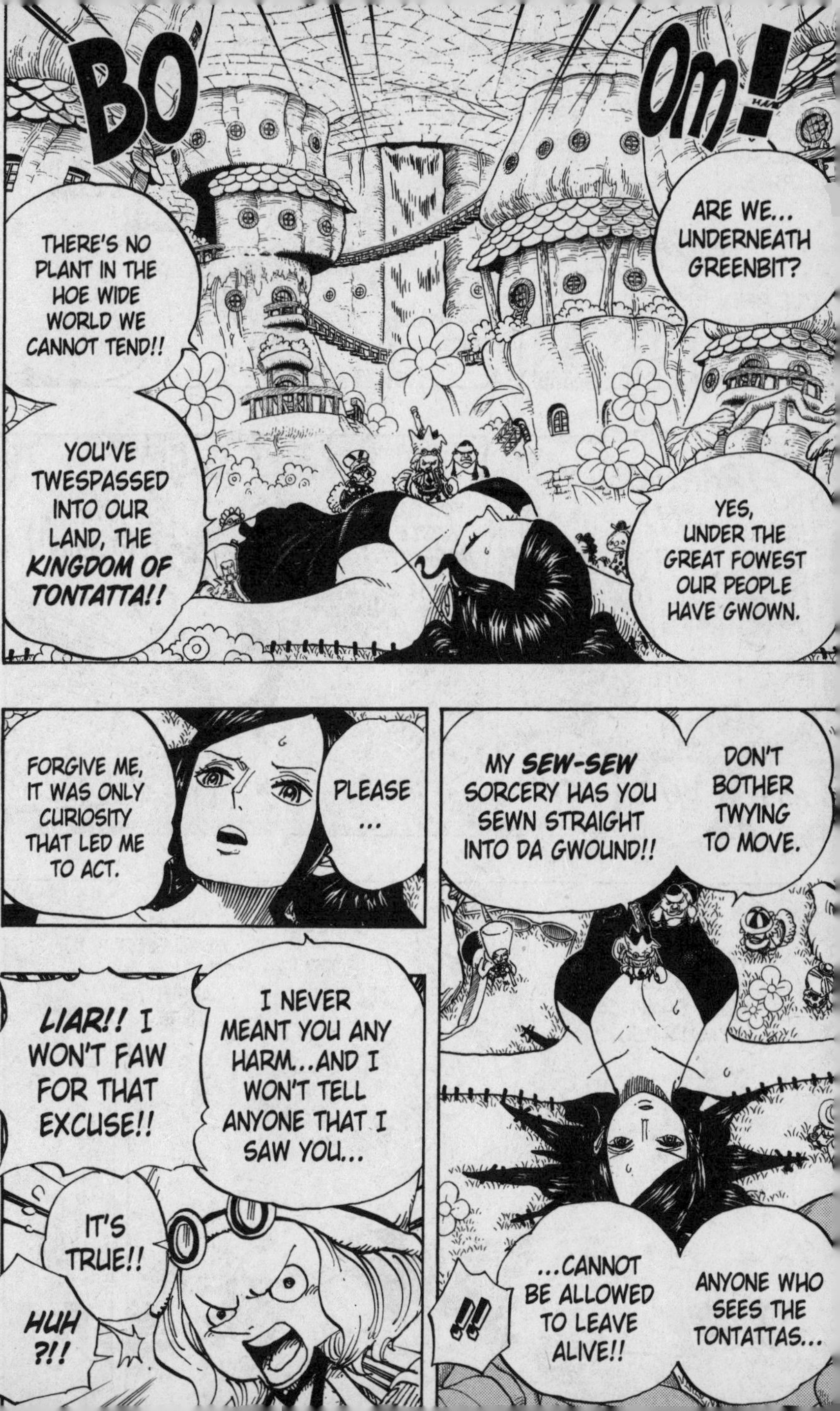
BOOM!
ARE WE... UNDERNEATH GREENBIT?
YES, UNDER THE GREAT FOWEST OUR PEOPLE HAVE GWOWN.
THERE'S NO PLANT IN THE HOE WIDE WORLD WE CANNOT TEND!!
YOU'VE TWESPASSED INTO OUR LAND, THE *KINGDOM OF TONTATTA!!*
DON'T BOTHER TWYING TO MOVE.
MY ***SEW-SEW*** SORCERY HAS YOU SEWN STRAIGHT INTO DA GWOUND!!
PLEASE ...
FORGIVE ME, IT WAS ONLY CURIOSITY THAT LED ME TO ACT.
I NEVER MEANT YOU ANY HARM...AND I WON'T TELL ANYONE THAT I SAW YOU...
LIAR!! I WON'T FAW FOR THAT EXCUSE!!
IT'S TRUE!!
HUH ?!!
ANYONE WHO SEES THE TONTATTAS...
...CANNOT BE ALLOWED TO LEAVE ALIVE!!
!!

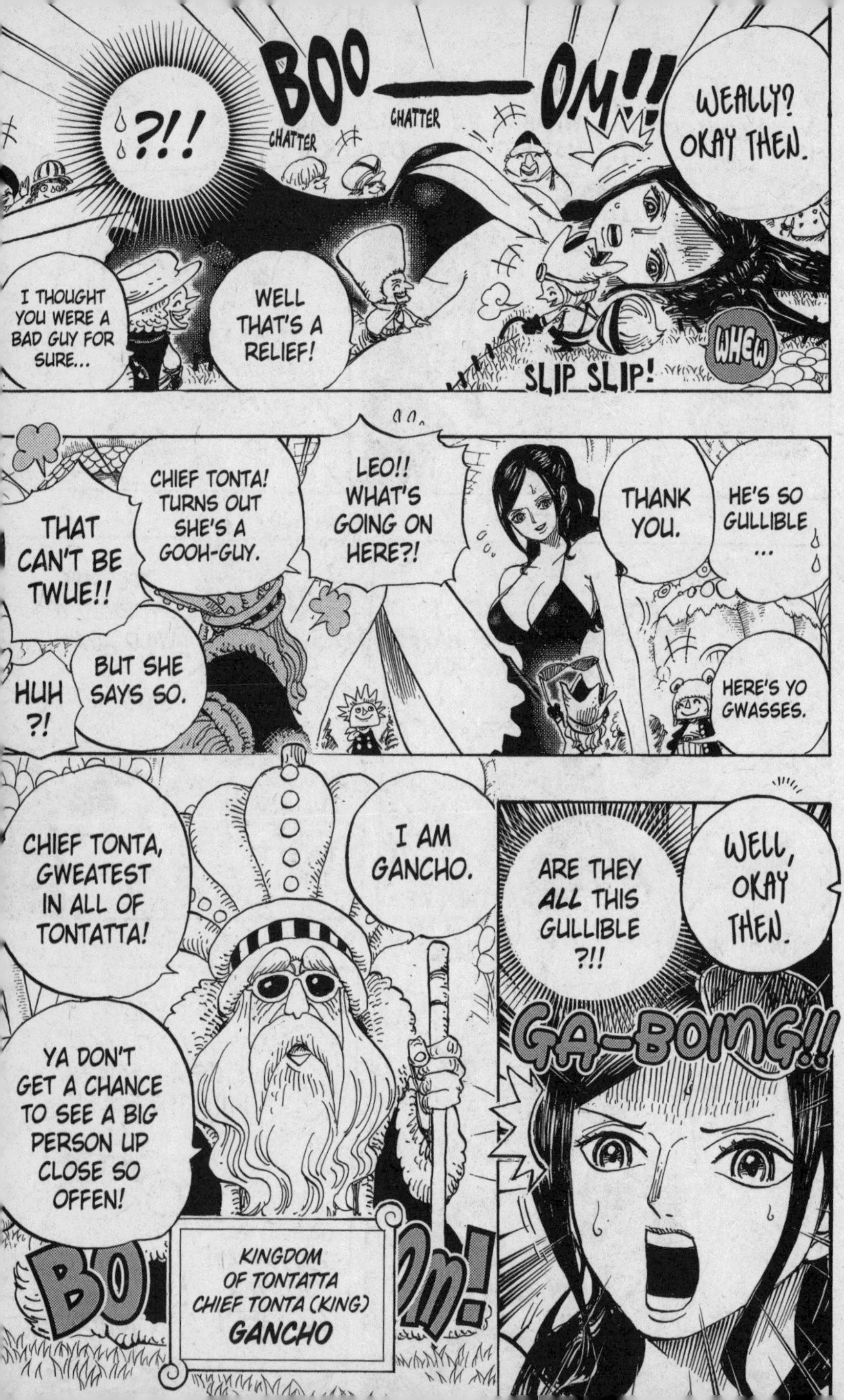
WEALLY? OKAY THEN.
BOO—OM!!
CHATTER
CHATTER
?!!
WHEW
SLIP SLIP!
WELL THAT'S A RELIEF!
I THOUGHT YOU WERE A BAD GUY FOR SURE...
HE'S SO GULLIBLE ...
THANK YOU.
HERE'S YO GWASSES.
LEO!! WHAT'S GOING ON HERE?!
CHIEF TONTA! TURNS OUT SHE'S A GOOH-GUY.
THAT CAN'T BE TWUE!!
BUT SHE SAYS SO.
HUH ?!
WELL, OKAY THEN.
ARE THEY ALL THIS GULLIBLE ?!!
GA-BOING!!
I AM GANCHO.
CHIEF TONTA, GWEATEST IN ALL OF TONTATTA!
YA DON'T GET A CHANCE TO SEE A BIG PERSON UP CLOSE SO OFFEN!
KINGDOM OF TONTATTA CHIEF TONTA (KING) GANCHO
BO—OM!

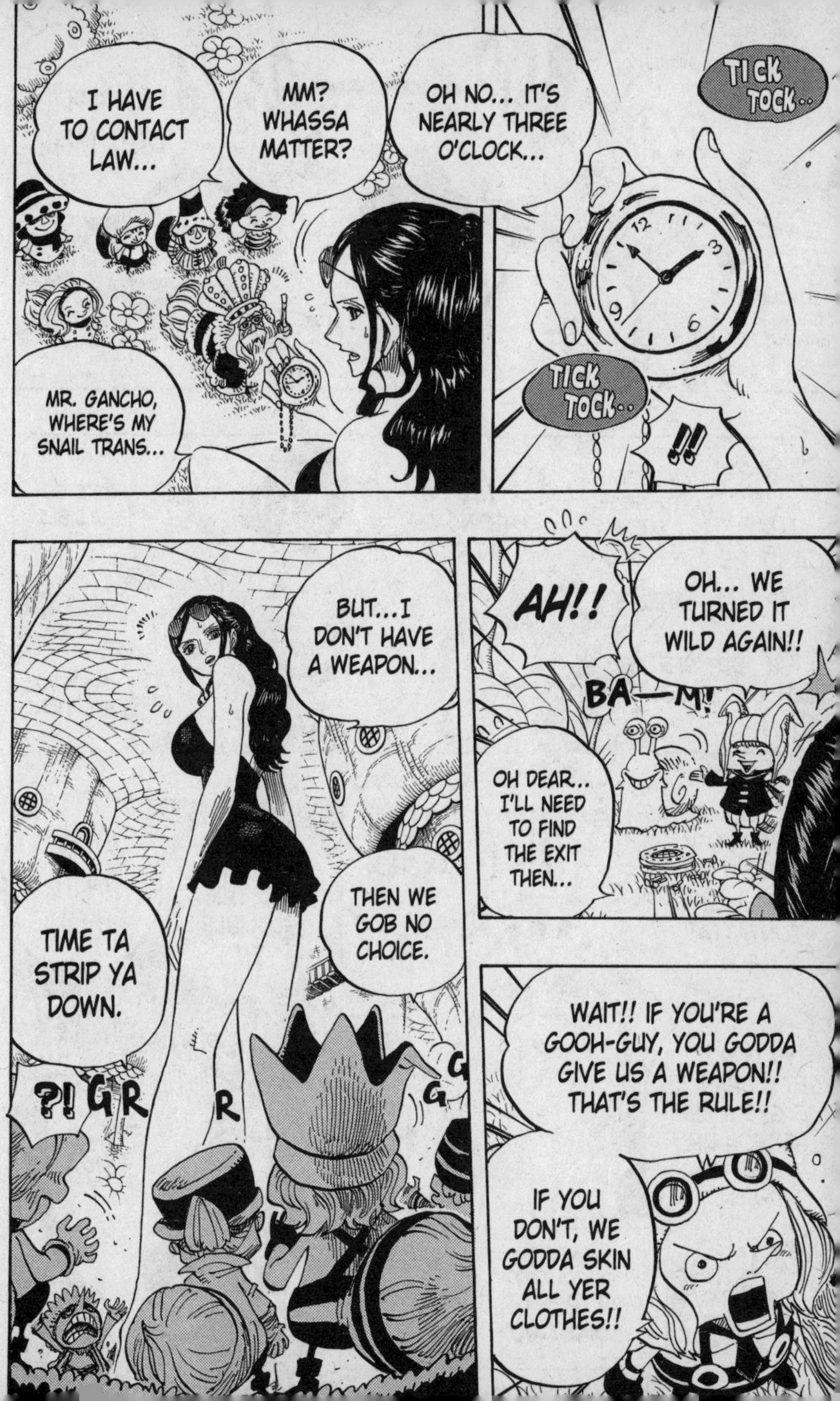
TICK TOCK..
TICK TOCK..
!!
OH NO... IT'S NEARLY THREE O'CLOCK...
MM? WHASSA MATTER?
I HAVE TO CONTACT LAW...
MR. GANCHO, WHERE'S MY SNAIL TRANS...
OH... WE TURNED IT WILD AGAIN!!
AH!!
BA—M!
OH DEAR... I'LL NEED TO FIND THE EXIT THEN...
WAIT!! IF YOU'RE A GOOH-GUY, YOU GODDA GIVE US A WEAPON!! THAT'S THE RULE!!
IF YOU DON'T, WE GODDA SKIN ALL YER CLOTHES!!
BUT...I DON'T HAVE A WEAPON...
THEN WE GOB NO CHOICE.
TIME TA STRIP YA DOWN.
?!
GRR
GG

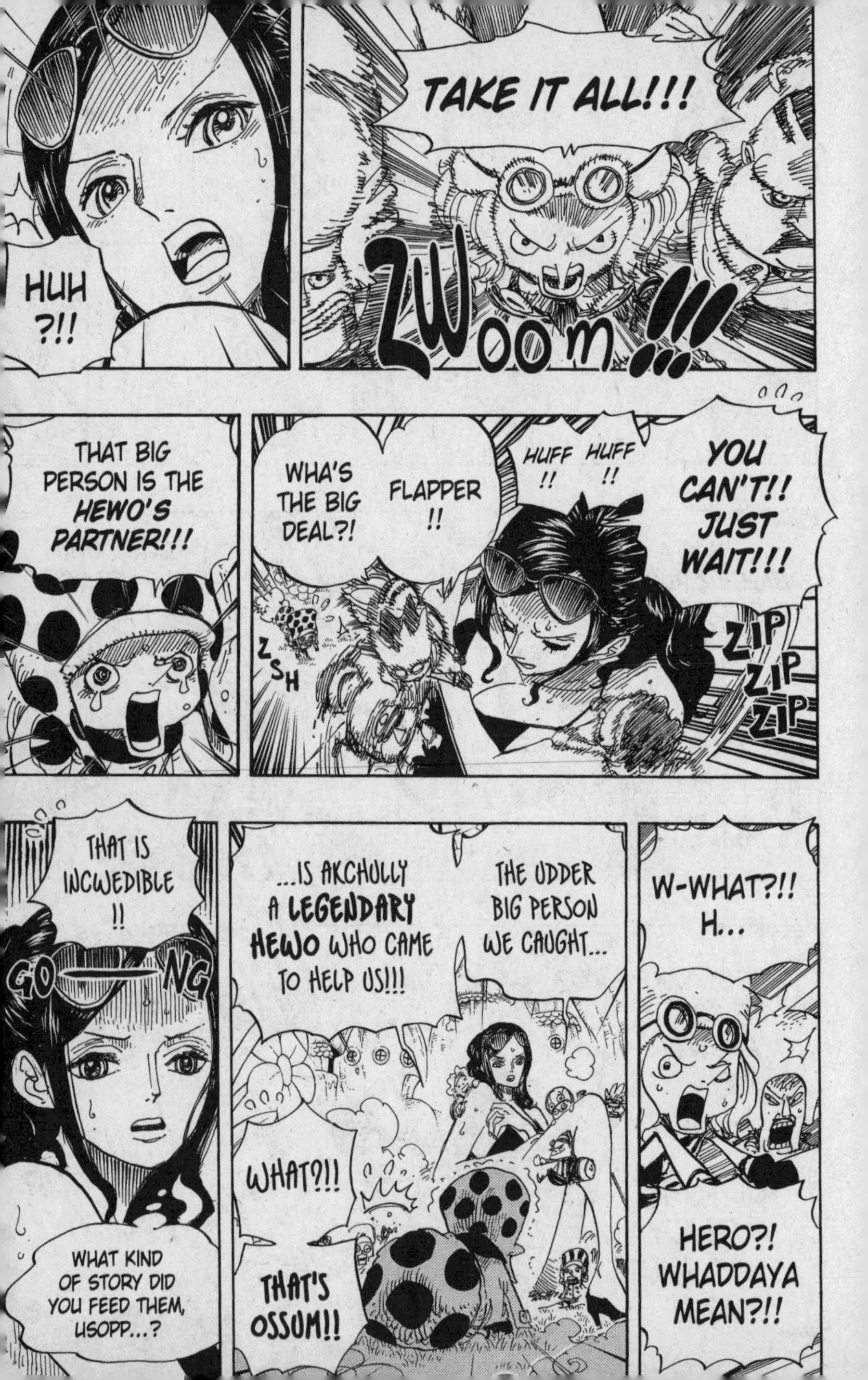
TAKE IT ALL!!!
ZWOOM!!!
HUH ?!!
YOU CAN'T!! JUST WAIT!!!
HUFF!! HUFF!!
FLAPPER!!
WHA'S THE BIG DEAL?!
ZIP ZIP ZIP
ZSH
THAT BIG PERSON IS THE HEWO'S PARTNER!!!
W-WHAT?!! H...
HERO?! WHADDAYA MEAN?!!
THE UDDER BIG PERSON WE CAUGHT...
...IS AKCHULLY A LEGENDARY HEWO WHO CAME TO HELP US!!!
WHAT?!!
THAT'S OSSUM!!
THAT IS INCWEDIBLE!!
GO—NG
WHAT KIND OF STORY DID YOU FEED THEM, USOPP...?

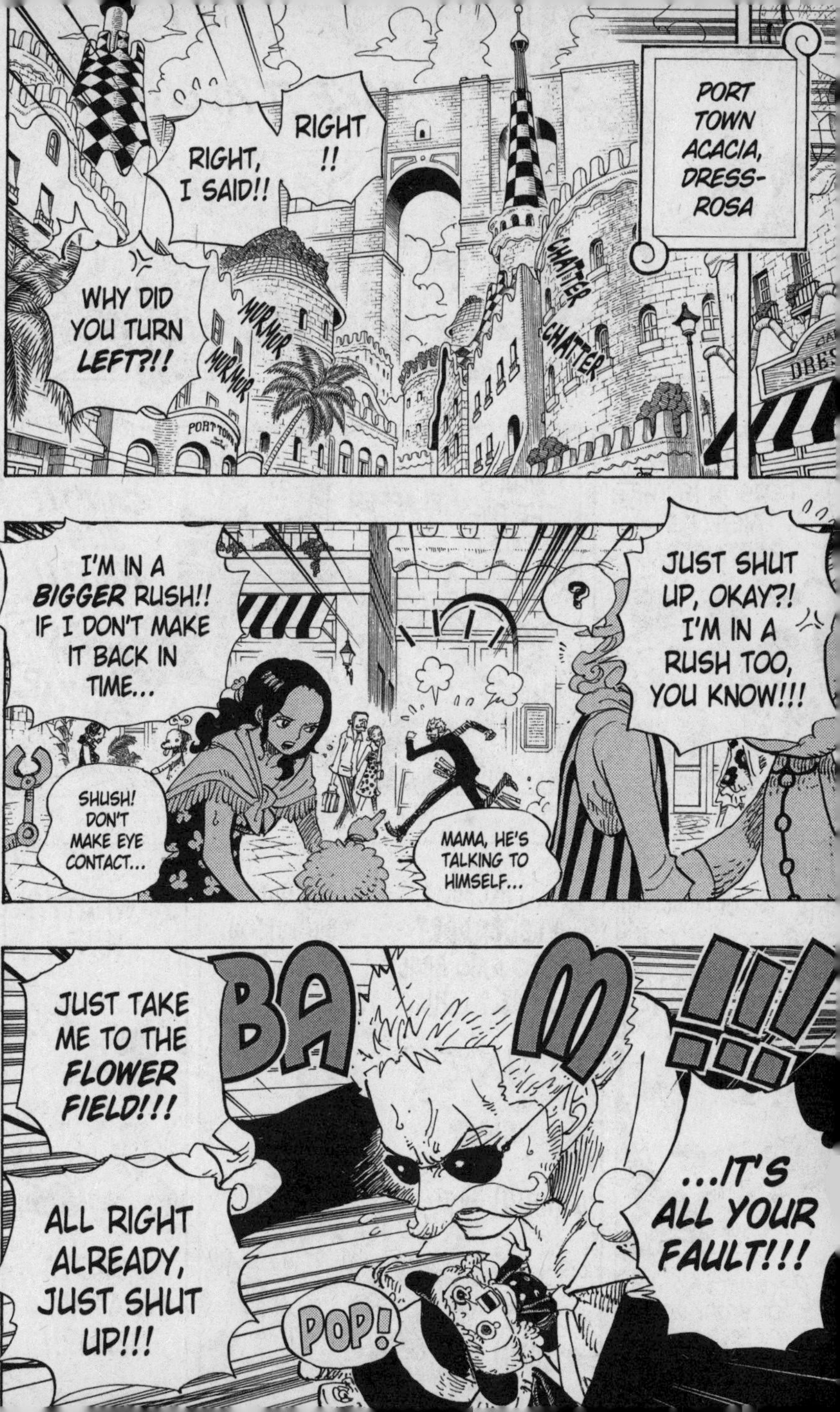
PORT TOWN ACACIA, DRESS-ROSA
RIGHT !!
RIGHT, I SAID!!
CHATTER CHATTER
MURMUR MURMUR
WHY DID YOU TURN LEFT?!!
JUST SHUT UP, OKAY?! I'M IN A RUSH TOO, YOU KNOW!!!
?
I'M IN A BIGGER RUSH!! IF I DON'T MAKE IT BACK IN TIME...
MAMA, HE'S TALKING TO HIMSELF...
SHUSH! DON'T MAKE EYE CONTACT...
BAM!!!
...IT'S ALL YOUR FAULT!!!
JUST TAKE ME TO THE FLOWER FIELD!!!
POP!
ALL RIGHT ALREADY, JUST SHUT UP!!!

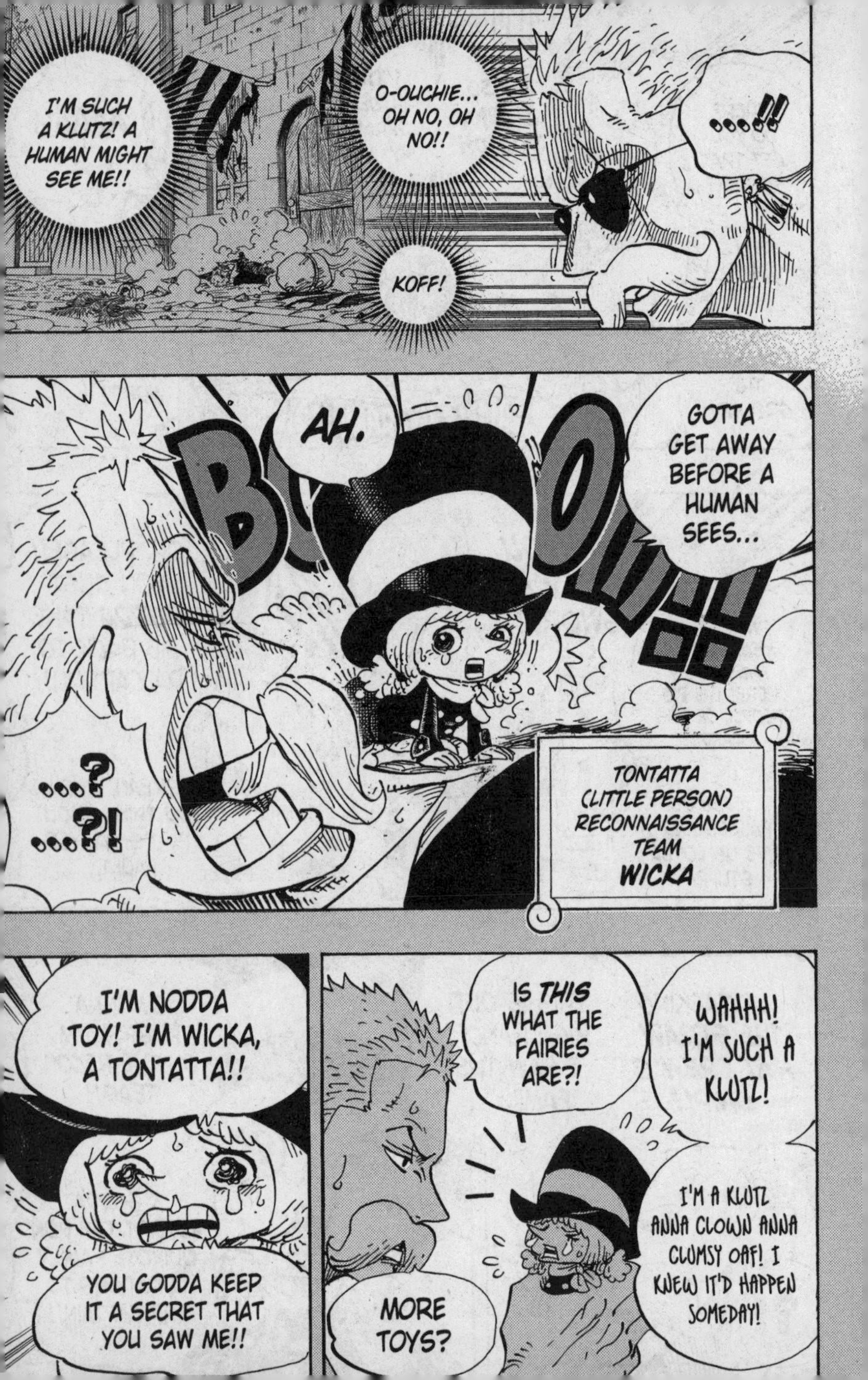
...!!
O-OUCHIE... OH NO, OH NO!!
KOFF!
I'M SUCH A KLUTZ! A HUMAN MIGHT SEE ME!!
GOTTA GET AWAY BEFORE A HUMAN SEES...
AH.
TONTATTA (LITTLE PERSON) RECONNAISSANCE TEAM WICKA
...?
...?!
WAHHH! I'M SUCH A KLUTZ!
IS THIS WHAT THE FAIRIES ARE?!
I'M A KLUTZ ANNA CLOWN ANNA CLUMSY OAF! I KNEW IT'D HAPPEN SOMEDAY!
MORE TOYS?
I'M NODDA TOY! I'M WICKA, A TONTATTA!!
YOU GODDA KEEP IT A SECRET THAT YOU SAW ME!!

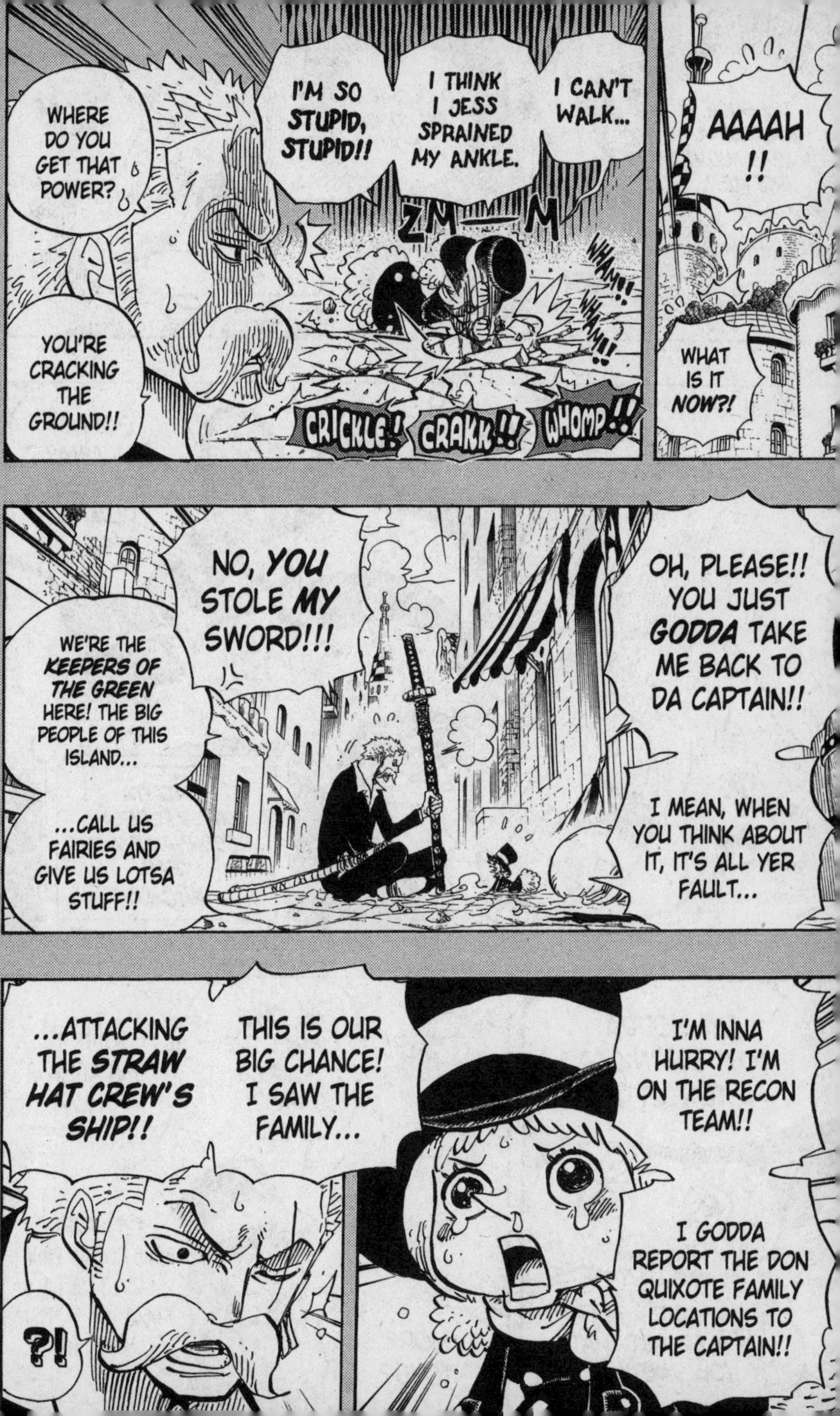
AAAAH!!
WHAT IS IT NOW?!
I CAN'T WALK...
I THINK I JESS SPRAINED MY ANKLE.
I'M SO STUPID, STUPID!!
ZM—M
WHAM!!
WHAM!!
WHOMP!!
CRAKK!!
CRICKLE!
WHERE DO YOU GET THAT POWER?
YOU'RE CRACKING THE GROUND!!
OH, PLEASE!! YOU JUST GODDA TAKE ME BACK TO DA CAPTAIN!!
I MEAN, WHEN YOU THINK ABOUT IT, IT'S ALL YER FAULT...
NO, YOU STOLE MY SWORD!!!
WE'RE THE KEEPERS OF THE GREEN HERE! THE BIG PEOPLE OF THIS ISLAND...
...CALL US FAIRIES AND GIVE US LOTSA STUFF!!
I'M INNA HURRY! I'M ON THE RECON TEAM!!
I GODDA REPORT THE DON QUIXOTE FAMILY LOCATIONS TO THE CAPTAIN!!
THIS IS OUR BIG CHANCE! I SAW THE FAMILY...
...ATTACKING THE STRAW HAT CREW'S SHIP!!
?!

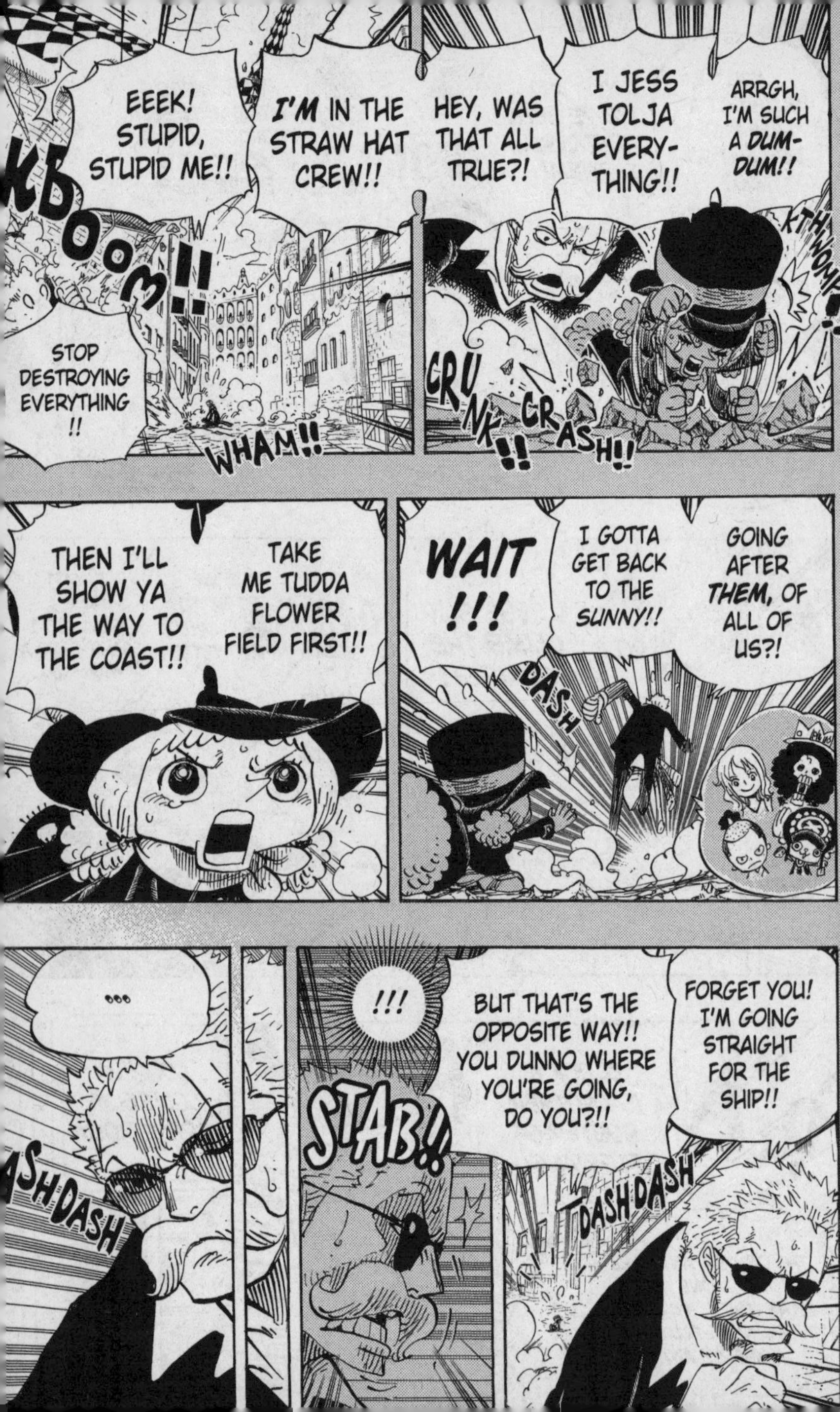
ARRGH, I'M SUCH A DUM-DUM!!
I JESS TOLJA EVERYTHING!!
HEY, WAS THAT ALL TRUE?!
KTHWOMP!!
CRUNK!!
CRASH!!
I'M IN THE STRAW HAT CREW!!
EEEK! STUPID, STUPID ME!!
KBOOOM!!
STOP DESTROYING EVERYTHING!!
WHAM!!
GOING AFTER THEM, OF ALL OF US?!
I GOTTA GET BACK TO THE SUNNY!!
WAIT!!!
DASH
TAKE ME TUDDA FLOWER FIELD FIRST!!
THEN I'LL SHOW YA THE WAY TO THE COAST!!
FORGET YOU! I'M GOING STRAIGHT FOR THE SHIP!!
DASH DASH
BUT THAT'S THE OPPOSITE WAY!! YOU DUNNO WHERE YOU'RE GOING, DO YOU?!!
!!!
STAB!!
...
DASH DASH

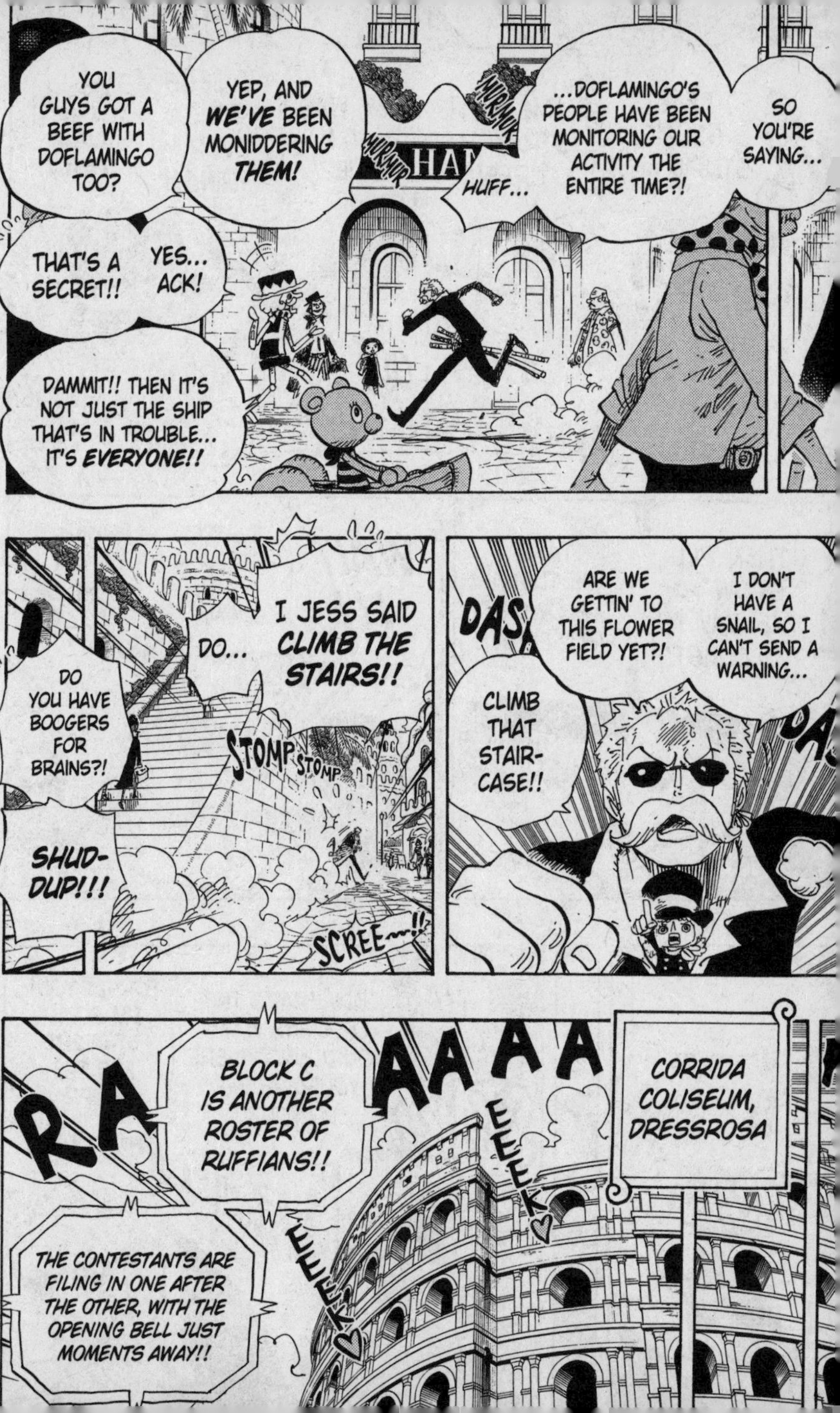
SO YOU'RE SAYING...
...DOFLAMINGO'S PEOPLE HAVE BEEN MONITORING OUR ACTIVITY THE ENTIRE TIME?!
HUFF...
MURMUR MURMUR
YEP, AND WE'VE BEEN MONIDDERING THEM!
YOU GUYS GOT A BEEF WITH DOFLAMINGO TOO?
YES... ACK!
THAT'S A SECRET!!
DAMMIT!! THEN IT'S NOT JUST THE SHIP THAT'S IN TROUBLE... IT'S EVERYONE!!
I DON'T HAVE A SNAIL, SO I CAN'T SEND A WARNING...
ARE WE GETTIN' TO THIS FLOWER FIELD YET?!
DAS
CLIMB THAT STAIR-CASE!!
I JESS SAID CLIMB THE STAIRS!!
DO...
DO YOU HAVE BOOGERS FOR BRAINS?!
STOMP STOMP
SHUD-DUP!!!
SCREE~~!!
CORRIDA COLISEUM, DRESSROSA
RAAAAA
BLOCK C IS ANOTHER ROSTER OF RUFFIANS!!
EEEEK
EEEEK
THE CONTESTANTS ARE FILING IN ONE AFTER THE OTHER, WITH THE OPENING BELL JUST MOMENTS AWAY!!

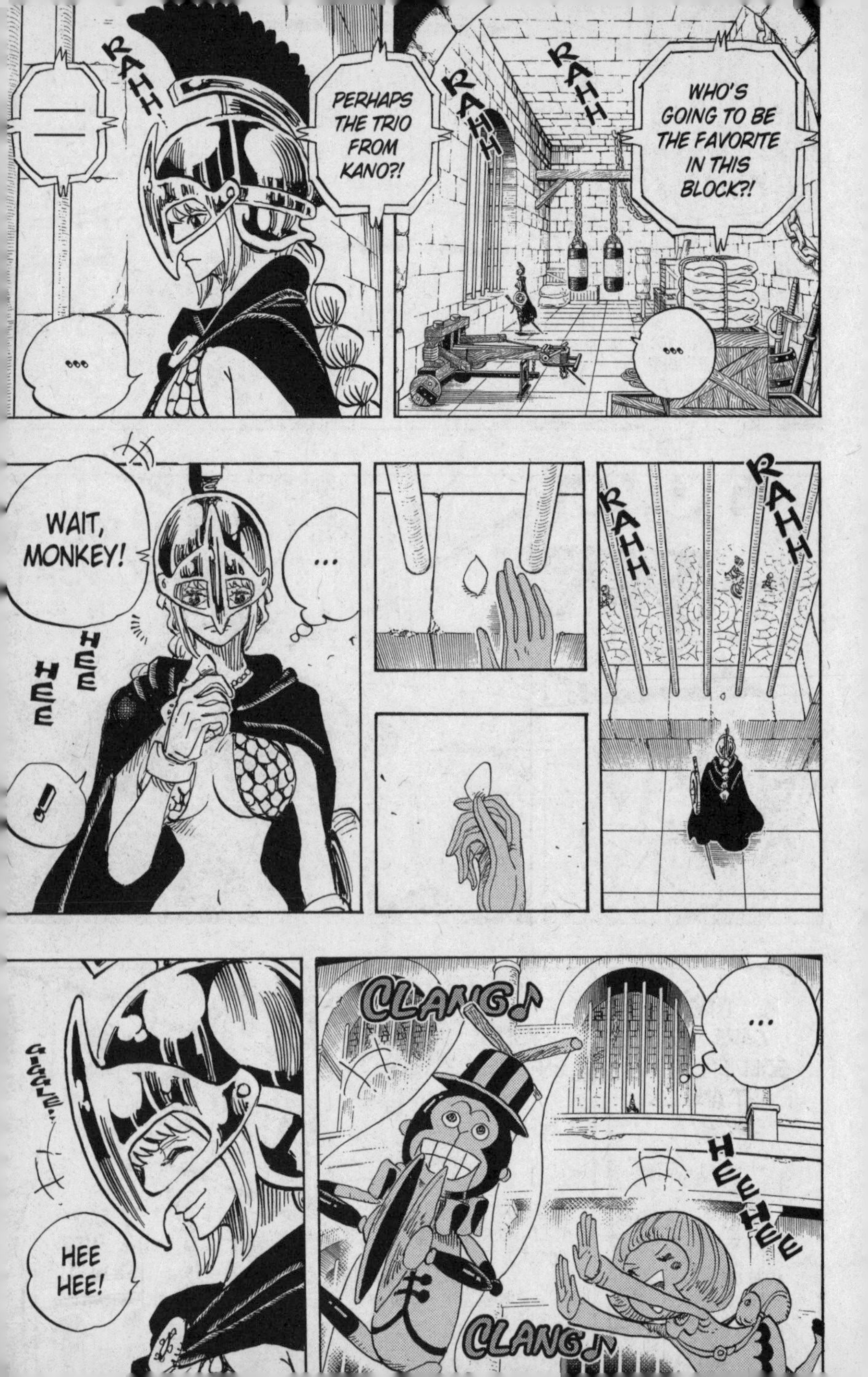
WHO'S GOING TO BE THE FAVORITE IN THIS BLOCK?!
RAHH
RAHH
PERHAPS THE TRIO FROM KANO?!
...
RAHH
——
...
RAHH
RAHH
...
WAIT, MONKEY!
HEE HEE
!
...
CLANG♪
HEEHEE
CLANG♪
GIGGLE...
HEE HEE!

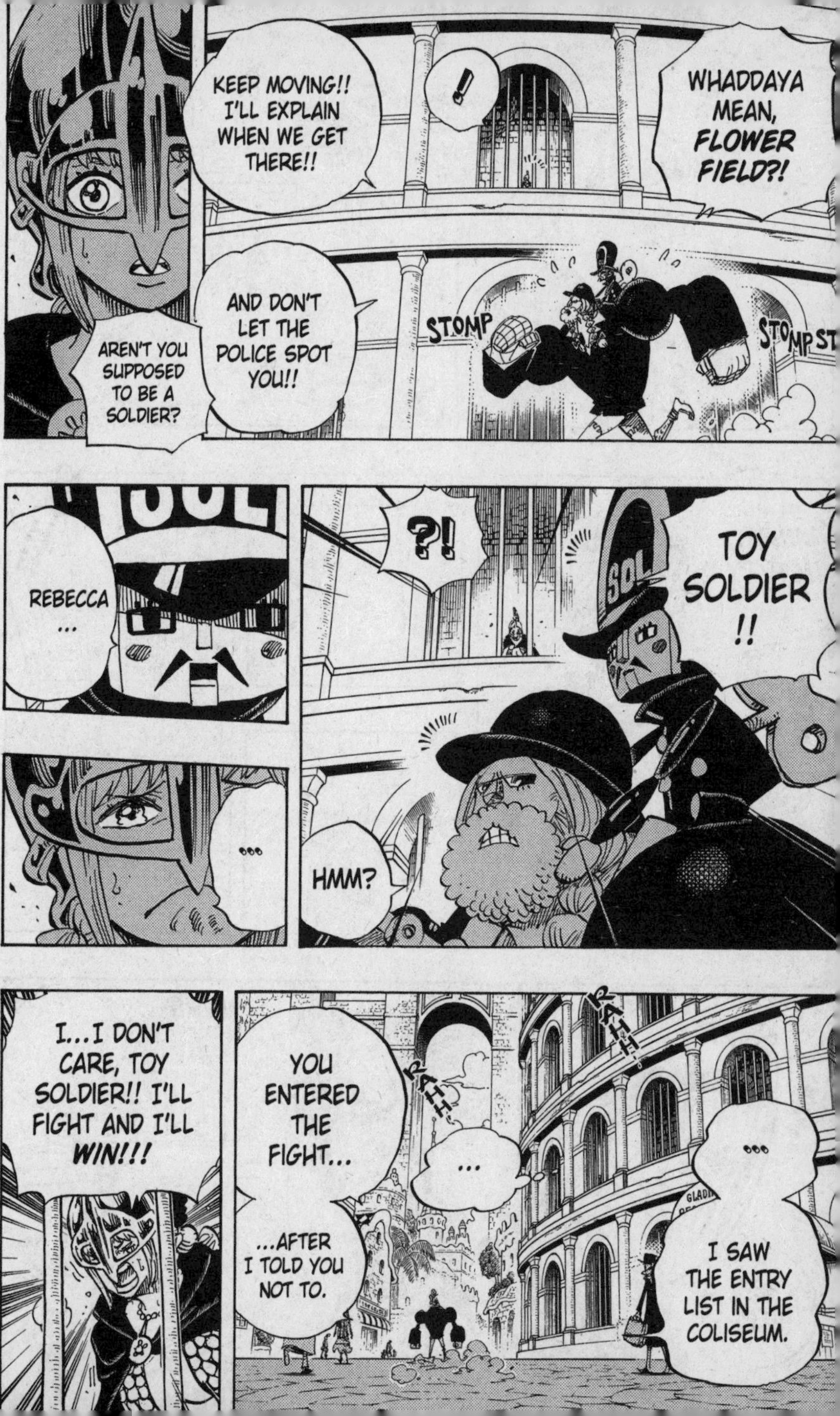
WHADDAYA MEAN, FLOWER FIELD?!
!
KEEP MOVING!! I'LL EXPLAIN WHEN WE GET THERE!!
AND DON'T LET THE POLICE SPOT YOU!!
STOMP
STOMP ST
AREN'T YOU SUPPOSED TO BE A SOLDIER?
TOY SOLDIER !!
?!
HMM?
REBECCA ...
...
I SAW THE ENTRY LIST IN THE COLISEUM.
...
RAHH
RAHH
...
YOU ENTERED THE FIGHT...
...AFTER I TOLD YOU NOT TO.
I...I DON'T CARE, TOY SOLDIER!! I'LL FIGHT AND I'LL WIN!!!

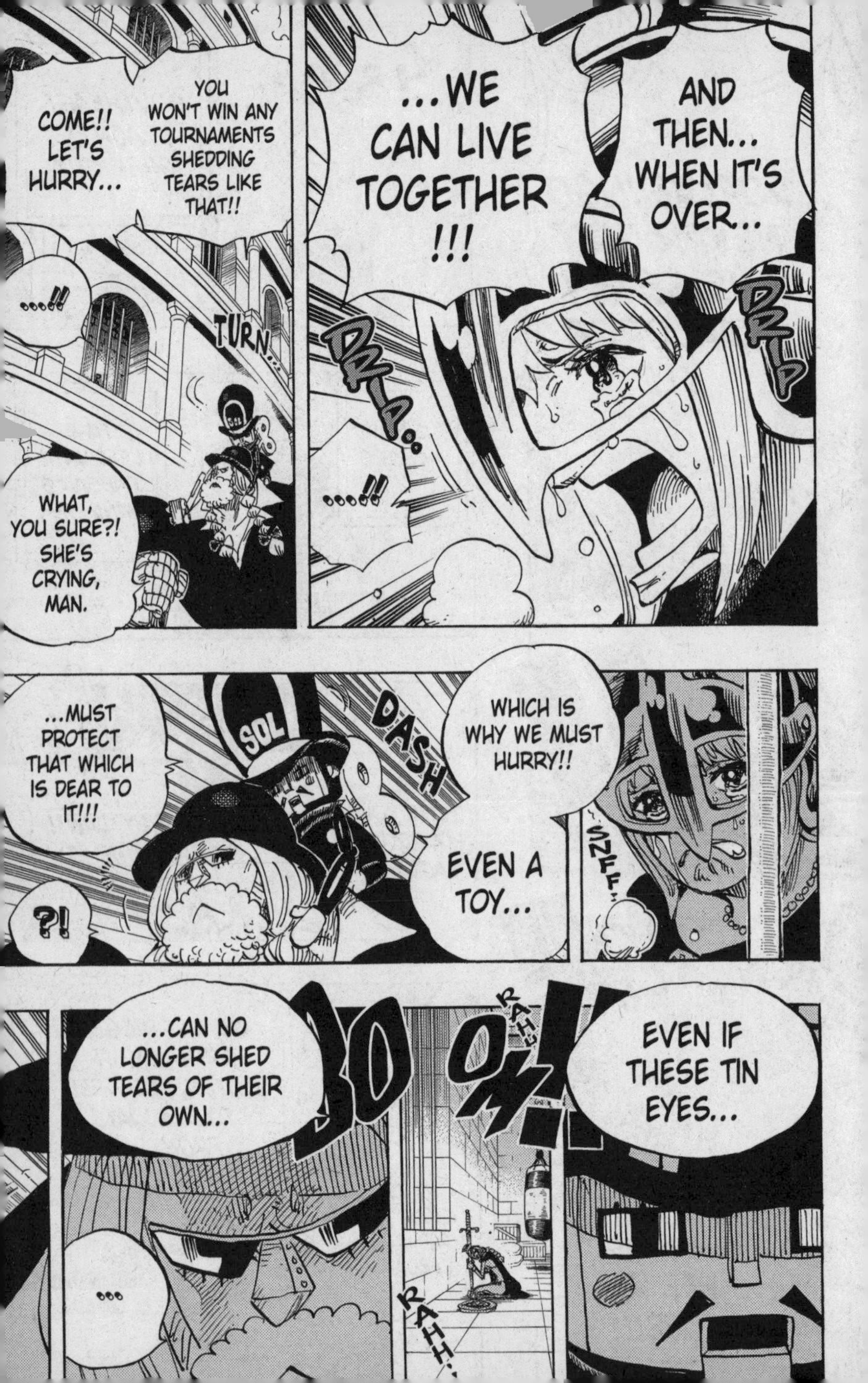
AND THEN... WHEN IT'S OVER...
...WE CAN LIVE TOGETHER !!!
DRIP
DRIP..
....!!
YOU WON'T WIN ANY TOURNAMENTS SHEDDING TEARS LIKE THAT!!
COME!! LET'S HURRY...
....!!
TURN...
WHAT, YOU SURE?! SHE'S CRYING, MAN.
SNFF
WHICH IS WHY WE MUST HURRY!!
DASH
EVEN A TOY...
...MUST PROTECT THAT WHICH IS DEAR TO IT!!!
?!
EVEN IF THESE TIN EYES...
BOOM!!
RAHH
...CAN NO LONGER SHED TEARS OF THEIR OWN...
RAHH!
...

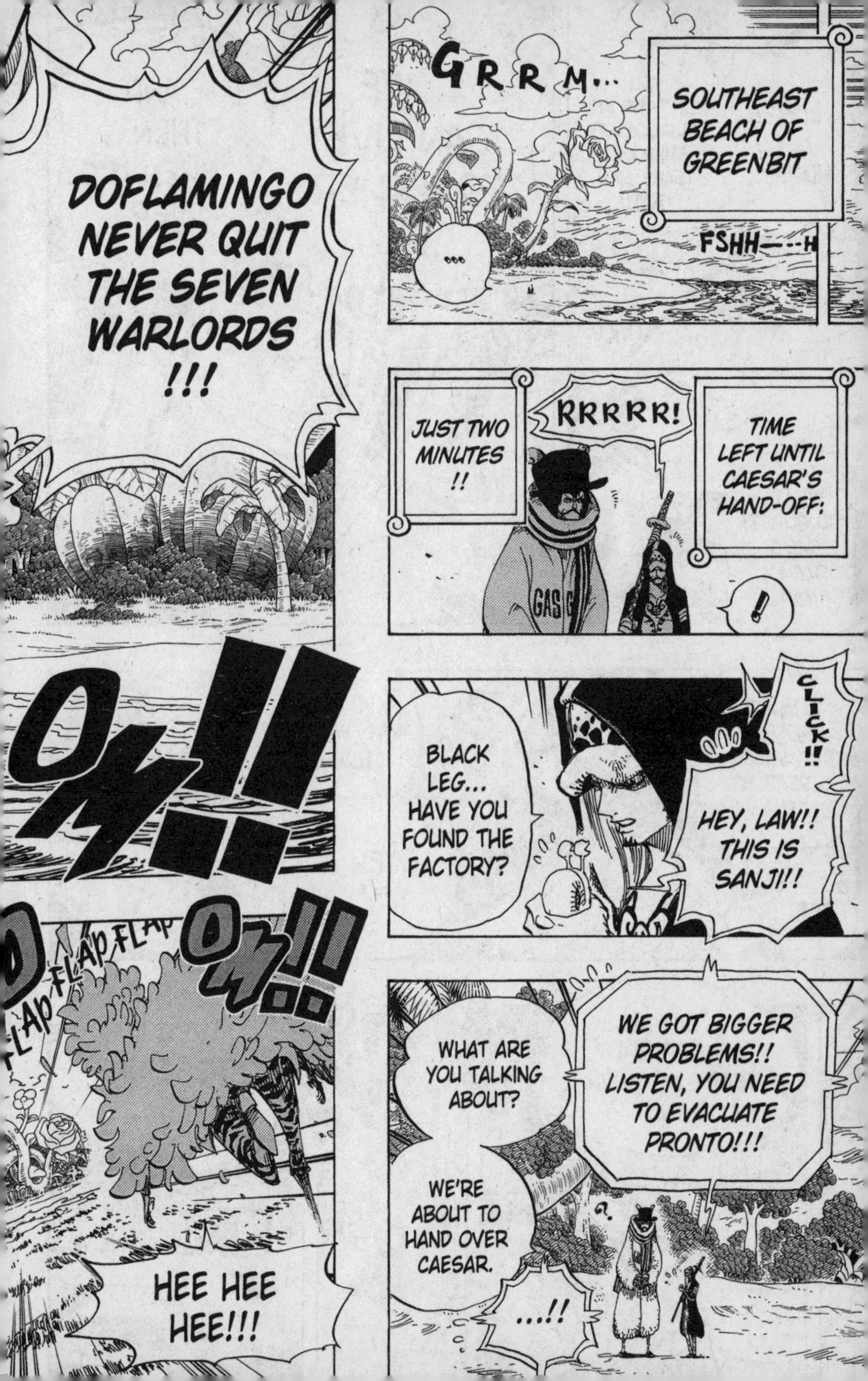
SOUTHEAST BEACH OF GREENBIT
GRRM...
FSHH---H
...
TIME LEFT UNTIL CAESAR'S HAND-OFF:
RRRRR!
JUST TWO MINUTES !!
!
CLICK!!
HEY, LAW!! THIS IS SANJI!!
BLACK LEG... HAVE YOU FOUND THE FACTORY?
WE GOT BIGGER PROBLEMS!! LISTEN, YOU NEED TO EVACUATE PRONTO!!!
WHAT ARE YOU TALKING ABOUT?
WE'RE ABOUT TO HAND OVER CAESAR.
...!!
DOFLAMINGO NEVER QUIT THE SEVEN WARLORDS !!!
OH!!
OW!!
FLAP FLAP FLAP FLAP
HEE HEE HEE!!!

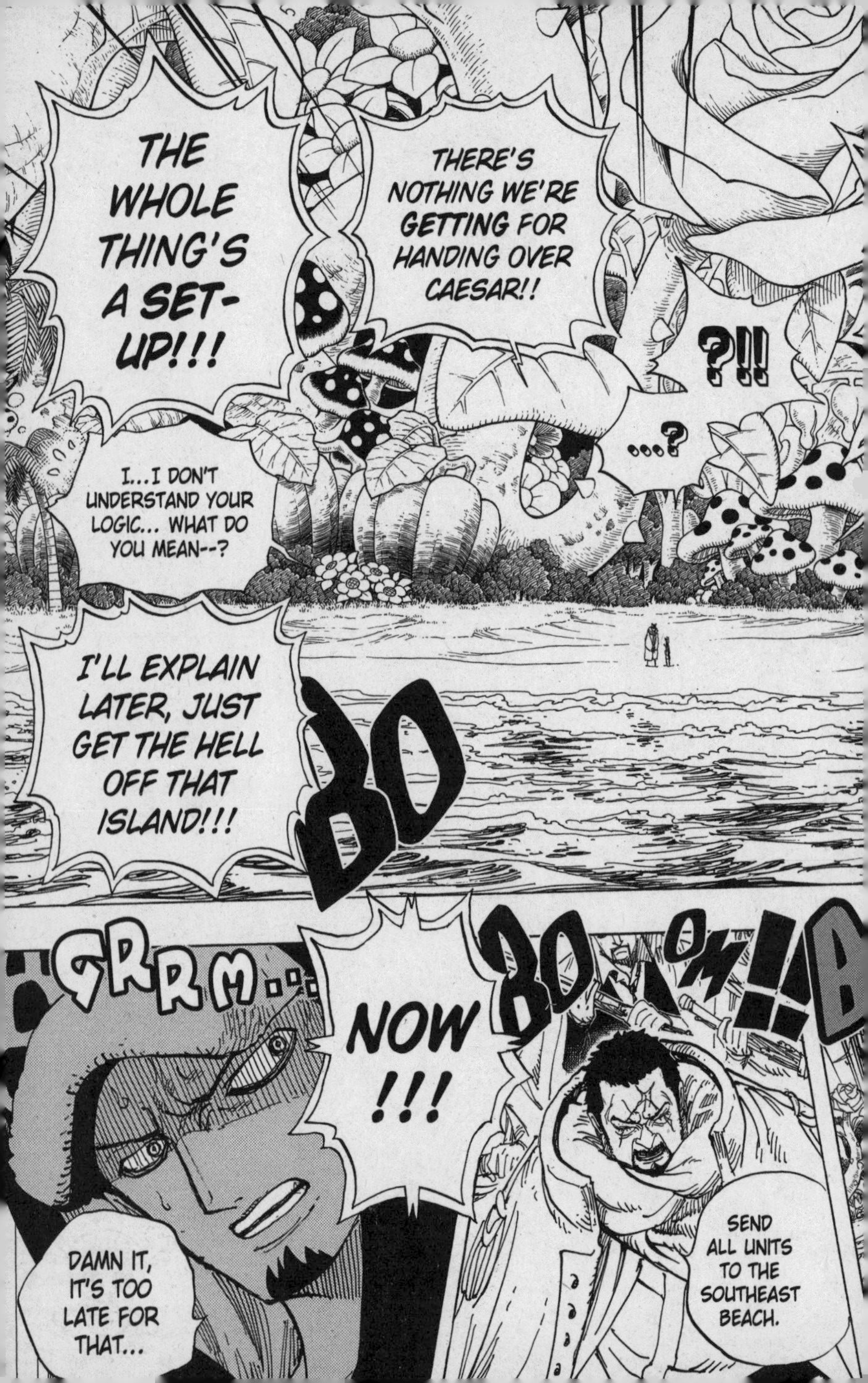

THERE'S NOTHING WE'RE GETTING FOR HANDING OVER CAESAR!!
THE WHOLE THING'S A SET-UP!!!
?!!
...?
I...I DON'T UNDERSTAND YOUR LOGIC... WHAT DO YOU MEAN--?
I'LL EXPLAIN LATER, JUST GET THE HELL OFF THAT ISLAND!!!
BO
BOOM!!
SEND ALL UNITS TO THE SOUTHEAST BEACH.
NOW!!!
GRRM...
DAMN IT, IT'S TOO LATE FOR THAT...

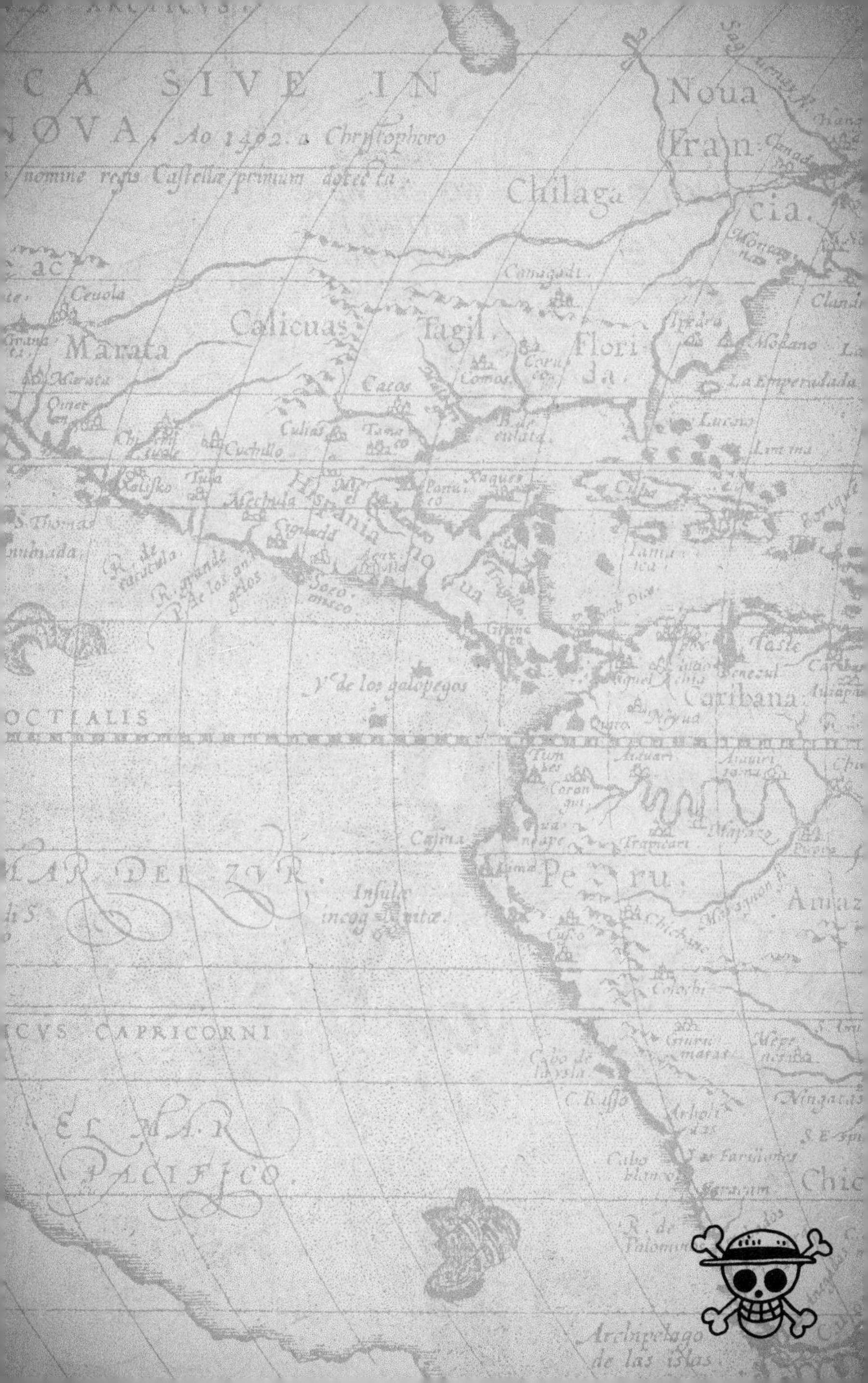

CA SIVE IN
NOVA, Ao 1462. a Christophoro
nomine regis Castella primum detecta.

Chilaga

Noua
Fran
cia.

ac
Ceuola
Marata
Morata
Quiet

Calicuas
Tagil
Flori
da.

Cacos

Culias
Tuna
Cuchillo

Hispania
NOua

Catisco
Tula

Soto
maior

de los galopegos

Cube

Caribana

OCCIALIS

MAR DEL ZVR.
Insulæ
incognitæ.

Pe ru.

Amaz

CVS CAPRICORNI

Cabo de
Sysla
C. Basso

Ningaria

EL MAR
PACIFICO.

Cabo
blanco

Chic

Archipelago
de las islas

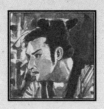

Puppies ♡ Birdies ♡ Piggies ♡

Isn't it cute when you call little things "-ies"?
Bunnies, kitties, horsies, koalies, Columbies, teddies, zebries,
Copernicies, Kobayashies...
Get ready, because adorable little volume 72
is about to startsies!!

– *Eiichiro Oda, 2013*

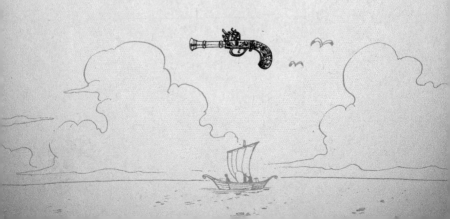

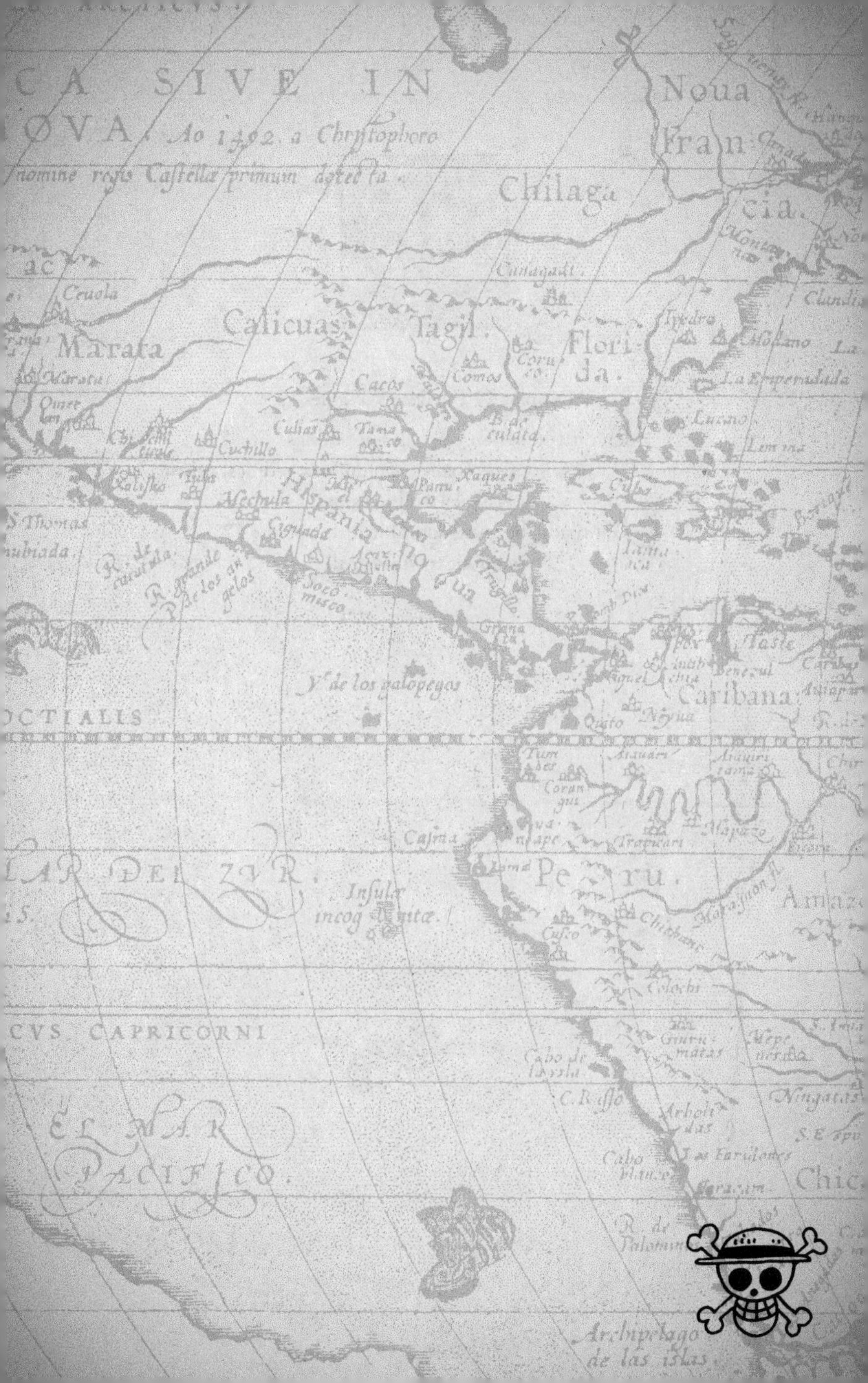

CA SIVE IN

Noua

MOVA, *Ao 1492 a Christophoro*

Fran-

nomine regis Castella primum detecta.

Chilaga

cia.

ac

Canagadi

Clundia

Ceuola

Calicuas

Tagil.

Thedra

Cibolano La

Marata

Florida.

La Emperialada

Marata

Cacos

Comos

Coru

Lucino

Omei

B. de

Culiaa

Tama

Lumina

Culias

Cuchillo

Hispania

Raques

Cala

S.Thomas

Asochula

Parru co

hubiada

Ciguad a

Acux

la

R.de

Sla

Tama

cucutua

Trugillo.

jca

R.grande

Socos

los gelos

musco

Grana

P.de

Y.de los galopegos

Taste

lucib

Caribas

 OCTIALIS

Benecul

Cinia

iguel etna

Caribana

Quito

Neyua

Tum

Aruaus

Aruqui

bez

tana

Chin

Coran

qui

Casina

nape

Trapucari

Mapa

LAR DEL ZVR.

Insula

Lima

Peru.

incog nita.

Cusco

Chipbase

Colochi

CVS CAPRICORNI.

Guru

Sipe

matas

nes dia

Cabo de

baxla

Ningatas

C.Raso

EL MAR

Arbol

S.E Spi

das

PACIFICO.

Cabo

las Faridones

blanco

Saracan

Chica

R.de

Palomas

Archipelago

de las islas

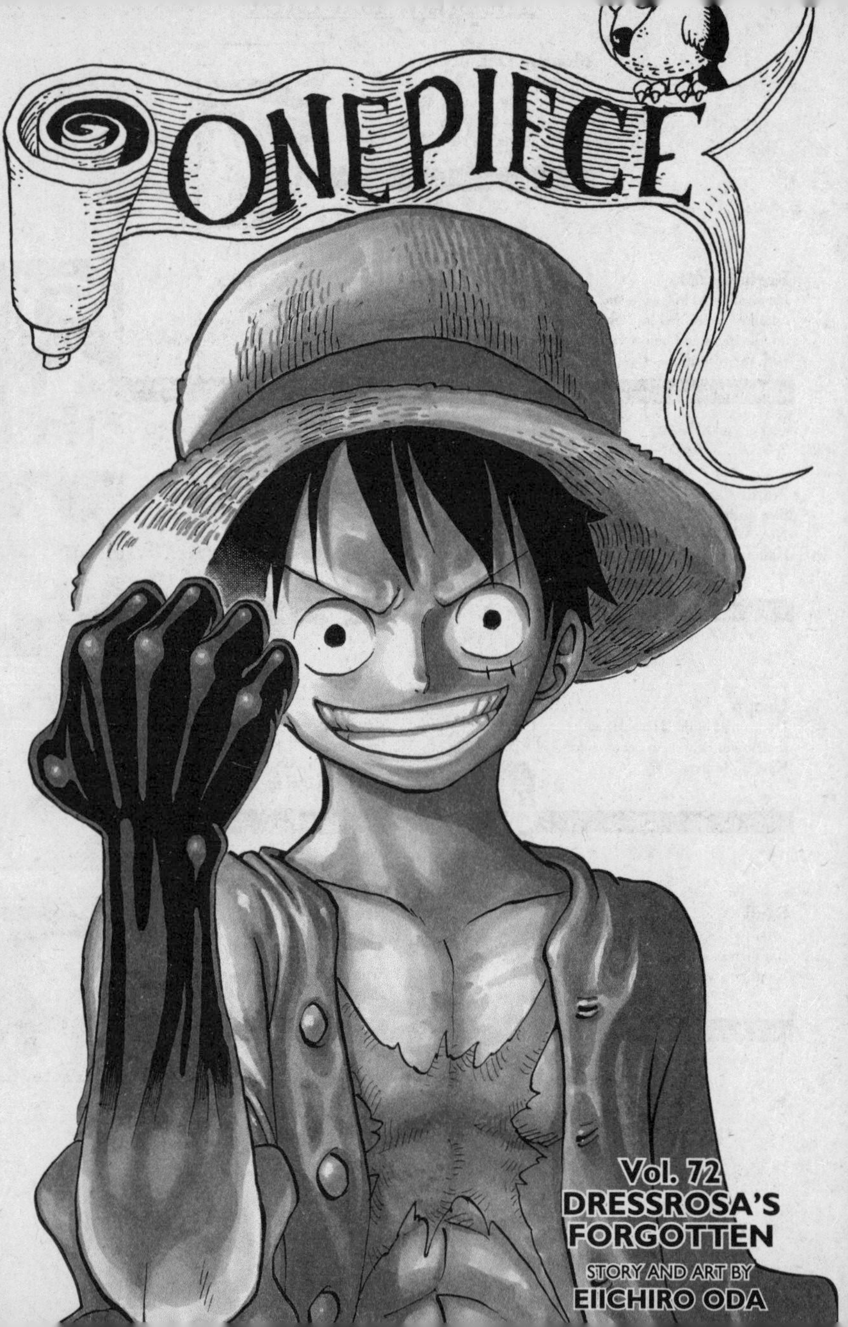
ONE PIECE

Vol. 72

DRESSROSA'S FORGOTTEN

STORY AND ART BY
EIICHIRO ODA

The Straw Hat Crew

Monkey D. Luffy

A young man who dreams of becoming the Pirate King. After training with Rayleigh, he and his crew head for the New World!

Captain, Bounty: 400 million berries

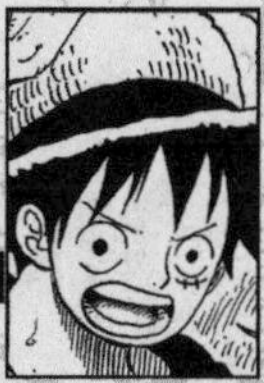

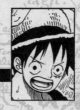

Roronoa Zolo

He swallowed his pride and asked to be trained by Mihawk on Gloom Island before reuniting with the rest of the crew.

Fighter, Bounty: 120 million berries

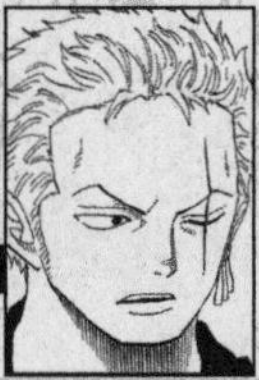

Tony Tony Chopper

After researching powerful medicine in Birdie Kingdom, he reunites with the rest of the crew.

Ship's Doctor, Bounty: 50 berries

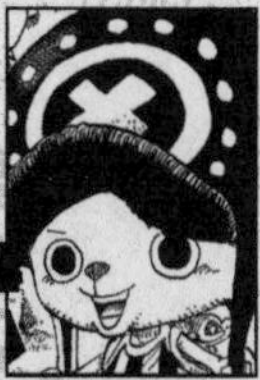

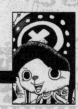

Nami

She studied the weather of the New World on the small Sky Island Weatheria, a place where weather is studied as a science.

Navigator, Bounty: 16 million berries

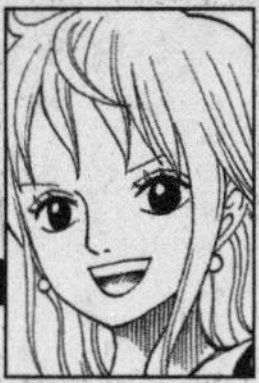

Nico Robin

She spent her time in Baltigo with the leader of the Revolutionary Army: Luffy's father, Dragon.

Archeologist, Bounty: 80 million berries

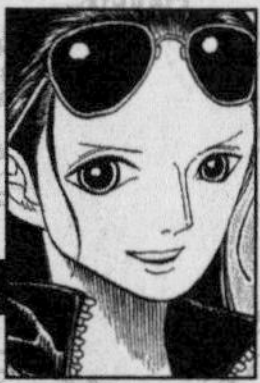

Usopp

He trained under Heracles at the Bowin Islands to become the King of Snipers.

Sniper, Bounty: 30 million berries

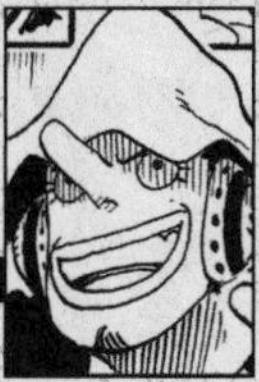

Franky

He modified himself in Future Land Baldimore and turned himself into Armored Franky before reuniting with the rest of the crew.

Shipwright, Bounty: 44 million berries

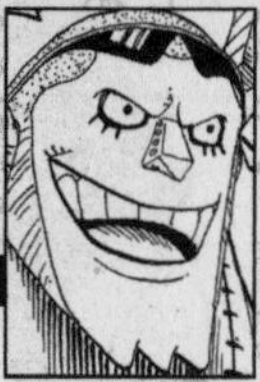

Sanji

After fighting the New Kama Karate masters in the Kamabakka Kingdom, he returned to the crew.

Cook, Bounty: 77 million berries

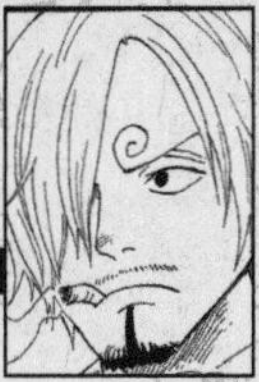

Brook

After being captured and used as a freak show by the Longarm Tribe, he became a famous rock star called "Soul King" Brook.

Musician, Bounty: 33 million berries

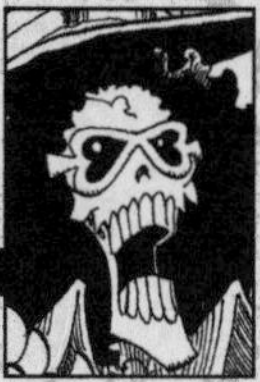

THE STORY OF ONE PIECE · VOLUME 72 ·

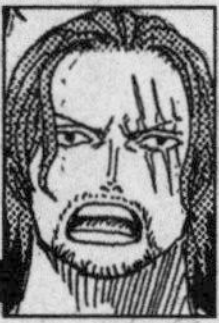

Shanks
One of the Four Emperors. He continues to wait for Luffy in the second half of the Grand Line, called the New World.
Captain of the Red-Haired Pirates

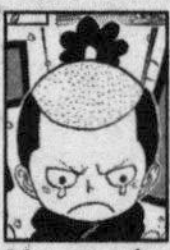

Momonosuke
Kin'emon's Son

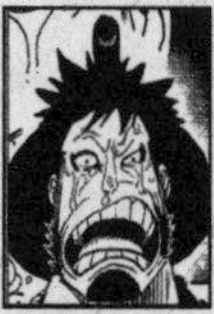

Foxfire Kin'emon
Samurai of Wano

Don Quixote Pirates

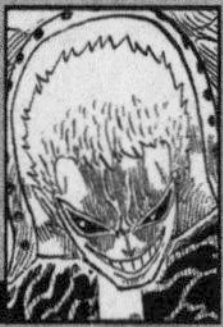

Don Quixote Doflamingo (Joker)
One of the Seven Warlords of the sea and a weapons broker. He works under the alias of "Joker."
Pirate, Warlord (former)

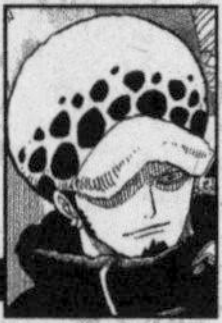

Trafalgar Law
The Surgeon of Death, wielder of the Op-Op Fruit's powers. Currently allied with Luffy.
Pirate, Warlord

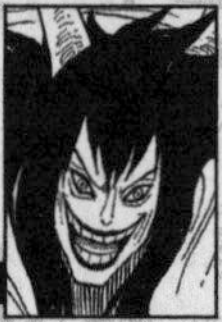

Master Caesar Clown
An authority on weapons of mass murder. Kidnapped by Law in an attempt to goad Doflamingo out of hiding.
Former government scientist

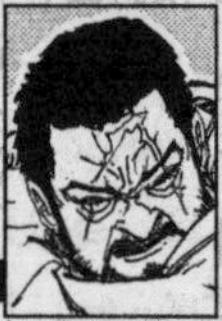

Fujitora (Issho)
A blind swordsman. One of the Three Admirals after Aokiji's departure.
Naval HQ Admiral

Tontatta Kingdom

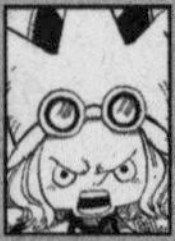

Leo
Warrior

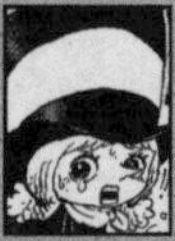

Wicka
Recon

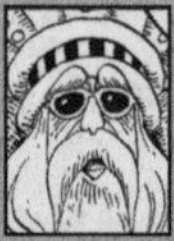

Gancho
King of the Tontattas

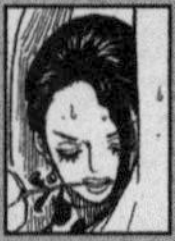

Violet
Dancer

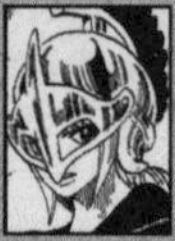

Rebecca
Gladiator

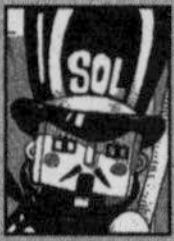
SOL

One-Legged Soldier
Toy

Having finished their two years of training, the Straw Hat crew reunites on the Sabaody Archipelago. They finally reach the final ocean, the New World, via Fish-Man Island!

The crew happens upon Trafalgar Law on the island of Punk Hazard, run by Caesar Clown. At Law's suggestion, they form a new pirate alliance that seeks to take down one of the Four Emperors. In order to draw Doflamingo's attention, they must first capture Caesar, who is producing the artificial Devil Fruit that Doflamingo sells to the Emperor, Kaido. They force Doflamingo to swear to leave the Seven Warlords and infiltrate his kingdom, Dressrosa. The crew splits up into three teams with distinct missions: destroying the factory, handing over Caesar and guarding the *Thousand Sunny*. Luffy's in the factory-destroying team, but he takes a detour to join a coliseum tournament offering Ace's Flame-Flame Fruit as a prize! Meanwhile, Law's team goes to hand over Caesar, but it's a trap! And now Usopp's team has been captured by little people?!

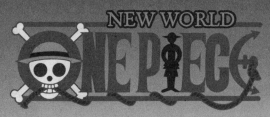

Vol. 72
Dressrosa's Forgotten

CONTENTS

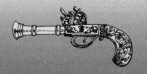

Chapter 712: VIOLET

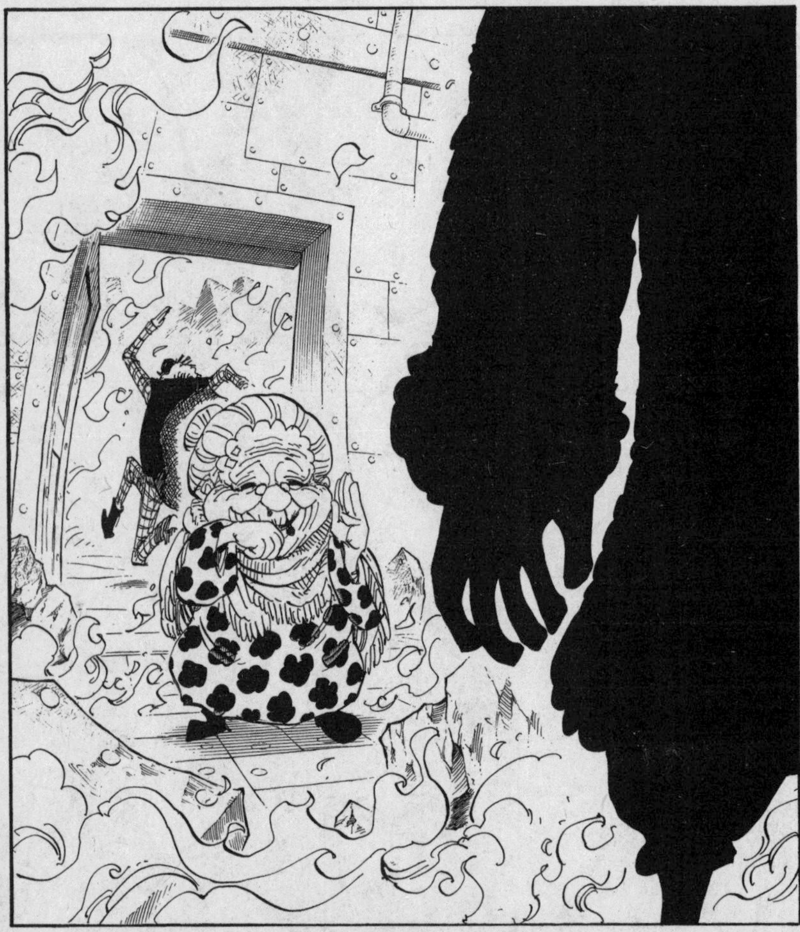

CARIBOU'S NEW WORLD KEE HEE HEE, VOL. 30:
"RUN, GABURU!" "IF YOU INSIST!!"

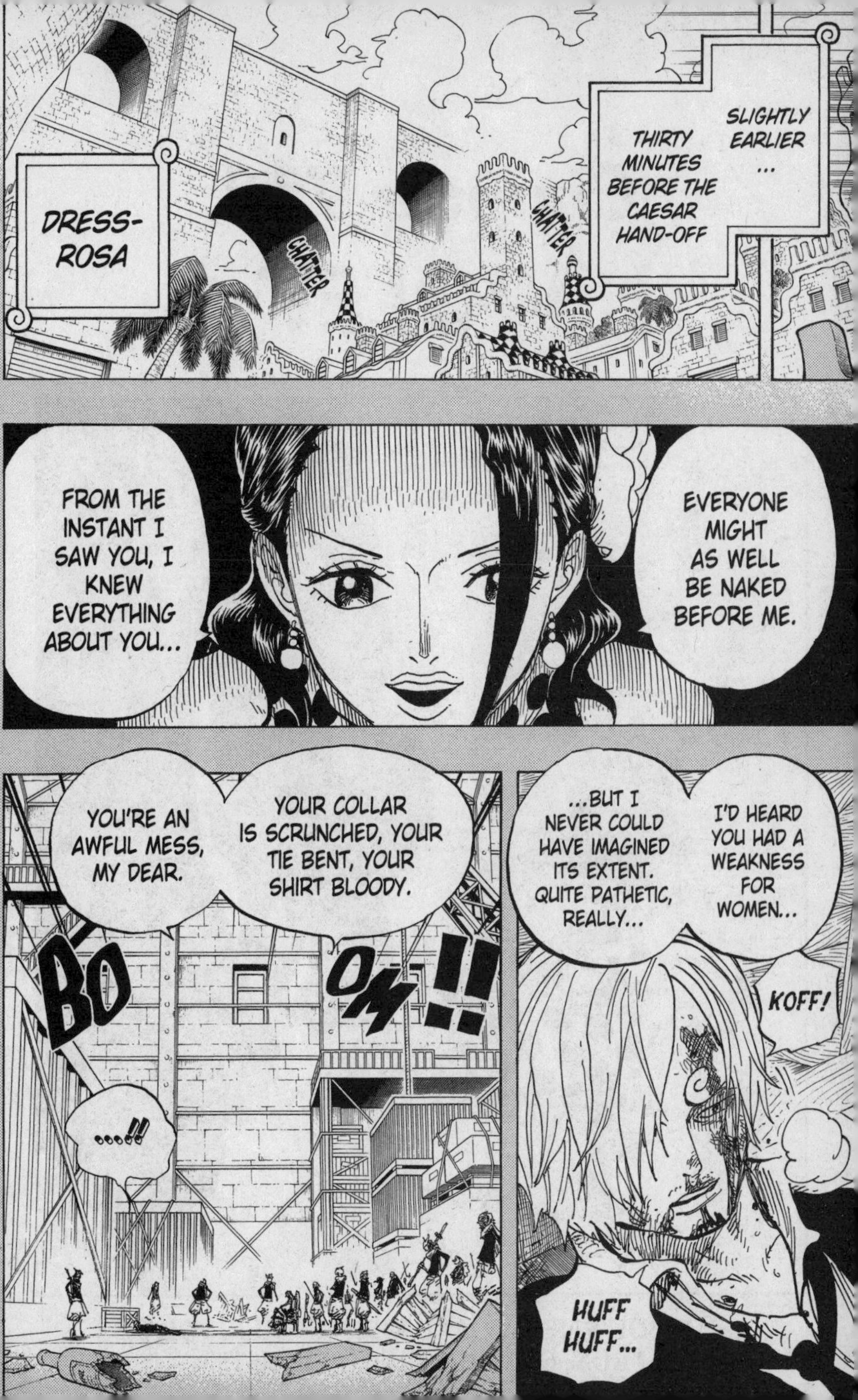
SLIGHTLY EARLIER ...
THIRTY MINUTES BEFORE THE CAESAR HAND-OFF
CHATTER
DRESS-ROSA
CHATTER
EVERYONE MIGHT AS WELL BE NAKED BEFORE ME.
FROM THE INSTANT I SAW YOU, I KNEW EVERYTHING ABOUT YOU...
I'D HEARD YOU HAD A WEAKNESS FOR WOMEN...
...BUT I NEVER COULD HAVE IMAGINED ITS EXTENT. QUITE PATHETIC, REALLY...
KOFF!
HUFF HUFF...
YOUR COLLAR IS SCRUNCHED, YOUR TIE BENT, YOUR SHIRT BLOODY.
YOU'RE AN AWFUL MESS, MY DEAR.
BOOM!!
...!!

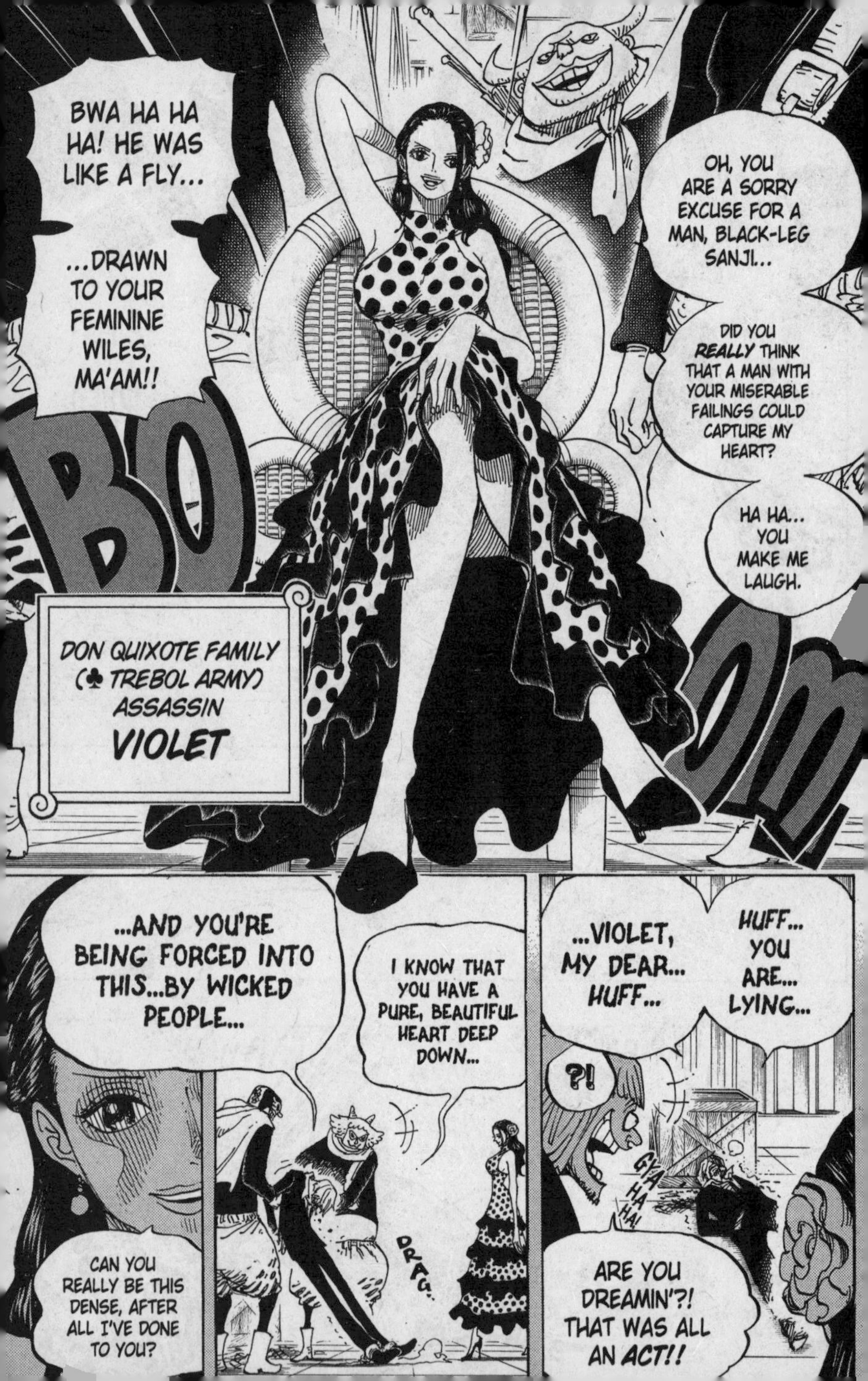
OH, YOU ARE A SORRY EXCUSE FOR A MAN, BLACK-LEG SANJI...
DID YOU *REALLY* THINK THAT A MAN WITH YOUR MISERABLE FAILINGS COULD CAPTURE MY HEART?
HA HA... YOU MAKE ME LAUGH.
BWA HA HA HA! HE WAS LIKE A FLY...
...DRAWN TO YOUR FEMININE WILES, MA'AM!!
BOOM
DON QUIXOTE FAMILY (♣ TREBOL ARMY) ASSASSIN
VIOLET
...VIOLET, MY DEAR... HUFF...
HUFF... YOU ARE... LYING...
?!
GYA HA HA HA!
ARE YOU DREAMIN'?! THAT WAS ALL AN *ACT*!!
I KNOW THAT YOU HAVE A PURE, BEAUTIFUL HEART DEEP DOWN...
DRAG...
...AND YOU'RE BEING FORCED INTO THIS...BY WICKED PEOPLE...
CAN YOU REALLY BE THIS DENSE, AFTER ALL I'VE DONE TO YOU?

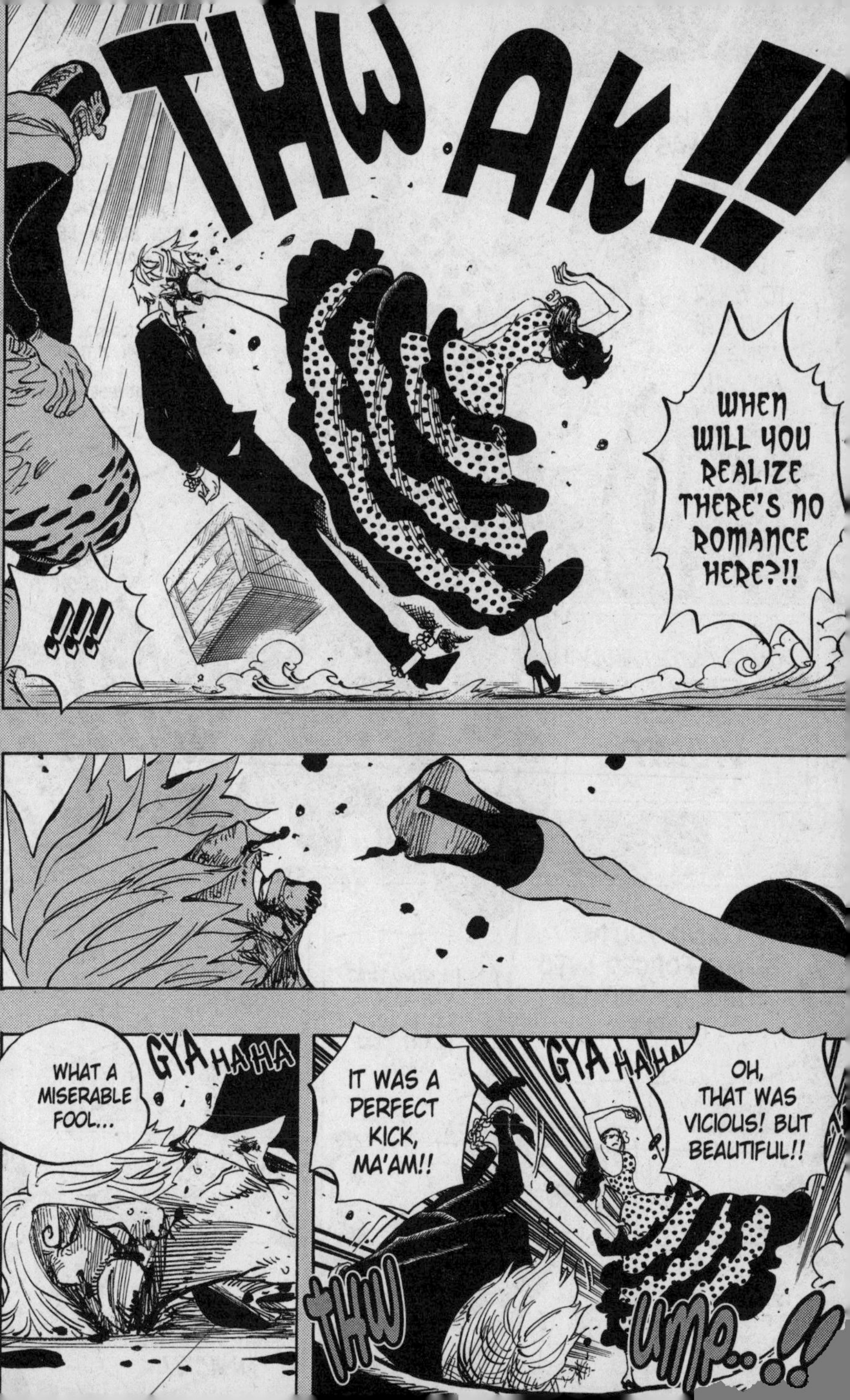
THWAK!!
WHEN WILL YOU REALIZE THERE'S NO ROMANCE HERE?!!
!!!
OH, THAT WAS VICIOUS! BUT BEAUTIFUL!!
GYA HAHA
IT WAS A PERFECT KICK, MA'AM!!
THUMP..!!
GYA HAHA
WHAT A MISERABLE FOOL...

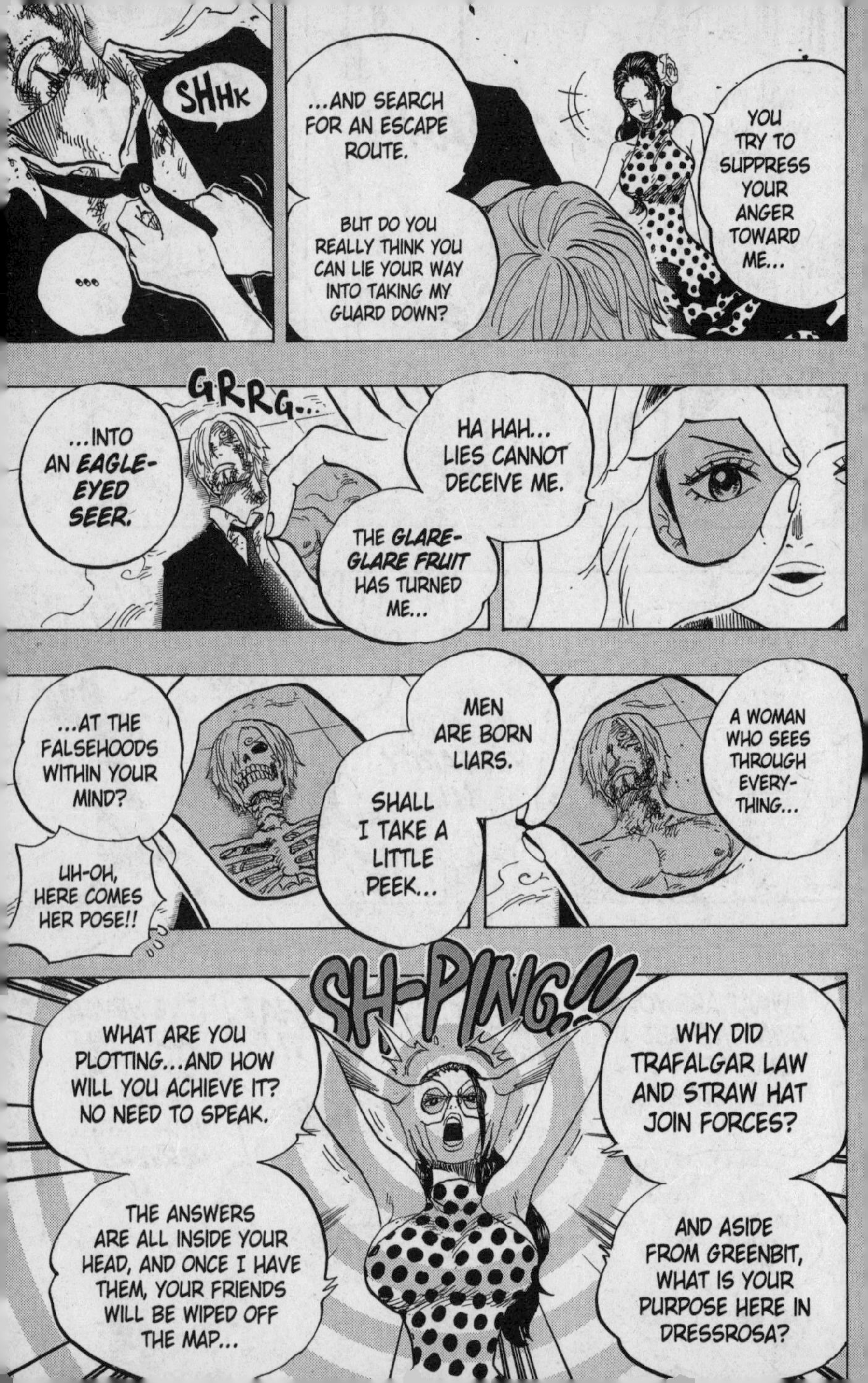
YOU TRY TO SUPPRESS YOUR ANGER TOWARD ME...
...AND SEARCH FOR AN ESCAPE ROUTE.
BUT DO YOU REALLY THINK YOU CAN LIE YOUR WAY INTO TAKING MY GUARD DOWN?
SHHK
...
HA HAH... LIES CANNOT DECEIVE ME.
THE GLARE-GLARE FRUIT HAS TURNED ME...
GRRG...
...INTO AN EAGLE-EYED SEER.
A WOMAN WHO SEES THROUGH EVERY-THING...
MEN ARE BORN LIARS.
SHALL I TAKE A LITTLE PEEK...
...AT THE FALSEHOODS WITHIN YOUR MIND?
UH-OH, HERE COMES HER POSE!!
SH-PING!!
WHY DID TRAFALGAR LAW AND STRAW HAT JOIN FORCES?
AND ASIDE FROM GREENBIT, WHAT IS YOUR PURPOSE HERE IN DRESSROSA?
WHAT ARE YOU PLOTTING...AND HOW WILL YOU ACHIEVE IT? NO NEED TO SPEAK.
THE ANSWERS ARE ALL INSIDE YOUR HEAD, AND ONCE I HAVE THEM, YOUR FRIENDS WILL BE WIPED OFF THE MAP...

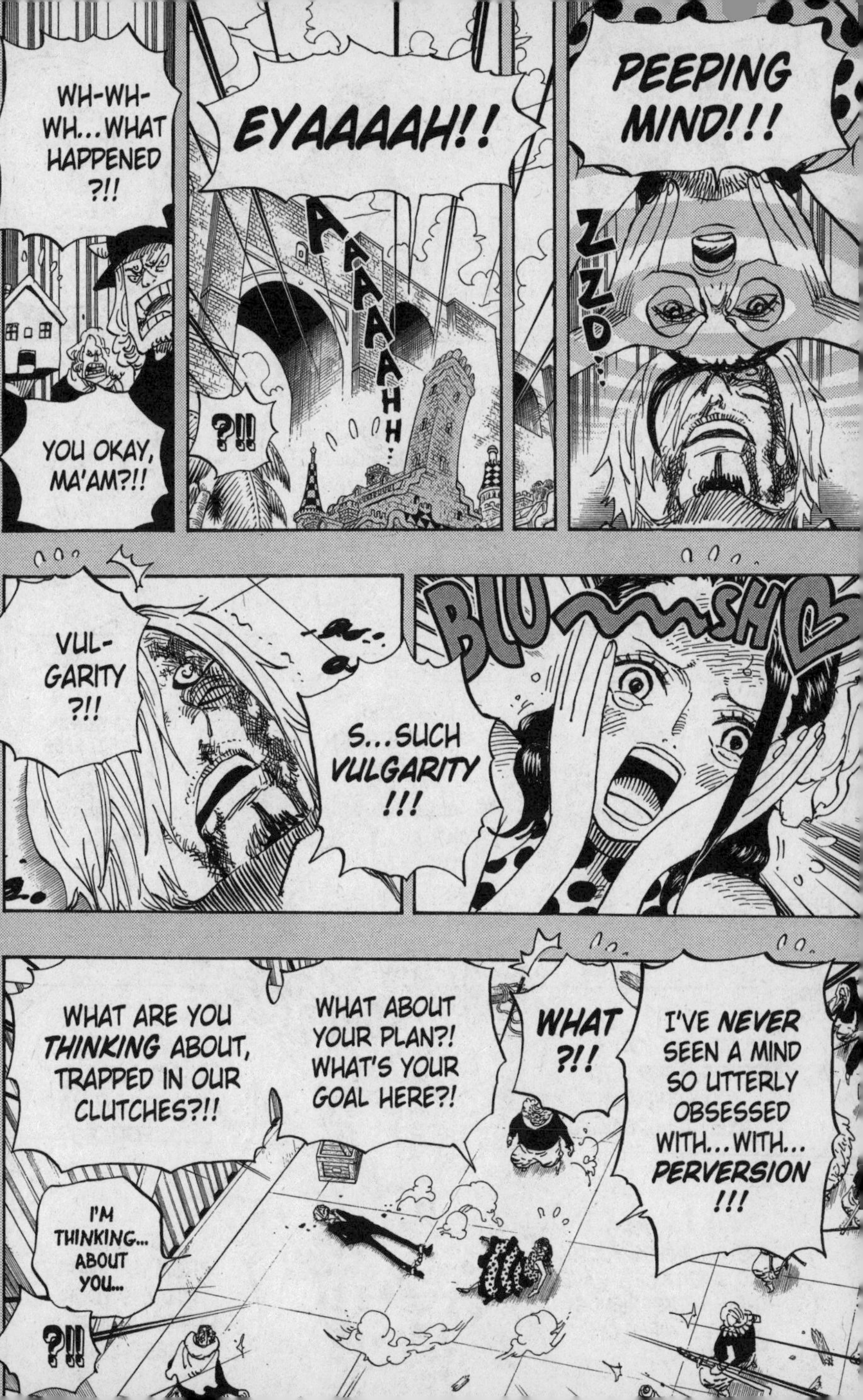
PEEPING MIND!!!
ZZZD
EYAAAAH!!
AAAAAHH
?!!
WH-WH-WH...WHAT HAPPENED ?!!
YOU OKAY, MA'AM?!!
BLU~~~SH
S...SUCH VULGARITY!!!
VUL-GARITY ?!!
I'VE NEVER SEEN A MIND SO UTTERLY OBSESSED WITH...WITH... PERVERSION!!!
WHAT ?!!
WHAT ABOUT YOUR PLAN?! WHAT'S YOUR GOAL HERE?!
WHAT ARE YOU THINKING ABOUT, TRAPPED IN OUR CLUTCHES?!!
I'M THINKING... ABOUT YOU...
?!!

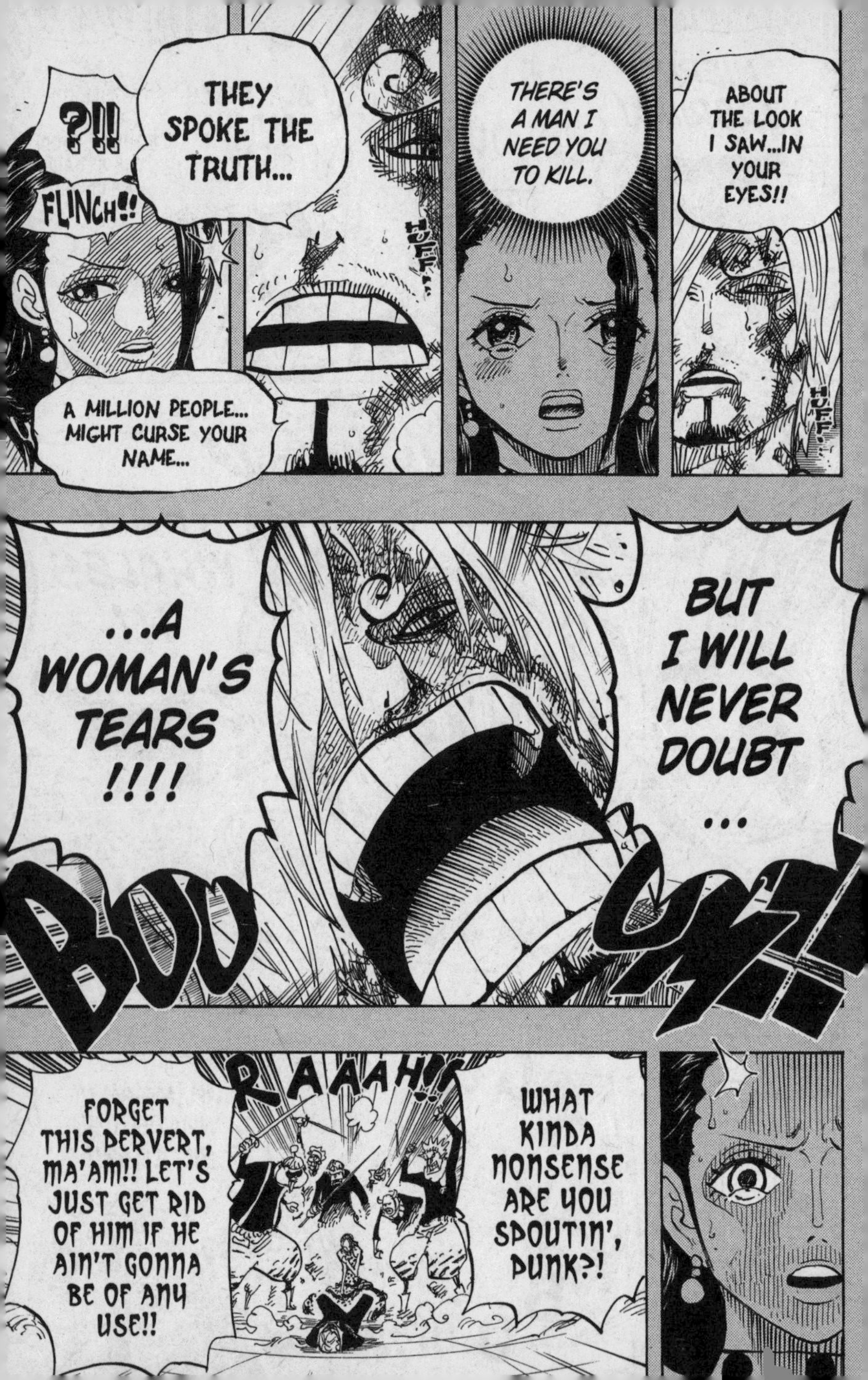
ABOUT THE LOOK I SAW...IN YOUR EYES!!
HUFF
THERE'S A MAN I NEED YOU TO KILL.
THEY SPOKE THE TRUTH...
HUFF
?!!
FLINCH!!
A MILLION PEOPLE... MIGHT CURSE YOUR NAME...
BUT I WILL NEVER DOUBT...
...A WOMAN'S TEARS!!!!
RAAAH!!
WHAT KINDA NONSENSE ARE YOU SPOUTIN', PUNK?!
FORGET THIS PERVERT, MA'AM!! LET'S JUST GET RID OF HIM IF HE AIN'T GONNA BE OF ANY USE!!

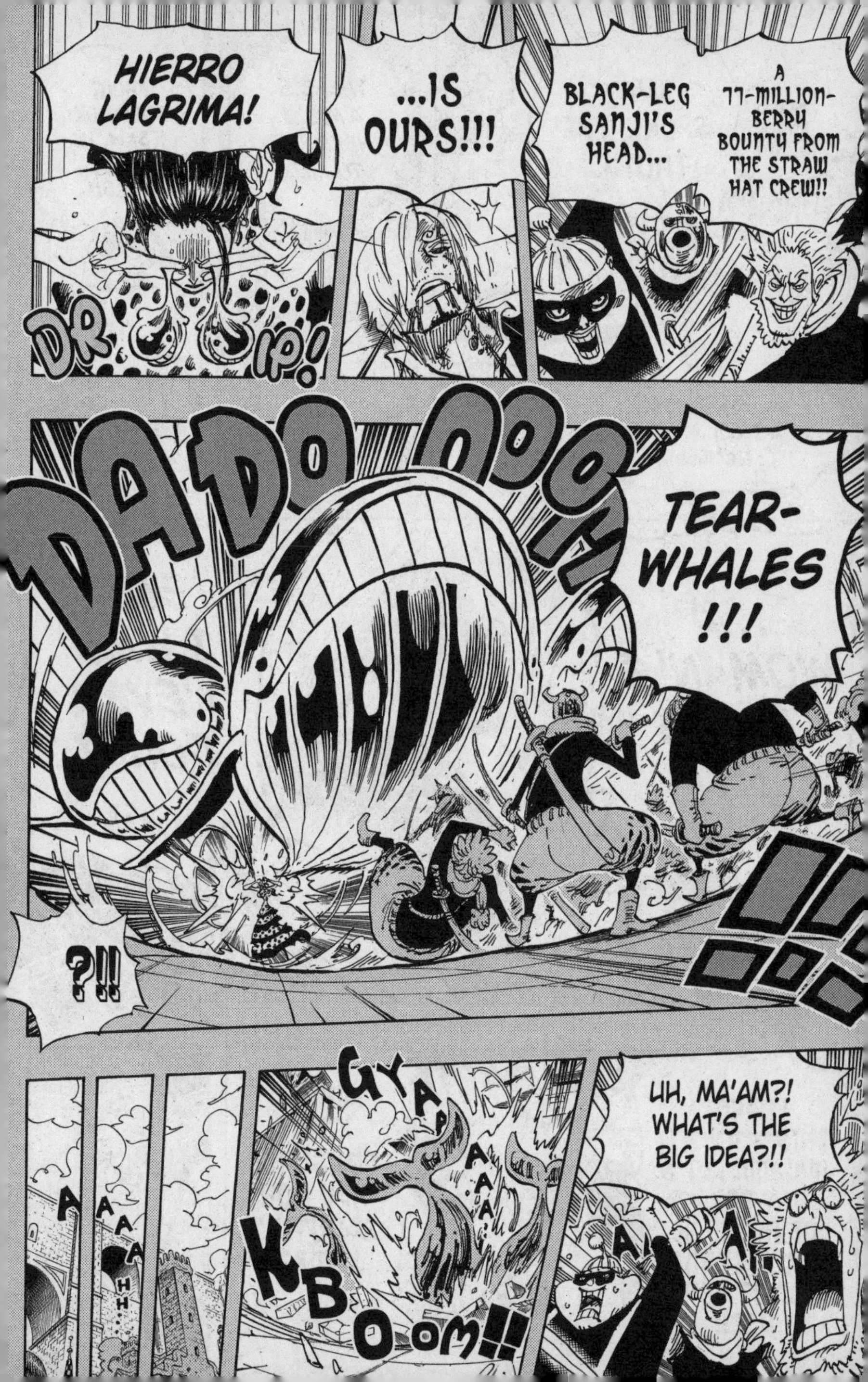
A 77-MILLION-BERRY BOUNTY FROM THE STRAW HAT CREW!!
BLACK-LEG SANJI'S HEAD...
...IS OURS!!!
HIERRO LAGRIMA!
DRIP!
TEAR-WHALES!!!
DADOOOOH
?!!
UH, MA'AM?! WHAT'S THE BIG IDEA?!!
GYAAAAAA
KBOOOM!!
AAAAHH...

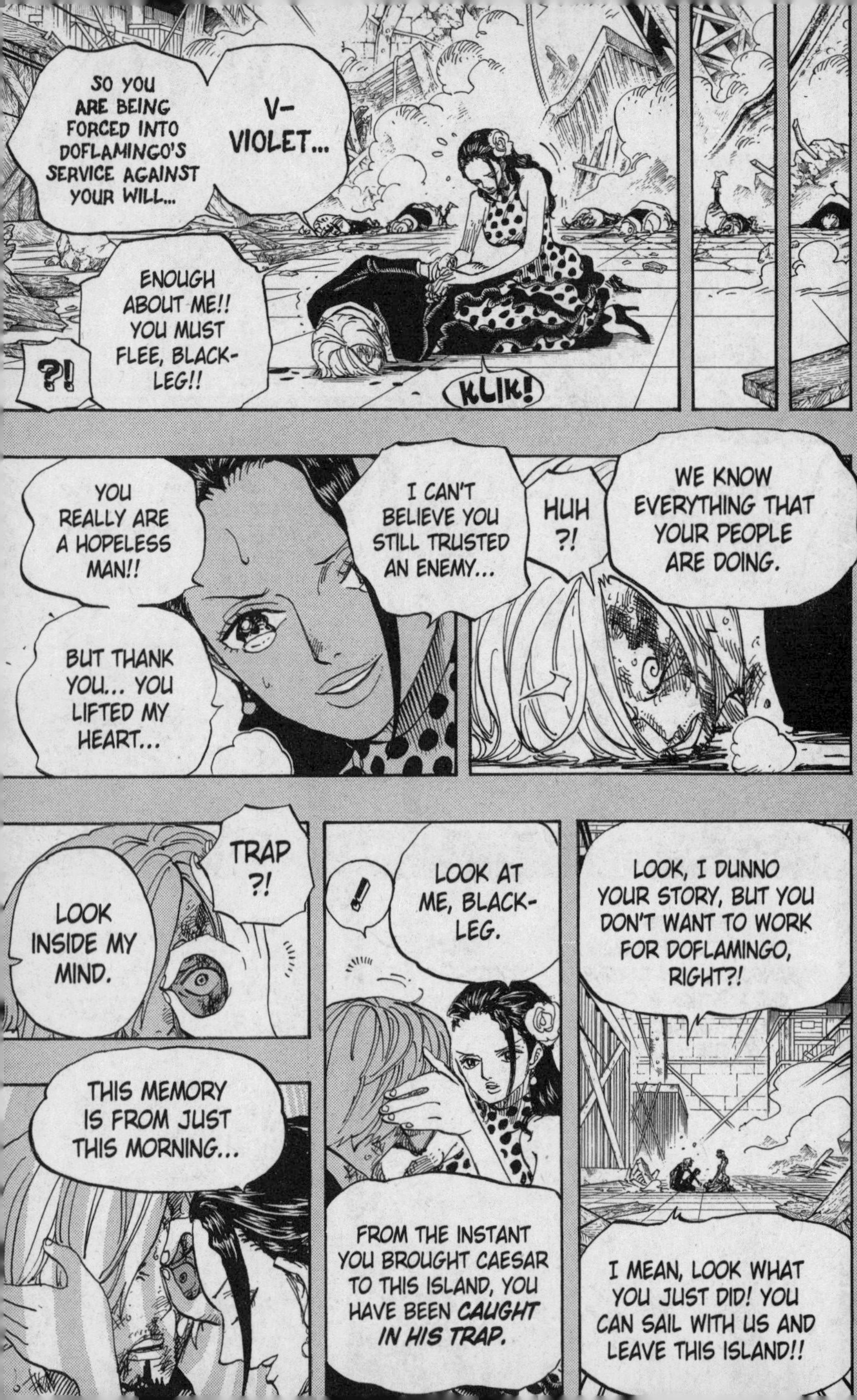
V-VIOLET...
SO YOU ARE BEING FORCED INTO DOFLAMINGO'S SERVICE AGAINST YOUR WILL...
KLIK!
ENOUGH ABOUT ME!! YOU MUST FLEE, BLACK-LEG!!
?!
WE KNOW EVERYTHING THAT YOUR PEOPLE ARE DOING.
HUH ?!
I CAN'T BELIEVE YOU STILL TRUSTED AN ENEMY...
YOU REALLY ARE A HOPELESS MAN!!
BUT THANK YOU... YOU LIFTED MY HEART...
LOOK, I DUNNO YOUR STORY, BUT YOU DON'T WANT TO WORK FOR DOFLAMINGO, RIGHT?!
I MEAN, LOOK WHAT YOU JUST DID! YOU CAN SAIL WITH US AND LEAVE THIS ISLAND!!
LOOK AT ME, BLACK-LEG.
!
FROM THE INSTANT YOU BROUGHT CAESAR TO THIS ISLAND, YOU HAVE BEEN *CAUGHT IN HIS TRAP.*
TRAP ?!
LOOK INSIDE MY MIND.
THIS MEMORY IS FROM JUST THIS MORNING...

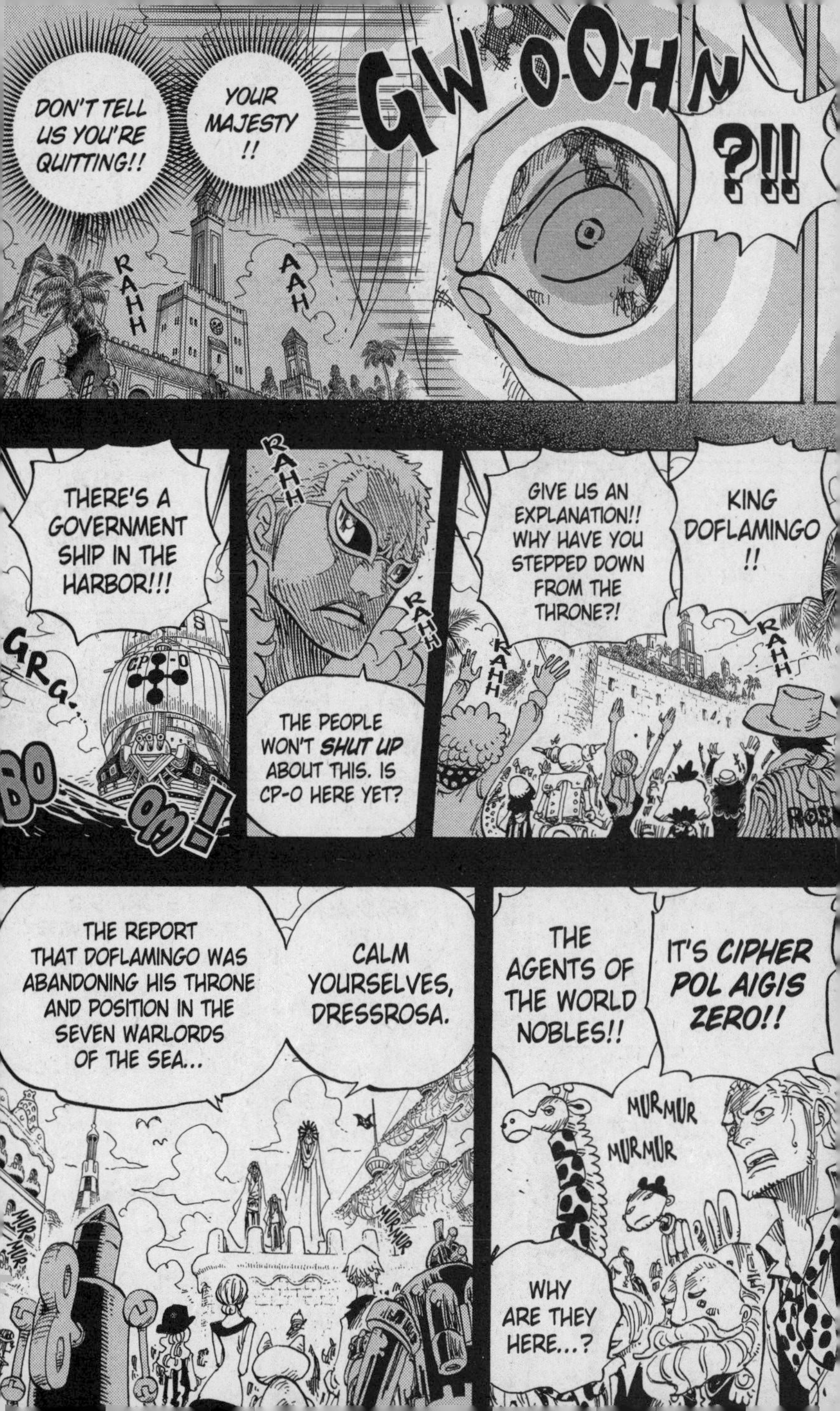
GWOOOHN
?!!
YOUR MAJESTY !!
DON'T TELL US YOU'RE QUITTING!!
AAH
RAHH
KING DOFLAMINGO !!
GIVE US AN EXPLANATION!! WHY HAVE YOU STEPPED DOWN FROM THE THRONE?!
RAHH
RAHH
RAHH
RAHH
THE PEOPLE WON'T *SHUT UP* ABOUT THIS. IS CP-0 HERE YET?
THERE'S A GOVERNMENT SHIP IN THE HARBOR!!!
GRG...
BOOM!
IT'S *CIPHER POL AIGIS ZERO!!*
THE AGENTS OF THE WORLD NOBLES!!
MURMUR
MURMUR
WHY ARE THEY HERE...?
CALM YOURSELVES, DRESSROSA.
THE REPORT THAT DOFLAMINGO WAS ABANDONING HIS THRONE AND POSITION IN THE SEVEN WARLORDS OF THE SEA...
MURMUR
MURMUR

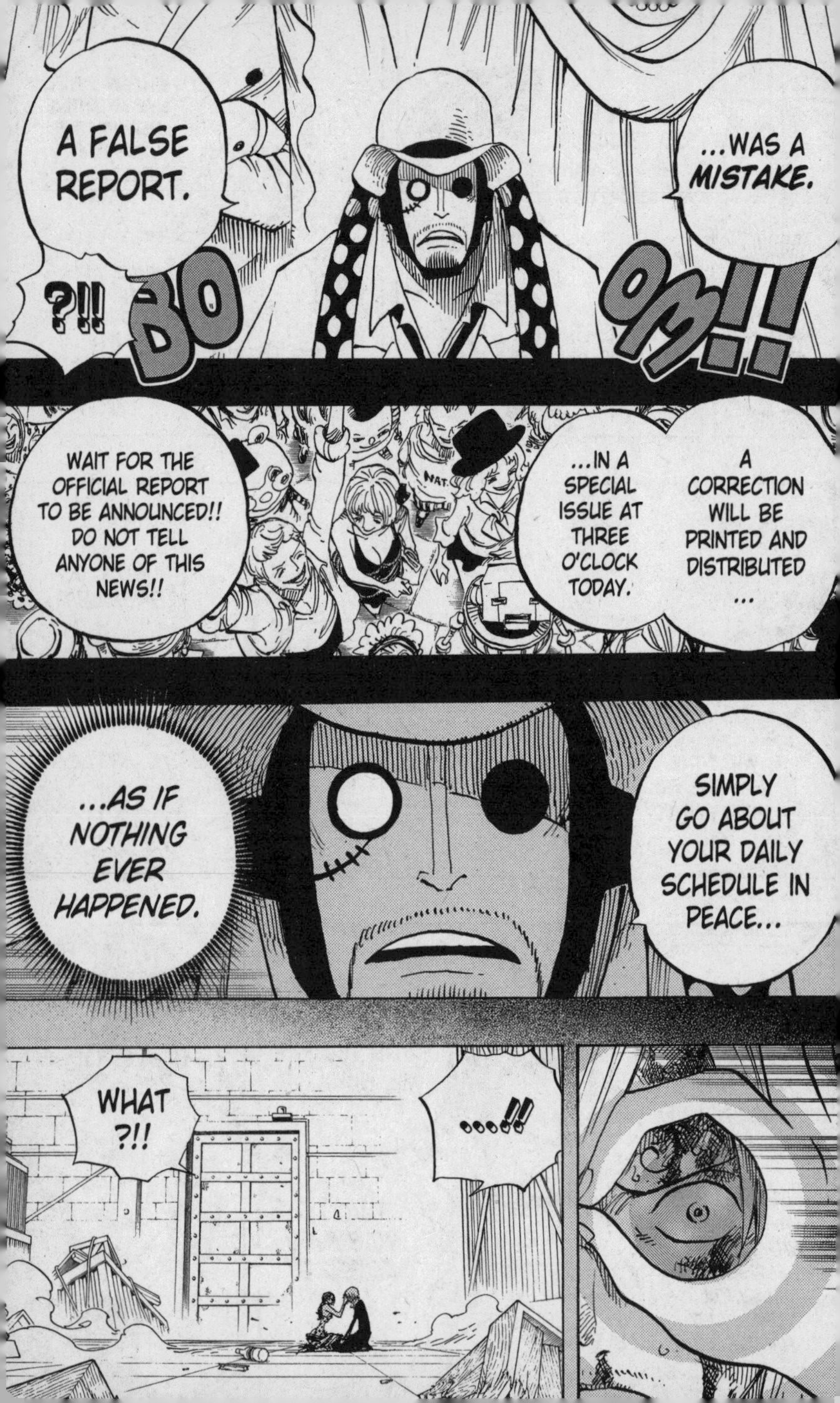
...WAS A MISTAKE.
A FALSE REPORT.
BOOM!!
?!!
A CORRECTION WILL BE PRINTED AND DISTRIBUTED ...
...IN A SPECIAL ISSUE AT THREE O'CLOCK TODAY.
WAIT FOR THE OFFICIAL REPORT TO BE ANNOUNCED!! DO NOT TELL ANYONE OF THIS NEWS!!
SIMPLY GO ABOUT YOUR DAILY SCHEDULE IN PEACE...
...AS IF NOTHING EVER HAPPENED.
...!!
WHAT?!!

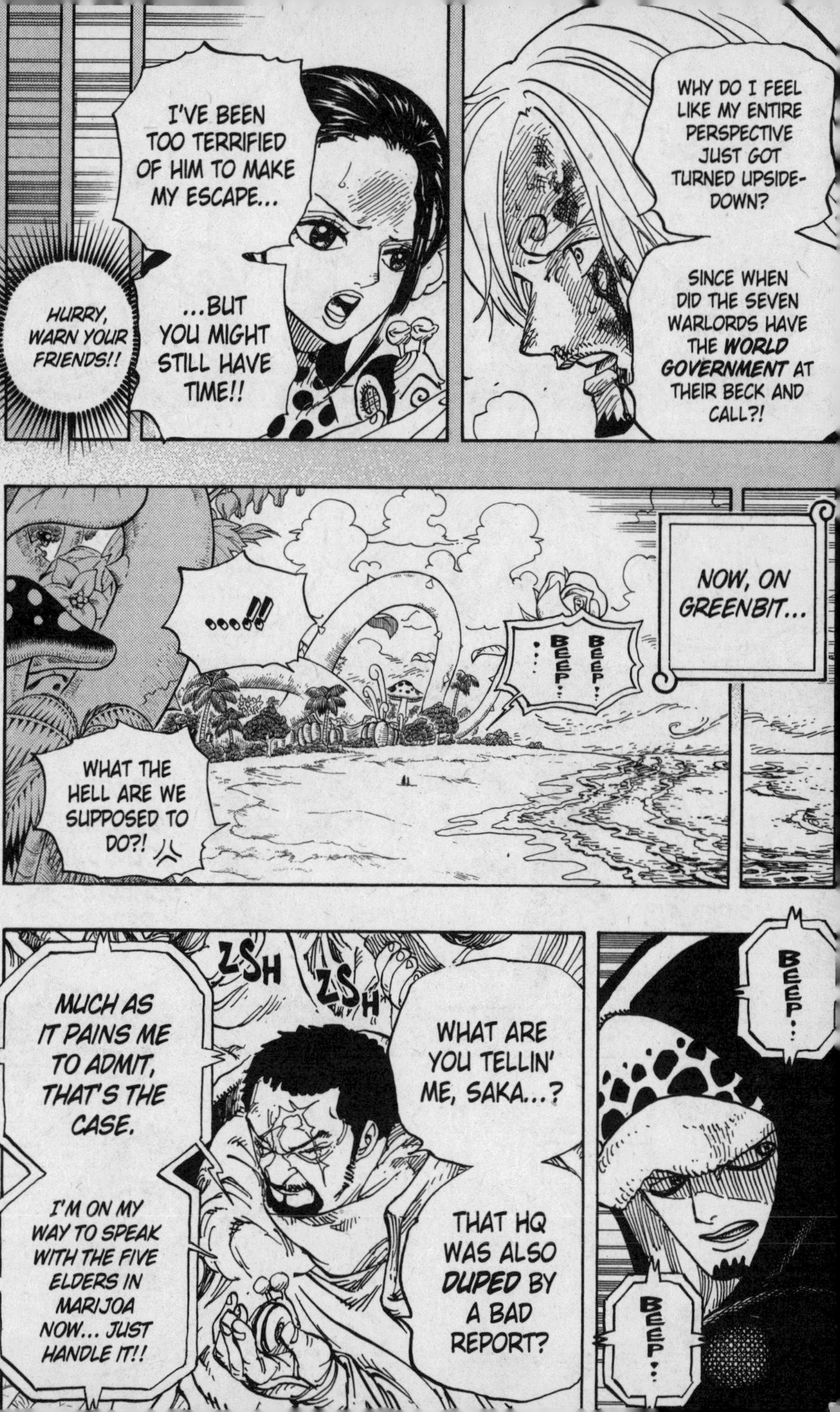

WHY DO I FEEL LIKE MY ENTIRE PERSPECTIVE JUST GOT TURNED UPSIDE-DOWN?
SINCE WHEN DID THE SEVEN WARLORDS HAVE THE WORLD GOVERNMENT AT THEIR BECK AND CALL?!
I'VE BEEN TOO TERRIFIED OF HIM TO MAKE MY ESCAPE...
...BUT YOU MIGHT STILL HAVE TIME!!
HURRY, WARN YOUR FRIENDS!!
NOW, ON GREENBIT...
BEEP...
BEEP...
....!!
WHAT THE HELL ARE WE SUPPOSED TO DO?!
BEEP...
BEEP...
ZSH
ZSH
WHAT ARE YOU TELLIN' ME, SAKA...?
MUCH AS IT PAINS ME TO ADMIT, THAT'S THE CASE.
THAT HQ WAS ALSO DUPED BY A BAD REPORT?
I'M ON MY WAY TO SPEAK WITH THE FIVE ELDERS IN MARIJOA NOW... JUST HANDLE IT!!

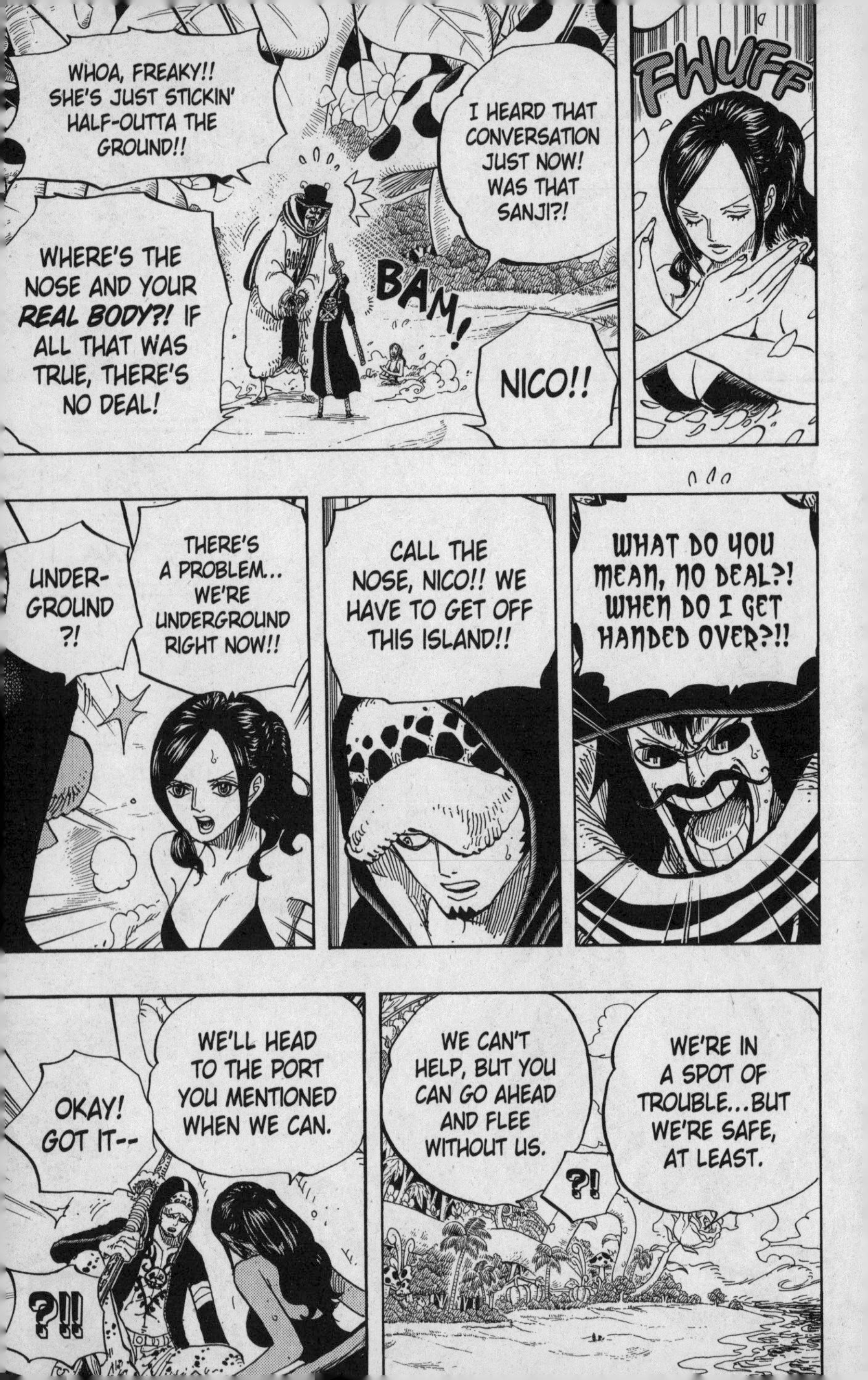
FWUFF
I HEARD THAT CONVERSATION JUST NOW! WAS THAT SANJI?!
WHOA, FREAKY!! SHE'S JUST STICKIN' HALF-OUTTA THE GROUND!!
BAM!
NICO!!
WHERE'S THE NOSE AND YOUR REAL BODY?! IF ALL THAT WAS TRUE, THERE'S NO DEAL!
WHAT DO YOU MEAN, NO DEAL?! WHEN DO I GET HANDED OVER?!!
CALL THE NOSE, NICO!! WE HAVE TO GET OFF THIS ISLAND!!
THERE'S A PROBLEM... WE'RE UNDERGROUND RIGHT NOW!!
UNDER-GROUND?!
WE'RE IN A SPOT OF TROUBLE...BUT WE'RE SAFE, AT LEAST.
WE CAN'T HELP, BUT YOU CAN GO AHEAD AND FLEE WITHOUT US.
?!
WE'LL HEAD TO THE PORT YOU MENTIONED WHEN WE CAN.
OKAY! GOT IT--
?!!

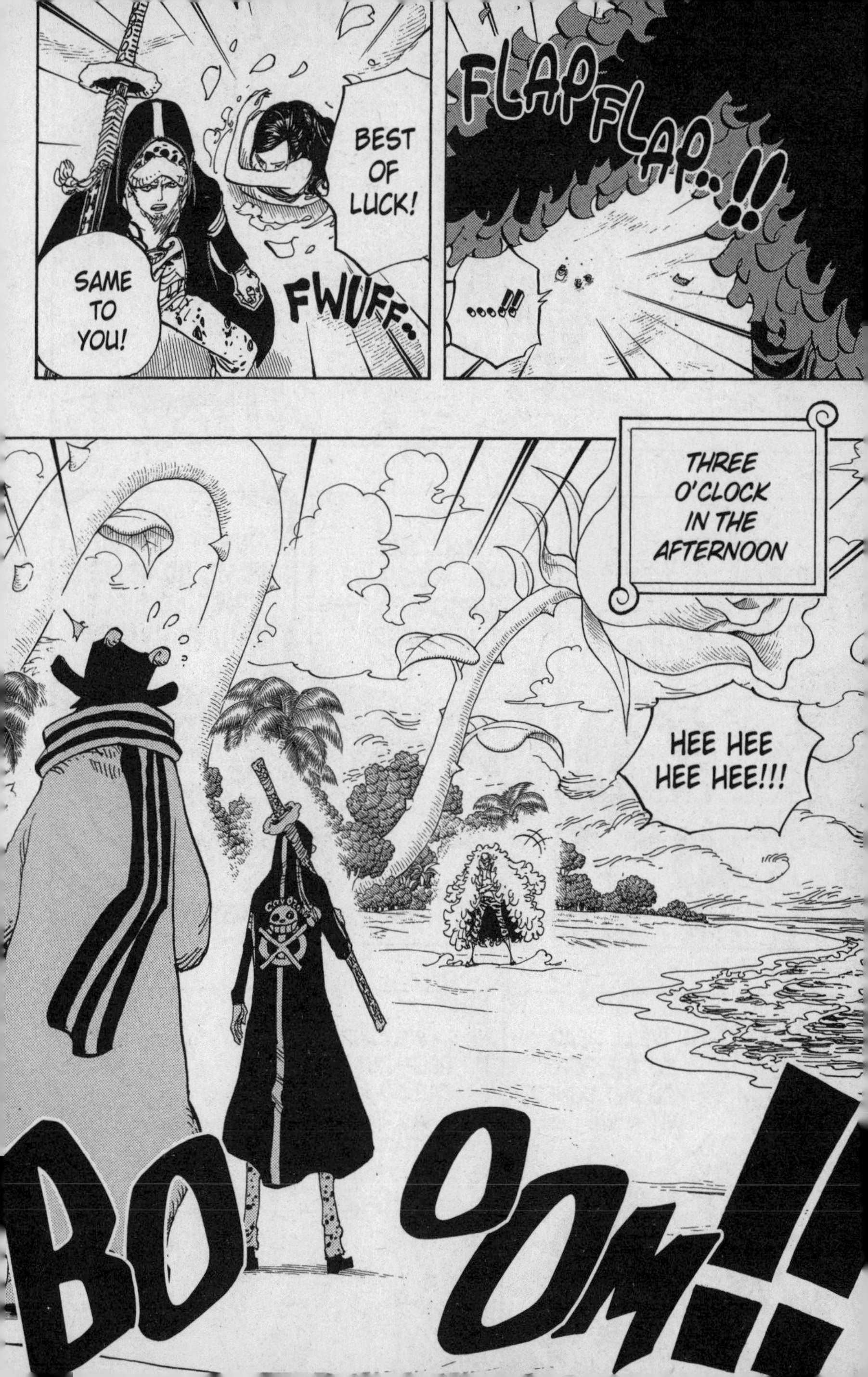
FLAP FLAP...!!
...!!
BEST OF LUCK!
FWUFF...
SAME TO YOU!
THREE O'CLOCK IN THE AFTERNOON
HEE HEE HEE HEE!!!
BOOOOM!!

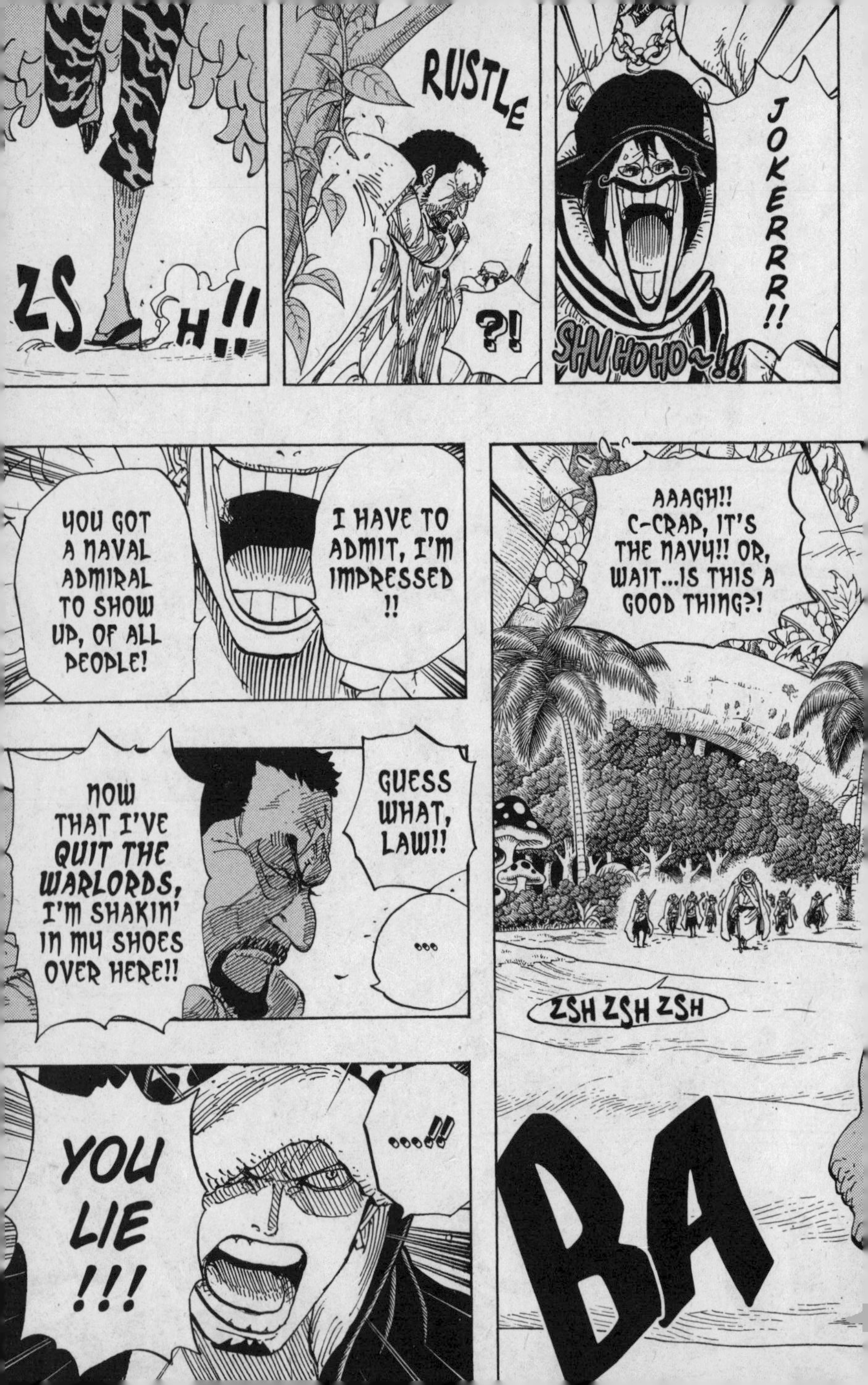
JOKERRR!!
SHU HO HO~!!
RUSTLE
?!
ZSH!!
AAAGH!! C-CRAP, IT'S THE NAVY!! OR, WAIT...IS THIS A GOOD THING?!
ZSH ZSH ZSH
BA
I HAVE TO ADMIT, I'M IMPRESSED!!
YOU GOT A NAVAL ADMIRAL TO SHOW UP, OF ALL PEOPLE!
GUESS WHAT, LAW!!
...
NOW THAT I'VE *QUIT THE WARLORDS*, I'M SHAKIN' IN MY SHOES OVER HERE!!
...!!
YOU LIE!!!

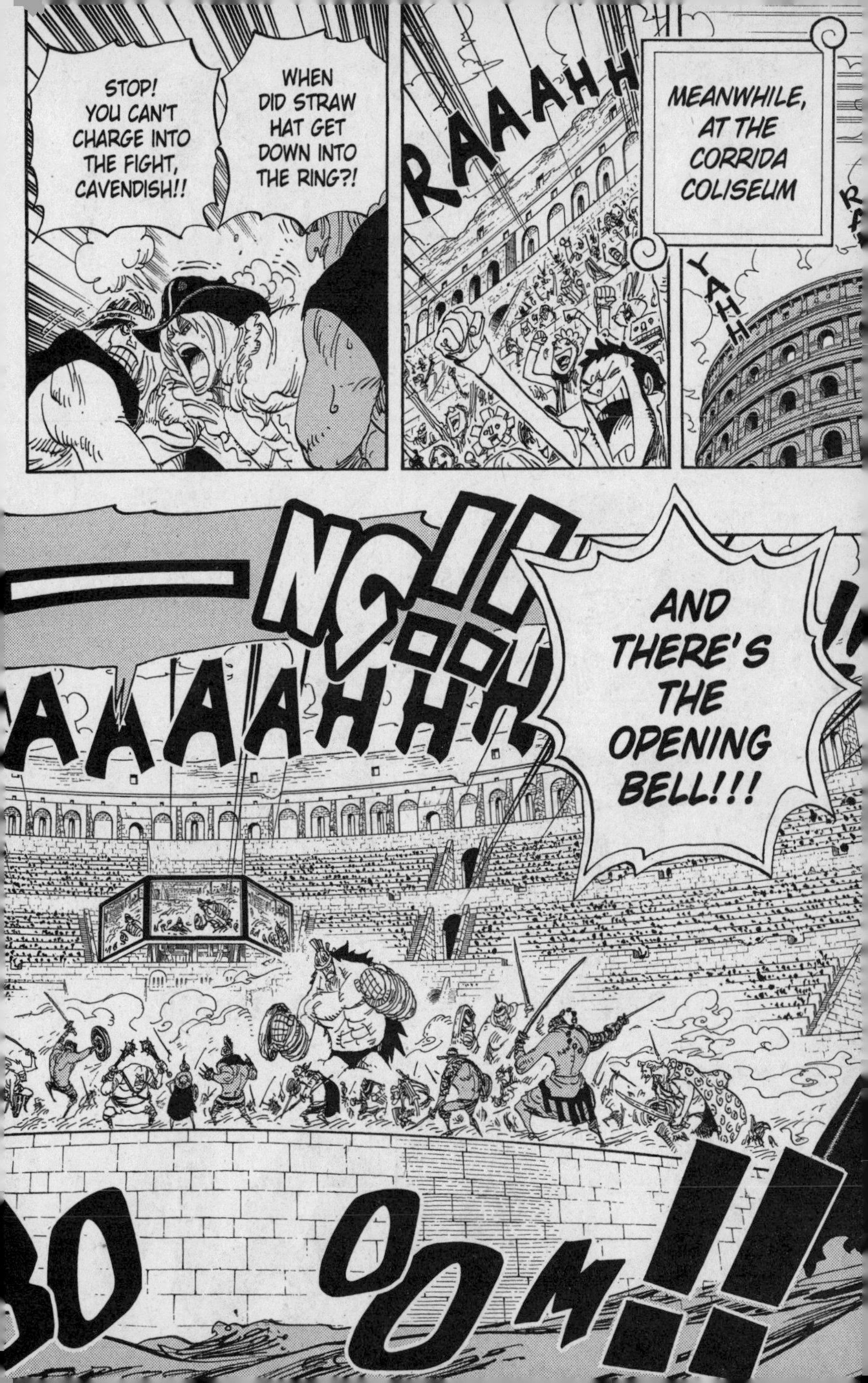

MEANWHILE, AT THE CORRIDA COLISEUM
YAHH
RAAAHH
WHEN DID STRAW HAT GET DOWN INTO THE RING?!
STOP! YOU CAN'T CHARGE INTO THE FIGHT, CAVENDISH!!
AND THERE'S THE OPENING BELL!!!

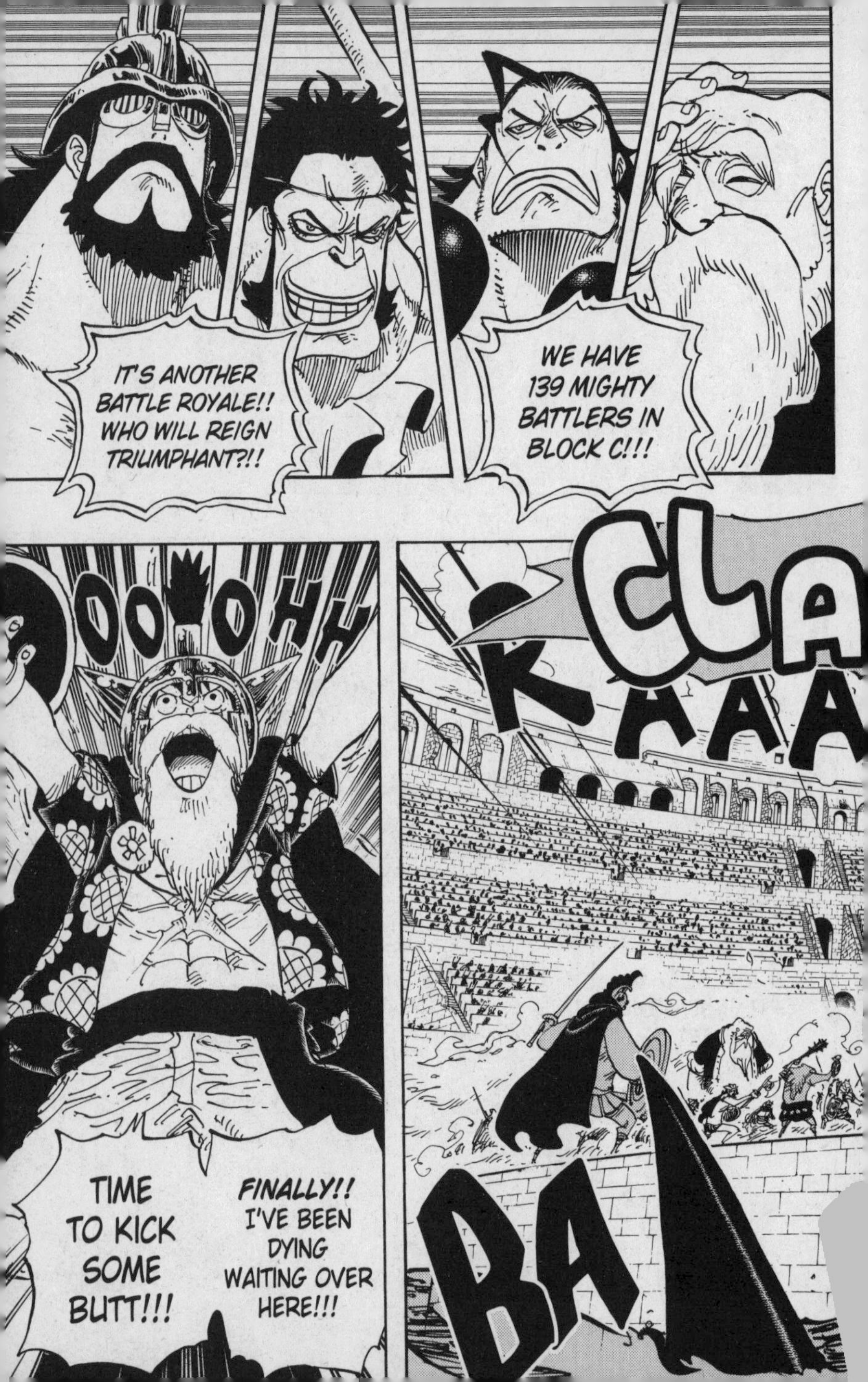

WE HAVE 139 MIGHTY BATTLERS IN BLOCK C!!!
IT'S ANOTHER BATTLE ROYALE!! WHO WILL REIGN TRIUMPHANT?!!
CLAKAAA
BA
OOO-OHH
FINALLY!! I'VE BEEN DYING WAITING OVER HERE!!!
TIME TO KICK SOME BUTT!!!

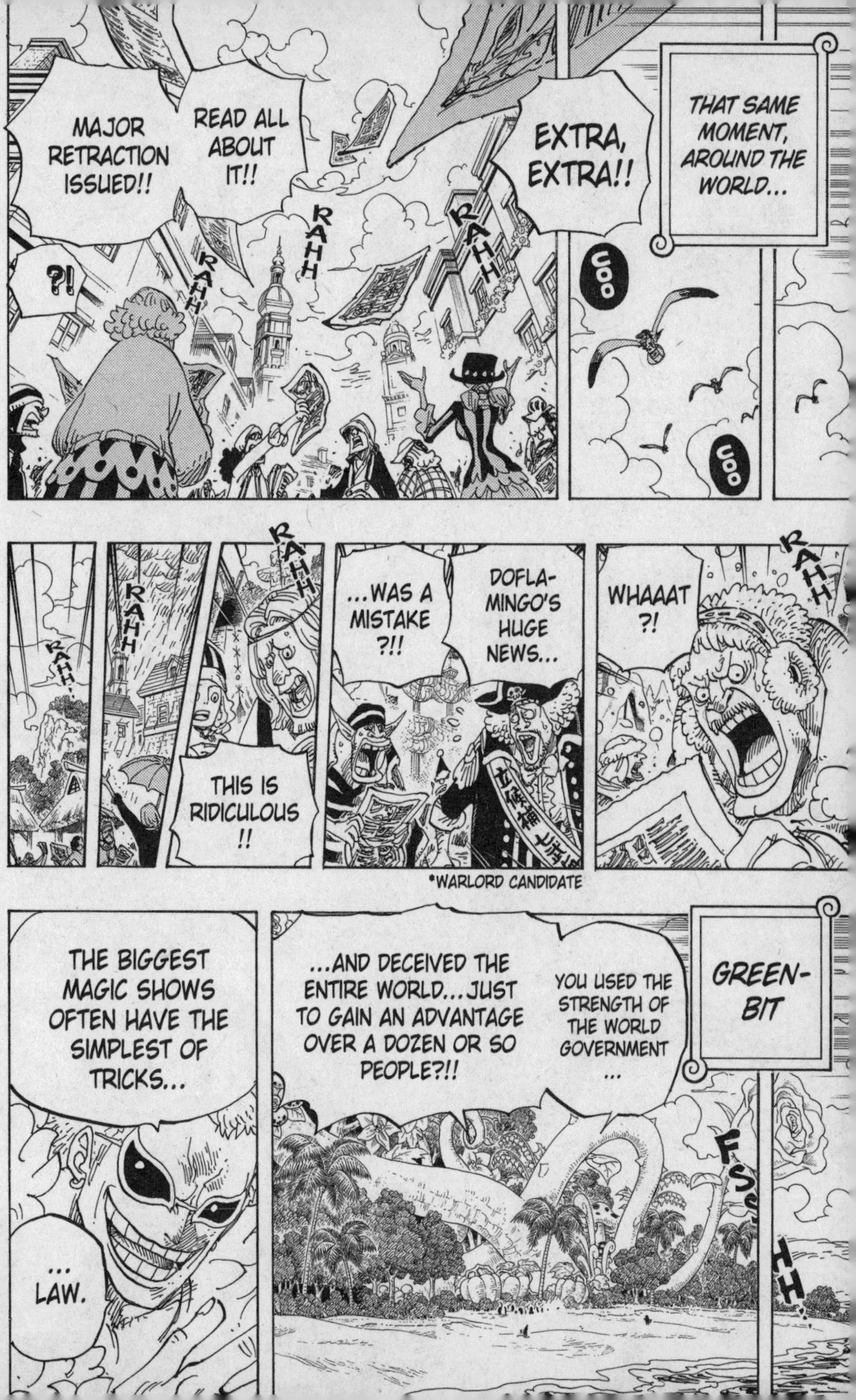
THAT SAME MOMENT, AROUND THE WORLD...
UOO
UOO
EXTRA, EXTRA!!
RAHH
READ ALL ABOUT IT!!
RAHH
MAJOR RETRACTION ISSUED!!
RAHH
?!
RAHH
WHAAAT?!
DOFLAMINGO'S HUGE NEWS...
...WAS A MISTAKE?!!
*WARLORD CANDIDATE
RAHH
THIS IS RIDICULOUS!!
RAHH
RAHH...
GREEN-BIT
FSSHH
YOU USED THE STRENGTH OF THE WORLD GOVERNMENT...
...AND DECEIVED THE ENTIRE WORLD...JUST TO GAIN AN ADVANTAGE OVER A DOZEN OR SO PEOPLE?!!
THE BIGGEST MAGIC SHOWS OFTEN HAVE THE SIMPLEST OF TRICKS...
...LAW.

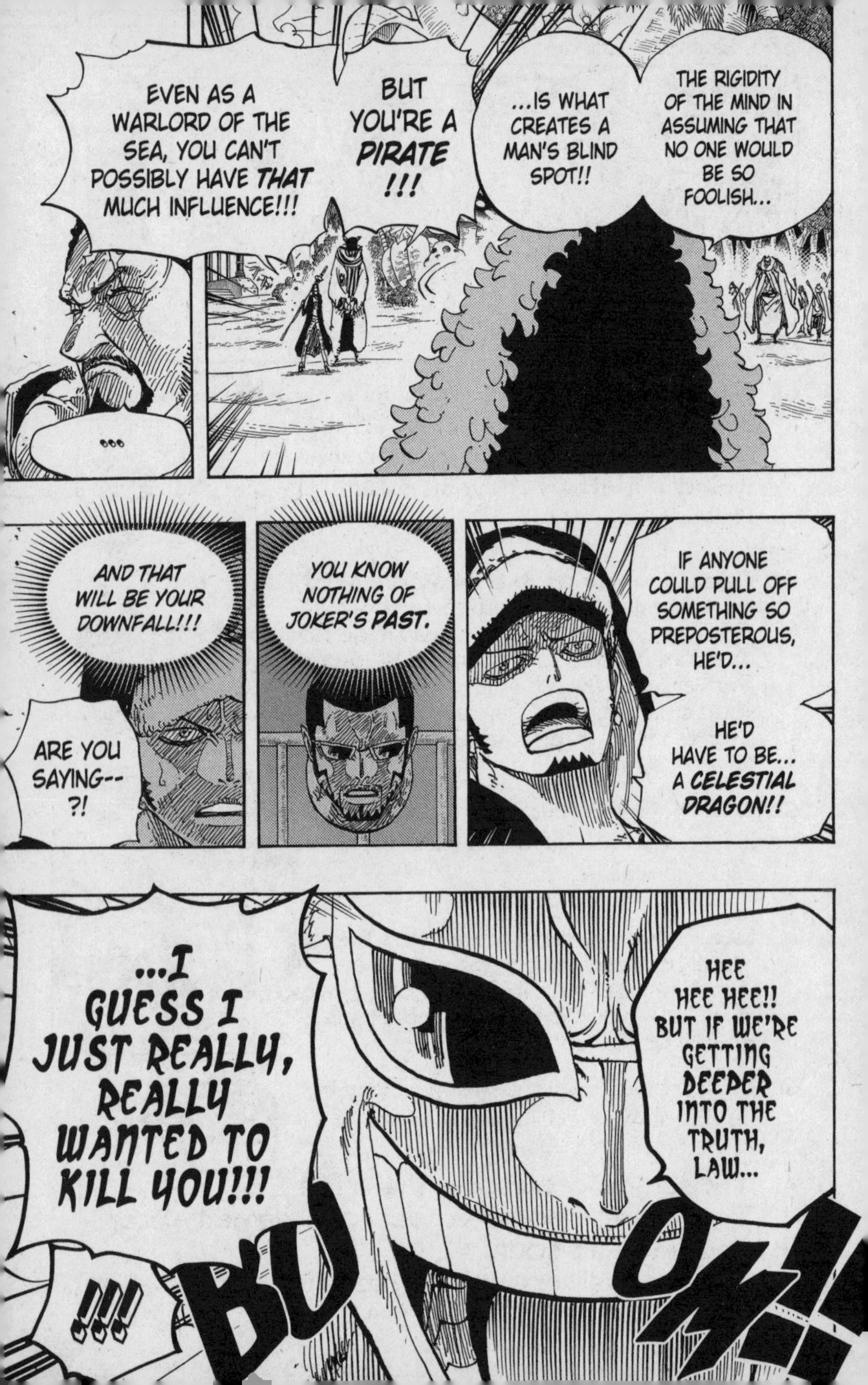
THE RIGIDITY OF THE MIND IN ASSUMING THAT NO ONE WOULD BE SO FOOLISH...
...IS WHAT CREATES A MAN'S BLIND SPOT!!
BUT YOU'RE A PIRATE!!!
EVEN AS A WARLORD OF THE SEA, YOU CAN'T POSSIBLY HAVE THAT MUCH INFLUENCE!!!
...
IF ANYONE COULD PULL OFF SOMETHING SO PREPOSTEROUS, HE'D...
HE'D HAVE TO BE... A CELESTIAL DRAGON!!
YOU KNOW NOTHING OF JOKER'S PAST.
AND THAT WILL BE YOUR DOWNFALL!!!
ARE YOU SAYING--?!
HEE HEE HEE!! BUT IF WE'RE GETTING DEEPER INTO THE TRUTH, LAW...
...I GUESS I JUST REALLY, REALLY WANTED TO KILL YOU!!!
BO
OM!!
!!!

SBS Question Corner

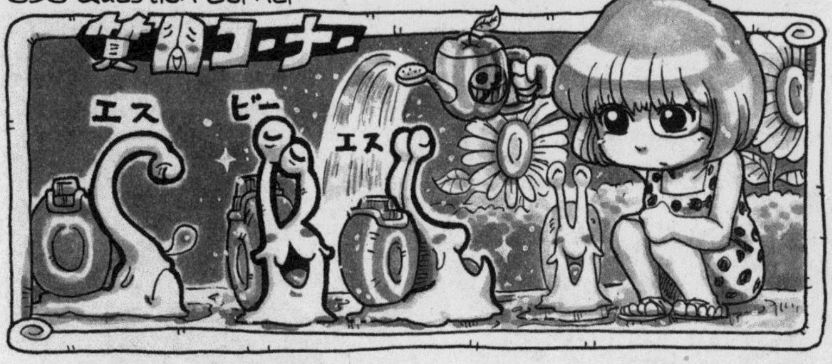
エス
ビー
エス

(Hippo Iron, Saitama)

Q: Odacchi, Odacchi, Odacchi, good morning. By the way, let's begin the SBS. And now, my question. On page 128 of Volume 31, the kids are asking for a story about the land of the dwarves, right? Right? Right? Please explain.

--Uekenger

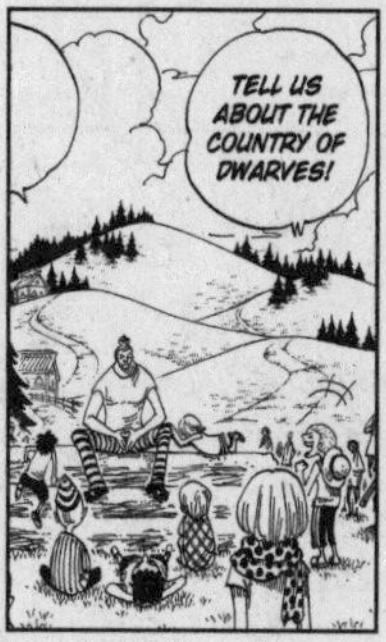
TELL US ABOUT THE COUNTRY OF DWARVES!

A: Geez, you've got the momentum of an avalanche, don't you? Starting the SBS, asking questions--I can't get a word in! I'm glad you found this, though. Perhaps you might find the answer to your question in Chapter 713, which starts right over there <--
Give it a read.

Q: When the crew left Punk Hazard, Franky's shirt said "JK" on it… But like, he makes such a gross JK (*joshi-kosei,* female high schooler)!!!

--Sanji Ikari

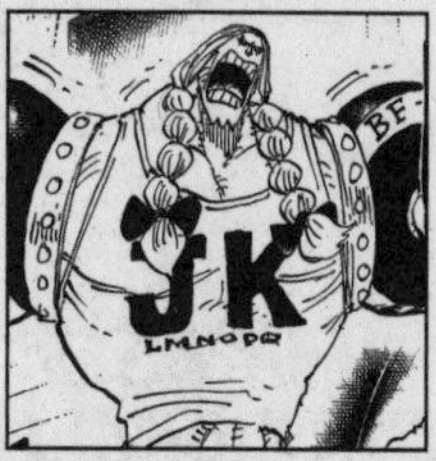
JK

A: Like OMG, I totally agree!! He's like, totally creepy!! But the more I see those braided pigtails, the more I think they look good on him...and that's like totally gross too!!

Q: Good day, Odacchi. Is this what you meant by the Ancient Weapon Pluton?

--Dobin

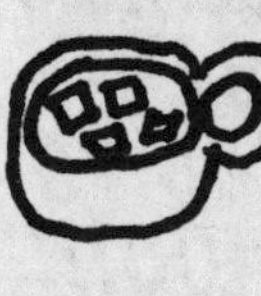

A: Those are croutons, right?!!
They're not ancient weapons named after gods in that soup...
They're just croutons, right?!! Σ(•□•)
Just crispy little pieces of bread, right?!

Chapter 713:
USOLAND

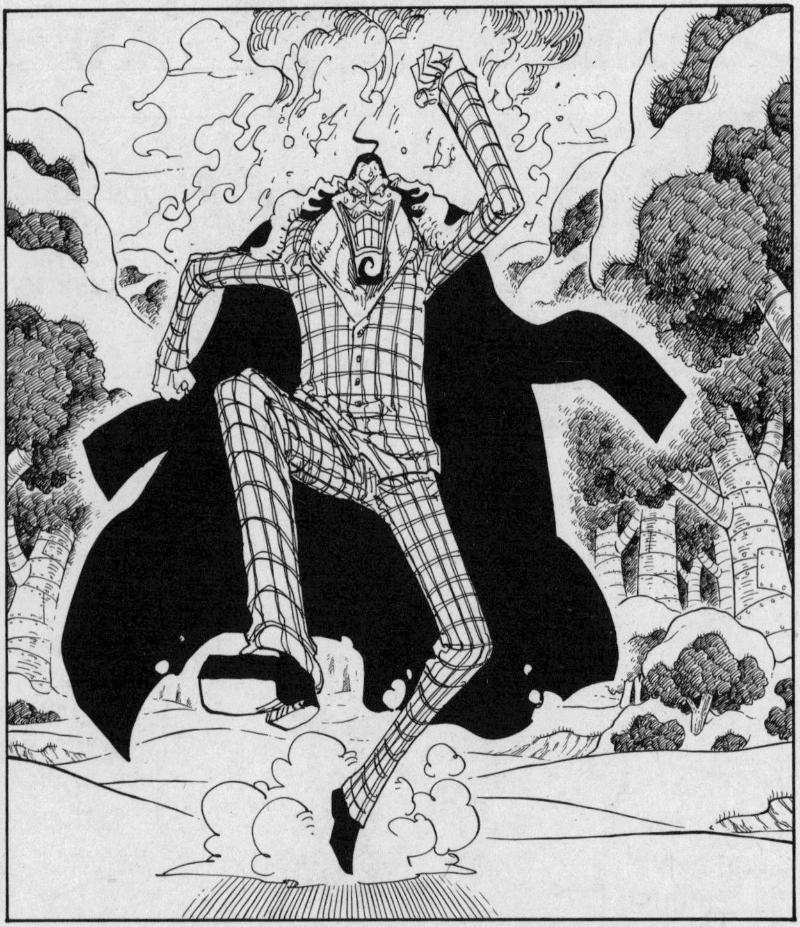

CARIBOU'S NEW WORLD KEE HEE HEE, VOL. 31:
"MAD DASH TO ESCAPE THE DEADLY PIRATE SCOTCH!!"

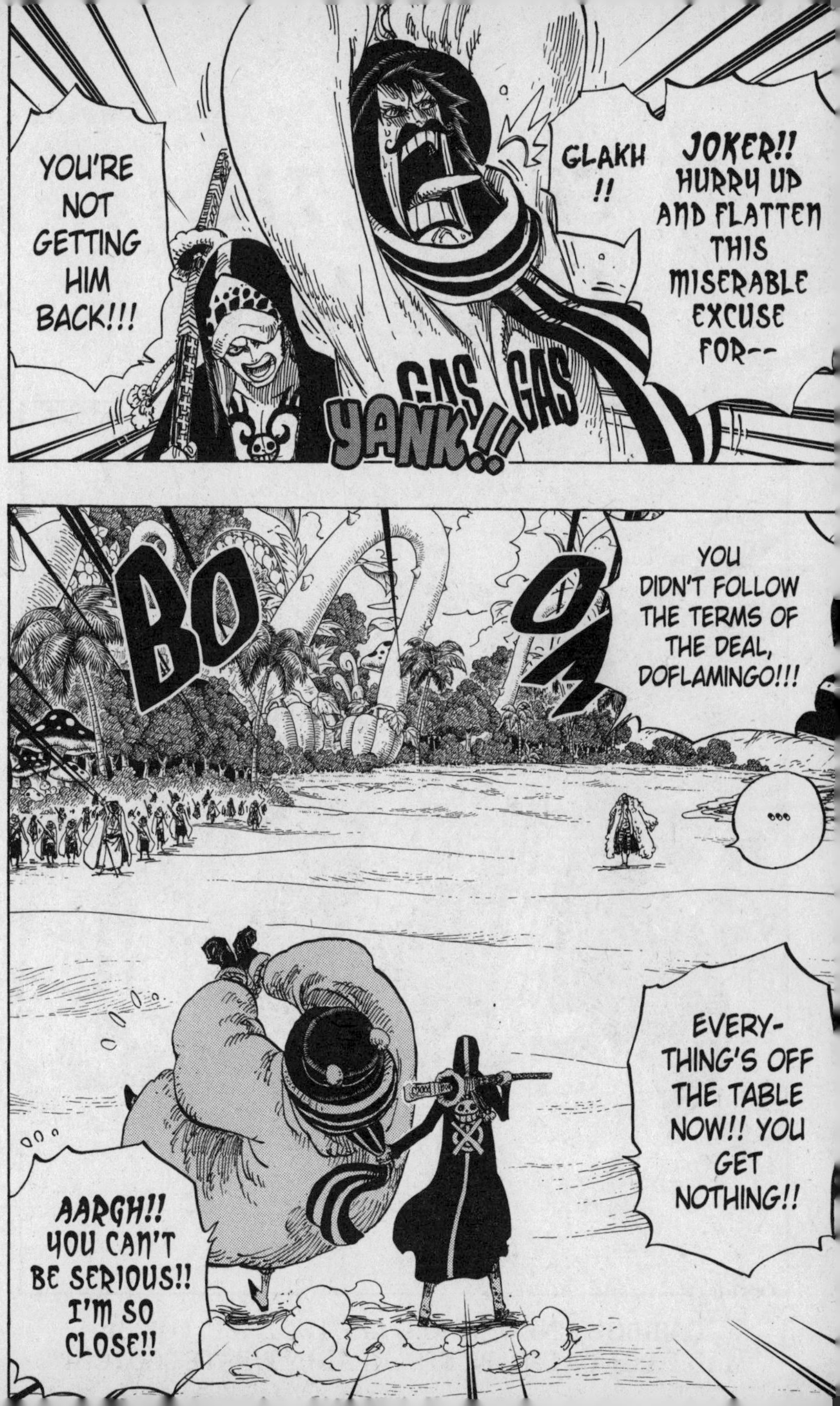
JOKER!! HURRY UP AND FLATTEN THIS MISERABLE EXCUSE FOR--
GLAKH !!
YOU'RE NOT GETTING HIM BACK!!!
GAS GAS
YANK!!
YOU DIDN'T FOLLOW THE TERMS OF THE DEAL, DOFLAMINGO!!!
...
BOOM
EVERY-THING'S OFF THE TABLE NOW!! YOU GET NOTHING!!
AARGH!! YOU CAN'T BE SERIOUS!! I'M SO CLOSE!!

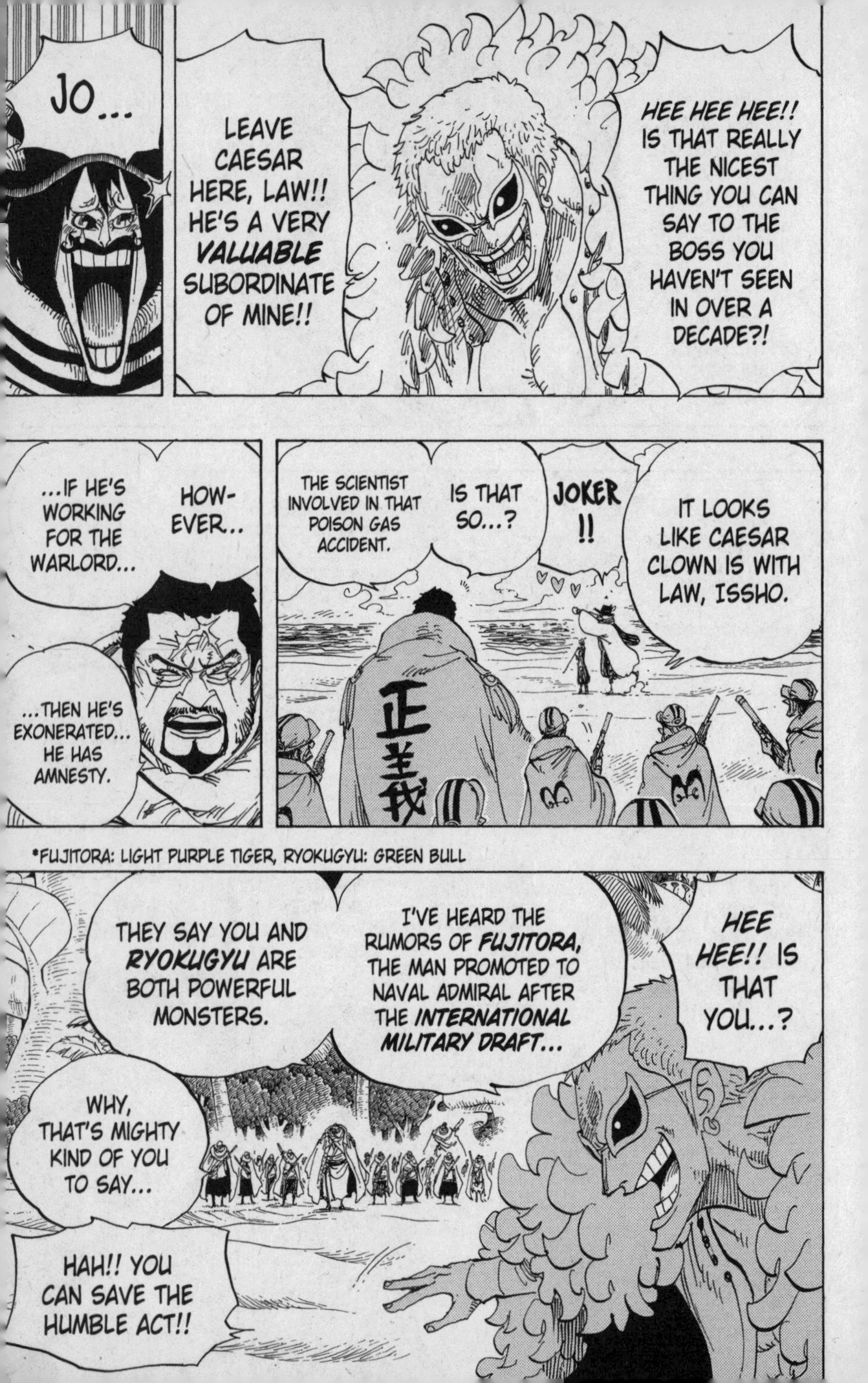
HEE HEE HEE!! IS THAT REALLY THE NICEST THING YOU CAN SAY TO THE BOSS YOU HAVEN'T SEEN IN OVER A DECADE?!
LEAVE CAESAR HERE, LAW!! HE'S A VERY VALUABLE SUBORDINATE OF MINE!!
JO...
IT LOOKS LIKE CAESAR CLOWN IS WITH LAW, ISSHO.
JOKER !!
IS THAT SO...?
THE SCIENTIST INVOLVED IN THAT POISON GAS ACCIDENT.
HOW-EVER...
...IF HE'S WORKING FOR THE WARLORD...
...THEN HE'S EXONERATED... HE HAS AMNESTY.
正義
HEE HEE!! IS THAT YOU...?
I'VE HEARD THE RUMORS OF FUJITORA, THE MAN PROMOTED TO NAVAL ADMIRAL AFTER THE INTERNATIONAL MILITARY DRAFT...
THEY SAY YOU AND RYOKUGYU ARE BOTH POWERFUL MONSTERS.
WHY, THAT'S MIGHTY KIND OF YOU TO SAY...
HAH!! YOU CAN SAVE THE HUMBLE ACT!!

*FUJITORA: LIGHT PURPLE TIGER, RYOKUGYU: GREEN BULL

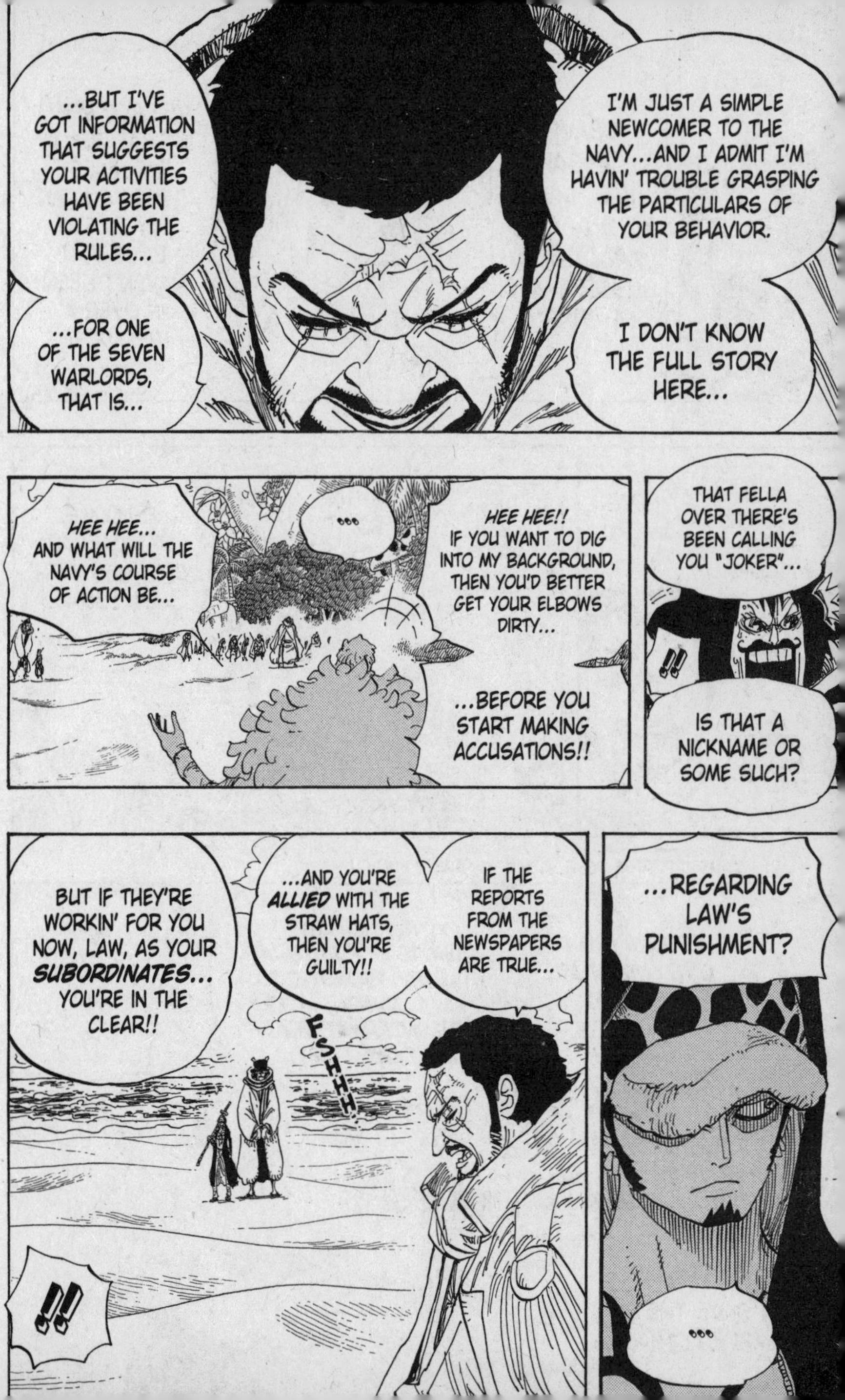
I'M JUST A SIMPLE NEWCOMER TO THE NAVY...AND I ADMIT I'M HAVIN' TROUBLE GRASPING THE PARTICULARS OF YOUR BEHAVIOR.
I DON'T KNOW THE FULL STORY HERE...
...BUT I'VE GOT INFORMATION THAT SUGGESTS YOUR ACTIVITIES HAVE BEEN VIOLATING THE RULES...
...FOR ONE OF THE SEVEN WARLORDS, THAT IS...
THAT FELLA OVER THERE'S BEEN CALLING YOU "JOKER"...
!!
IS THAT A NICKNAME OR SOME SUCH?
HEE HEE!! IF YOU WANT TO DIG INTO MY BACKGROUND, THEN YOU'D BETTER GET YOUR ELBOWS DIRTY...
...BEFORE YOU START MAKING ACCUSATIONS!!
...
HEE HEE... AND WHAT WILL THE NAVY'S COURSE OF ACTION BE...
...REGARDING LAW'S PUNISHMENT?
...
IF THE REPORTS FROM THE NEWSPAPERS ARE TRUE...
...AND YOU'RE ***ALLIED*** WITH THE STRAW HATS, THEN YOU'RE GUILTY!!
BUT IF THEY'RE WORKIN' FOR YOU NOW, LAW, AS YOUR ***SUBORDINATES...*** YOU'RE IN THE CLEAR!!
FSHHH
!!

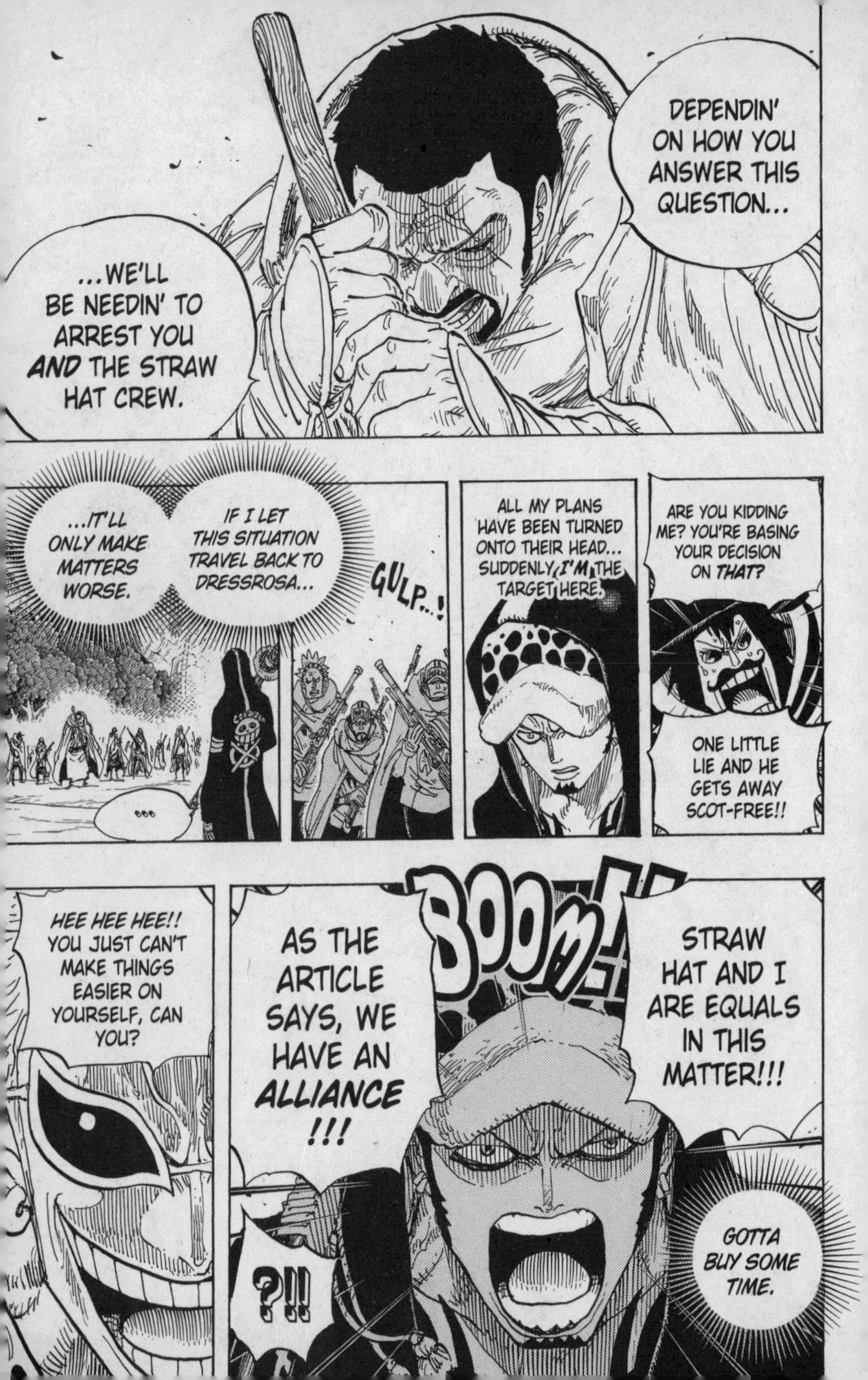

DEPENDIN' ON HOW YOU ANSWER THIS QUESTION...
...WE'LL BE NEEDIN' TO ARREST YOU *AND* THE STRAW HAT CREW.
ARE YOU KIDDING ME? YOU'RE BASING YOUR DECISION ON *THAT?*
ONE LITTLE LIE AND HE GETS AWAY SCOT-FREE!!
ALL MY PLANS HAVE BEEN TURNED ONTO THEIR HEAD... SUDDENLY *I'M* THE TARGET HERE.
GULP...!
IF I LET THIS SITUATION TRAVEL BACK TO DRESSROSA...
...IT'LL ONLY MAKE MATTERS WORSE.
...
BOOM!
STRAW HAT AND I ARE EQUALS IN THIS MATTER!!!
AS THE ARTICLE SAYS, WE HAVE AN *ALLIANCE*!!!
GOTTA BUY SOME TIME.
?!!
HEE HEE HEE!! YOU JUST CAN'T MAKE THINGS EASIER ON YOURSELF, CAN YOU?

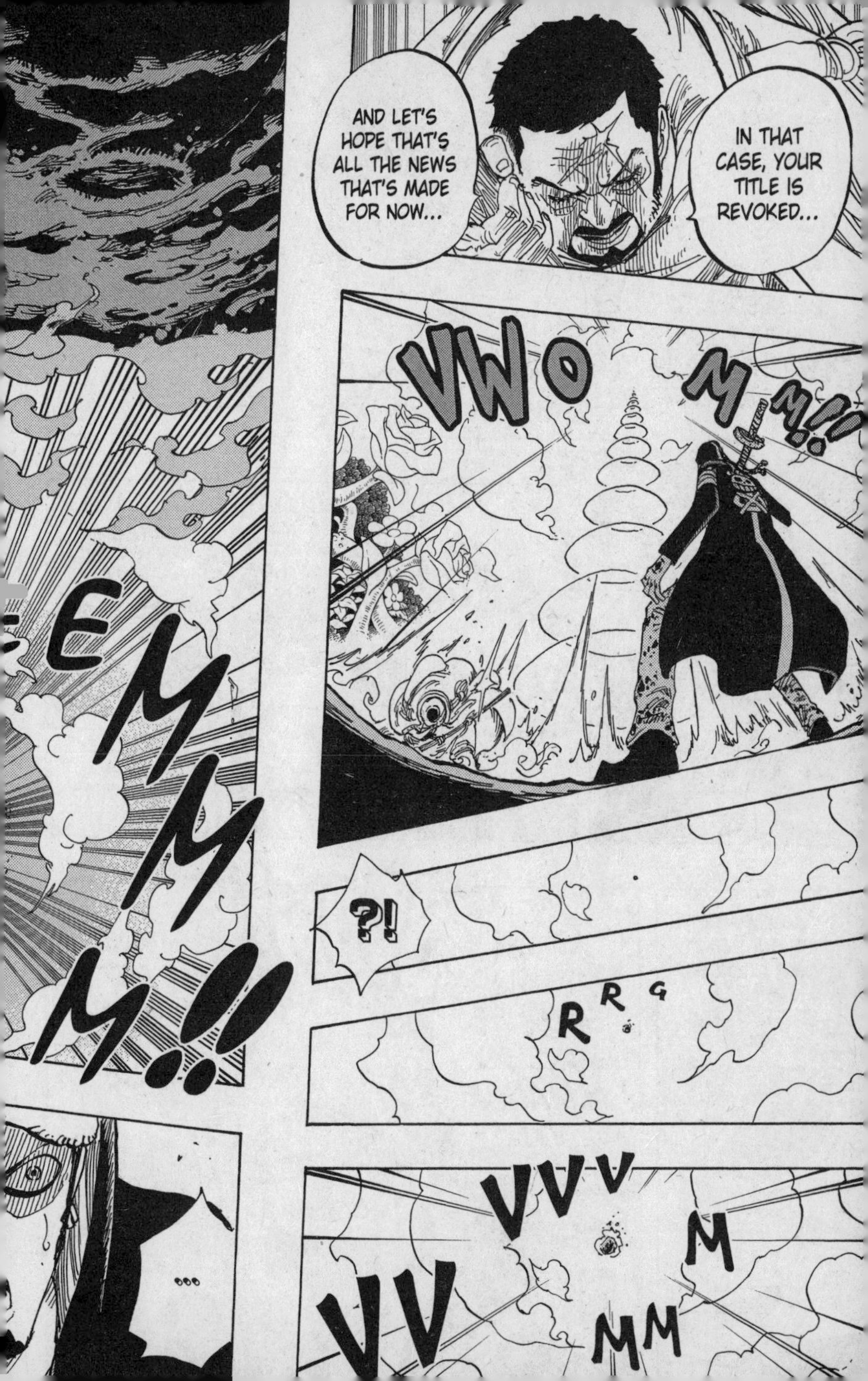
IN THAT CASE, YOUR TITLE IS REVOKED...
AND LET'S HOPE THAT'S ALL THE NEWS THAT'S MADE FOR NOW...
VWOMMM!!
?!
RRG
VVVVV
MMM
EMMM!!
...

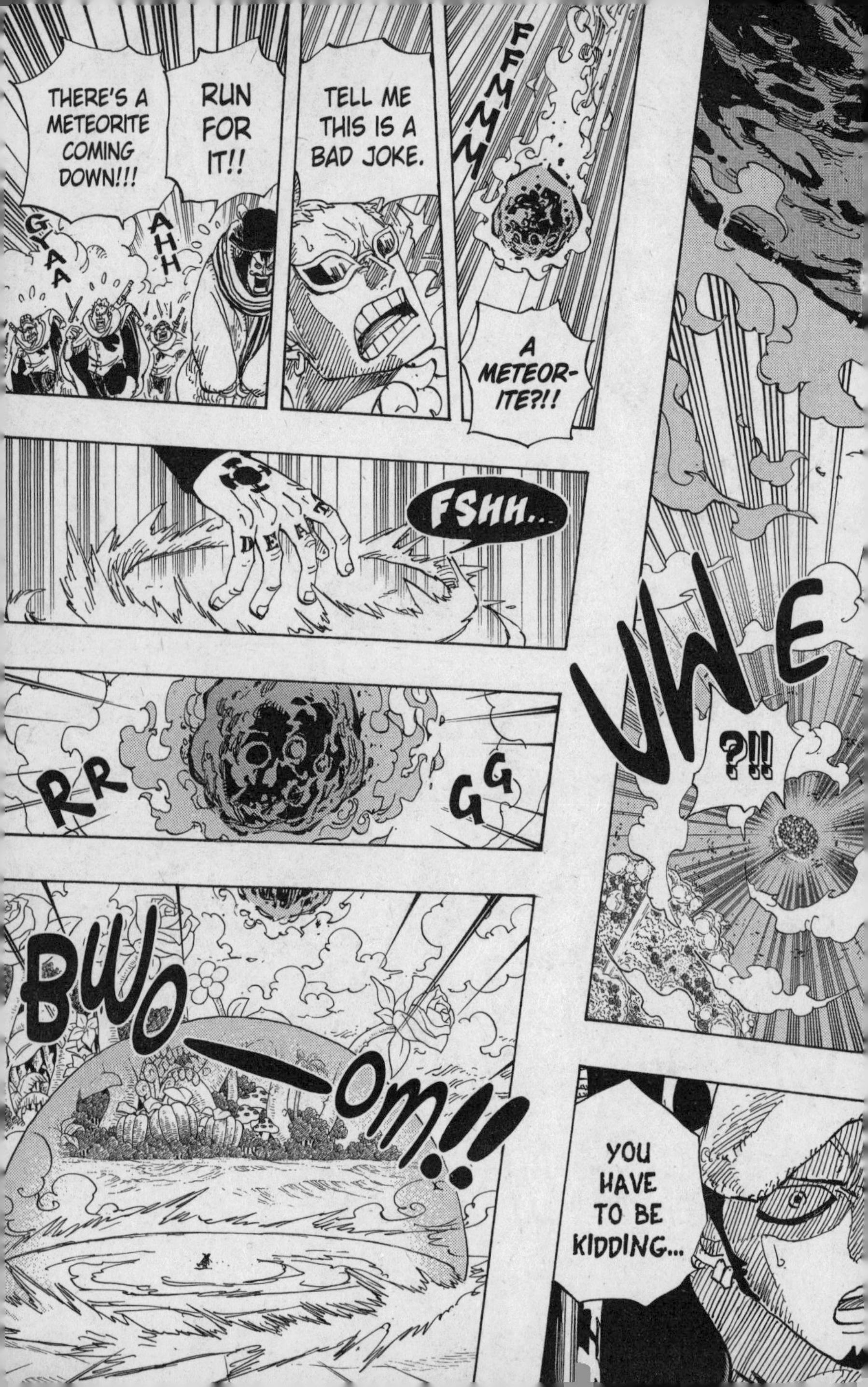
WHE
?!!
FFMMMM
A METEORITE?!!
TELL ME THIS IS A BAD JOKE.
RUN FOR IT!!
AHH
THERE'S A METEORITE COMING DOWN!!!
GYAA
FSHH...
RR
GG
BUO—OM!!
YOU HAVE TO BE KIDDING...

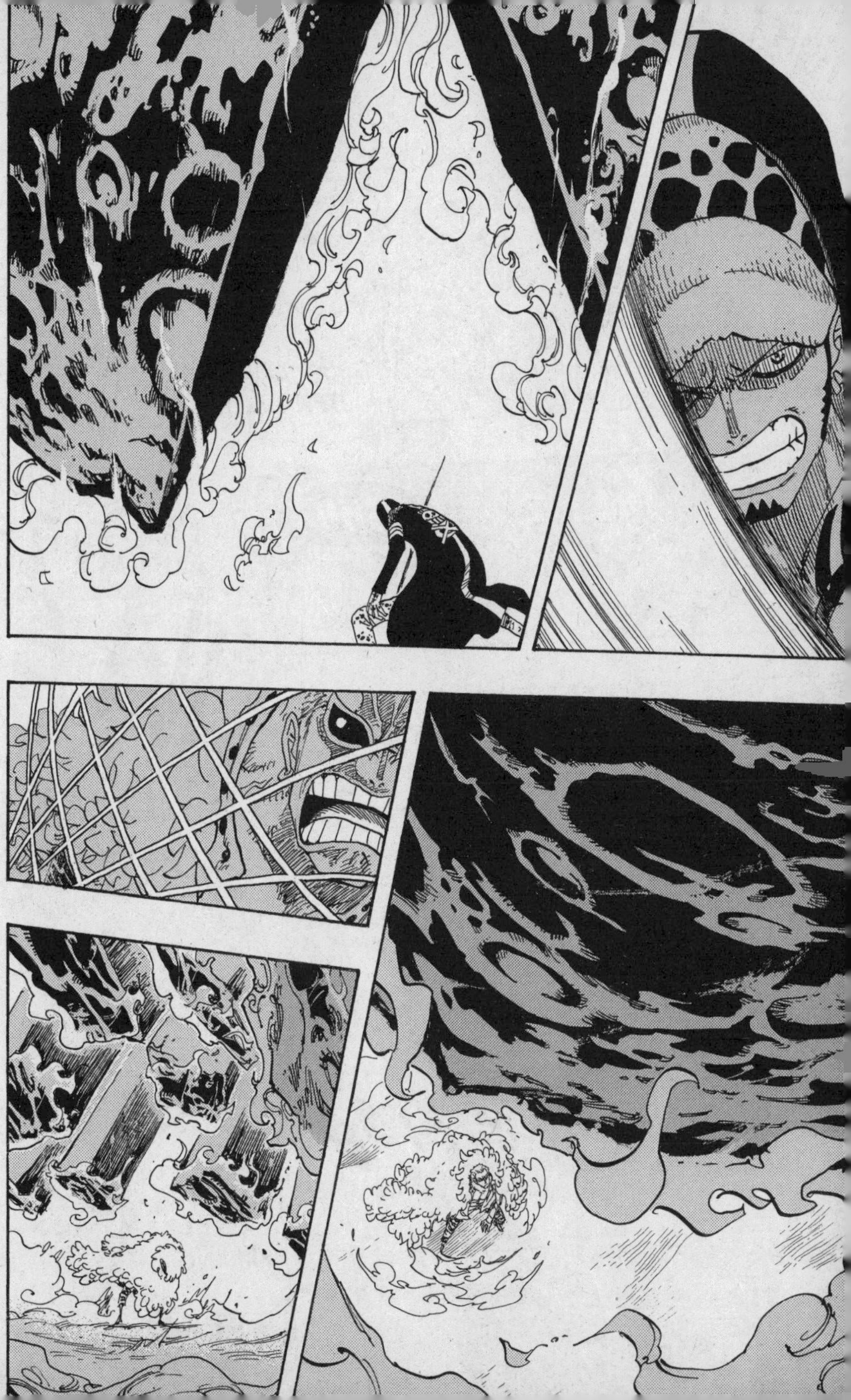

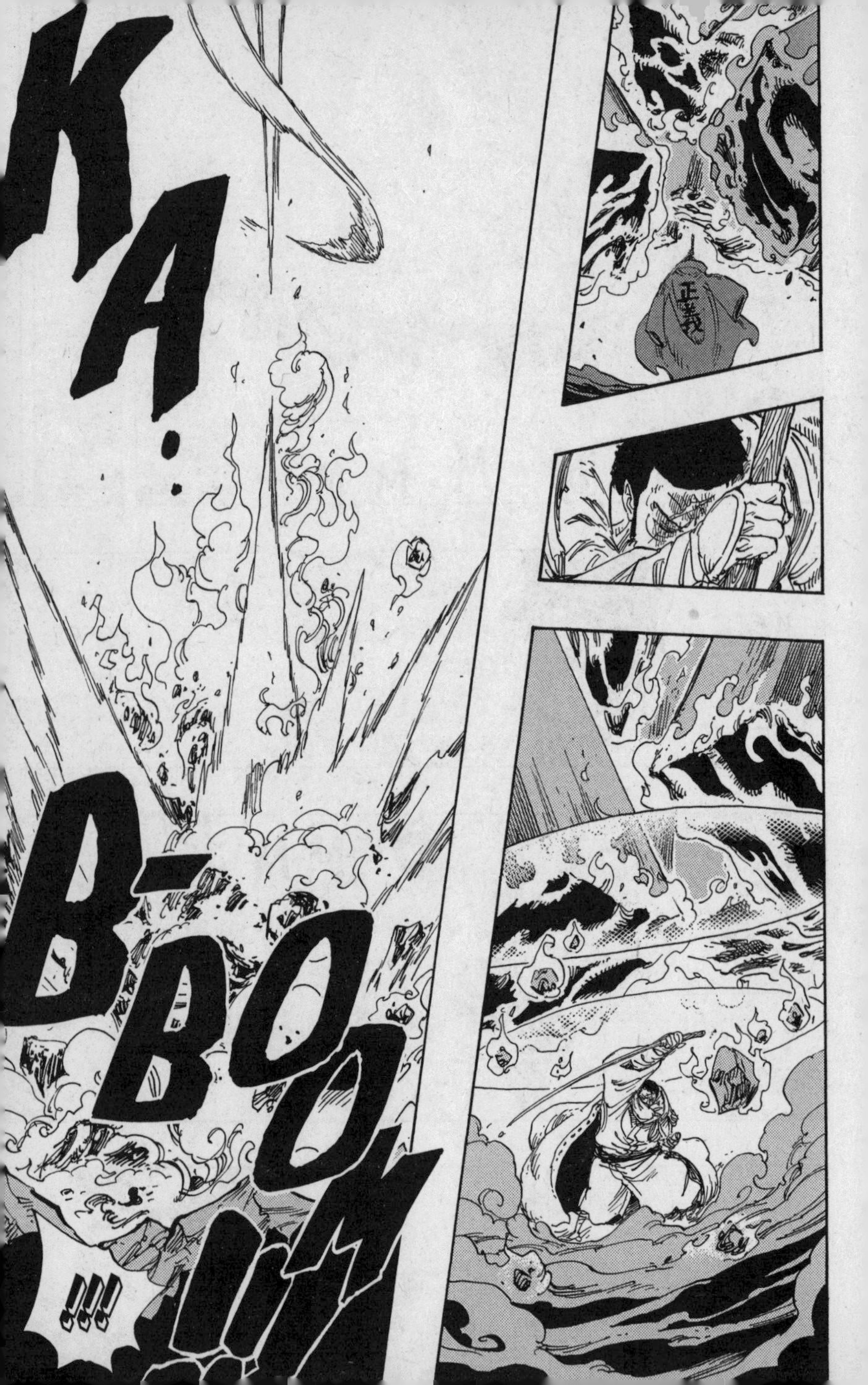
正義
KA- BBOOM!!!

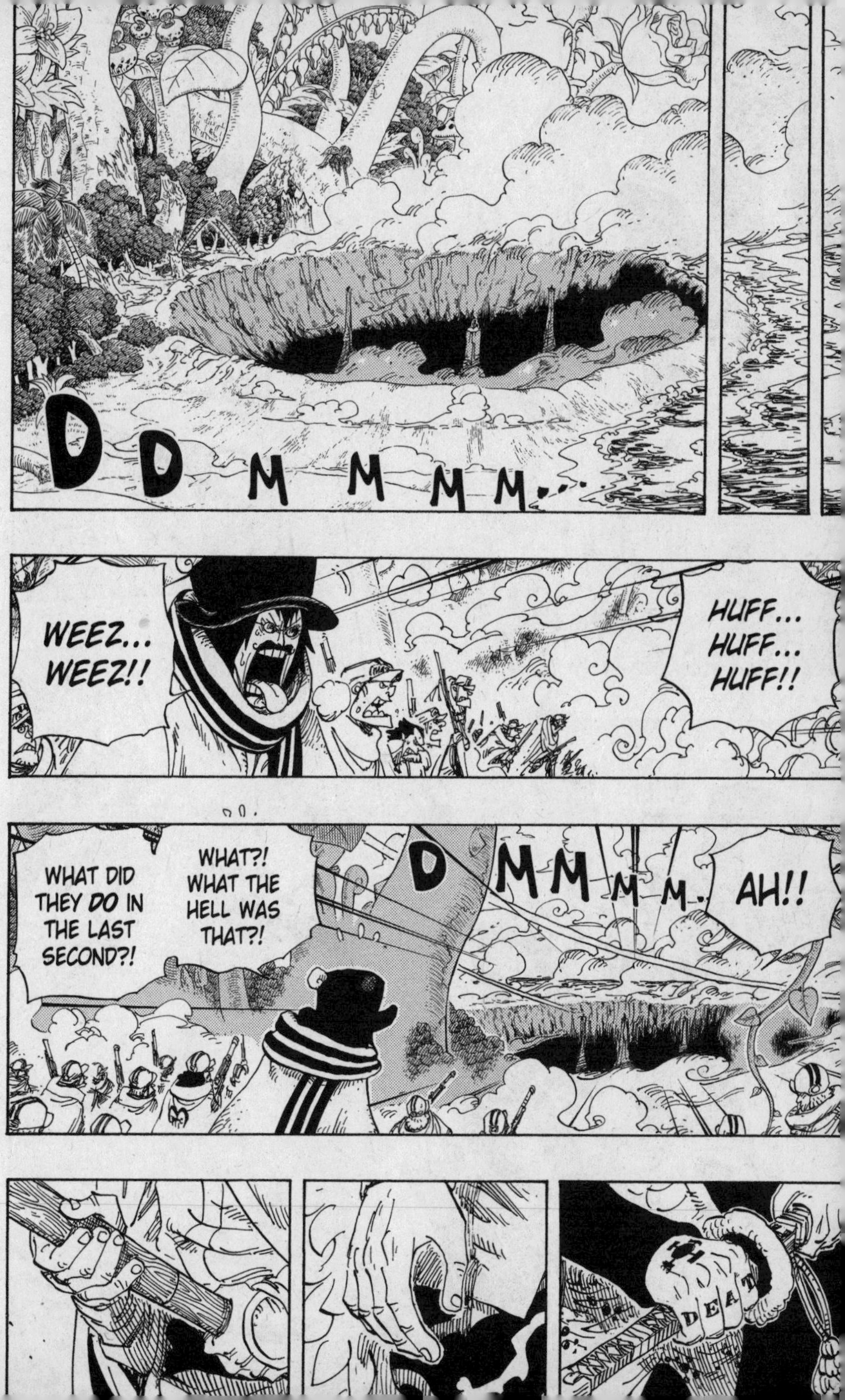
DDMMMM...
HUFF... HUFF... HUFF!!
WEEZ... WEEZ!!
AH!!
DMMMMM..
WHAT?! WHAT THE HELL WAS THAT?!
WHAT DID THEY DO IN THE LAST SECOND?!
DEAT

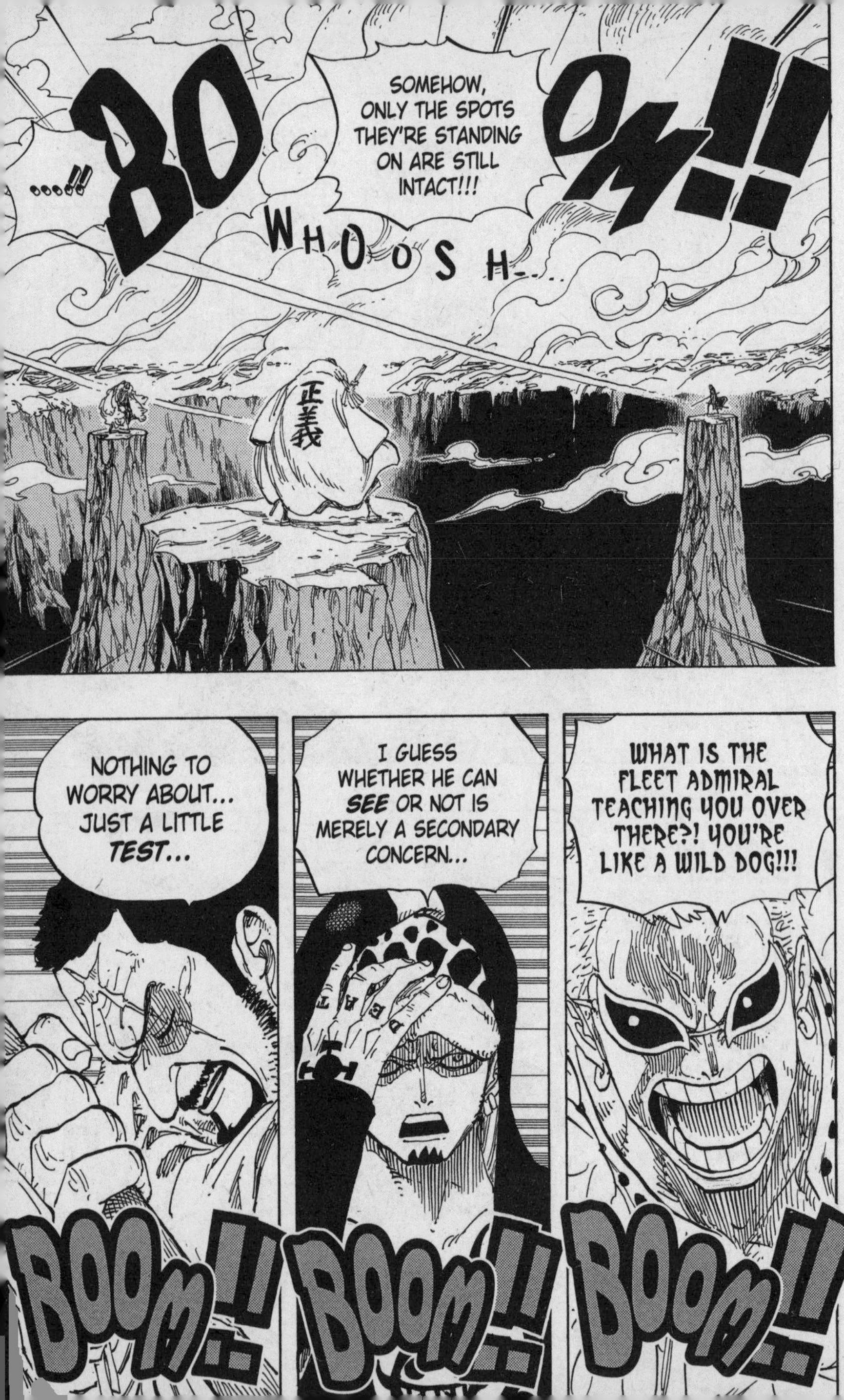
SOMEHOW, ONLY THE SPOTS THEY'RE STANDING ON ARE STILL INTACT!!!
BOOM!!
....!!
WHOOSH...
正義
WHAT IS THE FLEET ADMIRAL TEACHING YOU OVER THERE?! YOU'RE LIKE A WILD DOG!!!
BOOM!!
I GUESS WHETHER HE CAN SEE OR NOT IS MERELY A SECONDARY CONCERN...
BOOM!!
NOTHING TO WORRY ABOUT... JUST A LITTLE TEST...
BOOM!!

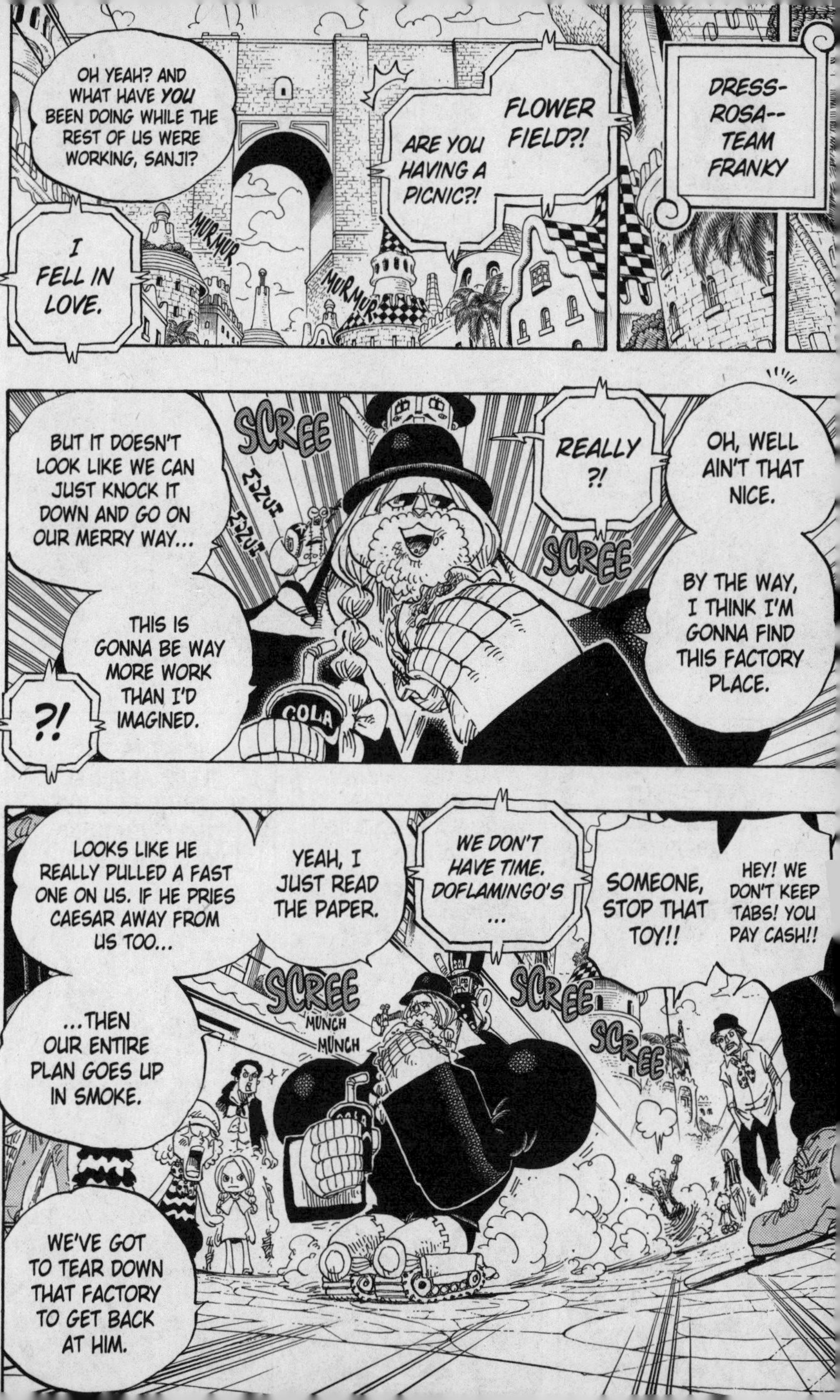
DRESS-ROSA-- TEAM FRANKY
FLOWER FIELD?!
ARE YOU HAVING A PICNIC?!
OH YEAH? AND WHAT HAVE YOU BEEN DOING WHILE THE REST OF US WERE WORKING, SANJI?
MURMUR
MURMUR
I FELL IN LOVE.
OH, WELL AIN'T THAT NICE.
REALLY ?!
SCREE
BUT IT DOESN'T LOOK LIKE WE CAN JUST KNOCK IT DOWN AND GO ON OUR MERRY WAY...
BY THE WAY, I THINK I'M GONNA FIND THIS FACTORY PLACE.
SCREE
THIS IS GONNA BE WAY MORE WORK THAN I'D IMAGINED.
?!
COLA
HEY! WE DON'T KEEP TABS! YOU PAY CASH!!
SOMEONE, STOP THAT TOY!!
WE DON'T HAVE TIME. DOFLAMINGO'S ...
YEAH, I JUST READ THE PAPER.
LOOKS LIKE HE REALLY PULLED A FAST ONE ON US. IF HE PRIES CAESAR AWAY FROM US TOO...
SCREE
SCREE
SCREE
MUNCH
MUNCH
...THEN OUR ENTIRE PLAN GOES UP IN SMOKE.
WE'VE GOT TO TEAR DOWN THAT FACTORY TO GET BACK AT HIM.

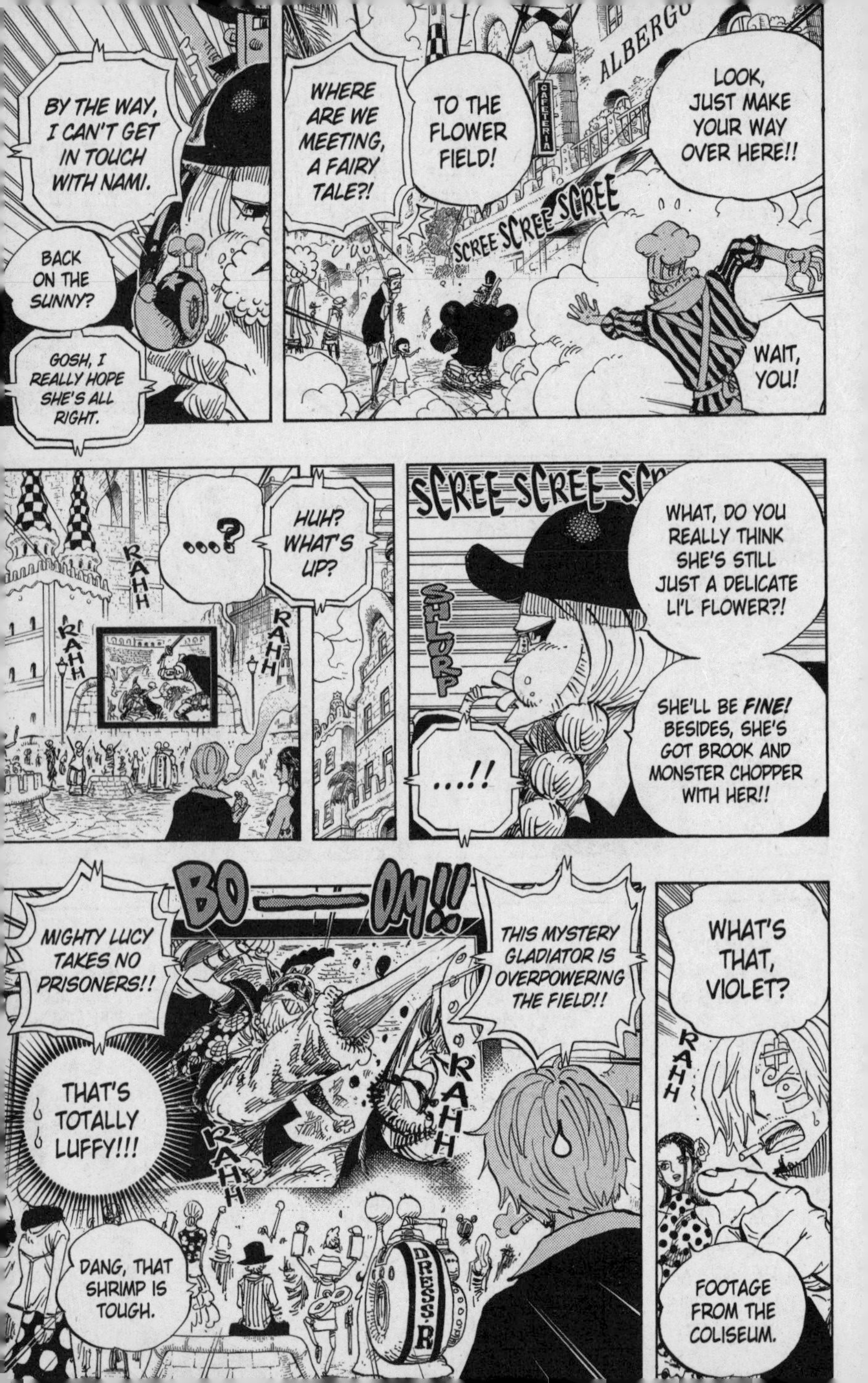
ALBERGO
CAFETERIA
LOOK, JUST MAKE YOUR WAY OVER HERE!!
TO THE FLOWER FIELD!
WHERE ARE WE MEETING, A FAIRY TALE?!
SCREE SCREE SCREE
WAIT, YOU!
BY THE WAY, I CAN'T GET IN TOUCH WITH NAMI.
BACK ON THE SUNNY?
GOSH, I REALLY HOPE SHE'S ALL RIGHT.
SCREE SCREE SCR
WHAT, DO YOU REALLY THINK SHE'S STILL JUST A DELICATE LI'L FLOWER?!
SHE'LL BE *FINE!* BESIDES, SHE'S GOT BROOK AND MONSTER CHOPPER WITH HER!!
SHLURP
...!!
HUH? WHAT'S UP?
...?
RAHH
RAHH
RAHH
RAHH
WHAT'S THAT, VIOLET?
RAHH
FOOTAGE FROM THE COLISEUM.
BO——OM!!
THIS MYSTERY GLADIATOR IS OVERPOWERING THE FIELD!!
MIGHTY LUCY TAKES NO PRISONERS!!
RAHH
THAT'S TOTALLY LUFFY!!!
RAHH
DRESS-R
DANG, THAT SHRIMP IS TOUGH.

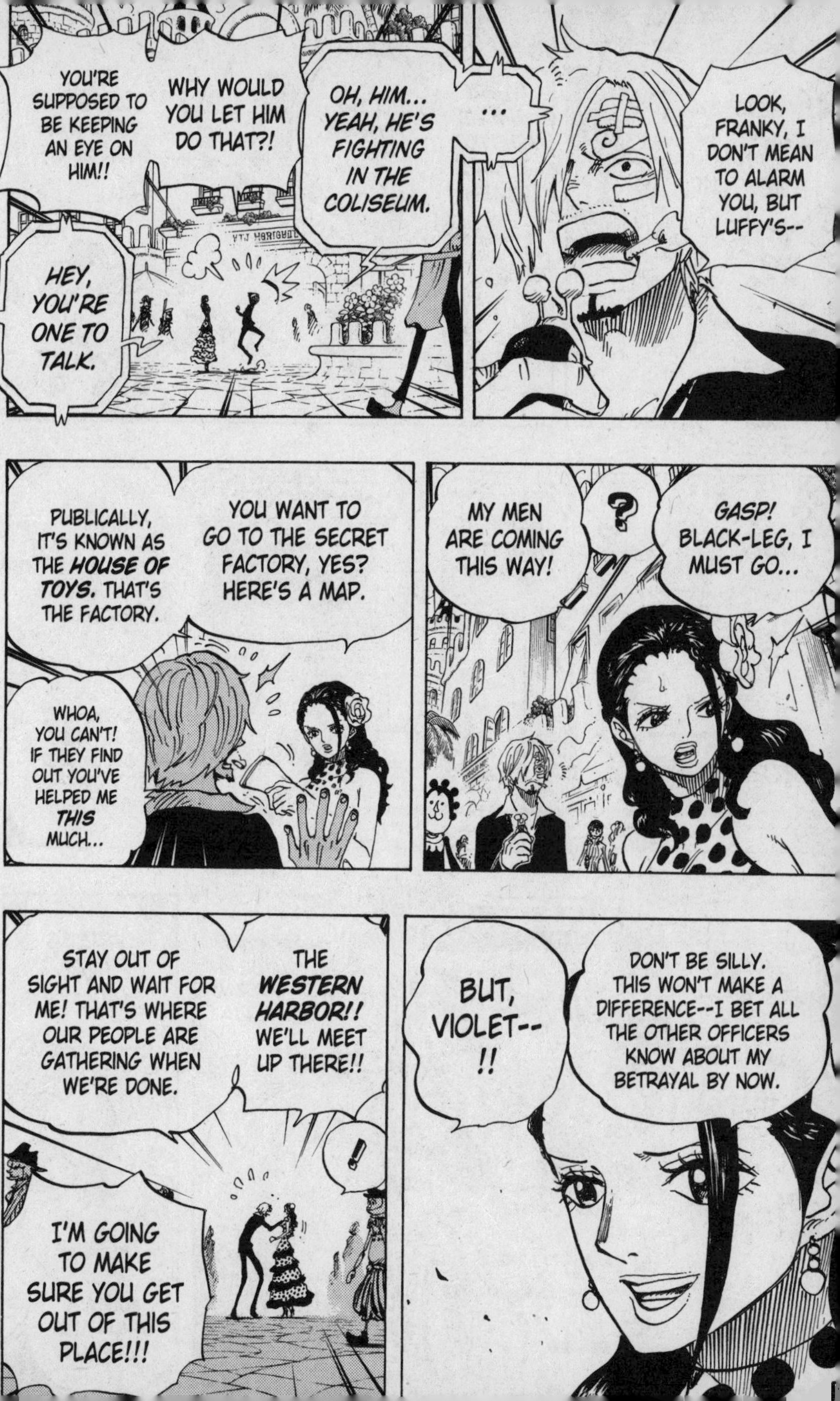
LOOK, FRANKY, I DON'T MEAN TO ALARM YOU, BUT LUFFY'S--
...
OH, HIM... YEAH, HE'S FIGHTING IN THE COLISEUM.
WHY WOULD YOU LET HIM DO THAT?!
YOU'RE SUPPOSED TO BE KEEPING AN EYE ON HIM!!
HEY, YOU'RE ONE TO TALK.
GASP! BLACK-LEG, I MUST GO...
?
MY MEN ARE COMING THIS WAY!
YOU WANT TO GO TO THE SECRET FACTORY, YES? HERE'S A MAP.
PUBLICALLY, IT'S KNOWN AS THE HOUSE OF TOYS. THAT'S THE FACTORY.
WHOA, YOU CAN'T! IF THEY FIND OUT YOU'VE HELPED ME THIS MUCH...
DON'T BE SILLY. THIS WON'T MAKE A DIFFERENCE--I BET ALL THE OTHER OFFICERS KNOW ABOUT MY BETRAYAL BY NOW.
BUT, VIOLET--!!
THE WESTERN HARBOR!! WE'LL MEET UP THERE!!
STAY OUT OF SIGHT AND WAIT FOR ME! THAT'S WHERE OUR PEOPLE ARE GATHERING WHEN WE'RE DONE.
!
I'M GOING TO MAKE SURE YOU GET OUT OF THIS PLACE!!!

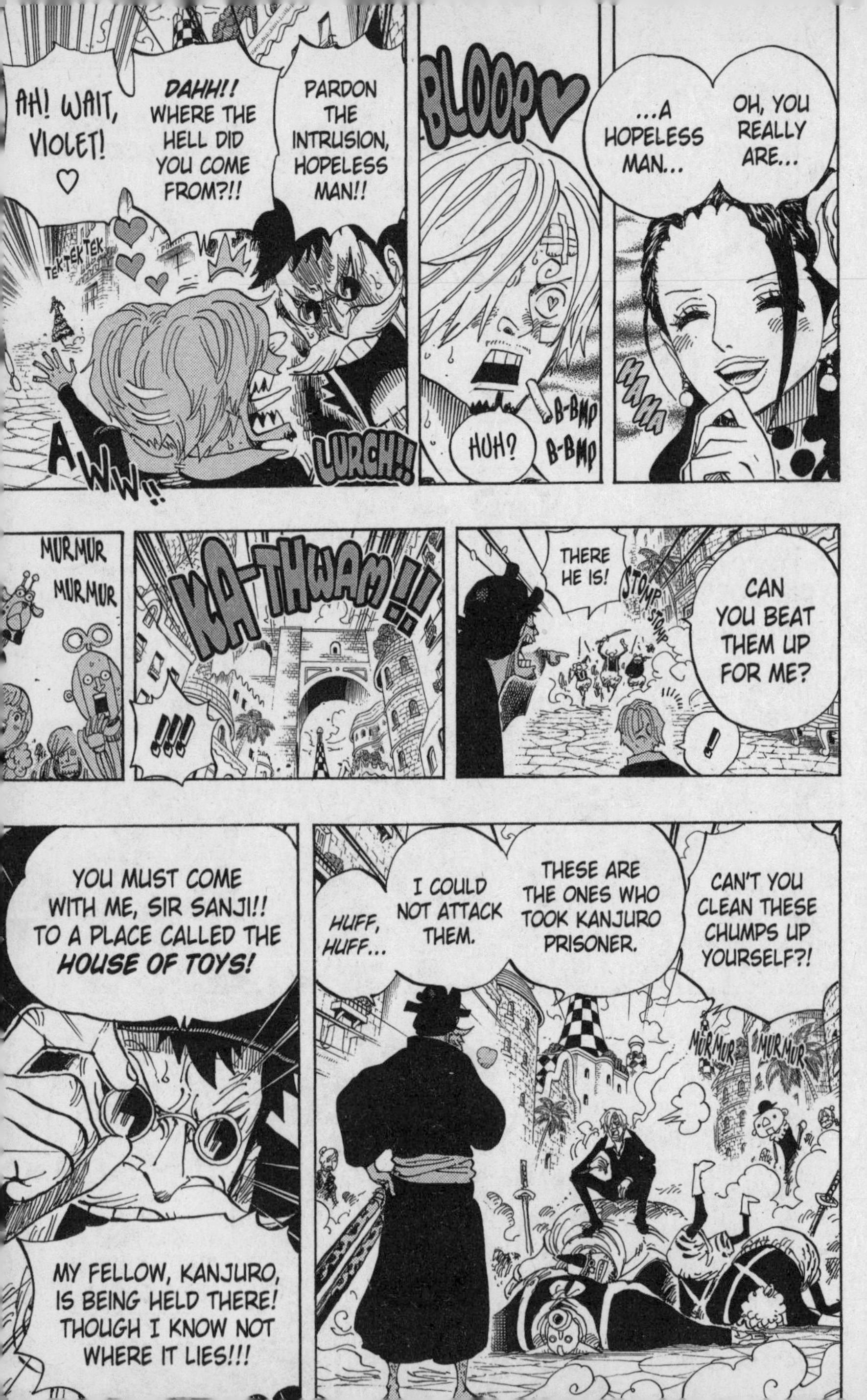
OH, YOU REALLY ARE...
...A HOPELESS MAN...
HAHA
BLOOP♥
B-BMP B-BMP
HUH?
PARDON THE INTRUSION, HOPELESS MAN!!
DAHH!! WHERE THE HELL DID YOU COME FROM?!!
AH! WAIT, VIOLET! ♡
TEKTEKTEK
LURCH!!
AWW!!
CAN YOU BEAT THEM UP FOR ME?
!
STOMP STOMP
THERE HE IS!
KA-THWAM!!
!!!
MURMUR
MURMUR
CAN'T YOU CLEAN THESE CHUMPS UP YOURSELF?!
THESE ARE THE ONES WHO TOOK KANJURO PRISONER.
I COULD NOT ATTACK THEM.
HUFF, HUFF...
MURMUR MURMUR
YOU MUST COME WITH ME, SIR SANJI!! TO A PLACE CALLED THE *HOUSE OF TOYS!*
MY FELLOW, KANJURO, IS BEING HELD THERE! THOUGH I KNOW NOT WHERE IT LIES!!!

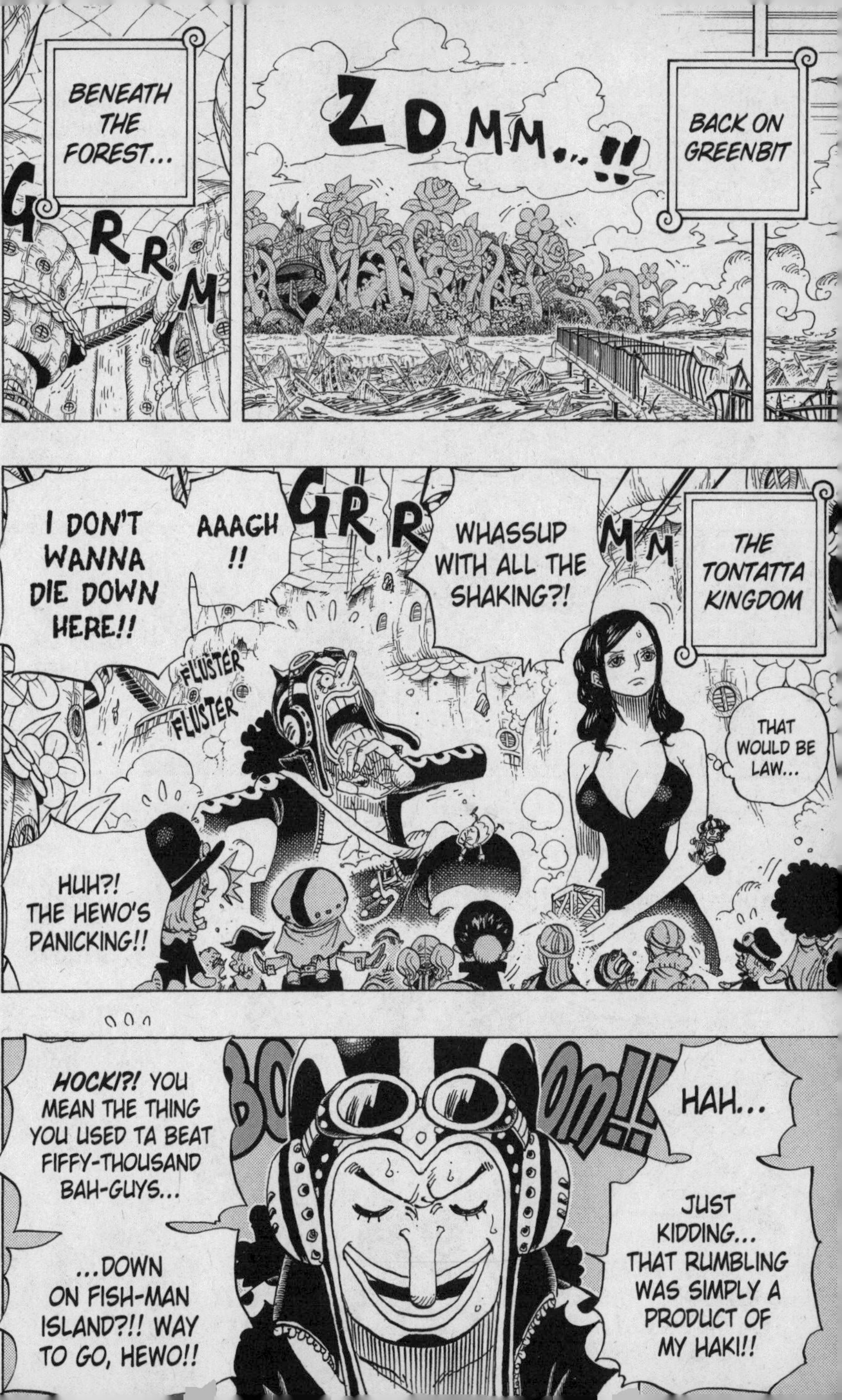
BACK ON GREENBIT
ZDMM...!!
BENEATH THE FOREST...
GRRRM
THE TONTATTA KINGDOM
THAT WOULD BE LAW...
WHASSUP WITH ALL THE SHAKING?!
GRRMM
AAAGH !!
I DON'T WANNA DIE DOWN HERE!!
FLUSTER FLUSTER
HUH?! THE HEWO'S PANICKING!!
HAH...
JUST KIDDING... THAT RUMBLING WAS SIMPLY A PRODUCT OF MY HAKI!!
BO OM!!
HOCKI?! YOU MEAN THE THING YOU USED TA BEAT FIFFY-THOUSAND BAH-GUYS...
...DOWN ON FISH-MAN ISLAND?!! WAY TO GO, HEWO!!

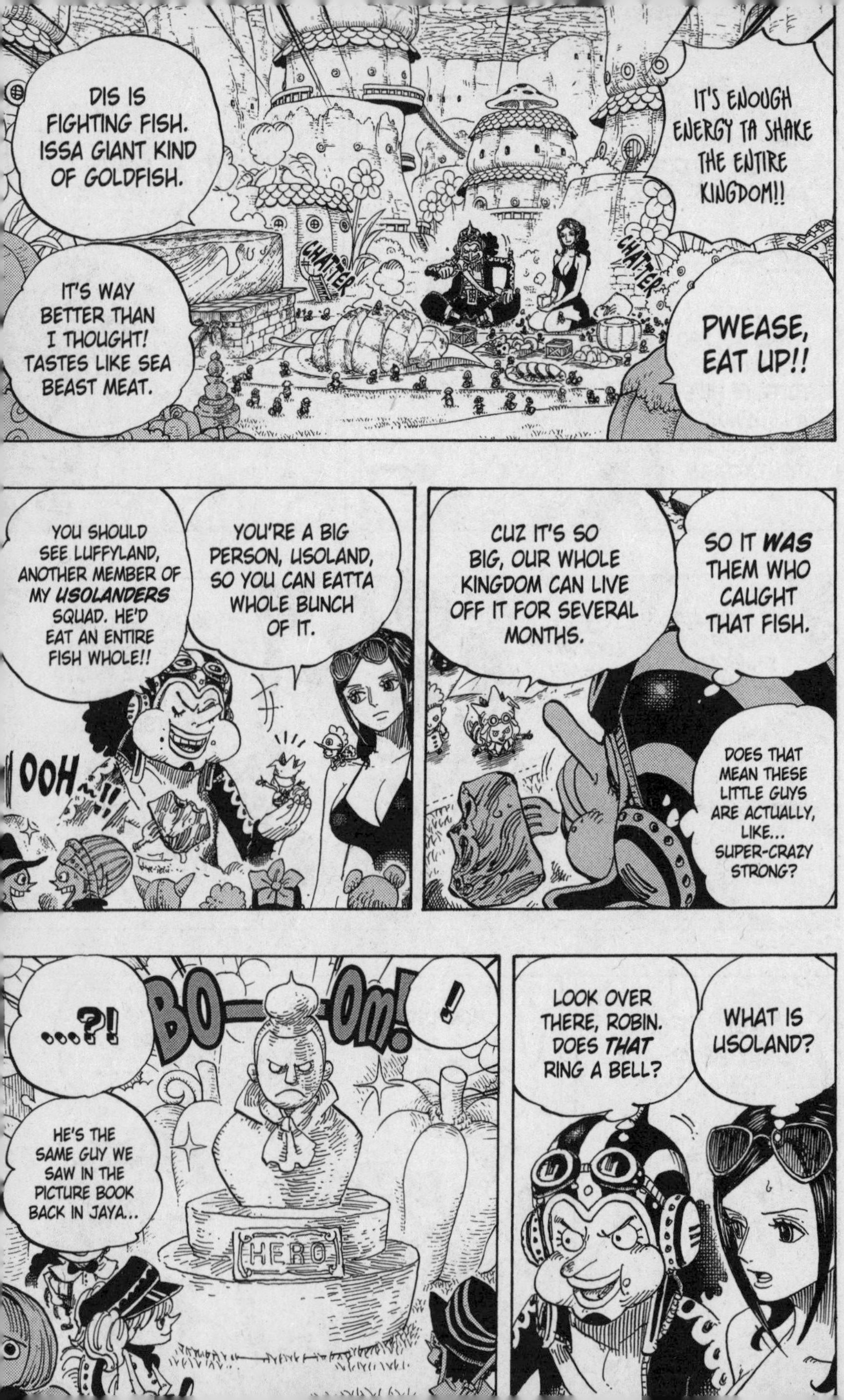
IT'S ENOUGH ENERGY TA SHAKE THE ENTIRE KINGDOM!!
DIS IS FIGHTING FISH. ISSA GIANT KIND OF GOLDFISH.
CHATTER
CHATTER
PWEASE, EAT UP!!
IT'S WAY BETTER THAN I THOUGHT! TASTES LIKE SEA BEAST MEAT.
SO IT *WAS* THEM WHO CAUGHT THAT FISH.
CUZ IT'S SO BIG, OUR WHOLE KINGDOM CAN LIVE OFF IT FOR SEVERAL MONTHS.
DOES THAT MEAN THESE LITTLE GUYS ARE ACTUALLY, LIKE... SUPER-CRAZY STRONG?
YOU'RE A BIG PERSON, USOLAND, SO YOU CAN EATTA WHOLE BUNCH OF IT.
YOU SHOULD SEE LUFFYLAND, ANOTHER MEMBER OF MY *USOLANDERS* SQUAD. HE'D EAT AN ENTIRE FISH WHOLE!!
OOH~!!
WHAT IS USOLAND?
LOOK OVER THERE, ROBIN. DOES *THAT* RING A BELL?
!
BO—OM!
...?!
HE'S THE SAME GUY WE SAW IN THE PICTURE BOOK BACK IN JAYA...
HERO

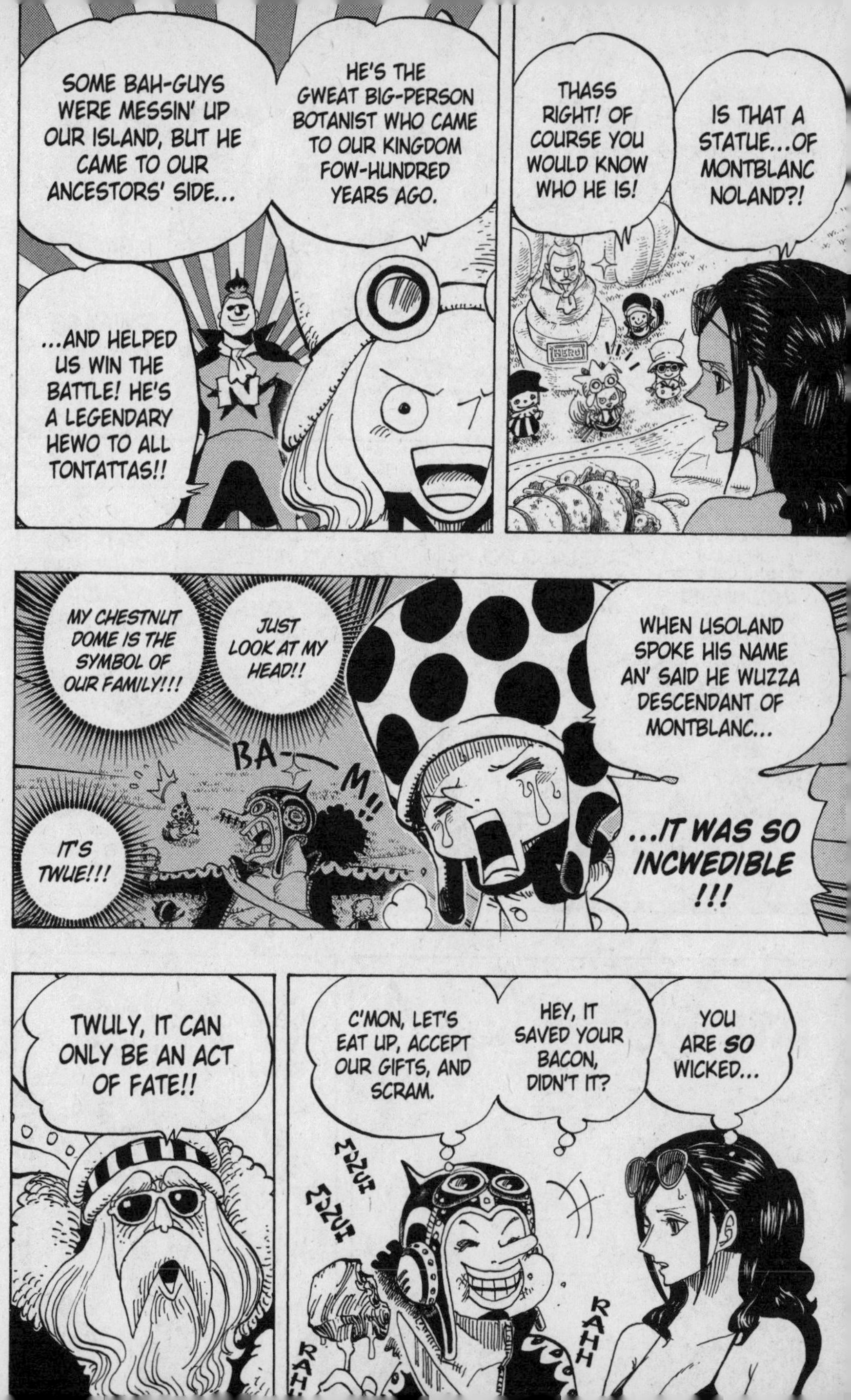
IS THAT A STATUE...OF MONTBLANC NOLAND?!
THASS RIGHT! OF COURSE YOU WOULD KNOW WHO HE IS!
HE'S THE GWEAT BIG-PERSON BOTANIST WHO CAME TO OUR KINGDOM FOW-HUNDRED YEARS AGO.
SOME BAH-GUYS WERE MESSIN' UP OUR ISLAND, BUT HE CAME TO OUR ANCESTORS' SIDE...
...AND HELPED US WIN THE BATTLE! HE'S A LEGENDARY HEWO TO ALL TONTATTAS!!
WHEN USOLAND SPOKE HIS NAME AN' SAID HE WUZZA DESCENDANT OF MONTBLANC...
...IT WAS SO INCWEDIBLE!!!
JUST LOOK AT MY HEAD!!
MY CHESTNUT DOME IS THE SYMBOL OF OUR FAMILY!!!
BA-M!!
IT'S TWUE!!!
YOU ARE SO WICKED...
HEY, IT SAVED YOUR BACON, DIDN'T IT?
C'MON, LET'S EAT UP, ACCEPT OUR GIFTS, AND SCRAM.
RAHH
RAHH
TWULY, IT CAN ONLY BE AN ACT OF FATE!!

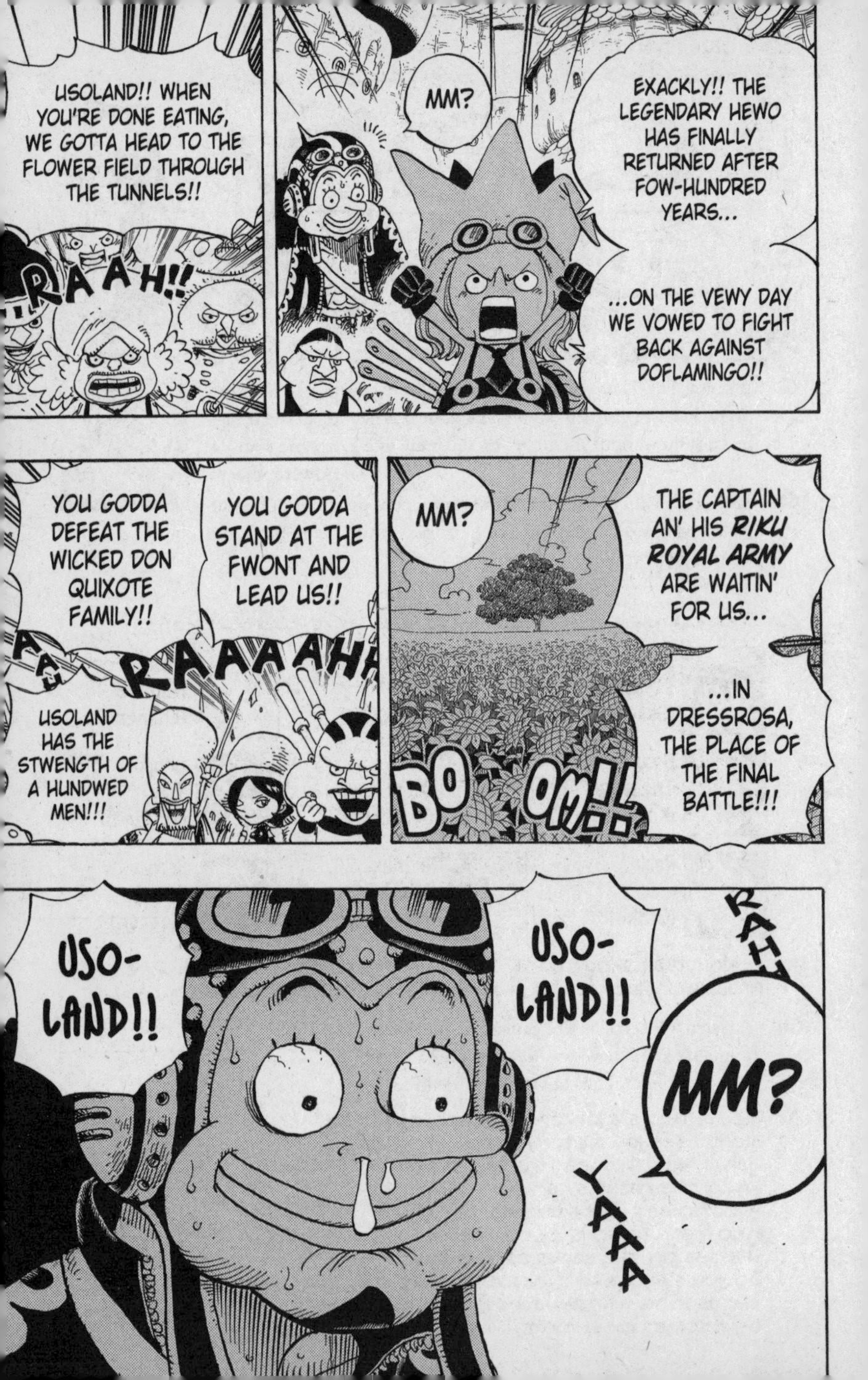
EXACKLY!! THE LEGENDARY HEWO HAS FINALLY RETURNED AFTER FOW-HUNDRED YEARS...
MM?
...ON THE VEWY DAY WE VOWED TO FIGHT BACK AGAINST DOFLAMINGO!!
USOLAND!! WHEN YOU'RE DONE EATING, WE GOTTA HEAD TO THE FLOWER FIELD THROUGH THE TUNNELS!!
RAAH!!
THE CAPTAIN AN' HIS *RIKU ROYAL ARMY* ARE WAITIN' FOR US...
MM?
...IN DRESSROSA, THE PLACE OF THE FINAL BATTLE!!!
BOOM!!
YOU GODDA STAND AT THE FWONT AND LEAD US!!
YOU GODDA DEFEAT THE WICKED DON QUIXOTE FAMILY!!
RAAAAAH
USOLAND HAS THE STWENGTH OF A HUNDWED MEN!!!
MM?
USO-LAND!!
USO-LAND!!
YAAAA

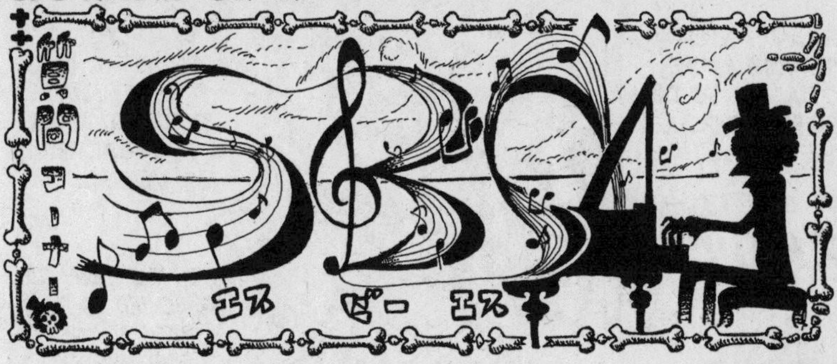

(Hiromitsu Shimojo, Gunma)

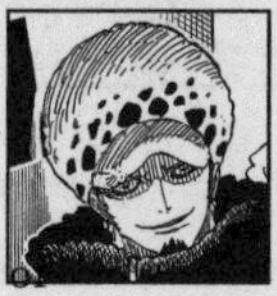

Q: It seems like Trafalgar Law, in the midst of his alliance with the Straw Hats, gives them some nicknames. What are all the things he calls the various members of the crew like Zoro and Franky?

--Edward Yacchi

Q: Mr. Oda, hello! If the Straw Hats were from different prefectures of Japan, what would they be? For example, would Nami be from Ehime? I'd love to hear from you!

--T. Rina

A: Tell you what, I'll answer these both at the same time.

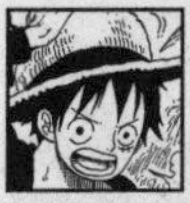

Luffy
Straw Hat
(Okinawa)

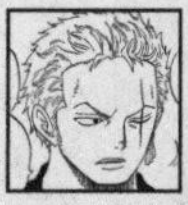

Zoro
Zoro
(Hokkaido)

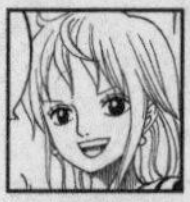

Nami
Nami
(Ehime)

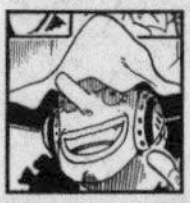

Usopp
The Nose
(Kanagawa)

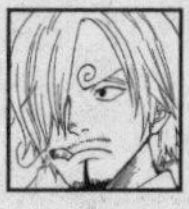

Sanji
Black-Leg
(Kyoto)

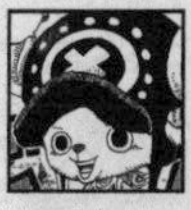

Chopper
Tony
(Toyama)

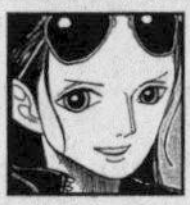

Robin
Nico
(Osaka)

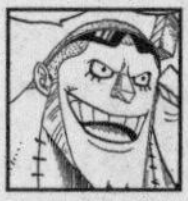

Franky
Robo
(Nagasaki)

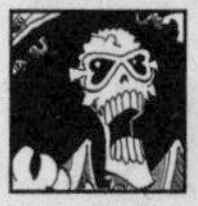

Brook
Boney
(Tottori)

A: I think that should do it. Some of those prefectures were probably influenced by the voice actors' hometowns (laughs).

Q: Odacchi, Odacchi!!! All I can see in the waves on p.154 of Volume 70 is bunnies!!! What have you done to me?!!!

--Law-Loving Y, Law-Loving A's Friend

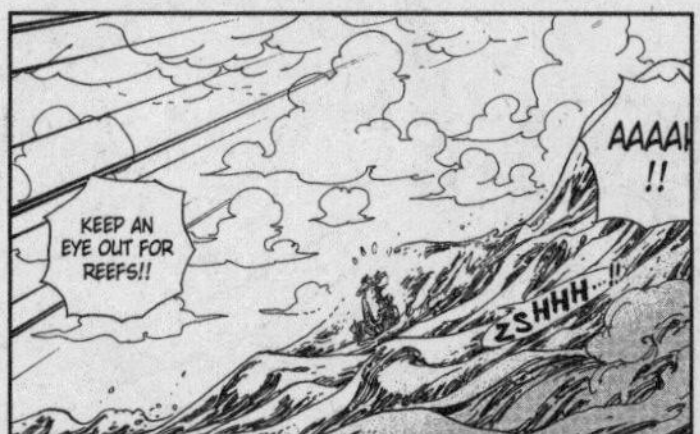
AAAAH!!
KEEP AN EYE OUT FOR REEFS!!
ZSHHH...!!

A: Geez, that's a long pen name!! I'd like to tell you a story from Papua New Guinea. It is said that when the rabbits ran out of food to eat, they tricked the fish into lining up so they could cross the sea on the backs of the fish. Do you suppose they made up that folk tale when they noticed the dancing white waves looked like rabbits? They do look like that sometimes, don't they?

Chapter 714:
LUCY AND MOOCY

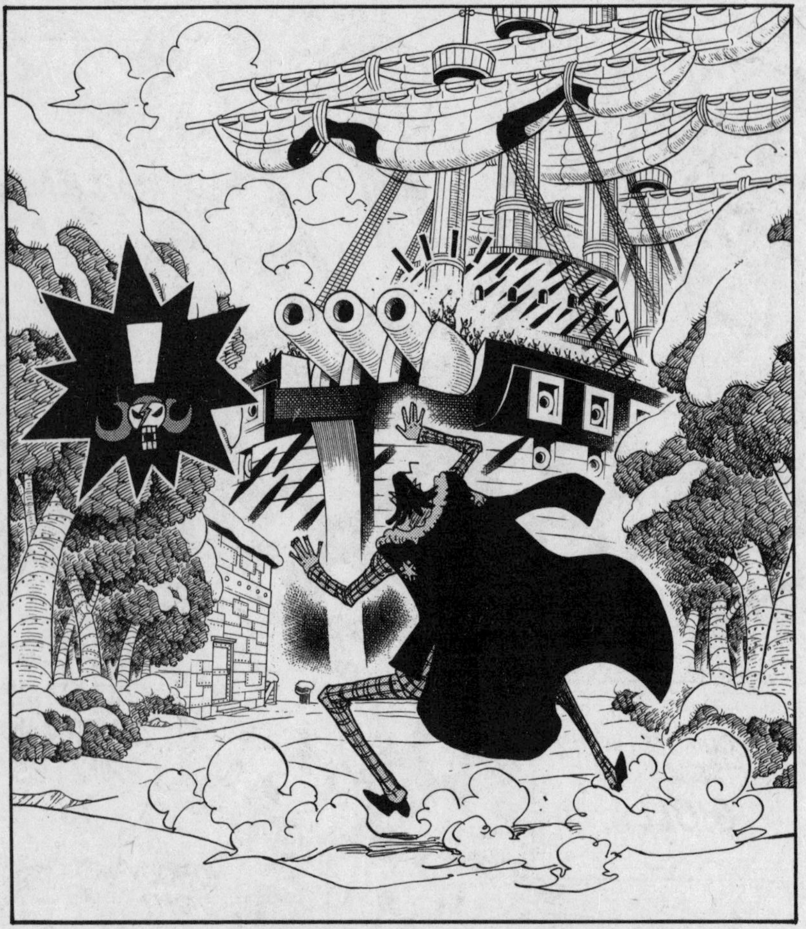

CARIBOU'S NEW WORLD KEE HEE HEE, VOL. 32:
"BACK AT THE PORT, MY ABANDONED LACKEYS"

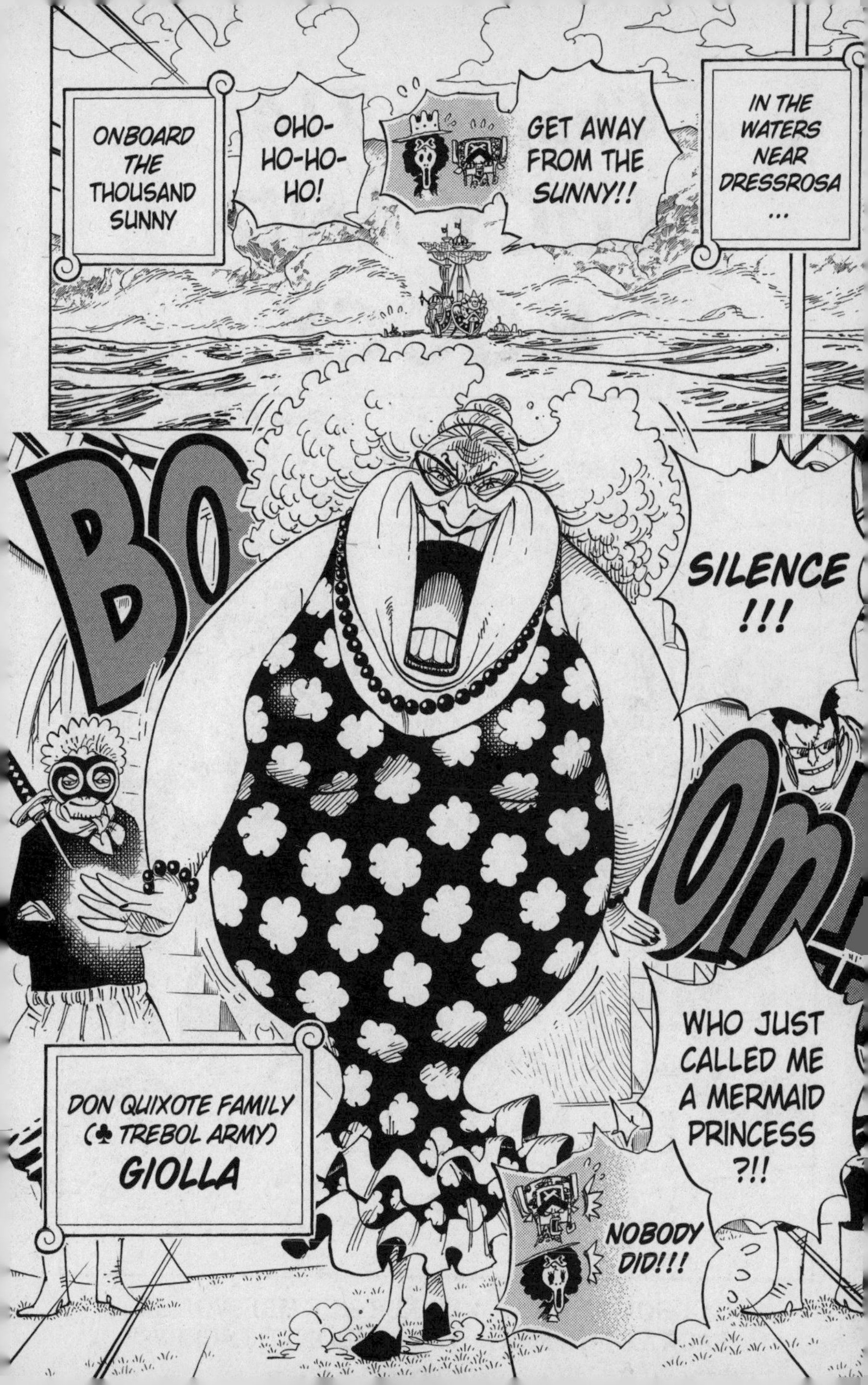
IN THE WATERS NEAR DRESSROSA ...
GET AWAY FROM THE SUNNY!!
OHO-HO-HO-HO!
ONBOARD THE THOUSAND SUNNY
SILENCE !!!
BO
OM
WHO JUST CALLED ME A MERMAID PRINCESS ?!!
NOBODY DID!!!
DON QUIXOTE FAMILY (♣ TREBOL ARMY) GIOLLA

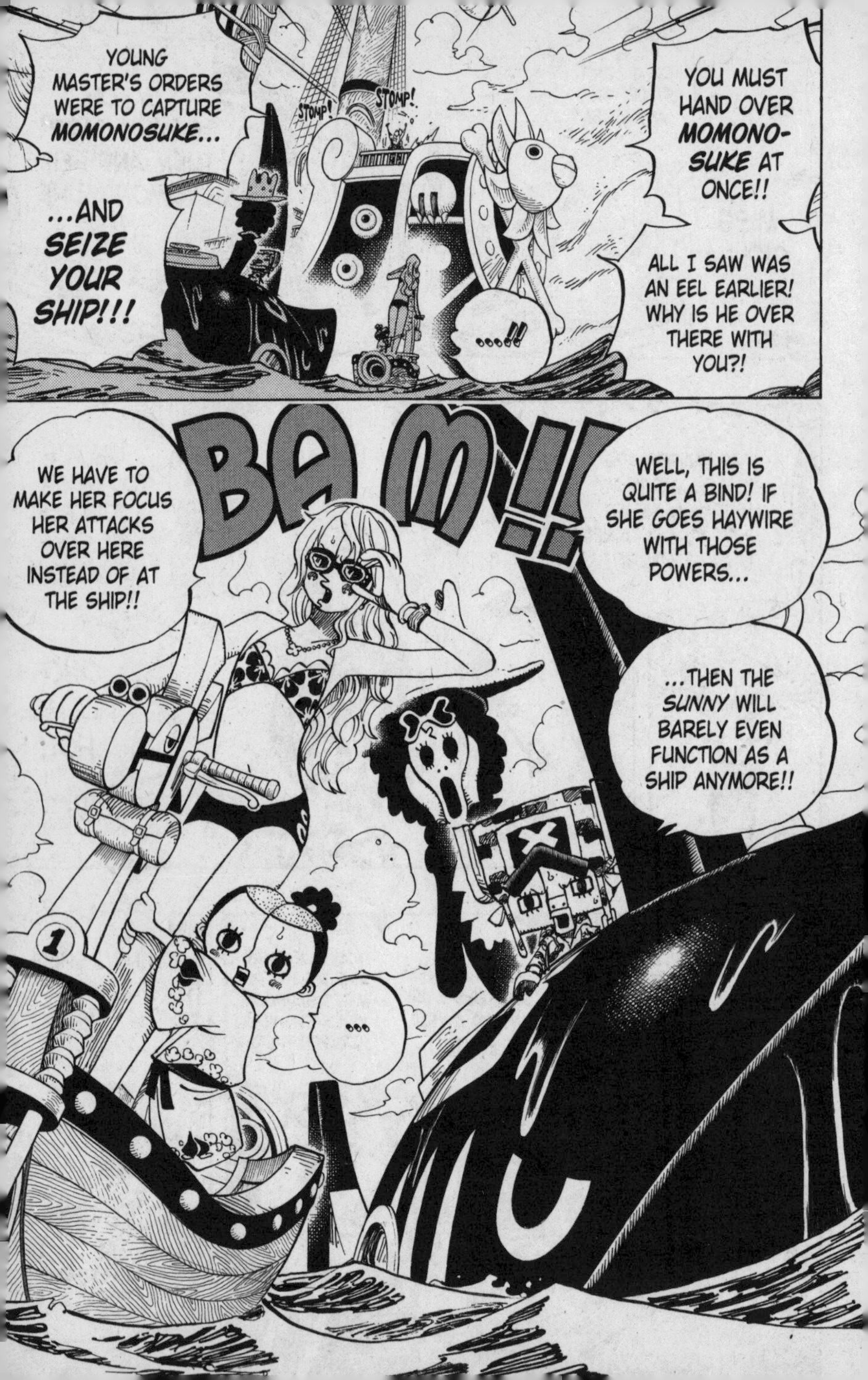

YOU MUST HAND OVER MOMONOSUKE AT ONCE!!
STOMP!
STOMP!
YOUNG MASTER'S ORDERS WERE TO CAPTURE MOMONOSUKE...
...AND SEIZE YOUR SHIP!!!
ALL I SAW WAS AN EEL EARLIER! WHY IS HE OVER THERE WITH YOU?!
....!!
BAM!!
WELL, THIS IS QUITE A BIND! IF SHE GOES HAYWIRE WITH THOSE POWERS...
...THEN THE SUNNY WILL BARELY EVEN FUNCTION AS A SHIP ANYMORE!!
WE HAVE TO MAKE HER FOCUS HER ATTACKS OVER HERE INSTEAD OF AT THE SHIP!!
...
1

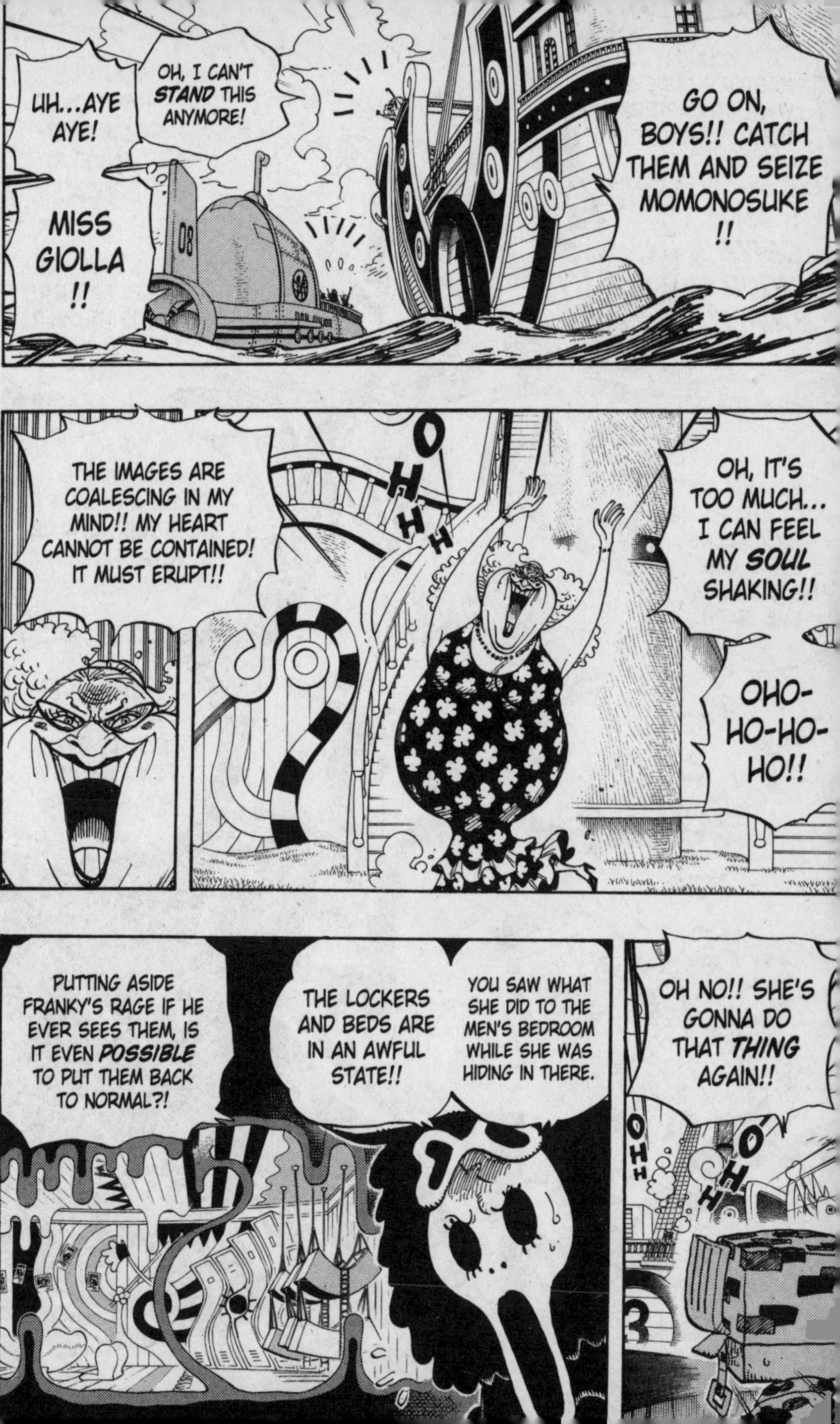
GO ON, BOYS!! CATCH THEM AND SEIZE MOMONOSUKE!!
OH, I CAN'T STAND THIS ANYMORE!
UH...AYE AYE!
MISS GIOLLA!!
OH, IT'S TOO MUCH... I CAN FEEL MY SOUL SHAKING!!
OHO-HO-HO-HO!!
OHHH
THE IMAGES ARE COALESCING IN MY MIND!! MY HEART CANNOT BE CONTAINED! IT MUST ERUPT!!
OH NO!! SHE'S GONNA DO THAT THING AGAIN!!
OHHH
OHHH
YOU SAW WHAT SHE DID TO THE MEN'S BEDROOM WHILE SHE WAS HIDING IN THERE.
THE LOCKERS AND BEDS ARE IN AN AWFUL STATE!!
PUTTING ASIDE FRANKY'S RAGE IF HE EVER SEES THEM, IS IT EVEN POSSIBLE TO PUT THEM BACK TO NORMAL?!

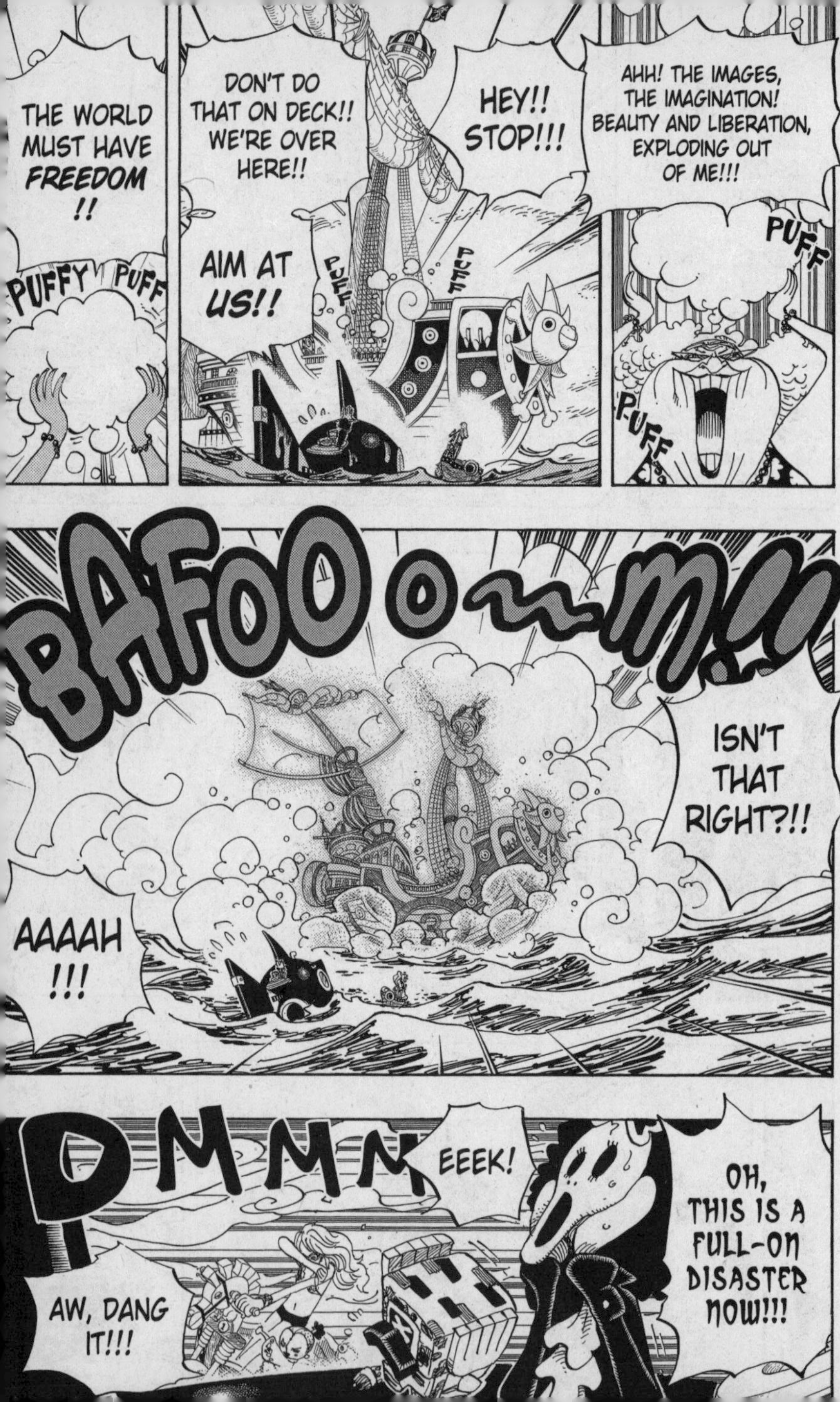
AHH! THE IMAGES, THE IMAGINATION! BEAUTY AND LIBERATION, EXPLODING OUT OF ME!!!
PUFF
P-UFF
HEY!! STOP!!!
DON'T DO THAT ON DECK!! WE'RE OVER HERE!!
AIM AT US!!
PUFF
PUFF
THE WORLD MUST HAVE FREEDOM !!
PUFF
PUFFY
BAFOOOOM!!
ISN'T THAT RIGHT?!!
AAAAH !!!
OH, THIS IS A FULL-ON DISASTER NOW!!!
EEEK!
DMMN
AW, DANG IT!!!

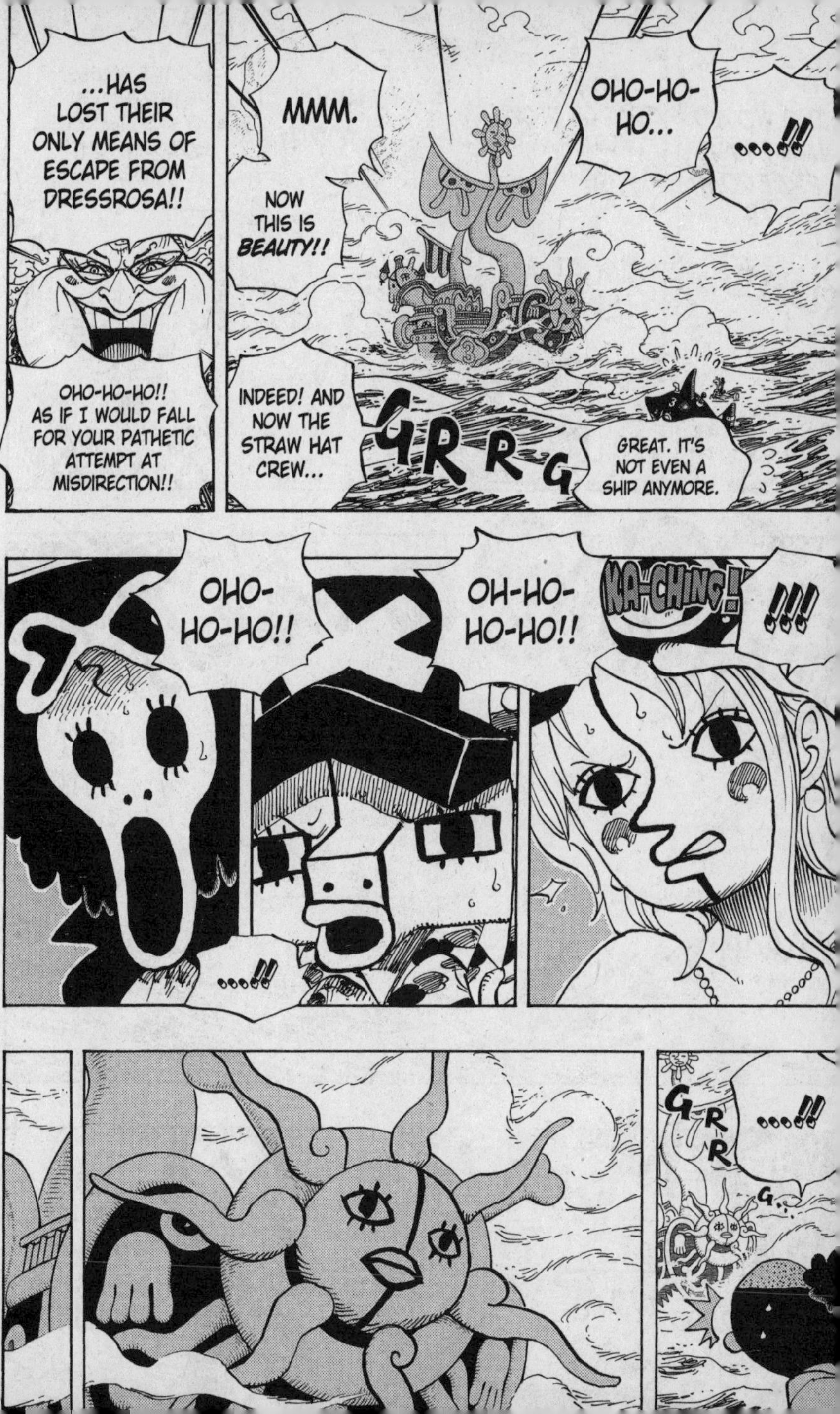
OHO-HO-HO...
...!!
MMM.
NOW THIS IS BEAUTY!!
GREAT. IT'S NOT EVEN A SHIP ANYMORE.
GRRG
INDEED! AND NOW THE STRAW HAT CREW...
...HAS LOST THEIR ONLY MEANS OF ESCAPE FROM DRESSROSA!!
OHO-HO-HO!! AS IF I WOULD FALL FOR YOUR PATHETIC ATTEMPT AT MISDIRECTION!!
!!!
KA-CHING!!
OH-HO-HO-HO!!
OHO-HO-HO!!
...!!
...!!
GRRG..

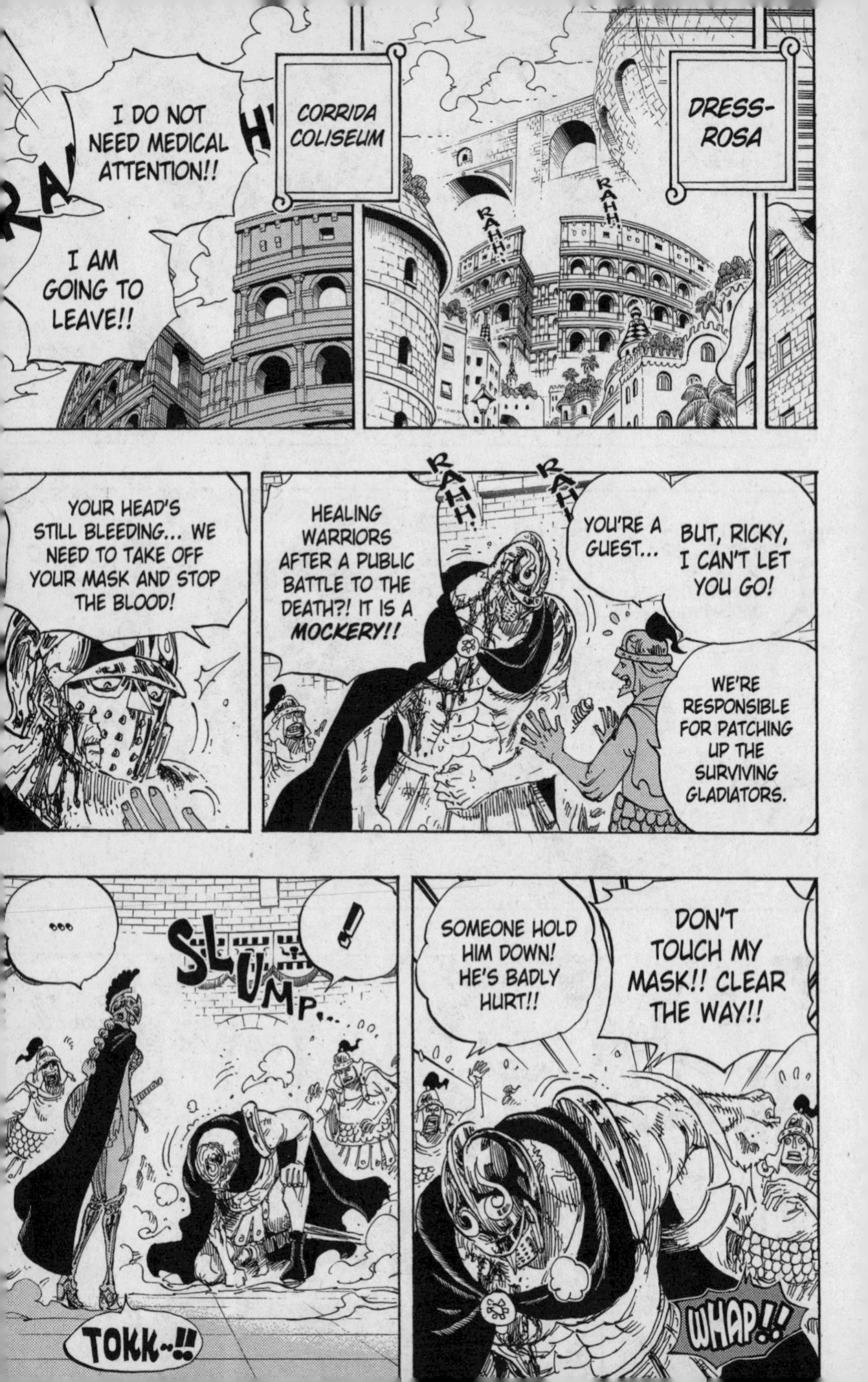
DRESS-ROSA
RAHH
RAHH
CORRIDA COLISEUM
I DO NOT NEED MEDICAL ATTENTION!!
I AM GOING TO LEAVE!!
RAHH
RAHH
BUT, RICKY, I CAN'T LET YOU GO!
WE'RE RESPONSIBLE FOR PATCHING UP THE SURVIVING GLADIATORS.
YOU'RE A GUEST...
HEALING WARRIORS AFTER A PUBLIC BATTLE TO THE DEATH?! IT IS A MOCKERY!!
YOUR HEAD'S STILL BLEEDING... WE NEED TO TAKE OFF YOUR MASK AND STOP THE BLOOD!
DON'T TOUCH MY MASK!! CLEAR THE WAY!!
SOMEONE HOLD HIM DOWN! HE'S BADLY HURT!!
WHAP!!
!
SLUMP...
...
TOKK-!!

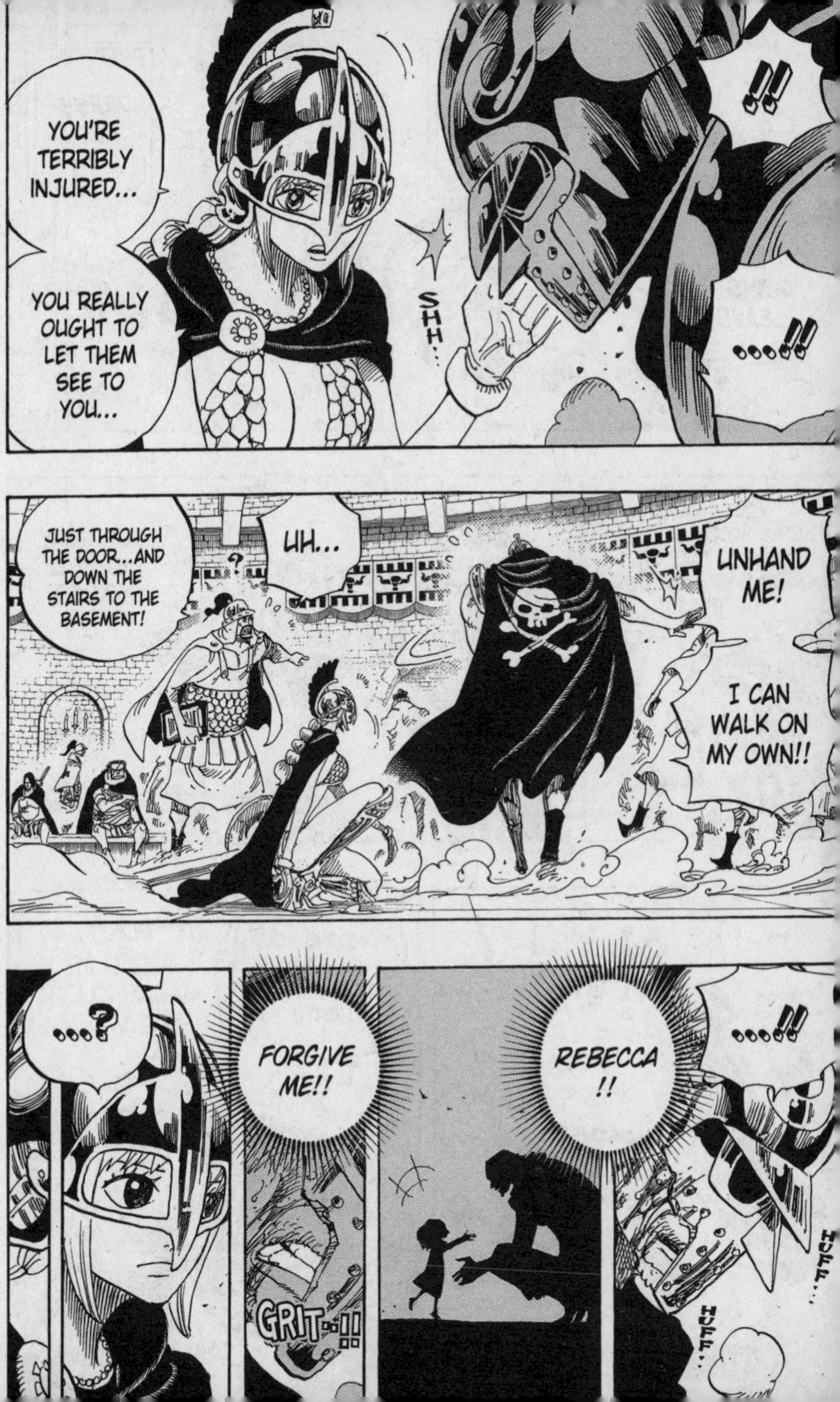
!!
...!!
SHH..
YOU'RE TERRIBLY INJURED...
YOU REALLY OUGHT TO LET THEM SEE TO YOU...
UNHAND ME!
I CAN WALK ON MY OWN!!
UH...
?
JUST THROUGH THE DOOR...AND DOWN THE STAIRS TO THE BASEMENT!
...!!
HUFF...
HUFF..
REBECCA!!
FORGIVE ME!!
GRIT..!!
...?

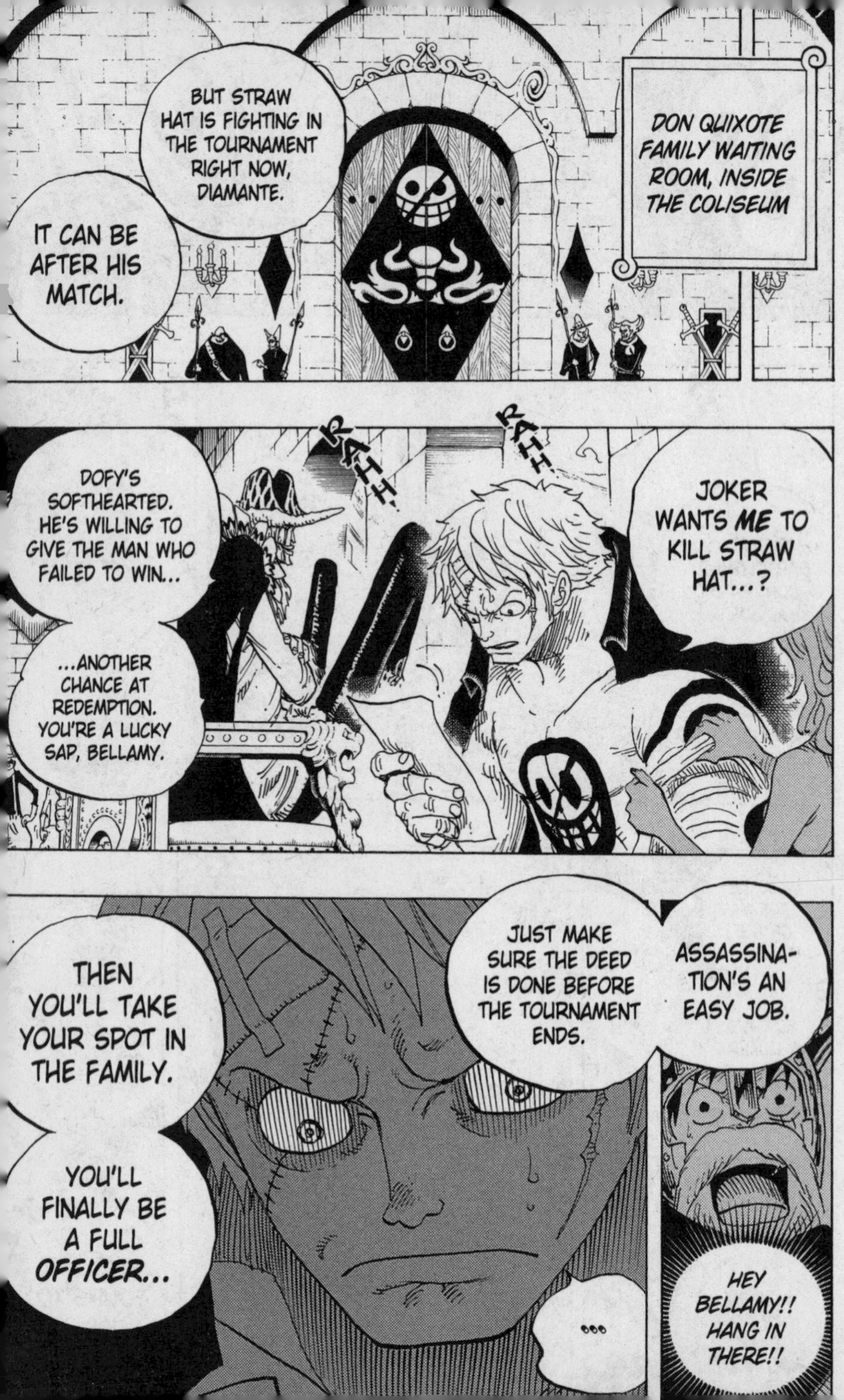
DON QUIXOTE FAMILY WAITING ROOM, INSIDE THE COLISEUM
BUT STRAW HAT IS FIGHTING IN THE TOURNAMENT RIGHT NOW, DIAMANTE.
IT CAN BE AFTER HIS MATCH.
RAHH
RAHH
JOKER WANTS *ME* TO KILL STRAW HAT...?
DOFY'S SOFTHEARTED. HE'S WILLING TO GIVE THE MAN WHO FAILED TO WIN...
...ANOTHER CHANCE AT REDEMPTION. YOU'RE A LUCKY SAP, BELLAMY.
ASSASSINATION'S AN EASY JOB.
JUST MAKE SURE THE DEED IS DONE BEFORE THE TOURNAMENT ENDS.
THEN YOU'LL TAKE YOUR SPOT IN THE FAMILY.
YOU'LL FINALLY BE A FULL *OFFICER*...
...
HEY BELLAMY!! HANG IN THERE!!

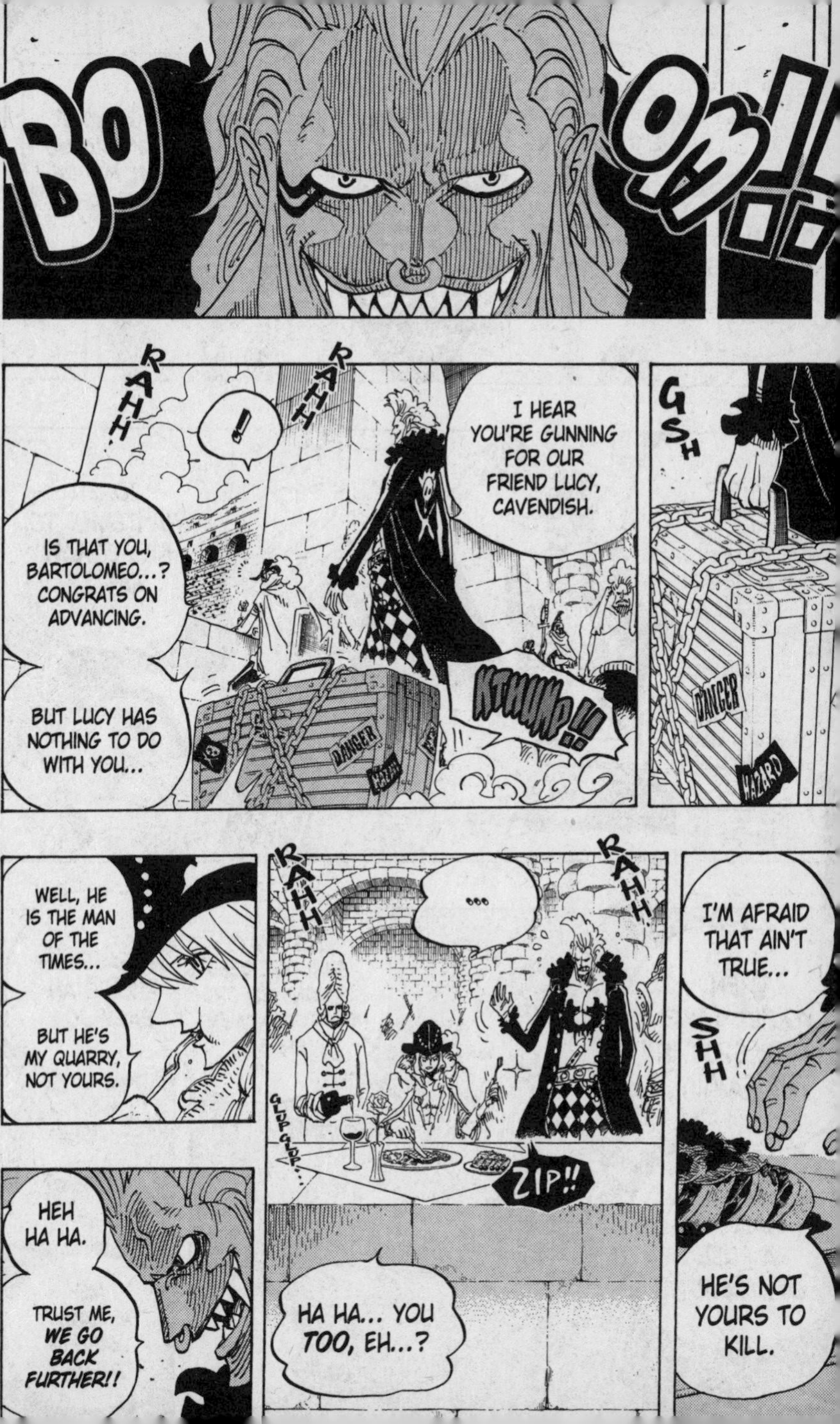
BOOM!!
GSH
I HEAR YOU'RE GUNNING FOR OUR FRIEND LUCY, CAVENDISH.
RAHH
RAHH
!
IS THAT YOU, BARTOLOMEO...? CONGRATS ON ADVANCING.
BUT LUCY HAS NOTHING TO DO WITH YOU...
KTHUMP!!
I'M AFRAID THAT AIN'T TRUE...
SHH
HE'S NOT YOURS TO KILL.
RAHH
...
RAHH
GLUP GLUP...
ZIP!!
WELL, HE IS THE MAN OF THE TIMES...
BUT HE'S MY QUARRY, NOT YOURS.
HA HA... YOU *TOO*, EH...?
HEH HA HA.
TRUST ME, ***WE GO BACK FURTHER!!***

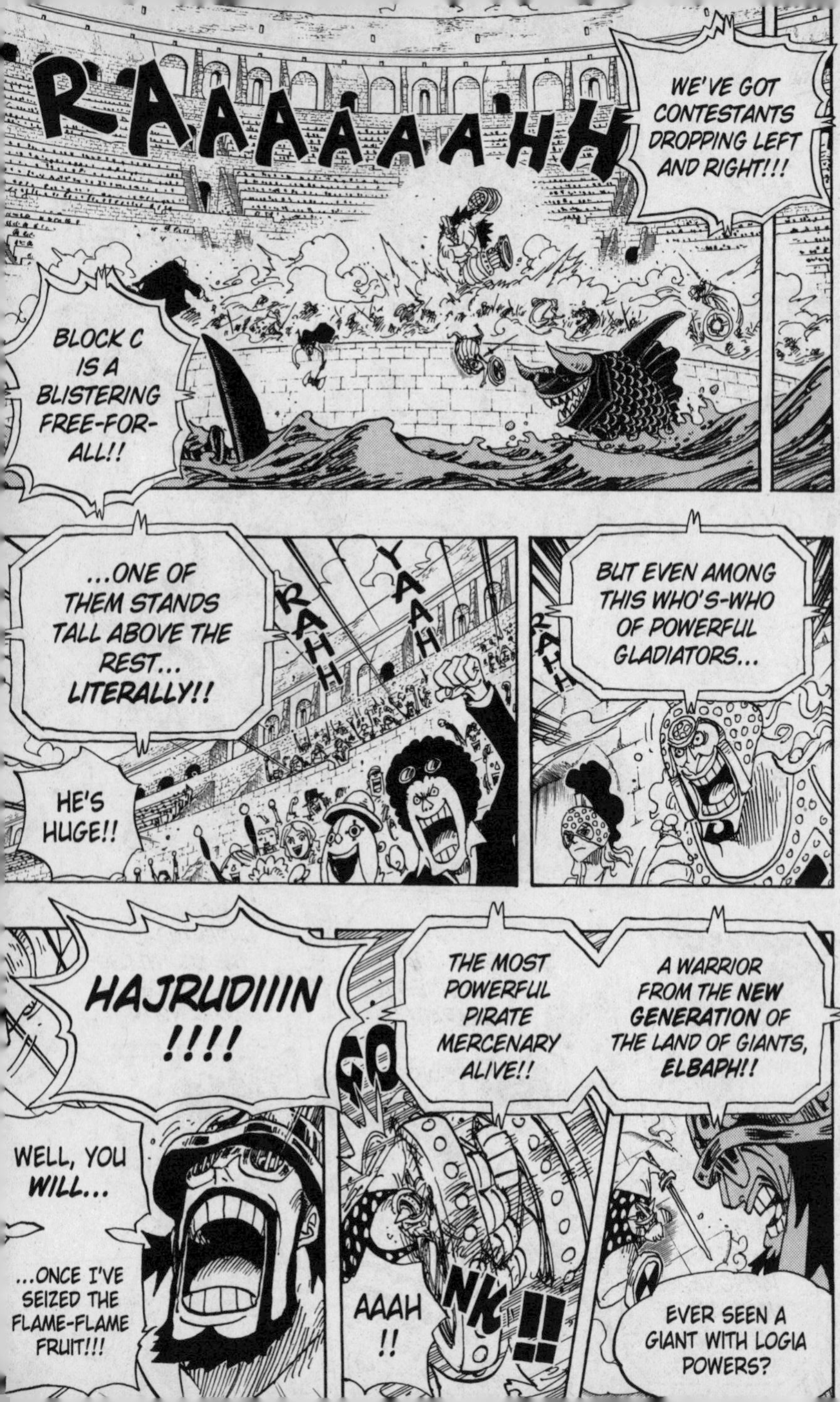
WE'VE GOT CONTESTANTS DROPPING LEFT AND RIGHT!!!
RAAAAAAHH
BLOCK C IS A BLISTERING FREE-FOR-ALL!!
BUT EVEN AMONG THIS WHO'S-WHO OF POWERFUL GLADIATORS...
RAHH
...ONE OF THEM STANDS TALL ABOVE THE REST... LITERALLY!!
YAAH
RAHH
HE'S HUGE!!
A WARRIOR FROM THE NEW GENERATION OF THE LAND OF GIANTS, ELBAPH!!
THE MOST POWERFUL PIRATE MERCENARY ALIVE!!
HAJRUDIIIN !!!!
EVER SEEN A GIANT WITH LOGIA POWERS?
GONK!!
AAAH !!
WELL, YOU WILL...
...ONCE I'VE SEIZED THE FLAME-FLAME FRUIT!!!

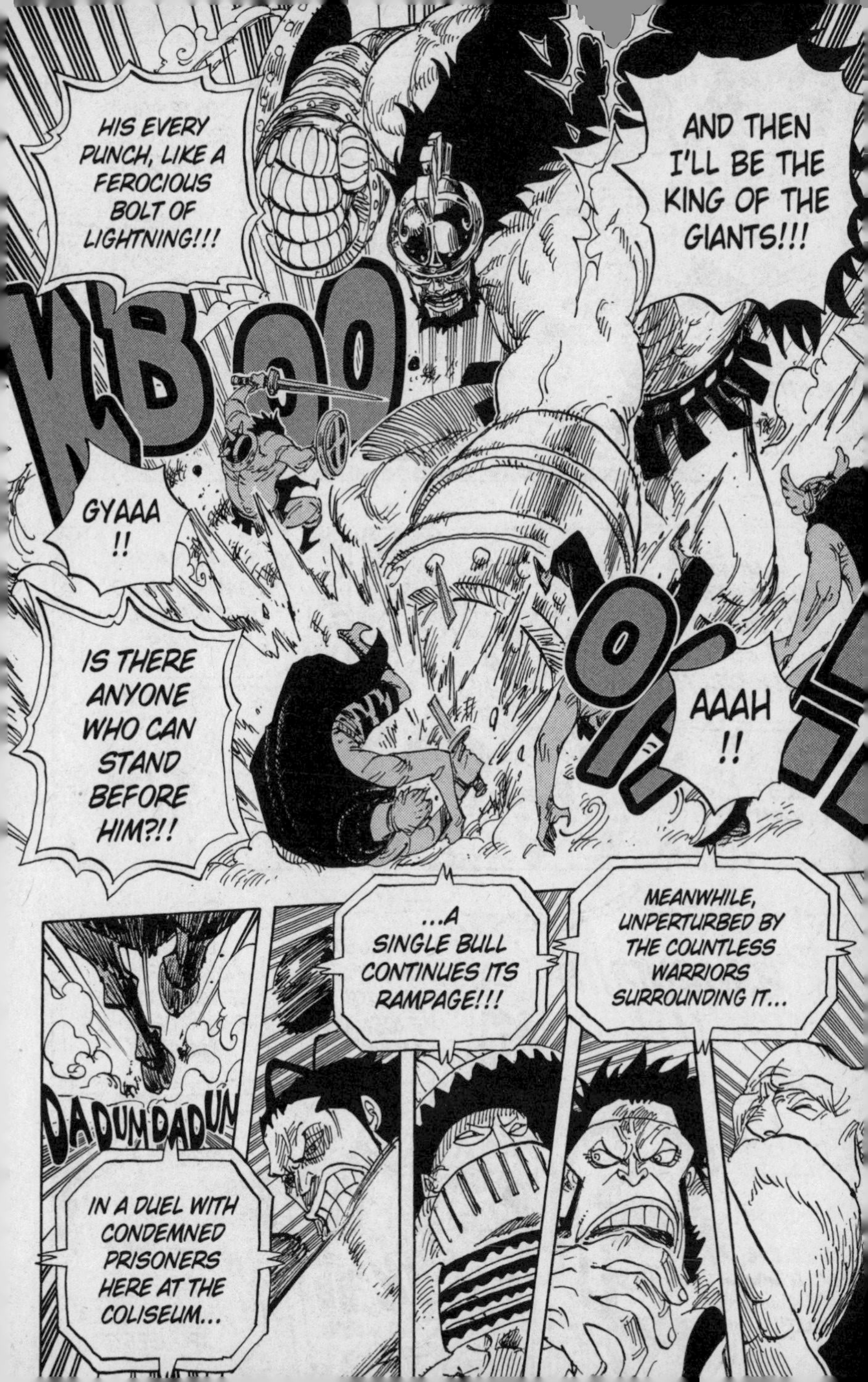
AND THEN I'LL BE THE KING OF THE GIANTS!!!
HIS EVERY PUNCH, LIKE A FEROCIOUS BOLT OF LIGHTNING!!!
GYAAA!!
AAAH!!
IS THERE ANYONE WHO CAN STAND BEFORE HIM?!!
MEANWHILE, UNPERTURBED BY THE COUNTLESS WARRIORS SURROUNDING IT...
...A SINGLE BULL CONTINUES ITS RAMPAGE!!!
DADUMDADUN
IN A DUEL WITH CONDEMNED PRISONERS HERE AT THE COLISEUM...

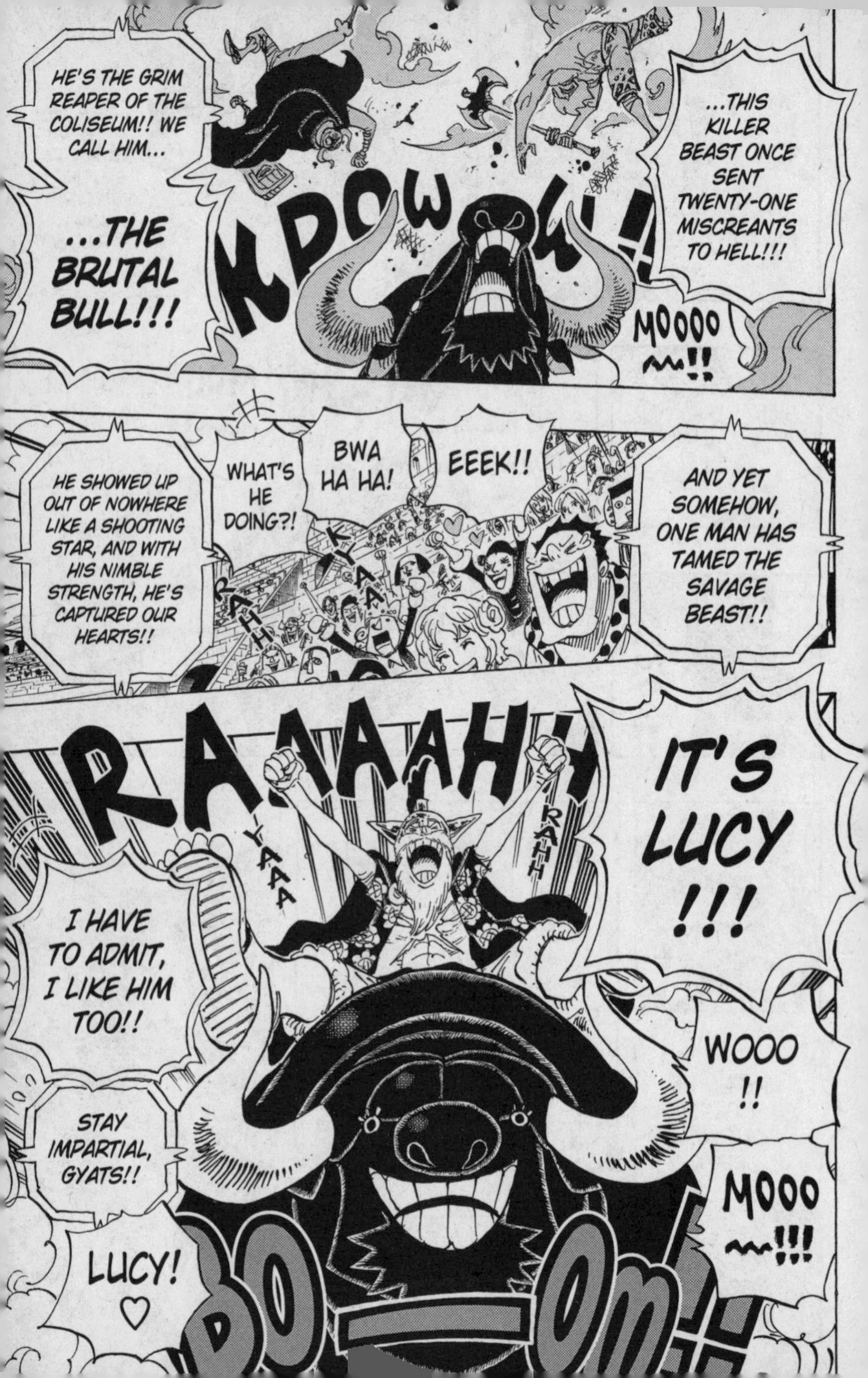
...THIS KILLER BEAST ONCE SENT TWENTY-ONE MISCREANTS TO HELL!!!
HE'S THE GRIM REAPER OF THE COLISEUM!! WE CALL HIM...
...THE BRUTAL BULL!!!
KDOW!!
MOOOO~!!
AND YET SOMEHOW, ONE MAN HAS TAMED THE SAVAGE BEAST!!
EEEK!!
BWA HA HA!
WHAT'S HE DOING?!
KYAA
HE SHOWED UP OUT OF NOWHERE LIKE A SHOOTING STAR, AND WITH HIS NIMBLE STRENGTH, HE'S CAPTURED OUR HEARTS!!
RAHH
IT'S LUCY!!!
RAAAAHH
RAHH
YAAA
I HAVE TO ADMIT, I LIKE HIM TOO!!
WOOO!!
STAY IMPARTIAL, GYATS!!
MOOO~!!!
LUCY! ♡
BOOOM!!

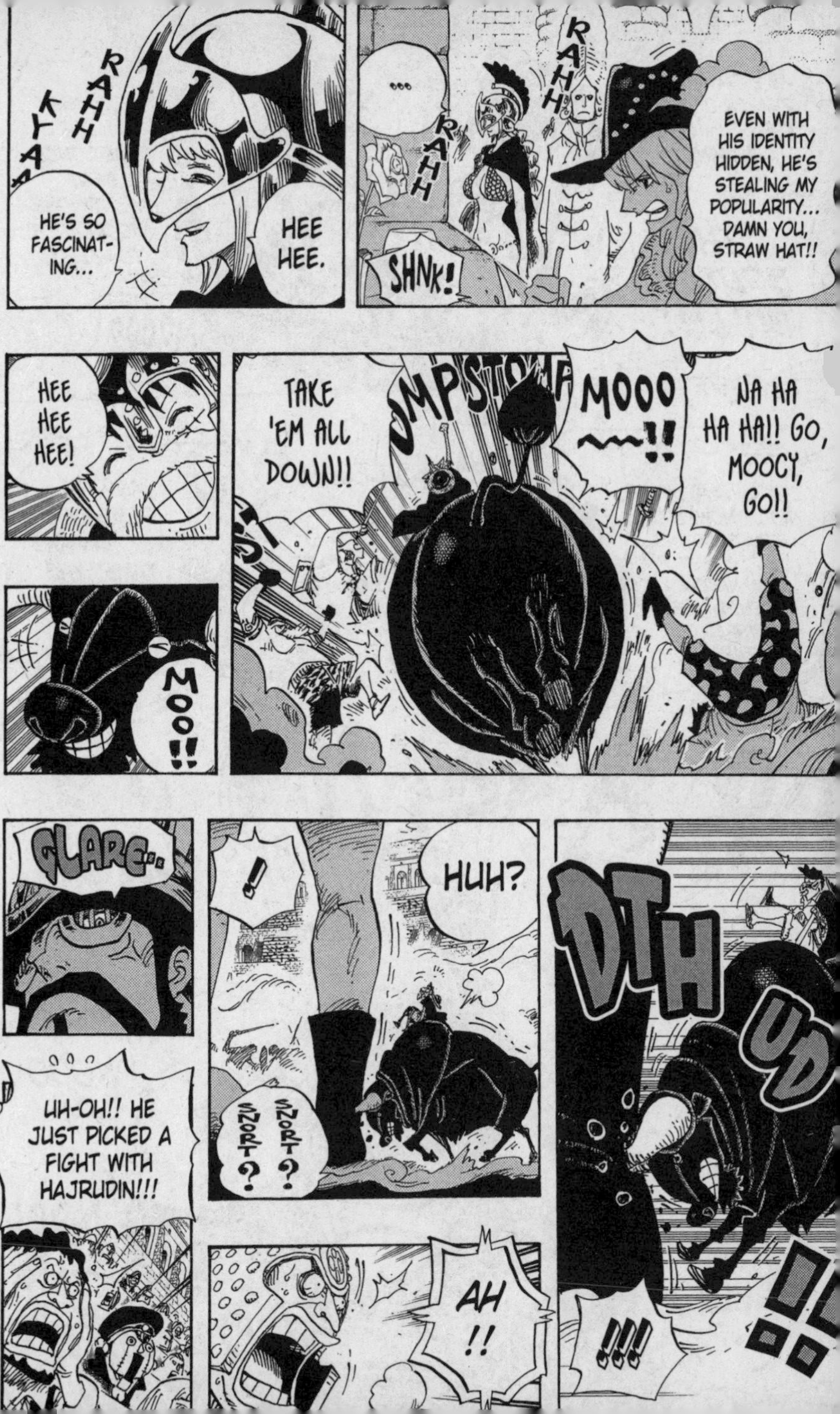
EVEN WITH HIS IDENTITY HIDDEN, HE'S STEALING MY POPULARITY... DAMN YOU, STRAW HAT!!
RAHH
RAHH
...
SHNK!
RAHH
KYAA
HEE HEE.
HE'S SO FASCINAT-ING...
NA HA HA HA!! GO, MOOCY, GO!!
MOOO ~~!!
TAKE 'EM ALL DOWN!!
HEE HEE HEE!
MOO!!
DTH UD
!!
!!!
HUH?
!
SNORT? SNORT?
AH !!
GLARE...
UH-OH!! HE JUST PICKED A FIGHT WITH HAJRUDIN!!!

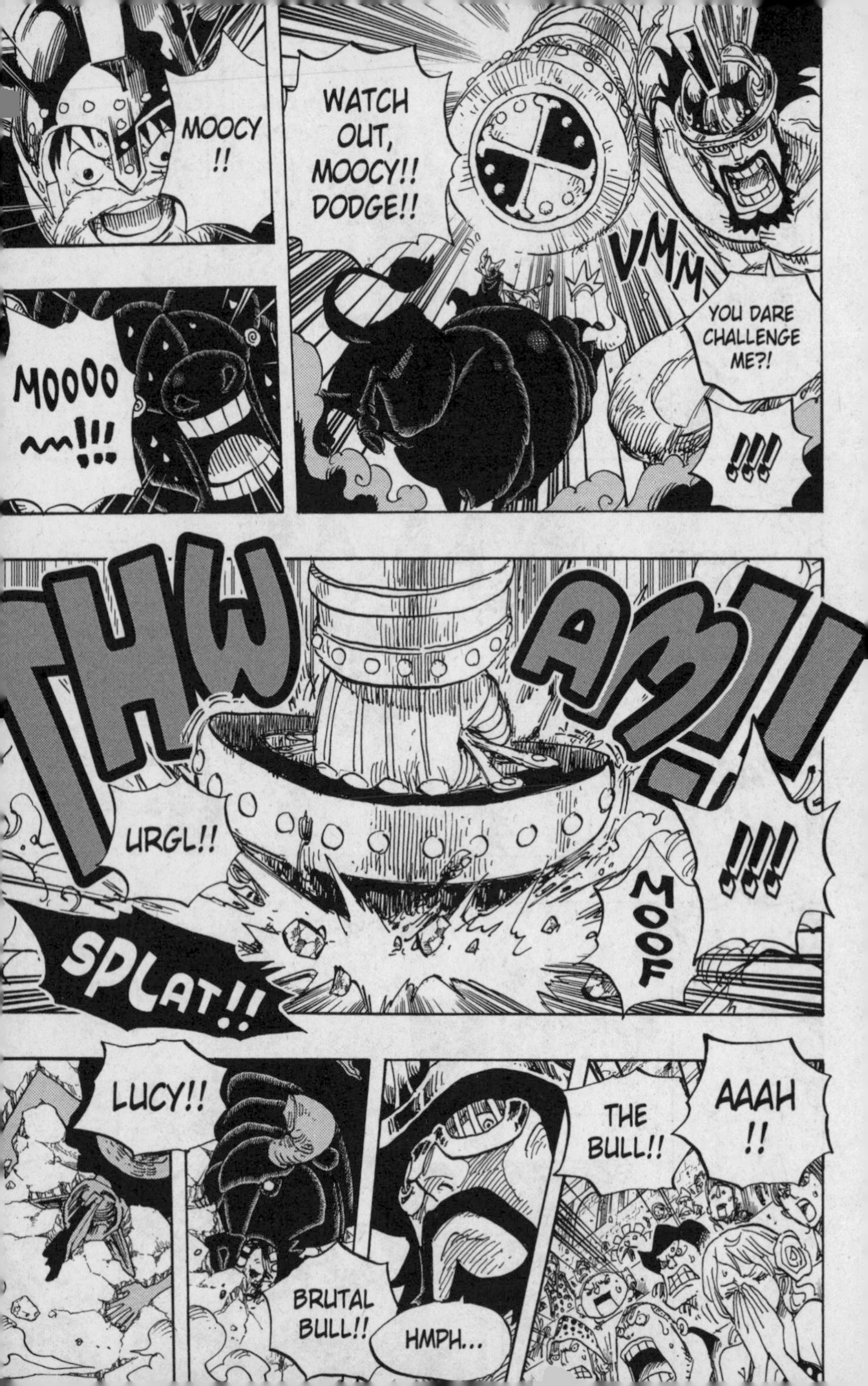
WATCH OUT, MOOCY!! DODGE!!
VMM
YOU DARE CHALLENGE ME?!
!!!
MOOCY!!
MOOOO~~!!!
THWAM!!
!!!
MOOF
URGL!!
SPLAT!!
AAAH!!
THE BULL!!
HMPH...
LUCY!!
BRUTAL BULL!!

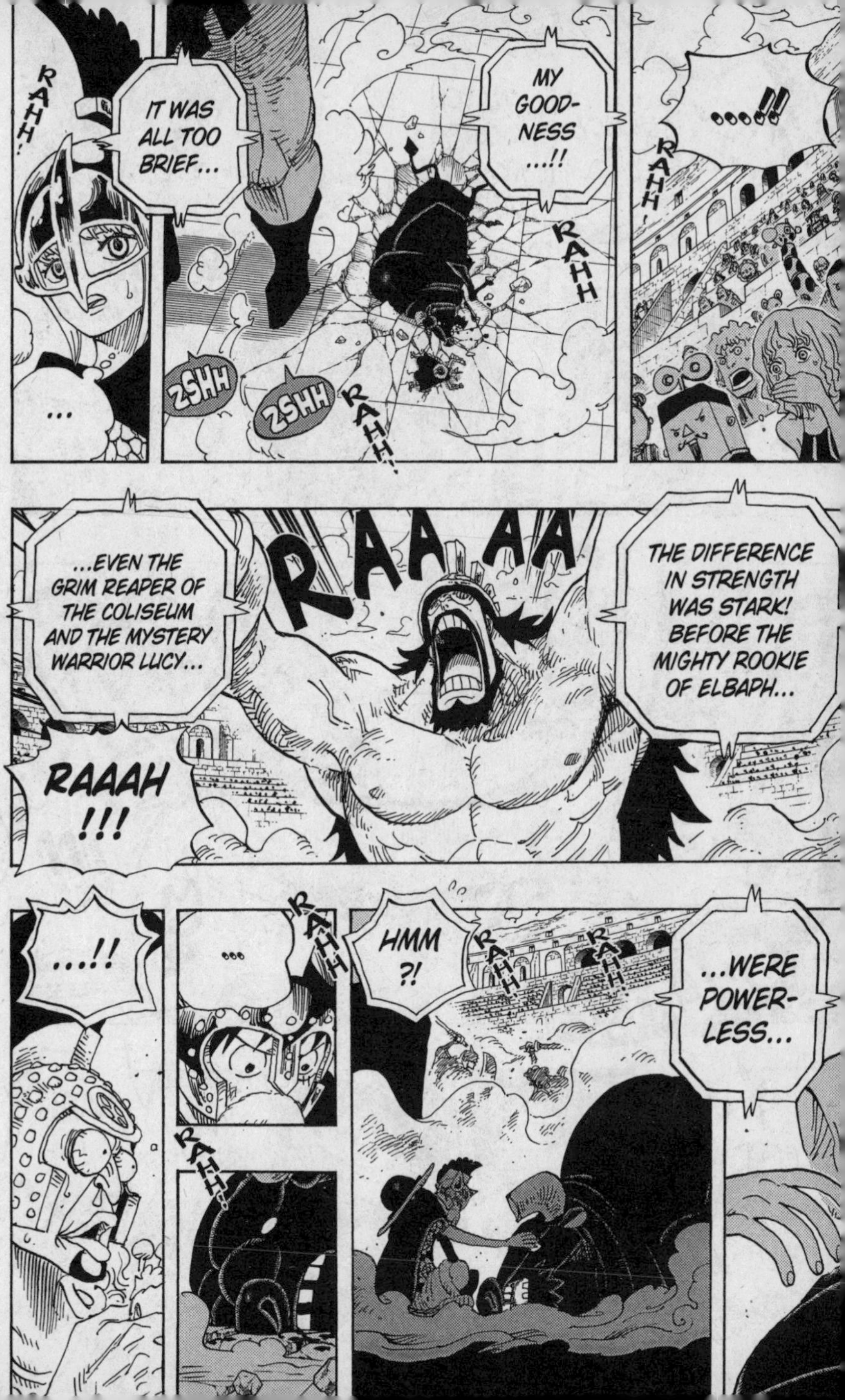

....!!
RAHH!
MY GOODNESS ...!!
RAHH
RAHH!
ZSHH
ZSHH
IT WAS ALL TOO BRIEF...
RAHH!
...
THE DIFFERENCE IN STRENGTH WAS STARK! BEFORE THE MIGHTY ROOKIE OF ELBAPH...
RAAAA
...EVEN THE GRIM REAPER OF THE COLISEUM AND THE MYSTERY WARRIOR LUCY...
RAAAH!!!
...WERE POWERLESS...
RAHH!
RAHH!
HMM ?!
RAHH
...
RAHH!
...!!

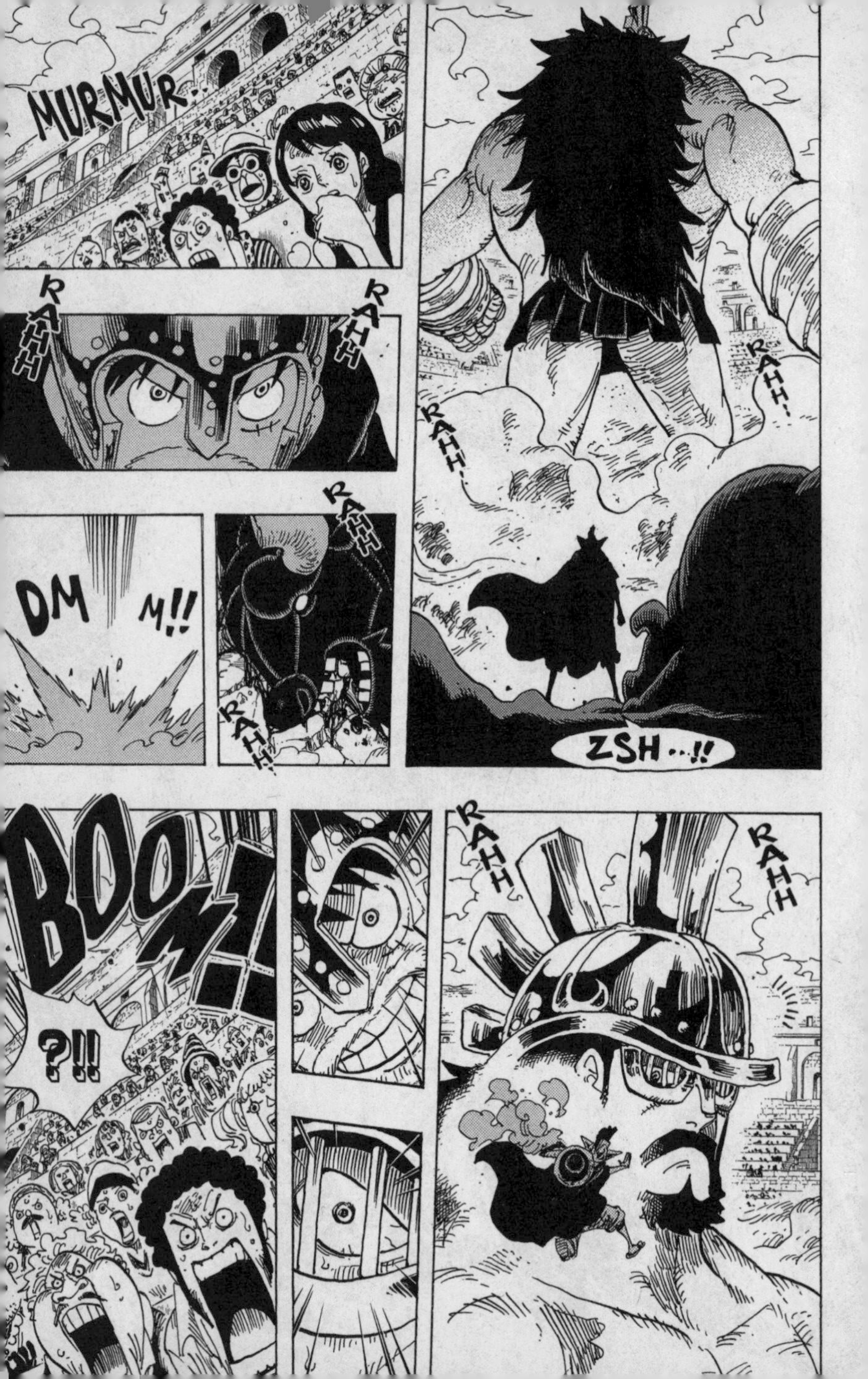
RAHH..
RAHH..
ZSH...!!
MURMUR
RAHH
RAHH
RAHH
RAHH..
DM M!!
RAHH
RAHH
BOOM!!
?!!

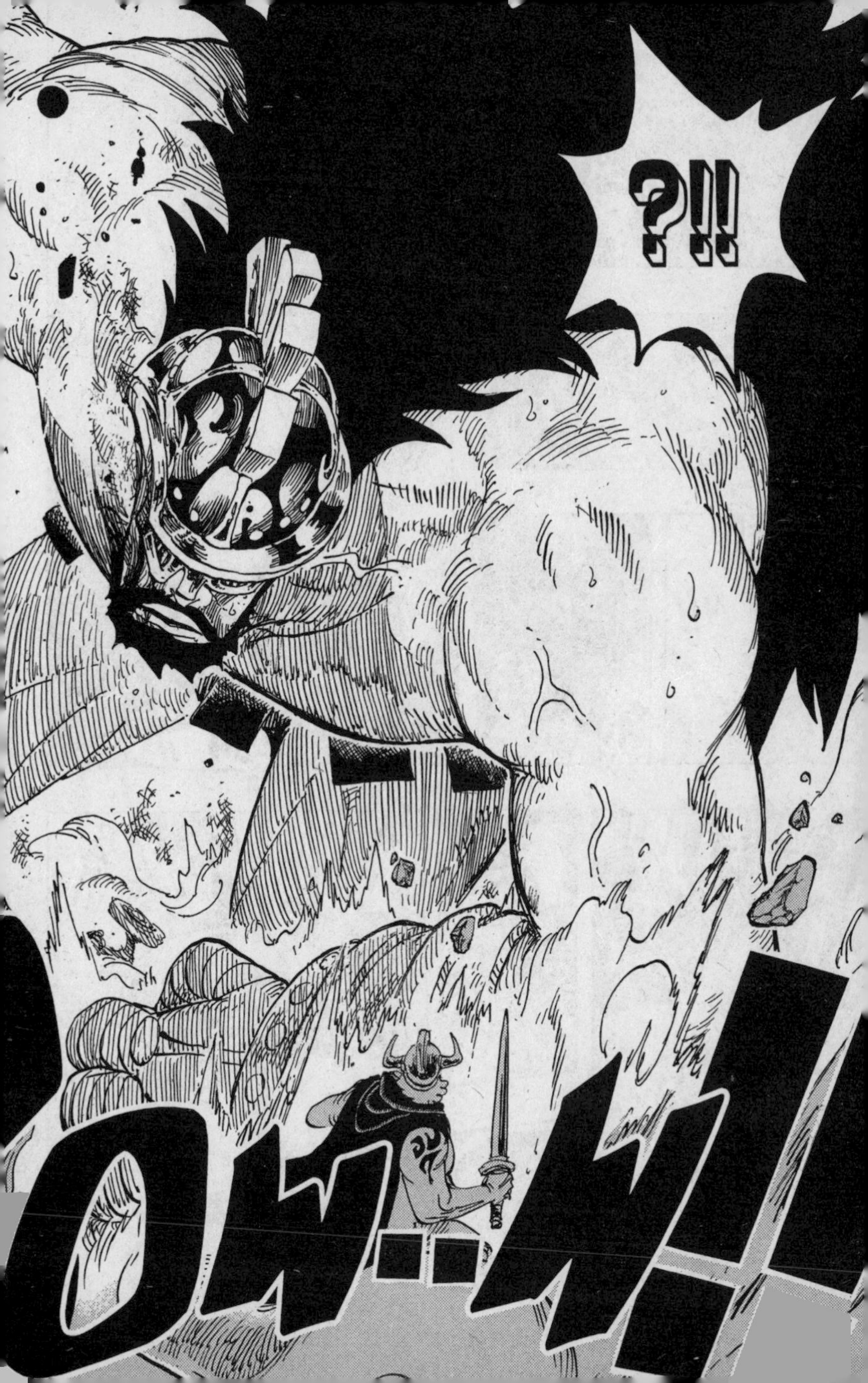
?!!
OW...W!!

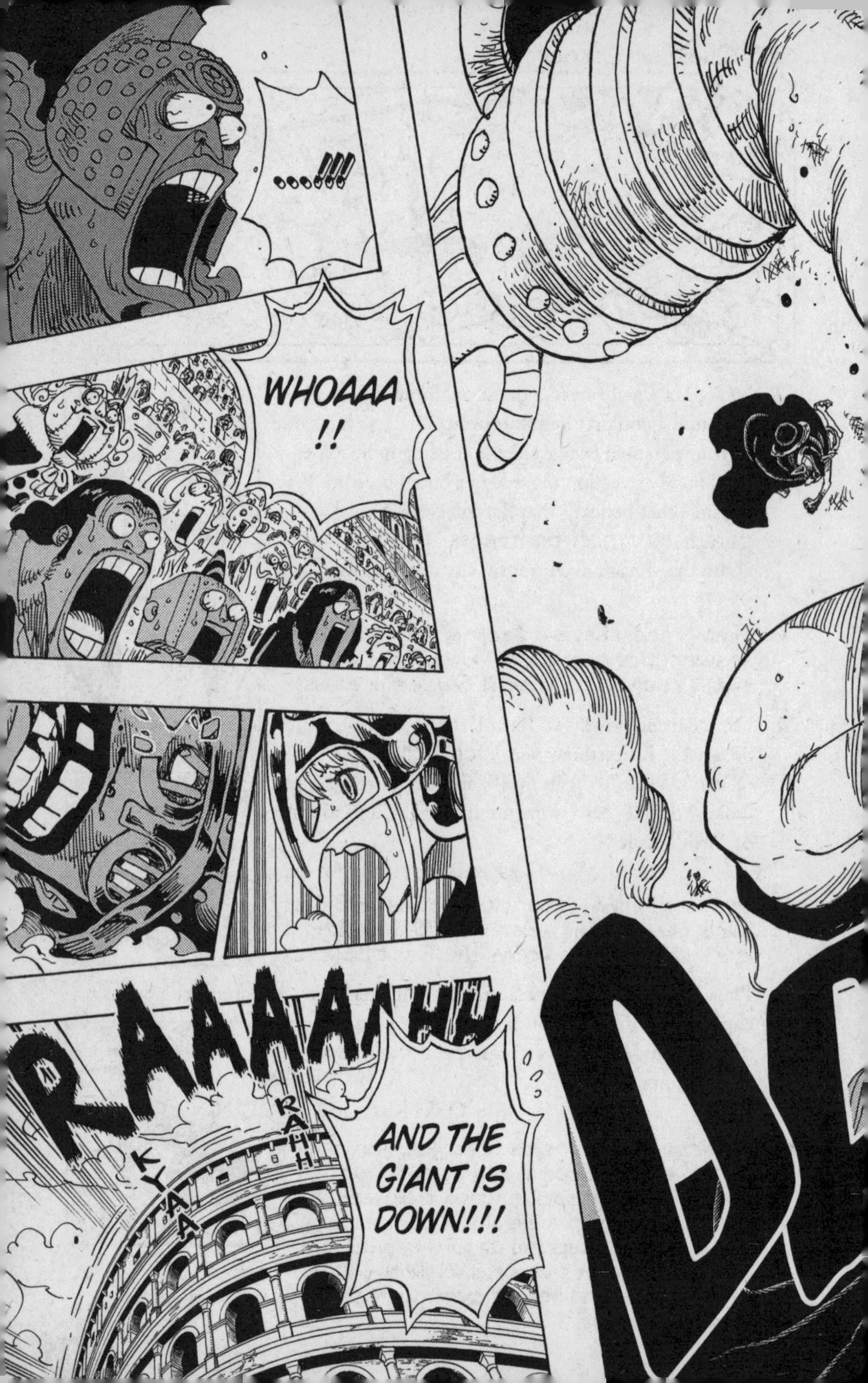
...!!!
WHOAAA !!
RAAAAAHH
KYAA
RAHH
AND THE GIANT IS DOWN!!!

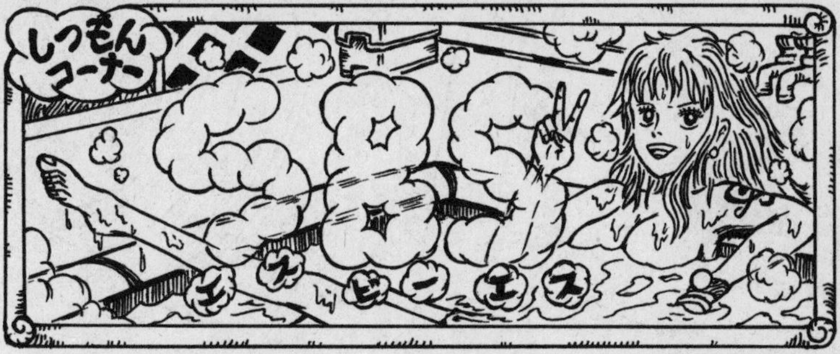
しつもん
コーナー
エスビーエス

(Sashinji, Chiba)

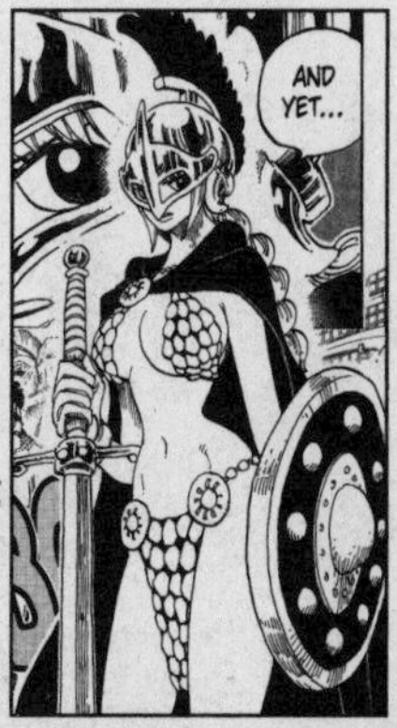
AND YET...

Q: Hello, Mr. Oda! I have a question about Rebecca the gladiator. I couldn't help but notice that, perhaps due to your personal tastes, she is exposing quite a lot of skin. My question regards her bikini bottom. Is it possible that beneath that flap of cloth is a paradise of non-pantyness? I'm so curious about this, I can't even put on any underwear.

--Tanpopo

A: Hmm, I see. I have a feeling that I shouldn't answer this question. I know the answer, but I'll keep it to myself! Sweet dreams!!

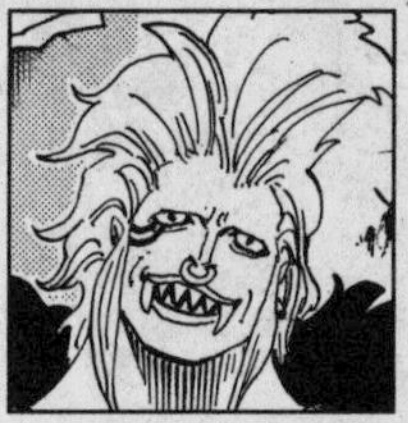

Q: Mr. Odacchi, howdy!☆ Bartolomeo's so cool, right? So what if his birthday was October 6th? (Y'know, since "to" can be 10, and "lo" is short for "roku," or six!) Also, what are his height, age and place of birth details?!

--*One Piece* is my reason for living

A: Birthday?! Hmm... I dunno, should I use that? Sure, I guess. His height is 7'3", he's 24 years old, and he's from the East Blue.

Q: I'm so jealous of Leo the Tontatta! ...my dad says. Apparently he wants to explore in Robin's region B too. Can you help him explore her boo...er, region B without my mom finding out?

--Orika Kakyoin

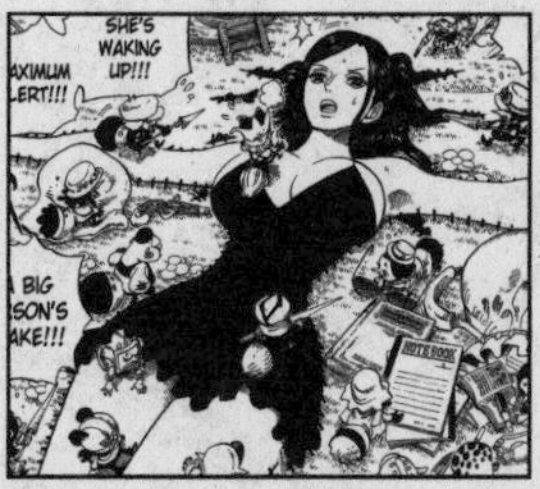
SHE'S WAKING UP!!!

A: At first I just wrote it as "Region Boobs" and laughed my butt off. But then my editor said it wasn't allowed, and we got into a big fight. Since I'm out of shape, I wound up with a skull fracture. What's wrong with the world that I'm the dang author and I can't even write what I want! I get no respect, I tell ya!

Chapter 715:
THE BATTLEGROUND OF BLOCK C

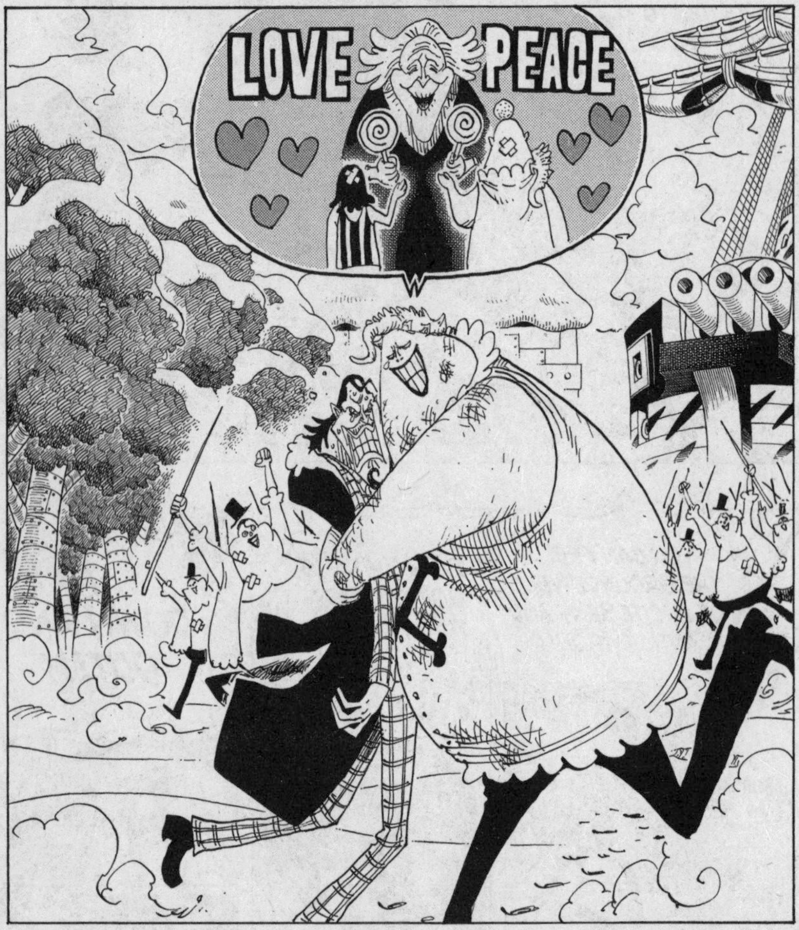
LOVE
PEACE

CARIBOU'S NEW WORLD KEE HEE HEE, VOL. 33: "REMEMBER WHAT OUR DEAD GRANDMA ALWAYS SAID: BROTHERS NEED TO GET ALONG!"

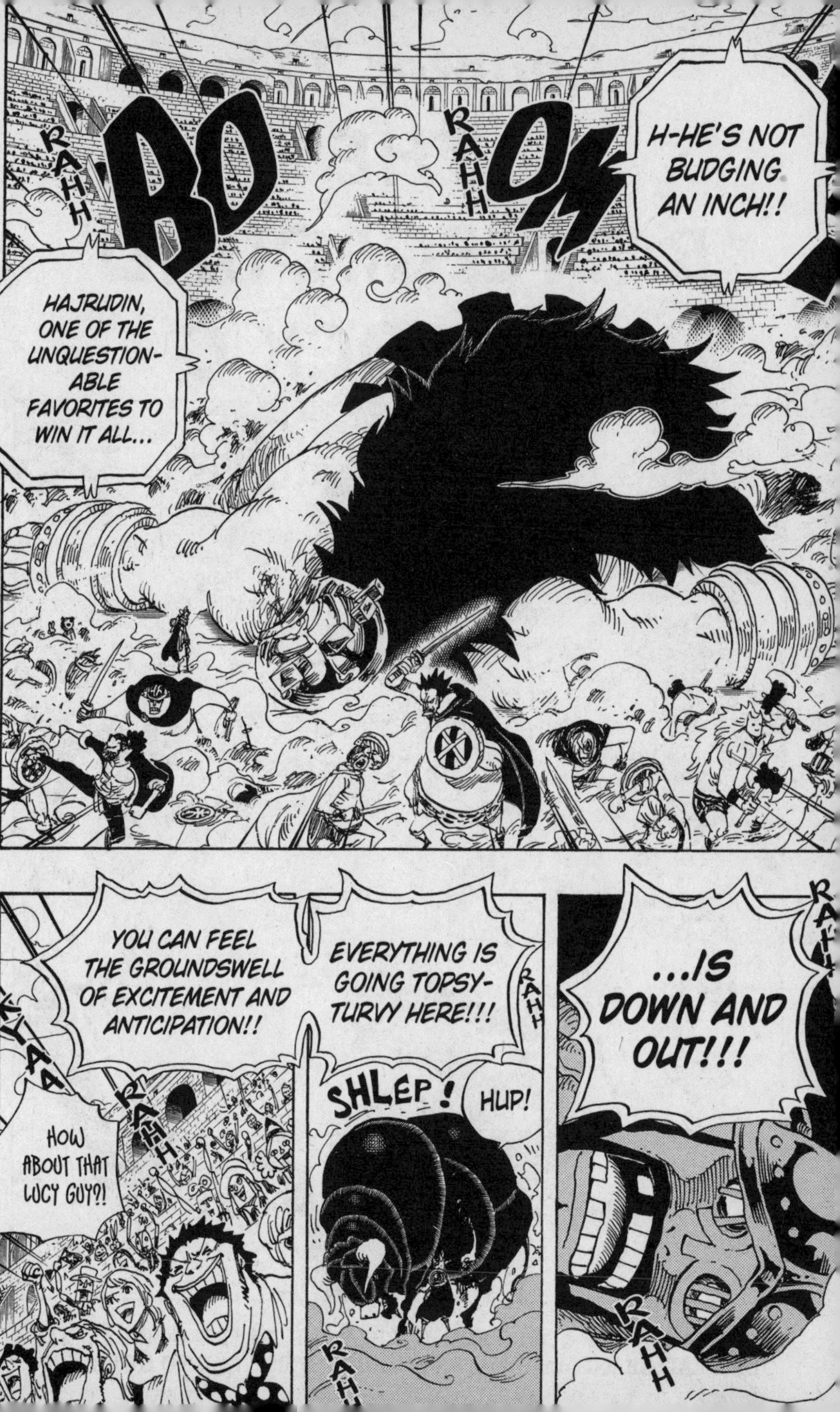
H-HE'S NOT BUDGING AN INCH!!
RAHH
BOOM
RAHH
HAJRUDIN, ONE OF THE UNQUESTION-ABLE FAVORITES TO WIN IT ALL...
...IS DOWN AND OUT!!!
RAHH
RAHH
EVERYTHING IS GOING TOPSY-TURVY HERE!!!
RAHH
HUP!
SHLEP!
RAHH
YOU CAN FEEL THE GROUNDSWELL OF EXCITEMENT AND ANTICIPATION!!
RAHH
KYAA
HOW ABOUT THAT LUCY GUY?!

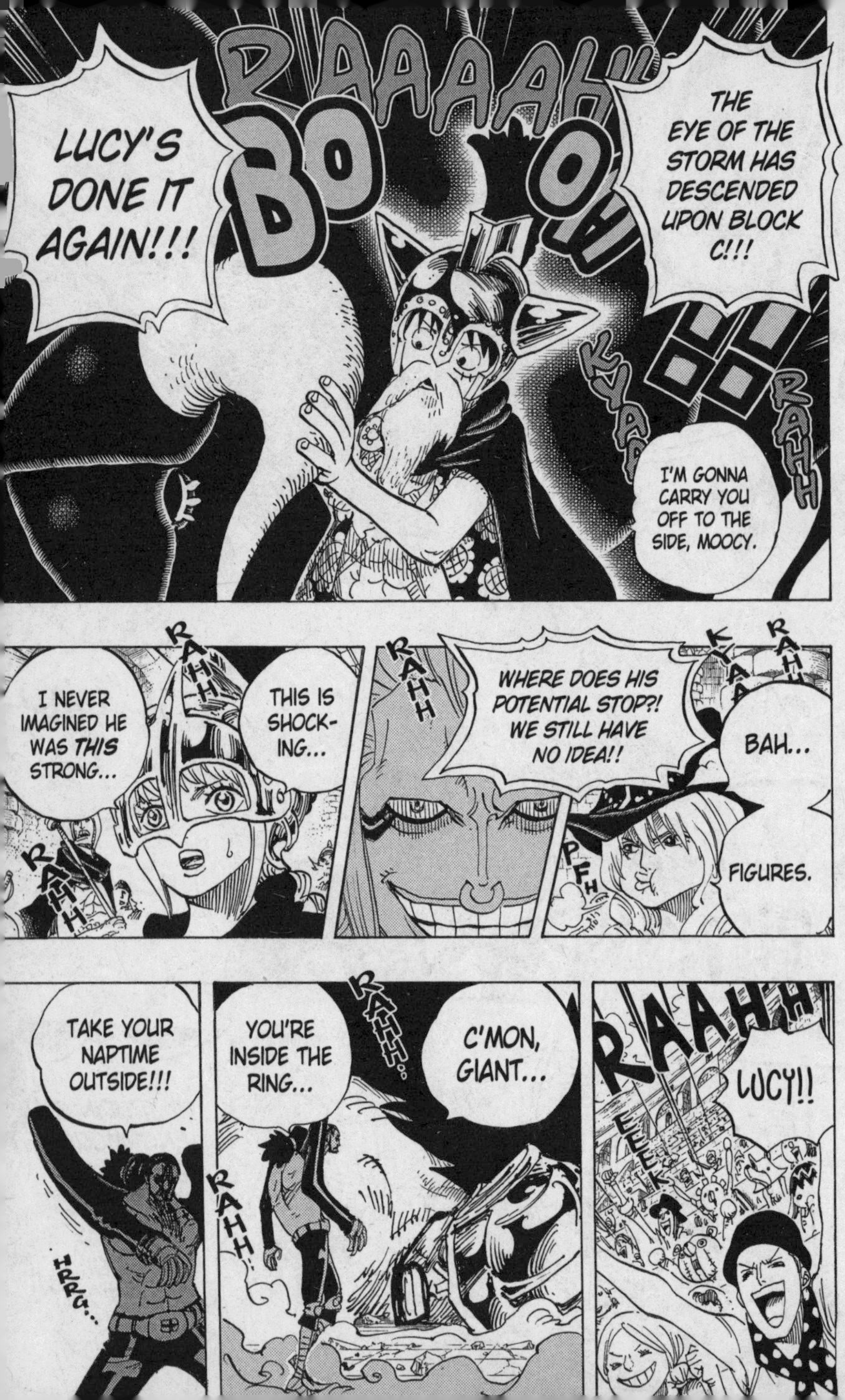
RAAAAH!!
THE EYE OF THE STORM HAS DESCENDED UPON BLOCK C!!!
BOOM
LUCY'S DONE IT AGAIN!!!
KYAA
RAHH
I'M GONNA CARRY YOU OFF TO THE SIDE, MOOCY.
RAHH
KYAA
BAH... FIGURES.
PFH
WHERE DOES HIS POTENTIAL STOP?! WE STILL HAVE NO IDEA!!
RAHH
THIS IS SHOCKING...
RAHH
I NEVER IMAGINED HE WAS *THIS* STRONG...
RAHH
RAAHH
LUCY!!
EEEEK
C'MON, GIANT...
RAHH
YOU'RE INSIDE THE RING...
RAHH
TAKE YOUR NAPTIME OUTSIDE!!!
HRRG...

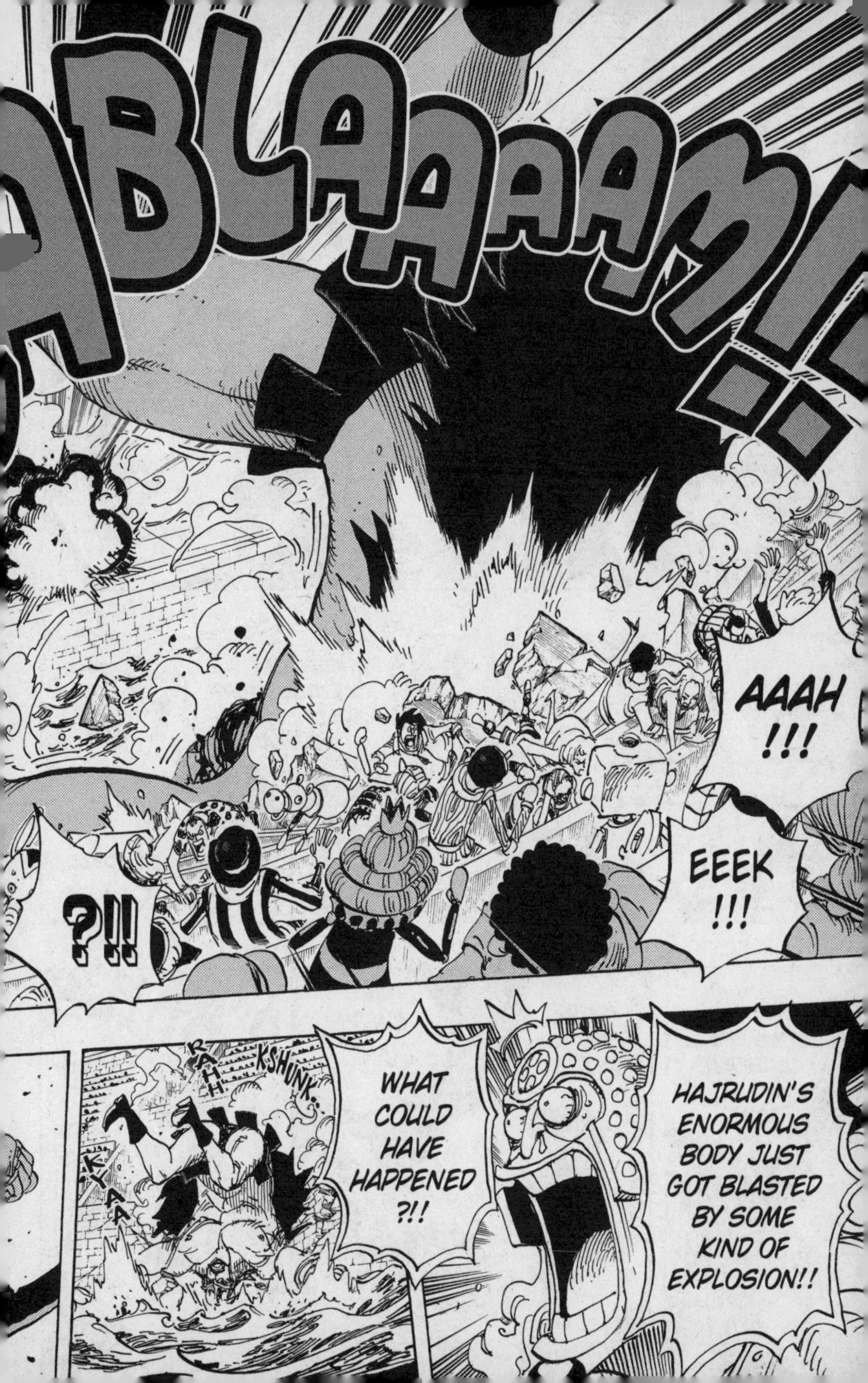
BLAAAAAM!!
AAAH!!!
EEEK!!!
?!!
HAJRUDIN'S ENORMOUS BODY JUST GOT BLASTED BY SOME KIND OF EXPLOSION!!
WHAT COULD HAVE HAPPENED?!!
KSHUNK
RAHH
KYAA

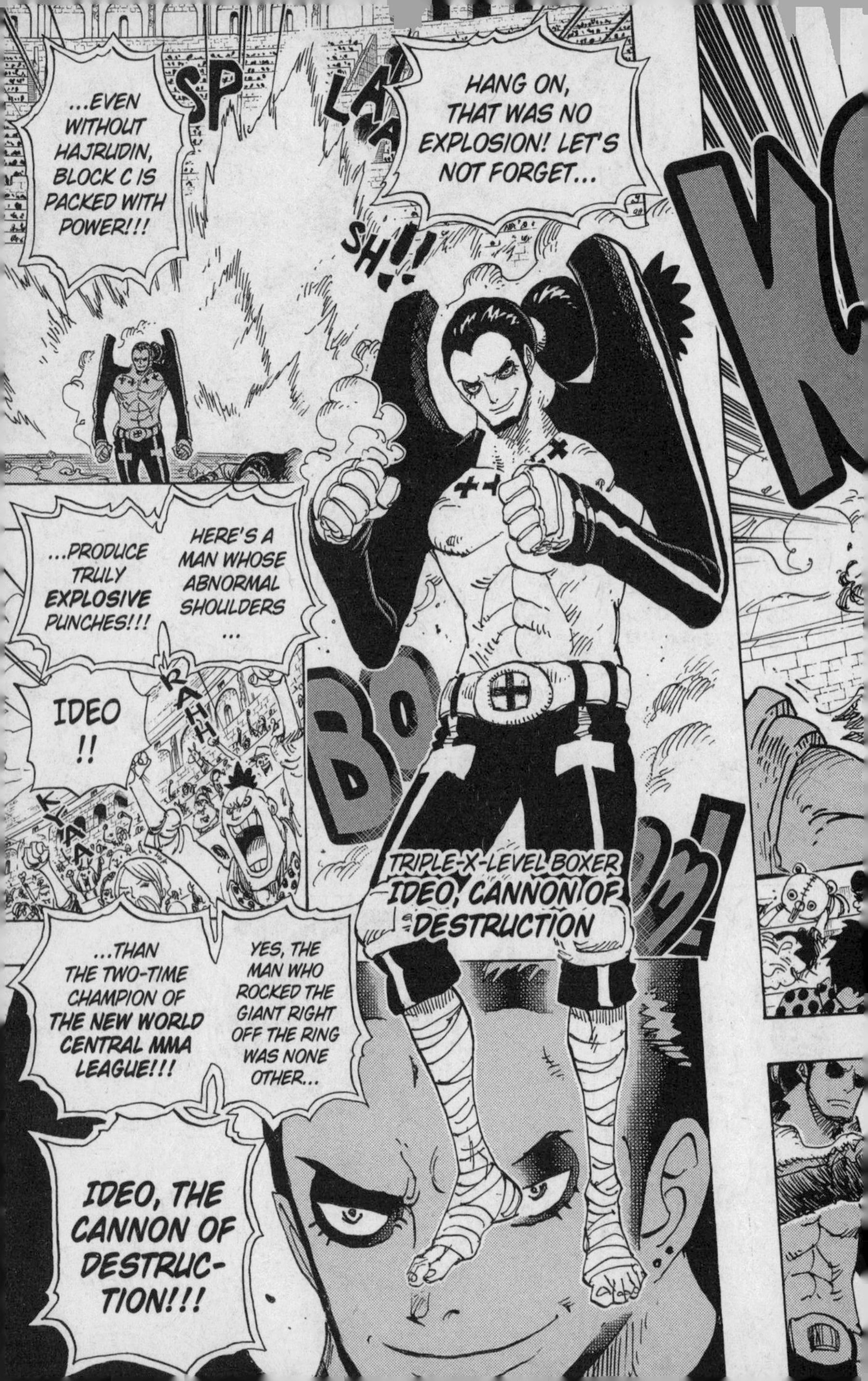
HANG ON, THAT WAS NO EXPLOSION! LET'S NOT FORGET...
SPLAAASH!!
BOOOM!
TRIPLE-X-LEVEL BOXER
IDEO, CANNON OF DESTRUCTION
...EVEN WITHOUT HAJRUDIN, BLOCK C IS PACKED WITH POWER!!!
HERE'S A MAN WHOSE ABNORMAL SHOULDERS ...
...PRODUCE TRULY EXPLOSIVE PUNCHES!!!
RAHH
IDEO !!
KYAA
YES, THE MAN WHO ROCKED THE GIANT RIGHT OFF THE RING WAS NONE OTHER...
...THAN THE TWO-TIME CHAMPION OF THE NEW WORLD CENTRAL MMA LEAGUE!!!
IDEO, THE CANNON OF DESTRUC-TION!!!

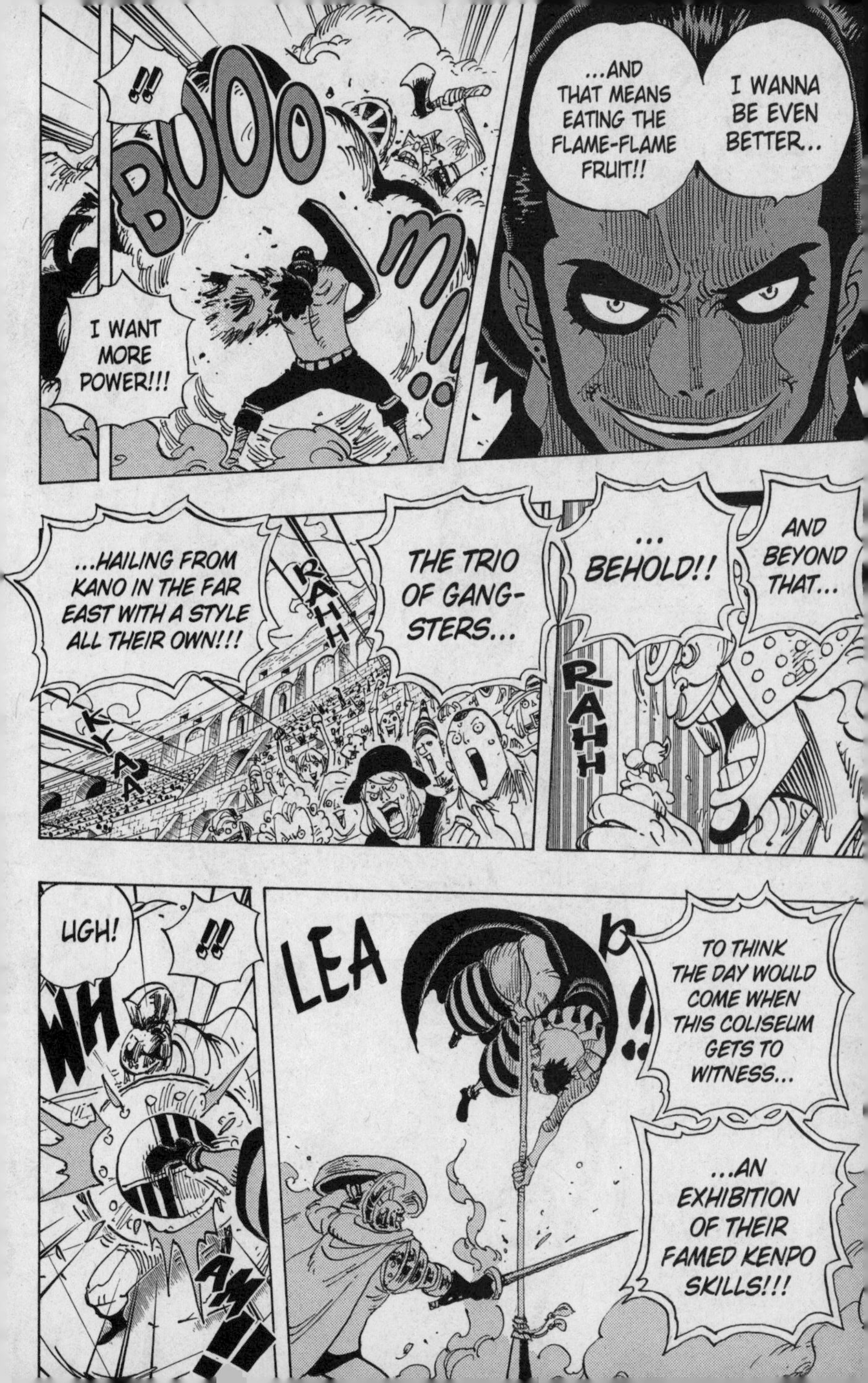
I WANNA BE EVEN BETTER...
...AND THAT MEANS EATING THE FLAME-FLAME FRUIT!!
!!
BUOOM...
I WANT MORE POWER!!!
AND BEYOND THAT...
... BEHOLD!!
RAHH
THE TRIO OF GANG-STERS...
RAHH
...HAILING FROM KANO IN THE FAR EAST WITH A STYLE ALL THEIR OWN!!!
KYAA
TO THINK THE DAY WOULD COME WHEN THIS COLISEUM GETS TO WITNESS...
...AN EXHIBITION OF THEIR FAMED KENPO SKILLS!!!
LEAP
!!
!!
UGH!

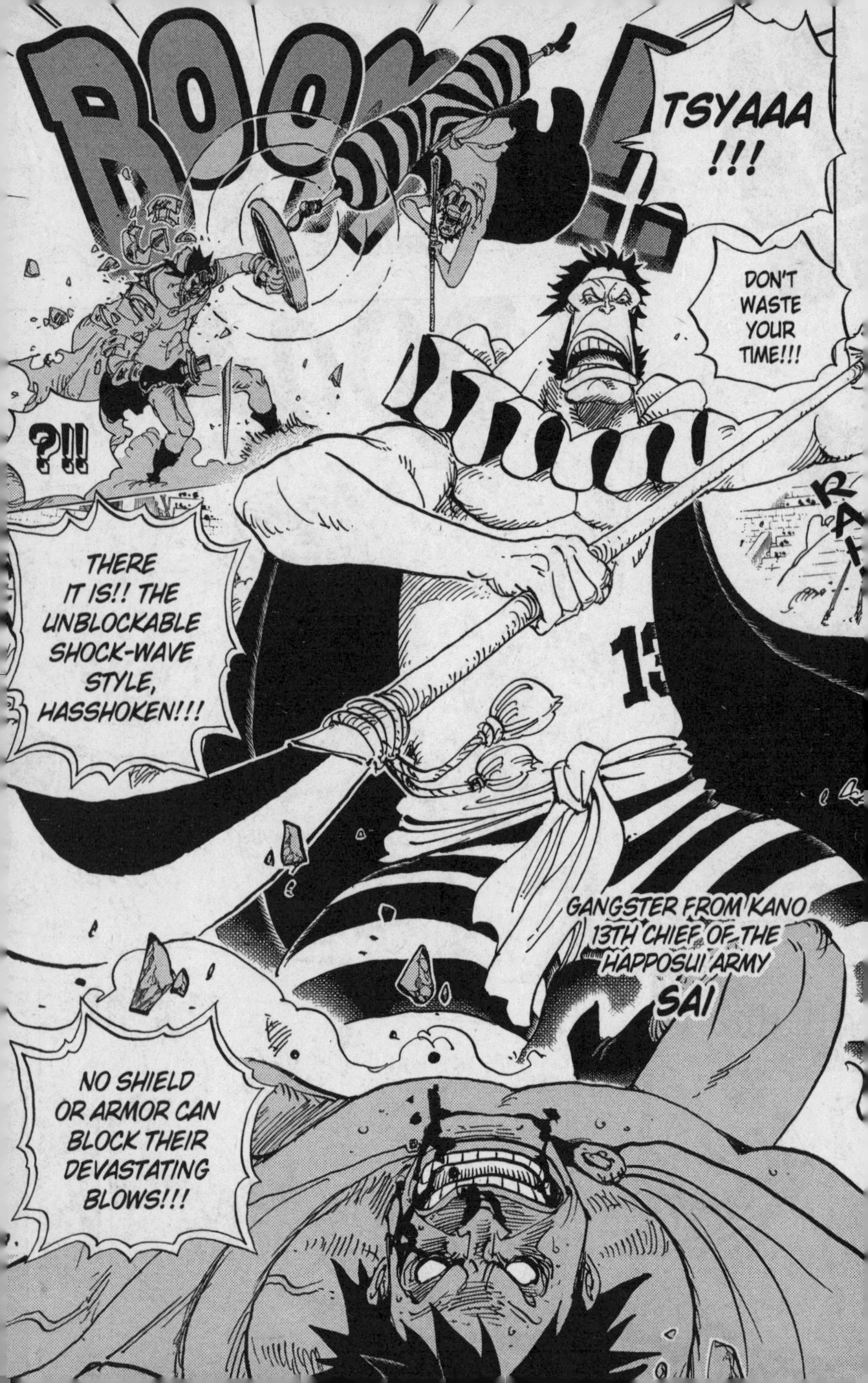
TSYAAA !!!
DON'T WASTE YOUR TIME!!!
BOOM
?!!
GANGSTER FROM KANO 13TH CHIEF OF THE HAPPOSUI ARMY SAI
THERE IT IS!! THE UNBLOCKABLE SHOCK-WAVE STYLE, HASSHOKEN!!!
NO SHIELD OR ARMOR CAN BLOCK THEIR DEVASTATING BLOWS!!!

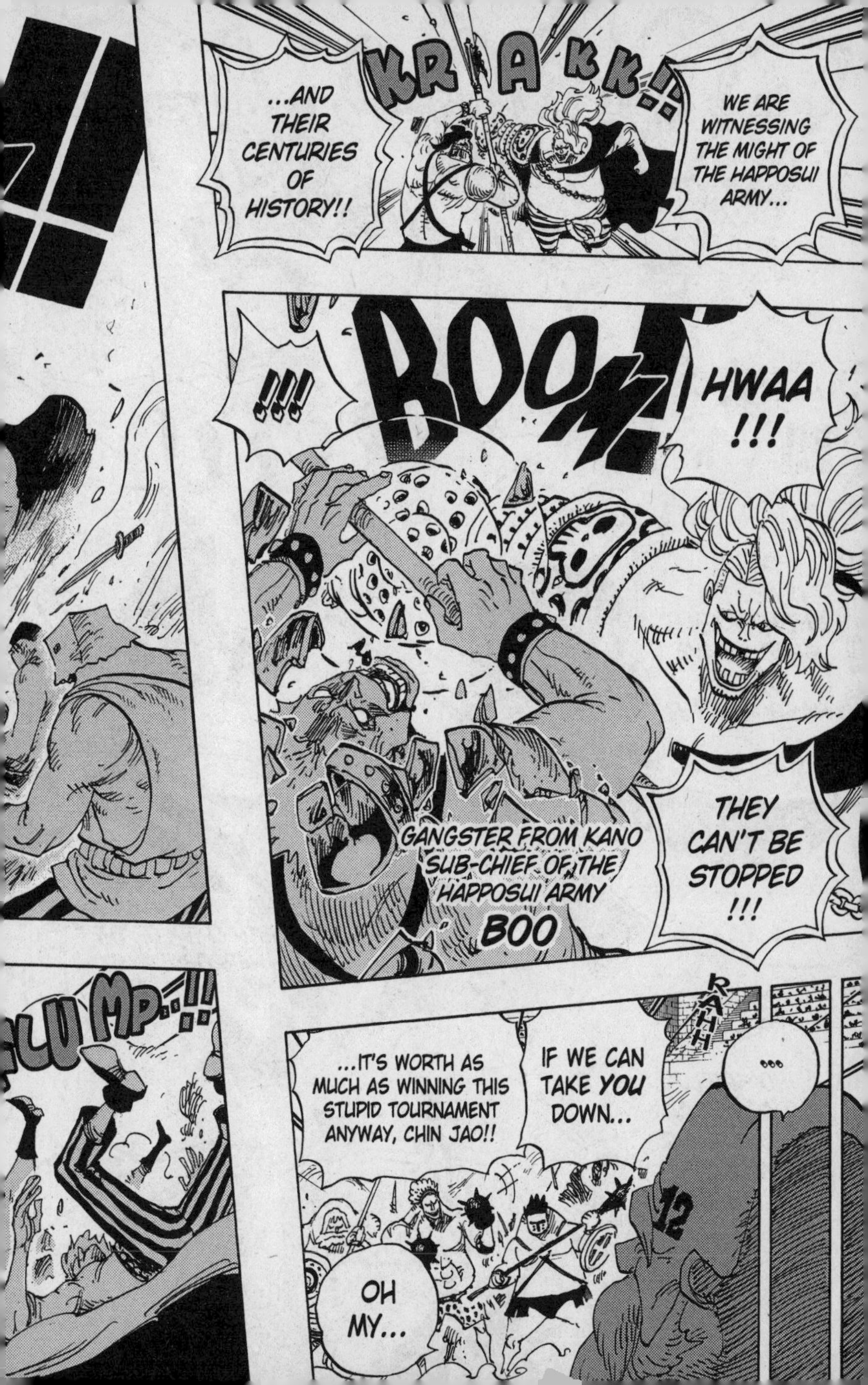
KRAKK!!
WE ARE WITNESSING THE MIGHT OF THE HAPPOSUI ARMY...
...AND THEIR CENTURIES OF HISTORY!!
BOOM
HWAA!!!
!!!
GANGSTER FROM KANO SUB-CHIEF OF THE HAPPOSUI ARMY BOO
THEY CAN'T BE STOPPED!!!
...
RAHH
IF WE CAN TAKE YOU DOWN...
...IT'S WORTH AS MUCH AS WINNING THIS STUPID TOURNAMENT ANYWAY, CHIN JAO!!
OH MY...
MP!!

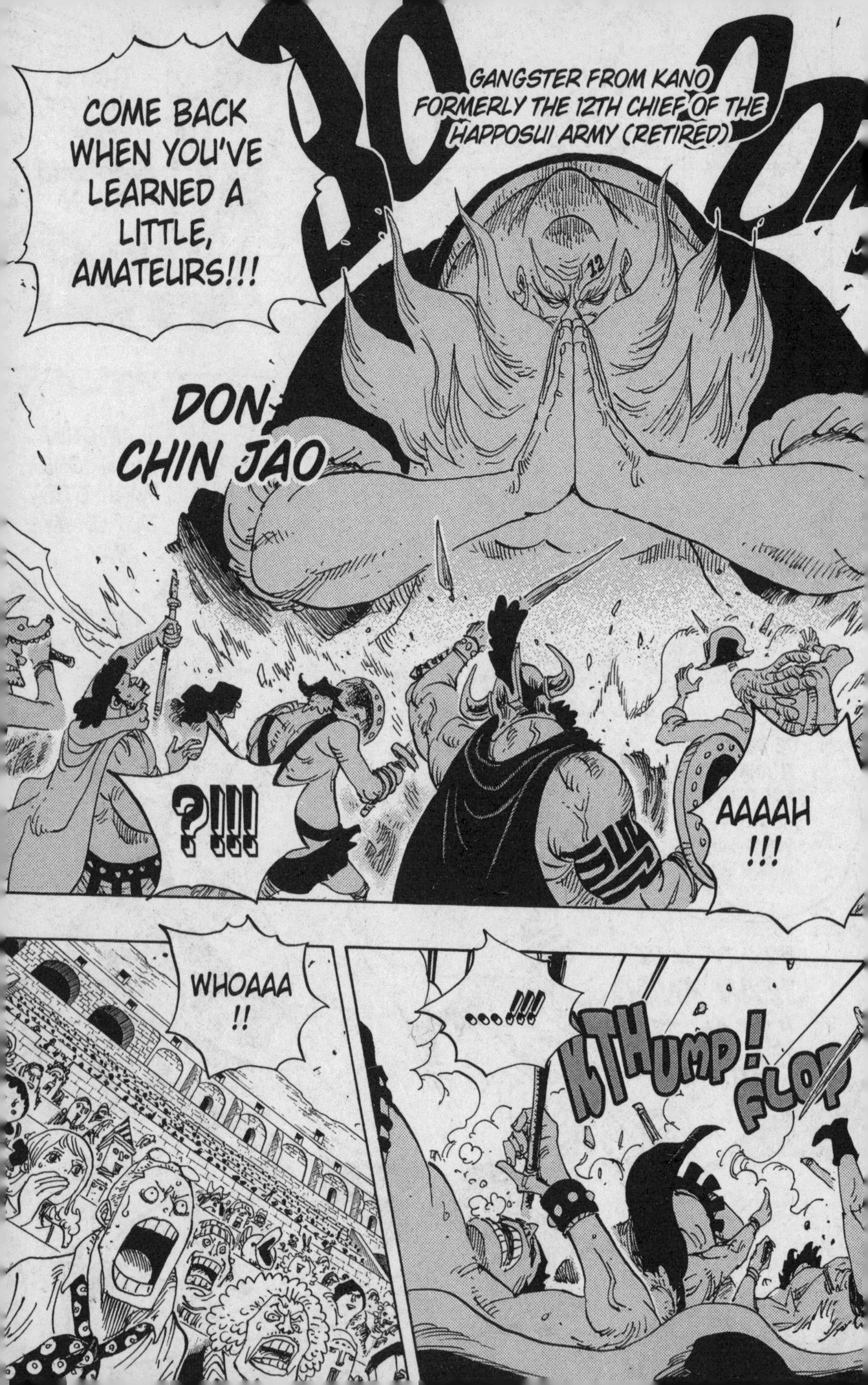
GANGSTER FROM KANO FORMERLY THE 12TH CHIEF OF THE HAPPOSUI ARMY (RETIRED)
COME BACK WHEN YOU'VE LEARNED A LITTLE, AMATEURS!!!
DON CHIN JAO
AAAAH !!!
?!!!
...!!!
KTHUMP!
FLOP
WHOAAA !!

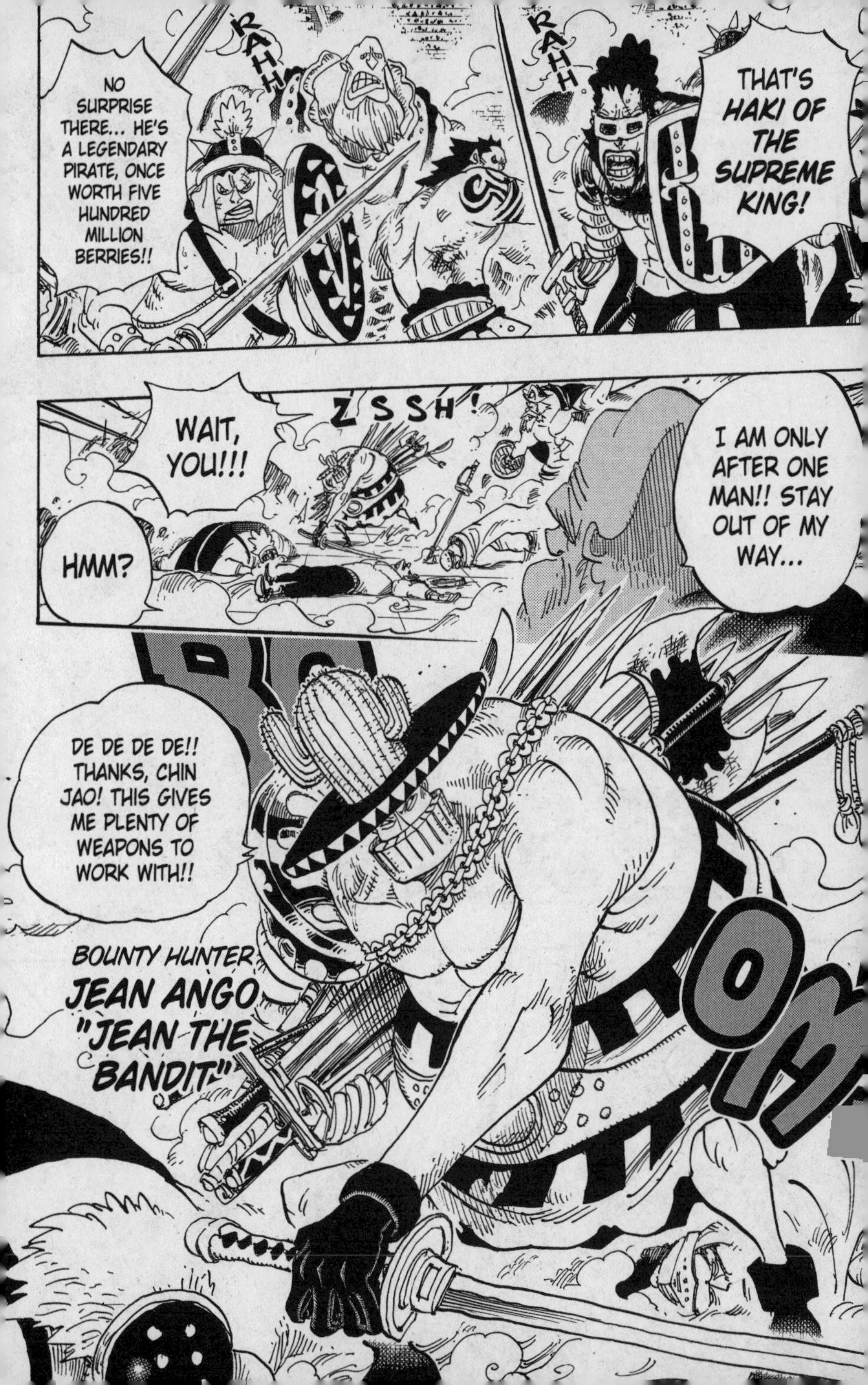
RAHH
THAT'S HAKI OF THE SUPREME KING!
RAHH
NO SURPRISE THERE... HE'S A LEGENDARY PIRATE, ONCE WORTH FIVE HUNDRED MILLION BERRIES!!
I AM ONLY AFTER ONE MAN!! STAY OUT OF MY WAY...
ZSSH!
WAIT, YOU!!!
HMM?
DE DE DE DE!! THANKS, CHIN JAO! THIS GIVES ME PLENTY OF WEAPONS TO WORK WITH!!
BOUNTY HUNTER JEAN ANGO "JEAN THE BANDIT"

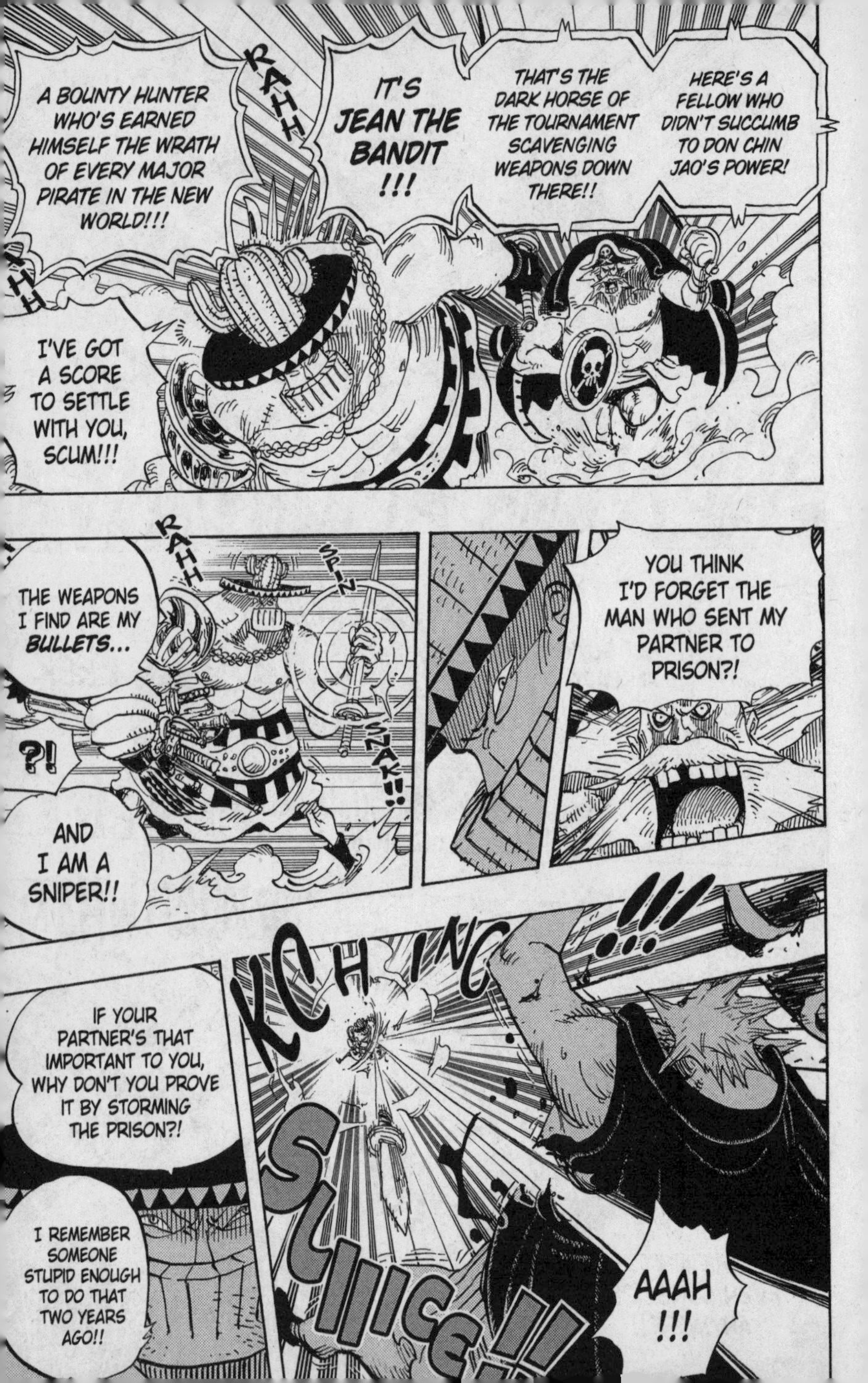
HERE'S A FELLOW WHO DIDN'T SUCCUMB TO DON CHIN JAO'S POWER!
THAT'S THE DARK HORSE OF THE TOURNAMENT SCAVENGING WEAPONS DOWN THERE!!
IT'S JEAN THE BANDIT!!!
RAHHH
A BOUNTY HUNTER WHO'S EARNED HIMSELF THE WRATH OF EVERY MAJOR PIRATE IN THE NEW WORLD!!!
I'VE GOT A SCORE TO SETTLE WITH YOU, SCUM!!!
YOU THINK I'D FORGET THE MAN WHO SENT MY PARTNER TO PRISON?!
RAHH
SPIN
THE WEAPONS I FIND ARE MY BULLETS...
SNAK!!
?!
AND I AM A SNIPER!!
...!!!
KCHING
IF YOUR PARTNER'S THAT IMPORTANT TO YOU, WHY DON'T YOU PROVE IT BY STORMING THE PRISON?!
SLIIICE!!
AAAH!!!
I REMEMBER SOMEONE STUPID ENOUGH TO DO THAT TWO YEARS AGO!!

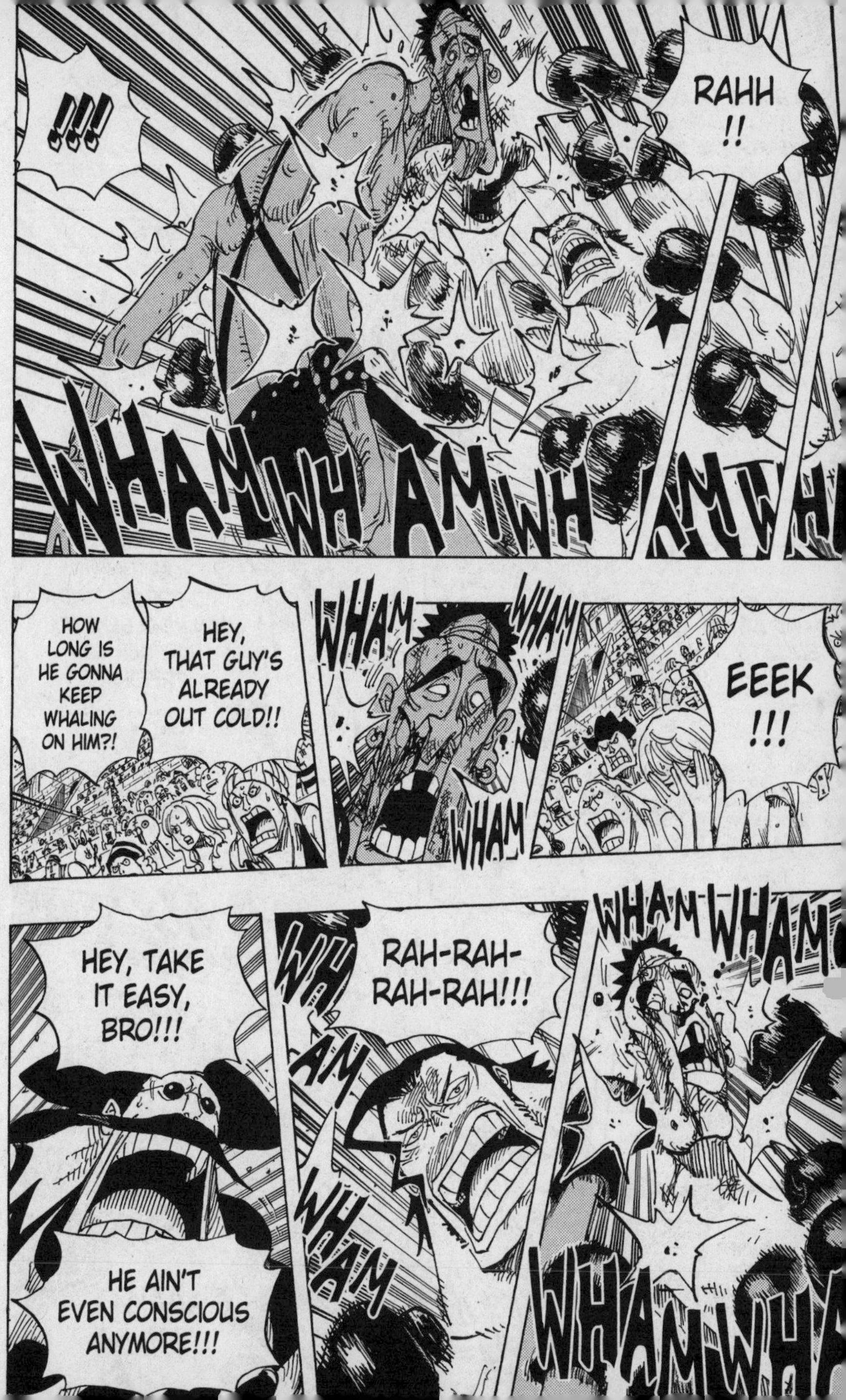
RAHH!!
!!!
WHAM WHAM WHAM WHAM
EEEK!!!
WHAM
WHAM
WHAM
HEY, THAT GUY'S ALREADY OUT COLD!!
HOW LONG IS HE GONNA KEEP WHALING ON HIM?!
WHAM WHAM
WHAM-WHA
RAH-RAH-RAH-RAH!!!
WHAM
WHAM
HEY, TAKE IT EASY, BRO!!!
HE AIN'T EVEN CONSCIOUS ANYMORE!!!

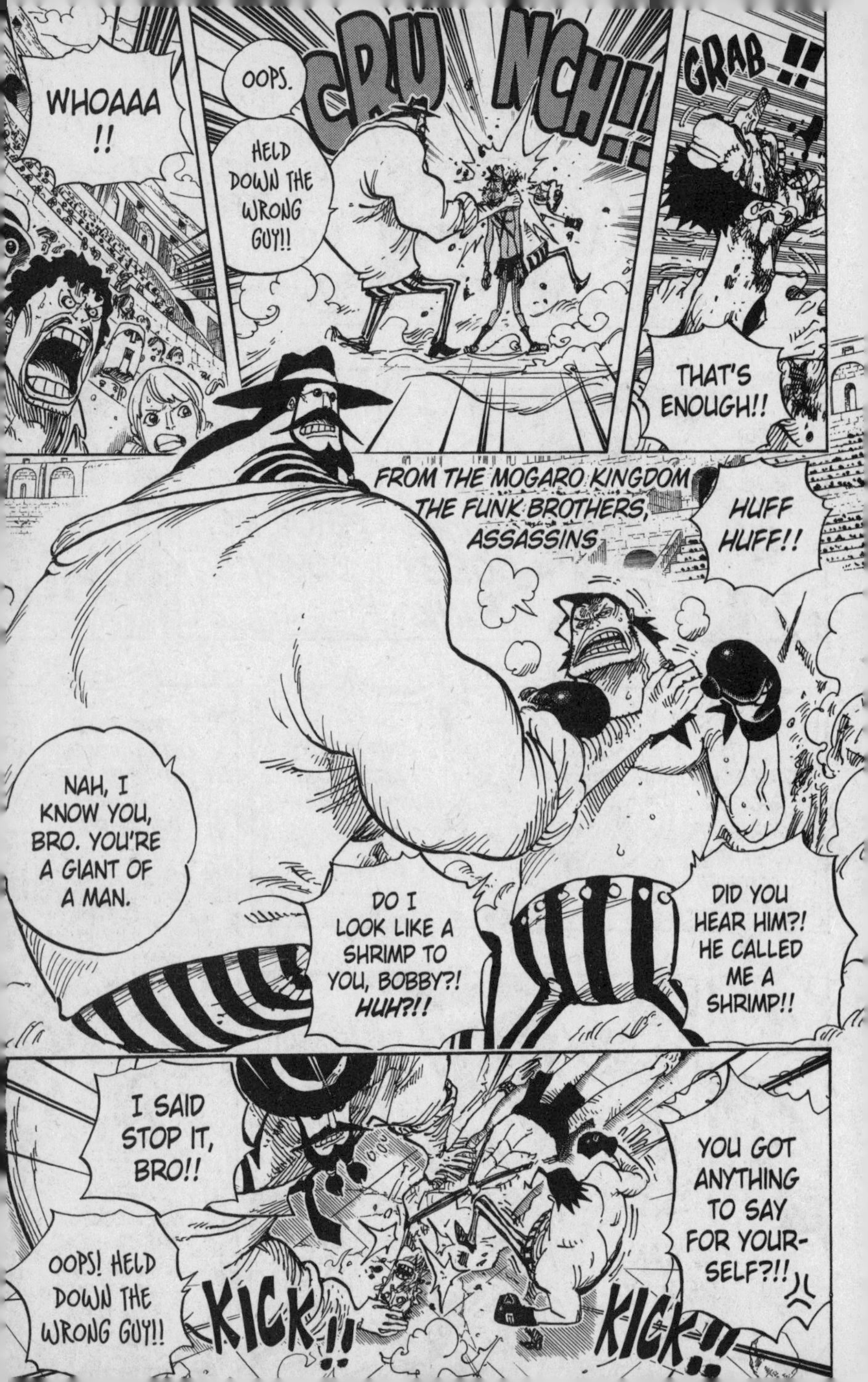
GRAB!!
THAT'S ENOUGH!!
CRUNCH!!
OOPS.
HELD DOWN THE WRONG GUY!!
WHOAAA!!
HUFF HUFF!!
FROM THE MOGARO KINGDOM THE FUNK BROTHERS, ASSASSINS
DID YOU HEAR HIM?! HE CALLED ME A SHRIMP!!
DO I LOOK LIKE A SHRIMP TO YOU, BOBBY?! HUH?!!
NAH, I KNOW YOU, BRO. YOU'RE A GIANT OF A MAN.
YOU GOT ANYTHING TO SAY FOR YOURSELF?!!
I SAID STOP IT, BRO!!
KICK!!
KICK!!
OOPS! HELD DOWN THE WRONG GUY!!

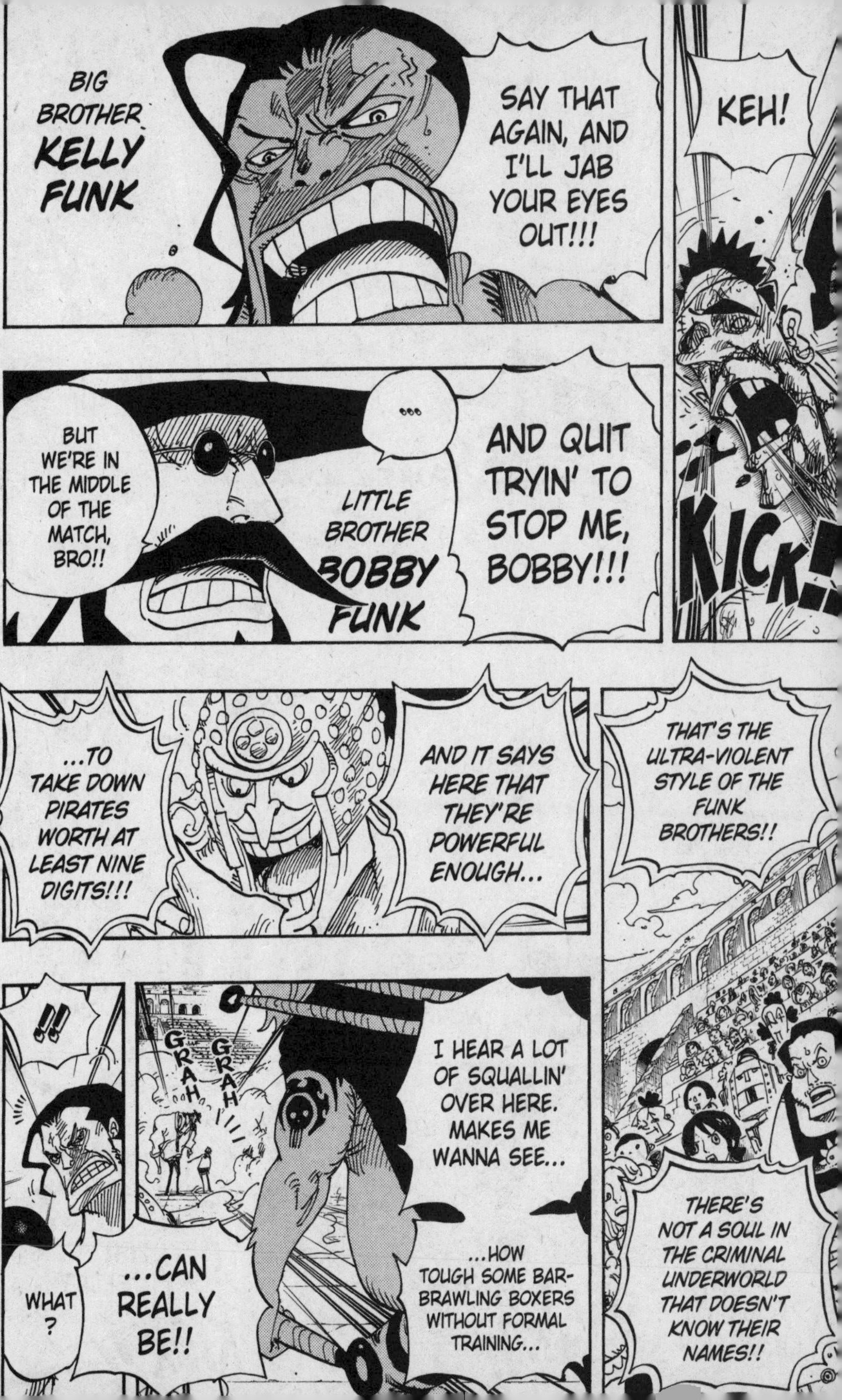
KEH!
KICK!!
SAY THAT AGAIN, AND I'LL JAB YOUR EYES OUT!!!
BIG BROTHER KELLY FUNK
...
AND QUIT TRYIN' TO STOP ME, BOBBY!!!
LITTLE BROTHER BOBBY FUNK
BUT WE'RE IN THE MIDDLE OF THE MATCH, BRO!!
THAT'S THE ULTRA-VIOLENT STYLE OF THE FUNK BROTHERS!!
THERE'S NOT A SOUL IN THE CRIMINAL UNDERWORLD THAT DOESN'T KNOW THEIR NAMES!!
AND IT SAYS HERE THAT THEY'RE POWERFUL ENOUGH...
...TO TAKE DOWN PIRATES WORTH AT LEAST NINE DIGITS!!!
I HEAR A LOT OF SQUALLIN' OVER HERE. MAKES ME WANNA SEE...
GRAH
GRAH
...HOW TOUGH SOME BAR-BRAWLING BOXERS WITHOUT FORMAL TRAINING...
...CAN REALLY BE!!
!!
WHAT ?

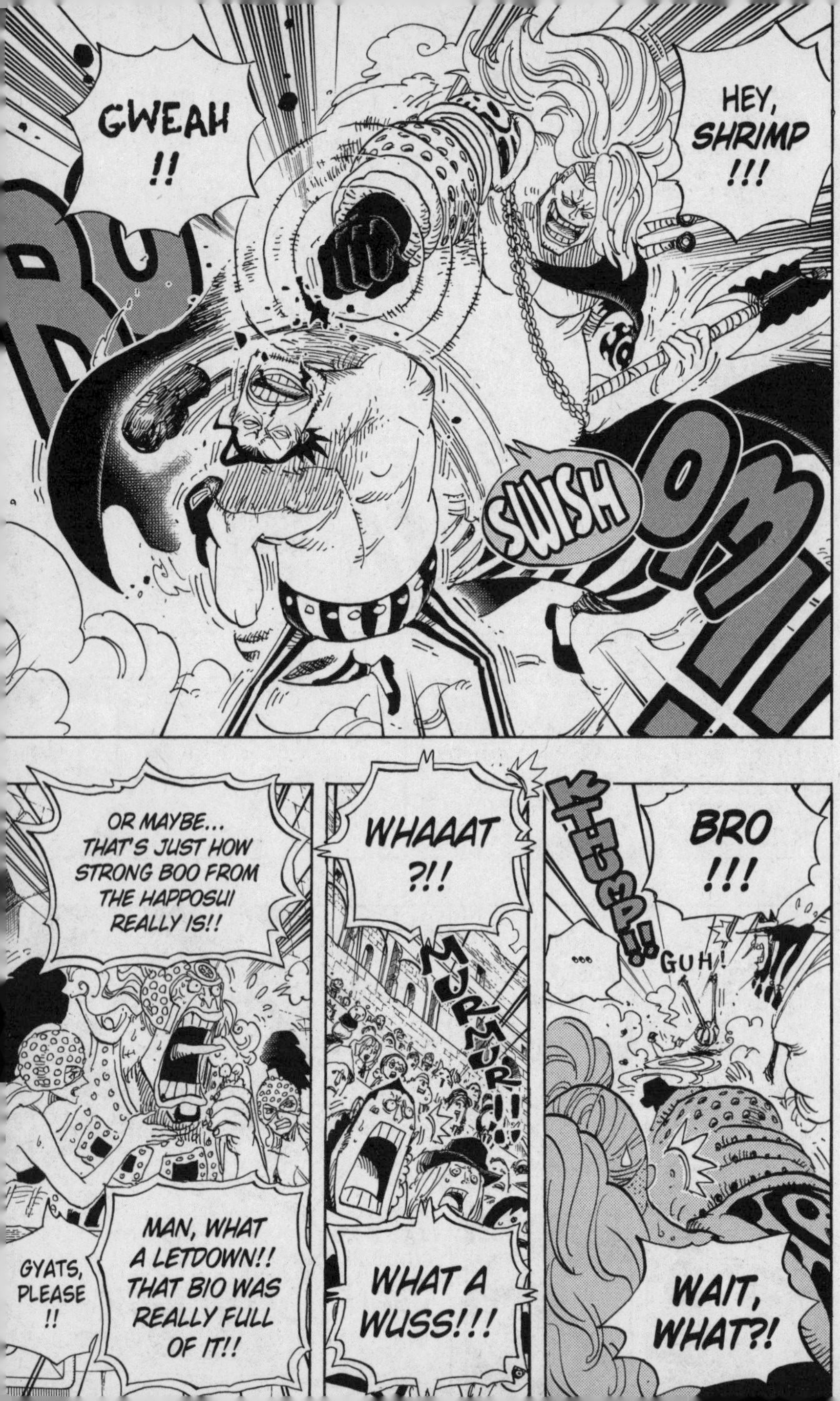
HEY, SHRIMP !!!
GWEAH !!
SWISH
BRO !!!
KTHUMP!!
...
GUH!
WAIT, WHAT?!
WHAAAT ?!!
MURMUR!!
WHAT A WUSS!!!
OR MAYBE... THAT'S JUST HOW STRONG BOO FROM THE HAPPOSUI REALLY IS!!
MAN, WHAT A LETDOWN!! THAT BIO WAS REALLY FULL OF IT!!
GYATS, PLEASE !!

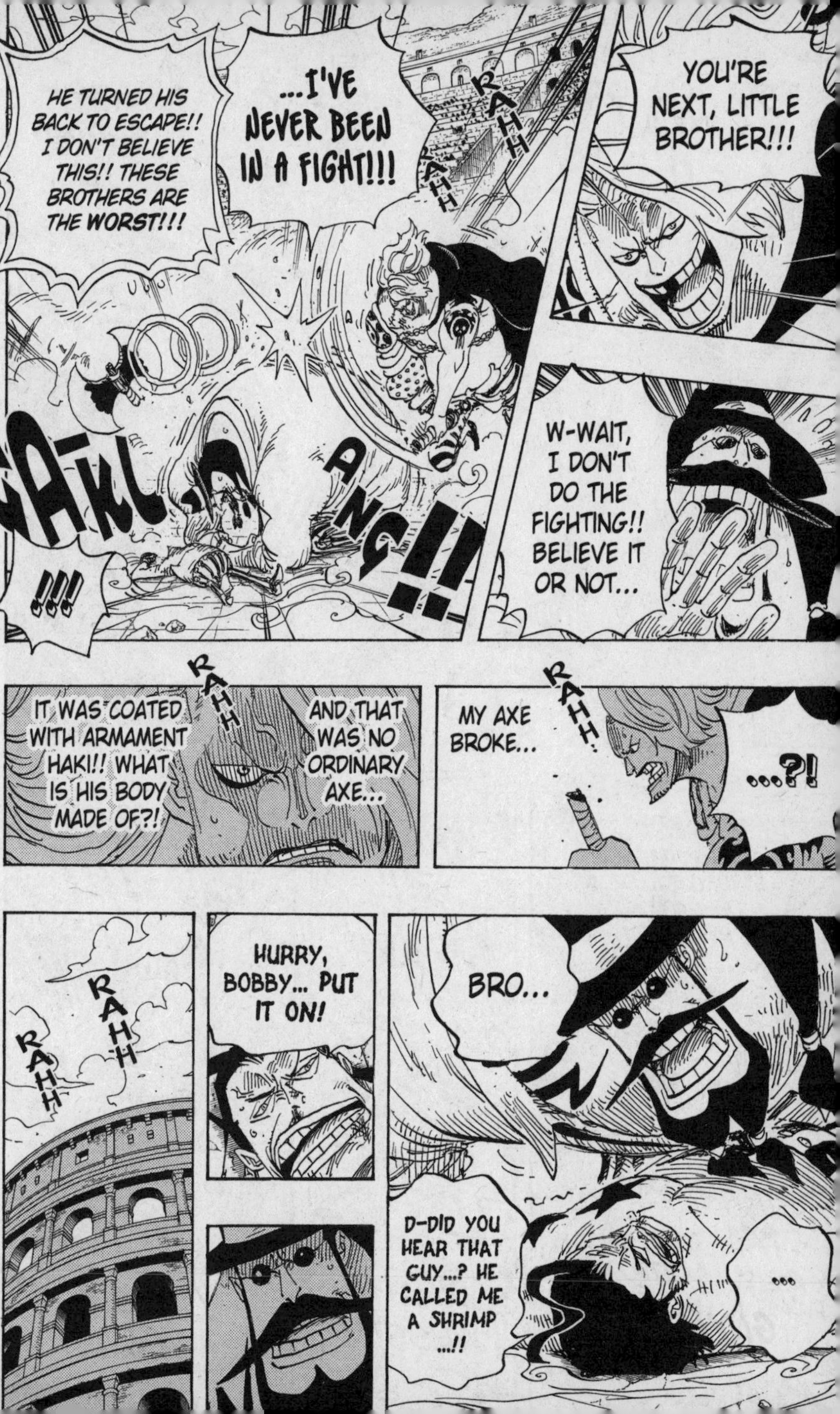
YOU'RE NEXT, LITTLE BROTHER!!!
W-WAIT, I DON'T DO THE FIGHTING!! BELIEVE IT OR NOT...
RAHH
RAHH
...I'VE NEVER BEEN IN A FIGHT!!!
HE TURNED HIS BACK TO ESCAPE!! I DON'T BELIEVE THIS!! THESE BROTHERS ARE THE WORST!!!
ANG!!
GAKI!!!
RAHH
MY AXE BROKE...
...?!
RAHH
AND THAT WAS NO ORDINARY AXE...
IT WAS COATED WITH ARMAMENT HAKI!! WHAT IS HIS BODY MADE OF?!
BRO...
D-DID YOU HEAR THAT GUY...? HE CALLED ME A SHRIMP ...!!
...
HURRY, BOBBY... PUT IT ON!
RAHH
RAHH

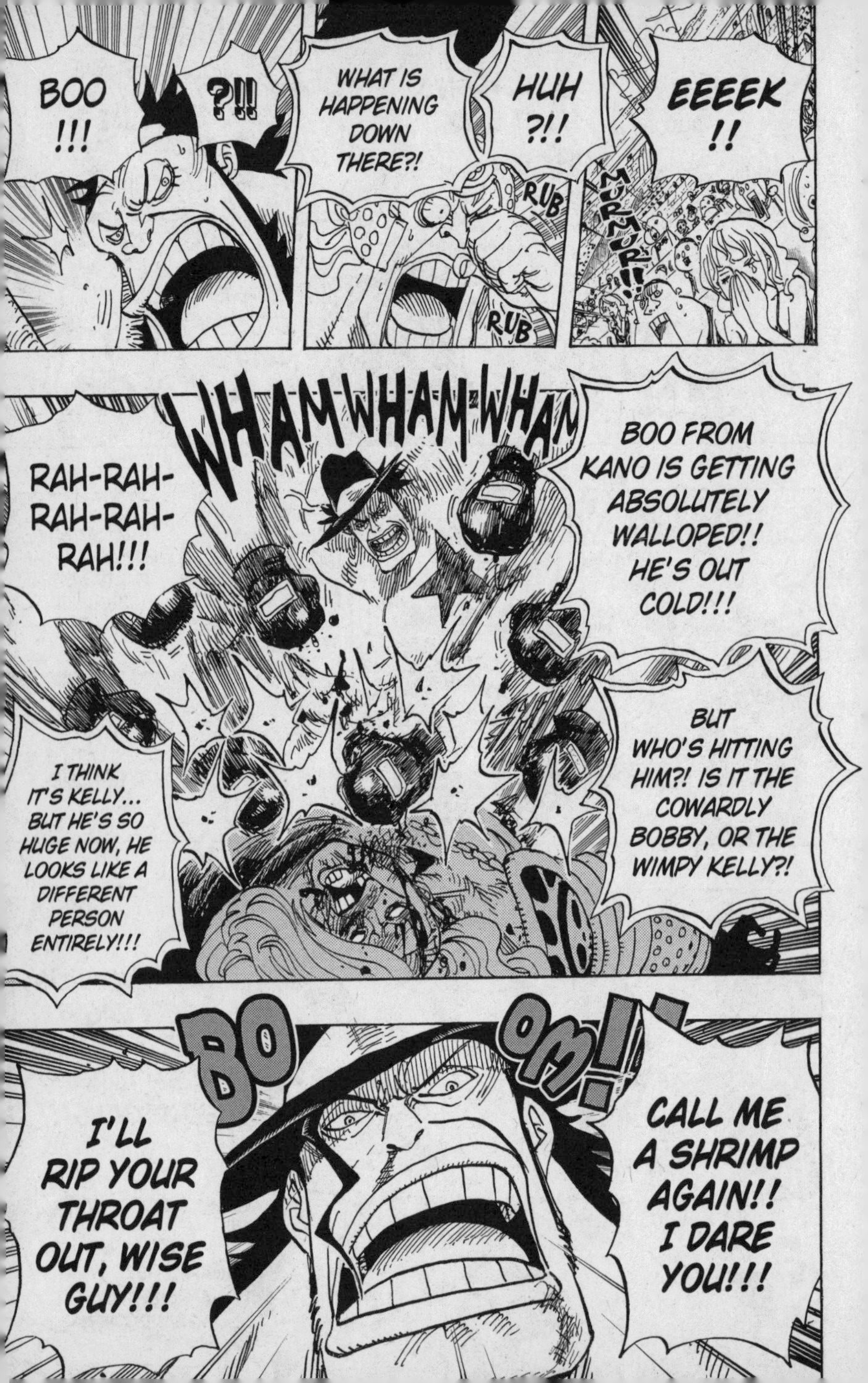
EEEEK !!
MURMUR!!
HUH ?!!
WHAT IS HAPPENING DOWN THERE?!
RUB
RUB
?!!
BOO !!!
BOO FROM KANO IS GETTING ABSOLUTELY WALLOPED!! HE'S OUT COLD!!!
WHAM WHAM WHAM
RAH-RAH-RAH-RAH-RAH!!!
BUT WHO'S HITTING HIM?! IS IT THE COWARDLY BOBBY, OR THE WIMPY KELLY?!
I THINK IT'S KELLY... BUT HE'S SO HUGE NOW, HE LOOKS LIKE A DIFFERENT PERSON ENTIRELY!!!
BOOM!!
CALL ME A SHRIMP AGAIN!! I DARE YOU!!!
I'LL RIP YOUR THROAT OUT, WISE GUY!!!

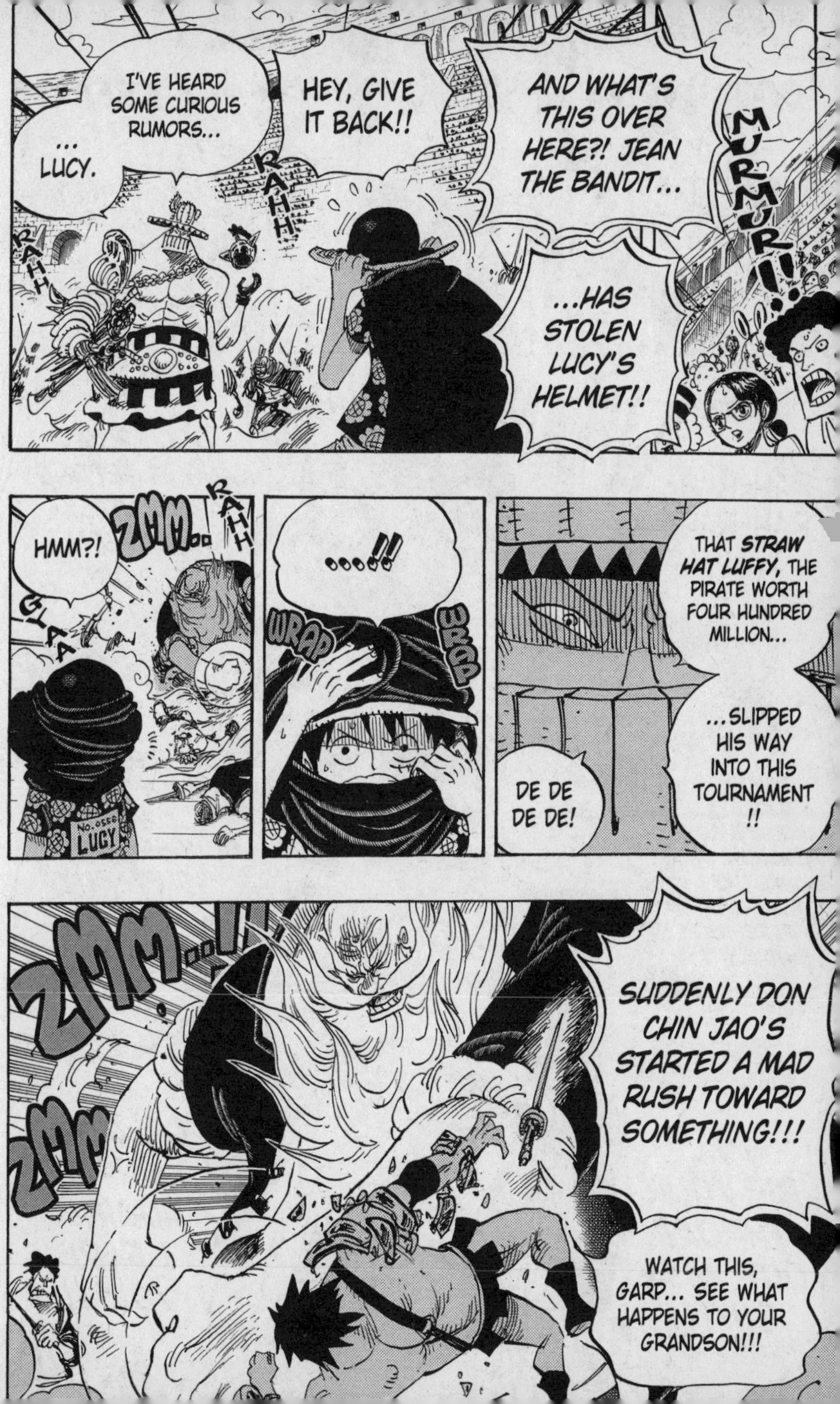
MURMUR!!
AND WHAT'S THIS OVER HERE?! JEAN THE BANDIT...
...HAS STOLEN LUCY'S HELMET!!
HEY, GIVE IT BACK!!
RAHH
I'VE HEARD SOME CURIOUS RUMORS...
... LUCY.
RAHH
THAT STRAW HAT LUFFY, THE PIRATE WORTH FOUR HUNDRED MILLION...
...SLIPPED HIS WAY INTO THIS TOURNAMENT!!
DE DE DE DE!
WRAP
WRAP
....!!
RAHH
ZMM..
HMM?!
GYAA
LUCY
SUDDENLY DON CHIN JAO'S STARTED A MAD RUSH TOWARD SOMETHING!!!
WATCH THIS, GARP... SEE WHAT HAPPENS TO YOUR GRANDSON!!!
ZMM..!!
ZMM

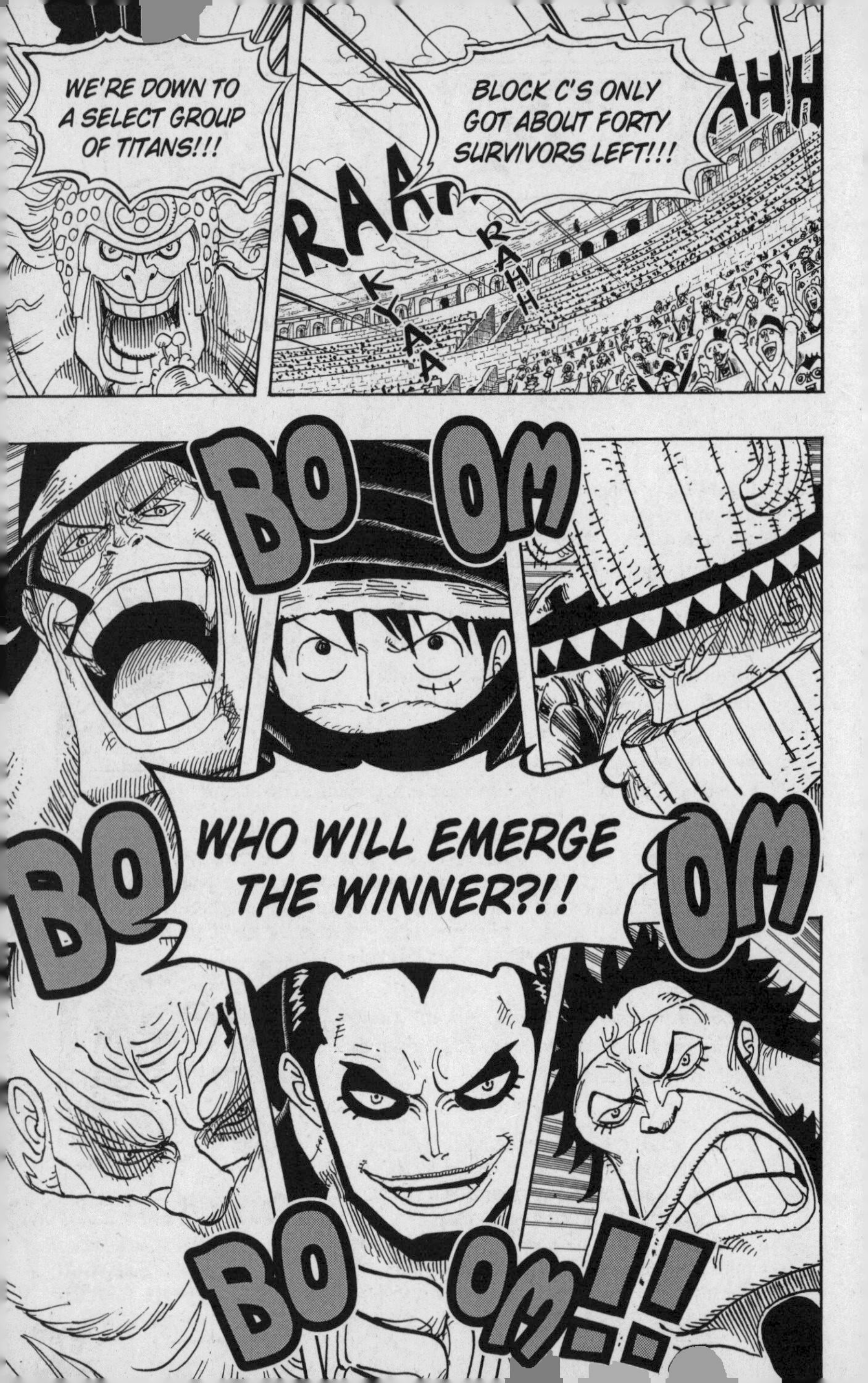
AHH
BLOCK C'S ONLY GOT ABOUT FORTY SURVIVORS LEFT!!!
RAAAH
RAHH
KYAAA
WE'RE DOWN TO A SELECT GROUP OF TITANS!!!
BOOM
BOOM
WHO WILL EMERGE THE WINNER?!!
BOOM!!

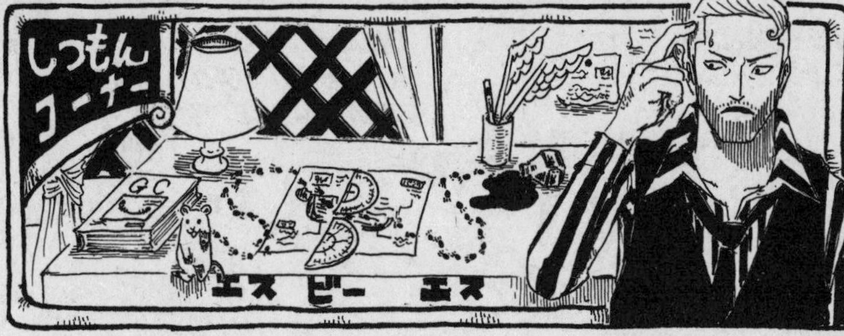
しつもんコーナー
エス ビー エス

(Coral, Fukuoka)

Q: Which one is a cat

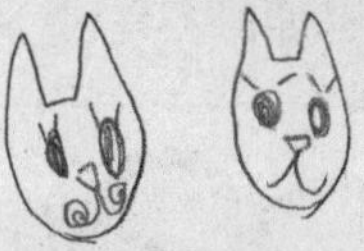

--Milk

A: Okay, um... Hmmm. Which one? Well...they both look like cats to me... Plus, if those aren't cats, what would they be? I'm gonna guess...the left one? Let's check the answer...
They didn't write an answer!!!

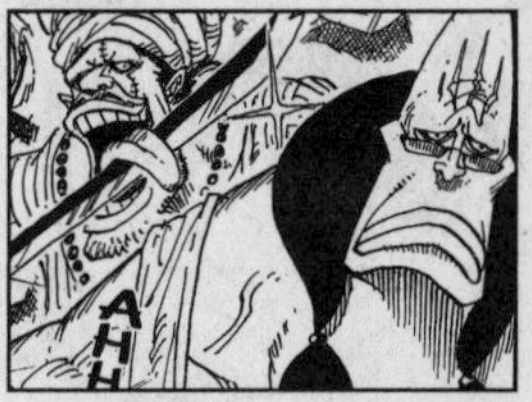

Q: Take this, Odacchi!! Western Lariat!!! And now, my question! In Chapter 704, you introduced the former bounty hunters Abdullah and Jeet. Are they former pro wrestlers, Abdullah the Butcher and Tiger Jeet Singh?! Abdullah's the one who gouged his forehead with forks!! You like pro wrestling, Odacchi? Are you in the pro-wrestling generation?

--Joker

A: That lariat hurt!! Well thanks, you just broke my neck. You're right, that is correct. Japan was in the midst of its pro wrestling craze when I was in elementary school. I loved that stuff, so this is my tribute to the greatest heels who ever menaced the ring, The Butcher and Jeet Singh!!

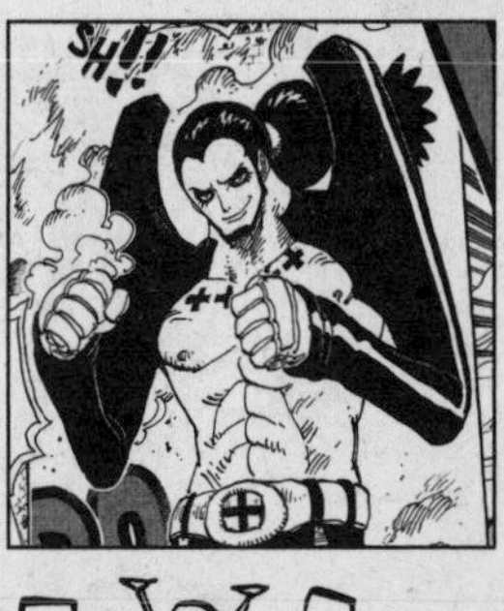

Q: Nice to meet you, Mr. Oda! I've been wondering, is Idea the Boxer based on *Ideon?* That got me really excited, despite my age.

--Astro Robo Sasa (age 38)

A: That's right. I took the idea from the old robot anime show, Ideon. Sorry, I had so many characters to introduce, I started having a bit too much fun with them. It was a robot with extended shoulders like this on the right. It was the very first plastic model I got as a kid.

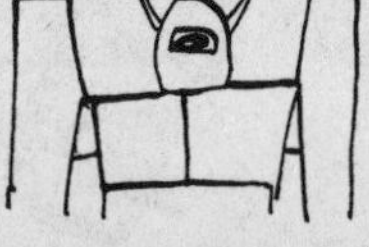

Ideon

Chapter 716:
DON CHIN JAO

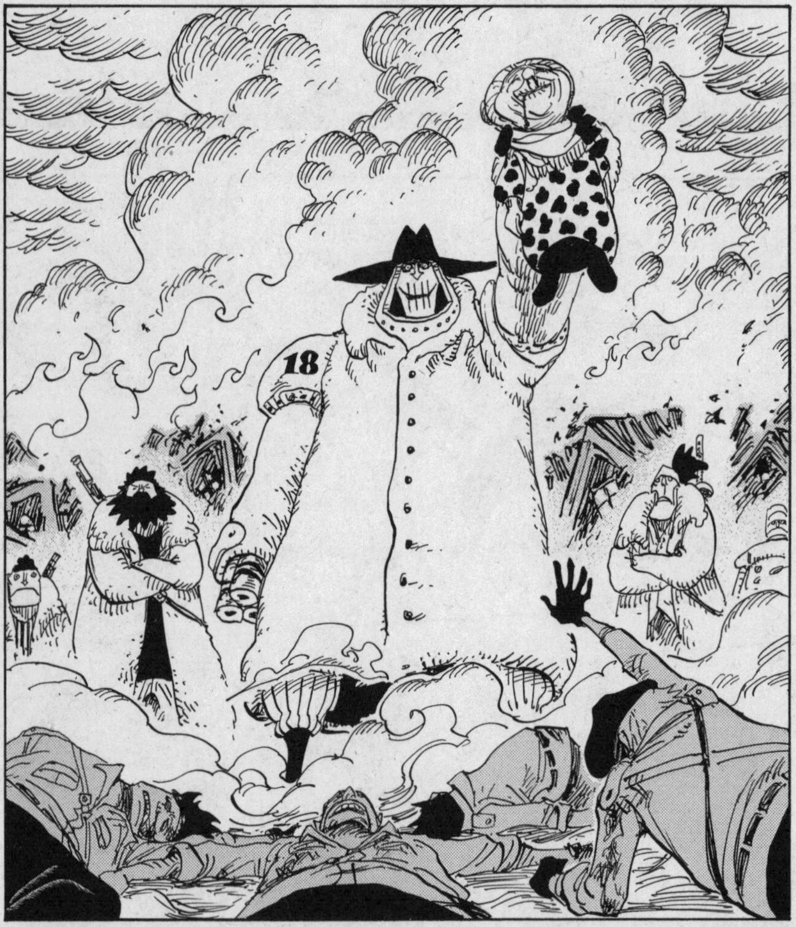
18

CARIBOU'S NEW WORLD KEE HEE HEE, VOL. 34: "BEHOLD THE FATE OF THE GRANDMOTHER OF REVOLUTION ARMY CAPTAIN GABURU"

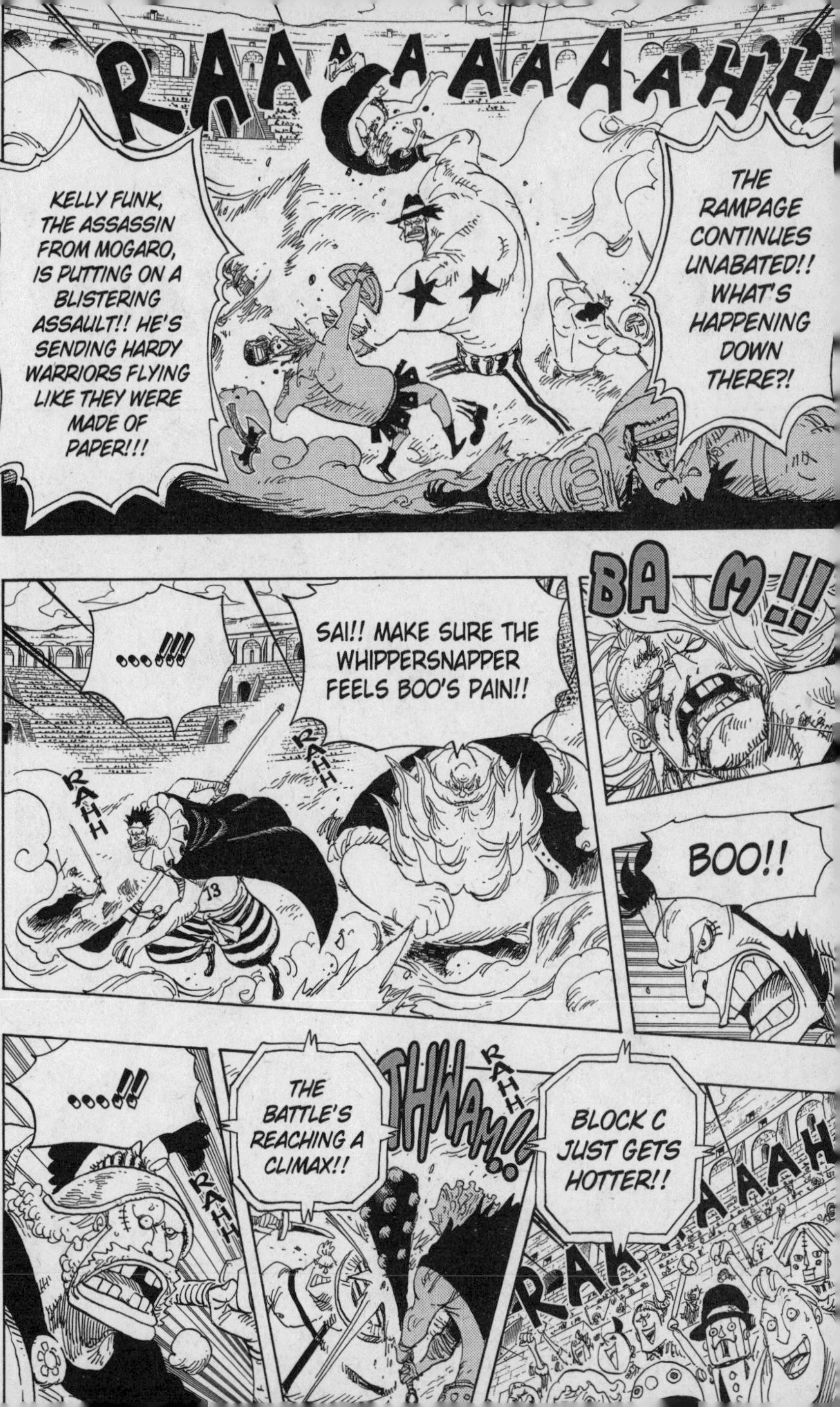
RAAAAAAAAAHH
THE RAMPAGE CONTINUES UNABATED!! WHAT'S HAPPENING DOWN THERE?!
KELLY FUNK, THE ASSASSIN FROM MOGARO, IS PUTTING ON A BLISTERING ASSAULT!! HE'S SENDING HARDY WARRIORS FLYING LIKE THEY WERE MADE OF PAPER!!!
BA-M!!
BOO!!
SAI!! MAKE SURE THE WHIPPERSNAPPER FEELS BOO'S PAIN!!
RAHH
...!!!
RAHH
BLOCK C JUST GETS HOTTER!!
RAAAAAAH
THWAM!!
RAHH
THE BATTLE'S REACHING A CLIMAX!!
...!!
RAHH

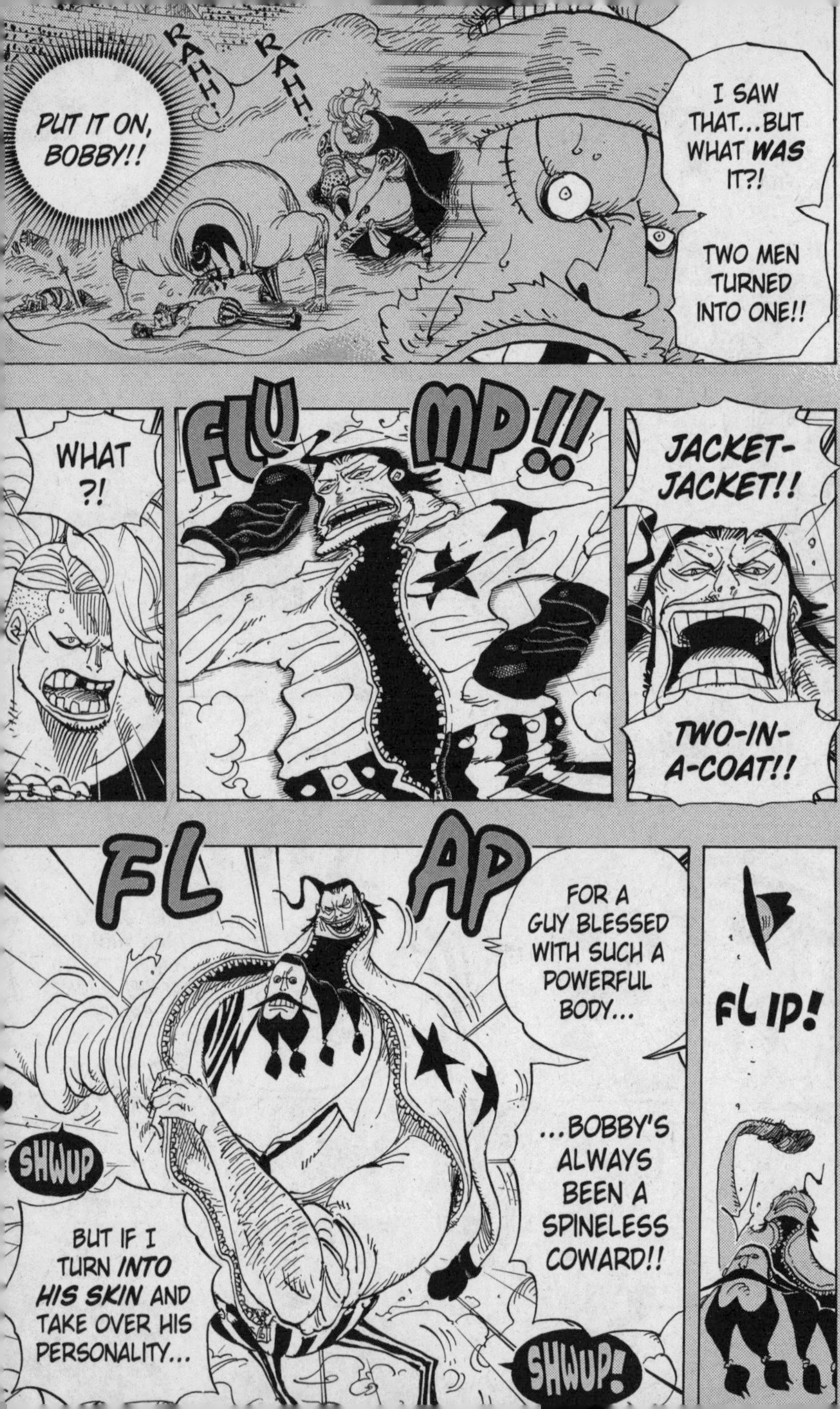
I SAW THAT...BUT WHAT WAS IT?!
TWO MEN TURNED INTO ONE!!
RAHH!
RAHH!
PUT IT ON, BOBBY!!
JACKET-JACKET!!
TWO-IN-A-COAT!!
FLUMP!!
WHAT?!
FLIP!
FLAP
FOR A GUY BLESSED WITH SUCH A POWERFUL BODY...
...BOBBY'S ALWAYS BEEN A SPINELESS COWARD!!
SHWUP
BUT IF I TURN INTO HIS SKIN AND TAKE OVER HIS PERSONALITY...
SHWUP!

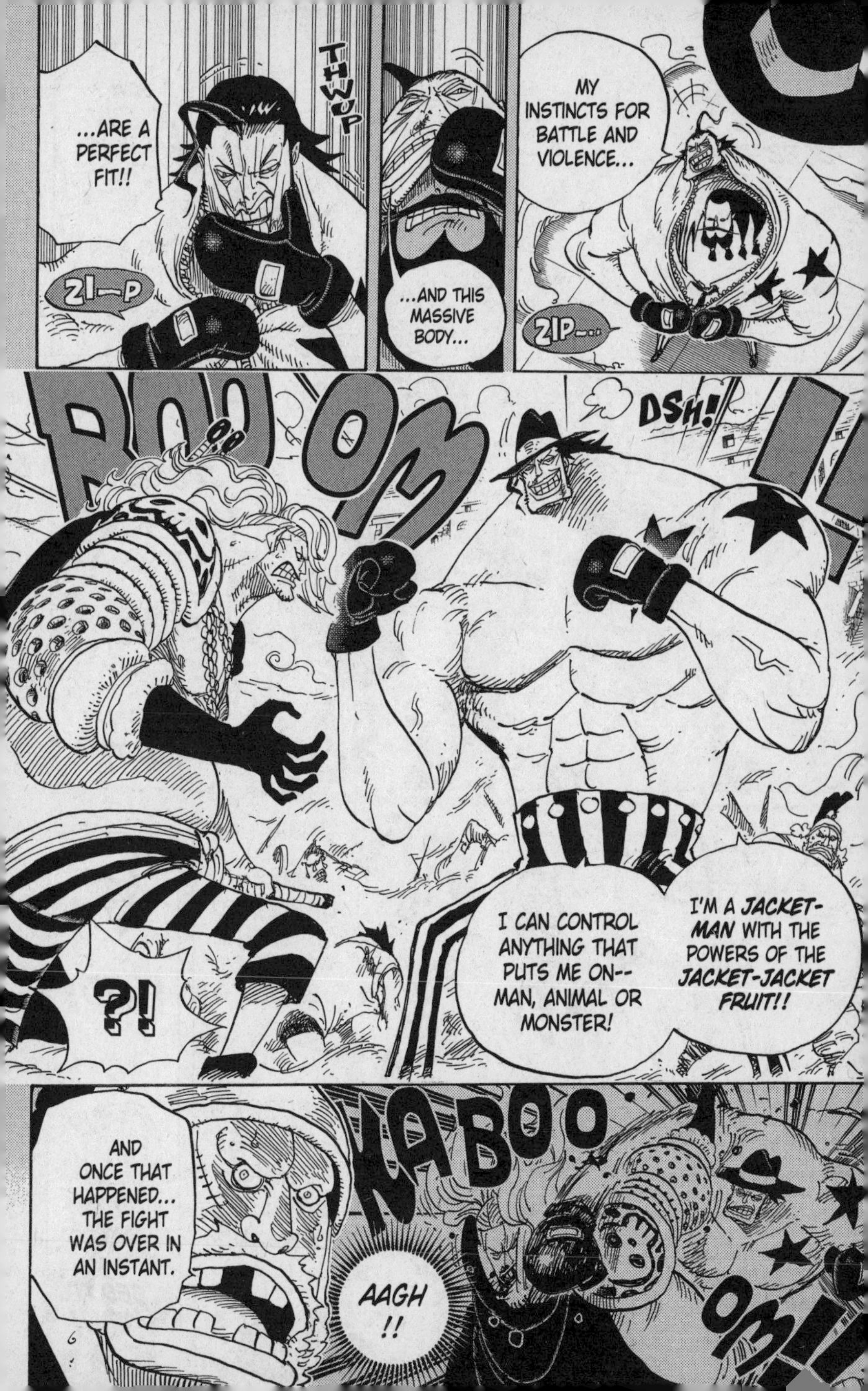
MY INSTINCTS FOR BATTLE AND VIOLENCE...
ZIP...
THWUP
...AND THIS MASSIVE BODY...
...ARE A PERFECT FIT!!
ZI--P
DSH!
BOOOM!!
I'M A *JACKET-MAN* WITH THE POWERS OF THE *JACKET-JACKET FRUIT!!*
I CAN CONTROL ANYTHING THAT PUTS ME ON-- MAN, ANIMAL OR MONSTER!
?!
KABOOOM!!
AAGH !!
AND ONCE THAT HAPPENED... THE FIGHT WAS OVER IN AN INSTANT.

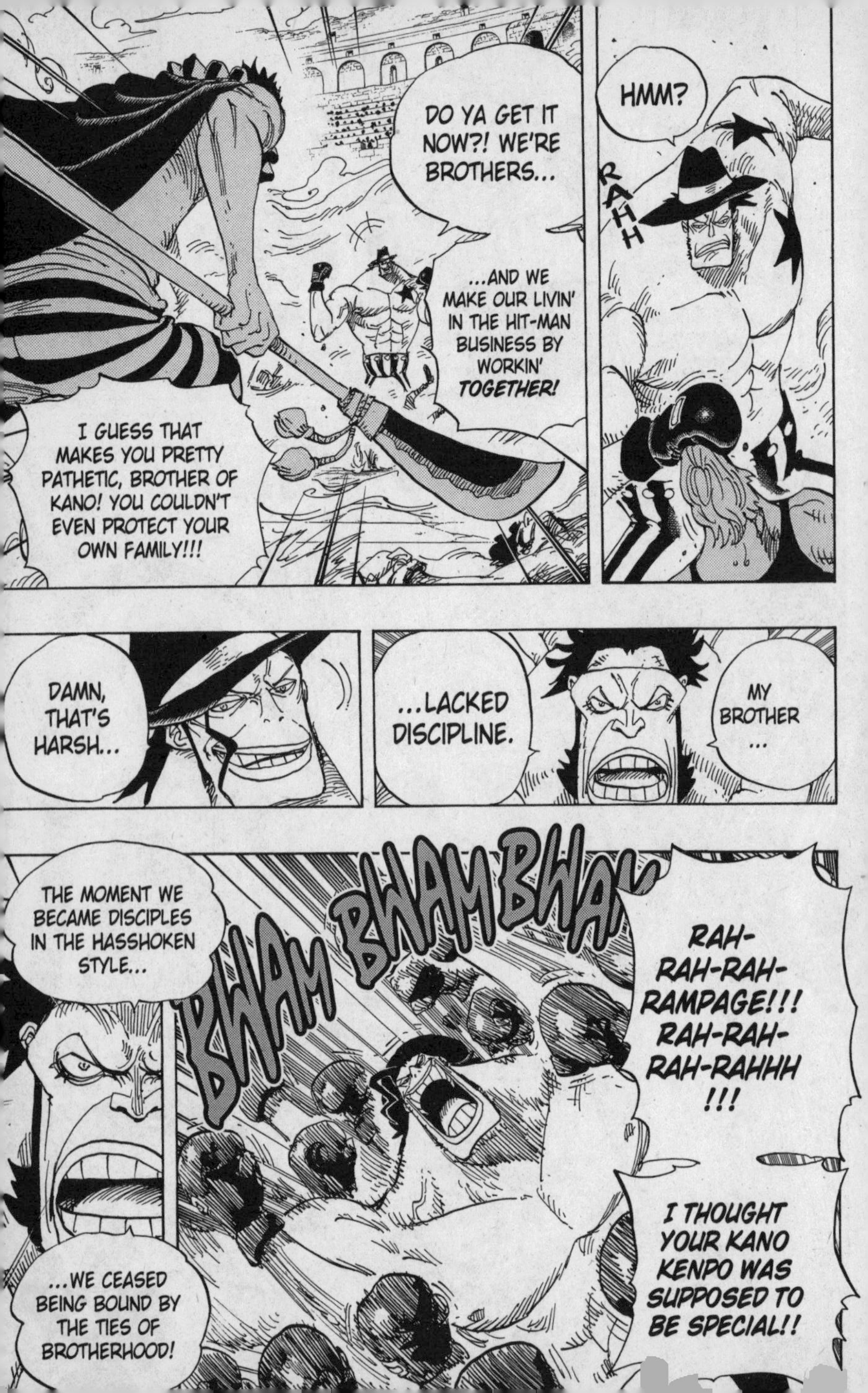
HMM?
RAHH
DO YA GET IT NOW?! WE'RE BROTHERS...
...AND WE MAKE OUR LIVIN' IN THE HIT-MAN BUSINESS BY WORKIN' *TOGETHER!*
I GUESS THAT MAKES YOU PRETTY PATHETIC, BROTHER OF KANO! YOU COULDN'T EVEN PROTECT YOUR OWN FAMILY!!!
MY BROTHER...
...LACKED DISCIPLINE.
DAMN, THAT'S HARSH...
RAH-RAH-RAH-RAMPAGE!!! RAH-RAH-RAH-RAHHH!!!
BHAM BHAM BHAM
THE MOMENT WE BECAME DISCIPLES IN THE HASSHOKEN STYLE...
I THOUGHT YOUR KANO KENPO WAS SUPPOSED TO BE SPECIAL!!
...WE CEASED BEING BOUND BY THE TIES OF BROTHERHOOD!

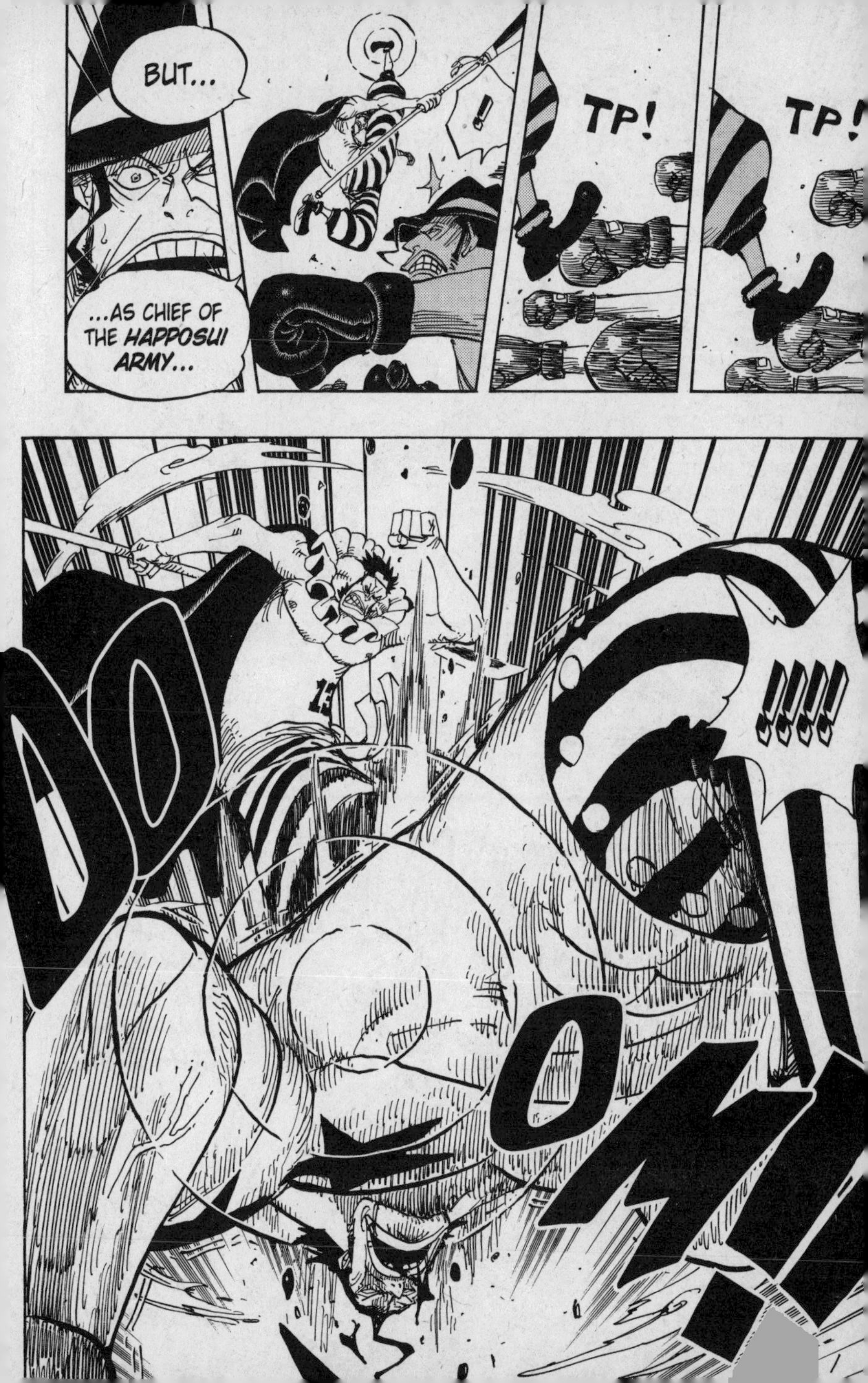
TP!
TP!
!
BUT...
...AS CHIEF OF THE *HAPPOSUI* ARMY...
!!!!
DOOM!!

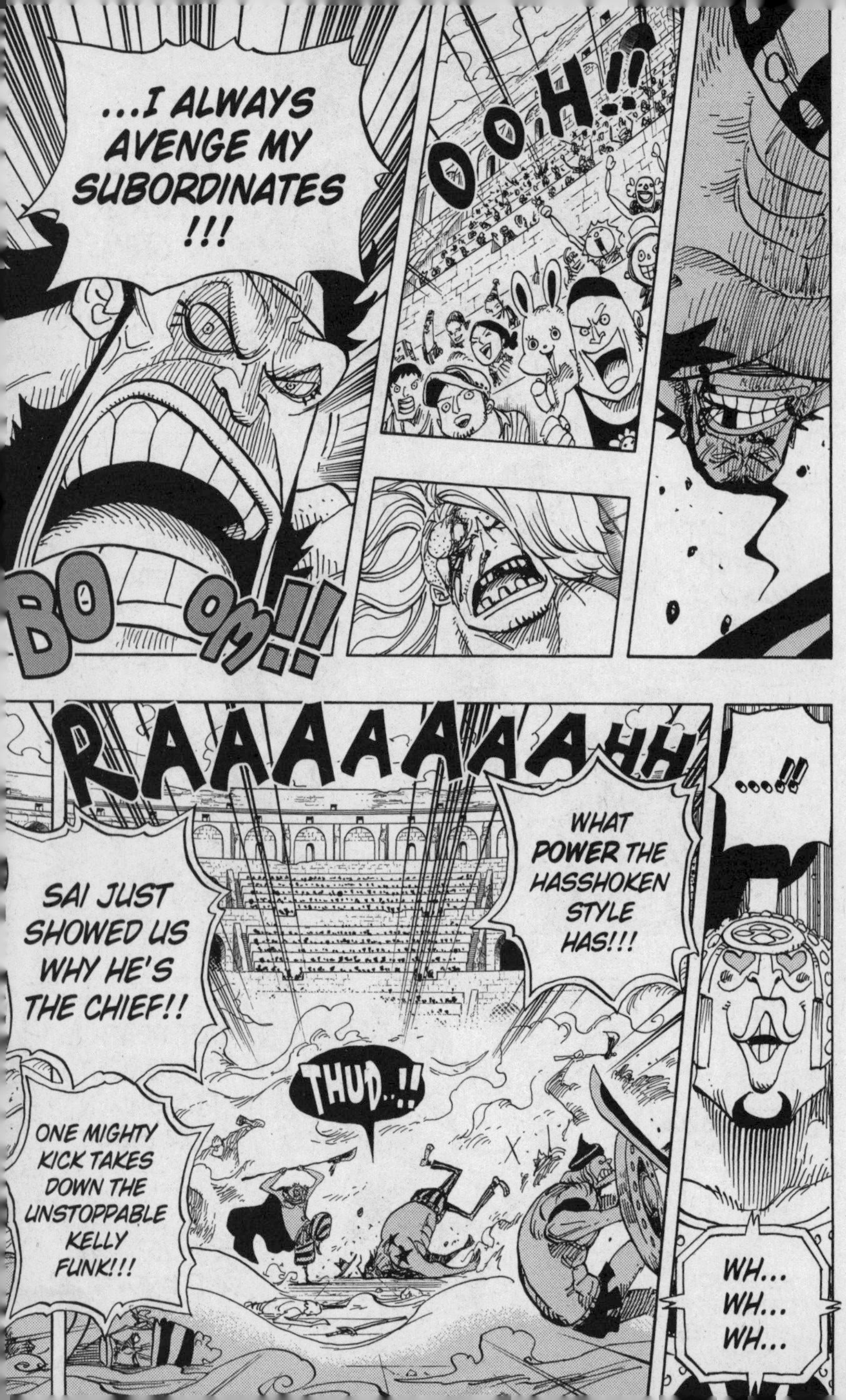
OOOH!!
...I ALWAYS AVENGE MY SUBORDINATES!!!
BOOM!!
...!!
WH... WH... WH...
RAAAAAAAHH
WHAT POWER THE HASSHOKEN STYLE HAS!!!
SAI JUST SHOWED US WHY HE'S THE CHIEF!!
THUD..!!
ONE MIGHTY KICK TAKES DOWN THE UNSTOPPABLE KELLY FUNK!!!

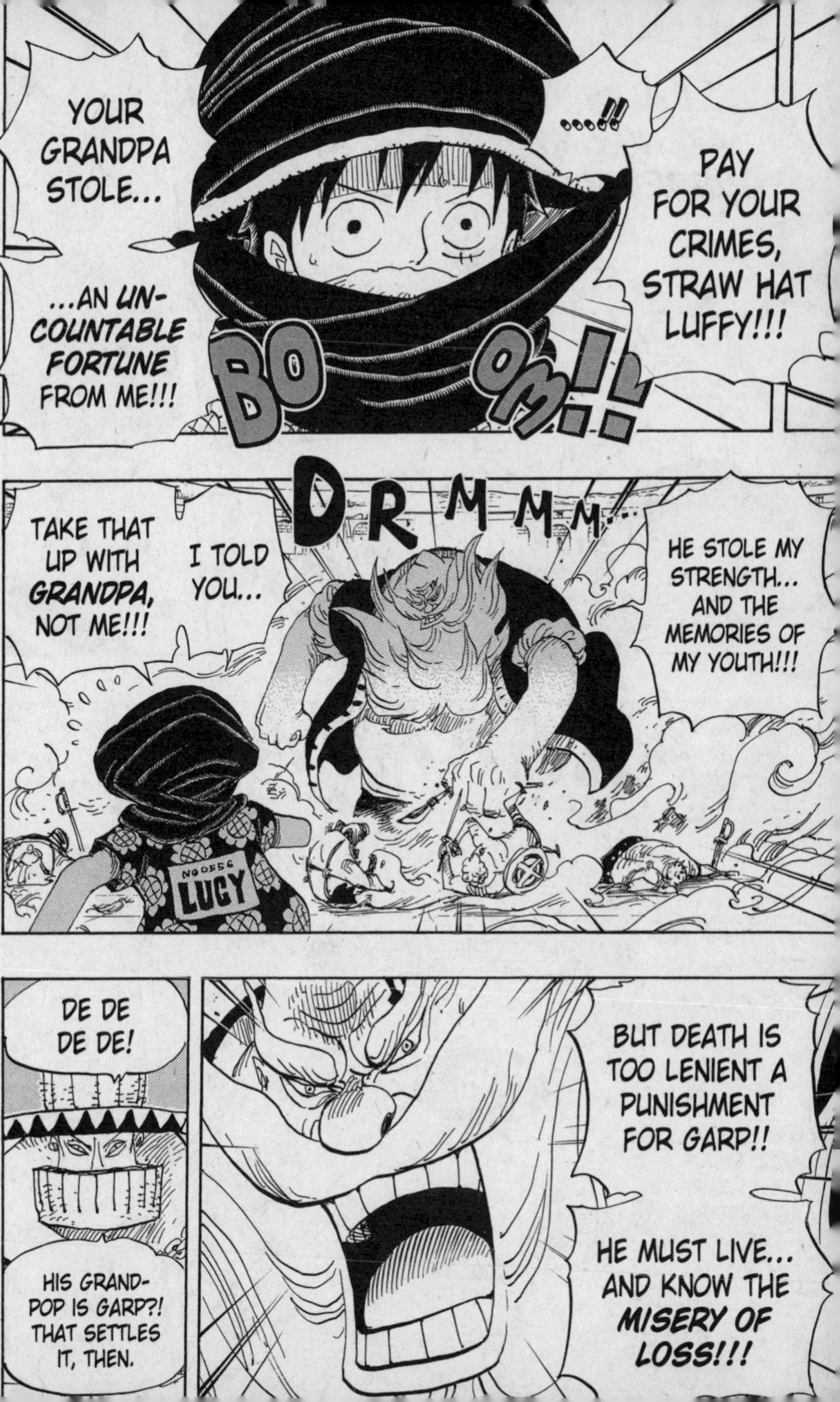
PAY FOR YOUR CRIMES, STRAW HAT LUFFY!!!
....!!
YOUR GRANDPA STOLE...
...AN UN-COUNTABLE FORTUNE FROM ME!!!
BOOM!!
DRMMM...
HE STOLE MY STRENGTH... AND THE MEMORIES OF MY YOUTH!!!
I TOLD YOU...
TAKE THAT UP WITH GRANDPA, NOT ME!!!
LUCY
BUT DEATH IS TOO LENIENT A PUNISHMENT FOR GARP!!
HE MUST LIVE... AND KNOW THE MISERY OF LOSS!!!
DE DE DE DE!
HIS GRAND-POP IS GARP?! THAT SETTLES IT, THEN.

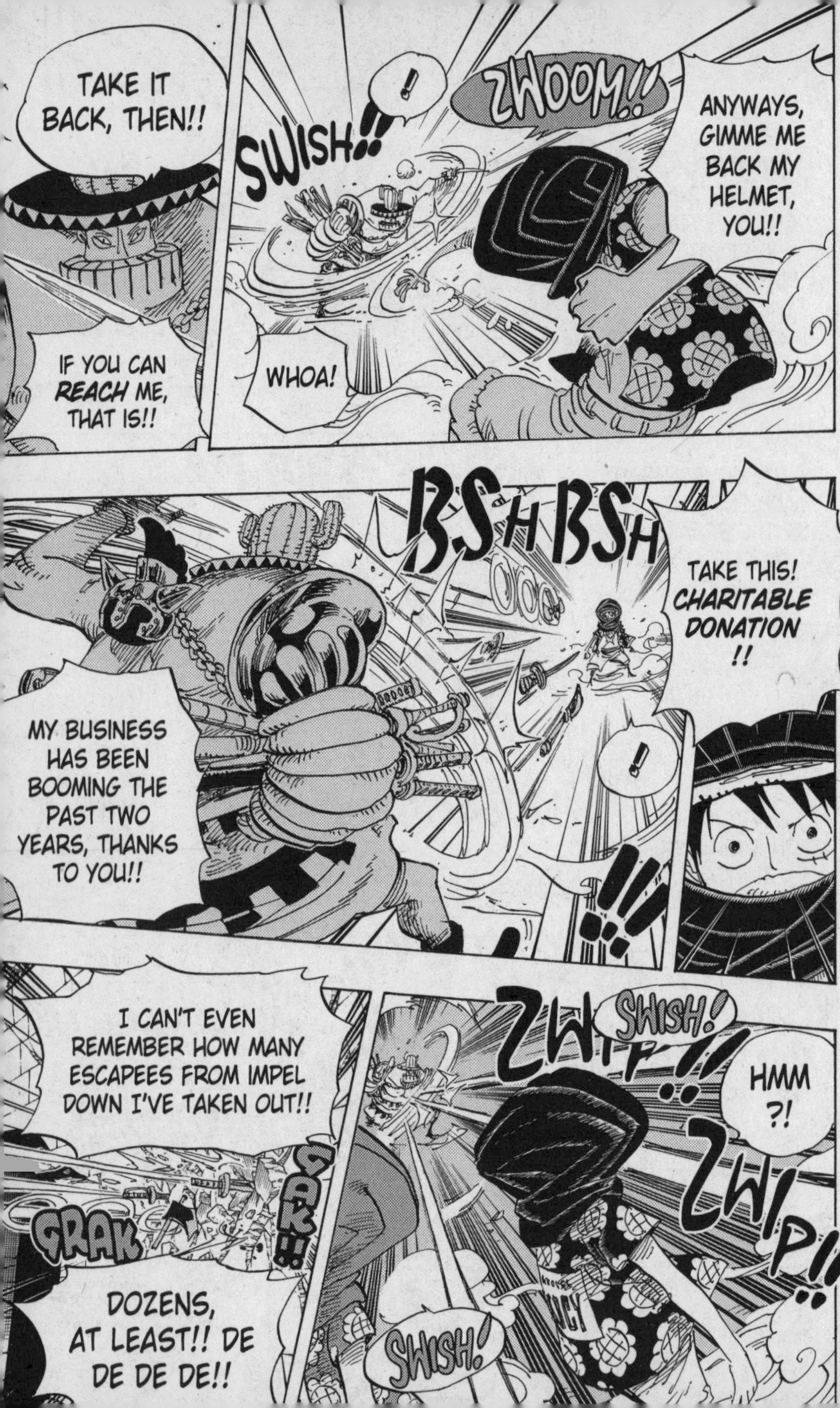
ANYWAYS, GIMME ME BACK MY HELMET, YOU!!
ZWOOM!!
!
SWISH!!
WHOA!
TAKE IT BACK, THEN!!
IF YOU CAN *REACH* ME, THAT IS!!
TAKE THIS! *CHARITABLE DONATION* !!
BSH BSH
!
MY BUSINESS HAS BEEN BOOMING THE PAST TWO YEARS, THANKS TO YOU!!
!!
HMM ?!
ZWIP!!
SWISH!
ZWIP!!
SWISH!
I CAN'T EVEN REMEMBER HOW MANY ESCAPEES FROM IMPEL DOWN I'VE TAKEN OUT!!
GAK!!
GRAK
DOZENS, AT LEAST!! DE DE DE DE!!

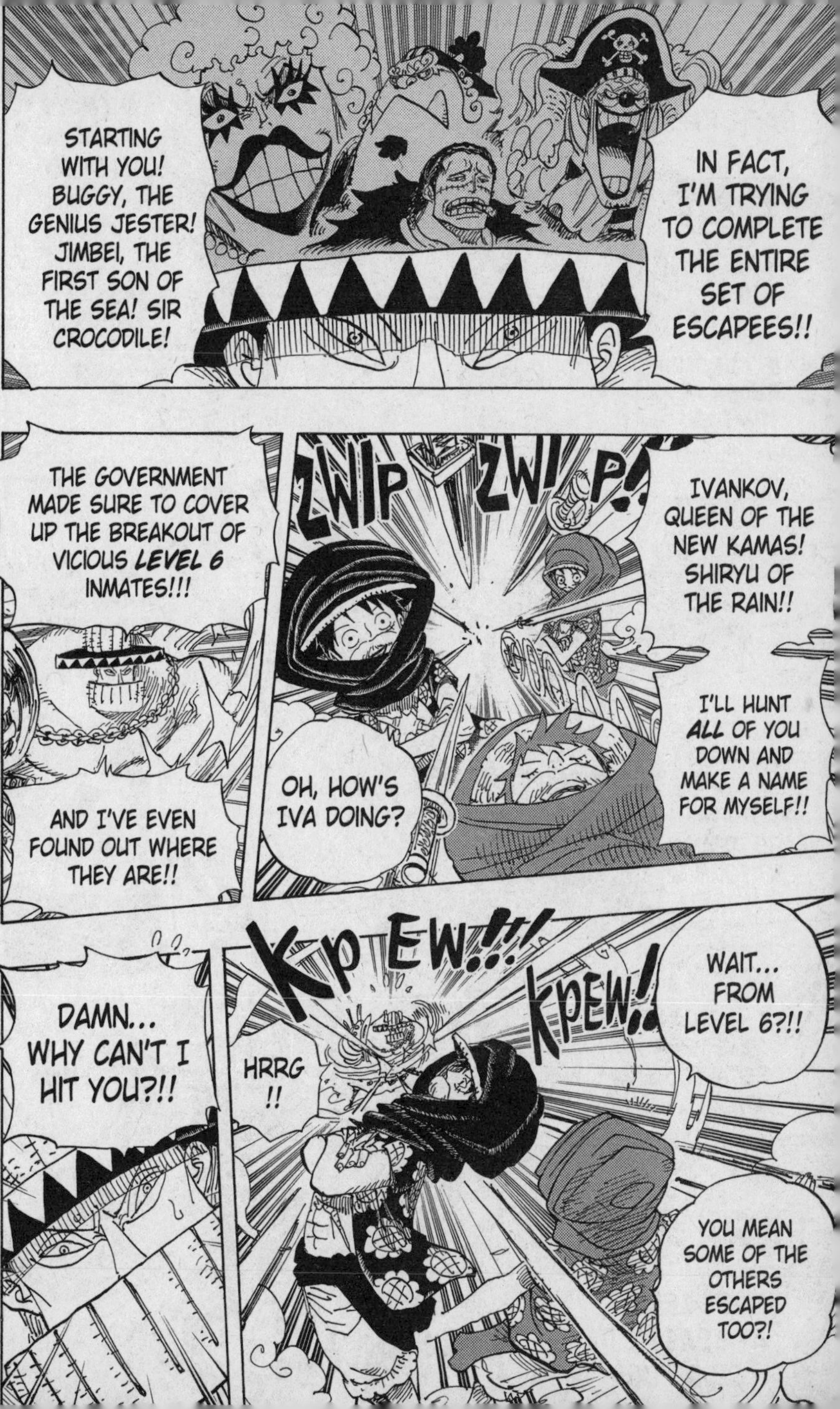
IN FACT, I'M TRYING TO COMPLETE THE ENTIRE SET OF ESCAPEES!!
STARTING WITH YOU! BUGGY, THE GENIUS JESTER! JIMBEI, THE FIRST SON OF THE SEA! SIR CROCODILE!
ZWIP ZWIP!
IVANKOV, QUEEN OF THE NEW KAMAS! SHIRYU OF THE RAIN!!
I'LL HUNT ALL OF YOU DOWN AND MAKE A NAME FOR MYSELF!!
OH, HOW'S IVA DOING?
THE GOVERNMENT MADE SURE TO COVER UP THE BREAKOUT OF VICIOUS LEVEL 6 INMATES!!!
AND I'VE EVEN FOUND OUT WHERE THEY ARE!!
WAIT... FROM LEVEL 6?!!
KPEW!!
KPEW!!!
HRRG!!
YOU MEAN SOME OF THE OTHERS ESCAPED TOO?!
DAMN... WHY CAN'T I HIT YOU?!!

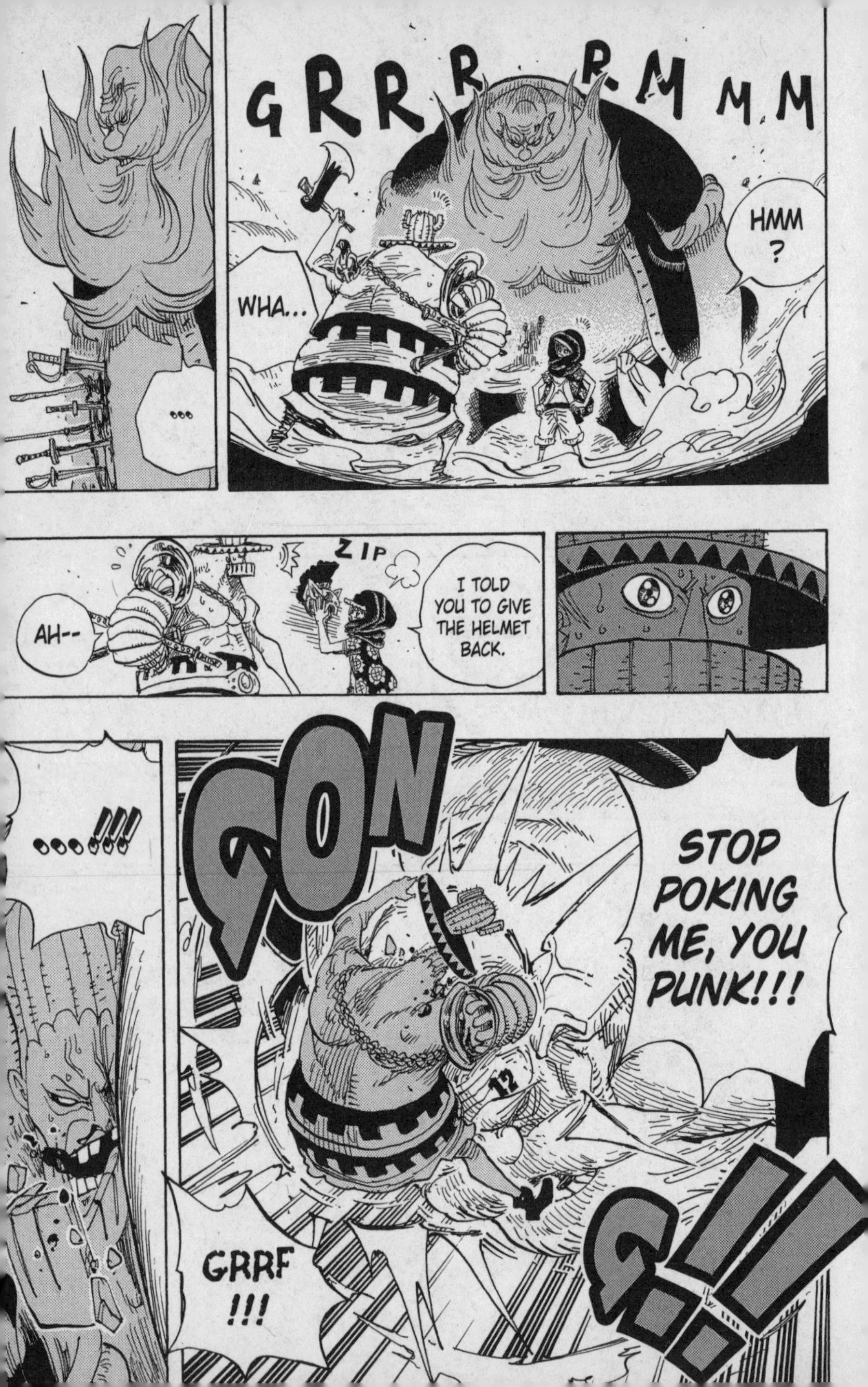
GRRRRMMM
HMM?
WHA...
...
ZIP
I TOLD YOU TO GIVE THE HELMET BACK.
AH--
STOP POKING ME, YOU PUNK!!!
GON
G!!
GRRF!!!
...!!!

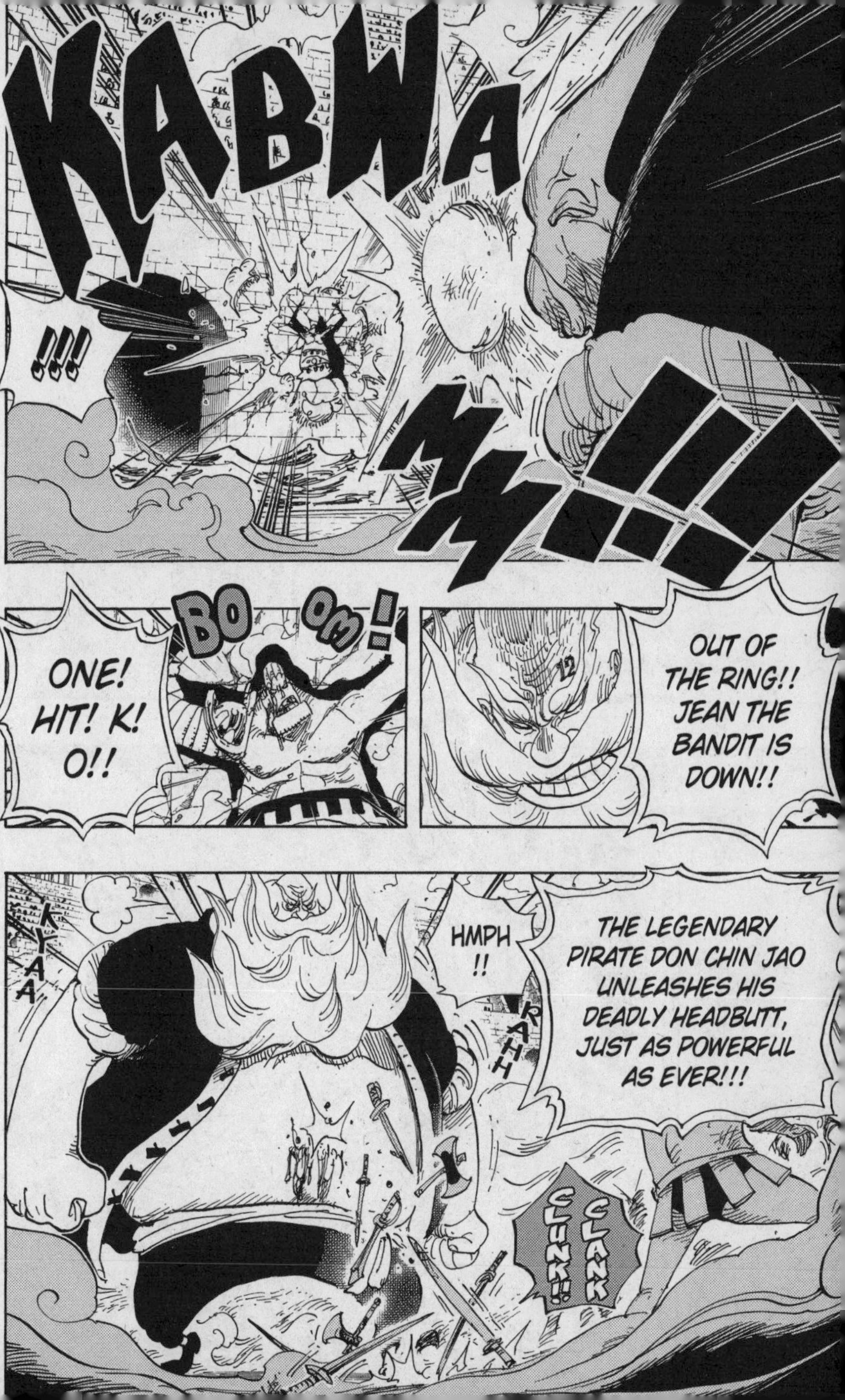
KABWAM!!!!
!!!
OUT OF THE RING!! JEAN THE BANDIT IS DOWN!!
BOOM!
ONE! HIT! K! O!!
THE LEGENDARY PIRATE DON CHIN JAO UNLEASHES HIS DEADLY HEADBUTT, JUST AS POWERFUL AS EVER!!!
RAHH
HMPH !!
KYAA
CLANK
CLUNK!!

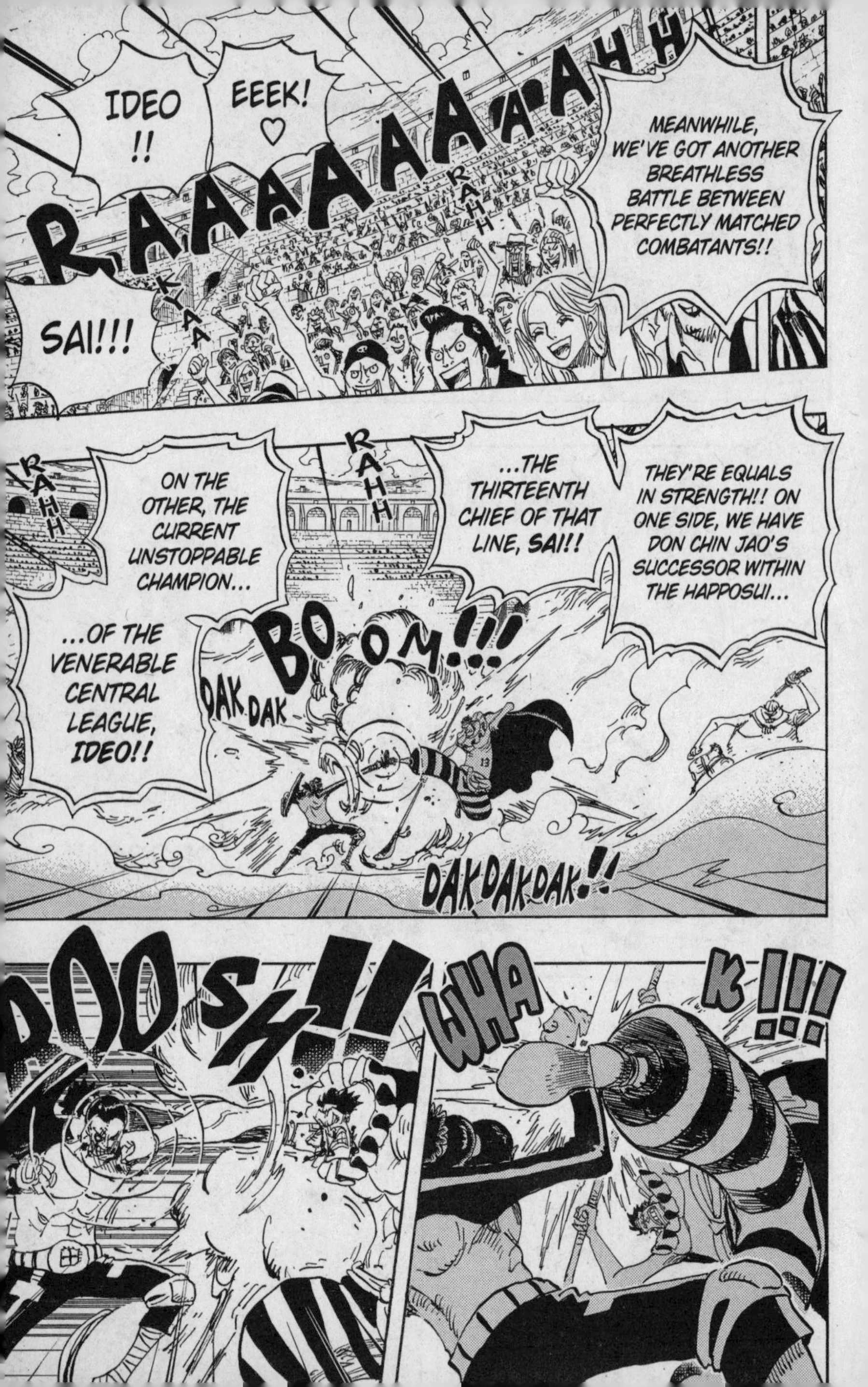
MEANWHILE, WE'VE GOT ANOTHER BREATHLESS BATTLE BETWEEN PERFECTLY MATCHED COMBATANTS!!
RAAAAAAAAHH
RAHH
EEEK! ♥
IDEO !!
KYAA
SAI!!!
THEY'RE EQUALS IN STRENGTH!! ON ONE SIDE, WE HAVE DON CHIN JAO'S SUCCESSOR WITHIN THE HAPPOSUI...
...THE THIRTEENTH CHIEF OF THAT LINE, SAI!!
RAHH
ON THE OTHER, THE CURRENT UNSTOPPABLE CHAMPION...
...OF THE VENERABLE CENTRAL LEAGUE, IDEO!!
RAHH
BOOM!!!
DAK DAK
DAKDAKDAK!!
WHAK!!!!
DOOSH!!

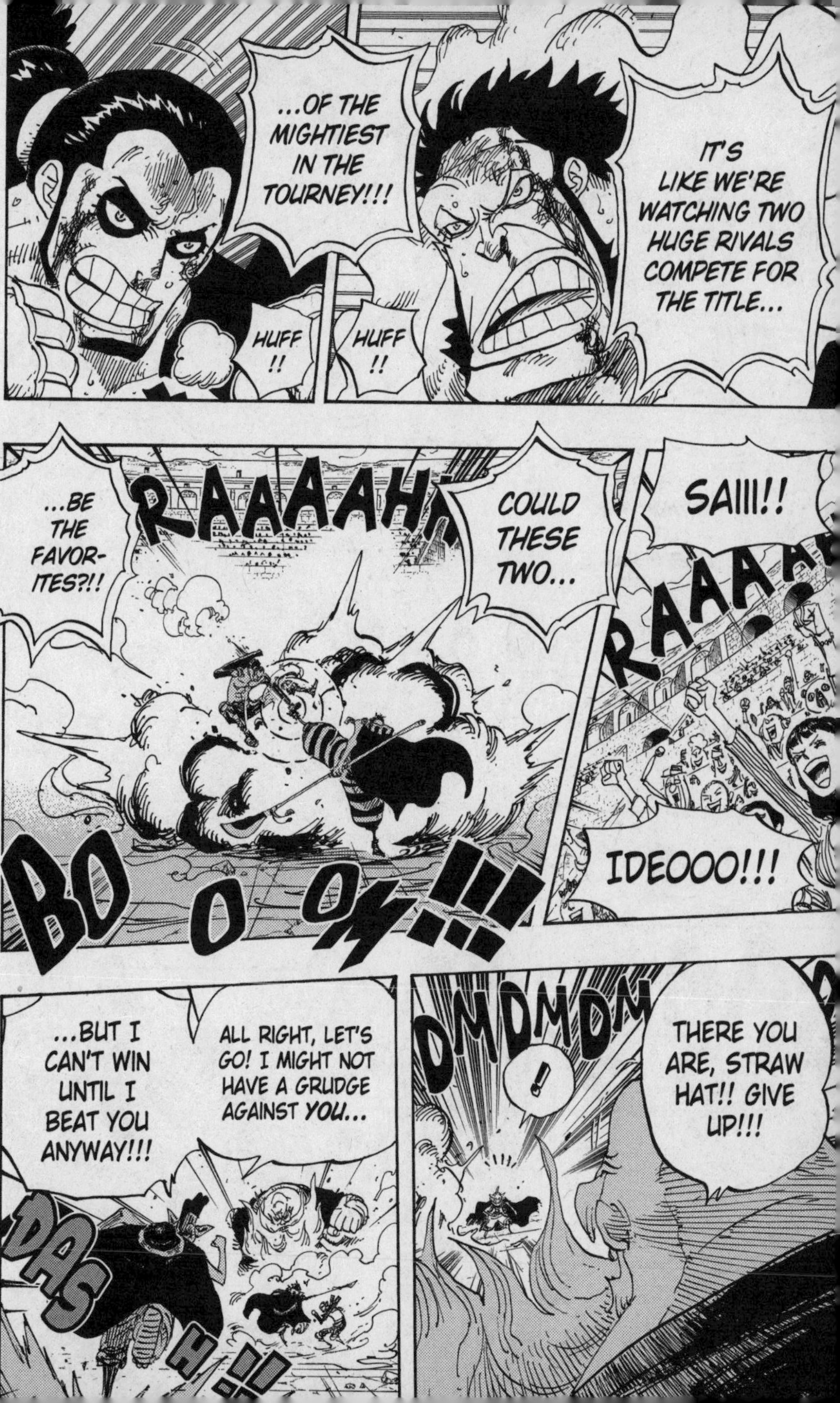
IT'S LIKE WE'RE WATCHING TWO HUGE RIVALS COMPETE FOR THE TITLE...
HUFF!!
...OF THE MIGHTIEST IN THE TOURNEY!!!
HUFF!!
SAIII!!
IDEOOO!!!
COULD THESE TWO...
...BE THE FAVORITES?!!
BOOOM!!!
THERE YOU ARE, STRAW HAT!! GIVE UP!!!
!
DMDMDM
ALL RIGHT, LET'S GO! I MIGHT NOT HAVE A GRUDGE AGAINST YOU...
...BUT I CAN'T WIN UNTIL I BEAT YOU ANYWAY!!!
DASH!!

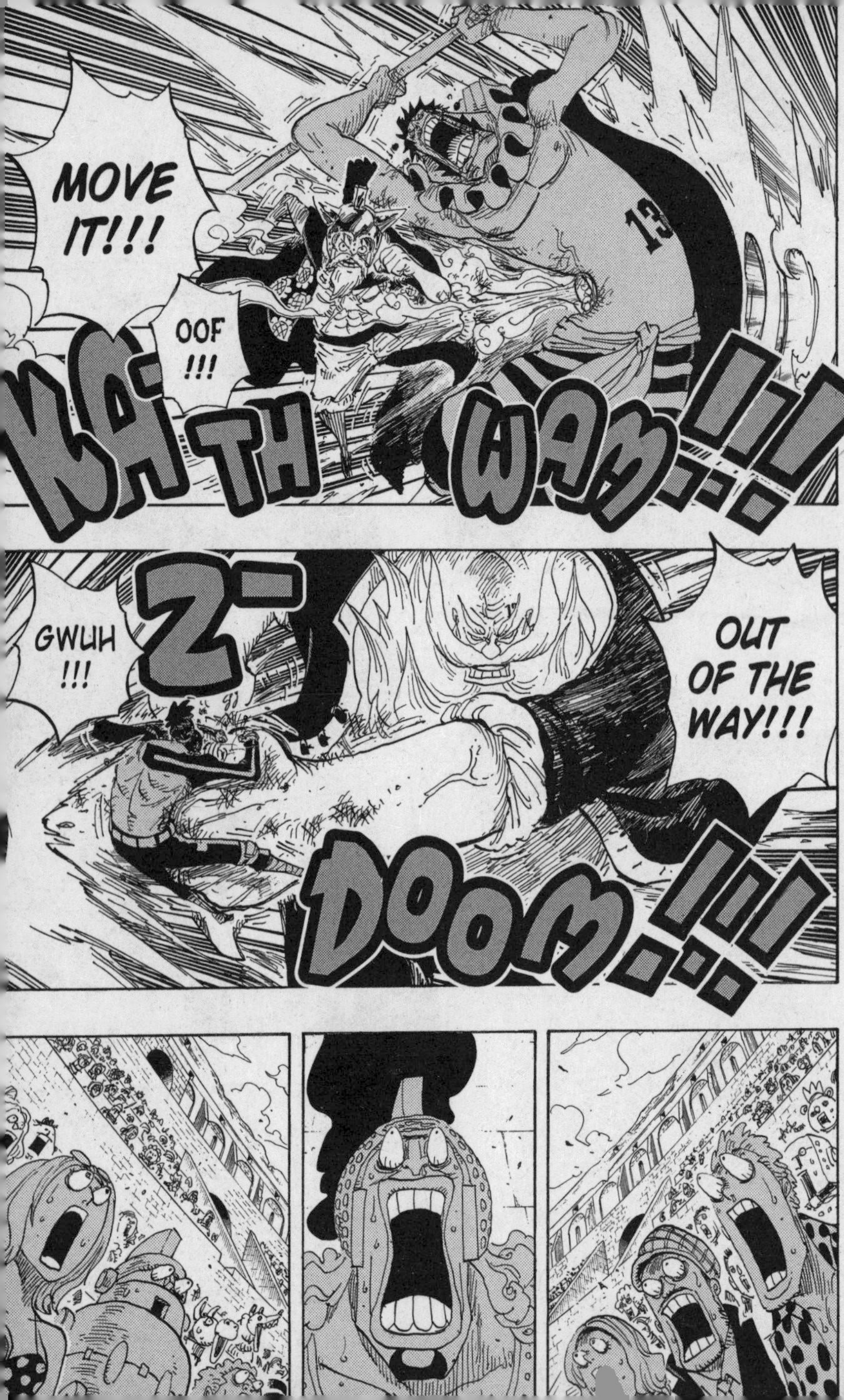

MOVE IT!!!
OOF!!!
KA-THWAM!!!
OUT OF THE WAY!!!
GWUH!!!
Z
DOOM!!!

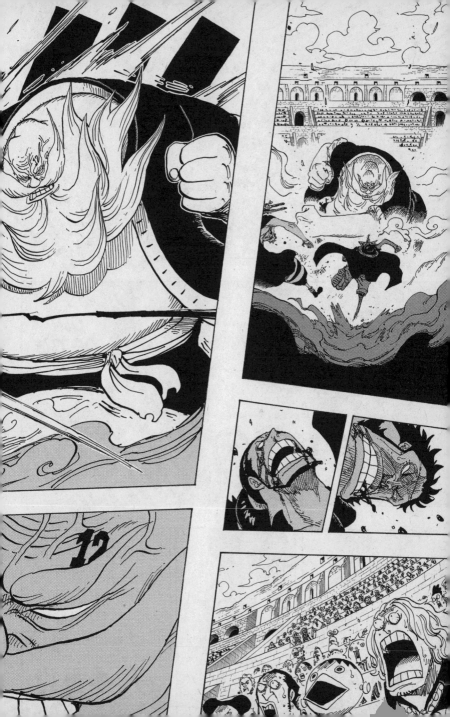

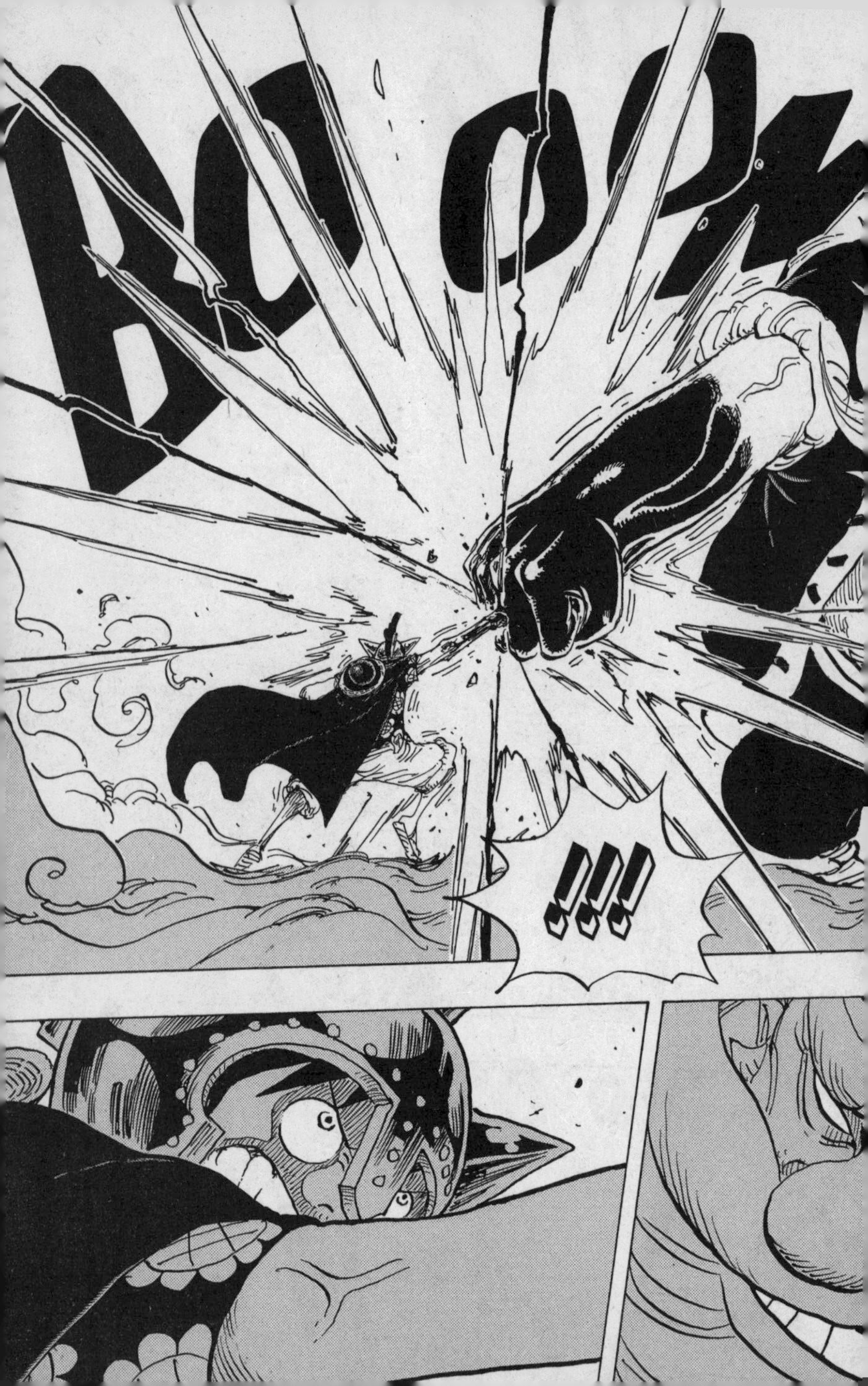
BOOOM
!!!

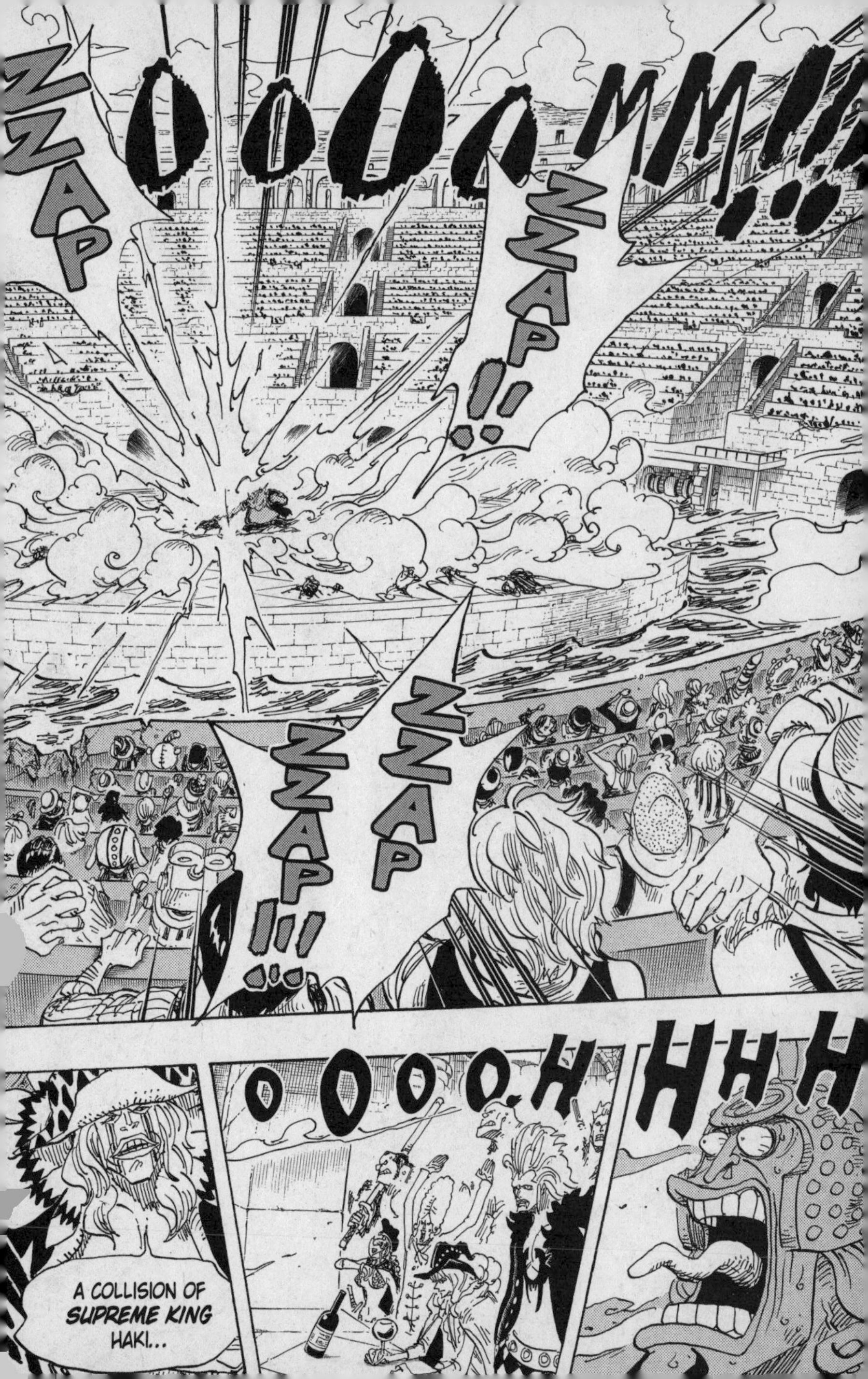
OOOOMM!!
ZZAP!!
ZZAP
ZZAP
ZZAP!!
OOOOHHHH
A COLLISION OF SUPREME KING HAKI...

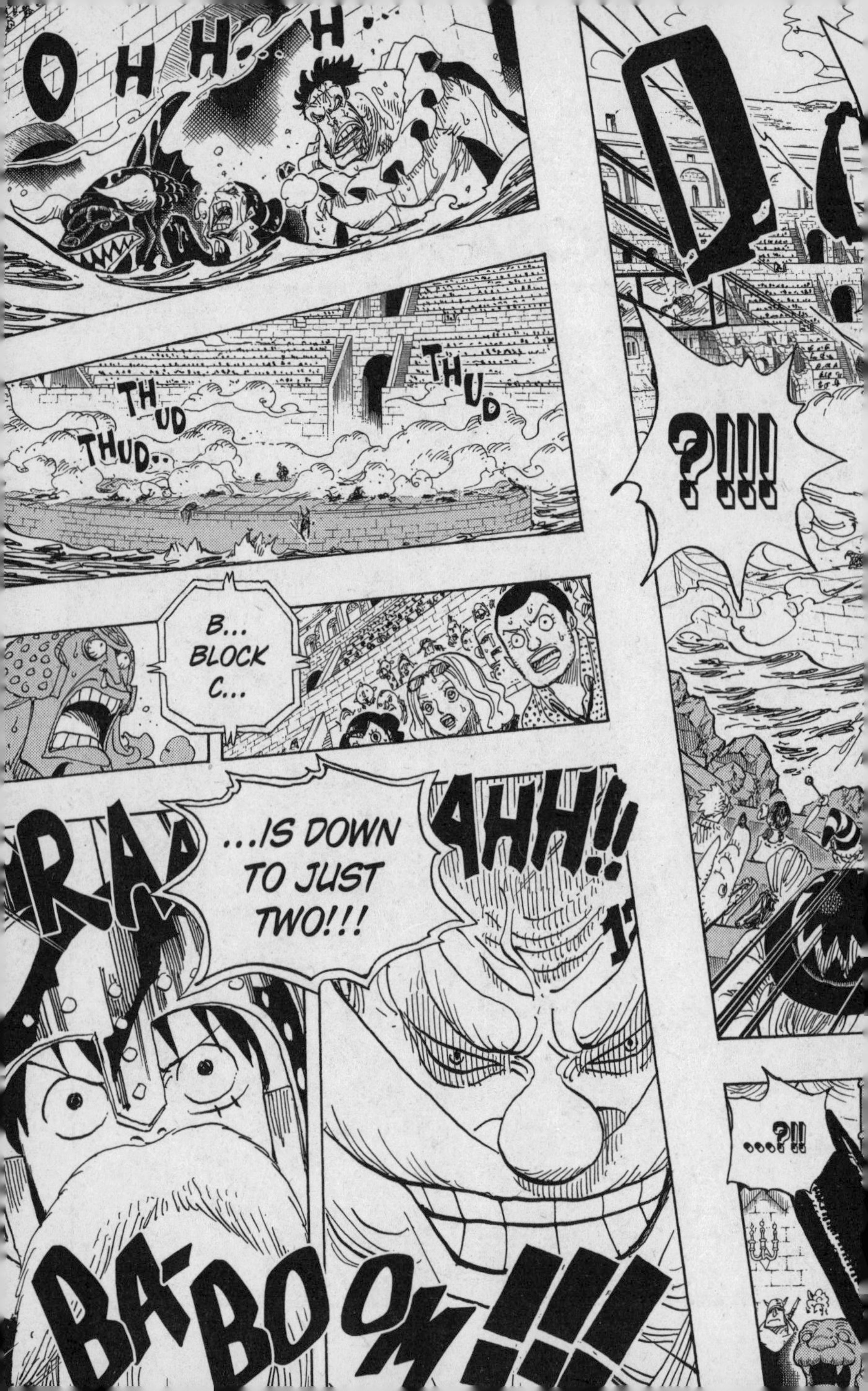
?!!!
OHHH...
THUD
THUD...
THUD
B... BLOCK C...
...IS DOWN TO JUST TWO!!!
RA
AHH!!
BA-BOOM!!!
...?!!

DRESSROSA'S FORGOTTEN

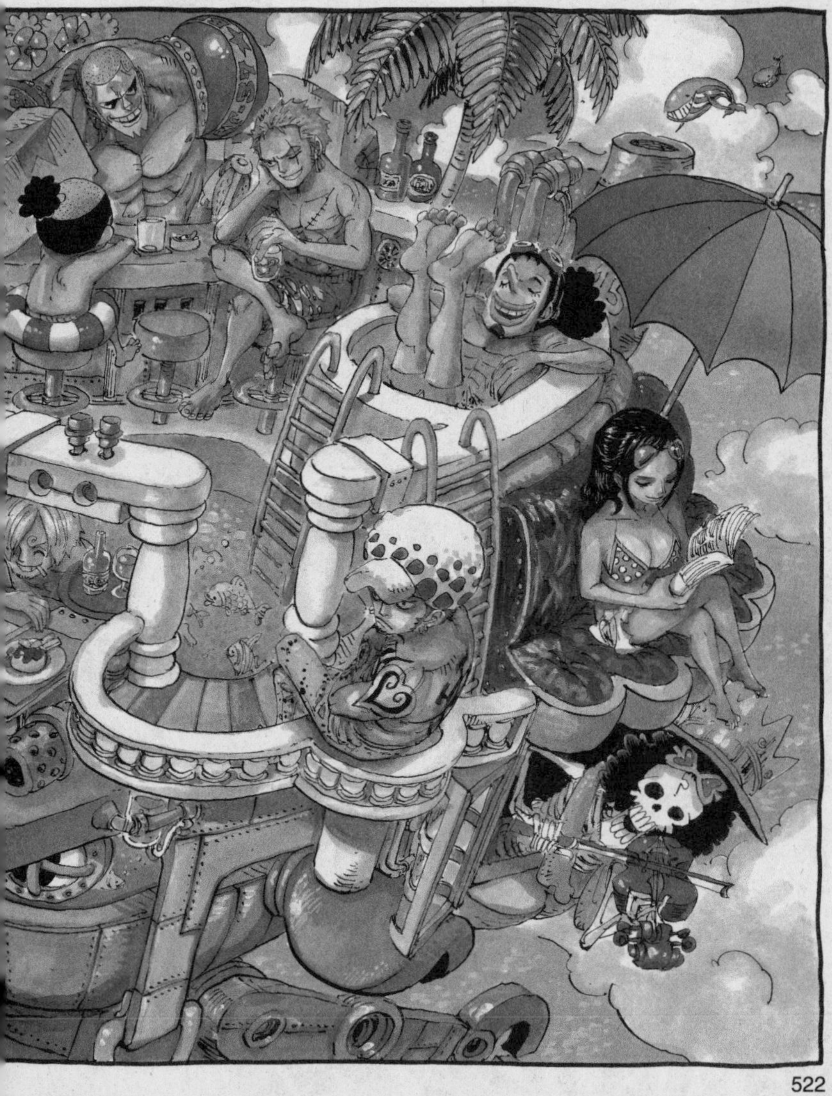

Chapter 717:

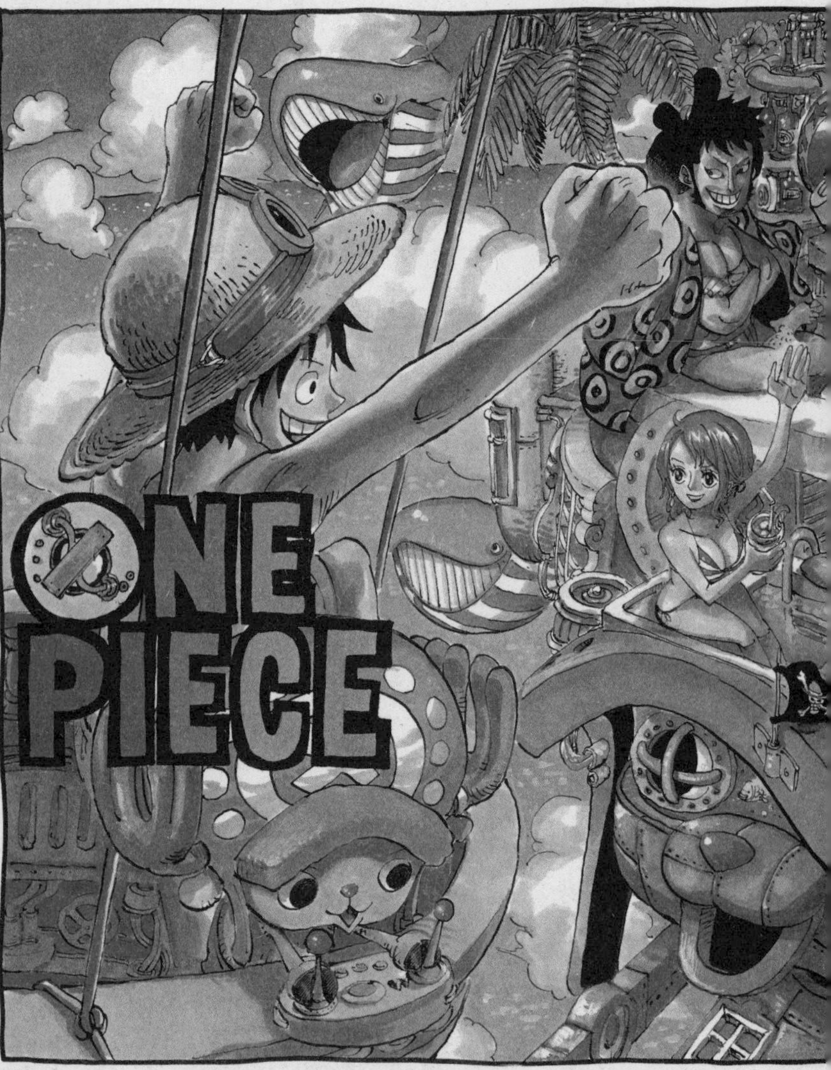
ONE PIECE

vol. 72
ONE PIECE

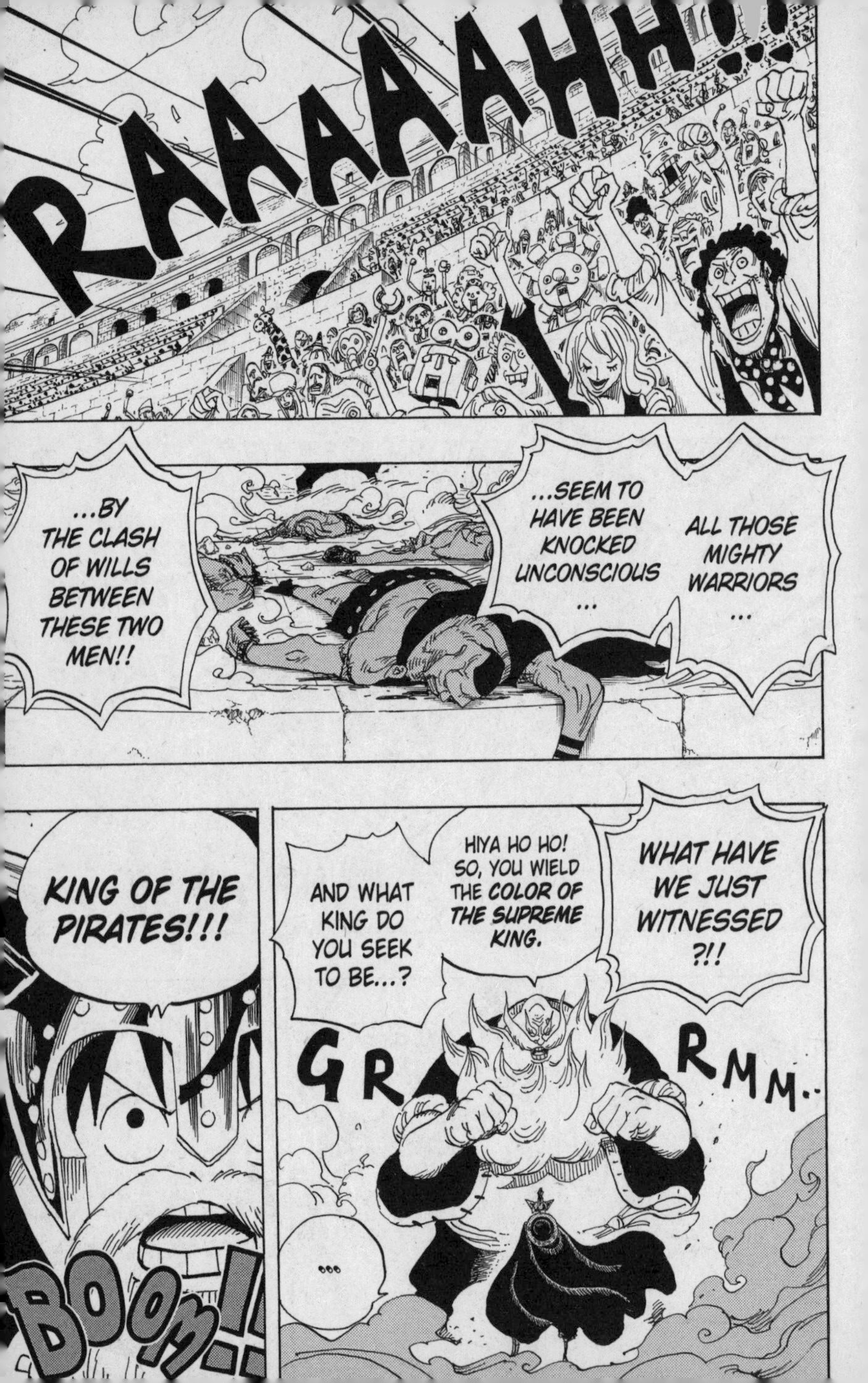
RAAAAAHH!!
ALL THOSE MIGHTY WARRIORS ...
...SEEM TO HAVE BEEN KNOCKED UNCONSCIOUS ...
...BY THE CLASH OF WILLS BETWEEN THESE TWO MEN!!
WHAT HAVE WE JUST WITNESSED ?!!
HIYA HO HO! SO, YOU WIELD THE COLOR OF THE SUPREME KING.
AND WHAT KING DO YOU SEEK TO BE...?
GRRMM..
...
KING OF THE PIRATES!!!
BOOM!!

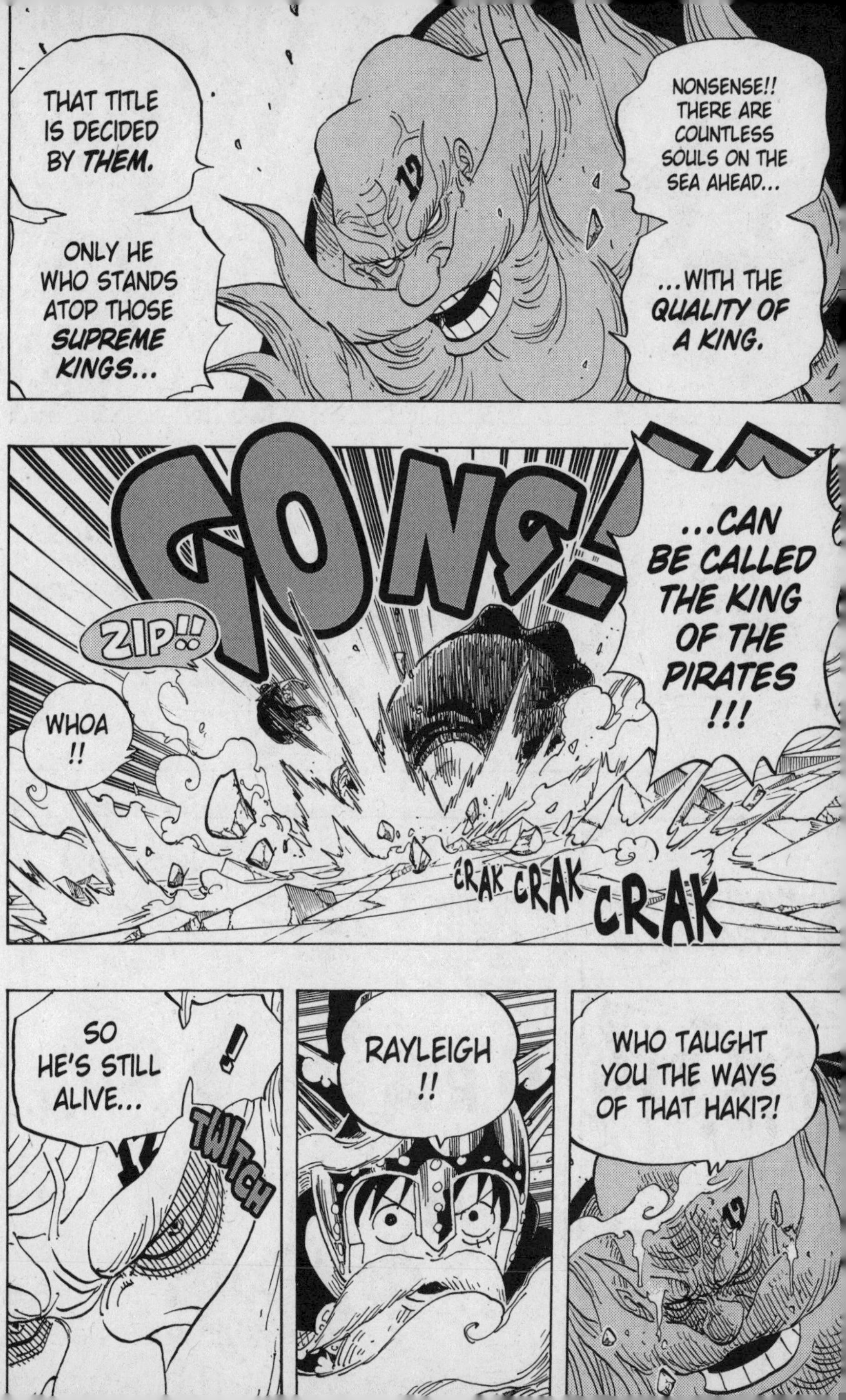
NONSENSE!! THERE ARE COUNTLESS SOULS ON THE SEA AHEAD...
...WITH THE QUALITY OF A KING.
THAT TITLE IS DECIDED BY THEM.
ONLY HE WHO STANDS ATOP THOSE SUPREME KINGS...
GONG!!
...CAN BE CALLED THE KING OF THE PIRATES!!!
ZIP!!
WHOA!!
CRAK CRAK CRAK
WHO TAUGHT YOU THE WAYS OF THAT HAKI?!
RAYLEIGH!!
!
SO HE'S STILL ALIVE...
TWITCH

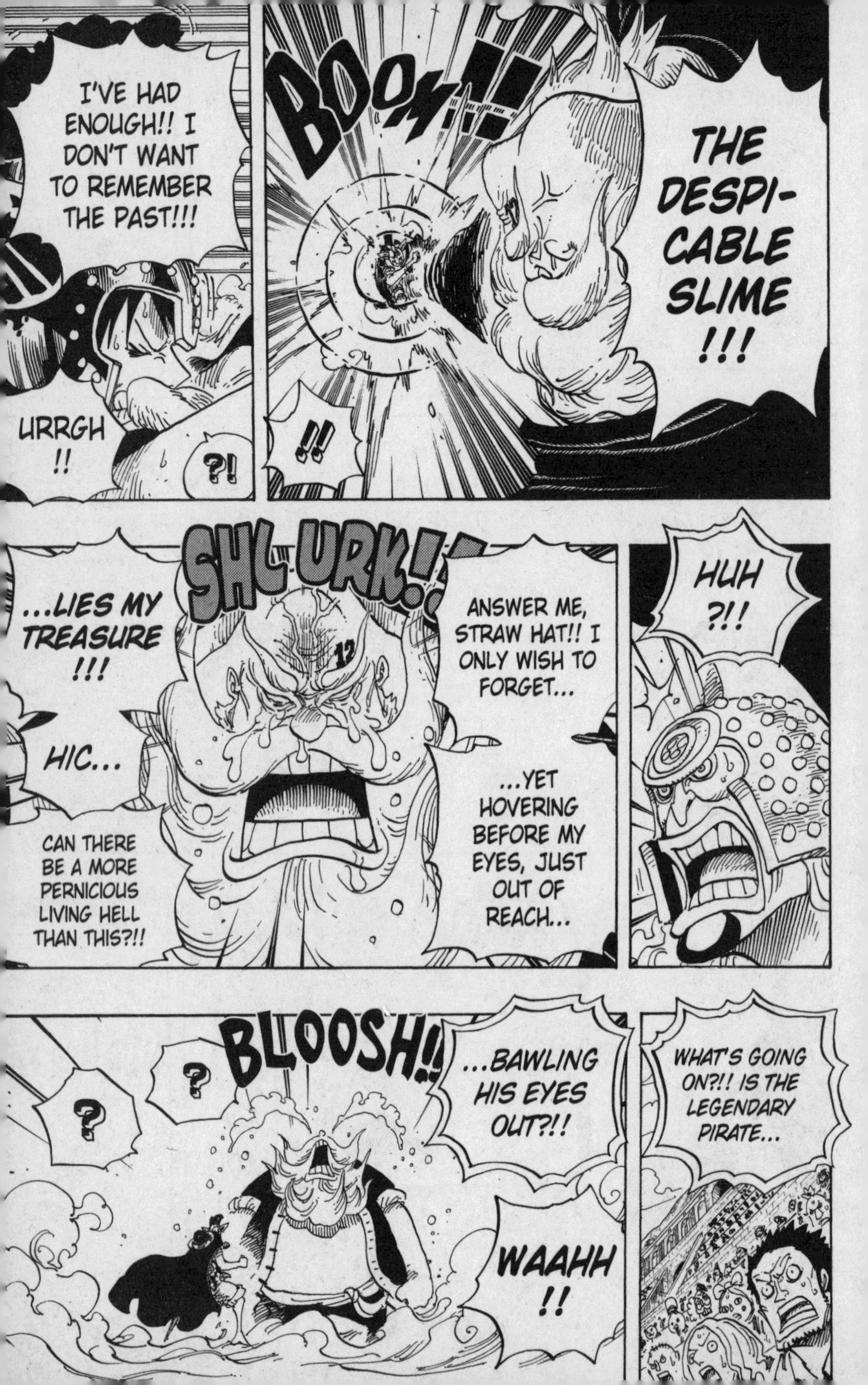
THE DESPI-CABLE SLIME!!!
BOOM!!
!!
I'VE HAD ENOUGH!! I DON'T WANT TO REMEMBER THE PAST!!!
URRGH!!
?!
HUH?!!
ANSWER ME, STRAW HAT!! I ONLY WISH TO FORGET...
SHLURK!!
...YET HOVERING BEFORE MY EYES, JUST OUT OF REACH...
...LIES MY TREASURE!!!
HIC...
CAN THERE BE A MORE PERNICIOUS LIVING HELL THAN THIS?!!
WHAT'S GOING ON?!! IS THE LEGENDARY PIRATE...
...BAWLING HIS EYES OUT?!!
BLOOSH!!
WAAHH!!
?
?

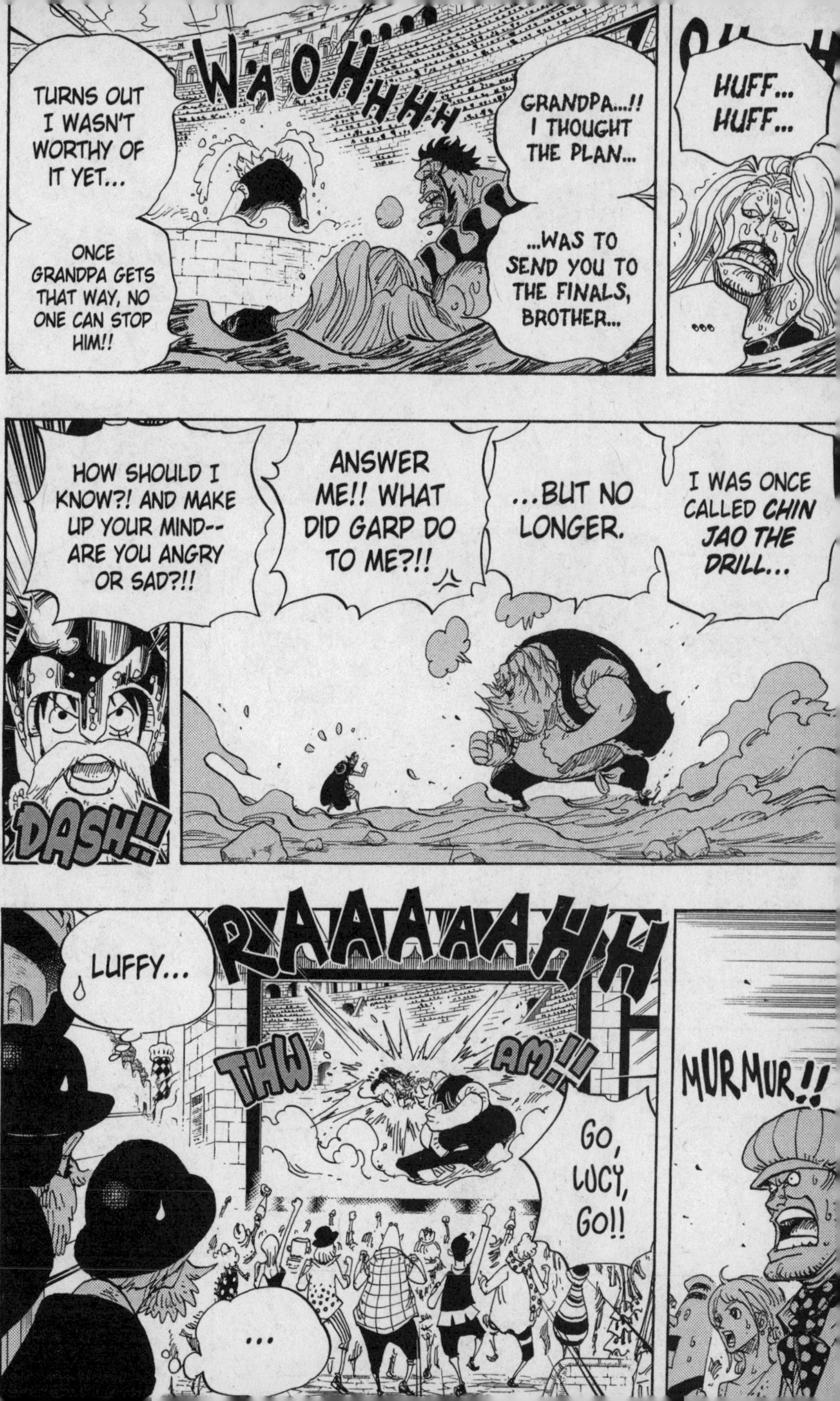
HUFF... HUFF...
...
WAOHHHH
GRANDPA...!! I THOUGHT THE PLAN...
...WAS TO SEND YOU TO THE FINALS, BROTHER...
TURNS OUT I WASN'T WORTHY OF IT YET...
ONCE GRANDPA GETS THAT WAY, NO ONE CAN STOP HIM!!
I WAS ONCE CALLED CHIN JAO THE DRILL...
...BUT NO LONGER.
ANSWER ME!! WHAT DID GARP DO TO ME?!!
HOW SHOULD I KNOW?! AND MAKE UP YOUR MIND-- ARE YOU ANGRY OR SAD?!!
DASH!!
MURMUR!!
RAAAAAAHH
THWAM!!
GO, LUCY, GO!!
LUFFY...
...

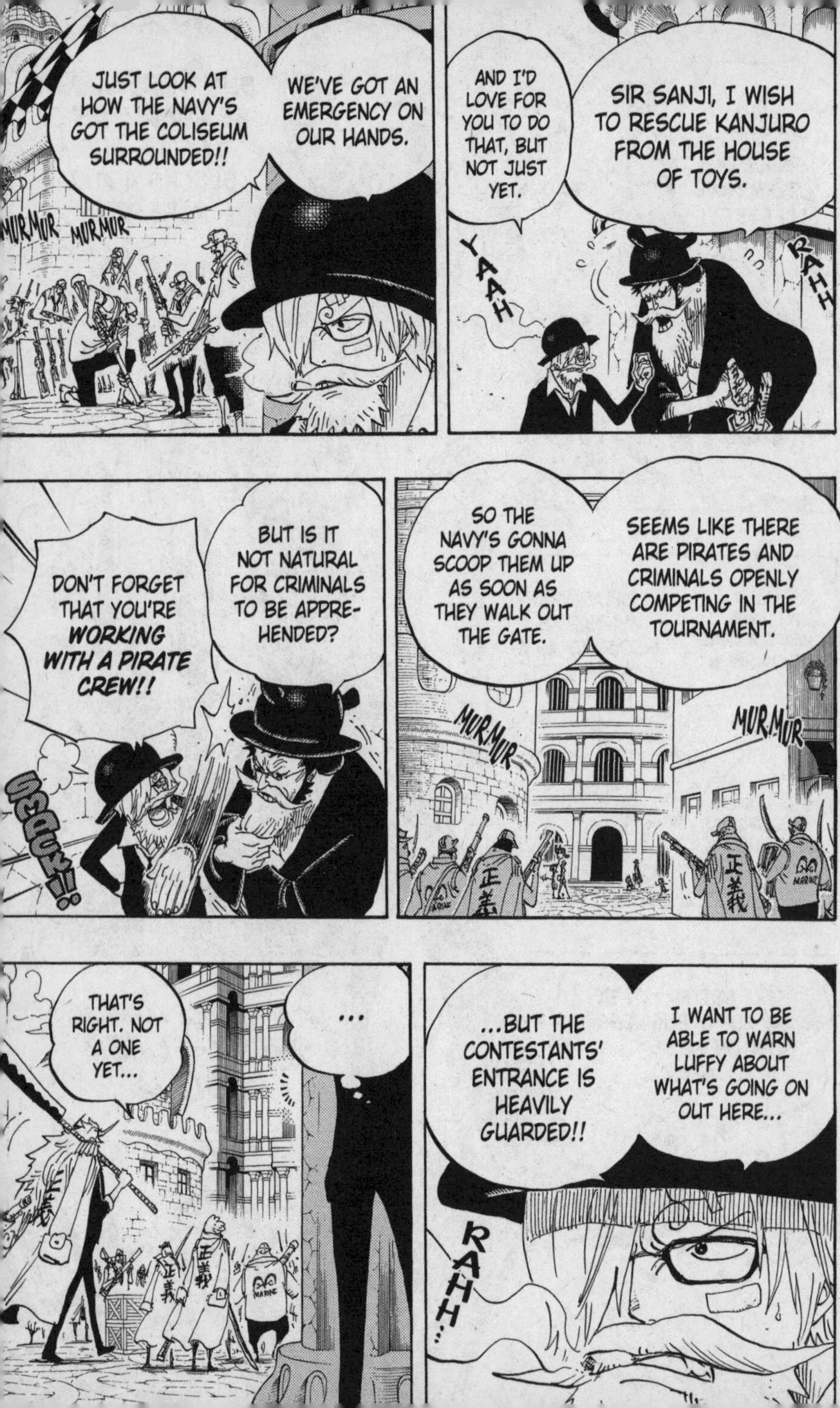
SIR SANJI, I WISH TO RESCUE KANJURO FROM THE HOUSE OF TOYS.
AND I'D LOVE FOR YOU TO DO THAT, BUT NOT JUST YET.
RAHH
YAAH
WE'VE GOT AN EMERGENCY ON OUR HANDS.
JUST LOOK AT HOW THE NAVY'S GOT THE COLISEUM SURROUNDED!!
MURMUR
MURMUR
SEEMS LIKE THERE ARE PIRATES AND CRIMINALS OPENLY COMPETING IN THE TOURNAMENT.
SO THE NAVY'S GONNA SCOOP THEM UP AS SOON AS THEY WALK OUT THE GATE.
MURMUR
MURMUR
BUT IS IT NOT NATURAL FOR CRIMINALS TO BE APPREHENDED?
DON'T FORGET THAT YOU'RE *WORKING WITH A PIRATE CREW!!*
SMACK!!
I WANT TO BE ABLE TO WARN LUFFY ABOUT WHAT'S GOING ON OUT HERE...
...BUT THE CONTESTANTS' ENTRANCE IS HEAVILY GUARDED!!
RAHH...
...
THAT'S RIGHT. NOT A ONE YET...

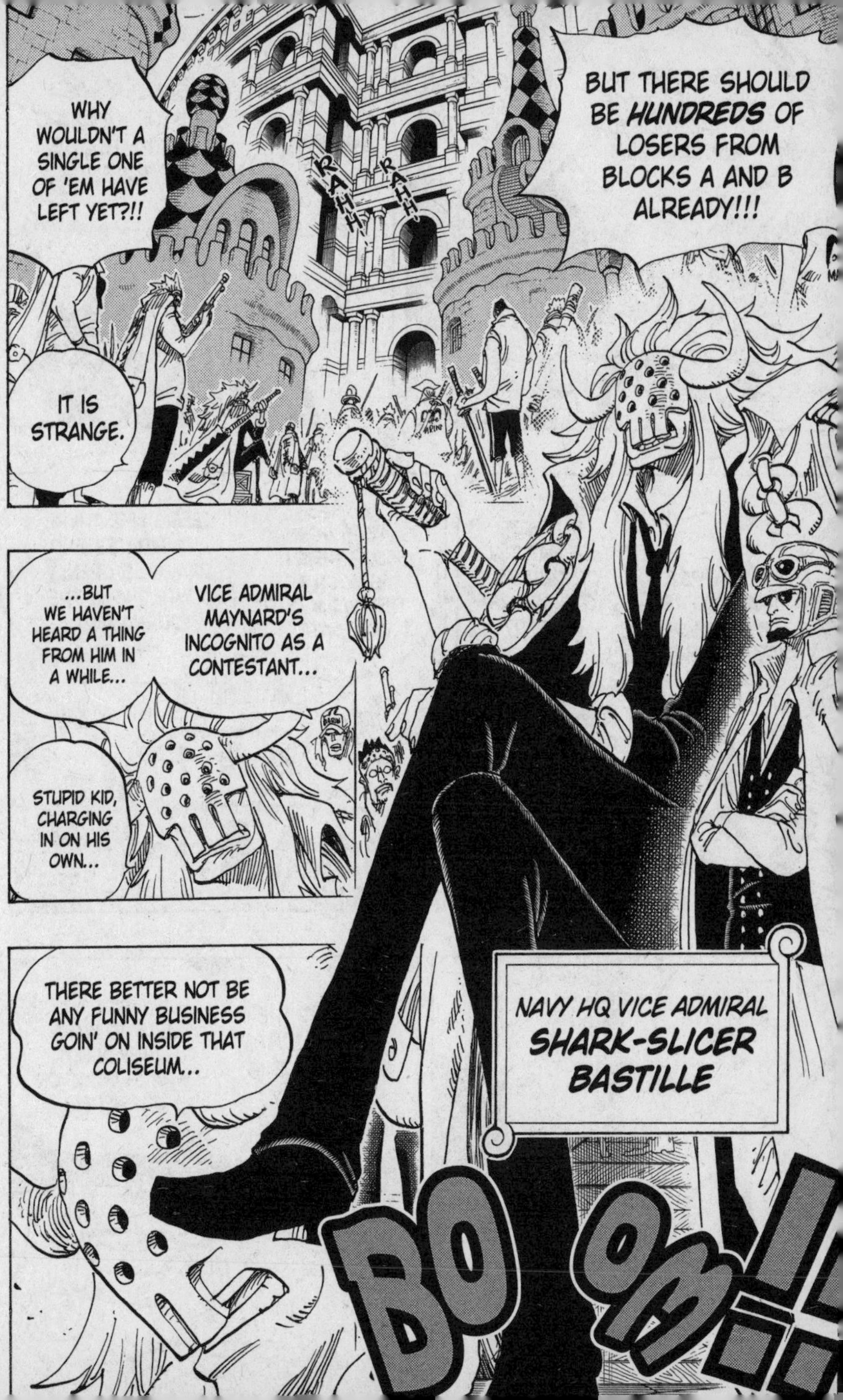
BUT THERE SHOULD BE HUNDREDS OF LOSERS FROM BLOCKS A AND B ALREADY!!!
RAHH
RAHH
WHY WOULDN'T A SINGLE ONE OF 'EM HAVE LEFT YET?!!
IT IS STRANGE.
VICE ADMIRAL MAYNARD'S INCOGNITO AS A CONTESTANT...
...BUT WE HAVEN'T HEARD A THING FROM HIM IN A WHILE...
STUPID KID, CHARGING IN ON HIS OWN...
NAVY HQ VICE ADMIRAL SHARK-SLICER BASTILLE
THERE BETTER NOT BE ANY FUNNY BUSINESS GOIN' ON INSIDE THAT COLISEUM...
BOOM!!

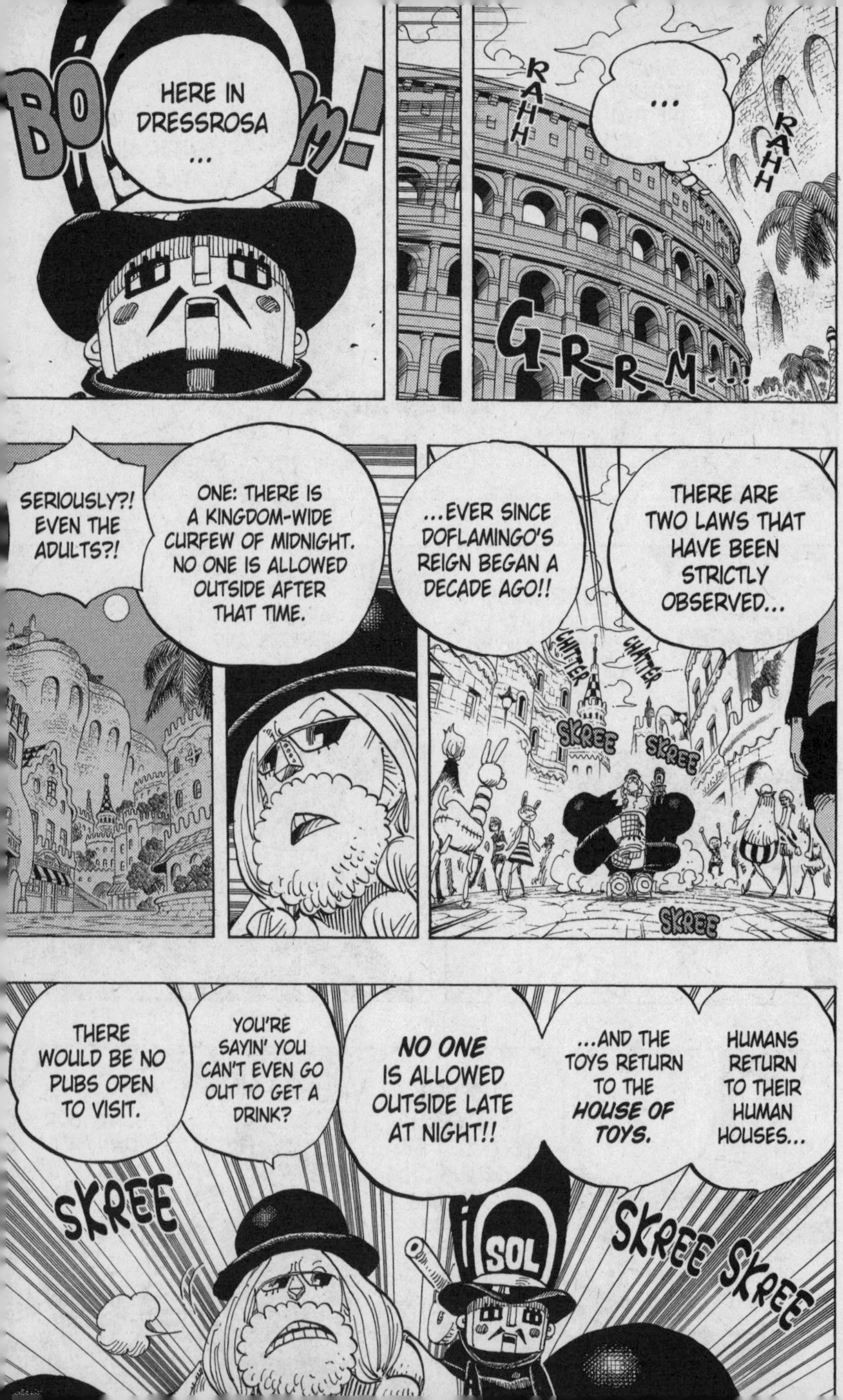
...
RAHH
RAHH
GRRRM...!
HERE IN DRESSROSA ...
BOOM!
THERE ARE TWO LAWS THAT HAVE BEEN STRICTLY OBSERVED...
...EVER SINCE DOFLAMINGO'S REIGN BEGAN A DECADE AGO!!
CHATTER
CHATTER
SKREE
SKREE
SKREE
ONE: THERE IS A KINGDOM-WIDE CURFEW OF MIDNIGHT. NO ONE IS ALLOWED OUTSIDE AFTER THAT TIME.
SERIOUSLY?! EVEN THE ADULTS?!
HUMANS RETURN TO THEIR HUMAN HOUSES...
...AND THE TOYS RETURN TO THE *HOUSE OF TOYS.*
NO ONE IS ALLOWED OUTSIDE LATE AT NIGHT!!
YOU'RE SAYIN' YOU CAN'T EVEN GO OUT TO GET A DRINK?
THERE WOULD BE NO PUBS OPEN TO VISIT.
SKREE SKREE
SOL
SKREE

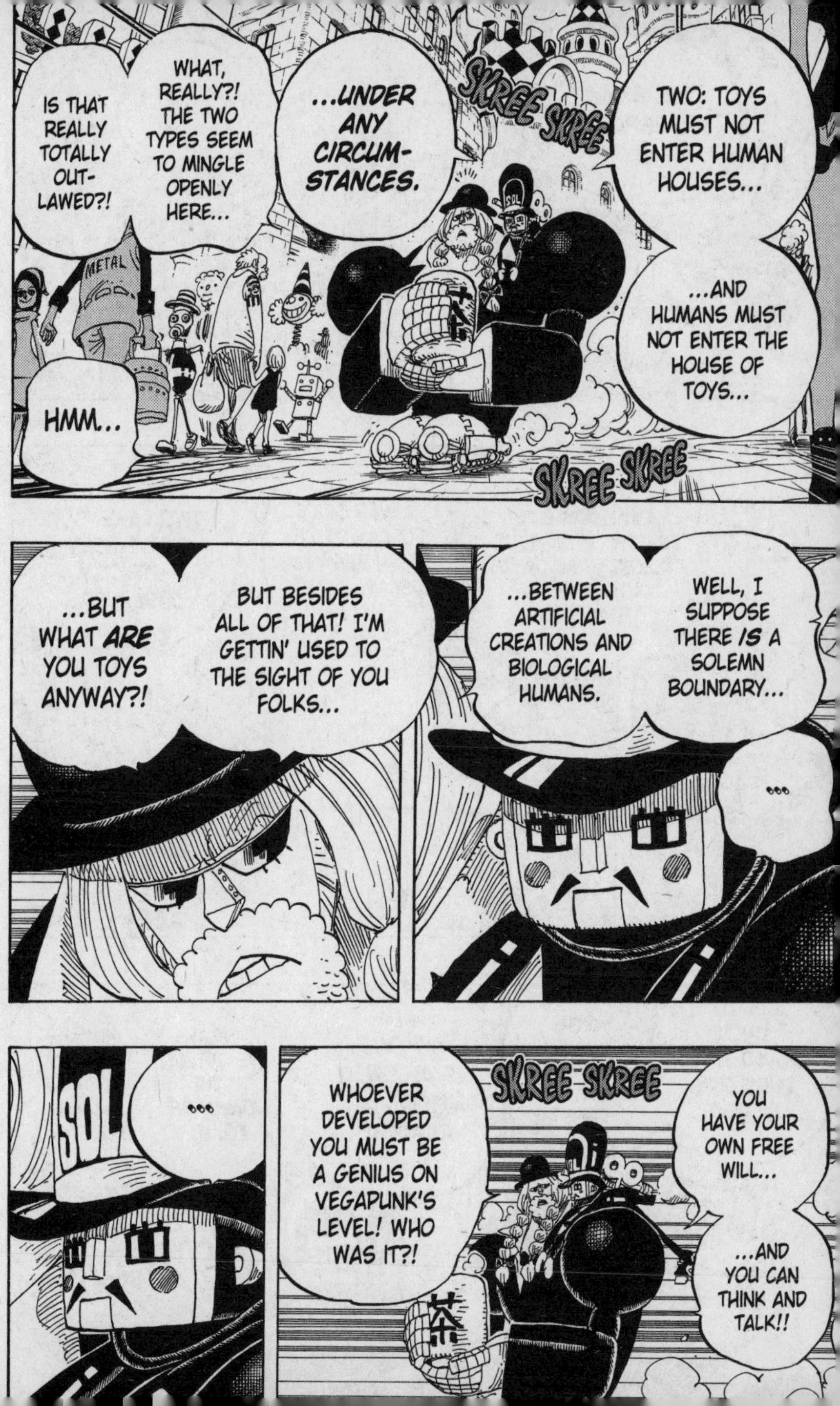
TWO: TOYS MUST NOT ENTER HUMAN HOUSES...
...AND HUMANS MUST NOT ENTER THE HOUSE OF TOYS...
...UNDER ANY CIRCUMSTANCES.
SKREE SKREE
SOL
METAL
WHAT, REALLY?! THE TWO TYPES SEEM TO MINGLE OPENLY HERE...
IS THAT REALLY TOTALLY OUT-LAWED?!
HMM...
SKREE SKREE
WELL, I SUPPOSE THERE IS A SOLEMN BOUNDARY...
...BETWEEN ARTIFICIAL CREATIONS AND BIOLOGICAL HUMANS.
...
BUT BESIDES ALL OF THAT! I'M GETTIN' USED TO THE SIGHT OF YOU FOLKS...
...BUT WHAT ARE YOU TOYS ANYWAY?!
SKREE SKREE
YOU HAVE YOUR OWN FREE WILL...
...AND YOU CAN THINK AND TALK!!
WHOEVER DEVELOPED YOU MUST BE A GENIUS ON VEGAPUNK'S LEVEL! WHO WAS IT?!
SOL
...

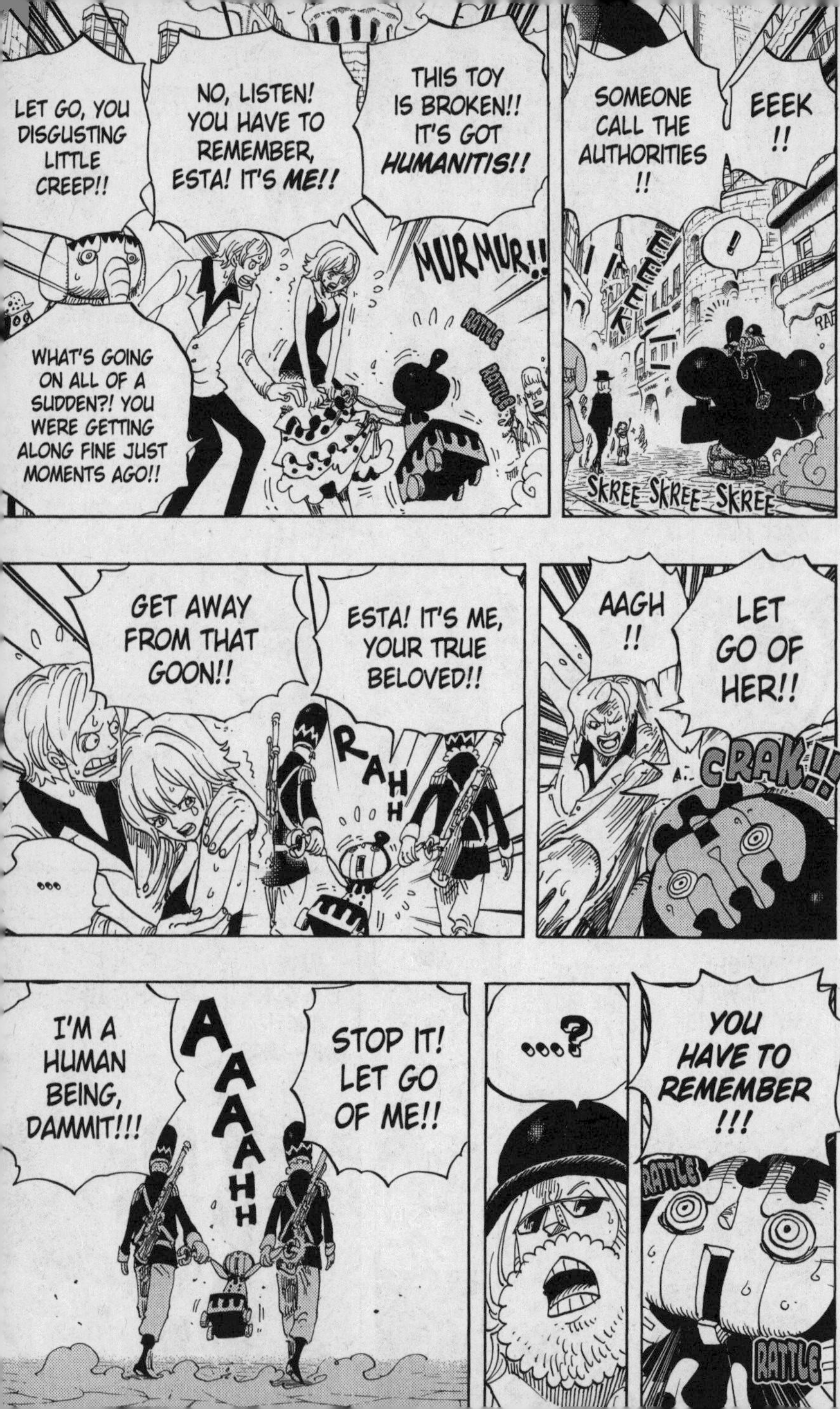
EEEK!!
SOMEONE CALL THE AUTHORITIES!!
!
SKREE SKREE SKREE
THIS TOY IS BROKEN!! IT'S GOT HUMANITIS!!
NO, LISTEN! YOU HAVE TO REMEMBER, ESTA! IT'S ME!!
LET GO, YOU DISGUSTING LITTLE CREEP!!
MURMUR!!
RATTLE
RATTLE
WHAT'S GOING ON ALL OF A SUDDEN?! YOU WERE GETTING ALONG FINE JUST MOMENTS AGO!!
LET GO OF HER!!
AAGH!!
CRAK!!
ESTA! IT'S ME, YOUR TRUE BELOVED!!
GET AWAY FROM THAT GOON!!
RAHH
...
YOU HAVE TO REMEMBER!!!
...?
RATTLE
RATTLE
STOP IT! LET GO OF ME!!
AAAAAHH
I'M A HUMAN BEING, DAMMIT!!!

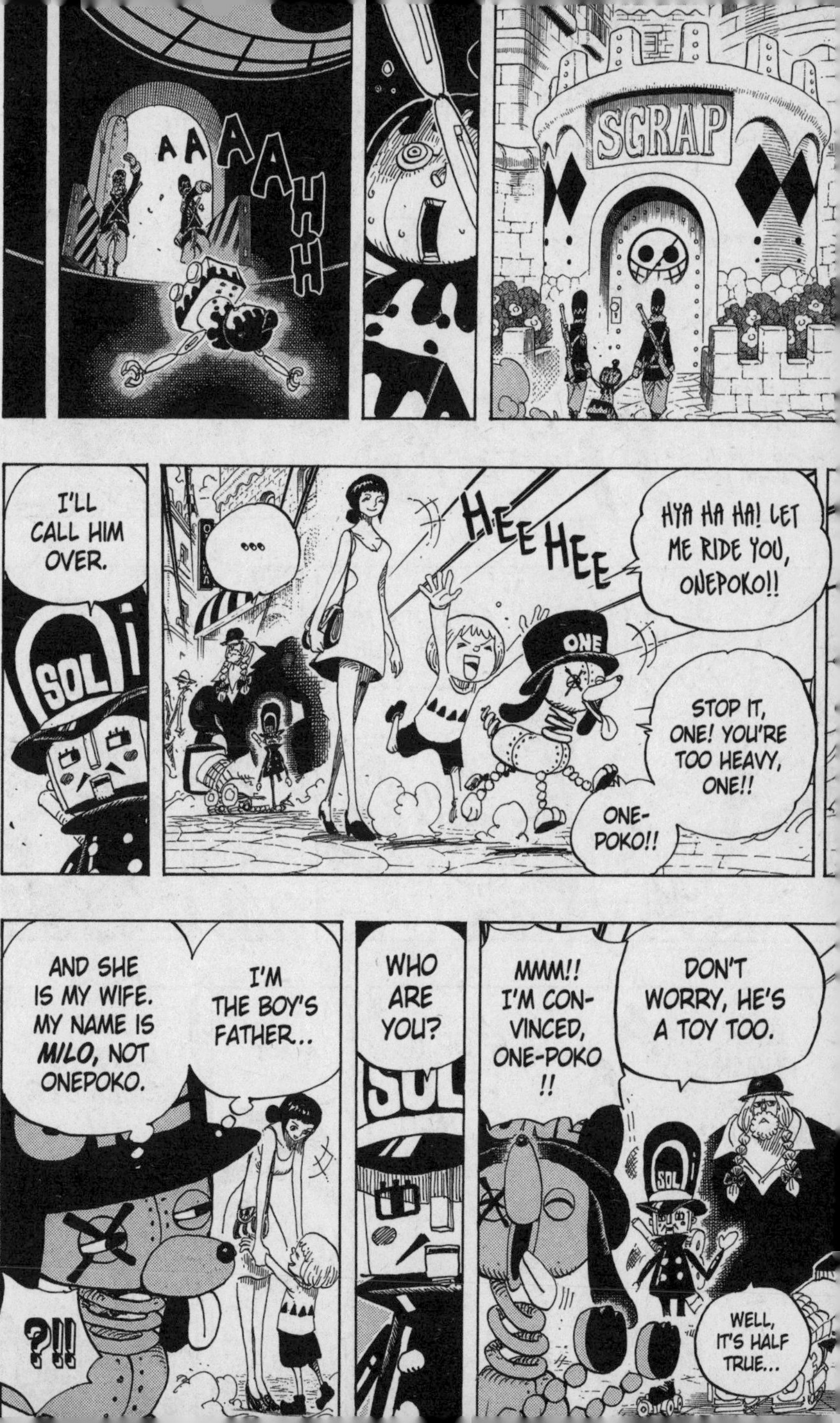
SCRAP
AAAAHHH
HYA HA HA! LET ME RIDE YOU, ONEPOKO!!
HEE HEE
ONE
STOP IT, ONE! YOU'RE TOO HEAVY, ONE!!
ONE-POKO!!
...
I'LL CALL HIM OVER.
SOL
DON'T WORRY, HE'S A TOY TOO.
MMM!! I'M CON-VINCED, ONE-POKO!!
SOL
WELL, IT'S HALF TRUE...
WHO ARE YOU?
I'M THE BOY'S FATHER...
AND SHE IS MY WIFE. MY NAME IS *MILO*, NOT ONEPOKO.
?!!

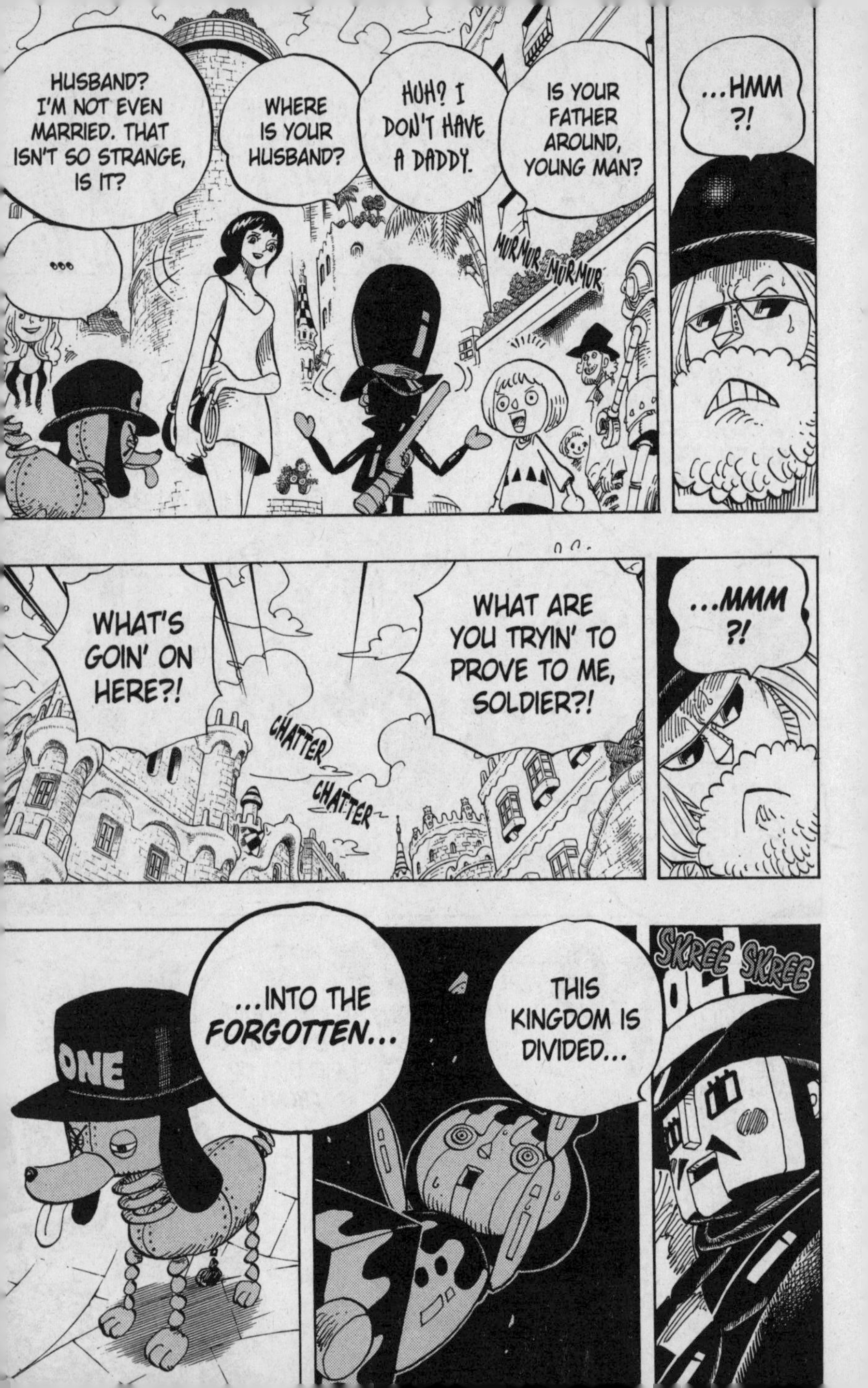
...HMM ?!
IS YOUR FATHER AROUND, YOUNG MAN?
HUH? I DON'T HAVE A DADDY.
WHERE IS YOUR HUSBAND?
HUSBAND? I'M NOT EVEN MARRIED. THAT ISN'T SO STRANGE, IS IT?
MURMUR MURMUR
...MMM ?!
WHAT ARE YOU TRYIN' TO PROVE TO ME, SOLDIER?!
WHAT'S GOIN' ON HERE?!
CHATTER CHATTER
SKREE SKREE
THIS KINGDOM IS DIVIDED...
...INTO THE FORGOTTEN...
ONE

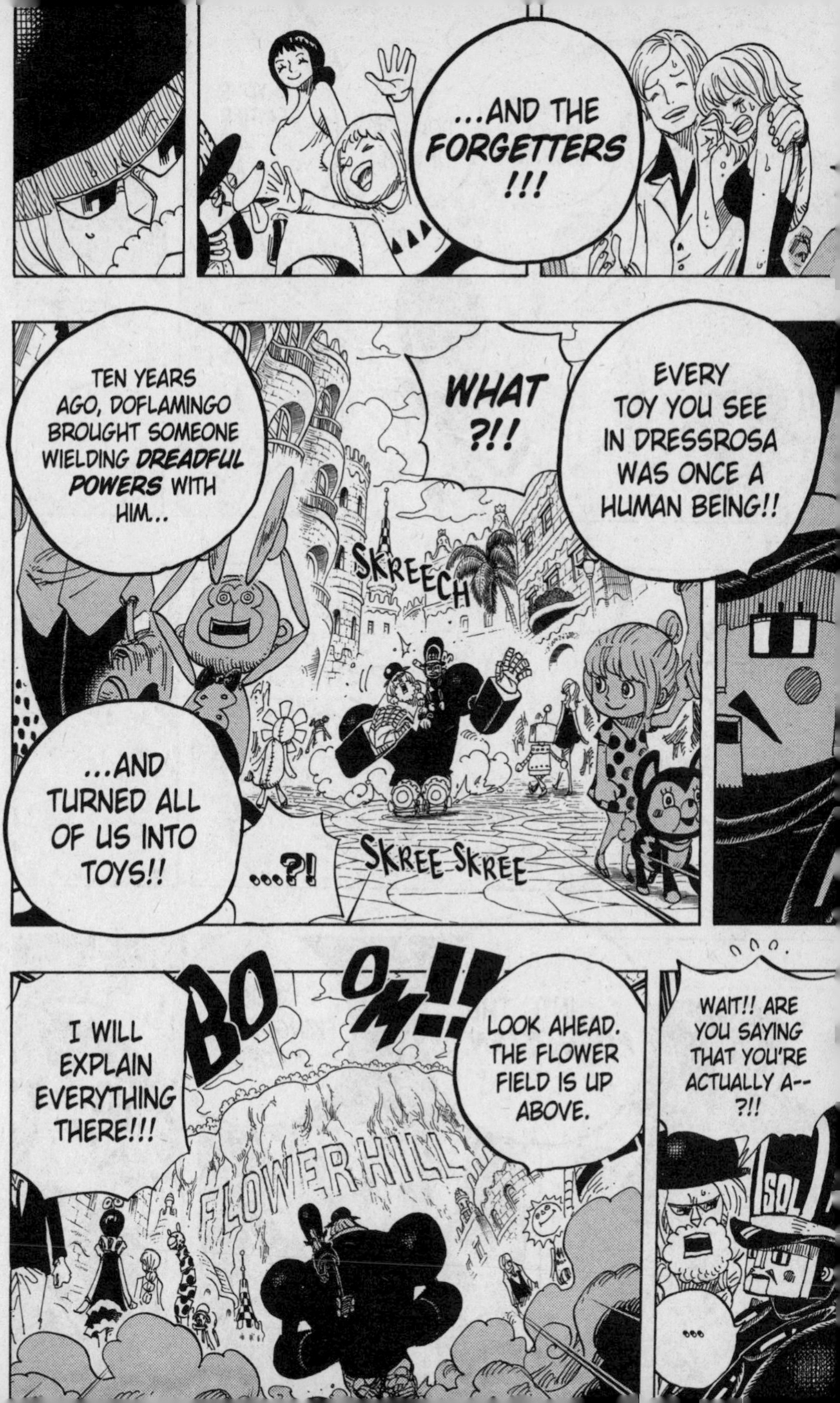
...AND THE FORGETTERS !!!
EVERY TOY YOU SEE IN DRESSROSA WAS ONCE A HUMAN BEING!!
WHAT ?!!
TEN YEARS AGO, DOFLAMINGO BROUGHT SOMEONE WIELDING DREADFUL POWERS WITH HIM...
SKREEECH
...AND TURNED ALL OF US INTO TOYS!!
SKREE SKREE
...?!
WAIT!! ARE YOU SAYING THAT YOU'RE ACTUALLY A-- ?!!
...
BOOM!!
LOOK AHEAD. THE FLOWER FIELD IS UP ABOVE.
I WILL EXPLAIN EVERYTHING THERE!!!
FLOWER HILL
SOL

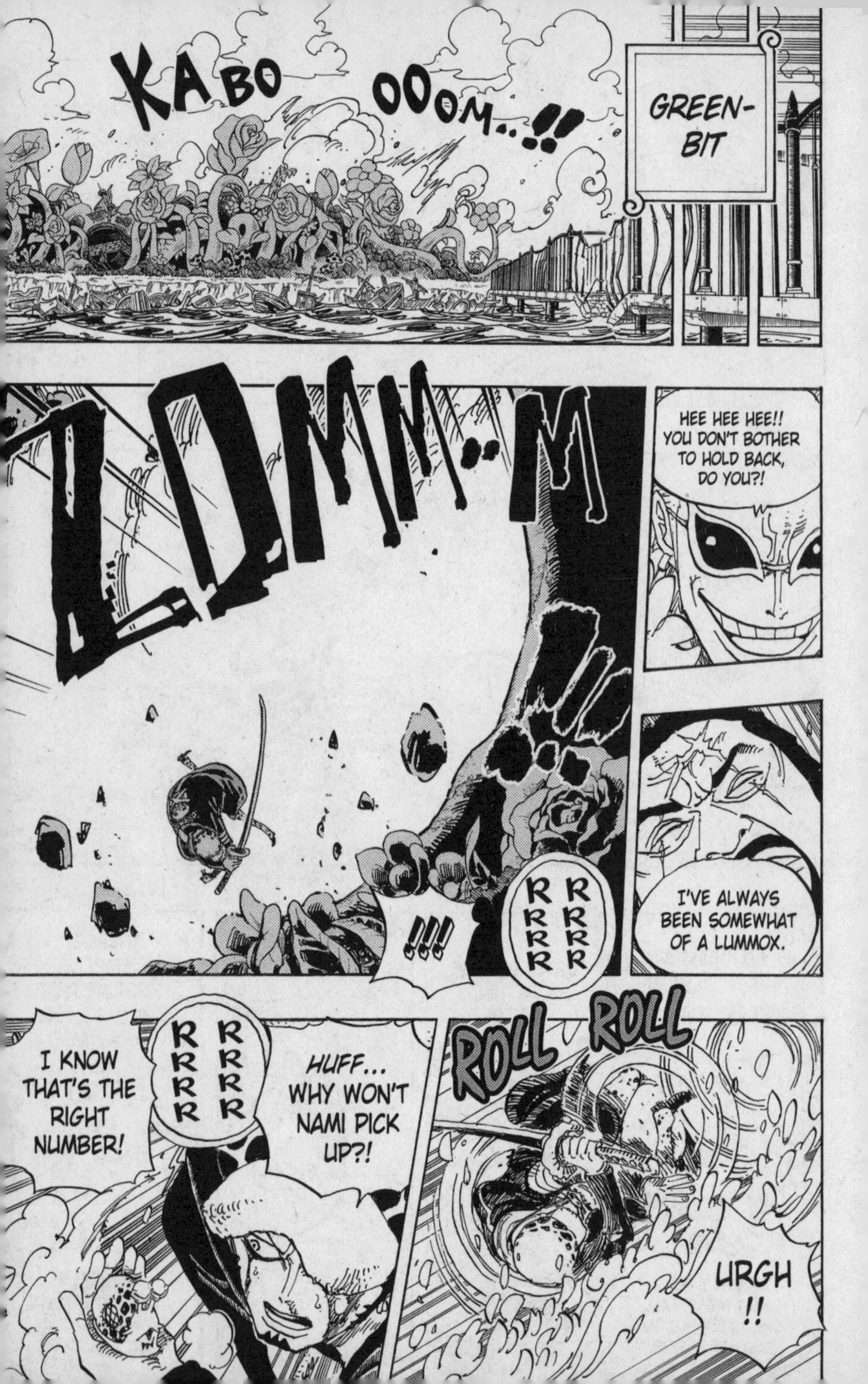
GREEN-BIT
KABOOOOM..!!
HEE HEE HEE!! YOU DON'T BOTHER TO HOLD BACK, DO YOU?!
I'VE ALWAYS BEEN SOMEWHAT OF A LUMMOX.
ZDMM..M
RRRR RRRR
!!!
ROLL ROLL
URGH!!
HUFF... WHY WON'T NAMI PICK UP?!
RRRR RRRR
I KNOW THAT'S THE RIGHT NUMBER!

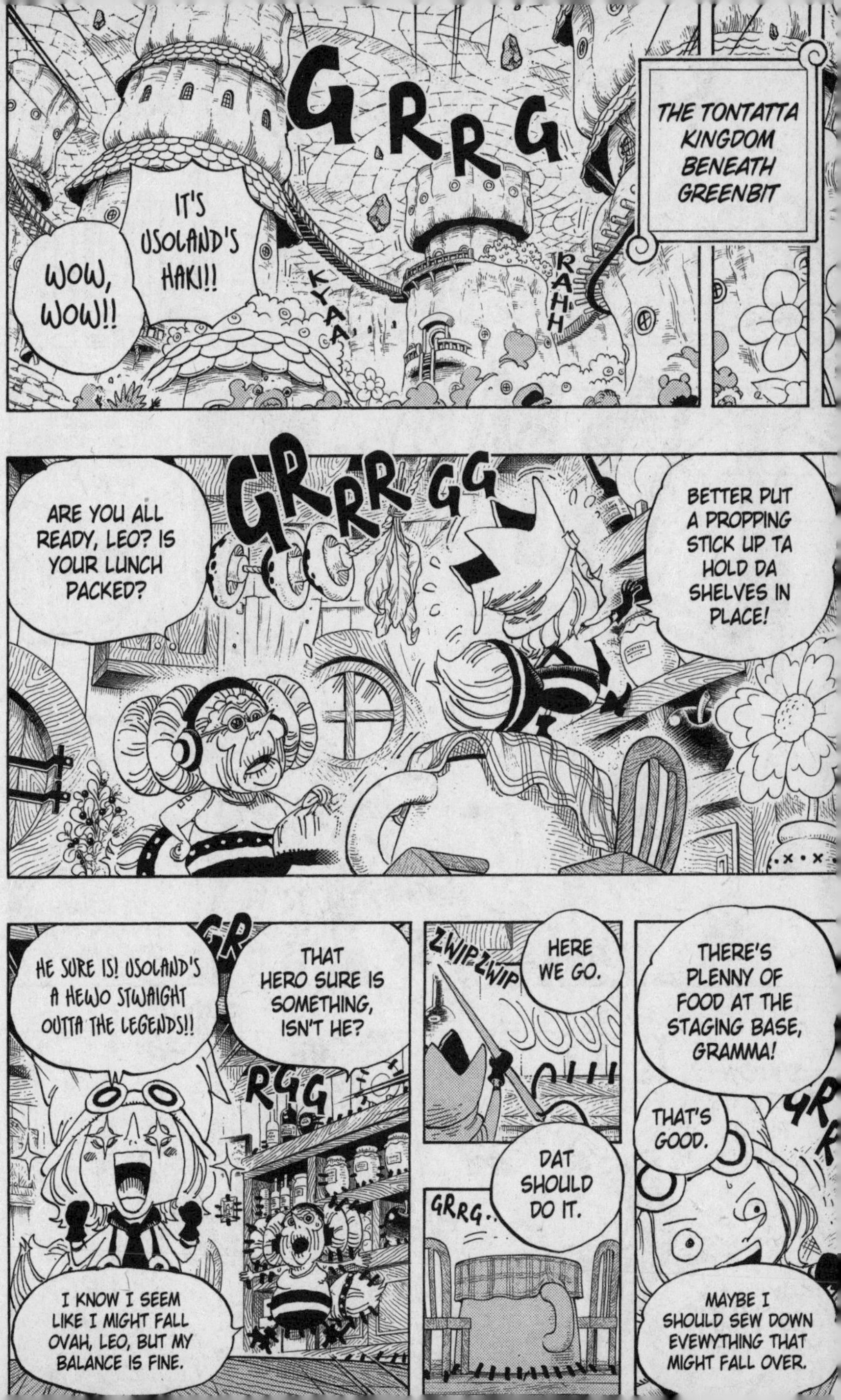
THE TONTATTA KINGDOM BENEATH GREENBIT
GRRG
RAHH
IT'S USOLAND'S HAKI!!
KYAA
WOW, WOW!!
BETTER PUT A PROPPING STICK UP TA HOLD DA SHELVES IN PLACE!
GRRRGG
ARE YOU ALL READY, LEO? IS YOUR LUNCH PACKED?
THERE'S PLENNY OF FOOD AT THE STAGING BASE, GRAMMA!
GRK
THAT'S GOOD.
MAYBE I SHOULD SEW DOWN EVEWYTHING THAT MIGHT FALL OVER.
HERE WE GO.
ZWIP ZWIP
DAT SHOULD DO IT.
GRRG..
THAT HERO SURE IS SOMETHING, ISN'T HE?
GR
HE SURE IS! USOLAND'S A HEWO STWAIGHT OUTTA THE LEGENDS!!
RGG
I KNOW I SEEM LIKE I MIGHT FALL OVAH, LEO, BUT MY BALANCE IS FINE.

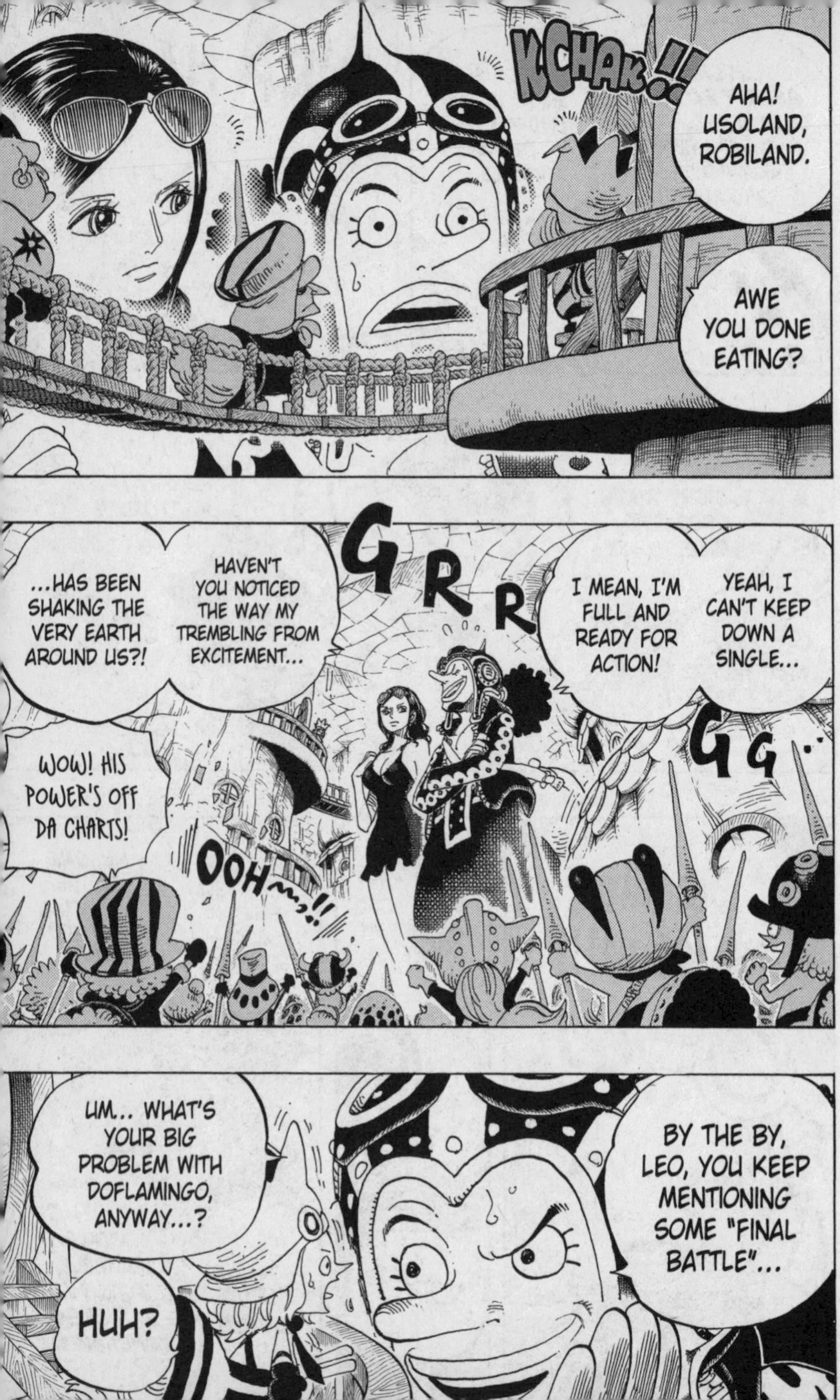
KCHAK!!
AHA! USOLAND, ROBILAND.
AWE YOU DONE EATING?
YEAH, I CAN'T KEEP DOWN A SINGLE...
I MEAN, I'M FULL AND READY FOR ACTION!
GRR
HAVEN'T YOU NOTICED THE WAY MY TREMBLING FROM EXCITEMENT...
...HAS BEEN SHAKING THE VERY EARTH AROUND US?!
GG...
WOW! HIS POWER'S OFF DA CHARTS!
OOH~!!
BY THE BY, LEO, YOU KEEP MENTIONING SOME "FINAL BATTLE"...
UM... WHAT'S YOUR BIG PROBLEM WITH DOFLAMINGO, ANYWAY...?
HUH?

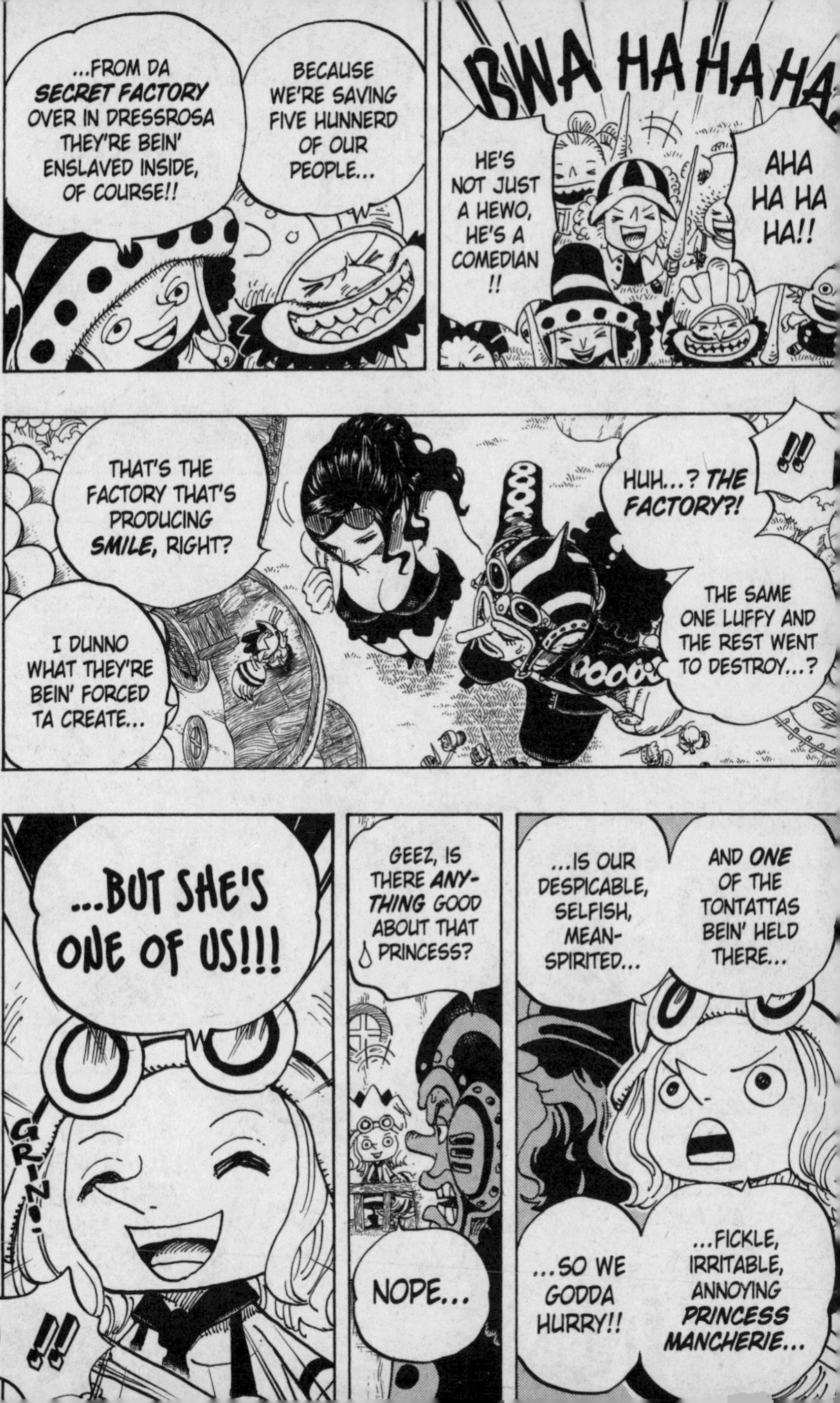
BWA HA HA HA HA
AHA HA HA HA!!
HE'S NOT JUST A HEWO, HE'S A COMEDIAN !!
BECAUSE WE'RE SAVING FIVE HUNNERD OF OUR PEOPLE...
...FROM DA SECRET FACTORY OVER IN DRESSROSA THEY'RE BEIN' ENSLAVED INSIDE, OF COURSE!!
!!
HUH...? THE FACTORY?!
THE SAME ONE LUFFY AND THE REST WENT TO DESTROY...?
THAT'S THE FACTORY THAT'S PRODUCING SMILE, RIGHT?
I DUNNO WHAT THEY'RE BEIN' FORCED TA CREATE...
AND ONE OF THE TONTATTAS BEIN' HELD THERE...
...IS OUR DESPICABLE, SELFISH, MEAN-SPIRITED...
...FICKLE, IRRITABLE, ANNOYING PRINCESS MANCHERIE...
...SO WE GODDA HURRY!!
GEEZ, IS THERE ANYTHING GOOD ABOUT THAT PRINCESS?
NOPE...
...BUT SHE'S ONE OF US!!!
GRIN
!!

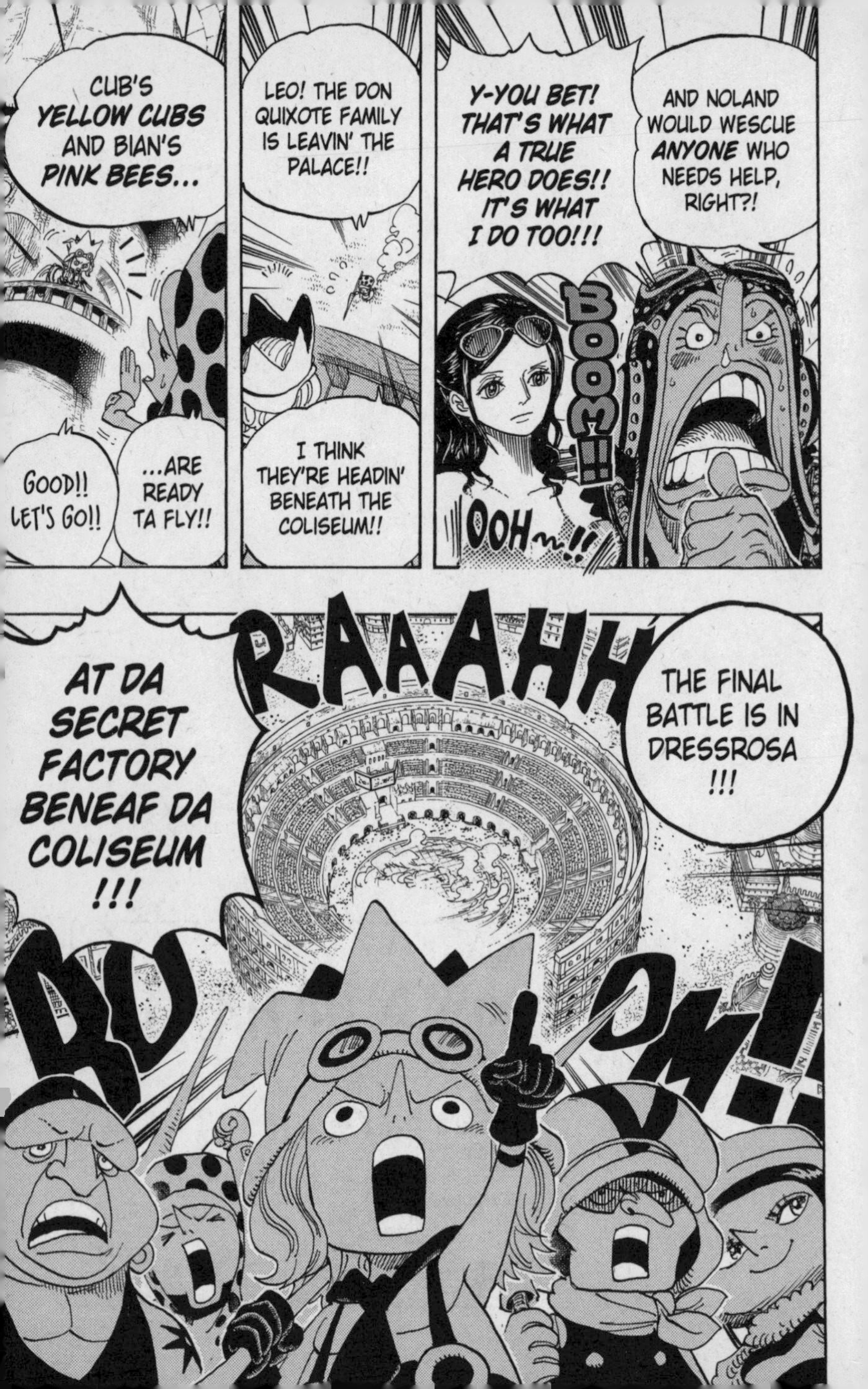

AND NOLAND WOULD WESCUE ANYONE WHO NEEDS HELP, RIGHT?!
Y-YOU BET! THAT'S WHAT A TRUE HERO DOES!! IT'S WHAT I DO TOO!!!
BOOM!!
OOH~!!
LEO! THE DON QUIXOTE FAMILY IS LEAVIN' THE PALACE!!
I THINK THEY'RE HEADIN' BENEATH THE COLISEUM!!
CUB'S YELLOW CUBS AND BIAN'S PINK BEES...
...ARE READY TA FLY!!
GOOD!! LET'S GO!!
THE FINAL BATTLE IS IN DRESSROSA!!!
RAAAHH
AT DA SECRET FACTORY BENEAF DA COLISEUM!!!
BOOM!!

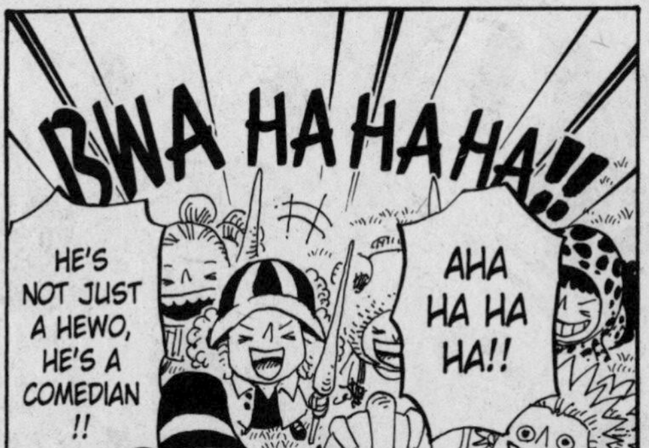
BWA HA HA HA HA!!
AHA HA HA HA!!
HE'S NOT JUST A HEWO, HE'S A COMEDIAN!!

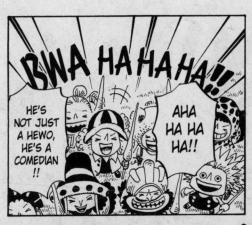

Chapter 718:
RIKU ARMY AT THE FLOWER FIELD

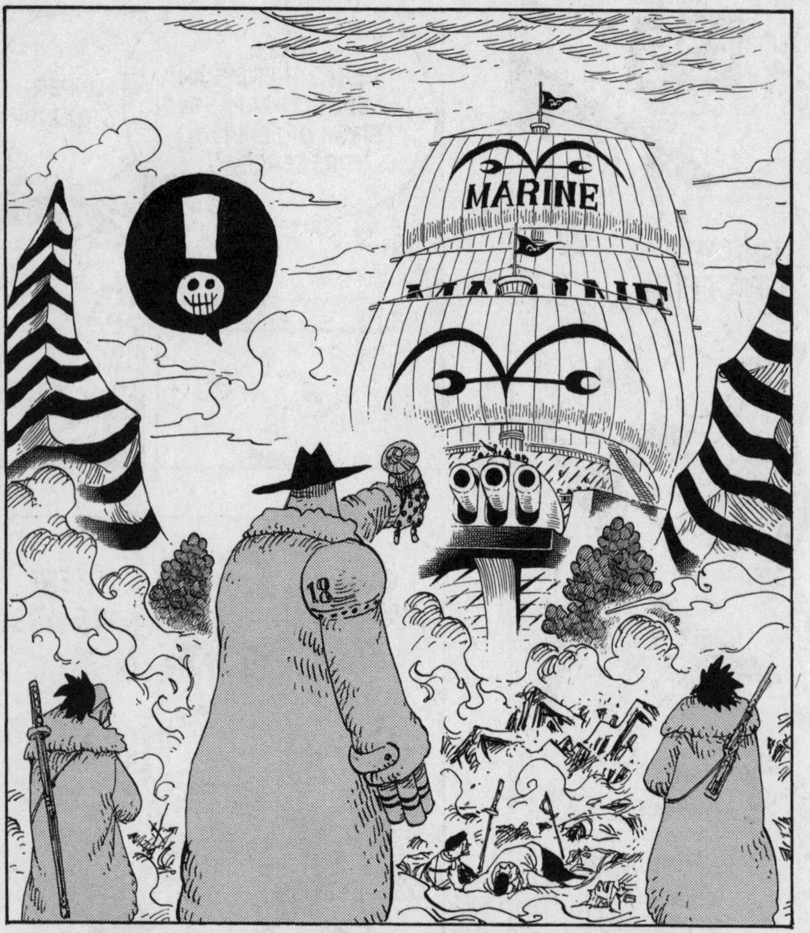
!
MARINE
18

CARIBOU'S NEW WORLD KEE HEE HEE, VOL. 35:
"A BATTLESHIP AT THE SHORE!!"

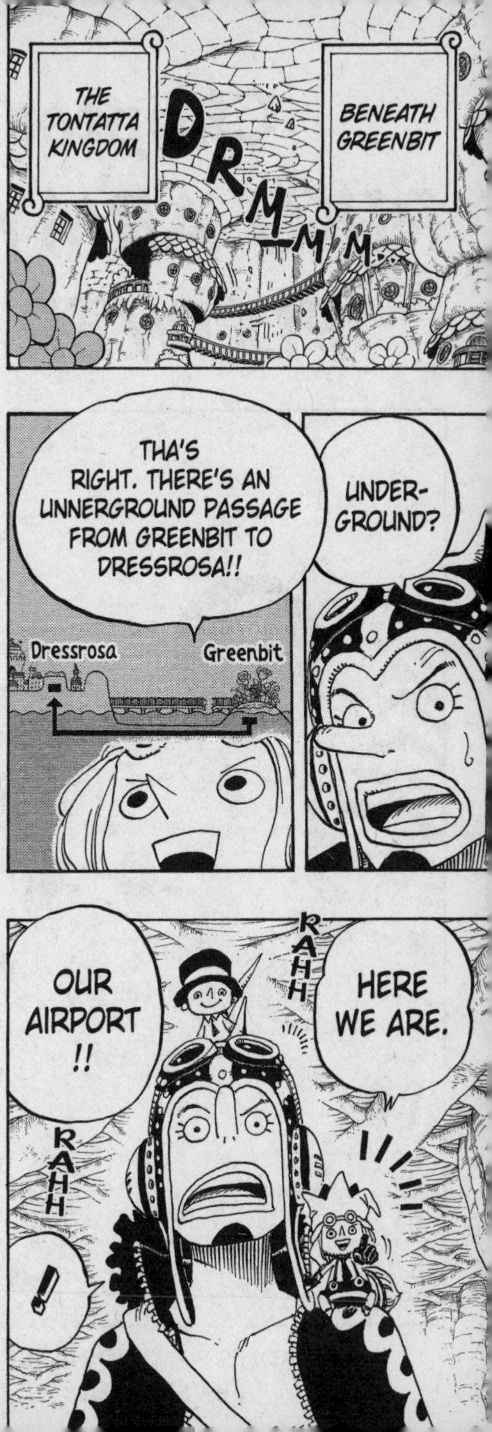
BENEATH GREENBIT
THE TONTATTA KINGDOM
DRMMMM
UNDER-GROUND?
THA'S RIGHT. THERE'S AN UNNERGROUND PASSAGE FROM GREENBIT TO DRESSROSA!!
Greenbit
Dressrosa
HERE WE ARE.
RAHH
OUR AIRPORT!!
RAHH
!

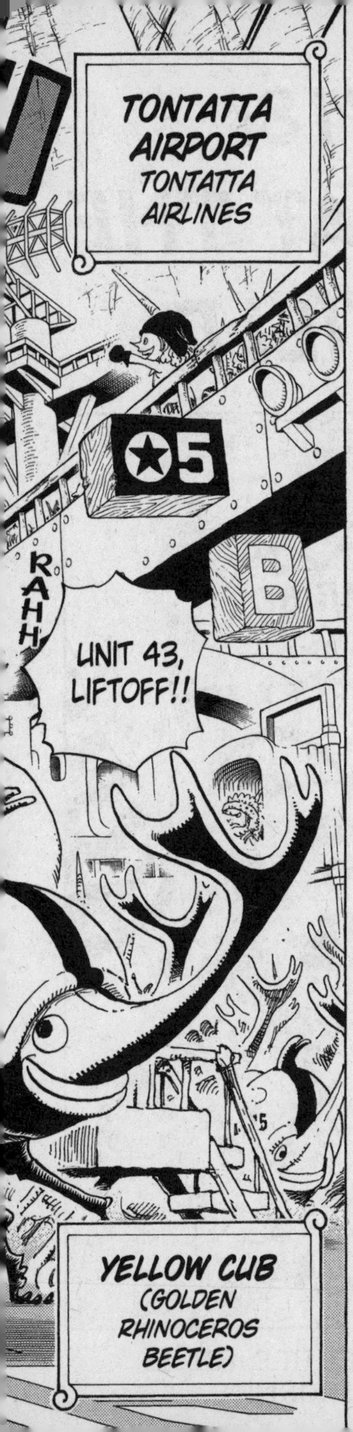
TONTATTA AIRPORT
TONTATTA AIRLINES
5
B
RAHH
UNIT 43, LIFTOFF!!
YELLOW CUB (GOLDEN RHINOCEROS BEETLE)

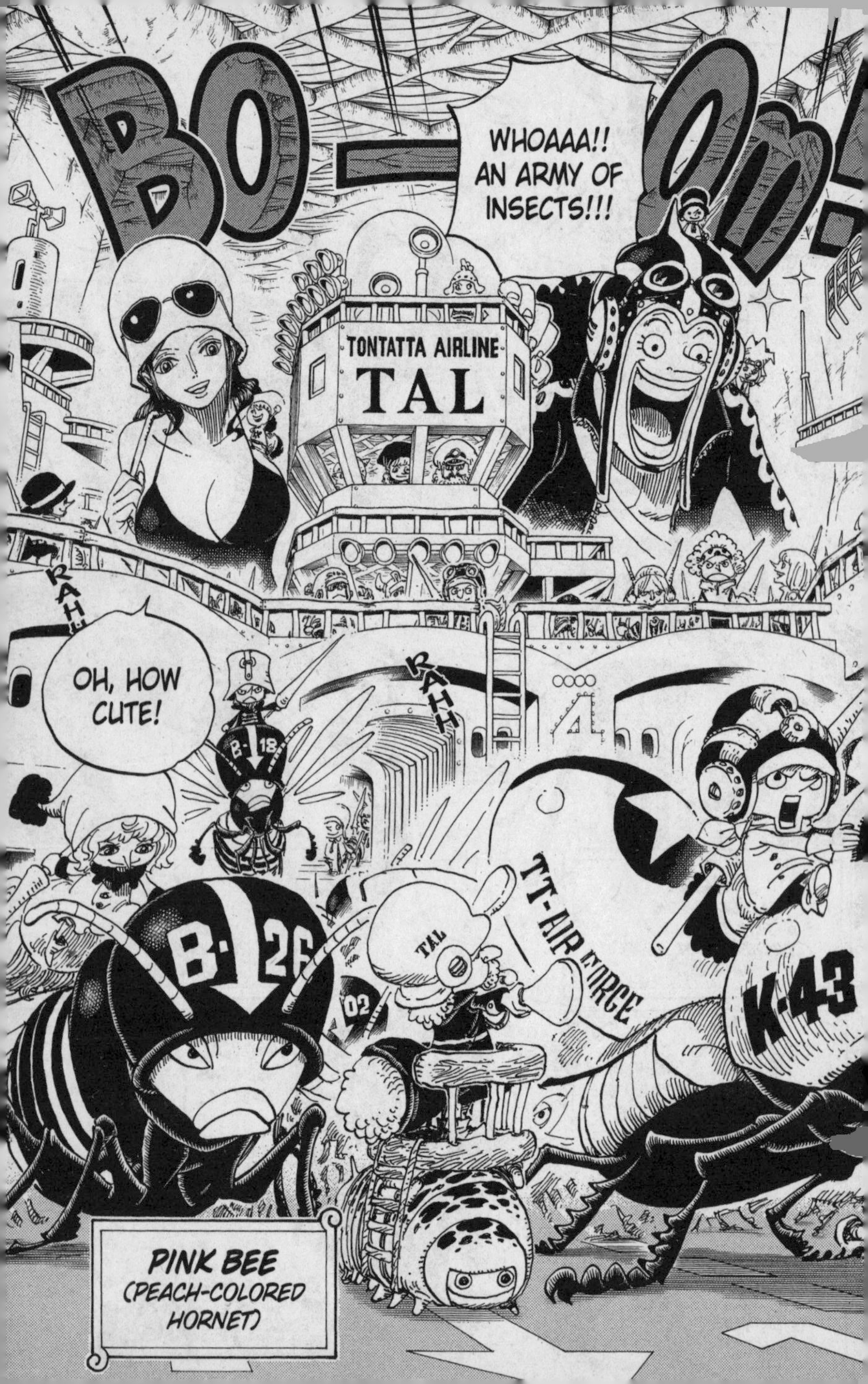
BO—OM!
WHOAAA!! AN ARMY OF INSECTS!!!
TONTATTA AIRLINE
TAL
4
K-43
TT-AIR FORCE
RAHH
TAL
02
RAHH
OH, HOW CUTE!
B-18
B-26
PINK BEE (PEACH-COLORED HORNET)

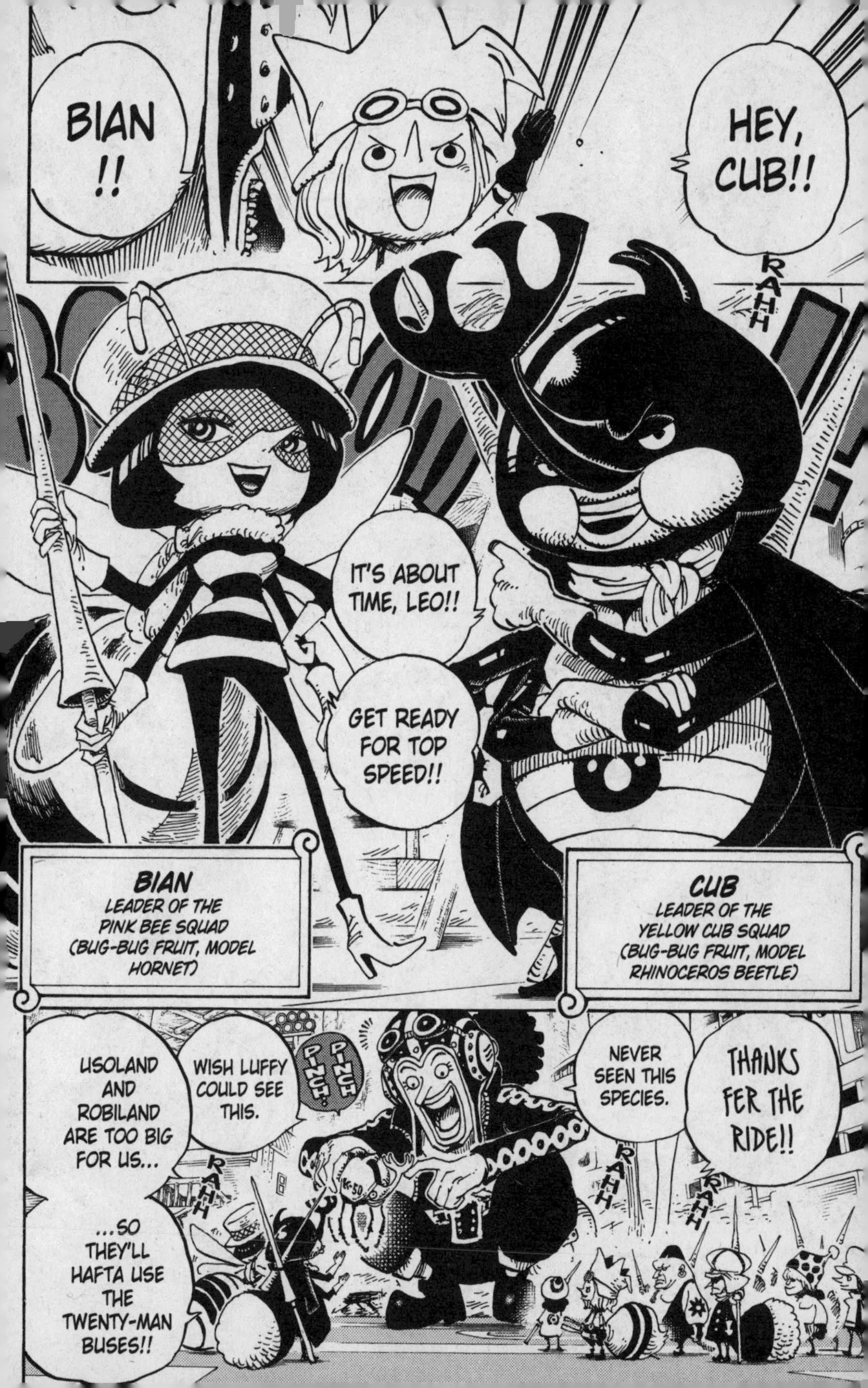
HEY, CUB!!
RAHH
BIAN!!
IT'S ABOUT TIME, LEO!!
GET READY FOR TOP SPEED!!
CUB
LEADER OF THE YELLOW CUB SQUAD (BUG-BUG FRUIT, MODEL RHINOCEROS BEETLE)
BIAN
LEADER OF THE PINK BEE SQUAD (BUG-BUG FRUIT, MODEL HORNET)
THANKS FER THE RIDE!!
RAHH
NEVER SEEN THIS SPECIES.
RAHH
PINCH PINCH
WISH LUFFY COULD SEE THIS.
USOLAND AND ROBILAND ARE TOO BIG FOR US...
RAHH
...SO THEY'LL HAFTA USE THE TWENTY-MAN BUSES!!

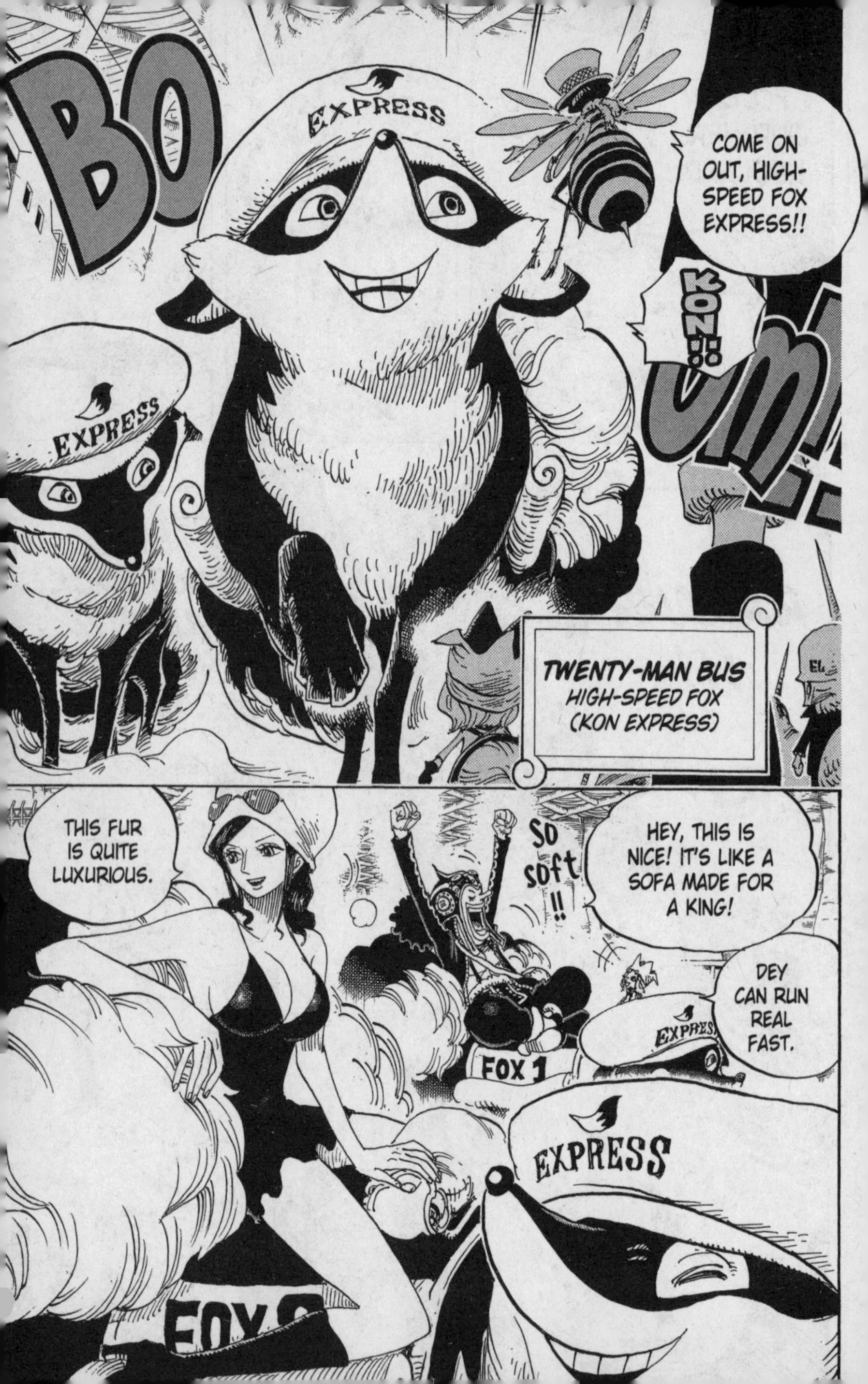
COME ON OUT, HIGH-SPEED FOX EXPRESS!!
KON!!
EXPRESS
EXPRESS
BO
TWENTY-MAN BUS
HIGH-SPEED FOX
(KON EXPRESS)
HEY, THIS IS NICE! IT'S LIKE A SOFA MADE FOR A KING!
DEY CAN RUN REAL FAST.
EXPRESS
SO soft!!
FOX 1
THIS FUR IS QUITE LUXURIOUS.
EXPRESS

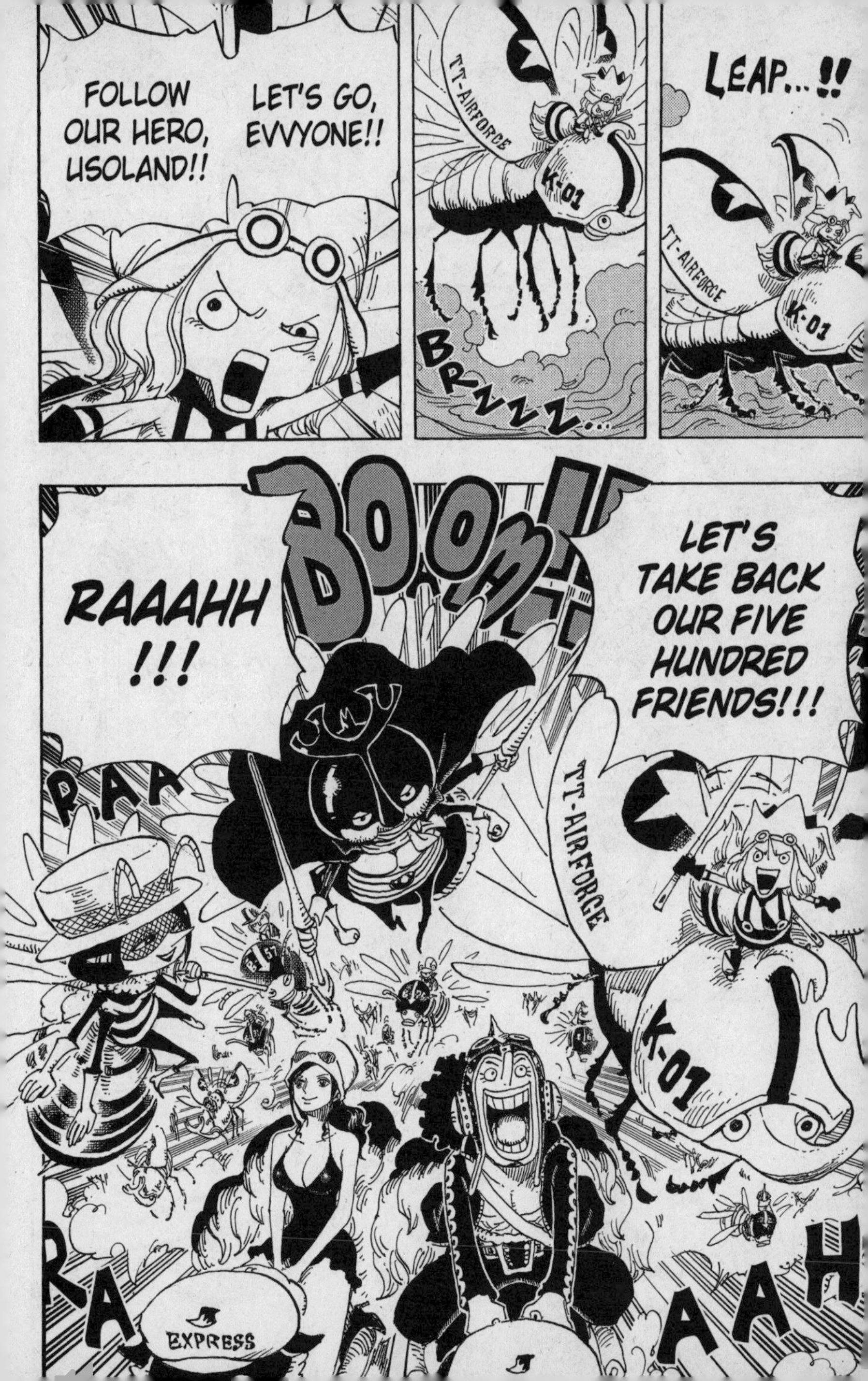
LEAP...!!
TT-AIRFORCE
K-01
TT-AIRFORCE
K-01
BRZZZZ...
LET'S GO, EVVYONE!!
FOLLOW OUR HERO, USOLAND!!
LET'S TAKE BACK OUR FIVE HUNDRED FRIENDS!!!
BOOM
RAAAHH !!!
RAA
TT-AIRFORCE
K-01
EXPRESS
RA
AAH

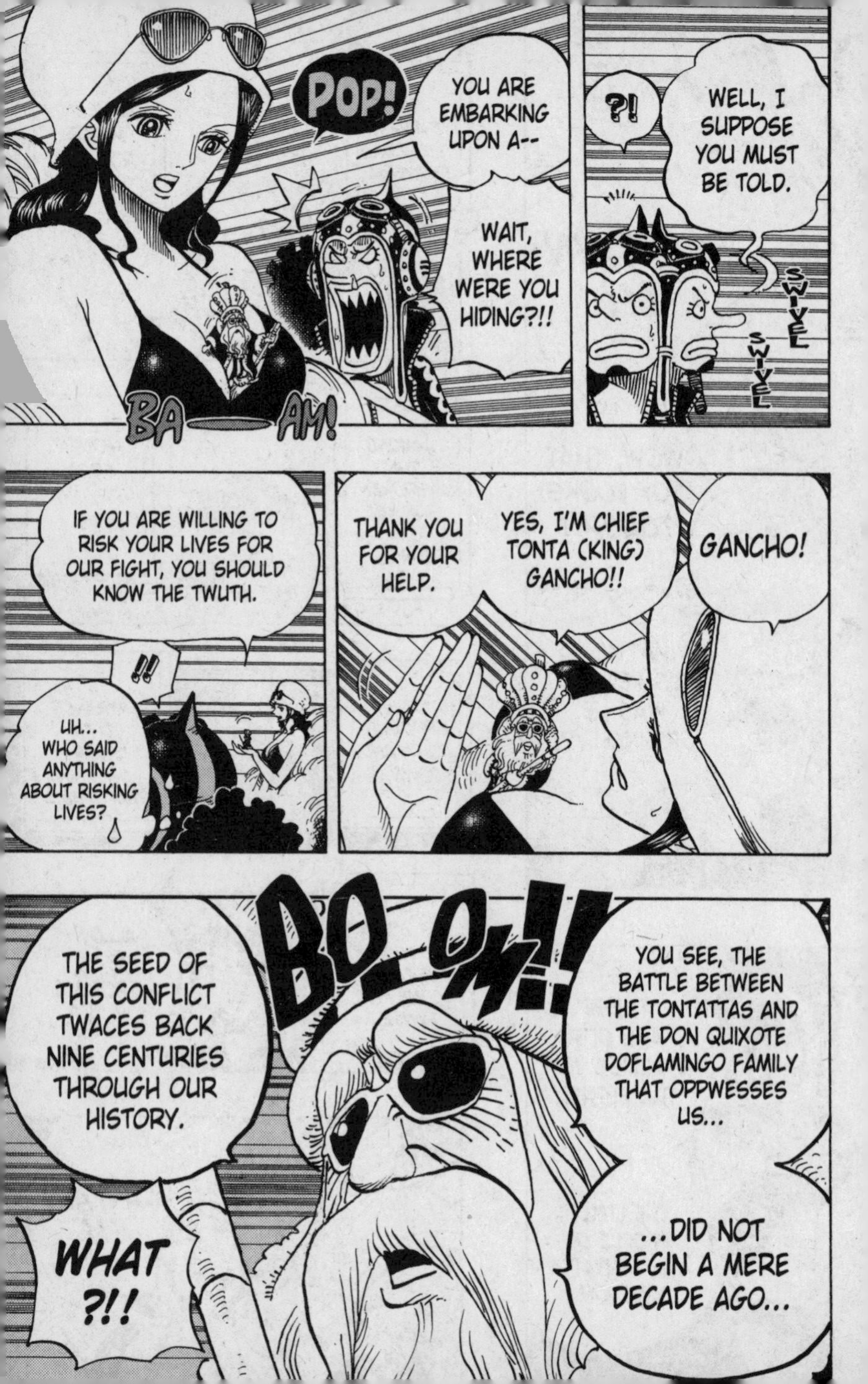
WELL, I SUPPOSE YOU MUST BE TOLD.
?!
SWIVEL
SWIVEL
YOU ARE EMBARKING UPON A--
POP!
WAIT, WHERE WERE YOU HIDING?!!
BA—AM!
GANCHO!
YES, I'M CHIEF TONTA (KING) GANCHO!!
THANK YOU FOR YOUR HELP.
IF YOU ARE WILLING TO RISK YOUR LIVES FOR OUR FIGHT, YOU SHOULD KNOW THE TWUTH.
!!
UH... WHO SAID ANYTHING ABOUT RISKING LIVES?
YOU SEE, THE BATTLE BETWEEN THE TONTATTAS AND THE DON QUIXOTE DOFLAMINGO FAMILY THAT OPPWESSES US...
...DID NOT BEGIN A MERE DECADE AGO...
BO—OM!!
THE SEED OF THIS CONFLICT TWACES BACK NINE CENTURIES THROUGH OUR HISTORY.
WHAT?!!

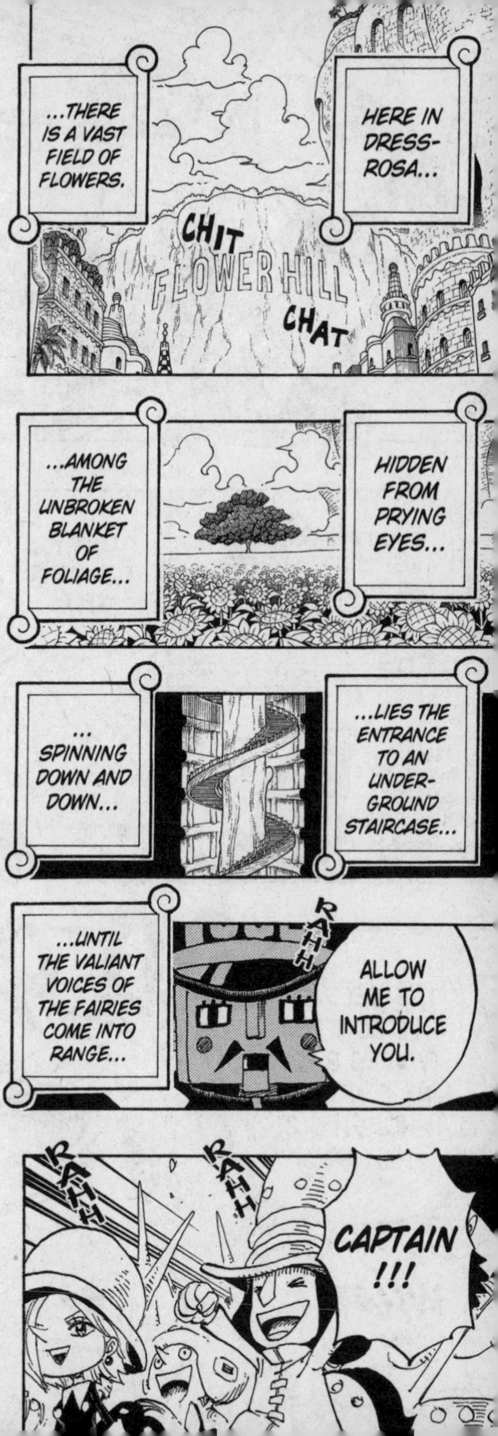
HERE IN DRESS-ROSA...
...THERE IS A VAST FIELD OF FLOWERS.
CHIT
FLOWER HILL
CHAT
HIDDEN FROM PRYING EYES...
...AMONG THE UNBROKEN BLANKET OF FOLIAGE...
...LIES THE ENTRANCE TO AN UNDER-GROUND STAIRCASE...
...SPINNING DOWN AND DOWN...
RAHH
ALLOW ME TO INTRODUCE YOU.
...UNTIL THE VALIANT VOICES OF THE FAIRIES COME INTO RANGE...
RAHH
RAHH
CAPTAIN!!!
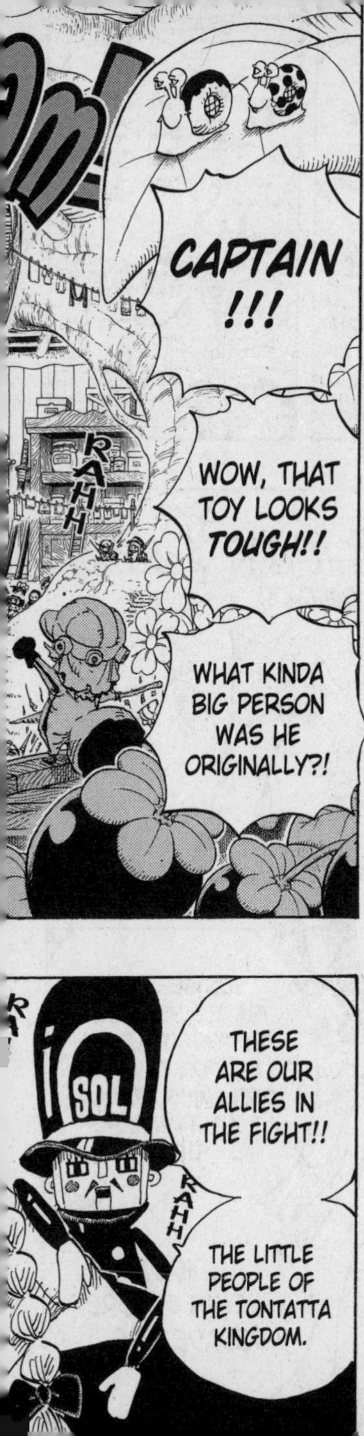
CAPTAIN!!!
RAHH
WOW, THAT TOY LOOKS TOUGH!!
WHAT KINDA BIG PERSON WAS HE ORIGINALLY?!
THESE ARE OUR ALLIES IN THE FIGHT!!
RAHH
THE LITTLE PEOPLE OF THE TONTATTA KINGDOM.

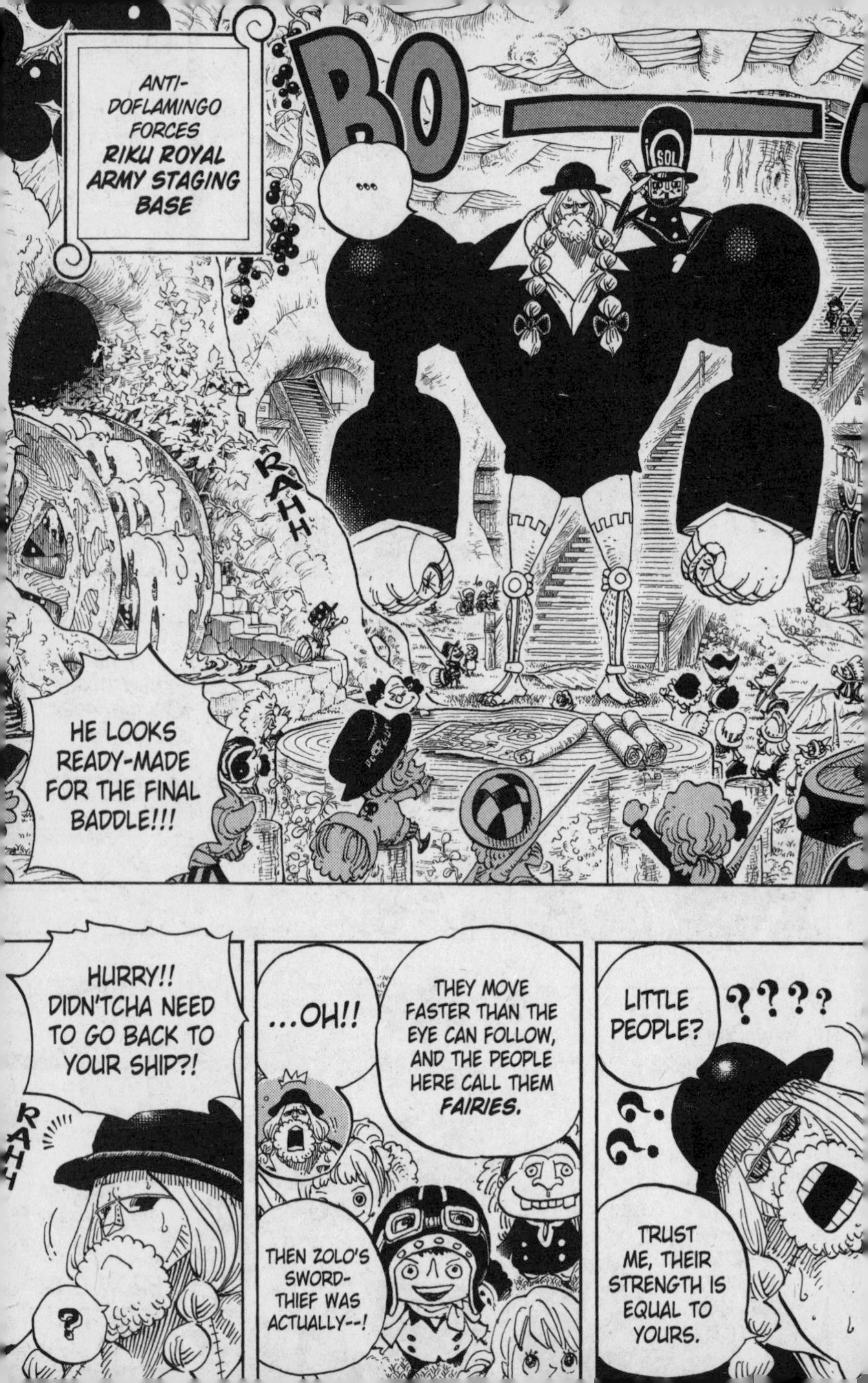

BO—T—
...
ANTI-DOFLAMINGO FORCES RIKU ROYAL ARMY STAGING BASE
RAHH
HE LOOKS READY-MADE FOR THE FINAL BADDLE!!!
LITTLE PEOPLE?
????
??
TRUST ME, THEIR STRENGTH IS EQUAL TO YOURS.
THEY MOVE FASTER THAN THE EYE CAN FOLLOW, AND THE PEOPLE HERE CALL THEM FAIRIES.
...OH!!
THEN ZOLO'S SWORD-THIEF WAS ACTUALLY--!
HURRY!! DIDN'TCHA NEED TO GO BACK TO YOUR SHIP?!
RAHH
?

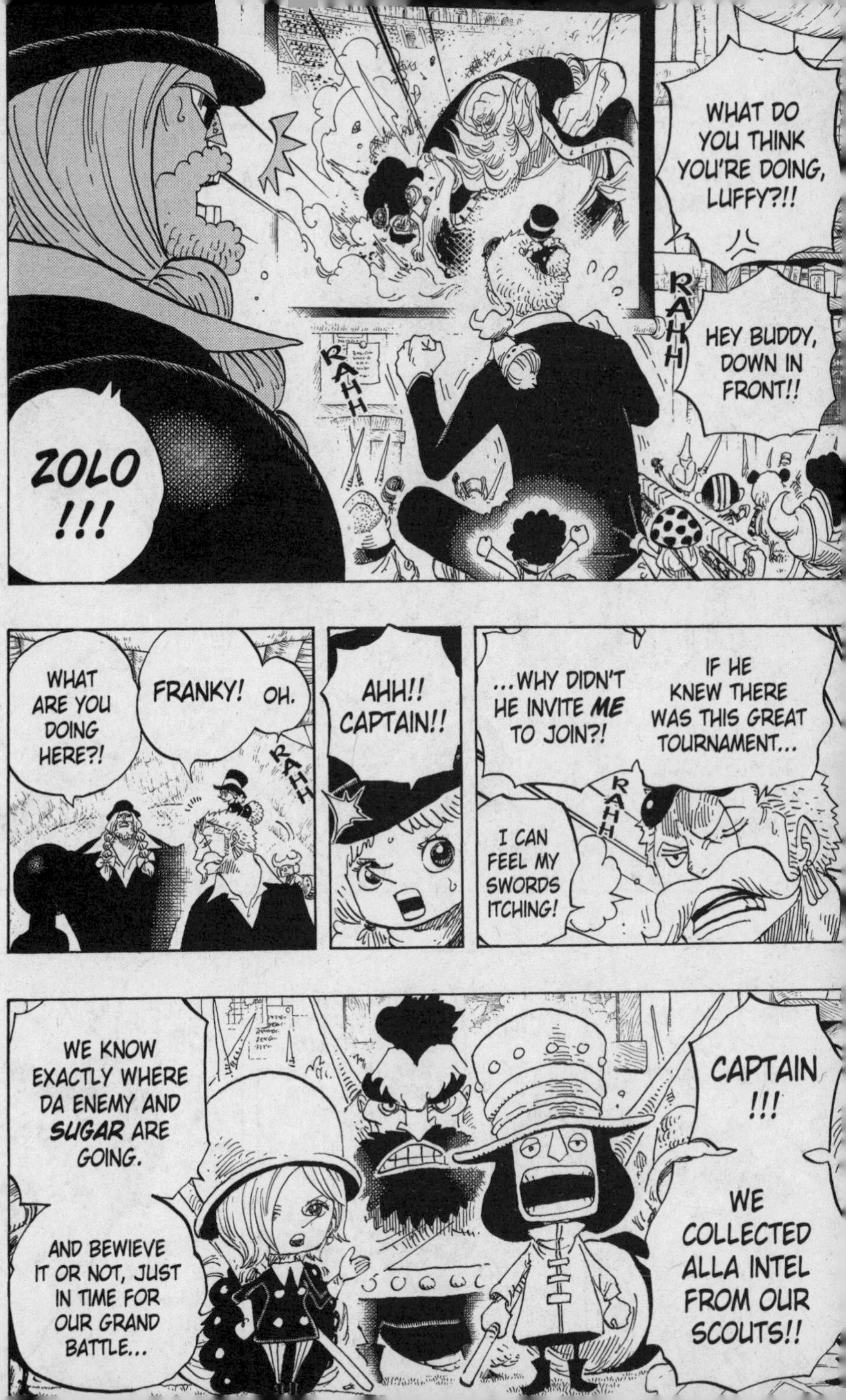
WHAT DO YOU THINK YOU'RE DOING, LUFFY?!!
RAHH
HEY BUDDY, DOWN IN FRONT!!
RAHH
ZOLO !!!
IF HE KNEW THERE WAS THIS GREAT TOURNAMENT...
...WHY DIDN'T HE INVITE *ME* TO JOIN?!
RAHH
I CAN FEEL MY SWORDS ITCHING!
AHH!! CAPTAIN!!
OH.
FRANKY!
WHAT ARE YOU DOING HERE?!
RAHH
CAPTAIN !!!
WE COLLECTED ALLA INTEL FROM OUR SCOUTS!!
WE KNOW EXACTLY WHERE DA ENEMY AND *SUGAR* ARE GOING.
AND BEWIEVE IT OR NOT, JUST IN TIME FOR OUR GRAND BATTLE...

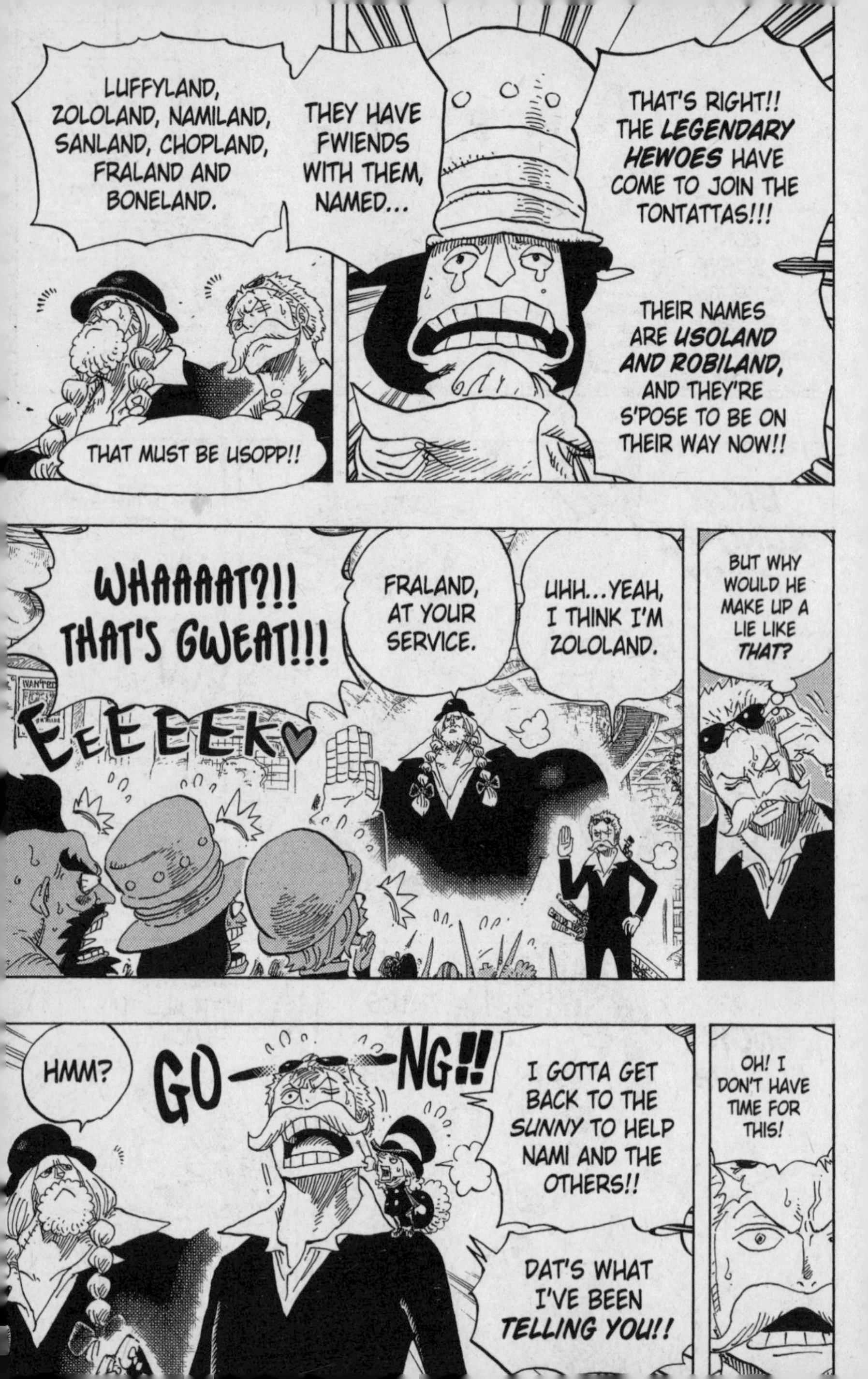
THAT'S RIGHT!! THE LEGENDARY HEWOES HAVE COME TO JOIN THE TONTATTAS!!!
THEIR NAMES ARE USOLAND AND ROBILAND, AND THEY'RE S'POSE TO BE ON THEIR WAY NOW!!
THEY HAVE FWIENDS WITH THEM, NAMED...
LUFFYLAND, ZOLOLAND, NAMILAND, SANLAND, CHOPLAND, FRALAND AND BONELAND.
THAT MUST BE USOPP!!
BUT WHY WOULD HE MAKE UP A LIE LIKE THAT?
UHH...YEAH, I THINK I'M ZOLOLAND.
FRALAND, AT YOUR SERVICE.
WHAAAAT?!! THAT'S GWEAT!!!
EEEEEK♥
OH! I DON'T HAVE TIME FOR THIS!
I GOTTA GET BACK TO THE SUNNY TO HELP NAMI AND THE OTHERS!!
GO——NG!!
HMM?
DAT'S WHAT I'VE BEEN TELLING YOU!!

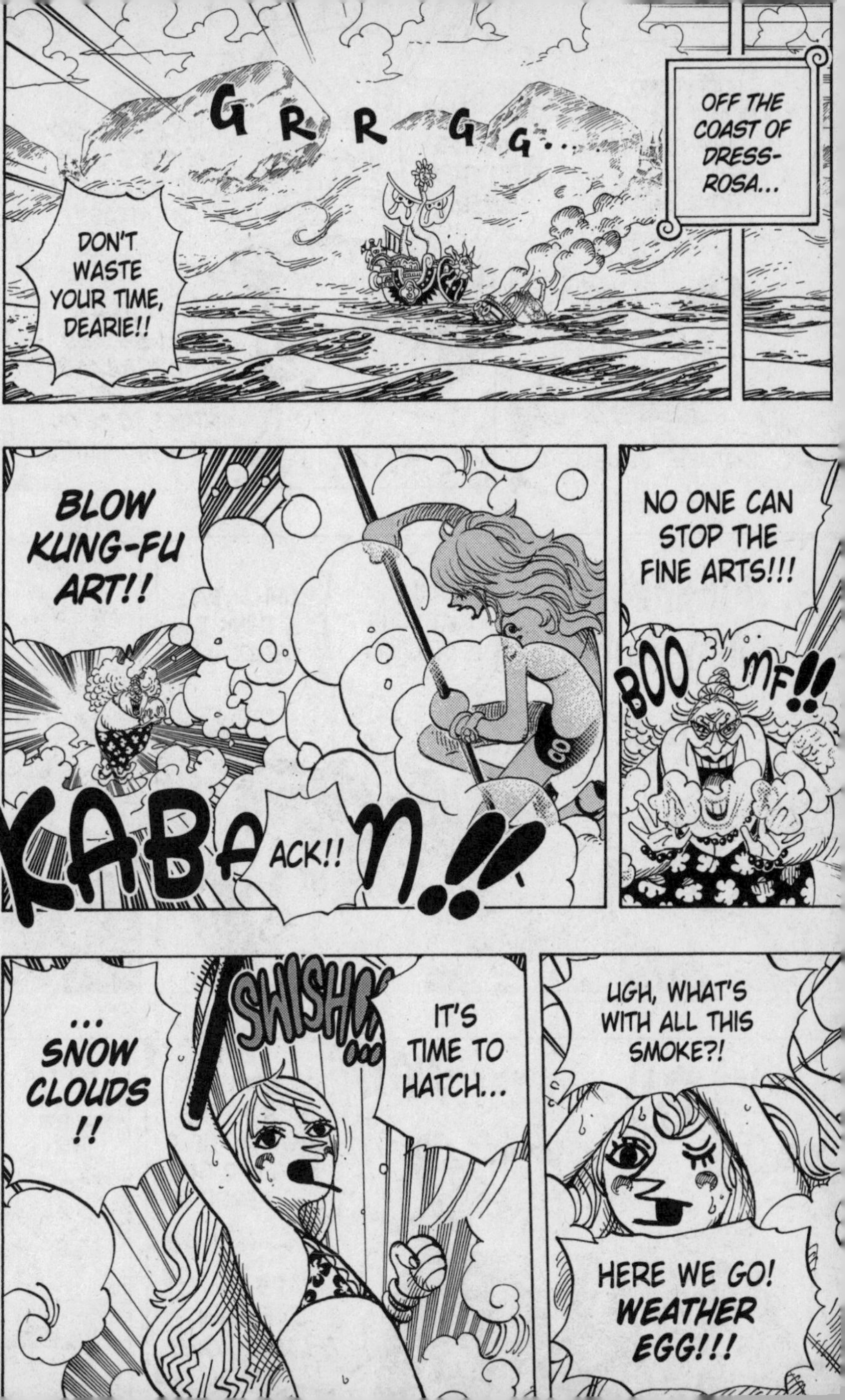
OFF THE COAST OF DRESS-ROSA...
GRRRGG...
DON'T WASTE YOUR TIME, DEARIE!!
NO ONE CAN STOP THE FINE ARTS!!!
BOOMF!!
BLOW KUNG-FU ART!!
KABAAN!!
ACK!!
UGH, WHAT'S WITH ALL THIS SMOKE?!
HERE WE GO! WEATHER EGG!!!
IT'S TIME TO HATCH...
SWISHOOO
... SNOW CLOUDS !!

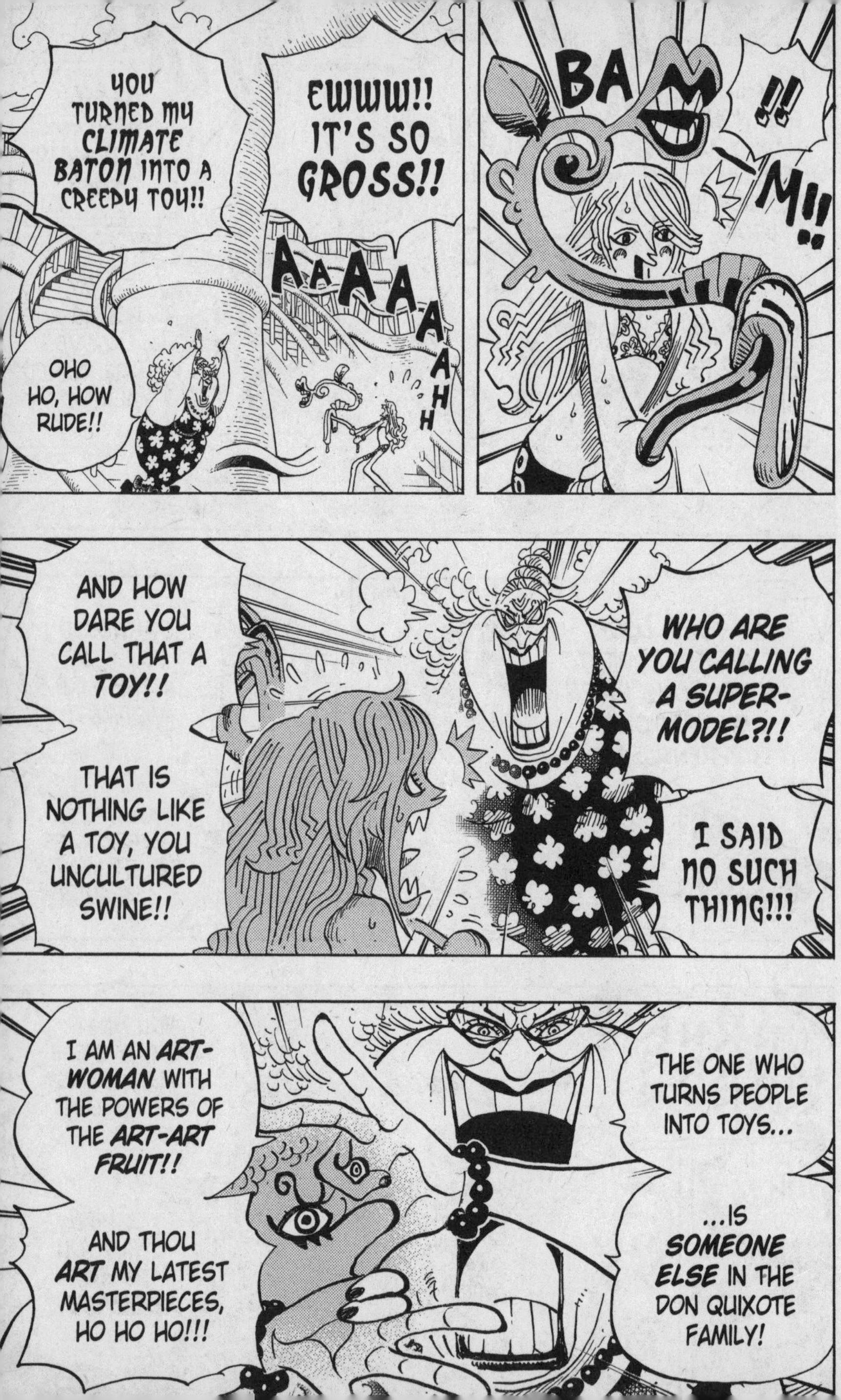
BAM!!
M!!
EWWW!! IT'S SO GROSS!!
YOU TURNED MY CLIMATE BATON INTO A CREEPY TOY!!
AAAAAAAHH
OHO HO, HOW RUDE!!
WHO ARE YOU CALLING A SUPER-MODEL?!!
I SAID NO SUCH THING!!!
AND HOW DARE YOU CALL THAT A TOY!!
THAT IS NOTHING LIKE A TOY, YOU UNCULTURED SWINE!!
THE ONE WHO TURNS PEOPLE INTO TOYS...
...IS SOMEONE ELSE IN THE DON QUIXOTE FAMILY!
I AM AN ART-WOMAN WITH THE POWERS OF THE ART-ART FRUIT!!
AND THOU ART MY LATEST MASTERPIECES, HO HO HO!!!

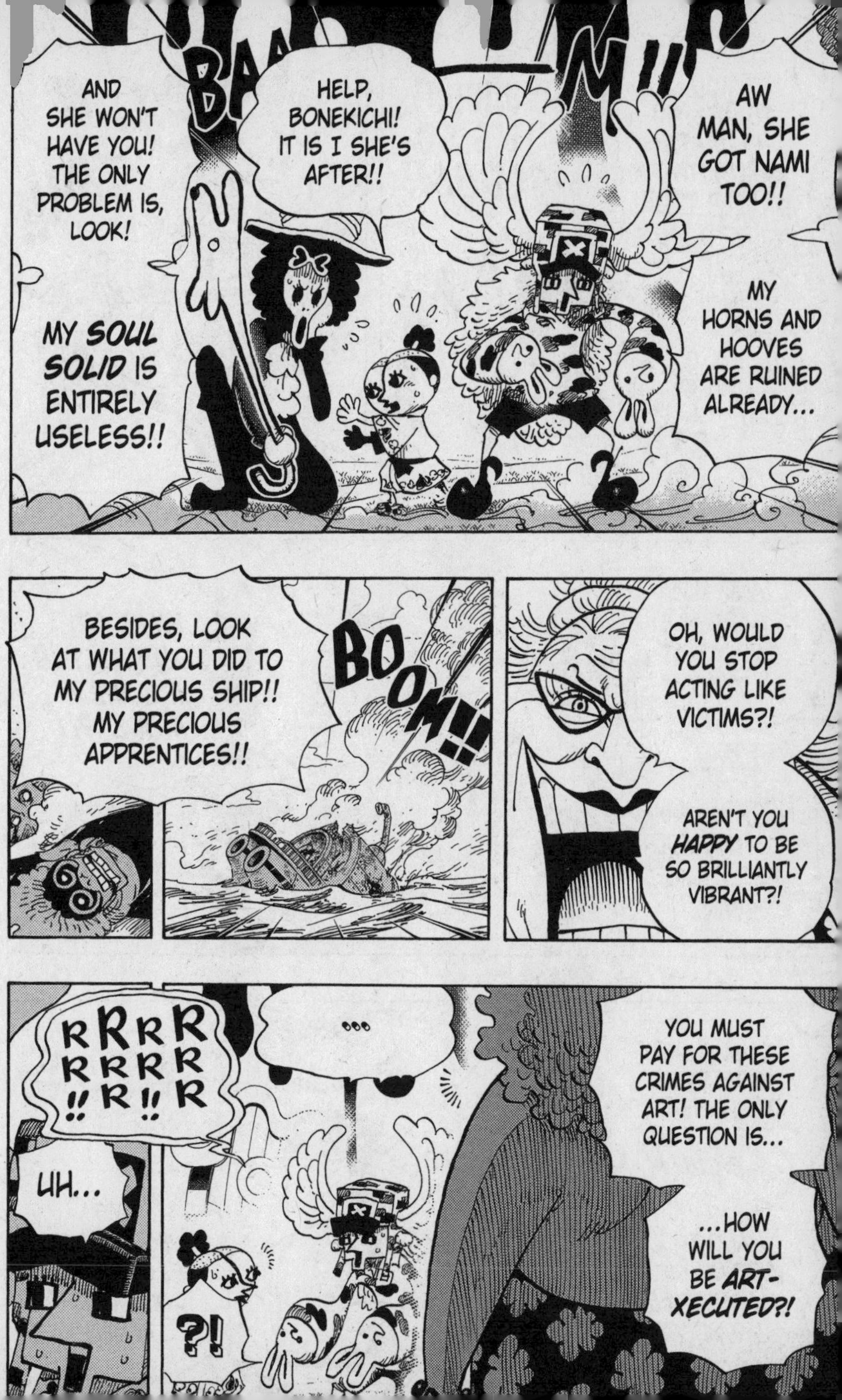
AW MAN, SHE GOT NAMI TOO!!
MY HORNS AND HOOVES ARE RUINED ALREADY...
HELP, BONEKICHI! IT IS I SHE'S AFTER!!
AND SHE WON'T HAVE YOU! THE ONLY PROBLEM IS, LOOK!
MY **SOUL SOLID** IS ENTIRELY USELESS!!
OH, WOULD YOU STOP ACTING LIKE VICTIMS?!
AREN'T YOU **HAPPY** TO BE SO BRILLIANTLY VIBRANT?!
BOOM!!
BESIDES, LOOK AT WHAT YOU DID TO MY PRECIOUS SHIP!! MY PRECIOUS APPRENTICES!!
YOU MUST PAY FOR THESE CRIMES AGAINST ART! THE ONLY QUESTION IS...
...HOW WILL YOU BE **ART-XECUTED?!**
...
?!
RRRRRRRRRRR!!R!!R
UH...

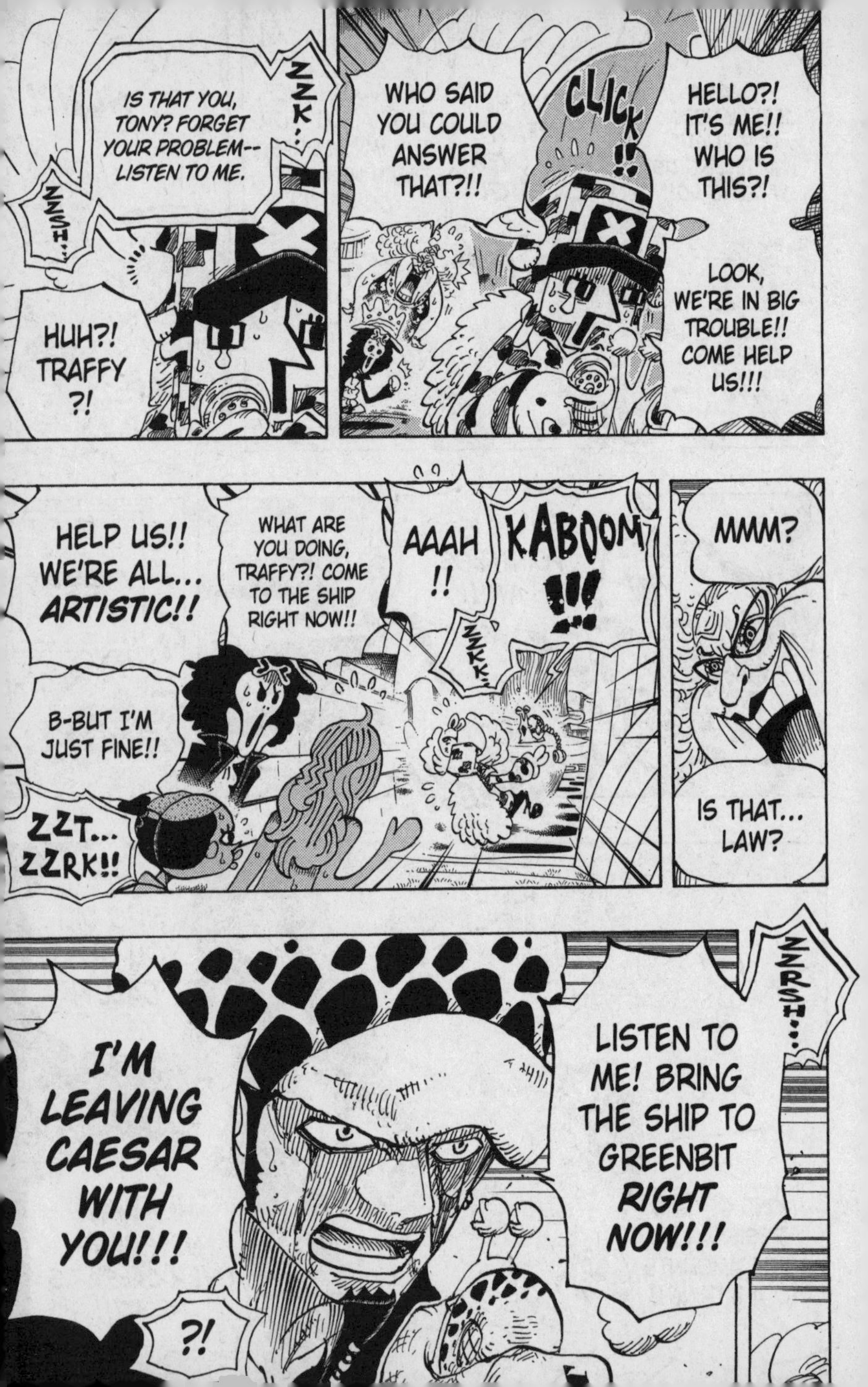
CLICK!!
HELLO?! IT'S ME!! WHO IS THIS?!
LOOK, WE'RE IN BIG TROUBLE!! COME HELP US!!!
WHO SAID YOU COULD ANSWER THAT?!!
ZZK...
IS THAT YOU, TONY? FORGET YOUR PROBLEM-- LISTEN TO ME.
ZZSH...
HUH?! TRAFFY ?!
MMM?
IS THAT... LAW?
KABOOM!!!
AAAH !!
ZZKK...
WHAT ARE YOU DOING, TRAFFY?! COME TO THE SHIP RIGHT NOW!!
HELP US!! WE'RE ALL... ARTISTIC!!
B-BUT I'M JUST FINE!!
ZZT... ZZRK!!
ZZRSH...
LISTEN TO ME! BRING THE SHIP TO GREENBIT RIGHT NOW!!!
I'M LEAVING CAESAR WITH YOU!!!
?!

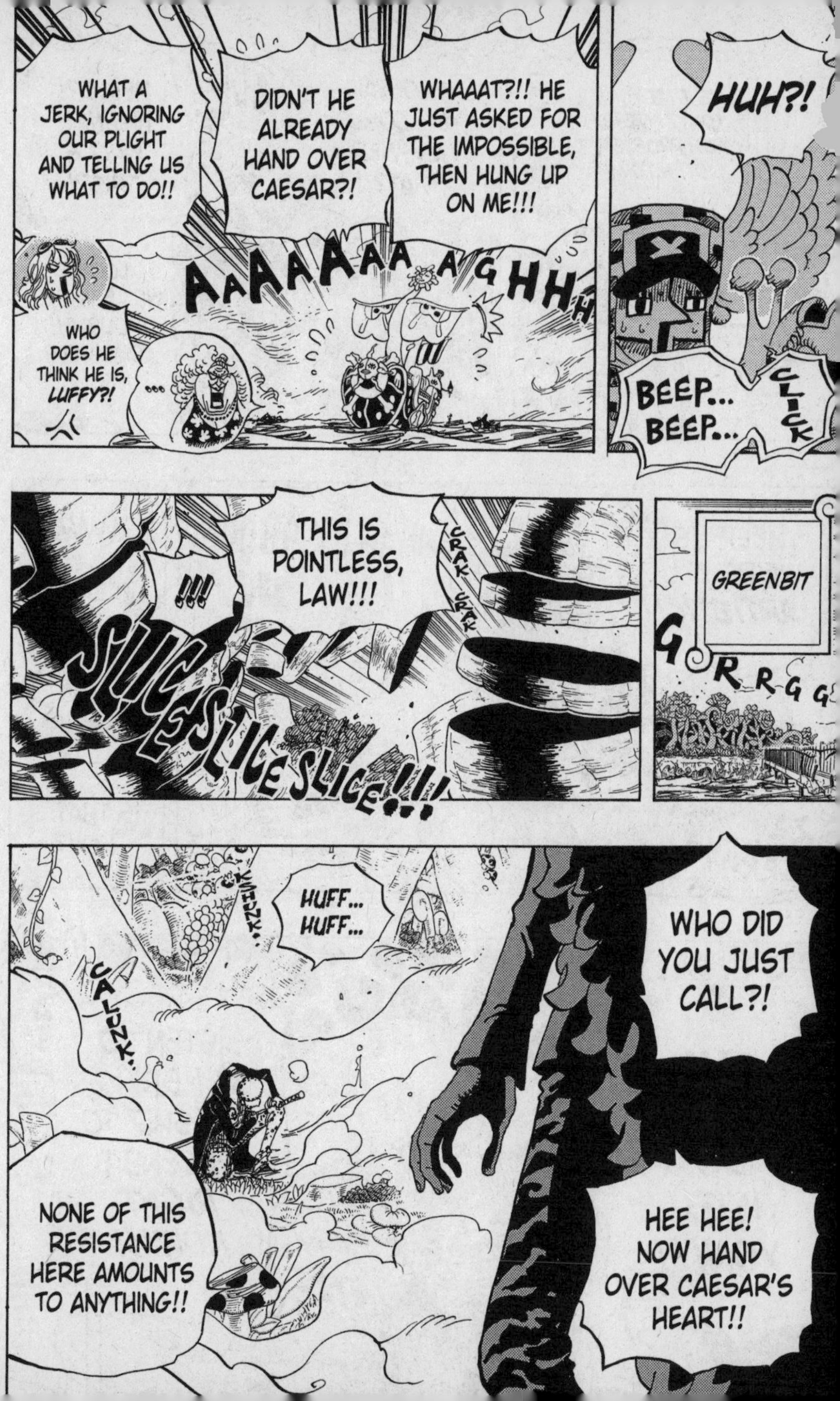
HUH?!
BEEP... BEEP...
CLICK
WHAAAT?!! HE JUST ASKED FOR THE IMPOSSIBLE, THEN HUNG UP ON ME!!!
DIDN'T HE ALREADY HAND OVER CAESAR?!
WHAT A JERK, IGNORING OUR PLIGHT AND TELLING US WHAT TO DO!!
AAAAAAAAGHHHH
WHO DOES HE THINK HE IS, LUFFY?!
...
GREENBIT
GRRRGGG
THIS IS POINTLESS, LAW!!!
CRAK
CRAK
!!!
SLICE SLICE SLICE SLICE!!!
WHO DID YOU JUST CALL?!
HEE HEE! NOW HAND OVER CAESAR'S HEART!!
HUFF... HUFF...
KSHUNK
CALUNK..
NONE OF THIS RESISTANCE HERE AMOUNTS TO ANYTHING!!

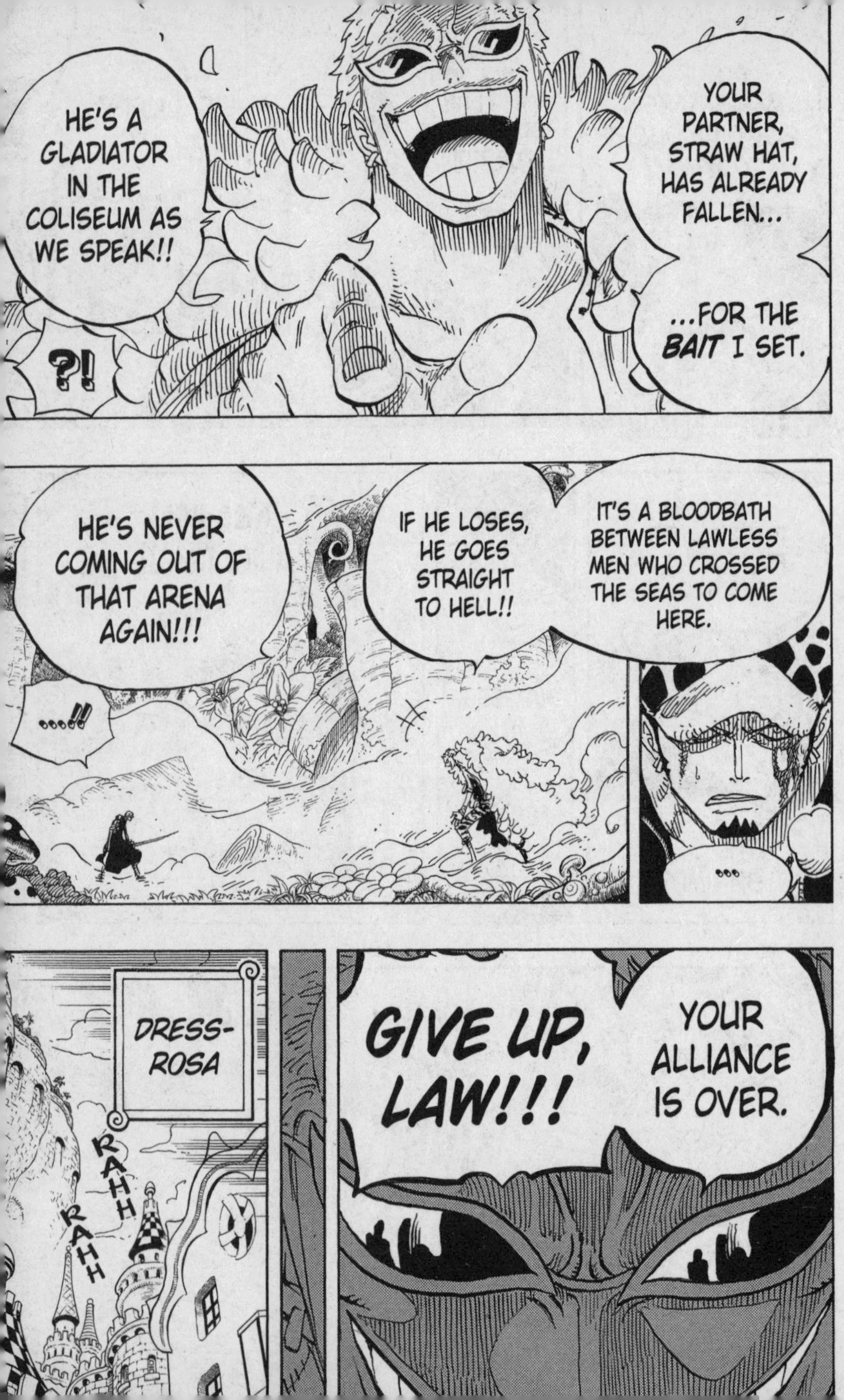
YOUR PARTNER, STRAW HAT, HAS ALREADY FALLEN...
...FOR THE *BAIT* I SET.
HE'S A GLADIATOR IN THE COLISEUM AS WE SPEAK!!
?!
IT'S A BLOODBATH BETWEEN LAWLESS MEN WHO CROSSED THE SEAS TO COME HERE.
...
IF HE LOSES, HE GOES STRAIGHT TO HELL!!
HE'S NEVER COMING OUT OF THAT ARENA AGAIN!!!
...!!
YOUR ALLIANCE IS OVER.
GIVE UP, LAW!!!
DRESS-ROSA
RAHH
RAHH

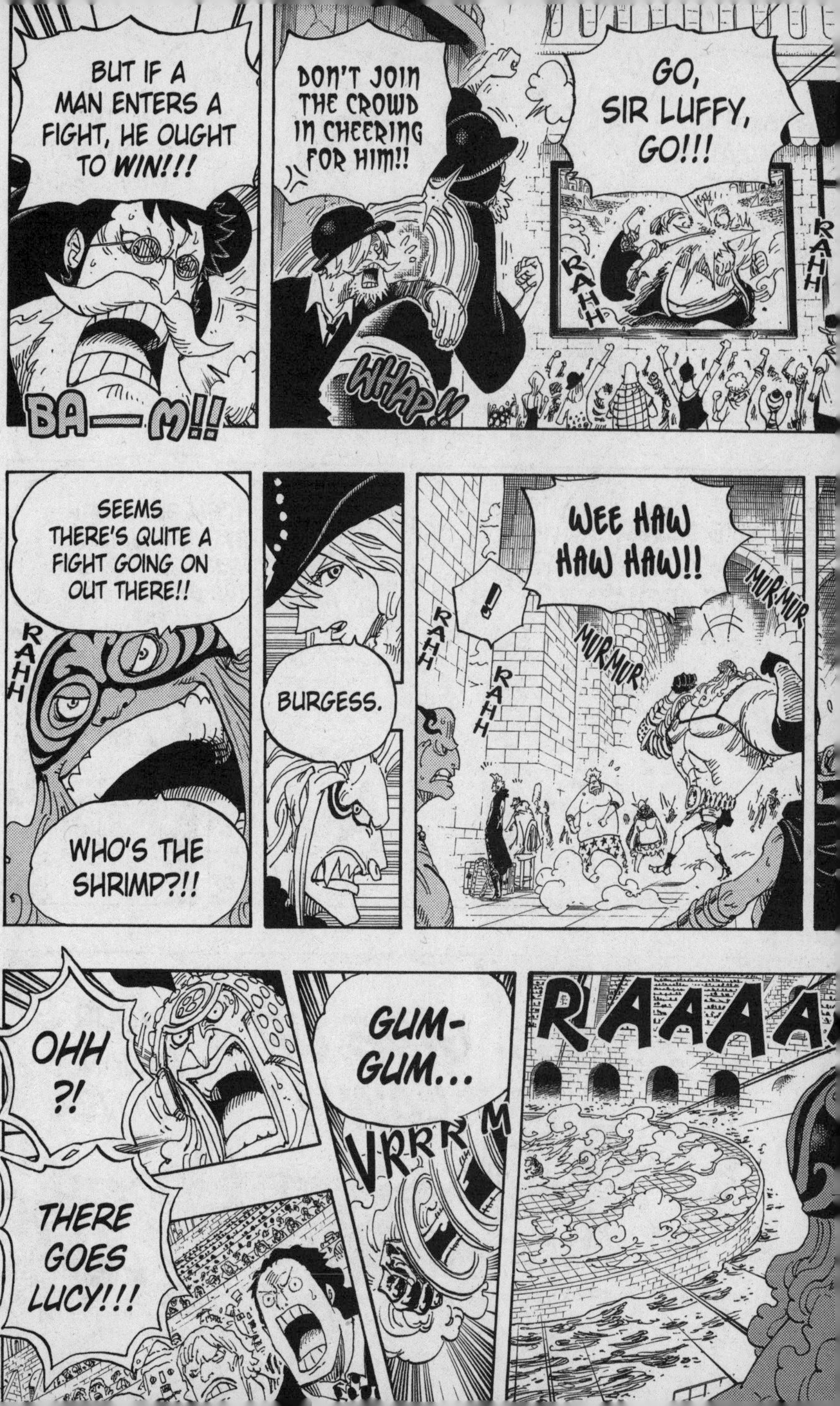
GO, SIR LUFFY, GO!!!
RAHH
RAHH
DON'T JOIN THE CROWD IN CHEERING FOR HIM!!
WHAP!!
BUT IF A MAN ENTERS A FIGHT, HE OUGHT TO WIN!!!
BA—M!!
WEE HAW HAW HAW!!
MURMUR
!
MURMUR
RAHH
RAHH
BURGESS.
SEEMS THERE'S QUITE A FIGHT GOING ON OUT THERE!!
RAHH
WHO'S THE SHRIMP?!!
RAAAA
GUM-GUM...
VRRRM
OHH ?!
THERE GOES LUCY!!!

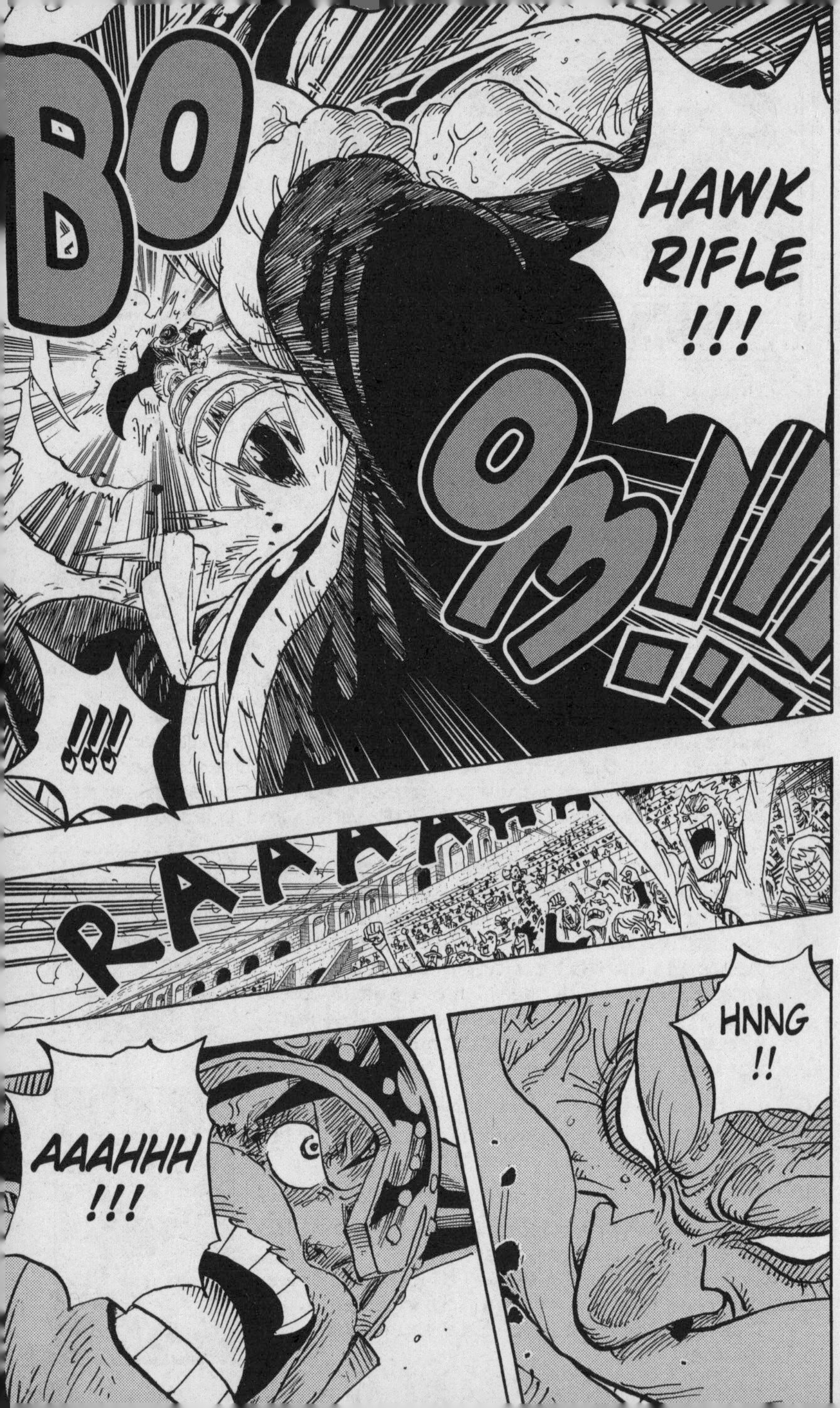
HAWK RIFLE !!!
BO
OM!!
!!!
RAAAAAHH
HNNG !!
AAAHHH !!!

SBS Question Corner

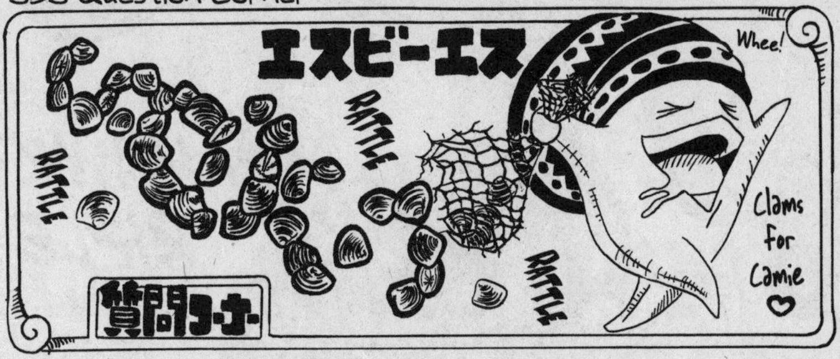

エスビーエス
Whee!
RATTLE
RATTLE
RATTLE
Clams for Camie ♡
質問コーナー

(Michi Nakahara, Tottori)

Q: Hello, Mr. Oda! I noticed that Dressrosa was based on our home of Spain, so I decided to send you this letter as the speaker for our group. Why did you choose Spain? If you ever have reason to visit Spain, I hope you will attend Barcelona's Salon Del Manga (a Spanish manga/anime convention). Nothing to be afraid of! Our women won't stab you!

--Voice of the Pirate King

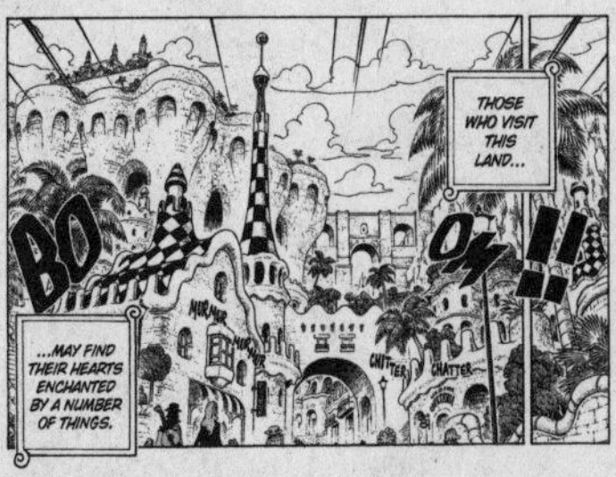

THOSE WHO VISIT THIS LAND...
BO
OM!!
MURMUR
CHITTER
CHATTER
...MAY FIND THEIR HEARTS ENCHANTED BY A NUMBER OF THINGS.

A: This is a condensed version of a letter I received from Spain. The Japanese was strange in a few places, so I think that must have come from one of those auto-translation sites. Thanks for the letter. You're right about Dressrosa. It's based on Spain, and ancient Greece for the coliseum parts. When I took a close look at Doflamingo and tried to think of what kind of country suited him, I arrived at the conclusion of Spain. I've mentioned lands of One Piece being inspired by real countries in the SBS before, but this is the first time I've gotten feedback from residents of that country. I can't be irresponsible in the way I draw, but if you do see anything that seems like a half-baked version of your culture or buildings, please forgive me. Remember, it's just a manga.

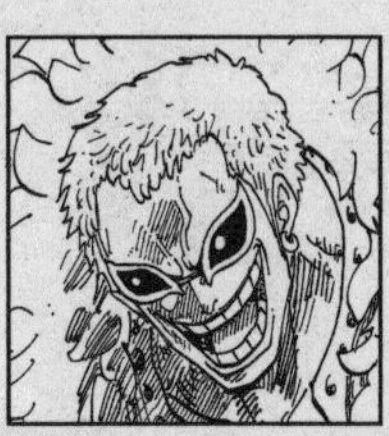

Q: I've been wondering for ages--would you draw gender-swapped versions of the Worst Generation for us? In fact, please do!!!

--Momokichi

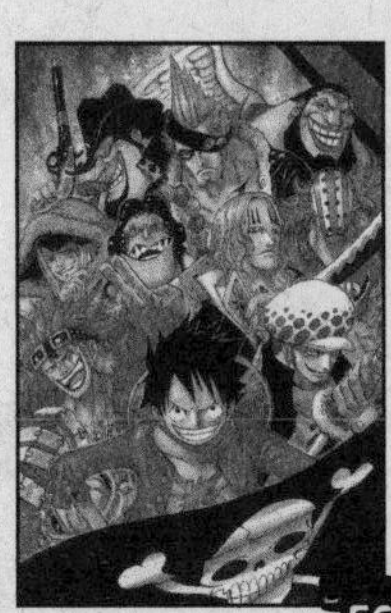

A: I got so many requests for this. I mean, I'll do it, but it's creepy, okay? Check it out on page 582. I haven't shown Blackbeard since the time skip yet, so he's not included. That's all for this SBS. See you next volume!!

Chapter 719:
OPEN, CHIN JAO

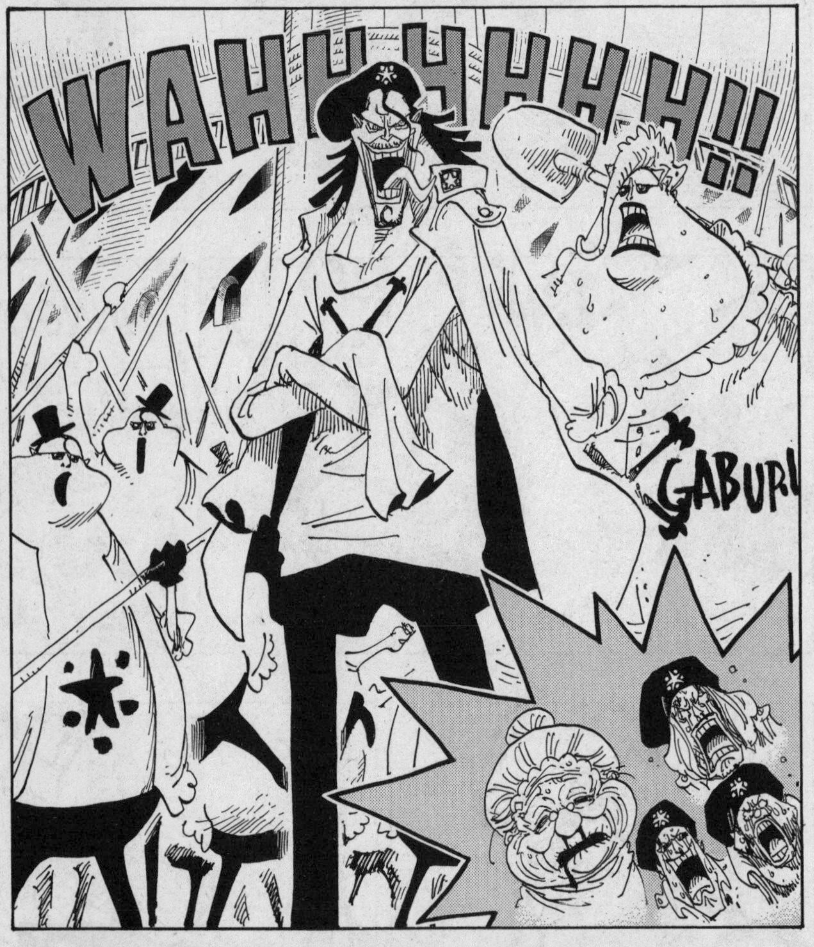
WAHHHHHHH!!
GABURI

CARIBOU'S NEW WORLD KEE HEE HEE, VOL. 36:
"CAPTAIN GABURU IS ALIVE AND ON THE SCENE!!!"

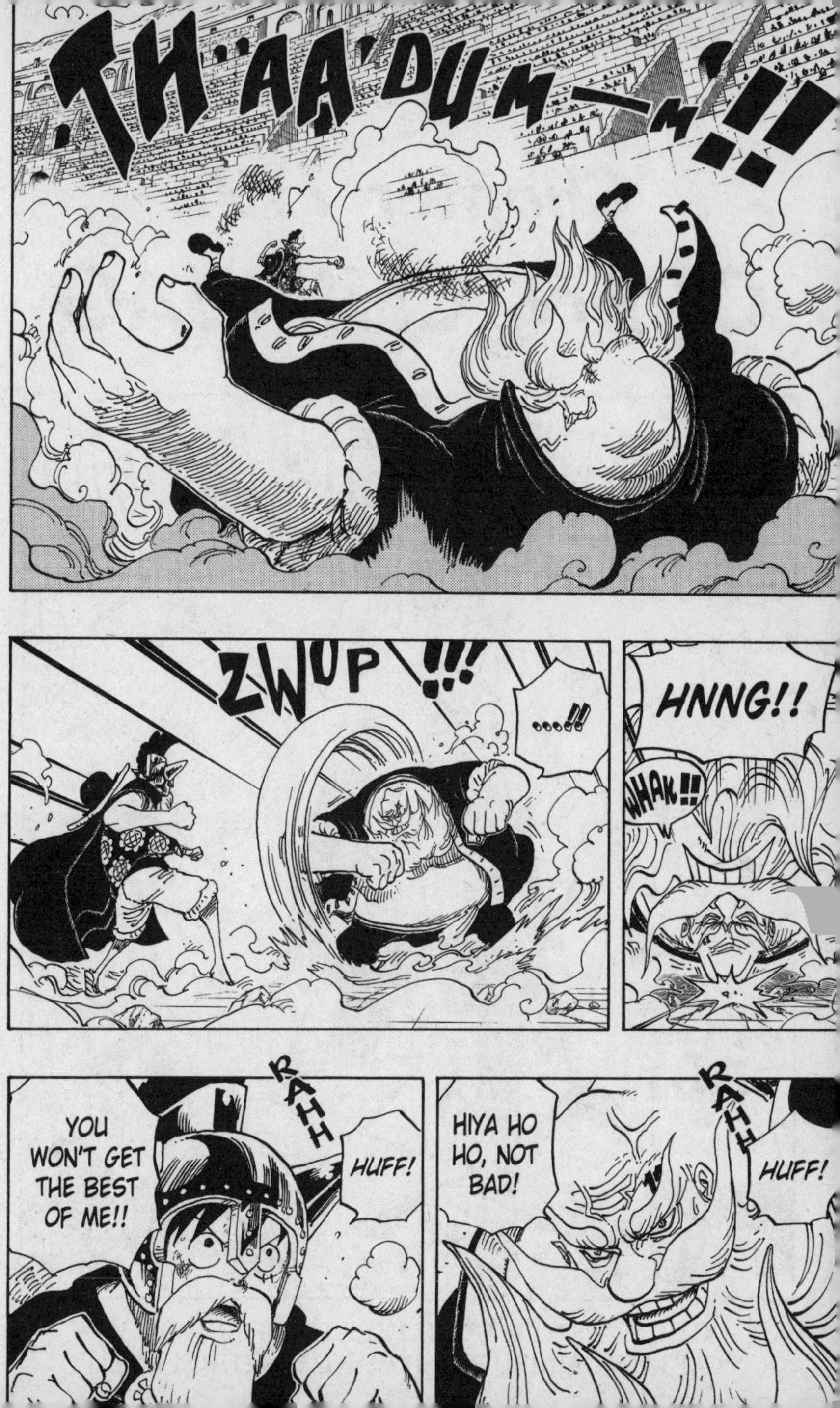
THAADUM—M!!
HNNG!!
WHAK!!
ZWOP!!!
...!!
RAHH
HUFF!
HIYA HO HO, NOT BAD!
RAHH
HUFF!
YOU WON'T GET THE BEST OF ME!!

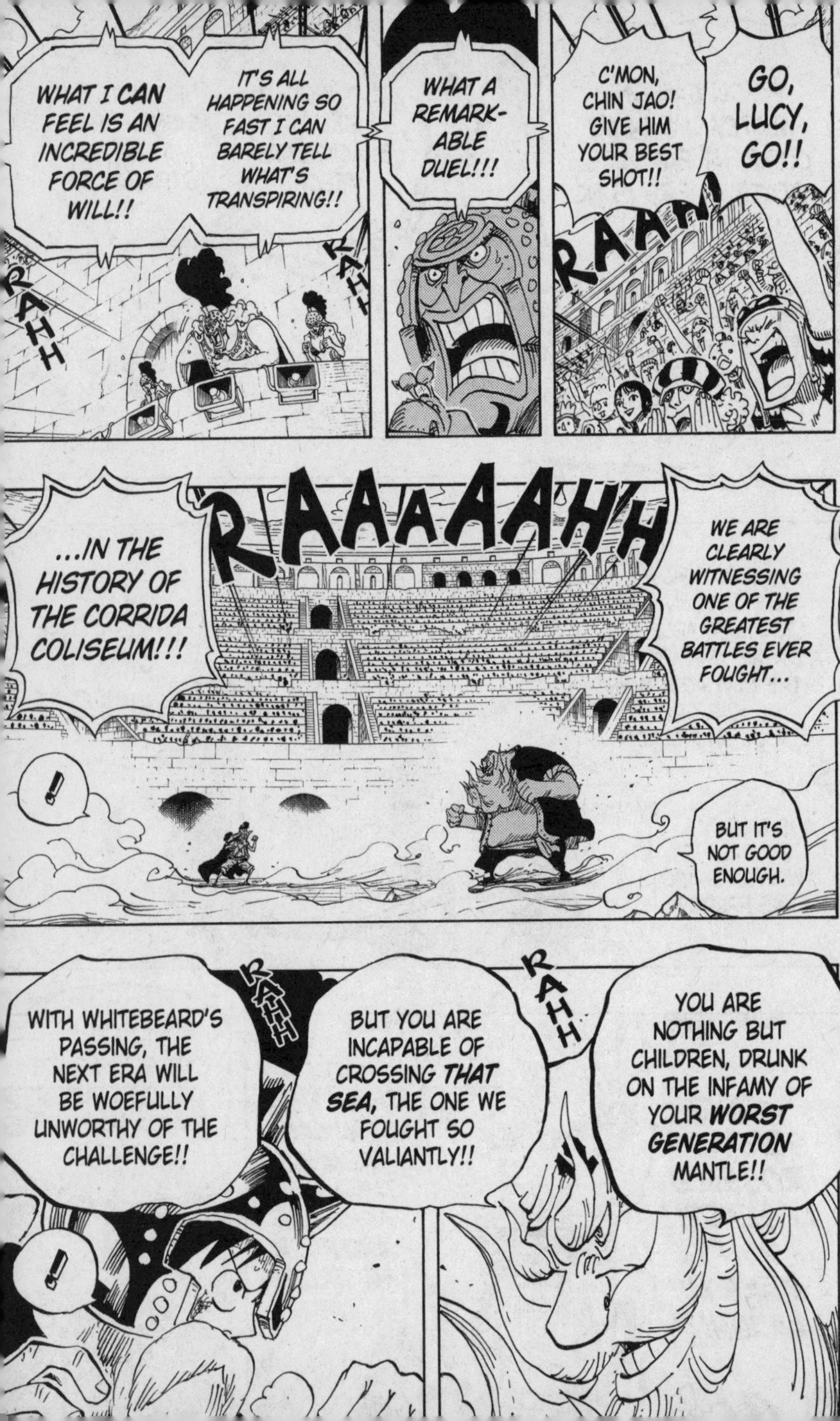
GO, LUCY, GO!!
C'MON, CHIN JAO! GIVE HIM YOUR BEST SHOT!!
RAAAH
WHAT A REMARKABLE DUEL!!!
RAHH
IT'S ALL HAPPENING SO FAST I CAN BARELY TELL WHAT'S TRANSPIRING!!
WHAT I CAN FEEL IS AN INCREDIBLE FORCE OF WILL!!
RAHH
WE ARE CLEARLY WITNESSING ONE OF THE GREATEST BATTLES EVER FOUGHT...
RAAAAAAHH
...IN THE HISTORY OF THE CORRIDA COLISEUM!!!
BUT IT'S NOT GOOD ENOUGH.
!
YOU ARE NOTHING BUT CHILDREN, DRUNK ON THE INFAMY OF YOUR WORST GENERATION MANTLE!!
RAHH
BUT YOU ARE INCAPABLE OF CROSSING THAT SEA, THE ONE WE FOUGHT SO VALIANTLY!!
RAHH
WITH WHITEBEARD'S PASSING, THE NEXT ERA WILL BE WOEFULLY UNWORTHY OF THE CHALLENGE!!
!

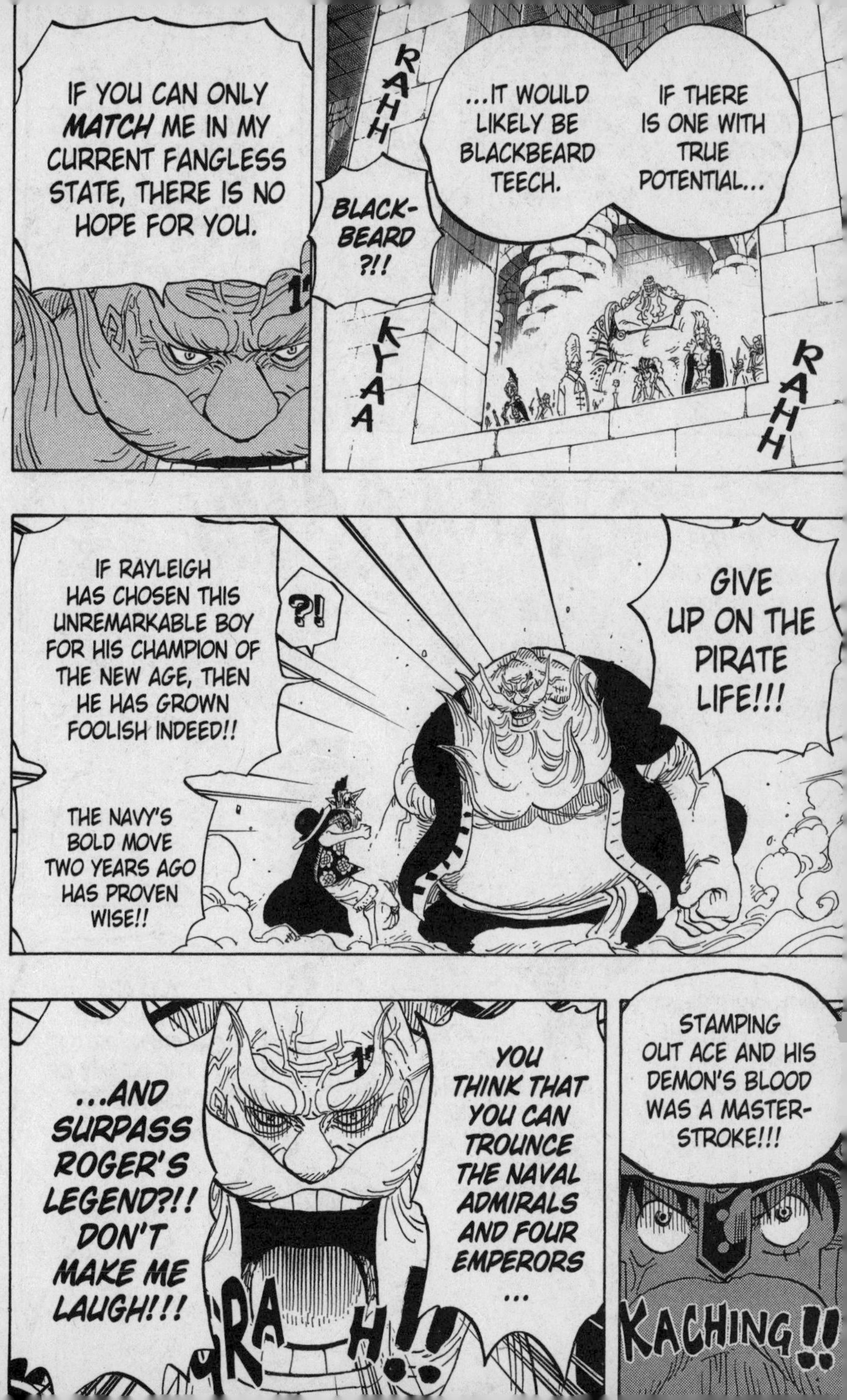
IF THERE IS ONE WITH TRUE POTENTIAL...
...IT WOULD LIKELY BE BLACKBEARD TEECH.
RAHH
BLACK-BEARD ?!!
KYAA
RAHH
IF YOU CAN ONLY MATCH ME IN MY CURRENT FANGLESS STATE, THERE IS NO HOPE FOR YOU.
GIVE UP ON THE PIRATE LIFE!!!
?!
IF RAYLEIGH HAS CHOSEN THIS UNREMARKABLE BOY FOR HIS CHAMPION OF THE NEW AGE, THEN HE HAS GROWN FOOLISH INDEED!!
THE NAVY'S BOLD MOVE TWO YEARS AGO HAS PROVEN WISE!!
STAMPING OUT ACE AND HIS DEMON'S BLOOD WAS A MASTER-STROKE!!!
KACHING!!
YOU THINK THAT YOU CAN TROUNCE THE NAVAL ADMIRALS AND FOUR EMPERORS ...
...AND SURPASS ROGER'S LEGEND?!! DON'T MAKE ME LAUGH!!!
RA-H!!

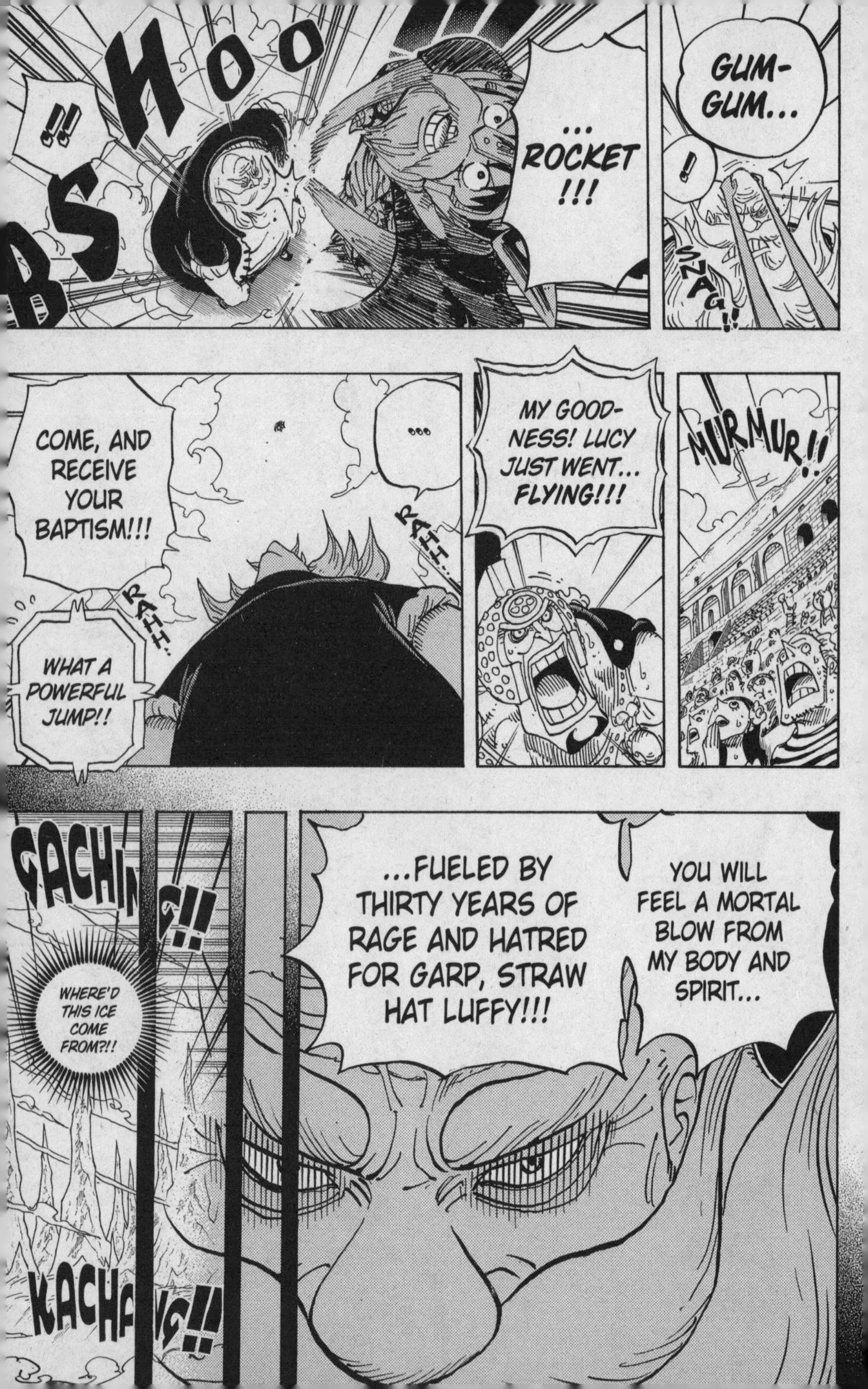
GUM-GUM...
!
SNAG!!
...ROCKET!!!
!!
BSHOO
MURMUR!!
MY GOODNESS! LUCY JUST WENT... FLYING!!!
...
COME, AND RECEIVE YOUR BAPTISM!!!
RAHH...
RAHH...
WHAT A POWERFUL JUMP!!
YOU WILL FEEL A MORTAL BLOW FROM MY BODY AND SPIRIT...
...FUELED BY THIRTY YEARS OF RAGE AND HATRED FOR GARP, STRAW HAT LUFFY!!!
WHERE'D THIS ICE COME FROM?!!

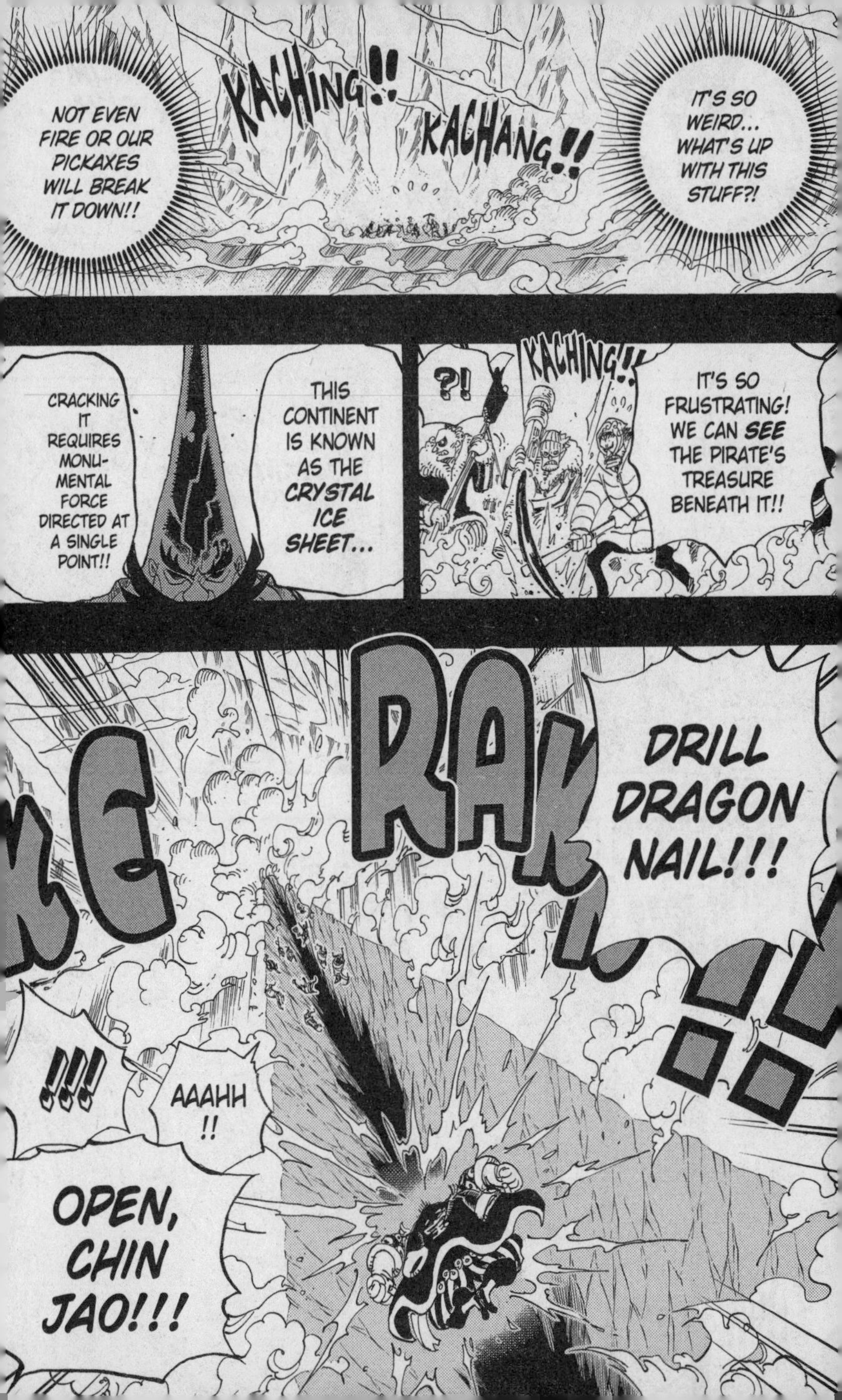
IT'S SO WEIRD... WHAT'S UP WITH THIS STUFF?!
KACHANG!!
KACHING!!
NOT EVEN FIRE OR OUR PICKAXES WILL BREAK IT DOWN!!
IT'S SO FRUSTRATING! WE CAN **SEE** THE PIRATE'S TREASURE BENEATH IT!!
KACHING!!
?!
THIS CONTINENT IS KNOWN AS THE **CRYSTAL ICE SHEET...**
CRACKING IT REQUIRES MONU-MENTAL FORCE DIRECTED AT A SINGLE POINT!!
DRILL DRAGON NAIL!!!
RAK
AAAHH !!
!!!
OPEN, CHIN JAO!!!

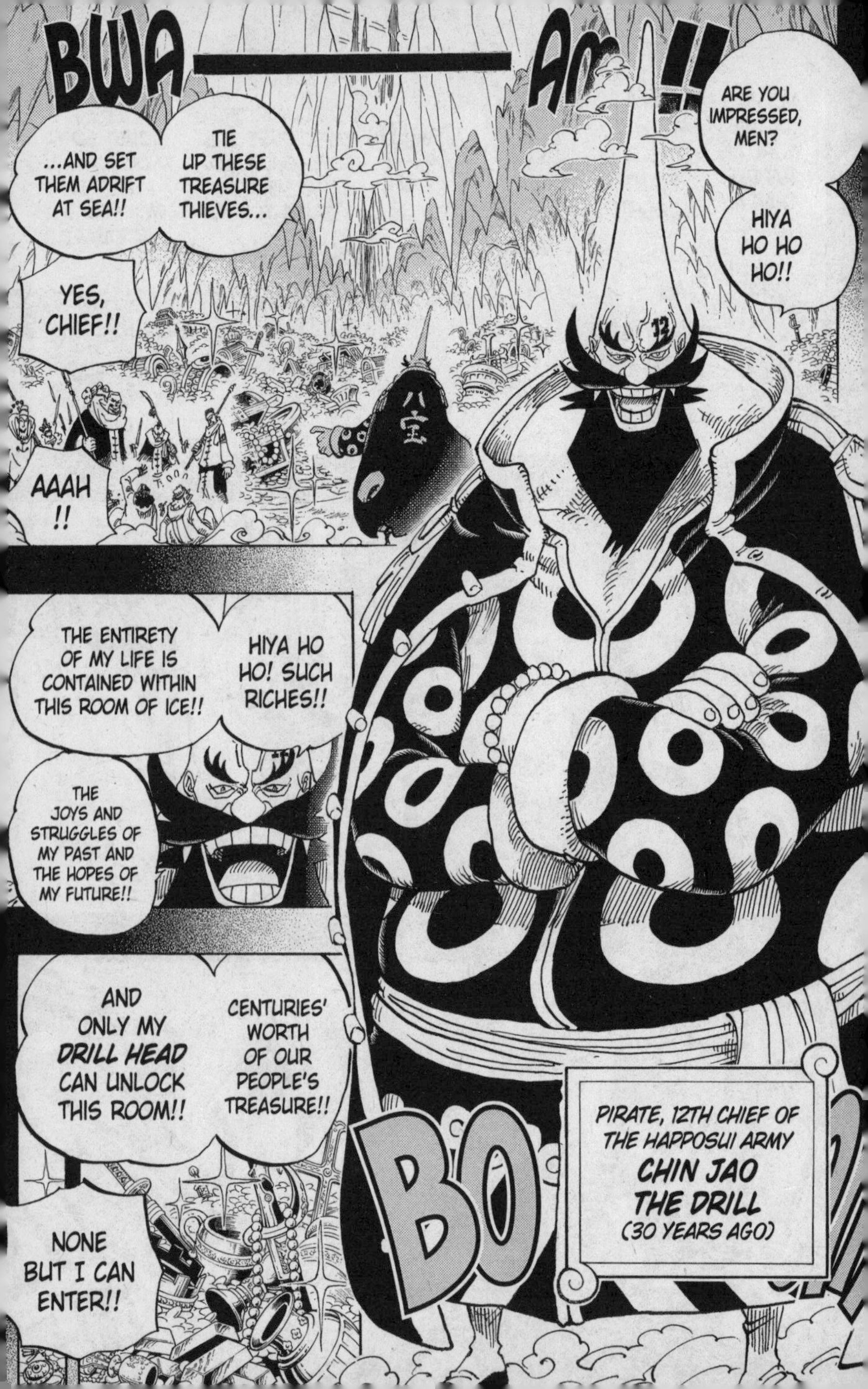
BWA——AM!!
ARE YOU IMPRESSED, MEN?
HIYA HO HO HO!!
TIE UP THESE TREASURE THIEVES...
...AND SET THEM ADRIFT AT SEA!!
YES, CHIEF!!
AAAH!!
BO
PIRATE, 12TH CHIEF OF THE HAPPOSUI ARMY
CHIN JAO THE DRILL
(30 YEARS AGO)
HIYA HO HO! SUCH RICHES!!
THE ENTIRETY OF MY LIFE IS CONTAINED WITHIN THIS ROOM OF ICE!!
THE JOYS AND STRUGGLES OF MY PAST AND THE HOPES OF MY FUTURE!!
CENTURIES' WORTH OF OUR PEOPLE'S TREASURE!!
AND ONLY MY DRILL HEAD CAN UNLOCK THIS ROOM!!
NONE BUT I CAN ENTER!!

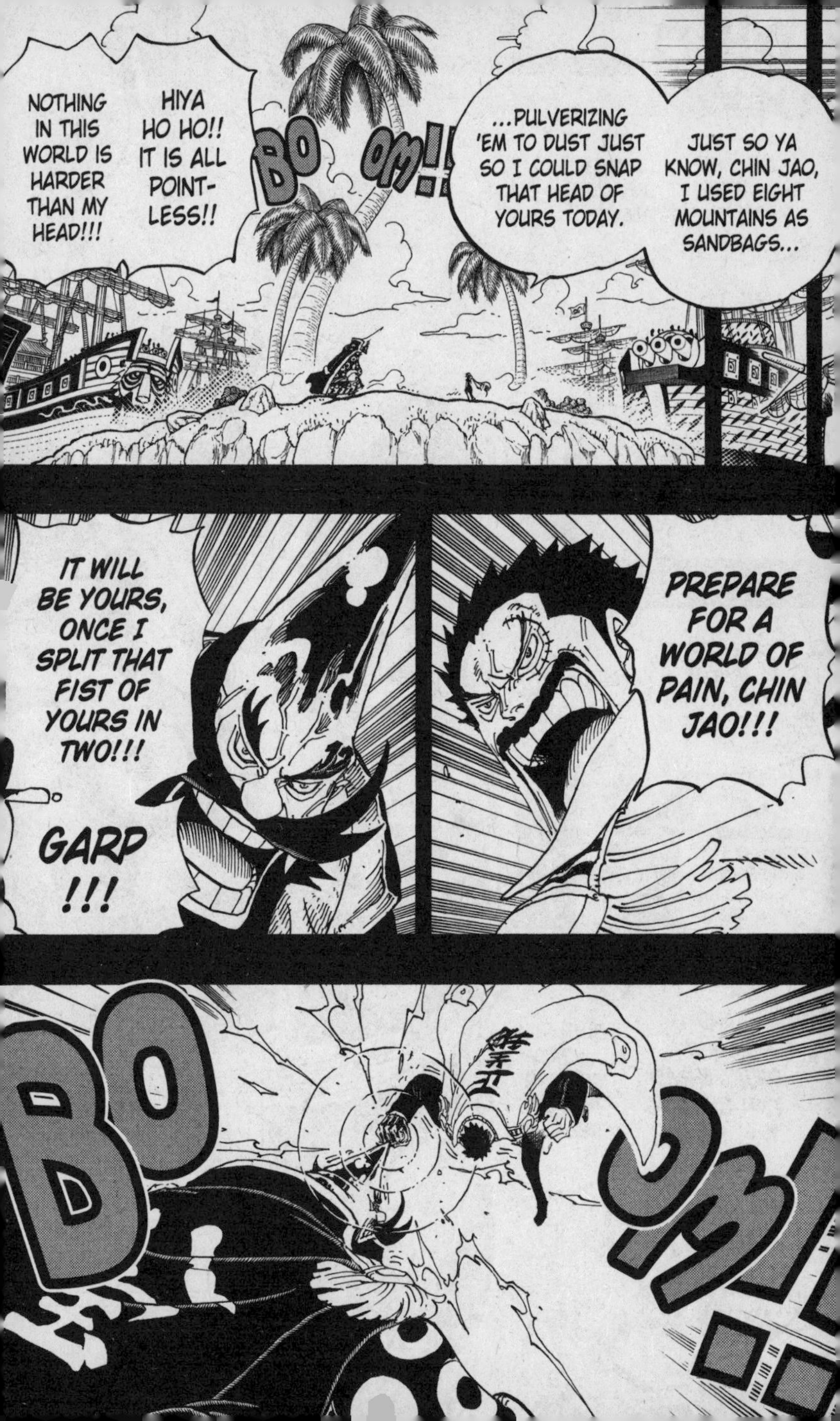
JUST SO YA KNOW, CHIN JAO, I USED EIGHT MOUNTAINS AS SANDBAGS...
...PULVERIZING 'EM TO DUST JUST SO I COULD SNAP THAT HEAD OF YOURS TODAY.
BOOM!!
HIYA HO HO!! IT IS ALL POINT-LESS!!
NOTHING IN THIS WORLD IS HARDER THAN MY HEAD!!!
PREPARE FOR A WORLD OF PAIN, CHIN JAO!!!
IT WILL BE YOURS, ONCE I SPLIT THAT FIST OF YOURS IN TWO!!!
GARP!!!
BOOM!!

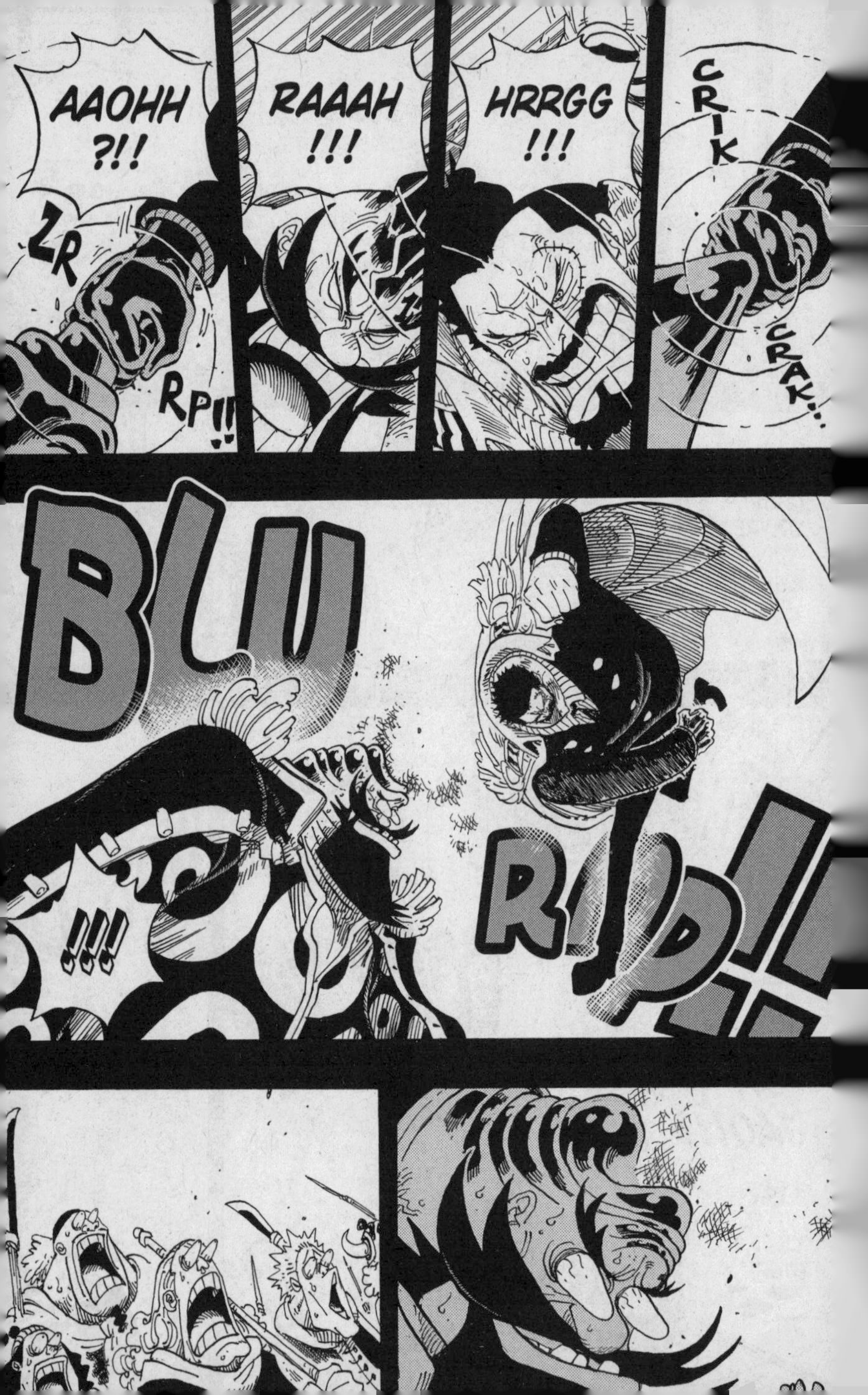
CRIK
CRAK...
HRRGG !!!
RAAAH !!!
AAOHH ?!!
ZR
RP!!
BLU
RP!!
!!!

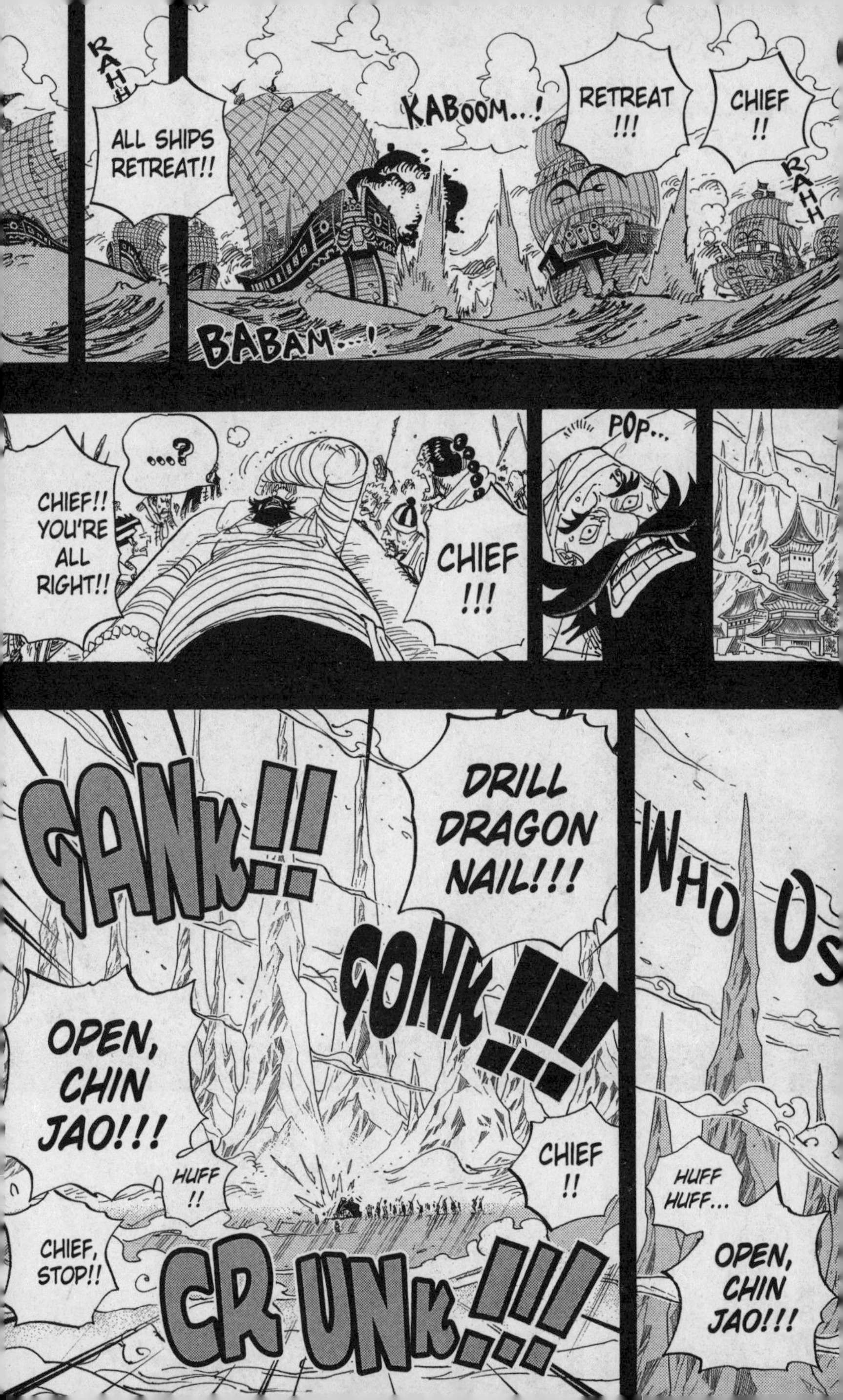
CHIEF !!
RAHH
RETREAT !!!
KABOOM...!
BABAM...!
RAHH
ALL SHIPS RETREAT!!
POP...
CHIEF !!!
...?
CHIEF!! YOU'RE ALL RIGHT!!
WHO OS
HUFF HUFF...
OPEN, CHIN JAO!!!
DRILL DRAGON NAIL!!!
GANK!!
GONK!!!
CHIEF !!
OPEN, CHIN JAO!!!
HUFF !!
CHIEF, STOP!!
CR UNK...!!!

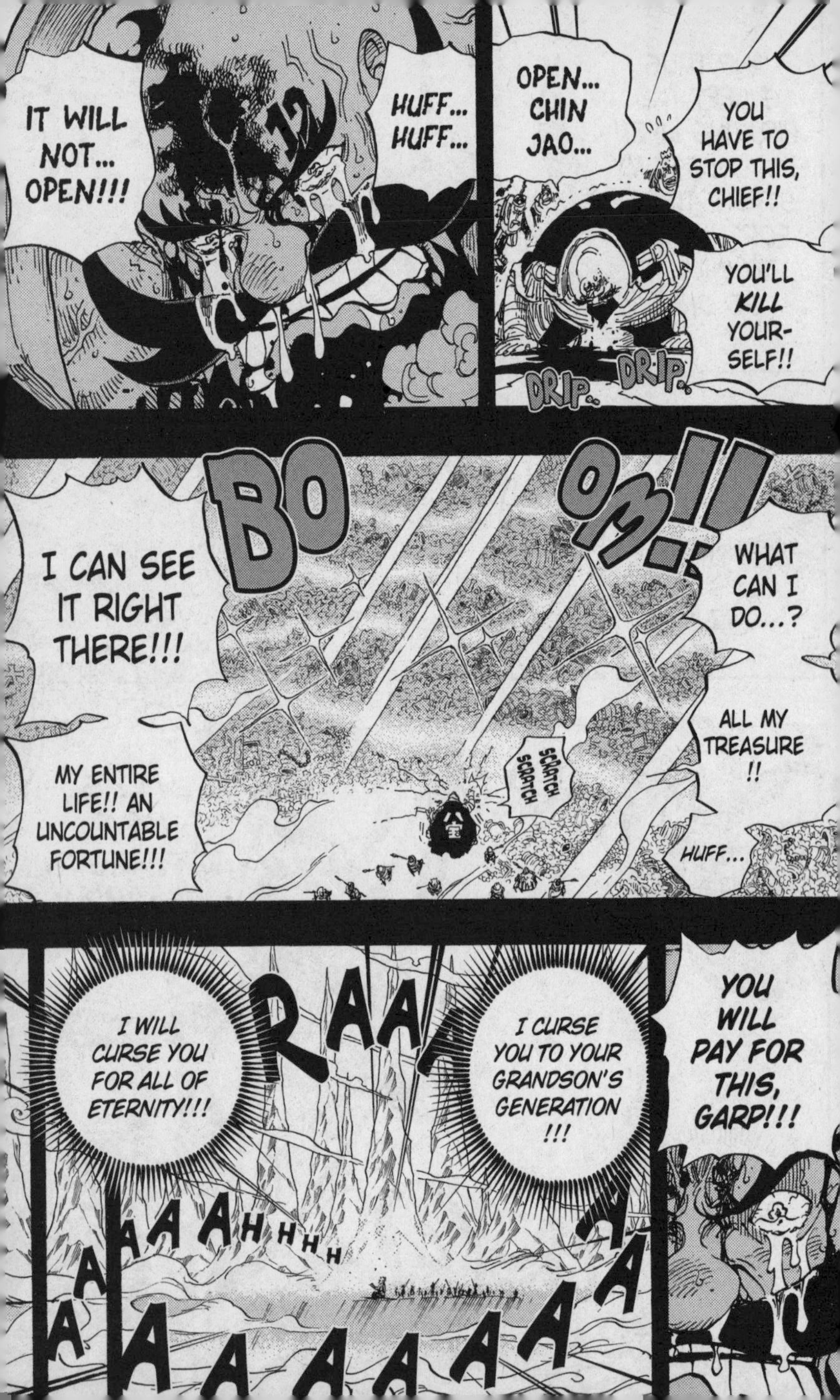
YOU HAVE TO STOP THIS, CHIEF!!
OPEN... CHIN JAO...
YOU'LL KILL YOURSELF!!
DRIP.. DRIP..
HUFF... HUFF...
IT WILL NOT... OPEN!!!
WHAT CAN I DO...?
BOOM!!
ALL MY TREASURE!!
I CAN SEE IT RIGHT THERE!!!
HUFF...
SCRATCH SCRATCH
MY ENTIRE LIFE!! AN UNCOUNTABLE FORTUNE!!!
YOU WILL PAY FOR THIS, GARP!!!
I CURSE YOU TO YOUR GRANDSON'S GENERATION!!!
RAAAAAAAAAAAAAAAAAAHHHHH
I WILL CURSE YOU FOR ALL OF ETERNITY!!!

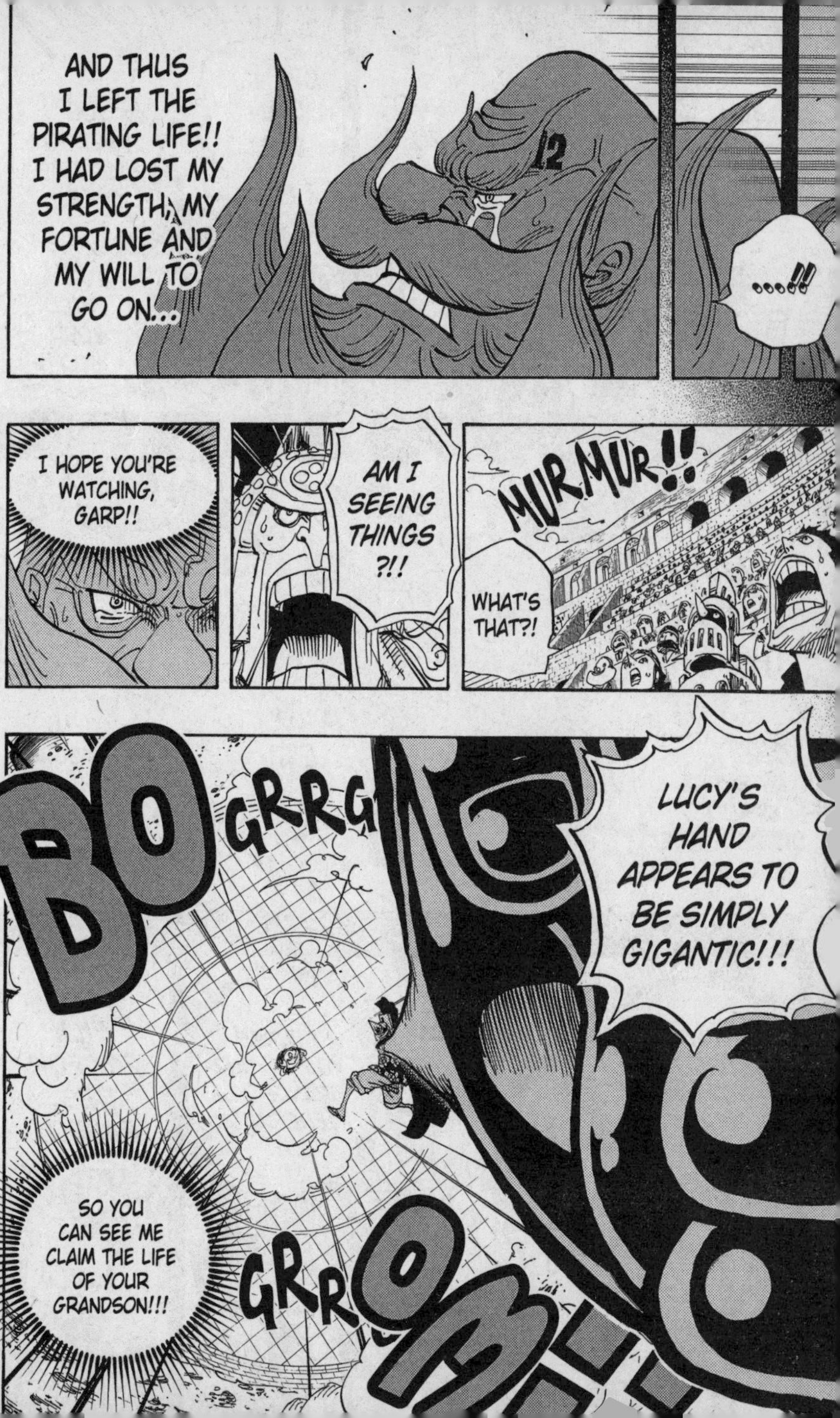
....!!
AND THUS I LEFT THE PIRATING LIFE!! I HAD LOST MY STRENGTH, MY FORTUNE AND MY WILL TO GO ON...
MURMUR!!
WHAT'S THAT?!
AM I SEEING THINGS?!!
I HOPE YOU'RE WATCHING, GARP!!
LUCY'S HAND APPEARS TO BE SIMPLY GIGANTIC!!!
BOGRRG
SO YOU CAN SEE ME CLAIM THE LIFE OF YOUR GRANDSON!!!
GRROMB

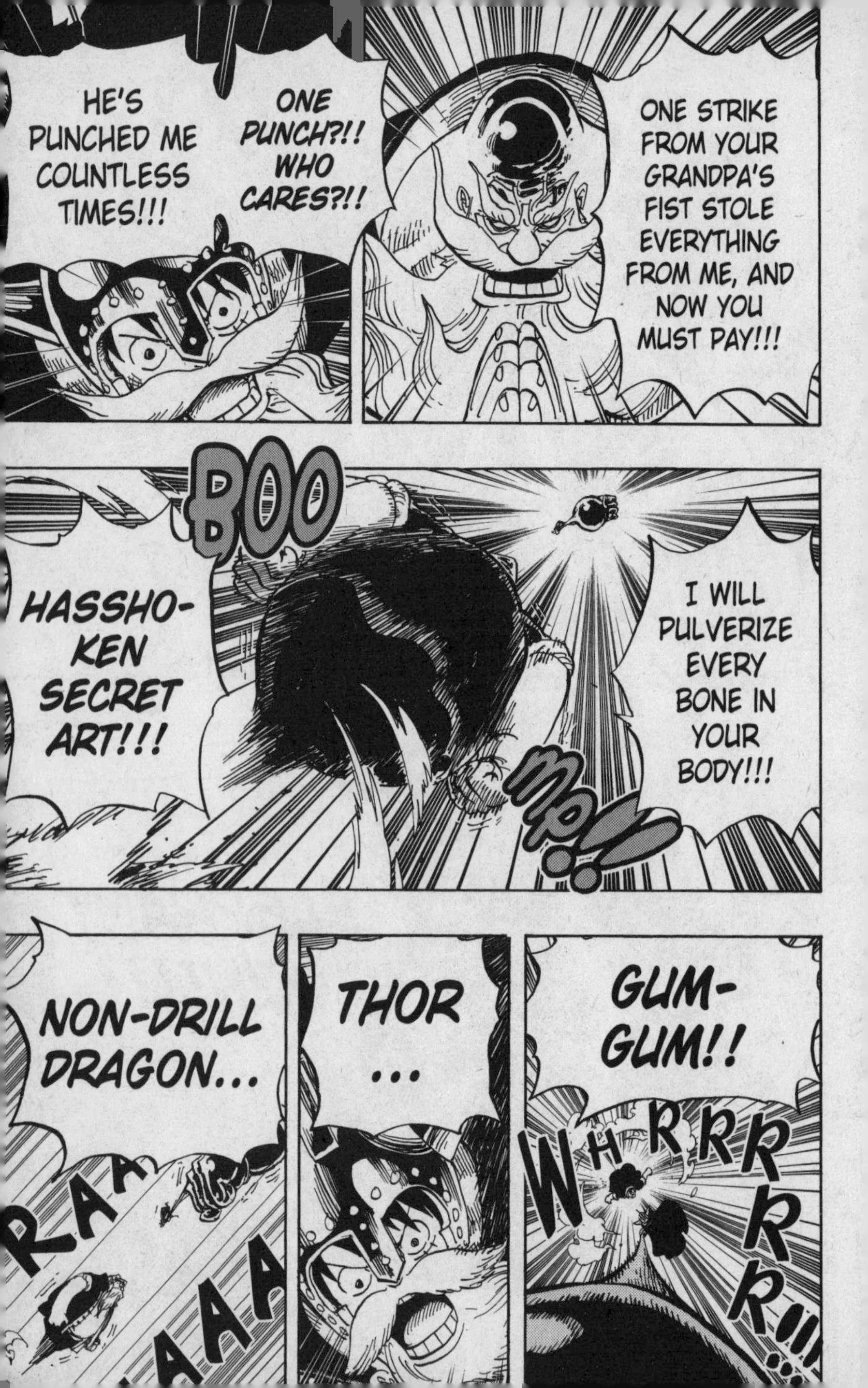
ONE STRIKE FROM YOUR GRANDPA'S FIST STOLE EVERYTHING FROM ME, AND NOW YOU MUST PAY!!!
ONE PUNCH?!! WHO CARES?!!
HE'S PUNCHED ME COUNTLESS TIMES!!!
I WILL PULVERIZE EVERY BONE IN YOUR BODY!!!
BOOmp!!
HASSHO-KEN SECRET ART!!!
GUM-GUM!!
WHRRRRRR!!!
THOR ...
NON-DRILL DRAGON...
RAAAAAA

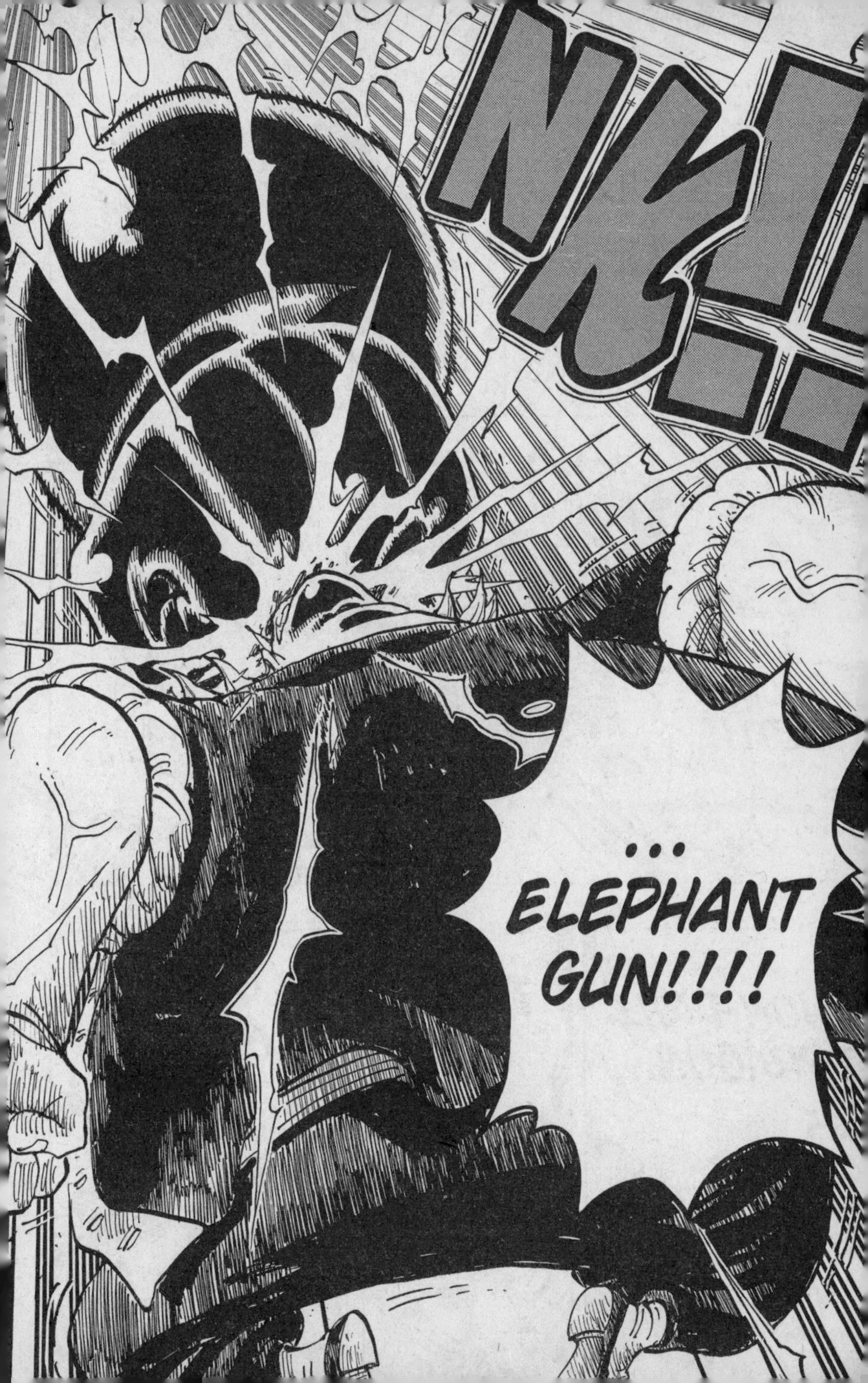
NN!!
...ELEPHANT GUN!!!!

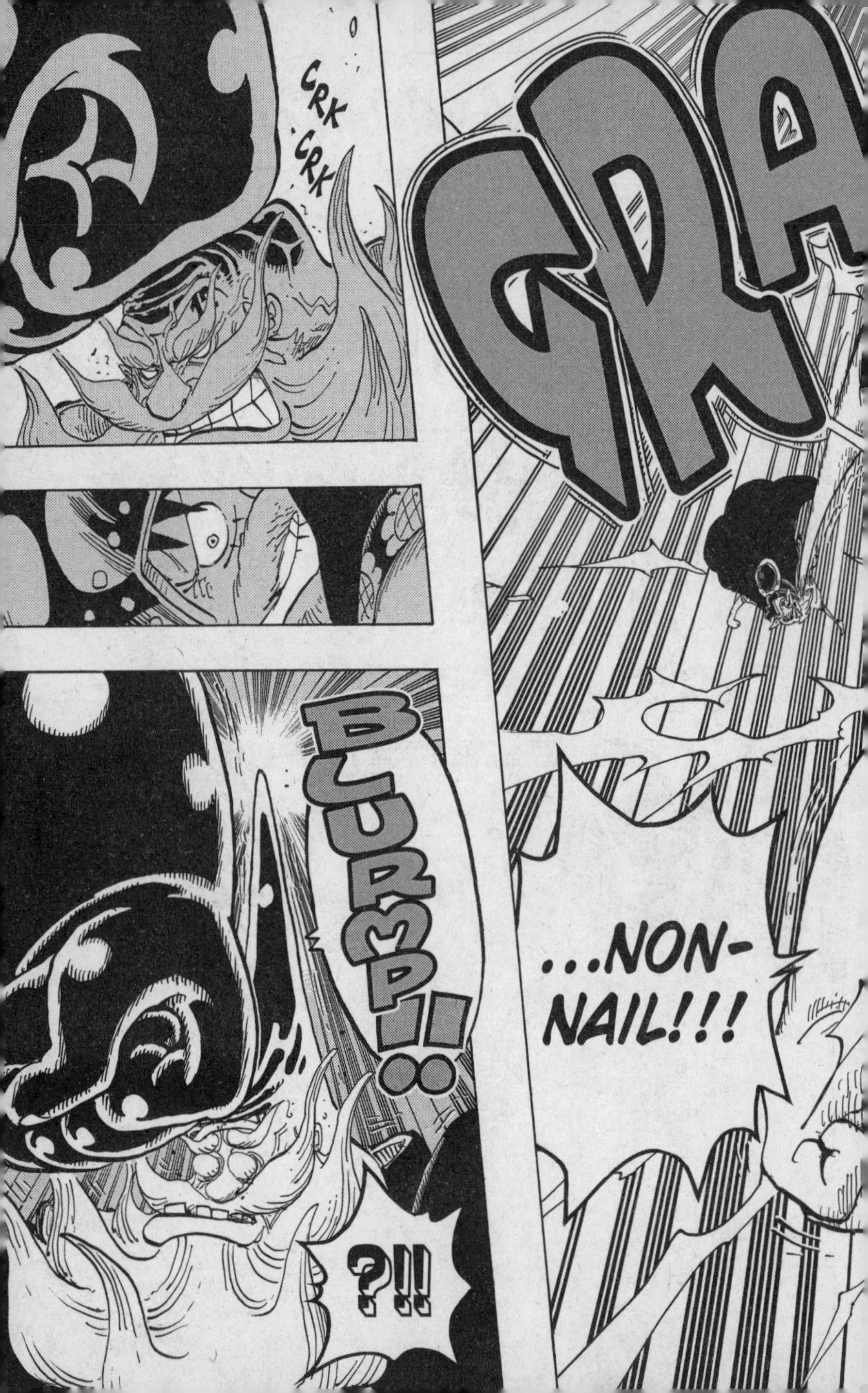
CRA
...NON-NAIL!!!
CRK CRK
BLUMP!!
?!!

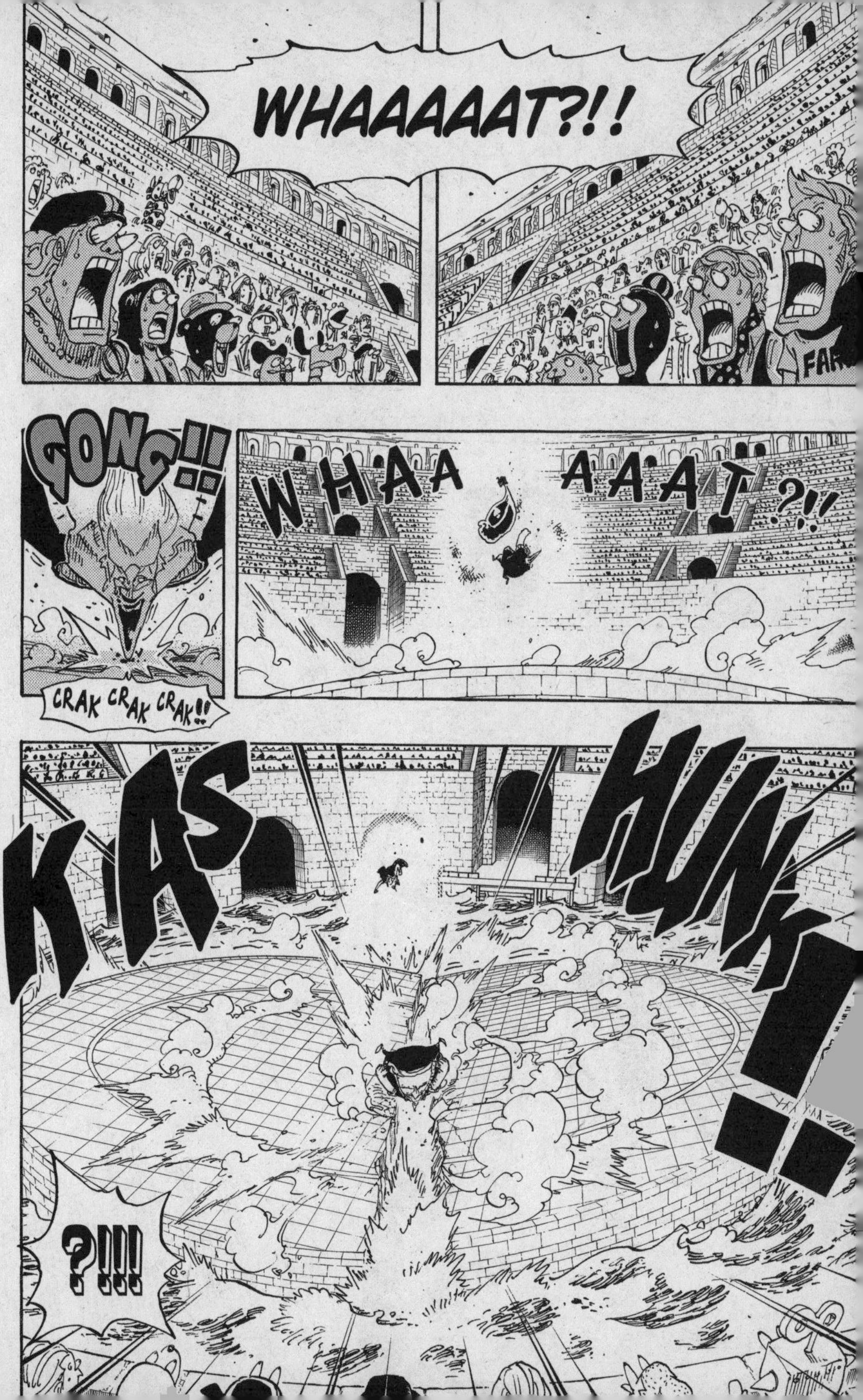
WHAAAAAT?!!
WHAA AAAT?!!
GONG!!
CRAK CRAK CRAK!!
KASHUNK!!
?!!!

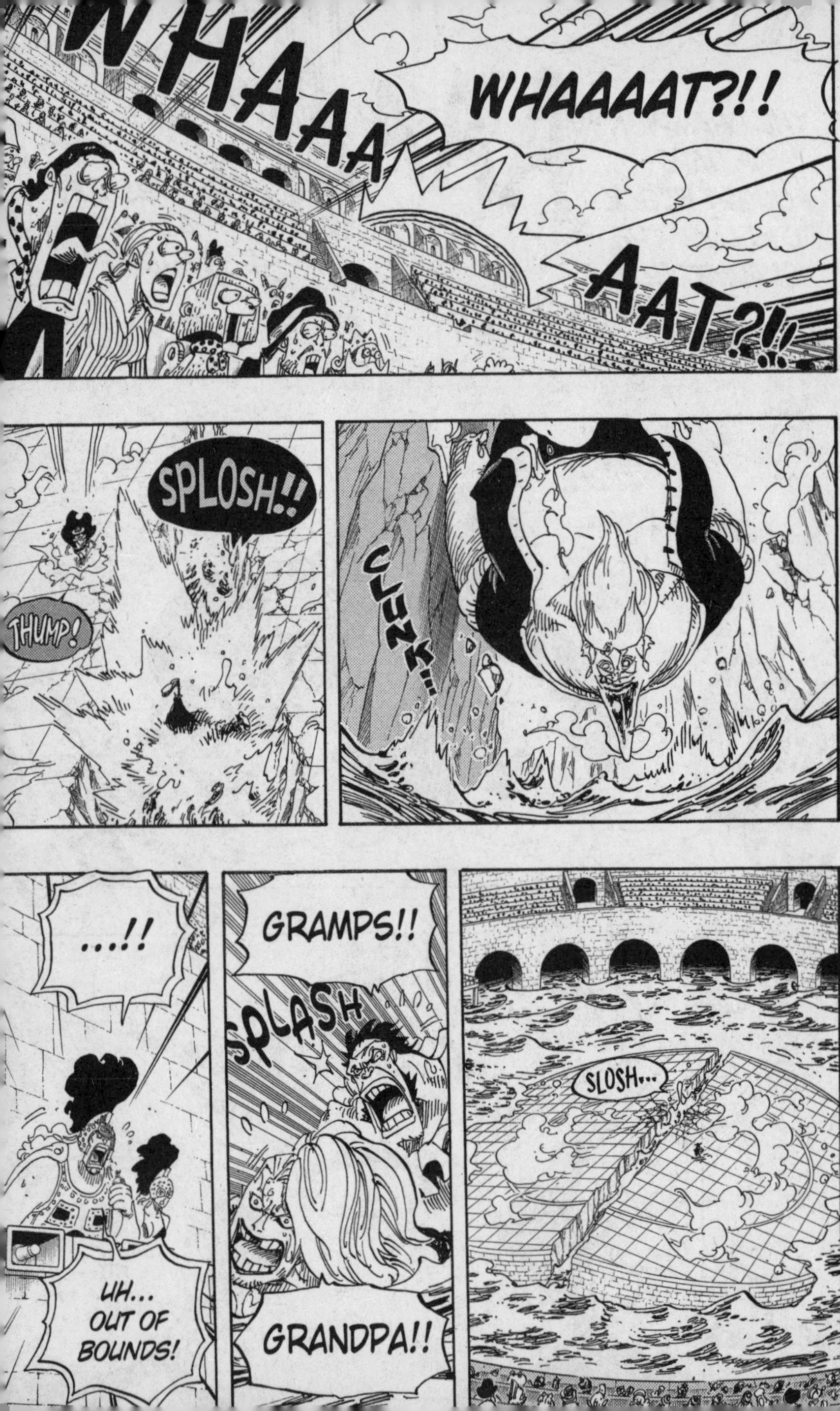
WHAAAAT?!!
WHAAAA
AAT?!!
CLUNK!!!
SPLOSH!!
THUMP!
SLOSH...
GRAMPS!!
SPLASH
GRANDPA!!
...!!
UH... OUT OF BOUNDS!

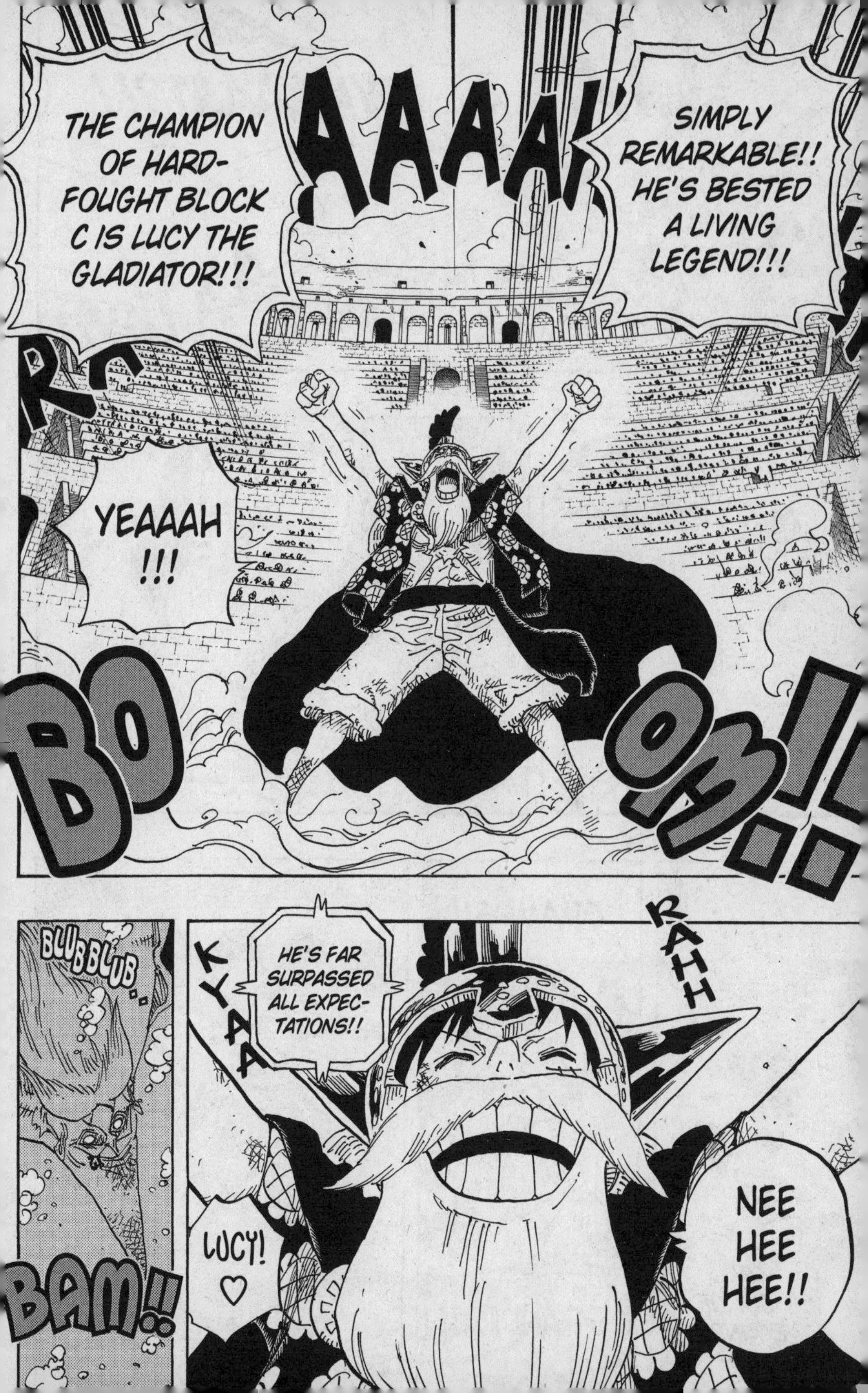
SIMPLY REMARKABLE!! HE'S BESTED A LIVING LEGEND!!!
THE CHAMPION OF HARD-FOUGHT BLOCK C IS LUCY THE GLADIATOR!!!
YEAAAH!!!
BOOM!!
RAHH
HE'S FAR SURPASSED ALL EXPEC-TATIONS!!
KYAA
NEE HEE HEE!!
LUCY! ♡
BLUBBLUB
BAM!!

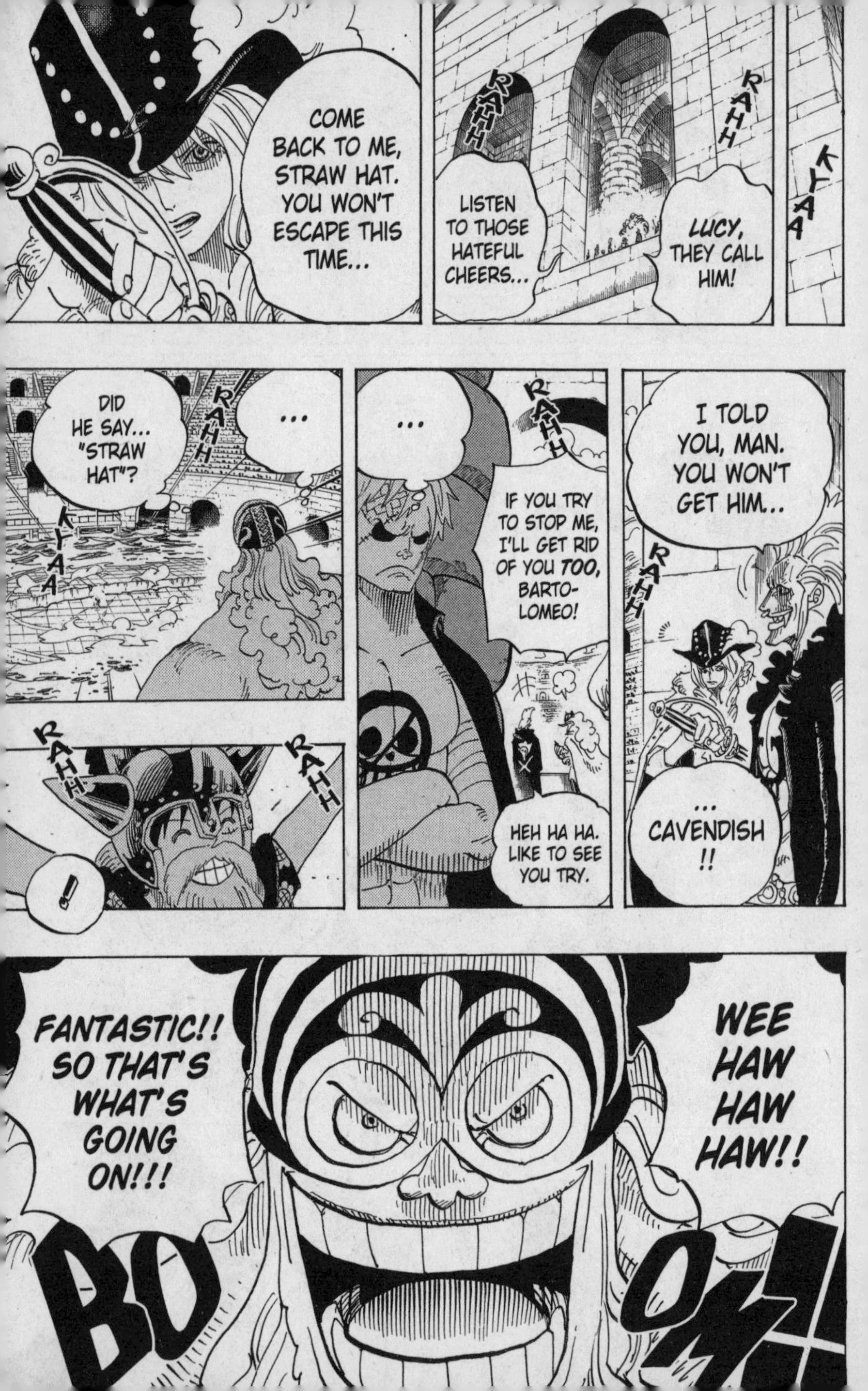

RAHH
KYAA
LUCY, THEY CALL HIM!
RAHH
LISTEN TO THOSE HATEFUL CHEERS...
COME BACK TO ME, STRAW HAT. YOU WON'T ESCAPE THIS TIME...
I TOLD YOU, MAN. YOU WON'T GET HIM..
RAHH
... CAVENDISH !!
RAHH
...
IF YOU TRY TO STOP ME, I'LL GET RID OF YOU *TOO*, BARTO-LOMEO!
HEH HA HA. LIKE TO SEE YOU TRY.
...
RAHH
DID HE SAY... "STRAW HAT"?
KYAA
RAHH
RAHH
!
WEE HAW HAW HAW!!
FANTASTIC!! SO THAT'S WHAT'S GOING ON!!!
BOOM!!

SBS Question Corner

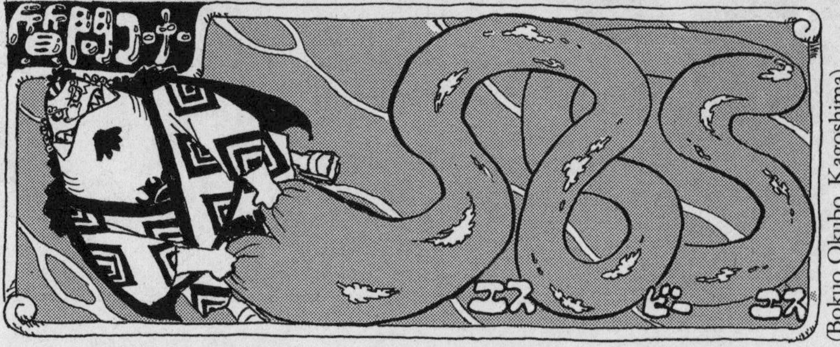

質問コーナー
SBS
エス ビー エス

(Bokuo Okubo, Kagoshima)

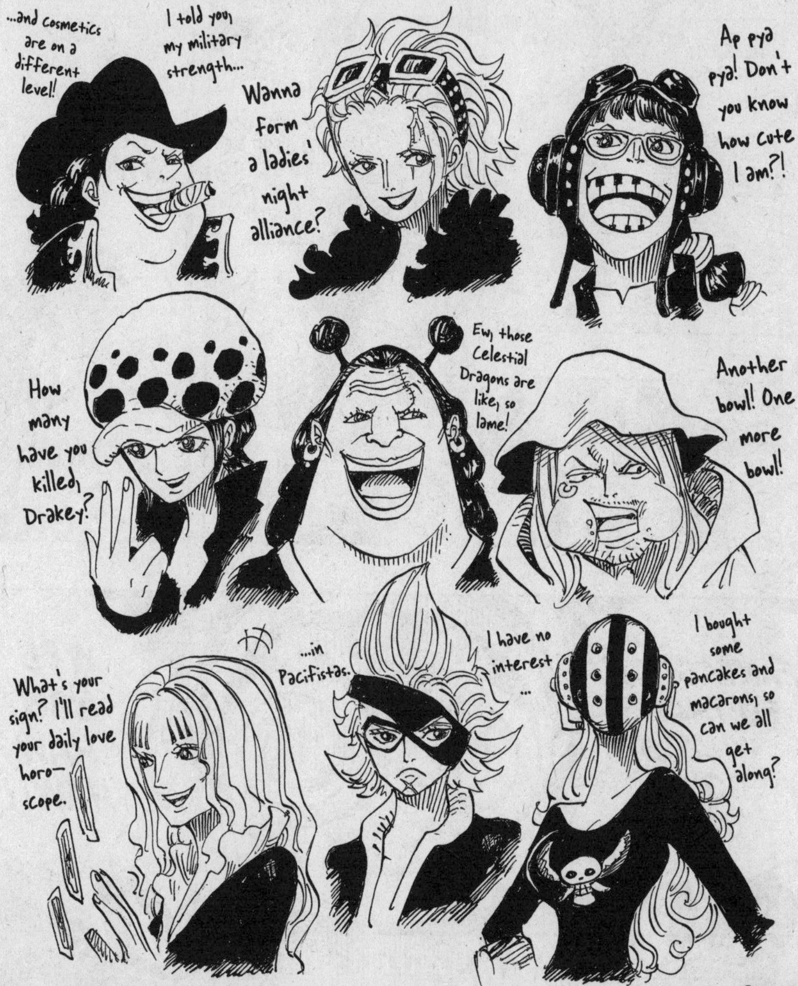

Ap pya pya! Don't you know how cute I am?!
Wanna form a ladies' night alliance?
I told you my military strength...
...and cosmetics are on a different level!
Another bowl! One more bowl!
Ew, those Celestial Dragons are like, so lame!
How many have you killed, Drakey?
I bought some pancakes and macarons, so can we all get along?
I have no interest ...
...in Pacifistas.
What's your sign? I'll read your daily love horoscope.

Chapter 720:
PRISONER-GLADIATORS

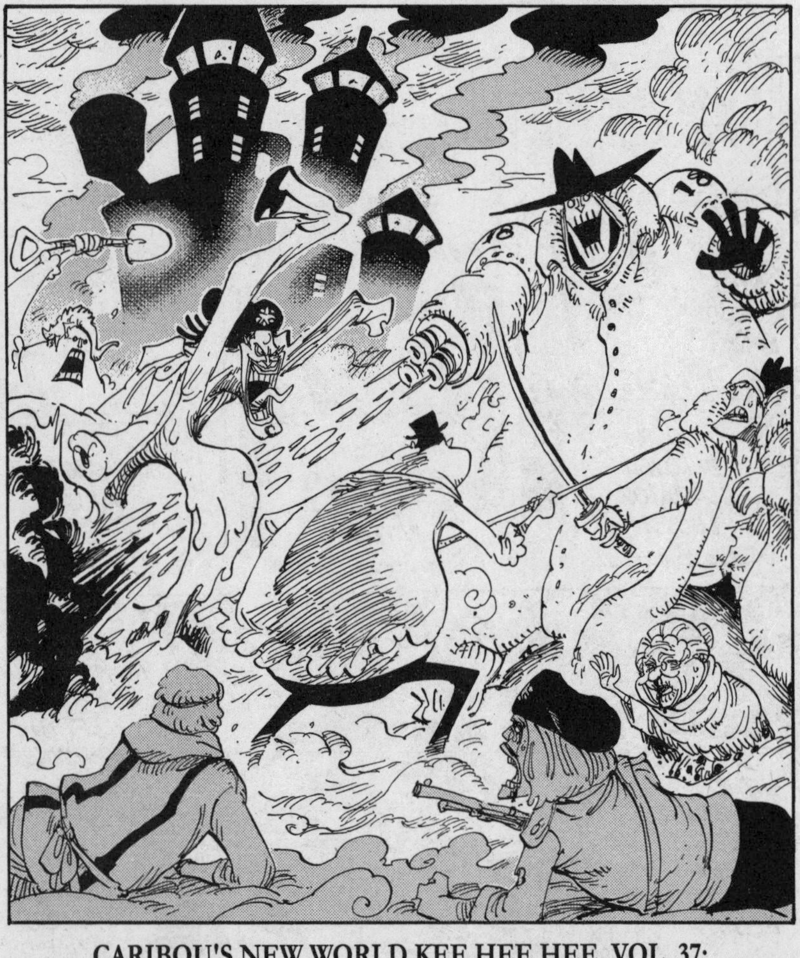

CARIBOU'S NEW WORLD KEE HEE HEE, VOL. 37:
"LIBERATE THE PROLETARIAT!! LIBERATE THE OLD HAG!!"

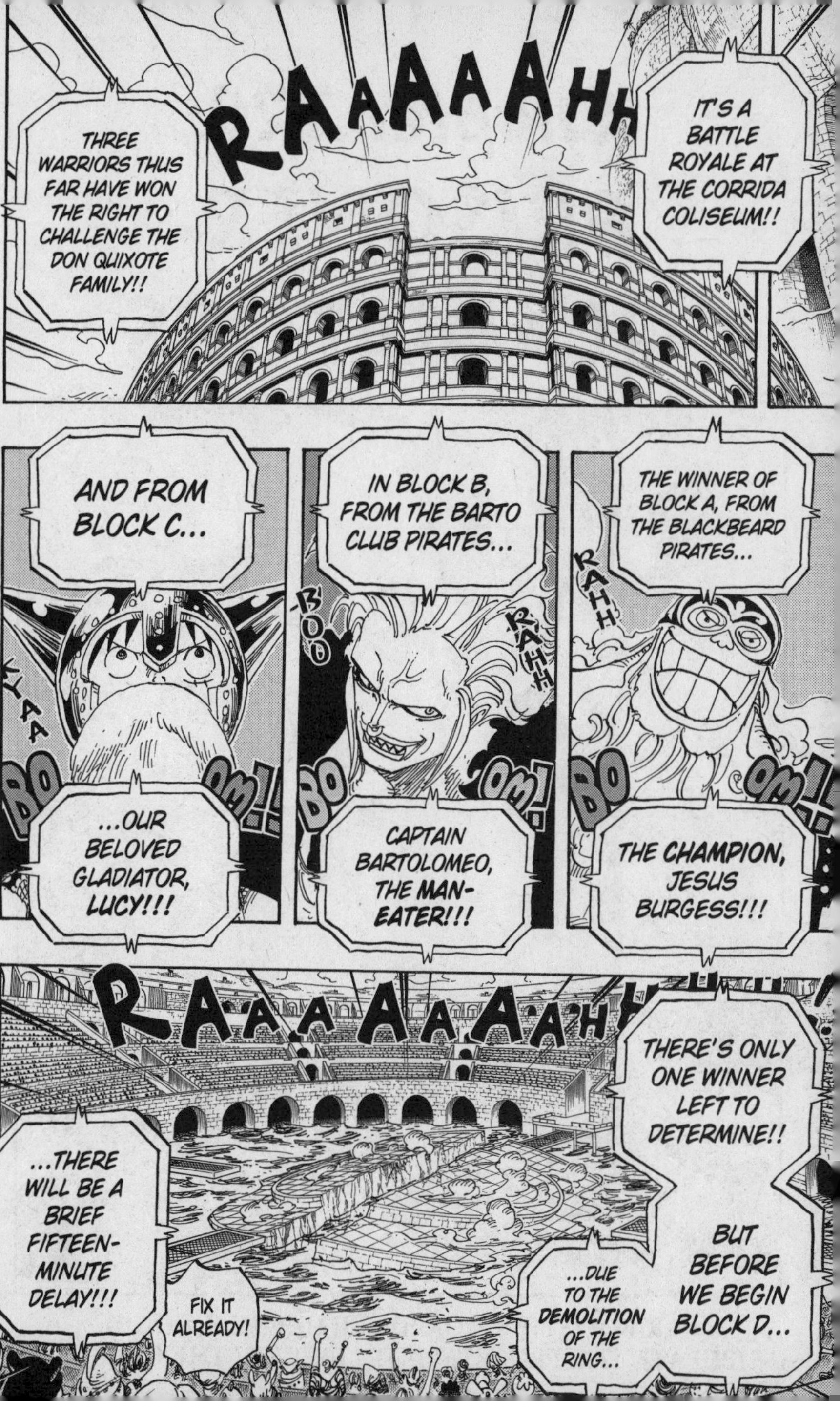
IT'S A BATTLE ROYALE AT THE CORRIDA COLISEUM!!
RAAAAAHH
THREE WARRIORS THUS FAR HAVE WON THE RIGHT TO CHALLENGE THE DON QUIXOTE FAMILY!!
THE WINNER OF BLOCK A, FROM THE BLACKBEARD PIRATES...
RAHH
BOOM!!
THE CHAMPION, JESUS BURGESS!!!
IN BLOCK B, FROM THE BARTO CLUB PIRATES...
BOO
RAHH
BOOM!
CAPTAIN BARTOLOMEO, THE MAN-EATER!!!
AND FROM BLOCK C...
KYAA
BOOM!!
...OUR BELOVED GLADIATOR, LUCY!!!
RAAAAAAAAHH
THERE'S ONLY ONE WINNER LEFT TO DETERMINE!!
BUT BEFORE WE BEGIN BLOCK D...
...DUE TO THE DEMOLITION OF THE RING...
...THERE WILL BE A BRIEF FIFTEEN-MINUTE DELAY!!!
FIX IT ALREADY!

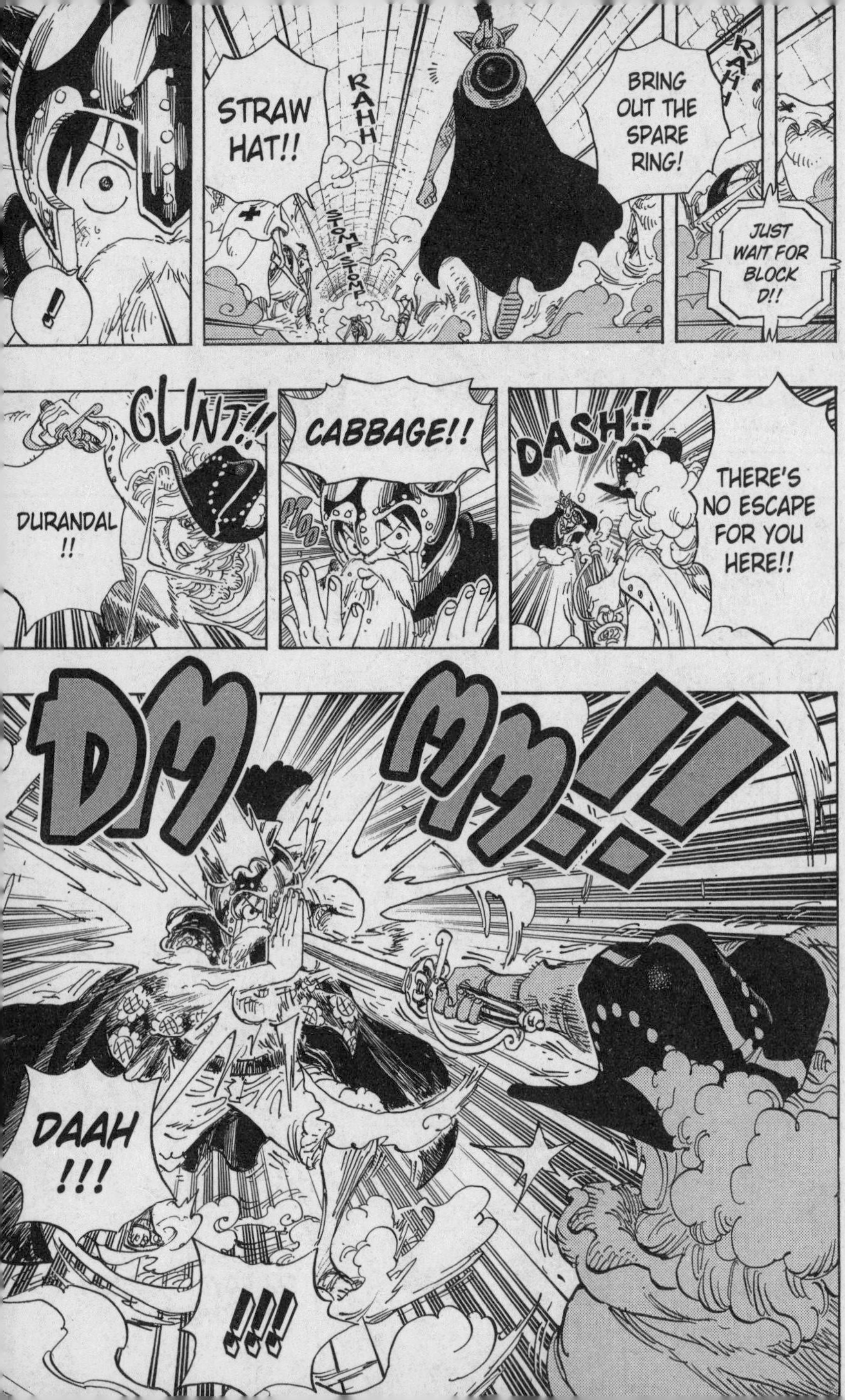
RAH!
BRING OUT THE SPARE RING!
JUST WAIT FOR BLOCK D!!
STRAW HAT!!
RAHH
STOMP STOMP
!
DASH!!
THERE'S NO ESCAPE FOR YOU HERE!!
CABBAGE!!
PTOO
GLINT!!
DURANDAL !!
DMMM!!
DAAH !!!
!!!

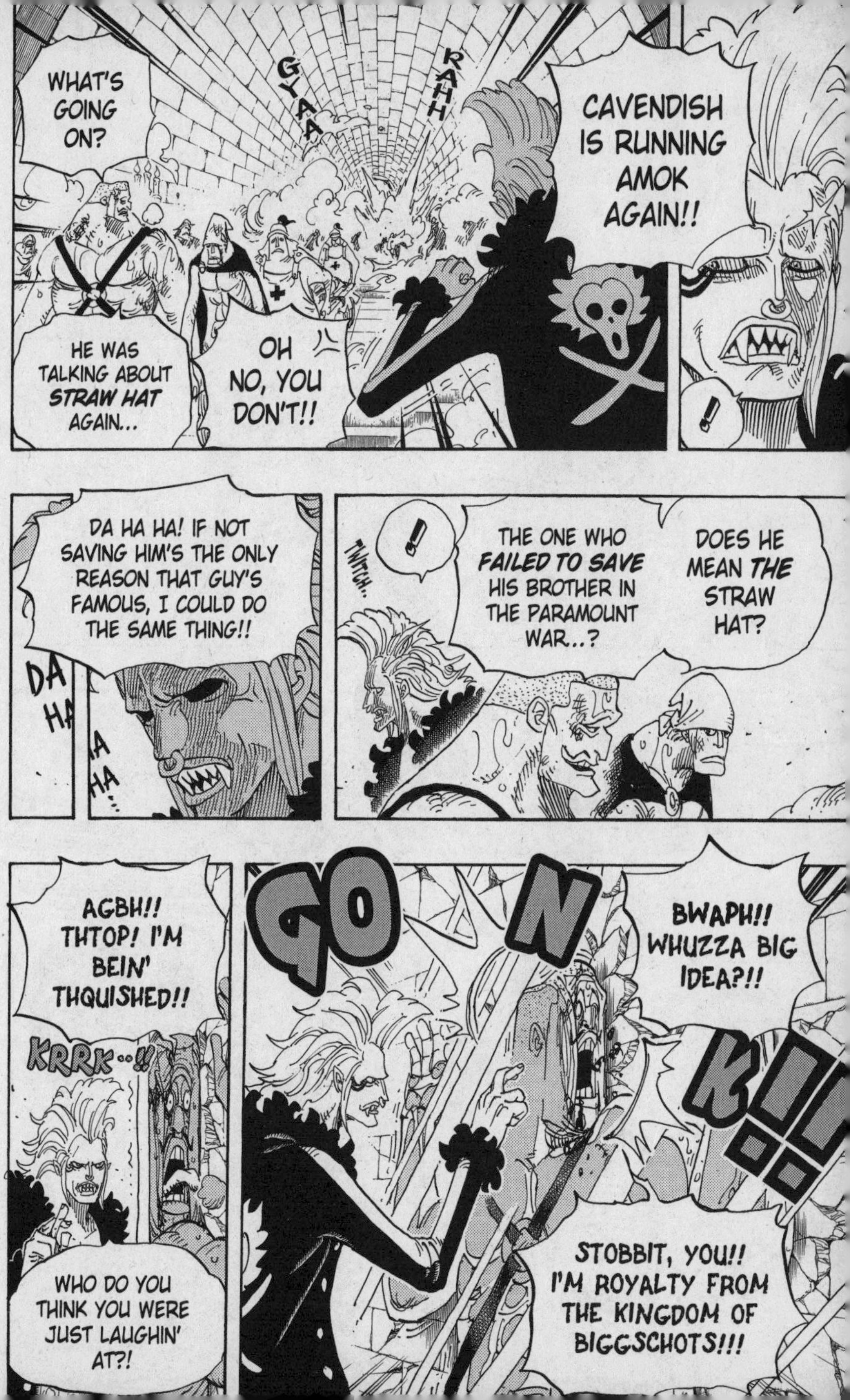
CAVENDISH IS RUNNING AMOK AGAIN!!
!
RAHH
GYAA
WHAT'S GOING ON?
OH NO, YOU DON'T!!
HE WAS TALKING ABOUT STRAW HAT AGAIN...
DOES HE MEAN THE STRAW HAT?
THE ONE WHO FAILED TO SAVE HIS BROTHER IN THE PARAMOUNT WAR..?
!
TWITCH...
DA HA HA! IF NOT SAVING HIM'S THE ONLY REASON THAT GUY'S FAMOUS, I COULD DO THE SAME THING!!
DA HA HA HA...
BWAPH!! WHUZZA BIG IDEA?!!
GONK!!
STOBBIT, YOU!! I'M ROYALTY FROM THE KINGDOM OF BIGGSCHOTS!!!
AGBH!! THTOP! I'M BEIN' THQUISHED!!
KRRK..!!
WHO DO YOU THINK YOU WERE JUST LAUGHIN' AT?!

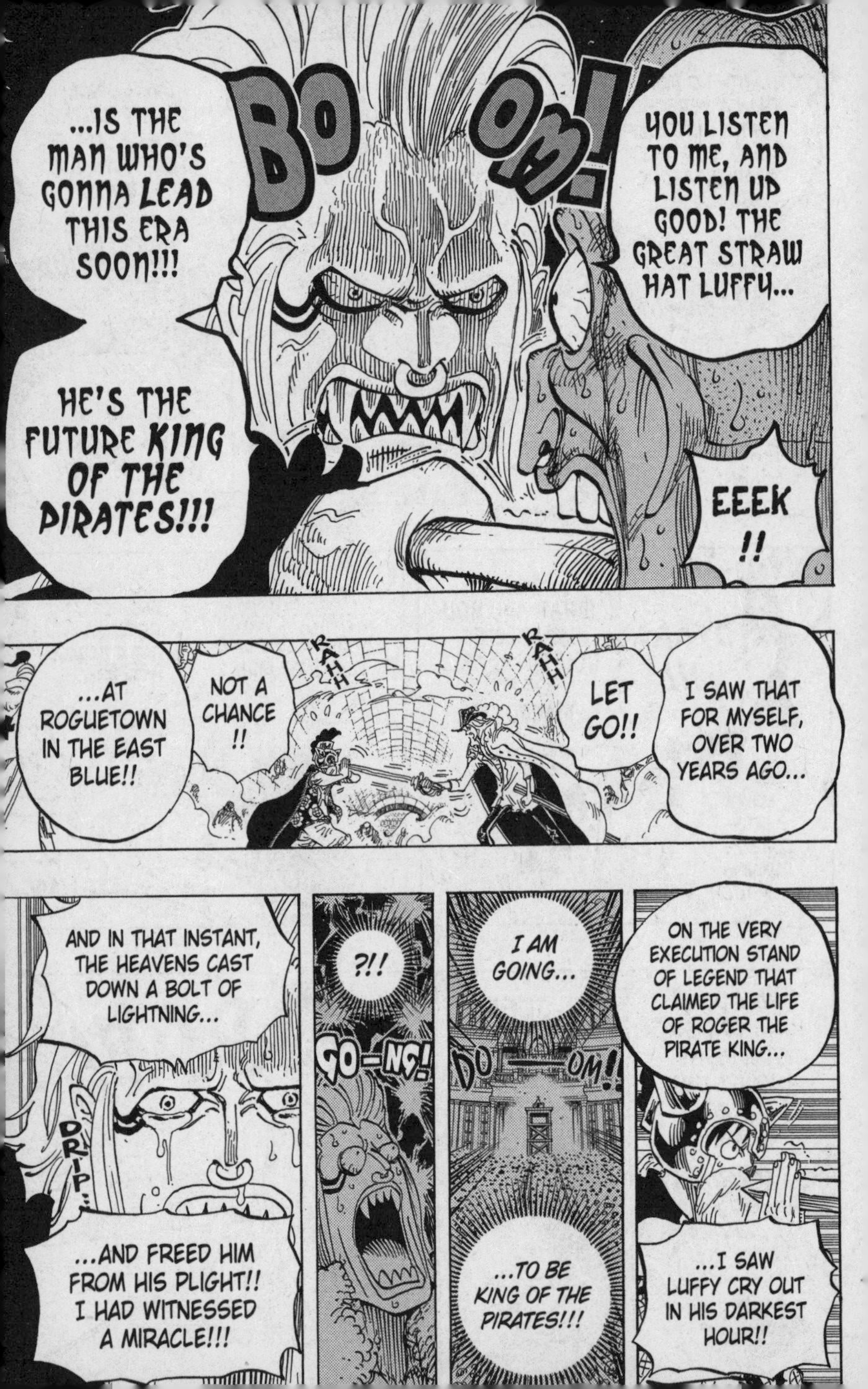

YOU LISTEN TO ME, AND LISTEN UP GOOD! THE GREAT STRAW HAT LUFFY...
BOOM!
...IS THE MAN WHO'S GONNA LEAD THIS ERA SOON!!!
HE'S THE FUTURE KING OF THE PIRATES!!!
EEEK !!
I SAW THAT FOR MYSELF, OVER TWO YEARS AGO...
LET GO!!
RAHH
RAHH
NOT A CHANCE !!
...AT ROGUETOWN IN THE EAST BLUE!!
ON THE VERY EXECUTION STAND OF LEGEND THAT CLAIMED THE LIFE OF ROGER THE PIRATE KING...
...I SAW LUFFY CRY OUT IN HIS DARKEST HOUR!!
I AM GOING...
DU—OM!!
...TO BE KING OF THE PIRATES!!!
?!!
GO-NG!
AND IN THAT INSTANT, THE HEAVENS CAST DOWN A BOLT OF LIGHTNING...
DRIP...
...AND FREED HIM FROM HIS PLIGHT!! I HAD WITNESSED A MIRACLE!!!

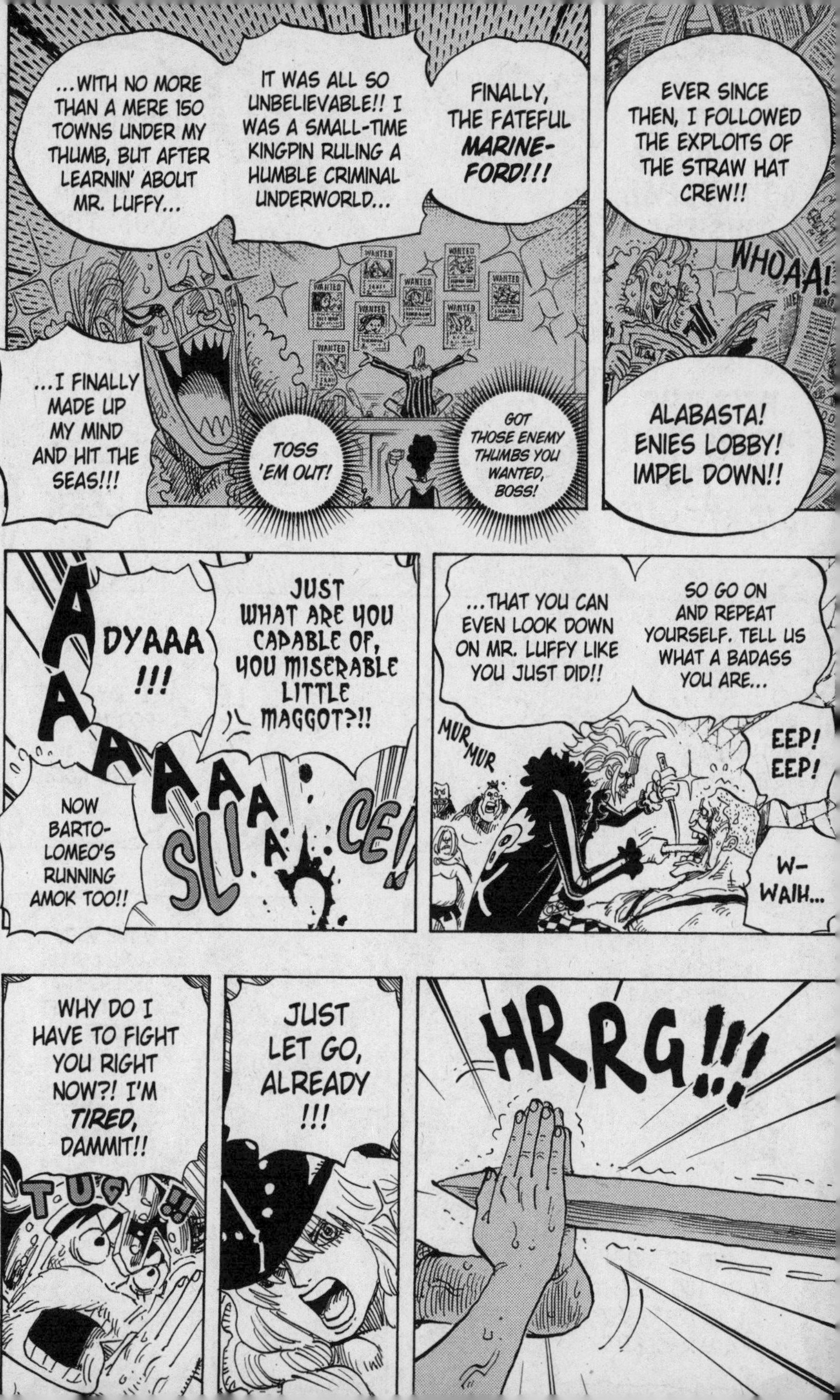
EVER SINCE THEN, I FOLLOWED THE EXPLOITS OF THE STRAW HAT CREW!!
WHOAA!
ALABASTA! ENIES LOBBY! IMPEL DOWN!!
FINALLY, THE FATEFUL MARINE-FORD!!!
IT WAS ALL SO UNBELIEVABLE!! I WAS A SMALL-TIME KINGPIN RULING A HUMBLE CRIMINAL UNDERWORLD...
...WITH NO MORE THAN A MERE 150 TOWNS UNDER MY THUMB, BUT AFTER LEARNIN' ABOUT MR. LUFFY...
GOT THOSE ENEMY THUMBS YOU WANTED, BOSS!
TOSS 'EM OUT!
...I FINALLY MADE UP MY MIND AND HIT THE SEAS!!!
SO GO ON AND REPEAT YOURSELF. TELL US WHAT A BADASS YOU ARE...
...THAT YOU CAN EVEN LOOK DOWN ON MR. LUFFY LIKE YOU JUST DID!!
EEP! EEP!
MUR MUR
W-WAIH...
JUST WHAT ARE YOU CAPABLE OF, YOU MISERABLE LITTLE MAGGOT?!!
ADYAAA!!!
SLICE!
NOW BARTO-LOMEO'S RUNNING AMOK TOO!!
HRRG!!!
JUST LET GO, ALREADY!!!
WHY DO I HAVE TO FIGHT YOU RIGHT NOW?! I'M TIRED, DAMMIT!!
TUG!!

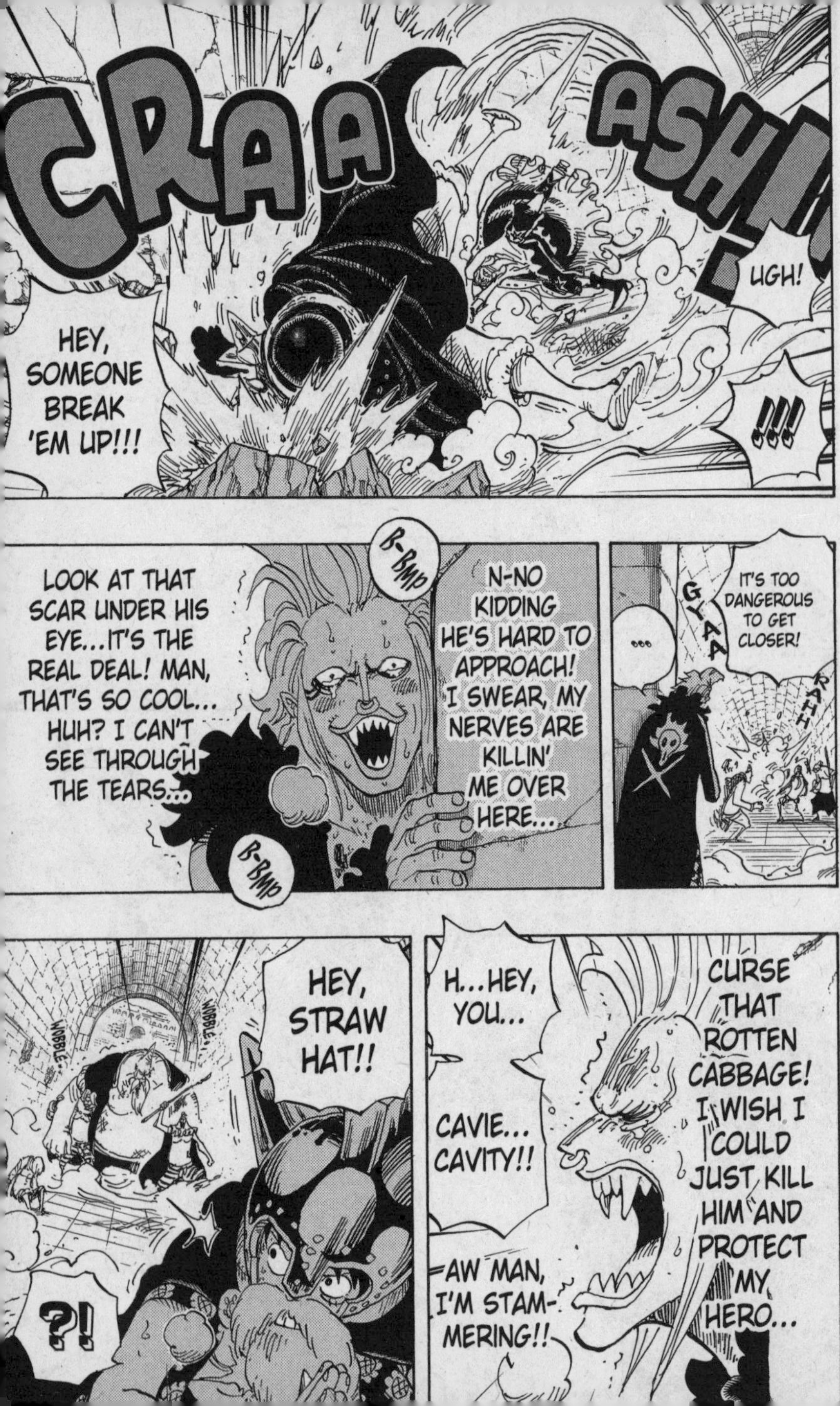
CRAA
ASH!
UGH!
!!!
HEY, SOMEONE BREAK 'EM UP!!!
IT'S TOO DANGEROUS TO GET CLOSER!
GYAA
RAHH
...
B-BMP
N-NO KIDDING HE'S HARD TO APPROACH! I SWEAR, MY NERVES ARE KILLIN' ME OVER HERE...
LOOK AT THAT SCAR UNDER HIS EYE...IT'S THE REAL DEAL! MAN, THAT'S SO COOL... HUH? I CAN'T SEE THROUGH THE TEARS...
B-BMP
CURSE THAT ROTTEN CABBAGE! I WISH I COULD JUST KILL HIM AND PROTECT MY HERO...
H...HEY, YOU...
CAVIE... CAVITY!!
AW MAN, I'M STAM-MERING!!
HEY, STRAW HAT!!
WOBBLE
WOBBLE
?!

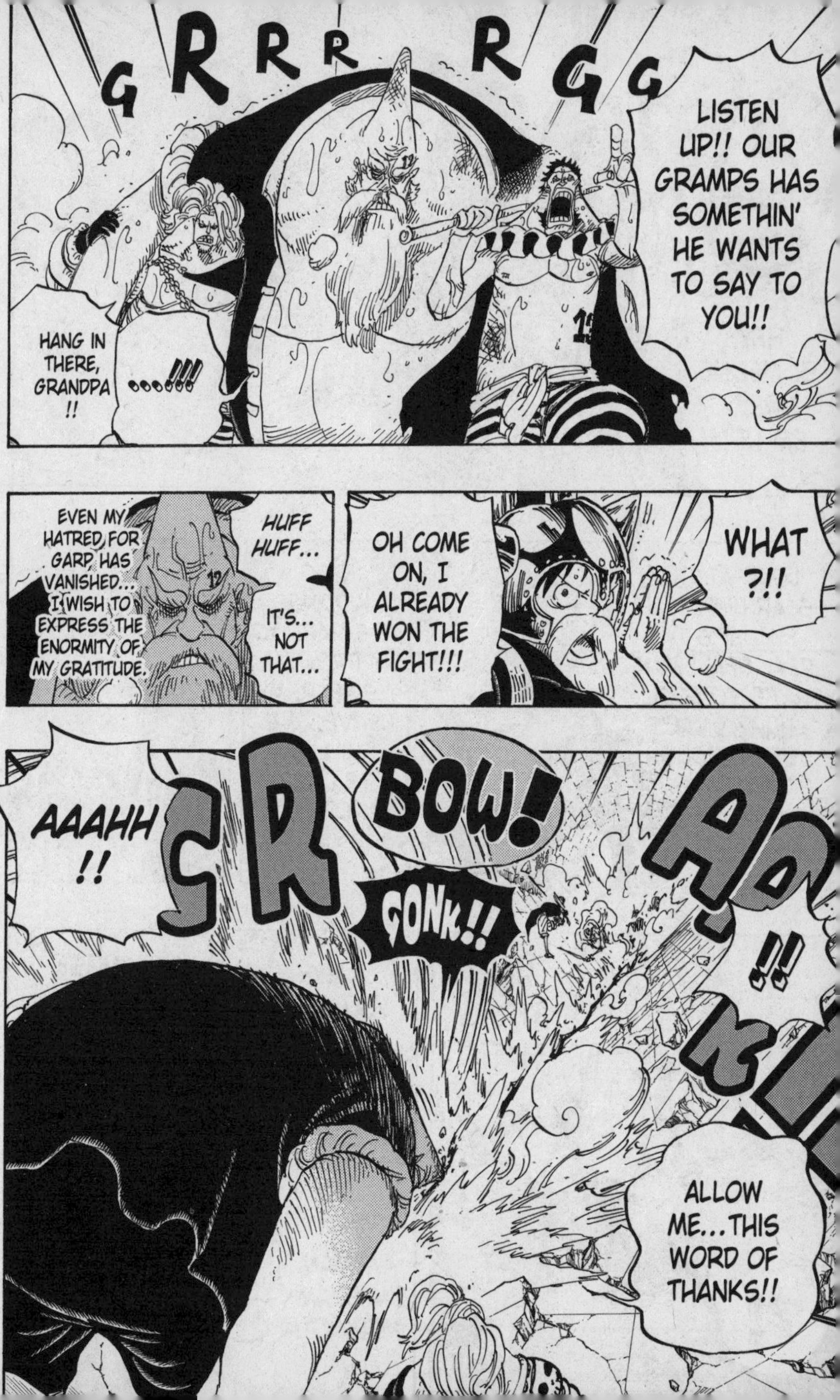
GRRRRGG
LISTEN UP!! OUR GRAMPS HAS SOMETHIN' HE WANTS TO SAY TO YOU!!
...!!!
HANG IN THERE, GRANDPA!!
WHAT?!!
OH COME ON, I ALREADY WON THE FIGHT!!!
HUFF HUFF...
IT'S... NOT THAT...
EVEN MY HATRED FOR GARP HAS VANISHED... I WISH TO EXPRESS THE ENORMITY OF MY GRATITUDE.
BOW!
GONK!!
AAAHH!!
ALLOW ME...THIS WORD OF THANKS!!

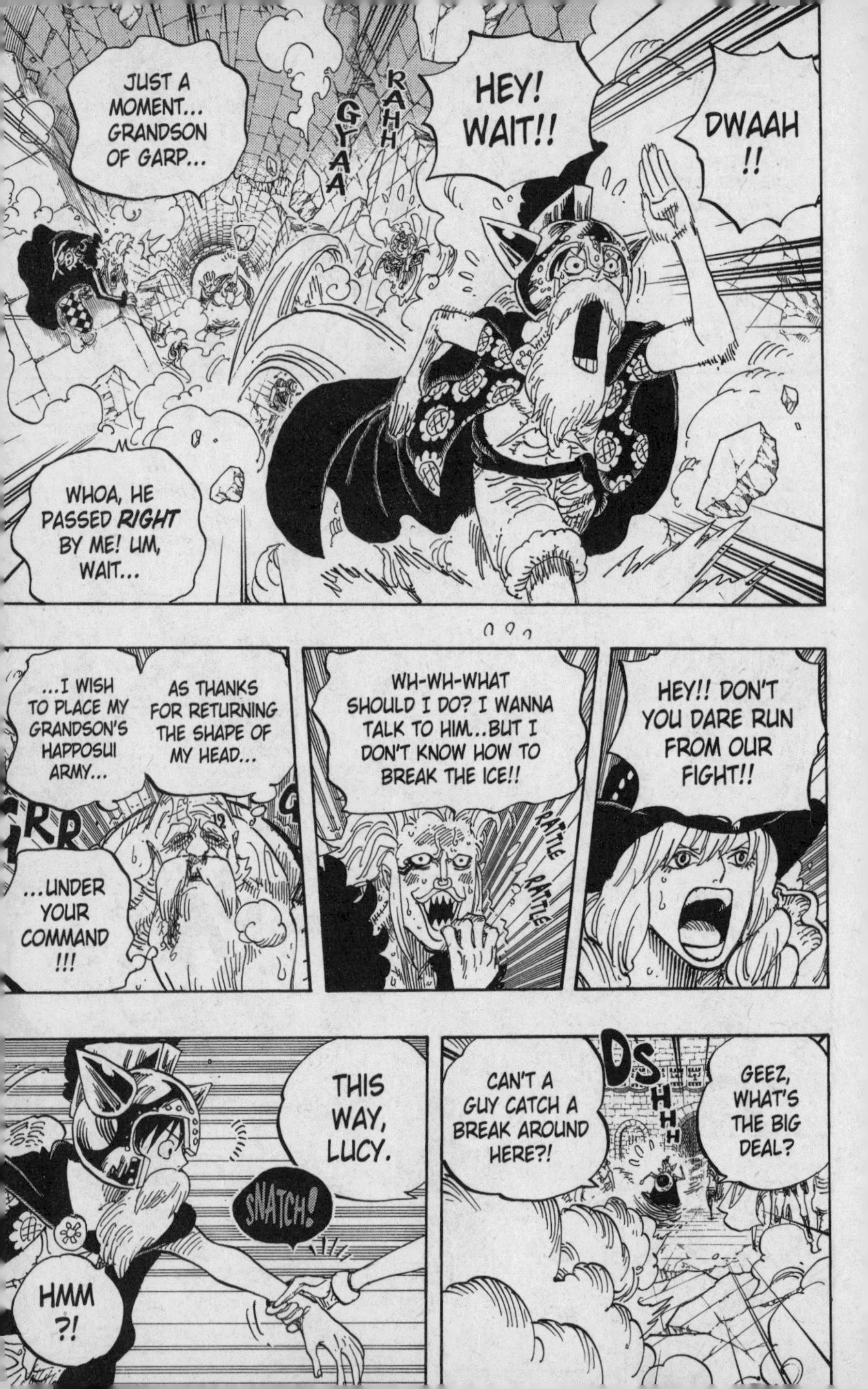
DWAAH !!
HEY! WAIT!!
RAHH
GYAA
JUST A MOMENT... GRANDSON OF GARP...
WHOA, HE PASSED *RIGHT* BY ME! UM, WAIT...
HEY!! DON'T YOU DARE RUN FROM OUR FIGHT!!
WH-WH-WHAT SHOULD I DO? I WANNA TALK TO HIM...BUT I DON'T KNOW HOW TO BREAK THE ICE!!
RATTLE
RATTLE
AS THANKS FOR RETURNING THE SHAPE OF MY HEAD...
...I WISH TO PLACE MY GRANDSON'S HAPPOSUI ARMY...
...UNDER YOUR COMMAND !!!
GEEZ, WHAT'S THE BIG DEAL?
DSHHH
CAN'T A GUY CATCH A BREAK AROUND HERE?!
THIS WAY, LUCY.
SNATCH!
HMM ?!

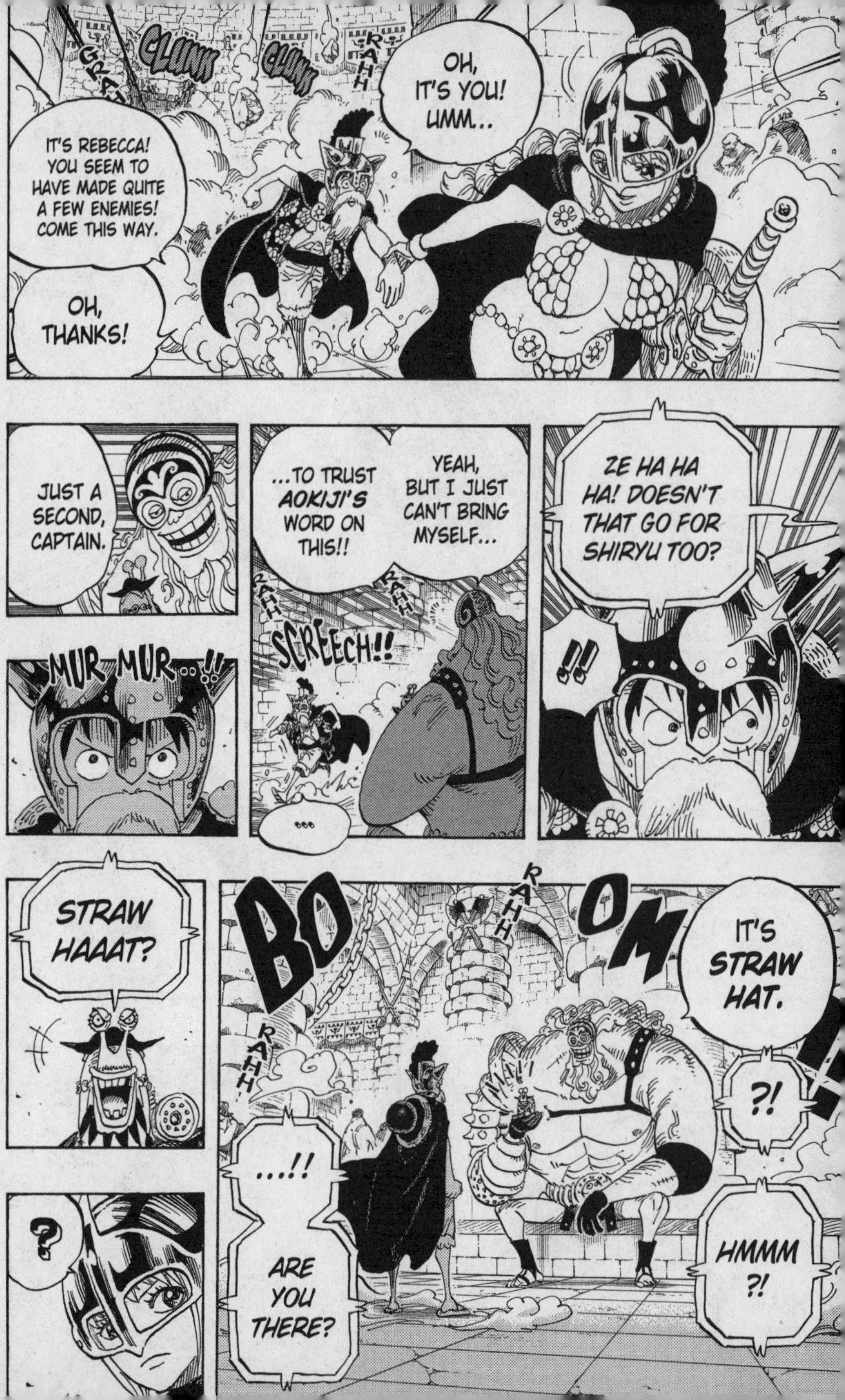
RAHH
CLUNK
CLUNK
GRAT
OH, IT'S YOU! UMM...
IT'S REBECCA! YOU SEEM TO HAVE MADE QUITE A FEW ENEMIES! COME THIS WAY.
OH, THANKS!
ZE HA HA HA! DOESN'T THAT GO FOR SHIRYU TOO?
!!
YEAH, BUT I JUST CAN'T BRING MYSELF...
...TO TRUST AOKIJI'S WORD ON THIS!!
RAHH
RAHH
SCREECH!!
...
JUST A SECOND, CAPTAIN.
MUR MUR..!!
OM
RAHH
BO
IT'S STRAW HAT.
?!
HMMM ?!
...!!
RAHH
ARE YOU THERE?
STRAW HAAAT?
?

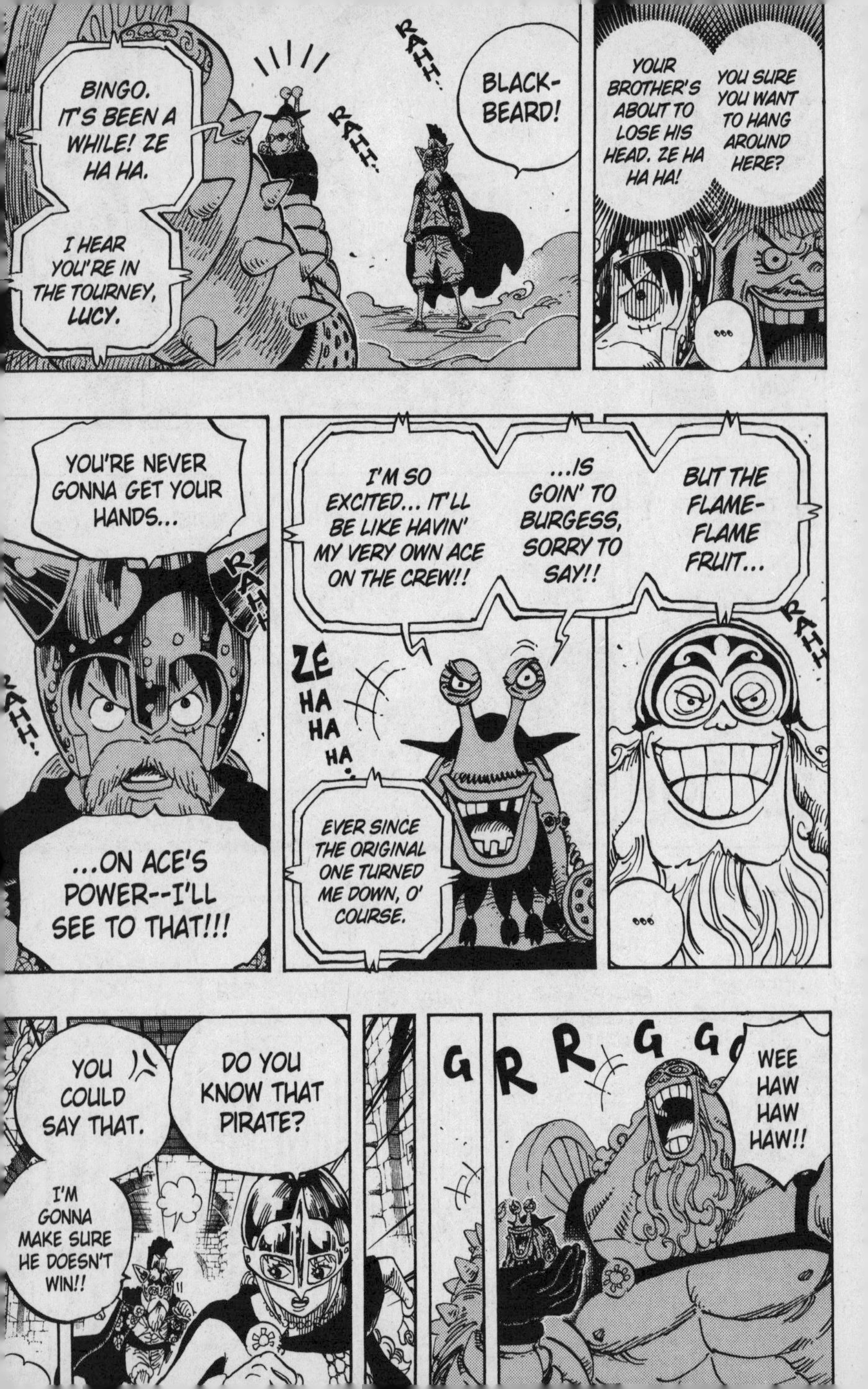
YOU SURE YOU WANT TO HANG AROUND HERE?
YOUR BROTHER'S ABOUT TO LOSE HIS HEAD. ZE HA HA HA!
...
BLACK-BEARD!
RAHH...
RAHH...
BINGO. IT'S BEEN A WHILE! ZE HA HA.
I HEAR YOU'RE IN THE TOURNEY, LUCY.
BUT THE FLAME-FLAME FRUIT...
RAHH
...
...IS GOIN' TO BURGESS, SORRY TO SAY!!
I'M SO EXCITED... IT'LL BE LIKE HAVIN' MY VERY OWN ACE ON THE CREW!!
ZE HA HA HA...
EVER SINCE THE ORIGINAL ONE TURNED ME DOWN, O' COURSE.
YOU'RE NEVER GONNA GET YOUR HANDS...
RAHH
RAHH...
...ON ACE'S POWER--I'LL SEE TO THAT!!!
WEE HAW HAW HAW!!
GRRGGG
DO YOU KNOW THAT PIRATE?
YOU COULD SAY THAT.
I'M GONNA MAKE SURE HE DOESN'T WIN!!

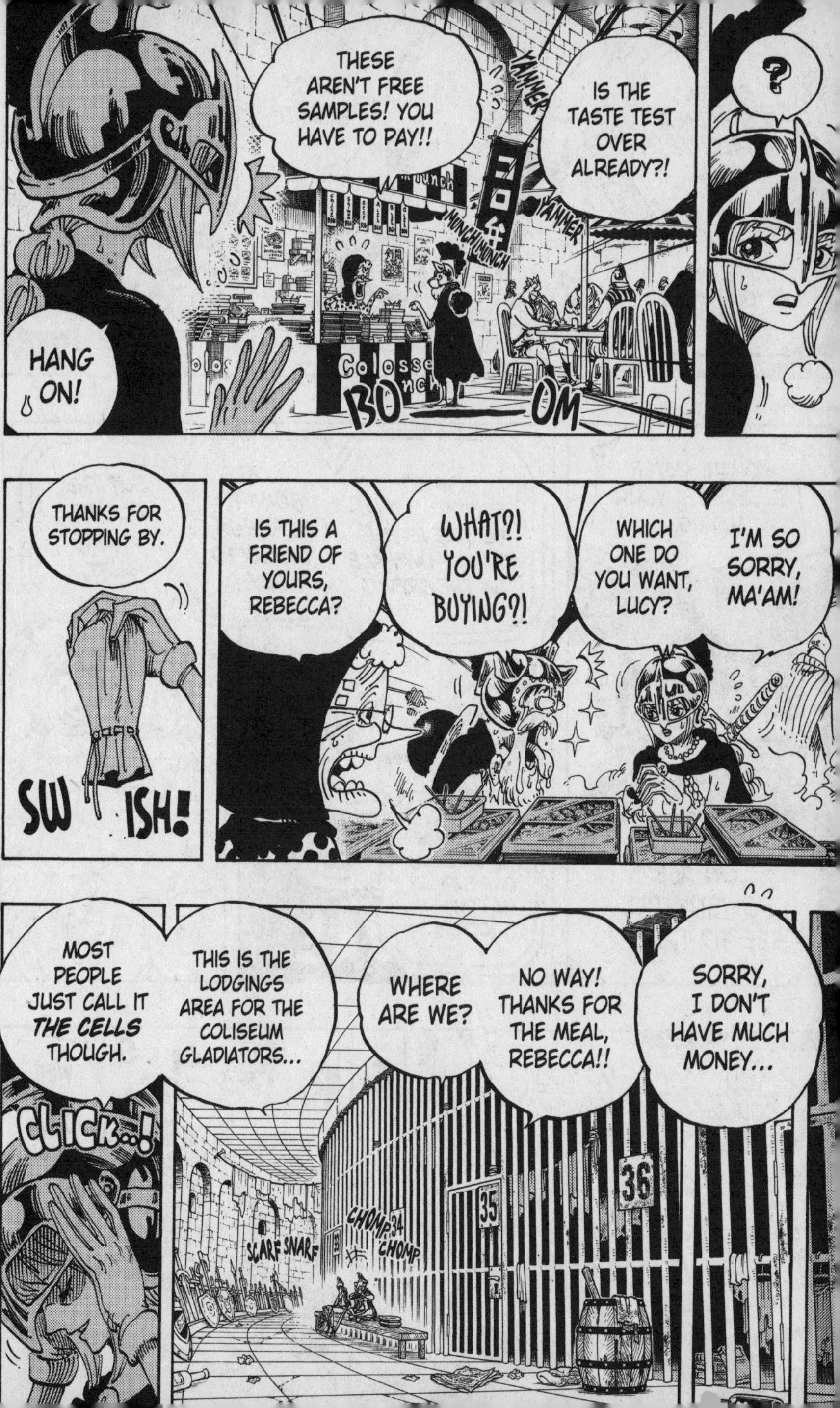
?
IS THE TASTE TEST OVER ALREADY?!
YAMMER YAMMER
THESE AREN'T FREE SAMPLES! YOU HAVE TO PAY!!
MUNCH MUNCH
BOOM
HANG ON!
I'M SO SORRY, MA'AM!
WHICH ONE DO YOU WANT, LUCY?
WHAT?! YOU'RE BUYING?!
IS THIS A FRIEND OF YOURS, REBECCA?
THANKS FOR STOPPING BY.
SWISH!
SORRY, I DON'T HAVE MUCH MONEY...
NO WAY! THANKS FOR THE MEAL, REBECCA!!
WHERE ARE WE?
THIS IS THE LODGINGS AREA FOR THE COLISEUM GLADIATORS...
MOST PEOPLE JUST CALL IT *THE CELLS* THOUGH.
36
35
CHOMP CHOMP
SCARF SNARF
CLICK..!

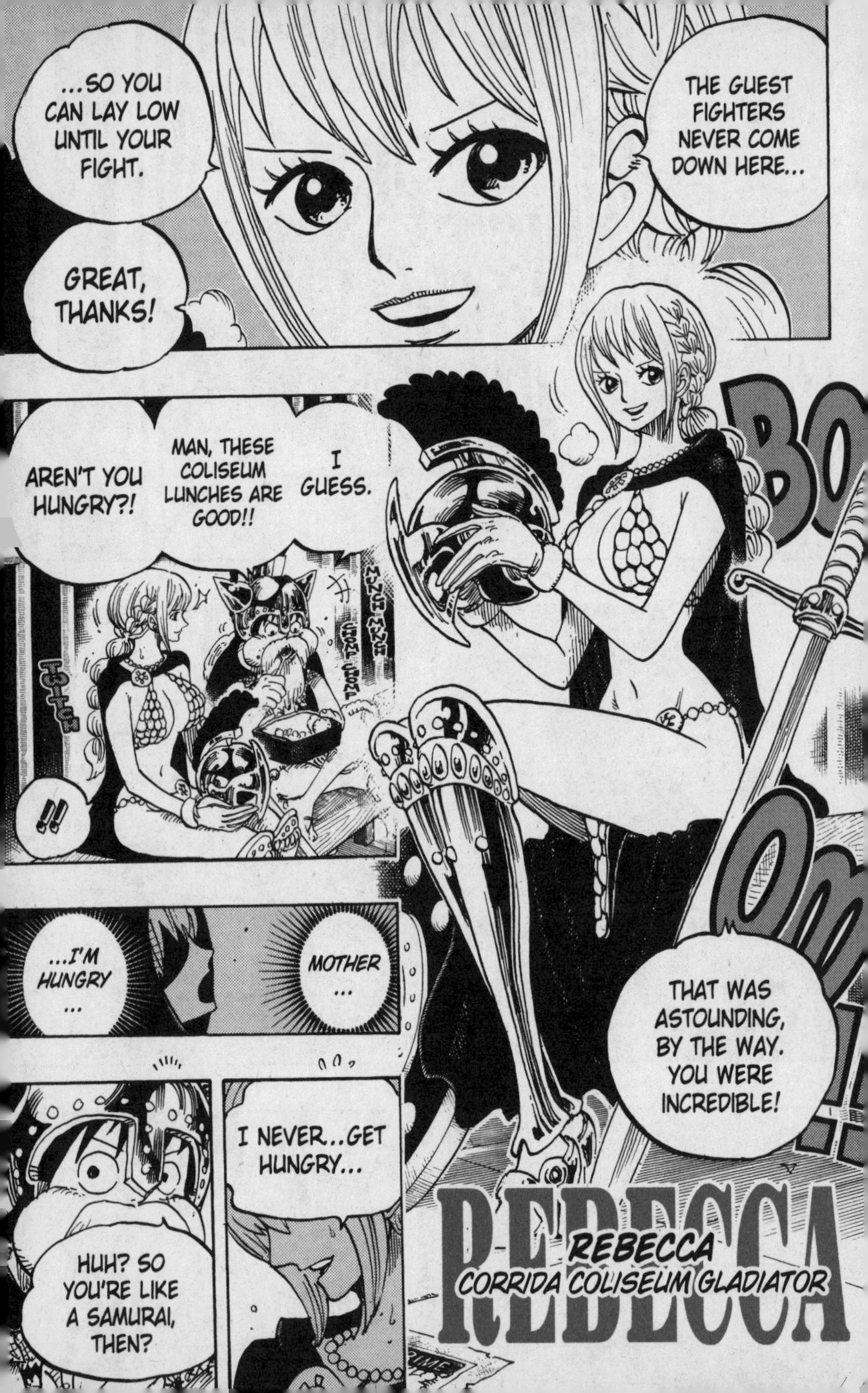
THE GUEST FIGHTERS NEVER COME DOWN HERE...
...SO YOU CAN LAY LOW UNTIL YOUR FIGHT.
GREAT, THANKS!
THAT WAS ASTOUNDING, BY THE WAY. YOU WERE INCREDIBLE!
REBECCA
REBECCA
CORRIDA COLISEUM GLADIATOR
I GUESS.
MAN, THESE COLISEUM LUNCHES ARE GOOD!!
AREN'T YOU HUNGRY?!
MUNCH MUNCH
CHOMP CHOMP
TWITCH
!!
MOTHER...
...I'M HUNGRY...
I NEVER...GET HUNGRY...
HUH? SO YOU'RE LIKE A SAMURAI, THEN?

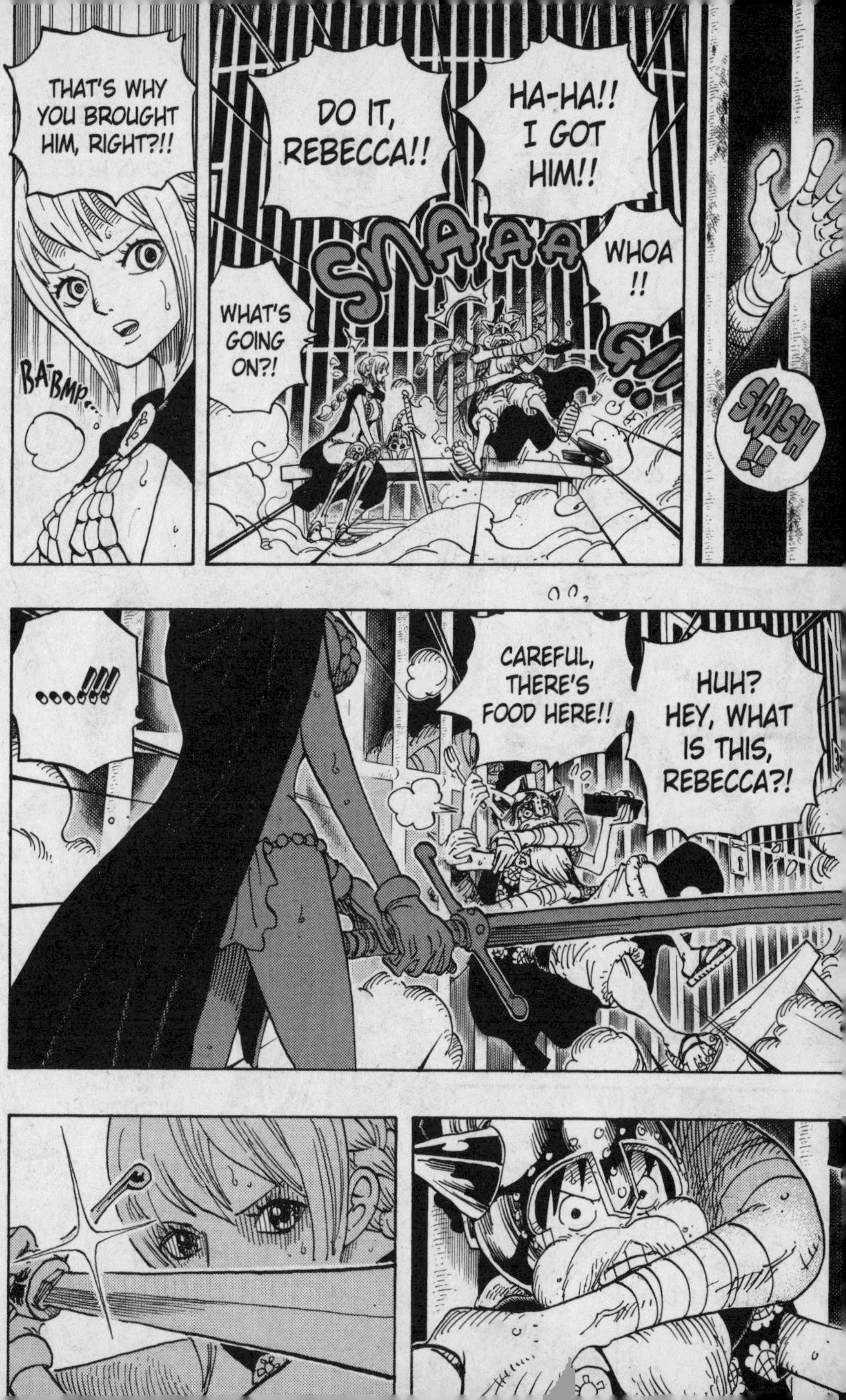
SWISH!!
HA-HA!! I GOT HIM!!
DO IT, REBECCA!!
WHOA!!
SNAAAAG!!
WHAT'S GOING ON?!
THAT'S WHY YOU BROUGHT HIM, RIGHT?!!
BA-BMP...
HUH? HEY, WHAT IS THIS, REBECCA?!
CAREFUL, THERE'S FOOD HERE!!
....!!!

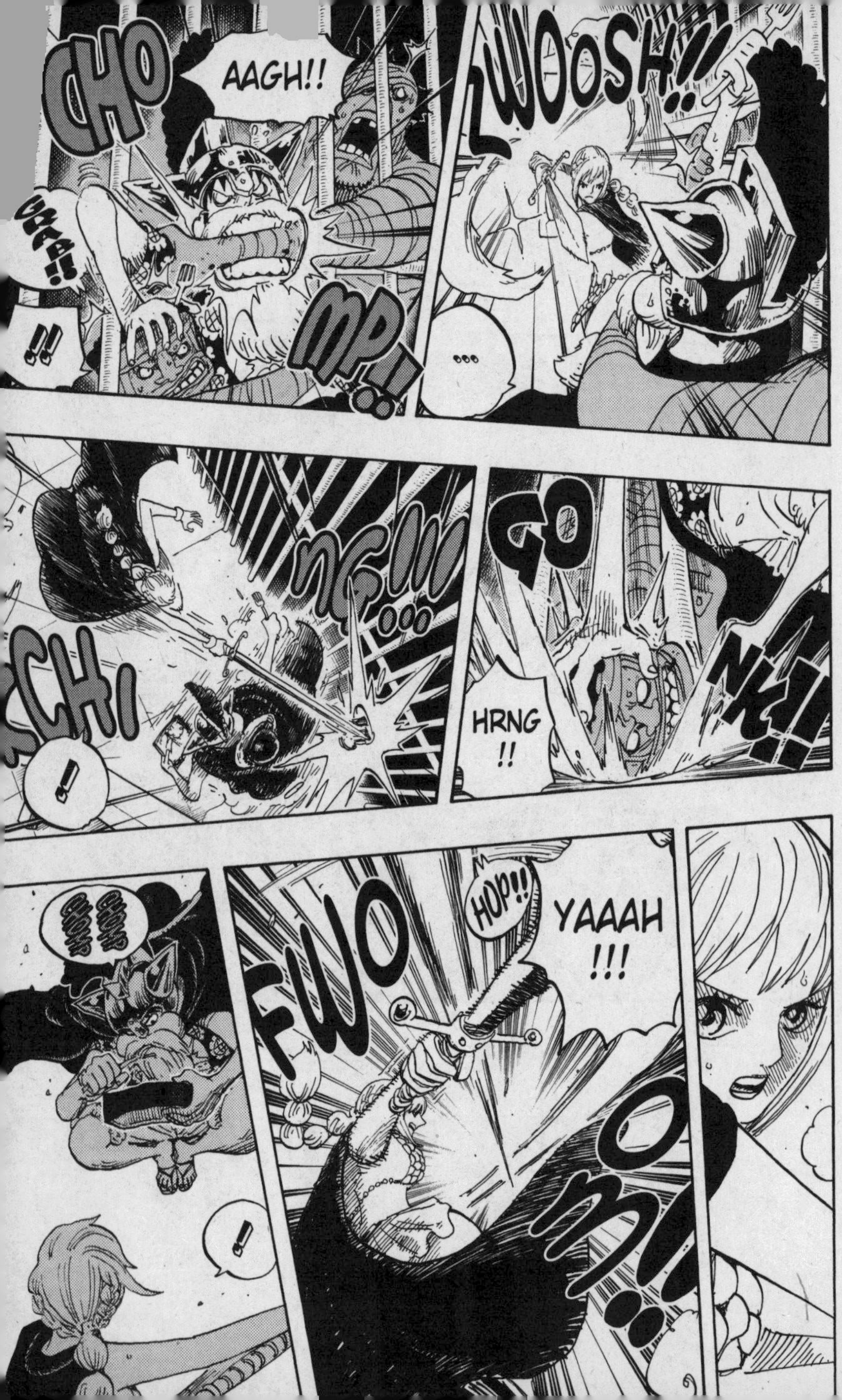
ZWOOSH!!
...
CHO
AAGH!!
GWAAH!!
!!
MP!!...
GO
NK!!
HRNG!!
NG!!!...
CHI
!
FWO
HOP!!
YAAAH!!!
OM!!...
CHOMP CHOMP
!

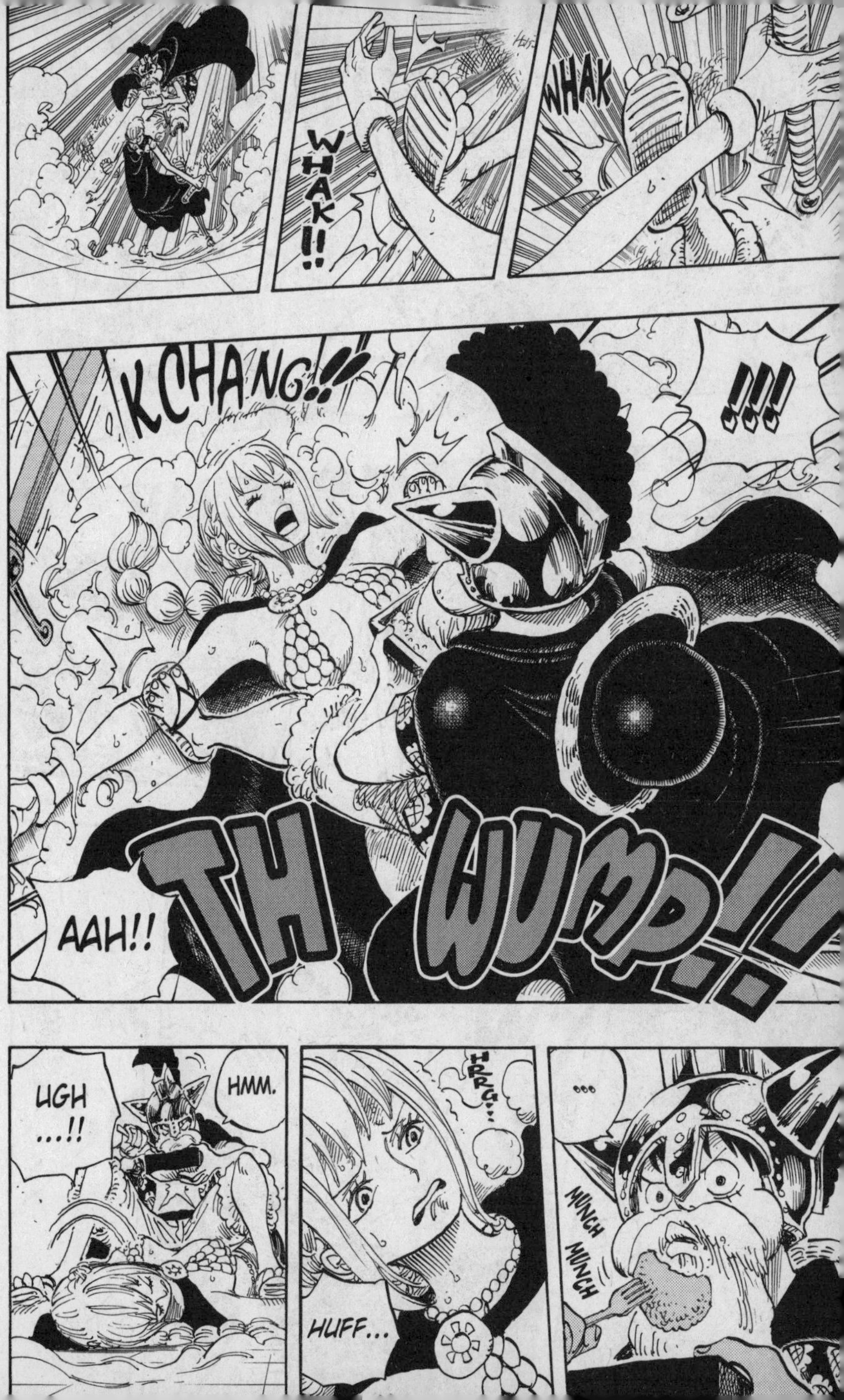
WHAK
WHAK!!
!!!
KCHANG!!
THWUMP!!
AAH!!
...
MUNCH
MUNCH
HRRG...
HUFF...
HMM.
UGH ...!!

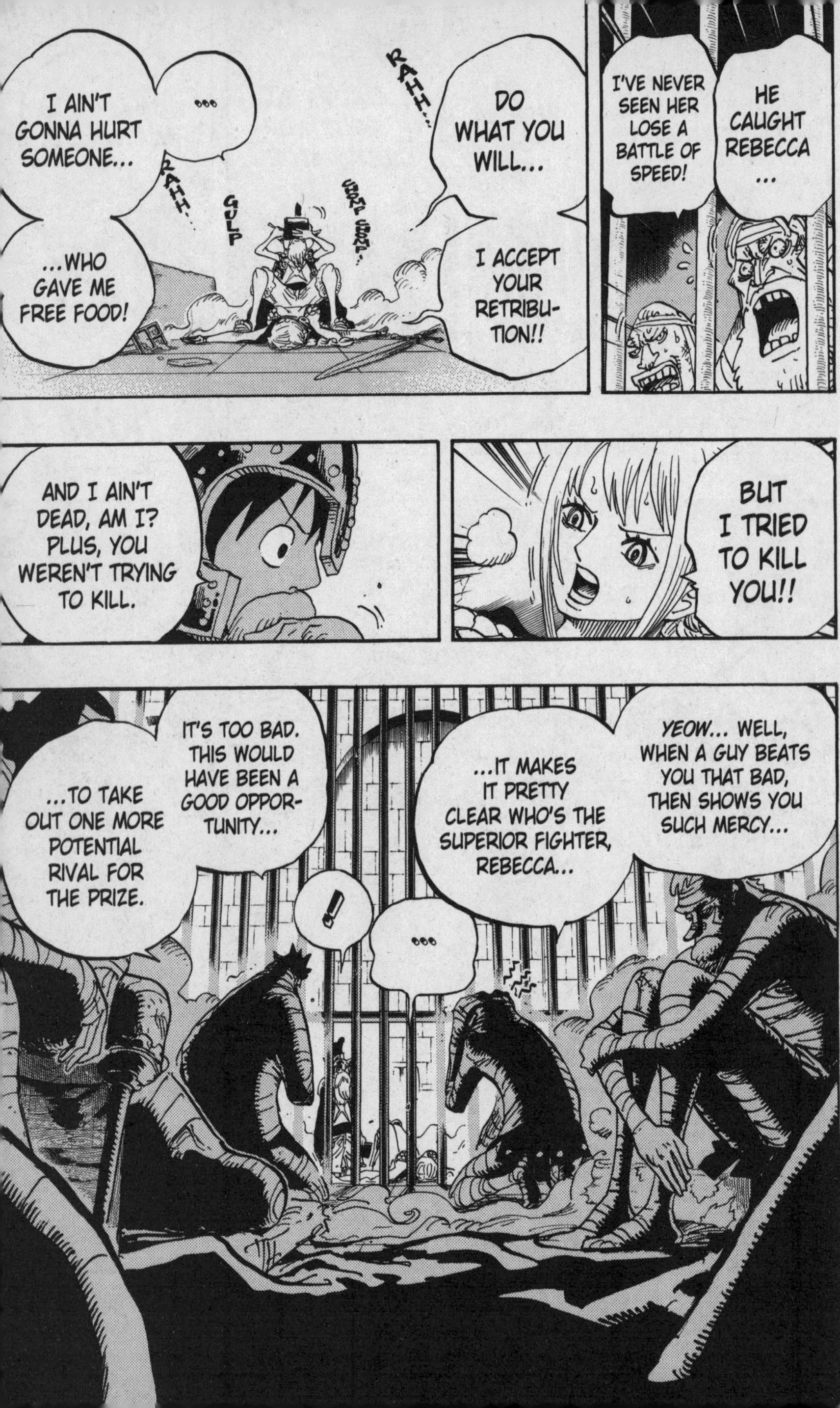

HE CAUGHT REBECCA...
I'VE NEVER SEEN HER LOSE A BATTLE OF SPEED!
DO WHAT YOU WILL...
RAHH...
I ACCEPT YOUR RETRIBUTION!!
CHOMP CHOMP
GULP
RAHH...
...
I AIN'T GONNA HURT SOMEONE...
...WHO GAVE ME FREE FOOD!
BUT I TRIED TO KILL YOU!!
AND I AIN'T DEAD, AM I? PLUS, YOU WEREN'T TRYING TO KILL.
YEOW... WELL, WHEN A GUY BEATS YOU THAT BAD, THEN SHOWS YOU SUCH MERCY...
...IT MAKES IT PRETTY CLEAR WHO'S THE SUPERIOR FIGHTER, REBECCA...
...
!
IT'S TOO BAD. THIS WOULD HAVE BEEN A GOOD OPPORTUNITY...
...TO TAKE OUT ONE MORE POTENTIAL RIVAL FOR THE PRIZE.

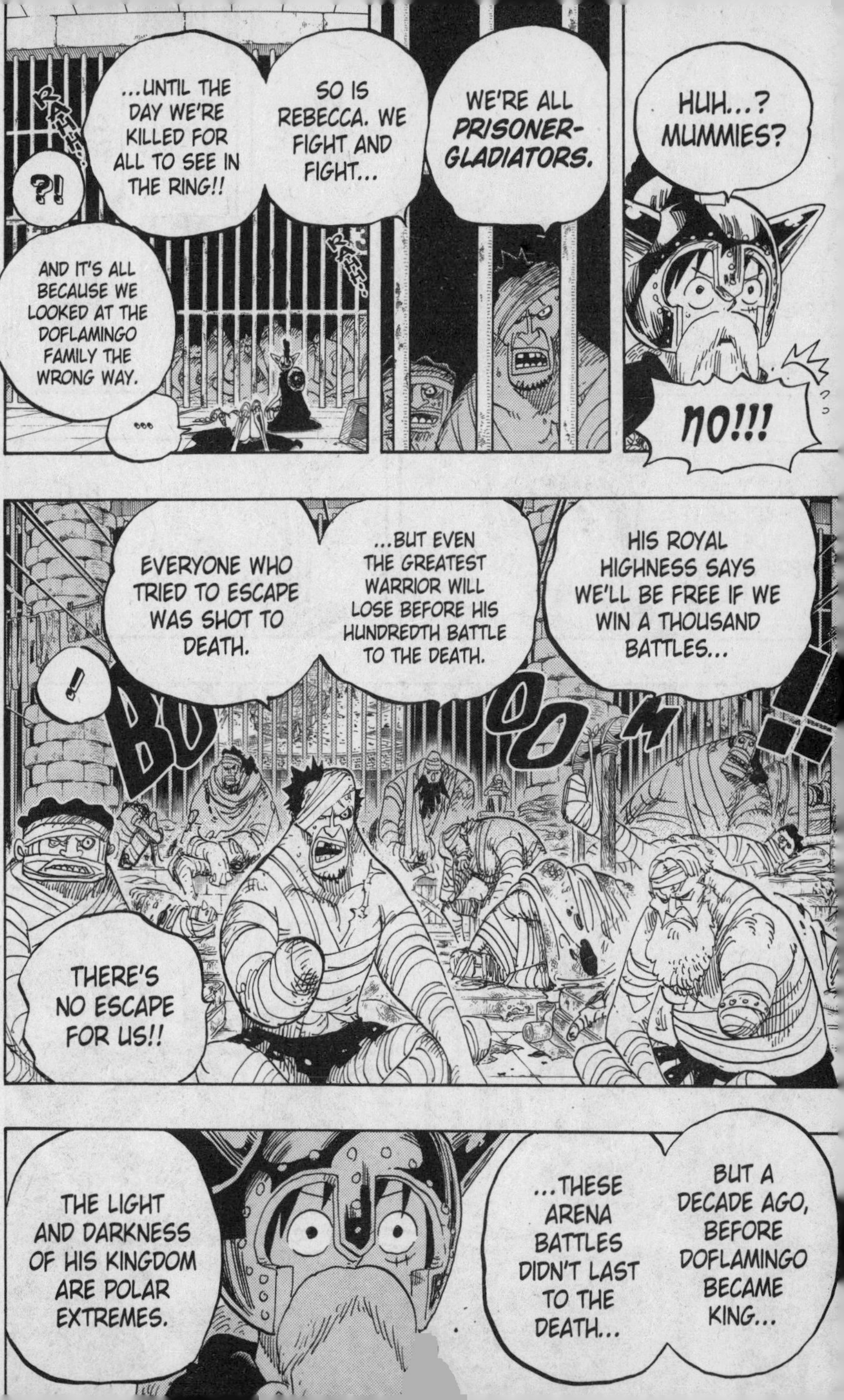

HUH...? MUMMIES?
NO!!!
WE'RE ALL PRISONER-GLADIATORS.
SO IS REBECCA. WE FIGHT AND FIGHT...
...UNTIL THE DAY WE'RE KILLED FOR ALL TO SEE IN THE RING!!
?!
AND IT'S ALL BECAUSE WE LOOKED AT THE DOFLAMINGO FAMILY THE WRONG WAY.
...
HIS ROYAL HIGHNESS SAYS WE'LL BE FREE IF WE WIN A THOUSAND BATTLES...
...BUT EVEN THE GREATEST WARRIOR WILL LOSE BEFORE HIS HUNDREDTH BATTLE TO THE DEATH.
EVERYONE WHO TRIED TO ESCAPE WAS SHOT TO DEATH.
!
BOOOM!!
THERE'S NO ESCAPE FOR US!!
BUT A DECADE AGO, BEFORE DOFLAMINGO BECAME KING...
...THESE ARENA BATTLES DIDN'T LAST TO THE DEATH...
THE LIGHT AND DARKNESS OF HIS KINGDOM ARE POLAR EXTREMES.

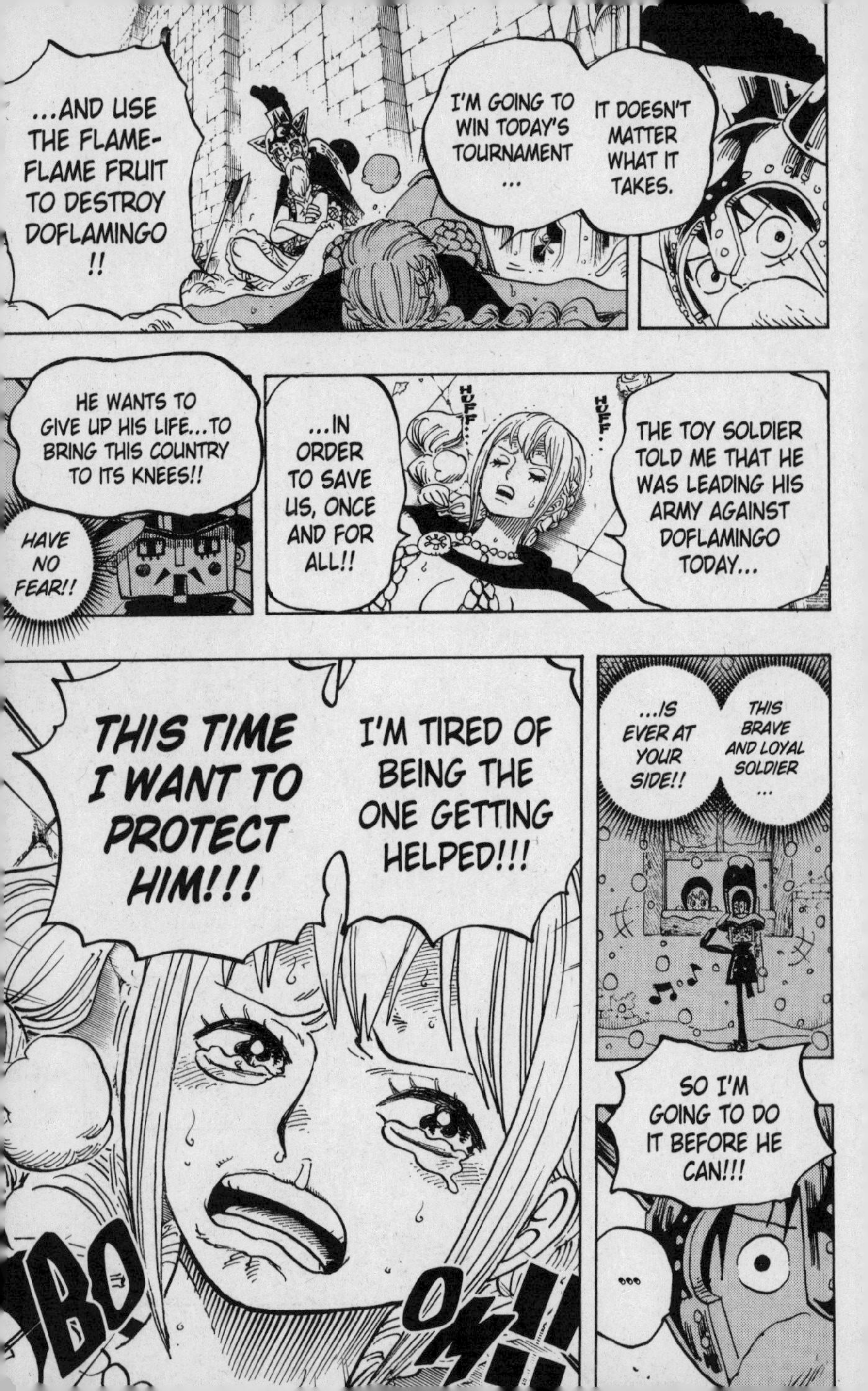
IT DOESN'T MATTER WHAT IT TAKES.
I'M GOING TO WIN TODAY'S TOURNAMENT ...
...AND USE THE FLAME-FLAME FRUIT TO DESTROY DOFLAMINGO !!
THE TOY SOLDIER TOLD ME THAT HE WAS LEADING HIS ARMY AGAINST DOFLAMINGO TODAY...
HUFF...
HUFF...
...IN ORDER TO SAVE US, ONCE AND FOR ALL!!
HE WANTS TO GIVE UP HIS LIFE...TO BRING THIS COUNTRY TO ITS KNEES!!
HAVE NO FEAR!!
THIS BRAVE AND LOYAL SOLDIER ...
...IS EVER AT YOUR SIDE!!
SO I'M GOING TO DO IT BEFORE HE CAN!!!
...
I'M TIRED OF BEING THE ONE GETTING HELPED!!!
THIS TIME I WANT TO PROTECT HIM!!!
OH!!
BO

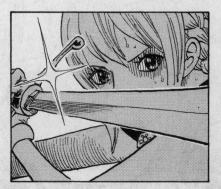

Chapter 721:
REBECCA AND THE SOLDIER

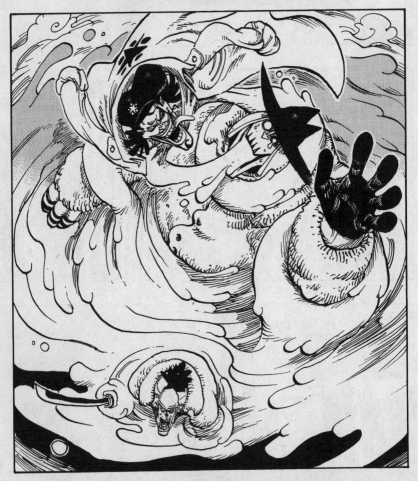

**CARIBOU'S NEW WORLD KEE HEE HEE, VOL. 38:
"TAKE OVER SCOTCH THE OPPRESSOR!!"**

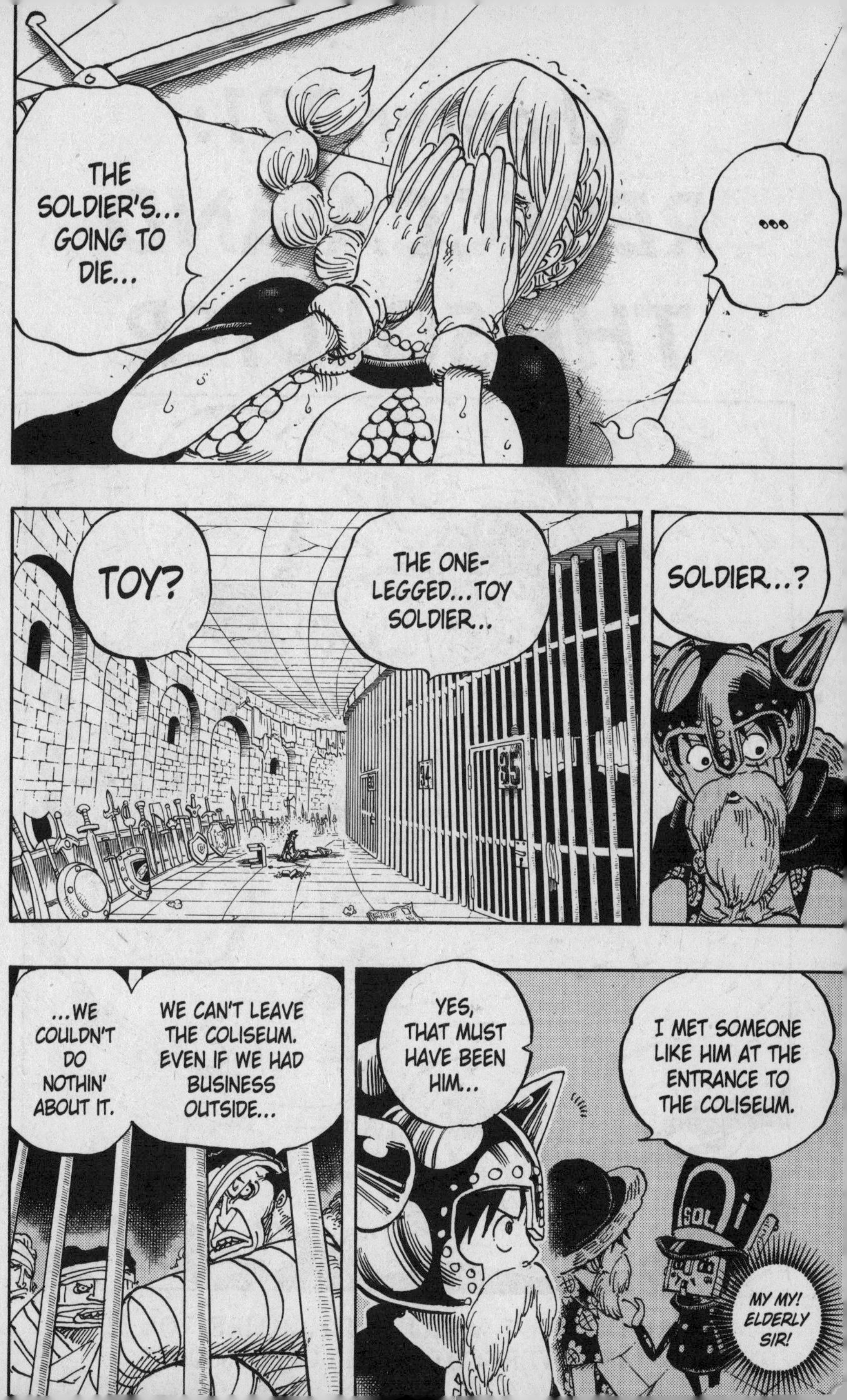
THE SOLDIER'S... GOING TO DIE...
...
SOLDIER...?
THE ONE-LEGGED...TOY SOLDIER..
TOY?
I MET SOMEONE LIKE HIM AT THE ENTRANCE TO THE COLISEUM.
YES, THAT MUST HAVE BEEN HIM...
MY MY! ELDERLY SIR!
WE CAN'T LEAVE THE COLISEUM. EVEN IF WE HAD BUSINESS OUTSIDE...
...WE COULDN'T DO NOTHIN' ABOUT IT.

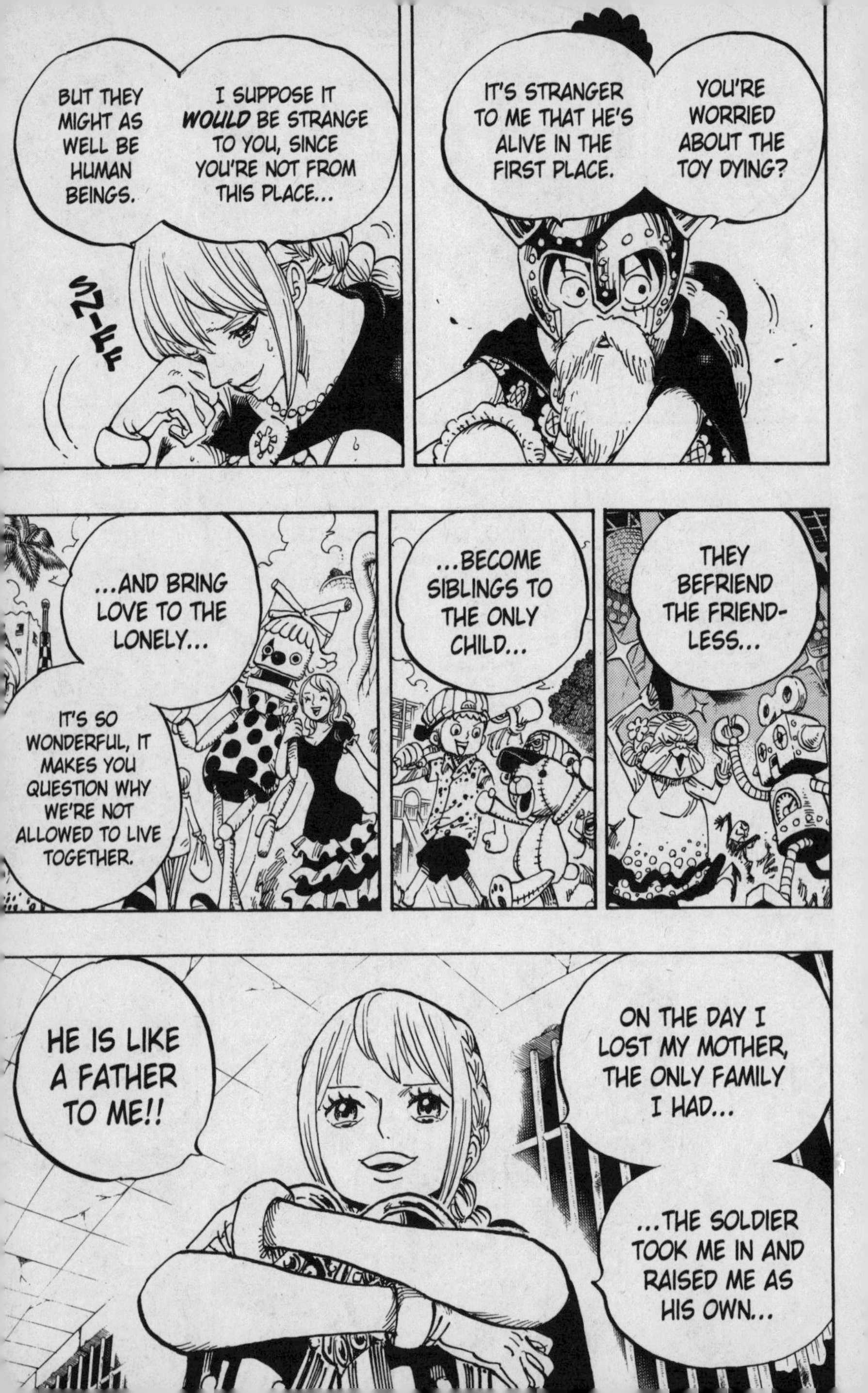
YOU'RE WORRIED ABOUT THE TOY DYING?
IT'S STRANGER TO ME THAT HE'S ALIVE IN THE FIRST PLACE.
I SUPPOSE IT *WOULD* BE STRANGE TO YOU, SINCE YOU'RE NOT FROM THIS PLACE...
BUT THEY MIGHT AS WELL BE HUMAN BEINGS.
SNIFF
THEY BEFRIEND THE FRIEND-LESS...
...BECOME SIBLINGS TO THE ONLY CHILD...
...AND BRING LOVE TO THE LONELY...
IT'S SO WONDERFUL, IT MAKES YOU QUESTION WHY WE'RE NOT ALLOWED TO LIVE TOGETHER.
ON THE DAY I LOST MY MOTHER, THE ONLY FAMILY I HAD...
...THE SOLDIER TOOK ME IN AND RAISED ME AS HIS OWN...
HE IS LIKE A FATHER TO ME!!

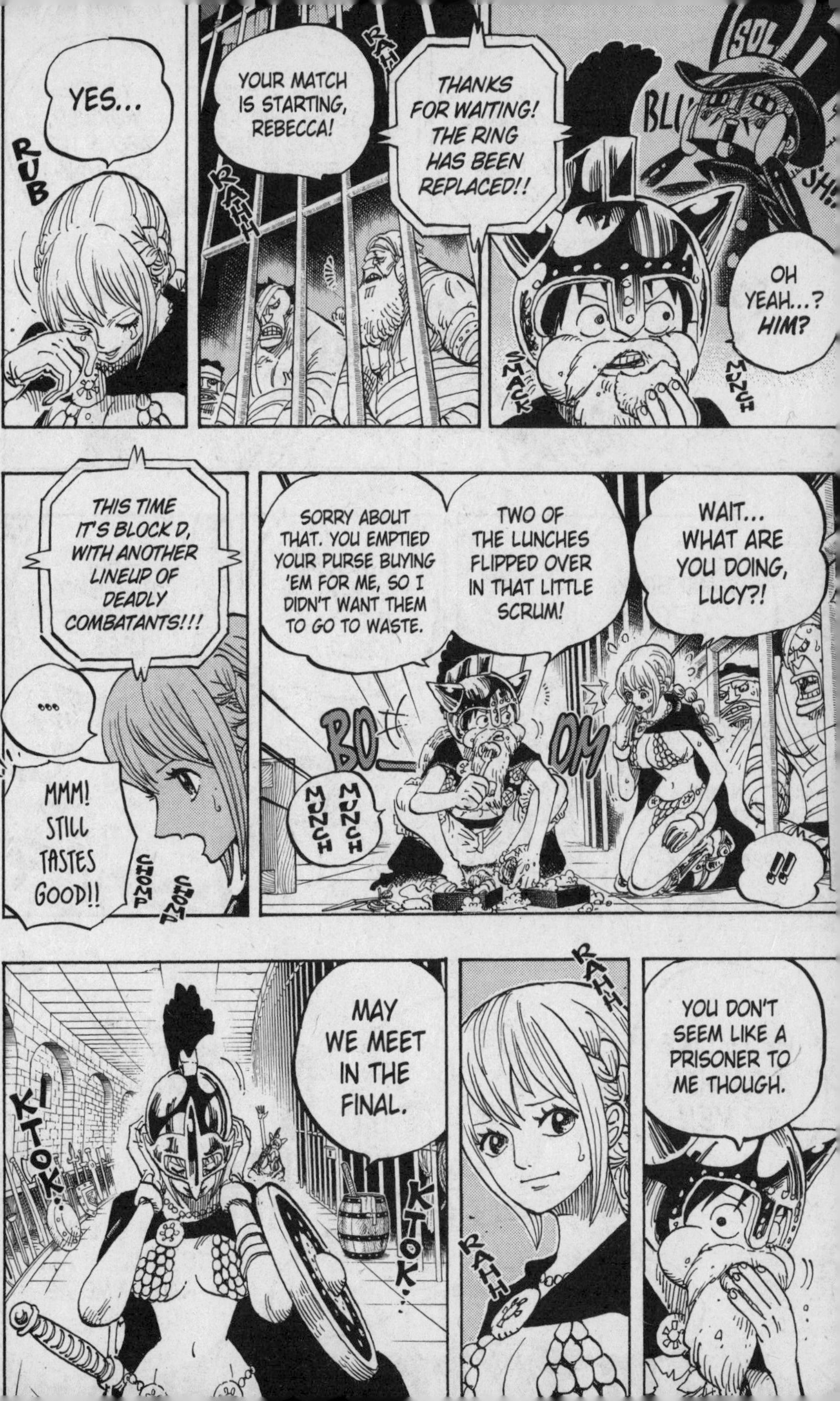
BLI
SH!!
OH YEAH...? HIM?
MUNCH
SMACK
THANKS FOR WAITING! THE RING HAS BEEN REPLACED!!
YOUR MATCH IS STARTING, REBECCA!
RAHH
RAHH
YES...
RUB
WAIT... WHAT ARE YOU DOING, LUCY?!
TWO OF THE LUNCHES FLIPPED OVER IN THAT LITTLE SCRUM!
SORRY ABOUT THAT. YOU EMPTIED YOUR PURSE BUYING 'EM FOR ME, SO I DIDN'T WANT THEM TO GO TO WASTE.
BO—OM
MUNCH MUNCH
!!
THIS TIME IT'S BLOCK D, WITH ANOTHER LINEUP OF DEADLY COMBATANTS!!!
...
MMM! STILL TASTES GOOD!!
CHOMP CHOMP
YOU DON'T SEEM LIKE A PRISONER TO ME THOUGH.
RAHH
RAHH
MAY WE MEET IN THE FINAL.
KTOK
KTOK

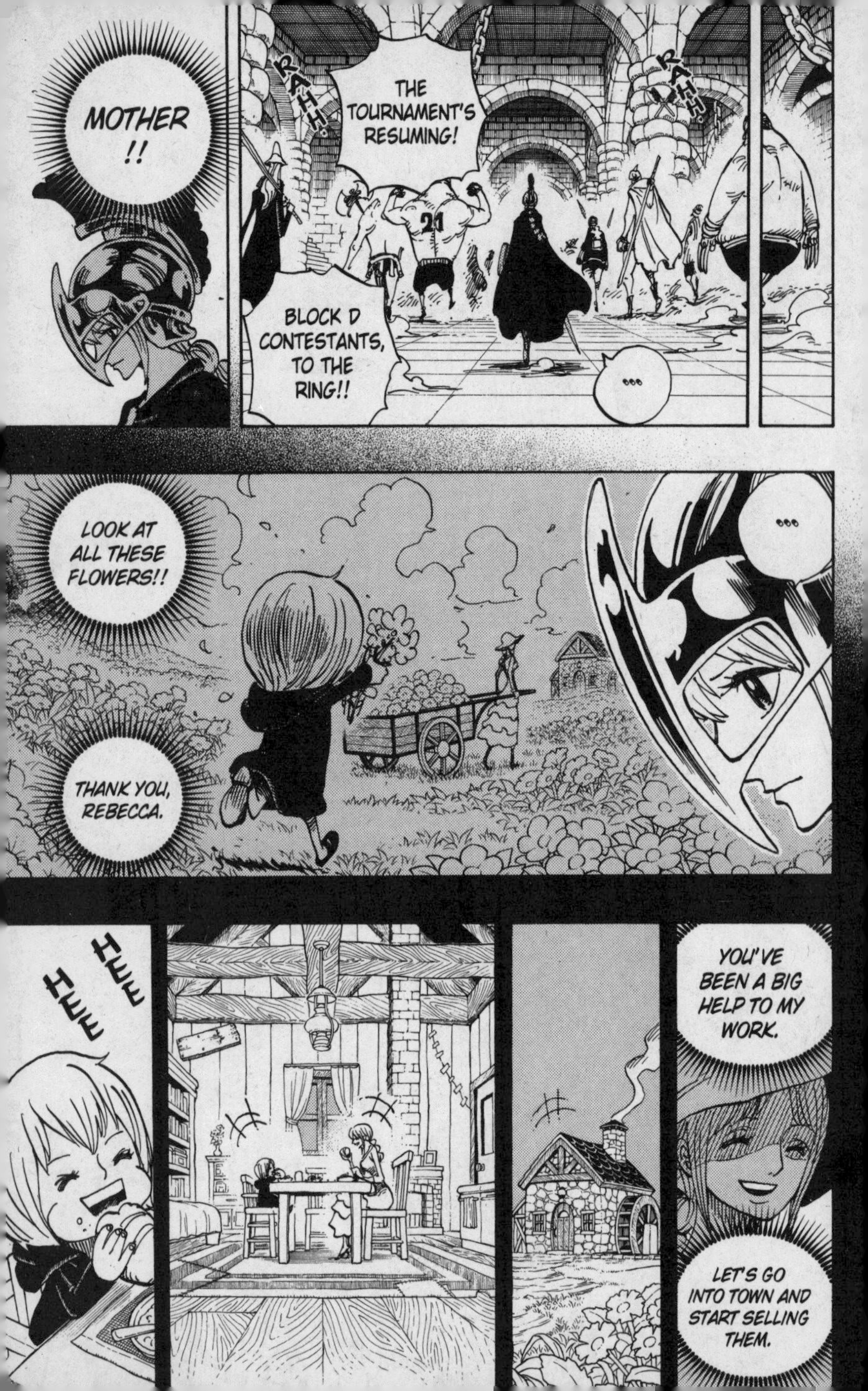
RAHH
THE TOURNAMENT'S RESUMING!
RAHH
BLOCK D CONTESTANTS, TO THE RING!!
...
MOTHER!!
...
LOOK AT ALL THESE FLOWERS!!
THANK YOU, REBECCA.
YOU'VE BEEN A BIG HELP TO MY WORK.
LET'S GO INTO TOWN AND START SELLING THEM.
HEE HEE

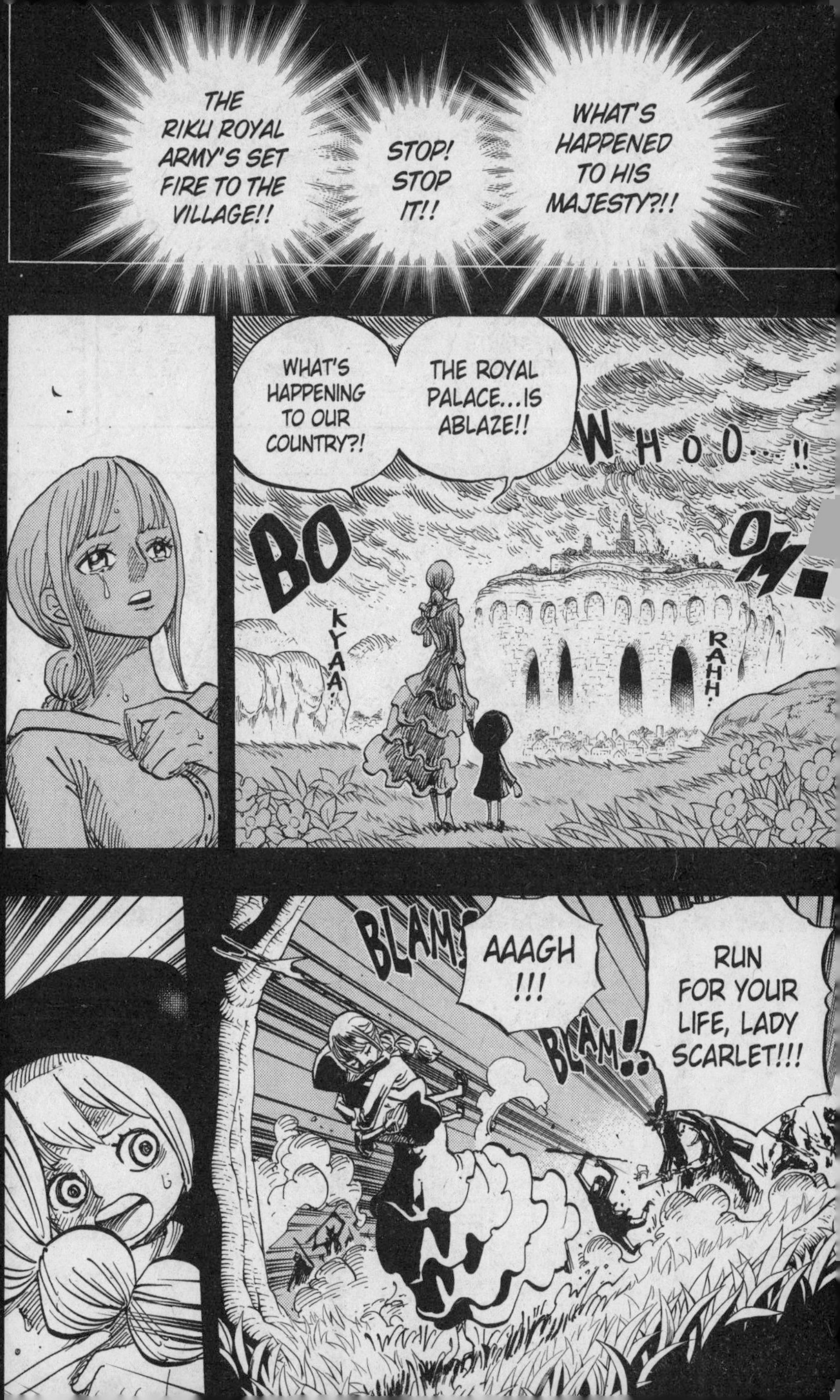
WHAT'S HAPPENED TO HIS MAJESTY?!!
STOP! STOP IT!!
THE RIKU ROYAL ARMY'S SET FIRE TO THE VILLAGE!!
WHOO...!!
OOM.
RAHH!
THE ROYAL PALACE...IS ABLAZE!!
WHAT'S HAPPENING TO OUR COUNTRY?!
BO
KYAA!
RUN FOR YOUR LIFE, LADY SCARLET!!!
BLAM!!
AAAGH !!!
BLAM!

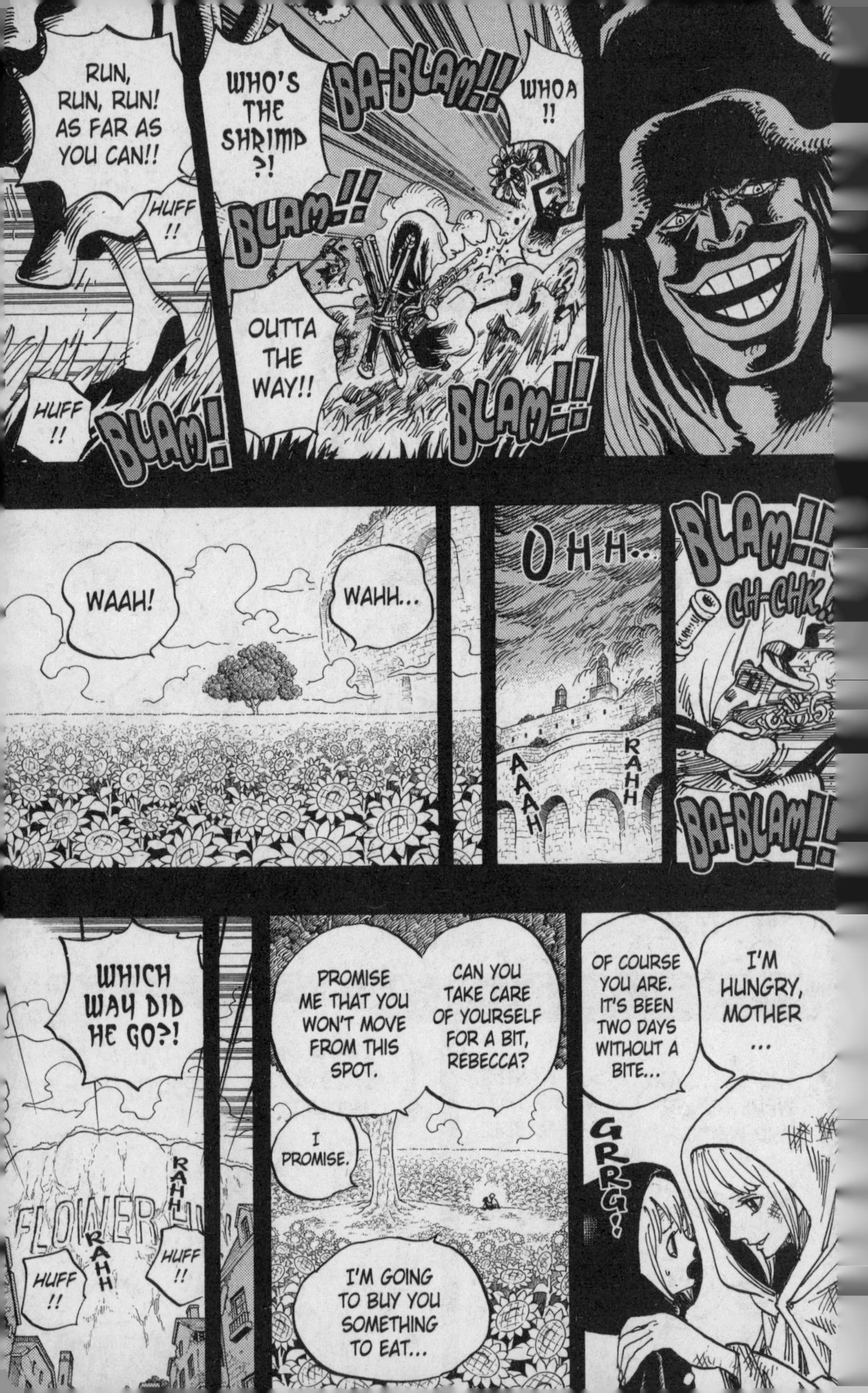
WHOA!!
BA-BLAM!!
WHO'S THE SHRIMP?!
BLAM!!
OUTTA THE WAY!!
BLAM!!
RUN, RUN, RUN! AS FAR AS YOU CAN!!
HUFF!!
HUFF!!
BLAM!
BLAM!!
CH-CHK..!
BA-BLAM!!
OHH...
RAHH
AAAH
WAHH...
WAAH!
I'M HUNGRY, MOTHER...
OF COURSE YOU ARE. IT'S BEEN TWO DAYS WITHOUT A BITE...
GRRRG...
CAN YOU TAKE CARE OF YOURSELF FOR A BIT, REBECCA?
PROMISE ME THAT YOU WON'T MOVE FROM THIS SPOT.
I PROMISE.
I'M GOING TO BUY YOU SOMETHING TO EAT...
WHICH WAY DID HE GO?!
RAHH
HUFF!!
FLOWER
RAHH
HUFF!!

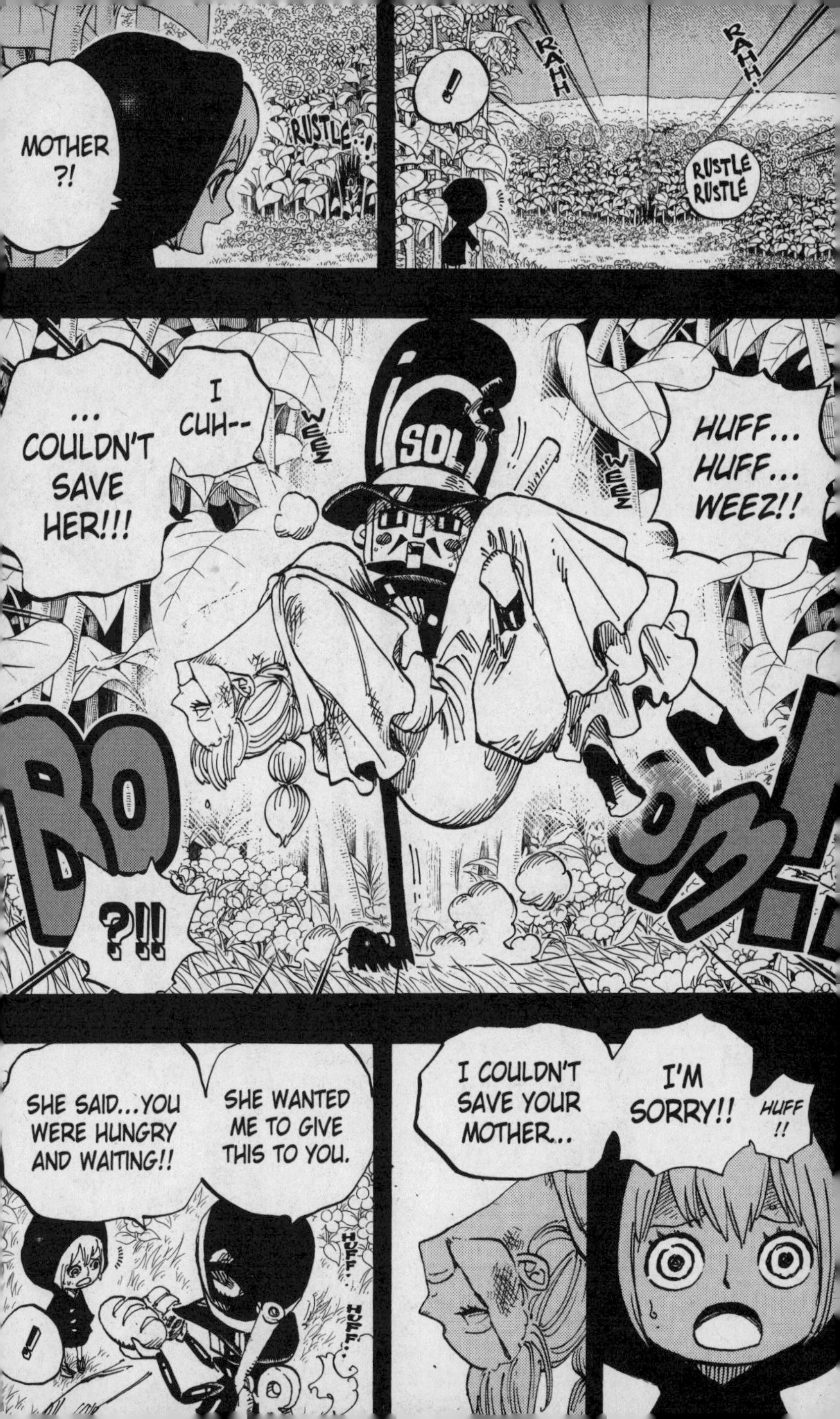
RAHH!
RAHH
!
RUSTLE RUSTLE
RUSTLE..!!
MOTHER ?!
HUFF... HUFF... WEEZ!!
WEEZ
SOL
BOOM!!
I CUH--
WEEZ
... COULDN'T SAVE HER!!!
?!!
HUFF !!
I'M SORRY!!
I COULDN'T SAVE YOUR MOTHER...
SHE WANTED ME TO GIVE THIS TO YOU.
SHE SAID...YOU WERE HUNGRY AND WAITING!!
HUFF..
HUFF..
!

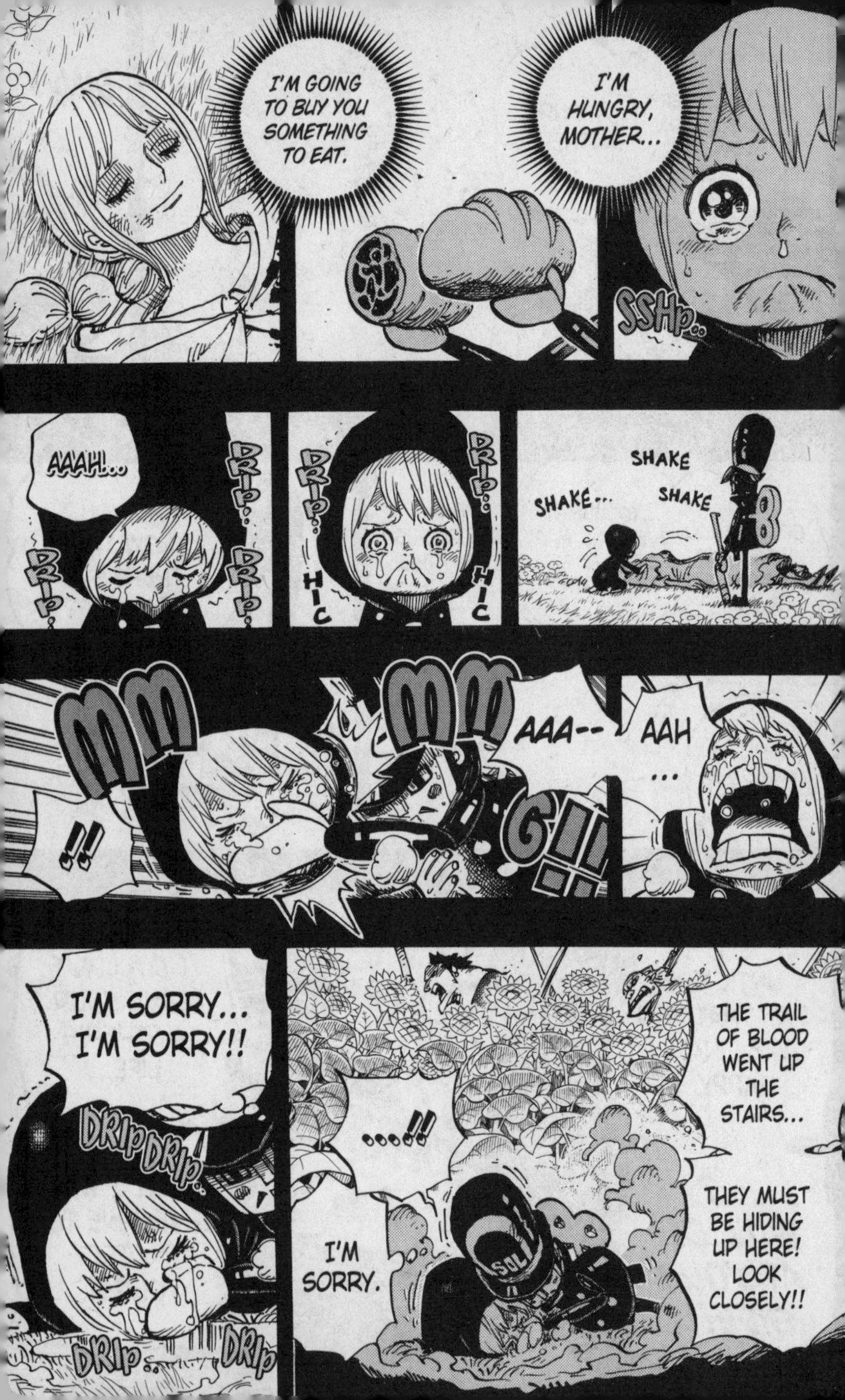
I'M HUNGRY, MOTHER...
SSHp..
I'M GOING TO BUY YOU SOMETHING TO EAT.
SHAKE
SHAKE
SHAKE...
DRIp..
DRIp..
HIC
HIC
AAAH...
DRIp..
DRIp
DRIp..
AAH
...
MM
AAA--
G!!
MM
!!
THE TRAIL OF BLOOD WENT UP THE STAIRS...
THEY MUST BE HIDING UP HERE! LOOK CLOSELY!!
....!!
I'M SORRY.
I'M SORRY... I'M SORRY!!
DRIp DRIp..
DRIp..
DRIp

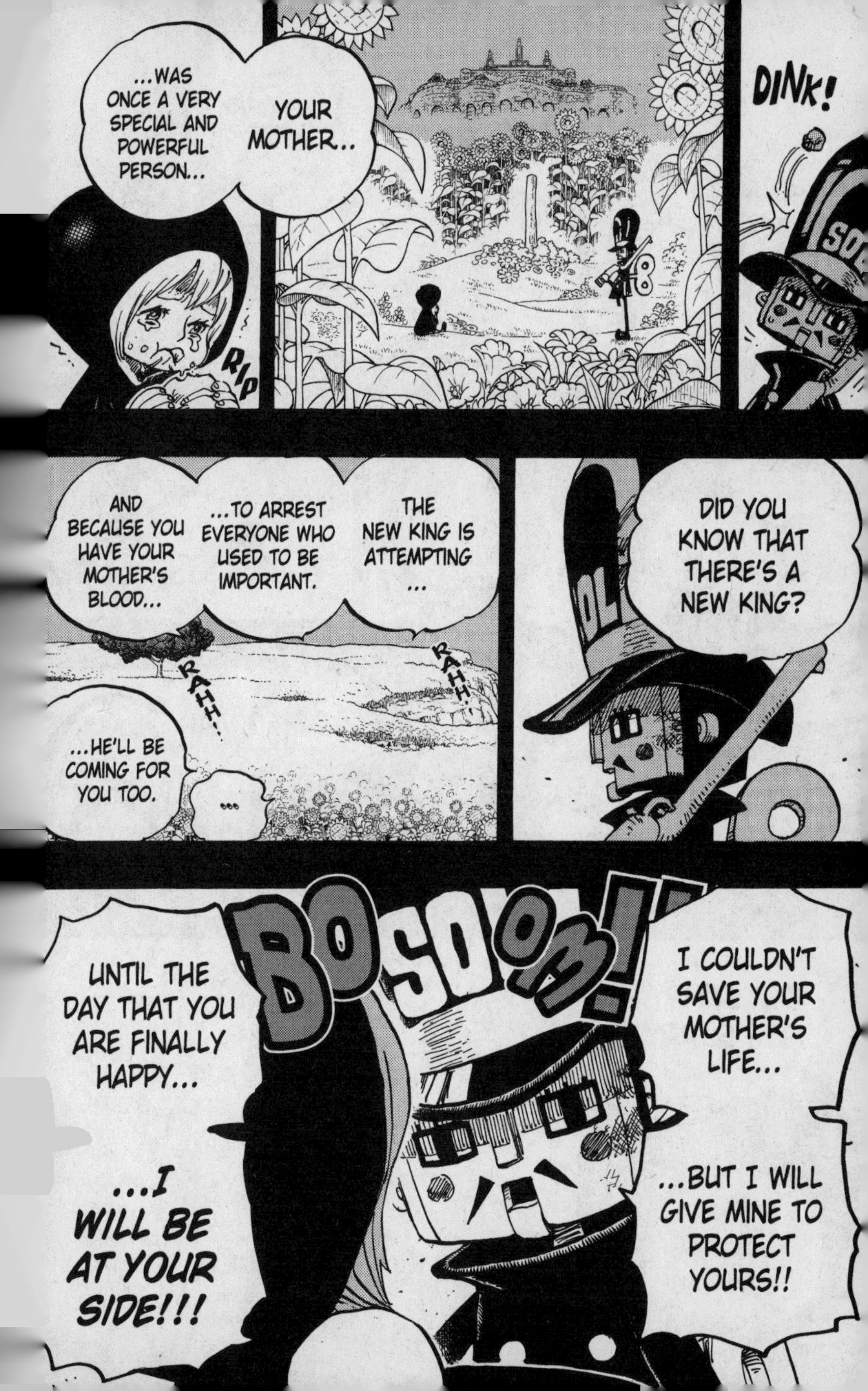
DINK!
YOUR MOTHER...
...WAS ONCE A VERY SPECIAL AND POWERFUL PERSON...
RIP
DID YOU KNOW THAT THERE'S A NEW KING?
THE NEW KING IS ATTEMPTING...
...TO ARREST EVERYONE WHO USED TO BE IMPORTANT.
AND BECAUSE YOU HAVE YOUR MOTHER'S BLOOD...
RAHH!
RAHH!
...HE'LL BE COMING FOR YOU TOO.
...
BOSOOM!!
I COULDN'T SAVE YOUR MOTHER'S LIFE...
...BUT I WILL GIVE MINE TO PROTECT YOURS!!
UNTIL THE DAY THAT YOU ARE FINALLY HAPPY...
...I WILL BE AT YOUR SIDE!!!

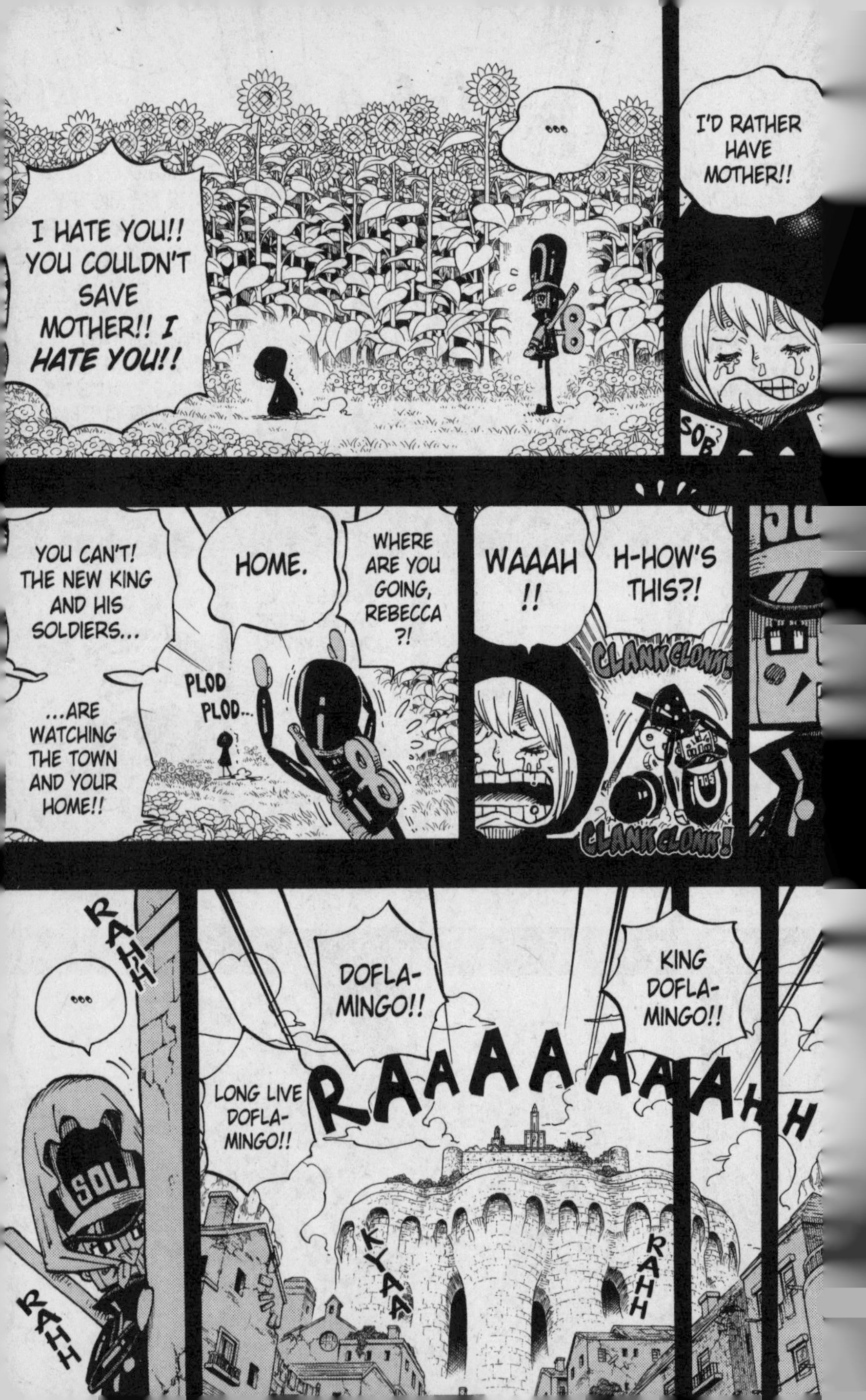
I'D RATHER HAVE MOTHER!!
SOB
...
I HATE YOU!! YOU COULDN'T SAVE MOTHER!! I HATE YOU!!
H-HOW'S THIS?!
CLANK CLONK!
WAAAH !!
CLANK CLONK!
WHERE ARE YOU GOING, REBECCA?!
HOME.
PLOD PLOD...
YOU CAN'T! THE NEW KING AND HIS SOLDIERS...
...ARE WATCHING THE TOWN AND YOUR HOME!!
KING DOFLAMINGO!!
DOFLAMINGO!!
RAAAAAAAAHH
LONG LIVE DOFLAMINGO!!
RAHH
KYAA
RAHH
...
RAHH

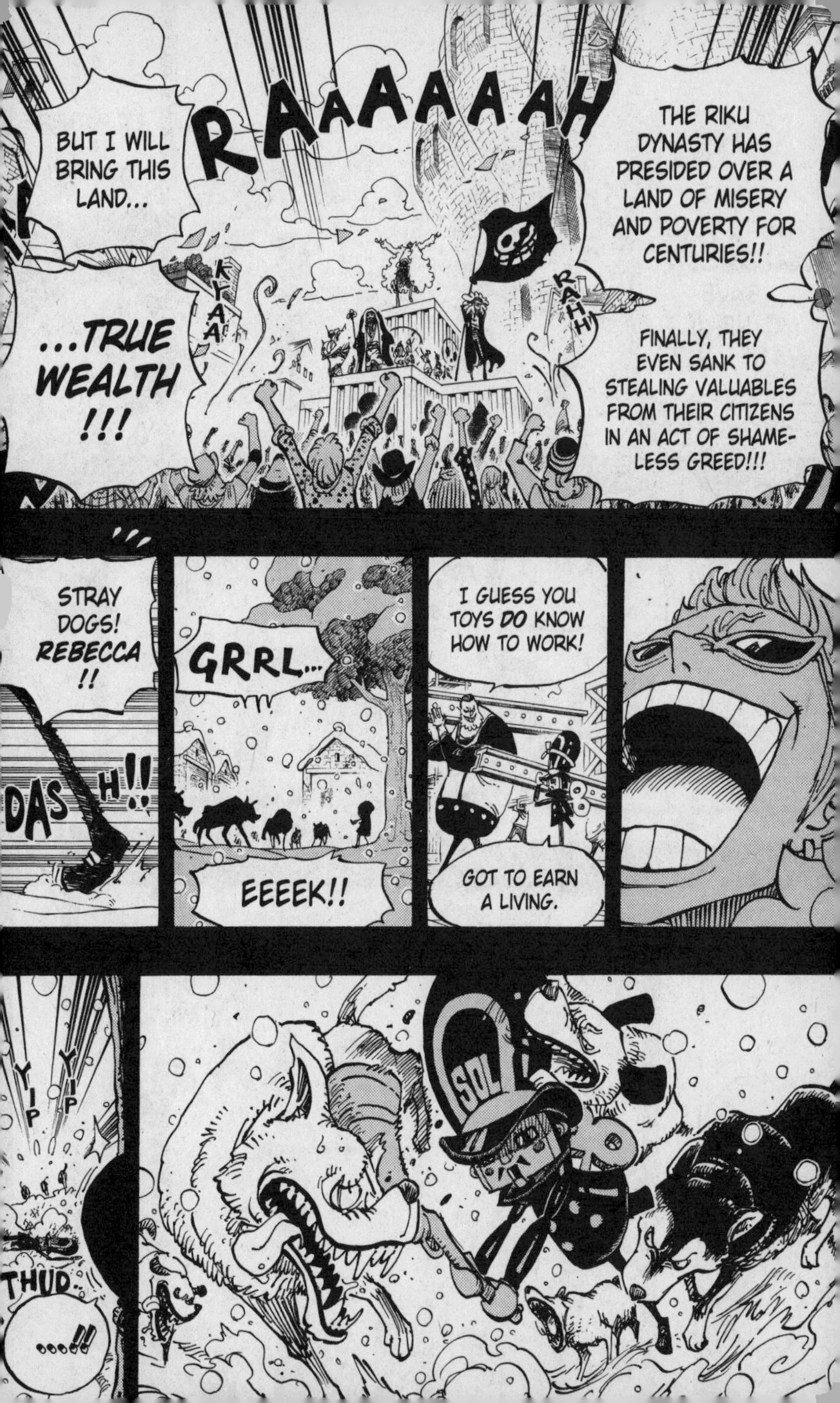
THE RIKU DYNASTY HAS PRESIDED OVER A LAND OF MISERY AND POVERTY FOR CENTURIES!!
FINALLY, THEY EVEN SANK TO STEALING VALUABLES FROM THEIR CITIZENS IN AN ACT OF SHAME-LESS GREED!!!
RAAAAAAH
RAHH
KYAA
BUT I WILL BRING THIS LAND...
...TRUE WEALTH !!!
I GUESS YOU TOYS DO KNOW HOW TO WORK!
GOT TO EARN A LIVING.
GRRL...
EEEEK!!
STRAY DOGS! REBECCA !!
DASH!!
YIP
YIP
THUD..
....!!

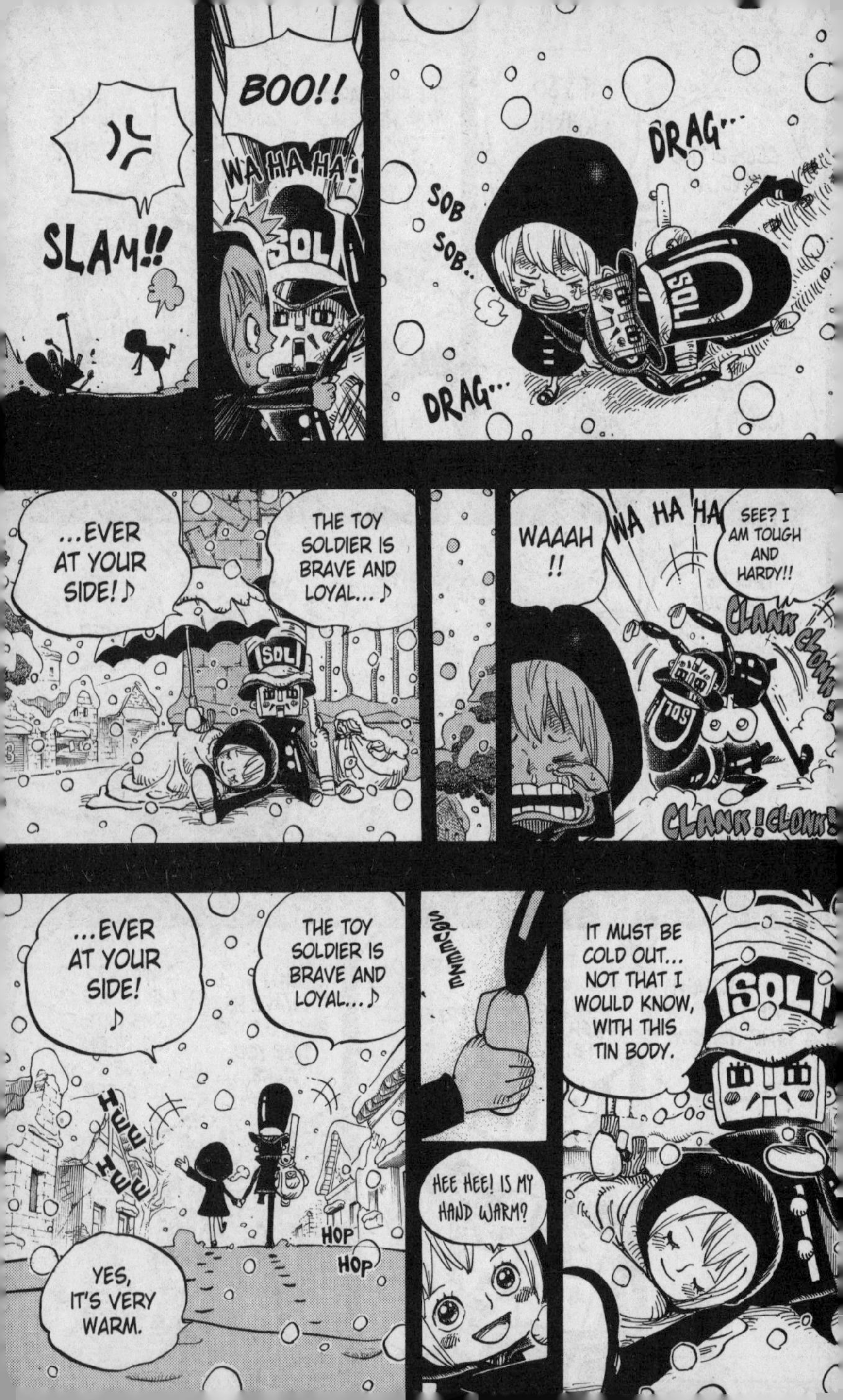

DRAG...
SOB SOB..
DRAG...
BOO!!
WA HA HA!
SLAM!!
WA HA HA
SEE? I AM TOUGH AND HARDY!!
WAAAH !!
CLANK CLONK
CLANK! CLONK!
THE TOY SOLDIER IS BRAVE AND LOYAL...♪
...EVER AT YOUR SIDE!♪
IT MUST BE COLD OUT... NOT THAT I WOULD KNOW, WITH THIS TIN BODY.
SQUEEEZE
HEE HEE! IS MY HAND WARM?
THE TOY SOLDIER IS BRAVE AND LOYAL...♪
...EVER AT YOUR SIDE! ♪
HEW HEW
HOP HOP
YES, IT'S VERY WARM.

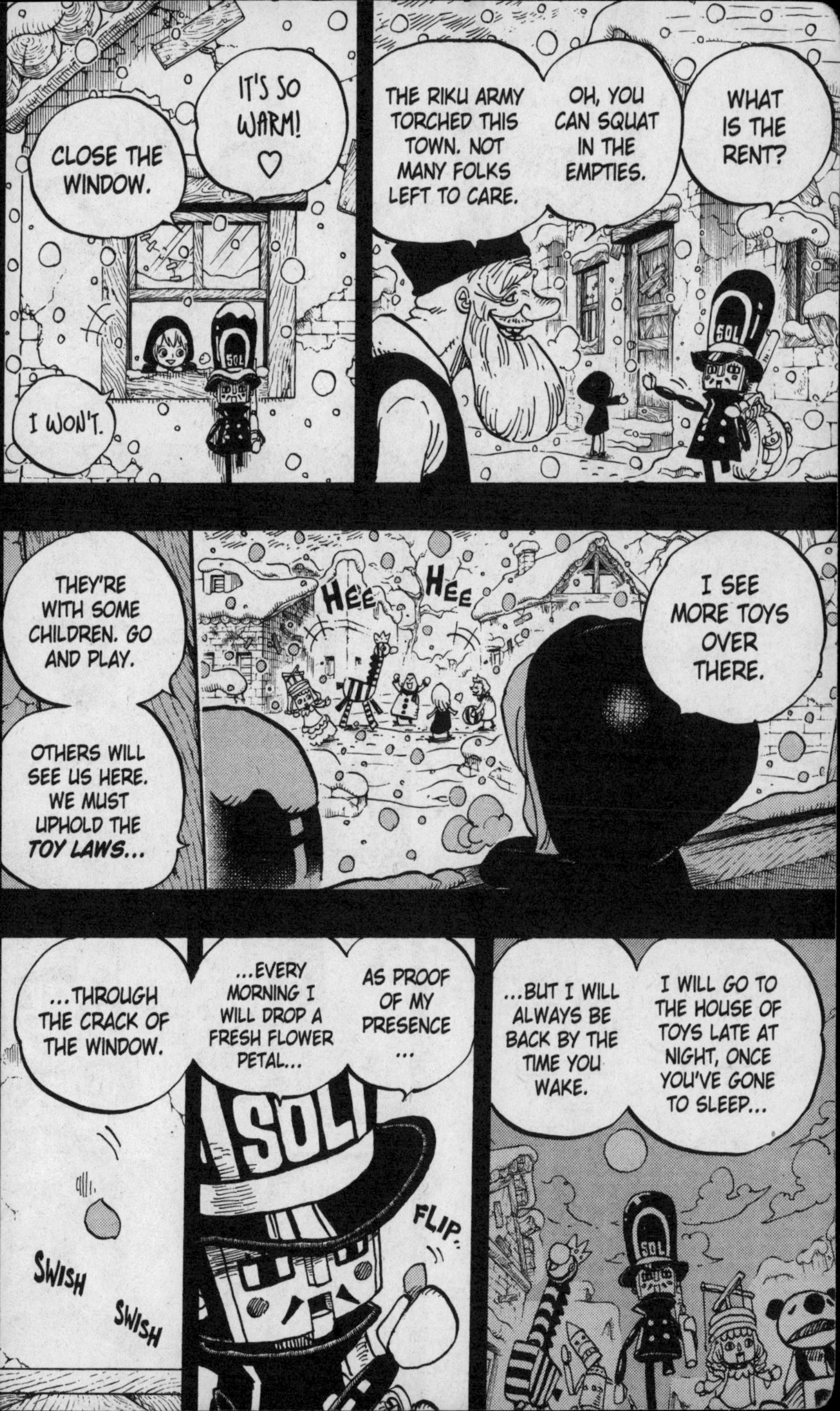
WHAT IS THE RENT?
OH, YOU CAN SQUAT IN THE EMPTIES.
THE RIKU ARMY TORCHED THIS TOWN. NOT MANY FOLKS LEFT TO CARE.
IT'S SO WARM! ♡
CLOSE THE WINDOW.
I WON'T.
I SEE MORE TOYS OVER THERE.
HEE
HEE
THEY'RE WITH SOME CHILDREN. GO AND PLAY.
OTHERS WILL SEE US HERE. WE MUST UPHOLD THE *TOY LAWS*...
I WILL GO TO THE HOUSE OF TOYS LATE AT NIGHT, ONCE YOU'VE GONE TO SLEEP...
...BUT I WILL ALWAYS BE BACK BY THE TIME YOU WAKE.
AS PROOF OF MY PRESENCE...
...EVERY MORNING I WILL DROP A FRESH FLOWER PETAL...
SOL
FLIP
...THROUGH THE CRACK OF THE WINDOW.
SWISH
SWISH

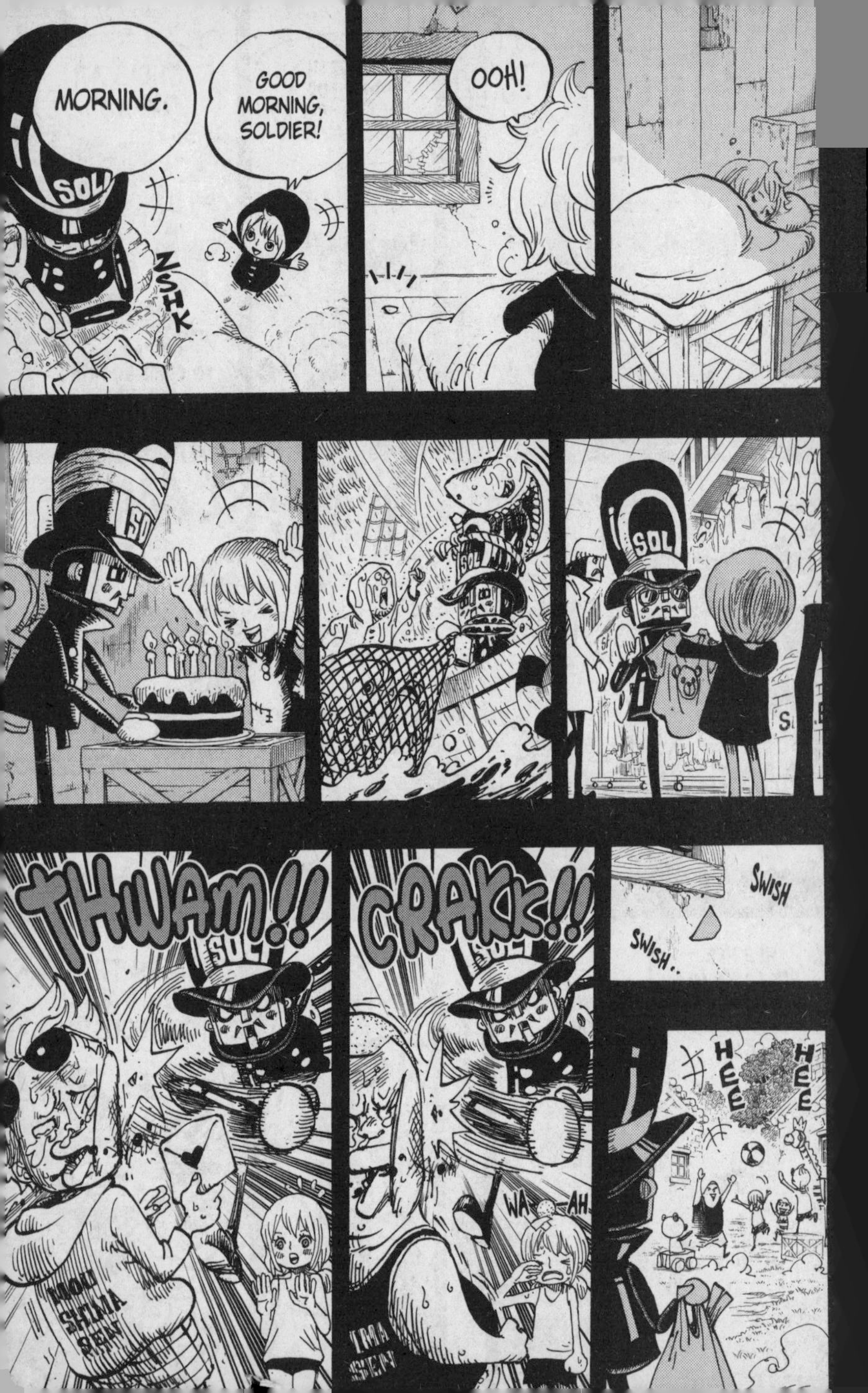
OOH!
GOOD MORNING, SOLDIER!
MORNING.
ZSHK
SOL
SOL
SOL
SWISH
SWISH..
HEE
HEE
CRAKK!!
WA--AH
THWAM!!
SOL
MOU SHIMA SEN

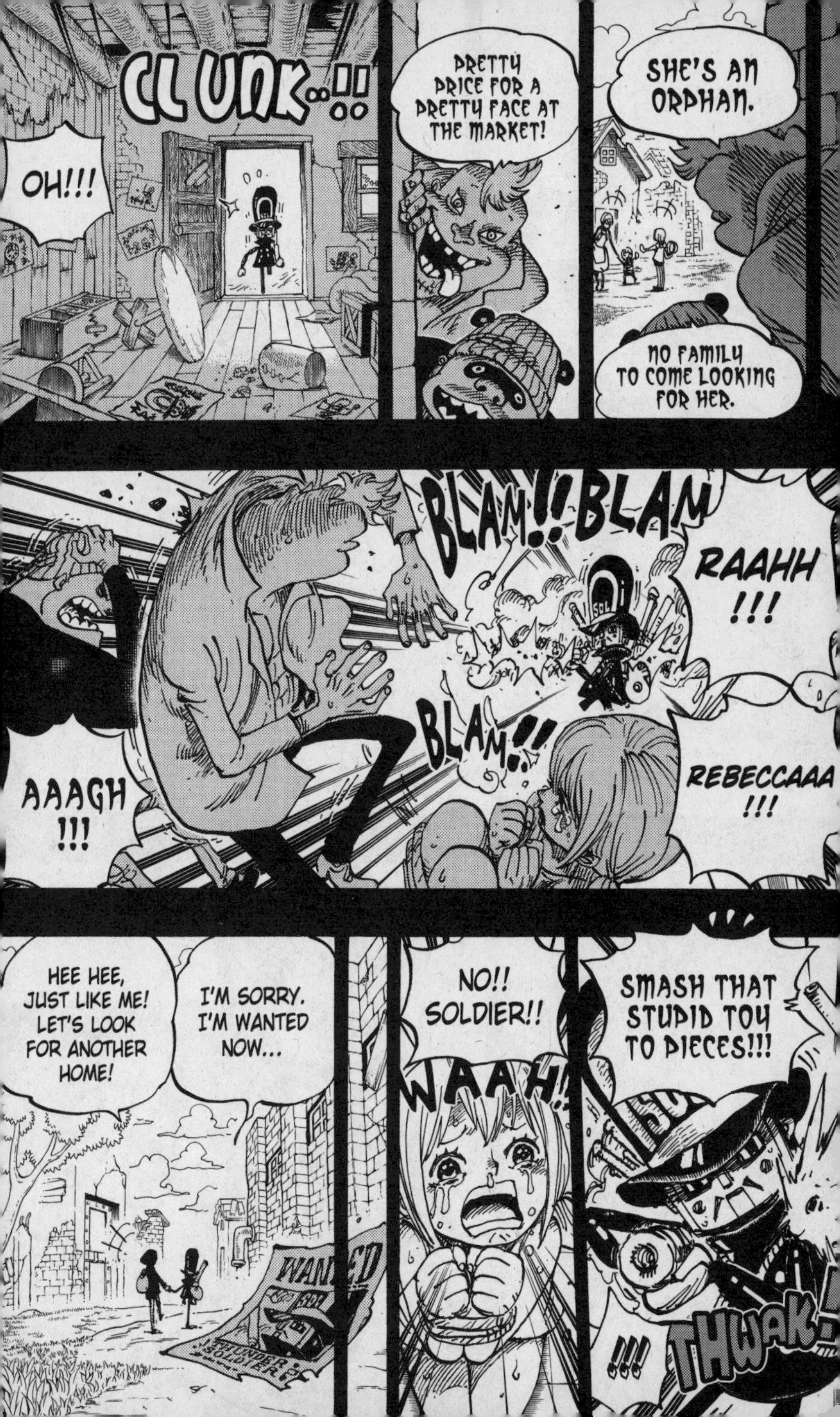
SHE'S AN ORPHAN.
NO FAMILY TO COME LOOKING FOR HER.
PRETTY PRICE FOR A PRETTY FACE AT THE MARKET!
CLUNK..!!
OH!!!
BLAM!! BLAM
RAAHH!!!
BLAM!!
REBECCAAA!!!
AAAGH!!!
SMASH THAT STUPID TOY TO PIECES!!!
THWAK..!
NO!! SOLDIER!!
WAAH!!
!!!
I'M SORRY. I'M WANTED NOW...
HEE HEE, JUST LIKE ME! LET'S LOOK FOR ANOTHER HOME!
WANTED
THUNDER SOLDIER

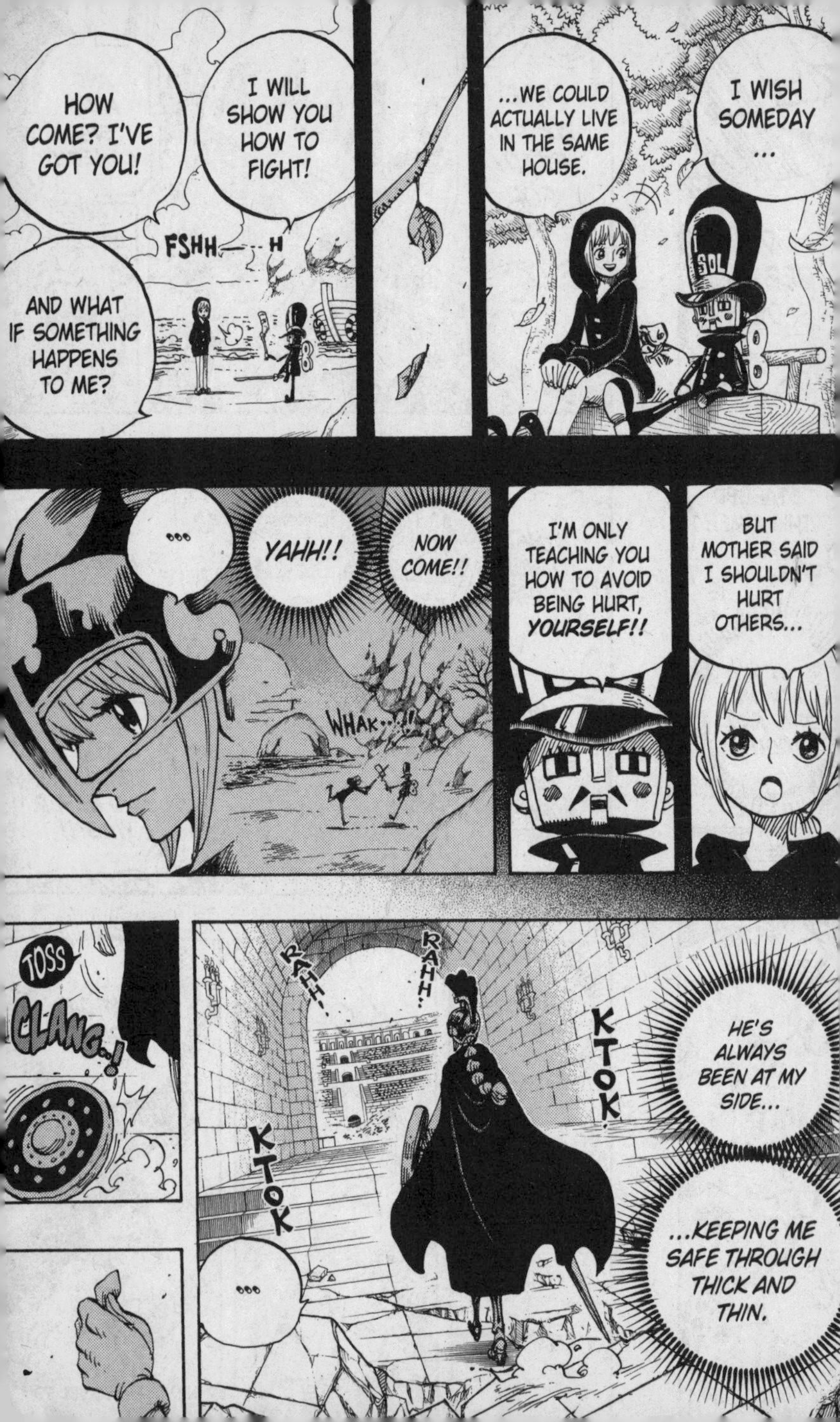
I WISH SOMEDAY ...
...WE COULD ACTUALLY LIVE IN THE SAME HOUSE.
I WILL SHOW YOU HOW TO FIGHT!
HOW COME? I'VE GOT YOU!
FSHH—H
AND WHAT IF SOMETHING HAPPENS TO ME?
BUT MOTHER SAID I SHOULDN'T HURT OTHERS...
I'M ONLY TEACHING YOU HOW TO AVOID BEING HURT, YOURSELF!!
NOW COME!!
YAHH!!
...
WHAK...!!
HE'S ALWAYS BEEN AT MY SIDE...
...KEEPING ME SAFE THROUGH THICK AND THIN.
KTOK
RAHH!
RAHH!
KTOK
...
TOSS
CLANG..!

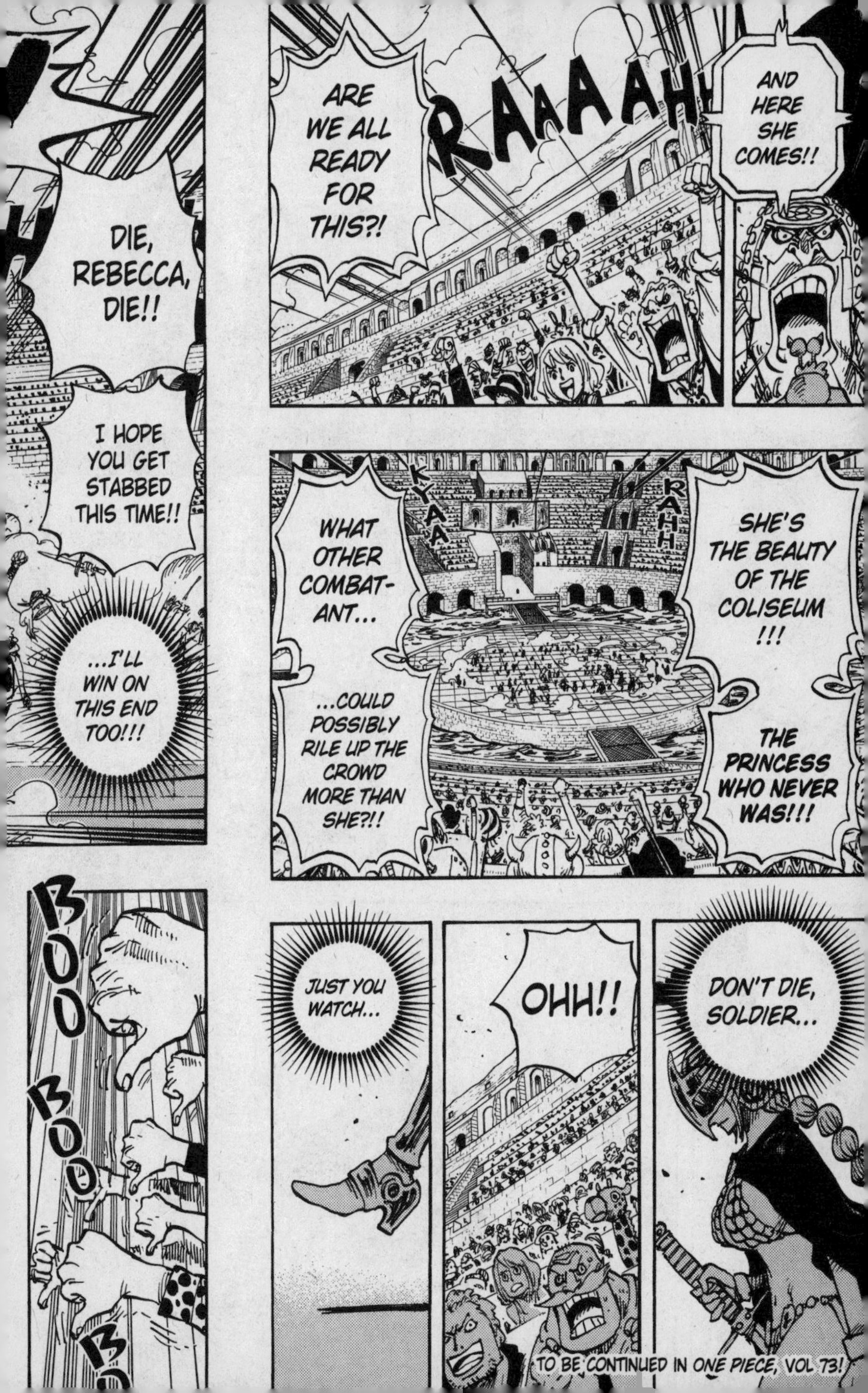
AND HERE SHE COMES!!
ARE WE ALL READY FOR THIS?!
RAAAAH
SHE'S THE BEAUTY OF THE COLISEUM!!!
THE PRINCESS WHO NEVER WAS!!!
RAHH
KYAA
WHAT OTHER COMBAT-ANT...
...COULD POSSIBLY RILE UP THE CROWD MORE THAN SHE?!!
DIE, REBECCA, DIE!!
I HOPE YOU GET STABBED THIS TIME!!
...I'LL WIN ON THIS END TOO!!!
DON'T DIE, SOLDIER...
OHH!!
JUST YOU WATCH...
BOO
BOO
TO BE CONTINUED IN ONE PIECE, VOL 73!

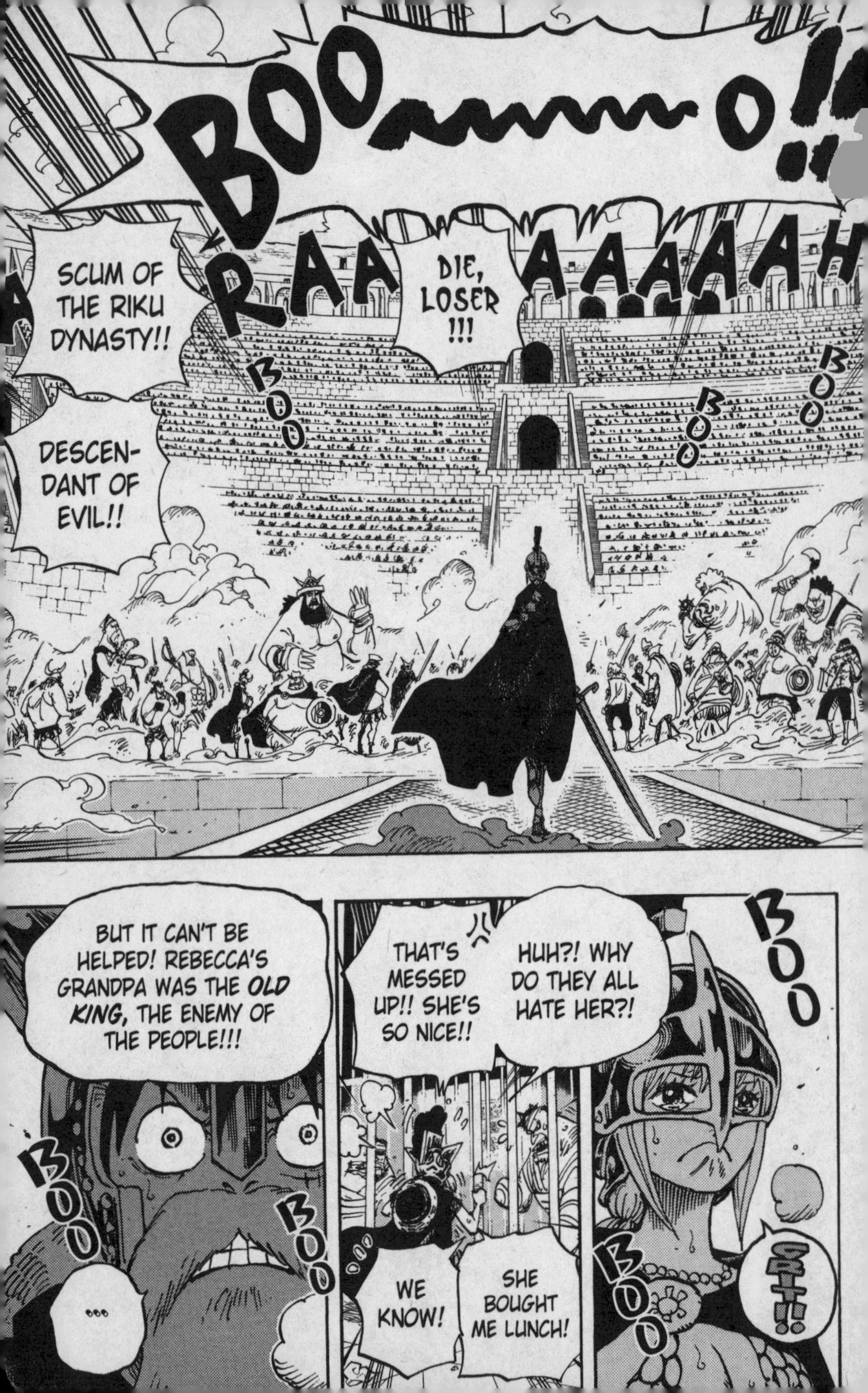
BOOOOOO!!
RAAAAAAAH
DIE, LOSER!!!
SCUM OF THE RIKU DYNASTY!!
DESCENDANT OF EVIL!!
BOO
BOO
BOO
BOO
GRIT!!
BOO
HUH?! WHY DO THEY ALL HATE HER?!
THAT'S MESSED UP!! SHE'S SO NICE!!
SHE BOUGHT ME LUNCH!
WE KNOW!
BUT IT CAN'T BE HELPED! REBECCA'S GRANDPA WAS THE *OLD KING*, THE ENEMY OF THE PEOPLE!!!
BOO
BOO
...

Black ✤ Clover

STORY & ART BY YŪKI TABATA

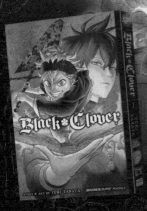

Asta is a young boy who dreams of becoming the greatest mage in the kingdom. Only one problem—he can't use any magic! Luckily for Asta, he receives the incredibly rare five-leaf clover grimoire that gives him the power of anti-magic. Can someone who can't use magic really become the Wizard King? One thing's for sure—Asta will never give up!

SHONEN JUMP

viz media
www.viz.com

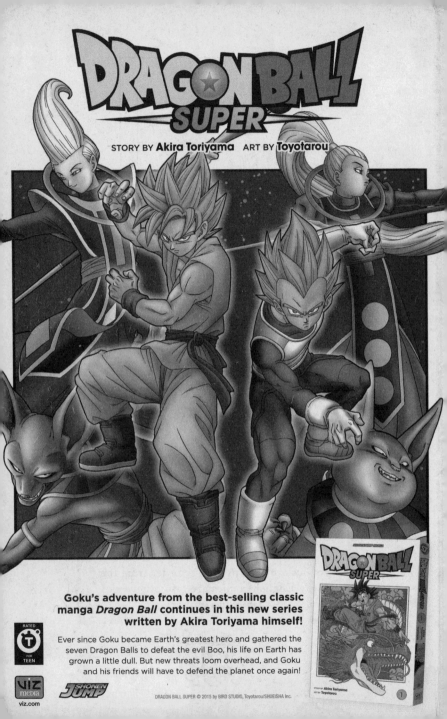

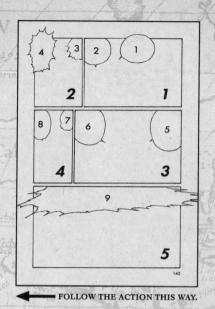

← **FOLLOW THE ACTION THIS WAY.**

THIS IS THE LAST PAGE!

One Piece has been printed in the original Japanese format in order to preserve the orientation of the original artwork.

Please turn it around and begin reading from right to left. Unlike English, Japanese is read right to left, so Japanese comics are read in reverse order from the way English comics are typically read. Have fun with it!